T0205737

More information about this series at http://www.springer.com/series/7410

Alexandra Boldyreva · Daniele Micciancio (Eds.)

Advances in Cryptology – CRYPTO 2019

39th Annual International Cryptology Conference
Santa Barbara, CA, USA, August 18–22, 2019
Proceedings, Part II

 Springer

Editors
Alexandra Boldyreva
Georgia Institute of Technology
Atlanta, GA, USA

Daniele Micciancio
University of California at San Diego
La Jolla, CA, USA

ISSN 0302-9743   ISSN 1611-3349   (electronic)
Lecture Notes in Computer Science
ISBN 978-3-030-26950-0   ISBN 978-3-030-26951-7   (eBook)
https://doi.org/10.1007/978-3-030-26951-7

LNCS Sublibrary: SL4 – Security and Cryptology

This Springer imprint is published by the registered company Springer Nature Switzerland AG
The registered company address is: Gewerbestrasse 11, 6330 Cham, Switzerland

Preface

The 39th International Cryptology Conference (Crypto 2019) was held at the University of California, Santa Barbara, California, USA, during August 18–22, 2019. It was sponsored by the International Association for Cryptologic Research (IACR). As in the previous year, a number of workshops took place on the days (August 17 and August 18, 2019) immediately before the conference. This year, the list of affiliated events included a Workshop on Attacks in Cryptography organized by Juraj Somorovsky (Ruhr University Bochum); a Blockchain Workshop organized by Rafael Pass (Cornell Tech) and Elaine Shi (Cornell); a Workshop on Advanced Cryptography Standardization organized by Daniel Benarroch (QEDIT) and Tancrède Lepoint (Google); a workshop on New Roads to Cryptopia organized by Amit Sahai (UCLA); a Privacy Preserving Machine Learning Workshop organized by Gilad Asharov (JP Morgan AI Research), Rafail Ostrovsky (UCLA) and Antigoni Polychroniadou (JP Morgan AI Research); and the Mathcrypt Workshop organized by Kristin Lauter (Microsoft Research), Yongsoo Song (Microsoft Research) and Jung Hee Cheon (Seoul National University).

Crypto continues to grow, year after year, and Crypto 2019 was no exception. The conference set new records for both submissions and publications, with a whopping 378 papers submitted for consideration. It took a Program Committee (PC) of 51 cryptography experts working with 333 external reviewers for over two months to select the 81 papers which were accepted for the conference.

As usual, papers were reviewed in the double-blind fashion, with each paper assigned to three PC members. Initially, papers received independent reviews, without any communication between PC members. After the initial review stage, authors were given the opportunity to comment on all available preliminary reviews. Finally, the PC discussed each submission, taking all reviews and author comments into account, and selecting the list of papers to be included in the conference program. PC members were limited to two submissions, and their submissions were held to higher standards. The two Program Chairs were not allowed to submit papers.

The PC recognized three papers and their authors for standing out amongst the rest. "Cryptanalysis of OCB2: Attacks on Authenticity and Confidentiality", by Akiko Inoue, Tetsu Iwata, Kazuhiko Minematsu and Bertram Poettering was voted Best Paper of the conference. Additionally, the papers "Quantum cryptanalysis in the RAM model: Claw-finding attacks on SIKE" by Samuel Jaques and John M. Schanck, and "Fully Secure Attribute-Based Encryption for t-CNF from LWE" by Rotem Tsabary, were voted Best Papers Authored Exclusively By Young Researchers.

Beside the technical presentations, Crypto 2019 featured a Rump session, and two invited talks by Jonathan Katz from University of Maryland, and Helen Nissenbaum from Cornell Tech.

We would like to express our sincere gratitude to all the reviewers for volunteering their time and knowledge in order to select a great program for 2019. Additionally, we are very appreciative of the following individuals and organizations for helping make Crypto 2019 a success:

- Muthu Venkitasubramaniam (University of Rochester) - Crypto 2019 General Chair
- Carmit Hazay (Bar-Ilan University) - Workshop Chair
- Jonathan Katz (University of Maryland) - Invited Speaker
- Helen Nissenbaum (Cornell Tech) - Invited Speaker
- Shai Halevi - Author of the IACR Web Submission and Review System
- Anna Kramer and her colleagues at Springer
- Whitney Morris and UCSB Conference Services

We would also like to say thank you to our numerous sponsors, the workshop organizers, everyone who submitted papers, the session chairs, and the presenters. Lastly, a big thanks to everyone who attended the conference at UCSB.

August 2019   Alexandra Boldyreva
                                                   Daniele Micciancio

CRYPTO 2019

The 39th International Cryptology Conference

University of California, Santa Barbara, CA, USA
August 18–22, 2019

Sponsored by the *International Association for Cryptologic Research*

General Chair

Muthu Venkitasubramaniam   University of Rochester, USA

Program Chairs

Alexandra Boldyreva   Georgia Institute of Technology, USA
Daniele Micciancio   University of California at San Diego, USA

Program Committee

Manuel Barbosa	INESC TEC, University of Porto, Portugal
Zvika Brakerski	Weizmann Institute of Science, Israel
Mark Bun	Simons Institute, Boston University, USA
Ran Canetti	Tel Aviv University, Israel, and Boston University, USA
Dario Catalano	University of Catania, Italy
Alessandro Chiesa	UC Berkeley, USA
Sherman S. M. Chow	Chinese University of Hong Kong, SAR China
Kai-Min Chung	Academia Sinica, Taiwan
Jean-Sebastien Coron	Luxembourg University, Luxembourg
Jean Paul Degabriele	TU Darmstadt, Germany
Nico Döttling	Cispa Helmholtz Center (i.G.), Germany
Orr Dunkelman	University of Haifa, Israel
Rosario Gennaro	City College, CUNY, USA
Tim Güneysu	Ruhr University Bochum, DFKI, Germany
Felix Günther	UC San Diego, USA
Siyao Guo	NYU Shanghai, China
Sean Hallgren	Pennsylvania State University, USA
Carmit Hazay	Bar-Ilan University, Israel
Susan Hohenberger	Johns Hopkins University, USA
Sorina Ionica	Université de Picardie, France
Bhavana Kanukurthi	Indian Institute of Science, India
Vladimir Kolesnikov	Georgia Institute of Technology, USA

Anja Lehmann	IBM Research Zurich, Switzerland
Vadim Lyubashevsky	IBM Research Zurich, Switzerland
Ilya Mironov	Google
Michael Naehrig	Microsoft Research
Svetla Nikova	KU Leuven, Belgium
Ryo Nishimaki	NTT Secure Platform Labs, Japan
Omer Paneth	MIT, USA
Charalampos Papamanthou	University of Maryland, USA
Chris Peikert	University of Michigan, USA
Giuseppe Persiano	University of Salerno, Italy
Christophe Petit	University of Birmingham, UK
Thomas Peyrin	Nanyang Technological University, Singapore
Benny Pinkas	Bar Ilan University, Israel
Bertram Poettering	Royal Holloway, University of London, UK
Mariana Raykova	Yale University, USA
Silas Richelson	UC Riverside, USA
Adeline Roux-Langlois	University Rennes, CNRS, IRISA, France
Peter Scholl	Aarhus University, Denmark
Dominique Schröder	Friedrich-Alexander-Universität, Germany
Thomas Shrimpton	University of Florida, USA
Damien Stehlé	ENS Lyon, France
Björn Tackmann	IBM Research Zurich, Switzerland
Keisuke Tanaka	Tokyo Institute of Technology, Japan
Eran Tromer	Tel Aviv University, Israel, and Columbia University, USA
Daniele Venturi	Sapienza, University of Rome, Italy
Xiao Wang	MIT, Boston University, USA
Xiaoyun Wang	Tsinghua University, China
Bogdan Warinschi	University of Bristol, UK
Mor Weiss	IDC Herzliya, Israel

Additional Reviewers

Ittai Abraham
Shweta Agrawal
Gorjan Alagic
Navid Alamati
Younes Talibi Alaoui
Martin Albrecht
Joel Alwen
Prabhanjan Ananth
Elena Andreeva
Benny Applebaum
Marcel Armour
Gal Arnon

Vivek Arte
Gilad Asharov
Tomer Ashur
Nuttapong Attrapadung
Benedikt Auerbach
Roberto Avanzi
Saikrishna
  Badrinarayanan
Josep Balasch
Foteini Baldimtsi
Marshall Ball
Achiya Bar-On

Paulo S. L. M. Barreto
James Bartusek
Carsten Baum
Gabrielle Beck
Amos Beimel
Sonia Belaid
Fabrice Benhamouda
Pauline Bert
Rishabh Bhadauria
Olivier Blazy
Jeremiah Blocki
Jonathan Bootle

Cecilia Boschini
Katharina Boudgoust
Florian Bourse
Elette Boyle
Jacqueline Brendel
Anne Broadbent
Wouter Castryck
Andrea Cerulli
Yilei Chen
Nai-Hui Chia
Ilaria Chillotti
Arka Rai Choudhuri
Michele Ciampi
Benoit Cogliati
Ran Cohen
Sandro Coretti
Craig Costello
Geoffroy Couteau
Jan Czajkowski
Dana Dachaman-Soled
Wei Dai
Anders Dalskov
Hannah Davis
Akshay Degwekar
Ioannis Demertzis
Patrick Derbez
David Derler
Itai Dinur
Mario Di Raimondo
Benjamin Dowling
Minxin Du
Léo Ducas
Yfke Dulek
Francois Dupressoir
Frédéric Dupuis
Stefan Dziembowski
Gautier Eberhart
Christoph Egger
Maria Eichlseder
Daniel Escudero
Antonio Faonio
Franz Aguirre Farro
Pooya Farshim
Omar Fawzi
Katharina Fech
Ben Fisch

Marc Fischlin
Emmanuel Fouotsa
Danilo Francati
Daniele Friolo
Ariel Gabizon
Tommaso Gagliardoni
Steven Galbraith
Chaya Ganesh
Lydia Garms
Romain Gay
Ran Gelles
Adela Georgescu
David Gerault
Essam Ghadafi
Satrajit Ghosh
Federico Giacon
Aarushi Goel
Junqing Gong
Alonso Gonzalez
Rishab Goyal
Vipul Goyal
Nicola Greco
Daniel Grosse
Zichen Gui
Tim Güneysu
Chethan Kamath Hosdurg
Mohammad Hajiabadi
Lucjan Hanzlik
Patrick Harasser
Carmit Hazay
Julia Hesse
Minki Hhan
Kuan-Yi Ho
Justin Holmgren
Akinori Hosoyamada
Patrick Hough
James Howe
Pavel Hubácek
Shih-Han Hung
Kathrin Hövelmanns
Takanori Isobe
Mitsugu Iwamoto
Malika Izabachène
Joseph Jaeger
Christian Janson
Dirmanto Jap

Stas Jarecki
Zhengzhong Jin
Charanjit Jutla
Guillaume Kaim
Mustafa Kairallah
Yael Kalai
Chethan Kamath
Marc Kaplan
Shuichi Katsumata
Shinagawa Kazumasa
Mojtaba Khalili
Dmitry Khovratovich
Ryo Kikuchi
Sam Kim
Elena Kirshanova
Fuyuki Kitagawa
Susumu Kiyoshima
Karen Klein
Michael Klooss
Kamil Kluczniak
Markulf Kohlweiss
Ilan Komargodski
Venkata Koppula
Evgenios Kornaropoulos
Takeshi Koshiba
Luke Kowalczyk
Stephan Krenn
Mukul Kulkarni
Ranjit Kumaresan
Gijs Van Laer
Russell W. F. Lai
Thalia Laing
Changmin Lee
Eysa Lee
Moon Sung Lee
Tancrède Lepoint
Jyun-Jie Liao
Han-Hsuan Lin
Huijia (Rachel) Lin
Helger Lipmaa
Qipeng Liu
Tianren Liu
Alex Lombardi
Patrick Longa
Julian Loss
Atul Luykx

Julio López
Fermi Ma
Jack P. K. Ma
Bernardo Magri
Mohammad Mahmoody
Christian Majenz
Hemanta Maji
Giulio Malavolta
Mary Maller
Nathan Manohar
Peter Manohar
Daniel Masny
Takahiro Matsuda
Alexander May
Sogol Mazaheri
Jeremias Mechler
Simon-Philipp Merz
Peihan Miao
Romy Minko
Takaaki Mizuki
Amir Moradi
Kirill Morozov
Travis Morrison
Nicky Mouha
Tamer Mour
Pratyay Mukherjee
Jörn Müller-Quade
Kartik Nayak
Gregory Neven
Ka-Lok Ng
Ruth Ng
Ngoc Khanh Nguyen
Ventzislav Nikov
Ariel Nof
Sai Lakshmi Bhavana
   Obbattu
Maciej Obremski
Tobias Oder
Sabine Oechsner
Wakaha Ogata
Miyako Ohkubo
Cristina Onete
Claudio Orlandi
Emmanuela Orsini
Carles Padro
Jiaxin Pan

Lorenz Panny
Dimitris Papadopoulos
Anat Paskin-Cherniavsky
Christopher Patton
Alice Pellet-Mary
Zack Pepin
Jeroen Pijnenburg
Oxana Poburinnaya
Antigoni Polychroniadou
Bart Preneel
Ben Pring
Emmanuel Prouff
Chen Qian
Luowen Qian
Willy Quach
Srinivasan Raghuraman
Adrián Ranea
Divya Ravi
Vincent Rijmen
Peter Rindal
Felix Rohrbach
Razvan Rosie
Dragos Rotaru
Ron Rothblum
Arnab Roy
Paul Rösler
Luisa Siniscalchi
Mohamed Sabt
Rajeev Anand Sahu
Cyprien de Saint Guilhem
Kazuo Sakiyama
Pratik Sarkar
Pascal Sasdrich
Alessandra Scafuro
Falk Schellenberg
Thomas Schneider
Tobias Schneider
Jacob Schuldt
Gregor Seiler
Sruthi Sekar
Karn Seth
Yannick Seurin
Aria Shahverdi
Abhishek Shetty
Sina Shiehian
Javier Silva

Siang Meng Sim
Mark Simkin
Luisa Siniscalchi
Fang Song
Pratik Soni
Katerina Sotiraki
Nicholas Spooner
Caleb Springer
Akshayaram Srinivasan
François-Xavier Standaert
Douglas Stebila
Damien Stehlé
Ron Steinfeld
Noah
   Stephens-Davidowitz
Christoph Striecks
Patrick Struck
Banik Subhadeep
Gelo Noel Tabia
Stefano Tessaro
Sri Aravinda Krishnan
   Thyagarajan
Mehdi Tibouchi
Elmar W. Tischhauser
Yosuke Todo
Junichi Tomida
Patrick Towa
Monika Trimoska
Itay Tsabary
Rotem Tsabary
Sulamithe Tsakou
Ida Tucker
Dominique Unruh
Bogdan Ursu
Vinod Vaikuntanathan
Kerem Varici
Prashant Vasudevan
Muthu
   Venkitasubramaniam
Fernando Virdia
Madars Virza
Ivan Visconti
Satyanarayana Vusirikala
Riad Wahby
Adrian Waller
Alexandre Wallet

Michael Walter
Haoyang Wang
Jiafan Wang
Meiqin Wang
Xiuhua Wang
Yuyu Wang
Gaven Watson
Hoeteck Wee
Weiqiang Wen

Harry W. H. Wong
Tim Wood
Joanne Woodage
Huangting Wu
Keita Xagawa
Shota Yamada
Takashi Yamakawa
Avishay Yanai
Kenji Yasunaga

Kevin Yeo
Eylon Yogev
Yu Yu
Mark Zhandry
Jiapeng Zhang
Yupeng Zhang
Yongjun Zhao
Yu Zheng

Sponsors

 CONCORDIUM

facebook findora FUJITSU

HACKMANIT   IBM Research   inpher

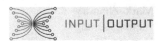

Contents – Part II

Leakage Resilience

Memory Hard Functions and Privacy Amplification

Attribute Based Encryption

Foundations

MPC Communication Complexity

The Communication Complexity
of Threshold Private Set Intersection

Satrajit Ghosh$^{(\boxtimes)}$ and Mark Simkin$^{(\boxtimes)}$

Aarhus University, Aarhus, Denmark
{satrajit,simkin}@cs.au.dk

Abstract. Threshold private set intersection enables Alice and Bob who hold sets S_A and S_B of size n to compute the intersection $S_A \cap S_B$ if the sets do not differ by more than some threshold parameter t. In this work, we investigate the communication complexity of this problem and we establish the first upper and lower bounds. We show that any protocol has to have a communication complexity of $\Omega(t)$. We show that an almost matching upper bound of $\tilde{\mathcal{O}}(t)$ can be obtained via fully homomorphic encryption. We present a computationally more efficient protocol based on weaker assumptions, namely additively homomorphic encryption, with a communication complexity of $\tilde{\mathcal{O}}(t^2)$. For applications like biometric authentication, where a given fingerprint has to have a large intersection with a fingerprint from a database, our protocols may result in significant communication savings.

Prior to this work, all previous protocols had a communication complexity of $\Omega(n)$. Our protocols are the first ones with communication complexities that mainly depend on the threshold parameter t and only logarithmically on the set size n.

1 Introduction

Private set intersection enables two mutually distrustful parties Alice and Bob to compute the intersection $S_A \cap S_B$ of their respective sets S_A and S_B without revealing any other information. Efficient protocols have numerous applications ranging from botnet detection [NMH+10], through online advertising [PSSZ15], to private contact discovery [Mar14]. The first solution to this problem was given by Meadows [Mea86] and since then, a long line of work [FNP04, KS05, DT10, DCW13, PSZ14, PSSZ15, KKRT16, HV17, KMP+17, RR17a, RR17b, CLR17, GN17, KLS+17, PSWW18] has considered the problem in the two-party, the multi-party, and the server-aided setting with both passive and active security. Beyond private set intersection, several works [KS05, HW06, CGT12, DD15, EFG+15, PSWW18] have also considered

S. Ghosh and M. Simkin—Supported by the European Unions's Horizon 2020 research and innovation program under grant agreement No 669255 (MPCPRO) and under grant agreement No 731583 (SODA) and the Independent Research Fund Denmark project BETHE.

A. Boldyreva and D. Micciancio (Eds.): CRYPTO 2019, LNCS 11693, pp. 3–29, 2019.
https://doi.org/10.1007/978-3-030-26951-7_1

protocols for privately computing the size of the set intersection, rather than the intersection itself. Freedman et al. [FNP04] proved a lower bound of $\Omega(n)$ on the communication complexity of any private set intersection protocol, where n is the size of the smallest input set. This lower bound directly extends to the case of protocols that only compute the intersection size and it constitutes a fundamental barrier to the efficiency of these protocols.

In certain scenarios we do not require the full power of private set intersection. For example, for the case of biometric authentication we may want to check whether a given fingerprint reading matches a fingerprint from a database. In this setting, we are neither interested in the concrete intersection nor in the exact size of the intersection. All we care about is a binary answer telling us whether the fingerprints have a large intersection or not. In the case of privacy-preserving ridesharing [HOS17] two users only want to share a ride if large parts of their trajectories on a map intersect. In this case, the users may be interested in the concrete intersection of their routes, but only if the intersection is large. Yet another example can be found in the online dating world, where two potential love birds Alice and Bob are only interested in learning the intersection of their dating preferences if the intersection thereof is sufficiently large. Speaking more abstractly, this problem is known as threshold private set intersection, where Alice and Bob hold sets of size n each and only want to learn the intersection if their sets do not differ by more than t elements. Only a few works [FNP04, HOS17, GN17, PSWW18, ZC18] have considered this problem and all of them present solutions, whose communication complexity scales at least linearly in the size of the smaller input set. This seems to be somewhat inherent to these works, since all of them start from a private set intersection protocol and then massage it until it becomes a threshold private set intersection protocol. In this work we ask:

What is the communication complexity of threshold private set intersection?

Answering this question is both theoretically and practically relevant. As explained above, threshold and regular private set intersection protocols have many applications. A better understanding of their communication complexities and their qualitative differences provides us with a better understanding of this research area. It enables us to pick the right tool for a given job and it allows us to have a firm understanding of the communication complexities that we can expect. From a practical perspective, overcoming the private set intersection lower bound of $\Omega(n)$ may result in significant efficiency gains for applications that only require threshold private set intersection. For example, in the biometric authentication setting one usually only allows for a very small difference between a stored and a given fingerprint. We show that using threshold private set intersection protocols, the communication complexity can be almost completely independent of the total size of the fingerprints and instead only depends on the maximum allowed difference between the two fingerprints.

1.1 Our Contribution

We initiate the study of sublinear (in the set size) threshold private set intersection and provide a first characterization of its communication complexity. We prove a lower bound of $\Omega(t)$ on the communication complexity of any protocol that computes the intersection of two sets that do not differ by more than t elements. We present an almost matching upper bound of $\tilde{\mathcal{O}}(t)$ based on fully homomorphic encryption. We show how to avoid the use of fully homomorphic encryption by presenting a computationally more efficient protocol based on weaker assumptions, namely additively homomorphic encryption, with communication complexity of $\tilde{\mathcal{O}}(t^2)$. For applications, where the set intersection has to be large and thus t is small, our protocols may result in significant improvements over the state-of-the-art in terms of communication complexity.

Along the way we also present a communication efficient protocol for private intersection cardinality testing, which privately computes whether two sets differ by more than a given threshold t or not. We believe that this protocol may be of independent interest. From a conceptual perspective, our paper highlights somewhat surprising connections between threshold private set intersection, set reconciliation protocols [MTZ03] from distributed systems, and sparse polynomial interpolation [BOT88], which have to the best of our knowledge not been known before.

What This Paper Is Not About. Most existing works on private set intersection aim to develop the most practically efficient protocols. At the same time, many basic theoretical questions about private set intersection remain unanswered. The goal of this work to provide first answers to one such question. We hope that the research direction initiated in this work will eventually lead to asymptotically optimal *and* practically efficient protocols. The results in this paper present several novel techniques to provide the first non-trivial feasibility results for sublinear threshold private set intersection, which we believe to be of theoretical importance, but we do not claim them to be practically useful yet.

1.2 Technical Overview

Our main threshold private set intersection protocol can be split into two subprotocols. One for testing, whether two given sets are "similar enough" and one for computing the set intersection of two such similar sets. Here we highlight some of the main ideas underlying our protocols.

Private Intersection Cardinality Testing. The goal of private intersection cardinality testing is to enable Alice and Bob, who hold sets S_A and S_B of elements from a field $\mathbb{F}_p$, to determine, whether their sets are similar or not. More formally, we have some similarity threshold parameter t and we would like to test whether $|(S_A \setminus S_B) \cup (S_B \setminus S_A)| \leq 2t$ without revealing any other information about the sets. Our solution to this problem is based on the idea of encoding sets as polynomials over a field as has been done in numerous previous works [BK89, MTZ03, FNP04, KS05]. However, in contrast to previous works, which encode the elements of a set into the roots of a polynomial, we encode the elements into separate monomials of a polynomial. Our encoding procedure encodes a set $S_A = \{a_1, \ldots, a_n\}$ as a polynomial $p_A(x) = \sum_{i=1}^{n} x^{a_i}$. The main idea behind this encoding is that, given two encoded sets $p_A(x)$ and $p_B(x)$, the number of monomials in the polynomial $p(x) = p_A(x) - p_B(x)$ corresponds to the size of the symmetric set difference between S_A and S_B. In particular, if $|(S_A \setminus S_B) \cup (S_B \setminus S_A)| \leq 2t$, then $p(x)$ has at most $2t$ monomials. Encoding the sets in such a way, allows us to make use of the polynomial sparsity test of Grigorescu et al. [GJR10], which itself is heavily based on the seminal work of Ben-Or and Tiwari [BOT88]. A polynomial $p(x)$ is called t-sparse if it has at most t monomials. Grigorescu et al. present a randomized algorithm that only requires $2t$ evaluations of $p(x)$ to determine, whether the polynomial is t-sparse or not. To obtain our private intersection cardinality test, we combine the ideas above with additively homomorphic encryption and the privacy-preserving linear algebra techniques of Kiltz et al. [KMWF07]. Our resulting protocol has a communication complexity of $\tilde{\mathcal{O}}(t^2)$.

Threshold Private Set Intersection. For the problem of threshold private set intersection, our starting point is the set reconciliation protocol by Minsky et al. [MTZ03], where Alice and Bob hold sets S_A and S_B and would like to compute the set union $S_A \cup S_B$ in a communication efficient manner. As shown by Minsky et al., Alice and Bob can do this with communication complexity proportional to the size of the symmetric set difference, that is, with communication complexity roughly $\tilde{\mathcal{O}}((|S_{A \setminus B}| + |S_{B \setminus A}|) \log p)$ bits. This is asymptotically close to optimal, since at the very least both parties need to exchange the data elements that are not part of the intersection $S_A \cap S_B$. The set reconciliation protocol by Minsky et al. starts by encoding both sets as monic polynomials, where the roots of the polynomial correspond to the elements of the set. For a set $S_A = \{a_1, \ldots, a_n\}$, the corresponding polynomial is $p_A(x) = \prod_{i=1}^{n}(x - a_i)$. The degree $\deg(p_A)$ of the polynomial equals the set size n and since p_A is monic, it can be interpolated from n evaluation points. The main observation behind Minsky et al.'s protocol is that

$$p(x) := \frac{p_A(x)}{p_B(x)} = \frac{p_{A \setminus B}(x)}{p_{B \setminus A}(x)}$$

If we divide the two polynomials representing the sets, then the common factors of $p_A(x)$ and $p_B(x)$ cancel out and what remains is a rational function[1], where the numerator represents the elements exclusively contained in S_A and the denominator represents the elements only contained in S_B. It is straightforward to see that if S_A and S_B do not differ by more than $2t$ elements, that is if $|S_{A \setminus B}| + |S_{B \setminus A}| \leq 2t$, then $\deg(p) = \deg(p_{A \setminus B}) + \deg(p_{B \setminus A}) \leq 2t$ and we can interpolate p from $2t$ evaluation points via rational function interpolation[2].

---

[1] A rational function is the fraction of two polynomials. See Sect. 2.1 for details.
[2] See [MTZ03] for details on rational function interpolation over a field.

The second observation behind Minsky et al.'s protocol is that we can compute evaluation points of $p(x)$ from evaluation points of $p_A(x)$ and $p_B(x)$. To evaluate p at location α, both Alice and Bob first separately evaluate $p_A(x)$ and $p_B(x)$ at α and then jointly compute $p(\alpha) = \frac{p_A(\alpha)}{p_B(\alpha)}$.

Based on these observations the set union protocol by Minsky et al. roughly works as follows. Let us assume that we already know that the sets do not differ by more than $2t$ elements. First, both Alice and Bob encode their sets as polynomials as described above. Both parties separately evaluate their polynomials on some pre-agreed set of evaluation points $\{\alpha_1, \ldots, \alpha_{2t}\}$ to obtain $\{p_A(\alpha_1), \ldots, p_A(\alpha_{2t})\}$ and $\{p_B(\alpha_1), \ldots, p_B(\alpha_{2t})\}$. After exchanging their sets of polynomial evaluations, both parties use rational interpolation to compute the function $p(x) = \frac{p_{A \setminus B}(x)}{p_{B \setminus A}(x)}$. Given $p(x)$, for example Alice, learns the denominator $p_{B \setminus A}(x)$ and computes an encoding of the set union $p_{A \cup B}(x) = p_A(x) \cdot p_{B \setminus A}(x)$. Importantly for us we observe that apart from computing the set union, Alice can also compute the set intersection by computing $p_{A \cap B}(x) = \frac{p_A(x)}{p_{A \setminus B}(x)}$. The key observation here is that in order to compute the intersection, it is sufficient for Alice to learn which elements are exclusive to her set. In case of a "large" intersection, this quantity is much smaller than the size of the sets or the size of the intersection.

Given Minsky et al.'s protocol, one possible approach towards constructing a sublinear private set intersection protocol (for similar sets) would be to combine it with a generic protocol for secure two-party computation. Both parties input evaluation points of their polynomials, using a secure computation protocol we interpolate $p(x)$, and finally output $p_{A \setminus B}(x)$ and $p_{B \setminus A}(x)$ to Alice and Bob respectively. Unfortunately, this does not seem to result in a practically or asymptotically efficient protocol. In order to interpolate $p(x)$, one would have to perform a gaussian elimination inside the secure computation protocol. For a system of linear equations with $\mathcal{O}(t)$ unknowns, this requires $\mathcal{O}(t^3)$ operations.

We take a very different approach. We only make minimal use of generic secure computation to obtain "noisy" evaluation points of p. Using these points, Alice can then in plain interpolate a rational function $\frac{p_{A \setminus B}(x)}{U(x)}$, where $U(x)$ is a uniformly random polynomial. From this polynomial Alice can learn $p_{A \setminus B}(x)$ and therefore $p_{A \cap B}(x)$, but nothing else beyond that.

2   Preliminaries

Notation. Let λ be the computational and κ the statistical security parameter. For a set S, we write $v \leftarrow S$ to denote that v is chosen uniformly at random from S. For a possibly randomized algorithm A, we write $v \leftarrow A(x)$ to denote a run of A on input x that produces output v. For $n \in \mathbb{N}$, we write $[n] := \{1, 2, \ldots, n\}$. We write $|S|$ for the number of elements in S. We use $\tilde{\mathcal{O}}(\cdot)$ as a variant of the big-O notation that ignores polylog factors.

Sets. Throughout most of the paper we will assume that the sets of Alice and Bob are of equal size n. We show how to deal with sets of different sizes in Sect. 6.4. We assume that the set elements come from a field $\mathbb{F}_p$, where p is a $\Theta(\kappa)$-bit prime.

Size of the Intersection vs. Size of the Symmetric Set Difference. We will measure the "similarity" of two sets S_A and S_B in terms of size of their symmetric set difference. In some scenarios it may be more convenient to measure the similarity of two sets in terms of intersection size. These two measures are equivalent. A *lower* bound t_{min} on the intersection set size $|S_A \cap S_B|$, corresponds to a *upper* bound $t_{max} = 2(n - t_{min})$ on the size of the symmetric set difference $|(S_A \setminus S_B) \cup (S_B \setminus S_A)|$.

2.1 Linear Algebra

We recall some terminology and definitions from linear algebra.

Matrices. Let $\mathbb{F}_p^{k \times k}$ be the set of k-by-k square matrices with entries from $\mathbb{F}_p$. A matrix $M \in \mathbb{F}_p^{k \times k}$ is said to be invertible, if there exists a matrix M^{-1}, such that $M \cdot M^{-1} = I$, where I is the identity matrix. A matrix that is not invertible is called singular. A matrix M is singular if and only if it has determinant 0.

Polynomials. Let $p(x) = \sum_{i=0}^{n} a_i x^i$ be a polynomial. We call $\{a_0, \ldots, a_n x^n\}$ the monomials and $\{a_0, \ldots, a_n\}$ the coefficients of the polynomial. The degree $\deg(p)$ of a polynomial $p(x)$ is the the largest i, such that the monomial $a_i x^i \neq 0$. A polynomial is said to be monic if for $i = \deg(p)$, we have $a_i = 1$. We write $\mathbb{F}_p[X]$ to denote the set of polynomials with coefficients from the field $\mathbb{F}_p$. A polynomial $p(x) \in \mathbb{F}_p[X]$ of degree d is uniquely defined and can be efficiently interpolated form $d + 1$ evaluation points $\{(\alpha_1, p(\alpha_1)), \ldots, (\alpha_{d+1}, p(\alpha_{d+1}))\}$ via Lagrange interpolation. If $p(x)$ is monic, then d points suffice. A polynomial $h(x) = \frac{p(x)}{q(x)}$, where $p(x), q(x)$ are polynomials of degree n and m, is called a rational polynomial or rational function. It can be interpolated, uniquely up to constants, from $n + m + 1$ points [MTZ03]. If $p(x)$ and $q(x)$ are monic, then $n + m$ points suffice. A polynomial $p(x)$ is said to be ℓ-sparse if has at most ℓ monomials, i.e. if $|\{a_i x^i \mid a_i \neq 0\}| \leq \ell$.

Our main construction in Sect. 6 will make use of an observation about polynomials due to Kissner and Song [KS05]. For the sake of concreteness we restate their lemma[3] here in a slightly less general fashion, which is tailored to our needs.

Lemma 1 ([KS05]). *Let p be a prime. Let $p(x), q(x) \in \mathbb{F}_p[X]$ be polynomials of degree $d \leq t$ with $\gcd(p(x), q(x)) = 1$. Let $R_1(x), R_2(x) \in \mathbb{F}_p[X]$ be two uniformly random polynomials of degree t. Then $U(x) = p(x) \cdot R_1(x) + q(x) \cdot R_2(x)$ is a uniformly random polynomial of degree at most $2t$.*

---

[3] The lemma we are referring to here is Lemma 2 in the paper of Kissner and Song.

Another basic observation about polynomials that we will need, is captured in Lemma 2. Simply speaking it states that for some given polynomial $p(x)$ of degree d_p and some uniformly random polynomial $R(x)$ of degree d_R, the probability that the polynomials share a common root negligible in the statistical security parameter κ.

Lemma 2. *Let p be a $\Theta(\kappa)$-bit prime. Let $p(x) \in \mathbb{F}_p[X]$ be an arbitrary but fixed non-zero polynomial of degree at most d_p and let $R(x) \in \mathbb{F}_p[X]$ be a uniformly random polynomial of degree at most d_R. Then*

$$\Pr[\gcd(p(x), R(x)) \neq 1] \leq \mathsf{negl}(\kappa)$$

Proof (sketch). The gcd of $p(x)$ and $R(x)$ equals to one if and only if the two polynomials share no common roots. A uniformly random polynomial $R(x)$ of degree d_R has at most d_R roots, which are distributed uniformly at random. The probability of picking one random root that is not a root of $p(x)$ is $1 - \frac{d_p}{p}$. It follows that

$$\Pr[\gcd(p(x), R(x)) \neq 1] = 1 - \Pr[\gcd(p(x), R(x)) = 1]$$
$$= 1 - (1 - \frac{d_p}{p})^{d_R}$$
$$\leq \mathsf{negl}(\kappa)$$

2.2 Secure Two-Party Computation

Our security definitions are given in the universal composability (UC) framework of Canetti [Can01]. We provide a brief overview here and refer the reader to [MQU07, CDN15] for a more complete summary of the security model.

We consider a two-party protocol Π that is supposed to implement some ideal functionality $\mathcal{F}$. Security is defined by comparing two processes. In the real process the two parties execute the protocol Π. The protocol itself is allowed to make use of an idealized functionality $\mathcal{G}$. An environment $\mathcal{Z}$ chooses the inputs of all parties, it models everything that is external to the protocol, and it represents the adversary, who attacks the protocol. $\mathcal{Z}$ may corrupt a party and get access to that party's internal tapes. In the ideal process, two dummy parties send their inputs to the ideal functionality $\mathcal{F}$ and get back the output of the computation. In such an ideal process, a simulator $\mathcal{S}$, also known as the ideal world adversary, emulates $\mathcal{Z}$'s view of a real protocol execution. $\mathcal{S}$ has full control of the corrupted dummy party. $\mathcal{S}$ emulates $\mathcal{Z}$'s view of that party as well as its communication with $\mathcal{G}$. At the end of both executions $\mathcal{Z}$ outputs a single bit. Let $\mathsf{REAL}_\lambda[\mathcal{Z}, \Pi, \mathcal{G}]$, respectively $\mathsf{IDEAL}_\lambda[\mathcal{Z}, S, \mathcal{F}]$, be the random variable denoting $\mathcal{Z}$'s final output bit in the real, respectively ideal, process. We say Π securely implements $\mathcal{F}$, if no environment $\mathcal{Z}$ can distinguish whether it has been part of a real or ideal process.

Definition 1. *Π securely implements functionality $\mathcal{F}$ with respect to a class of environments Env in the $\mathcal{G}$-hybrid model, if there exists a simulator $\mathcal{S}$ such that for all $\mathcal{Z} \in$ Env we have*

$$|\Pr[\mathsf{REAL}_\lambda[\mathcal{Z}, \Pi, \mathcal{G}] = 1] - \Pr[\mathsf{IDEAL}_\lambda[\mathcal{Z}, S, \mathcal{F}] = 1]| \leq \mathsf{negl}(\lambda)$$

In this paper, we focus on static passive adversaries. We consider environments $\mathcal{Z}$ that get full read-only access to a corrupted party's internal tapes. The corrupted party follows the protocol honestly.

2.3   Additively Homomorphic Encryption

We recall the definition of additively homomorphic encryption and the associated IND-CPA security notion.

Definition 2 (Public Key Encryption Scheme). *A public key encryption scheme $\mathcal{E} = (\mathsf{KeyGen}, \mathsf{Enc}, \mathsf{Dec})$ consists of three algorithms:*

$\mathsf{KeyGen}(1^\lambda)$: *The key generation algorithm takes as input the security parameter 1^λ and outputs a key pair $(\mathsf{sk}, \mathsf{pk})$.*

$\mathsf{Enc}(\mathsf{pk}, m)$: *The encryption algorithm takes as input the public key pk, a message $m \in \mathcal{M}$, and outputs a ciphertext c.*

$\mathsf{Dec}(\mathsf{sk}, c)$: *The decryption algorithm takes as input the secret key sk, the ciphertext $c' \in \mathcal{C}$, and outputs a plaintext m.*

We say $\mathcal{E}$ is additively homomorphic if we can add encrypted values and multiply them by plaintext constants. Concretely, if there exist operations $\boxplus$ and $\boxdot$, such that for any $a, b \in \mathcal{M}$ and any two ciphertexts $c_1 = \mathsf{Enc}(\mathsf{pk}, m_1)$ and $c_2 = \mathsf{Enc}(\mathsf{pk}, m_2)$, it holds that $(a \boxdot c_1) \boxplus (b \boxdot c_2) = \mathsf{Enc}(\mathsf{pk}, a \cdot m_1 + b \cdot m_2)$. For the sake of simplicity and readability we will use the same notation for algebraic operations on the plaintext and algebraic operations on the ciphertext space. We assume that it will be clear from the context which one is meant. Possible instantiations of such a cryptosystem are the Paillier cryptosystem [Pai99] or its generalization the Damgård-Jurik cryptosystem [DJ01]. We will furthermore assume that the message space of the encryption scheme is a field[4].

Definition 3 (Indistinguishability under Chosen Plaintext Attacks). *Let $\mathcal{E} = (\mathsf{KeyGen}, \mathsf{Enc}, \mathsf{Dec})$ be a (homomorphic) encryption scheme and let $\mathcal{A}$ be a PPT adversary. We say $\mathcal{E}$ is IND-CPA-secure if for all PPT adversaries $\mathcal{A}$ it holds that*

---

[4] For the case of the Paillier cryptosystem this is strictly speaking not the case, since not every element from the message space has an inverse. However, finding an element that does not have an inverse is as hard as breaking the security of the cryptosystem. Therefore, we can treat the message space as if it was an actual field.

$$\Pr \left[b = b' : \begin{array}{c} (\mathsf{sk}, \mathsf{pk}) \leftarrow \mathsf{KeyGen}(1^\lambda) \\ (m_0, m_1) \leftarrow \mathcal{A}(\mathsf{pk}) \\ b \leftarrow \{0,1\} \\ c \leftarrow \mathsf{Enc}(\mathsf{pk}, m_b) \\ b' \leftarrow \mathcal{A}(c) \end{array} \right] \leq \frac{1}{2} + \mathsf{negl}(x)$$

$\mathcal{F}_{\mathrm{OLE}}$

The sender has input $(a, b) \in \mathbb{F}^2$ and the receiver has input $x \in \mathbb{F}$.

- Upon receiving a message $(\mathtt{inputS}, (a, b))$ from the sender with a, b, store a and b.
- Upon receiving a message $(\mathtt{inputR}, x)$ from the receiver with x, store x.
- Compute $y = a \cdot x + b$ and send $(\mathtt{output}, y)$ to the receiver.

Fig. 1. Oblivious linear function evaluation functionality.

2.4 Oblivious Linear Function Evaluation

Oblivious linear function evaluation allows a receiver to obliviously evaluate a linear function that is only known to the sender. Concretely, the sender has two input values $a, b \in \mathbb{F}$ that determine a linear function $f(x) = a \cdot x + b$ over $\mathbb{F}$ and the receiver holds input $x \in \mathbb{F}$. The receiver will learn only $f(x)$, and the sender learns nothing about the evaluation point x. The corresponding ideal functionality $\mathcal{F}_{\mathrm{OLE}}$ is depicted in Fig. 1. Several efficient instantiations, both in the passive and malicious settings, exist [NP99, IPS09, ADI+17, GNN17].

3   Lower and Upper Bounds

To provide a better understanding of what is possible and what is not, we present upper and a lower bounds for the communication complexity of threshold private set intersection protocols. We prove unconditionally that any threshold private set intersection protocol has to have a communication complexity of $\Omega(t)$, where t is an upper bound on the size of the symmetric set difference. We show how to obtain an almost matching upper bound of $\tilde{\mathcal{O}}(t)$ using fully homomorphic encryption [RAD78, Gen09, BGV12]. Due to its computational complexity, this bound seems to be mainly of theoretical interest. We sketch a construction based on simpler assumptions, namely garbled circuits [Yao86], with a communication complexity of $\tilde{\mathcal{O}}(t^3)$. In light of these results, our main protocol, which we will describe in the following sections, places itself in between those bounds. It has a communication complexity of $\tilde{\mathcal{O}}(t^2)$ and is thus asymptotically more efficient than the garbled circuit solution. It is based on weaker assumptions, namely additively homomorphic encryption, and is computationally more efficient than the construction based on fully homomorphic encryption. A visual illustration of these results can be found in Fig. 2.

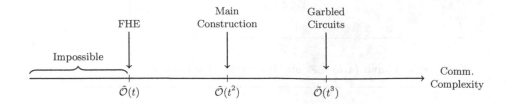

Fig. 2. An illustration what is possible and what is not in terms of communication complexity of threshold private intersection protocols. t is the upper bound on the symmetric set difference of the two sets.

Lower Bound for Threshold Private Set Intersection. To prove our lower bound for threshold private set intersection, we will make use of a known lower bound for the disjointness problem. In the disjointness problem, Alice and Bob hold two n-bit vectors a and b, and would like to compute the function

$$
\mathrm{Dis}(a, b) = \begin{cases} 0 & \text{if } \exists i : a_i = b_i = 1 \\ 1 & \text{Otherwise} \end{cases}
$$

A series of results [BFS86, KS92, Raz90, BYJKS04] have established that the communication complexity of this function is $\Theta(n)$. Freedman et al. [FNP04] observed that these results directly yield a lower bound of $\Omega(n)$ on the communication complexity of any set intersection protocol for sets of size n. We sketch how these results also provide a lower bound for threshold private set intersection. Assume towards contradiction that for sets of size n', which have an intersection of size at least $n' - t$, there exists a protocol Π that computes their intersection with communication complexity $o(t)$. We can use such a protocol to construct a private set intersection protocol for sets of size t with complexity $o(t)$ as follows. Assume Alice has input set S_A and Bob has input set S_B each of size t. The private set intersection protocol simply fixes a set S_D of $n' - t$ distinct dummy elements as part of the protocol description. Alice and Bob execute the threshold private set intersection protocol Π, where Alice uses $S_A \cup D$ and Bob uses $S_B \cup D$ as the input to Π. Since both parties use the same dummy elements, it is guaranteed that their inputs to Π have an intersection of size at least $n' - t$, which means that the protocol will always output the intersection $(S_A \cup S_D) \cap (S_B \cup S_D)$. From this output each party can locally compute $((S_A \cup S_D) \cap (S_B \cup S_D)) \setminus S_D = S_A \cap S_B$ to learn the desired intersection, which contradicts the lower bound of $\Omega(t)$ for computing the set intersection of S_A and

S_B. The lower bound for the communication complexity of threshold private set intersection follows.

Upper Bound from Fully Homomorphic Encryption. We sketch how to combine the set reconciliation protocol of Minsky et al. [MTZ03] with fully homomorphic encryption [RAD78, Gen09, BGV12] to obtain an almost matching upper bound of $\tilde{\mathcal{O}}(t)$. We provide a high-level description of the construction here and leave the details to the interested reader. Fully homomorphic encryption allows anyone to evaluate arbitrary circuits over encrypted data without being able to decrypt. Known instantiations are based on lattice based assumptions, such as learning with errors [BV11a] or the ring learning with errors [BV11b]. Fully homomorphic encryption leads to a conceptually very simple and communication efficient solution for general secure two party computation. Alice encrypts her data and sends it to Bob. Bob encrypts his data and homomorphically evaluates the desired function on their joint encrypted data. He sends back the result to Alice, who can decrypt the result of the computation. The communication complexity only depends on the size of the inputs and the size of the output, but importantly it does not depend on the size of the evaluated circuit.

Using fully homomorphic encryption, we let Alice and Bob execute a variation of Minsky et al.'s protocol. Alice encodes her set S_A as a polynomial $p_A(x) = \prod_{i=1}^{n}(x - a_i)$ and sends Bob encrypted evaluations $\{p_A(\alpha_1), \ldots, p_A(\alpha_{2t})\}$ as well as an additional encrypted evaluation $p_A(z)$ and the uniformly random z itself in the clear. Bob evaluates his set as a polynomial on the same points and then homomorphically interpolates the rational function $\frac{p_A(x)}{p_B(x)} = \frac{p_{A\backslash B}(x)}{p_{B\backslash A}(x)}$, where the gcd of numerator and denominator is 1, using the first $2t$ encrypted points to obtain a candidate polynomial p. Bob computes

$$(p(x), p_A(z), p_B(z), z) \mapsto \begin{cases} p_{A\backslash B}(x) & \text{if } p(z) = \frac{p_A(z)}{p_B(z)} \\ \bot & \text{Otherwise} \end{cases}$$

on the encrypted data and sends back the result to Alice. The correctness of this approach directly follows from the correctness of Minsky et al.'s protocol. Security follows from the security of fully homomorphic encryption. The total communication consists of Alice sending $2t + 1$ ciphertexts to Bob and him sending the coefficients of the polynomial in the numerator, i.e. t ciphertexts, to Alice. Assuming the ciphertexts are larger than the corresponding plaintexts by at most a multiplicative constant and assuming that the set elements are drawn from $\mathbb{F}_p$, we can conclude that the total communication complexity is $\mathcal{O}(t \log p)$ bits. Despite its nice communication complexity, this solution has two drawbacks. From a theoretical perspective, it relies on fully homomorphic encryption and thus can only be instantiated from lattice based assumptions. From a practical perspective, it does not seem to be anywhere near practical due to the fact that one has to homomorphically perform a rational polynomial interpolation on the ciphertexts, which leads to a high computational complexity.

Using Garbled Circuits. A simple, but asymptotically inefficient solution based on one-way functions and oblivious transfer can be obtained by using garbled circuits [Yao86] instead of fully homomorphic encryption. For garbled circuits, the communication complexity corresponds to the size of the circuit that is being evaluated. Following the same approach as above, the size of the circuit is dominated by the rational interpolation logic. Using gaussian elimination this step requires $\mathcal{O}(t^3)$ operations, which leads to a total communication complexity of at least $\tilde{\mathcal{O}}(t^3)$ bits.

4   Intersection Cardinality Testing

An important building block for our threshold private set intersection protocol in Sect. 6, is a intersection cardinality testing protocol, which enables two parties to check whether their sets differ by more than a given threshold $2t$ with communication complexity $\tilde{\mathcal{O}}(t)$. We present a non-private solution based on polynomial sparsity testing here and show how to obtain a privacy-preserving version thereof in Sect. 5. We believe that the non-private as well as the private intersection cardinality test may be of independent interest.

From a conceptual perspective, our protocol is very simple. It is basically a direct application of the polynomial sparsity test of Grigorescu et al. [GJR10] to an appropriate encoding of sets as polynomials. We encode a set $S_A = \{a_1, \ldots, a_n\}$ as a polynomial $p_A(x) = \sum_{i=1}^{n} x^{a_i}$. The main idea behind this encoding is that the sparsity of the polynomial $p_A(x) - p_B(x)$ corresponds to the size of the symmetric set difference of S_A and S_B. The protocol Π_{ICT}^{2t} is described in Fig. 3.

Theorem 1. *Let S_A and S_B be subsets of $\mathbb{F}_p$. Let $q > (4t^2 + 2t)(p-1)2^\kappa$ be a prime power. Π_{ICT}^{2t} has a communication overhead of $4t + 1$ field elements from $\mathbb{F}_q$. If $|S_{A\backslash B}| + |S_{B\backslash A}| \leq 2t$, then $\Pr[\Pi_{ICT}^{2t}$ outputs* similar$] = 1$ *and if $|S_{A\backslash B}| + |S_{B\backslash A}| > 2t$, then $\Pr[\Pi_{ICT}^{2t}$ outputs* similar$] \leq 1 - 2^{-\kappa}$.*

Proof. The original algorithm of Grigorescu et al. [GJR10] takes an arbitrary polynomial p as its input, computes the corresponding Hankel matrix H, and then computes the determinant thereof. We essentially directly apply their algorithm to the polynomial $p_C(x) = p_A(x) - p_B(x)$. We exploit the fact that we can compute the Hankel matrix H_C of $p_C(x)$ by first computing the Hankel matrices H_A and H_B. The correctness and the parameters of the randomized polynomial sparsity testing protocol directly follow from the test of Grigorescu et al.[5]

It remains to show that the sparsity of the computed polynomial does indeed reflect the size of the symmetric set difference. If S_A and S_B have an intersection of size k, then the polynomial $p_A(x) - p_B(x)$ will have exactly $2(n-k)$ monomials. Thus, if $|S_{A\backslash B}| + |S_{B\backslash A}| < 2t$, then $k > n - t$ and therefore $p_A(x) - p_B(x)$ will be a $2t$-sparse polynomial.   □

---

[5] See Theorem 3 in their work.

$$\Pi_{\text{ICT}}^{2t}$$

Alice and Bob have as input set $S_A = \{a_1, \ldots, a_n\} \in \mathbb{F}_p^n$ and $S_B = \{b_1, \ldots, b_n\} \in \mathbb{F}_p^n$ respectively.

Protocol:

1. Alice and Bob encode their sets as polynomials $p_A(x) = \sum_{i=1}^n x^{a_i}$ and $p_B(x) = \sum_{i=1}^n x^{b_i}$ in $\mathbb{F}_q[X]$.
2. Alice picks uniformly random $u \leftarrow \mathbb{F}_q$.
3. Alice computes the Hankel matrix

$$H_A = \begin{bmatrix} p_A(u^0) & p_A(u^1) & \cdots & p_A(u^{2t}) \\ p_A(u^1) & p_A(u^2) & \cdots & p_A(u^{2t+1}) \\ \vdots & \vdots & \ddots & \vdots \\ p_A(u^{2t}) & p_A(u^{2t+1}) & \cdots & p_A(u^{4t}) \end{bmatrix}$$

   and sends it along with u to Bob.
4. Bob, using his own Hankel matrix H_B, computes $H_C = H_A - H_B$.
5. If $\det(H_C) = 0$, then Bob outputs `similar`, otherwise he outputs `different`.

Fig. 3. Protocol for intersection cardinality testing based on the polynomial sparsity testing protocol of Grigorescu et al. [GJR10].

Efficiency. To get a better idea of what this theorem means in terms of concrete efficiency, it is worth looking at some common real world parameter settings. For instance, for sets of 64-bit integers, a statistical security parameter $\kappa = 40$, and a threshold t of size at most 2^{20}, we roughly require a 128-bit modulus q.

5   Private Intersection Cardinality Testing

We obtain a privacy-preserving version of the intersection cardinality test from Sect. 4 via a combination of homomorphic encryption and the matrix singularity test due to Kiltz et al. [KMWF07]. The singularity test enables Alice, who holds a encrypted matrix over a finite field, and Bob, who holds the decryption key, to test whether the matrix is singular or not. Recall, that a matrix being singular and it having determinant 0 are equivalent statements. Let $\mathcal{F}_{\text{INV}}$ be the corresponding ideal functionality, which either returns `singular` or `invertible`. Kiltz et al. show how to securely and efficiently implement such a functionality using additively homomorphic encryption.

Theorem 2 ([KMWF07]). *Let $M \in \mathbb{F}_q^{k \times k}$ be the encrypted matrix. Assuming* IND-CPA*-secure additively homomorphic encryption, the ideal functionality $\mathcal{F}_{\text{INV}}$ can be realized securely with communication complexity $\mathcal{O}(k^2 \log q \log k)$ in*

$\mathcal{O}(\log k)$ *rounds with security against a passive adversary. The protocol is correct with probability* $1 - \frac{k+1}{q}$, *which for a q chosen as in Theorem 1 is overwhelming in κ.*

For our choice of q (see Theorem 1) the protocol of Kiltz et al. fails with negligible (in κ) probability. In the following, for the sake of simplicity, we will assume that the corresponding ideal functionality $\mathcal{F}_{\mathrm{INV}}$ has perfect correctness. All of our protocols and proofs trivially extend to the case, where the ideal functionality errs with a negligible probability.

5.1   Ideal Functionality

The ideal functionality $\mathcal{F}_{\mathrm{PICT}}^{2t}$ for private intersection cardinality testing is depicted in Fig. 4. Alice and Bob send their input sets S_A and S_B to the ideal functionality, which checks whether the sets differ by more than $2t$ elements. It outputs **different** if this is the case and it outputs **similar** otherwise. Note that our ideal functionality is size hiding in the sense that the environment $\mathcal{Z}$ does not learn the size of the input sets of Alice or Bob.

$$\mathcal{F}_{\mathrm{PICT}}^{2t}$$

Alice and Bob have as input set S_A and S_B respectively.

- Upon receiving message $(\mathtt{inputA}, S_\mathrm{A})$ from Alice, store S_A.
- Upon receiving message $(\mathtt{inputB}, S_\mathrm{B})$ from Bob, store S_B.
- If $|(S_\mathrm{A} \setminus S_\mathrm{B}) \cup (S_\mathrm{B} \setminus S_\mathrm{A})| \leq 2t$, then the functionality outputs **similar**, otherwise **different**, to Alice and Bob.

Fig. 4. Ideal functionality for private intersection cardinality testing.

5.2   Protocol

Our private intersection cardinality test Π_{PICT}^{2t} closely follows its non-private counterpart Π_{ICT}^{2t} from Sect. 4. The main difference is that we now encrypt the Hankel matrix of Alice before sending it to Bob. Upon receiving Alice's encrypted matrix, Bob exploits the homomorphic properties of the encryption scheme to compute the Hankel matrix that corresponds to the polynomial encoding of the symmetric set difference. Using $\mathcal{F}_{\mathrm{INV}}$, Bob learns whether the matrix is singular or invertible and thus learns, whether the intersection of the two sets is large enough. The protocol Π_{PICT}^{2t} is depicted in Fig. 5.

$$\Pi_{\text{PICT}}^{2t}$$

Alice and Bob have as input set $S_A = \{a_1, \ldots, a_n\} \in \mathbb{F}_p^n$ and $S_B = \{b_1, \ldots, b_n\} \in \mathbb{F}_p^n$ respectively.

Protocol:

1. Alice and Bob encode their sets as polynomials $p_A(x) = \sum_{i=1}^n x^{a_i}$ and $p_B(x) = \sum_{i=1}^n x^{b_i}$ in $\mathbb{F}_q[X]$.
2. Alice picks uniformly random $u \leftarrow \mathbb{F}_q$.
3. Alice samples an encryption key $(\mathsf{sk}, \mathsf{pk}) \leftarrow \mathsf{KeyGen}(1^\lambda)$ and computes an encrypted version of her Hankel matrix

$$H_A = \begin{bmatrix} c_0 & c_1 & \cdots & c_{2t} \\ c_1 & c_2 & \cdots & c_{2t+1} \\ \vdots & \vdots & \ddots & \vdots \\ c_{2t} & c_{2t+1} & \cdots & c_{4t} \end{bmatrix}$$

where $c_i \leftarrow \mathsf{Enc}(pk, p_A(u^i))$.
4. Alice sends H_A, u, and pk to Bob.
5. Bob computes his own encrypted Hankel matrix H_B and computes $H_C = H_A - H_B$.
6. Alice sends sk and Bob sends H_C to the ideal functionality $\mathcal{F}_{\text{INV}}$.
7. If Bob gets back $\mathtt{singular}$ from $\mathcal{F}_{\text{INV}}$, then he sends $\mathtt{similar}$ to Alice and outputs $\mathtt{similar}$ himself, otherwise he sends and outputs $\mathtt{different}$.

Fig. 5. Protocol for private intersection cardinality testing.

5.3 Security

Theorem 3. *Let q be as in Theorem 1. Let $\mathcal{E} = (\mathsf{KeyGen}, \mathsf{Enc}, \mathsf{Dec})$ be a IND-CPA secure additively homomorphic encryption scheme. Then Π_{PICT}^{2t} securely implements $\mathcal{F}_{\text{PICT}}^{2t}$ in the $\mathcal{F}_{\text{INV}}$-hybrid model with security against a passive adversary and overwhelming (in κ) correctness.*

Proof. Either Alice or Bob can be corrupted. We consider the two cases separately.

Alice Corrupt. In this case, security holds trivially. The environment corrupting Alice learns nothing beyond the input and output of the computation.

Bob Corrupt. The simulator $\mathcal{S}$ sends Bob's input to the ideal functionality and obtains $\mathsf{result} \in \{\mathsf{similar}, \mathsf{different}\}$. $\mathcal{S}$ picks a uniformly random $u \leftarrow \mathbb{F}_q$ and samples an encryption key $(\mathsf{sk}, \mathsf{pk}) \leftarrow \mathsf{KeyGen}(1^\lambda)$. It computes $c_i \leftarrow \mathsf{Enc}(pk, 0)$ for $0 \leq i \leq 4t$.

$$H_A = \begin{bmatrix} c_0 & c_1 & \cdots & c_{2t} \\ c_1 & c_2 & \cdots & c_{2t+1} \\ \vdots & \vdots & \ddots & \vdots \\ c_{2t} & c_{2t+1} & \cdots & c_{4t} \end{bmatrix}$$

The simulator leaks u, pk, and H_A to $\mathcal{Z}$. At this point Bob would send some matrix H_C to the ideal functionality $\mathcal{F}_{\text{INV}}$, which is also simulated by $\mathcal{S}$. If result = similar, then the simulator leaks singular to $\mathcal{Z}$. Otherwise the simulator leaks invertible. The only difference between the environment's view in a real and a simulated protocol execution is the matrix H_A. In a real execution it contains encrypted evaluations of Alice's polynomial. In the simulated execution it contains encryptions of 0. Indistinguishability of the real and ideal process follows directly from the IND-CPA security of the encryption scheme.   □

Instantiating $\mathcal{F}_{\text{INV}}$ in Π_{PICT}^{2t} with the singularity test of Kiltz et al. [KMWF07], results in a protocol with a communication complexity of $\tilde{\mathcal{O}}(t^2)$ in the plain model.

Lemma 3. *The communication complexity of Π_{PICT}^{2t} is $\tilde{\mathcal{O}}(t^2)$ in the plain model.*

6   Threshold Private Set Intersection

In this section we present our threshold private set intersection protocol, which proceeds as follows. First, Alice and Bob use $\mathcal{F}_{\text{PICT}}^{2t}$ to determine whether their sets differ by more than $2t$ elements. If the ideal functionality outputs different, the parties output $\perp$. If it outputs similar, the parties engage in a secure set intersection protocol, which has a communication complexity of $\tilde{\mathcal{O}}(t)$ bits.

6.1   Ideal Functionality

The ideal functionality $\mathcal{F}_{\text{TPSI}}^{2t}$ for threshold private set intersection is depicted in Fig. 6. Alice and Bob send their input sets S_A and S_B to the ideal functionality, which checks whether the sets differ by more than $2t$ elements. If this is the case, the functionality returns $\perp$ to both parties. If this is not the case, the functionality returns the set intersection $S_A \cap S_B$ to both Alice and Bob.

6.2   Protocol

Our protocol loosely follows the approach of Minsky et al.'s [MTZ03] set reconciliation protocol. Assume that the sets of Alice and Bob do not differ by more than t elements. Both Alice and Bob encode their sets as polynomials over a field, where the roots of the polynomials are the elements of the corresponding set. Let $p_A(x) = \prod_{i=1}^{n}(x - a_i)$ and $p_B(x) = \prod_{i=1}^{n}(x - b_i)$ be those polynomials.

$$\mathcal{F}_{\text{TPSI}}^{2t}$$

Alice and Bob have as input sets S_A and S_B respectively.

- Upon receiving message $(\texttt{inputA}, S_A)$ from Alice, store S_A and leak $(\texttt{inputA}, |S_A|)$ to the environment $\mathcal{Z}$.
- Upon receiving message $(\texttt{inputB}, S_B)$ from Bob, store S_B and leak $(\texttt{inputB}, |S_B|)$ to the environment $\mathcal{Z}$.
- If $|(S_A \setminus S_B) \cup (S_B \setminus S_A)| \leq 2t$, then the functionality outputs $A \cap B$, otherwise $\perp$, to Alice and Bob.

Fig. 6. Threshold private set intersection functionality.

Ideally, we would like to directly apply Minsky et al.'s protocol to interpolate $\mathsf{p}(x) = \frac{\mathsf{p}_B(x)}{\mathsf{p}_A(x)} = \frac{\mathsf{p}_{B \setminus A}(x)}{\mathsf{p}_{A \setminus B}(x)}$ from which both Alice and Bob could compute the intersection of their sets. For example, Alice could extract[6] $\mathsf{p}_{A \setminus B}(x)$ from $\mathsf{p}(x)$ and compute the intersection function as $\frac{\mathsf{p}_A(x)}{\mathsf{p}_{A \setminus B}(x)}$. Unfortunately, Alice would learn more information than she should, since she could also simply extract $\mathsf{p}_{B \setminus A}(x)$ and learn Bob's entire set.

As discussed before, one possible solution is to use generic secure two-party computation for interpolating p and separating the numerator and denominator. Due to the complexity of the computational task, this does not seem to result in a asymptotically or practically efficient solution. Our protocol takes a different approach and only makes minimal use of generic secure two-party computation. We only use it to transform evaluation points of p into a noisy versions thereof. Using these noisy evaluation points, Alice and Bob can perform the interpolation in plain to compute the set intersection without learning the other party's input.

In our construction, we will make use of a noisy polynomial addition functionality functionality $\mathcal{F}_{\text{NPA}}^{(3t+1,\,t)}$, which takes the polynomials $\mathsf{p}_A(x)$ and $\mathsf{p}_B(x)$ of Alice and Bob as its input and outputs noisy evaluation points $\{\mathsf{V}(\alpha_1), \ldots, \mathsf{V}(\alpha_{3t+1})\}$, where $\mathsf{V}(x) = \mathsf{p}_A(x) \cdot \mathsf{R}_1(x) + \mathsf{p}_B(x) \cdot \mathsf{R}_2(x)$. The polynomials R_1 and R_2 are uniformly random polynomials of degree t. We show how to efficiently instantiate this functionality with communication complexity $\tilde{\mathcal{O}}(t)$ in Sect. 7. Our protocol is presented in Fig. 7.

6.3 Security

Theorem 4. *Protocol* Π_{TPSI}^{2t} *securely implements* $\mathcal{F}_{\text{TPSI}}^{2t}$ *in the* $(\mathcal{F}_{\text{PICT}}^{2t},$ $\mathcal{F}_{\text{NPA}}^{(3t+1,\,t)})$-*hybrid model with security against a passive adversary.*

---

[6] separating the numerator and denominator from a given rational function is easy here, because we obtain the coefficients of both separately during the interpolation step.

$$\Pi_{\mathrm{TPSI}}^{2t}$$

Alice and Bob have as input set $S_\mathsf{A} = \{a_1, \ldots, a_n\} \in \mathbb{F}_p^n$ and $S_\mathsf{B} = \{b_1, \ldots, b_n\} \in \mathbb{F}_p^n$ respectively.

The values $\alpha_1, \ldots, \alpha_{3t+1} \in \mathbb{F}_p$ are fixed and publicly known.

Protocol:

1. Alice and Bob send S_A and S_B to $\mathcal{F}_{\mathrm{PICT}}^{2t}$.
2. If $\mathcal{F}_{\mathrm{PICT}}^{2t}$ returns **different**, both parties output $\perp$.
3. Alice and Bob encode their sets as polynomials $\mathsf{p_A}(x) = \prod_{i=1}^n (x - a_i)$ and $\mathsf{p_B}(x) = \prod_{i=1}^n (x - b_i)$.
4. Alice and Bob send $\mathsf{p_A}(x)$ and $\mathsf{p_B}(x)$ to $\mathcal{F}_{\mathrm{NPA}}^{(3t+1,\,t)}$.
5. Both receive evaluation points $(\mathsf{V}(\alpha_1), \ldots, \mathsf{V}(\alpha_{3t+1}))$, where $\mathsf{V}(\alpha_i) = \mathsf{p_A}(\alpha_i) \cdot \mathsf{R}_1(\alpha_i) + \mathsf{p_B}(\alpha_i) \cdot \mathsf{R}_2(\alpha_i)$ and $\mathsf{R}_1, \mathsf{R}_2$ are uniformly random polynomials of degree t.
6. Alice computes $\mathsf{p}(\alpha_i) = \frac{\mathsf{V}(\alpha_i)}{\mathsf{p_A}(\alpha_i)} = \frac{\mathsf{U}(\alpha_i)}{\mathsf{p_{A\backslash B}}(\alpha_i)}$ for each $i \in [3t+1]$ and interpolates p with gcd of numerator and denominator being 1 from these points.
7. Alice performs the following steps (Bob works analogously):
   (a) Alice sets $S_{\mathsf{A}\cap\mathsf{B}} := S_\mathsf{A}$.
   (b) For each $a_i \in S_\mathsf{A}$, if $\mathsf{p_{A\backslash B}}(a_i) = 0$, Alices removes a_i from $S_{\mathsf{A}\cap\mathsf{B}}$.
   (c) Alice outputs $S_{\mathsf{A}\cap\mathsf{B}}$.

Fig. 7. Protocol for securely computing the intersection of two sets that do not differ by more than $2t$ points.

Proof. We first show that our protocol indeed produces the correct result and we then go on to prove its security.

Correctness. If S_A and S_B differ by more than $2t$ elements, then both parties output $\perp$ and terminate in step 2 of the protocol. If on the other hand $|(S_\mathsf{A} \backslash S_\mathsf{B}) \cup (S_\mathsf{B} \backslash S_\mathsf{A})| \leq 2t$, then since $|S_\mathsf{A}| = |S_\mathsf{B}|$, it follows that $|(S_\mathsf{A} \backslash S_\mathsf{B})| \leq t$ and $|(S_\mathsf{B} \backslash S_\mathsf{A})| \leq t$. Alice computes polynomial

$$
\begin{aligned}
\mathsf{p}(\alpha_i) = \frac{\mathsf{V}(\alpha_i)}{\mathsf{p_A}(\alpha_i)} &= \frac{\mathsf{p_A}(\alpha_i) \cdot \mathsf{R}_1(\alpha_i) + \mathsf{p_B}(\alpha_i) \cdot \mathsf{R}_2(\alpha_i)}{\mathsf{p_A}(\alpha_i)} \\
&= \frac{\mathsf{p_{A\cap B}}(\alpha_i) \cdot \mathsf{p_{A\backslash B}}(\alpha_i) \cdot \mathsf{R}_1(\alpha_i) + \mathsf{p_{A\cap B}}(\alpha_i) \cdot \mathsf{p_{B\backslash A}}(\alpha_i) \cdot \mathsf{R}_2(\alpha_i)}{\mathsf{p_{A\cap B}}(\alpha_i) \cdot \mathsf{p_{A\backslash B}}(\alpha_i)} \\
&= \frac{\mathsf{p_{A\backslash B}}(\alpha_i) \cdot \mathsf{R}_1(\alpha_i) + \mathsf{p_{B\backslash A}}(\alpha_i) \cdot \mathsf{R}_2(\alpha_i)}{\mathsf{p_{A\backslash B}}(\alpha_i)}
\end{aligned}
$$

The numerator is a polynomial of degree at most $2t$ and the denominator is a polynomial of degree at most t. It follows that she can interpolate $\mathsf{p}(x)$ from $3t+1$ points. The polynomial in the denominator encodes the elements that are only in Alice's set and thus she can learn the intersection by removing those elements from her set S_A. By Lemma 2 we are certain that, with overwhelming probability, no root in the denominator $p_{A\backslash B}$ will be cancelled out by accident from the remaining random numerator.

Security. We assume that Alice is corrupt. The proof, where Bob is corrupt is completely symmetrical. The simulator sends Alice's input set to the ideal functionality $\mathcal{F}_{\text{TPSI}}^{2t}$ and either obtains result $= \perp$ or the intersection result $= S_{A\cap B}$. In the first step of the protocol, Alice would send her set S_A to the ideal functionality $\mathcal{F}_{\text{PICT}}^{2t}$, which is simulated by the simulator $\mathcal{S}$. If result $= \perp$, then $\mathcal{S}$ returns different as the ideal functionality's answer to $\mathcal{Z}$. Otherwise, $\mathcal{S}$ answers with similar. In case the protocol did not terminate, Alice would continue by sending $p_A(x)$ to $\mathcal{F}_{\text{NPA}}^{(3t+1,\,t)}$. At this point, the simulator needs to construct a polynomial $V(x)$ for responding to Alice's query. In a real protocol execution the polynomial would be

$$V(x) = p_{A\cap B}(x) \underbrace{\left(p_{A\backslash B}(x) \cdot R_1(x) + p_{B\backslash A}(x) \cdot R_2(x) \right)}_{U(x):=}$$

Since $|S_A| = |S_B|$, it follows that $|S_{A\backslash B}| = |S_{B\backslash A}|$ and thus $\deg(p_{A\backslash B}) = \deg(p_{B\backslash A})$. Furthermore, we know that $\deg(p_{A\backslash B}(x)) = |S_A| - |S_{A\cap B}|$. From these observations we can conclude that the degree of $\deg(U) = |S_A| - |S_{A\cap B}| + t$. The simulator $\mathcal{S}$ picks a uniformly random polynomial $U(x)$ of that degree and for $1 \leq i \leq 3t+1$, it computes the polynomial evaluations $V(\alpha_i) = U(\alpha_i) \cdot p_{A\cap B}(\alpha_i)$ and leaks them to $\mathcal{Z}$ as the output of $\mathcal{F}_{\text{NPA}}^{(3t+1,\,t)}$. The environment's view in a real and in a simulated process only differs in the way we choose the polynomial $V(x)$. We know that $\deg(p_{A\backslash B}) = \deg(p_{B\backslash A}) \leq t$, that $\gcd(p_{A\backslash B}, p_{B\backslash A}) = 1$, and that $\deg(R_1) = \deg(R_2) = t$. Indistinguishability of the real and the simulated process directly follows from Lemma 1. $\qquad\square$

When instantiating the hybrids we use in Π_{TPSI}^{2t} with the protocols from Sects. 5 and 7, then we obtain a protocol with communication complexity $\tilde{\mathcal{O}}(t^2)$. To reduce the communication complexity of our Π_{TPSI}^{2t} protocol to $\tilde{\mathcal{O}}(t)$, it suffices to reduce the communication complexity of Π_{PICT}^{2t} from $\tilde{\mathcal{O}}(t^2)$ to $\tilde{\mathcal{O}}(t)$. Thus, in this context, our work reduces the problem of communication efficient threshold private set intersection to that of communication efficient private intersection cardinality testing.

Lemma 4. *The communication complexity of Π_{TPSI}^{2t} is $\tilde{\mathcal{O}}(t^2)$ in the plain model.*

6.4   Dealing with Sets of Different Sizes

Throughout the paper we have so far assumed that the sets of Alice and Bob are of the same size. This was done for the sake of simplicity, but is not necessary in general. Consider two sets S_A and S_B, where, without loss of generality, we assume that $|S_B| > |S_A|$. Independently of their actual intersection size, the symmetric set difference of the two sets will be at least $t_{\min} := |S_B| - |S_A|$. This means that the threshold parameter t in our privacy-preserving protocols would need to be at least t_{min}. Since the set sizes are known, we can simply pad S_A to the size of S_B with dummy elements and adapt our difference threshold to $t_{new} := t + |S_B| - |S_A| \leq 2t$ accordingly. The simple approach of padding the smaller set to the size of the larger one would thus increase the communication complexity of our protocols by at most a small constant factor. The relation between the size of the symmetric set difference and total set sizes is illustrated in Fig. 8.

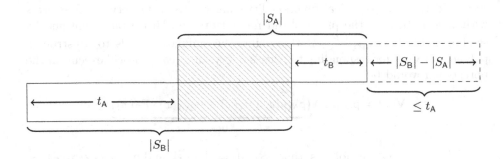

Fig. 8. An illustration of how the size of the symmetric set difference behaves for sets of different sizes. The set intersection between the sets S_A and S_B is indicated by the shaded gray area. The size of the symmetric set difference ($S_{A\setminus B} \cup S_{B\setminus A}$) is $t_A + t_B$. The dotted rectangle on the right illustrates the amount of padding we would have to perform to make the two sets be of the same size. Padding S_A to the size of S_B would increase the symmetric set difference by at most t_A.

7   Noisy Polynomial Addition

We show how to efficiently instantiate the noisy polynomial addition functionality $\mathcal{F}_{NPA}^{\ell, t}$ from Sect. 6 using oblivious linear function evaluation.

7.1   Ideal Functionality

The ideal functionality $\mathcal{F}_{NPA}^{\ell, t}$, depicted in Fig. 9, for noisy polynomial addition takes polynomials $p_A(x)$ and $p_B(x)$ of degree n from Alice and Bob as input, and returns back ℓ evaluation points of $p_A(x) \cdot R_1(x) + p_B(x) \cdot R_2(x)$, where $R_1(x)$ and $R_2(x)$ are uniformly random polynomials of degree t.

7.2   Protocol

Our starting point is a protocol by Ghosh and Nilges [GN17], which implements a very similar functionality in the $\mathcal{F}_{OLE}$-hybrid model. In their protocol the sender inputs a polynomial $p_A(x)$ and random polynomial $R(x)$, the receiver inputs a

---

$$\mathcal{F}_{\mathrm{NPA}}^{\ell,\,t}$$

Alice and Bob have inputs $p_A(x)$ and $p_B(x)$ of degree n.
Let $\{\alpha_1,\ldots,\alpha_\ell\}$ be a set of publicly known distinct points in $\mathbb{F}$.

- Upon receiving message $(\texttt{inputS}, p_A(x))$ from Alice, where $p_A(x) \in \mathbb{F}[X]$, store the polynomial $p_A(x)$.
- Upon receiving message $(\texttt{inputR}, p_B(x))$ from Bob, where $p_B(x) \in \mathbb{F}[X]$, store polynomial $p_B(x)$.
- Once both parties have submitted their polynomials, pick uniformly random polynomials $R_1(x), R_2(x) \in \mathbb{F}[X]$ of degree t and set $p(x) = p_A(x) \cdot R_1(x) + p_B(x) \cdot R_2(x)$.
- Send ℓ evaluation points $\{p(\alpha_1), \cdots, p(\alpha_\ell)\}$ to Alice and Bob.

Fig. 9. Noisy polynomial addition functionality.

polynomial $p_B(x)$ and gets back a noisy polynomial $p_A(x) + R(x) \cdot p_B(x)$. We use a modified version of their protocol to instantiate our $\mathcal{F}_{\mathrm{NPA}}^{\ell,\,t}$ functionality.

In our protocol, both Alice and Bob evaluate their input polynomials on the evaluation points $\{\alpha_1,\ldots,\alpha_\ell\}$. Alice picks two uniformly random polynomials $R_1^A(x), R_2^A(x)$ of degree t and a random polynomial $U_A(x)$ of degree ℓ. Bob picks two random polynomials $R_1^B(x), R_2^B(x)$ of degree t and a random polynomial $U_B(x)$ of degree ℓ. Now Alice and Bob will invoke the $\mathcal{F}_{\mathrm{OLE}}$ ideal functionality 2ℓ times, where Alice will act as the receiver in the first ℓ and as the sender in the last ℓ invocations. In the first ℓ instances, for each $i \in [\ell]$, Alice inputs evaluation points $p_A(\alpha_i)$, Bob inputs $(R_1^B(\alpha_i), U_B(\alpha_i))$, and Alice receives back $s_A(\alpha_i) = p_A(\alpha_i) \cdot R_1^B(\alpha_i) + U_B(\alpha_i)$. In the next ℓ instances, for each $i \in [\ell]$, Bob inputs $p_B(\alpha_i)$, Alice inputs $(R_2^A(\alpha_i), U_A(\alpha_i))$, and Bob receives back $s_B(\alpha_i) = p_B \cdot R_2^A(\alpha_i) + U_A(\alpha_i)$. For each $i \in [\ell]$, Alice sends $s_A'(\alpha_i) = s_A(\alpha_i) + p_A(\alpha_i) \cdot R_1^A(\alpha_i) - U_A(\alpha_i)$ to Bob, who can then compute

$$
\begin{aligned}
p_A(\alpha_i) \cdot R_1(\alpha_i) + p_B \cdot R_2(\alpha_i) &:= \\
s_B(\alpha_i) + s_A'(\alpha_i) + p_B(\alpha_i) \cdot R_2^B(\alpha_i) - U_B(\alpha_i) &= \\
p_A(\alpha_i) \cdot \left(R_1^A(\alpha_i) + R_1^B(\alpha_i)\right) + p_B \cdot \left(R_2^A(\alpha_i) + R_2^B(\alpha_i)\right)
\end{aligned}
$$

In a completely symmetrical fashion, Bob sends $s_B'(\alpha_i) = s_B(\alpha_i) + p_B(\alpha_i) \cdot R_1^B(\alpha_i) - U_B(\alpha_i)$ to Alice, who can then compute the same evaluation points of their noisy polynomial addition $p_A(\alpha_i) \cdot R_1(\alpha_i) + p_B \cdot R_2(\alpha_i)$. Our protocol is described formally in Fig. 10.

Theorem 5. $\Pi_{\mathrm{NPA}}^{\ell,\,t}$ *implements* $\mathcal{F}_{\mathrm{NPA}}^{\ell,\,t}$ *in the* $\mathcal{F}_{\mathrm{OLE}}$*-hybrid model with security against a passive adversary.*

$$\Pi_{\mathrm{NPA}}^{\ell,\, t}$$

Let $\{\alpha_1, \ldots, \alpha_\ell\}$ be a set of publicly known distinct points in $\mathbb{F}_p$. Alice and Bob have inputs $\mathsf{p}_\mathsf{A}(x) \in \mathbb{F}_p[X]$ and $\mathsf{p}_\mathsf{B}(x) \in \mathbb{F}_p[X]$ of degree n each.

Protocol:

1. Alice picks $\mathsf{R}_1^\mathsf{A}(x), \mathsf{R}_2^\mathsf{A}(x) \in \mathbb{F}_p[X]$ of degree t and $\mathsf{U}_\mathsf{A}(x) \in \mathbb{F}_p[X]$ of degree ℓ uniformly at random.
2. Bob picks $\mathsf{R}_1^\mathsf{B}(x), \mathsf{R}_2^\mathsf{B}(x) \in \mathbb{F}_p[X]$ of degree t and $\mathsf{U}_\mathsf{B}(x) \in \mathbb{F}[X]$ of degree ℓ uniformly at random.
3. For each $i \in [\ell]$
   - Alice sends $(\mathtt{inputR}, \mathsf{p}_\mathsf{A}(\alpha_i))$ to $\mathcal{F}_{\mathrm{OLE}}$.
   - Bob sends $(\mathtt{inputS}, (\mathsf{R}_1^\mathsf{B}(\alpha_i), \mathsf{U}_\mathsf{B}(\alpha_i)))$ to $\mathcal{F}_{\mathrm{OLE}}$.
   - Alice receives back $\mathsf{s}_\mathsf{A}(\alpha_i) = \mathsf{p}_\mathsf{A}(\alpha_i) \cdot \mathsf{R}_1^\mathsf{B}(\alpha_i) + \mathsf{U}_\mathsf{B}(\alpha_i)$.
4. For each $i \in [\ell]$
   - Bob sends $(\mathtt{inputR}, \mathsf{p}_\mathsf{B}(\alpha_i))$ to $\mathcal{F}_{\mathrm{OLE}}$.
   - Alice sends $(\mathtt{inputS}, (\mathsf{R}_2^\mathsf{A}(\alpha_i), \mathsf{U}_\mathsf{A}(\alpha_i)))$ to $\mathcal{F}_{\mathrm{OLE}}$.
   - Alice receives back $\mathsf{s}_\mathsf{B}(\alpha_i) = \mathsf{p}_\mathsf{B}(\alpha_i) \cdot \mathsf{R}_2^\mathsf{A}(\alpha_i) + \mathsf{U}_\mathsf{A}(\alpha_i)$.
5. For each $i \in [\ell]$, Alice sends to Bob

$$\mathsf{s}_\mathsf{A}'(\alpha_i) = \mathsf{s}_\mathsf{A}(\alpha_i) + \mathsf{p}_\mathsf{A}(\alpha_i) \cdot \mathsf{R}_1^\mathsf{A}(\alpha_i) - \mathsf{U}_\mathsf{A}(\alpha_i)$$

6. For each $i \in [\ell]$, Bob sends to Alice

$$\mathsf{s}_\mathsf{B}'(\alpha_i) = \mathsf{s}_\mathsf{B}(\alpha_i) + \mathsf{p}_\mathsf{B}(\alpha_i) \cdot \mathsf{R}_2^\mathsf{B}(\alpha_i) - \mathsf{U}_\mathsf{B}(\alpha_i)$$

7. Alice outputs the evaluation points

$$\mathsf{p}(\alpha_i) = \mathsf{s}_\mathsf{A}(\alpha_i) + \mathsf{s}_\mathsf{B}'(\alpha_i) + \mathsf{p}_\mathsf{A}(\alpha_i) \cdot \mathsf{R}_1^\mathsf{A}(\alpha_i) - \mathsf{U}_\mathsf{A}(\alpha_i)$$

8. Bob outputs the evaluation points

$$\mathsf{p}(\alpha_i) = \mathsf{s}_\mathsf{B}(\alpha_i) + \mathsf{s}_\mathsf{A}'(\alpha_i) + \mathsf{p}_\mathsf{B}(\alpha_i) \cdot \mathsf{R}_2^\mathsf{B}(\alpha_i) - \mathsf{U}_\mathsf{B}(\alpha_i)$$

Fig. 10. Protocol for computing evaluation points of the noisy polynomial addition of $\mathsf{p}_\mathsf{A}(x)$ and $\mathsf{p}_\mathsf{B}(x)$ in the $\mathcal{F}_{\mathrm{OLE}}$-hybrid model.

Proof (Sketch). We assume that Alice is corrupt. The proof, where Bob is corrupt is completely symmetrical. The simulator sends Alice's input p_A to the ideal functionality $\mathcal{F}_{\mathrm{NPA}}^{\ell,\, t}$ and gets back $\{\mathsf{p}(\alpha_1), \cdots, \mathsf{p}(\alpha_\ell)\}$. The simulator picks the polynomials $\mathsf{U}_\mathsf{B}(x)$ and $\mathsf{U}_\mathsf{A}(x)$ of degree ℓ uniformly at random. It then picks $\mathsf{p}_\mathsf{B}(x)$ of degree n and $\mathsf{R}_1^\mathsf{A}(x), \mathsf{R}_2^\mathsf{A}(x), \mathsf{R}_1^\mathsf{B}(x), \mathsf{R}_2^\mathsf{B}(x)$ of degree t uniformly at random under the constraint that

$$\mathsf{p}(\alpha_i) = \mathsf{p}_\mathsf{A}(\alpha_i) \cdot \left(\mathsf{R}_1^\mathsf{A}(\alpha_i) + \mathsf{R}_1^\mathsf{B}(\alpha_i)\right) + \mathsf{p}_\mathsf{B}(\alpha_i) \cdot \left(\mathsf{R}_2^\mathsf{A}(\alpha_i) + \mathsf{R}_2^\mathsf{B}(\alpha_i)\right)$$

Using these values the simulator computes $\mathsf{s}_\mathsf{A}(\alpha_i), \mathsf{s}_\mathsf{B}(\alpha_i), \mathsf{s}_\mathsf{A}'(\alpha_i), \mathsf{s}_\mathsf{B}'(\alpha_i)$ as in the protocol description.

During the first ℓ invocations of $\mathcal{F}_{\text{OLE}}$, Alice would send $(\text{inputR}, p_A(\alpha_i))$ to the ideal functionality $\mathcal{F}_{\text{OLE}}$. The simulator leaks $s_A(\alpha_i)$ to $\mathcal{Z}$ as the response that Alice would receive from $\mathcal{F}_{\text{OLE}}$. During the next ℓ invocations of $\mathcal{F}_{\text{OLE}}$ Alice would send $(\text{inputS}, (R_2^A(\alpha_i), U_A(\alpha_i)))$, but does not receive anything back, hence we do not need to simulate anything here. Finally we leak $s'_B(\alpha_i)$ to $\mathcal{Z}$ as the message that she would receive in step 6. The only difference between a real protocol execution and our simulation is the choice of $p_B(x)$, which in turn influences the value of $s'_B(\alpha_i)$. However, since

$$p(\alpha_i) = s_A(\alpha_i) + s'_B(\alpha_i) + p_A(\alpha_i) \cdot R_1^A(\alpha_i) - U_A(\alpha_i)$$

we have that

$$s'_B(\alpha_i) = p(\alpha_i) - p_A(\alpha_i) \cdot R_1^A(\alpha_i) - p_A(\alpha_i) \cdot R_1^B(\alpha_i) + U_A(\alpha_i) - U_B(\alpha_i)$$

At this point we observe that the values $s'_B(\alpha_i)$ are distributed uniformly at random, since we only learn ℓ evaluation points and since $U_B(x)$ is a uniformly random polynomial of degree ℓ, which is not known to Alice.   □

Efficiency. The communication complexity of $\Pi_{\text{NPA}}^{\ell, t}$ essentially depends on the communication complexity of the $\mathcal{F}_{\text{OLE}}$ functionality. Using a passively secure instantiations of $\mathcal{F}_{\text{OLE}}$ with constant communication overhead [NP99, IPS09, ADI+17], we obtain a instantiation for $\mathcal{F}_{\text{NPA}}^{\ell, t}$ with communication complexity $\mathcal{O}(\ell \log p)$.

8 Conclusion and Open Problems

In this work we have initiated the study of sublinear threshold private set intersection. We have established a lower bound, showing that any protocol has to have a communication complexity of at least $\Omega(t)$, where t is the maximum allowed size of the symmetric set difference. We have shown an almost matching upper bound of $\tilde{\mathcal{O}}(t)$ based on fully homomorphic encryption and we have shown how to obtain a protocol with communication complexity $\tilde{\mathcal{O}}(t^2)$ based on additively homomorphic encryption. Our work poses several exciting open questions. From a theoretical perspective, it remains an open problem to construct a protocol with communication complexity $\tilde{\mathcal{O}}(t)$ from weaker assumptions than fully homomorphic encryption. Since our intersection protocol in Sect. 6 already has the desired complexity, one "only" needs to find a protocol for private set intersection cardinality testing with the same communication complexity. From a practical perspective, it is an open question to develop protocols that are practically, rather than just asymptotically, efficient.

Acknowledgments. We would like to thank Ivan Damgård, Claudio Orlandi, and Tobias Nilges for the fruitful discussions that have helped shape the current work.

References

[ADI+17]   Applebaum, B., Damgård, I., Ishai, Y., Nielsen, M., Zichron, L.: Secure arithmetic computation with constant computational overhead. In: Katz, J., Shacham, H. (eds.) CRYPTO 2017. LNCS, vol. 10401, pp. 223–254. Springer, Cham (2017). https://doi.org/10.1007/978-3-319-63688-7_8

[BFS86]   Babai, L., Frankl, P., Simon, J.: Complexity classes in communication complexity theory (preliminary version). In: 27th FOCS, pp. 337–347. IEEE Computer Society Press, October 1986

[BGV12]   Brakerski, Z., Gentry, C., Vaikuntanathan, V.: (Leveled) fully homomorphic encryption without bootstrapping. In: Goldwasser, S. (ed.) ITCS 2012, pp. 309–325. ACM, January 2012

[BK89]   Blum, M., Kannan, S.: Designing programs that check their work. In: 21st ACM STOC, pp. 86–97. ACM Press, May 1989

[BOT88]   Ben-Or, M., Tiwari, P.: A deterministic algorithm for sparse multivariate polynominal interpolation (extended abstract). In: 20th ACM STOC, pp. 301–309. ACM Press, May 1988

[BV11a]   Brakerski, Z., Vaikuntanathan, V.: Efficient fully homomorphic encryption from (standard) LWE. In: Ostrovsky, R. (ed.) 52nd FOCS, pp. 97–106. IEEE Computer Society Press, October 2011

[BV11b]   Brakerski, Z., Vaikuntanathan, V.: Fully homomorphic encryption from ring-LWE and security for key dependent messages. In: Rogaway, P. (ed.) CRYPTO 2011. LNCS, vol. 6841, pp. 505–524. Springer, Heidelberg (2011). https://doi.org/10.1007/978-3-642-22792-9_29

[BYJKS04]   Bar-Yossef, Z., Jayram, T.S., Kumar, R., Sivakumar, D.: An information statistics approach to data stream and communication complexity. J. Comput. Syst. Sci. **68**(4), 702–732 (2004)

[Can01]   Canetti, R.: Universally composable security: a new paradigm for cryptographic protocols. In: 42nd FOCS, pp. 136–145. IEEE Computer Society Press, October 2001

[CDN15]   Cramer, R., Damgård, I., Nielsen, J.B.: Secure Multiparty Computation and Secret Sharing. Cambridge University Press, Cambridge (2015)

[CGT12]   De Cristofaro, E., Gasti, P., Tsudik, G.: Fast and private computation of cardinality of set intersection and union. In: Pieprzyk, J., Sadeghi, A.-R., Manulis, M. (eds.) CANS 2012. LNCS, vol. 7712, pp. 218–231. Springer, Heidelberg (2012). https://doi.org/10.1007/978-3-642-35404-5_17

[CLR17]   Chen, H., Laine, K., Rindal, P.: Fast private set intersection from homomorphic encryption. In: Thuraisingham, B.M., Evans, D., Malkin, T., Xu, D. (eds.) ACM CCS 17, pp. 1243–1255. ACM Press, October/November 2017

[DCW13]   Dong, C., Chen, L., Wen, Z.: When private set intersection meets big data: an efficient and scalable protocol. In: Sadeghi, A.-R., Gligor, V.D., Yung, M. (eds.) ACM CCS 2013, pp. 789–800. ACM Press, November 2013

[DD15]   Debnath, S.K., Dutta, R.: Secure and efficient private set intersection cardinality using bloom filter. In: Lopez, J., Mitchell, C.J. (eds.) ISC 2015. LNCS, vol. 9290, pp. 209–226. Springer, Cham (2015). https://doi.org/10.1007/978-3-319-23318-5_12

[DJ01]   Damgård, I., Jurik, M.: A generalisation, a simpli.cation and some applications of Paillier's probabilistic public-key system. In: Kim, K. (ed.) PKC 2001. LNCS, vol. 1992, pp. 119–136. Springer, Heidelberg (2001). https://doi.org/10.1007/3-540-44586-2_9

[DT10]   De Cristofaro, E., Tsudik, G.: Practical private set intersection protocols with linear complexity. In: Sion, R. (ed.) FC 2010. LNCS, vol. 6052, pp. 143–159. Springer, Heidelberg (2010). https://doi.org/10.1007/978-3-642-14577-3_13

[EFG+15] Egert, R., Fischlin, M., Gens, D., Jacob, S., Senker, M., Tillmanns, J.: Privately computing set-union and set-intersection cardinality via bloom filters. In: Foo, E., Stebila, D. (eds.) ACISP 2015. LNCS, vol. 9144, pp. 413–430. Springer, Cham (2015). https://doi.org/10.1007/978-3-319-19962-7_24

[FNP04]   Freedman, M.J., Nissim, K., Pinkas, B.: Efficient private matching and set intersection. In: Cachin, C., Camenisch, J.L. (eds.) EUROCRYPT 2004. LNCS, vol. 3027, pp. 1–19. Springer, Heidelberg (2004). https://doi.org/10.1007/978-3-540-24676-3_1

[Gen09]   Gentry, C.: Fully homomorphic encryption using ideal lattices. In: Mitzenmacher, M. (ed.) 41st ACM STOC, pp. 169–178. ACM Press, May/June 2009

[GJR10]   Grigorescu, E., Jung, K., Rubinfeld, R.: A local decision test for sparse polynomials. Inf. Process. Lett. **110**(20), 898–901 (2010)

[GN17]   Ghosh, S., Nilges, T.: An algebraic approach to maliciously secure private set intersection. Cryptology ePrint Archive, Report 2017/1064 (2017). https://eprint.iacr.org/2017/1064

[GNN17]   Ghosh, S., Nielsen, J.B., Nilges, T.: Maliciously secure oblivious linear function evaluation with constant overhead. In: Takagi, T., Peyrin, T. (eds.) ASIACRYPT 2017. LNCS, vol. 10624, pp. 629–659. Springer, Cham (2017). https://doi.org/10.1007/978-3-319-70694-8_22

[HOS17]   Hallgren, P.A., Orlandi, C., Sabelfeld, A.: PrivatePool: privacy-preserving ridesharing. In: 30th IEEE Computer Security Foundations Symposium, CSF 2017, Santa Barbara, CA, USA, 21–25 August 2017, pp. 276–291 (2017)

[HV17]   Hazay, C., Venkitasubramaniam, M.: Scalable multi-party private set-intersection. In: Fehr, S. (ed.) PKC 2017. LNCS, vol. 10174, pp. 175–203. Springer, Heidelberg (2017). https://doi.org/10.1007/978-3-662-54365-8_8

[HW06]   Hohenberger, S., Weis, S.A.: Honest-verifier private disjointness testing without random oracles. In: Danezis, G., Golle, P. (eds.) PET 2006. LNCS, vol. 4258, pp. 277–294. Springer, Heidelberg (2006). https://doi.org/10.1007/11957454_16

[IPS09]   Ishai, Y., Prabhakaran, M., Sahai, A.: Secure arithmetic computation with no honest majority. In: Reingold, O. (ed.) TCC 2009. LNCS, vol. 5444, pp. 294–314. Springer, Heidelberg (2009). https://doi.org/10.1007/978-3-642-00457-5_18

[KKRT16] Kolesnikov, V., Kumaresan, R., Rosulek, M., Trieu, N.: Efficient batched oblivious PRF with applications to private set intersection. In: Weippl, E.R., Katzenbeisser, S., Kruegel, C., Myers, A.C., Halevi, S. (eds.) ACM CCS 2016, pp. 818–829. ACM Press, October 2016

[KLS+17] Kiss, Á., Liu, J., Schneider, T., Asokan, N., Pinkas, B.: Private set intersection for unequal set sizes with mobile applications. Proc. Priv. Enhancing Technol. **2017**(4), 177–197 (2017)

[KMP+17] Kolesnikov, V., Matania, N., Pinkas, B., Rosulek, M., Trieu, N.: Practical multi-party private set intersection from symmetric-key techniques. In: Thuraisingham, B.M., Evans, D., Malkin, T., Xu, D. (eds.) ACM CCS 2017, pp. 1257–1272. ACM Press, October/November 2017

[KMWF07] Kiltz, E., Mohassel, P., Weinreb, E., Franklin, M.: Secure linear algebra using linearly recurrent sequences. In: Vadhan, S.P. (ed.) TCC 2007. LNCS, vol. 4392, pp. 291–310. Springer, Heidelberg (2007). https://doi.org/10.1007/978-3-540-70936-7_16

[KS92] Kalyanasundaram, B., Schintger, G.: The probabilistic communication complexity of set intersection. SIAM J. Discret. Math. **5**(4), 545–557 (1992)

[KS05] Kissner, L., Song, D.X.: Privacy-preserving set operations. In: Shoup, V. (ed.) CRYPTO 2005. LNCS, vol. 3621, pp. 241–257. Springer, Heidelberg (2005). https://doi.org/10.1007/11535218_15

[Mar14] Marlinspike, M.: The difficulty of private contact discovery (2014). https://signal.org/blog/contact-discovery

[Mea86] Meadows, C.A.: A more efficient cryptographic matchmaking protocol for use in the absence of a continuously available third party. In: Proceedings of the 1986 IEEE Symposium on Security and Privacy, Oakland, California, USA, 7–9 April 1986, pp. 134–137 (1986)

[MQU07] Müller-Quade, J., Unruh, D.: Long-term security and universal composability. In: Vadhan, S.P. (ed.) TCC 2007. LNCS, vol. 4392, pp. 41–60. Springer, Heidelberg (2007). https://doi.org/10.1007/978-3-540-70936-7_3

[MTZ03] Minsky, Y., Trachtenberg, A., Zippel, R.: Set reconciliation with nearly optimal communication complexity. IEEE Trans. Inf. Theory **49**(9), 2213–2218 (2003)

[NMH+10] Nagaraja, S., Mittal, P., Hong, C.-Y., Caesar, M., Borisov, N.: BotGrep: finding P2P bots with structured graph analysis. In: Proceedings of the 19th USENIX Security Symposium, Washington, DC, USA, 11–13 August 2010, pp. 95–110 (2010)

[NP99] Naor, M., Pinkas, B.: Oblivious transfer and polynomial evaluation. In: 31st ACM STOC, pp. 245–254. ACM Press, May 1999

[Pai99] Paillier, P.: Public-key cryptosystems based on composite degree residuosity classes. In: Stern, J. (ed.) EUROCRYPT 1999. LNCS, vol. 1592, pp. 223–238. Springer, Heidelberg (1999). https://doi.org/10.1007/3-540-48910-X_16

[PSSZ15] Pinkas, B., Schneider, T., Segev, G., Zohner, M.: Phasing: private set intersection using permutation-based hashing. In: 24th USENIX Security Symposium, USENIX Security 15, Washington, D.C., USA, 12–14 August 2015, pp. 515–530 (2015)

[PSWW18] Pinkas, B., Schneider, T., Weinert, C., Wieder, U.: Efficient Circuit-based PSI via Cuckoo hashing. In: Nielsen, J.B., Rijmen, V. (eds.) EUROCRYPT 2018. LNCS, vol. 10822, pp. 125–157. Springer, Cham (2018). https://doi.org/10.1007/978-3-319-78372-7_5

[PSZ14] Pinkas, B., Schneider, T., Zohner, M.: Faster private set intersection based on OT extension. In: Proceedings of the 23rd USENIX Security Symposium, San Diego, CA, USA, 20–22 August 2014, pp. 797–812 (2014)

[RAD78] Rivest, R.L., Adleman, L., Dertouzos, M.L.: On data banks and privacy homomorphisms. Found. Secur. Comput. **4**(11), 169–180 (1978)

[Raz90] Razborov, A.A.: Applications of matrix methods to the theory of lower bounds in computational complexity. Combinatorica **10**(1), 81–93 (1990)

[RR17a] Rindal, P., Rosulek, M.: Improved private set intersection against malicious adversaries. In: Coron, J.-S., Nielsen, J.B. (eds.) EUROCRYPT 2017. LNCS, vol. 10210, pp. 235–259. Springer, Cham (2017). https://doi.org/10.1007/978-3-319-56620-7_9

[RR17b]   Rindal, P., Rosulek, M.: Malicious-secure private set intersection via dual execution. In: Thuraisingham, B.M., Evans, D., Malkin, T., Xu, D. (eds.) ACM CCS 2017, pp. 1229–1242. ACM Press, October/November 2017

[Yao86]   Yao, A.C.-C.: How to generate and exchange secrets (extended abstract). In: 27th FOCS, pp. 162–167. IEEE Computer Society Press, October 1986

[ZC18]   Zhao, Y., Chow, S.S.M.: Can you find the one for me? Privacy-preserving matchmaking via threshold PSI. Cryptology ePrint Archive, Report 2018/184 (2018). https://eprint.iacr.org/2018/184

Adaptively Secure MPC with Sublinear Communication Complexity

Ran Cohen[1,2]([⊠]), Abhi Shelat[2]([⊠]), and Daniel Wichs[2]

[1] Boston University, Boston, USA
[2] Northeastern University, Boston, USA
{rancohen,wichs}@ccs.neu.edu, abhi@neu.edu

Abstract. A central challenge in the study of MPC is to balance between security guarantees, hardness assumptions, and resources required for the protocol. In this work, we study the cost of tolerating adaptive corruptions in MPC protocols under various corruption thresholds. In the strongest setting, we consider adaptive corruptions of an arbitrary number of parties (potentially all) and achieve the following results:

– A two-round secure function evaluation (SFE) protocol in the CRS model, assuming LWE and indistinguishability obfuscation (iO). The communication, the CRS size, and the online-computation are sublinear in the *size* of the function. The iO assumption can be replaced by secure erasures. Previous results required either the communication or the CRS size to be polynomial in the function size.

– Under the same assumptions, we construct a "Bob-optimized" 2PC (where Alice talks first, Bob second, and Alice learns the output). That is, the communication complexity and total computation of Bob are sublinear in the function size and in Alice's input size. We prove impossibility of "Alice-optimized" protocols.

– Assuming LWE, we bootstrap adaptively secure NIZK arguments to achieve proof size sublinear in the circuit size of the NP-relation.

On a technical level, our results are based on *laconic function evaluation (LFE)* (Quach, Wee, and Wichs, FOCS'18) and shed light on an interesting duality between LFE and FHE.

Next, we analyze adaptive corruptions of all-but-one of the parties and show a two-round SFE protocol in the threshold PKI model (where keys of a threshold FHE scheme are pre-shared among the parties) with communication complexity sublinear in the circuit size, assuming LWE and NIZK. Finally, we consider the honest-majority setting, and show a two-round SFE protocol with guaranteed output delivery under the same constraints.

R. Cohen—Research supported by the Northeastern University Cybersecurity and Privacy Institute Post-doctoral fellowship, NSF grant TWC-1664445, NSF grant 1422965, and by the NSF MACS project.

A. Shelat—Research supported by NSF grant TWC-1664445 and a Google Faculty fellowship.

D. Wichs—Research supported by NSF grants CNS-1314722, CNS-1413964, CNS-1750795 and the Alfred P. Sloan Research Fellowship.

© International Association for Cryptologic Research 2019
A. Boldyreva and D. Micciancio (Eds.): CRYPTO 2019, LNCS 11693, pp. 30–60, 2019.
https://doi.org/10.1007/978-3-030-26951-7_2

1   Introduction

After establishing feasibility in the 1980's [8, 28, 52, 76, 79], the rich literature of multi-party computation (MPC) has focused on several performance aspects of the problem. These aspects include: (a) studying the resources required in terms of communication rounds, total amount of communication, and total amount of computation, (b) minimizing the required complexity assumptions under the various notions, and most importantly, (c) enhancing the notion of security, starting from the simplest notion of static corruptions with semi-honest adversaries in a stand-alone model, to sequential, and concurrent composition, to adaptive corruptions of parties by a malicious adversary.

Recent results have considered a few of these questions simultaneously. Despite several decades of progress, many basic questions about feasibility and asymptotic optimality of MPC protocols remain. The focus of this paper is to study *the price of adaptive security* in light of recent round-optimal and low-communication protocols for the static-security setting.

Recall that *adaptive security* [7, 20] for an MPC protocol models the realistic threat in which the adversary can corrupt a party during the execution of a protocol—in particular, after seeing some of the transcript of a protocol. In contrast, with *static corruptions*, the adversary must choose which parties to corrupt *before* the protocol begins. In this simpler static case, the security argument relies on the fact that the inputs of the corrupted parties are known, and thus the simulator can "work around" these parties to generate a reasonable, and consistent transcript for the remaining parties. Indeed, adaptive security is known to be strictly stronger than static security [20, 22].

While the idea of allowing an adversary to corrupt parties at anytime during protocol executions seems natural, its technical formulation is captured by obliging the simulator in the security definition to support some specific tasks. In particular, the technical difficulty in achieving adaptive security is that the simulator must produce a transcript for the execution *before* knowing which parties are corrupted. In an extreme case, the protocol can already be completed, and the adversary can then *begin* to corrupt all of the parties, one by one.

Two main models are considered for adaptive corruptions. In the first and simpler one, it is assumed that parties can *securely erase* certain parts (and even all) of their random tapes.[1] In this setting, when simulating a party who gets corrupted, the simulator may not be required to provide random coins explaining all the messages previously sent by that party. In the second, *erasures-free* model, there are no assumptions about the ability to erase local information. When a party is corrupted in this adaptive security notion, the adversary can learn all of that party's inputs and internal random coins. In this case, a secure

---

[1] We note that in certain cases it is reasonable to erase the random coins, e.g., when encrypting a message it is normally fine not to store the encryption randomness; however, is some cases one cannot erase all of its random tape, e.g., when sending a public encryption key it is normally essential to store the decryption key. We refer the reader to [18, 20] for further discussion on secure erasures.

protocol requires a simulator that, after producing the transcript, can "explain" the transcript by generating the coins and inputs for a given party after they are corrupted. In particular, the simulator only learns the input of that party after the corruption (e.g., after the entire execution), and then must "explain" the transcript it produced beforehand in a way that is consistent with the given input.

As a result of these difficulties, most of the literature shows that achieving adaptive security is notoriously harder than achieving static security; in some cases there are outright impossibility results such as the case of fully homomorphic encryption [68], public-key encryption which cannot exist for arbitrary messages [72], constant-round MPC in the plain model (under black-box simulation) [47], MPC protocols with non-expander communication graphs [17], and composable broadcast protocols without an honest majority [62]. All of these lower bounds, with the exception of [47], hold also for the weaker adaptive setting with secure erasures.

1.1 Full Adaptivity: Adaptive Corruptions of All the Parties

We start by considering the strongest adversary that can adaptively corrupt, and arbitrarily control, any subset of the participating parties. We will focus on the resources required for securely evaluating a function, balancing between the number of rounds, the communication complexity, and the online-computational complexity (the work performed between the first and last messages).

The feasibility of *adaptively secure* MPC was established in the seminal CLOS protocol [21] in a resoundingly strong manner in the UC framework [19]. This paper established the notion of fully adaptive security as described above, in the stronger, erasures-free setting, when the adversary can corrupt *all* protocol parties after execution. They then achieved this notion with a brilliant, yet complicated protocol that worked in the *common random string* model.[2] However, that protocol's round complexity depended on the circuit *depth*, and its communication was polynomially larger than the *size* of the circuit being computed. Roughly 15 years later, Canetti et al. [27] constructed a constant-round protocol under standard assumptions, and recently Benhamouda et al. [10] constructed a 2-round protocol assuming 2-round adaptively secure oblivious transfer (OT). But again, both of these recent results require communication that is larger than the circuit size, and thus come at a larger cost than recent protocols for static corruptions that require two rounds and sublinear communication in the circuit size [71].

Another line of recent work overcomes the communication bottleneck, but at the cost of stronger assumptions and a large *common reference string*. Constant-round [24,38] and 2-round [26,46] protocols for adaptively secure MPC are known assuming indistinguishability obfuscation (iO) for circuits and one-way

---

[2] In the *common random string* model, all parties receive a uniformly random string generated in a trusted setup phase. In the *common reference string* model, the common string is sampled according to some pre-defined distribution.

functions (OWF). These protocols have sublinear communication ([24,38] in the semi-honest model, [26,46] in the malicious setting[3]), but require a large CRS (at least linear in the circuit size). In particular, the approach of these results is to place an obfuscated universal circuit into the common reference string which can compute any function of a given size. Thus, these results are more aptly described as *bounded-circuit-size* adaptively secure MPC. In contrast, we aim to study a setup model in which the reference string is smaller (preferably independent) of the size of the evaluated function.

Lastly, recent advances in the static setting [1,75] presented protocols with online-computation that only depends on the function's *depth* but not on its *size*. In the adaptive setting, on the contrary, all known protocols require computing the function during the online part of the computation.

We now present three results in the fully adaptive setting: a resource-efficient MPC protocol; feasibility and infeasibility results regarding one-sided-optimized two-party protocols; and NIZK protocols with a short proof.

Two-Round MPC with Low Communication and Online-Computation. Thus, the first result of this paper is to present a 2-round fully adaptively secure MPC that requires only sublinear communication (i.e., depends only on the inputs, outputs, and depth of the function), sublinear online-computation, and that uses a sublinear common reference string. To achieve our result, we combine the techniques from the recent work on *Laconic Function Evaluation* (LFE) [75] (that can be instantiated under a natural variant of the learning with errors assumption, called *adaptive LWE (ALWE)*.[4]) and *explainability compilers* [38]. In this sense, our answer to the main question regarding the cost of adaptive security versus static security shows a minimal cost to the communication complexity in the secure-erasures model, and the addition of complexity assumptions in the erasures-free setting: namely the need for sub-exponentially secure iO in order to implement the explainability compiler. Table 1 summarizes the performance characteristics of prior work in comparison to our new result.

Theorem 1 (adaptively secure MPC with sublinear communication, informal). *Assuming ALWE and secure erasures (alternatively, sub-exponential iO), every function can be securely computed by a 2-round protocol tolerating a malicious adversary that can adaptively corrupt all of the parties, such that the communication complexity, the online-computation complexity, and the size of the common reference string are sublinear in the function size.*

---

[3] The protocols in [24,38] use the CLOS compiler [21] to get malicious security. Since the communication of previously known adaptively secure ZK protocols depends on the NP relation (see [44,58,70] and references therein), the communication of the maliciously secure protocols depended on the CRS. Our short NIZK (Theorem 3) can be used to reduce the communication of [24,38] in the malicious setting as well.

[4] The basic construction in [75] holds under the standard LWE assumption; however, for the purpose of (semi-)malicious MPC, in which the inputs to the protocol can be chosen adaptively, after the CRS is published, we require the stronger variant.

To explain the key bottleneck in achieving our result, note that almost all known methods for succinct MPC in the static setting rely on *fully homomorphic encryption* [49].[5] The general template is for parties to encrypt and broadcast their inputs, independently evaluate the function on said inputs, and then jointly decrypt the output. The problem in the case of adaptive security is that the simulator must produce a transcript for such a protocol, consisting of the input ciphertexts and the output ciphertext, without knowing the inputs of any parties; later after corruption, the simulator would need to provide a decryption key that explains the ciphertexts for any given input and for the final output. Unfortunately, Katz et al. [68] showed that this exact task is not possible for all functions, even assuming secure erasures, since the existence of such a simulator would imply a compact circuit that can be used to compute the function.

To get around the impossibility of adaptively secure FHE, the key insight of our approach is to instead use a recent technique of laconic function evaluation (LFE) [75], itself an extension of the idea of laconic OT [29]. At a high level, LFE allows a party to publish a short *digest* of a function; later any party can encrypt an input to that function such that the resulting ciphertext is still small with respect to the *size* of the function. In particular, both the digest and the ciphertext size are proportional to the *depth* of the function. Because the computational cost of the decryption algorithm is proportional to evaluating the function, LFE avoids the impossibility argument for adaptive security from [68], while preserving the succinct communication pattern. LFE is in some sense a dual notion to FHE. We extend on this duality in the discussion on the two-party case below.

Our starting point follows the statically secure protocol from [75]. The idea is for the parties to each locally compute a digest of the function f (this is done deterministically, using a CRS for LFE parameters), and then use an MPC protocol (possibly not communication efficient) to jointly compute the encryption of the inputs $(x_1, \ldots, x_n)$. The communication and online-computation required are naturally proportional only to the encryption algorithm, which depends on the depth of the original function but not on its size. Finally, each of the parties can then locally decrypt the ciphertext with respect to the digest to recover the output.

Nonetheless, for adaptive security, it is unclear how to simulate the output ciphertext when possibly all n parties can be corrupted. To circumvent this barrier, we first observe that the protocol from [75] achieves adaptive security in the *erasures* model, without any additional assumptions, and then remove the erasures using the explainability compiler technique from [38]. Loosely speaking, an explainability compiler takes a randomized circuit C and compiles it to a circuit $\widetilde{C}$, computing the same function, along with an additional program Explain, such that given any input/output pair (x, y) the program Explain can produce coins r satisfying $y = \widetilde{C}(x; r)$.

---

[5] Another approach for compact MPC is using *function secret sharing (FSS)* [15, 16]. This approach does not seem to support adaptive corruptions.

Overall, this framework achieves all of the round, communication, and online-computation complexity goals, but it still requires a common reference string whose size is related to the *depth* of the function being computed, and further in the erasures-free setting, it relies on iO. In contrast, in the static corruption setting, only LWE is required.

Alice/Bob-Optimized Protocols. Consider a two-message protocol for two parties, where Alice sends the first message, Bob replies with the second, and only Alice learns the output. In this setting, it is possible for one party's total *computation* (and thus also total communication) to be proportional to the size of their input and output, while the other party "does all of the work" of securely evaluating the function. These protocol variants are designated as "optimized for Alice" or "optimized for Bob," depending on which party saves the work.

In the static-corruption setting, Alice-optimized protocols can be constructed assuming FHE, where Alice encrypts her input, Bob homomorphically evaluates the circuit and returns the encrypted result. Quach et al. [75] showed that Bob-optimized protocols can be constructed from LFE, where Alice compresses the function with her input hard-wired, sends the digest to Bob who replies with the encryption of his input. Therefore, in the static setting, FHE and LFE are dual notions with respect to the work-load of the computation. We next show that in the adaptive setting this duality breaks. On the one hand, we extend the impossibility result of FHE [68] to rule out adaptively secure 2-round Alice-optimized protocols (even assuming secure erasures). On the other hand, we construct an adaptively secure, semi-malicious,[6] Bob-optimized protocol from LFE and explainability compilers (alternatively, just from LFE assuming secure erasures). We note that any 2-round Bob-optimized protocol can be converted into a 3-round Alice-optimized protocol, which is the best one could hope for. Table 2 summarizes our results vis a vis prior work.

Theorem 2 (Alice/Bob-optimized protocols, informal).

1. *Assuming ALWE and secure erasures (alternatively, sub-exponential iO), there exists an adaptively secure semi-malicious 2PC, where the total communication and Bob's computation are sublinear in the function size and in Alice's input size.*
2. *There exists 2-party functions such that in any adaptively secure, semi-honest, 2-round protocol realizing them, Bob's message must grow linearly in his input, even assuming secure erasures.*

The key idea behind our Bob-optimized protocol is to use the same LFE approach put forth in [75] for static security, and strengthen it to tolerate adaptive corruptions. To support an adaptive corruption of Alice, the simulator will need to produce an *equivocal* first message, i.e., to simulate the digest without

---

[6] In the semi-malicious setting, the adversary follows the protocol as in the semi-honest case, but he can choose arbitrary random coins for corrupted parties.

Table 1. Round, communication, and online-computation of MPC tolerating any number of corruptions, for $f : (\{0,1\}^{\ell_{in}})^n \to \{0,1\}^{\ell_{out}}$ represented by a circuit C of depth d. *CRS* refers to a common random string, whereas *Ref* refers to a common *reference* string whose sampling coins are secret. (*) The results in [47] only hold in the stand-alone setting.

Protocol	Security (erasures)	Rounds	Communication	Online computation	Setup size	Setup type	Assumption
MW [71]	static	2	$\mathrm{poly}(\ell_{in}, \ell_{out}, d, \kappa, n)$	$\mathrm{poly}(|C|, \kappa)$	$\mathrm{poly}(\kappa, d)$	CRS	LWE, NIZK
QWW [75] ABJMS [1]	static	2	$\mathrm{poly}(\ell_{in}, \ell_{out}, d, \kappa, n)$	$\mathrm{poly}(\ell_{in}, \ell_{out}, d, \kappa, n)$	$\mathrm{poly}(\kappa, d)$	CRS	ALWE LWE
CLOS [21]	adaptive(no)	$O(d)$	$|C| \cdot \mathrm{poly}(\kappa, n)$	$\mathrm{poly}(|C|, \kappa)$	$\mathrm{poly}(\kappa)$	CRS	TDP, NCE dense-crypto
GS [47]*	adaptive(no)	$O(d)$	$|C| \cdot \mathrm{poly}(\kappa, n)$	$\mathrm{poly}(|C|, \kappa)$	-	-	CRH TDP, NCE dense-crypto
DKR [38] CGP [24]	adaptive(no)	$O(1)$	$|C| \cdot \mathrm{poly}(\kappa, n)$	$\mathrm{poly}(|C|, \kappa)$	$\mathrm{poly}(|C|, \kappa)$	Ref	OWF, iO
GP [46]	adaptive(no)	2	$\mathrm{poly}(\ell_{in}, \ell_{out}, \kappa, n)$	$\mathrm{poly}(|C|, \kappa)$	$\mathrm{poly}(|C|, \kappa)$	Ref	OWF, iO
CPV [27]	adaptive(no)	$O(1)$	$|C| \cdot \mathrm{poly}(\kappa, n)$	$\mathrm{poly}(|C|, \kappa)$	$\mathrm{poly}(\kappa)$	CRS	NCE dense-crypto
BLPV [10]	adaptive(no)	2	$|C| \cdot \mathrm{poly}(\kappa, n)$	$\mathrm{poly}(|C|, \kappa)$	$\mathrm{poly}(\kappa)$	Ref	adaptive 2-round OT
This work	adaptive(yes) adaptive(no)	2	$\mathrm{poly}(\ell_{in}, \ell_{out}, d, \kappa, n)$ $\mathrm{poly}(\ell_{in}, \ell_{out}, d, \kappa, n)$	$\mathrm{poly}(|C|, \kappa)$	$\mathrm{poly}(\kappa, d)$ $\mathrm{poly}(\ell_{in}, \ell_{out}, d, \kappa, n)$	CRS Ref	ALWE ALWE, iO

Table 2. Comparison of two-message semi-honest protocols for $f : \{0,1\}^{\ell_A} \times \{0,1\}^{\ell_B} \to \{0,1\}^{\ell_{\text{out}}}$. Alice talks first, Bob the second, and only Alice learns the output. For simplicity, multiplicative factors that are polynomial in the security parameter κ or the circuit depth d are suppressed.

Approach	Security (erasures)	CRS	Communication		Computation		Assumptions
			Alice	Bob	Alice	Bob	
GC [79]	static	-	ℓ_A	$|f|$	$|f|$	$|f|$	static OT
LOT [29]	static	$O(1)$	$O(1)$	$|f|$	$|f|$	$|f|$	DDH, etc.
FHE [49]	static	-	ℓ_A	ℓ_{out}	$\ell_A + \ell_{\text{out}}$	$|f|$	LWE
LFE [75]	static	$O(1)$	$O(1)$	$\ell_B + \ell_{\text{out}}$	$|f|$	$\ell_B + \ell_{\text{out}}$	ALWE
equivocal GC [27]	adaptive (no)	-	ℓ_A	$|f|$	$|f|$	$|f|$	adaptive OT
This work	adaptive (yes)	$O(1)$	$O(1)$	$\ell_B + \ell_{\text{out}}$	$|f|$	$\ell_B + \ell_{\text{out}}$	ALWE
	adaptive (no)	$\ell_B + \ell_{\text{out}}$	$O(1)$	$\ell_B + \ell_{\text{out}}$	$|f|$	$\ell_B + \ell_{\text{out}}$	ALWE and iO
	adaptive (yes)	$|f|$	$|f|$	$\ell_{\text{out}} + o(\ell_B)$	$|f|$	$|f|$	impossible

knowing the input value of Alice, and upon a later corruption of Alice generate appropriate random coins explaining the message. Our first technical contribution is to create an equivocal version of the LFE scheme of [75]. Similarly, to support an adaptive corruption of Bob, the simulator should be able to generate an equivocal second message, i.e., generate the ciphertext without knowing the input of Bob, and upon a later corruption of Bob provide appropriate random coins. This can be handled either assuming secure erasures, or using explainability compilers.

Succinct Adaptively Secure NIZK. Next, we consider the problem of constructing an adaptively secure non-interactive zero-knowledge protocol (NIZK) that is "succinct," i.e., the size of the proof and of the common reference string should be smaller than the size of the circuit relation. The best we can hope for is for the proof to be the size of the witness (as otherwise, the lower-bound of Gentry and Wichs [50] requires a non-standard complexity assumption). The first adaptively secure NIZK was constructed by Groth et al. [56], however it was not succinct. Gentry [49] and later Gentry et al. [51] combined FHE with a standard NIZK system to construct such schemes that are secure against static corruptions, and as observed in [51] also against adaptive corruptions in the secure-erasures setting. However, these schemes are not secure against adaptive corruptions in the erasure-free setting. In particular, they run into the FHE bottleneck for adaptive security by Katz et al. [68] described above.

Our main technique to overcome this lower bound is to use *homomorphic trapdoor functions (HTDF)* [53]. HTDF schemes are a primitive that conceptually unites homomorphic encryption and homomorphic signatures. In our usage, HTDF can be thought of as fully homomorphic commitment schemes which are equivocal (hence, statistically hiding), where a trapdoor can be used to open any commitment to any desired value. Using HTDF, the prover can commit to the witness (instead of encrypting it), evaluate the circuit over the commitments, and use adaptive but non-succinct NIZK (e.g., from [56]) to prove knowledge of the witness and that the result commits to 1. The verifier evaluates the circuits over the committed witness, and verifies the NIZK to ensure that the result is a

Table 3. NIZK arguments with security parameter κ, for circuit size $|C|$, depth d, and witness size $|w|$.

Protocol	Security (erasures)	CRS size	Proof size	Assumptions
Groth [55]	static	$|C| \cdot \text{poly}(\kappa)$	$|C| \cdot \text{poly}(\kappa)$	TDP
Groth [55]	static	$|C| \cdot \text{polylog}(\kappa) + \text{poly}(\kappa)$	$|C| \cdot \text{poly}(\kappa)$	Naccache-Stern
GOS [56]	adaptive (no)	$\text{poly}(\kappa)$	$|C| \cdot \text{poly}(\kappa)$	pairing based
Gentry [49]	adaptive (yes)	$\text{poly}(\kappa)$	$|w| \cdot \text{poly}(\kappa, d)$	LWE, NIZK
GGIPSS [51]	adaptive (yes)	$\text{poly}(\kappa)$	$|w| + \text{poly}(\kappa, d)$	LWE, NIZK
This work	adaptive (no)	$\text{poly}(\kappa)$	$|w| \cdot \text{poly}(\kappa, d)$	LWE, NIZK

commitment to 1. A summary of our results in comparison to prior work appears in Table 3.

Theorem 3 (short NIZK, informal). *Assuming LWE, if there exists adaptively secure NIZK arguments for NP, there exists adaptively secure NIZK arguments for NP with proof size sublinear in the circuit size of the NP relation.*

1.2 Adaptive Corruptions of a Strict Subset of the Parties

Recall that the notion of fully adaptive security allows the adversary to corrupt *all* of the parties in the execution—in which case the protocol offers no privacy of inputs. A criticism of this notion is that it may be too strong for certain applications. In fact, the motivation behind this strong notion arises mainly from its application to *composition* of protocols. Namely, in a larger protocol that involves more parties, participants of a sub-protocol may eventually *all* become corrupted, and thus security of the larger protocol will depend on the fully adaptive security of the subprotocol.

It is equally justifiable, however, to consider other protocol-design tasks in which the protocol needs only withstand a weaker adversary who can corrupt either all-but-one of the participants, or—weaker still—only a minority of the players. We next consider adaptive security in these two settings.

All-But-One Corruptions. When considering adaptive security for all-but-one corruptions, Ishai et al. [63] constructed a constant-round, information-theoretically secure protocol in the OT-hybrid model. Garg and Sahai [47] showed an elegant way to instantiate the trusted setup required for [63] using non-black-box techniques and thus constructed a constant-round MPC protocol in the plain model, under standard cryptographic assumptions. The communication in both of these protocols is super-linear in the circuit size.

In contrast, for the weaker notion of static security, Asharov et al. [3] presented a 2-round protocol with sublinear communication, albeit in the *threshold-PKI model*. The threshold-PKI model is a setup in which all the participants of the protocol are privately given individualized key shares corresponding to a public key. A single-round protocol for threshold PKI was also given in [3], yielding a 3-round protocol in a standard CRS setup. Mukherjee and Wichs [71] removed the need for this extra round, thereby presented a 2-round MPC with sublinear communication in the common random string model.

We can thus pose our main question regarding the *cost* of adaptive security for communication-optimal protocols. Recently, Damgård et al. [43] constructed an adaptively secure 3-round MPC protocol with sublinear communication complexity in the threshold-PKI model assuming LWE. Their main idea is to use a special threshold FHE scheme that enables equivocating encryptions of 0 to encryptions of 1. Initially, the parties broadcast encryptions of their inputs. Next, each party locally evaluates the circuit, and the parties re-randomize the evaluated ciphertext in the second round by broadcasting (special) encryptions of 0. The third round is a single-round threshold decryption protocol.

To simulate this protocol, the simulator uses the equivocal mode of the public key. This way, all ciphertexts in the first round are simulated as encryptions of 0. After extracting corrupted parties' inputs, and obtaining the output value, the simulator uses the re-randomizing round to carefully add non-zero encryptions, and force the joint ciphertext to be an encryption of the output. Finally, the threshold decryption protocol is simulated. We note that using the approach of [43] (which is based on [41]), the re-randomization round seems to be inherent, and so it is unclear how to obtain optimal two rounds using this technique.

Our result in this setting is to construct an adaptively secure 2-round MPC assuming non-committing encryption (NCE) and threshold equivocal FHE in the threshold-PKI setup model. The setup assumption can be instantiated using the recent 2-round protocol of [10], assuming 2-round adaptively secure OT, resulting in a 4-round variant in the CRS model. All of the necessary primitives can be instantiated from LWE in the semi-malicious setting, and security in the malicious case follows using NIZK. Table 4 summarizes the prior work and our contribution in this model.

Theorem 4 (all-but-one corruptions, informal). *Assuming LWE and adaptively secure NIZK, every function can be securely computed by a 2-round protocol in the threshold-PKI model tolerating a malicious adversary that can adaptively corrupt all-but-one of the parties such that the communication complexity is sublinear in the function size.*

Table 4. Comparison of maliciously secure MPC for $f : (\{0,1\}^{\ell_{in}})^n \rightarrow \{0,1\}^{\ell_{out}}$ represented by a circuit C of depth d, tolerating $n-1$ corruptions. (*) The results in [47] only hold in the stand-alone model.

Protocol	Security	Rounds	Communication	Assumptions	Setup
AJLTVW [3]	static	2	$\text{poly}(\ell_{in}, \ell_{out}, d, \kappa, n)$	LWE, NIZK	threshold PKI
		3			CRS
MW [71]	static	2	$\text{poly}(\ell_{in}, \ell_{out}, d, \kappa, n)$	LWE, NIZK	CRS
IPS [63]	adaptive	$O(1)$	$|C| + \text{poly}(d, \log|C|, \kappa, n)$	OT-hybrid	-
GS [47]	adaptive	$O(1)$	$|C| + \text{poly}(d, \log|C|, \kappa, n)$	CRH, TDP, NCE dense crypto	-
DPR [43]	adaptive	3	$\text{poly}(\ell_{in}, \ell_{out}, d, \kappa, n)$	LWE, NIZK	threshold PKI
This work	adaptive	2	$\text{poly}(\ell_{in}, \ell_{out}, d, \kappa, n)$	LWE, NIZK	threshold PKI
		4			CRS

Our protocol follows the template of [3], where every party encrypts his input in the first round, locally evaluates the circuit over the ciphertexts, uses its key-share to partially decrypt the result, and broadcasts the decrypted share (some additional "smudging" noise is sometimes required to protect the decryption share). The technical challenges are: (1) the ciphertexts in the first round must be created in an equivocal way, and (2) the simulation strategy used for the threshold decryption in [3] (and similarly in [71]) is inherently static, and does not translate in a straightforward way to the adaptive setting.

We overcome the first challenge by constructing a novel *threshold equivocal FHE* scheme. The scheme is equipped with an equivocal key-generation algorithm. All ciphertexts encrypted in this mode are "meaningless" and carry no information about the plaintext; a trapdoor can be used to equivocate any ciphertext to any message. We instantiate this FHE scheme using the *dual-mode* HTDF scheme of Gorbunov et al. [53] that can generate the homomorphic trapdoor functions in an extractable mode, corresponding to the standard (meaningful) mode of the FHE, and an equivocal mode, corresponding to the meaningless mode.

We proceed to explain the second challenge. As observed in [3,71], the threshold decryption protocol may leak some information about the shares of the secret key, and the simulator for the decryption protocol can be used to protect *exactly* one party. In the static setting, when the set of corrupted parties is known ahead of time, the simulator can choose one of the honest parties P_h as a special party for simulating the threshold decryption. This approach does not work in the adaptive setting since the party P_h may get corrupted after simulating the decryption protocol. The simulator cannot know in advance which party will be the last to remain honest. For this reason, we use a different simulation strategy which allows the simulator to "correct" his choice of the party that is simulated as honest for the decryption protocol. Technically, this is done by having each party send shares of zero to each other party over a secure channel (that can be instantiated via NCE). These shares are used to hide the partial decryptions without changing their values. Since shares exchanged between pairs of honest parties remain hidden from the eyes of the adversary, the simulator has more freedom to replace the special party P_h upon corruption, by another honest party, even after simulating the decryption protocol.

Thus, as it stands, the cost of adaptive security with respect to the best statically secure protocols is either the threshold-PKI setup assumption, or the requirement of 2 additional rounds. Removing either of these costs remains an interesting open question.

Honest-Majority Setting. In the honest-majority setting, it is possible to guarantee output delivery to all honest parties. Damgård and Ishai [39] demonstrated the feasibility of constructing adaptively secure protocols that use a constant number of rounds and only require one-way functions. However, the communication of their protocol is super-linear in the circuit size.

In the static-corruption setting, Asharov et al. [3] constructed the first protocol with sublinear communication using threshold FHE; their protocol requires 4 rounds in the threshold-PKI model and 5 rounds in the CRS model. Gordon et al. [54] reduced the round complexity to 2 in the threshold-PKI model or 3 in the CRS model. Recently, Ananth et al. [2] showed a 3-round protocol in the plain model with communication polynomial in the circuit size, and Badrinarayanan et al. [4] showed a similar result with sublinear communication. Moreover, this round complexity is tight because it is known that 2-round fair protocols are impossible in the CRS model [48,54,74].[7]

Our result in this setting is to construct an adaptively secure analogue of [3,4]. In particular, we construct a 2-round adaptively secure MPC with guaranteed output delivery and the same communication complexity as in the static case, assuming NCE and threshold equivocal FHE in the threshold-PKI model in the semi-malicious setting (all assumptions can be based on LWE). Security in the malicious case follows using NIZK. We can compile our 2-round protocol into a constant-round protocol in the plain with the same communication complexity by computing the threshold-PKI setup using the protocol of Damgård and Ishai [39].

Theorem 5 (honest majority, informal). *Assuming LWE and adaptively secure NIZK, every function can be securely computed with guaranteed output delivery by a 2-round protocol in the threshold-PKI model tolerating a malicious adversary that can adaptively corrupt a minority of the parties such that the communication complexity is sublinear in the function size.*

The 2-round protocol is based on the protocol from the all-but-one case, described in Sect. 1.2. The challenge lies in overcoming aborting parties to guarantee output delivery. We combine techniques from the threshold FHE of [54] that required $n/2$ decryption shares to reconstruct the output into our threshold equivocal FHE. The main idea is to share the decryption key using Shamir's secret sharing instead of additive secret sharing. Both Shamir's reconstruction and the decryption algorithm consist of linear operations, which make them compatible with each other. As observed by Gordon et al. [54] (see also [14]), the problem with a naïve use of this technique is that the "smudging noise" (used to protect partial decryptions from leakage) is multiplied by the Lagrange coefficients, which may cause an incorrect decryption. Following [54], we have each party secret shares his smudging noise using Shamir's scheme, in a way that is compatible with the reconstruction procedure. We show that this technique can support adaptive corruptions.

To conclude, in the threshold-PKI model, the price of adaptive security is *the same* as of static security in terms of assumptions, number of rounds, and communication complexity. In the plain model, the cost is an additional constant number of rounds. Table 5 summarizes prior work and our results.

---

[7] We emphasize that the lower bounds hold given a public-coin setup, where all parties get the same information, and does not hold given a private-coin setup such as threshold PKI.

Table 5. Comparison of maliciously secure MPC for $f : (\{0,1\}^{\ell_{in}})^n \to \{0,1\}^{\ell_{out}}$ represented by a circuit C of depth d, in the honest-majority setting.

Protocol	Security	Rounds	Communication	Assumptions	Setup
AJLTVW [3]	static	4 5	$\text{poly}(\ell_{in}, \ell_{out}, d, \kappa, n)$	LWE, NIZK	threshold PKI CRS
GLS [54]	static	2 3	$\text{poly}(\ell_{in}, \ell_{out}, d, \kappa, n)$	LWE, NIZK	threshold PKI CRS
ACGJ [2]	static	3	$|C| \cdot \text{poly}(\kappa, n)$	PKE and zaps	-
BJMS [4]	static	2 3	$\text{poly}(\ell_{in}, \ell_{out}, d, \kappa, n)$	LWE, zaps, dense crypto	threshold PKI -
DI [39]	adaptive	$O(1)$	$|C| \cdot \text{poly}(\kappa, n)$	OWF	-
This work	adaptive	2 $O(1)$	$\text{poly}(\ell_{in}, \ell_{out}, d, \kappa, n)$	LWE, NIZK	threshold PKI -

1.3 Additional Related Work

Adaptive security tolerating an arbitrary number of corruptions has been considered in various models, including protocols in the CRS model [10,21,27], the sunspot model [23], the key-registration model [6], the temper-proof hardware model [61], the super-polynomial simulation model [5,59], and more generally, based on UC-puzzles [37,78]. All of these protocols require super-linear communication complexity.

Adaptive security in the secure-erasures model was considered in [7,9,42, 60,64,69,73], and in the erasures-free model tolerating all-but-one corruptions in [43,57,63,66] as well as in the honest-majority setting [36,39,41]. With the exception of [43], all of these protocols also require super-linear communication complexity.

Garay et al. [45] considered information-theoretic MPC in the client-server setting, where a constant number of clients uses n servers that assist with the computation, and studied sublinear communication in the number of *servers*. They gave a complete characterization for semi-honest security with static corruptions and adaptive corruptions with or without erasures.

In the static setting, MPC with sublinear communication complexity over eventual-delivery asynchronous channels was constructed in [32]. We conjecture that our techniques can also be applied in the asynchronous setting to obtain adaptive security with low communication.

We note that since the protocol of Garg and Polychroniadou [46] has low communication complexity, and its CRS size depends on the circuit size, it is possible to use a more compact representation of the function, e.g., by a Turing machine (TM) (or a RAM program as considered in [26]), and obfuscate it using iO for Turing machines. Nonetheless, the solution provided in this paper is different in several qualitative aspects. First, to make the CRS independent of the computation at hand, it is preferred to obfuscate a *universal* TM, which receives the description of the concrete TM on its input tape; while iO for TM with *bounded* inputs exists under the same assumptions as iO for circuits [11, 12,25], iO for TM with *unbounded* inputs is only known under the stronger assumptions of public-coin differing-inputs obfuscation [65]. Second, it is not clear how to replace the iO for TM assumption by secure erasures. Third, the computation may require a large auxiliary information, e.g., access to a large database, whose description is independent of the TM; this may result with a large description of the function. In our solution, the obfuscated circuit is sublinear in the computation size even when a large auxiliary information is used.

1.4 Open Questions

Our main question is to study the price of adaptive security. Dramatic improvements in the answer to this question have emerged over the past 15 years, and this paper is able to establish almost zero cost in terms of round or communication. Our results, however, leave the following questions as future work.

- **Reducing setup assumptions.** Our results for fully adaptive, 2-round, protocols without erasures require a *common reference string*. Are there fully adaptively secure protocols with sublinear communication complexity in the common *random* string(even with super-constant number of rounds)?
- **Reducing hardness assumptions.** Are there fully adaptively secure protocols with sublinear communication without assuming secure erasures or explainability compilers/iO?
- **Improving setup assumptions/round complexity for all-but-one.** Our optimal-round protocol requires a pre-distribution of the FHE keys. We show a 4-round protocol in the CRS model (equivalently, in the plain model for semi-honest). Are there 2 or 3 round protocols with sublinear communication in the CRS model to match the results for static adversaries?

Paper Organization

In Sect. 3, we present our results on fully adaptive security, and in Sects. 4.1 and 4.2, we present our results on Bob- and Alice-optimized protocols. In Sect. 5, we consider the all-but-one corruption case, and in Sect. 6, the honest-majority case. We refer the reader to the full version of the paper [35] for formal definitions and complete proofs.

2   Preliminaries

Basic Notations. For $n \in \mathbb{N}$ let $[n] = \{1, \cdots, n\}$. We denote by κ the security parameter. Let poly denote the set all positive polynomials and let PPT denote a probabilistic algorithm that runs in *strictly* polynomial time. A function $\nu : \mathbb{N} \to \mathbb{R}$ is *negligible* if $\nu(\kappa) < 1/p(\kappa)$ for every $p \in$ poly and sufficiently large κ. Two distribution ensembles $X = \{X(a, \kappa)\}_{a \in \{0,1\}^*, \kappa \in \mathbb{N}}$ and $Y = \{Y(a, \kappa)\}_{a \in \{0,1\}^*, \kappa \in \mathbb{N}}$ are computationally indistinguishable (denoted $X \overset{c}{\equiv} Y$) if no PPT algorithm can tell the difference between them except with negligible probability (in κ).

Cryptographic Primitives. In this work, we consider secure protocols in various security settings that require different cryptographic primitives. We present formal definitions for all primitives in the full version [35]. An informal description of every primitive is given before it is used in the main body.

Security Model. We present our results in the UC framework. We refer the reader to [19] for a detailed description of the framework.

In our secure function evaluation protocols, we will consider two security notions. In the honest-majority setting, we will consider security with *guaranteed output delivery* [33], informally meaning that all honest parties will receive the correct output from the computation. In general, when an honest majority is not assumed this cannot be achieved [31], and the standard requirement is for *security with abort*, informally meaning that the adversary has the capability to first learn the output from the computation and later force all honest parties to output ⊥.

Guaranteed output delivery and security with abort are not to be confused with *guaranteed termination*, which means that the honest parties actually finish the protocol. We emphasize that UC protocols cannot provide guaranteed termination since the adversary has full control over the communication channels, and he can simply "hang" the computation. Therefore, following the convention of Canetti et al. [21], we exclude trivial protocols, and require that the properties of guaranteed output delivery or security with abort will hold when the environment provides sufficiently many activations to the parties, and the adversary delivers all messages.[8] In particular, unlike the stand-alone model, in the UC model even when a protocol guarantees output delivery, we allow the adversary to learn the output from the computation while the honest parties do not; however, if an honest party terminates it is guaranteed to receive the output. An alternative, is to work in the $\mathcal{F}_{\text{sync}}$-hybrid model [31] or to consider the framework of [67], which ensures guaranteed termination regardless of the adversary's actions (but, still, as long as the environment provides sufficiently many activations to the parties).

3   Sublinear Communication in the Fully Adaptive Setting

In this section, we consider the fully adaptive setting (where the adversary can corrupt all parties) and construct two-round secure protocols with sublinear communication and online-computation complexity (in the circuit size). Our starting point is the protocol of Quach et al. [75] that is based on *laconic function evaluation (LFE)*.

---

[8] Other properties such as *privacy* and *independence of inputs* are always required to hold.

3.1   Cryptographic Primitives Used in the Protocol

Laconic Function Evaluation. Informally, an LFE scheme consists of 4 algorithms. The CRS generation algorithm generates a common random string given the security parameter and function parameters (e.g., function depth and input length) crs ← LFE.crsGen(1^κ, params). The compression algorithm produces a small digest of a circuit digest$_C$ = LFE.Compress(crs, C; r). The encryption algorithm encrypts the input based on the digest ct ← LFE.Enc(crs, digest$_C$, x). The decryption algorithm decrypts the ciphertext using the random coins used in the compression y = LFE.Dec(crs, C, r, ct).

We require the LFE to be correct, i.e., using the notation above it holds that $y = C(x)$, and secure, meaning that the ciphertext can be simulated given the output value y without knowing the input x. LFE can be constructed with the function-hiding property, which ensures that the digest can be simulated based on the function parameters without knowing the function itself. If function hiding is not required (as is the case in this section) the compression algorithm can be made deterministic. We consider the "adaptive" version of LFE, where the inputs to the computation can be chosen *after* the CRS has been sampled. Quach et al. [75] constructed LFE schemes satisfying this property assuming *adaptive LWE*.

Explainability Compilers. Informally, an explainability compiler takes as input a description of a randomized algorithm Alg, and outputs two algorithms: $\widetilde{\mathsf{Alg}}$ and Explain. The first algorithm $\widetilde{\mathsf{Alg}}$ computes the same functionality as Alg. The second algorithm Explain takes an input/output pair (x, y) and produces random coins r such that $y = \widetilde{\mathsf{Alg}}(x; r)$.

Assuming iO for circuits and OWF, Dachman-Soled et al. [38] constructed explainability compilers with *selective* security, where the challenge input is selected independently of the compiled circuit. Explainability compilers with *adaptive* security, where the challenge input is selected based on the compiled circuit follows via complexity leveraging [13] assuming iO and OWF with subexponential security (see also [24]). Looking ahead, to support adaptive inputs from the environment, our protocol requires the latter variant.

3.2   Adaptive Security with Sublinear Communication: Secure-Erasures Setting

We will show that assuming LFE every function can be securely realized in the common *random* string model with secure erasures, by a 2-round protocol tolerating an arbitrary number of adaptive corruptions with sublinear communication, online-computation, and CRS size. In Sect. 3.3, we will show how to replace the secure-erasures assumption by assuming explainability compilers, in which case the protocol requires a common *reference* string.

The basis of our protocol is the 2-round protocol of Quach et al. [75, Thm. 6.2] in the common random string model, that is secure against $n - 1$ static corruptions and achieves sublinear communication and online-computation assuming the existence of LFE. The protocol from [75] is specified in a hybrid model with an ideally secure computation (with abort) of the function LFE.Enc (i.e., the $\mathcal{F}_{\text{sfe-abort}}^{\text{LFE.Enc}}$-hybrid model). That is, the ideal functionality receives $(\text{crs}, \text{digest}_f, x_i, r_i)$ from each party P_i and computes

$$\text{ct} = \text{LFE.Enc}(\text{crs}, \text{digest}_f, x_1, \ldots, x_n; \oplus_{i \in [n]} r_i).$$

In case of inconsistent inputs, or if the adversary sends abort, the functionality outputs $\perp$.

Given a circuit C_f computing f, the protocol of [75] is defined as follows:

- The common random string is computed as $\text{crs} \leftarrow \text{LFE.crsGen}(1^\kappa, f.\text{params})$.
- Upon receiving $(\text{input}, \text{sid}, x_i)$, every party P_i computes $\text{digest}_f = \text{LFE.Compress}(\text{crs}, C_f)$, samples a uniformly random $r_i \leftarrow \{0, 1\}^*$, and invokes the ideal functionality $\mathcal{F}_{\text{sfe-abort}}^{\text{LFE.Enc}}$ with $(\text{input}, \text{sid}, (\text{crs}, \text{digest}_f, x_i, r_i))$.
- Upon receiving $(\text{output}, \text{sid}, \text{ct})$ from the ideal functionality, party P_i checks that $\text{ct} \neq \perp$ (otherwise, P_i outputs $(\text{output}, \text{sid}, \perp)$), computes $y = \text{LFE.Dec}(\text{crs}, C_f, \text{ct})$, and outputs $(\text{output}, \text{sid}, y)$.

Proving security of the protocol against a static adversary corrupting all-but-one of the parties is straightforward. Namely, by definition of LFE schemes, the simulator can simulate the ciphertext ct based on the output y, and without knowing the input values, as $\text{ct} \leftarrow \text{Sim}_{\text{LFE}}(\text{crs}, C_f, \text{digest}_f, y)$. Furthermore, by the properties of LFE, the size of the circuit computing LFE.Enc is $\text{poly}(\kappa, \ell_{\text{in}}, \ell_{\text{out}}, d, n)$. By instantiating the ideal functionality using a statically secure 2-round protocol (e.g., the one from [71]), Quach et al. [75] achieved a statically secure protocol with sublinear communication and online-computational complexity.

A closer look at the protocol of [75] shows that it remains secure even facing adaptive corruptions of all-but-one of the parties, since a single honest party suffices to keep the randomness used for LFE.Enc hidden from the adversary. Furthermore, under the additional assumption of secure erasures, each party can erase his random coins r_i immediately after invoking $\mathcal{F}_{\text{sfe-abort}}^{\text{LFE.Enc}}$, and the protocol can satisfy adaptive corruptions of all the parties. By instantiating the functionality $\mathcal{F}_{\text{sfe-abort}}^{\text{LFE.Enc}}$ with the 2-round adaptively secure MPC from [10], we obtain the following theorem.

Theorem 6 (Theorem 1, secure-erasures version, restated). *Assume the existence of LFE schemes for P/poly, of 2-round adaptively and maliciously secure OT, and of secure erasures, and let $f : (\{0, 1\}^{\ell_{in}})^n \rightarrow \{0, 1\}^{\ell_{out}}$ be an n-party function of depth d.*

Then, $\mathcal{F}_{\text{sfe-abort}}^f$ can be UC-realized tolerating a malicious, adaptive PPT adversary by a 2-round protocol in the common random string model. The size of the common random string is $\text{poly}(\kappa, d)$, whereas the communication and online-computational complexity of the protocol are $\text{poly}(\kappa, \ell_{in}, \ell_{out}, d, n)$.

Note that following [10, 75], the assumptions in Theorem 6 hold under the adaptive LWE assumption.

3.3 Adaptive Security with Sublinear Communication: Erasures-Free Setting

In the erasures-free setting, it is unclear how to simulate the output ciphertext, and later upon learning all of the inputs values of the parties, explain the random coins that are used to generate it. We get around this barrier by using explainability compilers.

Two-Round Protocol Assuming Adaptive Explainability Compilers. We consider explainability compilers with adaptive security (where the challenge ciphertext is dynamically chosen) that can be realized by sub-exponentially secure iO and OWF. To define the common reference string for the protocol, we define the distribution $D_{\mathsf{lfe}}(\mathsf{params})$ that is parametrized by an LFE scheme and by the parameters of the function to be computed params. The distribution D_{lfe} computes $\mathsf{crs} \leftarrow \mathsf{LFE.crsGen}(1^\kappa, \mathsf{params})$ and $(\mathsf{LFE.Enc}, \mathsf{Explain}) \leftarrow \mathsf{Comp}(1^\kappa, \mathsf{LFE.Enc})$, and outputs the reference string $(\mathsf{crs}, \mathsf{LFE.Enc})$.

We would like to define the protocol in the $\mathsf{LFE.Enc}$-hybrid model; however, the function $\mathsf{LFE.Enc}$ is only given in the CRS and is not known before the protocol begins. To get around this technicality, we define the function $f_C((C_1, x_1, r_1), \ldots, (C_n, x_n, r_n))$ that receives a circuit C_i, a value x_i, and random coins r_i from each party, and outputs $C_1(x_1, \ldots, x_n; \oplus r_i)$ in case $C_1 = \ldots = C_n$, or $\bot$ otherwise (Fig. 1).

Theorem 7 (Theorem 1, erasures-free version, restated). *Assume the existence of LFE schemes for* P/poly, *of explainability compilers with adaptive security for* P/poly, *and of 2-round adaptively and maliciously secure OT, and let* $f : (\{0,1\}^{\ell_{in}})^n \rightarrow \{0,1\}^{\ell_{out}}$ *be a deterministic n-party function of depth d.*

Then, $\mathcal{F}^f_{\mathsf{sfe\text{-}abort}}$ *can be UC-realized in the* $\mathcal{F}^{D_{\mathsf{lfe}}}_{\mathsf{crs}}$-*hybrid model tolerating a malicious, adaptive PPT adversary by a 2-round protocol. The size of the common reference string, the communication complexity, and online-computational complexity of the protocol are* $\mathrm{poly}(\kappa, \ell_{in}, \ell_{out}, d, n)$.

The proof of the theorem follows from Lemma 1 (proven in the full version [35]) by instantiating the functionality $\mathcal{F}^{f_C}_{\mathsf{sfe\text{-}abort}}$, that is used to compute $\mathsf{LFE.Enc}$, using the 2-round protocol from [10] that requires 2-round adaptively and maliciously secure OT.

Lemma 1. *Assume the existence of LFE schemes for* P/poly, *and of explainability compilers with adaptive security for* P/poly, *and let* f *be a deterministic n-party function. Then, the protocol* π_{full} *UC-realizes* $\mathcal{F}^f_{\mathsf{sfe\text{-}abort}}$ *tolerating a malicious, adaptive PPT adversary in the* $(\mathcal{F}^{D_{\mathsf{lfe}}}_{\mathsf{crs}}, \mathcal{F}^{f_C}_{\mathsf{sfe\text{-}abort}})$-*hybrid model.*

4 Adaptively Secure Alice/Bob-Optimized Protocols

In this section, we consider 2-message protocols between Alice and Bob, with respective inputs $x_A \in \{0,1\}^{\ell_A}$ and $x_B \in \{0,1\}^{\ell_B}$, where only Alice learns the

---

Protocol π_{full}

- **Common Input:** An LFE scheme and a circuit C_f computing the function f.
- **Hybrid model:** The parties have access to the CRS functionality $\mathcal{F}_{\text{crs}}^{D_{\text{lfe}}(f.\text{params})}$ that outputs a crs for the LFE scheme and a circuit $\widehat{\text{LFE.Enc}}$, and to the SFE functionality $\mathcal{F}_{\text{sfe-abort}}^{fc}$.
- **The Protocol:**

1. Upon receiving $(\text{input}, \text{sid}, x_i)$, every party P_i invokes $\mathcal{F}_{\text{crs}}^{D_{\text{lfe}}(f.\text{params})}$ to get $(\text{crs}, \widehat{\text{LFE.Enc}})$, computes $\text{digest}_f = \text{LFE.Compress}(\text{crs}, C_f)$, samples a uniformly random $r_i \leftarrow \{0,1\}^*$, and invokes $\mathcal{F}_{\text{sfe-abort}}^{fc}$ with $(\text{input}, \text{sid}, (\widehat{\text{LFE.Enc}}, (\text{crs}, \text{digest}_f, x_i), r_i))$.
2. Upon receiving ct from the ideal functionality, party P_i checks that $\text{ct} \neq \bot$ (if so P_i outputs $(\text{output}, \text{sid}, \bot)$), computes $y = \text{LFE.Dec}(\text{crs}, C_f, \text{ct})$, and outputs $(\text{output}, \text{sid}, y)$.

Fig. 1. Two-round SFE with adaptive, malicious security

output $y = f(x_A, x_B)$. We say that a protocol is "Alice-optimized" if Alice's computation and the total communication of the protocol are proportional to $|x_A| + |y|$, while the computation complexity of Bob is proportional to $|f|$. We say that a protocol is "Bob-optimized" if Bob's computation and the total communication are proportional to $|x_B| + |y|$, while the computation complexity of Alice is proportional to $|f|$.

There exist insecure protocols which are Alice-optimized, where Alice sends her input to Bob who computes the function and returns the output to Alice. Similarly, there exist insecure protocols which are Bob-optimized, where Bob sends his input to Alice when she asks for it, and Alice computes the function on her own.

Assuming FHE [49], there exist statically secure Alice-optimized protocols, where Alice sends her encrypted input to Bob who homomorphically evaluates the function and returns the encrypted output to Alice. Alice's computation and the total communication of the protocol are $(|x_A| + |y|) \cdot \text{poly}(\kappa)$. Assuming function-hiding LFE [75], there exist statically secure Bob-optimized protocols, where Alice sends $\text{digest} \leftarrow \text{LFE.Compress}(\text{crs}, f_{x_A}(\cdot))$ to Bob, who replies with his encrypted input $\text{ct} \leftarrow \text{LFE.Enc}(\text{digest}, x_B)$, and finally Alice recovers the output. Bob's computation and the total communication of the protocol are $(|x_B| + |y|) \cdot \text{poly}(\kappa, d)$, where d is the depth of the function f.

The question we consider is whether there exist adaptively secure protocols which are Alice-optimized or Bob-optimized.

4.1 Adaptively Secure Bob-Optimized Protocol

The elegant protocol from [75] is secure in the common random string model tolerating a static corruption of one of the parties by a semi-malicious adversary (that can choose arbitrary random coins for the corrupted party, but acts honestly otherwise).

Adjusting this protocol to the adaptive setting requires overcoming a few obstacles. Namely, the simulator should be able to generate an equivocal first message, i.e., to simulate the digest without knowing the input value of Alice, and upon a later corruption of Alice generate appropriate random coins explaining the message. Similarly, the simulator should be able to generate an equivocal second message, i.e., generate the ciphertext without knowing the input of Bob, and upon a later corruption of Bob provide appropriate random coins.

To support an adaptive corruption of Alice, we enhance the LFE scheme to support an equivocal mode (see Sect. 4.1). In this mode, the CRS is generated along with a trapdoor information. The trapdoor can be used to explain a simulated digest as a compression of any circuit with the appropriate parameters. Similarly to Sect. 3, to support an adaptive corruption of Bob, we can use either secure erasures or explainability compilers.

Theorem 8 (Part 1 of Theorem 2, restated). *Assume the existence of equivocal, function-hiding LFE schemes for* P/poly *and of explainability compilers with adaptive security for* P/poly, *and let* $f : \{0,1\}^{\ell_A} \times \{0,1\}^{\ell_B} \to \{0,1\}^{\ell_{out}}$ *be a deterministic two-party function computable by a depth-d circuit.*

Then, $\mathcal{F}_{sfe}^f$ *can be UC-realized tolerating a semi-malicious, adaptive PPT adversary by a 2-message protocol in the common reference string model with secure channels. The size of the common reference string, the communication complexity (of both parties), and the computational complexity of Bob are* $(\ell_B + \ell_{out}) \cdot \mathrm{poly}(\kappa, d)$.

The proof of Theorem 8 follows from Lemma 3 below. In the secure-erasures setting, we can remove the explainability compilers assumption, and get the following corollary.

Corollary 1. *Assume the existence of equivocal, function-hiding LFE schemes for* P/poly *and let* f *be a two-party function as above. Then,* $\mathcal{F}_{sfe}^f$ *can be UC-realized in the secure-erasures model tolerating a semi-malicious, adaptive PPT adversary by a 2-message protocol in the common random string model with secure channels. The size of the common random string is* $\mathrm{poly}(\kappa, d)$, *and the communication complexity and computational complexity of Bob are* $(\ell_B + \ell_{out}) \cdot \mathrm{poly}(\kappa, d)$.

The secure channels can be instantiated over authenticated channels assuming NCE [20,30,34,40]; however, delivering Bob's public key to Alice requires either an additional communication round or a trusted setup.

Equivocal LFE. We start by extending the notion of LFE to support an equivocal mode.

Definition 1 (equivocal LFE). *A function-hiding LFE scheme Π is equivocal if there exists a PPT simulator* $(\mathsf{Sim}^1_{\text{EQUIV-FH}}, \mathsf{Sim}^2_{\text{EQUIV-FH}})$ *for the scheme Π such that for all stateful PPT adversary $\mathcal{A}$, it holds that*

$$\left| \Pr\left[\mathsf{Expt}^{\mathsf{EquivFH\text{-}real}}_{\Pi,\mathcal{A}}(\kappa) = 1 \right] - \Pr\left[\mathsf{Expt}^{\mathsf{EquivFH\text{-}ideal}}_{\Pi,\mathcal{A}}(\kappa) = 1 \right] \right| \leq \mathsf{negl}(\kappa),$$

for the experiments $\mathsf{Expt}^{\mathsf{EquivFH\text{-}real}}$ *and* $\mathsf{Expt}^{\mathsf{EquivFH\text{-}ideal}}$ *defined below:*

$\mathsf{Expt}^{\mathsf{EquivFH\text{-}real}}_{\Pi,\mathcal{A}}(\kappa)$	$\mathsf{Expt}^{\mathsf{EquivFH\text{-}ideal}}_{\Pi,\mathcal{A}}(\kappa)$
params $\leftarrow \mathcal{A}(1^\kappa)$	
crs $\leftarrow$ LFE.crsGen$(1^\kappa,$ params$)$	params $\leftarrow \mathcal{A}(1^\kappa)$
$C \leftarrow \mathcal{A}(\mathsf{crs})$	$(\mathsf{crs}, \mathsf{digest}, \mathsf{state}) \leftarrow \mathsf{Sim}^1_{\text{EQUIV-FH}}(1^\kappa, \mathsf{params})$
$\quad$ s.t. $C \in \mathcal{C}$ and $C.$params $=$ params	$C \leftarrow \mathcal{A}(\mathsf{crs})$
$r \leftarrow \{0,1\}^*$	$\quad$ s.t. $C \in \mathcal{C}$ and $C.$params $=$ params
digest $=$ LFE.Compress$(\mathsf{crs}, C; r)$	$r \leftarrow \mathsf{Sim}^2_{\text{EQUIV-FH}}(C, \mathsf{state})$
Output $\mathcal{A}(\mathsf{crs}, \mathsf{digest}, r)$	Output $\mathcal{A}(\mathsf{crs}, \mathsf{digest}, r)$

In the following lemma (proven in the full version [35] We show that the generic construction of function-hiding LFE from standard LFE presented in [75] can be adjusted to provide equivocality.

Lemma 2. *Assuming the existence of standard LFE schemes and semi-malicious, adaptively secure, 2-round OT, there exists a function-hiding, equivocal LFE scheme.*

We note that both LFE [75] and adaptively and maliciously (hence, also semi-maliciously) secure 2-round OT [10] can be instantiated assuming adaptive LWE. Hence, also equivocal FH-LFE can be instantiated assuming adaptive LWE (Fig. 2).

Protocol π_{bob}

- **Common Input:** An LFE scheme and a circuit C_f computing the function f.
- **Notation:** Define the algorithm LFE.Compress$_{\mathsf{crs}, C_f}(x)$ by hard-wiring crs and the circuit C_f to the compression algorithm LFE.Compress$(\mathsf{crs}, C_f(x, \cdot))$, and given input x compress the circuit $C_f(x, \cdot)$ with the input x hard-wired.
- **The Protocol:**

1. Upon receiving (input, sid, x_A), Alice samples uniformly at random $r_A \leftarrow \{0,1\}^*$, computes digest $=$ LFE.Compress$_{\mathsf{crs}, C_f}(x_A; r_A)$, and sends (sid, digest) to Bob.
2. Upon receiving (sid, digest) from Alice, and having received (input, sid, x_B), Bob computes ct $\leftarrow$ LFE.Enc$(\mathsf{crs}, \mathsf{digest}, x_B)$, and sends (sid, ct) to Alice.
3. Upon receiving a message (sid, ct) from Bob, Alice computes $y =$ LFE.Dec$(\mathsf{crs}, C, r_A, \mathsf{ct})$ and outputs (output, sid, y).

Fig. 2. 2-round, Bob-optimized protocol with adaptive, semi-malicious security

Semi-malicious Bob-Optimized Protocol. We proceed to our Bob-optimized protocol. Recall that the distribution $D_{\mathsf{lfe}}(\mathsf{params})$ samples a crs for the LFE scheme, computes $(\widetilde{\mathsf{LFE.Enc}}, \mathsf{Explain}) \leftarrow \mathsf{Comp}(1^\kappa, \mathsf{LFE.Enc})$, and outputs $(\mathsf{crs}, \widetilde{\mathsf{LFE.Enc}})$.

Lemma 3. *Consider the notations and assumptions in Theorem 8. Then, protocol π_{bob} securely realizes the functionality $\mathcal{F}_{\mathsf{sfe}}^f$ tolerating a semi-malicious, adaptive PPT adversary in the $(\mathcal{F}_{\mathsf{smt}}, \mathcal{F}_{\mathsf{crs}}^{D_{\mathsf{lfe}}(f.\mathsf{params})})$-hybrid model.*

The proof of Lemma 3 can be found in full version [35].

4.2 Impossibility of Adaptively Secure Alice-Optimized Protocol

We now turn to show that the impossibility of adaptively secure FHE from [68] can be extended to rule out adaptively secure Alice-optimized protocols. In fact, we prove a stronger impossibility showing that for some functions the size of Bob's message cannot be smaller than his input, even if Alice's message and the CRS are long. Intuitively, if the output of the function is simply Bob's input, then clearly Bob's message cannot be compressing. We show that this is the case even if the output is short.

For $n \in \mathbb{N}$, we define the two-party functionality $f_n(x_A, g_B) = (g_B(x_A), \lambda)$, where Alice has input $x_A \in \{0,1\}^{\log n}$, Bob has input a function $g_B : \{0,1\}^{\log n} \to \{0,1\}$, represented by its truth table as an n-bit string, and Alice learns the output $g_B(x_A)$.

Theorem 9 (Part 2 of Theorem 2, restated). *Let π_n be a 2-message protocol in the common reference string model for computing f_n, where Alice sends first the message m_1 and Bob replies with the message m_2. If the protocol tolerates a semi-honest, adaptive adversary in the secure-erasures model, then $|m_2| \geq n$.*

Intuitively, by adaptively corrupting Alice and equivocating her input, we can essentially recover $g_B(x_A)$ in any choice of x_A from the protocol transcript. This means that the Bob's response must encode the entire truth table of g_B, which is of size n. The formal proof of Theorem 9 can be found in the full version [35].

5 Adaptive Corruptions of All-But-One of the Parties

In this section, we prove an analogue result in the adaptive setting to the result of Asharov et al. [3], who showed how to compute any function tolerating all-but-one corruptions using a two-round protocol in the threshold-PKI model assuming threshold FHE, which in turn can be instantiated using LWE. Our construction relies on *threshold equivocal FHE* (defined in the full version [35]) that allows simulating ciphertexts for honest parties and explaining them properly upon later corruptions.

We note that the simulation technique used in [3] (and similarly in [71]) does not translate to the adaptive setting. As observed in [3,71], the threshold decryption protocol may leak some information about the shares of the secret key, and the simulator for the decryption protocol can be used to protect *exactly* one party. Since [3,71] considered static corruptions, the set of corrupted parties was known ahead of time, and the simulator could choose one of the honest parties P_h as a special party for the simulation. The decryption protocol was simulated with respect to P_h, as if he is the only honest party. For this reason, proving security of *exactly* $n-1$ corruptions in [71] was considerably simpler than proving security of *up to* $n-1$ corruptions.[9]

The simulation strategy that was used in [3,71] does not translate to the adaptive setting, since the party P_h that is chosen by the simulator may get corrupted after simulating the decryption protocol. The simulator cannot know in advance which party will be the last to remain honest. For this reason, we use a different simulation strategy, which allows the simulator to "correct" his choice of the party that is simulated as honest for the decryption protocol. Technically, this is done by having each party send shares of zero to each other party over a secure channel (that can be instantiated via NCE). These shares are used to hide the partial decryptions without changing their value. Since shares exchanged between pairs of honest parties remain hidden from the eyes of the adversary, the simulator has more freedom to replace the special party P_h upon corruption, by another honest party, even after simulating the decryption protocol.

5.1 Threshold Equivocal FHE

In the full version [35], we define *equivocal FHE* as an FHE scheme that is augmented with the capability to generate a public key in an "equivocal mode," allowing to explain any ciphertext as an encryption of any value. We show how to construct equivocal FHE from an HTDF scheme, which in turn can be based on LWE. This serves as a stepping stone for *threshold equivocal FHE* which is used in the construction below.

In a threshold FHE scheme, the key-generation and the decryption algorithms are in fact n-party protocols. We consider the simplest case of n-out-of-n threshold FHE and require a single round decryption protocol (following [3,43,54,71]). We note that threshold FHE for more general access structures are also known assuming LWE [14].

Definition 2 (TEFHE). *A threshold equivocal fully homomorphic encryption (TEFHE) is a seven-tuple of algorithms* (TEFHE.Gen, TEFHE.Enc, TEFHE.Eval, TEFHE.PartDec, TEFHE.FinDec, TEFHE.GenEquiv, TEFHE.Equiv) *satisfying the following properties:*

---

[9] We note that the same problem arises also in the threshold FHE scheme for more general access structures [14, Def. 5.5], where the simulation is defined only for *maximal* invalid party sets.

- TEFHE.Gen$(1^\kappa, 1^d) \to (\mathsf{pk}, \mathsf{sk}_1, \ldots, \mathsf{sk}_n)$: *on input the security parameter κ and a depth bound d, the key-generation algorithm outputs a public key* pk *and n secret key shares* $\mathsf{sk}_1, \ldots, \mathsf{sk}_n$.
- TEFHE.Enc$(\mathsf{pk}, \mu) \to \mathsf{ct}$: *on input a public key* pk *and a plaintext $\mu \in \{0,1\}$, the encryption algorithm outputs a ciphertext* ct.
- TEFHE.Eval$(\mathsf{pk}, C, \mathsf{ct}_1, \ldots, \mathsf{ct}_\ell) \to \mathsf{ct}$: *on input a public key* pk, *a circuit* C : $\{0,1\}^\ell \to \{0,1\}$, *and a tuple of ciphertexts* $(\mathsf{ct}_1, \ldots, \mathsf{ct}_\ell)$, *the homomorphic evaluation algorithm outputs a ciphertext* ct.
- TEFHE.PartDec$(i, \mathsf{sk}_i, \mathsf{ct}) \to \mathsf{p}_i$: *on input a secret key share* sk_i *and a ciphertext* ct, *the partial decryption algorithm outputs a partial decryption* p_i.
- TEFHE.FinDec$(\mathsf{pk}, \mathsf{p}_1, \ldots, \mathsf{p}_n) \to \tilde{\mu}$: *on input a public key* pk *and a set* $\{\mathsf{p}_i\}_{i \in [n]}$, *the final decryption algorithm outputs* $\tilde{\mu} \in \{0, 1, \bot\}$.
- TEFHE.GenEquiv$(1^\kappa, 1^d) \to (\mathsf{pk}, \mathsf{td})$: *on input the security parameter κ and a depth bound d, the equivocal key-generation algorithm outputs a public-key* pk *and a trapdoor* td.
- TEFHE.Equiv$(\mathsf{td}, \mathsf{ct}, m) \to r$: *on input a trapdoor* td, *a ciphertext* ct, *and a plaintext m, the equivocation algorithm outputs random coins r.*

We require the following properties:

1. The FHE scheme that is defined by setting the decryption key $\mathsf{sk} = (\mathsf{sk}_1, \ldots, \mathsf{sk}_n)$ and the decryption algorithm is composed of executing TEFHE.PartDec $(i, \mathsf{sk}_i, \mathsf{ct})$ for every $i \in [n]$ followed by TEFHE.FinDec$(\mathsf{pk}, \mathsf{p}_1, \ldots, \mathsf{p}_n)$ is a correct, compact, and secure equivocal FHE scheme for circuits of depth d.
2. Simulatability of partial decryption: there exists a PPT simulator $\mathrm{Sim}_{\mathrm{TEFHE}}$ such that on input $i \in [n]$, and all decryption keys except of the i'th one $\{\mathsf{sk}_j\}_{j \neq i}$ The following distributions are statistically close:

$$\{\mathsf{p}_i \mid \mathsf{p}_i \leftarrow \mathrm{TEFHE.PartDec}(i, \mathsf{sk}_i, \mathsf{ct})\} \overset{c}{\equiv} \{\mathsf{p}'_i \mid \mathsf{p}'_i \leftarrow \mathrm{Sim}_{\mathrm{TEFHE}}(i, \mathsf{ct}, \mu, \{\mathsf{sk}_j\}_{j \neq i})\},$$

where the keys are set as $(\mathsf{pk}, \mathsf{sk}_1, \ldots, \mathsf{sk}_n) \leftarrow \mathrm{TEFHE.Gen}(1^\kappa, 1^d)$, the ciphertext is set as $\mathsf{ct} \leftarrow \mathrm{TEFHE.Eval}(\mathsf{pk}, C, \mathsf{ct}_1, \ldots, \mathsf{ct}_\ell)$ for a circuit $C : \{0,1\}^\ell \to \{0,1\}$ and for $i \in [\ell]$ ciphertext $\mathsf{ct}_i \leftarrow \mathrm{TEFHE.Enc}(\mathsf{pk}, \mu_i)$ with $\mu_i \in \{0,1\}$, and $\mu = C(\mu_1, \ldots, \mu_\ell)$.

In the protocol, we will require some additional properties regarding the key-generation and threshold-decryption protocols.

Definition 3 (special TEFHE). *A special TEFHE is a TEFHE scheme satisfying the following properties:*

1. *On input 1^κ and 1^d, the key-generation algorithm* TEFHE.Gen *outputs* $(\mathsf{pk}, \mathsf{sk}_1, \ldots, \mathsf{sk}_n)$ *where the public key* pk *defines a prime number q, and each secret key* sk_i *is uniformly distributed in* $\mathbb{Z}_q^{n'}$ *for some $n' = \mathrm{poly}(\kappa, d)$.*
2. *The partial decryption algorithm* $\mathsf{p}_i \leftarrow \mathrm{TEFHE.PartDec}(i, \mathsf{sk}_i, \mathsf{ct})$ *operates by computing* $\mathsf{p}_i = \langle \mathsf{ct}, \mathsf{sk}_i \rangle + e \mod q$.
3. *For every $v_1, \ldots, v_n \in \mathbb{Z}_q$, the final decryption algorithm* TEFHE. PartDec$(\mathsf{pk}, \mathsf{p}_1, \ldots, \mathsf{p}_n)$ *satisfies the following* linearity *property*

$$\mathrm{TEFHE.FinDec}(\mathsf{pk}, \mathsf{p}_1 + v_1, \ldots, \mathsf{p}_n + v_n) = \mathrm{TEFHE.FinDec}(\mathsf{pk}, \mathsf{p}_1, \ldots, \mathsf{p}_n) + \sum_{i \in [n]} v_i.$$

Lemma 4. *Assuming LWE there exist special TEFHE schemes.*

The lemma is proved in the full version [35].

5.2 The Protocol

We define the protocol in the threshold-PKI hybrid model, where a trusted party generates the keys of the TEFHE scheme $(\mathsf{pk}, \mathsf{sk}_1, \ldots, \mathsf{sk}_n) \leftarrow \mathsf{TEFHE.Gen}(1^\kappa, 1^d)$ and $(\mathsf{pk}, \mathsf{sk}_i)$ to every P_i. In the full version [35], we probe the following theorem (Fig. 3).

Theorem 10. *Assume that special TEFHE exists, let $t < n$, and let $f : (\{0,1\}^{\ell_{in}})^n \to \{0,1\}^{\ell_{out}}$ be an efficiently computable function of depth d. Then, $\mathcal{F}^f_{\mathsf{sfe\text{-}abort}}$ can be UC-realized in the $(\mathcal{F}_{\mathsf{thresh\text{-}pki}}, \mathcal{F}_{\mathsf{smt}})$-hybrid model, tolerating an adaptive, semi-malicious, PPT t-adversary, by a two-round protocol with communication complexity $\mathrm{poly}(\ell_{in}, \ell_{out}, d, \kappa, n)$.*

Protocol $\pi_{\mathsf{allbutone}}$

- **Private Input:** Every party P_i, for $i \in [n]$, has private input $x_i \in \{0,1\}^{\ell_{in}}$.
- **Common Input:** A special TEFHE scheme Π and a circuit C_f of depth d.
- **The Protocol:**

1. Upon receiving $(\mathsf{input}, \mathsf{sid}, x_i)$, party P_i proceeds as follows:
   (a) Invoke $\mathcal{F}_{\mathsf{thresh\text{-}pki}}(\Pi, d)$ with $(\mathsf{init}, \mathsf{sid})$ to receive $(\mathsf{sid}, \mathsf{pk}, \mathsf{sk}_i)$. Let q be the prime associated with the public key pk (as per Definition 3).
   (b) Encrypt the input as $\mathsf{ct}_i \leftarrow \mathsf{TEFHE.Enc}(\mathsf{pk}, x_i)$.
   (c) Sample random $\mathsf{s}_i^1, \ldots, \mathsf{s}_i^n \leftarrow \mathbb{Z}_q$, conditioned on $\sum_{j=1}^n \mathsf{s}_i^j = 0 \mod q$.
   (d) Send $(\mathsf{sid}, \mathsf{ct}_i, \mathsf{s}_i^j)$ to P_j over a secure channel (via $\mathcal{F}_{\mathsf{smt}}$).
2. In case some party aborts, output $(\mathsf{output}, \mathsf{sid}, \bot)$ and halt. Otherwise, upon receiving $(\mathsf{sid}, \cdot)$ messages from all the parties, party P_i proceeds as follows:
   (a) Compute $\mathsf{ct} = \mathsf{TEFHE.Eval}(\mathsf{pk}, C_f, \mathsf{ct}_1, \ldots, \mathsf{ct}_n)$.
   (b) Partially decrypt the result as $\mathsf{p}_i = \mathsf{TEFHE.PartDec}(i, \mathsf{sk}_i, \mathsf{ct})$.
   (c) Set $\mathsf{m}_i = \mathsf{p}_i + \sum_{j=1}^n \mathsf{s}_j^i \mod q$ and send $(\mathsf{sid}, \mathsf{m}_i)$ to every party.
3. In case some party aborts, output $(\mathsf{output}, \mathsf{sid}, \bot)$ and halt. Otherwise, upon receiving $(\mathsf{sid}, \cdot)$ from all the parties, party P_i runs the final decrypt as $y = \mathsf{TEFHE.FinDec}(\mathsf{pk}, \{\mathsf{m}_1, \ldots, \mathsf{m}_n\})$ and outputs $(\mathsf{output}, \mathsf{sid}, y)$.

Fig. 3. 2-round MPC with semi-malicious security

Malicious Security with Sublinear Communication. Asharov et al. [3] provided a round-preserving compiler from semi-maliciously security to maliciously security in the static setting assuming NIZK. In the full version [35], we prove security of this compiler in the adaptive setting. We note that following the GMW paradigm, it is important that the semi-malicious protocol can be defined purely over a broadcast channel, however, the protocol in Sect. 5.2 uses secure channels. To resolve this issue, the secret shares of zero that were sent over secure point-to-point channels should be encrypted and transmitted over the broadcast channel. As we consider adaptive corruptions, we need to use non-committing encryption and each non-committing public key should be used to encrypt n elements in $\mathbb{Z}_q$. We consider the distribution of the NCE public keys as part of the threshold-PKI functionality. Alternatively, the public keys can be exchanged at the cost of an additional communication round.

Theorem 11 (Theorem 4, restated). *Assume the existence of special TEFHE schemes and NCE schemes, let $t < n$, and let $f : (\{0,1\}^{\ell_{in}})^n \rightarrow \{0,1\}^{\ell_{out}}$ be an efficiently computable function of depth d. Then, $\mathcal{F}^f_{\text{sfe-abort}}$ can be UC-realized in the $(\mathcal{F}_{\text{thresh-pki}}, \mathcal{F}_{\text{bc}}, \mathcal{F}_{\text{nizk}})$-hybrid model, tolerating an adaptive, malicious, PPT t-adversary, by a two-round protocol with communication complexity $\mathrm{poly}(\ell_{in}, \ell_{out}, d, \kappa, n)$.*

6   The Honest-Majority Setting

In this section, we show how to adjust the protocol from Sect. 5 that provides security with abort, into guaranteeing output delivery in the honest-majority setting. We apply some of the techniques from [54] on our adaptively secure protocol designed for the all-but-one setting, and achieve a matching result tolerating adaptive corruptions.

In the all-but-one case (Sect. 5) the decryption key was shared using additive secret sharing. As observed in [54], since the decryption of the GSW-based threshold FHE consists of linear operations, it is possible to use Shamir's secret sharing [77] instead. The problem with a naïve use of this idea is that when the partial decryptions are reconstructed, each decryption share is multiplied by the Lagrange coefficient, and thus also the smudging noise. This will result in blowing up the noise and may end up with an incorrect decryption. Gordon et al. [54] overcame this problem by having each party secret share (using Shamir's scheme) its smudging noise in the first round of the protocol, and parties added shares of the smudging noise of non-aborting parties in a way that is compatible with the decryption algorithm.[10]

In the full version [35], we adjust the definition of TEFHE to support $n/2$-out-of-n secret sharing, prove existence under LWE, and use it for proving the following theorem.

Theorem 12. *Assume the existence of special $n/2$-out-of-n TEFHE schemes, let $t < n/2$, and let $f : (\{0,1\}^{\ell_{in}})^n \rightarrow \{0,1\}^{\ell_{out}}$ be an efficiently computable function of depth d. Then, $\mathcal{F}^f_{\text{sfe-god}}$ can be UC-realized in the $(\mathcal{F}_{\text{thresh-pki}}, \mathcal{F}_{\text{smt}})$-hybrid model, tolerating an adaptive, semi-malicious, PPT t-adversary, by a two-round protocol with communication complexity $\mathrm{poly}(\ell_{in}, \ell_{out}, d, \kappa, n)$.*

Similarly to the previous section, using the semi-malicious to malicious compiler, we obtain the following corollary.

Theorem 13. *Consider the same assumptions as in Theorem 12. Then, $\mathcal{F}^f_{\text{sfe-god}}$ can be UC-realized in the $(\mathcal{F}_{\text{thresh-pki}}, \mathcal{F}_{\text{bc}}, \mathcal{F}_{\text{nizk}})$-hybrid model, tolerating an*

---

[10] Recently, Boneh et al. [14] showed that this problem can be overcome in a different way, by using a special secret sharing scheme that ensures the Lagrange coefficients are binary values.

adaptive, malicious PPT t-adversary, by a two-round protocol with communication complexity $\mathrm{poly}(\ell_{in}, \ell_{out}, d, \kappa, n)$.

References

1. Ananth, P., Badrinarayanan, S., Jain, A., Manohar, N., Sahai, A.: From FE combiners to secure MPC and back. IACR Cryptology ePrint Archive 2018/457 (2018)
2. Ananth, P., Choudhuri, A.R., Goel, A., Jain, A.: Round-optimal secure multiparty computation with honest majority. In: Shacham, H., Boldyreva, A. (eds.) CRYPTO 2018. LNCS, vol. 10992, pp. 395–424. Springer, Cham (2018). https://doi.org/10.1007/978-3-319-96881-0_14
3. Asharov, G., Jain, A., López-Alt, A., Tromer, E., Vaikuntanathan, V., Wichs, D.: Multiparty computation with low communication, computation and interaction via threshold FHE. In: Pointcheval, D., Johansson, T. (eds.) EUROCRYPT 2012, Part II. LNCS, vol. 7237, pp. 483–501. Springer, Heidelberg (2012). https://doi.org/10.1007/978-3-642-29011-4_29
4. Badrinarayanan, S., Jain, A., Manohar, N., Sahai, A.: Secure MPC: laziness leads to GOD. IACR Cryptology ePrint Archive 2018/580 (2018)
5. Barak, B., Sahai, A.: How to play almost any mental game over the net - concurrent composition via super-polynomial simulation. In: FOCS, pp. 543–552 (2005)
6. Canetti, R., Dodis, Y., Pass, R., Walfish, S.: Universally composable security with global setup. In: Vadhan, S.P. (ed.) TCC 2007. LNCS, vol. 4392, pp. 61–85. Springer, Heidelberg (2007). https://doi.org/10.1007/978-3-540-70936-7_4
7. Beaver, D., Haber, S.: Cryptographic protocols provably secure against dynamic adversaries. In: Rueppel, R.A. (ed.) EUROCRYPT 1992. LNCS, vol. 658, pp. 307–323. Springer, Heidelberg (1993). https://doi.org/10.1007/3-540-47555-9_26
8. Ben-Or, M., Goldwasser, S., Wigderson, A.: Completeness theorems for non-cryptographic fault-tolerant distributed computation (extended abstract). In: STOC, pp. 1–10 (1988)
9. Bendlin, R., Damgård, I., Orlandi, C., Zakarias, S.: Semi-homomorphic encryption and multiparty computation. In: Paterson, K.G. (ed.) EUROCRYPT 2011. LNCS, vol. 6632, pp. 169–188. Springer, Heidelberg (2011). https://doi.org/10.1007/978-3-642-20465-4_11
10. Benhamouda, F., Lin, H., Polychroniadou, A., Venkitasubramaniam, M.: Two-round adaptively secure multiparty computation from standard assumptions. In: Beimel, A., Dziembowski, S. (eds.) TCC 2018, Part I. LNCS, vol. 11239, pp. 175–205. Springer, Cham (2018). https://doi.org/10.1007/978-3-030-03807-6_7
11. Bitansky, N., Garg, S., Lin, H., Pass, R., Telang, S.: Succinct randomized encodings and their applications. In: STOC, pp. 439–448 (2015)
12. Bitansky, N., et al.: Indistinguishability obfuscation for RAM programs and succinct randomized encodings. SICOMP **47**(3), 1123–1210 (2018)
13. Boneh, D., Boyen, X.: Efficient selective-ID secure identity-based encryption without random oracles. In: Cachin, C., Camenisch, J.L. (eds.) EUROCRYPT 2004. LNCS, vol. 3027, pp. 223–238. Springer, Heidelberg (2004). https://doi.org/10.1007/978-3-540-24676-3_14
14. Boneh, D., et al.: Threshold cryptosystems from threshold fully homomorphic encryption. In: Shacham, H., Boldyreva, A. (eds.) CRYPTO 2018, Part I. LNCS, vol. 10991, pp. 565–596. Springer, Cham (2018). https://doi.org/10.1007/978-3-319-96884-1_19

15. Boyle, E., Gilboa, N., Ishai, Y.: Breaking the circuit size barrier for secure computation under DDH. In: Robshaw, M., Katz, J. (eds.) CRYPTO 2016, Part I. LNCS, vol. 9814, pp. 509–539. Springer, Heidelberg (2016). https://doi.org/10.1007/978-3-662-53018-4_19

16. Boyle, E., Gilboa, N., Ishai, Y.: Group-based secure computation: optimizing rounds, communication, and computation. In: Coron, J.-S., Nielsen, J.B. (eds.) EUROCRYPT 2017, Part II. LNCS, vol. 10211, pp. 163–193. Springer, Cham (2017). https://doi.org/10.1007/978-3-319-56614-6_6

17. Boyle, E., Cohen, R., Data, D., Hubáček, P.: Must the communication graph of MPC protocols be an expander? In: Shacham, H., Boldyreva, A. (eds.) CRYPTO 2018, Part III. LNCS, vol. 10993, pp. 243–272. Springer, Cham (2018). https://doi.org/10.1007/978-3-319-96878-0_9

18. Canetti, R.: Security and composition of multiparty cryptographic protocols. J. Cryptol. 13(1), 143–202 (2000)

19. Canetti, R.: Universally composable security: a new paradigm for cryptographic protocols. In: FOCS, pp. 136–145 (2001)

20. Canetti, R., Feige, U., Goldreich, O., Naor, M.: Adaptively secure multi-party computation. In: STOC, pp. 639–648 (1996)

21. Canetti, R., Lindell, Y., Ostrovsky, R., Sahai, A.: Universally composable twoparty and multi-party secure computation. In: STOC, pp. 494–503 (2002)

22. Canetti, R., Damgård, I., Dziembowski, S., Ishai, Y., Malkin, T.: Adaptive versus non-adaptive security of multi-party protocols. J. Cryptol. 17(3), 153–207 (2004)

23. Canetti, R., Pass, R., Shelat, A.: Cryptography from sunspots: how to use an imperfect reference string. In: FOCS, pp. 249–259 (2007)

24. Canetti, R., Goldwasser, S., Poburinnaya, O.: Adaptively secure two-party computation from indistinguishability obfuscation. In: Dodis, Y., Nielsen, J.B. (eds.) TCC 2015, Part II. LNCS, vol. 9015, pp. 557–585. Springer, Heidelberg (2015). https://doi.org/10.1007/978-3-662-46497-7_22

25. Canetti, R., Holmgren, J., Jain, A., Vaikuntanathan, V.: Succinct garbling and indistinguishability obfuscation for RAM programs. In: STOC, pp. 429–437 (2015)

26. Canetti, R., Poburinnaya, O., Venkitasubramaniam, M.: Better two-round adaptive multi-party computation. In: Fehr, S. (ed.) PKC 2017. LNCS, vol. 10175, pp. 396–427. Springer, Heidelberg (2017). https://doi.org/10.1007/978-3-662-54388-7_14

27. Canetti, R., Poburinnaya, O., Venkitasubramaniam, M.: Equivocating Yao: constant-round adaptively secure multiparty computation in the plain model. In: STOC, pp. 497–509 (2017)

28. Chaum, D., Crépeau, C., Damgård, I.: Multiparty unconditionally secure protocols (Abstract). In: Pomerance, C. (ed.) CRYPTO 1987. LNCS, vol. 293, pp. 11–19. Springer, Heidelberg (1988). https://doi.org/10.1007/3-540-48184-2_43

29. Cho, C., Döttling, N., Garg, S., Gupta, D., Miao, P., Polychroniadou, A.: Laconic oblivious transfer and its applications. In: Katz, J., Shacham, H. (eds.) CRYPTO 2017, Part II. LNCS, vol. 10402, pp. 33–65. Springer, Cham (2017). https://doi.org/10.1007/978-3-319-63715-0_2

30. Choi, S.G., Dachman-Soled, D., Malkin, T., Wee, H.: Improved non-committing encryption with applications to adaptively secure protocols. In: Matsui, M. (ed.) ASIACRYPT 2009. LNCS, vol. 5912, pp. 287–302. Springer, Heidelberg (2009). https://doi.org/10.1007/978-3-642-10366-7_17

31. Cleve, R.: Limits on the security of coin flips when half the processors are faulty (extended abstract). In: STOC, pp. 364–369 (1986)

58   R. Cohen et al.

32. Cohen, R.: Asynchronous secure multiparty computation in constant time. In: Cheng, C.-M., Chung, K.-M., Persiano, G., Yang, B.-Y. (eds.) PKC 2016. LNCS, vol. 9615, pp. 183–207. Springer, Heidelberg (2016). https://doi.org/10.1007/978-3-662-49387-8_8

33. Cohen, R., Lindell, Y.: Fairness versus guaranteed output delivery in secure multiparty computation. J. Cryptol. **30**(4), 1157–1186 (2017)

34. Cohen, R., Peikert, C.: On adaptively secure multiparty computation with a short CRS. In: Zikas, V., De Prisco, R. (eds.) SCN 2016. LNCS, vol. 9841, pp. 129–146. Springer, Cham (2016). https://doi.org/10.1007/978-3-319-44618-9_7

35. Cohen, R., Shelat, A., Wichs, D.: Adaptively secure MPC with sublinear communication complexity (2019). https://eprint.iacr.org/2018/1161

36. Cramer, R., Damgård, I., Dziembowski, S., Hirt, M., Rabin, T.: Efficient multiparty computations secure against an adaptive adversary. In: Stern, J. (ed.) EUROCRYPT 1999. LNCS, vol. 1592, pp. 311–326. Springer, Heidelberg (1999). https://doi.org/10.1007/3-540-48910-X_22

37. Dachman-Soled, D., Malkin, T., Raykova, M., Venkitasubramaniam, M.: Adaptive and concurrent secure computation from new adaptive, non-malleable commitments. In: Sako, K., Sarkar, P. (eds.) ASIACRYPT 2013, Part II. LNCS, vol. 8269, pp. 316–336. Springer, Heidelberg (2013). https://doi.org/10.1007/978-3-642-42033-7_17

38. Dachman-Soled, D., Katz, J., Rao, V.: Adaptively secure, universally composable, multiparty computation in constant rounds. In: Dodis, Y., Nielsen, J.B. (eds.) TCC 2015. LNCS, vol. 9015, pp. 586–613. Springer, Heidelberg (2015). https://doi.org/10.1007/978-3-662-46497-7_23

39. Damgård, I., Ishai, Y.: Constant-round multiparty computation using a black-box pseudorandom generator. In: Shoup, V. (ed.) CRYPTO 2005. LNCS, vol. 3621, pp. 378–394. Springer, Heidelberg (2005). https://doi.org/10.1007/11535218_23

40. Damgård, I., Nielsen, J.B.: Improved non-committing encryption schemes based on a general complexity assumption. In: Bellare, M. (ed.) CRYPTO 2000. LNCS, vol. 1880, pp. 432–450. Springer, Heidelberg (2000). https://doi.org/10.1007/3-540-44598-6_27

41. Damgård, I., Nielsen, J.B.: Universally composable efficient multiparty computation from threshold homomorphic encryption. In: Boneh, D. (ed.) CRYPTO 2003. LNCS, vol. 2729, pp. 247–264. Springer, Heidelberg (2003). https://doi.org/10.1007/978-3-540-45146-4_15

42. Damgård, I., Pastro, V., Smart, N., Zakarias, S.: Multiparty computation from somewhat homomorphic encryption. In: Safavi-Naini, R., Canetti, R. (eds.) CRYPTO 2012. LNCS, vol. 7417, pp. 643–662. Springer, Heidelberg (2012). https://doi.org/10.1007/978-3-642-32009-5_38

43. Damgård, I., Polychroniadou, A., Rao, V.: Adaptively secure multi-party computation from LWE (via Equivocal FHE). In: Cheng, C.-M., Chung, K.-M., Persiano, G., Yang, B.-Y. (eds.) PKC 2016. LNCS, vol. 9615, pp. 208–233. Springer, Heidelberg (2016). https://doi.org/10.1007/978-3-662-49387-8_9

44. Ganesh, C., Kondi, Y., Patra, A., Sarkar, P.: Efficient adaptively secure zero-knowledge from garbled circuits. In: Abdalla, M., Dahab, R. (eds.) PKC 2018. LNCS, vol. 10770, pp. 499–529. Springer, Cham (2018). https://doi.org/10.1007/978-3-319-76581-5_17

45. Garay, J., Ishai, Y., Ostrovsky, R., Zikas, V.: The price of low communication in secure multi-party computation. In: Katz, J., Shacham, H. (eds.) CRYPTO 2017, Part II. LNCS, vol. 10401, pp. 420–446. Springer, Cham (2017). https://doi.org/10.1007/978-3-319-63688-7_14

46. Garg, S., Polychroniadou, A.: Two-round adaptively secure MPC from indistinguishability obfuscation. In: Dodis, Y., Nielsen, J.B. (eds.) TCC 2015. LNCS, vol. 9015, pp. 614–637. Springer, Heidelberg (2015). https://doi.org/10.1007/978-3-662-46497-7_24

47. Garg, S., Sahai, A.: Adaptively secure multi-party computation with dishonest majority. In: Safavi-Naini, R., Canetti, R. (eds.) CRYPTO 2012. LNCS, vol. 7417, pp. 105–123. Springer, Heidelberg (2012). https://doi.org/10.1007/978-3-642-32009-5_8

48. Gennaro, R., Ishai, Y., Kushilevitz, E., Rabin, T.: On 2-round secure multiparty computation. In: Yung, M. (ed.) CRYPTO 2002. LNCS, vol. 2442, pp. 178–193. Springer, Heidelberg (2002). https://doi.org/10.1007/3-540-45708-9_12

49. Gentry, C.: Fully homomorphic encryption using ideal lattices. In: STOC, pp. 169–178 (2009)

50. Gentry, C., Wichs, D.: Separating succinct non-interactive arguments from all falsifiable assumptions. In: STOC, pp. 99–108 (2011)

51. Gentry, C., Groth, J., Ishai, Y., Peikert, C., Sahai, A., Smith, A.D.: Using fully homomorphic hybrid encryption to minimize non-interative zero-knowledge proofs. JCRYPTOL 28(4), 820–843 (2015)

52. Goldreich, O., Micali, S., Wigderson, A.: How to play any mental game or a completeness theorem for protocols with honest majority. In: STOC, pp. 218–229 (1987)

53. Gorbunov, S., Vaikuntanathan, V., Wichs, D.: Leveled fully homomorphic signatures from standard lattices. In: STOC, pp. 469–477 (2015)

54. Dov Gordon, S., Liu, F.-H., Shi, E.: Constant-round MPC with fairness and guarantee of output delivery. In: Gennaro, R., Robshaw, M. (eds.) CRYPTO 2015, Part II. LNCS, vol. 9216, pp. 63–82. Springer, Heidelberg (2015). https://doi.org/10.1007/978-3-662-48000-7_4

55. Groth, J.: Short pairing-based non-interactive zero-knowledge arguments. In: Abe, M. (ed.) ASIACRYPT 2010. LNCS, vol. 6477, pp. 321–340. Springer, Heidelberg (2010). https://doi.org/10.1007/978-3-642-17373-8_19

56. Groth, J., Ostrovsky, R., Sahai, A.: New techniques for noninteractive zero-knowledge. J. ACM 59(3), 11:1–11:35 (2012)

57. Hazay, C., Patra, A.: Efficient one-sided adaptively secure computation. J. Cryptol. 30(1), 321–371 (2017)

58. Hazay, C., Venkitasubramaniam, M.: On the power of secure two-party computation. In: Robshaw, M., Katz, J. (eds.) CRYPTO 2016, Part I. LNCS, vol. 9815, pp. 397–429. Springer, Heidelberg (2016). https://doi.org/10.1007/978-3-662-53008-5_14

59. Hazay, C., Venkitasubramaniam, M.: Composable adaptive secure protocols without setup under polytime assumptions. In: Hirt, M., Smith, A. (eds.) TCC 2016. LNCS, vol. 9985, pp. 400–432. Springer, Heidelberg (2016). https://doi.org/10.1007/978-3-662-53641-4_16

60. Hazay, C., Lindell, Y., Patra, A.: Adaptively secure computation with partial erasures. In: PODC, pp. 291–300 (2015)

61. Hazay, C., Polychroniadou, A., Venkitasubramaniam, M.: Constant round adaptively secure protocols in the tamper-proof hardware model. In: Fehr, S. (ed.) PKC 2017. LNCS, vol. 10175, pp. 428–460. Springer, Heidelberg (2017). https://doi.org/10.1007/978-3-662-54388-7_15

62. Hirt, M., Zikas, V.: Adaptively secure broadcast. In: Gilbert, H. (ed.) EUROCRYPT 2010. LNCS, vol. 6110, pp. 466–485. Springer, Heidelberg (2010). https://doi.org/10.1007/978-3-642-13190-5_24

63. Ishai, Y., Prabhakaran, M., Sahai, A.: Founding cryptography on oblivious transfer – efficiently. In: Wagner, D. (ed.) CRYPTO 2008. LNCS, vol. 5157, pp. 572–591. Springer, Heidelberg (2008). https://doi.org/10.1007/978-3-540-85174-5_32

64. Ishai, Y., Prabhakaran, M., Sahai, A.: Secure arithmetic computation with no honest majority. In: Reingold, O. (ed.) TCC 2009. LNCS, vol. 5444, pp. 294–314. Springer, Heidelberg (2009). https://doi.org/10.1007/978-3-642-00457-5_18

65. Ishai, Y., Pandey, O., Sahai, A.: Public-coin differing-inputs obfuscation and its applications. In: Dodis, Y., Nielsen, J.B. (eds.) TCC 2015, Part II. LNCS, vol. 9015, pp. 668–697. Springer, Heidelberg (2015). https://doi.org/10.1007/978-3-662-46497-7_26

66. Katz, J., Ostrovsky, R.: Round-optimal secure two-party computation. In: Franklin, M. (ed.) CRYPTO 2004. LNCS, vol. 3152, pp. 335–354. Springer, Heidelberg (2004). https://doi.org/10.1007/978-3-540-28628-8_21

67. Katz, J., Maurer, U., Tackmann, B., Zikas, V.: Universally composable synchronous computation. In: Sahai, A. (ed.) TCC 2013. LNCS, vol. 7785, pp. 477–498. Springer, Heidelberg (2013). https://doi.org/10.1007/978-3-642-36594-2_27

68. Katz, J., Thiruvengadam, A., Zhou, H.-S.: Feasibility and infeasibility of adaptively secure fully homomorphic encryption. In: Kurosawa, K., Hanaoka, G. (eds.) PKC 2013. LNCS, vol. 7778, pp. 14–31. Springer, Heidelberg (2013). https://doi.org/10.1007/978-3-642-36362-7_2

69. Lindell, Y.: Adaptively secure two-party computation with erasures. In: CT-RSA, pp. 117–132 (2009)

70. Lindell, Y., Zarosim, H.: Adaptive zero-knowledge proofs and adaptively secure oblivious transfer. J. Cryptol. **24**(4), 761–799 (2011)

71. Mukherjee, P., Wichs, D.: Two round multiparty computation via multi-key FHE. In: Fischlin, M., Coron, J.-S. (eds.) EUROCRYPT 2016, Part II. LNCS, vol. 9666, pp. 735–763. Springer, Heidelberg (2016). https://doi.org/10.1007/978-3-662-49896-5_26

72. Nielsen, J.B.: Separating random oracle proofs from complexity theoretic proofs: the non-committing encryption case. In: Yung, M. (ed.) CRYPTO 2002. LNCS, vol. 2442, pp. 111–126. Springer, Heidelberg (2002). https://doi.org/10.1007/3-540-45708-9_8

73. Nielsen, J.B., Nordholt, P.S., Orlandi, C., Burra, S.S.: A new approach to practical active-secure two-party computation. In: Safavi-Naini, R., Canetti, R. (eds.) CRYPTO 2012. LNCS, vol. 7417, pp. 681–700. Springer, Heidelberg (2012). https://doi.org/10.1007/978-3-642-32009-5_40

74. Patra, A., Ravi, D.: On the exact round complexity of secure three-party computation. In: Shacham, H., Boldyreva, A. (eds.) CRYPTO 2018, Part II. LNCS, vol. 10992, pp. 425–458. Springer, Cham (2018). https://doi.org/10.1007/978-3-319-96881-0_15

75. Quach, W., Wee, H., Wichs, D.: Laconic function evaluation and applications. In: FOCS, pp. 859–870 (2018)

76. Rabin, T., Ben-Or, M.: Verifiable secret sharing and multiparty protocols with honest majority (extended abstract). In: FOCS, pp. 73–85 (1989)

77. Shamir, A.: How to share a secret. Commun. ACM **22**(11), 612–613 (1979)

78. Venkitasubramaniam, M.: On adaptively secure protocols, pp. 455–475 (2014)

79. Yao, A.C.: How to generate and exchange secrets (extended abstract). In: FOCS, pp. 162–167 (1986)

Communication Lower Bounds for Statistically Secure MPC, With or Without Preprocessing

Ivan Damgård[✉], Kasper Green Larsen, and Jesper Buus Nielsen[✉]

Computer Science, Aarhus University, Aarhus, Denmark
{ivan,jbn}@cs.au.dk

Abstract. We prove a lower bound on the communication complexity of unconditionally secure multiparty computation, both in the standard model with $n = 2t + 1$ parties of which t are corrupted, and in the preprocessing model with $n = t + 1$. In both cases, we show that for any $g \in \mathbb{N}$ there exists a Boolean circuit C with g gates, where any secure protocol implementing C must communicate $\Omega(ng)$ bits, even if only passive and statistical security is required. The results easily extends to constructing similar circuits over any fixed finite field. This shows that for all sizes of circuits, the $O(n)$ overhead of all known protocols when t is maximal is inherent. It also shows that security comes at a price: the circuit we consider could namely be computed among n parties with communication only $O(g)$ bits if no security was required. Our results extend to the case where the threshold t is suboptimal. For the honest majority case, this shows that the known optimizations via packed secret-sharing can only be obtained if one accepts that the threshold is $t = (1/2 - c)n$ for a constant c. For the honest majority case, we also show an upper bound that matches the lower bound up to a constant factor (existing upper bounds are a factor $\lg n$ off for Boolean circuits).

1 Introduction

In secure multiparty computation (MPC) a set of n parties compute an agreed function on inputs held privately by the parties. The goal is that the intended result is the only new information released and is correct, even if t of the parties are corrupted by an adversary.

In this paper we focus on unconditional security where even an unbounded adversary cannot learn anything he should not, and we ask what is the minimal amount of communication one needs to compute a function securely. In particular: how does this quantity compare to the size of the inputs and to the

I. Damgård—Supported by the ERC Advanced Grant MPCPRO.

K. G. Larsen—Supported by a Villum Young Investigator grant and an AUFF starting grant. Part of this work was done while KGL was a long term visitor at the Simons Institute for Theory of Computing.

J. B. Nielsen—Supported by the Independent Research Fund Denmark project BETHE.

A. Boldyreva and D. Micciancio (Eds.): CRYPTO 2019, LNCS 11693, pp. 61–84, 2019.
https://doi.org/10.1007/978-3-030-26951-7_3

circuit size of the function? Since one can always compute the function without security by just sending the inputs to one party and let her compute the function, an interesting question is what overhead in communication (if any) is required for a secure protocol? An even harder question is if the communication must be larger than the circuit size of the function. Note that the questions only seem interesting for unconditional security: for computational security we can use homomorphic encryption to compute any function securely with only a small overhead over the input size.

There is a lot of prior work on lower bounding communication in interactive protocols, see for instance [Kus92, FY92, CK93, FKN94, KM97, KR94, BSPV99, GR03] (and see [DPP14] for an overview of these results). The previous work most relevant to us is [DPP14]. They consider a special model with three parties where only two have input and only the third party gets output, and consider perfect secure protocols. This paper was the first to show an explicit example of a function where the communication for a (perfectly) secure protocol must be larger than the input.

Later, in [DNOR16], a lower bound was shown on the *number of messages* that must be sent to compute a certain class of functions with statistical security. When the corruption threshold t is $\Theta(n)$, their bound is $\Omega(n^2)$. This of course implies that $\Omega(n^2)$ bits must be sent. However, we are interested in how the communication complexity relates to the input and circuit size of the function, so once the input size become larger than n^2 the bound from [DNOR16] is not interesting in our context.

In [DNPR16], lower bounds on communication were shown that grow with the circuit size. However, these bounds only hold for a particular class of protocols known as gate-by-gate protocols, and we are interested in lower bounds with no restrictions on the protocol.

In [IKM+13] the case of statistically secure 2-party computation with preprocessing is considered, where the parties are given access to correlated randomness at the start of the protocol. They show that the input size is (essentially) both an upper and a lower bound for the communication needed to compute a non-trivial function in this model, if one allows exponentially large preprocessed data. If one insists on the more practical case of polynomial size preprocessing, virtually all known protocols have communication proportional to the circuit size of the function. However, in [Cou18] it was shown (also for the 2PC case) that even with polynomial size preprocessed data, one can have communication smaller than the circuit size of the function, for a special class of so-called layered circuits.

1.1 Our Results

In this paper, we prove lower bounds for the model with n parties of which t are passively and statically corrupted. The network is synchronous, and we assume that the adversary can learn the length of any message sent (in accordance with the standard ideal functionality modeling secure channels which always leaks the message length). We consider statistically secure protocols in both the standard model with honest majority, $n = 2t + 1$ and the preprocessing model where $n = t + 1$ is possible.

To understand our results, note first that any function can be computed insecurely by sending the inputs to one party and let her compute the function. This takes communication S where S is the input size, assuming the output is short. What we show in both models is now that for any S, there exists a function f with input size S such that any protocol that evaluates f securely must communicate $\Omega(nS)$ bits. As mentioned, [DPP14] showed that such an overhead over the input size is sometimes required, we are the first to show that it grows with the number of players. So we see that security sometimes comes at a price, compared to an insecure solution.

However, we can say even more: we are able to construct functions f as we just claimed such that they can be evaluated by circuits of size $O(S)$. This means we also get the following: In both models, for any $g \in \mathbb{N}$ there exists a Boolean circuit C with g gates, where any protocol that evaluates C securely must communicate $\Omega(ng)$ bits. For the honest majority case, the result easily extends to constructing similar circuits over any fixed finite field. This shows that for all sizes of circuits, the $\Omega(n)$ overhead of all known protocols for maximal t is inherent. It is the first time it has been shown that there are circuits of all sizes which must suffer this $\Omega(n)$ overhead ([DNOR16] implies this result for circuits of size n).

The reader should note that since our result only talks about functions with linear size circuits, this leaves open the question of overhead over the circuit size when the circuit is much bigger than the inputs[1].

Our results extend to the case where the threshold t is suboptimal. Namely, if $n = 2t + s$, or $n = t + s$ for the preprocessing model, then the lower bound is $O(gn/s)$ and this shows that the improvement in communication that we know we can get for honest majority using so-called packed secret-sharing, can only be obtained if one accepts that the threshold t is $t = (1/2 - c)n$ for a constant c. In more detail, [DIK10] shows that for large n end even larger circuits of "sufficiently nice" shape, one can get a perfectly secure protocol with communication $\tilde{O}(g)$ for circuits with g gates (where the $\tilde{O}$ hides logarithmic factors in g and n). This protocol uses packed secret sharing which allows us to share a vector of $\Theta(n)$ field elements where each share is only one field element. We can therefore do $\Theta(n)$ secure arithmetic operations in parallel "for the price of one". This construction gives communication $\tilde{O}(g)$ but a corruption threshold much smaller than $n/2$. However, using the so-called *committee approach* (originally by Bracha but introduced for MPC in [DIK+08]), one can build a new protocol for the same function and similar complexity but now with threshold $t = (1/2 - c)n$ for an arbitrarily small constant c. Our results now imply that there is no way to improve the committee approach (or any other approach) to yield $t = (1/2 -$

---

[1] This is a much harder question of a completely different nature: for instance, if you are given a circuit to evaluate securely, there might exist a much smaller circuit computing the same function, so proving something on the overhead over the circuit size in general seems out of the question unless we are "magically" given the smallest circuit for the function in question.

$o(1))n$: the circuits we build in this paper are indeed "nice enough" to be handled by the protocol from [DIK10], so any hypothetical improvement as stated would yield a protocol contradicting our lower bound.

For honest majority, we also show an upper bound that matches the lower bound up to a constant factor for all values of $t < n/2$. This is motivated by the fact that the existing upper bound from [DN07] is a factor $\lg n$ off for Boolean circuits. We do this by exploiting recent results by Cascudo et al. [CCXY18] on so-called reverse multiplication friendly embeddings.

For dishonest majority with preprocessing, an upper bound for $t = n - 1$ was already known. Namely, by an easy generalization of the two party protocol from [IKM+13] (already mentioned there), one obtains communication complexity $O(nS)$ for any function where S is the input size, using an exponential amount of preprocessed data. This matches our lower bound up to a constant factor: for the functions we consider, circuit and input size are essentially the same, so our bound is $\Omega(ng) = \Omega(nS)$. This settles the question of communication complexity in the preprocessing model for maximal t and exponential size preprocessing. For the case of suboptimal values of t where $t = n - s$ we show an upper bound $O(tg/s)$ with polynomial size preprocessing, using a simple generalization of known protocols. We do not know if this can be strengthened to $\Omega(St/s)$ if one allows exponential size preprocessing.

On the technical side, what we show are actually lower bounds on the entropy of the messages sent on the network when the inputs have certain distributions. This then implies similar bounds in general on the average number of bits to send: an adversary who corrupts no one still learns the lengths of messages, and must not be able to distinguish between different distributions of inputs. Hence message lengths cannot change significantly when we change the inputs, otherwise the protocol is insecure.

To show our results, we start from a lower bound for the communication complexity of private information retrieval with or without preprocessing and one server. While such a bound follows from the results in [IKM+13], we give our own (much simpler) proof for self-containment. From this bound we show lower bounds for honest majority in the 3-party case and then finally "lift" the results to the multiparty case, while for dishonest majority we go directly from 2-party to multiparty. The observations we make in the 3-party case are related, at least in spirit, to what was done in [DPP14], indeed we also prove a lower bound for a case where 2 parties have input and the third has output. There are two important differences, however: first, we prove results for statistical security which is stronger than perfect security as in [DPP14] (because we show lower bounds). Second, while [DPP14] considers a very general class of functions, we consider a particular function (the inner product) which makes proofs simpler, but more importantly, we need the structure of this function to lift our results to the multiparty case.

The lifting is done using a simple but effective trick which is new to the best of our knowledge: loosely speaking, we start from a circuit computing, say $f(x_1, .., x_n)$ where the x_i's are the private inputs. Then we introduce an extra input bit b_i for P_i, and demand that her output be $b_i \cdot f(x_1, ..., x_n)$. By a reduction to the 3-party case, we can show that P_i must communicate a lot when $b_i = 1$ and $b_j = 0$ for $j \neq i$. Since now the identity of the party who gets the output is determined by the inputs, a secure protocol is not allowed to reveal this identity, and this forces all players to communicate a lot.

2 Preliminaries

2.1 Information Theory

We first recall the well-known Fano's inequality which implies that for a random variable X, if we are given the value of another random variable X' which is equal to X except with probability δ, then the uncertainly of X drops to 0 as $\delta \to 0$:

Lemma 1. *Let δ be the probability that $X \neq X'$ and $\mathcal{X}$ be the support set of X and X'. Then $\mathrm{H}(X \mid X') \leq h(\delta) + \delta(\lg |\mathcal{X}| - 1)$, where $h()$ is the binary entropy function.*

It is easy to see from this result that if δ is negligible in some security parameter while $\lg |\mathcal{X}|$ is polynomial, then $\mathrm{H}(X \mid X')$ is also negligible.

In the following we will use $\mathrm{D}(X, X')$ to denote the statistical distance between the distributions of X and X' with common support $\mathcal{X}$, that is:

$$\mathrm{D}(X, X') = \frac{1}{2} \sum_{x \in \mathcal{X}} |\Pr(X = x) - \Pr(X' = x)|$$

Now, from Lemmas 4.5 and 4.6 in [DPP98] it follows immediately that we can bound the change in entropy in terms of the distance;

Lemma 2. $|\mathrm{H}(X) - \mathrm{H}(X')| \leq \mathrm{D}(X, X')(\lg \mathcal{X} - \lg \mathrm{D}(X, X'))$.

The other result we need considers a case where we have two random variables X, Y and another pair X', Y' such that $\mathrm{D}((X, Y), (X', Y'))$ is bounded by some (small) δ. Then we can show that $\mathrm{H}(X \mid Y)$ is close to $\mathrm{H}(X' \mid Y')$:

Corollary 1. *Assume $\mathrm{D}((X, Y), (X', Y')) \leq \delta$, and let $\mathcal{XY}$ be the support set of X, Y. Then we have $|\mathrm{H}(X \mid Y) - \mathrm{H}(X' \mid Y')| \leq 2\delta(\lg |\mathcal{XY}| - \lg \delta)$.*

Proof. By the triangle inequality, it is easy to see that

$$\mathrm{D}(Y, Y') \leq \mathrm{D}((X, Y), (X', Y')).$$

Now we can use the above lemma and the triangle inequality again to calculate as follows:

$$\begin{aligned}
|\mathrm{H}(X|Y) - \mathrm{H}(X'|Y')| &= |\mathrm{H}(X, Y) - \mathrm{H}(Y) - (\mathrm{H}(X', Y') - \mathrm{H}(Y'))| \\
&\leq |\mathrm{H}(X, Y) - \mathrm{H}(X', Y')| + |\mathrm{H}(Y) - \mathrm{H}(Y')| \\
&\leq \delta(\lg |\mathcal{XY}| - \lg \delta) + \mathrm{D}(Y, Y')(\lg |\mathcal{Y}| - \lg \mathrm{D}(Y, Y')) \\
&\leq 2\delta(\lg |\mathcal{XY}| - \lg \delta).
\end{aligned}$$

$\square$

Again we can see that if δ is negligible in a security parameter while $|\mathcal{XY}|$ is polynomial, then the difference in conditional entropies is negligible.

2.2 Unconditionally Secure MPC

We look at a special case of MPC called secure function evaluation. There are n parties $P_1, \ldots, P_n$. They are connected by secure point-to-point channels in a synchronous network. Each of them has an input $x_i \in \{0,1\}^I$ in round 1. Eventually each P_i gives an output $y_i \in \{0,1\}^O$. We assume that $t < n/2$ of the parties can be corrupted. We consider only passive security. In this setting security basically means that the outputs are correct and that the distribution of the view of any t parties and be sampled given only their inputs and outputs.

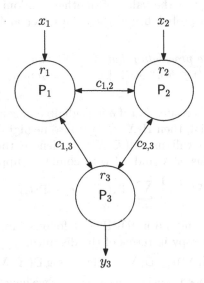

Fig. 1. A special case of the model where $n = 3$ and P_3 has no input and P_1, P_2 have no output.

We define security as in [Can00]. Here we give a few details for self containment. Each party P_i has a random tape r_i. In the pre-processing model or *correlated randomness model* $r = (r_1, \ldots, r_n)$ is drawn from a joint distribution R,

$$(r_1, \ldots, r_n) \leftarrow R.$$

In the *standard* model, each r_i is uniform and independent of everything else. We use

$$(y_1, \ldots, y_n) = \langle P_1(x_1; r_1), \ldots, P_n(x_n; r_n) \rangle$$

to denote a run of the protocol with input $x = (x_1, \ldots, x_n)$ and fixed random tapes, resulting in $P_i(x_i; r_i)$ outputting y_i. We use $c_{i,j}$ to denote the communication between $P_i(x_i; r_i)$ and $P_j(x_j; r_j)$. We let $c_{i,j} = c_{j,i}$. We let

$$\text{view}_i(x, r) = (x_i, r_i, c_{i,1}, \ldots, c_{i,n}, y_i).$$

This is all the values seen by P_i in the protocol. In Fig. 1, the model is illustrated for $n = 3$ and for the case where P_3 has no input and $\mathsf{P}_1, \mathsf{P}_2$ have no output.

For a set $C \subseteq \{\mathsf{P}_1, \ldots, \mathsf{P}_n\}$ and an input vector $\boldsymbol{x}$ we let

$$\text{view}_C(\boldsymbol{x}, \boldsymbol{r}) = (\boldsymbol{x}, \{(i, \text{view}_i(\boldsymbol{x}, \boldsymbol{r}))\}_{i \in C}, \boldsymbol{y}),$$

where $\boldsymbol{y} = (y_1, \ldots, y_n)$ and y_i is the output of P_i. We use $\text{view}_C \, \boldsymbol{x}$ to denote $\text{view}_C(\boldsymbol{x}, \boldsymbol{r})$ for a uniformly random $\boldsymbol{r}$.

We now define perfect correctness and perfect privacy.

Definition 1 (perfect correctness). *For all inputs $(x_1, \ldots, x_n)$ and all random tapes $(r_1, \ldots, r_n)$ it holds that*

$$\langle \mathsf{P}_1(x_1; r_1), \ldots, \mathsf{P}_n(x_n; r_n) \rangle = f(x_1, \ldots, x_n).$$

An adversary structure is a set $\mathcal{A}$ of subsets $C \subseteq \{\mathsf{P}_1, \ldots, \mathsf{P}_n\}$. It is usual to require that $\mathcal{A}$ is monotone but we do not do that here. For a simulator S and a set C of corrupted parties we define

$$\text{sim}_{C,S} \, \boldsymbol{x} = (\boldsymbol{x}, S\{(i, x_i, y_i)\}_{i \in C}, f\boldsymbol{x}).$$

The simulator might be randomized, and we use $\text{sim}_{C,S} \, \boldsymbol{x}$ to denote the distribution obtained by a random run.

Definition 2 (perfect privacy). *We say that a protocol for f has perfect privacy against $\mathcal{A}$ if there exists a simulator S such that for all inputs $\boldsymbol{x}$ and $\boldsymbol{y} = f\boldsymbol{x}$ and all $C \in \mathcal{A}$ it holds that the distributions $\text{sim}_{C,S} \, \boldsymbol{x}$ and $\text{view}_C \, \boldsymbol{x}$ are the same.*

Note that perfect privacy implies perfect correctness.

When working with statistical security we introduce a security parameter $\sigma \in \mathbb{N}$. The protocol and the simulator is allowed to depend on σ. We use

$$(y_1, \ldots, y_n) = \langle \mathsf{P}_1(\sigma, x_1; r_1), \ldots, \mathsf{P}_n(\sigma, x_n; r_n) \rangle$$

to denote a run of the protocol with fixed security parameter σ and fixed random tapes, resulting in $\mathsf{P}_i(\sigma, x_i; r_i)$ outputting y_i. We let

$$\text{view}_i(\boldsymbol{x}, \boldsymbol{r}, \sigma) = (\sigma, x_i, r_i, c_{i,1}, \ldots, c_{i,n}, y_i).$$

We use

$$(y_1, \ldots, y_n) \leftarrow \langle \mathsf{P}_1(\sigma, x_1), \ldots, \mathsf{P}_n(\sigma, x_n) \rangle$$

to denote a random run. In a random run, $\text{view}_i(\boldsymbol{x}, \sigma)$ becomes a random variable. For a simulator S, a set C of corrupted parties and security parameter σ we define

$$\text{sim}_{C,S}(\boldsymbol{x}, \sigma) = (\boldsymbol{x}, S(\{(i, x_i, y_i)\}_{i \in C}, \sigma), f\boldsymbol{x}).$$

We use $\mathrm{D}(V_1, V_2)$ to denote the statistical distance between the distributions of random variables V_1 and V_2. Statistical security is defined as usual: even given the inputs and outputs of honest parties, the simulated views of the corrupted parties are statistically close to the real views.

Definition 3 (negligible function). *We call a function* $\epsilon : \mathbb{N} \to \mathbb{R}$ *negligible if for all* $c \in \mathbb{N}$ *there exists* $n \in \mathbb{N}$ *such that*

$$\forall n > n_0 \, (\, \epsilon(n) < n^{-c} \,).$$

We use negl *to denote a generic negligible function, i.e., the term* negl *both takes the role as a function, but also has the implicit claim that this function is negligible.*

Definition 4 (statistical privacy). *We say that a protocol for f has statistical privacy against* $\mathcal{A}$ *if there exists a simulator S such that for all inputs* $\boldsymbol{x}$*, all values of* σ*,* $\boldsymbol{y} = f\boldsymbol{x}$*, and all* $C \in \mathcal{A}$ *it holds that*

$$\mathrm{D}(\mathrm{sim}_{C,S}(\boldsymbol{x}, \sigma), \mathrm{view}_C(\boldsymbol{x}, \sigma)).$$

is negligible (as a function of σ*).*

We call a protocol t-private if it is private for the adversary set consisting of all subsets of size at most t.

2.3   Private Information Retrieval

A special case of MPC is private information retrieval. The setting is illustrated in Fig. 2. The input of P_1 is a bit string $x_1 \in \{0,1\}^I$. The input of P_2 specifies an index $x_2 \in \{0, \ldots, I-1\}$. The output y_2 is bit number x_2 in x_1. In the correlated randomness setting the randomness can be sampled as any joint distribution $(r_1, r_2) \leftarrow R$ and r_i securely given to P_i. We call this pre-processing PIR (PP-PIR). In contrast, PIR takes place in the standard model where r_1, r_2 are independent and uniform.

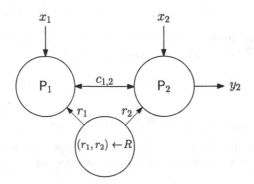

Fig. 2. PIR with pre-processing (PP-PIR).

Definition 5 (PIR). *We call π a perfect (PP-)PIR if it is perfectly correct and it is perfect $\{\{P_1\}\}$-private, i.e., the view of P_i can be simulated given just x_1. We call π a statistical (PP-)PIR if it is statistical $\{\{P_1\}\}$-private, i.e., the view of P_i can be simulated statistically given just x_1 and the protocol is statistically close to correct.*

We first (re)prove some basic facts about PIR. These results are known, at least in the folklore. However, we could not find a reference for the proof in the statistical security case, so we include proofs here for self-containment. Let $c_{1,2}$ denote the communication between P_1 and P_2. Then:

Lemma 3. *If π is a perfect PIR, then there exists a function x such that $x_1 = x(c_{1,2})$.*

Proof. The function postulated in the lemma can be implemented by computing each value $x_1[j]$ as follows: Given $c_{1,2}$, set $x_2 = j$ and iterate over all values of r_2, until one is found where where $(x_2, r_2, c_{1,2})$ is a possible value of P_2's view of π. More concretely, if P_2 starts from x_2, r_2 and we assume P_1 sent the messages in $c_{1,2}$ (with P_1 as sender), then P_2 would send the messages occurring in $c_{1,2}$ (with P_2 as sender). Once such an r_2 is found, output the value y that P_1 would output based on this view. It now follows immediately from perfect correctness that if the loop terminates, then $y = x_1[j]$. Moreover, perfect privacy implies that an r_2 as required for termination must exist: Given any view $x_1, r_1, c_{1,2}$ for P_1, then for any x_2 there must be an r_2 leading to this view. Otherwise, P_1 could exclude one or more values of x_2. $\square$

Lemma 4. *Assume that π is a statistical PIR. Let X_1, X_2 denote random variables describing uniformly random inputs to P_1, P_2. Let $C_{1,2}$ be the random variable describing $c_{1,2}$ after a random run on X_1, X_2. Then there exists a function x such that $\Pr[X_1 = x(C_{1,2})] = 1 - \text{negl}(\sigma)$.*

Proof. Let $C_{1,2}(x_2)$ denote $C_{1,2}$ when the input of P_2 is x_2. We now prove two claims.

Claim 1. There exists a function x_{x_2} such that

$$\Pr[X_1[x_2] = x_{x_2}(C_{1,2}(x_2))] = 1 - \text{negl}(\sigma).$$

Claim 2. For all x_2 and x_2' it holds that

$$D((X_1, C_{1,2}(x_2)), (X_1, C_{1,2}(x_2'))) = \text{negl}(\sigma).$$

Let us first see that if these claims are true, then we are done. By combining the claims we get that:

$$\Pr[X_1[x_2] = x_{x_2}(C_{1,2}(x_2'))] = 1 - \text{negl}(\sigma).$$

Now let $x(C) = (x_0(C), \ldots, x_{I-1}(C))$. Then by a union bound

$$\Pr[X_1 = x(C_{1,2}(x_2'))] = 1 - \text{negl}(\sigma),$$

as I is polynomial in σ. This holds for all x_2', so

$$\Pr[X_1 = x(C_{1,2})] = 1 - \mathrm{negl}(\sigma),$$

as desired.

Claim 1 follows from statistical correctness. Consider a random run of P_2 using input x_2 and uniformly random (r_1, r_2), resulting in communication $c_{1,2}$ and output y_2. We know that

$$\Pr[y_2 = X_1[x_2]] = 1 - \mathrm{negl}(\sigma).$$

Assume now that someone gave you the execution of the protocol but deleted x_1, r_1, r_2, and y_2, and hence left you with only $c_{1,2}$ and x_2. Consider now sampling a uniformly random x_1', r_1' and r_2' that are consistent with $c_{1,2}$ and x_2, i.e., running $\mathsf{P}_1(x_1'; r_1')$ and $\mathsf{P}_2(x_2; r_2')$ produced exactly the messages $c_{1,2}$. Let y_2' be the resulting output of $\mathsf{P}_2(x_2; r_2')$ when running $\mathsf{P}_1(x_1'; r_1')$ and $\mathsf{P}_2(x_2; r_2')$.

Then clearly y_2' and y_2 will have the same distribution. Namely, the distribution of the deleted x_1, r_1 and r_2 were also uniform, consistent with $c_{1,2}, x_2$. Hence

$$\Pr[y_2' = X_1[x_2]] = 1 - \mathrm{negl}(\sigma).$$

Let y be the function which samples y_2' from $c_{1,2}, x_2$ as described above. Let $x_{x_2}(\cdot) = y(\cdot, x_2)$. Then

$$\Pr[x_{x_2}(C_{1,2}(x_2)) = X_1[x_2]] = 1 - \mathrm{negl}(\sigma),$$

as desired.

Claim 2 follows directly from statistical privacy (P_1 does not learn x_2). Namely, we have that

$$\mathrm{sim}_{\{\mathsf{P}_1\}, S}(\boldsymbol{x}, \sigma) = ((X_1, x_2), S(X_1, \sigma), X_1[x_2])$$

and

$$\mathrm{view}_{\{\mathsf{P}_1\}}(\boldsymbol{x}, \sigma) = ((X_1, x_2), (X_1, C_{1,2}), X_1[x_2])$$

are statistically indistinguishable, so if we let $C_{1,2}'$ be the distribution of $C_{1,2}$ output by S, then

$$\mathrm{D}((X_1, C_{1,2}(x_2)), (X_1, C_{1,2}')) = \mathrm{negl}(\sigma)$$

for all x_2. Then use the triangle inequality:

$$\mathrm{D}((X_1, C_{1,2}(x_2)), (X_1, C_{1,2}(x_2'))) \leq$$
$$\mathrm{D}((X_1, C_{1,2}(x_2)), (X_1, C_{1,2}')) + \mathrm{D}((X_1, C_{1,2}'), (X_1, C_{1,2}(x_2'))) = \mathrm{negl}(\sigma).$$

$\square$

These results imply that the communication in single server PIR must be large: By Lemmas 4 and 1 we can conclude that $H(C_{1,2}) \geq I(X_1; C_{1,2}) = H(X_1) - H(X_1|C_{1,2}) \geq H(X_1) - \text{negl}(\sigma)$. We now show that a similar result holds for PP-PIR:

Lemma 5. *Assume that π is a statistical PP-PIR. Let X_1, X_2 denote random variables describing uniformly random inputs to P_1, P_2. Let $C_{1,2}$ be the random variable describing $c_{1,2}$ after a random run on X_1, X_2. Then $H(C_{1,2}) \geq H(X_1) - \text{negl}(\sigma)$.*

Proof. Let R be the function used to sample the correlated randomness (r_1, r_2), i.e., $(r_1, r_2) = R(r)$ for a uniformly random r. Notice that since (PP-)PIR does not impose any privacy restrictions on what P_2 learns, we can construct a secure PIR protocol π' from π as follows: P_2 runs R, sends r_1 to P_1, and then we run π. We can now apply Lemmas 4 and 1 to π' and conclude that $H(X_1|C_{1,2}, R_1) = \text{negl}(\sigma)$, here R_1 is a random variable describing the choice of r_1 and we note that the conversation in π' consists of r_1 and $c_{1,2}$. Since X_1 and R_1 are independent, we have $H(X_1) = H(X_1|R_1)$ and now the chain rule gives immediately that $H(C_{1,2}) \geq H(X_1) - \text{negl}(\sigma)$ as desired (intuitively, given R_1, the uncertainty on X_1 is maximal, but if we add $C_{1,2}$ the uncertainty drops to essentially 0, and so $C_{1,2}$ must contain information corresponding to the entropy drop). □

3   Lower Bounds Without Correlated Randomness

In this section we prove that there is an n-party function describable by a circuit C of size $|C|$ where each of the n parties have communication $\Theta(|C|)$, in the standard model. For the sake of presentation we present it via a series of simpler results, each highlighting one essential idea of the proof. We first give a function for three parties where one party must have high communication, proving the result first for perfect and then statistical security. Then we lift this up to an n-party function where there is a special *heavy* party. A heavy party has a short input and a short output, but still must have communication $\Theta(|C|)$ bits. Then we embed this function into a slightly more complicated one, where each party can obliviously choose to be the heavy party. This gives an n-party function where all parties must have communication $\Theta(|C|)$. This is because they must have communication $\Theta(|C|)$ when they are the heavy party, and a private protocol is not allowed to leak who is the heavy party. Throughout this series of results we assume maximal threshold $n = 2t + 1$ for simplicity. At the end we investigate how the bound behaves when $n = 2t + s$ for $1 \leq s \leq t$.

Our main theorem will be the following.

Theorem 1. *Let $n = 2t+s$. There exists a function $\widehat{\text{IP}}_{I,n}$ with circuit complexity $O(nI)$ such that in any statistically t-private protocol for $\widehat{\text{IP}}_{I,n}$ in the model without preprocessing, the average communication complexity is at least $\frac{Int}{2s} - \epsilon = \Theta(ntI)/s$ for a negligible ϵ.*

3.1 Lower Bound, Perfect Security, Three Parties

We start by considering a protocol for three parties of the form in Fig. 1. The input of P_1 is $x_1 \in \{0,1\}^I$, the input of P_2 is $x_2 \in \{0,1\}^I$. The output of P_3 is the inner product between x_1 and x_2, i.e., the single bit

$$y_3 = \bigoplus_{i=1}^{I} x_{1,i} x_{2,i}.$$

Denote this function by $\mathrm{IP}_{I,3}$.

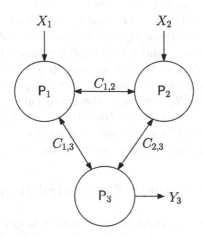

Fig. 3. A special case of the model where $n = 3$ and P_3 has no input and P_1, P_2 have no output, and where the inputs are uniformly random.

Theorem 2. *In any protocol for $\mathrm{IP}_{I,3}$ that is perfectly correct and perfectly private if P_1 or P_2 are corrupt, party P_3 will for random inputs have average communication complexity at least I.*

Proof. Assume that we have a protocol implementing $\mathrm{IP}_{I,3}$ with security as assumed. Let X_1 denote a random variable that is uniformly random on $\{0,1\}^I$. Let X_2 denote an independent random variable that is uniformly random on $\{0,1\}^I$. Let $C_{i,j}$ denote the communication between P_i and P_j in a random execution $\langle P_1(X_1), P_2(X_2), P_3 \rangle$ and let Y_3 denote output of P_3 in the random execution. See Fig. 3.

Below, we will first prove that the following two inequalities implies high communication for P_3:

$$H(X_1 \mid C_{1,2}, C_{1,3}, C_{2,3}) \leq \epsilon. \tag{1}$$

$$H(X_1 \mid C_{1,2}, C_{2,3}) \geq I - \epsilon. \tag{2}$$

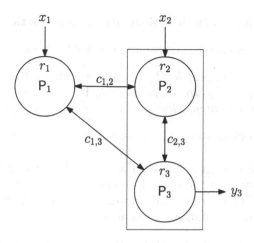

Fig. 4. Collapsing P_2 and P_3 into a single party.

These inequalities will be true with $\epsilon = 0$ for perfect security and for a negligible ϵ for statistical security. We will show that this implies:

$$H(C_{1,3}) \geq I - 2\epsilon, \tag{3}$$

To see this, we use the chain rule for conditional Shannon entropy:

$$I - \epsilon < H(X_1 \mid C_{1,2}, C_{2,3}) < H(X_1 C_{1,3} \mid C_{1,2} C_{2,3}) =$$
$$H(X_1 \mid C_{1,3} C_{1,2} C_{2,3}) + H(C_{1,3} \mid C_{1,2} C_{2,3}) \leq \epsilon + H(C_{1,3}).$$

We conclude that $H(C_{1,3}) \geq I - 2\epsilon$, i.e., P_3 must communicate on average at least $1 - 2\epsilon$ bits.

We now prove that for a perfectly secure protocol, (1) holds with $\epsilon = 0$. For this purpose, consider the 3-party protocol π' in Fig. 4, where we consider P_2 and P_3 as one party. We call P_1 the sender and (P_2, P_3) the receiver. Notice that x_2 can be taken to be any vector which is all-zero, except it has a 1 in position j. In that case it follows from perfect correctness of π that the receiver always learns the j'th bit of x_1. Furthermore, if π is perfectly private when P_1 is corrupted, then the sender learns nothing about j. This is because a corrupted sender learns only x_1 and r_1, exactly as in the protocol. So, if π is a perfectly correct and perfectly 1-private protocol for $IP_{3,I}$, then π' is a perfect PIR. Hence (1) follows from Lemma 3.

We then prove (2) for $\epsilon = 0$. To see this note that by perfect privacy when P_2 is corrupt, we can simulate $(C_{1,2}, C_{2,3})$ given X_2 as P_2 has no output. This implies that

$$H(X_1 \mid C_{1,2}, C_{2,3}) \geq H(X_1 \mid X_2) = I$$

as we wanted.

This completes the proof of Theorem 2. □

3.2   Lower Bound, Statistical Security, Three Parties

We now prove that essentially the same result holds also for statistical security.

Theorem 3. *In any protocol for* $IP_{I,3}$ *that is statistically correct and statistically private if* P_1 *or* P_2 *are corrupt, party* P_3 *will for random inputs have average communication complexity at least* $I - \epsilon$ *for a negligible* ϵ.

Proof. From the previous section it is clear that we only have to prove that (1) and (2) still hold.

As for (1), we clearly get a statistically secure PIR by considering P_2 and P_3 as one party, exactly as in the proof for perfect security. Then, by Lemma 4, it follows that given $C_{1,2}, C_{1,3}$ one can compute a guess at X'_1 such that $\Pr[X'_1 \neq X_1]$ is negligible. Then (1) follows by Lemma 1:

$$\mathrm{H}(X|C_{1,2}, C_{1,3}, C_{2,3}) \leq \mathrm{H}(X \mid C_{1,2}, C_{1,3}) \leq \mathrm{H}(X_1 \mid X'_1) \leq \epsilon$$

for a negligible ϵ.

As for (2), we exploit the fact that the protocol is statistically secure against a corrupt P_2. This means there exists a simulator that (using only x_2 as input) will simulate the view of P_2, including $c_{1,2}, c_{2,3}$. The definition of statistical security requires that the simulated view is statistically close to the real view even given the input x_1 (of the honest P_1). Note that here the distributions are taken only over the random coins of the parties and the simulator.

Now we run the protocol with a uniformly random X_1 as input for P_1, and a uniformly random input X_2 for P_2. As before we let $C_{1,2}, C_{2,3}$ denote the variables representing the communication in the real protocol while $C'_{1,2}, C'_{2,3}$ denote the simulated conversation. The statistical security now implies that

$$\mathrm{D}((X_1, (C_{1,2}, C_{2,3})), \ (X_1, (C'_{1,2}, C'_{2,3})))$$

is negligible—actually statistical security implies the stronger requirement that the distance be small for every fixed value of X_1 and X_2. Now (2) follows immediately from this and Corollary 1.

This completes the proof of Theorem 3. $\square$

3.3   Lower Bound, Statistical Security, n Parties, Maximal Resilience

We now generalize the bound to more parties. Assume that $n = 2t + 1$. We will call the parties $P_{1,1}, \ldots, P_{1,t}, P_{2,1}, \ldots, P_{2,t}, P_3$. We assume that P_3 only has output and the other parties only have inputs. Consider the following function $IP_{n,I}$, where each $P_{j,i}$ for $i = 1, \ldots, t; j = 1, 2$ has an input $x_{j,i} \in \{0, 1\}^I$ and no output, and where P_3 has no input and has an output $y_n \in \{0, 1\}$. The output y_n is the inner product between $x_{1,1} x_{1,2} \ldots, x_{1,t}$ and $x_{2,1} x_{2,2} \ldots, x_{2,t}$ computed in the field with two elements. See Fig. 5.

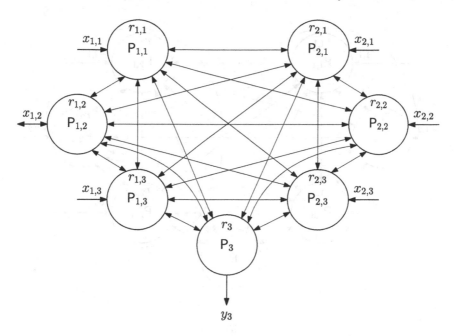

Fig. 5. A special case of the model where $n = 7$ and P_3 has no input and $P_{1,1}, P_{1,2}, P_{1,3}, P_{2,1}, P_{2,2}, P_{2,3}$ have no outputs.

Theorem 4. *Let $n = 2t + 1$. In any statistically t-private and statistically correct protocol for $\mathrm{IP}_{I,n}$ party P_3 will for all inputs have average communication complexity at least $tI - \epsilon$ for a negligible ϵ.*

Proof. Given a protocol for $\mathrm{IP}_{I,n}$, we can make a protocol for $\mathrm{IP}_{tI,3}$ by grouping parties together as in Fig. 6. Corrupting one party in $\mathrm{IP}_{tI,3}$ corrupts at most t parties in $\mathrm{IP}_{I,n}$. Therefore we can apply Theorem 3. $\square$

3.4 Stronger Lower Bound, Statistical Security, n Parties, Maximal Threshold

We now give a function where all parties need to have high communication complexity. We do this essentially by making a function where each party obliviously can choose to be the party P_3 in the proof of Theorem 4. Since nobody knows who plays the role of P_3 and P_3 needs to have high communication complexity, all parties must have high communication complexity.

Assume that $n = 2t + 1$. We will call the parties $P_{1,1}, \ldots, P_{1,t}, P_{2,1}, \ldots, P_{2,t}, P_3$. Consider the following function $\mathrm{IP}'_{n,I}$, where each $P_{j,i}$ for $i = 1, \ldots, t$; $j = 1, 2$ has an input $x_{j,i} \in \{0,1\}^I$ and an input $b_{j,i} \in \{0,1\}$, and where P_3 has input $b_3 \in \{0,1\}$. First compute y to be the inner product between $x_{1,1} x_{1,2} \ldots, x_{1,t}$ and $x_{2,1} x_{2,2} \ldots, x_{2,t}$. The output of P_3 is $y_3 = b_3 y$. The output of $P_{j,i}$ is $y_{j,i} = b_{j,i} y$.

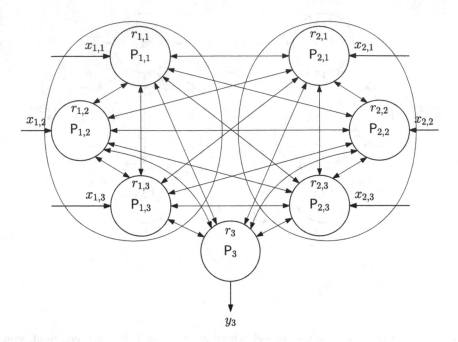

Fig. 6. Reduction from the n-party case to the 3-party case, maximal threshold $n = 2t + 1$.

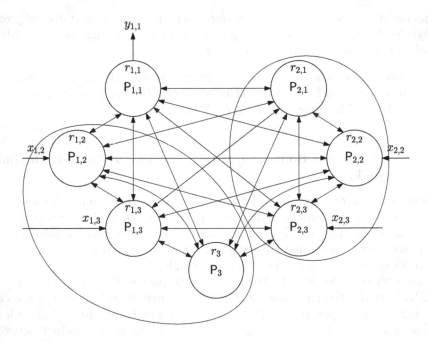

Fig. 7. Reduction from IP to IP$'$.

Theorem 5. *Let $n = 2t+1$. In any statistically t-private and statistically correct protocol for $\mathrm{IP}'_{I,n}$ the average total communication is at least $(n(t-1)I)/2 - \epsilon$ for a negligible ϵ.*

Proof. Assume we have such a protocol for $\mathrm{IP}'_{I,n}$. Notice that if we pick any input except that we hard-code the inputs $b_3 = 1$ and $b_{j,i} = 0$, then $\mathrm{IP}'_{I,n}$ is just $\mathrm{IP}_{I,n}$, so it follows trivially that for these inputs the communication complexity of P_3 is $tI - \epsilon$. And this holds for all possible inputs (by statistical security and by considering the case where no parties are corrupted), in particular also the inputs where we set all non-hardcoded inputs to be all-zero, i.e., $x_{j,i} = \mathbf{0}$ and $x_3 = \mathbf{0}$. Call this input vector $\boldsymbol{x}_3$.

Consider then hard-coded inputs where we make the change that $b_3 = 0$, $b_{1,1} = 1$, $b_{j,i} = 0$ for $(j,i) \neq (1,1)$, $x_{1,1} = \mathbf{0}$, and $x_{2,1} = \mathbf{0}$. If we have a secure protocol for $\mathrm{IP}'_{n,I}$ we of course also have one for the case with these hard-coded inputs. We can then via the reduction in Fig. 7 apply Theorem 3 to see that the communication complexity of $\mathsf{P}_{1,1}$ must be at least $(t-1)I - \epsilon$. Note that it is $t-1$ and not t as we had to get rid of the input of $\mathsf{P}_{1,1}$ to be able to reduce to the three-party case. The communication complexity of $\mathsf{P}_{1,1}$ is at least $(t-1)I - \epsilon$ for all ways to set the non-hardcoded inputs, so also when we set them to be all-zero. Call this input vector $\boldsymbol{x}_{1,1}$.

Similarly, define $\boldsymbol{x}_{j,i}$ to be the set of inputs where all inputs are 0 except that $b_{j,i} = 1$. We can conclude as above, that on this input $\mathsf{P}_{j,i}$ has communication complexity at least $(t-1)I - \epsilon$.

Consider then the input vector $\mathbf{0}$ where all inputs are 0. The only difference between for instance $\boldsymbol{x}_{j,i}$ and $\mathbf{0}$ is whether $b_{j,i} = 1$ or $b_{j,i} = 0$. Notice, however, that since all other inputs are 0, this change does not affect the output of any other party. Therefore their views cannot change by more than a negligible amount. This easily implies that the average amount of communication with $\mathsf{P}_{j,i}$ cannot change by more than a negligible amount. By linearity of expectation it follows that the average communication complexity of $\mathsf{P}_{j,i}$ cannot change by more than a negligible amount. So on input $\mathbf{0}$ party $\mathsf{P}_{j,i}$ will have average communication complexity negligibly close to $(t-I)I - \epsilon$. This holds for all parties. Therefore the average total communication is at least $(n(t-1)I)/2 - \epsilon/2$. It is not $(t-1)I$ as we would be counting each bit of communication twice (both at the sending and the receiving end). $\qquad\square$

3.5 Lower Bound, Statistical Security, n Parties, Sub-maximal Resilience

We now generalize our bound to the case with sub-maximal threshold, i.e., $n > 2t + 1$. Let $s = n - 2t$. We will first show that one group of s players must communicate a lot. We consider the function $\mathrm{IP}_{I,n,t}$, where each $\mathsf{P}_{j,i}$ for $i = 1,\ldots,t; j = 1,2$ has an input $x_{j,i} \in \{0,1\}^I$ and no output, and where $\mathsf{P}_{3,1},\ldots,\mathsf{P}_{3,s}$ have no input, and $\mathsf{P}_{3,1}$ has an output $y_n \in \{0,1\}$ which is the inner product of between $x_{1,1}x_{1,2}\ldots,x_{1,t}$ and $x_{2,1}x_{2,2}\ldots,x_{2,t}$ computed in the field with two elements. Call this function $\mathrm{IP}_{I,n,t}$. See Fig. 8.

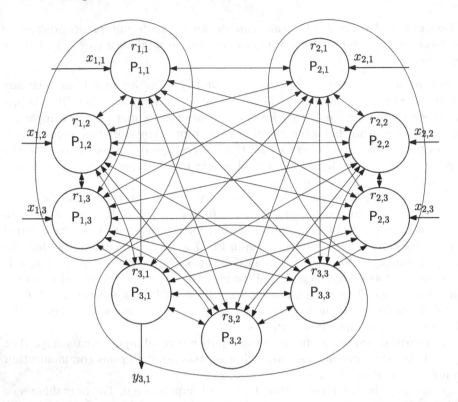

Fig. 8. Reduction from the n-party case to the 3-party case, sub-maximal threshold, here $n = 9$ and $t = 3$.

Theorem 6. *Let* $s = n - 2t$. *In any statistically* t-*private protocol for* $\mathrm{IP}_{I,n,t}$ *parties* $\mathsf{P}_{3,1}, \ldots, \mathsf{P}_{3,s}$ *will for all inputs have average total communication complexity at least* $tI - \epsilon$ *for a negligible* ϵ.

Proof. Given a protocol for $\mathrm{IP}_{I,n,t}$, we can make a 3-party protocol for $\mathrm{IP}_{tI,3}$ by grouping parties together as in Fig. 8. This protocol is secure against corruption of P_1 or P_2 since this corrupts at most t parties in the protocol for $\mathrm{IP}_{n,I,t}$. Therefore we can apply Theorem 3 (recall that to show that result, we only needed to corrupt P_1 or P_2). □

3.6 Stronger Lower Bound, Statistical Security, n Parties, Sub-maximal Threshold

Assume that $n = 2t + s$. Assume for simplicity that s is even and that s divides n. Let $n = 2T$.

We will call the parties $\mathsf{P}_{1,1}, \ldots, \mathsf{P}_{1,T}, \mathsf{P}_{2,1}, \ldots, \mathsf{P}_{2,T}$. Consider the function $\widehat{\mathrm{IP}}_{n,I}$. Each $\mathsf{P}_{j,i}$ for $i = 1, \ldots, t; j = 1, 2$ has an input $x_{j,i} \in \{0,1\}^I$ along with an input $b_{j,i} \in \{0,1\}$ and an output $y_{j,i} \in \{0,1\}$. The outputs are defined as follows.

First let y be the inner product between $x_{1,1}x_{1,2}\ldots, x_{1,T}$ and $x_{2,1}x_{2,2}\ldots, x_{2,T}$ computed in the field with two elements. Let $y_{j,i} = b_{j,i}y$.

We prove Theorem 1, which we recall here:

Theorem 7. *Let $n = 2t+s$. There exists a function $\widehat{IP}_{I,n}$ with circuit complexity $O(nI)$ such that in any statistically t-private protocol for $\widehat{IP}_{I,n}$ in the model without preprocessing, the average communication complexity is at least $\frac{Int}{2s} - \epsilon = \Theta(ntI)/s$ for a negligible ϵ.*

Proof. Assume we have a protocol for $\widehat{IP}_{I,n}$. Let $h = s/2$. We can group the parties into n/s groups of s parties, indexed by $g = 0, \ldots, n/s - 1$. In group G_g we put the parties $P_{1,hg+1}, \ldots, P_{1,hg+h}$ and $P_{2,hg+1}, \ldots, P_{2,hg+h}$.

For each g we can define three virtual parties P_1^g, P_2^g, P_3^g. We let $P_3^g = G_g$. We let $P_1^g = \{P_{1,1}, \ldots, P_{1,T}\} \setminus G_g$ and we let $P_2^g = \{P_{2,1}, \ldots, P_{2,T}\} \setminus G_g$. We then hardcode the inputs of the parties in G_g to be all-zero, except that we let $P_{1,hg+1}$ choose to be the heavy party by setting $b_{1,hg+1} = 1$. For all other parties, let them use $b_{j,i} = 0$. It follows by statistical security, as in the proof of Theorem 5, that the communication complexity for these hardcoded inputs must be the same as for some fixed input, say the all-0 one.

Note that $|P_1^g| = |P_2^g| = T - s/2 = t$. So if the protocol we start from is private against t corruptions, then the derived protocol for the three virtual parties is private against corruption of P_1^g or P_2^g. By Theorem 3, it follows that P_3^g must communicate at least $tI - \epsilon$ bits. There are n/s groups. Since the choice of g depends only on the private inputs, we can argue exactly as in the proof of Theorem 5 that all groups must communicate this much, so this gives a total communication of at least $(tIn/s)/2 - \epsilon/2$.

Finally, it is easy to see that the circuit complexity of $\widehat{IP}_{n,I}$ is $O(nI)$, since the cost of computing the function is dominated by the cost of computing the inner product. $\qquad\square$

4   Lower Bounds, Correlated Randomness

In this section, we consider lower bounds for protocols in the correlated randomness model and arrive at the following result:

Theorem 8. *Let $n = t + s$. There exists a function $PIR_{n,I}$ with circuit complexity $O(nI)$ such that in any statistically t-private protocol for $PIR_{n,I}$ in the preprocessing model, the average communication complexity is at least $\Theta(ntI)/s$.*

We sketch the proof of this result, the details are trivial to fill in, as they are extremely similar to the ideas in the previous section.

We define the function $PIR_{n,I}$ as follows: each party P_i has three inputs: $x_i \in \{0,1\}^I$, $z_i \in \{0,1\}^{\lg(nI)}$ and $b_i \in \{0,1\}$. To evaluate the function, set x to be the concatenation of all the x_i's and set $z = \oplus_{i=1}^n z_i$. Interpret z as an index that points to a bit in x which we denote $x[z]$. Then the output for P_i is $b_i \cdot x[z]$.

Assume first that we have a protocol π that computes $PIR_{I,n}$ with statistical security in the correlated randomness model when $t = n-1$ parties are corrupted. We consider the case $s > 1$ later.

For any fixed value $1 \leq i \leq n$, we can group the parties $\{P_j | j \neq i\}$ together to form one virtual party P_i^1, and let P_i play the role of a second virtual party P_i^2. Furthermore we hardcode the inputs as follows: $b_i = 1$ and $b_j = 0$ for $j \neq i$, and furthermore $z_j = 0^{\lg(nI)}$ for $j \neq i$. With this hardcoding we clearly obtain a PP-PIR where P_i^1 is the sender and P_i^2 is the receiver. It follows from Lemma 5 that the communication complexity for P_i^2 must be $\Omega(nI)$. Since this holds for any i, and since the communication pattern is not allowed to depend on the inputs, it follows as in the proof of Theorem 5 that all players must have this much communication always, so we see that the total communication complexity is $\Omega(n^2I)$.

Assume now that the threshold t is sub-optimal, i.e., $t = n - s$, where we assume for simplicity that s divides n. Now, given a protocol that computes $PIR_{I,n}$ in this setting, we can divide the set of players in n/s disjoint subsets of size s and show that each group of s players must have communication complexity $\Omega(nI)$. This follows similarly to what we just did, by hardcoding the inputs appropriately. As a result we get a lower bound of $\Omega(ntI/s)$ for this case.

Finally, we note that for any all large enough I (compared to n), the circuit complexity of $PIR_{n,I}$ is $O(nI)$. To see this, note that the cost of computing the function is dominated by computing $x[z]$ from x, z. This is known as the storage access function and is known to have a linear size circuit [Weg87].

5   Upper Bounds

5.1   Honest Majority

In this section, we prove upper bounds that match up to a constant factor the lower bounds we proved for the standard model with honest majority. At first sight this may seem like a trivial exercise: In [DN07] a passively secure protocol was presented that securely evaluates any arithmetic circuit C of size $|C|$ with communication complexity $O(n|C|)$ field elements. This seems to already match our lower bound. However, that protocol only works for a field $\mathbb{F}$ with more than n elements, and so cannot be directly used for the Boolean case.

One can partially resolve this by noticing that all our lower bounds hold for any finite field, in fact the proofs do not use the size of field at all. So if we consider instead the inner product function over a larger field $\mathbb{F}$, then the bounds match. But this is still not completely satisfactory because the result still holds only as long as $n < |\mathbb{F}|$.

To get a cleaner result, we can combine the protocol from [DN07] with a recent technique from [CCXY18] known as *reverse multiplication friendly embeddings* (RMFE). Such an embedding can be defined when we have a base field $\mathbb{F}$ and an extension field $\mathbb{K}$. Then the embedding consists of two $\mathbb{F}$-linear mappings S, T where $S : \mathbb{F}^k \mapsto \mathbb{K}$ and $T : \mathbb{K} \mapsto \mathbb{F}^k$. The defining property we need is that

$$T(S(\boldsymbol{a}) \cdot S(\boldsymbol{b})) = \boldsymbol{a} * \boldsymbol{b}$$

for any $a, b \in \mathbb{F}^k$, and where $a * b$ is the coordinate-wise (Schur) product.

So these mappings allow us to implement k multiplications in parallel in $\mathbb{F}$ by one multiplication in K. In [CCXY18] it is shown how to construct (families of) RMFE(s) such that $\mathbb{F} = \mathbb{F}_2$ and $\mathbb{K} = \mathbb{F}_{2^u}$ where u is $\Theta(k)$. So the encoding of a as an element in $\mathbb{K}$ comes with only a constant factor overhead. With these tools, we can prove:

Theorem 9. *There exists a perfect passive secure protocol for honest majority such that for any n and all large enough I, the protocol computes $IP'_{I,n}$ with communication complexity $O(n^2 I)$ bits.*

Remark 1. Since the protocol handles $n = 2t + 1$ this matches our upper bound in Theorem 5, up to a constant factor.

Proof. (Sketch) First we choose an RMFE by the above construction, so we have $S : \mathbb{F}^k \mapsto \mathbb{K}$ and $T : \mathbb{K} \mapsto \mathbb{F}^k$, we make the choice such that $n < |\mathbb{K}| = 2^u$. Then the protocol we build will work as long as $I \geq k$.

Recall that in the function $IP'_{I,n}$, which is defined at the start of Sect. 3.4, the first $2t$ parties get as input a vector consisting of I bits. We will call these the *vector parties*. In addition, each party also gets an input bit that decides if that party gets output. For convenience in this proof, we will denote the parties by a single index, so that P_j, for $j = 1..2t$ are the input parties, whereas P_n's only input is the bit b_n. Initially, each vector party will split his input vector into $\lceil I/k \rceil$ vectors of length k bits each, padding the last block with 0's if it is incomplete. By appropriate renumbering we can say that between them, the vector parties now hold k-bit vectors $x_1, ..., x_v$ and $y_1, ..., y_v$, where party P_j holds a subset of the x_i's if $1 \leq j \leq t$, and holds a subset of the y_i's if $t < j \leq 2t$. Let x be the concatenation of all the x_i's and y the concatenation of all y_i's. Now the desired output for party P_j, for all j, can be written as $b_j(x \cdot y)$ where $x \cdot y$ is the inner product.

Now, note that one way to compute $x \cdot y$ product is to first compute $z = \sum_i x_i * y_i$ and then add all coordinates in z (recall that $*$ denotes the Schur or coordinate-wise product). This is essentially the strategy we will follow.

Recall that each vector party P_j holds a subset of x_i's or a subset of y_i's. He applies S to each vector in his subset to get a set V_j of elements in $\mathbb{K}$. The parties will now use the V_j's as input to an instance of the protocol from [DN07]. This protocol can compute any arithmetic circuit over $\mathbb{K}$ and is based on Shamir secret sharing. It can therefore be used to compute securely $[\sum_i S(x_i) \cdot S(y_i)]$, which denotes a secret sharing of $\sum_i S(x_i) \cdot S(y_i)$, i.e., each party holds a share of the value.

Let $w = \sum_i S(x_i) \cdot S(y_i)$. Note that by linearity

$$T(w) = T(\sum_i S(x_i) \cdot S(y_i)) = \sum_i T(S(x_i) \cdot S(y_i)) = \sum_i x_i * y_i = z$$

So this means that the only remaining problem is the following: given a secret sharing of w, we need to securely compute $T(w)$ and add all coordinates of the resulting vector. The result of this will be $x \cdot y$, the result we want. If we think of $\mathbb{K}$ as a u-dimensional vector space over $\mathbb{F}$, the combined operation of applying T and adding the coordinates is an $\mathbb{F}$-linear mapping and hence has a matrix M over $\mathbb{F}$, actually with just 1 row. Therefore we will first compute sharings $[w_1], ..., [w_u]$ where he w_i's are the coordinates of w. This can be done by a standard method where we first create $[r], [r_1], ..., [r_u]$ for a random $r \in \mathbb{K}$ (by adding random contributions from all players). Then we open $w - r$, compute its coordinates in public and add them to $[r_1], ..., [r_u]$ to get $[w_1], ..., [w_u]$. Finally linearity of the secret sharing implies we apply M to the coordinates by only local computation to get a secret sharing of the result $[x \cdot y]$. We can assume that each party P_j has also secret shared a bit b_j where $b_j = 1$ if and only if he is to get the result. We can then compute $[b_j s]$ for each j and open this privately to P_j.

Let us compute the cost of all this: the main part of the computation is to compute $[w]$ from sharings of the inputs. This requires essentially $\lceil In/k \rceil$ secure multiplications which the protocol from [DN07] can do at communication cost $\lceil In/k \rceil \cdot n$ elements in $\mathbb{K}$. An element in $\mathbb{K}$ has u bits and u is $O(k)$. So the cost in bits is $O(In/k \cdot n \cdot k) = O(In^2)$. One easily sees that the cost of sharing the inputs initially is also $O(In^2)$. The final stage where we go from $[w]$ to the result does not depend on I and its cost can therefore be ignored for all large enough I.

$\square$

For values of t that are smaller than the maximal value, the protocol in the above proof can be optimized in a straightforward way using packed secret sharing. Concretely, if $n = 2t + \ell$, one can secret share a vector of ℓ values where shares are only 1 field element, so this saves a factor ℓ compared to the original protocol. This way, we easily obtain an upper bound matching the result from Theorem 1.

5.2 Dishonest Majority

In this section, we sketch a generalization of known protocols in the preprocessing model leading to an upper bound that matches our lower bound for the $PIR_{I,n}$ function.

Let us consider a passively secure variant of the well known SPDZ protocol for $n = t + 1$, i.e., the secret values are additively secret shared among the players (no authentication is needed because we consider passive security). Linear operations can be done with no communication and multiplications are done using multiplication triples that are taken from the preprocessed data. It is clear that such a protocol would work with any linear secret sharing scheme as long as corruption of t players gives no information the secret.

So for the case of $n = t + s$, we can use Shamir secret-sharing with polynomials of degree t. Using the packed secret-sharing technique we can then encode a vector of $\Theta(s)$ values as the secret, instead of one value. This allows us to perform $\Theta(s)$ multiplications in parallel while communicating only $O(n)$ field elements.

Namely, a multiplication involves opening two values, and this is done by sending shares to one player who reconstructs and sends the result to all parties.

Now, if we consider computing the $PIR_{I,n}$ function, the dominating part is to compute the storage access function (see Sect. 4). This function has a logarithmic depth layered circuit of size $O(In)$. We can therefore compute it by doing s operations in parallel at a time, leading to a communication complexity of $O(In^2/s)$ field elements.

One caveat is that this protocol will need a field with at least n elements, and the $PIR_{I,n}$ function is defined on binary values. This leads to an overhead factor of $\lg n$. However, using reverse multiplication friendly embeddings as in the previous subsection, we can get rid of this overhead.

Since we only need to consider $n > t \geq n/2$ in this model, we can assume that n is $\Theta(t)$, so a communication complexity of $O(In^2/s)$ bits matches our lower bound $\Omega(Int/s)$.

6   Conclusion and Future Work

In a nutshell, we have seen that nS where S is the input size, is a (up to a constant factor) lower bound on the communication complexity of unconditionally secure MPC, and for the particular functions we consider, this bound even equals the product of n and the circuit size of the function. For the dishonest majority case with preprocessing $O(nS)$ is also an upper bound (at least if one allows exponentially large storage for preprocessing).

Now, for honest majority, the obvious open problem is what happens for functions where the circuit size is much larger than the input: is there a lower bound that grows with the circuit size of the function (if we also require computational complexity polynomial in the circuit size)? Another question is whether our lower bound for suboptimal corruption threshold t is tight, in terms of the input size. Here $n = t + s$ and the bound is $\Omega(tS/s)$, so the question is if there is a matching upper bound, possibly by allowing exponential size preprocessing?

References

[BSPV99] Blundo, C., De Santis, A., Persiano, G., Vaccaro, U.: Randomness complexity of private computation. Comput. Complex. 8(2), 145–168 (1999)

[Can00] Canetti, R.: Security and composition of multiparty cryptographic protocols. J. Cryptol. 13(1), 143–202 (2000)

[CCXY18] Cascudo, I., Cramer, R., Xing, C., Yuan, C.: Amortized complexity of information-theoretically secure MPC revisited. In: Shacham, H., Boldyreva, A. (eds.) CRYPTO 2018. LNCS, vol. 10993, pp. 395–426. Springer, Cham (2018). https://doi.org/10.1007/978-3-319-96878-0_14

[CK93] Chor, B., Kushilevitz, E.: A communication-privacy tradeoff for modular addition. Inf. Process. Lett. 45(4), 205–210 (1993)

[Cou18] Couteau, G.: A note on the communication complexity of multiparty computation in the correlated randomness model. Cryptology ePrint Archive, Report 2018/465 (2018)

[DIK+08] Damgård, I., Ishai, Y., Krøigaard, M., Nielsen, J.B., Smith, A.D.: Scalable multiparty computation with nearly optimal work and resilience. In: Wagner, D. (ed.) CRYPTO 2008. LNCS, vol. 5157, pp. 241–261. Springer, Heidelberg (2008). https://doi.org/10.1007/978-3-540-85174-5_14

[DIK10] Damgård, I., Ishai, Y., Krøigaard, M.: Perfectly secure multiparty computation and the computational overhead of cryptography. In: Gilbert, H. (ed.) EUROCRYPT 2010. LNCS, vol. 6110, pp. 445–465. Springer, Heidelberg (2010). https://doi.org/10.1007/978-3-642-13190-5_23

[DN07] Damgård, I., Nielsen, J.B.: Scalable and unconditionally secure multiparty computation. In: Menezes, A. (ed.) CRYPTO 2007. LNCS, vol. 4622, pp. 572–590. Springer, Heidelberg (2007). https://doi.org/10.1007/978-3-540-74143-5_32

[DNOR16] Damgård, I., Nielsen, J.B., Ostrovsky, R., Rosén, A.: Unconditionally secure computation with reduced interaction. In: Fischlin, M., Coron, J.-S. (eds.) EUROCRYPT 2016. LNCS, vol. 9666, pp. 420–447. Springer, Heidelberg (2016). https://doi.org/10.1007/978-3-662-49896-5_15

[DNPR16] Damgård, I., Nielsen, J.B., Polychroniadou, A., Raskin, M.A.: On the communication required for unconditionally secure multiplication. In: Robshaw, M., Katz, J. (eds.) CRYPTO 2016. LNCS, vol. 9815, pp. 459–488. Springer, Heidelberg (2016). https://doi.org/10.1007/978-3-662-53008-5_16

[DPP98] Damgård, I., Pedersen, T.P., Pfitzmann, B.: Statistical secrecy and multibit commitments. IEEE Trans. Inf. Theory 44(3), 1143–1151 (1998)

[DPP14] Data, D., Prabhakaran, M.M., Prabhakaran, V.M.: On the communication complexity of secure computation. In: Garay, J.A., Gennaro, R. (eds.) CRYPTO 2014. LNCS, vol. 8617, pp. 199–216. Springer, Heidelberg (2014). https://doi.org/10.1007/978-3-662-44381-1_12

[FKN94] Feige, U., Kilian, J., Naor, M.: A minimal model for secure computation (extended abstract), pp. 554–563 (1994)

[FY92] Franklin, M.K., Yung, M.: Communication complexity of secure computation (extended abstract), pp. 699–710 (1992)

[GR03] Gál, A., Rosén, A.: Lower bounds on the amount of randomness in private computation, pp. 659–666 (2003)

[IKM+13] Ishai, Y., Kushilevitz, E., Meldgaard, S., Orlandi, C., Paskin-Cherniavsky, A.: On the power of correlated randomness in secure computation. In: Sahai, A. (ed.) TCC 2013. LNCS, vol. 7785, pp. 600–620. Springer, Heidelberg (2013). https://doi.org/10.1007/978-3-642-36594-2_34

[KM97] Kushilevitz, E., Mansour, Y.: Randomness in private computations. SIAM J. Discrete Math. 10(4), 647–661 (1997)

[KR94] Kushilevitz, E., Rosén, A.: A randomnesss-rounds tradeoff in private computation, pp. 397–410 (1994)

[Kus92] Kushilevitz, E.: Privacy and communication complexity. SIAM J. Discrete Math. 5(2), 273–284 (1992)

[Weg87] Wegener, I.: The complexity of Boolean functions (1987). https://eccc.weizmann.ac.il/static/books/The_Complexity_of_Boolean_Functions/

Communication-Efficient Unconditional MPC with Guaranteed Output Delivery

Vipul Goyal[1], Yanyi Liu[2], and Yifan Song[1(✉)]

[1] Carnegie Mellon University, Pittsburgh, USA
vipul@cmu.edu, yifans2@andrew.cmu.edu
[2] Tsinghua University, Beijing, China
yl2866@cornell.edu

Abstract. We study the communication complexity of unconditionally secure MPC with guaranteed output delivery over point-to-point channels for corruption threshold $t < n/3$. We ask the question: "is it possible to construct MPC in this setting s.t. the communication complexity per multiplication gate is linear in the number of parties?" While a number of works have focused on reducing the communication complexity in this setting, the answer to the above question has remained elusive for over a decade.

We resolve the above question in the affirmative by providing an MPC with communication complexity $O(Cn\kappa + n^3\kappa)$ where κ is the size of an element in the field, C is the size of the (arithmetic) circuit, and, n is the number of parties. This represents a strict improvement over the previously best known communication complexity of $O(Cn\kappa + D_M n^2\kappa + n^3\kappa)$ where D_M is the multiplicative depth of the circuit. To obtain this result, we introduce a novel technique called *4-consistent tuples of sharings* which we believe to be of independent interest.

1 Introduction

In secure multiparty computation (MPC), a set of n players wish to evaluate a function f on their private inputs. The function f is publicly known to all players and is assumed to be an arithmetic circuit C over some finite field. Very informally, the protocol execution should not leak anything about the individual inputs beyond what can already be inferred from the function output.

The notion of MPC was introduced in the beautiful work of Yao [Yao82]. Early feasibility results on MPC were obtained by Yao [Yao82] and Goldreich et al. [GMW87] in the computational setting where the adversary is assumed to have bounded computational resources. Subsequent works [BOGW88, CCD88] considered the unconditional (or information-theoretic) setting and showed a positive result for up to $t < n/3$ corrupted parties assuming point-to-point communication channels. If one assumes a broadcast channel in addition, it was

---

V. Goyal and Y. Song—Research supported in part by a JP Morgan Faculty Fellowship, a gift from Ripple, a gift from DoS Networks, a grant from Northrop Grumman, and, a Cylab seed funding award.

A. Boldyreva and D. Micciancio (Eds.): CRYPTO 2019, LNCS 11693, pp. 85–114, 2019.
https://doi.org/10.1007/978-3-030-26951-7_4

shown in [RBO89,Bea89] how to obtain positive results in the unconditional setting for up to $t < n/2$ corrupted parties. MPC plays a central role in cryptography, and, by now has been studied in a variety of different interesting settings. Examples include security against semi-honest adversaries vs malicious adversaries, unconditional security vs computational security, and, security with abort vs guaranteed output delivery.

In this work, we are interested in the communication complexity of unconditionally secure MPC with guaranteed output delivery. We assume that the parties are connected using point-to-point channels, the adversary is malicious (and may deviate from the protocol arbitrarily), and, the corruption threshold $t < n/3$ (to avoid the known negative results on Byzantine agreement [LSP82]). Indeed, the classical BGW protocol already gives a feasibility result in this setting by presenting an unconditional MPC with guaranteed output delivery for corruption threshold $t < n/3$. Several subsequent works have focused on improving the communication complexity of MPC in this setting. Note that the real world efficiency of MPC in the unconditional setting is typically dominated by its communication complexity (as opposed to the computational complexity). This is because the local computations required are typically simple: often just a series of linear operations. Representing the functionality as an arithmetic circuit, the addition gates are typically "free" requiring no communication at all. Hence, the communication complexity of the protocol depends upon the number of multiplication gates in the circuit.

In this paper, we ask the following natural question:

"Is it possible to construct unconditional MPC with guaranteed output delivery for $t < n/3$ s.t. the communication complexity per multiplication gate is linear in the number of parties?"

Having linear communication complexity is interesting as it means that the work done by a single party is independent of the number of parties participating in the computation, giving a fully scalable protocol. While a number of works have made significant progress, the answer to this question has remained elusive so far. Best known communication complexity for malicious adversaries in this setting comes from the construction in [BTH08]. The construction in [BTH08] has communication complexity $O(Cn\kappa + D_M n^2 \kappa + n^3 \kappa)$ where κ is the size of an element in the field, C is the circuit size and D_M is the multiplicative depth of the circuit. For circuits which are "narrow and deep" (i.e., the multiplicative depth D_M is not much smaller than the circuit size C), the communication complexity per multiplication gate can be as high as $O(n^2)$ elements. The factor of $D_M n^2 \kappa$ unfortunately appears in several papers studying this setting [DN07,BTH08], [DIK10,BSFO12]. This led Ben-Sasson, Fehr, and, Ostrovsky to ask the question whether this factor is inherent [BSFO12].

Building on a variety of previous works, it was shown in [DI06,HN06] that there exist cryptographic secure MPC protocols with linear communication complexity with guaranteed output delivery. In the unconditional setting, linear communication complexity protocols are known for passive adversaries [DN07].

However the question of obtaining an analogous construction against active adversaries has remained open for over a decade.

Our Results. In this work, we resolve the above question in the affirmative by providing an MPC with guaranteed output delivery, perfect security against a malicious adversary corrupting up to $t < n/3$ of the parties, and, using only point-to-point communication channels. The communication complexity of our construction is $O(Cn\kappa + n^3\kappa)$ which is a strict improvement over the previous best result of [BTH08]. Compared with the work [BTH08], our main contribution is removing the quadratic term related to the multiplicative depth of the circuit, while keeping the circuit-independent term as efficient as that in [BTH08]. To obtain this result, we introduce a novel technique which we call *4-consistent tuples of sharings*. Very informally, this technique allows us to increase the redundancy in an n-out-of-n sharing "on demand" such that if an adversary cheats and changes its share in the n-out-of-n sharing, it can be detected and either kicked out or added to a list of disputed parties. A high level overview of the key technical obstacle encountered by previous works, and, how we overcome it using 4-consistent tuples of sharings is given in Sect. 2.

Related Works. The notion of MPC was first introduced in [Yao82, GMW87] in 1980s. Feasibility results for MPC were obtained by [Yao82, GMW87, CDVdG87] under cryptographic assumptions, and by [BOGW88, CCD88] in the information-theoretic setting. Subsequently, a large number of works have focused on improving the efficiency of MPC protocols in various settings.

In this work, we focus on improving the asymptotic communication complexity of MPC for arithmetic circuits over a finite field with output delivery guarantee and security against an active adversary which may control up to $t < n/3$ parties, in the information-theoretical setting. After the pioneering work of Ben-Or et al. [BOGW88] which shows the feasibility in this setting, Hirt et al. [HMP00] introduced Party-Elimination Framework which is a general technique to efficiently transform a semi-honest protocol into a protocol providing unconditional security with minimal additional cost. With this technique, Hirt et al. constructed a MPC protocol with communication complexity $O(Cn^3\kappa + \text{poly}(n,\kappa))$ bits, where C is the size of the circuit and κ is the size of an element in the underlying field. A number of works [HM01, DN07, BTH08] then continued to improve the communication complexity by using this technique. The previous best result [BTH08] provided a protocol with perfect security with asymptotic communication complexity $O(Cn\kappa + D_M n^2\kappa + n^3\kappa)$ bits, where D_M is the multiplicative depth of the circuit. In a subsequent result [BSFO12] which focuses on the setting of security against up to $t < n/2$ corrupted parties assuming the existence of a broadcast channel, the authors raised the question whether the quadratic dependency w.r.t. the multiplicative depth is an inherent restriction. Our result answers this question by presenting the first construction which achieves linear communication per multiplication gate.

A number of works also focus on improving the communication efficiency of MPC with output delivery guarantee in the settings with different threshold on the number of corrupted parties. In the setting where $t < (1/3 - \epsilon)n$, secret sharing can be used to hide a batch of values, resulting in more efficient protocols. E.g., Damgard et al. [DIK10] introduced a protocol with communication complexity $O(C \log C \log n \cdot \kappa + D_M^2 \text{poly}(n, \log C)\kappa)$ bits. In the setting of honest majority (i.e., $t < 1/2n$), Hirt et al. [HN06] presented a protocol with communication complexity $O(Cn\kappa + n\mathcal{BC})$, where $\mathcal{BC}$ is the cost for broadcasting a bit by one party, by using threshold homomorphic encryption [Pai99] and assuming the existence of a broadcast channel. Ben-Sasson et al. [BSFO12] presented a protocol with communication complexity $O(Cn\kappa + D_M n^2 \kappa + n^7 \kappa)$ assuming the existence of a broadcast channel in the information-theoretical setting. More recent works in the computational setting have been able to obtain communication efficient MPC with output delivery guarantee in as low as 3 rounds, e.g., [BJMS18].

A rich line of works have focused on the performance of MPC in practice. Many concretely efficient MPC protocols were presented in [LP12, NNOB12, FLNW17] [ABF+17, LN17, CGH+18]. All of these works emphasized on the practical running time and only provided security with abort. Some of them were specially constructed for two parties [LP12, NNOB12] or three parties [FLNW17, ABF+17].

2   Technical Overview

Our goal is to construct an unconditionally secure MPC protocol with guaranteed output delivery against a fully malicious adversary which may corrupt $t < n/3$ parties. Our construction is for arithmetic circuits over a finite field, and, achieves a communication complexity per multiplication gate which is linear in the number of parties. The previous best result in this setting was obtained over a decade ago by [BTH08]. In this section, we present an overview of our main ideas.

How Previous Techniques Work: The communication complexity achieved by the construction in [BTH08] is $O(Cn\kappa + D_M n^2 \kappa + n^3 \kappa)$ where κ is the size of an element in the field, C is the circuit size and D_M is the multiplicative depth of the circuit. Our goal would be to eliminate the term $O(D_M n^2 \kappa)$ which would allow us to obtain a construction with linear communication complexity per multiplication gate.

We now take a closer look at the construction in [BTH08]. To improve the efficiency, several subroutines in [BTH08] handle a *batch* of $O(n)$ multiplication gates at one time. The overall cost of each such operation is $O(n^2)$ elements. In this way, the amortized cost per multiplication gate only comes out to $O(n)$ elements. While this seems to already give us the result we seek, a major limitation of the techniques in [BTH08] (as well as prior works) is that the batches must solely consist of multiplication gates *at the same depth in the circuit*. Since the communication cost for a batch is at least $O(n^2)$ field elements (even if the number of multiplication gates in the batch is significantly lower than n), and, the number of batches is at least the multiplicative depth D_M, the overall communication complexity cannot be lower than $O(D_M n^2 \kappa)$.

The fundamental reason why we can only handle multiplication gates from a single layer in any given batch is that the parties need to ensure that the result of computing a layer is correct before moving on to the next layer. To understand why this is the case, consider the following explicit attack.

The Key Bottleneck: We briefly describe the protocol for each multiplication gate in [BTH08]. Let x, y be the inputs of the multiplication gate. We use $[x]_d$ to denote a d-sharing of x. A d-sharing of x is the vector of shares obtained by applying a $(d+1)$-out-of-n secret sharing scheme on x. After a sharing is distributed, each party holds a single share. Now consider the evaluation of a multiplication gate. In the beginning, all parties hold shares of input wire values $[x]_t, [y]_t$. In addition, all parties also hold a random (Beaver) tuple of sharings $([a]_t, [b]_t, [c]_t)$ where $c = ab$ generated in the preparation phase. To compute the output sharing $[xy]_t$, the parties will go through the following steps:

1. All parties locally compute $[x+a]_t := [x]_t + [a]_t$ and $[y+b]_t := [y]_t + [b]_t$.
2. All parties reconstruct $[x+a]_t, [y+b]_t$ by using a reconstruction protocol discussed below.
3. On receiving $x+a, y+b$, all parties locally compute $[xy]_t = (x+a)(y+b) - (x+a)[b]_t - (y+b)[a]_t + [c]_t$.

Our first attempt is to let one party P_{king} collect all the shares from $[x+a]_t, [y+b]_t$, reconstruct $x+a, y+b$, and send the results back to all other parties. In this way, each multiplication gate only costs $O(n\kappa)$ bits even though we are evaluating a single multiplication gate. Even if some of the parties are corrupted, P_{king} can use error correction to recover the correct values. However, if P_{king} itself is corrupted, the honest parties may get incorrect results. In fact, P_{king} may even decide to send different values to different honest parties resulting in honest parties holding inconsistent shares. At this point, if without any further verification, one more multiplication gate is computed on the resulting output, we show that P_{king} can learn the (full) value on an internal wire of the circuit!

In more detail, suppose P_{king} is corrupted. For a sharing $[a]_t$, we use a_i to denote the i-th share of $[a]_t$. All parties are going to evaluate $x \cdot y$ and then $(xy) \cdot z$. We give an attack to allow the adversary to recover the value of y:

1. P_{king} receives all shares of $[x+a]_t$ and $[y+b]_t$ from all parties. P_{king} computes $(x+a)$ and $(y+b)$.
2. P_{king} selects a set of honest parties $\mathcal{H}'$ with size $|\mathcal{H}'| = n - t - 1$.
3. P_{king} sends $(x+a)$ and $(y+b)$ to parties which are not in $\mathcal{H}'$. For parties $P_j \in \mathcal{H}'$, P_{king} sends $(x+a+1)$ and $(y+b)$.
4. All parties locally compute $[xy]_t = (x+a)(y+b) - (x+a)[b]_t - (y+b)[a]_t + [c]_t$. For a party $P_j \in \mathcal{H}'$, the share of $[xy]_t$ it should hold is $(x+a)(y+b) - (x+a)b_j - (y+b)a_j + c_j$. However, since P_{king} sent $(x+a+1)$ instead of $(x+a)$ to P_j, the actual share P_j holds is $((x+a)(y+b) - (x+a)b_j - (y+b)a_j + c_j) + (y+b-b_j)$. This is equal to the correct share of $[xy]_t$ plus the value $(y+b-b_j)$. A party P_k which is not in $\mathcal{H}'$ holds the correct share of $[xy]_t$.

5. For the next multiplication gate, P_{king} receives shares of $[xy+a']_t$ and $[z+b']_t$ from all the parties. For $[xy+a']_t$, P_{king} uses the $(t+1)$ shares provided by parties (including those controlled by the adversary) that are not in $\mathcal{H}'$ to reconstruct $(xy+a')$. Then P_{king} computes the correct shares parties in $\mathcal{H}'$ should hold.

6. For each party $P_j \in \mathcal{H}'$, P_{king} computes the difference between the correct share of P_j and the real share P_j provided, which is $(y+b-b_j)$. Note that P_{king} learnt $y+b$ while evaluting the previous multiplication gate, and therefore, P_{king} learns the value of b_j.

7. The adversary uses the shares of $[b]_t$ held by corrupted parties and $\{b_j\}_{P_j \in \mathcal{H}'}$, the shares of parties in $\mathcal{H}'$, to reconstruct the value of b. Then it can compute y from $y+b$ and b. If y was the value on an input wire, the adversary has learnt an input value. Else it learnt an intermediate wire value in the circuit.

Using n-out-of-n Secret Sharing: The above attack works because of the inherent redundancy in a t-sharing. By only learning a small number of shares, the adversary can compute the correct values of the remaining shares, obtain the (incorrect) values for these shares, and finally, learn private information by comparing the incorrect values to the correct values. Our natural starting point to fix this problem would be to use a $(n-1)$-sharing (i.e., n-out-of-n sharing). In the preparation phase, we generate a random tuple of sharings $([a]_{t,n-1}, [b]_{t,n-1}, [c]_t)$ where $[a]_{t,n-1}$ denotes a t-sharing, and, an $(n-1)$-sharing of the same value a. The parties locally compute $[x+a]_{n-1} = [x]_t + [a]_{n-1}$ (instead of $[x+a]_t$). Now it can be shown that each share an honest party sends to P_{king} is uniformly distributed, and, the above attack ceases to work. The parties can safely evaluate *multiple layers of multiplication gates* without leaking any information to the adversary.

While this idea fixes the attack we outlined earlier, eliminating the redundancy unfortunately opens the door to a host of other attacks which we discuss next.

Checking the Reconstructions: An obvious issue with the above approach is now not only P_{king}, but *any* party can cheat by sending a wrong share to P_{king}. As before, a corrupted P_{king} can also send incorrect values and even different values to different parties. Therefore, we need to run a verification procedure to ensure every party behaved honestly. However before running a verification, all parties evaluate exactly $O(n)$ multiplication gates (even though they may not be at the same layer). The verification is thus done in batches.

First, the parties check whether (for each multiplication gate) they all received the same elements from P_{king}. This verification is done in batches and is based on techniques from prior works. If this check fails, a pair of disputed parties is identified and removed, and, all multiplication gates are re-evaluated. Otherwise, this check guarantees that the sharings of the output of all the multiplication gates held by honest parties are consistent (though not necessarily correct).

Next, the parties check whether the reconstructions of values $[x+a]_{n-1}$, $[y+b]_{n-1}$ are correct. Towards that end, we will use the reconstruction protocol from [BTH08] to reconstruct $[x+a]_t := [x]_t + [a]_t$, $[y+b]_t := [y]_t + [b]_t$, which guarantees that all honest parties get the correct results. If this second check passes, then all multiplication gates are correctly evaluated and all parties continue to evaluate the remaining multiplication gates.

However if the above check fails, we run into an obstacle. In [BTH08], failure of this check would necessarily imply the dishonesty of P_{king} (since the messages sent by other parties to P_{king}, even if maliciously generated, could be corrected by relying on the redundancy). Thus, P_{king} would be kicked out and the whole batch would be executed again. However in our setting, there are two possibilities: (1) at least one corrupted parties sent a wrong share to P_{king}, or, (2) P_{king} distributed wrong results. Even if one is given that P_{king} behaved honestly, it is hard for anybody (including P_{king}) to tell which party sent the wrong share. This is because the shares do not have any redundancy and it is possible to change the secret without getting detected by just changing a single share.

Without loss of generality, let $(x^{i^*} + a^{i^*})$ be the first wrong value reconstructed by P_{king} (the parties learn i^* as part of the above check).

Increasing Redundancy Using 4-Consistent Tuples: Observe that if a party supplied an incorrect share of $[x^{i^*} + a^{i^*}]_{n-1}$, then since $(x^{i^*} + a^{i^*})$ was shared using a $(n-1)$-sharing, the only way to detect who is cheating would be to go back to how these shares were generated, recompute the correct share for each party, and, see which party supplied an incorrect share. Note that $[x^{i^*} + a^{i^*}]_{n-1} = [x^{i^*}]_t + [a^{i^*}]_{n-1}$ and $[x^{i^*}]_t$ is a t-sharing. Therefore, we focus on the generation process of $[a^{i^*}]_{n-1}$.

The generation of $[a^i]_{n-1}$ is done in batches as follows [BTH08]. Each party P_i first randomly generates $[s^i]_{t,n-1}$ for a random element s^i and distributes the sharings to all other parties (i.e., j-th share to P_j). Then all parties extract the randomness by using a hyper-invertible matrix M and locally computing $([a^1]_{t,n-1}, \ldots, [a^n]_{t,n-1}) = M([s^1]_{t,n-1}, \ldots, [s^n]_{t,n-1})$. In particular, $[a^{i^*}]_{n-1} = M_{i^*}([s^1]_{n-1}, \ldots, [s^n]_{n-1})$, where M_{i^*} is the i^*-th row of M.

Our first attempt to resolve this problem is as follows. The sharing $[s^i]_t$ can be seen as the "redundant" version of the sharing $[s^i]_{n-1}$. Similarly, the matrix $([s^1]_t, \ldots, [s^n]_t)$ can be seen as the redundant version of $([s^1]_{n-1}, \ldots, [s^n]_{n-1})$. The parties can generate the redundant version of $[a^{i^*}]_{n-1}$ as $[a^{i^*}]_t = M_{i^*}([s^1]_t, \ldots, [s^n]_t)$. The parties can now send the shares from $[x^{i^*} + a^{i^*}]_t$ to P_{king}. These shares cannot be modified by the adversary because of the large redundancy present. However what if a party cheated while sending shares from $[x^{i^*} + a^{i^*}]_{n-1}$ but not while sending shares from $[x^{i^*} + a^{i^*}]_t$? The goal of detecting who cheated still continues to evade us.

To resolve this problem, we wish to create a redundant version of the matrix $([s^1]_{n-1}, \ldots, [s^n]_{n-1})$ in a way such that from this version, the *entire* matrix can be recovered. That is, for each i, we should be able to recover the entire sharing $[s^i]_{n-1}$ as opposed to just the secret s^i (even if the adversary tampers with the shares it holds). Towards that end, our idea would be to actually convert this given matrix into *three* separate matrices such that each row of these matrices is a carefully chosen t-sharing. Even if the adversary tampers with its shares arbitrarily in each of these 3 matrices and the original matrix, these 3 matrices can be entirely recovered and then, be used to recover the original matrix. We now give more details.

All parties first agree on a partition of the set of all parties $\mathcal{P} = \mathcal{P}_1 \bigcup \mathcal{P}_2 \bigcup \mathcal{P}_3$ such that $|\mathcal{P}_1|, |\mathcal{P}_2|, |\mathcal{P}_3| \leq t + 1$. For the first matrix, the columns held by parties in $\mathcal{P}_1$ are the same as the original matrix and the remaining columns are randomly sampled such that each row of the matrix is a t-sharing. It can always be achieved since for each row, only up to $t+1$ values are fixed (i.e., copied from the original matrix). Similarly, for the second and the third matrices, the columns held by parties in $\mathcal{P}_2$ and $\mathcal{P}_3$ are the same as the original matrix respectively. The remaining columns are randomly sampled such that each row of these two matrices is a t-sharing. To recover the original matrix from these 3 matrices, we simply pick the columns held by parties in $\mathcal{P}_1$ from the first matrix, the columns held by parties in $\mathcal{P}_2$ from the second matrix and the columns held by parties in $\mathcal{P}_3$ from the third matrix. In case the adversary tampers with up to t columns of each matrix, all the 3 matrices can be recovered using error correction and then the original matrix can be recovered.

We now focus on the i-th row of these four matrices (including the original one). Denote these by $([_0 s^i]_{n-1}, [_1 s^i]_t, [_2 s^i]_t, [_3 s^i]_t)$ (recall that each row of each matrix is a sharing). Together with the t-sharing $[_0 s^i]_t := [s^i]_t$, we call such 4 sharings $([_0 s^i]_t, [_1 s^i]_t, [_2 s^i]_t, [_3 s^i]_t)$ a 4-consistent tuple of sharings. More formally, we say a tuple of sharings $([_0 s]_t, [_1 s]_t, [_2 s]_t, [_3 s]_t)$ is 4-consistent w.r.t. a partition of $\mathcal{P} = \mathcal{P}_1 \bigcup \mathcal{P}_2 \bigcup \mathcal{P}_3$ where $|\mathcal{P}_1|, |\mathcal{P}_2|, |\mathcal{P}_3| \leq t + 1$, if the $(n-1)$-sharing $[s]_{n-1}$, where the k-th share of $[s]_{n-1}$ equals the k-th share of $[_j s]_t$ for all $j \in \{1, 2, 3\}$ and $P_k \in \mathcal{P}_j$, satisfies that $s = {_0 s}$.

We prove that 4-consistency is preserved under linear operations. In more detail, by applying M_{i^*} to the 3 new matrices, we are able to obtain three t-sharings $[_1 a^{i^*}]_t, [_2 a^{i^*}]_t, [_3 a^{i^*}]_t$ such that these would entirely allow one to recover all shares of $[a^{i^*}]_{n-1}$ and make sure $[a^{i^*}]_{n-1}$ and $[a^{i^*}]_t$ are sharings of the same value a^{i^*}. We stress that these 3 sharings not only allow us to recover all shares of $[a^{i^*}]_{n-1}$, but, in fact, also provide sufficient redundancy to make sure that an adversary controlling up to t parties cannot cause the recovery procedure to fail.

Using 4-Consistent Tuples to Detect the Cheaters: How do the parties generate these 4 matrices, and, ensure 4-consistency? Each party P_i generates the sharings $[s^i]_{t,n-1}$ and distributes them as before. P_i generates three additional t-sharings $[_1 s^i]_t, [_2 s^i]_t, [_3 s^i]_t$ such that for $j \in \{1, 2, 3\}$ and $P_k \in \mathcal{P}_j$, the k-th share of $[_j s^i]_t$ equals the k-th share of $[s^i]_{n-1}$. P_i then distributes $[_j s^i]_t$ to all parties which are not in $\mathcal{P}_j$ (because parties in $\mathcal{P}_j$ have already received their shares when P_i distributed $[s^i]_{n-1}$) for every $j \in \{1, 2, 3\}$. Let $[_0 s^i]_t := [s^i]_t$.

Next, all parties must check whether each party P_i distributed a valid 4-consistent tuple of sharings $([_0 s^i]_t, [_1 s^i]_t, [_2 s^i]_t, [_3 s^i]_t)$. We develop subroutines to do it efficiently by checking a batch of them each time. (If the check fails, a pair of disputed parties is identified and removed.)

Recall that $[a^{i^*}]_{n-1} = M_{i^*}([s^1]_{n-1}, \ldots, [s^n]_{n-1})$. To verify whether parties in $\mathcal{P}_j$ provided correct shares when reconstructing $x^{i^*} + a^{i^*}$, all parties (locally) compute

$$[_j d^{i^*}]_t := [x^{i^*}]_t + [_j a^{i^*}]_t$$
$$= [x^{i^*}]_t + M_{i^*}([_j s^1]_t, \ldots, [_j s^n]_t)$$

The computed shares are then sent to P_{king}. Observe that for $P_k \in \mathcal{P}_j$, the k-th shares of $[_j s^1]_t, \ldots, [_j s^n]_t$ are exactly the k-th shares of $[s^1]_{n-1}, \ldots, [s^n]_{n-1}$. On receiving all shares of $[_j d^{i^*}]_t$, P_{king} is able to recover all shares of $[_j d^{i^*}]_t$ even if several of the received shares are incorrect. This allows P_{king} to recover correct shares from $[x^{i^*}]_t + [_j a^{i^*}]_{n-1}$ for all $P_k \in \mathcal{P}_j$. P_{king} can now check whether a party in $\mathcal{P}_j$ behaved honestly by sending the correct share earlier. Therefore, in the end, P_{king} claims that some party P_k is corrupted and all parties treat (P_{king}, P_k) as a pair of disputed parties.

On the Proof of Security: We point out that it is non-trivial to prove the security of our construction. Recall that each party P_i generates a tuple of t-sharings to encode its randomness when generating $[a^{i^*}]$ (i.e., to encode $[s^i]_{n-1}$). In general, a t-sharing can only be used to hide one value since the adversary might have t shares and just need one more to reconstruct all shares and the secret value. However, we use a t-sharing to encode up to $t+1$ values, and, the values held by honest parties should remain unknown to the adversary. Therefore, one must be careful in using 4-consistent tuples to ensure that the simulator is able to obtain an identical view. For more details, we refer the readers to Appendix A in the full version of this paper.

Efficiency: In each batch, $O(n)$ multiplication gates are first evaluated. Then all parties check whether the results are correct. When a pair of disputed parties is identified, these two parties are removed and all these $O(n)$ multiplication gates will be reevaluated. Our protocol costs $O(n^2 \kappa)$ bits for the entire batch. Therefore, on average, each multiplication only costs $O(n\kappa)$ bits. For each failure, at least one corrupted party is removed. Thus the number of reevaluations is bounded by $O(n)$, which means that reevaluations cost at most $O(n^3\kappa)$. Hence, the communication complexity of the overall protocol is $O(Cn\kappa + n^3\kappa)$.

3 Preliminary

3.1 Model

We consider a set of parties $\mathcal{P} = \{P_1, P_2, ..., P_n\}$ where each party can provide inputs, receive outputs, and participate in the computation. For every pair of parties, there exists a secure (private and authentic) synchronous channel so that they can directly send messages to each other.

We focus on functions which can be represented as arithmetic circuits over a finite field $\mathbb{F}$ (with $|\mathbb{F}| \geq 2n$) with input, addition, multiplication, random, and output gates. Let $\kappa = \log |\mathbb{F}|$ be the size of an element in $\mathbb{F}$.

An adversary is able to corrupt at most $t < n/3$ parties, provide inputs to corrupted parties, and receive all messages sent to the corrupted parties. Corrupted parties can deviate from the protocol arbitrarily. We denote the set of corrupted parties by $\mathcal{C}$.

Each party P_i is assigned with a unique non-zero field element $\alpha_i \in \mathbb{F}\backslash\{0\}$ as the identity.

3.2 Byzantine Agreement

Byzantine agreement allows all honest parties to reach a binary consensus. A protocol for byzantine agreement takes a bit from each party as input, and all honest parties will reach to a consensus if at most t parties are corrupted. Furthermore, if all honest parties hold the same bit b in the beginning, then all honest parties agree on b finally.

In our protocol, we use a byzantine agreement protocol to let all parties reach a binary consensus and let one party broadcast one bit to all other parties. Broadcast allows a party (as a sender) to send a bit b to the remaining parties and all parties eventually receive the same bit b' where $b = b'$ when the sender is honest. An easy way to instantiate broadcast is to let the party send the bit b to all other parties, and then all parties run a byzantine agreement protocol to reach a consensus on the bit b' they received.

With $t < n/3$, both consensus and broadcast can be achieved by a perfect byzantine agreement protocol communicating $O(n^2)$ bits [BGP92, CW92].

3.3 Party-Elimination Framework

Party-Elimination was first introduced in [HMP00]. It is a general strategy to achieve perfect security efficiently.

The basic idea is to divide the computations into several segments. For each segment, all active parties first evaluate this segment and then check the correctness of the evaluation. It is guaranteed that at least one honest party will discover that the segment is evaluated incorrectly if any corrupted parties deviate from the protocol. After the check is completed, all active parties reach a consensus on whether this segment is successfully evaluated. In the case of success, all active parties continue to evaluate the next segment. In the case of failure, all active parties run another protocol to locate two active parties such that at least one of them is corrupted. Then these two parties are eliminated from the set of active parties. The same segment is evaluated again.

Therefore, each failure results in a reduction in the number of corrupted parties and only a bounded number ($O(n)$) of failures may happen.

We use $\mathcal{P}_{\text{active}}$ to denote the set of parties which are active currently. Only parties in $\mathcal{P}_{\text{active}}$ can participate in the remaining computations. We use $\mathcal{C}_{\text{active}} \subset \mathcal{P}_{\text{active}}$ for the set of active corrupted parties. Let n' be the size of $\mathcal{P}_{\text{active}}$. We use t' for the maximum possible number of the corrupted parties in $\mathcal{P}_{\text{active}}$.

Each time a pair of disputed parties is identified, these two parties are removed from $\mathcal{P}_{\text{active}}$ and hence $\mathcal{C}_{\text{active}}$. It results in $n' := n' - 2$ and $t' := t' - 1$. Initially we have $n = n', t = t'$. Let $T = n' - 2t'$. Therefore, T remains unchanged during the whole protocol.

We directly borrow the instantiation of Party-Elimination Framework used in [BTH08]. We build a compiler which takes a procedure π as input and outputs a procedure or a protocol π' which either outputs the original result of π or outputs a pair of disputed parties which contains at least one corrupted party. In the rest of the constructions, each party maintains a happy-bit. Formally,

---

Procedure 1 PARTY-ELIMINATION(π)

1: Initialization Phase:
   All parties initially set their happy-bits to happy.
2: Computation Phase:
   All parties run the procedure π.
3: Fault Detection Phase:
   1. Each party sends its happy-bit to all other parties.
   2. For each party, if at least one of the happy-bits it receives is unhappy, sets its happy-bit to be unhappy.
   3. All parties run a consensus protocol on their respective happy-bits. If the result is happy, all parties take the result of π as the output and halt. Otherwise, run the following steps.
4: Fault Localization Phase:
   1. All parties agree on a referee $P_r \in \mathcal{P}_{\text{active}}$. Every other party sends everything it generated, sent, and received in the Computation Phase and Fault Detection Phase to P_r.
   2. On receiving all information from other parties, P_r simulates the Computation Phase and Fault Detection Phase. P_r broadcasts either $(P_i, \text{corrupt})$ (in the case P_i does not follow the procedure) or $(\ell, P_i, P_k, v, v', \text{disputed})$ where ℓ is the index of the message where P_i should have sent v to P_k while P_k claimed to have received $v' \neq v$.
      (a) If $(P_i, \text{corrupt})$ is broadcast, all parties set $E = \{P_r, P_i\}$.
      (b) Otherwise, P_i and P_k broadcast whether they agree with P_r. If P_i disagrees, set $E = \{P_r, P_i\}$; if P_k disagrees, set $E = \{P_r, P_k\}$; otherwise, set $E = \{P_i, P_k\}$.
   3. All parties take E as the output and halt.

We point out that the happy-bits are used in π and therefore, the value of a happy-bit reflects whether this party is satisfied with the execution of π.

After a procedure π is compiled by PARTY-ELIMINATION, parties will communicate with each other in Fault Detection Phase and Fault Localization Phase, which adds some communication cost to π'. Parties will communicate $O(n^2)$ elements in Fault Detection Phase to distribute happy-bits and reach the consensus. Let $m(\pi)$ be the total elements communicated in π, the overhead of the Fault Localization Phase will then be $O(m(\pi) + n^2)$. In total, the overall communication complexity is $O(m(\pi) + n^2)$ elements or $O(m(\pi)\kappa + n^2\kappa)$ bits.

3.4 Hyper-Invertible Matrix

We adopt the definition of hyper-invertible matrices from [BTH08].

Definition 1 ([BTH08]). *An r-by-c matrix M is hyper-invertible if for any index sets $R \subseteq \{1, 2, ..., r\}$ and $C \subseteq \{1, 2, ..., c\}$ with $|R| = |C| > 0$, the matrix M_R^C is invertible, where M_R denotes the matrix consisting of the rows $i \in R$ of M, M^C denotes the matrix consisting of the columns $j \in C$ of M, and $M_R^C = (M_R)^C$.*

We point out a very useful property of hyper-invertible matrices, which is a more generalized version compared with that shown in [BTH08].

Lemma 1. *Let M be a hyper-invertible r-by-c matrix and $(y_1, ..., y_r) = M(x_1, ..., x_c)$. Then for any sets of indices $A \subseteq \{1, 2, ..., c\}$ and $B \subseteq \{1, 2, ..., r\}$ such that $|A| + |B| = c$, there exists a linear function $f : \mathbb{F}^c \to \mathbb{F}^r$ which takes $\{x_i\}_{i \in A}, \{y_j\}_{j \in B}$ as inputs and outputs $\{x_i\}_{i \notin A}, \{y_j\}_{j \notin B}$.*

3.5 Secret Sharing

In our protocol, we use the standard Shamir secret sharing scheme [Sha79]. We adopt the notion of d-shared in [BTH08].

Definition 2 ([BTH08]). *We say that a value s is (correctly) d-shared (among the parties in $\mathcal{P}_{\text{active}}$) if every honest party $P_i \in \mathcal{P}_{\text{active}}$ is holding a share s_i of s, such that there exists a degree-d polynomial $p(\cdot)$ with $p(0) = s$ and $p(\alpha_i) = s_i$ for every $P_i \in \mathcal{P}_{\text{active}}$. The vector $(s_1, s_2, ..., s_{n'})$ of shares is called a d-sharing of s, and is denoted by $[s]_d$. A (possibly incomplete) set of shares is called d-consistent if these shares lie on a degree-d polynomial.*

For every function $f : \mathbb{F}^m \to \mathbb{F}^{m'}$, by writing $f([x^{(1)}]_d, [x^{(2)}]_d, ..., [x^{(m)}]_d)$, we mean f is applied on $(x_i^{(1)}, x_i^{(2)}, ..., x_i^{(m)})$ for every $i \in \{1, 2, ..., n'\}$. Especially, when we say all parties in $\mathcal{P}_{\text{active}}$ locally compute $f([x^{(1)}]_d, [x^{(2)}]_d, ..., [x^{(m)}]_d)$, each party P_i computes $f(x_i^{(1)}, x_i^{(2)}, ..., x_i^{(m)})$.

We point out that Shamir secret sharing scheme is linear, i.e., for every two d-sharing $[u]_d, [v]_d, [c_1 u + c_2 v]_d = c_1[u]_d + c_2[v]_d$. We also heavily use the following two facts: in the case $t' < (n' - d)/2$, a d-sharing $[u]_d$ is correctable with at most t' errors, e.g., by Berlekamp-Welch Algorithm; in the case $t' < n' - d$, a d-sharing $[u]_d$ is detectable with at most t' errors, due to the fact that two different degree-d polynomials $f_1(\cdot), f_2(\cdot)$ over $\mathbb{F}$ can have at most d points where two polynomials are equal. Particularly, a t-sharing is always correctable in our setting since $n' - 2t' = T = n - 2t > t$ and therefore $t' < (n' - t)/2$.

We say a t-sharing $[v]_t$ is correct (or v is correctly t-shared) if all shares held by honest parties lie on a degree-t polynomial. As we mentioned above, a correct t-sharing is always recoverable.

In our protocol, we use $[s]_{d_1, d_2}$ to represents two sharings of the same value s, one is d_1-sharing and the other one is d_2-sharing. We use $[s]_{d_1, d_2, d_3}$ to represent three sharings of the same value s, d_1-sharing, d_2-sharing and d_3-sharing respectively.

3.6 Batched Reconstruction

We directly borrow the procedure from [BTH08] to reconstruct a batch of d-sharings. The procedure RECONS takes T d-sharings as input and reconstructs each sharing to all parties.

Procedure 2 RECONS$(\mathcal{P}_{\text{active}}, d, [s^1]_d, [s^2]_d, \ldots, [s^T]_d)$ [BTH08]

1: All parties agree on n' different values $\beta_1, \beta_2, \ldots, \beta_{n'} \in \mathbb{F}$.
2: Expansion:
    For every $j \in \{1, 2, \ldots, n'\}$, all parties (locally) expand $[s^1]_d, [s^2]_d, \ldots, [s^T]_d$ into an error correction code $[u^1]_d, [u^2]_d, \ldots, [u^{n'}]_d$ as:

$$[u^j]_d = [s^1]_d + [s^2]_d \beta_j + [s^3]_d \beta_j^2 + \ldots + [s^T]_d \beta_j^{T-1}$$

3: Collecting shares of $[u^i]_d$:
    For every party P_i, all other parties send their shares of $[u^i]_d$ to P_i.
4: Each party P_i tries to reconstruct u^i from the shares it received:
    P_i checks whether there exists a degree-d polynomial f such that at least $\min\{d + t' + 1, n'\}$ of the shares lie on it. If not, P_i sets its happy-bit to **unhappy**. P_i sends the value $u^i = f(0)$ or $\perp$ (in the case that f does not exist) to other parties.
5: On receiving $u^1, \ldots, u^{n'}$, each party P_i tries to reconstruct and output $s^1, \ldots, s^T$:
    If there exists a degree-$(T-1)$ polynomial g such that at least $T + t'$ values of $u^1, u^2, \ldots, u^{n'}$ lie on it, P_i computes $s^1, s^2, \ldots, s^T$ from any T of them. Otherwise, P_i sets its happy-bit to **unhappy** and sets $s^j = \perp$ for all $j \in \{1, \ldots, T\}$. P_i takes $s^1, \ldots, s^T$ as output.

We point out two facts about the procedure RECONS, which are shown in [BTH08].

1. If $d < T = n' - 2t'$ and all d-sharings are correct, then RECONS always successfully reconstructs the sharings to parties in $\mathcal{P}_{\text{active}}$. As we mentioned before, a d-sharing is correctable with at most t' errors when $t' < (n' - d)/2$, which is equivalent to $d < n' - 2t' = T$.
2. If $d < n' - t'$ and all d-sharings are correct, then either all sharings are correctly reconstructed or at least one happy-bit of an honest party is **unhappy**.

The procedure RECONS will reconstruct $T = \Omega(n)$ sharings while communicating $O(n^2)$ elements to collect shares of $[u^i]_d$ in Step 3 and distributed the reconstructed u^i to all parties. Thus, the overall communication complexity is $O(n^2 \kappa)$ bits. Note that for each sharing, the communication complexity to reconstruct it is $O(n)$ elements in average.

3.7 Input Gates

We directly use the result in [BTH08] where they provided a protocol for input gates with communication complexity $O(c_I n \kappa + n^3 \kappa)$ bits, where c_I is the number of input gates in the circuit. The formal functionality appears in $\mathcal{F}_{\text{input}}$.

Functionality 3 $\mathcal{F}_{\text{input}}(c_I)$

1: $\mathcal{F}_{\text{input}}$ receives inputs, which are denoted by $v^1, v^2, \ldots, v^{c_I} \in \mathbb{F}$, from all parties including honest and corrupted parties. $\mathcal{F}_{\text{input}}$ initially sets $\text{state}_j = 1$ for $j \in \{1, \ldots, c_I\}$.

2: From $j = 1$ to c_I, $\mathcal{F}_{\text{input}}$ asks $\mathcal{S}$ what to do next:
  - On receiving $(P_i, P_k, \text{disputed})$ where $\mathcal{C}_{\text{active}} \bigcap \{P_i, P_k\} \neq \emptyset$, $\mathcal{F}_{\text{input}}$ sets $\mathcal{P}_{\text{active}} := \mathcal{P}_{\text{active}} \backslash \{P_i, P_k\}$ and $\mathcal{C}_{\text{active}} := \mathcal{C}_{\text{active}} \backslash \{P_i, P_k\}$.
  - On receiving $(v^j, \text{corrupted})$ where v^j is sent by a corrupted party, $\mathcal{F}_{\text{input}}$ sets $\text{state}_j = 0, \mathcal{P}^j = \mathcal{P}_{\text{active}}, \mathcal{C}^j = \mathcal{C}_{\text{active}}$ and then handle $j := j + 1$.
  - On receiving $\{v_s^j\}_{P_s \in \mathcal{C}_{\text{active}}}$, $\mathcal{F}_{\text{input}}$ sets $\mathcal{P}^j = \mathcal{P}_{\text{active}}, \mathcal{C}^j = \mathcal{C}_{\text{active}}$ and then handle $j := j + 1$.

3: For each $j \in \{1, \ldots, c_I\}$, if $\text{state}_j = 1$, $\mathcal{F}_{\text{input}}$ computes a random t-sharing $[v^j]_t$ of the input v^j received in the first step, such that for all $P_s \in \mathcal{C}^j$, the s-th share of $[v^j]_t$ is v_s^j. If $\text{state}_j = 0$, $\mathcal{F}_{\text{input}}$ sets $[v^j]_t = [0]_0$.

4: For every $j \in \{1, \ldots, c_I\}$ and $P_i \in \mathcal{P}^j$, $\mathcal{F}_{\text{input}}$ sends v_i^j to P_i. $\mathcal{F}_{\text{input}}$ also sends $\mathcal{P}_{\text{active}}$ to all parties.

We refer the reader to the appendix of [BTH08] for the construction of a protocol which instantiates $\mathcal{F}_{\text{input}}$.

4   4-Consistency

In our protocol, we first use random $(n'-1)$-sharings to help evaluate the circuit. Indeed, there is no redundancy in a $(n'-1)$-sharing: to reconstruct the value, all shares from $\mathcal{P}_{\text{active}}$ are needed. However, it makes the sharing vulnerable and the verification becomes much harder due to the lack of redundancy, e.g., every party is able to change the value by changing its own share without being detected.

Therefore, we need a tool to let each party commit their shares *after* evaluating the circuit to help verifying the honesty. To this end, we introduce the notion 4-consistency. Recall that t is the maximum number of corrupted parties an adversary can control and n' is the number of active parties.

Definition 3. *For a partition π of $\mathcal{P}_{\text{active}} = \mathcal{P}_1 \bigcup \mathcal{P}_2 \bigcup \mathcal{P}_3$ such that $|\mathcal{P}_1|, |\mathcal{P}_2|, |\mathcal{P}_3| \leq t + 1$, a tuple of t-sharings $[\![r]\!] = ([_0 r]_t, [_1 r]_t, [_2 r]_t, [_3 r]_t)$ is a 4-consistent tuple w.r.t. π if $_0 r = r$ and there exists a degree-$(n'-1)$ polynomial $p(\cdot)$ with $p(0) = r$ and for all $P_i \in \mathcal{P}_j$, $p(\alpha_i)$ is the i-th share of the sharing $[_j r]_t$.*

In fact, the vector $(p(\alpha_1), p(\alpha_2), \ldots, p(\alpha_{n'}))$ is a $(n'-1)$-sharing of r by definition. We denote it as $[r]_{n'-1}$. In our construction, $[r]_{t, n'-1}$ is first generated to do evaluation. Then, in the verification step, $[_1 r]_t, [_2 r]_t, [_3 r]_t$ are generated to commit the shares of $[r]_{n'-1}$. This is due to the fact that t-sharings are correctable (as we explained in Sect. 3.5). Therefore, each share of $[r]_{n'-1}$ can be recovered no matter how corrupted parties change their shares.

Lemma 2. *4-consistency is preserved under linear combinations*

Proof. We show that, for every two 4-consistent tuples $[\![r]\!], [\![s]\!]$ which are w.r.t. π and constants c_1, c_2,

$$[\![c_1 r + c_2 s]\!] := c_1 [\![r]\!] + c_2 [\![s]\!]$$
$$= (c_1 [_0 r]_t + c_2 [_0 s]_t, c_1 [_1 r]_t + c_2 [_1 s]_t, c_1 [_2 r]_t + c_2 [_2 s]_t, c_1 [_3 r]_t + c_2 [_3 s]_t)$$

is still 4-consistent w.r.t. π.

To see this, by the linearity of Shamir secret sharing scheme, each entry of the resulting tuple is still a t-sharing. Especially, $c_1 [_0 r]_t + c_2 [_1 s]_t = [c_1 (_0 r) + c_2 (_0 s)]_t$ and $c_1 r + c_2 s = c_1 (_0 r) + c_2 (_0 s)$.

Let $p(\cdot), q(\cdot)$ be the polynomials such that $p_1(0) = r, p_2(0) = s$ and for every $j \in \{1, 2, 3\}$ and $P_i \in \mathcal{P}_j$, $p_1(\alpha_i), p_2(\alpha_i)$ are the i-th shares of the sharings $[_j r]_t, [_j s]_t$ respectively (as per the definition). Let $p_3 = c_1 p_1 + c_1 p_2$. Then $p_3(0) = c_1 p_1(0) + c_2 p_2(0) = c_1 r + c_2 s$. For every $P_i \in \mathcal{P}_j$, $p_3(\alpha_i) = c_1 p_1(\alpha_i) + c_2 p_2(\alpha_i)$ which is exactly the i-th share of $c_1 [_j r]_t + c_2 [_j s]_t$. □

We say a 4-consistent tuple $[\![r]\!] = ([_0 r]_t, [_1 r]_t, [_2 r]_t, [_3 r]_t)$ is correct if (1) each of the t-sharings is correct and (2) after correcting possible wrong shares held by corrupted parties, it is 4-consistent.

5 Building Block

In this section, we introduce several building blocks which will be utilized in the full protocol.

5.1 Random Triple-Sharings

The following procedure, TRIPLESHARERANDOM($\mathcal{P}_{\text{active}}, d_1, d_2, d_3$), is used to generate and distribute T random triple-sharings $\{[r^i]_{d_1, d_2, d_3}\}_{i=1}^{T}$ where $r^1, \ldots, r^T$ are sampled uniformly from $\mathbb{F}$ and $d_1, d_2, d_3 \geq t'$. It finally outputs either T valid random triple-sharings or a pair of disputed parties. The ideal functionality is described in $\mathcal{F}_{\text{triple}}$.

Functionality 4 $\mathcal{F}_{\text{triple}}(d_1, d_2, d_3)$

1: On receiving $(P_i, P_k, \text{disputed})$, where $\mathcal{C}_{\text{active}} \cap \{P_i, P_k\} \neq \emptyset$, from $\mathcal{S}$, $\mathcal{F}_{\text{triple}}$ sends $(P_i, P_k, \text{disputed})$ to all parties.

2: On receiving $(\{r_s^{1, d_1}, r_s^{1, d_2}, r_s^{1, d_3}\}_{P_s \in \mathcal{C}_{\text{active}}}, \ldots, \{r_s^{T, d_1}, r_s^{T, d_2}, r_s^{T, d_3}\}_{P_s \in \mathcal{C}_{\text{active}}})$ from $\mathcal{S}$, $\mathcal{F}_{\text{triple}}$ samples $r^1, r^2, \ldots, r^T$ uniformly from $\mathbb{F}$. Then $\mathcal{F}_{\text{triple}}$ randomly generates $[r^1]_{d_1, d_2, d_3}, \ldots, [r^T]_{d_1, d_2, d_3}$ such that for every $j \in \{1, \ldots, T\}$ and $P_s \in \mathcal{C}_{\text{active}}$, the s-th shares of $[r^j]_{d_1, d_2, d_3}$ are $r_s^{j, d_1}, r_s^{j, d_2}, r_s^{j, d_3}$ respectively. For every $j \in \{1, \ldots, T\}$ and $P_i \in \mathcal{P}_{\text{active}}$, $\mathcal{F}_{\text{triple}}$ sends the i-th shares of $[r^j]_{d_1, d_2, d_3}$ to P_i.

The basic construction is very similar to the protocol which generates random double-sharings in [BTH08]. The only difference is that we generate triple-sharings instead of double-sharings.

In the beginning of the computation, all parties will agree on a constant hyper-invertible matrix M of size $n' \times n'$, which will be employed to extract randomness. The first step of the protocol is to let each party P_i distribute a triple-sharing $[s^i]_{d_1,d_2,d_3}$ of a random value s^i. Then apply the hyper-invertible matrix M on them, i.e., $([r^1]_{d_1,d_2,d_3}, \ldots, [r^{n'}]_{d_1,d_2,d_3}) = M([s^1]_{d_1,d_2,d_3}, \ldots, [s^{n'}]_{d_1,d_2,d_3})$.

For the last $2t'$ triple-sharings, each of them is reconstructed by a different party. Each party who reconstructs one of the triple-sharings checks whether they are valid and sets its happy-bit to **unhappy** if the triple-sharing is invalid. Finally, all parties take the remaining $T = n' - 2t'$ triple-sharings as output.

It guarantees that either the output (i.e., $[r^1]_{d_1,d_2,d_3}, \ldots, [r^T]_{d_1,d_2,d_3}$) is correct or at least one happy-bit of an honest party is **unhappy**.

Formally,

Procedure 5 TRIPLESHARERANDOM($\mathcal{P}_{\text{active}}, d_1, d_2, d_3$)

1: All parties agree on a hyper-invertible matrix M of size $n' \times n'$.
2: Parties distribute their own randomness:
   Each party P_i samples $s^i \in \mathbb{F}$ uniformly. Then randomly generate $[s^i]_{d_1,d_2,d_3}$. For each other party P_j, P_i sends the j-th shares of $[s^i]_{d_1,d_2,d_3}$ to P_j.
3: Extracting randomness from honest parties:
   All parties locally compute
   $$([r^1]_{d_1,d_2,d_3}, \ldots, [r^{n'}]_{d_1,d_2,d_3}) = M([s^1]_{d_1,d_2,d_3}, \ldots, [s^{n'}]_{d_1,d_2,d_3})$$
4: Check the correctness:
   1. For $j \in \{T+1, \ldots, n'\}$, all parties send their shares of $[r^j]_{d_1,d_2,d_3}$ to P_j.
   2. P_j checks whether the triple-sharing it received is valid, i.e., all shares of $[r^j]_{d_1}, [r^j]_{d_2}, [r^j]_{d_3}$ lie on degree-d_1, degree-d_2, degree-d_3 polynomials g_1, g_2, g_3 respectively, and $g_1(0) = g_2(0) = g_3(0)$. If not, P_j sets its happy-bit to **unhappy**.
5: All parties take the first T triple-sharings $[r_1]_{d_1,d_2,d_3}, \ldots, [r_T]_{d_1,d_2,d_3}$ as output.

In procedure TRIPLESHARERANDOM, parties communicate $O(n^2)$ elements to distribute randomness in Step 2 and check correctness in Step 4. Thus, the overall communication complexity is $O(n^2\kappa)$ bits. Note that the communication complexity for generating each random triple sharing is $O(n)$ elements.

Let   TRIPLESHARERANDOM-PE   :=PARTY-ELIMINATION(TRIPLESHARE RANDOM). Then TRIPLESHARERANDOM-PE securely computes $\mathcal{F}_{\text{triple}}$.

Lemma 3 ([BTH08]). *The protocol* TRIPLESHARERANDOM-PE *computes* $\mathcal{F}_{triple}$ *with perfect security when* $|\mathcal{C}_{\text{active}}| < |\mathcal{P}_{\text{active}}|/3$.

The overall communication complexity of TRIPLESHARERANDOM-PE is $O(n^2\kappa)$ bits.

5.2   Random Multiplication Tuples

The procedure GENERATETUPLES($\mathcal{P}_{\text{active}}$) is used to generate T correctly and independently random tuples $([a]_{t,n'-1}, [b]_{t,n'-1}, [c]_t)$, which we call multiplication tuples, where a, b are uniformly random and $c = ab$. It outputs either T random multiplication tuples or a pair of disputed parties. The ideal functionality is described in $\mathcal{F}_{\text{multi-tuple}}$.

Functionality 6 $\mathcal{F}_{\text{multi-tuple}}(\mathcal{P}_{\text{active}})$

1: On receiving $(P_i, P_k, \text{disputed})$, where $\mathcal{C}_{\text{active}} \cap \{P_i, P_k\} \neq \emptyset$, from $\mathcal{S}$, $\mathcal{F}_{\text{multi-tuple}}$ sends $(P_i, P_k, \text{disputed})$ to all parties.
2: On receiving

$$(\{a_s^{1,t}, a_s^{1,n'-1}, b_s^{1,t}, b_s^{1,n'-1}, c_s^{1,t}\}_{P_s \in \mathcal{C}_{\text{active}}}, \ldots, \{a_s^{T,t}, a_s^{T,n'-1}, b_s^{T,t}, b_s^{T,n'-1}, c_s^{T,t}\}_{P_s \in \mathcal{C}_{\text{active}}})$$

from $\mathcal{S}$, $\mathcal{F}_{\text{multi-tuple}}$ samples $a^1, \ldots, a^T, b^1, \ldots, b^T$ uniformly from $\mathbb{F}$ and computes $c^1 = a^1 b^1, \ldots, c^T = a^T b^T$. Then $\mathcal{F}_{\text{multi-tuple}}$ randomly generates

$$([a^1]_{t,n'-1}, [b^1]_{t,n'-1}, [c^1]_t), \ldots, ([a^T]_{t,n'-1}, [b^T]_{t,n'-1}, [c^T]_t)$$

such that for every $j \in \{1, \ldots, T\}$ and $P_s \in \mathcal{C}_{\text{active}}$, the s-th shares of $([a^j]_{t,n'-1}, [b^j]_{t,n'-1}, [c^j]_t)$ are $(a_s^{1,t}, a_s^{1,n'-1}, b_s^{1,t}, b_s^{1,n'-1}, c_s^{1,t})$ respectively. For every $j \in \{1, \ldots, T\}$ and $P_i \in \mathcal{P}_{\text{active}}$, $\mathcal{F}_{\text{multi-tuple}}$ sends the i-th shares of $([a^j]_{t,n'-1}, [b^j]_{t,n'-1}, [c^j]_t)$ to P_i.

The basic construction is very similar to the protocol which generates random triples in [BTH08]. The difference is that we generate triple-sharings $[a]_{t',t,n'-1}, [b]_{t',t,n'-1}, [r]_{t,2t',n'-1}$ instead of double-sharings $[a]_{t',t}, [b]_{t',t}, [r]_{t,2t'}$ in the beginning. However $[a]_{n'-1}, [b]_{n'-1}$ are directly output and $[r]_{n'-1}$ is discarded.

GENERATETUPLES($\mathcal{P}_{\text{active}}$) first invokes TRIPLESHARERANDOM to generate random triple sharings $[a^1]_{t',t,n'-1}, \ldots, [a^T]_{t',t,n'-1}, [b^1]_{t',t,n'-1}, \ldots, [b^T]_{t',t,n'-1}$ and $[r^1]_{t,2t',n'-1}, \ldots, [r^T]_{t,2t',n'-1}$. For every $i \in \{1, \ldots, T\}$, $[a^i]_{t'}, [b^i]_{t'}$ are used to compute $[c^i]_{2t'} = [a^i]_{t'}[b^i]_{t'}$ locally and $[r^i]_{t,2t'}$ is used to generate $[c^i]_t$.

Procedure 7 GENERATETUPLES($\mathcal{P}_{\text{active}}$)

1: Generate random triple-sharings:
   All parties invoke TRIPLESHARERANDOM($\mathcal{P}_{\text{active}}, t', t, n' - 1$) two times to generate $[a^1]_{t',t,n'-1}, \ldots, [a^T]_{t',t,n'-1}$ and $[b^1]_{t',t,n'-1}, \ldots, [b^T]_{t',t,n'-1}$. Then invoke TRIPLESHARERANDOM($\mathcal{P}_{\text{active}}, t, 2t', n' - 1$) to generate $[r^1]_{t,2t',n'-1}, \ldots, [r^T]_{t,2t',n'-1}$.
2: For $j \in \{1, \ldots, T\}$, all parties locally compute $[c^j]_{2t'} = [a^j]_{t'}[b^j]_{t'}$ where $c^j = a^j b^j$. Since each party directly multiplies its shares, the result is a $2t'$-sharing.
3: For $j \in \{1, \ldots, T\}$, the parties in $\mathcal{P}_{\text{active}}$ locally compute $[d^j]_{2t'} = [c^j]_{2t'} - [r^j]_{t'}$.
4: Invoke RECONS($\mathcal{P}_{\text{active}}, 2t', [d^1]_{2t'}, \ldots, [d^T]_{2t'}$) to reconstruct $d^1, \ldots, d^T$.
5: For $j \in \{1, \ldots, T\}$, the parties in $\mathcal{P}_{\text{active}}$ locally compute $[c^j]_t = d^j + [r^j]_t$.
6: Output the T tuples $([a^1]_{t,n'-1}, [b^1]_{t,n'-1}, [c^1]_t), \ldots, ([a^T]_{t,n'-1}, [b^T]_{t,n'-1}, [c^T]_t)$.

As parties only communicate with each other when invoking TRIPLESHARERANDOM and RECONS, the communication complexity of GENERATETUPLES is thus $O(n^2 \kappa)$ bits. Note that the communication cost of each random multiplication tuple is $O(n)$ elements.

Let GENERATETUPLES-PE := PARTY-ELIMINATION(GENERATETUPLES). Then GENERATETUPLES-PE securely computes $\mathcal{F}_{\text{multi-tuple}}$.

Lemma 4 ([BTH08]).   *The protocol* GENERATETUPLES-PE *computes* $\mathcal{F}_{multi\text{-}tuple}$ *with perfect security when* $|\mathcal{C}_{\text{active}}| < |\mathcal{P}_{\text{active}}|/3$.

The overall communication complexity of GENERATETUPLES-PE is $O(n^2\kappa)$ bits.

5.3   Generating 4-Consistent Tuples

The procedure QUADRUPLESHARERANDOM$(\mathcal{P}_{\text{active}}, \mathcal{P}_1, \mathcal{P}_2, \mathcal{P}_3)$ is used to generate T correct and random 4-consistent tuples $[\![r]\!] = ([_0r]_t, [_1r]_t, [_2r]_t, [_3r]_t)$. The procedure takes $\mathcal{P}_{\text{active}}$, and a partition $\mathcal{P}_{\text{active}} = \mathcal{P}_1 \bigcup \mathcal{P}_2 \bigcup \mathcal{P}_3$, where $|\mathcal{P}_1|, |\mathcal{P}_2|, |\mathcal{P}_3| \leq t+1$, as input. It outputs either T correct random 4-consistent tuples or a pair of disputed parties. The ideal functionality is described in $\mathcal{F}_{4\text{-consistency}}$.

Functionality 8 $\mathcal{F}_{4\text{-consistency}}(\mathcal{P}_{\text{active}}, \mathcal{P}_1, \mathcal{P}_2, \mathcal{P}_3)$

1: On receiving $(P_i, P_k, \text{disputed})$, where $\mathcal{C}_{\text{active}} \bigcap \{P_i, P_k\} \neq \emptyset$, from $\mathcal{S}$, $\mathcal{F}_{4\text{-consistency}}$ sends $(P_i, P_k, \text{disputed})$ to all parties.
2: On receiving $(\{_0r_s^1, {_1}r_s^1, {_2}r_s^1, {_3}r_s^1\}_{P_s \in \mathcal{C}_{\text{active}}}, \dots, \{_0r_s^T, {_1}r_s^T, {_2}r_s^T, {_3}r_s^T\}_{P_s \in \mathcal{C}_{\text{active}}})$ from $\mathcal{S}$, $\mathcal{F}_{4\text{-consistency}}$ randomly generates

$$[\![r^1]\!], \dots, [\![r^T]\!]$$

such that for every $j \in \{1, \dots, T\}$ and $P_s \in \mathcal{C}_{\text{active}}$, the s-th shares of $[\![r^j]\!]$ are $(_0r_s^j, {_1}r_s^j, {_2}r_s^j, {_3}r_s^j)$ respectively. For every $j \in \{1, \dots, T\}$ and $P_i \in \mathcal{P}_{\text{active}}$, $\mathcal{F}_{4\text{-consistency}}$ sends the i-th shares of $[\![r^j]\!]$ to P_i.

The construction of QUADRUPLESHARERANDOM is similar to TRIPLESHARERANDOM by the following means: First, each party deals a random 4-consistent tuple, and then a hyper-invertible matrix is applied to extract the randomness. For the last $2t'$ out of n' 4-consistent tuples, they will then be reconstructed to check whether corrupted parties cheated in the computation. Finally, the remaining $n' - 2t' = T$ 4-consistent tuples will be output.

Procedure 9 QUADRUPLESHARERANDOM$(\mathcal{P}_{\text{active}}, \mathcal{P}_1, \mathcal{P}_2, \mathcal{P}_3)$

1: All parties agree on a hyper-invertible matrix M.
2: Parties distribute their own randomness:
   Each party P_i generates a random 4-consistent tuple
   $[\![s^i]\!] = ([_0s^i]_t, [_1s^i]_t, [_2s^i]_t, [_3s^i]_t)$. For each other party P_j, P_i sends the j-th shares of $[\![s^i]\!]$ to P_j.
3: Extracting randomness from honest parties:
   All parties locally compute

$$([\![r^1]\!], \dots, [\![r^{n'}]\!]) = M([\![s^1]\!], \dots, [\![s^{n'}]\!]).$$

4: Check the correctness:
   1. For $j \in \{T+1, \dots, n'\}$, all parties send their shares of $[\![r^j]\!]$ to P_j.

2. P_j checks whether the 4-consistent tuple $[\![r^j]\!]$ is valid. If not, P_j sets its happy-bit to **unhappy**.
5: All parties take the first T tuples $[\![r^1]\!], \ldots, [\![r^T]\!]$ as output.

Parties communicate $O(n^2)$ elements to deal n' and reconstruct $2t'$ 4-consistent tuples, so the overall communication complexity is $O(n^2\kappa)$ bits. Note that in average, the communication cost for each 4-consistent tuple is $O(n)$ elements.

Let QuadrupleShareRandom-PE := Party-Elimination(Quadruple ShareRandom). Then QuadrupleShareRandom-PE securely computes $\mathcal{F}_{\text{4-consistency}}$.

Lemma 5. *The protocol* QuadrupleShareRandom-PE *computes* $\mathcal{F}_{\text{4-consistency}}$ *with perfect security when* $|\mathcal{C}_{\text{active}}| < |\mathcal{P}_{\text{active}}|/3$.

The overall communication complexity of QuadrupleShareRandom-PE is $O(n^2\kappa)$ bits.

5.4   Random 0-Sharings

The protocol ZeroShareRandom is used to generate T random t-sharings of 0. It outputs either T correct and random t-sharings of 0 or a pair of disputed parties. The ideal functionality is described in $\mathcal{F}_{\text{zero}}$.

Functionality 10 $\mathcal{F}_{\text{zero}}(\mathcal{P}_{\text{active}})$

1: On receiving $(P_i, P_k, \text{disputed})$, where $\mathcal{C}_{\text{active}} \cap \{P_i, P_k\} \neq \emptyset$, from $\mathcal{S}$, $\mathcal{F}_{\text{zero}}$ sends $(P_i, P_k, \text{disputed})$ to all parties.
2: On receiving $(\{r_s^1\}_{P_s \in \mathcal{C}_{\text{active}}}, \ldots, \{r_s^T\}_{P_s \in \mathcal{C}_{\text{active}}})$ from $\mathcal{S}$, $\mathcal{F}_{\text{zero}}$ randomly generates $[0^1]_t, \ldots, [0^T]_t$ such that for all $j \subset \{1, \ldots, T\}$ and $P_s \in \mathcal{C}_{\text{active}}$, the s-th share of $[0^j]_t$ is r_s^j. For all $j \in \{1, \ldots, T\}$ and $P_i \in \mathcal{P}_{\text{active}}$, $\mathcal{F}_{\text{4-consistency}}$ sends the i-th shares of $[0^1]_t, \ldots, [0^T]_t$ to P_i.

ZeroShareRandom first invokes $\mathcal{F}_{\text{triple}}(t, t, t)$ to generate T random triple-sharings $[r]_{t,t,t}$. Then computes $[0]_t$ by subtracting the first t-sharing of r from the second t-sharing of r. Formally,

---
Protocol 11 ZeroShareRandom($\mathcal{P}_{\text{active}}$)

1: Generate random triple-sharings:
   All parties invoke $\mathcal{F}_{\text{triple}}(t, t, t)$ to generate $[r^1]_{t,t,t}, \ldots, [r^T]_{t,t,t}$. If $\mathcal{F}_{\text{triple}}$ outputs $(P_i, P_k, \text{disputed})$, all parties halt. We write each triple-sharings $[r^j]_{t,t,t}$ as $([a^j]_t, [b^j]_t, [c^j]_t)$ where $r^j = a^j = b^j = c^j$ to distinguish these three t-sharings of the same value r^j.
2: For $j \in \{1, \ldots, T\}$, all parties locally compute $[0^j]_t = [b^j]_t - [a^j]_t$. All parties take $[0^1]_t, \ldots, [0^T]_t$ as output.

As we invoke $\mathcal{F}_{\text{triple}}(t, t, t)$ to generate T random sharings of 0 from T random triple-sharings, the overall communication complexity is $O(n^2\kappa)$ bits. And in average, the communication cost for each random t-sharing of 0 is $O(n)$ elements.

5.5   Check Consistency

The procedure CHECKCONSISTENCY is used to check whether a party P_{king} sent T same elements to all other parties. It outputs either $\bot$ or a disputed pairs.

We may think P_{king} distributes T 0-sharings (which are essentially constant values) to all other parties. Suppose these sharings are $[d^1]_0, \dots, [d^T]_0$. In the beginning, all parties agree on a hyper-invertible matrix M of size $(T + t') \times T$. Then all parties (locally) compute $([r^1]_0, \dots, [r^{T+t'}]_0) = M([d^1]_0, \dots, [d^T]_0)$. Each 0-sharing is reconstructed by a different party and each party who reconstructs one of the 0-sharing checks whether it is valid and sets its happy-bit to unhappy if not. Note that at least T sharings are checked by honest parties. If all honest parties are satisfied with the execution, by the property of hyper-invertible matrices, all honest parties received the same T elements from P_{king}.

However, in the fault-location phase, just providing all information in the computation phase is not enough. To find a pair of disputed parties, P_{king} should send these T elements to the referee. Formally,

---

Procedure 12 CHECKCONSISTENCY($\mathcal{P}_{\text{active}}, P_{\text{king}}, [d^1]_0, \dots, [d^T]_0$)

1: Initialization Phase:
   All parties initially set their happy-bits to happy.
2: Computation Phase:
   1. All parties agree on a hyper-invertible matrix M of size $(T + t') \times T$.
   2. All parties locally compute $([r^1]_0, \dots, [r^{T+t'}]_0) = M([d^1]_0, \dots, [d^T]_0)$.
   3. For $j \in \{1, \dots, T + t'\}$, all parties send their shares of $[r^j]_0$ to P_j.
   4. P_j checks whether $[r^j]_0$ it receives is valid, i.e., all shares of $[r^j]_0$ are equal. If not, P_j sets its happy-bit to unhappy.
3: Fault Detection Phase:
   1. Each party sends their happy-bit to all other parties.
   2. For each party, if at least one of the happy-bits it receives is unhappy, set its happy-bit to be unhappy.
   3. All parties run a consensus protocol on their respective happy-bits. If the result is happy, all parties halt. Otherwise, run the following steps.
4: Fault Localization Phase:
   1. All parties agree on a referee $P_r \in \mathcal{P}_{\text{active}}$. Every other party sends everything it generated, sent and received in the Computation Phase and Fault Detection Phase to P_r. P_{king} sends $d^1, \dots, d^T$ to P_r.
   2. On receiving all information from other parties, P_r simulates the Computation Phase and Fault Detection Phase. P_r broadcasts either $(P_i, \text{corrupt})$ (in the case P_i does not follow the procedure) or $(\ell, P_i, P_k, v, v', \text{disputed})$ where ℓ is the index of the message where P_i should have sent v to P_k while P_k claimed to have received $v' \neq v$.
      (a) If $(P_i, \text{corrupt})$ is broadcast, all parties set $E = \{P_r, P_i\}$.
      (b) Otherwise, P_i and P_k broadcast whether they agree with P_r. If P_i disagrees, set $E = \{P_r, P_i\}$; if P_k disagrees, set $E = \{P_r, P_k\}$; otherwise, set $E = \{P_i, P_k\}$.
   3. All parties take E as output and halt.

In the computation phase of CHECKCONSISTENCY, all parties send $O(n^2)$ elements. The remaining step is the same as PARTY-ELIMINATION except that P_{king} needs to send additional $O(n)$ elements to P_r in the fault localization phase. The overall communication complexity is $O(n^2\kappa)$ bits.

5.6   Check 4-Consistency

The procedure CHECK4CONSISTENCY is used to check whether each party distributed a correct 4-consistent tuple. The privacy is preserved when invoking this procedure. It outputs either $\perp$ or a pair of disputed parties.

In the beginning, all parties agree on a hyper-invertible matrix M of size $(T+t')\times T$. Then, all parties invoke $\mathcal{F}_{\text{4-consistency}}$ several times to generate enough number of random tuples of 4-consistent sharings. Each random 4-consistent tuple is associated to one input 4-consistent tuple and it is reconstructed to the dealer of the input tuple. Instead of checking the original one, we will check the summation of these two tuples.

Every time, up to T tuples are checked. All parties locally apply M on these T tuples to get $T + t'$ tuples. Each tuple is then reconstructed by a different party. Each party who reconstructs the tuple of sharings checks whether it is 4-consistent and sets its happy-bit to unhappy if not. Note that at least T tuples are checked by honest parties. If all honest parties are satisfied with the execution, by the property of hyper-invertible matrices and the linearity of 4-consistent sharings, these T tuples are correct and 4-consistent.

However, in the fault-location phase, the dealer cannot provide the original tuple of sharings to the referee. Instead, the dealer provides the new tuple which is the summation of the original one and a random one. Note that the original tuple is generated by the dealer which should be 4-consistent and the random tuple is 4-consistent guaranteed by $\mathcal{F}_{\text{4-consistency}}$.

Procedure 13 CHECK4CONSISTENCY$(\mathcal{P}_{\text{active}}, \mathcal{P}_1, \mathcal{P}_2, \mathcal{P}_3, \{[\![s^j]\!]\}_{j=1}^{n'})$

1: Initialization Phase:

      All parties initially set their happy-bits to happy.

2: Pre-Computation Phase:

    1. All parties agree on a hyper-invertible matrix M of size $(T + t') \times T$.

    2. From $j = 1$ to $\lceil n'/T\rceil$:

        All parties call $\mathcal{F}_{\text{4-consistency}}$ to generate T random tuples of 4-consistent sharings $[\![r^{T(j-1)+1}]\!], \ldots, [\![r^{T(j-1)+T}]\!]$. If $\mathcal{F}_{\text{4-consistency}}$ outputs $(P_i, P_k, \text{disputed})$, all parties take $(P_i, P_k, \text{disputed})$ as output and halt.

    3. For $j \in \{1, \ldots, n'\}$, all parties send their shares of $[\![r^j]\!]$ to P_j.

    4. For $j \in \{1, \ldots, n'\}$, all parties compute

$$[\![u^j]\!] := [\![s^j]\!] + [\![r^j]\!]$$

3: Computation Phase:

    For $l > n'$, we set $[\![u^l]\!] := ([0]_0, [0]_0, [0]_0, [0]_0)$. For $j \in \{1, \ldots \lceil n'/T\rceil\}$:

1. All parties locally compute $(\llbracket v^1 \rrbracket, \dots, \llbracket v^{T+t'} \rrbracket) = M(\llbracket u^{T(j-1)+1} \rrbracket, \dots, \llbracket u^{T(j-1)+T} \rrbracket)$.

2. For $k \in \{1, \dots, T+t'\}$, all parties send their shares of $\llbracket v^k \rrbracket$ to P_k.

3. P_k checks whether the 4-consistent tuple it received is valid. If not, P_k sets its happy-bit to unhappy.

4: Fault Detection Phase:

1. Each party sends their happy-bit to all other parties.

2. For each party, if at least one of the happy-bits it receives is unhappy, set its happy-bit to be unhappy.

3. All parties run a consensus protocol on their respective happy-bits. If the result is happy, all parties halt. Otherwise, run the following steps.

5: Fault Localization Phase:

1. All parties agree on a referee $P_r \in \mathcal{P}_{\text{active}}$. Every other party sends everything it generated, sent and received in the Computation Phase and Fault Detection Phase to P_r. Each party P_i also sends $\llbracket u^i \rrbracket$ to P_r.

2. On receiving all information from other parties, P_r simulates the Computation Phase and Fault Detection Phase. P_r broadcasts either $(P_i, \text{corrupt})$ (in the case P_i does not follow the procedure) or $(\ell, P_i, P_k, v, v', \text{disputed})$ where ℓ is the index of the message where P_i should have sent v to P_k while P_k claimed to have received $v' \neq v$.

   (a) If $(P_i, \text{corrupt})$ is broadcast, all parties set $E = \{P_r, P_i\}$.

   (b) Otherwise, P_i and P_k broadcast whether they agree with P_r. If P_i disagrees, set $E = \{P_r, P_i\}$; if P_k disagrees, set $E = \{P_r, P_k\}$; otherwise, set $E = \{P_i, P_k\}$.

3. All parties take E as output and halt.

In the pre-computation phase of CHECK4CONSISTENCY, all parties invoke $\mathcal{F}_{\text{4-consistency}}$ $\lceil n'/T \rceil = O(1)$ times and send $O(n^2)$ elements to reconstruct n' $\llbracket r^j \rrbracket$-s to different parties. In total, $O(n^2)$ elements are sent.

In the computation phase, all parties send $O(n^2)$ elements to reconstruct $T + t'$ $\llbracket v^k \rrbracket$-s to different parties each round and $\lceil n'/T \rceil = O(1)$ rounds are executed. The remaining step is the same as PARTY-ELIMINATION except that, in the fault localization phase, each party P_i should send $\llbracket u^i \rrbracket$-s to P_r, which contains $O(n^2)$ elements in total. The overall communication complexity is $O(n^2\kappa)$ bits.

6   Protocol

In this section, we formally describe our construction. The main protocol is divided into several parts. In the first part, all input gates are handled by $\mathcal{F}_{\text{input}}$. We refer the reader to Sect. 3.7. The second part generates random shares for all random gates. In the third part, the circuit is divided into segments where each segment contains exactly T multiplication gates. Then each segment is evaluated sequentially. The last part handles the output gates.

6.1   Random Gates

The functionality $\mathcal{F}_{\text{rand}}$ is used to generate random sharings of uniform elements in $\mathbb{F}$. We use c_R for the number of random gates in the circuit.

Functionality 14 $\mathcal{F}_{\text{rand}}(c_R)$

1: From $j = 1$ to c_R, $\mathcal{F}_{\text{rand}}$ asks $\mathcal{S}$ what to do next:
  – On receiving $(P_i, P_k, \text{disputed})$ where $\mathcal{C}_{\text{active}} \bigcap \{P_i, P_k\} \neq \emptyset$, $\mathcal{F}_{\text{rand}}$ sets $\mathcal{P}_{\text{active}} := \mathcal{P}_{\text{active}} \backslash \{P_i, P_k\}$ and $\mathcal{C}_{\text{active}} := \mathcal{C}_{\text{active}} \backslash \{P_i, P_k\}$.
  – On receiving $\{v_s^j\}_{P_s \in \mathcal{C}_{\text{active}}}$, $\mathcal{F}_{\text{rand}}$ sets $\mathcal{P}^j = \mathcal{P}_{\text{active}}, \mathcal{C}^j = \mathcal{C}_{\text{active}}$ and continue to handle $j := j + 1$.
2: For every $j \in \{1, \ldots, c_R\}$, $\mathcal{F}_{\text{rand}}$ generates a random value $v^j \in \mathbb{F}$ and computes a random t-sharing $[v^j]_t$ such that for all $P_s \in \mathcal{C}^j$, the s-th share of $[v^j]_t$ is v_s^j.
3: For every $j \in \{1, \ldots, c_R\}$ and $P_i \in \mathcal{P}^j$, $\mathcal{F}_{\text{rand}}$ sends v_i^j to P_i. $\mathcal{F}_{\text{rand}}$ also sends $\mathcal{P}_{\text{active}}$ to all parties.

The formal instantiation of $\mathcal{F}_{\text{rand}}$ is described below.

Protocol 15 $\text{RAND}(\mathcal{P}_{\text{active}}, c_R)$

1: From $j = 1$ to $\lceil c_R/T \rceil$, do the follows:
  1. All parties in $\mathcal{P}_{\text{active}}$ call $\mathcal{F}_{\text{triple}}(n' - 1, t, t')$.
  2. If $\mathcal{F}_{\text{triple}}$ outputs $(P_i, P_k, \text{disputed})$, all parties set $\mathcal{P}_{\text{active}} := \mathcal{P}_{\text{active}} \backslash \{P_i, P_k\}$ and P_i, P_k halt. Repeat this step.
  3. Otherwise, all $(n' - 1)$-sharings and t'-sharings are discarded. Denote the T t-sharings as $[v^{T(j-1)+1}]_t, \ldots, [v^{T(j-1)+T}]_t$. All parties in $\mathcal{P}_{\text{active}}$ continue to handle $j := j + 1$.
2: All parties take $[v^1]_t, \ldots, [v^{c_R}]_t$ as output and the remaining sharings are discarded.

We now show that RAND securely computes $\mathcal{F}_{\text{rand}}$.

Lemma 6. *The protocol* RAND *computes* $\mathcal{F}_{rand}$ *with perfect security when* $|\mathcal{C}_{\text{active}}| < |\mathcal{P}_{\text{active}}|/3$.

Proof. Let $\mathcal{A}$ be the adversary in the real world. We show the existence of $\mathcal{S}$:
  From $j = 1$ to $\lceil c_R/T \rceil$, $\mathcal{S}$ does the follows:

1. $\mathcal{S}$ emulates $\mathcal{F}_{\text{triple}}(n' - 1, t, t')$.
2. On receiving $(P_i, P_k, \text{disputed})$, where $\mathcal{C}_{\text{active}} \bigcap \{P_i, P_k\} \neq \emptyset$, from $\mathcal{A}$, $\mathcal{S}$ sets $\mathcal{P}_{\text{active}} := \mathcal{P}_{\text{active}} \backslash \{P_i, P_k\}$ and $\mathcal{C}_{\text{active}} := \mathcal{C}_{\text{active}} \backslash \{P_i, P_k\}$. $\mathcal{S}$ sends $(P_i, P_k, \text{disputed})$ to $\mathcal{F}_{\text{rand}}$. Repeat the loop from the beginning.
3. On receiving $(\{r_s^{1,n'-1}, r_s^{1,t}, r_s^{1,t'}\}_{P_s \in \mathcal{C}_{\text{active}}}, \{r_s^{T,n'-1}, r_s^{T,t}, r_s^{T,t'}\}_{P_s \in \mathcal{C}_{\text{active}}})$ from $\mathcal{A}$, for $i = 1, 2, \ldots, T$, $\mathcal{S}$ sets $\{v_s^{T(j-1)+i}\}_{P_s \in \mathcal{C}_{\text{active}}} = \{r_s^{i,t}\}_{P_s \in \mathcal{C}_{\text{active}}}$.
4. From $i = 1$ to T, if $T(j-1) + i \leq T$, $\mathcal{S}$ sends $\{v_s^{T(j-1)+i}\}_{P_s \in \mathcal{C}_{\text{active}}}$ to $\mathcal{F}_{\text{rand}}$.

Note that $\mathcal{S}$ does not send any message to $\mathcal{A}$. The view of $\mathcal{A}$ in either world is just empty. $\qquad\square$

Note that, each time we repeat Step 1.2, at least one corrupted party is removed from $\mathcal{P}_{\text{active}}$. Thus, we will repeat Step 1.2 at most $t = O(n)$ times. Therefore, $\mathcal{F}_{\text{triple}}$ is invoked at most $\lceil c_R/T \rceil + O(n)$ times.

By using TRIPLESHARERANDOM-PE to instantiate $\mathcal{F}_{\text{triple}}$ in RAND, the overall communication complexity is $O((\lceil c_R/T \rceil + O(n))n^2\kappa) = O(c_R n\kappa + n^3\kappa)$ bits.

6.2   Addition and Multiplication Gates

The circuit is first divided into several segments such that each segment seg contains T multiplication gates. All segments are evaluated sequentially. If a segment is evaluated successfully, then in the end, every output wire of this segment is a correct t-sharing. Otherwise, a pair of disputed parties is recognized. We first describe the procedure for evaluating one segment.

Procedure 16 EVAL($\mathcal{P}_{\text{active}}$, seg)

1: Initialization:

   All parties agree on a party P_{king} and a partition of $\mathcal{P}_{\text{active}} = \mathcal{P}_1 \bigcup \mathcal{P}_2 \bigcup \mathcal{P}_3$ such that $|\mathcal{P}_1|, |\mathcal{P}_2|, |\mathcal{P}_3| \leq t + 1$.

2: Generate multiplication tuples:

   All parties invoke GENERATETUPLES-PE($\mathcal{P}_{\text{active}}$). If the result is $(P_i, P_k, \text{disputed})$, all parties take it as output and halt. Otherwise, run the following steps.

3: Evaluate seg:

   For every addition gate, all parties apply addition on their own shares.

   For every multiplication gate, a multiplication tuple generated in the first step is associated with it. We use $[x]_t, [y]_t$ for the input wires and $([a]_{t,n'-1}, [b]_{t,n'-1}, [c]_t)$ for the multiplication tuple.

   1. All parties compute $[d]_{n'-1} := [x]_t + [a]_{n'-1}$ and $[e]_{n'-1} := [y]_t + [b]_{n'-1}$.
   2. All parties send their shares of $[d]_{n'-1}$ and $[e]_{n'-1}$ to P_{king}.
   3. P_{king} reconstructs the d and e. Then send these two elements back to all other parties.
   4. All parties compute $[z]_t := de - d[b]_t - e[a]_t + [c]_t$.

4: Check the consistency of P_{king}:

   Let $d^1, \ldots, d^T, e^1, \ldots, e^T$ be the elements P_{king} distributed in the last step. We view that step as P_{king} distributing $[d^1]_0, \ldots, [d^T]_0, [e^1]_0, \ldots, [e^T]_0$.

   1. All parties invoke the procedure CHECKCONSISTENCY($\mathcal{P}_{\text{active}}, P_{\text{king}}, [d^1]_0, \ldots, [d^T]_0$). If the result is $(P_i, P_k, \text{disputed})$, all parties take it as output and halt.
   2. All parties invoke the procedure CHECKCONSISTENCY($\mathcal{P}_{\text{active}}, P_{\text{king}}, [e^1]_0, \ldots, [e^T]_0$). If the result is $(P_i, P_k, \text{disputed})$, all parties take it as output and halt.

5: Recompute all reconstructions:

   We use $([x^1]_t, [y^1]_t), \ldots, ([x^T]_t, [y^T]_t)$ for the input wires of the multiplication gates in seg and $([a^1]_{t,n'-1}, [b^1]_{t,n'-1}, [c^1]_t), \ldots, ([a^T]_{t,n'-1}, [b^T]_{t,n'-1}, [c^T]_t)$ for the multiplication tuples associated with the multiplication gates.

1. For $j \in \{1, \ldots, T\}$, all parties compute $[d^j]_t = [x^j]_t + [a^j]_t, [e^j]_t = [y^j]_t + [b^j]_t$.

2. Invoke $\text{RECONS}(\mathcal{P}_{\texttt{active}}, t, [d^1]_t, \ldots, [d^T]_t)$ and $\text{RECONS}(\mathcal{P}_{\texttt{active}}, t, [e^1]_t, \ldots, [e^T]_t)$.

3. On receiving $d^1, \ldots, d^T, e^1, \ldots, e^T$, each party checks that whether they are correctly reconstructed by $P_{\texttt{king}}$ in step 4. If they are all correct, take the shares of each output wires of seg as output and halt. Otherwise, find the first value which is incorrect. Without loss of generality, suppose d^{i^*} is the first incorrect value. Then do the following check.

6: Commit randomness used in GENERATETUPLES-PE:

   For $P_i \in \mathcal{P}_{\texttt{active}}$, let $[s^i]_{t,n'-1}$ denote the t-sharing and $(n'-1)$-sharing of s^i that P_i distributed in TRIPLESHARERANDOM (which is used in GENERATETUPLES-PE).

   1. For party P_i, it randomly generates $[_1 s^i]_t, [_2 s^i]_t, [_3 s^i]_t$ such that for $j \in \{1, 2, 3\}$ and $P_k \in \mathcal{P}_j$, the k-th share of $[_j s^i]_t$ (i.e., $_j s_k^i$) is the same as that of $[s^i]_{n'-1}$.

   2. For $j \in \{1, 2, 3\}$ and $P_k \in \mathcal{P}_{\texttt{active}} \backslash \mathcal{P}_j$, P_i sends the k-th share of $[_j s^i]_t$ to P_k.

7: Check 4-Consistency:

   Let $[_0 s^i]_t := [s^i]_t$ and $[\![s^i]\!]$ denote the tuple of sharings $([_0 s^i]_t, [_1 s^i]_t, [_2 s^i]_t, [_3 s^i]_t)$.

   1. All parties invoke the procedure

   $$\text{CHECK4CONSISTENCY}(\mathcal{P}_{\texttt{active}}, \mathcal{P}_1, \mathcal{P}_2, \mathcal{P}_3, \{[\![s^j]\!]\}_{j=1}^{n'})$$

   2. If the result is $(P_i, P_k, \text{disputed})$, all parties take it as output and halt. Otherwise, run the following steps.

8: Find a disputed pair of parties:

   Let M be the invertible matrix used in TRIPLESHARERANDOM. Let M_{i^*} be the i^*-th row of M. Then $[a^{i^*}]_{n'-1} = M_{i^*}([s^1]_{n'-1}, \ldots, [s^{n'}]_{n'-1})$.

   1. For $j \in \{1, 2, 3\}$, all parties compute

   $$[_j d^{i^*}]_t = [x^{i^*}]_t + M_{i^*}([_j s^1]_t, \ldots, [_j s^{n'}]_t)$$

   2. For $j \in \{1, 2, 3\}$, all parties send their shares of $[_j d^{i^*}]_t$ to $P_{\texttt{king}}$.

   3. $P_{\texttt{king}}$ finds j^* and k^* where the k^*-th share of $[_{j^*} d^{i^*}]_t$ is not the value he received from P_{k^*} in Step 3. $P_{\texttt{king}}$ broadcasts $(k^*, \text{corrupt})$.

   4. All parties take $\{P_{\texttt{king}}, P_{k^*}, \text{disputed}\}$ as output and halt.

Now, we analyze the correctness of EVAL. The first two steps are straightforward. For Step 3, every addition gate can be computed locally by all parties. To evaluate a multiplication gate, we use a random multiplication tuple. Instead of using random t-sharings in [BTH08], we use random $(n'-1)$-sharings (namely $[a]_{n'-1}$ and $[b]_{n'-1}$) to hide the t-sharings (namely $[x]_t$ and $[y]_t$). In this way, the messages that $P_{\texttt{king}}$ receives from honest parties are uniformly random. It prevents a malicious $P_{\texttt{king}}$ to gain addition knowledge from the shares of honest parties. Indeed, if all parties behave honestly, then all parties will get a random t-sharing $[z]_t$ where $z = xy$.

However, a corrupted party may send an incorrect share to P_{king} or a malicious P_{king} may send incorrect values back to all other parties. To detect such malicious behaviors, we first check whether P_{king} sent the same values in Step 4. It is vital since it directly decides whether the shares of $[z]_t$ held by honest parties are consistent or not.

If all parties confirm that P_{king} sent the same values to all other parties (at least to all honest parties), the next step is to check whether these reconstructed values are correct. This time, all parties use $[a]_t$ and $[b]_t$ instead of $[a]_{n'-1}$ and $[b]_{n'-1}$. Note that for each input wire of multiplication gates, all parties have already held a *correct* t-sharings, which is guaranteed by Step 4. Thus, we can reconstruct all t-sharings $[a]_t + [x]_t$ and $[b]_t + [y]_t$ for multiple layers of multiplication gates, which were evaluated in this segment, in parallel. If all reconstructions are the same as those in Step 3, then we confirm that this segment is evaluated successfully.

If all parties find at least one of the reconstructions is incorrect, then there must be some corrupted party which doesn't follow the protocol. All parties focus on the first incorrect one. Without loss of generality, we assume it is d^{i^*}.

The main difficulty is that the redundancy is not enough to identify a pair of disputed parties. Therefore, in Step 6, all parties commit their randomness used in generating $[a^{i^*}]_{t',t,n'-1}$, namely $[s^1]_{t',t,n'-1}, \ldots [s^{n'}]_{t',t,n'-1}$. Note that correct t'-sharings and t-sharings have already had enough redundancy in the sense that all parties can correct all shares no matter how corrupted parties change their shares. Therefore, we require that each party P_i commits $[s^i]_{n'-1}$ by using several t-sharings $[_1 s^i]_t, [_2 s^i]_t, [_3 s^i]_t$. Together with $[_0 s^i]_t = [s^i]_t$, the tuple of these 4 sharings forms a 4-consistent tuple.

In Step 7, all parties check whether these tuples are 4-consistent.

In the last step, for every $j \in \{1, 2, 3\}$, all parties compute

$$[_j d^{i^*}]_t = [x^{i^*}]_t + M_{i^*}([_j s^1]_t, \ldots, [_j s^{n'}]_t)$$

Note that for $P_i \in \mathcal{P}_j$, the i-th share of $[_j d^{i^*}]_t$ is exactly the share P_i should have sent to P_{king} and this time, P_i cannot change its share without being caught. P_{king} collects all shares of $[_1 d^{i^*}]_t, [_2 d^{i^*}]_t, [_3 d^{i^*}]_t$ and is able to broadcast a corrupted party. All party then view P_{king} and the party it broadcast as a pair of disputed parties.

Now we analyze the communication complexity of EVAL.

In Step 2, GENERATETUPLES-PE is invoked one time and the communication complexity is $O(n^2 \kappa)$ bits. In Step 3, for each multiplication gate, P_{king} receives from and sends to other parties $O(n)$ elements in total, which costs $O(n\kappa)$ bits. In Step 4, CHECKCONSISTENCY is invoked two times and the communication complexity is $O(n^2 \kappa)$ bits. In Step 5, RECONS is invoked two times and the communication complexity is $O(n^2 \kappa)$ bits. In Step 6, all parties send $O(n^2)$ elements to distribute $[_1 s^i]_t, [_2 s^i]_t, [_3 s^i]_t$. In Step 7, CHECK4CONSISTENCY is invoked one time and the communication complexity is $O(n^2 \kappa)$ bits. In Step 8, all parties send $O(n)$ elements to P_{king} to reconstruct $[_1 d^{i^*}]_t, [_2 d^{i^*}]_t, [_3 d^{i^*}]_t$ to P_{king}. Then another $O(n^2)$ elements are sent to let P_{king} broadcast a corrupted party.

Therefore, the overall complexity is $O(n^2 \kappa)$ bits.

6.3 Output Gates

The procedure OUTPUT helps reconstruct t-sharings to the parties specified by the output gates under the guarantee that, for each sharing associated with the output gates, the shares held by parties in $\mathcal{P}_{\text{active}} \setminus \mathcal{C}_{\text{active}}$ are consistent.

Procedure 17 OUTPUT($\mathcal{P}_{\text{active}}$)

   All output gates are divided into several segments of size T. All segments are executed *sequentially*. For each segment:
1: All parties repeat the following steps until success:
   1. All parties call $\mathcal{F}_{\text{zero}}$.
   2. If $\mathcal{F}_{\text{zero}}$ outputs $(P_i, P_k, \text{disputed})$, all parties set $\mathcal{P}_{\text{active}} := \mathcal{P}_{\text{active}} \setminus \{P_i, P_k\}$. Redo the loop.
   3. If $\mathcal{F}_{\text{zero}}$ outputs T t-sharings of 0, break the loop.
2: Each output gate consumes one $[0]_t$ generated in the last step. For each output gate, $[s]_t$ denotes the t-sharing and $P_{i^*} \in \mathcal{P}$, the party who receives s. All parties in $\mathcal{P}_{\text{active}}$ compute $[s]_t := [s]_t + [0]_t$ and send their shares of $[s]_t$ to P_{i^*}.
3: Each receiver P_{i^*} reconstructs s from the shares it receives in the last step.

   Let c_O be the number of output gates in the circuit. Then all output gates are divided into $\lceil c_O / T \rceil$ segments. Note that each time $\mathcal{F}_{\text{zero}}$ outputs a pair of disputed parties, at least one corrupted party is removed from $\mathcal{P}_{\text{active}}$. Thus $\mathcal{F}_{\text{zero}}$ will be *rerun* at most $O(n)$ times. $\mathcal{F}_{\text{zero}}$ will be invoked at most $O(n) + \lceil c_O / T \rceil$ times. For each output gate, all parties send $O(n)$ elements to the designated party to reconstruct the output. Therefore, by using ZEROSHARERANDOM to instantiate $\mathcal{F}_{\text{zero}}$, the overall communication complexity is $O(c_O n \kappa + n^3 \kappa)$ bits.

6.4 Main Protocol

Now, we are ready to present the main protocol. In the protocol, all parties first invoke $\mathcal{F}_{\text{input}}$ to securely share their inputs. Then $\mathcal{F}_{\text{rand}}$ is invoked to generate random sharings for random gates.

Let c_M denote the number of multiplication gates. The circuit is divided into $\lceil c_M / T \rceil$ segments such that each segment contains T multiplication gates. Segments are evaluated sequentially based on their topological order. For each segment **seg**, the procedure EVAL is invoked. If the result is a pair of disputed parties, then these two parties are removed from $\mathcal{P}_{\text{active}}$ and all parties in $\mathcal{P}_{\text{active}}$ reevaluate **seg**. Otherwise, the protocol continues to evaluate the next segment.

Finally, OUTPUT is invoked to reconstruct the outputs to designated parties.

Protocol 18 MAIN

1: Input gates:
   All parties invoke $\mathcal{F}_{\text{input}}(c_I)$.
2: Rand gates:
   All parties invoke $\mathcal{F}_{\text{rand}}(c_R)$.
3: Evaluation:
   1. All parties agree on a partition $(\text{seg}_1, \text{seg}_2, \ldots, \text{seg}_{\lceil c_M/T \rceil})$ of the circuit such that the number of multiplication gates of each segment is T.
   2. From $j = 1$ to $\lceil c_M/T \rceil$:
      (a) All parties run the procedure EVAL$(\mathcal{P}_{\text{active}}, \text{seg}_j)$.
      (b) If the output is $(P_i, P_k, \text{disputed})$, all parties set $\mathcal{P}_{\text{active}} :=$ $\mathcal{P}_{\text{active}} \backslash \{P_i, P_k\}$ and repeat the loop.
      (c) Otherwise, set $j := j + 1$ and continue to handle the next segment.
4: Output gates:
   All parties invoke the procedure OUTPUT$(\mathcal{P}_{\text{active}})$.

Now we analyze the communication complexity of MAIN.

For Step 3, each time EVAL outputs a pair of disputed parties, at least one corrupted party is removed from $\mathcal{P}_{\text{active}}$. Thus, EVAL will be *rerun* at most $O(n)$ times. In total, EVAL will be invoked $O(n) + \lceil c_M/T \rceil$ times. The overall communication complexity of this step is $O(c_M n \kappa + n^3)$ bits.

Let $C = c_I + c_R + c_M + c_O$. Then the overall communication complexity of MAIN is $O(Cn\kappa + n^3 \kappa)$ bits.

Theorem 1. *Let $\mathbb{F}$ be a finite field of size $|\mathbb{F}| \geq 2n$ and C be an arithmetic circuit over $\mathbb{F}$. Protocol MAIN evaluates C with perfect security against an active adversary which corrupts at most $t < n/3$ parties.*

We provide the full proof of Theorem 1 in the full version of this paper in Appendix B.

References

[ABF+17] Araki, T., et al.: Optimized honest-majority MPC for malicious adversaries - breaking the 1 billion-gate per second barrier. In: 2017 IEEE Symposium on Security and Privacy (SP), pp. 843–862. IEEE (2017)

[Bea89] Beaver, D.: Multiparty protocols tolerating half faulty processors. In: Brassard, G. (ed.) CRYPTO 1989. LNCS, vol. 435, pp. 560–572. Springer, New York (1990). https://doi.org/10.1007/0-387-34805-0_49

[BGP92] Berman, P., Garay, J.A., Perry, K.J.: Bit optimal distributed consensus. In: Baeza-Yates, R., Manber, U. (eds.) Computer Science, pp. 313–321. Springer, Heidelberg (1992). https://doi.org/10.1007/978-1-4615-3422-8_27

[BJMS18] Badrinarayanan, S., Jain, A., Manohar, N., Sahai, A.: Threshold multi-key FHE and applications to MPC. Cryptology ePrint Archive, Report 2018/580 (2018). https://eprint.iacr.org/2018/580

[BOGW88] Ben-Or, M., Goldwasser, S., Wigderson, A.: Completeness theorems for non-cryptographic fault-tolerant distributed computation. In: Proceedings of the Twentieth Annual ACM Symposium on Theory of Computing, pp. 1–10. ACM (1988)

[BSFO12] Ben-Sasson, E., Fehr, S., Ostrovsky, R.: Near-linear unconditionally-secure multiparty computation with a dishonest minority. In: Safavi-Naini, R., Canetti, R. (eds.) CRYPTO 2012. LNCS, vol. 7417, pp. 663–680. Springer, Heidelberg (2012). https://doi.org/10.1007/978-3-642-32009-5_39

[BTH08] Beerliová-Trubíniová, Z., Hirt, M.: Perfectly-secure MPC with linear communication complexity. In: Canetti, R. (ed.) TCC 2008. LNCS, vol. 4948, pp. 213–230. Springer, Heidelberg (2008). https://doi.org/10.1007/978-3-540-78524-8_13

[CCD88] Chaum, D., Crépeau, C., Damgard, I.: Multiparty unconditionally secure protocols. In: Proceedings of the Twentieth Annual ACM Symposium on Theory of Computing, pp. 11–19. ACM (1988)

[CDVdG87] Chaum, D., Damgård, I.B., van de Graaf, J.: Multiparty computations ensuring privacy of each party's input and correctness of the result. In: Pomerance, C. (ed.) CRYPTO 1987. LNCS, vol. 293, pp. 87–119. Springer, Heidelberg (1988). https://doi.org/10.1007/3-540-48184-2_7

[CGH+18] Chida, K., et al.: Fast large-scale honest-majority MPC for malicious adversaries. In: Shacham, H., Boldyreva, A. (eds.) CRYPTO 2018. LNCS, vol. 10993, pp. 34–64. Springer, Cham (2018). https://doi.org/10.1007/978-3-319-96878-0_2

[CW92] Coan, B.A., Welch, J.L.: Modular construction of a byzantine agreement protocol with optimal message bit complexity. Inf. Comput. 97(1), 61–85 (1992)

[DI06] Damgård, I., Ishai, Y.: Scalable secure multiparty computation. In: Dwork, C. (ed.) CRYPTO 2006. LNCS, vol. 4117, pp. 501–520. Springer, Heidelberg (2006). https://doi.org/10.1007/11818175_30

[DIK10] Damgård, I., Ishai, Y., Krøigaard, M.: Perfectly secure multiparty computation and the computational overhead of cryptography. In: Gilbert, H. (ed.) EUROCRYPT 2010. LNCS, vol. 6110, pp. 445–465. Springer, Heidelberg (2010). https://doi.org/10.1007/978-3-642-13190-5_23

[DN07] Damgård, I., Nielsen, J.B.: Scalable and unconditionally secure multiparty computation. In: Menezes, A. (ed.) CRYPTO 2007. LNCS, vol. 4622, pp. 572–590. Springer, Heidelberg (2007). https://doi.org/10.1007/978-3-540-74143-5_32

[FLNW17] Furukawa, J., Lindell, Y., Nof, A., Weinstein, O.: High-throughput secure three-party computation for malicious adversaries and an honest majority. In: Coron, J.-S., Nielsen, J.B. (eds.) EUROCRYPT 2017. LNCS, vol. 10211, pp. 225–255. Springer, Cham (2017). https://doi.org/10.1007/978-3-319-56614-6_8

[GMW87] Goldreich, O., Micali, S., Wigderson, A.: How to play any mental game. In: Proceedings of the Nineteenth Annual ACM Symposium on Theory of Computing, pp. 218–229. ACM (1987)

[HM01] Hirt, M., Maurer, U.: Robustness for free in unconditional multi-party computation. In: Kilian, J. (ed.) CRYPTO 2001. LNCS, vol. 2139, pp. 101–118. Springer, Heidelberg (2001). https://doi.org/10.1007/3-540-44647-8_6

[HMP00] Hirt, M., Maurer, U., Przydatek, B.: Efficient secure multi-party computation. In: Okamoto, T. (ed.) ASIACRYPT 2000. LNCS, vol. 1976, pp. 143–161. Springer, Heidelberg (2000). https://doi.org/10.1007/3-540-44448-3_12

[HN06] Hirt, M., Nielsen, J.B.: Robust multiparty computation with linear communication complexity. In: Dwork, C. (ed.) CRYPTO 2006. LNCS, vol. 4117, pp. 463–482. Springer, Heidelberg (2006). https://doi.org/10.1007/11818175_28

[LN17] Lindell, Y., Nof, A.: A framework for constructing fast MPC over arithmetic circuits with malicious adversaries and an honest-majority. In: Proceedings of the 2017 ACM SIGSAC Conference on Computer and Communications Security, pp. 259–276. ACM (2017)

[LP12] Lindell, Y., Pinkas, B.: Secure two-party computation via cut-and-choose oblivious transfer. J. Cryptol. **25**(4), 680–722 (2012)

[LSP82] Lamport, L., Shostak, R., Pease, M.: The byzantine generals problem. ACM Trans. Program. Lang. Syst. **4**(3), 382–401 (1982)

[NNOB12] Nielsen, J.B., Nordholt, P.S., Orlandi, C., Burra, S.S.: A new approach to practical active-secure two-party computation. In: Safavi-Naini, R., Canetti, R. (eds.) CRYPTO 2012. LNCS, vol. 7417, pp. 681–700. Springer, Heidelberg (2012). https://doi.org/10.1007/978-3-642-32009-5_40

[Pai99] Paillier, P.: Public-key cryptosystems based on composite degree residuosity classes. In: Stern, J. (ed.) EUROCRYPT 1999. LNCS, vol. 1592, pp. 223–238. Springer, Heidelberg (1999). https://doi.org/10.1007/3-540-48910-X_16

[RBO89] Rabin, T., Ben-Or, M.: Verifiable secret sharing and multiparty protocols with honest majority. In: Proceedings of the Twenty-First Annual ACM Symposium on Theory of Computing, STOC 1989, pp. 73–85. ACM, New York (1989)

[Sha79] Shamir, A.: How to share a secret. Commun. ACM **22**(11), 612–613 (1979)

[Yao82] Yao, A.C.: Protocols for secure computations. In: 23rd Annual Symposium on Foundations of Computer Science, SFCS 2008, pp. 160–164. IEEE (1982)

Symmetric Cryptanalysis

Efficient Collision Attack Frameworks for RIPEMD-160

Fukang Liu[1,6], Christoph Dobraunig[2,3], Florian Mendel[4], Takanori Isobe[5,6], Gaoli Wang[1(✉)], and Zhenfu Cao[1(✉)]

[1] Shanghai Key Laboratory of Trustworthy Computing,
East China Normal University, Shanghai, China
liufukangs@163.com, {glwang,zfcao}@sei.ecnu.edu.cn
[2] Graz University of Technology, Graz, Austria
[3] Radboud University, Nijmegen, The Netherlands
cdobraunig@cs.ru.nl
[4] Infineon Technologies AG, Ludwigsburg, Germany
florian.mendel@gmail.com
[5] National Institute of Information and Communications Technology, Tokyo, Japan
[6] University of Hyogo, Kobe, Japan
takanori.isobe@ai.u-hyogo.ac.jp

Abstract. RIPEMD-160 is an ISO/IEC standard and has been applied to generate the Bitcoin address with SHA-256. Due to the complex dual-stream structure, the first collision attack on reduced RIPEMD-160 presented by Liu, Mendel and Wang at Asiacrypt 2017 only reaches 30 steps, having a time complexity of 2^{70}. Apart from that, several semi-free-start collision attacks have been published for reduced RIPEMD-160 with the start-from-the-middle method. Inspired from such start-from-the middle structures, we propose two novel efficient collision attack frameworks for reduced RIPEMD-160 by making full use of the weakness of its message expansion. Those two frameworks are called dense-left-and-sparse-right (DLSR) framework and sparse-left-and-dense-right (SLDR) framework. As it turns out, the DLSR framework is more efficient than SLDR framework since one more step can be fully controlled, though with extra 2^{32} memory complexity. To construct the best differential characteristics for the DLSR framework, we carefully build the linearized part of the characteristics and then solve the corresponding nonlinear part using a guess-and-determine approach. Based on the newly discovered differential characteristics, we provide colliding messages pairs for the first practical collision attacks on 30 and 31 (out of 80) steps of RIPEMD-160 with time complexity $2^{35.9}$ and $2^{41.5}$ respectively. In addition, benefiting from the partial calculation, we can attack 33 and 34 (out of 80) steps of RIPEMD-160 with time complexity $2^{67.1}$ and $2^{74.3}$ respectively. When applying the SLDR framework to the differential characteristic used in the Asiacrypt 2017 paper, we significantly improve the time complexity by a factor of 2^{13}. However, it still cannot compete with the results obtained from the DLSR framework. To the best of our knowledge, these are the best collision attacks on reduced RIPEMD-160 with respect to the number of steps, including the first colliding message pairs for 30 and 31 steps of RIPEMD-160.

© International Association for Cryptologic Research 2019
A. Boldyreva and D. Micciancio (Eds.): CRYPTO 2019, LNCS 11693, pp. 117–149, 2019.
https://doi.org/10.1007/978-3-030-26951-7_5

Keywords: Hash function · RIPEMD-160 · Start-from-the-middle · Collision attack · Collision

1   Introduction

A cryptographic hash function is a function which takes arbitrary long messages as input and output a fixed-length hash value. Traditionally, such a cryptographic hash function has to fulfill the three basic requirements of collision resistance, preimage resistance and second preimage resistance in order to be considered secure. Most standardized hash functions, like SHA-1, SHA-2, HAS-160, or RIPEMD-160 are based on the Merkle-Damgård paradigm [3, 22] which iterates a compression function with fixed-size input to compress arbitrarily long messages. Furthermore, the aforementioned hash functions have in common that their compression function is built by utilization of additions, rotations, xor and boolean functions in an unbalanced Feistel network. This way of designing hash functions has been greatly threatened, starting with a series of results as well as advanced message modification techniques by Wang et al. [28–31].

Before Wang et al. proposed a series of collision attacks on MD-SHA hash family, there existed substantial efforts to analyze the security of MD-SHA hash functions. Historically, the start-from-the-middle structure was first exploited by den Boer et al. at Eurocrypt 1993 to break the compression function of MD5 [6]. Later at FSE 1996, Dobbertin applied the start-from-the-middle approach to break full MD4 [7]. Since the target is the hash function rather than the compression function, the initial value must be consistent with its definition of the primitive, which is costly under the start-from-the-middle structure. To overcome this obstacle, Dobbertin introduced a connecting phase to connect the correct initial value with the starting point in the middle by exploiting the property of the round boolean function and the freedom of message words [7]. As will be shown, our SLDR framework is almost the same with Dobbertin's structure to break MD4. Moreover, the neutral bits introduced by Biham and Chen [1] at Crypto 2004 serve as an important tool to analyze MD-SHA hash family as well till now. A message bit is neutral up to step n if flipping this bit does not influence the differential characteristic conditions up to step n with a high probability. Due to the low diffusion of SHA-0/SHA-1's step functions, there exist many neutral bits up to a few steps.

Soon after Wang et al. presented their exciting work on MD4/MD5/SHA-0/SHA-1, where all the differential characteristics were hand-crafted, De Cannière and Rechberger invented the first automatic search tool to solve the nonlinear part of the differential characteristic of SHA-1 with the guess-and-determine technique [5]. With such a guess-and-determine technique, Mendel et al. designed a tool to find the differential characteristic of SHA-2 at Asiacrypt 2011 [18]. Later, tools to solve the nonlinear characteristics of SHA-2, RIPEMD-128 and RIPEMD-160 progressed well and a series of results were published [10, 11, 16, 17, 19–21]. After Wang et al. presented the differential characteristic as well as the corresponding sufficient conditions used to break MD5 in [30], cryptographers soon observed that the differential characteristic conditions were not sufficient in [30]. Specifically, Stevens revealed that the differential rotations must hold if the differential characteristic hold [24]. Consequently, Stevens further investigated the influence of the carry and added some extra bit conditions to have the differential rotations hold with probability close to 1. A highly-related work is the recently proposed method to theoretically calculate the probability of the step function of RIPEMD-160 at Asiacrypt 2017 [16], where the authors introduced the influence of the modular difference propagation and also presented how to add extra conditions for RIPEMD-160 to ensure the modular difference propagates correctly.

The very first theoretical collision attack on full SHA-1 was achieved by Wang et al. at Crypto 2005 [29], which required about 2^{69} calls to SHA-1's compression function. However, practical collisions were still out-of-reach. After a decade's effort, Stevens et al. presented the first practical collision of full SHA-1 at Crypto 2017 [25]. In that work, Stevens et al. utilized the SHA-1 collision search GPU framework [13] and the speed-up techniques such as neutral bits and boomerangs and finally found the practical collision of SHA-1. Boomerangs were introduced by Joux and Peyrin at Crypto 2007 [12] to speed up the collision search for SHA-1. It consists in carefully selecting a few bits that are all flipped together in a way that this effectively flips only one state bit in the first 16 steps, and therefore the diffusion of uncontrollable changes is greatly slowed down.

The RIPEMD family can be considered as a subfamily of the MD-SHA-family, since, for instance, RIPEMD [2] consists of two MD4-like functions computed in parallel with totally 48 steps. The security of RIPEMD was first put into question by Dobbertin [8] and a practical collision attack on it was proposed by Wang et al. [28]. In order to reinforce the security of RIPEMD, Dobbertin, Bosselaers and Preneel [9] proposed two strengthened versions of RIPEMD in 1996, which are RIPEMD-128 and RIPEMD-160 with 128/160 bits output and 64/80 steps, respectively. In order to make both computation branches more distinct from each other, not only different constants, but also different rotation values, message expansions and boolean functions are used for RIPEMD-128 and RIPEMD-160 in both of their branches.

Due to the complicated structure of the dual-stream RIPEMD-128 and RIPEMD-160, collision attacks on the two primitives progressed slowly. For RIPEMD-128, a practical collision attack on 38 steps was achieved at FSE 2012 with a new structure [19]. Later, a practical collision attack on 40 steps was achieved at CT-RSA 2014 [26]. A break-through was made at Eurocrypt 2013, when Landelle and Peyrin employed the start-from-the-middle approach to break the compression function of full RIPEMD-128 [14]. As for RIPEMD-160, no collision attack was presented before Asiacrypt 2017 [16]. However, several results of semi-free-start collision attacks on the compression function of RIPEMD-160 were obtained with the start-from-the-middle approach [17,21], only one of them started from the first step and the remaining started from the middle, further showing the difficulty to cryptanalyze the collision resistance of RIPEMD-160. In the work of [21], a partial calculation to ensure that more uncontrolled bit conditions hold was also introduced with a few statements. Later, a thorough discussion was presented at ToSC 2017 [27].

At Asiacrypt 2017, the authors proposed a strategy to mount collision attacks on the dual-stream RIPEMD-160 [16]. Specifically, they inserted the difference at the message word m_{15}, which is used to update the last internal state of the left branch in the first round. Then, they utilized the search tool [21] to find a differential characteristic whose left branch was linear and sparse and the right branch was as sparse as possible. At last, they applied single-step and multi-step message modification only to the dense right branch to make as many bit conditions as possible hold in a very traditional way, i.e. starting modification from the first step. Typically, multi-step message modification requires a lot of complicated hand-crafted work for different discovered differential characteristics and therefore is very time-consuming. This motivates us to come up with two efficient collision attack frameworks.

Since SHA-3 does not provide the 160-bit digest and the first collision of full SHA-1 has been presented [25], as an ISO/IEC standard, RIPEMD-160 is often used as a drop-in replacement of SHA-1 and therefore worth analyzing. For instance, RIPEMD-160 and SHA-256 have been used to generate the Bitcoin address. For completeness, we list some related work of RIPEMD-160 in Table 1.

This paper is organized as follows. The preliminaries of this paper are introduced in Sect. 2, including some notations, description of RIPEMD-160, start-from-the-middle structure to find collisions, single-step message modification, and how to estimate the probability of the uncontrolled part. In Sect. 3, the details of the two efficient collision attack frameworks are explained. Then, we will show how to construct suitable differential characteristics for the DLSR framework and report the newly discovered 30/31/33/34-step differential characteristics in Sect. 4. The application of the frameworks to the differential characteristics is shown in Sect. 5. Finally, our paper is summarized in Sect. 6.

Table 1. Summary of preimage and collision attack on RIPEMD-160.

Target	Attack Type	Steps	Time	Memory	Ref
comp. function	preimage	31	2^{148}	2^{17}	[23]
hash function	preimage	31	2^{155}	2^{17}	[23]
comp. function	semi-free-start collision	36[a]	low	negligible	[17]
	semi-free-start collision	36	$2^{70.4}$	2^{64}	[21]
	semi-free-start collision	36	$2^{55.1}$	2^{32}	[16]
	semi-free-start collision	42[a]	$2^{75.5}$	2^{64}	[21]
	semi-free-start collision	48[a]	$2^{76.4}$	2^{64}	[27]
hash function	collision	30	2^{70}	negligible	[16]
	collision	30[b]	2^{57}	negligible	Appendix A
	collision	30	$2^{35.9}$	2^{32}	Sect. 5.1
	collision	31	$2^{41.5}$	2^{32}	Sect. 5.2
	collision	33	$2^{67.1}$	2^{32}	Sect. 5.3
	collision	34	$2^{74.3}$	2^{32}	Sect. 5.4

[a] An attack starting at an intermediate step.
[b] Based on the differential characteristic in [16].

Our Contributions. With the start-from-the-middle structure, we propose two efficient collision attack frameworks for reduced RIPEMD-160. For the sake of clearness, we differentiate the two frameworks by dense-left-and-sparse-right (DLSR) framework and sparse-left-and-dense-right (SLDR) framework. The two frameworks significantly simplify the procedure of finding collisions after a differential characteristic is discovered and provide an efficient way to choose the best differential characteristic from many candidates discovered by a search tool. To the best of our knowledge, we obtained the best collision attacks on reduced RIPEMD-160 with respect to the number of steps, including the first practical attack. Specifically, the contribution of this paper can be summarized as follows.

- Two novel efficient collision attack frameworks for reduced RIPEMD-160 are proposed. The DLSR framework is much more efficient than SLDR framework since one more step can be fully controlled, though with extra 2^{32} memory complexity.
- With a guess-and-determine technique, new 30/31/33/34-step differential characteristics of RIPEMD-160 are discovered, whose left branch is dense and right branch is linear and sparse.
- By applying the DLSR framework to the newly discovered 30-step and 31-step differential characteristics, practical collision attacks on 30 and 31 steps of RIPEMD-160 are achieved. The instances of collision are provided as well.
- With the partial calculation technique that fully exploits the property of the round boolean function of RIPEMD-160 and the differential characteristic conditions, we introduce a clever way to dynamically choose the value of free message words under the DLSR framework. Thus, based on the newly discovered 33-step and 34-step differential characteristics, we can mount collision attack on 33 and 34 steps of RIPEMD-160 with time complexity $2^{67.1}$ and $2^{74.3}$ respectively.
- Applying the SLDR framework to the discovered 30-step differential characteristic of Liu, Mendel and Wang [16], we improve the collision attack on 30 steps of RIPEMD-160 by a factor of 2^{13}.

2 Preliminaries

In this section, several preliminaries of this paper will be introduced.

2.1 Notation

For a better understanding of this paper, we introduce the following notations.

1. $\gg$, $\lll$, $\ggg$, $\oplus$, $\vee$, $\wedge$ and $\neg$ represent respectively the logic operation: *shift right, rotate left, rotate right, exclusive or, or, and, negate.*
2. $\boxplus$ and $\boxminus$ represent respectively the modular addition and modular substraction on 32 bits.
3. $M = (m_0, m_1, ..., m_{15})$ and $M' = (m'_0, m'_1, ..., m'_{15})$ represent two 512-bit message blocks.

4. K_j^l and K_j^r represent the constant used at the left and right branch for round j.
5. Φ_j^l and Φ_j^r represent respectively the 32-bit boolean function at the left and right branch for round j.
6. s_i^l and s_i^r represent respectively the rotation constant used at the left and right branch during step i.
7. $\pi_1(i)$ and $\pi_2(i)$ represent the index of the message word used at the left and right branch during step i.
8. X_i, Y_i represent respectively the 32-bit internal state of the left and right branch updated during step i for compressing M.
9. V^j represent the $(j+1)$-th bit of V (V can be $X_i, Y_i, Q_i, F...$), where the least significant bit is the 1st bit and the most significant bit is the 32nd bit. For example, X_i^0 represents the least significant bit of X_i.
10. $V^{p\sim q}(0 \leq q < p \leq 31)$ represents the $(q+1)$-th bit to the $(p+1)$-th bit of the 32-bit word V (V can be $X_i, Y_i, Q_i, F...$). For example, $X_i^{1\sim 0}$ represents the two bits X_i^1 and X_i^0 of X_i.

Moreover, we adopt the concept of generalized conditions in [5]. Some related notations for differential characteristics are presented in Table 2.

Table 2. Notations for differential characteristics

(x,x^*)	(0,0)	(1,0)	(0,1)	(1,1)	(x,x^*)	(0,0)	(1,0)	(0,1)	(1,1)
?	✓	✓	✓	✓	3	✓	✓	−	−
−	✓	−	−	✓	5	✓	−	✓	−
x	−	✓	✓	−	7	✓	✓	✓	−
0	✓	−	−	−	A	−	✓	−	✓
u	−	✓	−	−	B	✓	✓	−	✓
n	−	−	✓	−	C	−	−	✓	✓
1	−	−	−	✓	D	✓	−	✓	✓
♯	−	−	−	−	E	−	✓	✓	✓

• x represents one bit of the first message and x^* represents the same bit of the second message.

2.2 Description of RIPEMD-160

RIPEMD-160 is a 160-bit hash function that uses the Merkle-Damgård construction as domain extension algorithm: the hash function is built by iterating a 160-bit compression function H which takes as input a 512-bit message block M_i and a 160-bit chaining variable CV_i:

$$CV_{i+1} = H(CV_i, M_i)$$

where a message to hash is padded beforehand to a multiple of 512 bits and the first chaining variable is set to the predetermined initial value IV, that is $CV_0 = IV$. We refer to [9] for a detailed description of RIPEMD-160.

The RIPEMD-160 compression function is a wider version of RIPEMD-128 and is based on MD5, but with the particularity that it consists of two different and almost independent parallel instances of it. We differentiate the two computation branches by left and right branch. The compression function consists of 80 steps divided into 5 rounds of 16 steps each in both branches.

Initialization. The 160-bit input chaining variable CV_i is divided into five 32-bit words h_i ($i = 0, 1, 2, 3, 4$), initializing the left and right branch 160-bit internal state in the following way:

$$X_{-4} = h_0^{\ggg 10}, \quad X_{-3} = h_4^{\ggg 10}, \quad X_{-2} = h_3^{\ggg 10}, \quad X_{-1} = h_2, \quad X_0 = h_1.$$
$$Y_{-4} = h_0^{\ggg 10}, \quad Y_{-3} = h_4^{\ggg 10}, \quad Y_{-2} = h_3^{\ggg 10}, \quad Y_{-1} = h_2, \quad Y_0 = h_1.$$

Particularly, CV_0 corresponds to the following five 32-bit words:

$X_{-4} = Y_{-4} = \text{0xc059d148}$, $X_{-3} = Y_{-3} = \text{0x7c30f4b8}$, $X_{-2} = Y_{-2} = \text{0x1d840c95}$, $X_{-1} = Y_{-1} = \text{0x98badcfe}$, $X_0 = Y_0 = \text{0xefcdab89}$.

Message Expansion. The 512-bit input message block is divided into 16 message words m_i of size 32 bits. Each message word m_i will be used once in every round in a permuted order π for both branches.

Step Function. At round j, the internal state is updated in the following way.

$$LQ_i = X_{i-5}^{\lll 10} \boxplus \Phi_j^l(X_{i-1}, X_{i-2}, X_{i-3}^{\lll 10}) \boxplus m_{\pi_1(i)} \boxplus K_j^l,$$
$$X_i = X_{i-4}^{\lll 10} \boxplus (LQ_i)^{\lll s_i^l},$$
$$RQ_i = Y_{i-5}^{\lll 10} \boxplus \Phi_j^r(Y_{i-1}, Y_{i-2}, Y_{i-3}^{\lll 10}) \boxplus m_{\pi_2(i)} \boxplus K_j^r,$$
$$Y_i = Y_{i-4}^{\lll 10} \boxplus (RQ_i)^{\lll s_i^r},$$

where $i = (1, 2, 3, ..., 80)$ and $j = (0, 1, 2, 3, 4)$. The details of the boolean functions and round constants for RIPEMD-160 are displayed in Table 3. The other parameters can be found in the specification [9].

Table 3. Boolean Functions and Round Constants in RIPEMD-160

Round j	ϕ_j^l	ϕ_j^r	K_j^l	K_j^r	Function	Expression
0	XOR	ONX	0x00000000	0x50a28be6	XOR(x,y,z)	$x \oplus y \oplus z$
1	IFX	IFZ	0x5a827999	0x5c4dd124	IFX(x,y,z)	$(x \wedge y) \oplus (\neg x \wedge z)$
2	ONZ	ONZ	0x6ed9eba1	0x6d703ef3	IFZ(x,y,z)	$(x \wedge z) \oplus (y \wedge \neg z)$
3	IFZ	IFX	0x8f1bbcdc	0x7a6d76e9	ONX(x,y,z)	$x \oplus (y \vee \neg z)$
4	ONX	XOR	0xa953fd4e	0x00000000	ONZ(x,y,z)	$(x \vee \neg y) \oplus z$

Finalization. A finalization and a feed-forward is applied when all 80 steps have been computed in both branches. The five 32-bit words h'_i composing the output chaining variable are computed in the following way.

$$h'_0 = h_1 \boxplus X_{79} \boxplus Y_{78}^{\lll 10},$$
$$h'_1 = h_2 \boxplus X_{78}^{\lll 10} \boxplus Y_{77}^{\lll 10},$$
$$h'_2 = h_3 \boxplus X_{77}^{\lll 10} \boxplus Y_{76}^{\lll 10},$$
$$h'_3 = h_4 \boxplus X_{76}^{\lll 10} \boxplus Y_{80},$$
$$h'_4 = h_0 \boxplus X_{80} \boxplus Y_{79}.$$

2.3   Start-from-the-Middle Structure

The start-from-the-middle structure was first used to break the compression function of MD5 [6]. However, when applying such a structure to find collisions, an extra phase is essential to match the correct initial value. Historically, Dobbertin was the first to use it to find real collisions [7]. In order to match the correct initial value of MD4, Dobbertin introduced a connecting phase in the framework. Exploiting the property of the boolean function and the freedom degree of message words, Dobbertin could achieve a connection with a very low cost. Due to the high cost once there is no efficient approach to achieve a connection, the start-from-the-middle structure is generally applied to find semi-free-start or free-start collisions, which do not require the match with the predefined initial value. Although such a structure has been used to find collisions in [10,15], the situation is much simpler than Dobbertin's work [7]. Specifically, since the length of the middle part is short, only a few message words are fixed [10,15] and the connection can be achieved trivially.

Formally, suppose there are r consecutive internal states $s_1, s_2, ..., s_r$ to be connected, which are updated with the messages words $m_{w_1}, m_{w_2}, ..., m_{w_r}$ respectively. In [7], one of $m_{w_1}, m_{w_2}, ..., m_{w_r}$ is fixed so as to extend the length of the middle part. Therefore, an efficient approach to solve it is non-trivial. For the start-from-the-middle structure used in [10,15] to find real collisions, none of $m_{w_1}, m_{w_2}, ..., m_{w_r}$ are fixed in order to obtain a solution of the middle part. In this situation, they could achieve connection trivially when computing from the first step, i.e. obtain the value of m_{w_i} according to the already computed $s_i, s_{i-1}, ..., s_{i-r}$. However, the length of the middle part is greatly limited, thus leaving more uncontrolled conditions in such a situation. Or else, the authors made a tradeoff and finally determined not to consider the complex situation.

As will be shown in our two frameworks, we also use the start-from-the-middle approach to find real collisions in a complex situation similar to Dobbertin's work [7]. Our motivation is to ensure that as many conditions as possible hold in the second round, which sometimes is almost impossible with multi-step message modification or requires sophisticated and time-consuming manual work. Therefore, in the SLDR framework, one of the message words used to update the internal states to be connected will be fixed. In the DLSR framework, we even fix two of the message words used to update the internal states to be connected, thus greatly extending the controllable part of the differential characteristic and leaving fewer uncontrolled conditions. Fortunately, because of the property of the round boolean function and the weakness of the message expansion of RIPEMD-160, we can manage to achieve a connection with a low cost for the two frameworks.

2.4   Single-Step Message Modification

Since only single-step message modification [28] will be used in this paper, we give a brief description of it. Generally, single-step message modification can ensure all the conditions in the first round for most MD-SHA-like hash functions. The implied reason is that the message words are used for the first time in the first round. Therefore, the attackers can randomly choose values for the internal states while satisfying the conditions in the first round, i.e. randomly choose values for the free bits of internal states. Then, the corresponding message words can be computed according to the already fixed internal states in the first round. For the sake of clearness, we take the step function of RIPEMD-160 as instance.

Suppose the following pattern represents the conditions on X_i.

$$X_i = \text{-11- ---- ---- -1-- 1--- n-un -u-- --11.}$$

Then, we can first choose a random value for X_i and then correct it in the following way to ensure the conditions on it hold.

$$X_i \leftarrow X_i \wedge \texttt{0xfffff0ff},$$
$$X_i \leftarrow X_i \vee \texttt{0x60048243}.$$

If there are two-bit conditions on X_i, we then check them and correct them. Suppose $X_i^4 = X_{i-1}^4$ is one two-bit condition, we first check whether $X_i^4 = X_{i-1}^4$ holds. If it does not hold, we simply flip X_i^4. In this way, all conditions on X_i can hold. Finally, we compute the corresponding message word to update X_i with $X_i, X_{i-1}, ..., X_{i-5}$. The above description of single-step message modification is different from the original one [28], but the implied idea is the same.

2.5   Propagation of Modular Difference

At Asiacrypt 2017, theoretical calculation of the probability of the step function of RIPEMD-160 was described by introducing the influence of the propagation of modular difference [16]. The complete description of the calculation procedure is complex. Generally, the authors divided the problem into two parts. The first part is to calculate the characteristics of Q_i (LQ_i/RQ_i for the left/right branch) which satisfies an equation like $(Q_i \boxplus c_0)^{\lll s} = Q_i^{\lll s} \boxplus c_1$ (c_0 and c_1 are constants) to ensure the correct propagation of modular difference. Then, they calculate the probability that the bit conditions on the internal state (X_i/Y_i for left/right branch) hold under the condition that Q_i satisfies the equation $(Q_i \boxplus c_0)^{\lll s} = Q_i^{\lll s} \boxplus c_1$. In other words, they considered the dependency between the bit conditions and the propagation of modular difference and this obviously is a more accurate assumption.

In this paper, since the dense part of the differential characteristic will be first fixed and the remaining part is very sparse and short, we can simply assume the independency between the bit conditions and the propagation of modular difference. Thus, the product of the probability of correct propagation of modular difference and the probability of bit conditions will represent the final probability of the uncontrolled part. Specifically, supposing Q_i (LQ_i/RQ_i for left/right branch) satisfies the equation $(Q_i \boxplus c_0)^{\lll s} = Q_i^{\lll s} \boxplus c_1$ with probability p and there are q bit conditions on the corresponding internal state (X_i/Y_i for left/right branch), then the final probability is $p \times 2^{-q}$. According to our experiments, such an assumption is reasonable and almost consistent with the experiments.

Calculating the probability $(Q_i \boxplus c_0)^{\lll s} = Q_i^{\lll s} \boxplus c_1$ can be found in Daum's Ph.D thesis [4], which was well illustrated in [16] with the help of a table. Due to the space limitation, we refer the readers to Table 3 in [16].

3   Efficient Collision Attack Frameworks

In this section, we will present the details of the two efficient collision attack frameworks. Both frameworks aim at ensuring as many conditions as possible in an efficient way for specific strategies to construct differential characteristics. For the SLDR framework, the differential characteristic is constructed by inserting a difference at the message word m_{15}, which is used to update the last internal state in the first round on the left branch. Moreover, the differential characteristic on the left branch should be linear and sparse. For the DLSR framework, the differential characteristic is constructed by inserting difference at the message word m_{12}, which is used to update the last internal state in the first round on the right branch. In addition, the differential characteristic on the right branch should be linear and sparse. For both frameworks, the linear and sparse branch remains fully probabilistic. The differential characteristic patterns for SLDR and DLSR framework are depicted in Fig. 1.

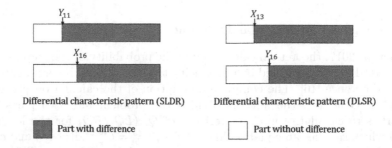

Differential characteristic pattern (SLDR)   Differential characteristic pattern (DLSR)

■ Part with difference   □ Part without difference

Fig. 1. Illustration of the differential characteristic patterns for both frameworks

3.1   SLDR Collision Attack Framework

Since m_{15} is firstly used to update Y_{11}, for the strategy to build differential characteristic by inserting difference only at m_{15} and making the left branch sparse at Asiacrypt 2017 [16], the following two observations can be obtained.

Observation 1. *There is no condition on Y_i ($1 \leq i \leq 8$).*

Observation 2. *The first internal state with difference on the right branch is Y_{11}. When considering the difference propagating to Y_{12}, we are actually considering the difference propagation of $Y_{11} \oplus (Y_{10} \vee \neg Y_9^{\lll 10})$ where only Y_{11} has differences. If all the bits$(p_i, p_{i+1}, ..., p_j)$ with difference in Y_{11} are flipped by adding conditions $Y_{10}^{p_i} = 1, Y_{10}^{p_{i+1}} = 1, ..., Y_{10}^{p_j} = 1$ when constructing the differential characteristic, there will not be conditions on Y_9 either.*

The above two observations motivate us to consider the start-from-the-middle structure to find collisions. Therefore, we carefully investigated the message expansion on the right branch and finally found an efficient collision attack framework for such a strategy to construct differential characteristics.

The overview of SLDR attack framework is illustrated in Fig. 2. Such a framework contains 4 steps, as specified below and illustrated in Fig. 3.

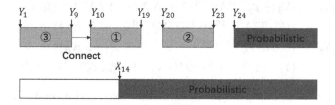

Fig. 2. Overview of SLDR collision attack framework for RIPEMD-160

Step 1. Generate a starting point (Preparation)

Y_{10}	Y_{11}	Y_{12}	Y_{13}	Y_{14}	Y_{15}	Y_{16}	Y_{17}	Y_{18}	Y_{19}
m_6	m_{15}	m_8	m_1	m_{10}	m_3	m_{12}	m_6	m_{11}	m_3

Connect

Step 2. Compute forward from the middle

Y_{20}	Y_{21}	Y_{22}	Y_{23}
m_7	m_0	m_{13}	m_5

Step 3. Compute forward from the first step

Y_1	Y_2	Y_3	Y_4	Y_5	Y_6	Y_7	Y_8	Y_9
m_5	m_{14}	m_7	m_0	m_9	m_2	m_{11}	m_4	m_{13}

Fig. 3. Specification of SLDR collision attack framework for RIPEMD-160. Message words in red at Step 1 and Step 3 represent their values will be fixed.

Step 1: Fix the internal states located in the middle part from Y_{10} to Y_{19}, which can be easily finished via single-step message modification since only m_3 is used twice to update the internal states. Specifically, randomly choose values for Y_i ($10 \leq i \leq 18$) while keeping their conditions hold via single-step message modification since $(m_3, m_{12}, m_6, m_{11})$ are used for the first time. Then, we reuse m_3 to compute Y_{19} and check its condition. If the condition does not hold, choose another solution of Y_i ($10 \leq i \leq 18$) and repeat until we find a solution of Y_i ($10 \leq i \leq 19$). We call a solution of Y_i ($10 \leq i \leq 19$) a starting point.

Step 2: Apply single-step message modification to ensure the conditions on Y_i ($20 \leq i \leq 23$) since their corresponding message words (m_7, m_0, m_{13}, m_5) are used for the first time.

Step 3: Randomly choose values for the free message words m_{14} and m_9. Compute from the first step until Y_5. Then achieve connection in Y_{10}, whose corresponding message word m_6 has been fixed in the starting point. The costly condition $Y_7 = 0$ is used to ensure Y_{10} is irrelevant to Y_8, which can be satisfied by consuming the freedom degree of m_2.

$$Y_7 = 0.$$
$$Y_6 = ((Y_7 \boxminus Y_3^{\lll 10})^{\ggg 15} \boxminus (m_{11} \boxplus K_0^r)) \oplus (Y_5 \vee \overline{Y_4^{\lll 10}}).$$
$$m_2 = (Y_6 \boxminus Y_2^{\lll 10})^{\ggg 15} \boxminus (ONX(Y_5, Y_4, Y_3^{\lll 10}) \boxplus Y_1^{\lll 10} \boxplus K_0^r).$$
$$Y_9 = ((Y_{10} \boxminus Y_6^{\lll 10})^{\ggg 7} \boxminus (Y_5^{\lll 10} \boxplus m_6 \boxplus K_0^r)) \oplus \texttt{0xffffffff}.$$
$$Y_8 = ((Y_9 \boxminus Y_5^{\lll 10})^{\ggg 7} \boxminus (Y_4^{\lll 10} \boxplus m_{13} \boxplus K_0^r)) \oplus (Y_7 \vee Y_6^{\lll 10}),$$
$$m_4 = (Y_8 \boxminus Y_4^{\lll 10})^{\ggg 5} \boxminus (ONX(Y_7, Y_6, Y_5^{\lll 10}) \boxplus Y_3^{\lll 10} \boxplus K_0^r).$$

Compute m_{15}, m_8, m_1, m_{10} to achieve connection in Y_i ($11 \leq i \leq 14$). More specifically, m_{15} is computed by Y_i ($6 \leq i \leq 11$), m_8 is computed by Y_i ($7 \leq i \leq 12$), m_1 is computed by Y_i ($8 \leq i \leq 13$) and m_{10} is computed by Y_i ($9 \leq i \leq 14$).

Step 4: All message words have been fixed after connection. Then we verify the probabilistic parts in both branches. If they do not hold, return Step 2 until we find colliding messages. The degree of freedom is provided by m_0, m_5, m_7, m_9, m_{13} and m_{14}.

Such a general framework can ensure all the bit conditions on Y_i ($10 \leq i \leq 23$) trivially, which is almost impossible via multi-step message modification once the conditions are dense. However, more attention should be paid when applying it to a specific differential characteristic. In this framework, Y_7 is fixed to zero to achieve an efficient connection in Y_{10}, thus resulting in $RQ_{11} = Y_{11}^{\ggg s_{11}^r}$. If the differential characteristic conditions on Y_{11} always make RQ_{11} fail to satisfy its corresponding equation, this framework cannot be applied directly. Although we can fix some bits of Y_7 to one to solve it, this will influence the success probability of connection. Therefore, when constructing the differential characteristic, such a bad case should be considered and avoided.

3.2 DLSR Collision Attack Framework

Now, we consider an opposite strategy to construct differential characteristics by inserting difference only at m_{12} and making the right branch sparse. In this way, X_{13} is the first internal state with difference. To propagate the difference in X_{13} to X_{14}, we are actually propagating the difference of $X_{13} \oplus X_{12} \oplus X_{11}^{\lll 10}$. Since there is no difference in X_{11} or X_{12} and it is an XOR operation, there will be always conditions on X_{11} and X_{12}. However, there will not be conditions on X_i ($1 \leq i \leq 10$). This also motivates us to consider the start-from-the-middle approach.

The overview of DLSR framework is shown in Fig. 4. The attack procedure can be divided into four steps as well, as illustrated in Fig. 5.

Step 1: Fix the internal states located in the middle part from X_{11} to X_{23}, which can be easily finished via single-step message modification since only m_{15} is used twice to update the internal states. If there are too many bit conditions on X_{23}, we can firstly fix the internal states from X_{12} to X_{23} via single-step message modification since all the corresponding message words (m_7, m_4, m_{13}, m_1, m_{10}, m_6 and m_{15}) are used for the first time. Then, we compute X_{11} by using X_i ($12 \leq i \leq 16$) and m_{15}. At last, we check the conditions on X_{11} and the modular difference of X_{15}. If they do not hold, choose another solution of X_i ($12 \leq i \leq 23$) via single-step message modification and repeat until we can find a solution for the starting point X_i ($11 \leq i \leq 23$). After a starting point is fixed, we have to achieve connection in five consecutive internal states X_i ($11 \leq i \leq 15$). However, m_{10} and m_{13} have been already fixed. Thus, an efficient approach to achieve connection in X_{11} and X_{14} is quite important and non-trivial.

To achieve connection in X_{14}, we pre-compute a solution set $\mathbf{S}$ for (X_9, X_{10}) according to the following equation by exhausting all possible values of X_9. For each X_9, compute the corresponding X_{10} and store X_9 in a two-dimensional array with $X_9 \oplus X_{10}$ denoting the row number. Both the time complexity and memory complexity of the pre-computation are 2^{32}.

$$X_{14} = X_{10}^{\lll 10} \boxplus (XOR(X_{13}, X_{12}, X_{11}^{\lll 10}) \boxplus X_9^{\lll 10} \boxplus m_{13} \boxplus K_0^l)^{\lll 7}.$$

Step 2: Apply single-step message modification to ensure the conditions on X_{24} since its corresponding message word m_3 is not fixed in the starting point and is used for the first time. We have to stress that we have considered the influence of the propagation of modular difference and have added extra bit conditions to control its correct propagation with probability 1.

Step 3: Randomly choose values for the free message words m_0, m_2 and m_5. Compute from the first step until X_8 and then achieve connection in X_{11} and X_{14} as follows. First, we calculate the value of **var**.

$$\mathbf{var} = ((X_{11} \boxminus X_7^{\lll 10})^{\ggg 14} \boxminus (X_6^{\lll 10} \boxplus m_{10} \boxplus K_0^l)) \oplus X_8^{\lll 10}.$$

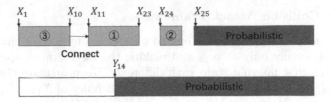

Fig. 4. Overview of DLSR collision attack framework for RIPEMD-160

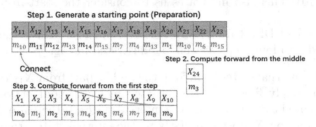

Fig. 5. Specification of DLSR collision attack framework for RIPEMD-160. Message words in red at Step 1 and Step 3 represent their values will be fixed.

Second, find solutions of (X_9, X_{10}) from **S** which satisfy $X_9 \oplus X_{10} = $ **var**. The corresponding solutions are stored in the row numbered **var**. In this way, each solution of (X_9, X_{10}) will ensure the connection in X_{11} and X_{14}. At last, compute m_8 and m_9 as follows to ensure X_9 and X_{10} can be the computed value for connection. Since there are 2^{32} valid pairs of (X_9, X_{10}) in **S** and **var** is a random 32-bit variable, we expect one solution of (X_9, X_{10}) for a random **var** on average.

$$m_8 = (X_9 \boxminus X_5^{\lll 10})^{\ggg 11} \boxminus (XOR(X_8, X_7, X_6^{\lll 10}) \boxplus X_4^{\lll 10} \boxplus K_0^l).$$
$$m_9 = (X_{10} \boxminus X_6^{\lll 10})^{\ggg 13} \boxminus (XOR(X_9, X_8, X_7^{\lll 10}) \boxplus X_5^{\lll 10} \boxplus K_0^l).$$

Compute m_{11}, m_{12} and m_{14} to achieve connection in X_{12}, X_{13} and X_{15}. Specifically, m_{11} is computed by X_i ($7 \leq i \leq 12$), and m_{12} is computed by X_i ($8 \leq i \leq 13$), and m_{14} is computed by X_i ($10 \leq i \leq 15$).

Step 4: All message words have been fixed after connection. Then we verify the probabilistic part in both branches. If they do not hold, return Step 2 until we find colliding messages. The degree of freedom is provided by m_0, m_2, m_3 and m_5.

However, observe that there will be difference in X_{13} and X_{14} when inserting difference at m_{12}. Therefore, $LQ_{13} = (X_{13} \boxminus X_9^{\lll 10})^{\ggg 6}$ and $LQ_{14} = (X_{14} \boxminus X_{10}^{\lll 10})^{\ggg 7}$ have to satisfy their corresponding equations to ensure the correct propagation of modular difference. Since X_9 and X_{10} cannot be controlled, we have to verify whether LQ_{13} and LQ_{14} satisfy their corresponding equations when obtaining a solution of (X_9, X_{10}). A way to reduce the verifying phase is to filter the wrong pair of (X_9, X_{10}) in the pre-computing phase. However, we cannot expect one solution of (X_9, X_{10}) for a random **var** anymore. In other words, whatever the case is, the influence of the correct propagation of modular difference of X_{13} and X_{14} must be taken into account when estimating the success probability.

Therefore, under our DLSR framework, except the modular difference of X_{13} and X_{14}, all the conditions on X_i $(11 \leq i \leq 24)$ can hold trivially with an efficient method, which sometimes is almost impossible with multi-step message modification or at least very time-consuming and requires sophisticated manual work, especially when the conditions are dense in the second round. For the dense left branch, since there is no condition on X_i $(1 \leq i \leq 10)$, we only need focus on the the uncontrolled conditions on internal states X_i $(i \geq 25)$ and the modular difference of X_{13} and X_{14}. Thus, to construct the best differential characteristic for this framework, there should be minimum active bits in X_i $(i \geq 23)$ and the modular difference of X_{13} and X_{14} should hold with a high probability. Moreover, to select the best differential characteristic from many discovered candidates, we only need to analyze the probability of the conditions on X_i $(i \geq 25)$, consisting of the number of bit conditions and the influence of the modular difference propagation, as well as the probability of the correct propagation of the modular difference of X_{13} and X_{14}. Obviously, we significantly simplify the procedure to construct and select differential characteristics as well as find collisions with the DLSR framework.

3.3 Comparison

Under the SLDR framework, we can only control until Y_{23} by adding an extra costly condition $Y_7 = 0$ to achieve efficient connection. For the DLSR framework, we can control until X_{24} by consuming extra 2^{32} memory to achieve efficient connection. Hence, the SLDR framework has the obvious advantage of having no memory requirement. However, when there is sufficient memory available, there is a great advantage to leverage the DLSR framework, since we can control the internal state until the 24th step. In other words, one more step can be fully controlled with the DLSR framework, thus having the potential to leave fewer uncontrolled conditions. It should be noted that the number of steps that can be controlled highly depends on the message expansion. Thus, we rely on the specifics of RIPEMD-160's message expansion and extend to more steps as well as find an efficient approach to achieve connection in the complex situation.

A direct application of the SLDR framework to the 30-step differential characteristic in [16] will improve the collision attack by a factor of 2^{11}. With a partial calculation technique, two more uncontrolled bit conditions can be controlled. Thus, the collision attack on 30 steps of RIPEMD-160 is improved to 2^{57}. Actually, the 30-step differential characteristic in [16] is not perfect under our

SLDR framework since there are three bit conditions on Y_9. Although the three bit conditions can be eliminated by generating a new differential characteristic with **Observation 2** taken into account, the time complexity is still too high. As will be shown, we can attack 30 steps of RIPEMD-160 with time complexity $2^{35.9}$ under the DLSR framework. Therefore, considering its improving factor, we decided not to generate a new differential characteristic for the SLDR framework and we refer the readers to Appendix A for the details of the improvement for the collision attack at Asiacrypt 2017 [16]. The source code to verify the correctness of the SLDR framework is available at https://github.com/Crypt-CNS/Improved_Collision_Attack_on_Reduced_RIPEMD-160.git.

Actually, not only the framework but also the characteristic of the fully probabilistic branch has influences on the final effect of the collision attack. Taking the two factors into consideration, we finally determined to utilize the DLSR framework.

4   Differential Characteristics

As stated in the previous section, to construct the best differential characteristic for the DLSR framework, the uncontrolled part should hold with a high probability. To achieve this, according to the boolean function IFX used in the second round on the left branch, we have to control that there are a few active bits in X_i ($i \geq 23$) so that the number of bit conditions on X_i ($i \geq 25$) is minimal. Suppose we will analyze the collision resistance of t steps of RIPEMD-160. According to the finalization phase of the compression function of RIPEMD-160, to achieve a minimal number of active bits in X_i ($i \geq 23$), it is better to let only one of $Y_{t-1}, Y_{t-2}, Y_{t-3}, Y_{t-4}$ have differences and $\Delta Y_t = 0$. In this way, only one of $X_t, X_{t-1}, X_{t-2}, X_{t-3}$ has differences and $\Delta X_{t-4} = 0$.

Based on such a strategy to construct differential characteristics, we firstly determine the characteristics on the fully probabilistic right branch for 30/31/33/34 steps of RIPEMD-160, which can be found in Tables 11, 12, 13 and 14 respectively.

Then, we construct the sparse characteristics on the left branch starting from X_{23} for 30/31/33/34 steps of RIPEMD-160, which are displayed in Table 4.

At last, we utilize a search tool [11,18–21] to solve the nonlinear characteristic located at X_i ($11 \leq i \leq 22$) based on a guess-and-determine technique [5]. To choose the best nonlinear characteristic from many candidates, we only need focus on the conditions on X_i ($i \geq 25$), consisting of the number of bit conditions and the probability of the correct propagation of the modular difference, as well as the probability that LQ_{13} and LQ_{14} satisfy their corresponding equations. The best 30-step, 31-step, 33-step and 34-step differential characteristics for RIPEMD-160 that we eventually determined are displayed in Tables 11, 12, 13 and 14 respectively. To save space, we only list the uncontrolled two-bit conditions located at the fully probabilistic right branch and X_i ($i \geq 25$), which

Table 4. Sparse characteristics on the left branch

i	30 steps of RIPEMD-160	31 steps of RIPEMD-160
23	u - u - -	- - - - - - - n - - n - - - - - - - - - - - - - - - - - -
24	- - - - - - - - - - - - - - - - - - n - - n - - - - - - - -	- u - u -
25	- -	- -
26	- -	- -
27	- -	- -
28	- -	- -
29	- - n - n	- - - - - - - - - u - - u - - - - - - - - - - - - - -
30	- -	- -
31	- -	- -

i	33 steps of RIPEMD-160	34 steps of RIPEMD-160
23	- - - - - - - u - - u - - - - - - - - - n - - - - - - - - -	- n - - - - - - - - - - u - - - - - - - - - - u -
24	- - u - - - - - - - - u - - - - - - - - - - - - - - - u - -	- - - n - - - - - - - - - - - - - - - - u - - n - - - - - - -
25	- - - - - - - - - - - - - - - - n - - n - - - - - - - - -	- - - - - - - - - - - n - - u - - - - - - - - - - - -
26	- - - - - - - - - - - u - - u - - - - - - - - - - - - - -	- - - u - - n -
27	n - - n -	- - - - - - - - - - - - - - - - - - - n - - u - - - - - -
28	- - - - - - - - - - - - - - u - - u - - - - - - - - -	- - - - - - - - - u - - n - - - - - - - - - - - - - -
29	- -	- -
30	- -	- -
31	- -	- -
32	- -	- -
33	- - u - u	- u - - n - - - - - -
34		- -

cannot be denoted by generalized conditions. The two-bit conditions located at X_i ($11 \leq i \leq 24$) as well as the equations to ensure the correct propagation of modular difference of X_i ($15 \leq i \leq 24$) are not listed in the four tables since all these conditions can hold trivially under the DLSR framework. In addition, from the differential characteristics and the corresponding starting points in next section, it is not difficult to extract all these information.

If we construct characteristic for 32 steps of RIPEMD-160 in a similar way, there will be many bit conditions in X_i ($i \geq 23$), which is even greater than that of 33 steps. This is because $\Delta X_{28} \neq 0$ and $\Delta X_{29} \neq 0$. Therefore, for the attack with high time complexity, we only provide the results for more steps.

Thanks to the efficiency of our DLSR framework, once a differential characteristic for collision attack is determined, the uncontrolled probability can be calculated immediately. Therefore, for each characteristic in Tables 11, 12, 13 and 14, we also present the corresponding total uncontrolled probability in these tables, consisting of the number of bit conditions on the right branch and X_i ($i \geq 25$), as well as the equations to ensure the correct propagation of modular difference on the right branch and of X_{13}, X_{14} and X_i ($i \geq 25$). The probability estimated in these four tables represents the success probability to find the collision when the DLSR framework is directly applied to the differential characteristics.

For the best 34-step differential characteristic given in Table 14, a direct application of the DLSR framework is infeasible since it is beyond the birthday attack. However, by benefiting from the partial calculation, which fully exploits the property of the round boolean function and the existing differential characteristic conditions, we significantly improve this probability. Such a technique will be also used to improve the collision attack on 31 and 33 steps of RIPEMD-160. The details will be explained in next section. It should be noted that the effect of partial calculation highly depends on the existing differential characteristic conditions. Therefore, when selecting differential characteristics from many candidates, we actually have taken the effect of partial calculation into account as well.

5 Application

5.1 Practical Collision Attack on 30 Steps of RIPEMD-160

By applying the DLSR framework to the discovered 30-step differential characteristic in Table 11, we can mount collision attack on 30 steps of RIPEMD-160 with time complexity $2^{35.9}$ and memory complexity 2^{32}. It should be noted that there are sufficient free bits in m_0, m_2, m_3 and m_5 to generate a collision. The collision is displayed in Table 5. For completeness, the starting point can be found in Table 7.

5.2 Collision Attack on 31 Steps of RIPEMD-160

According to Table 12, the time complexity to mount collision attack on 31 steps is $2^{42.5}$ if the DLSR framework is directly applied. However, we can make it slightly better with partial calculation technique by using the property of the boolean function IFX. This is based on the following observation.

Table 5. Collision for 30 steps of RIPEMD-160

M	1fbb5316 8ad15821 bf04a498 b85ed58f 4d2d28f6 977b64cd 8c7769dc 961cce16 9d7a5bc6 f6519d38 37316e69 206d429 2f451be9 e748c57f 5c73a141 e753c86
M'	1fbb5316 8ad15821 bf04a498 b85ed58f 4d2d28f6 977b64cd 8c7769dc 961cce16 9d7a5bc6 f6519d38 37316e69 206d429 2f449be9 e748c57f 5c73a141 e753c86
hash value	cdcf5aec cf44ca54 70a8cdbb e1fd7e6d bea2687d

Table 6. Collision for 31 steps of RIPEMD-160

M	3d604874 ff13f724 d60f43b4 c02645eb a9df768c 172f15dc d8cfa4bb edb8f36f c898dd5e 71c62ade d13c6647 bfa932ef fc2b5325 fc5c01e5 5f7658c8 e5e50cc1
M'	3d604874 ff13f724 d60f43b4 c02645eb a9df768c 172f15dc d8cfa4bb edb8f36f c898dd5e 71c62ade d13c6647 bfa932ef fc2bd325 fc5c01e5 5f7658c8 e5e50cc1
hash value	5244127c c976d649 362154bb 59070fc 8e5212e1

Table 7. Starting points for differential characteristics

30 steps	31 steps
$m_1 = $ 0x8ad15821,	$m_1 = $ 0xff13f724,
$m_4 = $ 0x4d2d28f6, $m_6 = $ 0x8c7769dc,	$m_4 = $ 0xa9df768c, $m_6 = $ 0xd8cfa4bb,
$m_7 = $ 0x961cce16, $m_{10} = $ 0x37316e69,	$m_7 = $ 0xedb8f36f, $m_{10} = $ 0xd13c6647,
$m_{13} = $ 0xe748e57f, $m_{15} = $ 0xe753c86.	$m_{13} = $ 0xfc5c01e5, $m_{15} = $ 0xe5e50cc1.
X_{11} 111111000110000011000001011110001	X_{11} 01011100111011101010100010101010
X_{12} 011010101011011111100011001000101	X_{12} 01010101010111001010110111110101
X_{13} 1000111011u10000000101011010110	X_{13} 1101nuuuuuu00000111000111110110
X_{14} 010n111010101110011001000000001000	X_{14} 101u0010100010000101101011100101
X_{15} 1n000100111100001001110101u11101	X_{15} 0u1000101001001001011001111110101
X_{16} 10101111110000001n110110u0n0110	X_{16} 00100000010001001n1100101nn1001
X_{17} n0000100101u011011000101011011101	X_{17} u00101010101100nuuuu0100110101nu
X_{18} 01100n001100110000unnu01nun00101	X_{18} 0011010110u100101u001nun1n111001
X_{19} 1100001u00n1nuun0un0100000010nun	X_{19} 0nu1100un1011110101110u000001111
X_{20} 1u1nn0u011u00110110110101nu1100n	X_{20} 010110111uu11001nn1un00101n10011
X_{21} 100111011000101000001011un100u0uu	X_{21} 01n11n111001101010011101010001000
X_{22} 1001011111uuu00n0011u10010001000	X_{22} 000001100111unnnnnnnnn01u111100
X_{23} u1101000111100011010000110100u11	X_{23} 1001001n11n001000011110101011011100
X_{24} 011--1----1------110n01n-----0--	X_{24} 1u10001111111---0-1001101011011u1

33 steps	34 steps
$m_1 = $ 0xf2470729,	$m_1 = $ 0x58a0be2,
$m_4 = $ 0xd19ebad5, $m_6 = $ 0x1f2c0d0e,	$m_4 = $ 0x8d38c100, $m_6 = $ 0x7214c160,
$m_7 = $ 0xc4f488a9, $m_{10} = $ 0x236883a,	$m_7 = $ 0xea755943, $m_{10} = $ 0xa6a0ee3e,
$m_{13} = $ 0x8425047b, $m_{15} = $ 0x6458c5e3.	$m_{13} = $ 0xb9e9de76, $m_{15} = $ 0xb949ab42.
X_{11} 10010000100111110011110000011111	X_{11} 10111101110000100001001101000001000
X_{12} 00101100110001010110101110010100	X_{12} 01010101001011011010101000000010
X_{13} 0101100111n00010011011111010101111	X_{13} 11000011nuu11010010001010000010101
X_{14} 110u0110110001011110110000111	X_{14} 110n000000001011010000100100000000
X_{15} 1u00001001100111111011100101u11101	X_{15} 0n00101110001101101110000u000n0
X_{16} 0111111000000000100n10011un1u0001	X_{16} 00000011001001000001n0111u00uu0110
X_{17} n0010111111n1110000u010110u00011	X_{17} u00100010110100n0uuu101n1000101n
X_{18} 000unn1unnn1011101u1u11unn001111	X_{18} 0101110100uu10110111101110nuu1011u
X_{19} u0nn101111un110u01011001000u0101	X_{19} u1nuun01010n01011nnuu0100010101n
X_{20} 0u101110u111001s0nn0n1n0u1110u011	X_{20} 1001u00u0uu1u11u0001u11u100u000u
X_{21} n1n110000uu1u10100n1000n010001un	X_{21} u1nu0010u1000u001000nu10u100nu10
X_{22} 0100unn010101111000111nunnnu0un	X_{22} 010010001001000uuu00uu0uu011nu101
X_{23} 00110111u11u10101101010n00100001	X_{23} 0n01010111001u0011111111110101u1
X_{24} 11u0101101011u01000101-111100--u	X_{24} 100n011--11111110101-u00n1010111

Observation 3. Let $F = X_{25}X_{24} \oplus \overline{X_{25}}X_{23}^{\lll 10}$, then

$$F^i = \begin{cases} X_{24}^i & (X_{24}^i = X_{23}^{i-10}) \\ X_{24}^i & (X_{25}^i = 1) \\ X_{23}^{i-10} & (X_{25}^i = 0). \end{cases}$$

Note that X_{26} is updated by the free message word m_0 and X_i ($21 \leq i \leq 24$) can be fully controlled. Although X_{25} cannot be controlled and unknown, we can use partial calculation to ensure several bit conditions on X_{26} hold.

Specifically, consider the 31-step differential characteristic in Table 12. We write $X_{25}, X_{24}, X_{23}^{\lll 10}$ in binary as follows for a better understanding. Consider the following calculation of F, we can know several bits of F if the conditions on X_{25} hold, where a denotes that the bit value is possible to be determined by carefully choosing values of X_{24} and X_{23}, and b denotes that the bit value cannot be determined with existing differential characteristic conditions.

$$X_{25} = \text{10-- ---- ---- ---- ---- ---- ---- -10-.}$$
$$X_{24} = \text{1u10 0011 1111 1--0 -1-0 1-01 0--- --u1.}$$
$$X_{23}^{\lll 10} = \text{n001 0001 1110 1-11 01-- ---0 ---- -n-1.}$$
$$F = \text{10bb 00b1 111b 1aab a1aa aaab aaaa aaa1.}$$

Consider the calculation of $sum_0 = X_{21}^{\lll 10} \boxplus K_1^l$ after adding four bit conditions on X_{21}. In this way, the higher 12 bits of sum_0 are constant.

$$X_{21}^{\lll 10} = \text{0110 1010 0110 010- 0--0 0-01 n1-n ---0.}$$
$$K_1^l = \text{0101 1010 1000 0010 0111 1001 1001 1001.}$$
$$sum_0 = \text{1100 0100 1110 bbbb bbbb bbbb bbbb bbb1.}$$

Then, we consider the calculation of $sum_1 = sum_0 \boxplus m_0$ by pre-fixing the pattern of m_0 as follows.

$$sum_0 = \text{1100 0100 1110 bbbb bbbb bbbb bbbb bbb1.}$$
$$m_0 = \text{0-11 110- ---- ---- ---- ---- ---- ----.}$$
$$sum_1 = \text{0b00 00bb bbbb bbbb bbbb bbbb bbbb bbbb.}$$

Next, we consider the calculation of $sum_2 = sum_1 \boxplus F$ as follows.

$$sum_1 = \text{0b00 00bb bbbb bbbb bbbb bbbb bbbb bbbb.}$$
$$F = \text{10bb 00b1 111b 1aab a1aa aaab aaaa aaa1.}$$
$$sum_2 = \text{1bbb 0bbb bbbb bbbb bbbb bbbb bbbb bbbb.}$$

At last, consider the calculation of X_{26} after adding three extra bit conditions on X_{22}.

$$X_{26} = X_{22}^{\lll 10} \boxplus (F \boxplus X_{21}^{\lll 10} \boxplus K_1^l \boxplus m_0)^{\lll 12} = X_{22}^{\lll 10} \boxplus sum_2^{\lll 12}.$$
$$sum_2^{\lll 12} = \text{bbbb bbbb bbbb bbbb bbbb 1bbb 0bbb bbbb.}$$
$$X_{22}^{\lll 10} = \text{11un nnnn nnnn n0-u ---- 0000 01-1 10-1.}$$
$$X_{26} = \text{bbbb bbbb bbbb bbbb bbbb 1bbb bbbb bbbb.}$$

Therefore, $X_{26}^{11} = 1$ can hold with probability 1. In the same procedure to perform the partial calculation, if we choose the following pattern of m_0, $X_{26}^{11} = 1$ can always hold as well.

$$m_0 = \text{0100 000- ---- ---- ---- ---- ---- ----.}$$

It should be noted that m_0 is randomly chosen at the third step when applying the DLSR framework. Therefore, with our partial calculation, we can choose the value for m_0 in a clever way to have the condition $X_{26}^{11} = 1$ always hold. Therefore, the time complexity of a collision attack on 31 steps of RIPEMD-160 is improved to $2^{41.5}$.

According to the above analysis, it is not difficult to observe that such an approach to make only one bit condition hold is costly since at least 6 bits of

m_0 have to be fixed. In the case when there are sufficient free bits in the free message words, such a method is feasible. However, when the success probability is low, we have to carefully consume the degree of freedom. As will be shown in the collision attack on 33/34 steps of RIPEMD-160, we dynamically choose a value for m_0 to save the degree of freedom. Moreover, partial calculation will show its significant effect to decrease the time complexity when attacking 33 and 34 steps of RIPEMD-160.

Verification. Both the correctness of the framework and the partial calculation are fully verified. The collision for 31 steps of RIPEMD-160 is displayed in Table 6 and the corresponding starting point is provided in Table 7.

5.3   Collision Attack on 33 Steps of RIPEMD-160

If we directly apply the DLSR framework to the discovered 33-step differential characteristic in Table 13, the time complexity is $2^{71.6}$ and the memory complexity is 2^{32}. With the partial calculation, we can choose m_0 in a clever way to ensure more uncontrolled bit conditions hold.

Write X_{25}, X_{24}, $X_{23}^{\lll 10}$ in binary according to Table 13 as follows for a better understanding. Thus, several bits of $F = X_{25}X_{24} \oplus \overline{X_{25}}X_{23}^{\lll 10}$ can be known if the conditions on X_{25} hold based on **Observation 3**.

$$X_{25} = \texttt{-11- ---- ---- -1-- 1--- n--n ---- --11.}$$
$$X_{24} = \texttt{11u0 10-- 0--1 1u01 0001 01-1 1110 0--u.}$$
$$X_{23}^{\lll 10} = \texttt{1u10 --1- 0-01 0n00 100- 0100 1-01 1-u1.}$$
$$F = \texttt{1110 aaaa 0aa1 b10b 000a 01a0 1abb baa1.}$$

Consider the calculation of X_{26},

$$X_{26} = X_{22}^{\lll 10} \boxplus (F \boxplus X_{21}^{\lll 10} \boxplus K_1^l \boxplus m_0)^{\lll 12}.$$

Observe that the higher 12 bits of F can be fully fixed by properly setting values for X_{24} and X_{23}. Moreover, $X_{21}^{\lll 10} \boxplus K_1^l$ and $X_{22}^{\lll 10}$ are all constants after a starting point is found. Therefore, it is feasible to have a clever choice of the higher 12 bits of m_0 rather than in a random way to ensure the conditions on the lower 12 bits of X_{26}. To explain more precisely, we firstly present the starting point of the 33-step differential characteristic in Table 7.

From this starting point, the following information can be extracted.

$$F \wedge \texttt{0xfffc0000} = \texttt{1110 1011 0101 b100 0000 0000 0000 0000.}$$
$$X_{21}^{\lll 10} \boxplus K_1^l = \texttt{0100 1110 1100 0011 1001 0010 1111 1010.}$$

Then, we add some extra conditions on m_0 to ensure that there is always a carry from the 20th bit to 21st bit when calculating $F \boxplus X_{21}^{\lll 10} \boxplus K_1^l \boxplus m_0$. The reason why there is a carry is as follows. Suppose $sum_3 = X_{21}^{\lll 10} \boxplus K_1^l \boxplus m_0$. When m_0

satisfies such a pattern, $sum_3^{19\sim18} = 11_2$. Since $F^{18} = 1$, there will be always carry from the 20th bit when calculating $F \boxplus sum_3$.

$$F \wedge \texttt{0xfffc0000} = \texttt{1110 1011 0101 b100 0000 0000 0000 0000}.$$
$$X_{21}^{\lll 10} \boxplus K_1^l = \texttt{0100 1110 1100 0011 1001 0010 1111 1010}.$$
$$m_0 = \texttt{---- ---- ---- 101- ---- ---- ---- ----}.$$

Therefore,

$$(F \wedge \texttt{0xfff00000}) \boxplus ((X_{21}^{\lll 10} \boxplus K_1^l) \wedge \texttt{0xfff00000}) \boxplus \texttt{0x100000} = \texttt{0x3a200000}.$$

Moreover, to ensure that the modular difference of X_{26} can hold with a probability close to 1, we add an extra bit condition $X_{26}^9 = 1$. The reason can be found in the following calculation of $LQ_{26}^{\lll 12} = X_{26} \boxminus X_{22}^{\lll 10}$. In this way, $LQ_{26}^{31\sim30} = 00_2$ can hold with probability 1, thus resulting $(LQ_{26} \boxplus \texttt{0x407fff7e})^{\lll 12} = LQ_{26}^{\lll 12} \boxplus \texttt{0xfff7e408}$ holds with a probability close to 1.

$$X_{26} = \texttt{---1 ---- ---- -u-- u--- 1010 1--- ----}.$$
$$X_{22}^{\lll 10} = \texttt{1011 ---- 0--- -nun nnu0 un0- 0-un n010}.$$
$$LQ_{26}^{\lll 12} = \texttt{---- ---- ---- ---- ---- 00-- ---- ----}.$$

After the above preparation, we give a complete description of how to choose m_0 in a clever way to ensure the bit conditions on the lower 12 bits of X_{26}. After choosing values for X_{24} via single-step message modification and computing the corresponding m_3, we will determine the value of m_0 according to the following procedure.

step 1: Randomly choose values for the lower 12 bits of X_{26} while keeping the conditions on this part hold.

step 2: Compute the lower 12 bits of $X_{26} \boxminus X_{22}^{\lll 10}$. Then, the higher 12 bits of LQ_{26} are known.

step 3: Based on $LQ_{26} = m_0 \boxplus F \boxplus X_{21}^{\lll 10} \boxplus K_1^l$, we can compute the higher 12 bits of m_0 since the higher 12 bits of LQ_{26} and $F \boxplus X_{21}^{\lll 10} \boxplus K_1^l$ as well as the carry from the 20-th bit are all known. The remaining free bits of m_0 are set to a random value.

In this way, we can ensure that 4 extra bit conditions on X_{26} and the modular difference of it hold. Therefore, the time complexity of collision attack on 33 steps of RIPEMD-160 becomes $2^{71.6-4.5} = 2^{67.1}$. It should be noted that there are sufficient free bits in m_0, m_2, m_3 and m_5 to generate a collision even though m_0 is not fully random anymore. Specifically, it is equivalent to fixing 8 bits of m_0.

Verification. Our program has verified the correctness of the above optimizing strategy of partial calculation. Moreover, due to the low time complexity of the left branch after applying such a strategy, we can find a group solution of message words to ensure the dense left branch as shown in Table 8.

Table 8. Solution of dense left branch

Solution for 33-step left branch							
m_0	0xdc0b0468	m_1	0xf2470729	m_2	0xee83478c	m_3	0x3c25962
m_4	0xd19ebad5	m_5	0x1aed1d2b	m_6	0x1f2c0d0e	m_7	0xc4f488a9
m_8	0x586e5bed	m_9	0x1a444ebb	m_{10}	0x236883a	m_{11}	0xd38ea539
m_{12}	0x61e4d55f	m_{13}	0x8425047b	m_{14}	0xe8649646	m_{15}	0x6458c5e3
Solution for 34-step left branch							
m_0	0xc2056cdf	m_1	0x58a0be2	m_2	0xe114b874	m_3	0xb7f045ff
m_4	0x8d38c100	m_5	0x4e926b96	m_6	0x7214c160	m_7	0xea755943
m_8	0x496a5788	m_9	0x857f0518	m_{10}	0xa6a0ee3e	m_{11}	0xcd1f88a9
m_{12}	0x14a4951c	m_{13}	0xb9e9de76	m_{14}	0x65df3f3a	m_{15}	0xb949ab42

5.4 Collision Attack on 34 Steps of RIPEMD-160

The best 34-step differential characteristic is displayed in Table 14. A direct application of the DLSR framework to this differential characteristic is infeasible since the uncontrolled part holds with probability $2^{-81.4}$. Fortunately, we can exploit the partial calculation of X_{26} as above to ensure a lot of bit conditions on X_{26} hold. Different from the 33-step differential characteristic where the lower 12 bits of X_{26} can be controlled with probability 1, only the higher 20 bits of X_{26} can be controlled with probability 2^{-2} for the discovered 34-step differential characteristic. However, there are a lot of conditions on the higher 20 bits of X_{26}. Therefore, there is a great advantage if exploiting such a strategy even though it succeeds with probability 2^{-2}. The details will be explained in the following, which share many similarities with the procedure for the 33-step differential characteristic.

Let $F = X_{25}X_{24} \oplus \overline{X_{25}}X_{23}^{\lll 10}$. We write $X_{25}, X_{24}, X_{23}^{\lll 10}$ in binary according to Table 14 as follows. Thus, many bits of F can be controlled by properly choosing values for the free bits of X_{24} and X_{23}.

$$X_{25} = \texttt{---1 ---- --n- -u0- ---- 00-1 1--- ----.}$$
$$X_{24} = \texttt{100n 011- -111 111- -10- -u00 n10- -111.}$$
$$X_{23}^{\lll 10} = \texttt{001u -01- 1-11 -101 011- u1-n -1-- ----.}$$
$$F = \texttt{b0b0 ab1a aa11 a10a a1ba 11a0 01aa aaaa.}$$

Consider the calculation of X_{26},

$$X_{26} = X_{22}^{\lll 10} \boxplus (F \boxplus X_{21}^{\lll 10} \boxplus K_1^l \boxplus m_0)^{\lll 12}.$$

Observe that there are only two possible values for the lower 20 bits of F depending on X_{25}^{13} after setting values for X_{24} and X_{23} properly. Moreover, $X_{21}^{\lll 10} \boxplus K_1^l$ and $X_{22}^{\lll 10}$ are all constants after a starting point is found. Therefore, it is feasible to have a clever choice of the lower 20 bits of m_0 rather than in a random way to ensure the conditions on the higher 20 bits of X_{26}. To explain more precisely, we firstly present the starting point of the 34-step differential characteristic in Table 7.

From this starting point, the following information can be extracted.

$$F \wedge \text{0x000fffff} = 0000\ 0000\ 0000\ 1101\ 01b1\ 1100\ 0101\ 0111.$$
$$X_{21}^{\lll 10} \boxplus K_1^l = 0110\ 1100\ 1001\ 1101\ 1001\ 0100\ 1110\ 0100.$$

Therefore, $(F \boxplus X_{21}^{\lll 10} \boxplus K_1^l) \wedge \text{0x000fffff}$ can only take two possible values, which are 0xaf13b and 0xb113b.

Moreover, it should be observed that the modular difference of X_{26} holds with a very low probability of $2^{-3.1}$. Therefore, adding extra bit conditions to control the modular difference is vital as well. We add four extra bit conditions $X_{26}^{31} = 1$, $X_{26}^{30} = X_{22}^{20}$, $X_{26}^{29} = 0$ and $X_{26}^{27} = 0$, all of which are located at the higher 20 bits of X_{26}. The reason can be found in the following calculation of $LQ_{26}^{\lll 12} = X_{26} \boxminus X_{22}^{\lll 10}$. In this way, $LQ_{26}^{19 \sim 16} = 0000_2$ can hold with probability 1, thus resulting $(LQ_{26} \boxplus \text{0xe06be})^{\lll 12} = LQ_{26}^{\lll 12} \boxplus \text{0xe06be000}$ holds with probability 1.

$$X_{26} = \text{1-0u 0-n- --00 -11- ---- ---- -1-- ----.}$$
$$X_{22}^{\lll 10} = \text{1-n0 uuu0 -uu0 uu01 1nu1 01-1 00-0 --0-.}$$
$$LQ_{26}^{\lll 12} = \text{0000 ---- ---- ---- ---- ---- ---- ----.}$$

Since we are trying to control the higher 20 bits of X_{26}, the influence of the carry from the 12th bit must be taken into account when calculating $X_{22}^{\lll 10} \boxplus LQ_{26}^{\lll 12}$. The carry behaves randomly since m_0 is random and the higher 12 bits of $F \boxplus X_{21}^{\lll 10} \boxplus K_1^l$ are random. However, since $X_{22}^{1 \sim 0} = 01_2$, there is a bias that there is no carry from the 12th bit. Therefore, in the implementation, we always assume there is no carry, which holds with probability slightly higher than 2^{-1}.

After the above preparation, we give a complete description of how to choose m_0 in a clever way to ensure the 10 bit conditions on the higher 20 bits of X_{26}. After choosing values for X_{24} via single-step message modification and computing the corresponding m_3, we will determine the value of m_0 in the following procedure.

step 1: Randomly choose values of the higher 20 bits of X_{26} while keeping the 10 bit conditions on this part hold.

step 2: Compute the higher 20 bits of $X_{26} \boxminus X_{22}^{\lll 10}$ by assuming there is no carry from the 12th bit. Then, the lower 20 bits of LQ_{26} are known.

step 3: Based on $LQ_{26} = m_0 \boxplus F \boxplus X_{21}^{\lll 10} \boxplus K_1^l$, we can compute the lower 20 bits of m_0 since the lower 20 bits of LQ_{26} and $F \boxplus X_{21}^{\lll 10} \boxplus K_1^l$ are known. Randomly choose one value of the 20 bits of $F \boxplus X_{21}^{\lll 10} \boxplus K_1^l$ from the two possible values and compute the corresponding lower 20 bits of m_0. The remaining free bits of m_0 are set to a random value.

In this way, we can ensure that 6 bit conditions on X_{26} and the modular difference of it hold. Therefore, the time complexity of collision attack on 33 steps of RIPEMD-160 is improved to $2^{81.4-9.1+2} = 2^{74.3}$. It should be noted that there are sufficient free bits in m_0, m_2, m_3 and m_5 to generate a collision even though m_0 is not fully random anymore. Specifically, it is equivalent to fixing 10 bits of m_0.

Verification. The above partial calculation to ensure 10 bit conditions on the higher 20 bits of X_{26} has been verified with the program, which is consistent with our estimated success probability $2^{-1-1} = 2^{-2}$. In addition, we also found a solution for the dense left branch as shown in Table 8.

Experiment Details. The verification is briefly described above. To make this paper more complete, we give a relatively detailed description of our experiments. For the efficiency of the search, we store the solutions for (X_9, X_{10}) in RAM. However, due to the memory limit of our PC (Linux system) or Linux server, we could only store 2^{28} solutions for (X_9, X_{10}) in a two-dimensional dynamic array in RAM for one program, thus resulting that the success probability of connection becomes 2^{-4}.

Therefore, for our DLSR framework, we count the total times T_1 to start from Step 2 (where we start choosing another random values for free message words) and the total times T_2 to start verifying the probabilistic part X_i ($i \geq 25$) and Y_j ($j \geq 14$) after the connection succeeds. It is found that $T_1/T_2 = 17$, which is consistent with the success probability of connection. Obviously, it is expected that the total number of attempts to find the collision is T_2 when all the 2^{32} solutions can be stored in RAM for one program.

To find the collision for 30 steps of RIPEMD-160 in this paper, $T_2 = $ 0x4c11e4a5 and $T_1/T_2 = 17$. To find the collision for 31 steps of RIPEMD-160 in this paper, $T_2 = $ 0xfa3bab4a47 and $T_1/T_2 = 17$.

Note that the estimated probability to find the collision for 30/31 steps of RIPEMD-160 is $2^{-35.9}$ and $2^{-41.5}$ when all the 2^{32} solutions can be stored in RAM. Therefore, according the value of T_2, we believe that the estimated probability is reasonable. Similar experiments have been conducted for the collision attack on 33 and 34 steps of RIPEMD-160. The source code can be found at https://github.com/Crypt-CNS/DLSR_Framework_RIPEMD160.

6   Conclusion

Inspired from the start-from-the-middle approach, we discovered two efficient collision frameworks for reduced RIPEMD-160 by making full use of the weakness of message expansion. With the DLSR framework, we achieved the first practical collision attack on 30 and 31 steps of RIPEMD-160. Benefiting from the partial calculation techniques, the random message word can be chosen in a clever way so as to ensure more uncontrolled bit conditions hold. In this way, with the newly discovered 33-step and 34-step differential characteristics, collision attack on 33 and 34 steps of RIPEMD-160 can be achieved with time complexity $2^{67.1}$ and $2^{74.3}$ respectively. When applying the SLDR framework to the differential characteristic at Asiacrypt 2017, the time complexity is significantly improved, though it still cannot compete with the result obtained from the DLSR framework.

Acknowledgements. We thank the anonymous reviewers of CRYPTO 2019 for their insightful comments and suggestions. Fukang Liu and Zhenfu Cao are supported by National Natural Science Foundation of China (Grant No. 61632012, 61672239). In addition, Fukang Liu is also supported by Invitation Programs for Foreigner-based Researchers of the National Institute of Information and Communications Technology (NICT). Takanori Isobe is supported by Grant-in-Aid for Scientific Research (B) (KAKENHI 19H02141) for Japan Society for the Promotion of Science. Gaoli Wang is supported by the National Natural Science Foundation of China (No. 61572125) and National Cryptography Development Fund (No. MMJJ20180201).

A   Application of the SLDR Framework

A direct application of this framework to the 30-step differential characteristic in [16] will improve the collision attack by a factor of 2^{11}. The constraints on RQ_i and the starting point are displayed in Tables 9 and 10 respectively.

Observe that m_{14} is randomly chosen in the SLDR framework and used to update Y_{25}. When the starting point is extended to Y_{20}, $sum_0 = Y_{20}^{\lll 10} \boxplus K_1^T = \texttt{0xf45c8129}$ is constant. Let $F = IFZ(Y_{24}, Y_{23}, Y_{22}^{\lll 10}) = (Y_{24} \wedge Y_{22}^{\lll 10}) \oplus (Y_{23} \wedge \overline{Y_{22}^{\lll 10}})$. Adding six extra bit conditions on Y_{23} ($Y_{23}^{26 \sim 24} = 000_2$) and Y_{22} ($Y_{22}^{16 \sim 14} = 000_2$) will make $F^{26 \sim 24} = 000_2$. Then, adding four bit conditions on m_{14} ($m_{14}^{26 \sim 23} = 1000_2$) will make $RQ_{25}^{26 \sim 25} = 00_2$ since $RQ_{25} = F \boxplus sum_0 \boxplus m_{14}$. In this way, the condition $Y_{25}^{1 \sim 0} = 01_2$ can always hold. Since all the newly added conditions can be fully controlled under this framework, two more probabilistic bit conditions are controlled, thus improving the collision attack by a factor of 2^{13} in total. A solution for the dense right branch is as follows: $m_0 = \texttt{0x284ca581}$, $m_1 = \texttt{0x55fd6120}$, $m_2 = \texttt{0x694b052c}$, $m_3 = \texttt{0xd5f43d9f}$, $m_4 = \texttt{0xa064a7c8}$, $m_5 = \texttt{0xb9f7b3cd}$, $m_6 = \texttt{0x1221b7bb}$, $m_7 = \texttt{0x42156657}$, $m_8 = \texttt{0x121ecfee}$, $m_9 = \texttt{0xce7a7105}$, $m_{10} = \texttt{0xf2d47e6f}$, $m_{11} = \texttt{0xf567ac2e}$, $m_{12} = \texttt{0x20d0d1cb}$, $m_{13} = \texttt{0x9d928b7d}$, $m_{14} = \texttt{0x5c6ff19b}$, $m_{15} = \texttt{0xc306e50f}$.

Table 9. Starting point for the differential characteristic presented at Asiacrypt'17

Y_{10}	01110000001111110100000010001010	Y_{16}	1111n1uu000n1n110001n1111nuuuuuu
Y_{11}	10110111000011011001000000nuuuu	Y_{17}	1u10111un110111100u10unnn0nnn011
Y_{12}	nuuuuuuuuuuuuuuuuu0n0n00100001100	Y_{18}	010010000n1011111n00001001000001
Y_{13}	0unn1uu0111110100nuunn11011011un	Y_{19}	1u00010110010010010101001000011101
Y_{14}	010000111111111110nu101011nu1111	Y_{20}	00000001011001100000000nu110101100
Y_{15}	000010111100u1u11010000u11010101		

Table 10. Information of RQ_i

Equation: $(RQ_i \boxplus in)^{\lll \text{shift}} = RQ_i^{\lll \text{shift}} \boxplus out$									
i	shift	in	out	Pr.	i	shift	in	out	Pr.
11	8	0x1000000	0x1	1[a]	26	7	0x1000800	0x80040000	$\approx 2^{-1}$
12	11	0x15	0xa800	0.999	27	12	0x7ffc0000	0xbffff800	$\approx 2^{-1.4}$
13	14	0x6ffba800	0xea001bff	$\approx 2^{-1}$	28	7	0x0	0x0	1
24	11	0xffffff00	0xfff80000	0.999	29	6	0xc0000000	0xfffffff0	$\approx 2^{-0.4}$
25	7	0x80000	0x4000000	$\approx 2^{-0.02}$	30	15	0x10	0x80000	0.999

[a] The condition $Y_7 = 0$ makes it hold with probability 1.

B   Differential Characteristics

We present the differential characteristics used for collision attack in this section.

Table 11. 30-Step differential characteristic

i	X	$\pi_1(i)$	Y	$\pi_2(i)$
1	--------------------------------	0	--------------------------------	5
2	--------------------------------	1	--------------------------------	14
3	--------------------------------	2	--------------------------------	7
4	--------------------------------	3	--------------------------------	0
5	--------------------------------	4	--------------------------------	9
6	--------------------------------	5	--------------------------------	2
7	--------------------------------	6	--------------------------------	11
8	--------------------------------	7	--------------------------------	4
9	--------------------------------	8	--------------------------------	13
10	--------------------------------	9	--------------------------------	6
11	---0--------------------------	10	--------------------------------	15
12	--1---------------------------	11	--------------------------------	8
13	--------u--0-----------------	12	--------------------------------	1
14	---n-1----------------1---	13	-----------------0-----------	10
15	-n000----1-10000 1001-1--01u1----	14	-----------------1-----------	3
16	-010111--11-0---011n1----0u0n0110	15	----------u-----------------	12
17	n----1-010-u----11000101 01011---	7	--------------------------------	6
18	0--00n-011001100 00unnu--nun--101	4	----------1------------------	11
19	-100001u00n-nuun 0un0100-000--nun	13	----------1------------------	3
20	-u-nn-u011u00110 110110-01nu1100n	1	u-------------------------------	7
21	----11011-0----0---101-un100u0uu	10	--------------------------------	0
22	10------uuu--n0--1u10-100--000	6	1----------------------------0	13
23	u----001-110001-1----u--	15	1----------------------------1	5
24	011--1---1-----110n0-n----0--	3	----------------------un--------	10
25	--------------00-00--------	12	--------------------------------	14
26	--------0--1-----------------	0	-----------------0-01---------	15
27	--------------------------------	9	----------------1-11---------	8
28	--------------------------------	5	--------u-un-----------------	12
29	-n-------------------------n	2	--------------------------------	4
30	--------------------------------	14	--------------------------------	9

Other uncontrolled bit conditions on the left branch	$X_{28}^{29} = X_{27}^{19}, X_{28}^{0} = X_{27}^{22}$.
Other uncontrolled bit conditions on the right branch	$Y_{18}^{31} = Y_{17}^{31}, Y_{22}^{9} = Y_{21}^{9}, Y_{26}^{20} = Y_{25}^{20}, Y_{26}^{19} = Y_{25}^{19}$.
Modular difference	$(RQ_{16} \boxplus 0xffff8000)^{\lll 6} = RQ_{16}^{\lll 6} \boxplus 0xffe00000$. Pr. : Negligible. $(RQ_{28} \boxplus 0xffff8000)^{\lll 7} = RQ_{28}^{\lll 7} \boxplus 0xffc00000$. Pr. : Negligible. $(LQ_{13} \boxplus 0xffff8000)^{\lll 6} = LQ_{13}^{\lll 6} \boxplus 0xffe00000$. Pr. : Negligible. $(LQ_{14} \boxplus 0x200000)^{\lll 7} = LQ_{14}^{\lll 7} \boxplus 0x10000000$. Pr. : $2^{-0.1}$. $(LQ_{25} \boxplus 0x458)^{\lll 7} = LQ_{25}^{\lll 7} \boxplus 0x22c00$. Pr. : Negligible. $(LQ_{26} \boxplus 0xfffdc200)^{\lll 12} = LQ_{26}^{\lll 12} \boxplus 0xdc200000$. Pr. : $2^{-0.3}$. $(LQ_{27} \boxplus 0x24000000)^{\lll 15} = LQ_{27}^{\lll 15} \boxplus 0x1200$. Pr. : $2^{-0.3}$. $(LQ_{28} \boxplus 0xffffee00)^{\lll 9} = LQ_{28}^{\lll 9} \boxplus 0xffdc0000$. Pr. : Negligible. $(LQ_{29} \boxplus 0x240000)^{\lll 11} = LQ_{29}^{\lll 11} \boxplus 0x20000001$. Pr. : $2^{-0.2}$.
Total uncontrolled probability	$2^{-(10+0.9+25)} = 2^{-35.9}$

Table 12. 31-Step differential characteristic

i	X	$\pi_1(i)$	Y	$\pi_2(i)$
		$\Delta m_{12} = 2^{15}$		
1	--------------------------------	0	--------------------------------	5
2	--------------------------------	1	--------------------------------	14
3	--------------------------------	2	--------------------------------	7
4	--------------------------------	3	--------------------------------	0
5	--------------------------------	4	--------------------------------	9
6	--------------------------------	5	--------------------------------	2
7	--------------------------------	6	--------------------------------	11
8	--------------------------------	7	--------------------------------	4
9	--------------------------------	8	--------------------------------	13
10	--------------------------------	9	--------------------------------	6
11	--------------------------------	10	--------------------------------	15
12	---1-----------0----------------	11	--------------------------------	8
13	----nuuu uuu--------------------	12	--------------------------------	1
14	---u0------------------1-0---	13	-------------------0------------	10
15	-u------10---110010-----11-0---	14	-------------------1------------	3
16	-0-0----------00-n-1----1nn--01	15	-------------n------------------	12
17	u--------01---nuuuu01-0-101--nu	7	--------------------------------	6
18	00-----11-u----01u001nun-n-1-001	4	----------1---------------------	11
19	-nu1100un10-1----0-110u0-0------	13	----------1---------------------	3
20	010------1uu110-1nn-un-0--1n1-01-	1	n-------------------------------	7
21	01n--n---0011--010-11-010-0--00-	10	--------------------------------	0
22	0-0--110-111unnn nnnnnnn0-u-----0	6	1------------------------------0	13
23	-0------n-1n001000111101-1101----	15	1------------------------------1	5
24	1u100011 11111--0-1-01-010-----u1	3	--------------------nu----------	10
25	10----------------------------10-	12	--------------------------------	14
26	--------------------1--1--------	0	--------------------0-01--------	15
27	--------------------------------	9	---------------------1-11-------	8
28	--------------------------------	5	---------n-nu-------------------	12
29	--------u--u-------------------	2	--------------------------------	4
30	--------0--0--------------------	14	--------------------------------	9
31	--------------------------------	11	--------------------------------	1

Other uncontrolled bit conditions on the left branch	$X_{28}^{19} = X_{27}^{9}$, $X_{28}^{22} = X_{27}^{12}$.		
Other uncontrolled bit conditions on the right branch	$Y_{18}^{31} = Y_{17}^{31}$, $Y_{22}^{9} = Y_{21}^{9}$, $Y_{26}^{20} = Y_{25}^{20}$, $Y_{26}^{19} = Y_{25}^{19}$, $Y_{30}^{0} = Y_{29}^{0}$, $Y_{30}^{29} = Y_{29}^{29}$, $Y_{30}^{30} = Y_{29}^{30}$.		
	$(RQ_{16} \boxplus \text{0x8000})^{\lll 6} = RQ_{16}^{\lll 6} \boxplus \text{0x200000}$.		Pr. : Negligible.
	$(RQ_{28} \boxplus \text{0x8000})^{\lll 7} = RQ_{28}^{\lll 7} \boxplus \text{0x400000}$.		Pr. : Negligible.
	$(LQ_{13} \boxplus \text{0x8000})^{\lll 6} = LQ_{13}^{\lll 6} \boxplus \text{0x200000}$.		Pr. : Negligible.
	$(LQ_{14} \boxplus \text{0xffe00000})^{\lll 7} = LQ_{14}^{\lll 7} \boxplus \text{0xf0000000}$.		Pr. : $2^{-0.1}$.
Modular difference	$(LQ_{25} \boxplus \text{0xdfffffff})^{\lll 7} = LQ_{25}^{\lll 7} \boxplus \text{0xffffff70}$.		Pr. : $2^{-0.2}$.
	$(LQ_{26} \boxplus \text{0x90})^{\lll 12} = LQ_{26}^{\lll 12} \boxplus \text{0x90000}$.		Pr. : Negligible.
	$(LQ_{27} \boxplus \text{0xfff70000})^{\lll 15} = LQ_{27}^{\lll 15} \boxplus \text{0x7ffffffc}$.		Pr. : $2^{-1.1}$.
	$(LQ_{28} \boxplus \text{0x80000004})^{\lll 9} = LQ_{28}^{\lll 9} \boxplus \text{0x900}$.		Pr. : $2^{-1.1}$.
	$(LQ_{29} \boxplus \text{0xfffff700})^{\lll 11} = LQ_{29}^{\lll 11} \boxplus \text{0xffb80000}$.		Pr. : Negligible.
Total uncontrolled probability	$2^{-(12+2.5+28)} = 2^{-42.5}$		

Table 13. 33-Step differential characteristic

i	X	$\pi_1(i)$	Y	$\pi_2(i)$
\(\Delta m_{12} = 2^{15}\)				
1	--------------------------------	0	--------------------------------	5
2	--------------------------------	1	--------------------------------	14
3	--------------------------------	2	--------------------------------	7
4	--------------------------------	3	--------------------------------	0
5	--------------------------------	4	--------------------------------	9
6	--------------------------------	5	--------------------------------	2
7	--------------------------------	6	--------------------------------	11
8	--------------------------------	7	--------------------------------	4
9	--------------------------------	8	--------------------------------	13
10	--------------------------------	9	--------------------------------	6
11	--------------------------------	10	--------------------------------	15
12	-----------------------1----	11	--------------------------------	8
13	----------n--0--------11--0-0---	12	--------------------------------	1
14	---u---------------------001--	13	--------------------0------	10
15	-u000-------0-----1--1--1u--1--	14	----------------------1----	3
16	-111-------0-0-100n10--1un1u0-01	15	----------n-------------	12
17	n0-1-1-1111n11--0-0u01-110u0----	7	--------------------------------	6
18	000unn1unnn1--1101u1u1-unn00-1-1	4	------------1-------------	11
19	u0nn10-111un1--u01011001000u0-01	13	------------1-------------	3
20	0u101110u1110010nn0n-n0u-110u011	1	n-------------------------------	7
21	n1n-100-0uu1u--100n1-00n01000-un	10	--------------------------------	0
22	0-0-unn0101011----0----nunnnu0un	6	1------------------------------0	13
23	001-011-u11u10--1-0-010n00100-01	15	1------------------------------1	5
24	11u010--0--11u01000101-111100--u	3	------------------------nu----	10
25	-11----------1--1---n--n------11	12	--------------------------------	14
26	---1--------u--u---10-01-------	0	----------------------0-01----	15
27	n--n------1--0--0--------------	9	------------------------1-11---	8
28	0--1--1-------------u--u-------	5	------------------n-nu-----	12
29	-----------------0-10-1------	2	--------------------------------	4
30	----------1--1------------------	14	----------1--1-----	9
31	--------------------------------	11	--1------------------------------1	1
32	--------------------------------	8	--n------------------------------n	2
33	--u-----------------------------u	3	--------------------------------	15

Other uncontrolled bit conditions on the left branch	$X_{26}^{31} = X_{25}^{21},\ X_{27}^{11} = X_{26}^{1},\ X_{27}^{8} = X_{26}^{30}$.
Other uncontrolled bit conditions on the right branch	$Y_{18}^{31} = Y_{17}^{31},\ Y_{22}^{9} = Y_{21}^{9},\ Y_{26}^{20} = Y_{25}^{20},\ Y_{26}^{19} = Y_{25}^{19},\ Y_{30}^{0} = Y_{29}^{0},\ Y_{30}^{29} = Y_{29}^{29},\ Y_{30}^{30} = Y_{29}^{30}$,
Modular difference	$(RQ_{16} \boxplus \text{0x8000})^{\lll 6} = RQ_{16}^{\lll 6} \boxplus \text{0x200000}.$ Pr. : Negligible.
	$(RQ_{28} \boxplus \text{0x8000})^{\lll 7} = RQ_{28}^{\lll 7} \boxplus \text{0x400000}.$ Pr. : Negligible.
	$(LQ_{13} \boxplus \text{0x8000})^{\lll 6} = LQ_{13}^{\lll 6} \boxplus \text{0x200000}.$ Pr. : Negligible.
	$(LQ_{14} \boxplus \text{0xffe00000})^{\lll 7} = LQ_{14}^{\lll 7} \boxplus \text{0xf0000000}.$ Pr. : $2^{-0.1}$.
	$(LQ_{25} \boxplus \text{0x33ef815})^{\lll 7} = LQ_{25}^{\lll 7} \boxplus \text{0x9f7c0a81}.$ Pr. : $2^{-1.5}$.
	$(LQ_{26} \boxplus \text{0x407fff7e})^{\lll 12} = LQ_{26}^{\lll 12} \boxplus \text{0xfff7e408}.$ Pr. : $2^{-0.5}$.
	$(LQ_{27} \boxplus \text{0x39ff8})^{\lll 15} = LQ_{27}^{\lll 15} \boxplus \text{0xcffc0002}.$ Pr. : $2^{-0.3}$.
	$(LQ_{28} \boxplus \text{0xc007fffe})^{\lll 9} = LQ_{28}^{\lll 9} \boxplus \text{0xffffb80}.$ Pr. : $2^{-0.6}$.
	$(LQ_{29} \boxplus \text{0xfffffb80})^{\lll 11} = LQ_{29}^{\lll 11} \boxplus \text{0xffdc0000}.$ Pr. : Negligible.
	$(LQ_{30} \boxplus \text{0x240000})^{\lll 7} = LQ_{30}^{\lll 7} \boxplus \text{0x12000000}.$ Pr. : $2^{-0.2}$.
	$(LQ_{31} \boxplus \text{0xee000000})^{\lll 13} = LQ_{31}^{\lll 13} \boxplus \text{0xffffffdc0}.$ Pr. : $2^{-0.2}$.
	$(LQ_{32} \boxplus \text{0x240})^{\lll 12} = LQ_{32}^{\lll 12} \boxplus \text{0x240000}.$ Pr. : Negligible.
	$(LQ_{33} \boxplus \text{0xffdc0000})^{\lll 11} = LQ_{33}^{\lll 11} \boxplus \text{0xdfffffff}.$ Pr. : $2^{-0.2}$.
Total uncontrolled probability	$2^{-(31+3+3.6+34)} = 2^{-71.6}$

Table 14. 34-Step differential characteristic

		$\Delta m_{12} = 2^{15}$		
i	X	$\pi_1(i)$	Y	$\pi_2(i)$
1	--------------------------------	0	--------------------------------	5
2	--------------------------------	1	--------------------------------	14
3	--------------------------------	2	--------------------------------	7
4	--------------------------------	3	--------------------------------	0
5	--------------------------------	4	--------------------------------	9
6	--------------------------------	5	--------------------------------	2
7	--------------------------------	6	--------------------------------	11
8	--------------------------------	7	--------------------------------	4
9	--------------------------------	8	--------------------------------	13
10	--------------------------------	9	--------------------------------	6
11	--------------------------------	10	--------------------------------	15
12	--------------10-----0----	11	--------------------------------	8
13	--------nuu1-0----------0-----	12	--------------------------------	1
14	-1-n00---00101101-0010---------	13	------------------0--------	10
15	-n0010----1100----------0--u000n-	14	------------------------1----	3
16	-00-0----010010--1n0111u-0uu0110	15	------------n---------------	12
17	u00100---110100n0uuu101n1-00101n	7	--------------------------------	6
18	0101101-00uu-01101110-10nuu1-11u	4	--------1-------------------	11
19	u1nuun01010n01-11nnuu0100010--1n	13	---------1------------------	3
20	1001u00n0nu1u11u0001n11n100u000u	1	u---------------------------	7
21	u1nu001-u1-00u001--0nu10u100nu-0	10	--------------------------------	0
22	-100-0--0-1-n0uuu0-uu0uu011nu101	6	1----------------------------0	13
23	-n-1------001u-01-1-11-101011-u1	15	1---------------------------1	5
24	100n011--111111-10--u00n10--111	3	----------------------un--------	10
25	---1------n--u0-----00-11-----	12	--------------------------------	14
26	---u--n---00-11----------1------	0	------------------0-01------	15
27	1-----0--------------n--u-----	9	----------------1-11--------	8
28	---------u-n--------0----1---	5	---------n-un---------------	12
29	---------0-10-1----------------	2	--------------------------------	4
30	1-1------------------------	14	---------1-1----------------	9
31	---------------------------	11	--1-----------------------1	1
32	----------------0--0--------	8	-u------------------------n	2
33	---------------------u--n-----	3	-1------------------------1	15
34	----------------------------	10	--------------------------------	5

Other uncontrolled bit conditions on the left branch	$X_{25}^{25} = X_{24}^{15}, X_{26}^9 = X_{25}^{31}, X_{27}^{18} = X_{26}^8, X_{27}^{21} = X_{26}^{11}.$	
Other uncontrolled bit conditions on the right branch	$Y_{18}^{31} = Y_{17}^{31}, Y_{22}^9 = Y_{21}^9, Y_{26}^{20} = Y_{25}^{20}, Y_{26}^{19} = Y_{25}^{19}, Y_{30}^0 = Y_{29}^0, Y_{30}^{29} = Y_{29}^{29}, Y_{30}^{30} = Y_{29}^{30}.$	
Modular difference	$(RQ_{16} \boxplus 0x8000)^{\lll 6} = RQ_{16}^{\lll 6} \boxplus 0x200000.$	Pr. : Negligible.
	$(RQ_{28} \boxplus 0x8000)^{\lll 7} = RQ_{28}^{\lll 7} \boxplus 0x400000.$	Pr. : Negligible.
	$(LQ_{13} \boxplus 0x8000)^{\lll 6} = LQ_{13}^{\lll 6} \boxplus 0x200000.$	Pr. : Negligible.
	$(LQ_{14} \boxplus 0x200000)^{\lll 7} = LQ_{14}^{\lll 7} \boxplus 0x10000000.$	Pr. = $2^{-0.1}$.
	$(LQ_{25} \boxplus 0x84201be3)^{\lll 7} = LQ_{25}^{\lll 7} \boxplus 0x100df1c2.$	Pr. = $2^{-1.2}$.
	$(LQ_{26} \boxplus 0xe06be)^{\lll 12} = LQ_{26}^{\lll 12} \boxplus 0xe06be000.$	Pr. = $2^{-3.1}$.
	$(LQ_{27} \boxplus 0x11802000)^{\lll 15} = LQ_{27}^{\lll 15} \boxplus 0x100008c0.$	Pr. = $2^{-0.2}$.
	$(LQ_{28} \boxplus 0xdffff900)^{\lll 9} = LQ_{28}^{\lll 9} \boxplus 0xfff1ffc0.$	Pr. = $2^{-0.2}$.
	$(LQ_{29} \boxplus 0xfff20000)^{\lll 11} = LQ_{29}^{\lll 11} \boxplus 0x90000000.$	Pr. = $2^{-0.9}$.
	$(LQ_{30} \boxplus 0x70000000)^{\lll 7} = LQ_{30}^{\lll 7} \boxplus 0x38.$	Pr. = $2^{-0.9}$.
	$(LQ_{31} \boxplus 0xffffffc8)^{\lll 13} = LQ_{31}^{\lll 13} \boxplus 0xfff90000.$	Pr. : Negligible.
	$(LQ_{32} \boxplus 0x70000)^{\lll 12} = LQ_{32}^{\lll 12} \boxplus 0x70000000.$	Pr. = $2^{-0.9}$.
	$(LQ_{33} \boxplus 0x90000000)^{\lll 11} = LQ_{33}^{\lll 11} \boxplus 0xfffffc80.$	Pr. = $2^{-0.9}$.
Total uncontrolled probability	$2^{-8.4-37-36} = 2^{-81.4}$	

References

1. Biham, E., Chen, R.: Near-collisions of SHA-0. In: Franklin, M. (ed.) CRYPTO 2004. LNCS, vol. 3152, pp. 290–305. Springer, Heidelberg (2004). https://doi.org/10.1007/978-3-540-28628-8_18

2. Bosselaers, A., Preneel, B. (eds.): Integrity Primitives for Secure Information Systems. LNCS, vol. 1007. Springer, Heidelberg (1995). https://doi.org/10.1007/3-540-60640-8

3. Damgård, I.B.: A design principle for hash functions. In: Brassard, G. (ed.) CRYPTO 1989. LNCS, vol. 435, pp. 416–427. Springer, New York (1990). https://doi.org/10.1007/0-387-34805-0_39

4. Daum, M.: Cryptanalysis of Hash functions of the MD4-family. Ph.D. thesis, Ruhr University Bochum (2005)

5. De Cannière, C., Rechberger, C.: Finding SHA-1 characteristics: general results and applications. In: Lai, X., Chen, K. (eds.) ASIACRYPT 2006. LNCS, vol. 4284, pp. 1–20. Springer, Heidelberg (2006). https://doi.org/10.1007/11935230_1

6. den Boer, B., Bosselaers, A.: Collisions for the compression function of MD5. In: Helleseth, T. (ed.) EUROCRYPT 1993. LNCS, vol. 765, pp. 293–304. Springer, Heidelberg (1994). https://doi.org/10.1007/3-540-48285-7_26

7. Dobbertin, H.: Cryptanalysis of MD4. In: Gollmann, D. (ed.) FSE 1996. LNCS, vol. 1039, pp. 53–69. Springer, Heidelberg (1996). https://doi.org/10.1007/3-540-60865-6_43

8. Dobbertin, H.: RIPEMD with two-round compress function is not collision-free. J. Cryptol. 10(1), 51–70 (1997)

9. Dobbertin, H., Bosselaers, A., Preneel, B.: RIPEMD-160: a strengthened version of RIPEMD. In: Gollmann, D. (ed.) FSE 1996. LNCS, vol. 1039, pp. 71–82. Springer, Heidelberg (1996). https://doi.org/10.1007/3-540-60865-6_44

10. Dobraunig, C., Eichlseder, M., Mendel, F.: Analysis of SHA-512/224 and SHA-512/256. In: Iwata, T., Cheon, J.H. (eds.) ASIACRYPT 2015. LNCS, vol. 9453, pp. 612–630. Springer, Heidelberg (2015). https://doi.org/10.1007/978-3-662-48800-3_25

11. Eichlseder, M., Mendel, F., Schläffer, M.: Branching heuristics in differential collision search with applications to SHA-512. In: Cid, C., Rechberger, C. (eds.) FSE 2014. LNCS, vol. 8540, pp. 473–488. Springer, Heidelberg (2015). https://doi.org/10.1007/978-3-662-46706-0_24

12. Joux, A., Peyrin, T.: Hash functions and the (amplified) boomerang attack. In: Menezes, A. (ed.) CRYPTO 2007. LNCS, vol. 4622, pp. 244–263. Springer, Heidelberg (2007). https://doi.org/10.1007/978-3-540-74143-5_14

13. Karpman, P., Peyrin, T., Stevens, M.: Practical free-start collision attacks on 76-step SHA-1. In: Gennaro, R., Robshaw, M. (eds.) CRYPTO 2015. LNCS, vol. 9215, pp. 623–642. Springer, Heidelberg (2015). https://doi.org/10.1007/978-3-662-47989-6_30

14. Landelle, F., Peyrin, T.: Cryptanalysis of full RIPEMD-128. In: Johansson, T., Nguyen, P.Q. (eds.) EUROCRYPT 2013. LNCS, vol. 7881, pp. 228–244. Springer, Heidelberg (2013). https://doi.org/10.1007/978-3-642-38348-9_14

15. Leurent, G.: Message freedom in MD4 and MD5 collisions: application to APOP. In: Biryukov, A. (ed.) FSE 2007. LNCS, vol. 4593, pp. 309–328. Springer, Heidelberg (2007). https://doi.org/10.1007/978-3-540-74619-5_20

16. Liu, F., Mendel, F., Wang, G.: Collisions and semi-free-start collisions for round-reduced RIPEMD-160. In: Takagi, T., Peyrin, T. (eds.) ASIACRYPT 2017. LNCS, vol. 10624, pp. 158–186. Springer, Cham (2017). https://doi.org/10.1007/978-3-319-70694-8_6

17. Mendel, F., Nad, T., Scherz, S., Schläffer, M.: Differential attacks on reduced RIPEMD-160. In: Gollmann, D., Freiling, F.C. (eds.) ISC 2012. LNCS, vol. 7483, pp. 23–38. Springer, Heidelberg (2012). https://doi.org/10.1007/978-3-642-33383-5_2

18. Mendel, F., Nad, T., Schläffer, M.: Finding SHA-2 characteristics: searching through a minefield of contradictions. In: Lee, D.H., Wang, X. (eds.) ASIACRYPT 2011. LNCS, vol. 7073, pp. 288–307. Springer, Heidelberg (2011). https://doi.org/10.1007/978-3-642-25385-0_16

19. Mendel, F., Nad, T., Schläffer, M.: Collision attacks on the reduced dual-stream hash function RIPEMD-128. In: Canteaut, A. (ed.) FSE 2012. LNCS, vol. 7549, pp. 226–243. Springer, Heidelberg (2012). https://doi.org/10.1007/978-3-642-34047-5_14

20. Mendel, F., Nad, T., Schläffer, M.: Improving local collisions: new attacks on reduced SHA-256. In: Johansson, T., Nguyen, P.Q. (eds.) EUROCRYPT 2013. LNCS, vol. 7881, pp. 262–278. Springer, Heidelberg (2013). https://doi.org/10.1007/978-3-642-38348-9_16

21. Mendel, F., Peyrin, T., Schläffer, M., Wang, L., Wu, S.: Improved cryptanalysis of reduced RIPEMD-160. In: Sako, K., Sarkar, P. (eds.) ASIACRYPT 2013. LNCS, vol. 8270, pp. 484–503. Springer, Heidelberg (2013). https://doi.org/10.1007/978-3-642-42045-0_25

22. Merkle, R.C.: One way hash functions and DES. In: Brassard, G. (ed.) CRYPTO 1989. LNCS, vol. 435, pp. 428–446. Springer, New York (1990). https://doi.org/10.1007/0-387-34805-0_40

23. Ohtahara, C., Sasaki, Y., Shimoyama, T.: Preimage attacks on the step-reduced RIPEMD-128 and RIPEMD-160. IEICE Trans. 95-A(10), 1729–1739 (2012)

24. Stevens, M.: Fast collision attack on MD5. Cryptology ePrint Archive, Report 2006/104 (2006). https://eprint.iacr.org/2006/104

25. Stevens, M., Bursztein, E., Karpman, P., Albertini, A., Markov, Y.: The first collision for full SHA-1. In: Katz, J., Shacham, H. (eds.) CRYPTO 2017. LNCS, vol. 10401, pp. 570–596. Springer, Cham (2017). https://doi.org/10.1007/978-3-319-63688-7_19

26. Wang, G.: Practical collision attack on 40-Step RIPEMD-128. In: Benaloh, J. (ed.) CT-RSA 2014. LNCS, vol. 8366, pp. 444–460. Springer, Cham (2014). https://doi.org/10.1007/978-3-319-04852-9_23

27. Wang, G., Shen, Y., Liu, F.: Cryptanalysis of 48-step RIPEMD-160. IACR Trans. Symmetric Cryptol. 2017(2), 177–202 (2017)

28. Wang, X., Lai, X., Feng, D., Chen, H., Yu, X.: Cryptanalysis of the hash functions MD4 and RIPEMD. In: Cramer, R. (ed.) EUROCRYPT 2005. LNCS, vol. 3494, pp. 1–18. Springer, Heidelberg (2005). https://doi.org/10.1007/11426639_1

29. Wang, X., Yin, Y.L., Yu, H.: Finding collisions in the full SHA-1. In: Shoup, V. (ed.) CRYPTO 2005. LNCS, vol. 3621, pp. 17–36. Springer, Heidelberg (2005). https://doi.org/10.1007/11535218_2
30. Wang, X., Yu, H.: How to break MD5 and other hash functions. In: Cramer, R. (ed.) EUROCRYPT 2005. LNCS, vol. 3494, pp. 19–35. Springer, Heidelberg (2005). https://doi.org/10.1007/11426639_2
31. Wang, X., Yu, H., Yin, Y.L.: Efficient collision search attacks on SHA-0. In: Shoup, V. (ed.) CRYPTO 2005. LNCS, vol. 3621, pp. 1–16. Springer, Heidelberg (2005). https://doi.org/10.1007/11535218_1

Improving Attacks on Round-Reduced Speck32/64 Using Deep Learning

Aron Gohr[(✉)]

Bundesamt für Sicherheit in der Informationstechnik (BSI), Bonn, Germany
aron.gohr@bsi.bund.de

Abstract. This paper has four main contributions. First, we calculate the predicted difference distribution of Speck32/64 with one specific input difference under the Markov assumption completely for up to eight rounds and verify that this yields a globally fairly good model of the difference distribution of Speck32/64. Secondly, we show that contrary to conventional wisdom, machine learning can produce very powerful cryptographic distinguishers: for instance, in a simple low-data, chosen plaintext attack on nine rounds of Speck, we present distinguishers based on deep residual neural networks that achieve a mean key rank roughly five times lower than an analogous classical distinguisher using the full difference distribution table. Thirdly, we develop a highly selective key search policy based on a variant of Bayesian optimization which, together with our neural distinguishers, can be used to reduce the remaining security of 11-round Speck32/64 to roughly 38 bits. This is a significant improvement over previous literature. Lastly, we show that our neural distinguishers successfully use features of the ciphertext pair distribution that are invisible to all purely differential distinguishers even given unlimited data.

While our attack is based on a known input difference taken from the literature, we also show that neural networks can be used to rapidly (within a matter of minutes on our machine) find good input differences without using prior human cryptanalysis. Supplementary code and data for this paper is available at https://github.com/agohr/deep_speck.

Keywords: Deep Learning · Differential cryptanalysis · Speck

1 Introduction

1.1 Motivation and Goals of This Paper

Deep Learning has led to great improvements recently on a number of difficult tasks ranging from machine translation [7,40] and autonomous driving [13] to playing various abstract board games at superhuman level [16,37,38]. In cryptography, practical work using machine learning techniques has mostly focused on side-channel analysis [31,34,35]. On a theoretical level, it has long been recognized that cryptography and machine learning are naturally linked fields, see e.g.

© International Association for Cryptologic Research 2019
A. Boldyreva and D. Micciancio (Eds.): CRYPTO 2019, LNCS 11693, pp. 150–179, 2019.
https://doi.org/10.1007/978-3-030-26951-7_6

the survey of the subject given in [36]. Many cryptographic tasks can be naturally framed as learning tasks and consequently cryptographic hardness assumptions may for instance yield examples for distributions that are by design difficult to learn. However, not much work as been done on machine-learning based cryptanalysis. This paper is the first to show that neural networks can be used to produce attacks quite competitive to the published state of the art against a round-reduced version of a modern block cipher.

1.2 Contributions and Structure of This Paper

Main Results. This paper tries to teach neural networks to exploit differential properties of round-reduced Speck. To this end, we train neural networks to distinguish the output of Speck with a given input difference from random data. To test the strength of these machine-learned distinguishers, we first calculate the expected efficiency of some multiple-differential distinguishers for round-reduced Speck32/64 that use the full Markov model of Speck32/64, i.e. all differential characteristics following a given input difference. This is the strongest form of differential distinguishing attack known that does not involve key search and to the best of our knowledge, the efficiency of distinguishing attacks of this kind has not been studied before for any Speck variant. A fairly high detection efficiency is achieved for up to about eight rounds past our chosen input difference.

Our neural distinguishers achieve better overall classification accuracy than these very strong baselines (see Table 2 for details). As an additional performance metric, we construct a simple partial key recovery attack on nine rounds of Speck using only 128 chosen plaintexts where the two types of distinguisher can be directly compared. In this test, we try to recover one subkey. The mean rank of this subkey is roughly five times lower with the neural distinguishers than with the difference distribution table. We explore this further by designing a cryptographic task in which the adversary has to distinguish two ciphertext pair distributions that have exactly the same ciphertext difference distribution. We find that our neural distinguishers perform fairly well in this game without any retraining, reinforcing the observation that the neural distinguishers use features not represented in the difference distribution table.

In order to allow for a direct comparison to existing literature, we also construct a partial key recovery attack against 11 (out of 22) rounds of Speck32/64 based on a lightweight version of our neural distinguishers. The attack is expected to recover the last two subkeys after $2^{14.5}$ chosen-plaintext queries at a computational complexity equivalent to about 2^{38} Speck encryptions; expected average wall time to recovery of the last two subkeys on a desktop computer under single-threaded CPU-only execution is about 15 min in our proof of concept implementation. The closest comparison to this in the literature might be the attack on Speck32/64 reduced to 11 rounds presented in [19], which needs an expected 2^{14} chosen plaintexts to recover a Speck key with a computational effort of about 2^{46} reduced Speck evaluations. For a summary, see Table 1.

All experiments reported in this paper have been performed with a full implementation of Speck32/64, i.e. including the real key schedule. However, there is no evidence that the neural distinguishers use any properties of the key schedule. In particular, our 11-round key recovery attack has been tested also against reduced Speck32/64 with the free key schedule (independent and uniformly distributed subkeys), with no difference in performance compared to the real key schedule.

While other authors have tried to use neural networks for cryptanalytic tasks (see e.g. [6,15,17,18,26,28] and the references cited therein), this paper is to the best of our knowledge the first work that compares cryptanalysis performed by a deep neural network to solving the same problems with strong, well-understood conventional cryptanalytic tools. It is also to the best of our knowledge the first paper to combine neural networks with strong conventional cryptanalysis techniques and the first paper to demonstrate a neural network based attack on a symmetric cryptographic primitive that improves upon the published state of the art.

The comparison with traditional techniques serves in this paper both a benchmarking purpose and heuristically also as an additional safeguard against possible flaws in experimental setup. In the examples here considered, the performance of our deep neural networks is competitive with results obtained classically.

Table 1. Summary of key recovery attacks on 11 round Speck32/64. Computational complexity is given in terms of Speck evaluations on a modern CPU, i.e. assuming full utilisation of SIMD parallelism for fast key search.

Type	Complexity	Data	Source
Single-trail differential	2^{46}	2^{14} CP	[19]
Neural multiple differential	2^{38}	$2^{14.5}$ CP	This paper, Sect. 4

Structure of the Paper. In Sect. 2, we give a short overview of the Speck family of block ciphers and fix some notations.

In Sect. 3, we systematically develop new high-gain random-or-real differential distinguishers for round-reduced Speck based on an approach similar to that used on KATAN32 in [3]. For five to eight rounds of Speck32/64, we calculate for the first time the full distribution of differences within the Markov model for Speck induced by the input difference 0x0040/0000 up to double precision rounding error. See Table 2 for details.

Section 4 contains our main results on using neural networks for cryptanalysis: we develop strong neural distinguishers against Speck reduced to up to eight rounds and show key recovery attacks competitive with classical methods for 9 and 11 rounds. We further show that using few shot learning techniques, fairly strong distinguishers against up to six rounds of Speck can be trained from very small data sets (see Fig. 2) and with very little computation. We use this further to automatically *find* good input differences for Speck32/64 without using prior human cryptanalysis.

In Sect. 5, we further investigate the capabilities of our networks by introducing a differential cryptanalytic task which we call the *real differences experiment* where the distinguishers of Sect. 3 are made useless. In this model, the adversary has to distinguish a real ciphertext $C = (C_0, C_1)$ obtained by encrypting two blocks of data P_0, P_1 with a known plaintext difference Δ from ciphertext that has additionally been bitwise-added with a random masking value $K_{out} \in \{0, 1\}^b$, where b is the block size of the primitive considered.

We show that our best neural models for the main distinguishing task discussed in Sect. 4 have discovered ways to win in this experiment significantly more often than random guessing without any retraining, although for the five-round case retraining is found to be quite helpful in extending this advantage. We also discuss a concrete example of a ciphertext pair that is misclassified by traditional differential distinguishers.

In Sect. 6 we discuss our results and possible extensions of this work.

1.3   Related Work

Related Cryptographic Work. Speck has since its publication [9] received a fair amount of analysis, see e.g. [8] for a review. We focus only on those works that are most relevant to the present paper.

The differential cryptanalysis of Speck was first studied by Abed, List, Lucks and Wenzel in [2]. They constructed efficient differential characteristics for round-reduced versions of all members of the Speck family of ciphers and showed how to use these for key recovery. For Speck32/64, the round 3 difference of their 9-round characteristic is used in the present work as the input difference required by our differential distinguishers.

In [19], Dinur improved the analysis given in [2] by using a two-round guess and determine attack to speed up key recovery and extend the number of rounds that can be attacked. The two-round guess and determine stage of this attack takes as input a bitwise input difference and the cipher output two rounds later and returns all possible solutions for the subkeys used in these final rounds. In Sect. 3, we use this two-round attack to construct a practical distinguisher for Speck reduced to five rounds that exploits the nonuniformity of the ciphertext pair distribution perfectly in the setting where only the input difference but not the input values to the cipher are known.

Biryukov and Velichkov proposed in [11] a framework for the automatic search for optimal single differential characteristics of Speck and further improved on the differential characteristics found in [2]. They also showed that Speck is not a Markov cipher. This latter finding is reinforced by our finding that neural distinguishers on Speck can for a nontrivial number of rounds outperform in terms of prediction accuracy all purely differential distinguishers.

Differential attacks are most useful in the chosen plaintext setting, as the adversary needs to see the output of the primitive under study given plaintext inputs with a particular chosen difference. The most powerful attacks against round-reduced Speck that have been put forward in the known plaintext setting come from linear cryptanalysis [5, 30].

Multiple differential cryptanalysis as an extension of truncated differential cryptanalysis was first studied by Blondeau and Gerard in [12]. A multiple-differential attack framework for block ciphers with small block size which (under the assumption that the relevant differential transition probabilities can be calculated correctly) exploits the difference between the wrong-key and right-key difference distributions perfectly was developed by Albrecht and Leander [3] and used to provide new cryptanalytic results on the KATAN32 block cipher, significantly extending the number of rounds that can be shown to be attackable.

Prior Work on Machine Learning and Data Driven Techniques in Cryptanalysis. A number of works have explored the use of machine learning and broadly applicable statistical techniques for cryptanalytic purposes previously. We give a brief review here.

For the purpose of this review, precomputation attacks are generally viewed as not being machine learning. Likewise, side channel attacks and other ways of exploiting the implementation of a mechanism are considered not to be cryptanalysis in the sense here discussed.

Laskari, Meletiou, Stamatiou and Vrahatis [28] reported some success (in terms of search tree size, not necessarily in terms of execution time) compared to the baseline given by unoptimized brute force search in applying evolutionary computing methods to the problem of recovering additional subkey bits in four- and six round reduced DES subsequent to a classical differential attack.

Klimov, Mityagin and Shamir used genetic algorithms and neural networks to break a proposed public-key scheme itself based on neural networks [25]. The same protocol was broken in the same paper also using two other methods.

A few authors have looked at the possibility of using machine learning directly to distinguish between or to otherwise attack unreduced modern ciphers. From a cryptographic point of view, this is clearly expected to be impossible, at least unless mode-of-operation or other implementation issues make it feasible. This is e.g. also the conclusion reached by Chou, Lin and Chen [15], who perform some experiments along these lines and give a review of the literature.

Gomez, Huang, Zhang, Li, Osama and Kaiser [20] used unsupervised learning using neural networks to achieve code book recovery for short-period Vigenere ciphers in a setting in which neither parallel text nor information on the enciphering mechanism was available to the network during training. Their motivation was primarily to work towards unsupervised learning techniques for machine translation.

Abadi and Andersen [1] trained two neural networks to protect their communications from a third network that was trying to read their traffic. They showed that the two networks were in this setting able to use a pre-shared secret to shut out the adversary. However, neither analysis of humanly designed primitives nor human cryptanalysis of the communication method developed by the networks was performed.

Rivest in [36] reviewed various connections between machine learning and cryptography. He also suggested some possible directions of research in cryptanalytic applications of machine learning.

Greydanus reported that recurrent neural networks can in a black box setting learn to simulate a restricted version of Enigma [21].

Purely data driven attacks have been used with good success e.g. against RC4 by Paterson, Poettering and Schuldt [32]. They basically learn from a very large amount of RC4 keystream examples a Bayesian model of single-byte and two-byte biases of RC4. This model is then used to derive some plaintext data given on the order of millions of encryptions of the same plaintext.

2 The Speck Family of Block Ciphers

2.1 Notations and Conventions

Bitwise addition will in the sequel be denoted by $\oplus$, modular addition modulo 2^n by $\boxplus$, and bitwise rotation of a fixed-size word by $\lll$ for rotation to the left and $\ggg$ for rotation to the right. Here, k will be the word size of the primitive in question, which in the case of Speck32/64 is 16.

In this paper, differential cryptanalysis will always mean cryptanalysis with regards to bitwise differences in the adversary-controlled input to the cipher under study. Let hence $F : \{0,1\}^n \to \{0,1\}^m$ be a map. Then, a *differential transition* for F is a pair $(\Delta_{\text{in}}, \Delta_{\text{out}}) \in \{0,1\}^n \times \{0,1\}^m$. The probability $P(\Delta_{\text{in}} \to \Delta_{\text{out}})$ of the differential transition $F : \Delta_{\text{in}} \to \Delta_{\text{out}}$ is defined as

$$P(\Delta_{\text{in}} \to \Delta_{\text{out}}) := \frac{\text{Card}(\{x \in \{0,1\}^n : F(x) \oplus F(x \oplus \Delta_{\text{in}}) = \Delta_{\text{out}}\})}{2^n}. \quad (1)$$

In the description of differential attacks, it is sometimes necessary to specify specific ciphertext or plaintext differences or ciphertext/plaintext states. A single Speck block (or the difference between two blocks, depending on context) will in this paper be described by a pair of hexadecimal numbers. For instance, for Speck32/64, a state difference in which only the most significant bit is set will be written as 0x8000/8000.

For a primitive iteratively constructed by repeated application of a simpler building block (i.e. a round function), a *differential characteristic* or *differential trail* will be a sequence of differential transitions, given by a sequence of differences $\Delta_0, \Delta_1, \ldots, \Delta_n$. When the same concepts are applied to key-dependent function families (e.g. block ciphers), any key dependence of the differential probability will usually be suppressed, although such key-dependencies can make a difference for security evaluation and although they are known to exist in ARX primitives (see e.g. [4]).

As introduced by Lai, Massey and Murphy [27], a *Markov cipher* is an iterated block cipher in which the probability of the individual differential transitions is independent of the concrete plaintext values if the subkeys applied to each round are chosen in a uniformly random manner. It is common to suppress the effect of initial or final keyless permutations on the assessment of the Markov property, because the details of message modifying the data that goes into these initial or final permutations are outside the scope of differential cryptanalysis. In the case of Speck, the first round up to and excluding the first subkey addition is for instance a fixed initial permutation on the plaintext.

A *differential attack* is any cryptographic attack that uses nonrandom properties of the output of a cryptographic primitive when it is being given input data with a known difference distribution. The most general form of differential attack that has been formally discussed in the literature are *multiple differential attacks* [12], where information from an arbitrary set of differential transitions is exploited in order to maximise the gain of the resulting attack.

In this paper, we will see both attacks that only use the information contained in observed ciphertext *differences* and the full information contained in output ciphertext *pairs*. We will in the sequel call the former *purely differential* attacks and the latter *general differential* attacks.

A *distinguisher* is a classifier C that accepts as input d data sampled independently from a finite event space Ω according to one of n probability distributions $\mathcal{D}_i, i = 1, \ldots, n$, and outputs a guess of i for the submitted input item d. Here, i is chosen at each trial with a probability p_i from the set $\{1, 2, \ldots, n\}$. The selection method for i together with the distributions $\mathcal{D}_i$ is known in advance and is in this paper called an *experiment*.

2.2   A Short Description of Speck

Speck is an iterated block cipher designed by Beaulieu, Treatman-Clark, Shors, Weeks, Smith and Wingers [9] for the NSA with the aim of building a cipher efficient in software implementations in IoT devices [8]. It is an ARX construction, meaning that it is a composition of the basic functions of modular addition (mod 2^k), bitwise rotation, and bitwise addition applied to k-bit words. In [9], various versions of Speck were proposed, which differ from each other by the values of some rotation constants, the number of rounds suggested, as well as by the block and key sizes used. Generally, Speckn/m will denote Speck with n bit block size and m bits key size.

The round function $F : \mathbb{F}_2^k \times \mathbb{F}_2^{2k} \to \mathbb{F}_2^{2k}$ of Speck is very simple. It takes as input a k-bit subkey K and a cipher state consisting of two k-bit words (L_i, R_i) and produces from this the next round state (L_{i+1}, R_{i+1}) as follows:

$$L_{i+1} := ((L_i \ggg \alpha) \boxplus R_i) \oplus K, R_{i+1} := (R_i \lll \beta) \oplus L_{i+1}, \tag{2}$$

where α, β are constants specific to each member of the Speck cipher family ($\alpha = 7, \beta = 2$ for Speck32/64 and $\alpha = 8, \beta = 3$ for the other variants).

The round function is applied a fixed number of times (for 22 rounds in the case of Speck32/64) to produce from the plaintext input the ciphertext output. The subkeys for each round are generated from a master key by a non-linear key schedule that uses as its main building block also this round function. Some details of the key schedule differ between different versions of Speck due to the different number of words in the master key. The key schedule will not be analyzed in this paper and we therefore refer to [9] for further information.

3   Multiple Differential Attacks on Speck32/64

3.1   Pure Differential Distinguishers

Setting. Multiple differential attacks [12] build cryptographic distinguishers by using a set S of differential transitions for some cryptographic function F to characterise its behaviour. The basic idea is that each transition $\Delta_i \rightarrow \delta_j$ in S has associated with it a probability p_{ij} of being observed given the experimental setting the cipher is being studied in and another probability $\tilde{p}_{ij}$ in some situation that is being distinguished against. Given some observed data $\mathcal{O}$ from the experiment, Bayesian inference can then be used to determine e.g. if the observed data comes from the real or the random experiment.

Calculating Differential Transition Probabilities. We use algorithm 2 in [29] to compute the differential behaviour of the nonlinear component of Speck32/64, which is simply modular addition modulo 2^{16}. This gives us an efficient way to access arbitrary entries of the single-round differential transition matrix $A \in \mathbb{R}^{2^{32} \times 2^{32}}$ of Speck. Given an input difference distribution $v_i \in \mathbb{R}^{2^{32}}$ for round i of Speck, we calculate the distribution at the input of round $i + 1$ by setting $v_{i+1} := A v_i$.

Starting from the input difference $\Delta = 0x0040/0000$, i.e. the round 3 difference of the differential characteristic given in Table 7 of [2], we have calculated the full predicted induced output distribution of Speck32/64 for up to 8 rounds in this way. The required sparse matrix-vector multiplications and the on-the-fly calculation of the relevant matrix entries took around 300 core-days of computing time in our implementation and produced about 34 gigabytes of distribution data for each round, which was saved to disk for further study. The input difference Δ is used in most distinguishers developed in the remainder of this paper. It transitions deterministically to the low-weight difference $0x8000/8000$ and has been chosen for being a very good starting point for truncated differential cryptanalysis in a low-data setting.

Cryptographic Tasks. In this section, we set out to distinguish reduced-round Speck output with the input difference Δ from random data. Our distinguishers will use the full predicted output difference distribution for the number of rounds considered. We will denote by Di the resulting distinguisher for i rounds. Hence, D5 will e.g. be the resulting five-round distinguisher and the corresponding distinguishing problem will be referred to as the *D5 task*.

Classification. To distinguish between examples of real ciphertext pairs and examples generated at random, we assume that random ciphertext pair differences are distributed according to the uniform distribution on nonzero ciphertext blocks. We classify an observed output difference δ as real if the predicted probability of observing it in the real distribution is $> 1/(2^{32} - 1)$ and as random otherwise. This exploits the non-uniformity of the output difference distribution perfectly if our prediction of this distribution does not contain errors. The reported true positive rates and accuracies for the distinguishers defined by the predicted output distribution were calculated under the assumption that the true output distribution is the predicted one.

Sources of Error. This kind of calculation works only if the cipher under study does not deviate too strongly from the Markov property. Also, in our calculation we used double-precision arithmetic, which introduces rounding errors. We have therefore tested the validity of this model in three ways:

1. We checked empirically that the highest-probability transition found by our model for eight rounds $(0x0040/0000 \rightarrow 0x0280/0080)$ is empirically observed with the expected probability of $2^{-26.015}$. This was found to be the case.
2. We checked empirically that the predicted true positive rates of our differential distinguishers match observed values on a size 10^6 test set from the real distribution. This was also the case within experimental error margins. The corresponding experiment for true negative rates was not performed, as the random distribution is a priori known exactly, so given the distinguisher, there is no error in predicting its accuracy on random samples.
3. We approximated the true difference distribution of Speck32/64 also empirically using 100 billion samples in each case. The resulting distinguishers were clearly inferior to our theoretical model.

These experiments indicate that our model captures the difference distribution of round-reduced Speck32/64 for the considered input difference quite well.

Distinguisher Accuracy and Key Rank. Accuracy as well as true positive and true negative rate results are summarised in the next section, specifically in Table 2. Computing the full difference distribution table of Speck32/64 yields fairly strong distinguishers for at least up to eight rounds (better results than presented here may be possible with other input differences). Statistics on key ranking in the context of a simple key recovery attack can be found in Table 3.

3.2   Differential Distinguishers Using the Full Distribution of Ciphertext Pairs

Setting and Motivation. The distinguishers so far considered in this paper observe a ciphertext pair that has been generated from a known input difference (but unknown input plaintext pairs) and try to guess based on the ciphertext difference whether the observed pair has been generated by reduced Speck encryption or randomly chosen. It is clear that one could improve on this by considering not only the difference data for an observed ciphertext pair, but the entire data observed. However, this is more difficult, because calculating the full distribution of ciphertext pairs for the real distribution is not feasible. The goal of this section is to determine, for differential distinguishers on five-round Speck with the input difference used in the previously studied distinguishers, how much of an advantage the adversary might gain in still exploiting this additional information.

A Perfect Differential Distinguisher for Speck32/64 Reduced to Five Rounds. We have developed a perfect distinguisher for the D5 task. Given an observed ciphertext pair $C := (C_0, C_1)$ and an input difference Δ, the likelihood $P(C|\text{real})$ that we would observe (C_0, C_1) under the real distribution for a block cipher E of block size b and key size k given uniformly random key and plaintext data is given by $2^{-(b+k)}N$, where N is the number of key and plaintext pairs (K, P) such that $E_K(P) = C_0$ and $E_K(P \oplus \Delta) = C_1$. But N is just the number $N_{\text{keys}}(C)$ of keys that decrypt C into a plaintext pair with difference Δ. On the other hand, $P(C|\text{random}) = 1/(2^{2b} - 2^b)$, so applying Bayes' theorem again, for perfect classification we need to determine whether $N_{\text{keys}}(C) > 2^{b+k}/(2^{2b} - 2^b) \approx 2^{b+k-2b}$ or not. For Speck32/64, we hence check whether $N_{\text{keys}} > 2^{32}$.

For the D5 task, it is possible to do this in practice by enumerating the possible round-3 differential states and then launching the two-round attack from [19] for each of these intermediate differences, enumerating the subkeys sk_5 and sk_4 used in rounds 4 and 5. After obtaining candidate round 3 output, we note that the round 1 output difference is known (the input difference transitions deterministically to 0x8000/8000) and use the two round attack again to recover the first two subkeys. We stop after $2^{32} + 1$ solutions have been found or the key space has been exhausted, whichever comes first. We tested this distinguisher on a test set of 10000 examples. 9456 of these were correctly classified, for an overall accuracy of about 95%. Replacing key search on the first two rounds with a (much faster) estimate of the number of solutions based on the 3-round difference distribution table did not lead to a statistically significant loss in performance.

4   Neural Distinguishers for Reduced Speck32/64

4.1   Overview

In this section, we will use neural networks to develop distinguishing attacks that try to solve the same problems as those presented previously. We only report results on our best neural models. The computational effort used in searching for a good architecture was not excessive; all machine learning experiments here reported were performed on a single workstation. Some other choices of architecture yield results that are also comparable or superior to the distinguishers presented in the previous section. One example of a simpler network architecture with still reasonable performance is shown in the github repository.

4.2   Network Structure

Input Representation. A pair (C_0, C_1) of ciphertexts for Speck32/64 can be written as a sequence of four sixteen-bit words (w_0, w_1, w_2, w_3), mirroring the word-oriented structure of the cipher. In our networks, the w_i are directly interpreted as the row-vectors of a 4×16-matrix and the input layer consists of 64 units likewise arranged in a 4×16 array.

Overall Network Structure. Our best network is a residual tower of two-layer convolutional neural networks preceded by a single bit-sliced convolution and followed by a densely connected prediction head. Deep residual networks were first introduced in [22] for image recognition and have been successful since in a number of other applications, for instance strategic board games [38,39]. The results reported for five and six rounds use a depth-10 residual tower; for seven and eight round Speck, our final models use just a single residual block.

Initial Convolution. The input layer is connected in channels-first mode to one layer of bit-sliced, e.g. width 1, convolutions with 32 output channels. Batch normalization is applied to the output of these convolutions. Finally, rectifier nonlinearities are applied to the outputs of batch normalization and the resulting 32×16 matrix is passed to the main residual tower.

Convolutional Blocks. Each convolutional block consists of two layers of 32 filters. Each layer applies first the convolutions, then a batch normalization, and finally a rectifier layer. At the end of the convolutional block, a skip connection then adds the output of the final rectifier layer of the block to the input of the convolutional block and passes the result to the next block.

Prediction Head. The prediction head consists of two hidden layers and one output unit. The first and second layer are densely connected layers with 64 units. The first of these layers is followed by a batch normalization layer and a rectifier layer; the second hidden layer does not use batch normalization but is simply a densely connected layer of 64 relu units. The final layer consists of a single output unit using a sigmoid activation.

Rationale. The use of the initial width-1 convolutional layer is intended to make the learning of simple bit-sliced functions such as bitwise addition easier. The number of filters in the initial convolution is meant to expand the data to the format required by the residual tower. The choice of the input channels is motivated by a desire to make the word-oriented structure of the cipher known to the network. The use of a densely connected prediction head reflects the fact that for a nontrivial number of rounds, we do not expect the input data to show strong spatial symmetries, so any attempt to extract local features from the data using a spatially symmetric pooling layer of some sort is probably futile. The size of the layers was determined by experiment, although we tried only a few settings. The depth of the residual tower was chosen so as to allow for integration of input data over the whole input string within the convolutional layers. However, even a design with just one residual block achieves reasonably good (clearly superior to a purely differential distinguisher) results.

4.3 Training Real vs Random Classifiers

Data Generation. Training and validation data was generated by using the Linux random number generator (/dev/urandom) to obtain uniformly distributed keys K_i and plaintext pairs P_i with the input difference $\Delta = 0x0040/0000$ as well as a vector of binary-valued real/random labels Y_i. To produce training or validation data for k-round Speck, the plaintext pair P_i was then encrypted for k rounds if Y_i was set, while otherwise the second plaintext of the pair was replaced with a freshly generated random plaintext.

In this way, data sets consisting of 10^7 samples were generated for training. Preprocessing was performed to transform the data so obtained into the format required by the network. Data generation is very cheap. On a standard PC, it takes a few seconds to generate a data set of size 10^7 in our implementation.

Basic Training Pipeline. Training was run for 200 epochs on the dataset of size 10^7. The datasets were processed in batches of size 5000. The last 10^6 samples were withheld for validation. Optimization was performed against mean square error loss plus a small penalty based on L2 weights regularization (with regularization parameter $c = 10^{-5}$) using the Adam algorithm [24] with default parameters in Keras [14]. A cyclic learning rate schedule was used, setting the learning rate l_i for epoch i to $l_i := \alpha + \frac{(n-i) \bmod (n+1)}{n} \cdot (\beta - \alpha)$, with $\alpha = 10^{-4}, \beta = 2 \cdot 10^{-3}$ and $n = 9$. The networks obtained at the end of each epoch were stored and the best network by validation loss was evaluated against a test set of size 10^6 not used in training or validation.

Improving the Distinguishers by Key Search. We tested whether the distinguishers obtained can be improved by key search. To this end, a size one million test set for Speck reduced to seven rounds was generated as previously described. Each ciphertext pair c in the test set was then evaluated by performing brute force key search on the last round, grading the resulting partial decryptions using a six-round neural distinguisher, and combining the results into a score for the ciphertext pair c by transforming the scores into real-vs-random likelihood ratios and averaging. Algorithm 1 gives details on the method used.

Using Key Search as a Teacher for a Fast Neural Distinguisher. The size one million sample set so obtained was further used as a training target for a single-block distinguisher against seven rounds of Speck. Training was performed from a randomly initialized network state for 300 epochs at batch size 5000 with a single learning rate drop from 0.001 to 0.0001 at epoch 200. Data on the resulting distinguisher can be found in Tables 2 and 3.

Algorithm 1. KeyAveraging: Deriving a differential distinguisher against a block cipher E^{r+1} reduced to $r + 1$ rounds for input difference Δ from a corresponding distinguisher $\mathcal{D}$ against E^r. A sample is predicted to come from the real distribution if and only if the output value of the algorithm is ≥ 0.5.

Require: Observed output ciphertext pair $C_0, C_1 \in \{0,1\}^b$
1: $D_i \leftarrow [\text{DecryptOneRound}(C_i, k) \text{ for } k \in \text{Subkeys}]$
2: $v_k \leftarrow \mathcal{D}(D_0[k], D_1[k])$ for all $k \in \text{Subkeys}$
3: $v_k \leftarrow v_k/(1 - v_k)$ for all $k \in \text{Subkeys}$
4: $v \leftarrow \text{Average}([v_k, k \in \text{Subkeys}])$
5: $v \leftarrow v/(1 + v)$
6: **return** v

Training an 8-Round Distinguisher. For 8 rounds, the training scheme described above fails, i.e. the model does not learn to approximate any useful function. We still succeeded in training an 8-round distinguisher slightly superior to the difference distribution table by using several stages of pre-training. First, we retrained our best seven-round distinguisher to recognize 5-round Speck32/64 with the input difference $0x8000/840a$ (the most likely difference to appear three rounds after the input difference $0x0040/0000$). This was done on 10^7 examples for ten epochs with a batch size of 5000 and a learning rate of 10^{-4}. Then, we trained the distinguisher so obtained to recognize 8-round Speck with the input difference $0x0040/0000$ by processing 10^9 freshly generated examples once with batch size 10000, keeping the learning rate constant. Finally, learning rate was dropped twice to 10^{-5} and finally to 10^{-6} after processing another 10^9 fresh examples each, again with a batch size of 10000.

Training Cost. A single epoch of training according to the basic training schedule for one of our ten-block networks takes about 150 s on a single GTX 1080 Ti graphics card at batch size 5000. A full training cycle can therefore be run in less than a day, and results superior to the difference distribution table can be obtained in less than fifteen minutes after starting the training cycle for our neural distinguishers against 5 to 7 rounds.

4.4   Results

Test Set Accuracy. We summarize data on our best models in Table 2. N5 and N6 are networks with ten residual blocks trained using the basic training method. N7 was trained to predict output of the KeyAveraging algorithm used with a six-round single-block neural distinguisher derived by knowledge distillation from N6 (see the paragraph on inference speed below for further details). N8 was derived from N7 using the staged training method described in Sect. 4.3. The neural distinguishers achieve higher accuracies than the purely differential baselines discussed in the previous section on all tasks. The accuracy of the key search based distinguishers was not matched, as expected. Validation losses were only slightly lower than training losses at the end of training, suggesting that

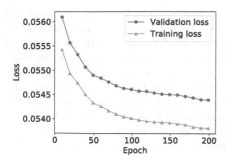 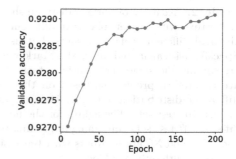

Fig. 1. Training a neural network to distinguish 5-round Speck32/64 output for the input difference $\Delta = 0x0040/0$ from random data. *(left)* Training and validation loss by epoch. *(right)* Validation accuracy. *(both)* Only data for epochs with lowest learning rate is shown. Intermediate epochs contained excursions to low performance. Full learning history for this run is available from supplementary data.

only mild overfitting took place. An example learning history for a five-round network is shown in Fig. 1. Algorithm 1 was tried on the seven round problem and did slightly improve prediction accuracy: ground truth was matched in 62.7% of the test sample.

If encryption is performed with fixed keys, a mild key dependency of distinguisher performance is observed, in line with previous work on Speck [4]. For instance, with 100 random keys, we found that true positive rates for the 7-round distinguisher empirically varied between 57.1 and 49.7%. See the github repository for code and data on this.

Key Ranking. We can extend all of the distinguishers here discussed by one round at no additional cost by using the fact that the first subkey addition happens after the first application of nonlinearity in Speck. An adversary in the chosen-plaintext setting can easily inject plaintext differences of their choosing into the output of the first round of Speck. A simple attack on 9-round Speck can then be performed as follows:

1. Request encryptions for n chosen plaintext pairs $P_1, \ldots, P_n$ such that the output difference of the first round will be $\Delta = 0x0040/0000$. Obtain the corresponding ciphertext pairs $C_1, \ldots, C_n$.
2. For each value of the final subkey k, decrypt the C_i under k to get C_i^k. Let δ_i^k be the difference of the ciphertext pair C_i^k.
3. Use a 7-round differential distinguisher to get scores Z_i^k for each partially decrypted ciphertext pair.
4. For each k, combine the scores Z_i^k into one score v_k.
5. Sort the keys in descending order according to their score v_k.

We have implemented this attack both with the 7-round distinguisher derived from the difference distribution of 7-round Speck with the given input difference and with our 7-round neural distinguisher. In the case of the neural distinguisher, we used the formula

Table 2. Accuracy of various distinguishers against Speck32/64 using two blocks of ciphertext with chosen plaintext difference $0x0040/0000$ for Nr rounds. D5-D8 are classical differential distinguishers that use the entire difference distribution table of Speck32/64 (calculated under the Markov assumption). N5-N8 are neural distinguishers solving the same distinguishing task. The accuracies of the D5-D8 distinguishers are theoretical predictions based on the assumption that they correctly predict the difference distribution, but have been empirically confirmed within 2σ error margins on size 10^6 test sets. The figures for the neural distinguishers were obtained by testing on size 10^6 test sets containing approximately 500000 positive and negative examples each. N5 and N6 are networks with ten residual blocks, while N7 and N8 are smaller networks with only one block.

Nr	Distinguisher	Accuracy	True Positive Rate	True Negative Rate
5	D5	0.911	0.877	0.947
5	N5	$0.929 \pm 5.13 \cdot 10^{-4}$	$0.904 \pm 8.33 \cdot 10^{-4}$	$0.954 \pm 5.91 \cdot 10^{-4}$
6	D6	0.758	0.680	0.837
6	N6	$0.788 \pm 8.17 \cdot 10^{-4}$	$0.724 \pm 1.26 \cdot 10^{-3}$	$0.853 \pm 1.00 \cdot 10^{-3}$
7	D7	0.591	0.543	0.640
7	N7	$0.616 \pm 9.7 \cdot 10^{-4}$	$0.533 \pm 1.41 \cdot 10^{-3}$	$0.699 \pm 1.30 \cdot 10^{-3}$
8	D8	0.512	0.496	0.527
8	N8	$0.514 \pm 1.00 \cdot 10^{-3}$	$0.519 \pm 1.41 \cdot 10^{-3}$	$0.508 \pm 1.42 \cdot 10^{-3}$

$$v_k := \sum_{i=1}^{n} \log_2(Z_i^k/(1 - Z_i^k)) \tag{3}$$

to combine the scores of individual decrypted ciphertext pairs into a score for the key; in the case of the difference distribution table, we set

$$v_k := \sum_{i=1}^{n} \log_2(P(\delta_i^k)), \tag{4}$$

where $P(\delta_i^k)$ is the probability according to the difference distribution table of observing the output difference δ_i^k in the output of Speck32/64 reduced to seven rounds given the input difference Δ. This is comparable, since in both cases we can up to a constant multiplicative factor heuristically treat the summed terms as logarithms of real-vs-random likelihood ratios[1].

We chose $n = 64$ for this experiment. In this setting, we found that the neural distinguishers achieved much better key ranking (Table 3).

It is worth noting the following:

Proposition 1. *Assume that E is any Speck variant with a free key schedule and that $\mathcal{A}$ is an attack that tries to recover the Speck key used using purely*

---

[1] As an implementation remark, note that with the neural networks *used in this paper*, the individual terms in the sum of Eq. 3 are up to a scale factor just the neural network outputs before application of the final sigmoid activation.

Table 3. Statistics on a key recovery attack on 9-round Speck32/64. The same attack using 128 chosen plaintexts is executed using both a distinguisher based on the difference distribution table and a neural distinguisher against Speck32/64 reduced to 7 rounds. All values reported are based on 1000 trials of the respective attacks. Reported error bars around the mean are for a 2σ confidence interval, where σ is calculated based on the observed standard deviation of the key rank. The rank of a key is defined as the number of subkeys ranked higher, i.e. rank zero corresponds to successful key recovery. When several keys were ranked equally, the right key was assumed to be in a random position among the equally ranked keys. Key rank data on all runs as well as data on runs with 64 and 256 chosen plaintexts is available from the github repository.

Distinguisher	Mean of key rank	Median key rank	Success rate
D7	263.9 ± 77.7	9.0	0.13
N7	52.1 ± 34.7	1.0	0.358

differential methods, i.e. assume that it gets as input plaintext differences $P_0 \oplus P_1, P_0 \oplus P_2, \ldots, P_0 \oplus P_n$ as well as ciphertexts $C_0, C_1, \ldots, C_n$. Then full key recovery can never be successful with a success rate beyond 50%.

Proof. To see this, consider any pair of ciphertexts C_0, C_1 and a Speck subkey k. Suppose that $E_k^{-1}(C_0) \oplus E_k^{-1}(C_1) = \delta$, where E_k denotes single-round encryption under the subkey k. Flip the most significant bit of k and call the resulting new subkey k'. Then it is straightforward to verify that $E_{k'}^{-1}(C_0) \oplus E_{k'}^{-1}(C_1) = \delta$ as well. The proposition follows by applying this reasoning to the first round of E.

Hence, purely differential distinguishers for Speck always produce pairs (or larger groups) of equally ranked subkeys until the key schedule can be used to rule out candidate keys.

However, already with 256 chosen plaintexts our 9-round attack does in fact yield a success rate of about 70% if a neural distinguisher is used. This is only possible because our neural distinguishers are not purely differential distinguishers. See Sect. 5 for further evidence of this.

Inference Speed. The deep residual architecture described yields networks that are still reasonably efficient to evaluate. On a single machine using a GTX 1080 Ti graphics card we were able to process roughly 200000 ciphertext pairs per second with our deeper networks (10 residual blocks). For single-block networks, we reach about one million ciphertext pairs per second on the same hardware. For seven and eight rounds of Speck, the best networks here presented are single-block networks; for five and six rounds, one can produce networks that are almost as good as the ten-block architecture by using a simple form of knowledge distillation [23]. For instance, a single-block network with 92.7% accuracy on the D5 task can be obtained by training against the output of our ten-block network for 30 epochs on a size 10^7 training dataset with a single learning rate drop from 0.001 to 0.0001 at epoch 20.

Disagreement with Difference Distribution Table. For five-round Speck, we generated a size one million test set and calculated for each example both the relevant entry of the difference distribution table for Speck32/64 using the Markov model of Speck, and the output of a five-round one-block neural predictor. Exactly half of the test sample was generated using the real distribution, with the other half being drawn at random. We used this data set to study disagreements between the neural predictor and the difference distribution table.

Disagreement between both predictors was observed in 48826 samples, of which the majority was from the random distribution (about 57%). Our neural network chose the classification corresponding to ground truth in 67% of these cases of disagreement.

However, exploitation of information that can be obtained reliably from the difference distribution table was not perfect. For instance, 1549 of our samples were found to correspond to impossible differential transitions. Two of these were misclassified by the neural network as coming from the real distribution, although in both cases the confidence level returned by the neural network output was low (56% and 53% respectively).

On the other hand, the neural network also successfully identified output pairs that could not have appeared in the real distribution. For instance, the lowest neural network score on the set of disagreements was obtained for the output pair $(c_0, c_1) := (0xc65d2696, 0xa6a37b2a)$. This corresponds to an output difference of 0x60fe/5dbc, and the transition $0x0040/0000 \rightarrow 0x60fe/5dbc$ for five rounds has a transition probability of about 2^{-26} according to the Markov model. Accordingly, the predictor based on the difference distribution table assigns a 98% probability to this output pair being from the real distribution, whereas our neural distinguisher returns an almost zero score. Performing optimized key search, we found that there is in fact no key that links this output pair to a possible intermediate difference in round 3. Indeed, the sample had come from the random distribution in our test set.

Few-Shot Learning of Cryptographic Distributions. Few-shot learning is the ability of people (and sometimes machines) to learn to recognize objects of a certain category or to solve certain problems after having been shown only a few or even just *one* example. We tested if our neural networks can successfully perform few-shot learning of a cryptographic distribution given knowledge of another related distribution by performing the following experiment: a fresh neural network with one residual block was first trained to recognize Speck reduced to three rounds with a fixed but randomly chosen input difference. Training consisted of a single epoch of 2000 descent steps with batch size 5000, which on our hardware corresponds to about a minute of training time. We then accessed the output of the second-to-last layer of this network, treating it as a representation of the input data. We generated small samples (only real examples, specifically between 1 and 50 of them) of the output distribution for six rounds of Speck with the chosen input difference of our main distinguishers. Each example set so created was complemented by the same number of samples drawn from the random distribution. The resulting example set S was sent through the neural network to obtain the corresponding set $S' \subset \mathbb{R}^{64}$ of internal representation vectors. Ridge regression (with regularization parameter $\alpha = 1$) was used to create from this small training set a linear predictor $L : \mathbb{R}^{64} \to \mathbb{R}$ for the six-round distribution minimizing the squared error between labels and predictions on S'. We classified an example $x \in S'$ as real if $L(x) > 0.5$ and as random otherwise. This predictor was then tested on a size 50000 test set to determine its accuracy. This worked well even with a single-figure number of examples. Figure 2 gives detailed results, Algorithm 2 summarizes the algorithm used.

Algorithm 2. TrainByTransfer: Training a distinguisher for a block cipher with block size b reduced to r rounds E^r with input difference δ by transfer learning given an auxiliary neural distinguisher N for input difference Δ and E^s.

Require: N, r, δ, n
1: $X_0 \leftarrow n$ samples drawn from the real output distribution of E^r with input difference δ.
2: $Y_0 \leftarrow (1, 1, ..., 1) \in \mathbb{R}^n$
3: $X_1 \leftarrow n$ samples drawn uniformly at random from $\{0, 1\}^{2b}$.
4: $Y_1 \leftarrow 0 \in \mathbb{R}^n$.
5: $N' \leftarrow N[-2]$, where $N[-2]$ denotes the output of the second-to-last layer of N.
6: $Z, Y \leftarrow N'(X_0 || X_1), Y_0 || Y_1$
7: $L \leftarrow$ RidgeRegression(Z, Y)
8: **return** $L \circ N'$

Training a new distinguisher using Algorithm 2 is very efficient. For instance, retraining on a thousand example training set takes about a millisecond on our platform.

Deriving Good Input Differences Without Human Knowledge. This few-shot learning capability allows us to very quickly derive a rough lower bound for the effectiveness of truncated differential distinguishers for Speck for a given input difference and a given number of rounds. Concretely, given a pre-trained network for three-round Speck and a random input difference δ, we can quickly train a distinguisher for another random input difference δ' and evaluate its accuracy on a small test set. Starting with a random δ', we then use Algorithm 3 to optimize δ' for test set accuracy of the resulting distinguishers. Using $\alpha = 0.01, t = 2000$, and test and training datasets of size 1000 for each new input difference to be tested, we need less than two minutes of computing time for the training of the initial three-round distinguisher and about 15 s for each full run of Algorithm 3 on our platform. The initial difference of our main neural distinguishers is usually found within a few random restarts of the greedy optimizer and extending the number of rounds to be attacked, one can then easily show using transfer learning that at least six rounds of Speck can be distinguished with fairly high gain.

It seems likely that other generic optimization algorithms, e.g. suitable variants of Monte Carlo Tree Search, might work even better.

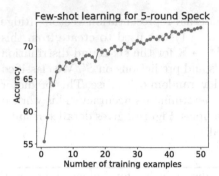
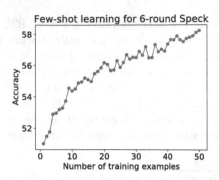

Fig. 2. Few-shot learning on the D5 and D6 tasks using a pre-trained classifier to preprocess the input data. Algorithm 2 was used with a fixed auxiliary network trained to distinguish Speck32/64 reduced to three rounds with a random fixed input difference. The number of training examples supplied was varied from 1 to 50. The accuracy figures shown are an average over 100 runs for each training set size, where for each training run a fresh training set of the indicated size was generated on the fly. Accuracy was measured against a fixed test set of size 50000. Measured accuracy is above guessing at 2σ significance level even for a single training example.

Algorithm 3. GreedyOptimizerWithExplorationBias: Given a function $F : \{0,1\}^b \to R$, try to find $x \in \{0,1\}^b$ which maximises F.

Require: F, number t of iterations, exploration factor α, input bit size b
1: $x \leftarrow \text{Rand}(0, 2^b - 1)$
2: $v_{\text{best}} \leftarrow F(x)$
3: $x_{\text{best}} \leftarrow x$
4: $v \leftarrow v_{\text{best}}$
5: $H \leftarrow$ hashtable with default value 0
6: **for** $i \in \{1, \ldots, t\}$ **do**
7:    $H[x] \leftarrow H[x] + 1$
8:    $r \leftarrow \text{Rand}(0, b - 1)$
9:    $x_{new} \leftarrow x \oplus (1 \ll r)$
10:   $v_{\text{new}} = F(x_{\text{new}})$
11:   **if** $v_{\text{new}} - \alpha \log_2(H[x_{\text{new}}]) > v - \alpha \log_2(H[x])$ **then**
12:     $v, x \leftarrow v_{\text{new}}, x_{\text{new}}$
13:   **end if**
14:   **if** $v_{\text{new}} > v_{\text{best}}$ **then**
15:     $v_{\text{best}}, x_{\text{best}} \leftarrow v, x$
16:   **end if**
17: **end for**
18: **return** x_{best}

4.5   Key Recovery Attack

To showcase the utility of our neural distinguishers as research tools, we have constructed a partial-key recovery attack based on the N7 and N6 distinguisher that is competitive to the best attacks previously known from the literature on

Speck32/64 reduced to 11 rounds, i.e. in particular to the 11-round attack of [19]. The attack proposed by Dinur has a computational complexity approximately equivalent to 2^{46} Speck evaluations. The attack is expected to succeed after querying 2^{13} chosen-plaintext pairs and obtaining the corresponding ciphertexts. Attacks on 12 to 14 rounds were also proposed in [19], naturally with substantially larger computational and data complexities.

Our eleven-round attack, in contrast, is expected to succeed with a computational complexity of roughly 2^{38} Speck evaluations if it is executed on a CPU. Its data complexity is slightly higher than that of the attack in [19]; however, computational complexity is reduced by a factor of more than 200.

Basic Attack Idea

Overview. The idea of our attack is to extend our neural 7-round distinguisher to a 9-round distinguisher by prepending a two-round differential transition $\delta \rightarrow$ 0x0040/0000 that is passed as desired with a probability of about 1/64. The 9-round distinguisher is then extended by another round at no additional cost by asking for encryptions of ciphertext pairs P_0, P_1 that encrypt to the desired input difference δ after one round of Speck encryption; this is easy, since no key addition happens in Speck before the first nonlinear operation.

The signal from this distinguisher will be rather weak. We therefore boost it by using k (probabilistic) neutral bits [10] to create from each plaintext pair a plaintext structure consisting of 2^k plaintext pairs that are expected to pass the initial two-round differential together. For each plaintext structure, we decrypt the resulting ciphertexts under all final subkeys and rank each partially decrypted ciphertext structure using our neural distinguisher. If the resulting score is beyond a threshold c_1, we attempt to decrypt another round and grade the resulting partially-decrypted ciphertexts using a six-round neural distinguisher. A key guess is returned if the resulting score for the partially decrypted ciphertext structure then exceeds another threshold c_2.

Ranking a Partial Decryption. To combine scores returned for individual ciphertext pairs in a ciphertext structure into a score for the structure, we use Eq. (3) as in the previously described 9-round attack.

Attack Parameters. This basic idea can be turned into a practical key recovery attack on 11-round Speck. The initial difference $(0x211/0xa04)$ and the neutral bits set consisting of bits 14,15,20,21,22,23 of the cipher state work well, even though bits 14,15 and 23 are not totally neutral. Using $c_1 = 15, c_2 = 100$ one obtains an attack that succeeds on average within about 20 minutes of computing time on a machine equipped with a GTX 1080 Ti graphics card, or in about 12 hours on a single core of a modern CPU. In one hundred trials, a key guess was output after processing on average $2^{13.2}$ ciphertext pairs. Recovery of both true last subkeys was successful in 81 cases; the final subkey was correctly guessed in 99 cases. In the one remaining case, the second-to-last subkey was correct and the guess for the last subkey was incorrect in one bit.

Improved Attack. This basic attack can be accelerated in various ways. Here, we focus on the following ideas:

1. The wrong key randomization hypothesis does not hold when only one round of trial decryption is performed, especially in a lightweight cipher. We use this to introduce an efficient key search policy using a generic optimization algorithm.
2. It is inefficient to spend the same amount of computation on every ciphertext structure. We use a generic method (an automatic exploitation versus exploration tradeoff based on upper confidence bounds) to focus our key search on the most promising ciphertext structures.

With these improvements, we can build an attack that recovers the final two subkeys of Speck32/64 reduced to 11 rounds with a success probability of about 50% from ciphertext corresponding to 12800 chosen plaintexts in about 8 min running in single-threaded mode on a single CPU core.[2]

Bayesian Optimization. Bayesian optimization [33] is a method that is commonly used for the optimization of black box functions f that are expensive to evaluate. Examples are found in many domains; the tuning of hyperparameters of machine learning models is one common example. It uses prior knowledge about the function to be optimized to construct a probabilistic model of the function that is easy to optimize. Knowledge about the model parameters is adjusted to accomodate input from function evaluations $f(x_0), f(x_1), \ldots, f(x_n)$. An *acquisition function* is then used to decide which points of the function to query next in order to improve in the most effective way possible knowledge about the maximum.

In this work, we use Bayesian optimization to build an effective key search policy for reduced-round Speck. This key search policy drastically reduces the number of trial decryptions used by our basic attack, at the cost of a somewhat expensive optimization step. The basic idea of our key search policy is that the expected response of our distinguisher upon wrong-key decryption will depend on the bitwise difference between the trial key and the real key. This *wrong-key response profile* can be captured in a precomputation. Given some trial decryptions, the optimization step then tries to come up with a new set of key hypotheses to try. These new key hypotheses are chosen such that they maximize the probability of the observed distinguisher responses.

Model Assumptions. Let C_0, C_1 be a ciphertext pair and let k be the real subkey used in the final round of encryption. Let $\delta \in \mathbb{F}_2^{16}$ and let $k' = k \oplus \delta$ be a wrong key. Denote the response of our distinguisher D to decryption by the key k' by $R_{D,\delta}(C_0, C_1) := D(E_{k'}^{-1}(C_0), E_{k'}^{-1}(C_1))$. We can then view $R_{D,\delta}$ as a random

---

[2] Running the same code with different parameters, other attacks can be obtained. The code repository, for instance, contains parameters for a 12-round attack that is practical on a single PC (with the parameters used, average runtime is under an hour on a GeForce GTX 1080 Ti GPU and success rate is ≈40%).

variable depending on δ induced by the ciphertext pair distribution and compute its mean μ_δ and standard deviation σ_δ. If we average the distinguisher response over all elements of a ciphertext structure of size n as used in our attack, the average can be expected to approximately follow a normal distribution[3] with mean μ_δ and standard deviation $\sigma_\delta/\sqrt{n}$.

Wrong Key Randomization. We calculated the wrong key response profile for our six- and seven round distinguishers for Speck32/64. To calculate the $r + 1$-round wrong key response profile, we generated 3000 random keys and message input pairs P_0, P_1 for each δ and encrypted for $r + 1$ rounds to obtain ciphertexts C_0, C_1. Denoting the final subkey of each encryption operation by k, we then performed single-round decryption to get $E_{k\oplus\delta}^{-1}(C_0), E_{k\oplus\delta}^{-1}(C_1)$ and had the resulting partially decrypted ciphertext pair rated by an r-round neural distinguisher. μ_δ and σ_δ were then calculated as empirical mean and standard deviation over these 3000 trials. The wrong key response profile for seven rounds is shown in Fig. 3. A lot of non-random structure is evident. The shape of the curves for σ_δ and for six rounds is similar.

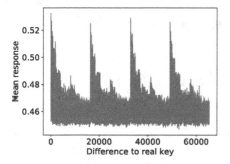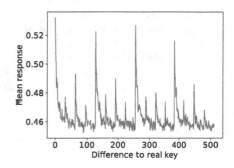

Fig. 3. Wrong key response profile (only μ_δ shown) for 8-round Speck32/64 and our 7-round neural distinguisher. For each difference δ between trial key and right key, 3000 ciphertext pairs with the input difference $0x0040/0000$ were encrypted for 8 rounds of Speck using randomly generated keys and then decrypted for one round using a final subkey at difference δ to the right key. Differences are shown on the x-axis, while mean response over the 3000 pairs tried is shown in the y-axis.

Using the Wrong-Key Response Profile for Key Search. Given our model assumptions and observations of the distinguisher response $r_0, r_1, \ldots, r_{n-1}$ for keys $k_0, k_1, \ldots, k_{n-1}$, we can view the r_i as values obtained from an n-dimensional normal distribution. The parameters of this normal distribution depend on the bitwise differences of the k_i to the real last subkey k, specifically on $\mu_{k\oplus k_i}$ and

---

[3] Note that for our neural networks, this argument can be slightly strengthened if the final sigmoid activation is removed, since then distinguisher output on an individual ciphertext pair is just a linear combination of 64 somewhat independent intermediate network units.

$\sigma_{k\oplus k_i}$. It is easy to see that the probability density at the observed values is maximised by minimizing the weighted euclidean distance $\sum_{i=0}^{n-1}(m_i - \mu_{k\oplus k_i})^2/\sigma_{k\oplus k_i}^2$. Our algorithm first generates a set of random key candidates, then scores those keys by decrypting the ciphertext structure currently under study, then calculates the average distinguisher response on the tried keys, and finds a new set of key candidates that bring the precomputed wrong key response profile in line with the observed values as well as possible. This is iterated for a few cycles. Algorithm 4 sums up the algorithm.

Algorithm 4. BayesianKeySearch: efficiently find a list of plausible key candidates given a ciphertext structure satisfying the initial differential of our attack.

Require: Ciphertext structure $C = C_0, \ldots C_{m-1}$, neural distinguisher N, number of candidates to be generated n, number of iterations l.

1: $S := \{k_0, k_1, \ldots, k_{n-1}\} \leftarrow$ choose at random without replacement from the set of all subkey candidates.
2: $L \leftarrow \{\}$
3: **for** $j \in \{0, 1, \ldots, l-1\}$: **do**
4:     $P_{i,k} \leftarrow Decrypt(C_i, k)$ for all $i \in \{0, 1, \ldots, m-1\}$, $k \in S$.
5:     $v_{i,k} \leftarrow N(P_{i,k})$ for all i,k
6:     $w_{i,k} \leftarrow \log_2(v_{i,k}/(1-v_{i,k}))$ for all $i \in \{0, \ldots, m-1\}, k \in S$
7:     $w_k \leftarrow \sum_{i=1}^{n} v_{i,k}$ for all$k \in S$
8:     $L \leftarrow L||[(k, w_k)$ for $k \in S]$
9:     $m_k \leftarrow \sum_{i=0}^{n-1} v_{i,k}/n$ for $k \in \{k_0, \ldots, k_{n-1}\}$
10:     $\lambda_k \leftarrow \sum_{i=0}^{n-1}(m_{k_i} - \mu_{k_i \oplus k})^2/\sigma_{k_i \oplus k}^2$ for $k \in \{0, 1, \ldots, 2^{16} - 1\}$:
11:     $S \leftarrow \text{argsort}_k(\lambda)[0 : n-1]$
12: **end for**
13: **return** L

All keys tried and their scores w_k on the current ciphertext structure are stored. Keys that obtain a score above a cutoff threshold c_1 are expanded by repeating the process for one further round, i.e. Algorithm 4 is used with a six-round neural distinguisher and its associated wrong key response profile. If one of the resulting key candidates scores above another threshold c_2, we determine that the search will be terminated, but the processing of the current search node is finished before the best pair of subkeys found for the last two rounds is returned.

Before we return a key, we perform a small verification search with hamming radius two around the two subkey candidates that are currently best. This removes remaining bit errors in the key guess. If the verification search yields an improvement, it is repeated with the new best key guess.

Given t ciphertext structures, our algorithm is first tried on each structure. If no solution is found, since Algorithm 4 is probabilistic, we continue for a preset number of iterations it before returning the highest-scoring pair of subkeys for the last two rounds. During these additional iterations, we have to actively decide which ciphertext structures we will spend our computational budget on.

We treat this as a multi-armed bandit problem and solve it using a standard exploration-exploitation technique, namely Upper Confidence Bounds (UCB). The order of the ciphertext structures to be tested in this phase depends on the highest distinguisher score obtained in the last-key search for the structures so far and on the number of visits they have received in our search. Specifically, denote by $w^i_{\max}$ the highest distinguisher score obtained so far for the ith ciphertext structure, by n_i the number of previous iterations in which the ith ciphertext structure has been selected, and by j the number of the current iteration. We calculate a priority score

$$s_i := w^i_{\max} + \alpha \cdot \sqrt{\log_2(j)/n_i} \tag{5}$$

and pick the ciphertext structure with the highest priority score for further processing. The visit count and the best result for this ciphertext structure are updated after the iteration has finished. We set α to $\sqrt{n_c}$, where n_c is the number of ciphertext structures available.

Results. In the trials subsequently described, we use 100 ciphertext structures of 64 chosen plaintext pair encryptions each, the cutoff parameters $c_1 = 5$, $c_2 = 10$, the UCB exploration term $\alpha = 10$, an iteration count for the Bayesian key search policy of $l = 5$ and candidate number $n = 32$, and an iteration budget for the main loop it = 500. Given a hundred ciphertext structures, our implementation outputs a key guess in approximately eight minutes on average (measured average in 100 trials: 500.68 s) when running on a single thread of our machine with no graphics card usage. This key guess is not always correct, but if it is not, this is easily apparent from the scores returned. When a fast graphics card is used, performance of our proof of concept implementation is not limited by the speed of neural network evaluation, but by the key search policy. The key search policy tries with the settings mentioned only 160 keys when processing a ciphertext structure.

We count a key guess as successful if the last round key was guessed correctly and if the second round key is at hamming distance at most two of the real key. Under these conditions, the attack was successful in 521 out of 1000 trials; recovery of the first round key was successful in 521 cases and in all of these cases, the second round key guess was wrong for at most two bits within the most significant nibble. For comparison, the attack presented in [19] is expected to succeed with the same data complexity in about 55% of all trials. In the simple model where in case of failure we request ciphertext values for another 100 plaintext structures, we expect that this attack will on average use $2^{14.5}$ chosen plaintexts until success, slightly more than [19].

Computational Complexity. We estimate that a highly optimized, fully SIMD-parallelized implementation of Speck32/64 could perform brute force key search on our system at a speed of about 2^{28} keys per second per core. Adjusting for the empirically measured success rate of our attack we expect to need about 1000 s on average to execute the key recovery algorithm on a single core of our system. This yields an estimated computational attack complexity of 2^{38} Speck encryptions until a solution is found. The additional effort needed for full-key recovery is negligible, since at that point a good ciphertext structure has been found and the same attack can be launched on that single ciphertext structure with distinguishers for less rounds of Speck.

5 The Real Differences Experiment

5.1 Summary

In this section, we design a cryptographic experiment in which the adversary has to do differential cryptanalysis in a setting where the random and the real difference distribution are the same. We show that our neural distinguishers are successful in this experiment and compare their efficiency to solving the same problem by key search in the case of five-round Speck.

5.2 Experiment

Motivation. We have seen in the previous section that our best neural distinguishers are better at recognizing Speck32/64 reduced up to eight rounds than a distinguisher based on the full difference distribution table. We have also seen that the Markov model at least predicts its own distinguishing success rate fairly well and have seen some evidence that the neural distinguishers exploit features outside the difference distribution table, e.g. from the fact that our neural distinguishers break Proposition 1. This section looks at that topic in isolation.

To this end, we introduce a differential cryptographic distinguishing task in which perfect knowledge of the differential distribution of a primitive under study does not in itself allow the adversary to do better than random guessing.

Experimental Setup. First, 10^6 samples were drawn from the real distribution for the D5, D6, D7 and D8 tasks. Then, half of these samples were randomized in the following way: for an output ciphertext pair $C = (C_0, C_1) \in \mathbb{F}_2^{2b}$ to be randomized, a blinding value $K \in \mathbb{F}_2^b$ was generated uniformly at random by reading from /dev/urandom. This value was bitwise-added to both ciphertexts to produce the randomized ciphertext $\tilde{C} = (C_0 \oplus K, C_1 \oplus K)$.

The resulting 10^6 samples of randomized or non-randomized ciphertext pairs were preprocessed as previously described and the results were passed to the appropriate pretrained neural network for classification as random or real. No further training took place.

Rationale. The distribution of difference values is clearly the same in both the random and the real sample in this experiment. On the other hand, in the random sample any information about the ciphertext other than the difference between the two ciphertext blocks given is perfectly hidden, as the blinding makes the results of the random sampling uniformly distributed on the hyperplane given by each possible difference.

Adapting Key Search. For reference, the key search based distinguisher on five rounds from Sect. 3 was modified to work in the real differences setting. In this setting, an exact solution by counting the keys leading to a decryption with the desired input difference seems infeasible, as both random and real examples are expected to regularly have a very high number of solutions. We therefore calculate two approximations to N_{keys}.

First, we calculate $A_{\text{rand}} := 2^{64} \cdot DP(\Delta C)$, where $DP(\Delta C)$ is the differential probability of observing the output difference of the ciphertext pair C as given by the Markov model of Speck.

Second, denoting by $\mathcal{D}_{\text{mid}}$ the set of possible round 3 differences, by $P(\delta)$ the probability of observing the round 3 difference δ, and by $N_\delta(C)$ the number of solutions for the final two subkeys that decrypt our observed ciphertext pair C to the round 3 difference δ, we compute $A_{\text{real}} := 2^{32} \cdot \sum_{\delta \in \mathcal{D}_{\text{mid}}} P(\delta) \cdot N_\delta(C)$.

C is then predicted as real if $A_{\text{real}} > A_{\text{rand}}$ and as random otherwise.

Results. Our best networks were found to solve the real differences task measurably better than random guessing without ever having explicitly been trained for it. Training on the real differences task was tried in the five-round case and expanded this advantage considerably. Predictably, however, key search yielded clearly superior distinguishing power. See Table 4 for details.

Table 4. Performance of neural distinguishers in the real differences experiment. For comparison, the performance of a key search based distinguisher and a version of the N5 network retrained to this task are also given. Test set size is 10^6 for the neural distinguishers and 10^4 for Search.

Nr	Distinguisher	Accuracy
5	N5	$0.707 \pm 9.10 \cdot 10^{-4}$
6	N6	$0.606 \pm 9.77 \cdot 10^{-4}$
7	N7	$0.551 \pm 9.95 \cdot 10^{-4}$
8	N8	$0.507 \pm 1.00 \cdot 10^{-3}$
5	Search	$0.810 \pm 7.84 \cdot 10^{-3}$
5	N5 retrained	$0.762 \pm 8.51 \cdot 10^{-4}$

These tests show that ciphertext pairs are not evenly distributed within their respective difference equivalence classes. Indeed, using neural distinguishers as a search tool it is easy to find examples of ciphertext pairs with relatively high-likelihood differences which have very little chance of appearing in the ciphertext pair distribution of reduced Speck. One such example has already been discussed in Sect. 4.4. For another, consider the output pair (0x58e0bc4, 0x85a4ff6c). It has the ciphertext difference 0x802a/f4a8, which is a high probability output difference for five round Speck given our input difference ($p \approx 2^{-15.3}$ according to the full Markov model, which matches empirical trials well here). However, the pair decrypts to our input difference with a much lower likelihood, around $2^{-35.3}$ according to our calculations.

Constraining the Additional Signal. If we constrain the blinding values used in the real differences experiment to be of the form aa, where a is any 16-bit word, our distinguishers fail. This is consistent with the observation that the distinguishers do not exploit the key schedule, as addition of a blinding value of this form is equivalent to changing the final subkey used in encryption. It also suggests that the networks exploit a strictly more fine-grained partition of the output pairs into equivalence classes than the difference equivalence classes. We find that intra-class variance of distinguisher output is very low for these equivalence classes and that also the input representations generated by the penultimate network layer show tight clustering.

6   Conclusions

We have tested in this paper whether neural networks can be used to develop statistical tests that efficiently exploit differential properties of a symmetric primitive that has been weakened sufficiently by round reduction to allow for attacks to be carried out in a low data setting. In the setting considered, this works reasonably well: our distinguishers offer classification accuracy superior to the difference distribution table for the primitive in question and use less memory, even if inference speed is of course low compared to the simple memory lookup needed with a precomputed difference distribution table. We consider it interesting that this much knowledge about the differential distribution of round-reduced Speck can be extracted from a few million examples by black-box methods.

The time needed to train a network from the ground up to an accuracy level beyond the difference distribution table is on the order of minutes in our trials when a single fast graphics card is available. Our networks start training with no cryptographic knowledge beyond the word-structure of the cipher, making our approach fairly generic. The transfer learning capabilities shown in this paper demonstrate that finding good input differences from scratch is likewise possible using our networks with minimal input of prior cryptographic knowledge. Our distinguishers have various novel properties, most notably the ability to differentiate between ciphertext pairs within the same difference class.

In the context of this study, it certainly helped that Speck32/64 is a small blocksize, lightweight primitive. However, this is true both for the optimisation of conventional attacks and for the application of machine learning.

Given that the present work is an initial case study, we would not be surprised if our results could be improved. Various directions for further research suggest themselves. For instance, it would be interesting if a reasonably generic way were found to give the model to be trained more prior knowledge about the cipher or to enable the researcher to more easily extract knowledge from a trained model.

Small improvements to network performance are also completely expected to be possible within the architecture and setting given by this paper.

It would be interesting to see the effect of giving the network cryptographic knowledge in the form of precomputed features. We did some tests along these lines, for instance by giving the prediction head a classification derived from the difference distribution table as an additional input, but this was only marginally helpful.

The use of Bayesian optimization and related methods for key search could be of more general interest whenever an attack exploits a statistical distinguisher with high evaluation cost. This could be a neural network, but for instance ordinary statistical distinguishers that need to be evaluated on very large sets of ciphertexts to be effective may also be examples.

We do not think that machine learning methods will supplant traditional cryptanalysis. However, we do think that our results show that neural networks can learn to do cryptanalysis at a level that is interesting for a cryptographer and that ML methods can be a useful addition to the cryptographic evaluators' tool box. We expect that similar to other general-purpose tools used in cryptography such as SAT solvers or Groebner basis methods, machine learning will not solve cryptography but usefully complement and support conventional dedicated methods of doing research on the security of symmetric constructions.

Acknowledgments. The author wishes to thank the anonymous reviewers for their questions and comments, as they helped him to improve the present paper.

References

1. Abadi, M., Andersen, D.G.: Learning to protect communications with adversarial neural cryptography. arXiv preprint arXiv:1610.06918 (2016)
2. Abed, F., List, E., Lucks, S., Wenzel, J.: Differential cryptanalysis of round-reduced SIMON and SPECK. In: Cid, C., Rechberger, C. (eds.) FSE 2014. LNCS, vol. 8540, pp. 525–545. Springer, Heidelberg (2015). https://doi.org/10.1007/978-3-662-46706-0_27
3. Albrecht, M.R., Leander, G.: An all-in-one approach to differential cryptanalysis for small block ciphers. In: Knudsen, L.R., Wu, H. (eds.) SAC 2012. LNCS, vol. 7707, pp. 1–15. Springer, Heidelberg (2013). https://doi.org/10.1007/978-3-642-35999-6_1
4. Ankele, R., Kölbl, S.: Mind the gap – a closer look at the security of block ciphers against differential cryptanalysis. In: Cid, C., Jacobson, M. (eds.) SAC 2018. LNCS, vol. 11349, pp. 163–190. Springer, Cham (2019). https://doi.org/10.1007/978-3-030-10970-7_8
5. Ashur, T., Bodden, D.: Linear cryptanalysis of reduced-round SPECK. In: Proceedings of the 37th Symposium on Information Theory in the Benelux, Werkgemeenschap voor Informatie-en Communicatietheorie (2016)
6. Awad, W.S., El-Alfy, E.-S.: Computational intelligence in cryptology. In: Improving Information Security Practices through Computational Intelligence, pp. 28–45 (2015)
7. Bahdanau, D., Cho, K., Bengio, Y.: Neural machine translation by jointly learning to align and translate. arXiv preprint arXiv:1409.0473 (2014)

8. Beaulieu, R., Shors, D., Smith, J., Treatman-Clark, S., Weeks, B., Wingers, L.: SIMON and SPECK: block ciphers for the Internet of Things. IACR Cryptology ePrint Archive 2015/585 (2015)
9. Beaulieu, R., Treatman-Clark, S., Shors, D., Weeks, B., Smith, J., Wingers, L.: The SIMON and SPECK lightweight block ciphers. In: 52nd ACM/EDAC/IEEE Design Automation Conference (DAC), 2015, pp. 1–6. IEEE (2015)
10. Biham, E., Chen, R.: Near-collisions of SHA-0. In: Franklin, M. (ed.) CRYPTO 2004. LNCS, vol. 3152, pp. 290–305. Springer, Heidelberg (2004). https://doi.org/10.1007/978-3-540-28628-8_18
11. Biryukov, A., Velichkov, V., Le Corre, Y.: Automatic search for the best trails in ARX: application to block cipher SPECK. In: Peyrin, T. (ed.) FSE 2016. LNCS, vol. 9783, pp. 289–310. Springer, Heidelberg (2016). https://doi.org/10.1007/978-3-662-52993-5_15
12. Blondeau, C., Gérard, B.: Multiple differential cryptanalysis: theory and practice. In: Joux, A. (ed.) FSE 2011. LNCS, vol. 6733, pp. 35–54. Springer, Heidelberg (2011). https://doi.org/10.1007/978-3-642-21702-9_3
13. Chen, C., Seff, A., Kornhauser, A., Xiao, J.: Deepdriving: learning affordance for direct perception in autonomous driving. In: 2015 IEEE International Conference on Computer Vision (ICCV), pp. 2722–2730. IEEE (2015)
14. Chollet, F., et al. Keras (2015). https://keras.io
15. Chou, J.-W., Lin, S.-D., Cheng, C.-M.: On the effectiveness of using state-of-the-art machine learning techniques to launch cryptographic distinguishing attacks. In: Proceedings of the 5th ACM Workshop on Security and Artificial Intelligence, pp. 105–110. ACM (2012)
16. Clark, C., Storkey, A.: Training deep convolutional neural networks to play go. In: International Conference on Machine Learning, pp. 1766–1774 (2015)
17. Danziger, M., Henriques, M.A.A.: Improved cryptanalysis combining differential and artificial neural network schemes. In: 2014 International Telecommunications Symposium (ITS), pp. 1–5. IEEE (2014)
18. de Mello, F., Xexéo, J.: Identifying encryption algorithms in ECB and CBC modes using computational intelligence. J. Univ. Comput. Sci. **24**(1), 25–42 (2018)
19. Dinur, I.: Improved differential cryptanalysis of round-reduced speck. In: Joux, A., Youssef, A. (eds.) SAC 2014. LNCS, vol. 8781, pp. 147–164. Springer, Cham (2014). https://doi.org/10.1007/978-3-319-13051-4_9
20. Gomez, A.N., Huang, S., Zhang, I., Li, B.M., Osama, M., Kaiser, L.: Unsupervised cipher cracking using discrete GANs. In International Conference on Learning Representations (2018)
21. Greydanus, S.: Learning the enigma with recurrent neural networks. arXiv preprint arXiv:1708.07576 (2017)
22. He, K., Zhang, X., Ren, S., Sun, J.: Deep residual learning for image recognition. In: Proceedings of the IEEE Conference on Computer Vision and Pattern Recognition, pp. 770–778 (2016)
23. Hinton, G., Vinyals, O., Dean, J.: Distilling the knowledge in a neural network. arXiv preprint: arXiv 1503.02531 (2015)
24. Kingma, D.P., Ba, J.: Adam: a method for stochastic optimization. arXiv preprint arXiv:1412.6980 (2014)
25. Klimov, A., Mityagin, A., Shamir, A.: Analysis of neural cryptography. In: Zheng, Y. (ed.) ASIACRYPT 2002. LNCS, vol. 2501, pp. 288–298. Springer, Heidelberg (2002). https://doi.org/10.1007/3-540-36178-2_18
26. Lagerhjelm, L.: Extracting information from encrypted data using deep neural networks. Master's thesis, Umeå University (2018)

27. Lai, X., Massey, J.L., Murphy, S.: Markov ciphers and differential cryptanalysis. In: Davies, D.W. (ed.) EUROCRYPT 1991. LNCS, vol. 547, pp. 17–38. Springer, Heidelberg (1991). https://doi.org/10.1007/3-540-46416-6_2

28. Laskari, E.C., Meletiou, G.C., Stamatiou, Y.C., Vrahatis, M.N.: Cryptography and cryptanalysis through computational intelligence. In: Nedjah, N., Abraham, A., Mourelle, L.M. (eds.) Computational Intelligence in Information Assurance and Security. Studies in Computational Intelligence, vol. 57, pp. 1–49. Springer, Heidelberg (2007). https://doi.org/10.1007/978-3-540-71078-3_1

29. Lipmaa, H., Moriai, S.: Efficient algorithms for computing differential properties of addition. In: Matsui, M. (ed.) FSE 2001. LNCS, vol. 2355, pp. 336–350. Springer, Heidelberg (2002). https://doi.org/10.1007/3-540-45473-X_28

30. Liu, Y., Kai, F., Wang, W., Sun, L., Wang, M.: Linear cryptanalysis of reduced-round SPECK. Inf. Process. Lett. **116**(3), 259–266 (2016)

31. Maghrebi, H., Portigliatti, T., Prouff, E.: Breaking cryptographic implementations using deep learning techniques. In: Carlet, C., Hasan, M.A., Saraswat, V. (eds.) SPACE 2016. LNCS, vol. 10076, pp. 3–26. Springer, Cham (2016). https://doi.org/10.1007/978-3-319-49445-6_1

32. Paterson, K.G., Poettering, B., Schuldt, J.C.N.: Big bias hunting in amazonia: large-scale computation and exploitation of RC4 biases (invited paper). In: Sarkar, P., Iwata, T. (eds.) ASIACRYPT 2014. LNCS, vol. 8873, pp. 398–419. Springer, Heidelberg (2014). https://doi.org/10.1007/978-3-662-45611-8_21

33. Pelikan, M., Goldberg, D.E., Cantú-Paz, E.: BOA: the bayesian optimization algorithm. In: Proceedings of the 1st Annual Conference on Genetic and Evolutionary Computation, vol. 1, pp. 525–532. Morgan Kaufmann Publishers Inc. (1999)

34. Picek, S., Heuser, A., Guilley: Template attack vs bayes classifier. Technical report, Cryptology ePrint Archive, Report 2017/531/2017 (2016)

35. Picek, S., Samiotis, I.P., Kim, J., Heuser, A., Bhasin, S., Legay, A.: On the performance of convolutional neural networks for side-channel analysis. In: Chattopadhyay, A., Rebeiro, C., Yarom, Y. (eds.) SPACE 2018. LNCS, vol. 11348, pp. 157–176. Springer, Cham (2018). https://doi.org/10.1007/978-3-030-05072-6_10

36. Rivest, R.L.: Cryptography and machine learning. In: Imai, H., Rivest, R.L., Matsumoto, T. (eds.) ASIACRYPT 1991. LNCS, vol. 739, pp. 427–439. Springer, Heidelberg (1993). https://doi.org/10.1007/3-540-57332-1_36

37. Silver, D., et al.: Mastering the game of go with deep neural networks and tree search. Nature **529**(7587), 484–489 (2016)

38. Silver, D., et al.: A general reinforcement learning algorithm that masters chess, shogi, and go through self-play. Science **362**(6419), 1140–1144 (2018)

39. Silver, D., et al.: Mastering the game of go without human knowledge. Nature **550**(7676), 354 (2017)

40. Wu, Y., et al.: Google's neural machine translation system: bridging the gap between human and machine translation. arXiv preprint arXiv:1609.08144 (2016)

Correlation of Quadratic Boolean Functions: Cryptanalysis of All Versions of Full MORUS

Danping Shi[1,2], Siwei Sun[1,2,3(✉)], Yu Sasaki[4], Chaoyun Li[5], and Lei Hu[1,2,3]

[1] State Key Laboratory of Information Security,
Institute of Information Engineering, Chinese Academy of Sciences,
Beijing, China
{shidanping,sunsiwei,hulei}@iie.ac.cn
[2] Data Assurance and Communication Security Research Center,
Chinese Academy of Sciences, Beijing, China
[3] School of Cyber Security, University of Chinese Academy of Sciences,
Beijing, China
[4] NTT Secure Platform Laboratories, Tokyo, Japan
sasaki.yu@lab.ntt.co.jp
[5] imec-COSIC, Department Electrical Engineering (ESAT), KU Leuven,
Leuven, Belgium
chaoyun.li@esat.kuleuven.be

Abstract. We show that the correlation of any quadratic Boolean function can be read out from its so-called *disjoint quadratic form*. We further propose a polynomial-time algorithm that can transform an arbitrary quadratic Boolean function into its disjoint quadratic form. With this algorithm, the exact correlation of quadratic Boolean functions can be computed efficiently.

We apply this method to analyze the linear trails of MORUS (one of the seven finalists of the CAESAR competition), which are found with the help of a generic model for linear trails of MORUS-like key-stream generators. In our model, any tool for finding linear trails of block ciphers can be used to search for trails of MORUS-like key-stream generators. As a result, a set of trails with correlation 2^{-38} is identified for all versions of full MORUS, while the correlations of previously published best trails for MORUS-640 and MORUS-1280 are 2^{-73} and 2^{-76} respectively (ASIACRYPT 2018). This significantly improves the complexity of the attack on MORUS-1280-256 from 2^{152} to 2^{76}. These new trails also lead to the first distinguishing and message-recovery attacks on MORUS-640-128 and MORUS-1280-128 with surprisingly low complexities around 2^{76}.

Moreover, we observe that the condition for exploiting these trails in an attack can be more relaxed than previously thought, which shows that the new trails are superior to previously published ones in terms of both correlation and the number of ciphertext blocks involved.

Keywords: Quadratic Boolean function · Disjoint quadratic form · Correlation attack · CAESAR competition · MORUS · MILP

© International Association for Cryptologic Research 2019
A. Boldyreva and D. Micciancio (Eds.): CRYPTO 2019, LNCS 11693, pp. 180–209, 2019.
https://doi.org/10.1007/978-3-030-26951-7_7

1   Introduction

The notion of authenticated encryption (AE), which provides both confidentiality and authenticity, was first introduced by Bellare and Namprempre around 2000 [4,5]. It was further developed and evolved into the notion of authenticated encryption with associated data (AEAD) [25–27] to capture the settings of real-world communication networks, where the authenticity of some public information (e.g., packet header) must be ensured. Informally, an AEAD is a secret-key scheme involving an encryption algorithm and a decryption algorithm. Its encryption algorithm receives a plaintext or message M, an associated data A, and a secret key K, and produces a ciphertext C and a tag T. The authenticity of the message and associated data can be checked against the tag T. We refer the reader to [25] for a more rigorous treatment of the definition of AEAD.

The CAESAR competition (the Competition for Authenticated Encryption: Security, Applicability, and Robustness) was announced at the Early Symmetric-key Crypto workshop 2013 [13] and also on-line at [7]. After several years of intensive analysis and comparison of the 57 submissions, the finalists were announced at FSE 2018. In this work, our target is one of the seven finalists—MORUS [35], which provides three main variants: MORUS-640 with a 128-bit key, and MORUS-1280 with either a 128-bit or a 256-bit key.

Related Work. Apart from the analysis provided by the designers, MORUS has received extensive third-party cryptanalysis. These cryptanalysis include differential cryptanalysis [12,23,29], linear cryptanalysis [19], SAT-based cryptanalysis [11], cube cryptanalysis [19,28], state-recovery [17,34] and key-recovery attacks [12], as well as attacks in the nonce-reuse setting [23]. However, these attacks either target round-reduced versions of MORUS, or are launched in the nonce-reuse setting which is contradicting to the nonce-respect assumption assumed by the designers. Therefore, none of these analysis violates the security claims of MORUS.

A major breakthrough on the cryptanalysis of MORUS was made at ASIACRYPT 2018 [2]. In this work, based on rotational-invariant linear approximations, Ashur et al. transfered linear approximations for a state-reduced version of MORUS (named as MiniMORUS) to linear approximations for MORUS. Linear approximations in the ciphertext bits with correlation 2^{-73} and 2^{-76} were identified for MORUS-640 and MORUS-1280 respectively. The approximation of MORUS-1280 leads to distinguishing attacks and message-recovery attacks on the full MORUS-1280 with 256-bit key. Since it requires about $2^{2\times76} = 2^{152}$ encryptions to exploit the correlation, MORUS-1280 with 128-bit keys remain immune to these attacks. Similarly, to exploit the correlation of MORUS-640, it requires about 2^{146} encryptions, which means MORUS-640-128 is also immune to these attacks.

Our Contribution. In this work, we investigate the problem of computing the correlation of quadratic Boolean functions. By transforming a quadratic

Boolean function into its so-called *disjoint quadratic form*, we propose, to the best of our knowledge, the first *polynomial time* algorithm that can determine the correlation of an arbitrary quadratic Boolean function, while in previous work (e.g., [2]), such correlations are computed with exhaustive or quite ad-hoc approaches which intrinsically limits their effectiveness.

Equipped with this new weapon, we set out to search for more complex rotational invariant linear trails of MORUS, and then compute their correlations with the new method. To this end, we set up a model for finding linear trails of MORUS-like key-stream generators, such that most existing search tools can be applied. The model we proposed is generic and can be applied to many other schemes, which is of independent interest. Eventually, using MILP based approach, we identify trails of all versions of MORUS which lead to significant improvement over the previous attack on MORUS-1280-256 presented by Ashur et al. [2]. Generally, the complexity is reduced from 2^{152} to 2^{76}. Moreover, these trails result in the first attacks on full MORUS-640 and MORUS-1280 with 128-bit key. A summary of the results are given in Table 1, from which we can see that the attack is not marginal and the complexities are approaching the boundary of practical attacks. We verify the attacks on a reduced version of MORUS. Also, following Ashur et al.'s approach [2], we verify all trail fragments for all versions of full MORUS.

Along the way, we make an interesting observation that the condition imposed on Ashur et al.'s attack can be relaxed. Specifically, the attacks actually only require that enough plaintexts with a common prefix of certain size are encrypted, rather than the same plaintext is encrypted enough times as stated in [2]. This observation motivates us to find trails involving a smaller number of ciphertext blocks, since the common-prefix assumption does occur in some practical protocols.

At this point, we would like to mention that even after Ashur et al.'s work [2], many researchers are not sure if MORUS will stay in the competition given the high complexities of the attacks and the status of MORUS-640-128 and MORUS-1280-128. However, we think that the new attacks breaking all versions of full MORUS with complexity around 2^{76} severely shake the security confidence of MORUS and should deserve more attentions. Finally, our technique is purely linear, and most of the attacks presented in our paper are known-plaintext attacks, where we do not rely on any property of the output of the initialization process except its randomness. Hence, it is interesting to see how to improve our analysis by applying the differential-linear framework [3,18].

The exact linear trails we used can be found in an extended version of the paper at https://eprint.iacr.org/2019/172, and the source code is available at https://github.com/siweisun/attack_morus.

Organization. In Sect. 2, we give a brief visualized description of the authenticated encryption scheme MORUS. Then in Sect. 3, we show how to compute the correlation of a quadratic Boolean function by transforming it into the so-called disjoint quadratic form. A generic model for finding linear trails of MORUS-like

Table 1. A summary of the results, where the span indicates the number of ciphertext blocks involved in the linear approximations.

Target	Linear masks of the ciphertext blocks	Span	|Correlation|	Data	Time	Source
MiniMORUS-640	08000000 04000105 8800a002 00105040 00080000	5	2^{-16}	2^{32}	2^{32}	[2]
	10000000 08000202 00004103 00002000	4	2^{-8}	2^{16}	2^{16}	Sect. 5
MiniMORUS-1280	00080000000000000 00800202000000001 0008406020000090 0004040000108000 0000000001000000	5	2^{-16}	2^{32}	2^{32}	[2]
	00000000010000 400000002010000 00000022000804 000000000008000	4	2^{-8}	2^{16}	2^{16}	Sect. 5
MORUS-640-128	10000000 10000000 10000000 10000000 08000202 08000202 08000202 08000202 00004103 00004103 00004103 00004103 00002C00 00002000 00002000 00002000	4	2^{-38}	2^{76}	2^{76}	Sect. 5
MORUS-1280-128	0000000000010000 0000000000010000 0000000000010000 0000000000010000 4000000020100000 4000000020100000 4000000020100000 4000000020100000 0000000220000804 0000000220000804 0000000220000804 0000000220000804 0000000000008000 0000000000008000 0000000000008000 0000000000008000	4	2^{-38}	2^{76}	2^{76}	Sect. 5
MORUS-1280-256	0008000000000000 0008000000000000 0008000000000000 0008000000000000 0080000202000001 0080000202000001 0080000202000001 0080000202000001 0008406020000090 0008406020000090 0008406020000090 0008406020000090 0004040000100800 0004040000100800 0004040000100800 0004040000100800 0000000001000000 0000000001000000 0000000001000000 0000000001000000	5	2^{-76}	2^{152}	2^{152}	[2]
	0000000000010000 0000000000010000 0000000000010000 0000000000010000 4000000020100000 4000000020100000 4000000020100000 4000000020100000 0000000220000804 0000000220000804 0000000220000804 0000000220000804 0000000000008000 0000000000008000 0000000000008000 0000000000008000	4	2^{-38}	2^{76}	2^{76}	Sect. 5

key-stream generators is constructed in Sect. 4, which is employed in Sect. 5 to search for linear trails of MORUS with high absolute correlations, leading to attacks on all versions of full MORUS. Section 6 discusses the condition of the attacks presented in the previous section and clarifies why trails involving a smaller number of ciphertext blocks are preferred. We propose some open problems and conclude in Sect. 7.

2   Specification of **MORUS** and **MiniMORUS**

We give a brief description of MORUS and MiniMORUS, which largely follows the notations used by Ashur et al. [2] to facilitate cross checking.

2.1   **MORUS**

MORUS is a family of AEAD schemes [35] whose interfaces are shown in Fig. 1. The encryption algorithm of MORUS operates on a $5q$-bit state composed of five q-bit registers ($q \in \{128, 256\}$), and each register is divided into four $q/4$-bit words as shown in Fig. 2, where we use $S_{i,j}$ to denote the jth bit of the ith register S_i of the $5q$-bit state S. The three recommended parameter sets of MORUS are listed in Table 2. Note that when the exact key size is not important, we use MORUS-640 and MORUS-1280 to denote the versions with 640-bit state and 1280-bit state, respectively.

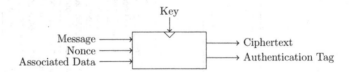

Fig. 1. The high-level structure of the encryption algorithm of an AEAD scheme

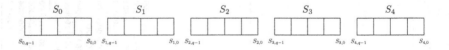

Fig. 2. A view of the MORUS internal state

During the encryption process of MORUS, a function

$$\texttt{StateUpdate} : \mathbb{F}_2^{5q} \times \mathbb{F}_2^{q} \to \mathbb{F}_2^{5q}$$

is repeatedly executed on the internal state. Each call to the `StateUpdate` function is called a step. We denote the state at the very beginning of the encryption

Table 2. The three variants of MORUS, where the sizes are measured in bits

Name	State size (5q)	Register size (q)	Word size (q/4)	Key size	Tag size
MORUS-640-128	640	128	32	128	128
MORUS-1280-128	1280	256	64	128	128
MORUS-1280-256	1280	256	64	256	128

process by $S^{-16} = S_0^{-16} \parallel S_1^{-16} \parallel S_2^{-16} \parallel S_3^{-16} \parallel S_4^{-16}$. After a series of steps, a sequence of states is produced:

$$S^{-16} \xrightarrow{\text{StateUpdate}} S^{-15} \xrightarrow{\text{StateUpdate}} \cdots \xrightarrow{\text{StateUpdate}} S^0 \xrightarrow{\text{StateUpdate}} \cdots$$

Therefore, we can use the notion $S^t = S_0^t \parallel S_1^t \parallel S_2^t \parallel S_3^t \parallel S_4^t$ to reference the state at step t. The detail of the StateUpdate function is shown in the following equations:

$$
\begin{aligned}
S_0^{t+1} &\leftarrow (S_0^t \oplus (S_1^t \cdot S_2^t) \oplus S_3^t) \lll_w b_0, & S_3^t &\leftarrow S_3^t \lll b_0', \\
S_1^{t+1} &\leftarrow (S_1^t \oplus (S_2^t \cdot S_3^t) \oplus S_4^t \oplus m_i) \lll_w b_1, & S_4^t &\leftarrow S_4^t \lll b_1', \\
S_2^{t+1} &\leftarrow (S_2^t \oplus (S_3^t \cdot S_4^t) \oplus S_0^t \oplus m_i) \lll_w b_2, & S_0^t &\leftarrow S_0^t \lll b_2', \\
S_3^{t+1} &\leftarrow (S_3^t \oplus (S_4^t \cdot S_0^t) \oplus S_1^t \oplus m_i) \lll_w b_3, & S_1^t &\leftarrow S_1^t \lll b_3', \\
S_4^{t+1} &\leftarrow (S_4^t \oplus (S_0^t \cdot S_1^t) \oplus S_2^t \oplus m_i) \lll_w b_4, & S_2^t &\leftarrow S_2^t \lll b_4',
\end{aligned}
$$

where $\lll_w b_i$ means rotation inside every w-bit ($w = q/4$) word of the register to the left by b_i bits, and $\lll$ is the ordinary left bitwise rotation operation. The concrete values for the rotation offsets are listed in Table 3, and we refer the readers to Fig. 3 for a visualization of the StateUpdate function.

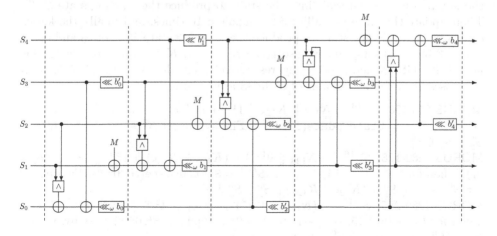

Fig. 3. The StateUpdate function of MORUS

Table 3. Rotation constants b_i for $\lll_w$ and b_i' for $\lll$ in round i of StepUpdate

Cipher	Rotation offsets for $\lll_w$					Rotation offsets for $\lll$				
	b_0	b_1	b_2	b_3	b_4	b_0'	b_1'	b_2'	b_3'	b_4'
MORUS-640-128	5	31	7	22	13	32	64	96	64	32
MORUS-1280-128	13	46	38	7	4	64	128	192	128	64
MORUS-1280-256	13	46	38	7	4	64	128	192	128	64

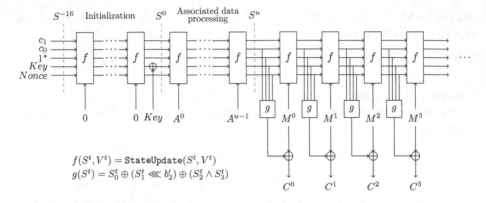

$$f(S^t, V^t) = \texttt{StateUpdate}(S^t, V^t)$$
$$g(S^t) = S_0^t \oplus (S_1^t \lll b_2') \oplus (S_2^t \wedge S_3^t)$$

Fig. 4. The encryption algorithm of MORUS

The encryption algorithm of MORUS can be divided into four phases. A visualized description of the encryption algorithm of MORUS without the finalization phase can be found in Fig. 4.

Initialization. The initialization of every MORUS instance starts by loading the key and nonce materials into the state to produce the starting state S^{-16}. Then update the state by calling StateUpdate 16 times, and finally the key is exclusive-ored into the state to produce the resulting state S^0. Let c_0 and c_1 be two 128-bit constants, and we use N_{128}, K_{128}, and K_{256} to denote the 128-bit nonce, 128-bit key and 256-bit key, respectively. The details of the initialization processes for different versions of MORUS are given in the following.

MORUS-640-128: $S^{-16} = N_{128} \parallel K_{128} \parallel 1^{128} \parallel c_0 \parallel c_1$. Then for $t = -16, -15, \cdots, -1$, $S^{t+1} = \texttt{StateUpdate}(S^t, 0^{128})$. Finally, we set $S^0 \leftarrow S_0^0 \parallel S_1^0 \oplus K_{128} \parallel S_2^0 \parallel S_3^0 \parallel S_4^0$.

MORUS-1280-128: $S^{-16} = (N_{128} \parallel 0^{128}) \parallel (K_{128} \parallel K_{128}) \parallel 1^{256} \parallel 0^{256} \parallel (c_0 \parallel c_1)$. Then for $t = -16, -15, \cdots, -1$, $S^{t+1} = \texttt{StateUpdate}(S^t, 0^{256})$. Finally, we set $S^0 \leftarrow S_0^0 \parallel S_1^0 \oplus (K_{128} \parallel K_{128}) \parallel S_2^0 \parallel S_3^0 \parallel S_4^0$.

MORUS-1280-256: $S^{-16} = (N_{128} \parallel 0^{128}) \parallel K_{256} \parallel 1^{256} \parallel 0^{256} \parallel (c_0 \parallel c_1)$. Then for $t = -16, -15, \cdots, -1$, $S^{t+1} = \texttt{StateUpdate}(S^t, 0^{256})$. Finally, we set $S^0 \leftarrow S_0^0 \parallel S_1^0 \oplus K_{256} \parallel S_2^0 \parallel S_3^0 \parallel S_4^0$.

Associated Data Processing. If there is no associated data, this process is omitted. Otherwise, the associated data is padded with zeros when necessary to form a multiple of q-bit (register size) block. Then the state is updated with the associated data A as $S^{t+1} = \texttt{StateUpdate}(S^t, A^t)$, for $t = 0, \cdots, u - 1$, where $u = \lceil |A|/q \rceil$ is the number of q-bit blocks of the (padded) associated data A.

Encryption. The plaintext is processed in q-bit blocks to update the state and generate the ciphertext block at the same time. Similar to associated data processing, the plaintext is padded with zeros if the last block is fractional. For $t = 0, \cdots, v - 1$, the following is performed.

$$C^t = M^t \oplus S_0^{u+t} \oplus (S_1^{u+t} \lll b_2') \oplus (S_2^{u+t} \wedge S_3^{u+t}),$$
$$S^{u+t+1} = \texttt{StateUpdate}(S^{u+t}, M^t),$$

where $v = \lceil |M|/q \rceil$ is the number of q-bit blocks of the padded plaintext.

Finalization. The authentication tag T is generated in the finalization phase by calling $\texttt{StateUpdate}$ ten more times. Since our attacks are completely irrelevant to how the tag is generated, we omit its details.

2.2 MiniMORUS and Rotational Invariance

MiniMORUS, proposed by Ashur et al. [2], is a family of helper constructions derived from MORUS. For every MORUS instance with a $5q$ bit state, there is a MiniMORUS instance with $5 \cdot (q/4)$-bit state. To be more specific, each register in MiniMORUS contains a single word of $w = q/4$ bits. Therefore, the word-oriented rotations in the $\texttt{StateUpdate}$ function of MORUS are removed in MiniMORUS, and the rotations within words ($\lll_\omega b_i$) are equivalent to ordinary bit-wise rotations ($\lll b_i$) in MiniMORUS. We refer the reader to Figs. 5 and 3 for a comparison.

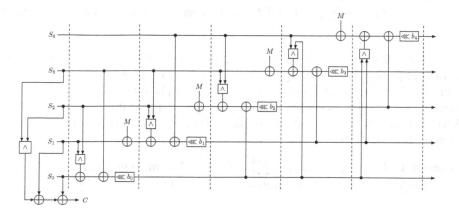

Fig. 5. The $\texttt{StateUpdate}$ function of MiniMORUS.

Obviously, MiniMORUS can be regarded as a reduced version of MORUS. Therefore, it is easier to search for linear trails of MiniMORUS. When a linear trail of MiniMORUS is identified, we can consider the trail for MORUS where the bits involved in every $q/4$-bit register of MiniMORUS are copied into all the four $q/4$-bit words in the corresponding register of MORUS. To put it simply, we only consider trails of MORUS involving the same bits within each word of one register. This kind of patterns are invariant under word-wise rotations. Therefore, the trails for MiniMORUS can be regarded as truncated representations of the trails for MORUS with rotational invariant patterns. We refer the reader to [2] for more details.

3   Correlation of Quadratic Boolean Functions

In this section, we give a brief introduction of necessary background of Boolean functions, prove that the correlation of a quadratic Boolean function can be read out from its disjoint quadratic form, and show how to convert an arbitrary quadratic Boolean function into its so-call *disjoint quadratic term* with a polynomial time algorithm.

Let $f : \mathbb{F}_2^n \to \mathbb{F}_2$ be a Boolean function with algebraic normal form (ANF)

$$f(\boldsymbol{x}) = \sum_{\boldsymbol{u} \in \mathbb{F}_2^n} a_{\boldsymbol{u}} \boldsymbol{x}^{\boldsymbol{u}},$$

where $\boldsymbol{x} = (x_1, \cdots, x_n), \boldsymbol{u} = (u_1, \cdots, u_n), a_{\boldsymbol{u}} \in \mathbb{F}_2$, and $\boldsymbol{x}^{\boldsymbol{u}} = \prod_{i=1}^n x_i^{u_i}$. The degree of the Boolean function f is defined as

$$\deg(f) = \max_{\boldsymbol{u} \in \mathbb{F}_2^n : a_{\boldsymbol{u}} \neq 0} wt(\boldsymbol{u}),$$

where $wt(\boldsymbol{u})$ is the Hamming weight of $\boldsymbol{u}$.

Definition 1 (Correlation). *The correlation of an n-variable Boolean function f is* $\mathrm{cor}(f) = \frac{1}{2^n} \sum_{\boldsymbol{x} \in \mathbb{F}_2^n} (-1)^{f(\boldsymbol{x})}$, *and the weight of the correlation is defined as* $- \log_2 |\mathrm{cor}(f)|$.

In the following, we use $\mathrm{Var}(f)$ to denote the set of variables involved in the Boolean function f. For example, if $h = x_1 x_2 + x_1 x_3 + 1$ and $g = x_2 x_3 x_4 + x_3 x_4$, then $\mathrm{Var}(h) = \{x_1, x_2, x_3\}$ and $\mathrm{Var}(g) = \{x_2, x_3, x_4\}$. Note that the variables are treated as symbolic objects. A variable x_i is *degenerate* if it does not appear in the ANF of f, i.e., $x_i \notin \mathrm{Var}(f)$. For example, if $f(x_1, x_2, x_3, x_4, x_5) = x_1 + x_2 x_3 + x_4$, then x_5 is degenerate.

Lemma 1. *Let $g(x_1, \cdots, x_n) = \sum_{t=1}^k f_t$ be a Boolean function such that the k sets $\mathrm{Var}(f_t)$ for $1 \leq t \leq k$ are mutually disjoint. Then $\mathrm{cor}(g) = \prod_{t=1}^k \mathrm{cor}(f_t)$.*

Proof. Let f_t be a Boolean function with n_t variables for $1 \leq t \leq k$, and $m = n - n_1 - \cdots - n_k$. According to Definition 1, we have

$$
\mathrm{cor}(g) = \frac{1}{2^n} \sum_{x \in \mathbb{F}_2^n} (-1)^{g(x)} = \sum_{x \in \mathbb{F}_2^n} \frac{(-1)^{(f_1 + f_2 + \cdots + f_k)(x)}}{2^n}
$$

$$
= \sum_{x_1 \in \mathbb{F}_2^{n_1}} \frac{(-1)^{f_1(x_1)}}{2^{n_1}} \cdots \sum_{x_k \in \mathbb{F}_2^{n_k}} \frac{(-1)^{f_k(x_1)}}{2^{n_k}} \cdot \sum_{x \in \mathbb{F}_2^m} \frac{(-1)^0}{2^m}
$$

$$
= \prod_{t=1}^{k} \mathrm{cor}(f_t),
$$

as desired. ☐

Example 1. $\mathrm{cor}(x_1 x_2 + x_3 x_4) = \mathrm{cor}(x_1 x_2) \cdot \mathrm{cor}(x_3 x_4) = 2^{-2}$.

Corollary 1. *Let $f(x_1, \cdots, x_n)$ be a Boolean function, and $f = g + x_j$ such that $x_j \notin \mathrm{Var}(g)$ is a separated linear term. Then $\mathrm{cor}(f) = 0$.*

Example 2. $\mathrm{cor}(x_1 x_2 + x_2 x_3 x_4 + x_3 x_5 + x_6) = \mathrm{cor}(x_1 x_2 + x_2 x_3 x_4 + x_3 x_5) \cdot \mathrm{cor}(x_6) = \mathrm{cor}(x_1 x_2 + x_2 x_3 x_4 + x_3 x_5) \cdot 0 = 0$.

Lemma 2. *Let $f(x, y) = xy + ax + by$ be a Boolean function and $a, b \in \mathbb{F}_2$ are constants. Then $\mathrm{cor}(f) = (-1)^{ab} \cdot 2^{-1}$.*

Proof. Prove by exhaustive analysis of a and b with Definition 1. ☐

Definition 2. *Two Boolean functions $f(x)$ and $g(x)$ are called cogredient if there exists an invertible matrix M, such that $g(x) = f(xM)$.*

Lemma 3. *Let $f(x)$ and $g(x)$ be two Boolean functions cogredient to each other. Then $\mathrm{cor}(f) = \mathrm{cor}(g)$.*

Proof. Since $f(x)$ and $g(x)$ are cogredient to each other, $g(x) = f(xM)$ for some invertible matrix M. The result follows from the following equation

$$
\mathrm{cor}(g) = \frac{1}{2^n} \sum_{x \in \mathbb{F}_2^n} (-1)^{g(x)} = \frac{1}{2^n} \sum_{x \in \mathbb{F}_2^n} (-1)^{f(xM)}
$$

$$
= \frac{1}{2^n} \sum_{x M^{-1} \in \mathbb{F}_2^n} (-1)^{f(x)} = \frac{1}{2^n} \sum_{x \in \mathbb{F}_2^n} (-1)^{f(x)}.
$$

☐

Lemma 3 implies that the correlation of a Boolean function is invariant by applying an invertible linear transformation to the input variables. Also, it is sufficient to consider functions with constant term 0 since $\mathrm{cor}(f) = -\mathrm{cor}(f + 1)$ for any f.

Definition 3 (Quadratic form). *A Boolean function f is quadratic if* $\deg(f) = 2$. *A quadratic Boolean function is called a quadratic form if its constant term is 0. Hence, a quadratic form can be written as*

$$f(x_1, \cdots, x_n) = \sum_{1 \leq i \leq j \leq n} a_{i,j} x_i x_j = Q_f(x_1, \cdots, x_n) + L_f(x_1, \cdots, x_n)$$

where $a_{i,j} \in \mathbb{F}_2$, Q_f contains all quadratic terms of f while L_f consists of all linear terms of f.

Let $f(x_1, \cdots, x_n)$ be a quadratic Boolean function. For $i \in \{1, \cdots, n\}$, we use $\sigma(f, x_i)$ to denote the number of terms of Q_f involving variable x_i.

Definition 4 (Disjoint quadratic form). *Let $f(x_1, \cdots, x_n)$ be a quadratic form. A term $x_i x_j$ of f is a separated quadratic term if $\sigma(f, x_i) = \sigma(f, x_j) = 1$. In particular, f is disjoint if all its quadratic terms are separated quadratic terms.*

Example 3. The two functions $x_1 x_2 + x_3 x_4$ and $x_1 x_3 + x_2 x_4 + x_2 + x_5$ are both disjoint quadratic forms, while $x_1 x_2 + x_2 x_3$ is not a disjoint quadratic form.

Lemma 4. *Let $f = x_{i_1} x_{i_2} + \cdots + x_{i_{2k-1}} x_{i_{2k}} + x_{j_1} + \cdots + x_{j_s}$ be a disjoint quadratic form. Then*

$$\mathrm{cor}(f) = \begin{cases} (-1)^{\sum_{t=1}^{k} \mathrm{Coef}_f(x_{i_{2t-1}}) \mathrm{Coef}_f(x_{i_{2t}})} \cdot 2^{-k} & \{j_1, \cdots, j_s\} \subseteq \{i_1, \cdots, i_{2k}\} \\ 0 & \{j_1, \cdots, j_s\} \not\subseteq \{i_1, \cdots, i_{2k}\} \end{cases}$$

where $\mathrm{Coef}_f(\boldsymbol{x}^u)$ denotes the coefficient of the monomial $\boldsymbol{x}^u$ in the ANF of f.

Proof. It follows from Lemma 1, Corollary 1, and Lemma 2.   □

With Lemma 4, it is easy to obtain the correlation of a disjoint quadratic form. In the remainder of this section, we will present an efficient algorithm for converting any given quadratic form to a cogredient disjoint quadratic form. Hence, we can efficiently compute the correlation of any given quadratic form. Before diving into the details of the algorithm, we first introduce some useful notations and subroutines employed in Algorithm 1.

Subroutine 1 (PickIndex). *Given a quadratic Boolean function $f(\boldsymbol{x})$ with $\boldsymbol{x} = (x_1, \cdots, x_n)$, PickIndex($f$) returns the index t of x_t, where t is the smallest integer $t \in \{1, \cdots, n\}$, such that $\sigma(f, x_t) \geq \sigma(f, x_{t'})$ for all $t' \in \{1, \cdots, n\}$.*

Example 4. Let $n = 3$, $f(\boldsymbol{x}) = x_1 x_2 + x_2 x_3 + x_3$. Then PickIndex($f$) = 2.

Subroutine 2 (Substitute). *Given a Boolean function $f(\boldsymbol{x}) = f(x_1, \cdots, x_n)$ and an $n \times n$ invertible matrix M, Substitute(f, M) returns the Boolean function $f(\boldsymbol{x}M)$.*

Example 5. Let $f = x_1 x_2 + x_2 x_3 + x_3$, and $M = \begin{bmatrix} 1 & 0 & 0 \\ 1 & 1 & 0 \\ 0 & 1 & 1 \end{bmatrix}$. Then Substitute($f, M$) gives $f(\boldsymbol{x}M) = (x_1 + x_2)(x_2 + x_3) + (x_2 + x_3)x_3 + x_3 = x_1 x_2 + x_1 x_3 + x_2$.

In Algorithm 1, for a given Boolean function $f(x_1, \cdots, x_n)$, we repeatedly use a substitution of variables of the form:

$$\begin{cases} x_u \leftarrow x_{t_1} + x_{t_2} + \cdots + x_{t_m} \\ x_j \leftarrow x_j, \quad \forall j \in \{1, \cdots, n\} - \{u\} \end{cases},$$

where $m \geq 2$, $u \in \{t_1, \cdots, t_m\}$, and $t_1 < t_2 < \cdots < t_m$. This substitution can be reformulated in the matrix form as $\boldsymbol{x} \leftarrow \boldsymbol{x} I_{u \leftarrow t_1, \cdots, t_m}$, where $I_{u \leftarrow t_1, \cdots, t_m}$ is obtained from the $n \times n$ identity matrix I by substituting the u-th column with a column vector whose t_j-th entry is 1 for $1 \leq j \leq m$ and other entries are 0. Note that we always have $I_{u \leftarrow t_1, \cdots, t_m} = I_{u \leftarrow t_1, \cdots, t_m}^{-1}$.

Algorithm 1: Transform to disjoint quadratic form

Input: A quadratic form $f(\boldsymbol{x}) = f(x_1, \cdots, x_n)$
Output: An invertible matrix M and a disjoint quadratic form $\hat{f}(\boldsymbol{x})$ such that $\hat{f}(\boldsymbol{x}) = f(\boldsymbol{x}M)$

1 /* Initialization */
2 $M \leftarrow I$ /* I is the $n \times n$ identity matrix */
3 $\hat{f}(\boldsymbol{x}) \leftarrow f(x_1, \cdots, x_n)$
4 $v \leftarrow$ PickIndex($\hat{f}$)

5 /* Transformation */
6 **while** $\sigma(\hat{f}, x_v) \geq 2$ **do**
7     $m \leftarrow \sigma(\hat{f}, x_v)$ /* The number of quadratic terms involving x_v */
8   Find all $t_1 < t_2 < \cdots < t_m$, such that $x_v x_{t_i}$ is a term of $\hat{f}$.

9     $\hat{f} \leftarrow$ Substitute($\hat{f}, I_{t_1 \leftarrow t_1, \cdots, t_m}$)
10     $M \leftarrow I_{t_1 \leftarrow t_1, \cdots, t_m} \cdot M$

11   **if** $\sigma(\hat{f}, x_{t_1}) \geq 2$ **then**
12        $k \leftarrow \sigma(\hat{f}, x_{t_1})$
13   Find all $s_1 < s_2 < \cdots < s_k$, such that $x_{t_1} x_{s_i}$ is a term of $\hat{f}$.

14        $\hat{f} \leftarrow$ Substitute($\hat{f}, I_{v \leftarrow s_1, \cdots, s_k}$)
15        $M \leftarrow I_{v \leftarrow s_1, \cdots, s_k} \cdot M$
16   **end**
17     $v \leftarrow$ PickIndex($\hat{f}$)
18 **end**

19 **return** M and $\hat{f}$

Example 6. Let $\hat{f} \leftarrow f(x_1, x_2, x_3, x_4, x_5) = x_1 x_2 + x_1 x_5 + x_2 x_3 + x_2 x_4 + x_1 + x_2$. Then $\sigma(\hat{f}, x_1) = 2$, $\sigma(\hat{f}, x_2) = 3$, $\sigma(\hat{f}, x_3) = 1$, $\sigma(\hat{f}, x_4) = 1$, and $\sigma(\hat{f}, x_5) = 1$. Thus, $v \leftarrow$ PickIndex($\hat{f}$) = 2. Now we extract the common factor $x_v = x_2$ in $Q_{\hat{f}}$:

$$\hat{f}(\boldsymbol{x}) = x_2(x_1 + x_3 + x_4) + x_1 x_5 + x_1 + x_2.$$

Then we apply the following substitution of variables:

$$\begin{cases} x_1 \leftarrow x_1 + x_3 + x_4 \\ x_j \leftarrow x_j, \quad j \in \{1, \cdots, 5\} - \{1\} \end{cases} . \tag{1}$$

This variable substitution gives $\hat{f} \leftarrow x_2 x_1 + (x_1 + x_3 + x_4)x_5 + (x_1 + x_3 + x_4) + x_2 = x_1 x_2 + x_1 x_5 + x_3 x_5 + x_4 x_5 + x_1 + x_2 + x_3 + x_4$. Then we need to check whether x_1 (the variable corresponding to a sum of the original variables rather than a single x_j) appears multiple times in $Q_{\hat{f}}$. Since $\sigma(\hat{f}, x_1) = 2$ (x_1 appears multiple times), we extract the common factor: $\hat{f} = x_1(x_2 + x_5) + x_3 x_5 + x_4 x_5 + x_1 + x_2 + x_3 + x_4$. Then we apply the variable substitution:

$$\begin{cases} x_2 \leftarrow x_2 + x_5 \\ x_j \leftarrow x_j, \quad j \in \{1, \cdots, 5\} - \{2\} \end{cases} . \tag{2}$$

This variable substitution gives $\hat{f} \leftarrow x_1 x_2 + x_3 x_5 + x_4 x_5 + x_1 + (x_2 + x_5) + x_3 + x_4 = x_1 x_2 + x_3 x_5 + x_4 x_5 + x_1 + x_2 + x_3 + x_4 + x_5$. At this point (a whole **while** loop is done), we can observe that $x_1 x_2$ is a separated quadratic term of $\hat{f}$. Actually, as shown in Theorem 1, every execution of the **while** loop will make one quadratic term separated. Then $\texttt{PickIndex}(\hat{f})$ returns 5, and we have $\hat{f} = x_1 x_2 + (x_3 + x_4)x_5 + x_1 + x_2 + x_3 + x_4 + x_5$. Applying the substitution

$$\begin{cases} x_3 \leftarrow x_3 + x_4 \\ x_j \leftarrow x_j, \quad j \in \{1, \cdots, 5\} - \{3\} \end{cases} , \tag{3}$$

gives $\hat{f} = x_1 x_2 + x_3 x_5 + x_1 + x_2 + x_3 + x_5$, which is a disjoint quadratic form. It follows from Eqs. (1)–(3) that

$$M = \begin{bmatrix} 1&0&0&0&0 \\ 0&1&0&0&0 \\ 0&0&1&0&0 \\ 0&0&1&1&0 \\ 0&0&0&0&1 \end{bmatrix} \cdot \begin{bmatrix} 1&0&0&0&0 \\ 0&1&0&0&0 \\ 0&0&1&0&0 \\ 0&0&0&1&0 \\ 0&1&0&0&1 \end{bmatrix} \cdot \begin{bmatrix} 1&0&0&0&0 \\ 0&1&0&0&0 \\ 1&0&1&0&0 \\ 1&0&0&1&0 \\ 0&0&0&0&1 \end{bmatrix} = \begin{bmatrix} 1&0&0&0&0 \\ 0&1&0&0&0 \\ 1&0&1&0&0 \\ 0&0&1&1&0 \\ 0&1&0&0&1 \end{bmatrix} .$$

It is readily to verify that $\hat{f} = f(\boldsymbol{x}M)$. Consequently, according to Lemma 3, the correlation of f is $(-1)^{1 \cdot 1 + 1 \cdot 1} \cdot 2^{-2} = 2^{-2}$.

To show the validity of Algorithm 1, we present the following result.

Lemma 5. *For any input quadratic form $f(\boldsymbol{x}) = f(x_1, \cdots, x_n)$ of Algorithm 1, each* **while** *loop will generate at least one separated quadratic terms.*

Proof. Let $\hat{f} = x_v(x_{t_1} + x_{t_2} + \cdots + x_{t_m}) + g$, where $v = \texttt{PickIndex}(\hat{f})$ and $t_1, t_2, \cdots, t_m$ be all the indices such that $x_{t_i} x_v$ is a term of $\hat{f}$ with $t_1 < t_2 < \cdots < t_m$. Then we have $\sigma(g, x_v) = 0$ according to the way we choose t_i's. After the variable substitution $\boldsymbol{x} \leftarrow \boldsymbol{x} \cdot I_{t_1 \leftarrow t_1, \cdots, t_m}$, we have

$$\hat{f} \leftarrow x_v x_{t_1} + g(\boldsymbol{x} \cdot I_{t_1 \leftarrow t_1, \cdots, t_m}).$$

Since x_v is unchanged under $I_{t_1 \leftarrow t_1, \cdots, t_m}$, we have $\sigma(\hat{f}, x_v) = 1 + \sigma(g, x_v) = 1$.

If $\sigma(\hat{f}, x_{t_1}) = 1$, then $x_v x_{t_1}$ is a separated quadratic term. Otherwise, we have $\sigma(\hat{f}, x_{t_1}) \geq 2$. Assume that the current $\hat{f}$ can be written as $\hat{f} = x_{t_1}(x_v + x_{s_1} + \cdots + x_{s_k}) + h$, where $s_1, s_2, \cdots, s_k$ are all the indices such that $x_{t_1} x_{s_i}$ is a term of $\hat{f}$ and $s_1 < s_2 < \cdots < s_k$. It implies that $\sigma(h, x_{t_1}) = 0$. Further, we have $\sigma(h, x_v) = 0$ since $\sigma(h, x_v) \leq \sigma(g, x_v) = 0$. Then the transformation $\boldsymbol{x} \leftarrow I_{v \leftarrow s_1, \cdots, s_k}$ carries the function $\hat{f}$ into

$$\hat{f} \leftarrow x_v x_{t_1} + h(\boldsymbol{x} \cdot I_{v \leftarrow s_1, \cdots, s_k}).$$

Thus, we have $\sigma(\hat{f}, x_{t_1}) = 1$ and $\sigma(\hat{f}, x_v) = 1$. This means that $x_v x_{t_1}$ is a separated quadratic term.   □

Theorem 1. *Given a quadratic form $f(\boldsymbol{x}) = f(x_1, \cdots, x_n)$, Algorithm 1 outputs a disjoint quadratic form $\hat{f}(\boldsymbol{x})$ and an invertible $n \times n$ matrix M, such that $\hat{f}(\boldsymbol{x}) = f(\boldsymbol{x}M)$. Moreover, Algorithm 1 has time complexity $\mathcal{O}(n^{3.8})$ and memory complexity $\Omega(n^2)$.*

Proof. According to Lemma 5, each **while** loop will generate at least one separated quadratic term. Hence, after at most $n/2$ **while** loops, all quadratic terms of the current $\hat{f}$ are disjoint quadratic terms.

Now we briefly analyze the complexity of Algorithm 1. From the above analysis, Algorithm 1 will have $n/2$ **while** loops in the worst case. This implies that the time complexity is upper bounded by the n matrix multiplications. Therefore, the time complexity of the algorithm can be estimated as $\mathcal{O}(n^{1+2.8})$, where we take $\mathcal{O}(n^{2.8})$ as the time complexity of the multiplication two $n \times n$ matrices [30]. It is readily seen that the memory complexity is $\Omega(n^2)$.   □

To sum up, with Lemma 3, Lemma 4, and Algorithm 1, we can compute the correlation of any quadratic Boolean function with polynomial time complexity.

4   Exploitable Linear Approximations of MORUS-like Key Stream Generators

We consider a typical stream cipher construction shown in Fig. 6. A partially unknown state S^U (initialized with a secret key and some public values) is processed by an initialization algorithm. Then a vectorial Boolean function $\mathcal{G}$ is applied to the state S^0 to produce one key stream word Z^0. For $0 \leq i < k$, a state update function is employed to obtain a new state $S^{i+1} = \mathcal{F}(S^i)$, from which a key stream word $Z^{i+1} = \mathcal{G}(S^{i+1})$ is extracted.

For this kind of stream ciphers, a generic attack based on linear cryptanalysis (e.g., [24]) can be applied, whose goal is to find a sequence of linear masks $(\lambda_0, \cdots, \lambda_k)$ for the key-stream blocks Z^i, such that the absolute value of the correlation $\text{cor}\left(\sum_{i=0}^{k} \lambda_i Z^i\right)$ can be maximized, where the number of ciphertext

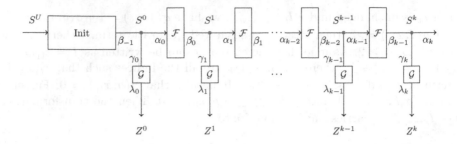

Fig. 6. Linear trails for MORUS-like key-stream generator

blocks involved in the linear approximation is called the *span*. In what follows, we establish a model in which finding $(\lambda_0, \cdots, \lambda_k)$ is *conceptually* the same as finding linear trails of a block cipher with additional constraints imposed on some linear masks at some special positions. With this model, existing tools [8, 14, 22, 31, 33] for finding good linear trails of block ciphers can be applied to search for $(\lambda_0, \cdots, \lambda_k)$.

Definition 5. *A linear trail of the key stream generator shown in Fig. 6:*

$$(\beta_{-1}, \gamma_0, \lambda_0, \alpha_0, \beta_0, \cdots, \alpha_{k-1}, \beta_{k-1}, \gamma_k, \lambda_k, \alpha_k)$$

is said to be exploitable if and only if $\beta_{-1} = 0$, $\alpha_k = 0$, and $\alpha_i + \gamma_i + \beta_{i-1} = 0$ for $0 \leq i \leq k$.

The motivation behind Definition 5 is that when the following equations

$$\begin{cases} \beta_{-1} = 0 \\ \alpha_k = 0 \\ \alpha_i + \gamma_i + \beta_{i-1} = 0, & 0 \leq i \leq k \\ \gamma_i S^i + \lambda_i Z^i = 0, & 0 \leq i \leq k \\ \alpha_i S^i + \beta_i S^{i+1} = 0, & 0 \leq i \leq k-1 \end{cases} \quad (4)$$

hold simultaneously, we have

$$\sum_{i=0}^{k} \lambda_i Z^i = \sum_{i=0}^{k} \gamma_i S^i = \beta_{-1} S^0 + \sum_{i=0}^{k-1} (\alpha_i S^i + \beta_i S^{i+1}) + \alpha_k S^k = 0. \quad (5)$$

Although in Definition 5 we require $\beta_{-1} = 0$, in fact, any characteristic starting with some $\beta_i = 0$ that follows the same pattern specified in Definition 5 across several consecutive ciphertext blocks can be exploited.

In this work, the MILP-based approach [14, 31, 33] is employed to search for linear trails of MORUS. One solution of the MILP model is a linear characteristic satisfying additional constraints specified in Definition 5. The objective function of the model is to minimize the number of active AND gates. The trails produced by the models are only *locally consistent*, and thus we cannot guarantee their global soundness with respect to optimality and validity, since the models are constructed under the assumption that all AND gates are independent.

Let us inspect a toy example where $f = f_1 + f_2 = x_1 x_2 + x_1 x_3 + x_2$ and

$$\begin{cases} f_1(x_1, x_2, x_3) = x_1 x_2 + x_2 \\ f_2(x_1, x_2, x_3) = x_1 x_3 \end{cases}.$$

The reader can check that in this case $\text{cor}(f_1) = \text{cor}(f_2) = 2^{-1}$, but $\text{cor}(f) = 0$, which implies that the sum of biased Boolean functions may be balanced. *Therefore, global consistency of the full trail cannot be ensured by local consistency.* To be more concrete, we show a real example. Table 4 presents an invalid linear trail generated by our MILP model whose span is 3. Note that in this paper, we show our trails in their linear-mask representations. There is a correspondence between the linear-mask representation and the trail-equation representation used in [2]. The five linear masks between α_0 and β_0 listed in Table 4 are the linear masks in the positions shown in Fig. 5 marked with dashed lines. Each row of the linear masks determines which AND gates are activated, and each active AND gate produces one equation containing one product term. By adding up these equations, we can reproduce the trail-equation representations used in [2]. In this work, we always need to convert the linear-mask representation into the trail-equation representation, which is required to determine its overall correlation by using the method proposed in Sect. 3.

For the sake of completeness, we give a complete example of the conversion process based on the trail shown in Table 4. From the linear masks, we can get the following equations:

$$C_{30}^0 \oplus S_{0,30}^0 \oplus S_{1,30}^0 = S_{2,30}^0 \cdot S_{3,30}^0$$
$$C_{22}^0 \oplus S_{0,22}^0 \oplus S_{1,22}^0 = S_{2,22}^0 \cdot S_{3,22}^0$$
$$S_{0,30}^0 \oplus S_{0,3}^1 \oplus S_{3,30}^0 = S_{1,30}^0 \cdot S_{2,30}^0$$
$$S_{0,22}^0 \oplus S_{0,27}^1 \oplus S_{3,22}^0 = S_{1,22}^0 \cdot S_{2,22}^0$$
$$S_{1,22}^0 \oplus S_{1,21}^1 \oplus S_{4,22}^0 = S_{2,22}^0 \cdot S_{3,22}^0$$
$$S_{4,22}^0 \oplus S_{4,3}^1 \oplus S_{2,22}^1 = S_{0,22}^1 \cdot S_{1,22}^1$$
$$C_{29}^1 \oplus S_{0,29}^1 \oplus S_{1,29}^1 = S_{2,29}^1 \cdot S_{3,29}^1$$
$$C_{27}^1 \oplus S_{0,27}^1 \oplus S_{1,27}^1 = S_{2,27}^1 \cdot S_{3,27}^1$$
$$C_{22}^1 \oplus S_{0,22}^1 \oplus S_{1,22}^1 = S_{2,22}^1 \cdot S_{3,22}^1$$
$$C_{21}^1 \oplus S_{0,21}^1 \oplus S_{1,21}^1 = S_{2,21}^1 \cdot S_{3,21}^1$$
$$C_3^1 \oplus S_{0,3}^1 \oplus S_{1,3}^1 = S_{2,3}^1 \cdot S_{3,3}^1$$
$$S_{0,29}^1 \oplus S_{0,2}^2 \oplus S_{3,29}^1 = S_{1,29}^1 \cdot S_{2,29}^1$$
$$S_{0,22}^1 \oplus S_{0,27}^2 \oplus S_{3,22}^1 = S_{1,22}^1 \cdot S_{2,22}^1$$

$$S_{0,21}^1 \oplus S_{0,26}^2 \oplus S_{3,21}^1 = S_{1,21}^1 \cdot S_{2,21}^1$$
$$S_{1,27}^1 \oplus S_{1,26}^2 \oplus S_{4,27}^1 = S_{2,27}^1 \cdot S_{3,27}^1$$
$$S_{1,3}^1 \oplus S_{1,2}^2 \oplus S_{4,3}^1 = S_{2,3}^1 \cdot S_{3,3}^1$$
$$S_{2,27}^1 \oplus S_{2,2}^2 \oplus S_{0,27}^2 = S_{3,27}^1 \cdot S_{4,27}^1$$
$$C_{26}^2 \oplus S_{0,26}^2 \oplus S_{1,26}^2 = S_{2,26}^2 \cdot S_{3,26}^2$$
$$C_2^2 \oplus S_{0,2}^2 \oplus S_{1,2}^2 = S_{2,2}^2 \cdot S_{3,2}^2$$

Adding up the above equations gives the trail equation:

$$C_{30}^0 \oplus C_{22}^0 \oplus C_{29}^1 \oplus C_{27}^1 \oplus C_{22}^1 \oplus C_{21}^1 \oplus C_3^1 \oplus C_{26}^2 \oplus C_2^2$$
$$= S_{2,22}^1 \cdot S_{3,22}^1 \oplus S_{1,22}^1 \cdot S_{2,22}^1 \oplus S_{2,22}^1 \oplus S_{3,22}^1 \oplus S_{1,22}^1$$
$$\oplus S_{2,21}^1 \cdot S_{3,21}^1 \oplus S_{1,21}^1 \cdot S_{2,21}^1 \oplus S_{3,21}^1$$
$$\oplus S_{2,29}^1 \cdot S_{3,29}^1 \oplus S_{1,29}^1 \cdot S_{2,29}^1 \oplus S_{3,29}^1 \oplus S_{1,29}^1$$
$$\oplus S_{2,30}^0 \cdot S_{3,30}^0 \oplus S_{1,30}^0 \cdot S_{2,30}^0 \oplus S_{3,30}^0 \oplus S_{1,30}^0$$
$$\oplus S_{1,22}^0 \cdot S_{2,22}^0$$
$$\oplus S_{0,22}^1 \cdot S_{1,22}^1$$
$$\oplus S_{3,27}^1 \cdot S_{4,27}^1 \oplus S_{4,27}^1$$
$$\oplus S_{2,26}^2 \cdot S_{3,26}^2$$
$$\oplus S_{2,2}^2 \cdot S_{3,2}^2 \oplus S_{2,2}^2$$
$$\oplus S_{3,22}^0$$
$$\oplus S_{2,27}^1.$$

The right-hand side of the equation is a quadratic Boolean function. Thus by applying the method shown in Sect. 3, we can obtain its correlation. However, for this special case, we know that its correlation is zero without converting it into the disjoint quadratic form, since the variable $S_{2,27}^1$ never appears in any other term of the quadratic Boolean function. Thus, according to Corollary 1, the correlation of $C_{30}^0 \oplus C_{22}^0 \oplus C_{29}^1 \oplus C_{27}^1 \oplus C_{22}^1 \oplus C_{21}^1 \oplus C_3^1 \oplus C_{26}^2 \oplus C_2^2$ is zero.

At this point, we emphasize that Definition 5 is only used as a mental helper to identify *potentially* good trails. Since in practice, we apply search tools that produce "good" linear trails assuming the independencies of the rounds or components within $\mathcal{F}$ and $\mathcal{G}$. However, these assumptions are generally not true as illustrated by the above example. Therefore, the outputs of the search tools are not reliable. We must *recompute the correlation of the full trail* by using dedicated methods which are suitable to the target under consideration. For instance, using the method presented in Sect. 3, we automatically detect such inconsistencies shown in the above examples.

Table 4. An invalid trail of MiniMORUS-640 with span 3

Round	Linear masks
0	α_0 40400000 40400000 00000000 40400000 00000000
	08000008 00400000 00000000 00000000 00000000
	08000008 00200000 00000000 00000000 00400000
	08000008 00200000 00000000 00000000 00400000
	08000008 00200000 00000000 00000000 00400000
	β_0 08000008 00200000 00400000 00000000 00000008
	γ_0 40400000 40400000 00000000 40400000 00000000
	λ_0 40400000
1	α_1 20600000 28400008 00400000 20600000 00000008
	0c000004 08000008 00000000 00000000 00000008
	0c000004 04000004 08000000 00000000 08000000
	04000004 04000004 00000004 00000000 00000000
	04000004 04000004 00000004 00000000 00000000
	β_1 04000004 04000004 00000004 00000000 00000000
	γ_1 28600008 28600008 00000000 20600000 00000000
	λ_1 28600008
2	γ_2 04000004 04000004 00000004 00000000 00000000
	λ_2 04000004

5   Searching for Linear Approximations of MORUS

By setting the plaintext to zero message as in [2], MiniMORUS and MORUS fit exactly into the model established in Sect. 4. Hence, linear trails of MiniMORUS and MORUS can be searched by using any existing tools for finding linear approximations. In our work, we apply the MILP-based approach, where the constraints imposed on the linear trails are encoded into MILP models.

In practice, we must determine the number of ciphertext blocks involved in the final linear combination of the ciphertext bits before we can set up the MILP model. First, we theoretically show that there is no useful linear approximation for MORUS involving only one ciphertext block. Let λ_0 be a linear mask of the key-stream generator shown in Fig. 6 for one ciphertext block. Then we have

$$\lambda_0 Z^0 = \bigoplus_{j,\lambda_{0,j}=1} (S_{0,j}^0 \oplus (S_{1,j+b_2'}^0 \oplus S_{2,j}^0 \cdot S_{3,j}^0))$$

$$= \bigoplus_{j,\lambda_{0,j}=1} S_{0,j}^0 \oplus \bigoplus_{j,\lambda_{0,j}=1} (S_{1,j+b_2'}^0 \oplus S_{2,j}^0 \cdot S_{3,j}^0).$$

Since the variable $S_{0,j}^0$ does not appear in other terms, we have $\mathrm{cor}(\lambda_0 Z^0) = 0$ according to Corollary 1.

Since the linear trails used in [2] span across 5 ciphertext blocks, we decide to only search for rotational invariant trails with spans greater than 1 and less than 6 (models for larger spans will have more variables which are difficult to solve). The best trails we found are of span 4, and the trails for MiniMORUS-640 and MORUS-640 are listed in Tables 5 and 6, respectively.

As an illustration, let us compute the correlation of the trail of MiniMORUS-640 shown in Table 5. Firstly, according to the linear masks shown in Table 5, we write down the following equations which hold with probability 1.

Table 5. A linear trail of MiniMORUS-640 with correlation -2^{-8}

Round	Linear masks
0	α_0 10000000 10000000 00000000 10000000 00000000
	00000002 00000000 00000000 00000000 00000000
	00000002 00000000 00000000 00000000 00000000
	00000002 00000000 00000000 00000000 00000000
	00000002 00000000 00000000 00000000 00000000
	β_0 00000002 00000000 00000000 00000000 00000000
	γ_0 10000000 10000000 00000000 10000000 00000000
	λ_0 10000000
1	α_1 08000200 08000202 00000002 08000200 00000000
	00004001 00000002 00000002 00000000 00000000
	00004001 00000001 00000000 00000000 00000002
	00004001 00000001 00000000 00000000 00000002
	00004001 00000001 00000000 00000000 00000002
	β_1 00004003 00000003 00000002 00000000 00004000
	γ_1 08000202 08000202 00000002 08000200 00000000
	λ_1 08000202
2	α_2 00000100 00004100 00000000 00000100 00004000
	00002000 00004000 00000000 00000000 00004000
	00002000 00002000 00000000 00000000 00000000
	00002000 00002000 00000000 00000000 00000000
	00002000 00002000 00000000 00000000 00000000
	β_2 00002000 00002000 00000000 00000000 00000000
	γ_2 00004103 00004103 00000002 00000100 00000000
	λ_2 00004103
3	γ_3 00002000 00002000 00000000 00000000 00000000
	λ_3 00002000

$$C_{28}^0 \oplus S_{0,28}^0 \oplus S_{1,28}^0 = S_{2,28}^0 \cdot S_{3,28}^0$$

$$S_{0,28}^0 \oplus S_{0,1}^1 \oplus S_{3,28}^0 = S_{1,28}^0 \cdot S_{2,28}^0$$

$$C_{27}^1 \oplus S_{0,27}^1 \oplus S_{1,27}^1 = S_{2,27}^1 \cdot S_{3,27}^1$$

$$C_9^1 \oplus S_{0,9}^1 \oplus S_{1,9}^1 = S_{2,9}^1 \cdot S_{3,9}^1$$

$$C_1^1 \oplus S_{0,1}^1 \oplus S_{1,1}^1 = S_{2,1}^1 \cdot S_{3,1}^1$$

$$S_{0,27}^1 \oplus S_{0,0}^2 \oplus S_{3,27}^1 = S_{1,27}^1 \cdot S_{2,27}^1$$

$$S_{0,9}^1 \oplus S_{0,14}^2 \oplus S_{3,9}^1 = S_{1,9}^1 \cdot S_{2,9}^1$$

$$S_{1,1}^1 \oplus S_{1,0}^2 \oplus S_{4,1}^1 = S_{2,1}^1 \cdot S_{3,1}^1$$

$$S_{4,1}^1 \oplus S_{4,14}^2 \oplus S_{2,1}^2 = S_{0,1}^2 \cdot S_{1,1}^2$$

$$C_{14}^2 \oplus S_{0,14}^2 \oplus S_{1,14}^2 = S_{2,14}^2 \cdot S_{3,14}^2$$

$$C_8^2 \oplus S_{0,8}^2 \oplus S_{1,8}^2 = S_{2,8}^2 \cdot S_{3,8}^2$$

$$C_1^2 \oplus S_{0,1}^2 \oplus S_{1,1}^2 = S_{2,1}^2 \cdot S_{3,1}^2$$

$$C_0^2 \oplus S_{0,0}^2 \oplus S_{1,0}^2 = S_{2,0}^2 \cdot S_{3,0}^2$$

$$S_{0,8}^2 \oplus S_{0,13}^3 \oplus S_{3,8}^2 = S_{1,8}^2 \cdot S_{2,8}^2$$

$$S_{1,14}^2 \oplus S_{1,13}^3 \oplus S_{4,14}^2 = S_{2,14}^2 \cdot S_{3,14}^2$$

$$C_{13}^3 \oplus S_{0,13}^3 \oplus S_{1,13}^3 = S_{2,13}^3 \cdot S_{3,13}^3$$

Table 6. A linear trail of MORUS-640 with correlation 2^{-38}, where "*4" stands for 4 copies of the same bit string

Round		Linear masks
0	α_0	10000000*4 10000000*4 00000000*4 10000000*4 00000000*4
		00000002*4 00000000*4 00000000*4 00000000*4 00000000*4
		00000002*4 00000000*4 00000000*4 00000000*4 00000000*4
		00000002*4 00000000*4 00000000*4 00000000*4 00000000*4
		00000002*4 00000000*4 00000000*4 00000000*4 00000000*4
	β_0	00000002*4 00000000*4 00000000*4 00000000*4 00000000*4
	γ_0	10000000*4 10000000*4 00000000*4 10000000*4 00000000*4
	λ_0	10000000*4
1	α_1	08000200*4 08000202*4 00000002*4 08000200*4 00000000*4
		00004001*4 00000002*4 00000002*4 00000000*4 00000000*4
		00004001*4 00000001*4 00000000*4 00000000*4 00000002*4
		00004001*4 00000001*4 00000000*4 00000000*4 00000002*4
		00004001*4 00000001*4 00000000*4 00000000*4 00000002*4
	β_1	00004003*4 00000003*4 00000002*4 00000000*4 00004000*4
	γ_1	08000202*4 08000202*4 00000002*4 08000200*4 00000000*4
	λ_1	08000202*4
2	α_2	00000100*4 00004100*4 00000000*4 00000100*4 00004000*4
		00002000*4 00004000*4 00000000*4 00000000*4 00004000*4
		00002000*4 00002000*4 00000000*4 00000000*4 00000000*4
		00002000*4 00002000*4 00000000*4 00000000*4 00000000*4
		00002000*4 00002000*4 00000000*4 00000000*4 00000000*4
	β_2	00002000*4 00002000*4 00000000*4 00000000*4 00000000*4
	γ_2	00004103*4 00004103*4 00000002*4 00000100*4 00000000*4
	λ_2	00004103*4
3	γ_3	00002000*4 00002000*4 00000000*4 00000000*4 00000000*4
	λ_3	00002000*4

Combining the above equations, we obtain an equation whose left-hand side involves only cipher-text bits, while the right-hand side of the equation can be regarded as a quadratic Boolean function.

$$C_{28}^0 \oplus C_{27}^1 \oplus C_9^1 \oplus C_1^1 \oplus C_{14}^2 \oplus C_8^2 \oplus C_1^2 \oplus C_0^2 \oplus C_{13}^3$$
$$= S_{2,28}^0 \cdot S_{3,28}^0 \oplus S_{1,28}^0 \cdot S_{2,28}^0 \oplus S_{3,28}^0 \oplus S_{1,28}^0$$
$$\oplus S_{2,9}^1 \cdot S_{3,9}^1 \oplus S_{1,9}^1 \cdot S_{2,9}^1 \oplus S_{3,9}^1 \oplus S_{1,9}^1$$
$$\oplus S_{2,27}^1 \cdot S_{3,27}^1 \oplus S_{1,27}^1 \cdot S_{2,27}^1 \oplus S_{3,27}^1 \oplus S_{1,27}^1$$
$$\oplus S_{2,8}^2 \cdot S_{3,8}^2 \oplus S_{1,8}^2 \cdot S_{2,8}^2 \oplus S_{3,8}^2 \oplus S_{1,8}^2$$
$$\oplus S_{0,1}^2 \cdot S_{1,1}^2 \oplus S_{0,1}^2 \oplus S_{1,1}^2$$
$$\oplus S_{2,1}^2 \cdot S_{3,1}^2 \oplus S_{2,1}^2$$
$$\oplus S_{2,0}^2 \cdot S_{3,0}^2$$
$$\oplus S_{2,13}^3 \cdot S_{3,13}^3$$

The right-hand side of the above equation can be transformed into its disjoint quadratic form with the method presented in Sect. 3.

$$S_{2,28}^0 \cdot S_{3,28}^0 \oplus S_{1,28}^0 \cdot S_{2,28}^0 \oplus S_{3,28}^0 \oplus S_{1,28}^0$$
$$\oplus S_{2,9}^1 \cdot S_{3,9}^1 \oplus S_{1,9}^1 \cdot S_{2,9}^1 \oplus S_{3,9}^1 \oplus S_{1,9}^1$$

$$\oplus S_{2,27}^1 \cdot S_{3,27}^1 \oplus S_{1,27}^1 \cdot S_{2,27}^1 \oplus S_{3,27}^1 \oplus S_{1,27}^1$$
$$\oplus S_{2,8}^2 \cdot S_{3,8}^2 \oplus S_{1,8}^2 \cdot S_{2,8}^2 \oplus S_{3,8}^2 \oplus S_{1,8}^2$$
$$\oplus S_{0,1}^2 \cdot S_{1,1}^2 \oplus S_{0,1}^2 \oplus S_{1,1}^2$$
$$\oplus S_{2,1}^2 \cdot S_{3,1}^2 \oplus S_{2,1}^2$$
$$\oplus S_{2,0}^2 \cdot S_{3,0}^2$$
$$\oplus S_{2,13}^3 \cdot S_{3,13}^3$$
$$= (S_{2,28}^0 \oplus 1)(S_{1,28}^0 \oplus S_{3,28}^0)$$
$$\oplus (S_{2,9}^1 \oplus 1)(S_{1,9}^1 \oplus S_{3,9}^1)$$
$$\oplus (S_{2,27}^1 \oplus 1)(S_{1,27}^1 \oplus S_{3,27}^1)$$
$$\oplus (S_{2,8}^2 \oplus 1)(S_{1,8}^2 \oplus S_{3,8}^2)$$
$$\oplus (S_{0,1}^2 \oplus 1)(S_{1,1}^2 \oplus 1)$$
$$\oplus S_{2,1}^2(S_{3,1}^2 \oplus 1)$$
$$\oplus S_{2,0}^2 \cdot S_{3,0}^2$$
$$\oplus S_{2,13}^3 \cdot S_{3,13}^3 \oplus 1$$

Therefore, the correlation of $C_{28}^0 \oplus C_{27}^1 \oplus C_9^1 \oplus C_1^1 \oplus C_{14}^2 \oplus C_8^2 \oplus C_1^2 \oplus C_0^2 \oplus C_{13}^3$ is -2^{-8}. Similarly, we can compute the correlations of the trails of MORUS-640, MiniMORUS-1280, and MORUS-1280.

Before going any further, we would like to give some insight into the trails of MiniMORUS to show how the linear approximations covering different parts of the cipher eventually eliminate all internal variables, leading to approximations involving only ciphertext variables. The following discussion is similar to the Sect. 4 of [2]. Several fragments are common between [2] and ours. We recommend the reader to review the Fig. 2 of [2] before reading the following part.

We can use the variables of C^t to approximate the variables of S_0^{t+1}, denoted by $C^t \rightarrow S_0^{t+1}$. At the same time, $C^{t+1}, S_0^{t+1}, S_1^{t+2} \rightarrow S_4^{t+1}$. These approximations are visualized in Fig. 7a and b, Note that two AND operations are involved in Fig. 7a, in which one is approximated to S_3 and the other is approximated to S_1. This seems to require weight 2. This trail fragment is the same as one of the fragments in [2], and [2] explains that there is another way of approximating those two AND operations: one is approximated to $S_3 \oplus S_2$ and the other is approximated to $S_2 \oplus S_1$. Two ways of the approximation form a hull effect, which makes its weight 1.

Figure 7b was also used in [2], which involves two AND operations. Those AND operations take the same input variables, S_2 and S_3. Hence those two deterministically cancel each other, which makes the weight of this fragment 0.

Basically, by combining the fragments in Fig. 7a to d, 1 bit of S_4^{t+1} is approximated from the ciphertext bits. We do the same to approximate 1 bit of S_4^{t+2} by sliding the steps by 1. Figure 7e to h are for this approximation. Hence by removing the step indices, Fig. 7e to h are exact copies of Fig. 7a to d.

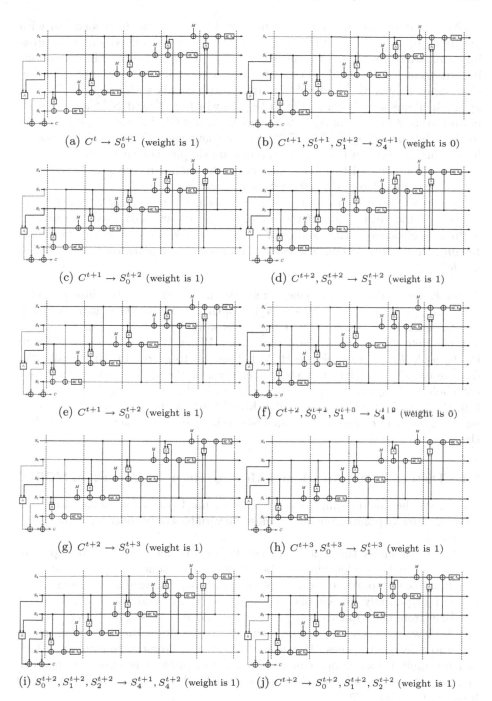

(a) $C^t \to S_0^{t+1}$ (weight is 1)

(b) $C^{t+1}, S_0^{t+1}, S_1^{t+2} \to S_4^{t+1}$ (weight is 0)

(c) $C^{t+1} \to S_0^{t+2}$ (weight is 1)

(d) $C^{t+2}, S_0^{t+2} \to S_1^{t+2}$ (weight is 1)

(e) $C^{t+1} \to S_0^{t+2}$ (weight is 1)

(f) $C^{t+2}, S_0^{t+2}, S_1^{t+2} \to S_4^{t+2}$ (weight is 0)

(g) $C^{t+2} \to S_0^{t+3}$ (weight is 1)

(h) $C^{t+3}, S_0^{t+3} \to S_1^{t+3}$ (weight is 1)

(i) $S_0^{t+2}, S_1^{t+2}, S_2^{t+2} \to S_4^{t+1}, S_4^{t+2}$ (weight is 1)

(j) $C^{t+2} \to S_0^{t+2}, S_1^{t+2}, S_2^{t+2}$ (weight is 1)

Fig. 7. MiniMORUS linear trail fragments

Note that the linear trail up to here, which has weight 6, is identical with [2]. Ashur et al. [2] iterated this approximation twice and added 4 more approximations, which makes the weight of their trail $(6 \times 2) + 4 = 16$. The core of our improvement lies in the detection of a rather complicated new approximation that approximates S_4^{t+1} and S_4^{t+2} by ciphertext bits only with weight 2. The new approximations are shown in Fig. 7i to j, in which S_4^{t+1} and S_4^{t+2} are approximated to the 3-bit sum of S_0^{t+2}, S_1^{t+2} and S_2^{t+2}, and C^{t+2} are also approximated to the 3-bit sum of $S_0^{t+2}, S_1^{t+2}, S_2^{t+2}$. The previous work [2] found the attack by hand thus the most of the approximations are simple such that 2 internal state bits are approximated to 1-bit of another state. thanks to the generic model in Sect. 4, we could detect this efficient approximation

We stress that the trail fragments are only used to shed insight on the full trails, and the verification of these trail fragments are only used to provided additional evidence of the validity of the analysis. *We never use trail fragments to compute the correlation. The correlation must be computed on the full trail as whole.*

Remark. we would like to make a remark on the effect of the in-word rotation ($\lll_w$) offsets (b_i, $i \in \{0, \cdots, 4\}$) of MORUS on the linear trails we find. In [2], Ashur et al. assumes that the trails work for any choice of b_i without any concrete discussion of the actual effect. We randomly choose 50 different $(b_0, b_1, b_2, b_3, b_4)$'s and generate 50 MILP models to search for their trails. We do observe slight variance of the correlations of the trails we find for different choices of $(b_0, b_1, b_2, b_3, b_4)$. For example, in the case of $(b_0, b_1, b_2, b_3, b_4) = (16, 31, 23, 3, 17)$, we identify a trail of MORUS-640 with correlation 2^{-34}, meaning that under our current cryptanalysis technique, this version is weaker than the original design.

5.1   Distinguishing Attack and Message-Recovery Attack on MORUS

So far, for the sake of simplicity, we have assumed that all message blocks are zero. As already pointed out in [2], message variables only contribute linearly to the trails.

Therefore, under the condition that the involved message bits are kept constants, the trails we identified can be employed to mount two types of attacks. The first one is a (partially) known-plaintext distinguishing attack, where a large number of partially known plaintexts are encrypted, and then we can detect the bias from the ciphertexts. The second one is a message-recovery attack, in which we can recover some unknown plaintext bits if the same plaintext is encrypted for many times. The scenario in which the message-recovery attack can be applied does happen in practice. For example, the same message can be encrypted with different IVs and potentially different keys in the so-called broadcast setting [1, 20].

For the message-recovery attacks, we rely on the approach proposed by Matsui [21]. For example, if the correlation of the trail employed in our message-recovery attack is 2ρ, we would encrypt a (unknown) message approximately n

times with different nonces or keys. Let T_b be the number of encryptions such that the linear combination (derived from the trail) of the ciphertext bits is equal to $b \in \{0,1\}$. Then we guess the value of the linear combination $\mathcal{L}(M)$ of the message M according to the following rule:

$$\mathcal{L}(M) = \begin{cases} 0, & \text{if } T_0 > T_1 \text{ and } \rho > 0, \\ 1, & \text{if } T_0 > T_1 \text{ and } \rho < 0, \\ 1, & \text{if } T_1 > T_0 \text{ and } \rho > 0, \\ 0, & \text{if } T_1 > T_0 \text{ and } \rho < 0. \end{cases}$$

The success probability of the procedure can be estimated as $\int_{-2\sqrt{n}|\rho|}^{\infty} \frac{1}{\sqrt{2\pi}} e^{-x^2/2} dx$, which would be greater than 84.1% if we set $n > \frac{1}{4}|\rho|^{-2}$ [21]. Therefore, if the correlation of the underlying approximation is 2^{-c}, we need about 2^{2c} encryptions to mount the attack.

On the Data Complexity. As pointed out by Ashur et al. [2], the data complexities of the attacks could be slightly lowered by using multiple linear trails [6,15,16]. Actually, given any trail found in this paper, we can derive another trail with the same correlation by rotating the masks within words by a common offset. If we assume independency, we could run $q/4$ (the word size) copies of the trail in parallel on the same encrypted blocks, which would save a factor of 2^5 on the data complexity for MORUS-640, and 2^6 for MORUS-1280.

5.2 Verification of the Attacks

To confirm the validity of our analysis, we experimentally verify the trails or trail fragments. For MiniMORUS, we are able to fully verify the correlations. Experiments show that the weights of the correlations of

$$C_{28}^0 \oplus C_{27}^1 \oplus C_9^1 \oplus C_1^1 \oplus C_{14}^2 \oplus C_8^2 \oplus C_1^2 \oplus C_0^2 \oplus C_{13}^3$$

and

$$C_{16}^0 \oplus C_{62}^1 \oplus C_{29}^1 \oplus C_{20}^1 \oplus C_{33}^2 \oplus C_{29}^2 \oplus C_{11}^2 \oplus C_2^2 \oplus C_{15}^3$$

for MiniMORUS-640 and MiniMORUS-1280 are 7.7919 and 8.1528 respectively, which are quite close to 8, the theoretically predicted correlation.

For MORUS, the correlation of the best trails we find is 2^{-38}, indicating that about 2^{76} encryptions have to be performed to verify the full trail, which is out of our reach. Following the approach presented in [2], we decompose the full trail into trail fragments according to Fig. 7, and every fragment is verified independently.

For MORUS-640 and MORUS-1280, the full trails can be divided into five trail fragments shown in Tables 7 and 8, respectively. We independently verify these trail fragments and the results are given in Fig. 8a and b. Again, the results fit the theoretical analysis very well.

Table 7. The five trail fragments of MORUS-640

	Trail fragment	Weight
χ_1	$C^0_{\{124,92,60,28\}} \oplus C^1_{\{97,65,33,1\}} = S^1_{4,\{97,65,33,1\}} \oplus S^2_{1,\{96,64,32,0\}}$	7
χ_2	$C^1_{\{123,91,59,27\}} \oplus C^2_{\{96,64,32,0\}} = S^2_{1,\{96,64,32,0\}}$	8
χ_3	$C^2_{\{104,72,40,8\}} \oplus C^3_{\{109,77,45,13\}} = S^3_{1,\{109,77,45,13\}}$	8
χ_4	$C^1_{\{105,73,41,9\}} \oplus C^2_{\{110,78,46,14\}} = S^3_{1,\{109,77,45,13\}} \oplus S^2_{4,\{110,78,46,14\}}$	7
χ_5	$C^2_{\{97,65,33,1\}} = S^1_{4,\{97,65,33,1\}} \oplus S^2_{4,\{110,78,46,14\}}$	8

Table 8. The five trail fragments of MORUS-1280

	Trail fragment	Weight
χ_1	$C^0_{\{208,144,80,16\}} \oplus C^1_{\{221,157,93,29\}} = S^1_{4,\{221,157,93,29\}} \oplus S^2_{1,\{203,139,75,11\}}$	7
χ_2	$C^1_{\{254,190,126,62\}} \oplus C^2_{\{203,139,75,11\}} = S^2_{1,\{203,139,75,11\}}$	8
χ_3	$C^2_{\{194,130,66,2\}} \oplus C^3_{\{207,143,79,15\}} = S^3_{1,\{207,143,79,15\}}$	8
χ_4	$C^1_{\{212,148,84,20\}} \oplus C^2_{\{225,161,97,33\}} = S^3_{1,\{207,143,79,15\}} \oplus S^2_{4,\{225,161,97,33\}}$	7
χ_5	$C^2_{\{221,157,93,29\}} = S^1_{4,\{221,157,93,29\}} \oplus S^2_{4,\{225,161,97,33\}}$	8

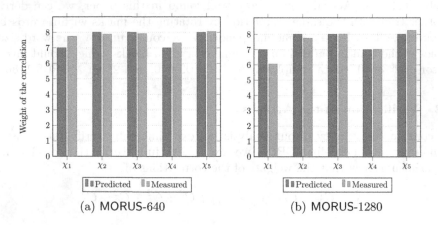

(a) MORUS-640   (b) MORUS-1280

Fig. 8. Experimental verification of the trail fragments of MORUS-640 and MORUS-1280

6 Searching for Trails with Smaller Spans

In [2], it is said that ciphertext correlations like those presented in previous sections can be exploited only when the same message is encrypted enough times:

> "... they can be leveraged to mount an attack in the broadcast setting, where the same message is encrypted multiple times with different IVs and potentially different keys [20]. In particular, the broadcast setting appears in practice in man-in-the-browser attacks against HTTPS connections following the BEAST model [10]. "

However, we find that this strong condition can be relaxed. Let us recall Fig. 4, and consider a trail with a 4-block span. If we encrypt a set of n-block ($n > 4$) messages sharing a common 4-block prefix $M^0 \parallel M^1 \parallel M^2 \parallel M^3$, then our analysis presented in previous sections is *completely irrelevant* with those message blocks beyond this common prefix. In fact, if we encrypt $M^0 \parallel M^1 \parallel M^2 \parallel M^3$ and $M^0 \parallel M^1 \parallel M^2 \parallel M^3 \parallel \cdots \parallel M^{n-1}$ with the same key, nonce, and associated data, the same intermediate values and ciphertexts will be produced within the 4-block span. Therefore, we can draw the conclusion that *the correlations involving k-block ciphertext can be leveraged to mount an attack if enough messages with a k-block common prefix are encrypted with different IV $\parallel$ key.*

Note that the above condition is strictly weaker than that presented in ASIACRYPT 2018 [2], and this setting does occur in practice. For example, when ARP packets are encrypted in WPA2-AES enabled WIFI networks, they share a 16-byte common prefix (8-byte LLC header and 8-byte ARP request header) [9]. This 16-byte common prefix extends to 22 bytes if the attacker is able to control the following 6-byte MAC address, which is not difficult to carry out [32]. Therefore, trails with smaller spans are more preferable, which motivates us to search for linear trails with smaller spans. The best trail with respect to the number of ciphertext blocks involved (span) we find is a trail of MORUS-640 with correlation 2^{-79}, whose span is 3 (see Table 9). However, the correlation is too low to be used in an attack.

The discussion of this section also indicates that the trails we find are superior to the ones presented in [2] in terms of both correlation and span. Moreover, since given a trail found in this paper, we can derive another trail with the same correlation by rotationally shift the masks within words by a common offset, we can identify the shifting offset minimizing the number of trailing zeros in the masks of the last block, which may further reduce the size of the common

Table 9. A linear trail of MORUS-640 with correlation 2^{-79} whose span is 3

Round		Linear masks				
0	α_0	00002520*4	00002520*4	00002020*4	00002520*4	00000000*4
		0004a400*4	00000000*4	00002020*4	00000000*4	00000000*4
		0004a400*4	00000000*4	00002020*4	00000000*4	00000000*4
		00048420*4	00000000*4	00101000*4	00000020*4	00000020*4
		00048400*4	00000020*4	00101000*4	08000000*4	00000020*4
	β_0	00048420*4	00000000*4	00101020*4	08000000*4	00040000*4
	γ_0	00002520*4	00002520*4	00002020*4	00002520*4	00000000*4
	λ_0	00002520*4				
1	α_1	00009420*4	00041000*4	00140020*4	08041000*4	00040000*4
		00128400*4	00040000*4	00140400*4	08048420*4	00040000*4
		00128400*4	00020000*4	00100400*4	08008420*4	00000000*4
		00028000*4	00020000*4	08020000*4	08008020*4	00000000*4
		08028020*4	08028020*4	08020000*4	08020020*4	00000000*4
	β_1	08028020*4	08028020*4	08020000*4	08020020*4	00000000*4
	γ_1	00041000*4	00041000*4	00041000*4	00041000*4	00000000*4
	λ_1	00041000*4				
2	γ_2	08028020*4	08028020*4	08020000*4	08020020*4	00000000*4
	λ_2	08028020*4				

prefix. For example, by shifting the trail of MORUS-640-1280 shown in Table 6, we obtain a trail shown in Table 10 requiring only 481-bit common prefix when used in an attack.

To take it one step further, the positions of the identical message blocks required in the attack do not need to be located at the beginning. A common suffix works as well as a common prefix, and any four consecutive common blocks work.

Table 10. A linear trail of MORUS-640 with correlation 2^{-38}

Round		Linear masks				
0	α_0	00004000*4	00004000*4	00000000*4	00004000*4	00000000*4
		00080000*4	00000000*4	00000000*4	00000000*4	00000000*4
		00080000*4	00000000*4	00000000*4	00000000*4	00000000*4
		00080000*4	00000000*4	00000000*4	00000000*4	00000000*4
		00080000*4	00000000*4	00000000*4	00000000*4	00000000*4
	β_0	00080000*4	00000000*4	00000000*4	00000000*4	00000000*4
	γ_0	00004000*4	00004000*4	00000000*4	00004000*4	00000000*4
	λ_0	00004000*4				
1	α_1	08002000*4	08082000*4	00000000*4	08082000*4	00000000*4
		00040001*4	00080000*4	00000000*4	00080000*4	00000000*4
		00040001*4	00040000*4	00000000*4	00000000*4	00080000*4
		00040001*4	00040000*4	00000000*4	00000000*4	00080000*4
		00040001*4	00040000*4	00000000*4	00000000*4	00080000*4
	β_1	000c0001*4	000c0000*4	00080000*4	00000000*4	00000001*4
	γ_1	08082000*4	08082000*4	00000000*4	08082000*4	00000000*4
	λ_1	08082000*4				
2	α_2	04000000*4	04000001*4	00000000*4	04000000*4	00000001*4
		80000000*4	00000001*4	00000000*4	00000000*4	00000001*4
		80000000*4	80000000*4	00000000*4	00000000*4	00000000*4
		80000000*4	80000000*4	00000000*4	00000000*4	00000000*4
		80000000*4	80000000*4	00000000*4	00000000*4	00000000*4
	β_2	80000000*4	80000000*4	00000000*4	00000000*4	00000000*4
	γ_2	040c0001*4	040c0001*4	00080000*4	04000000*4	00000000*4
	λ_2	040c0001*4				
3	γ_3	80000000*4	80000000*4	00000000*4	00000000*4	00000000*4
	λ_3	80000000*4				

7 Conclusion and Open Problems

In this work, we propose a polynomial-time algorithm for computing the correlation of a quadratic Boolean function based on its disjoint quadratic form. This method is employed to determine the correlations of the linear trails of MiniMORUS and MORUS we find by solving MILP problems derived from a generic helper model for MORUS-like key-stream generators.

As a result, a set of trails involving four blocks of ciphertext with correlation 2^{-38} is identified for all versions of full MORUS, which leads to the first distinguishing and message-recovery attacks on MORUS-640-128 and MORUS-1280-128. We also observe that the condition specified in [2] to launch the attacks can be relaxed, and this relaxation shows that our trails are superior to those presented in previous work not only in terms of correlation, but also in terms of the numbers of ciphertext blocks involved.

At this point, it is natural to ask some open questions. Firstly, is it possible to compute the correlation of Boolean functions with degrees higher than two efficiently? We believe that an efficient algorithm solving this problem would have a significant effect for cryptanalysis. Secondly, can we find good trails for MORUS which are not rotationally invariant?

Acknowledgment. The authors thank the anonymous reviewers for many helpful comments.The work is supported by the National Key R&D Program of China (Grant No. 2018YFB0804402), the Chinese Major Program of National Cryptography Development Foundation (Grant No. MMJJ20180102), the National Natural Science Foundation of China (61732021, 61802400, 61772519, 61802399), and the Youth Innovation Promotion Association of Chinese Academy of Sciences. Chaoyun Li is supported by the Research Council KU Leuven: C16/15/058, OT/13/071, and by European Union's Horizon 2020 research and innovation programme (No. H2020-MSCA-ITN-2014-643161 ECRYPT-NET).

References

1. AlFardan, N.J., Bernstein, D.J., Paterson, K.G., Poettering, B., Schuldt, J.C.N.: On the security of RC4 in TLS. In: Proceedings of the 22th USENIX Security Symposium, Washington, DC, USA, 14–16 August 2013, pp. 305–320 (2013)
2. Ashur, T., et al.: Cryptanalysis of MORUS. In: Peyrin, T., Galbraith, S. (eds.) ASIACRYPT 2018. LNCS, vol. 11273, pp. 35–64. Springer, Cham (2018). https://doi.org/10.1007/978-3-030-03329-3_2
3. Bar-On, A., Dunkelman, O., Keller, N., Weizman, A.: DLCT: a new tool for differential-linear cryptanalysis. IACR Cryptology ePrint Archive 2019/256 (2019). https://eprint.iacr.org/2019/256. Accepted to EUROCRYPT 2019
4. Bellare, M., Namprempre, C.: Authenticated encryption: relations among notions and analysis of the generic composition paradigm. In: Okamoto, T. (ed.) ASIACRYPT 2000. LNCS, vol. 1976, pp. 531–545. Springer, Heidelberg (2000). https://doi.org/10.1007/3-540-44448-3_41
5. Bellare, M., Namprempre, C.: Authenticated encryption: relations among notions and analysis of the generic composition paradigm. J. Cryptology **21**(4), 469–491 (2008)
6. Biryukov, A., De Cannière, C., Quisquater, M.: On multiple linear approximations. In: Franklin, M. (ed.) CRYPTO 2004. LNCS, vol. 3152, pp. 1–22. Springer, Heidelberg (2004). https://doi.org/10.1007/978-3-540-28628-8_1
7. CAESAR: Call for Submission. http://competitions.cr.yp.to/
8. Dobraunig, C., Eichlseder, M., Mendel, F.: Heuristic tool for linear cryptanalysis with applications to CAESAR candidates. In: Iwata, T., Cheon, J.H. (eds.) ASIACRYPT 2015. LNCS, vol. 9453, pp. 490–509. Springer, Heidelberg (2015). https://doi.org/10.1007/978-3-662-48800-3_20
9. Domonkos, T.P., Lueg, L.: Taking a different approach to attack WPA2-AES, or the born of the CCMP known-plain-text attack (2010). https://www.hwsw.hu/kepek/hirek/2011/05/wpa2aes_ccmp_known_plaintext.pdf
10. Duong, T., Rizzo, J.: Here come the ⊕ ninjas. Ekoparty (2011)

11. Dwivedi, A.D., Kloucek, M., Morawiecki, P., Nikolic, I., Pieprzyk, J., Wójtowicz, S.: SAT-based cryptanalysis of authenticated ciphers from the CAESAR competition. In: Proceedings of the 14th International Joint Conference on e-Business and Telecommunications (ICETE 2017), SECRYPT, Madrid, Spain, 24–26 July 2017, vol. 4, pp. 237–246 (2017)

12. Dwivedi, A.D., Morawiecki, P., Wójtowicz, S.: Differential and rotational cryptanalysis of round-reduced MORUS. In: Proceedings of the 14th International Joint Conference on e-Business and Telecommunications (ICETE 2017), SECRYPT, Madrid, Spain, 24–26 July 2017, vol. 4, pp. 275–284 (2017)

13. Early Symmetric Crypto workshop ESC (2013). https://www.cryptolux.org/mediawiki-esc2013/index.php/ESC_2013

14. Fu, K., Wang, M., Guo, Y., Sun, S., Hu, L.: MILP-based automatic search algorithms for differential and linear trails for speck. In: Peyrin, T. (ed.) FSE 2016. LNCS, vol. 9783, pp. 268–288. Springer, Heidelberg (2016). https://doi.org/10.1007/978-3-662-52993-5_14

15. Kaliski Jr., B.S., Robshaw, M.J.B.: Linear cryptanalysis using multiple approximations. In: Desmedt, Y.G. (ed.) CRYPTO 1994. LNCS, vol. 839, pp. 26–39. Springer, Heidelberg (1994). https://doi.org/10.1007/3-540-48658-5_4

16. Kaliski Jr., B.S., Robshaw, M.J.B.: Linear cryptanalysis using multiple approximations and FEAL. In: Preneel, B. (ed.) FSE 1994. LNCS, vol. 1008, pp. 249–264. Springer, Heidelberg (1995). https://doi.org/10.1007/3-540-60590-8_19

17. Kales, D., Eichlseder, M., Mendel, F.: Note on the robustness of CAESAR candidates. IACR Cryptology ePrint Archive 2017/1137 (2017). http://eprint.iacr.org/2017/1137

18. Langford, S.K., Hellman, M.E.: Differential-linear cryptanalysis. In: Desmedt, Y.G. (ed.) CRYPTO 1994. LNCS, vol. 839, pp. 17–25. Springer, Heidelberg (1994). https://doi.org/10.1007/3-540-48658-5_3

19. Li, Y., Wang, M.: Cryptanalysis of MORUS. Des. Codes Cryptography (2018). https://doi.org/10.1007/s10623-018-0501-6

20. Mantin, I., Shamir, A.: A practical attack on broadcast RC4. In: Matsui, M. (ed.) FSE 2001. LNCS, vol. 2355, pp. 152–164. Springer, Heidelberg (2002). https://doi.org/10.1007/3-540-45473-X_13

21. Matsui, M.: Linear cryptanalysis method for DES cipher. In: Helleseth, T. (ed.) EUROCRYPT 1993. LNCS, vol. 765, pp. 386–397. Springer, Heidelberg (1994). https://doi.org/10.1007/3-540-48285-7_33

22. Matsui, M.: On correlation between the order of S-boxes and the strength of DES. In: De Santis, A. (ed.) EUROCRYPT 1994. LNCS, vol. 950, pp. 366–375. Springer, Heidelberg (1995). https://doi.org/10.1007/BFb0053451

23. Mileva, A., Dimitrova, V., Velichkov, V.: Analysis of the authenticated cipher MORUS (v1). In: Pasalic, E., Knudsen, L.R. (eds.) BalkanCryptSec 2015. LNCS, vol. 9540, pp. 45–59. Springer, Cham (2016). https://doi.org/10.1007/978-3-319-29172-7_4

24. Minaud, B.: Linear biases in AEGIS keystream. In: Joux, A., Youssef, A.M. (eds.) SAC 2014. LNCS, vol. 8781, pp. 290–305. Springer, Cham (2014). https://doi.org/10.1007/978-3-319-13051-4_18

25. Rogaway, P.: Authenticated-encryption with associated-data. In: Proceedings of the 9th ACM Conference on Computer and Communications Security, CCS 2002, Washington, DC, USA, 18–22 November 2002, pp. 98–107 (2002)

26. Rogaway, P.: Nonce-based symmetric encryption. In: Roy, B., Meier, W. (eds.) FSE 2004. LNCS, vol. 3017, pp. 348–358. Springer, Heidelberg (2004). https://doi.org/10.1007/978-3-540-25937-4_22

27. Rogaway, P., Shrimpton, T.: A provable-security treatment of the key-wrap problem. In: Vaudenay, S. (ed.) EUROCRYPT 2006. LNCS, vol. 4004, pp. 373–390. Springer, Heidelberg (2006). https://doi.org/10.1007/11761679_23

28. Salam, M.I., Simpson, L., Bartlett, H., Dawson, E., Pieprzyk, J., Wong, K.K.: Investigating cube attacks on the authenticated encryption stream cipher MORUS. In: 2017 IEEE Trustcom/BigDataSE/ICESS, Sydney, Australia, 1–4 August 2017, pp. 961–966 (2017)

29. Shi, T., Guan, J., Li, J., Zhang, P.: Improved collision cryptanalysis of authenticated cipher MORUS. In: Artificial Intelligence and Industrial Engineering-AIIE, pp. 429–432 (2016)

30. Strassen, V.: Gaussian elimination is not optimal. Numer. Math. **13**(4), 354–356 (1969)

31. Sun, S., Hu, L., Wang, P., Qiao, K., Ma, X., Song, L.: Automatic security evaluation and (related-key) differential characteristic search: application to SIMON, PRESENT, LBlock, DES(L) and other bit-oriented block ciphers. In: Sarkar, P., Iwata, T. (eds.) ASIACRYPT 2014. LNCS, vol. 8873, pp. 158–178. Springer, Heidelberg (2014). https://doi.org/10.1007/978-3-662-45611-8_9

32. Tews, E., Weinmann, R.-P., Pyshkin, A.: Breaking 104 bit WEP in less than 60 seconds. In: Kim, S., Yung, M., Lee, H.-W. (eds.) WISA 2007. LNCS, vol. 4867, pp. 188–202. Springer, Heidelberg (2007). https://doi.org/10.1007/978-3-540-77535-5_14

33. Todo, Y., Isobe, T., Meier, W., Aoki, K., Zhang, B.: Fast correlation attack revisited. In: Shacham, H., Boldyreva, A. (eds.) CRYPTO 2018. LNCS, vol. 10992, pp. 129–159. Springer, Cham (2018). https://doi.org/10.1007/978-3-319-96881-0_5

34. Vaudenay, S., Vizár, D.: Under pressure: security of CAESAR candidates beyond their guarantees. IACR Cryptology ePrint Archive 2017/1147 (2017). http://eprint.iacr.org/2017/1147

35. Wu, H., Huang, T.: The authenticated cipher MORUS (v2). Submission to CAESAR: Competition for Authenticated Encryption. Security, Applicability, and Robustness (Round 3 and Finalist) (2016). https://competitions.cr.yp.to/round3/morusv2.pdf

Low-Memory Attacks Against Two-Round Even-Mansour Using the 3-XOR Problem

Gaëtan Leurent[(✉)] and Ferdinand Sibleyras[(✉)]

Inria, Paris, France
{gaetan.leurent,ferdinand.sibleyras}@inria.fr

Abstract. The iterated Even-Mansour construction is an elegant construction that idealizes block cipher designs such as the AES. In this work we focus on the simplest variant, the 2-round Even-Mansour construction with a single key. This is the most minimal construction that offers security beyond the birthday bound: there is a security proof up to $2^{2n/3}$ evaluations of the underlying permutations and encryption, and the best known attacks have a complexity of roughly $2^n/n$ operations.

We show that attacking this scheme with block size n is related to the 3-XOR problem with element size $\ell = 2n$, an important algorithmic problem that has been studied since the nineties. In particular the 3-XOR problem is known to require at least $2^{\ell/3}$ queries, and the best known algorithms require around $2^{\ell/2}/\ell$ operations: this roughly matches the known bounds for the 2-round Even-Mansour scheme.

Using this link we describe new attacks against the 2-round Even-Mansour scheme. In particular, we obtain the first algorithms where both the data and the memory complexity are significantly lower than 2^n. From a practical standpoint, previous works with a data and/or memory complexity close to 2^n are unlikely to be more efficient than a simple brute-force search over the key. Our best algorithm requires just λn known plaintext/ciphertext pairs, for some constant $0 < \lambda < 1$, $2^n/\lambda n$ time, and $2^{\lambda n}$ memory. For instance, with $n = 64$ and $\lambda = 1/2$, the memory requirement is practical, and we gain a factor 32 over brute-force search. We also describe an algorithm with asymptotic complexity $\mathcal{O}(2^n \ln^2 n/n^2)$, improving the previous asymptotic complexity of $\mathcal{O}(2^n/n)$, using a variant of the 3-SUM algorithm of Baran, Demaine, and Pǎtraşcu.

Keywords: Even-Mansour · Cryptanalysis · 3-XOR

1 Introduction

The Even-Mansour construction [12] is a very simple and elegant way to design a block cipher E from a public permutation P, defined as $E_k(x) = P(x \oplus k_1) \oplus k_2$. In the random permutation model, this construction has been proven secure as

A. Boldyreva and D. Micciancio (Eds.): CRYPTO 2019, LNCS 11693, pp. 210–235, 2019.
https://doi.org/10.1007/978-3-030-26951-7_8

long as $D \cdot Q \leq 2^n$, with n the block size, D the data complexity (online queries to the encryption function) and Q the number of evaluation of the permutation (offline queries). In particular, the time T needed by an attacker is lower bounded by Q, therefore attacks must satisfy $D \cdot T \geq 2^n$. We also have a number of attacks matching this bound, such as [7] with chosen plaintext or [11] using just known plaintext: when balancing online and offline queries, these attacks require only $2^{n/2}$ queries and $2^{n/2}$ computations (including all the computations required by the attack, in addition to permutation queries). A single-key version of the Even-Mansour construction has also been proposed with the same security [10], defined as $E_k(x) = P(x \oplus k) \oplus k$.

More recently, this construction was generalized to the iterated Even-Mansour scheme, also called key-alternating cipher [3]. The r-round construction uses r independent permutations and $r + 1$ keys, and can be considered as an idealization of concrete SPN ciphers:

$$E_k(x) = P_r\Big(\cdots P_2\big(P_1(x \oplus k_0) \oplus k_1\big) \cdots \Big) \oplus k_r$$

This construction was first proven to be secure up to $2^{2n/3}$ queries for $r \geq 2$ [3], and later improved to $2^{nr/(r+1)}$ queries [6,17].

As in the single-round case, the requirement to have independent keys and independent permutations can be relaxed without reducing the security. In particular, two single-key variants of the 2-round Even-Mansour have been proposed [5]:

EMIP : $E_k(x) = P_2\big(P_1(x \oplus k) \oplus k\big) \oplus k$

EMSP : $E_k(x) = P\big(P(x \oplus k) \oplus \pi(k)\big) \oplus k,$ with π a linear orthomorphism.

The EMIP construction (Fig. 1) uses two independent permutations, while the EMSP construction uses a single permutation, and a fixed linear orthomorphism (a linear operation such that both $x \mapsto \pi(x)$ and $x \mapsto x \oplus \pi(x)$ are invertible, such as multiplication by a constant in a field).

There are simple key-recovery attacks matching the $2^{nr/(r+1)}$ bound on the number of queries given in [3], but even with $r = 2$ the best known attacks require about $2^n/n$ operations (in addition to the queries). Attacks against the 3-round Even-Mansour construction have also been given in [8], with complexity close to $2^n/n$, and no attack better than 2^n is known for $r > 3$.

In this paper we focus on the most simple instances, the 2-round variants of EMIP and EMSP, collectively denoted as 2EM, and we look for better attacks than what is currently known, with a focus on low memory and low data.

Previous Works. The first non-trivial attack against an iterated Even-Mansour construction was described by Nikolic, Wang, and Wu in [19] against the two-round EMIP construction $P_2\big(P_1(x \oplus k) \oplus k\big) \oplus k$, using multi-collisions. The main idea is to consider the function $\phi : u \mapsto P_1(u) \oplus u$, and to evaluate it on a large number of points, so as to identify a particular value v that occurs

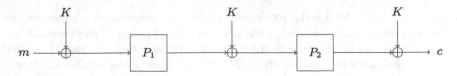

Fig. 1. Single key two-round Even-Mansour scheme (2EM) EMIP variant

more frequently than others (at least t times). Then, for each known plaintext pair $(x, E(x))$, the attacker assumes that $\phi(x \oplus k) = v$, *i.e.* $P_1(x \oplus k) \oplus k = x \oplus v$; this gives a key candidate $P_2(x \oplus v) \oplus E(x)$. Since the assumption holds for at least t values of x, the expected complexity is $2^n/t$.

According to the asymptotic analysis performed in [18], the optimal choice is to set $t = \Theta(n/\ln n)$. A value with this number of repetitions is expected after evaluating ϕ roughly $2^n/n$ times, so that the total complexity of this attack is $2^n \ln n/n$, asymptotically smaller than 2^n.

This attack was later improved by Dinur, Dunkelman, Keller and Shamir [8]. In particular, they describe a variant with lower online complexity using N_v different values v_i that appear t times each, with a smaller value of t. Each online pair $(x, E(x))$ is then used to make a key guess with every v_i, which reduces the data complexity to $2^n/N_v t$. They didn't evaluate this strategy asymptotically, but they computed that $N_v = 2^n \mu^t e^{-t}/t!$ multi-collisions should be found, when evaluating a fraction μ of the domain. In particular, with $\mu = 1/n$ and $t = o(n/\ln n)$, we have an upper bound on the data complexity: $2^n/N_v \leq n^{2t} = \exp(2t \ln n)$, which is asymptotically smaller than $2^{\lambda n}$ for any $\lambda > 0$. The time complexity is still $2^n/t$. Variants of the attack that can applied to Even-Mansour schemes with a linear key-schedule, such as EMSP are also given in [9].

Dinur *et al.* also proposed attacks against a more general construction with 3 independent keys, using multi-collisions to find differential properties of the random permutation. However this attack only reaches time complexity $\mathcal{O}(2^n/\sqrt{n/\ln n})$.

All those attacks require a large pre-processing step to discover multi-collisions: a t-collision is only expected after $2^{n(t-1)/t}$ evaluations of ϕ. Moreover, the best known algorithm to locate multi-collisions requires a memory of size $2^{n(t-2)/t}$ [16]. Therefore, multi-collision based techniques intrinsically require time and memory close to 2^n (asymptotically, we need to have t approaching infinity in order to gain a non-constant advantage over brute-force attacks).

In the journal version of their paper, Dinur *et al.* show an interesting side-result on EMIP. They describe an alternative attack with low memory using linear algebra [9, Section 4.2]. In this attack, they evaluate $\phi : u \mapsto P_1(u) \oplus u$ on a small set of λn values $(0 < \lambda < 1/3)$, and they look for linear relations that are satisfied by all $\phi(u)$ in the set: $L(\phi(u)) = 0$ with $n - \lambda n$ equations. Then, for a given plaintext pair $(x, E(x))$, if $x \oplus k$ is in the set, this implies linear relations on $z = k \oplus P_1(x \oplus k)$, the input of P_2: $L(z) = L(x)$. Finally, using structures for x and z, a match can be identified using linear relations on the key (following from the assumption that $x \oplus k$ is in the set), using $k = P_2(z) \oplus E(x)$. The full details of the attack are given in [9]. This attack only requires a memory of size $2^{\lambda n}$ to store the structures, but it requires $2^n/\lambda n$ chosen plaintext pairs. However, this approach is not applicable to 3EM or 2EM with independent keys, which are the main focus of their work.

More recently, Isobe and Shibutani [14] introduced Meet-in-the-Middle techniques to attack the 2-round Even-Mansour construction. The basic variant of their attack uses a function f depending on a bits of the key k_f (with a in the order of $\ln n$), and a function g depending on the remaining $n - a$ bits k_g. Furthermore, they use a starting point such that a output bits of f are actually independent of the key k_f. This allows them to do the matching over P_2 using just k_g. The attack requires time and data 2^{n-a}, with chosen plaintexts.

The function f is such that it is equivalent to looking for partial multi-collisions in ϕ while imposing a structure on the inputs: they fix $n-a$ bits of u and hope that a outputs bits of $\phi(u)$ will be independent of the remaining a bits of u. For this to work the parameter a must satisfy $a \cdot (2^a - 1) \leq n - a$, and Isobe and Shibutani only give concrete parameters for some values of n. Asymptotically, the maximal value of a can be found by solving $a \cdot (2^a - 1) = n - a$; since $a \lll n$ and $1 \lll 2^a$, we have $a \approx W(n \ln 2)/\ln 2 \approx \log n - \log \log n$, using the Lambert W function.

They also describe a low data-complexity variant of the attack, where the starting point is dynamically chosen so that $a + d$ bits of the plaintext are fixed. This reduces the data complexity to 2^{n-d-a}, while the time complexity is still 2^{n-a}. The parameters are more constrained and must satisfy $a \cdot 2^a + d \leq n - a$. If we want to achieve a data complexity of $2^{\lambda n}$ for a constant $0 < \lambda < 1$, we can set $d = n - \lambda n$, and $a - \log \lambda + \log n \quad \log \log n$. This gives a time complexity of $2^n \log n/\lambda n$.

Finally, they give a time-optimized attack where $b = a + c$ output bits of f are independent of k_f (instead of just a). This reduces the number of queries and memory needed for the matching to 2^{n-b}, but the attack still requires 2^{n-a} memory accesses and chosen plaintext. The parameters must satisfy $b \cdot 2^a + b - a \leq n - b$, but the authors only give concrete values for some choices of n, and no asymptotic analysis. However, we can observe that we must have $b \cdot 2^a \leq n$; in particular, if we want an attack with an advantage that is not asymptotically bounded, we need to have a approaching infinity and therefore b/n approaching zero (this attack cannot reduce the memory to $2^{\lambda n}$ with $\lambda < 1$). In particular, the optimal parameters satisfy $b \cdot 2^a + b - a = n - b$, with $b \lll n$ and $a \lll 2^a$, hence $b \cdot 2^a \approx n$. Therefore we have a complexity of roughly 2^{n-b} in queries and memory, and $b 2^n/n$ in time and data, with $\log n \leq b \lll n$.

All those attacks are summarized in Tables 1 and 2. We point out that the complexity reported in [14] is lower than listed here, because the authors assume that a memory access to a large table is significantly cheaper than the evaluation of the public permutations P_i. Given that a public permutation can obviously be implemented with a table lookup if memory is fast and cheap, we assume that a memory access to a table of size roughly 2^n cannot be faster than the evaluation of the P_i permutations.

Table 1. Comparison of attacks against 2EM. Asymptotic complexity, up to constants. "Data" denotes encryption queries, while "Queries" denotes calls to the public permutations P_i. $0 < \lambda < 1$; $\log n \leq \beta \lll n$; KP: Known plaintext; CP: Chosen plaintext.

Ref	Data		Queries	Time	Memory	Comment
[19]	$2^n \ln n/n$	KP	$2^n \ln n/n$	$2^n \ln n/n$	$2^n \ln n/n$	Multi-collisions
[8]	$2^n \sqrt{\ln n/n}$	CP	$2^n \sqrt{\ln n/n}$	$2^n \sqrt{\ln n/n}$	$2^n \sqrt{\ln n/n}$	Diff. m-c (indep. keys)
[8]	$2^{\lambda n}$	KP	$2^n \ln n/n$	$2^n \ln n/n$	$2^n \ln n/n$	Multi-collisions
[9]	$2^n/\lambda n$	CP	$2^n/\lambda n$	$2^n/\lambda n$	$2^{\lambda n}$	Linear algebra
[14]	$2^n \ln n/n$	CP	$2^n \ln n/n$	$2^n \ln n/n$	$2^n \ln n/n$	MitM
	$2^{\lambda n}$	CP	$2^n \ln n/n$	$2^n \ln n/n$	$2^n \ln n/n$	MitM
	$2^n \beta/n$	CP	$2^n/2^\beta$	$2^n \beta/n$	$2^n/2^\beta$	MitM
Section 3.3	n	KP	$2^n/\sqrt{n}$	$2^n/\sqrt{n}$	$2^n/\sqrt{n}$	3XOR [15]
Section 4.1	2^d	KP	$2^{n-d/2}$	$2^n/n$	$2^{n-d/2}$	Clamping + 3XOR [4]
Section 4.3	2^d	KP	$2^{n-d/2}$	$2^n \ln^2 n/n^2$	$2^{n-d/2}$	Clamping + 3XOR [1]
Section 4.4	λn	KP	$2^n/\lambda n$	$2^n/\lambda n$	$2^{\lambda n}$	Low Data Filter

Our Results. The main results of the paper are the three key-recovery attacks on EMIP given in Sect. 4 whose complexities are summarized in Tables 1 and 2. To the best of our knowledge these are the first attacks on EMIP to significantly reduce simultaneously the data and the memory complexities below 2^n. The first attack, Sect. 4.1, shows that we can achieve the best computational time complexity known so far, that is $\mathcal{O}(2^n/n)$, while using just as much data and queries as the best known distinguisher which is optimal in the balanced case ($2^{2n/3}$ calls to E, P_1 and P_2) with a memory usage not exceeding the number of queries. The next attack in Sect. 4.3 works exactly the same way only it is using another generic 3-XOR algorithm which improves the asymptotic time complexity to $\mathcal{O}(2^n \ln^2 n/n^2)$ that beats the best one known so far. However this 3-XOR algorithm is believed to be impractical for realistic block sizes, notably for $n = 64$. And the third attack in Sect. 4.4 uses very low data, λn, and possibly low memory, $2^{\lambda n}$, for some $\lambda < 1$ while keeping a competitive asymptotic time complexity of $\mathcal{O}(2^n/\lambda n)$.

We also present some security reduction notably showing that adding a linear key schedule does not protect against generic attacks on EMIP. This effectively extends the scope of our attacks in particular showing they can also be applied to the EMSP variant. We also explain the link between the 3-XOR problem and the key-recovery attacks on EMIP showing how one can help us solve the other which justifies our approach. Then we exhibit a symmetry in the Even-Mansour construction that shows how, in the chosen ciphertext attack (CPA) model, an attacker can always swap the number of queries he is making to E, P_1 and P_2 to optimize on the most available resources. This implicitly extends these and previous attacks to adapt to many different data and query complexity profiles.

Lastly we generalize our approach to show that a single key r rounds Even-Mansour scheme can be rewritten as a structured $(r + 1)$-XOR problem with words of size rn. Interestingly both the single key r rounds Even-Mansour and

Table 2. Comparison of attacks against 2EM with $n = 64$. The complexity unit is one evaluation of the cipher; we assume that computing P_1 or P_2 costs $1/2$, and that a memory access to a large table also costs $1/2$. The time complexity also includes the time necessary to generate the data.

Ref	Data		Queries	Time	Memory	Comment
[19]	$2^{58.7}$	KP	$2^{60.5}$	$2^{60.9}$	2^{60}	Multi-collisions
[8]	2^{45}	KP	$2^{60.7}$	$2^{60.7}$	2^{60}	Multi-collisions
[9]	2^{60}	CP	2^{59}	$2^{60.6}$	2^{16}	Linear algebra
[14]	2^{60}	CP	2^{60}	$2^{61.3}$	2^{60}	MitM
	2^{8}	CP	2^{62}	$2^{62.6}$	2^{62}	MitM
	2^{61}	CP	2^{57}	$2^{61.7}$	2^{58}	MitM
Section 3.3	2^{6}	KP	2^{61}	2^{62}	2^{61}	3XOR
Section 4.1	2^{42}	KP	2^{43}	2^{58}	2^{42}	Clamping + 3XOR [4], bal. case
	2^{14}	KP	2^{57}	$2^{58.6}$	2^{57}	optim. data
Section 4.2	2^{35}	CP	2^{57}	$2^{58.6}$	2^{35}	optim. memory & swap $E \leftrightarrow P_1$
Section 4.3	2^{42}	KP	2^{43}	N.A	N.A	Clamping + 3XOR [1], bal. case
Section 4.4	2^{5}	KP	2^{59}	2^{60}	2^{32}	Low Data Filter $\lambda = 1/2$
	2^{4}	KP	2^{60}	2^{61}	2^{16}	$\lambda = 1/4$

the $(r + 1)$-XOR problem with words of size rn have a simple information theoretic solver using $2^{\frac{r \cdot n}{r+1}}$ queries though solving these uses more computations than a brute-force solution for $r \geq 4$.

Practical Considerations. In a practical setting, the data complexity and the memory complexity are important considerations. In particular, an attack with complexity $2^n/n$ is unlikely to be more efficient than a brute-force attack if it requires almost 2^n data, or almost 2^n memory. As mentioned above, some of the previous attacks can reduce the data complexity to $2^{\lambda n}$ for an arbitrary $\lambda > 0$, and the attack from [9, Section 4.2] can reduce the memory to $2^{\lambda n}$, but so far none of them can simultaneously reduce the data and memory complexity below $2^{\lambda n}$ for $\lambda < 1$.

Besides, multi-collision based attacks can use a sequential memory (such as a hard drive) and sort values to locate collisions while the Meet-in-the-Middle attacks require random access memory, with $\Theta(2^n \ln n/n)$ accesses to a table of size $\Theta(2^n \ln n/n)$.

On the other hand the linear algebra techniques we use in our attacks will require algorithmic tricks very close to what was done by Bouillaguet, Delaplace and Fouque [4] for the 3-XOR problem. In particular the values we deal with are sufficiently random to be sorted linearly and the right matrix multiplication in GF(2) LM for an exponentially large matrix L can be computed with a number of operations linear in the size of L. Many constant time optimizations are therefore omitted in this work which justify that right multiplications, sorting and merging two big lists L_1 and L_2 take time and space $\mathcal{O}(|L_1| + |L_2|)$. This is consistent with previous cryptanalysis on EMIP.

For the cost of queries to the oracles E, P_1 and P_2 we mainly follow the convention established by Dinur *et al.* [9] which states that an online query to E costs 1 unit of computation implying that P_1 and P_2 cost $1/2$. The main advantage is that it makes it easy to compare with the brute-force solution that would use 2^n computations. The disadvantage is that it makes it hard to combine with the computations used for simple operations: an evaluation of a cryptographically secure permutation should cost more than a XOR operation.

We give concrete complexity values for $n = 64$ in Table 2 with the assumption that a combination of some linear time operations does not exceed the cost of computing a permutation that is $1/2$ time unit. Concretely, iteratively right multiplying, sorting and merging two lists L_1, L_2 costs $|L_1|/2 + |L_2|/2$. We believe this makes an honest comparison with previous works though they may use other assumptions.

Organization of the Paper. First, in Sect. 2, we show some reductions that extend our results and justify our approach. Then in Sect. 3 we take a close look on previous works done on the 3-XOR Problem to show how it can help the cryptanalysis of EMIP. Lastly, in Sect. 4, we devise three dedicated algorithms for EMIP each having their own particular complexity trade-off. Also we extend our approach in Sect. 5 to the r rounds iterated Even-Mansour construction.

Notations. We denote the block size of the Even-Mansour scheme (*i.e.* the width of the public permutations) as n, and the concatenation of n-bit blocks x and y as $x\|y$. When x and y fit together in one block, we use $x|y$ to denote their concatenation. We use $L[i]$ to denote element i of list L, $x_{[i]}$ to denote bit i of x, $x_{[i:j]}$ to denote bits i to $j - 1$, 0 to denote a zero GF(2) matrix and I to denote an identity GF(2) matrix. When L is a list of ℓ n-bit values, we identify it with a $\ell \times n$ matrix where the elements of L are the rows of the matrix. Finally, we use a curly brace for systems of equations.

2   Security Reductions

We start with some general observations about the security of iterated Even-Mansour schemes. In particular, we show that we can focus on the EMIP construction without loss of generality, how to reduce the security of this construction to an instance of the 3-XOR problem, and how to reorder the oracles to achieve many different trade-offs.

Some previous works already implicitly took advantage of such reductions. For example Isobe and Shibutani [14] realised that their recent attack on EMIP is also applicable to EMSP and Dinur *et al.* [9] realised that they could reorder the oracles for their cryptanalysis of reduced round LED. We formally show here that these tricks are in fact real security reductions and do not depend on the approach used.

2.1 Removing the Key Schedule

There are several variants of single-key multiple-round Even-Mansour studied in the literature. The most general form uses two independent permutations, and an arbitrary key schedule (see Fig. 2):

$$E_k(x) = P_2\big(P_1(x \oplus \gamma_0(k)) \oplus \gamma_1(k)\big) \oplus \gamma_2(k).$$

According to the analysis of [5], there is a class of good key schedules where the γ_i's are public linear bijective functions. In the following, we focus on this class of key schedules, *i.e.* we assume that the $\gamma_i \in \mathsf{GL}(\mathbb{F}_2^n)$. In order to simplify the analysis, we reduce the security of this construction to the security of the EMIP variant without a key schedule.

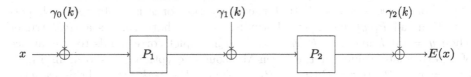

Fig. 2. Linear key-schedule 2-round Even-Mansour.

The main trick is to rewrite the addition of the subkey $\gamma_i(k)$ as the application of the inverse γ_i^{-1}, the addition of k and the application of the forward γ_i:

$$x \oplus \gamma_i(k) = \gamma_i\big(\gamma_i^{-1}(x \oplus \gamma_i(k))\big)$$
$$= \gamma_i\big(\gamma_i^{-1}(x) \oplus k\big)$$

which works thanks to γ_i being linear. Then we define E', P_1', P_2' as follows:

$$P_1'(x) = \gamma_1^{-1}\big(P_1(\gamma_0(x))\big) \quad P_2'(x) = \gamma_2^{-1}\big(P_2(\gamma_1(x))\big) \quad E'(x) = \gamma_2^{-1}\big(E(\gamma_0(x))\big)$$

Thanks to the previous relation, E', P_1', P_2' is actually an instance of EMIP with the same key k (see Fig. 3):

$$E'(x) = P_2'\big(P_1'(x \oplus k) \oplus k\big) \oplus k.$$

Therefore, any attack against EMIP can be used on E', P_1', P_2', and break the initial construction with a key schedule. In particular, a key-recovery attack against EMIP will recover the key of the more general scheme of 2EM.

In the following we only consider the EMIP variant without a key schedule, but thanks to this reduction our attacks can be applied to many other 2EM variants, including the EMSP construction of [5].

Definition 1 (EMIP key recovery). *Given oracle access to three permutations E, P_1, P_2 and their inverses, with the promise that there exist k such that $E(x) = P_2\big(P_1(x \oplus k) \oplus k\big) \oplus k$, recover k.*

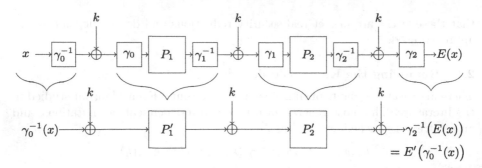

Fig. 3. Reduction of linear key schedule 2EM to EMIP.

2.2   Reduction to 3-XOR

Instead of directly focusing on a key-recovery attack, we focus on locating a triplet of values x, y, z such that the encryption of x is evaluated with permutation call $P_1(y)$ and $P_2(z)$. Formally, we say that x, y, z is a *right* triplet when $y = x \oplus k$ and $z = P_1(y) \oplus k$. A right triplet corresponds to a sequence of intermediate values in the Even-Mansour encryption, as shown in Fig. 4: $\big(x, y = x \oplus k, P_1(y), z = P_1(y) \oplus k, P_2(z), E(x) = P_2(z) \oplus k\big)$; we call this sequence a *path*.

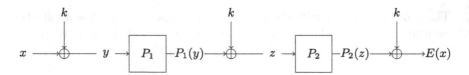

Fig. 4. A right triplet gives a path of EMIP

Since the permutations P_1 and P_2 are public, it is easy to compute a path given the key. Recovering the key from a path is also easy (we have $k = x \oplus y$), but it is hard to identify a right triplet corresponding to a path without the key. By definition a triplet is right when it follows the relation $\mathcal{R}$ defined as:

$$\mathcal{R}(x, y, z) := \begin{cases} x \oplus y = k \\ P_1(y) \oplus z = k \\ P_2(z) \oplus E(x) = k \end{cases} \tag{1}$$

$$\Rightarrow \begin{cases} x \oplus y = P_1(y) \oplus z \\ x \oplus y = P_2(z) \oplus E(x) \end{cases} \tag{2}$$

Notice that we can't directly observe (1) since we don't know k but we can easily verify the implied relation (2).

We claim that if one takes a random triplet combination and observes that it respects (2), then it is a right triplet with good probability. Indeed there are 2^n possible paths (one for every possible input x) implying as many right triplets and 2^{3n} possible triplet combinations; thus a random triplet will be right with probability 2^{-2n}. Since (2) is a $2n$-bit relation, a random but false triplet respects (2) also with probability 2^{-2n}. Therefore we can expect roughly as many right triplets than false triplets that respect (2), thus the first one we find is right with probability $\Omega(1)$. So from now on and for simplicity we will focus on filtering and recovering a triplet that simply respects (2). This means that our algorithms fails to recover the key on some instances, but they have a constant (non-zero) probability of success. In order to improve the success probability arbitrarily close to one, it is easy to test the triplets, and continue the attack until we find a right triplet (alternatively, the whole attack can just be repeated).

In order to simplify the analysis, the condition (2) can be rewritten as:

$$\begin{cases} (x \qquad) \oplus (y \oplus P_1(y)) \oplus (z \qquad) = 0 \\ (x \oplus E(x)) \oplus (y \qquad) \oplus (P_2(z)) = 0 \end{cases}$$

Therefore, finding a triplet satisfying (2) is equivalent to solving an instance of the 3-XOR problem, defined as:

$$\begin{aligned} f_0(x) &:= x \qquad \| x \oplus E(x) \\ f_1(y) &:= y \oplus P_1(y) \| y \\ f_2(z) &:= z \qquad \| P_2(z) \end{aligned} \tag{3}$$

The 3-XOR Problem is a well known algorithmic problem; it is a special case of k-XOR problem analyzed by Wagner as the generalized birhtday problem [20].

Definition 2 (3-XOR problem). *Given three functions f_0, f_1, f_2, find three inputs (x_0, x_1, x_2) such that $f_0(x_0) \oplus f_1(x_1) \oplus f_2(x_2) = 0$.*

We usually focus on functions f_0, f_1, f_2 that are chosen at random. Equivalently, we can be given lists L_0, L_1, L_2 (of random elements) instead of functions. The presentation with functions makes it more clear that the adversary can choose how many queries he makes to each of the functions.

EMIP Key Recovery from the 3-XOR Problem. From the previous discussion, solving the 3-XOR instance defined by (3) gives a triplet satisfying $\mathcal{R}$, which has a high probability of being a right triplet and revealing the key. Evaluating each of the f_i functions requires a single computation of a permutation. However evaluating f_0 must be done online (using an oracle call to E) because it depends on the key, while evaluating f_1 and f_2 can be done offline as the permutations are public and computable at will by the attacker. As per our adopted convention, an evaluation of f_0—that is a call to E—costs 1 unit of computation and an evaluation of f_1 or f_2 costs $1/2$.

We denote the list of values of f_i evaluated by an attacker as L_i. Therefore, the data complexity of an attack is equal to $D = |L_0|$. The time complexity is the amount of computation required to break the scheme. In the computational model, it will depend on the algorithm used and be denoted as T. In the information theoretic model we only look at the number of calls to the permutations and denote it Q, with $Q = (|L_1| + |L_2|)/2$. We will discuss both models.

As seen from the description in (3), we can choose some parts of the values in L_i. However, if we only use random values of x, y, z to build the lists, we obtain a random 3-XOR instance with words of size $w = 2n$. It is known that to find a solution of a 3-XOR problem with good probability, the lists size should respect $|L_0| \times |L_1| \times |L_2| \geq 2^w$. In the information theoretic setting this gives a key recovery attack with $D \times Q^2 = 2^{2n}$. This is the exact same complexity trade-off as the information theoretic distinguisher described by Gaži [13]. In particular it is known that this trade-off is proven optimal in the balanced case $D = Q = 2^{2n/3}$ [5].

2.3   Symmetry Between E, P_1 and P_2

In the 3-XOR problem the 3 functions behave essentially in the same way; if one has a solver using a few evaluations f_0 and lots of evaluations of f_1 and f_2, then the same solver could decide to use lots of queries to f_0 and f_1 and use fewer f_2 queries (just by permuting the functions). In our case, a natural choice is to minimize the number of evaluations of f_0, because they correspond to online queries. This ensures that we have $D \leq Q$. While this is easy to do with a 3-XOR approach, it is not obvious whether this can be done in general for an Iterated Even-Mansour key recovery. We now show that in the chosen ciphertext setting an attacker can actually permute the functions E, P_1 and P_2, and minimize the amount of online queries.

We assume that we are given an instance E, P_1, P_2 of EMIP, i.e. we have oracle access to E, P_1, P_2 denoting forward computations of the permutations, and E^{-1}, P_1^{-1}, P_2^{-1} denoting backward computations. We use a black-box solver $\mathcal{S}(E, E^{-1}, P_1, P_1^{-1}, P_2, P_2^{-1})$ that uses α calls to E/E^{-1} (online queries), β calls to P_1/P_1^{-1} and γ calls to P_2/P_2^{-1} and outputs the key k.

The trick is that we can rewrite the EMIP instance E, P_1, P_2, by permuting the oracles. For instance we have $P_1(x) = k \oplus P_2^{-1}(k \oplus E(k \oplus x))$ (directly from the definition of E), which gives the following EMIP instance with the same secret key k:

$$E' = P_1 \qquad\qquad P_1' = E \qquad\qquad P_2' = P_2^{-1}.$$

Therefore, we can use the solver as $\mathcal{S}(P_1, P_1^{-1}, E, E^{-1}, P_2^{-1}, P_2)$ to recover k using β online queries. Similarly, we can write $P_2(x) = k \oplus E(k \oplus P_1^{-1}(k \oplus x))$; therefore, we can use the solver as $\mathcal{S}(P_2, P_2^{-1}, P_1^{-1}, P_1, E, E^{-1})$ to recover k using γ online queries.

We could further use E^{-1} to rewrite P_1^{-1} and P_2^{-1} in the same fashion and obtain all the possible trade-off between α, β and γ. The point is that, given any solver $\mathcal{S}$, it is always up to the attacker to choose what is the most accessible data. From here onward all of our discussed trade-off will have $|L_0| \leq \min(|L_1|, |L_2|)$ to lower the query complexity but one can remember it is an arbitrary choice.

In particular, this trick can be applied to the attack of [9, Section 4.2]. Indeed, this attack uses λn queries to P_1, with $0 < \lambda < 1/3$ and $2^n/\lambda n$ queries to E and P_2. Using this trick we can reduce the data complexity from $2^n/\lambda n$ to λn, without affecting the other parameters. Actually, the attack presented in Sect. 4.4 can be seen as an improved variant of this modified attack (using known plaintext rather than chosen plaintext).

3   2EM Attacks from 3-XOR Algorithms

In this section we explore the link between 2EM key recovery and the 3-XOR problem. First, we review existing approaches to solve the 3-XOR problem, and we show that previous 2EM attacks can be reinterpreted in a 3-XOR framework. Then we describe new attacks against 2EM based on the reduction of the previous Section. In this section, we focus on a generic 3-XOR instance given by three w-bit function f_0, f_1 and f_2, or three lists L_0, L_1, L_2.

3.1   3-XOR Algorithms

The Birthday Problem, that is the problem of finding collisions among two lists, has been well studied and proven useful in a number of cryptanalysis. In 2002, Wagner proposed a natural extension of this problem, the Generalized Birthday Problem [20], that is the problem of finding collisions among k lists. Here we refer to this problem as the k-XOR problem. In particular Wagner left the hard case of $k = 3$ as an open problem. His best algorithm would just take one value of the first function and solve the classical Birthday Problem among the two others, with complexity $2^{w/2}$.

Subsequent works tried to address this open problem. Two main approaches managed to improve the time complexity of the 3-XOR: an approach based on partial multi-collisions by Nikolic and Sasaki [18] and an approach using linear algebra by Joux [15]. Unfortunately, those two solutions seem hard to combine.

Multi-collisions Algorithms. Nikolic and Sasaki [18] introduced a multi-collision algorithm for the 3-XOR problem as follows. First, compute many outputs of f_0 and look for the most frequent $w/2$-bit prefix α appearing. Store all the values with this fixed prefix in a list L_0 (a partial multi-collision for f_0). Then evaluate f_1 and f_2, $2^{w/2}/\sqrt{|L_0|}$ times each, and store the results in lists L_1 and L_2. Sort the lists, and look for pairs with a difference α in the first $w/2$ bits. An average, there should be $2^{w/2}/|L_0|$ such pairs, and there is a high probability that one of them sums to a value in L_0. According to their analysis, the optimal attack uses around $2^{w/2}/w$ evaluations of f_0, resulting in a multi-collision of size $\Theta(w/\ln(w))$; therefore this algorithm solves the 3-XOR problem with complexity $\mathcal{O}\big(2^{w/2}/\sqrt{w/\ln(w)}\big)$.

Linear Algebra. The second approach, introduced by Joux [15], uses linear algebra and reaches a slightly better complexity of $\mathcal{O}(2^{w/2}/\sqrt{w})$. This attack uses just $w/2$ evaluations of f_0 stored in a list L_0, and $2^{w/2}/\sqrt{w/2}$ evaluations of f_1 (resp. f_2) stored in a list L_1 (resp. L_2). Instead of collecting values in L_0 with a common prefix, we use Gaussian reduction to find a non-singular matrix M such that the elements of $L_0 \cdot M$ start with $w/2$ zeroes.[1] Then we focus on a modified 3-XOR instance:

$$L_0' = L_0 \cdot M \qquad L_1' = L_1 \cdot M \qquad L_2' = L_2 \cdot M.$$

The new instance has the same solutions ($L_0'[h] \oplus L_1'[i] \oplus L_2'[j] = 0 \Leftrightarrow L_0[h] \oplus L_1[i] \oplus L_2[j] = 0$), but the elements of L_0 start with $w/2$ zeroes. Therefore, as in the previous attack, we can efficiently find the solution after sorting the lists L_1 and L_2.

This approach was later generalized by Bouillaguet, Delaplace and Fouque [4], in order to deal with instances of the 3-XOR problem where the size of the lists is limited: given three lists with $|L_0| \cdot |L_1| \cdot |L_2| = 2^w$, they solve the 3-XOR problem with complexity $\mathcal{O}(|L_0| \cdot (|L_1| + |L_2|)/w)$. In particular, with three lists of size $2^{w/3}$ this gives a time complexity of $\mathcal{O}(2^{2w/3}/w)$.

In addition, this algorithm can be combined with the clamping trick of Bernstein to reduce the memory: the attacker first filters the lists L_i to keep only values that start with $w/4$ zero bits, and solves a shorter 3-XOR instance on $3w/4$ bits. If the initial lists have $2^{w/2}$ elements, the filtered lists still have $2^{w/4}$ elements, which is sufficient to expect a solution. This gives an algorithm with time $\mathcal{O}(2^{w/2})$ and memory only $\mathcal{O}(2^{w/3})$. Arguably, this is more practical that algorithms using $\mathcal{O}(2^{w/2}/w)$ memory.

BDP Algorithm. Even before these two approaches, Baran, Demaine and Pătraşcu [1] proposed an algorithm for the 3-SUM problem (using modular additions instead of XORs) with the asymptotical complexity of $\mathcal{O}(2^{w/2} \cdot \ln^2(w)/w^2)$. This algorithm has been adapted to the 3-XOR problem by Bouillaguet et al. [4] with the same complexity. This is best known asymptotic complexity for the 3-XOR problem, even though the algorithm is highly impracticable for realistic values of w. We nevertheless use this algorithm to cryptanalyse 2EM in Sect. 4.3.

3.2 Revisiting Previous Cryptanalysis

Interestingly all attacks so far on 2EM use the same techniques as developed against the 3-XOR problem. Most of the attack are based on multi-collisions [8, 9,19], and the MitM attack by Isobe and Shibutani [14] can also be interpreted as looking for a structured partial multi-collision, as seen in Sect. 1. On the other hand, the attack from [9, Section 4.2] uses linear algebra.

---

[1] For instance, we write L_0 as a block matrix $\begin{bmatrix} A & B \end{bmatrix}$ with two $w/2 \times w/2$ sub-matrices. If B is non-singular, we can use $M = \begin{bmatrix} I & 0 \\ B^{-1}A & B^{-1} \end{bmatrix}$.

Using the Reduction to 3-XOR. As explained in Sect. 2.2, we can use an attack against 3-XOR to build a key-recovery against 2EM in a generic way. In particular, this reduction gives attacks similar to the known attacks on 2EM if we start from multi-collision algorithms to solve 3-XOR. More precisely, the reduction leads to a 3-XOR instance with $w = 2n$, defined as:

$$f_0(x) := x \qquad \| x \oplus E(x) \qquad (3)$$
$$f_1(y) := y \oplus P_1(y) \| y$$
$$f_2(z) := z \qquad \| P_2(z)$$

If we directly apply the previous algorithm the time complexity will be $\mathcal{O}\big(2^n/\sqrt{n/\ln(n)}\big)$. Concretely the most natural way would be to search for prefix multi-collisions offline in f_1 as it is computationally intensive. Because of the definition of f_1, the second half y won't repeat but $(y \oplus P_1(y))$ should repeat roughly as often as a random function (assuming that P_1 is a random permutation). Indeed previous works [8,19] also use repetitions in the values of $(y \oplus P_1(y))$ in their attacks.

Improved Attack from Multi-collisions. We can actually improve this attack and obtain an attack equivalent to the previous works from [8,19], by using the special structure of the 3-XOR instance (3). After building a partial multi-collision L_1 with $\Theta(n/\ln(n))$ values of f_1 starting with α, we look for pairs with $\big(f_0(x) \oplus f_2(z)\big)_{[0:n]} = \alpha$. Because of the structure of f_0 and f_2, we can just use $z = x \oplus \alpha$ for each known plaintext x. Therefore we have $|L_0| = |L_2|$ pairs partially colliding to a predefined value. Each couple gives a full collision if the second n-bit part corresponds to one of the elements in L_1; this happens with probability $n/\ln(n) \cdot 2^{-n}$. Thus this attack requires lists of size $D = Q = \mathcal{O}\big(2^n/(n/\ln(n))\big)$ in order to succeed with high probability in the KPA model.

We see that because we can choose parts of the inputs our problem may be easier than the purely random 3-XOR case. However generic algorithms are a good start to find dedicated cryptanalysis of 2EM. Moreover, the best known attacks against 2EM [8,19] can actually be reinterpreted in this way.

In this paper, we will give new attacks against 2EM starting from this 3-XOR presentation, and using algorithms based on the linear algebra approach.

3.3 A Key Recovery Algorithm

Now we describe a key recovery algorithm simply using the linear algebra 3-XOR algorithm by Joux [15] on the 3-XOR instance obtained by the reduction from 2EM. Using this algorithms as a black box, we have a time complexity of $\mathcal{O}(2^n/\sqrt{n})$ (since $w = 2n$). This is not as good as the best known 2EM key recovery, but this will lay the ground for the more efficient algorithms in Sect. 4.

The full attack can be written as Algorithm **GA**:

GA1. Compute $f_1(y) = (y \oplus P_1(y))\|y$ for Q different values y and store them in L_1.

GA2. Compute $f_2(z) = z\|P_2(z)$ for Q different values z and store them in L_2.

GA3. Observe and find a set of n pairs of plaintext/ciphertext $(x, E(x))$ such that all $\{f_0(x) = x\|(x \oplus E(x))\}$ are linearly independent and store $x\|(x \oplus E(x))$ in L_0.

GA4. See L_0 as a $n \times 2n$ matrix. Use column reduction to find a $2n \times 2n$ transformation matrix M s.t. $L_0 M = [0_{n \times n}\|I_n]$.[2]

GA5. Right-multiply the lists with the transformation matrix:
$L'_0 \leftarrow L_0 M$; $L'_1 \leftarrow L_1 M$; $L'_2 \leftarrow L_2 M$.

GA6. Sort and find partial collisions in L'_1 and L'_2 on the first n−bit half. For each partial collisions $L'_1[i] \oplus L'_2[j]$ check whether the second n-bit half differs only on the hth bit for some h. If yes go to GA7. If no solution found, algorithm fails.

GA7. A solution to the 3-XOR problem $(L_0[h], L_1[i], L_2[j])$ has been found. Output $k = x \oplus y$ with x the first half of $L_0[h]$ and y the second half of $L_1[i]$.

The main idea is that, since the transformation matrix M is linear, solving the 3-XOR problem for L'_0, L'_1, L'_2 yields the same solutions as L_0, L_1, L_2. Using the transformed lists is easier as we exploit the fact that $L'_0 = [0_{n \times n}\|I_{n \times n}]$ which is always possible to ensure after step GA3.

Step GA3 will cost only n queries as n random words of size $2n$ will be linearly independent with very high probability. Note that because we just need to observe these, this attack works in the KPA setting.

Analysis. The query complexity Q is also the size of the lists L_1 and L_2. There are Q^2 pairs each XORing to one of the n elements of L_0 with probability $n/2^{2n}$ as they are taken randomly. Thus the probability of step GA6 succeeding is $(n \cdot Q^2)/2^{2n}$.

Therefore for a constant success probability we fix $(n \cdot Q^2)/2^{2n} = \Theta(1)$. This leads to the following complexities: $Q = \mathcal{O}(2^n/\sqrt{n})$, $T = \mathcal{O}(2^n/\sqrt{n})$ and $D = \mathcal{O}(n)$.

We recall here that sorting random values and performing a right matrix multiplication $L_1 M$ (resp. $L_2 M$) on an exponentially large L_i are both computed in time linear with the size of L_i [4]. As for the computation of M, it is of polynomial time in n and therefore negligible.

Q is the query complexity and we find the relation $DQ^2 = 2^{2n}$ as expected. Memory-wise we need to store the full lists L_1 and L_2 so the memory complexity will also be $Q = \mathcal{O}(2^n/\sqrt{n})$.

Steps GA1 and GA2 concentrate all the permutation's evaluations but can be done as a pre-processing step.

---

[2] We write $L_0 = [A\ B]$. If B is non-singular, we can use $M = \begin{bmatrix} I & 0 \\ B^{-1}A & B^{-1} \end{bmatrix}$.

4   Improved Attacks from the 3-XOR Problem

In the previous section we saw how tools to solve the 3-XOR problem could prove very useful for the 2EM key recovery attacks. But the cryptanalysis allows us to do some tweaks and have better results than simply applying the generic solutions.

In this section we will first show how to add a simple filter to Algorithm **GA** to mount an attack following the trade-off curve $DQ^2 = 2^{2n}$ while improving the time complexity of $T = 2^n/n$ (matching the best known 2EM attacks) and memory not exceeding Q. We also show how using the same filter but with the BDP algorithm adapted for the 3-XOR can give the best asymptotic time complexity so far, $T = \mathcal{O}(\frac{2^n \cdot \ln^2(n)}{n^2})$, though that largely remains theoretical.

Then we describe a very low data and low memory key recovery attack that essentially tweaks the previous Algorithm **GA** to a version that uses, for some parameter $0 < \lambda < 1$, few queries, $D = \lambda n$, time $Q = T = 2^n/\lambda n$ and memory $2^{\lambda n}$. This actually beats the best information theoretic distinguisher known so far in this range of very low data ($DQ^2 < 2^{2n}$).

4.1   Clamping to a Smaller 3-XOR Instance

We first describe an efficient algorithm with a large trade-off space with parameter $D = |L_0| = 2^d$ and $Q = |L_1| = |L_2| = 2^{n-d/2}$ and time complexity $\mathcal{O}(2^n/n)$ (independently of D and Q). This algorithm is built from the 3-XOR algorithm of [4], but we take advantage of the structure of the 3-XOR problem to reduce the time complexity below $\mathcal{O}(2^n/\sqrt{n})$ (reached by Algorithm GA). Indeed, our 3-XOR instance is given as:

$$
\begin{aligned}
f_0(x) &:= x && \| x \oplus E(x) \\
f_1(y) &:= y \oplus P_1(y) \| y \\
f_2(z) &:= z && \| P_2(z)
\end{aligned}
\tag{3}
$$

We can use a variant of the clamping trick of Bernstein [2] to simplify this instance. For a parameter d, we consider the $2^{n-d/2}$ values y with $y_{[0:d/2]} = 0$ and we evaluate f_1 on those values. This gives a list L_1 with $|L_1| = 2^{n-d/2}$ such that all values have $d/2$ zero bits ($L_1[i]_{[n:n+d/2]} = 0$). Similarly, we consider all values z' with $z'_{[0:d/2]} = 0$, and we evaluate f_2 on $z = P_2^{-1}(z')$ to build a list L_2 with $L_2[j]_{[n:n+d/2]} = 0$. Finally, we consider 2^d known plaintexts x, and we keep the values with $(x \oplus E(x))_{[0:d/2]} = 0$ in a list L_0. We expect to have $|L_0| = 2^{d/2}$. We now have three lists with $L_i[u]_{[n:n+d/2]} = 0$, so we can consider this as a 3-XOR problem on $w = 2n - d/2$ bits. We have $|L_0| \cdot |L_1| \cdot |L_2| = 2^{2n-d/2} = 2^w$; therefore there is on average one solution, and the algorithm of Bouillaguet *et al.* [4] finds it with complexity $\mathcal{O}(|L_0| \cdot (|L_1| + |L_2|)/w) = \mathcal{O}(2^n/n)$.

When writing the full details, we have Algorithm **CL**:

CL1. Compute $f_1(y) = (y \oplus P_1(y)) \| y$ for all y such that $y_{[0:d/2]} = 0$. Remove bits $[n : n + d/2]$ (fixed to 0) and store the $(2n - d/2)$-bit values in L_1.

CL2. Compute $f_2(P_2^{-1}(z')) = P_2^{-1}(z') \| z'$ for all z' such that $z'_{[0:d/2]} = 0$. Remove bits $[n : n + d/2]$ (fixed to 0) and store the $(2n - d/2)$-bit values in L_2.

CL3. Until a solution is found do:

  CL3.1. Capture and filter a set of n pairs of plaintext/ciphertext $(x, E(x))$ such that $(x \oplus E(x))_{[0:d/2]} = 0$ and all $\{f_0(x) = x \| (x \oplus E(x))\}$ are linearly independent. Remove bits $[n : n + d/2]$ (fixed to 0) and store the $(2n - d/2)$-bit values in L_0.

  CL3.2. See L_0 as an $n \times (2n - d/2)$ matrix. Use column reduction to find the $(2n - d/2) \times (2n - d/2)$ transformation matrix M such that $L_0 M = [0_{n \times (n - d/2)} \| I_n]$.

  CL3.3. Right-multiply the lists with the transformation matrix:
$L'_0 \leftarrow L_0 M; \quad L'_1 \leftarrow L_1 M; \quad L'_2 \leftarrow L_2 M.$

  CL3.4. Sort and find partial collisions in L'_1 and L'_2 on the] first $(n - d/2)$-bit prefix. For each partial collisions $L'_1[i] \oplus L'_2[j]$ check whether the second n-bit part differs only on the hth bit for some h. If yes go to CL4. If no solution found, loop on CL3.

CL4. A solution to the 3-XOR problem $(L_0[h], L_1[i], L_2[j])$ has been found. Output $k = x \oplus y$ with x the first n-bit of $L_0[h]$ and y made of $d/2$ zeros followed with the last $n - d/2$ bits of $L_1[i]$.

In steps CL1 and CL2 we only fixed the $d/2$ first bits so that we have lists of size $2^{n-d/2}$. Step CL2 still constructs the usual L_2 as a collection of $z \| P_2(z)$ only we need to fix the values of $P_2(z) = z'$ and compute the value $z = P_2^{-1}(z')$ using the inverse.

Then all of this works very much like Algorithm **GA** the main difference begin at step CL3.1 where we filter the observed pairs. Indeed we look for a triplet such that $x \oplus y = z' \oplus E(x)$ so fixing bits of y and z' fixes bits of $(x \oplus E(x))$.

4.2   Complexity Analysis

Data Complexity. The data complexity depends on the number of plaintext/ciphertext pairs we will expect to observe before we find a solution. One way to see it is to count the number of observable right triplets. Initially there are 2^n right triplets but we restrict ourselves to triplets such that $y_{[0:d/2]} = 0$ and $P_2(z)_{[0:d/2]} = 0$, a d-bit filter, so on average will remain 2^{n-d} right triplets. Therefore the moment we observe an x belonging to one of these right triplets it will necessarily pass the filter, give a solution and finish the algorithm. This happens with probability $2^{n-d}/2^n = 2^{-d}$ therefore we expect solution after $D = 2^d$ pairs $(x, E(x))$.

Memory Complexity. The largest lists in memory are L_1 and L_2 that require, in the balanced case, $\mathcal{O}(2^{n-d/2})$ blocks of memory.

Query Complexity. The offline query complexity is also the size of L_1 and L_2, that is $2^{n-d/2} = Q$. In particular, we use as much data as the best known distinguisher with $D \cdot Q^2 = 2^n$. Notice that for the balanced case $D = Q = 2^{2n/3}$ this attack is optimal in the information theoretic model as Chen et al. [5] proved that $\mathcal{O}(2^{2n/3})$ is a lower bound.

Time Complexity. First we need to compute both lists L_1 and L_2 requiring to compute $2^{n-d/2}$ permutations each (this can be a precomputation). We expect the algorithm to succeed after 2^d pairs $(x, E(x))$ with good probability. Thanks to the $d/2$-bit filter in step CL3.1 only $2^{d/2}$ pairs are expected to be processed by batches of n values. Therefore we expect to do $2^{d/2}/n$ loops CL3 before we finish. Each loop consists of computing a small transformation matrix, applying it to the big lists L_1 and L_2, sorting them and looking for prefix collisions. All of these costs are linear in the lists size, $2^{n-d/2}$, or in the number of expected $(n - d/2)$-bit prefix collisions in CL3.4 that is $|L_1| \cdot |L_2|/2^{n-d/2} = 2^{n-d/2}$. Therefore each loop costs $\mathcal{O}(2^{n-d/2})$ and is expected to be performed $2^{d/2}/n$ times for a total computational time complexity of $T = \mathcal{O}(2^n/n)$. This computational time is independent of d.

Discussion. Algorithm **CL** achieves a computational time complexity of $T = 2^n/n$ while using as much information as the best known information theoretic attack with $D \cdot Q^2 = 2^{2n}$. In particular this is information theoretically optimal in the balanced case $D = Q = 2^{2n/3}$ that is for $d = 2n/3$. This attack works with known plaintexts, and there is no obvious way to improve it using chosen plaintext.

For most of the choices of d, evaluations of the cipher and the permutations is not the dominant cost of the algorithm. In this analysis we assume that operations on n-bit words and memory access to lists L_1 and L_2 cost $\theta(1)$ evaluations of the cipher, but if we assume instead that they cost much less than one evaluation (as done in [14]) the attack is even more interesting.

To optimize the memory complexity that is $2^{n-d/2}$, we need to choose a fairly high value d. In that case the data complexity $D = 2^d$ becomes problematic but we can swap the number of online call to E with the number of offline calls to P_1, effectively swapping f_0 and f_1, thanks to the symmetry highlighted in Sect. 2.3. This gives a data and memory complexity of $2^{n-d/2}$, a query complexity of $Q = 2^{n-d/2-1} + 2^{d-1}$ and the time remains $T = \mathcal{O}(2^n/n)$. This becomes a Chosen Plaintext attack because step CL1 requires to choose part of inputs. Concrete values for $n = 64$ for such trade-off are given in Table 2 as "optim. memory & swap $E \leftrightarrow P_1$".

4.3 Using Baran-Demaine-Pătraşcu's 3-SUM Algorithm

Since the previous algorithm just uses a 3-XOR algorithm as a black box after clamping, we can also use it with the BDP algorithm adapted to 3-XOR [4]. In fact, any 3-XOR algorithm could be used after clamping which implies that an improved random 3-XOR algorithm would lead to an improved 2EM cryptanalysis. This adapted BDP algorithm has a better asymptotic complexity, with a speed-up of $\frac{w^2}{\ln^2(w)}$ compared to the quadratic algorithm.

This results in a key-recovery attack against 2EM with asymptotic time complexity $\mathcal{O}(2^n \cdot \ln^2(n)/n^2)$. This is asymptotically better than the best known 2EM key recoveries. However, as shown in [4], it is not practical for realistic word sizes w. Indeed the dominant term in the complexity of the BDP algorithm is $\mathcal{O}(|L_0| \cdot |L_1|/m^2)$ with $m = \Theta(n/\ln(n))$. Following the analysis of Bouillaguet et al., we have more concretely $m \simeq n/(112 \ln(n))$. Therefore, in order to have $m^2 > n$, we would need $n > 2.75 \times 10^6$.

4.4   Very Low Data Algorithm

The previous Algorithm **CL** can reach a low data complexity (with a small parameter d) that would be a multiple of n, or a relatively low memory complexity (close to $2^{n/2}$ with a large d), and having both close to $2^{n/2}$ requires chosen plaintexts. We now describe a new algorithm that combines a very low data complexity and a low memory. This algorithm uses only $D = \lambda n$ known plaintexts for $0 < \lambda < 1$, and has a time complexity $T = \mathcal{O}(2^n/\lambda n)$ while using only a memory of size $2^{\lambda n}$. Moreover, we have $D \cdot Q = 2^n$ and $D \cdot Q^2 = \mathcal{O}(2^{2n}/\lambda n)$, that is the best information theoretical trade-off so far between online and offline queries.

This will be algorithm **LD** with parameter $0 < \lambda < 1$ (typically, we have $\lambda = 1/2$):

LD1. Observe and find a set of λn pairs of plaintext/ciphertext $(x, E(x))$ such that all $\{(x \oplus E(x))_{[n-\lambda n:n]}\}$ are linearly independent and store $f_0(x) = x \| (x \oplus E(x))$ in L_0.

LD2. See L_0 as a three concatenated λn-line matrices:

$$L_0 = [\underbrace{A}_{n} \| \underbrace{B}_{n-\lambda n} \| \underbrace{C}_{\lambda n}]$$

Define the $n \times n$ small transformation matrix M_s:

$$M_s = \begin{bmatrix} I & 0 \\ C^{-1}B & C^{-1} \end{bmatrix} \qquad M_s^{-1} = \begin{bmatrix} I & 0 \\ B & C \end{bmatrix}$$

and the $2n \times 2n$ big transformation matrix M:

$$M = \left[\left(M_s \begin{bmatrix} 0 \\ A \end{bmatrix} \right) M_s \right] = \begin{bmatrix} I & 0 & 0 \\ 0 & I & 0 \\ C^{-1}A & C^{-1}B & C^{-1} \end{bmatrix}$$

LD3. Right-multiply the list L_0 with the big transformation matrix:
$$L_0' \leftarrow L_0 M = [\underbrace{0}_{n} \| \underbrace{0}_{n-\lambda n} \| \underbrace{I}_{\lambda n}]$$

LD4. Until a solution is found pick a new $(n - \lambda n)$-bit value α and do:

    LD4.1. For all λn-bit value u compute $f_1([\alpha|u] \cdot M_s^{-1}) = [\alpha|u] \cdot M_s^{-1} \oplus P_1([\alpha|u] \cdot M_s^{-1}) \| [\alpha|u] \cdot M_s^{-1}$. Store them in L_1.

    LD4.2. For all λn-bit value u compute $f_2(P_2^{-1}([\alpha|u] \cdot M_s^{-1})) = P_2^{-1}([\alpha|u] \cdot M_s^{-1}) \| [\alpha|u] \cdot M_s^{-1}$. Store them in L_2

    LD4.3. Modify the lists with the big transformation matrix:
$$L_1' \leftarrow L_1 M; \quad L_2' \leftarrow L_2 M.$$
    Note that all elements of L_1' and L_2' have bits $[n : n + \lambda n]$ set to α.

    LD4.4. Sort and find partial collisions in L_1' and L_2' on the first n-bit half. For each partial collisions $L_1'[i] \oplus L_2'[j]$ check whether the second half differs on a single bit h with $n - \lambda n < h \leq n$. If yes go to LD5. If no solution found, continue to loop on LD4.

LD5. A solution to the 3-XOR problem $(L_0[h - (n - \lambda n)], L_1[i], L_2[j])$ has been found. Output $k = x \oplus y$ with x the first half of $L_0[h - (n - \lambda n)]$ and y the second half of $L_1[i]$.

We again use the property that finding a solution for the 3-XOR in the modified lists yield the same solution in the original lists.

With the way we defined the big transformation matrix M in LD2 and the fact that we applied M_s^{-1} to the inputs in steps LD4.1 and LD4.2, when we perform step LD4.3 we get the values $f_1([\alpha|u] \cdot M_s^{-1}) \cdot M = [\alpha|u] \cdot M_s^{-1} \oplus P_1([\alpha|u] \cdot M_s^{-1}) \oplus (0|(u \cdot A)) \| [\alpha|u]$ and $f_2(P_2^{-1}([\alpha|u] \cdot M_s^{-1})) \cdot M = P_2^{-1}([\alpha|u] \cdot M_s^{-1}) \oplus (0|(u \cdot A)) \| [\alpha|u]$ stored in L_1' and L_2' respectively. Thus the right-hand side of both lists reverts to the form $\{\alpha|u\}$ with fixed α and for all u. Therefore we get an $(n - \lambda n)$-bit collision for free on α matching with zeroes in L_0'.

4.5   Complexity Analysis

For this attack, in each loop we pick a value α and build L_1, L_2 of size $2^{\lambda n}$. Then we have a solution among the $2^{2\lambda n}$ pairs if one of them XORs to one of the λn values of L_0. Since we have a collision on $(n - \lambda n)$-bit value α for free, one couple gives a solution with probability $\lambda n \cdot 2^{-(n+\lambda n)}$. Thus each loop gives a solution with probability $2^{2\lambda n} \cdot \lambda n \cdot 2^{-(n+\lambda n)} = \lambda n \cdot 2^{\lambda n - n}$. For a constant probability of success we will need to perform around $\frac{2^{n - \lambda n}}{\lambda n}$ iterations.

Data Complexity. Step LD1 completely determines the data complexity of the algorithm. We capture λn plaintext/ciphertext pairs and we get a linearly independent set of values with good probability. Therefore $D = \lambda n$ is the data complexity.

Memory Complexity. The list L_0 and the matrices take a space polynomial in n and therefore negligible. The lists L_1 and L_2 are always of size $2^{\lambda n}$. Therefore the memory complexity is $\mathcal{O}(2^{\lambda n})$.

Query Complexity. The computation of the public permutations are all done in steps LD4.1 and LD4.2 to build lists of size $2^{\lambda n}$. We pass through this step at each loop meaning that the total offline query complexity is:

$$Q = 2^{\lambda n} \cdot \frac{2^{n-\lambda n}}{\lambda n} = \frac{2^n}{\lambda n}$$

Time Complexity. Again, computations of the matrices in step LD2 are essentially polynomial in n so negligible. Step LD4.3 performs right-multiplications on large matrices and step LD4.4 is about sorting and merging which makes those steps linear given that the merged list is of reasonable size. Here we have a partial collision on n bits with probability 2^{-n} therefore there will be around $2^{2\lambda n} \cdot 2^{-n} = 2^{2\lambda n - n}$ partial collisions that is less than the size of the lists ($2^{\lambda n}$) therefore step LD4.4 has also a linear cost. The computational time complexity is therefore also led by the query complexity that is $T = \frac{2^n}{\lambda n}$.

Acceptable Range. Notice that the previous reasoning to derive the time complexity is only applicable when we do need more than one loop to finish the algorithm as it makes no sense to multiply by half-a-round. So all those trade-off depending on λ are constraints by:

$$\frac{2^{n-\lambda n}}{\lambda n} \geq 1 \Leftrightarrow \lambda \leq \frac{W(2^n \ln 2)}{n \ln 2} = 1 - \frac{\ln(n \ln 2)}{n \ln 2} + o(1)$$

(using the Lambert W function)

Discussion. This attack works in the KPA setting as we only need to observe pairs of plaintext/ciphertext, and we need to observe surprisingly few of them, λn pairs are sufficient.

The memory requirement, $\mathcal{O}(2^{\lambda n})$, can also go quite low as we choose the parameter λ but this comes at the cost of no pre-computation possible as we need the transformation matrix to get the right inputs to the public permutations.

The computational time complexity $T = 2^n/\lambda n$ compares well with previous cryptanalysis done on this subject. So far there were no key recovery attack on 2EM with a better asymptotic complexity than $\mathcal{O}(2^n/n)$.

In the information theoretic model, trade-off between D and Q is important as a designer can always arbitrarily limit the maximum value of D by, for example, rekeying in order to achieve a certain security goal. In this regard, this algorithm has a better trade-off between the data and query complexity than the best known generic distinguisher by Gaži [13] that has the trade-off $DQ^2 = 2^{2n}$. Here $DQ^2 = 2^{2n}/\lambda n$ thus being the best known key recovery, and also the best distinguisher, for the acceptable range of λn.

In fact the proof by Chen et al. [5] says nothing for low data range $D \leq 2^{n/4}$ and the best proof is therefore inherited from the original one round Even-Mansour scheme that lower-bounds the trade-off with $DQ \geq 2^n$. Gap between the best known distinguisher and the proof in this range is still an open problem but Algorithm **LD**, which has the trade-off $DQ = 2^n$—and also $DT = 2^n$—for any λ, proves for the first time the optimality of the original proof of the trade-off between D and Q for the acceptable range of λ that is for $1 \leq D \leq \frac{W(2^n \ln 2)}{\ln 2}$.

Previous Work. We can see this cryptanalysis as an advanced version of the attack by Dinur *et al.* using linear algebra [9, Section 4.2]. We can list three main differences that make this attack an improvement over the previous one. First, as already mentioned in Sect. 2.3, we use the symmetry between E, P_1, P_2 to reduce the data complexity from $2^n/\lambda n$ to λn. Then the use of the big transformation matrix M, that essentially performs a Gaussian elimination over the whole $2n$-bit words, makes the attack works with known plaintexts while Dinur *et al.* required chosen plaintexts (even after applying the symmetry trick). Finally, the resulting n-bit filter of step LD4.4 allows for a larger acceptable range of λ than the previous attack that needed $\lambda < 1/3$ to limit the number of partial collisions.

5   Extension to r Rounds

The approach can be generalized to attack multiple rounds. In fact the cryptanalysis of a single key r-round EM scheme can be written as a $(r + 1)$-XOR problem with words of size rn. Even though for $r \geq 4$ generic algorithms won't directly provide interesting attacks with competitive computational complexity, this elegantly rewrites the known generic distinguisher on rEM and may be a good start to look for dedicated cryptanalysis.

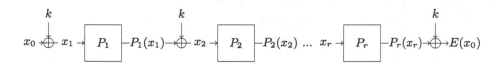

Fig. 5. A right tuple gives a path of rEM

Definition 3 (k-XOR problem). *Given k functions $f_0, f_1, f_2, ..., f_k$, find k inputs $(x_0, x_1, x_2, ..., x_k)$ such that $f_0(x_0) \oplus f_1(x_1) \oplus f_2(x_2) \oplus ... \oplus f_k(x_k) = 0$.*

Extended Relation. To see that we follow the same reasoning as in Sect. 2.2 but for the r-round EM, Fig. 5, and look for an $(r + 1)$-tuple $(x_0, x_1, ..., x_r)$ satisfying the generalized relation $\mathcal{R}$:

$$\mathcal{R}(x_0, x_1, x_2, ..., x_r) := \begin{cases} x_0 \oplus x_1 = k \\ P_i(x_i) \oplus x_{i+1} = k, & 1 \le i \le r-1 \\ P_r(x_r) \oplus E(x_0) = k \end{cases} \tag{4}$$

$$\Rightarrow \begin{cases} x_0 \oplus x_1 = P_1(x_1) \oplus x_2 \\ P_i(x_i) \oplus x_{i+1} = P_{i+1}(x_{i+1}) \oplus x_{i+2}, & 1 \le i \le r-2 \\ P_{r-1}(x_{r-1}) \oplus x_r = P_r(x_r) \oplus E(x_0) \end{cases}$$

$$\tag{5}$$

Again we cannot directly observe $\mathcal{R}$ but we can observe the implied relation 5 which is an rn-bit filter and is enough so that a random $(r+1)$-tuple satisfying Filter 5 is a right tuple with good probability.

Define Lists. Now we can define $r + 1$ lists of r n-bit entries such that solving the $(r + 1)$-XOR problem on those lists over all entries trivially gives a solution to 5:

$$L_0[h] := \begin{cases} x_0 & , h = 1 \\ 0 & , 2 \le h \le r - 1 \\ E(x_0) & , h = r \end{cases} \qquad L_1[h] := \begin{cases} x_1 \oplus P_1(x_1) & , h = 1 \\ P_1(x_1) & , h = 2 \\ 0 & , h \ge 3 \end{cases}$$

$$\underset{2 \le i \le r-1}{L_i[h]} := \begin{cases} 0 & , h \le i - 2 \\ x_i & , h = i - 1 \\ x_i \oplus P_i(x_i) & , h = i \\ P_i(x_i) & , h = i + 1 \\ 0 & , h \ge i + 2 \end{cases} \qquad L_r[h] := \begin{cases} 0 & , h \le r - 2 \\ x_r & , h = r - 1 \\ x_r \oplus P_r(x_r) & , h = r \end{cases}$$

see example for $r = 5$ in Table 3. Thus this indeed defines an $(r + 1)$-XOR problem with rn-bit words even though it is more structured than the purely random k-XOR problem. Upon its resolution we have a successful key recovery with good probability when guessing $k = x_0 \oplus x_1$.

Generic Cryptanalysis. Even though the problem is structured this allows us to use generic algorithms for the k-XOR problem to perform a cryptanalysis. With purely random functions it is known that the lower bounds of queries for the rn-bit words $(r + 1)$-XOR problem is $\mathcal{O}(2^{\frac{rn}{r+1}})$. Interestingly this exactly coincides with the lower bound queries for the single key r-round Even-Mansour scheme [3]. Using generic algorithms allows a cryptanalysis using $D = Q = \mathcal{O}(2^{\frac{rn}{r+1}})$ therefore being optimal in query complexity. In fact the approach can be thought as similar to the simple known distinguisher but instead of looking for contradictory paths we directly look for a correct path (that implies a right tuple) and guess the key.

Table 3. Cryptanalysis of 5EM.

Lists' construction for a cryptanalysis using the 6-XOR problem.				
$L_0 \ni \{\ x_0$	.	.	.	$E(x_0)\}$
$L_1 \ni \{\ x_1 \oplus P_1(x_1)$	$P_1(x_1)$	.	.	. $\}$
$L_2 \ni \{\ x_2$	$x_2 \oplus P_2(x_2)$	$P_2(x_2)$	.	. $\}$
$L_3 \ni \{\ .$	x_3	$x_3 \oplus P_3(x_3)$	$P_3(x_3)$	. $\}$
$L_4 \ni \{\ .$	.	x_4	$x_4 \oplus P_4(x_4)$	$P_4(x_4)\}$
$L_5 \ni \{\ .$	.	.	x_5	$x_5 \oplus P_5(x_5)\}$

Limitation. The computational time complexity of generic algorithms by Wagner for this problem is $T = \mathcal{O}\left(r \cdot 2^{\frac{rn}{\lfloor \log(r+1)\rfloor + 1}}\right)$ [20]. For $r = 2$ and 3 rounds this is just $\mathcal{O}(2^n)$ and we could improve from there in the 2EM case. For the 3EM case Dinur *et al.* [9] showed that we can have a complexity below $\mathcal{O}(2^n)$ using multicollisions and while it is fairly straightforward to rewrite the same attack in the 4-XOR context it is also non-trivial to improve this.

On the other hand the complexity is way over 2^n for $r \geq 4$ rounds. Therefore this is mainly an information theoretic attack. However the lists here have a strong structure, see Table 3, with many bits to 0 which opens the question of a dedicated algorithm with competitive computational time/memory trade-off.

6   Conclusion

In this paper we presented a 3-XOR approach to key-recovery attacks on single-key two-round Even-Mansour. That allows us to gain a better understanding of previous works and devise competitive algorithms using linear algebra techniques that have been initially developed for the random 3-XOR problem.

These attacks have a particularly interesting data and memory complexities. In particular, we give the first attacks where both the data and memory complexity are below $\mathcal{O}(2^{n-\varepsilon})$ for $\varepsilon > 0$, while achieving the best known time complexity of $\mathcal{O}(2^n/n)$. Previous attacks with a similar time complexity required either a very large memory or very large data, making them unlikely to be useful in practice. We also give an attack that improves the asymptotic time complexity to $\mathcal{O}(2^n \cdot \ln^2(n)/n^2)$, although it is not applicable for practical values of n. As another interesting result, we show a very low data attack that beats the best known distinguisher, and actually matches the proven lower bound for single round Even-Mansour construction, with $DT = 2^n$.

All those attacks are shown on the 2EM construction with no key schedule and independent permutations, but we prove that an attack on this variant of 2EM leads to an attack on the more general 2EM with a linear key schedule. Additionally we show that the 2EM construction has an implicit symmetry that allows to blindly swap the number of calls one makes to each oracle during an attack; this automatically allows new trade-offs between the parameters.

Iterated Even-Mansour schemes are idealized SPN networks and understanding their security is important because many block ciphers, including the AES, are based on this design. In this work we focused on the two-round construction linking it to the 3-XOR problem such that a future improvement of the random 3-XOR algorithms will improve our cryptanalysis. But we can also extend this approach to r-round constructions and the $(r + 1)$-XOR problem with a particular structure. We detail this link in Sect. 5 but additional work is required to build competitive key-recovery attacks from that.

Acknowledgement. Part of this work was supported by the French DGA.

References

1. Baran, I., Demaine, E.D., Pătraşcu, M.: Subquadratic algorithms for 3SUM. Algorithmica **50**(4), 584–596 (2008). https://doi.org/10.1007/s00453-007-9036-3
2. Bernstein, D.J.: Better price-performance ratios for generalized birthday attacks. In: Workshop Record of SHARCS, vol. 7, p. 160 (2007)
3. Bogdanov, A., Knudsen, L.R., Leander, G., Standaert, F.-X., Steinberger, J., Tischhauser, E.: Key-alternating ciphers in a provable setting: encryption using a small number of public permutations. In: Pointcheval, D., Johansson, T. (eds.) EUROCRYPT 2012. LNCS, vol. 7237, pp. 45–62. Springer, Heidelberg (2012). https://doi.org/10.1007/978-3-642-29011-4_5
4. Bouillaguet, C., Delaplace, C., Fouque, P.A.: Revisiting and improving algorithms for the 3XOR problem. IACR Trans. Symmetric Cryptol. **2018**(1), 254–276 (2018)
5. Chen, S., Lampe, R., Lee, J., Seurin, Y., Steinberger, J.: Minimizing the two-round Even-Mansour cipher. In: Garay, J.A., Gennaro, R. (eds.) CRYPTO 2014. LNCS, vol. 8616, pp. 39–56. Springer, Heidelberg (2014). https://doi.org/10.1007/978-3-662-44371-2_3
6. Chen, S., Steinberger, J.: Tight security bounds for key-alternating ciphers. In: Nguyen, P.Q., Oswald, E. (eds.) EUROCRYPT 2014. LNCS, vol. 8441, pp. 327–350. Springer, Heidelberg (2014). https://doi.org/10.1007/978-3-642-55220-5_19
7. Daemen, J.: Limitations of the Even-Mansour construction. In: Imai, H., Rivest, R.L., Matsumoto, T. (eds.) ASIACRYPT 1991. LNCS, vol. 739, pp. 495–498. Springer, Heidelberg (1993). https://doi.org/10.1007/3-540-57332-1_46
8. Dinur, I., Dunkelman, O., Keller, N., Shamir, A.: Key recovery attacks on 3-round Even-Mansour, 8-step LED-128, and full AES^2. In: Sako, K., Sarkar, P. (eds.) ASIACRYPT 2013. LNCS, vol. 8269, pp. 337–356. Springer, Heidelberg (2013). https://doi.org/10.1007/978-3-642-42033-7_18
9. Dinur, I., Dunkelman, O., Keller, N., Shamir, A.: Key recovery attacks on iterated Even-Mansour encryption schemes. J. Cryptol. **29**(4), 697–728 (2016)
10. Dunkelman, O., Keller, N., Shamir, A.: Minimalism in cryptography: the Even-Mansour scheme revisited. In: Pointcheval, D., Johansson, T. (eds.) EUROCRYPT 2012. LNCS, vol. 7237, pp. 336–354. Springer, Heidelberg (2012). https://doi.org/10.1007/978-3-642-29011-4_21
11. Dunkelman, O., Keller, N., Shamir, A.: Slidex attacks on the Even-Mansour encryption scheme. J. Cryptol. **28**(1), 1–28 (2015)

12. Even, S., Mansour, Y.: A construction of a cipher from a single pseudorandom permutation. In: Imai, H., Rivest, R.L., Matsumoto, T. (eds.) ASIACRYPT 1991. LNCS, vol. 739, pp. 210–224. Springer, Heidelberg (1993). https://doi.org/10.1007/3-540-57332-1_17

13. Gaži, P.: Plain versus randomized cascading-based key-length extension for block ciphers. In: Canetti, R., Garay, J.A. (eds.) CRYPTO 2013. LNCS, vol. 8042, pp. 551–570. Springer, Heidelberg (2013). https://doi.org/10.1007/978-3-642-40041-4_30

14. Isobe, T., Shibutani, K.: New key recovery attacks on minimal two-round Even-Mansour ciphers. In: Takagi, T., Peyrin, T. (eds.) ASIACRYPT 2017. LNCS, vol. 10624, pp. 244–263. Springer, Cham (2017). https://doi.org/10.1007/978-3-319-70694-8_9

15. Joux, A.: Algorithmic Cryptanalysis, 1st edn. Chapman & Hall/CRC, Boca Raton (2009)

16. Joux, A., Lucks, S.: Improved generic algorithms for 3-collisions. In: Matsui, M. (ed.) ASIACRYPT 2009. LNCS, vol. 5912, pp. 347–363. Springer, Heidelberg (2009). https://doi.org/10.1007/978-3-642-10366-7_21

17. Lampe, R., Patarin, J., Seurin, Y.: An asymptotically tight security analysis of the iterated Even-Mansour cipher. In: Wang, X., Sako, K. (eds.) ASIACRYPT 2012. LNCS, vol. 7658, pp. 278–295. Springer, Heidelberg (2012). https://doi.org/10.1007/978-3-642-34961-4_18

18. Nikolić, I., Sasaki, Y.: Refinements of the k-tree algorithm for the generalized birthday problem. In: Iwata, T., Cheon, J.H. (eds.) ASIACRYPT 2015. LNCS, vol. 9453, pp. 683–703. Springer, Heidelberg (2015). https://doi.org/10.1007/978-3-662-48800-3_28

19. Nikolić, I., Wang, L., Wu, S.: Cryptanalysis of round-reduced LED. In: Moriai, S. (ed.) FSE 2013. LNCS, vol. 8424, pp. 112–129. Springer, Heidelberg (2014). https://doi.org/10.1007/978-3-662-43933-3_7

20. Wagner, D.: A generalized birthday problem. In: Yung, M. (ed.) CRYPTO 2002. LNCS, vol. 2442, pp. 288–304. Springer, Heidelberg (2002). https://doi.org/10.1007/3-540-45708-9_19

(Post) Quantum Cryptography

How to Record Quantum Queries, and Applications to Quantum Indifferentiability

Mark Zhandry[(⊠)]

Princeton University & NTT Research, Princeton, USA
mzhandry@princeton.edu

Abstract. The quantum random oracle model (QROM) has become the standard model in which to prove the post-quantum security of random-oracle-based constructions. Unfortunately, none of the known proof techniques allow the reduction to record information about the adversary's queries, a crucial feature of many classical ROM proofs, including all proofs of indifferentiability for hash function domain extension.

In this work, we give a new QROM proof technique that overcomes this "recording barrier". We do so by giving a new "compressed oracle" which allows for efficient on-the-fly simulation of random oracles, roughly analogous to the usual classical simulation. We then use this new technique to give the first proof of quantum indifferentiability for the Merkle-Damgård domain extender for hash functions. We also give a proof of security for the Fujisaki-Okamoto transformation; previous proofs required modifying the scheme to include an additional hash term. Given the threat posed by quantum computers and the push toward quantum-resistant cryptosystems, our work represents an important tool for efficient post-quantum cryptosystems.

1 Introduction

The random oracle model [BR93] has proven to be a powerful tool for heuristically proving the security of schemes that otherwise lacked a security proof. In the random oracle model (ROM), a hash function H is modeled as a truly random function that can only be evaluated by querying an oracle for H. A scheme is secure in the ROM if it can be proven secure in this setting. Of course, random oracles cannot be efficiently realized; in practice, the random oracle is replaced with a concrete efficient hash function. The hope is that the ROM proof will indicate security in the real world, provided there are no structural weaknesses in the concrete hash function.

Meanwhile, given the looming threat of quantum computers [IBM17], there has been considerable interest in analyzing schemes for so called "post-quantum" security [NIS17, Son14, ATTU16, CBH+17, YAJ+17, CDG+17, CDG+15]. Many of the proposed schemes are random oracle schemes; Boneh et al. [BDF+11] argue that the right way of modeling the random oracle in the quantum setting

© International Association for Cryptologic Research 2019
A. Boldyreva and D. Micciancio (Eds.): CRYPTO 2019, LNCS 11693, pp. 239–268, 2019.
https://doi.org/10.1007/978-3-030-26951-7_9

is to use the quantum random oracle model, or QROM. Such a model allows a quantum attacker to query the random oracle on a quantum superposition of inputs. The idea is that a real-world quantum attacker, who knows the code for the concrete hash function, can evaluate the hash function in superposition in order to perform tasks such as Grover search [Gro96] or collision finding [BHT98]. In order to accurately capture such real-world attacks, it is crucial to model the random oracle to allow for such superposition queries. The quantum random oracle model has been used in a variety of subsequent works to prove the post-quantum security of cryptosystems [BDF+11, Zha12b, Zha15, TU16, Eat17].

The Recording Barrier. Unfortunately, proving security in the quantum random oracle model can be extremely difficult. Indeed, in the classical random oracle model, one can copy down the adversary's queries as a means to learning what points the adversary is interested in. Many classical security proofs crucially use this information in order to construct a new adversary which solves some hard underlying problem, reaching a contradiction. In the quantum setting, such copying is impossible by no-cloning. One can try to record some information about the query, but this amounts to a measurement of the adversary's query state which can be detected by the adversary. A mischievous adversary may refuse to continue if it detects such a measurement, rendering the adversary useless for solving the underlying problem. Because of the difficulty in reading an adversary's query, it also becomes hard to adaptively program the random oracle, another common classical proof technique.

This difficulty has led authors to develop new quantum-sound proof techniques to replace classical techniques, such as Zhandry's small-range distributions [Zha12a] or Targhi and Unruh's extraction technique [TU16]. These proof techniques choose the oracle from a careful distribution that allows for proofs to go through. However, every such proof technique always chooses a classical oracle at the beginning of the experiment, and leave the oracle essentially unchanged through the entire execution. The inability to change the oracle seems inherent, since if the proof gives the adversary different oracles during different queries, this is potentially easily detectable (even by classical adversaries).[1]

Constraining the oracles to be fixed functions seems to limit what can be proved using such non-recording techniques. For example, Dagdelen, Fischlin, and Gagliardoni [DFG13] show that such natural proof techniques are likely incapable of proving the security of Fiat-Shamir[2]. This leads to a natural question: *Is it possible to record information about an adversary's quantum query without the adversary detecting.*

---

[1] The one exception we are aware of is Unruh's adaptive programming [Unr15]. This proof does change the oracle adaptively, but only inputs for which adversary's queries have only negligible "weight". Thus, the change is not detectable. The following discussion also applies to Unruh's technique.

[2] We note that if the underlying building blocks are strengthened, Fiat-Shamir was proven secure by Unruh [Unr16].

Enter Indifferentiability. The random oracle model (quantum or otherwise) assumes the adversary treats the hash function as a monolithic object. Unfortunately, hash functions in practice are usually built from smaller building blocks, called compression functions. If one is not careful, hash functions built in this way are vulnerable to attacks such as length-extension attacks. Coron et al. [CDMP05] show that a hash function built from a compression function can be as good as a monolithic oracle in many settings if it satisfies a notion of *indifferentiability*, due to Maurer, Renner, and Holenstein [MRH04]. Roughly, in indifferentiability, an adversary A has oracle access to both h and H, and the adversary is trying to distinguish two possible worlds. In the "real world", h is a random function, and H is built from h according to the hash function construction. In the "ideal world", H is a random function, and h is simulated so as to be consistent with H. A hash function is indifferentiable from a random oracle if no efficient adversary can distinguish the two worlds.

Coron et al.'s proof of indifferentiability for Merkle-Damgard requires the simulator to remember the queries that the adversary has made. This is actually inherent for any domain extender, by a simple counting argument discussed below. In the quantum setting, such recording presents a serious issue, as recording a query is equivalent (from the adversary's point of view) to measuring the query. As any measurement will disturb the quantum system, such measurement may be detectable to the adversary. Note that in the case where A is interacting with a truly random h, there is no measurement happening. Therefore, if such a measurement can be detected, the adversary can distinguish the two cases, breaking indifferentiability.

Example. To illustrate what might go wrong, we will use the simple example from Coron et al. [CDMP05]. Here, we will actually assume access to two independent compression functions $h_0, h_1 : \{0,1\}^{2n} \to \{0,1\}^n$. We will define $H : \{0,1\}^{3n} \to \{0,1\}^n$ as $H(x,y) = h_1(h_0(x), y)$, where $x \in \{0,1\}^{2n}, y \in \{0,1\}^n$.

To argue that H is indifferentiable from a random oracle, Coron et al. use the following simulator S, which has access to H, and tries to implement the oracles h_0, h_1. S works as follows:

- S keeps databases D_0, D_1, which will contain tuples (x,y). D_b containing (x,y) means that S has set $h_b(x) = y$.
- h_0 is implemented on the fly: every query on x looks up $(x,y) \in D_0$, and returns y if it is found; if no such pair is found, a random y is chosen and returned, and (x,y) is added to D_0.
- By default, h_1 is answered randomly on the fly as in h_0. However, it needs to make sure that $h_1(h_0(x), y)$ always evaluates to $H(x,y)$, else it is trivial to distinguish the two worlds. Therefore, on a query (z,y), h_1 will check if there is a pair (x,z) in D_0 for some x. If so, it will reasonably guess that the adversary is trying to evaluate $H(x,y)$, and respond by making a query to $H(x,y)$. Otherwise it will resort to the default simulation.

Note that by defining the simulator in this way, if the adversary ever tries to evaluate H on (x,z) by first making a query x to h_0 to get y, and then making a query (y, z) to h_1, the simulator will correctly set the output of h_1 to $H(x, z)$, so that the adversary will get a result that is consistent with H. However, note that it is crucial that S wrote down the queries made to h_0, or else it will not know which point to query H when simulating h_1.

Now consider a quantum adversary. A quantum query to, say, h_0 will be the following operation:

$$\sum_{x \in \{0,1\}^{2n}, u \in \{0,1\}^n} \alpha_{x,u} |x, u\rangle \mapsto \sum_{x \in \{0,1\}^{2n}, u \in \{0,1\}^n} \alpha_{x,u} |x, u \oplus h_0(x)\rangle$$

Now, imagine our simulator trying to answer queries to h_0 in superposition. For simplicity, suppose this is the first query to h_0, so D_0 is empty. The natural approach is to just have S store its database D_0 in superposition, performing a map that may look like $|x, u\rangle \mapsto |x, u \oplus y\rangle \otimes |x, y\rangle$, where y is chosen randomly, and everything to the right of the $\otimes$ is the simulators state.

But now consider the following query by an adversary. It sets up the uniform superposition $\sum_{x,u} |x, u\rangle$ and queries. In the case where h_0 is a classical function, then this state becomes

$$\sum_{x,u} |x, u \oplus h_0(x)\rangle = \sum_{x,u} |x, u\rangle$$

Namely, the state is unaffected by making the query. In contrast, the simulated query would result in

$$\sum_{x,u} |x, u \oplus y\rangle \otimes |x, y\rangle$$

Here, the adversary's state is now entangled with the simulator's. It is straightforward to detect this entanglement by applying the Quantum Fourier Transform (QFT) to the adversary's x registers, and then measuring the result. In the case where the adversary is interacting with a random h_0, the QFT will result in a 0. In the simulated case, the QFT will result in a random string. These two cases are therefore easily distinguishable.

To remedy this issue, prior works in the quantum regime have abandoned on-the-fly simulation, instead opting for stateless simulation. Here, the simulator commits to a function to implement the oracle in the very beginning, and then sticks with this implementation throughout the entire experiment. Moreover, the simulator never records any information about the adversary's query, lest the adversary detect the entanglement with the simulator. This will certainly fix the issue above, and by carefully choosing the right implementations prior works have shown how to translate many classical results into the quantum setting.

However, for indifferentiability, choosing a single fixed function for h_0 introduces new problems. Now when the adversary makes a query to h_1, the simulator needs to decide if the query represents an attempt at evaluating H, and if so, it must program the output of h_1 accordingly. However, without knowing what inputs the adversary has queried to h_0, it seems impossible for the simulator to determine which point the adversary is interested in. For example, if the adversary queries h_1 on (y, z), there will be roughly 2^n possible x that gave rise to this y (since h_0 is compressing). Therefore, the simulator must choose from one of 2^n inputs of the form (x, z) on which to query H.

To make matters even more complicated, an adversary can submit the uniform superposition $\sum_x |x, 0\rangle$, resulting in the state $\sum_x |x, h_0(x)\rangle$, which causes it to "learn" $y = h_0(x)$. At this point, the simulator should be ready to respond to an h_1 query on (y, z) by using x, meaning the simulator *must* be entangled with x. Then, at some later time, the adversary can query again on the state $\sum_x |x, h_0(x)\rangle$, resulting in the original state $\sum_x |x, 0\rangle$ again. The adversary can test that it received the correct state using the quantum Fourier transform. Therefore, after this later query, the simulator must be un-entangled with x. Even more complex strategies are possible, where the adversary can compute and un-compute h_0 in stages, so as to try to hide what it is doing from any potential simulator.

These issues are much more general than just the simple domain extender above. Indeed, even classically domain extension with a *stateless* simulator is *impossible*, by the following simple argument. Suppose there is a hash function $H : \{0,1\}^M \to \{0,1\}^N$ built from a compression function $h : \{0,1\}^m \to \{0,1\}^n$ as $H = C^h$ for an oracle circuit C. Let $L = M + \log_2 N, \ell = m + \log_2 n$. Then L, ℓ represent the logarithm of the size of the truth tables for H, h. Since we are domain extending, we are interested in the case where $L \gg \ell$. Suppose even $L \geq \ell + 0.001$.

Suppose toward contradiction that h can be simulated statelessly, which we will represent as Sim^H (since the function can make H queries). Then h has a truth table of size 2^ℓ. In the real world, H agrees with C^h on all inputs; therefore in order for indifferentiability to hold, in the simulated world a uniformly random H must agree with $C^h = C^{\mathsf{Sim}^H}$ on an overwhelming fraction of inputs. But this is clearly impossible, as it would allow us to compress the random truth table of H: simply output the truth table for Sim^H, along with the ϵ fraction of input/output pairs where H and C^{Sim^H} disagree. The total length of this compressed truth table is $2^\ell + (\epsilon 2^M)(MN) = 2^\ell + \epsilon N 2^L$. As ϵ is negligible (and therefore much smaller than $1/N$) the compressed truth table will be smaller than 2^L, the size of the truth table for H. But since H is a random function its truth table cannot be compressed, reaching a contradiction.

Therefore, any simulator for indifferentiability, regardless of the scheme, *must* inherently store information about the adversary. But the existing QROM techniques are utterly incapable of such recording. We therefore ask: *Is indifferentiable domain extension even possible?*

1.1 This Work

In this work, perhaps surprisingly, we answer the question above in the affirmative. Namely, we give a new *compressed oracle technique*, which allows for recording the adversary's queries in a way that the adversary can never detect. The intuition is surprisingly simple: an adversary interacting with a random oracle can be thought of as being entangled with a uniform superposition of oracles.

As entanglement is symmetric, if the adversary ever has any information about the oracle, the *oracle must also have information about the adversary*. Therefore a simulator can always record *some* information about the adversary, if done carefully.

We then use the technique to prove the indifferentiability of the Merkle-Damgård construction. We believe our new technique will be of independent interest; for example our technique can be used to prove the security of the Fujisaki-Okamoto transformation [FO99], and also gives very short proofs of several quantum query lower bounds.

The Compressed Oracle Technique. In order to prove indifferentiability, we devise a new way of analyzing quantum query algorithms

Consider an adversary interacting with an oracle $h : \{0,1\}^m \to \{0,1\}^n$. It is well established that the usual quantum oracle mapping $|x, y\rangle \mapsto |x, y \oplus h(x)\rangle$ is equivalent to the "phase" oracle, which maps $|x, u\rangle \mapsto (-1)^{u \cdot h(x)}|x, u\rangle$ (we discuss this equivalence in Sect. 3). For simplicity, in this introduction we will focus on the phase oracle, which is without loss of generality.

Next, we note that the oracle h being chosen at random is equivalent (from the adversary's point of view) to h being in uniform superposition $\sum_h |h\rangle$. Indeed, the superposition can be reduced to a random h by measuring, and measuring the h registers (which is outside of A's view) is undetectable to A. To put another way, the superposition over h is a *purification* of the adversary's mixed state.

Therefore, we will imagine the h oracle as containing $\sum_h |h\rangle$. When A makes a query on $\sum_{x,u} \alpha_{x,u}|x, u\rangle$, the joint system of the adversary and oracle are

$$\sum_{x,u} \alpha_{x,u}|x, u\rangle \otimes \sum_h |h\rangle$$

The query introduces a phase term $(-1)^{u \cdot h(x)}$, so the joint system becomes

$$\sum_{x,u} \alpha_{x,u}|x, u\rangle \otimes \sum_h |h\rangle(-1)^{u \cdot h(x)}$$

We normally think of the phase as being returned to the adversary, but the phase really affects the entire system, so it is equivalent to think of the phase as being added to the oracle's state.

Now, we will think of h as a vector of length $2^m \times n$ by simply writing down h's truth table. We will think of each x, u pair as a point function $P_{x,u}$ which outputs u on x and 0 elsewhere. Using our encoding of functions as vectors, we can write $u \cdot h(x)$ as $P_{x,u} \cdot h$. We can therefore write the post-query state as

$$\sum_{x,u} \alpha_{x,u}|x, u\rangle \otimes \sum_h |h\rangle(-1)^{h \cdot P_{x,u}}$$

In general, the state after making q queries can be written as

$$\sum_{x_1,\ldots,x_q,u_1,\ldots,u_q} \alpha_{x_1,\ldots,x_q,u_1,\ldots,u_q}|\psi_{x_1,\ldots,x_q,u_1,\ldots,u_q}\rangle \otimes \sum_h |h\rangle(-1)^{h \cdot (P_{x_1,u_1}+\cdots+P_{x_q,u_q})}$$

Next, notice that by applying the Quantum Fourier transform to h, the h registers will now contain $(P_{x_1,u_1} + \cdots + P_{x_q,u_q})$ mod 2. Working in the Fourier domain, we see that each query simply adds $P_{x,u}$ (modulo 2) to the result. In the Fourier domain, the initial state is 0.

Therefore, from A's point of view, it is indistinguishable whether the oracle for h is a random oracle, or it is implemented as follows:

- The oracle keeps as state a vector $D \in \{0,1\}^{n \times 2^m}$, initially set to 0.
- On any oracle query, the oracle performs the map $|x, u\rangle \otimes |D\rangle \mapsto |x, u\rangle \otimes |D \oplus P(x, u)\rangle$

Thus, with this remarkably simple change in perspective, the oracle can actually be implemented by recording and updating phase information about the queries being in made.

We can now take this a couple steps further. Notice that after q queries, D is non-zero on at most q inputs (since it is the sum of q point functions). Therefore, we can store the database in an extremely compact form, namely the list of (x, y) pairs where $y = D(x)$ and $y \neq 0$. Notice that this allows us to efficiently simulate a random oracle, without an a priori bound on the number of queries. Previously, simulating an unbounded number of queries efficiently required computational assumptions, and simulation was only computationally secure. In contrast, simulating random oracles exactly required $2q$-wise independent functions [Zha12b] and hence required knowing q up front. We therefore believe this simulation will have independent applications for the efficient simulation of quantum oracles. We will call this the compressed Fourier oracle.

We can then take our compressed Fourier oracle, and convert it back into a primal-domain oracle. Namely, for each (x, y) pair, we perform the QFT on the y registers. The result is a superposition of databases of (x, w) pairs, where w roughly represents $h(x)$. For any pair not in the database, $h(x)$ is implicitly a uniform superposition of inputs independent of the adversary's view. We call this the compressed standard oracle. It intuitively represents what the adversary knows about the function h: if (x, y) is in the database then the adversary "knows" $h(x) = y$, and otherwise, the adversary "knows" nothing about $h(x)$. In Sect. 3, we show how to directly obtain the compressed standard oracle.

Applying Compressed Oracles to Indifferentiability. The compressed standard oracle offers a simple way to keep track of the queries the adversary has made. In particular, it tracks exactly the kind of information needed in the classical indifferentiability proof above, namely whether or not a particular value has been queried by the adversary, and what the value of the oracle at that point is. We use this to give a quantum indifferentiability proof for Merkle-Damgård construction using prefix-free encodings [CDMP05].

To illustrate our ideas, consider our simple example above with h_0, h_1 and H. Our simulator will simulate h_0 as in the compressed standard oracle, keeping a (superposition over) lists D_0 of (x, y) pairs. Next, our simulator must handle h_1 queries. When given a phase query $|y, z\rangle$, the simulator does the following. If first looks for a pair (x, y') in D_0 with $y' = y$. If one is found, it reasonably guesses that the adversary is interested in computing $H(x,z)$, and so it makes a query on (x,z) to H. Otherwise, it is reasonable to guess that the adversary is not trying to compute H on any input, since the adversary does not "know" any inputs to h_0 that would result in a query to h_1 on (y,z).

While the above appears to work, we need to make sure the simulator does not disturb the compressed oracle. Unfortunately, some disturbance is necessary. Indeed, determining the value of $h_0(x)$ is a measurement in the primal domain. On the other hand, the update procedure for the compressed oracles needs to decide whether or not x belongs in the database, and this corresponds to a measurement in the *Fourier* domain (since in the Fourier domain, $h_0(x)$ must be non-zero). These two measurements do not commute, so by the uncertainty principle it is impossible to perform both measurements perfectly.

Nonetheless, we show that the errors are small. Intuitively, we observe that the simulator does not actually need to know the entire value of $h_0(x)$, just whether or not it is equal to y. We call such information a "test". Similarly, the compressed oracle implementation just needs to know whether or not $h_0(x)$ is equal to 0, but in the Fourier domain.

Now, these primal and Fourier tests still do not commute. Fortunately, they "almost" commute, which we formalize in the full version [Zha18]. The intuition is that, if a primal test of the form "is $h_0(x) = y$" has a non-negligible chance of succeeding, $h_0(x)$ must be very "far" from the uniform superposition. This is because a uniform superposition puts an exponentially small weight on every outcome. Recall that the uniform superposition maps to $h_0(x) = 0$ in the Fourier domain. Thus by being "far" from uniform, the Fourier domain test has a negligibly-small chance of succeeding. Therefore, one of the two tests is always "almost" determined, meaning the measurement negligibly affects the state. This means that, no matter what initial state is, the two tests "almost" commute.

Thus, the simulator can perform these tests without perturbing the state significantly. This shows that h_0 queries are correctly simulated; we also need to show that h_1 queries are correctly simulated and consistent with H. The intuition above suggests that h_1 should be consistent with H, and indeed in Sect. 5 we show this using a careful sequence of hybrids. Then in the full version [Zha18], we use the same ideas to prove the indifferentiability of Merkle-Damgård.

The Power of Forgetting. Surprisingly, our simulator ends up strongly resembling the classical simulator. It is natural to ask, therefore, how the simulator gets around the difficulties outlined above.

First, notice that if we translate the query $\sum_{x,u} |x,u\rangle$ in our example to a phase query, it becomes $\sum_x |x,0\rangle$. This query has no effect on the oracle's state. This means the oracle remains un-entangled with the adversary, as desired.

Second, a query $\sum_x |x,0\rangle$ becomes $\sum_{x,u} |x,u\rangle$ for a phase query. Consider applying the query to the compressed Fourier oracle. The joint quantum system of the adversary and simulator becomes

$$\sum_{x,u \neq 0} |x,u\rangle|\{(x,u)\}\rangle + \sum_x |x,0\rangle|\{\}\rangle$$

A similar expression holds for the compressed standard oracle. Note that the simulator can clearly tell (whp) that the adversary has queried on x. Later, when the adversary queries on the same state a second time, (x, u) will get mapped to $(x, 0)$, and will hence be removed from the database. Thus, after this later query, the database contains no information about x. Hence, the adversary is un-entangled with x, and so it's tests will output the correct value.

Ultimately then, the key difference between our simulator and the natural quantum analog of the classical simulator is that our simulator must be ready to *forget* some of the oracle points it simulated previously. By implementing h_0 as a compressed oracle, it will forget *exactly* when it needs to so that the adversary can never detect that it is interacting with a simulated oracle.

Other Results. We expect our compressed oracle technique will have applications beyond indifferentiability. Here, we list two additional sets of results we are able to obtain using our technique:

Post-quantum Security of Fujisaki-Okamoto. The Fujisaki-Okamoto transformation [FO99] transforms a weak public key encryption scheme into a public key encryption scheme that is secure against *chosen ciphertext attacks*, in the random oracle model. Unfortunately, the classical proof does not work in quantum random oracle model, owing to similar issues with indifferentiability proofs. Namely, in one step of the proof, the reduction looks at the queries made by the adversary in order to decrypt chosen ciphertext queries. This is crucial to allow the reduction to simulate the view of the adversary without requiring the secret decryption key. But in the quantum setting, it is no longer straightforward to read the adversary's queries without disrupting its state.

Targhi and Unruh [TU16] previously modified the transformation by including an additional random oracle hash in the ciphertext. In the proof, the hash function is set to be injective, and the reduction can invert the hash in order to decrypt.

In the full version [Zha18], we show how to adapt our compressed oracle technique to prove the security of the original transform without the extra hash. In addition, we show security against even *quantum* chosen ciphertext queries, thus proving security in the stronger model of Boneh and Zhandry [BZ13]. We note that recently, Jiang et al. [JZC+18] proved the security of the FO transformation when used as a key encapsulation mechanism. Their proof is tight, whereas ours is somewhat loose. On the other hand, we note that their proof does not apply if FO is used directly as an encryption scheme, and does not apply in the case of quantum chosen ciphertext queries.

Simple Quantum Query Complexity Lower Bounds. We also show that our compressed oracles can be used to give very simple and optimal quantum query complexity lower bounds for problems for *random functions*, such as pre-image search, collision finding, and more generally k-SUM.

Our proof strategy is roughly as follows. First, since intuitively the adversary has no knowledge of values of h outside of D, except with very small probability any successful algorithm will output points in D. Therefore it suffices to bound the number of queries required to get D to contain a pre-image/collision/k-sum.

For pre-image search, we re-prove the optimal lower bound of $\Omega(2^{n/2})$ queries of [BBBV97], but for random functions; note that pre-image search for random functions and worst-case functions is equivalent using simple reductions. The proof appears superficially similar to [BBBV97]: we show that each query can increase the "amplitude" on "good" databases by a small $O(2^{-n/2})$ amount. After q queries, this amplitude becomes $O(q/2^{n/2})$, which we then square to get the probability of a "good" database. The proof is only slightly over a page once the compressed oracle formalism has been given.

We then re-prove the optimal collision lower bound of $\Omega(2^{n/3})$ queries for random functions, matching the worst case bound [AS04] and the more recent average case bound [Zha15]. Remarkably, our proof involves only a few lines of modification to the pre-image lower bound. We show that the amplitude on "good" databases increases by $O(\sqrt{q} \times 2^{n/2})$ for each query, where the extra $\sqrt{q}$ intuitively comes from the fact that the database has size at most q, giving q opportunities for a collision every time a new entry is added to the database[3].

In contrast to our very simple extension, the prior collision bounds involved very different techniques and were much more complicated. Also note that prior works could not prove directly that finding collisions were hard. Instead, they show that distinguishing a function with many collisions from an injective function was hard. This then only works directly for expanding functions, which are of little interest to cryptographers. Zhandry [Zha15] shows for random functions a reduction from expanding functions to compressing functions, giving the desired lower bound for compressing functions. Our proof, in contrast, works directly with functions of arbitrary domain and range. These features suggests that our proof technique is fundamentally different than those of prior works.

By generalizing our collision bound slightly, we can obtain an $\Omega(2^{n/(k+1)})$ lower bound for finding a set of distinct points $x_1, \ldots, x_k$ such that $\sum_i H(x_i) = 0$. This bound is tight as long as $n \leq km$ by adapting the collision-finding algorithm of [BHT98] to this problem. Again, our proof is obtained by modifying just a few lines of the pre-image search proof.

1.2   Related Works

Ristenpart, Shacham, and Shrimpton [RSS11] shows that indifferentiability is insufficient for replacing a concrete hash function with a random oracle in the setting of multi-stage games. Nonetheless, Mittelbach [Mit14] shows that indifferentiability can still be useful in these settings. Exploring the quantum analogs of these results is an interesting direction for future research.

---

[3] and the square root comes from the fact that the norm of the sum of q unit vectors of disjoint support is $\sqrt{q}$.

2   Preliminaries

Distinguishing Quantum States. The density matrix captures all statistical information about a mixed state. That is, if two states have the same density matrix, then they are perfectly indistinguishable.

For density matrices ρ, ρ' that are not identical, we define the trace distance as $T(\rho, \rho') = \frac{1}{2} \sum_i |\lambda_i|$, where λ_i are the eigenvalues of $\rho - \rho'$. The trace distance captures the maximum distinguishing advantage amongst all possible measurements of the state.

We will need the following Theorem of Bennett et al. (which we have slightly improved, see full version [Zha18] for the improved proof):

Lemma 1 ([BBBV97]). *Let $|\phi\rangle$ and $|\psi\rangle$ be quantum states with Euclidean distance ϵ. Then $T(|\phi\rangle\langle\phi|, |\psi\rangle\langle\psi|) = \epsilon\sqrt{1 - \epsilon^2/4} \leq \epsilon$.*

We will also need the following relaxation of commuting operations:

Definition 1. *Let U_0, U_1 be unitaries over the same quantum system. We say that U_0, U_1 ϵ-almost commute if, for any initial state ρ, the images of ρ under $U_0 U_1$ and $U_1 U_0$ are at most ϵ-far in trace distance.*

3   Oracle Variations

Here, we describe several oracle variations. The oracles will all be equivalent; the only difference is that the oracle registers and/or the query registers are encoded in different ways between queries. We start with the usual quantum random oracle, which comes in two flavors that we call the *standard oracle* and *phase oracle*. Then we will give our *compressed standard and phase oracles*.

Standard Oracle. Here, the oracle $H : \{0,1\}^m \rightarrow \{0,1\}^n$ is represented as its truth table: a vector of size 2^m where each component is an n-bit string.

The oracle takes as input a state consisting of three sets of registers: m-qubit x registers representing inputs to the function, n-qubit y registers for writing the response, and $n2^m$-qubit H registers containing the truth table of the actual function. The x, y registers come from the adversary, and the H registers are the oracle's state, which is hidden from the adversary accept by making queries. On basis states $|x, y\rangle \otimes |H\rangle$, the oracle performs the map $|x, y\rangle \otimes |H\rangle \mapsto |x, y \oplus H(x)\rangle \otimes |H\rangle$.

For initialization, the oracle H will be initialized to the uniform superposition over all H: $\frac{1}{\sqrt{2^{m \times 2^n}}} \sum_H |H\rangle$. We will call this oracle StO.

The only difference between StO and the usual quantum random oracle model is that, in the usual model, H starts out as a uniformly chosen random function rather than a superposition (that is, the H registers are the completely mixed state). We will call the oracle with this different initialization StO′.

Lemma 2. *StO and StO′ are perfectly indistinguishable. That is, for any adversary A making oracle queries, let $A^{StO}()$ and $A^{StO'}()$ denote the algorithm interfacing with StO and StO′, respectively. Then $\Pr[A^{StO}() = 1] = \Pr[A^{StO'}() = 1]$.*

Proof. This can be seen by tracing out the oracle registers. The mixed state of the adversary in both cases will be identical.   □

Thus, our initialization is equivalent to H being a uniformly random oracle.

Phase Oracle. We will also consider the well-known phase model of oracle queries. This model technically offers a different interface to the adversary, but can be mapped to the original oracle by simple Hadamard operations.

The oracle takes as input a state consisting of three sets of registers: x registers representing inputs to the function, z phase registers, and H registers containing the truth table of the actual function. On basis states $|x, y\rangle \otimes |H\rangle$, it performs the map $|x, z\rangle \otimes |H\rangle \mapsto (-1)^{y \cdot H(x)}|x, z\rangle \otimes |H\rangle$.

For initialization, H is the uniform superposition as before. We will call this oracle PhO. Analogous to the above, this is equivalent to the case where H is uniformly random. The following Lemma is implicit in much of the literature on quantum-accessible oracles:

Lemma 3. *For any adversary A making queries to* StO, *let B be the adversary that is identical to A, except it performs the Hadamard transformation* $H^{\otimes n}$ *to the response registers before and after each query. Then* $\Pr[A^{\mathsf{StO}}() = 1] = \Pr[B^{\mathsf{PhO}}() = 1]$.

Compressed Standard Oracles. We now define our compressed standard oracles. The intuition for our compressed standard oracle is the following. Let $|\tau\rangle$ be the uniform superposition. In the standard (uncompressed) oracle, suppose for each of the 2^m output registers, we perform the computation mapping $|\tau\rangle \mapsto |\tau\rangle|1\rangle$ and $|\phi\rangle \mapsto |\phi\rangle|0\rangle$ for any $|\phi\rangle$ orthogonal to $|\tau\rangle$. In other words, this computation tests whether or not the state of the output registers is 0 in the Fourier basis. We will write the output of the computation in some auxiliary space. Now the state of the oracle is a superposition over truth tables, and a superposition over vectors in $\{0, 1\}^{2^m}$ containing the output of the tests. A straightforward exercise (and a consequence of our analysis below) shows that if we perform these tests after q queries, all vectors in the test vector superposition have at most q positions containing a 0. The reason is, roughly, if we do the tests before any queries the vector will be identically 1 since we had a uniform superposition (which is 0 in the Fourier basis). Then, each query affects only one position of the superposition, increasing the number of 0's by at most 1.

Also notice that anywhere the vector contains a 1, the corresponding truth table component contains exactly the uniform superposition $|\tau\rangle$. Anywhere the vector contains a 0, the corresponding truth table component contains a state that is guaranteed to be orthogonal to $|\tau\rangle$.

What we can do then is compress this overall state. We will simply write down all the positions where the test vector contained a 0, and keep track of the truth table component for that position. Everywhere else we can simply ignore since we know what the truth table contains. The result is a (superposition over) database consisting of at most q input/output pairs.

In more detail, a database D will be a collection of (x, y) pairs, where $(x, y) \in D$ means the function has been specified to have value y on input x. We will write $D(x) = y$ in this case. If, for an input x there is no pair $(x, y) \in D$, then we will write $D(x) = \bot$, indicating that the function has not been specified. We will maintain that a database D only contains at most one pair for a given x.

Concretely, if we have an upper bound t on the number of specified points, a database D will be represented an element of the set S^t, where $S = (\{0, 1\}^m \cup \{\bot\}) \times \{0, 1\}^n$. Each value in S is an (x, y) pair; if $x \neq \bot$ the pair means $D(x) = y$, and $x = \bot$ means the pair is unused. For $x_1 < x_2 < \cdots < x_\ell$ and $y_1, \ldots, y_\ell$, the database representing that input x_i has been set to y_i for $i \in [\ell]$, with all other points unspecified, will be represented as:

$$((x_1, y_1), (x_2, y_2), \ldots, (x_\ell, y_\ell), (\bot, 0^n), \ldots, (\bot, 0^n))$$

where the number of $(\bot, 0^n)$ pairs is equal to $t - \ell$.

After query q, the state of the oracle will be a superposition of databases in this form, using the upper bound $t = q$. So initially the state is empty. We will maintain several invariants:

- For any database in the support of the superposition, for any (x, y) pair where $x = \bot$, we have that $y = 0^n$. All $(\bot, 0^n)$ pairs are at the end of the list.
- For any database in the support of the superposition, if (x, y) occurs before (x', y'), it must be that $x < x'$.
- For any of the ℓ positions that have been specified, the y registers are in a state that is orthogonal to the uniform superposition $|\tau\rangle$ (indicating that in the Fourier domain, the registers do *not* contain 0).

We also need to describe several procedures on databases. Let $|D|$ be the number of pairs $(x, y) \in D$ for $x \neq \bot$. For a database D with $|D| < t$ and $D(x) = \bot$, write $D \cup (x, y)$ to be the new database obtained by adding the pair (x, y) to D, inserting in the appropriate spot to maintain the ordering of the x values. Since $|D|$ was originally less than t, there will be at least one $(\bot, 0^n)$ pair, which is deleted. Therefore, the overall number of pairs (including $\bot$s) in D and $D \cup \{(x, y)\}$ are the same.

Before describing how to process a query, we need to describe a local decompression procedure $\mathsf{StdDecomp}_x$ which acts on databases. This is a unitary operation. It suffices to describe its action on a set of orthonormal states. Let t be the current upper bound on the number of set points.

- For D such that $D(x) = \bot$ and $|D| < t$,

$$\mathsf{StdDecomp}_x |D\rangle = \frac{1}{\sqrt{2^n}} \sum_y |D \cup (x, y)\rangle$$

That is, $\mathsf{StdDecomp}_x$ inserts into D the pair $(x, |\tau\rangle)$. This corresponds to decompressing the value of the database at position x

– For D such that $D(x) = \bot$ and $|D| = t$, $\mathsf{StdDecomp}_x|D\rangle = |D\rangle$. This means, if there is no room to expand for decompression, $\mathsf{StdDecomp}_x$ does nothing. Note that these states are illegal and $\mathsf{StdDecomp}_x$ will never by applied to such states.

– For a D' such that $D'(x) = \bot$ and $|D'| < t$,

$$\mathsf{StdDecomp}_x\left(\sum_y (-1)^{z \cdot y}|D' \cup (x, y)\rangle\rangle\right) = \sum_y (-1)^{z \cdot y}|D' \cup (x, y)\rangle\rangle \text{ for } z \neq 0$$

$$\mathsf{StdDecomp}_x\left(\frac{1}{\sqrt{2^n}}\sum_y |D' \cup (x, y)\rangle\rangle\right) = |D'\rangle$$

In other words, if D already is specified on x, and moreover if the corresponding y registers are in a state orthogonal to $|\tau\rangle$ (meaning they do not contain 0 in the Fourier domain), then there is no need to decompress and $\mathsf{StdDecomp}_x$ is the identity. On the other hand, if D is specified at x and the corresponding y registers are in the state $|\tau\rangle$, $\mathsf{StdDecomp}_x$ will remove x and the y register superposition from D.

Note that the left-hand sides of last two cases form an orthonormal basis for the span of $|D\rangle$ such that $D(x) \neq \bot$. The left-hand sides of the first two cases form an orthonormal basis for the remaining D. Thus, $\mathsf{StdDecomp}_x$ is defined on an orthonormal basis, which by linearity defines it on all states. The right-hand sides are the same basis states just in a different order. As such, this operation maps orthogonal states to orthogonal states, and is therefore unitary. Note that $\mathsf{StdDecomp}_x$ is actually an involution, as applying it twice results in the identity. Let $\mathsf{StdDecomp}$ be the related unitary operating on a quantum system over x, y, D states, defined by it's action on the computational basis states as:

$$|x, y\rangle \otimes |D\rangle = |x, y\rangle \otimes \mathsf{StdDecomp}_x|D\rangle$$

In other words, in superposition it applies $\mathsf{StdDecomp}_x$ to $|D\rangle$, where x is taken from the x registers.

For some additional notation, we will take $y \oplus \bot = y$ and $y \cdot \bot = 0$. Let $\mathsf{Increase}$ be theprocedure which initializes a new register $|(\bot, 0^n)\rangle\rangle$ and appends it to the end. In other words, $\mathsf{Increase}|x, y\rangle \otimes |D\rangle = |x, y\rangle \otimes |D\rangle|(\bot, 0^n)\rangle\rangle$, where $|D\rangle|(\bot, 0^n)\rangle\rangle$ is interpreted as a database computing the same partial function as D, but with the upper bound on number of points increased by 1.

Let $\mathsf{CStO}', \mathsf{CPhsO}'$ be unitaries defined on the computational basis states as

$$\mathsf{CStO}'|x, y\rangle \otimes |D\rangle = |x, y \oplus D(x)\rangle \otimes |D\rangle$$

$$\mathsf{CPhsO}'|x, y\rangle \otimes |D\rangle = (-1)^{y \cdot D(x)}|x, y\rangle \otimes |D\rangle$$

Finally, we describe the CStO and CPhsO oracles:

$$\mathsf{CStO} = \mathsf{StdDecomp} \circ \mathsf{CStO}' \circ \mathsf{StdDecomp} \circ \mathsf{Increase}$$

$$\mathsf{CPhsO} = \mathsf{StdDecomp} \circ \mathsf{CPhsO}' \circ \mathsf{StdDecomp} \circ \mathsf{Increase}$$

In other words, increase the bound on the number of specified points, then uncompress at x (which is ensured to have enough space since we increased the bound), apply the query (which is ensured to be specified since we decompressed), and then re-compress.

Lemma 4. CStO *and* StO *are perfectly indistinguishable.* CPhsO *and* PhO *are perfectly indistinguishable. That is, for any adversary A, we have* $\Pr[A^{\mathsf{CStO}}() = 1] = \Pr[A^{\mathsf{StO}}() = 1]$, *and for any adversary B, we have* $\Pr[B^{\mathsf{CPhsO}}() = 1] = \Pr[A^{\mathsf{PhO}}() = 1]$.

Proof. We prove the case for CStO and StO, the other case being almost identical. We prove security through a sequence of hybrids.

Hybrid 0. In this case, the adversary interacts with StO. That is, the oracle's database is initialized to the uniform superposition over all H, and each query performs the unitary mapping $|x, y\rangle \otimes |H\rangle \mapsto |x, y \oplus H(x)\rangle \otimes |H\rangle$.

Hybrid 1. In this hybrid, we use a slightly different way of representing the function H. Instead of writing H as a truth table, we represent it as a complete database $D = ((0, H(0)), (1, H(1)), \ldots, (2^m - 1, H(2^m - 1)))$. Here, the upper bound on the number of determined points is exactly 2^m. The oracle's state starts out as

$$\frac{1}{\sqrt{2^{n2^m}}} \sum_H |((0, H(0)), (1, H(1)), \ldots, (2^m - 1, H(2^m - 1)))\rangle$$

The update procedure for each query is simply CStO′, meaning that each query maps $|x, y\rangle \otimes |((0, H(0)), (1, H(1)), \ldots, (2^m - 1, H(2^m - 1)))\rangle$ to $|x, y \oplus H(x)\rangle \otimes |((0, H(0)), (1, H(1)), \ldots, (2^m - 1, H(2^m - 1)))\rangle$.

Hybrid 1 is identical to **Hybrid 0**, except that we have inserted the input points $1, \ldots, 2^m - 1$ into the oracle's state, which has no effect on the adversary.

Hybrid 2. Next, introduce a global decompression procedure StdDecomp′, which applies $\mathsf{StdDecomp}_x$ for all x in the domain, one at a time from 0 up to $2^m - 1$.

We observe that when the upper bound on determined points is 2^m, then $\mathsf{StdDecomp}_x$ commutes with $\mathsf{StdDecomp}_{x'}$ for any x, x'. This readily follows from the fact that when the upper bound is $t = 2^m$, $D(x) = \bot$ implies $|D| < t$.

In **Hybrid 2**, the oracle starts out as the empty database with upper bound 2^m. Then, each query is implemented as $\mathsf{StdDecomp}' \circ \mathsf{CStO}' \circ \mathsf{StdDecomp}'$.

Notice that StdDecomp′ only affects the oracle's registers and therefore commutes with the any computation on the adversary's side. Also notice that between each two queries, StdDecomp′ is applied twice and that it is an involution. Therefore the two applications cancel out. At the beginning, StdDecomp′ is applied to an empty database, which maps it to the uniform superposition

$$\frac{1}{\sqrt{2^{n2^m}}} \sum_H |((0, H(0)), (1, H(1)), \ldots, (2^m - 1, H(2^m - 1)))\rangle$$

before the first application of CStO′. Therefore, this hybrid is perfectly indistinguishable from **Hybrid 1**.

Hybrid 3. This hybrid applies StdDecomp ∘ CStO′ ∘ StdDecomp for each query.

To prove indistinguishability from **Hybrid 2**, consider a database D with upper bound 2^m but where $|D| = \ell$ for some $\ell \leq 2^m$. Notice that for any D' in the support of $\mathsf{StdDecomp}_{x'} |D\rangle$, $D'(x) = D(x)$ for all $x \neq x'$. This means

$$\mathsf{CStO'} \circ \mathsf{StdDecomp}_{x'} (|x, y\rangle \otimes |D\rangle)) = \mathsf{StdDecomp}_{x'} (|x, y \oplus D(x)\rangle \otimes |D\rangle)$$
$$= \mathsf{StdDecomp}_{x'} \circ \mathsf{CStO'}(|x, y\rangle \otimes |D\rangle)$$

In other words, when the query register contains $x \neq x'$, $\mathsf{StdDecomp}_{x'}$ and $\mathsf{CStO'}$ commute. Therefore,

$$\mathsf{StdDecomp'} \circ \mathsf{CStO'} \circ \mathsf{StdDecomp'}(|x, y\rangle \otimes |D\rangle)$$
$$= \mathsf{StdDecomp}_x \circ \mathsf{CStO'} \circ \mathsf{StdDecomp}_x(|x, y\rangle \otimes |D\rangle)$$
$$= \mathsf{StdDecomp} \circ \mathsf{CStO'} \circ \mathsf{StdDecomp}(|x, y\rangle \otimes |D\rangle)$$

This shows that **Hybrid 2** and **Hybrid 3** are identical.

Hybrid 4. Finally, this hybrid is the compressed standard oracle: the oracle's state starts out empty, and CStO is applied for each query.

To prove equivalence, first notice that for any x, y, D, $\mathsf{StdDecomp} \circ \mathsf{CStO'} \circ \mathsf{StdDecomp}(|x, y\rangle \otimes |D\rangle)$ has support on databases D' such that $|D'| \leq |D| + 1$. Indeed, all D' are defined on the same inputs except for possibly the input x.

This means that after q queries in **Hybrid 3**, the oracle's registers only have support on D containing at most q defined points; the remaining $\geq 2^m - q$ points are all $(\perp, 0^n)$. Therefore, we can discard all but the first q pairs in D, without affecting the adversary's state. The result is identical to **Hybrid 4**.   □

In the full version [Zha18], we give several more oracle variations; while not used in this work, they may be useful in other settings. These variations also provide an alternative way to arrive at the compressed standard oracles.

3.1   A Useful Lemma

Here, we provide a lemma which relates the adversary's knowledge of an oracle output to the probability that point appears in the compressed oracle database. This lemma is proved in the full version [Zha18], and follows from a straightforward (albeit delicate) analysis off the action of CStO.

Lemma 5. *Consider a quantum algorithm A making queries to a random oracle H and outputting tuples $(x_1, \ldots, x_k, y_1, \ldots, y_k, z)$. Let R be a collection of such tuples. Suppose with probability p, A outputs a tuple such that (1) the tuple is in R and (2) $H(x_i) = y_i$ for all i. Now consider running A with the oracle CStO, and suppose the database D is measured after A produces its output. Let p' be the probability that (1) the tuple is in R, and (2) $D(x_i) = y_i$ for all i (and in particular $D(x_i) \neq \perp$). Then $\sqrt{p} \leq \sqrt{p'} + \sqrt{k/2^n}$.*

4   Quantum Query Bounds Using Compressed Oracles

In this section, we re-prove several known query complexity lower bounds, as well as provide some new bounds. All these bounds follow from simple applications of our compressed oracles.

4.1   Optimality of Grover Search

Here, we re-prove that the quadratic speed-up of Grover search is optimal. Specifically, we prove that for a random function $H : \{0,1\}^m \to \{0,1\}^n$, any q query algorithm has a success probability of at most $O(q^2/2^n)$ for finding a pre-image of 0^n (or any fixed value).

Theorem 1. *For any adversary making q queries to CStO or CPhsO and an arbitrary number of database read queries, if the database D is measured after the q queries, the probability it contains a pair of the form $(x, 0^n)$ is at most $O(q^2/2^n)$.*

Proof. Let $0^n \in D$ mean that D contains a pair of the form $(x, 0^n)$. The compressed oracle's database starts out empty, so the probability $0^n \in D$ is zero. We will show that the probability cannot rise too much with each query. We consider compressed phase queries, CPhsO. Compressed standard queries are handled analogously. Consider the joint state of the adversary and oracle just before the qth CPhsO query:

$$|\psi\rangle = \sum_{x,y,z,D} \alpha_{x,y,z,D} |x,y,z\rangle \otimes |D\rangle$$

Where D represents the compressed phase oracle, x, y as the query registers, and z as the adversary's private storage. Define P as the projection onto the span of basis states $|x,y,z\rangle \otimes |D\rangle$ such that $0^n \in D$. Our goal will be to relate the norms of $P|\psi\rangle$ (the magnitude before the query) to $P \cdot \mathsf{CPhsO}|\psi\rangle$ (the magnitude after the query).

Define projections Q onto states such that (1) $0^n \notin D$ (meaning the database does not yet contain 0^n), (2) $y \neq 0$ (meaning CPhsO will affect D), and (3) $D(x) = \bot$ (meaning D has not yet been specified at x). Define projection R onto states such that $0^n \notin D$, $y \neq 0$ and $D(x) \neq \bot$; projection S onto states such that $0^n \notin D$, $y = 0$. Then $P + Q + R + S = \mathbf{I}$.

Consider $Q|\psi\rangle$. CPhsO maps basis states $|x,y,z\rangle \otimes |D\rangle$ in the support of $Q|\psi\rangle$ to $|x,y,z\rangle \otimes \frac{1}{\sqrt{2^n}} \sum_w (-1)^{y \cdot w} |D \cup (x,w)\rangle$. Since $0^n \notin D$, applying P to this state will yield $|x,y,z\rangle \otimes \frac{1}{\sqrt{2^n}} |D \cup (x,0^n)\rangle$. Notice that the images of the different basis states are orthogonal. Therefore, $\|P \cdot \mathsf{CPhsO} \cdot Q|\psi\rangle\| = \frac{1}{\sqrt{2^n}} \|Q|\psi\rangle\|$.

For basis vectors in the support of R, we must have $D(x) \notin \{\bot, 0^n\}$. Let D' be the database with x removed, and write $D = D' \cup (x,w)$ for $w = D(x)$. Then some algebraic manipulations show that $\mathsf{CPhsO}|x,y,z\rangle \otimes |D' \cup (x,w)\rangle$ is:

$$|x, y, z\rangle \otimes \left((-1)^{y \cdot w} \left(|D' \cup (x, w)\rangle + \frac{1}{\sqrt{2^n}} |D'\rangle \right) \right.$$

$$\left. + \frac{1}{2^n} \sum_{y'} (1 - (-1)^{y \cdot w} - (-1)^{y \cdot y'}) |D' \cup (x, y')\rangle \right)$$

Then $P \cdot \mathsf{CPhsO} |x, y, z\rangle \otimes |D' \cup (x, w)\rangle = \frac{-(-1)^{y \cdot w}}{2^n} |x, y, z\rangle \otimes |D' \cup (x, 0^n)\rangle$. Write $R|\psi\rangle = \sum_{x,y,z,D',w} \alpha_{x,y,z,D',w} |x, y, z\rangle \otimes |D' \cup (x, w)\rangle$. Then $\|P \cdot \mathsf{CPhsO} \cdot R|\psi\rangle\|^2$ is equal to:

$$\frac{1}{4^n} \sum_{x,y,z,D'} \|\sum_w \alpha_{x,y,z,D',w} (-1)^{y \cdot w}\|^2 \leq \frac{1}{2^n} \sum_{x,y,z,D',w} \|\alpha_{x,y,z,D',w}\|^2 = \frac{1}{2^n} \|R|\psi\rangle\|^2$$

Finally, $\|P \cdot \mathsf{CPhsO} \cdot P|\psi\rangle\| \leq \|P|\psi\rangle\|$ and $\mathsf{CPhsO} \cdot S|\psi\rangle = S|\psi\rangle$. Putting it all together, we have that $\|P \cdot \mathsf{CPhsO}|\psi\rangle\| \leq \|P|\psi\rangle\| + \frac{1}{\sqrt{2^n}} (\|Q|\psi\rangle\| + \|R|\psi\rangle\|) \leq \|P|\psi\rangle\| + \frac{1}{\sqrt{2^n}}$.

Therefore, after q queries, we have that the projection onto D containing a zero has norm at most $q/\sqrt{2^n}$. Now, the probability the database in $|\psi\rangle$ contains a 0^n is just the square of this norm, which is at most $\frac{q^2}{2^n}$.   □

The following is obtained by combining Theorem 1 with Lemma 5:

Corollary 1. *After making q quantum queries to a random oracle, the probability of finding a pre-image of 0^n is at most $O(q^2/2^n)$.*

Proof. We will assume the adversary always makes a final query on it's output x, and outputs $(x, H(x))$. This comes at the cost of at most 1 query, so it does not affect the asymptotic result. Then we can use the relation $R(x, y)$ which accepts if and only if $y = 0^n$. In the second experiment of Lemma 5, the only way for the adversary to win is to have the database contain a pre-image of 0^n. As such, Theorem 1 shows $p' = O(q^2/2^n)$. Then Lemma 5 shows that $p = O(q^2/2^n)$, which is exactly the probability the adversary outputs a pre-image of 0^n when interacting with the real random oracle.

4.2 Collision Lower Bound

Theorem 2. *For any adversary making q queries to CStO or CPhsO and an arbitrary number of database read queries, if the database D is measured after the q queries, the resulting database will contain a collision with probability at most $O(q^3/2^n)$.*

Proof. The proof involves changing just a few lines of the proof of Theorem 1. We define P to project onto databases D containing a collision, and re-define Q, R, S accordingly. Write $Q|\psi\rangle = \sum_{x,y,z,D} \alpha_{x,y,z,D} |x, y, z\rangle \otimes |D\rangle$. Then

$$P \cdot \mathsf{CPhsO} \cdot Q|\psi\rangle = \sum_{x,y,z,D} \alpha_{x,y,z,D} |x, y, z\rangle \otimes \frac{1}{\sqrt{2^n}} \sum_{w \in D} |D \cup (x, w)\rangle$$

We can write this as the $\frac{1}{\sqrt{2^n}} \sum_i |\phi_i\rangle$, where $|\phi_i\rangle$ is the partial sum which sets w to be the ith element in D (provided it exists). The $|\phi_i\rangle$ are orthogonal, and satisfy $\||\phi_i\rangle\| \leq \|Q|\psi\rangle\|$. Moreover, after q queries D has size at most q, and so there are at most q of the $|\phi_i\rangle$. Therefore, $\|P \cdot \mathsf{CPhsO} \cdot Q|\psi\rangle\| \leq \sqrt{q/2^n}\|Q|\psi\rangle\|$.

By a similar argument, $\|P \cdot \mathsf{CPhsO} \cdot R|\psi\rangle\| \leq \sqrt{q/2^n}\|R|\psi\rangle\|$. Putting everything together, this shows that the norm of $P|\psi\rangle$ increases by at most $\sqrt{q/2^n}$ with each query. Therefore, after q queries, the total norm is at most $\sqrt{q^3/2^n}$, giving a probability of $q^3/2^n$. $\square$

Corollary 2. *After making q quantum queries to a random oracle, the probability of finding a collision is at most $O(q^3/2^n)$.*

4.3 More General Settings

We can easily generalize even further. Let R be a relation on ℓ-tuples over $\{0,1\}^n$. Say that R is *satisfied* on a database D if D contains ℓ distinct pairs (x_i, y_i) such that $R(y_1, \ldots, y_\ell) = 1$. Let $k(q)$ be the maximum number of y that can be added to an unsatisfied database of size at most $q - 1$ to make it satisfied.

Theorem 3. *For any adversary making q queries to* CStO *or* CPhsO *and an arbitrary number of database read queries, if the database D is measured after the q queries, the resulting database will be satisfied with probability at most $O(q^2 k(q)/2^n)$.*

For the k-sum problem, there are at most $\binom{q}{k-1}$ incomplete tuples that can be completed by adding a new point. As such, $k(q) \leq \binom{q}{k-1} \leq q^{k-1}$. This gives:

Corollary 3. *After making q quantum queries to a random oracle, the probability of finding k distinct inputs x_i such that $\sum_i H(x_i) = 0^n$ is at most $O(q^{k+1}/2^n)$.*

5 Indifferentiability of A Simple Domain Extender

5.1 Definitions

Let $h : \{0,1\}^m \rightarrow \{0,1\}^n$ be a random oracle, and let $C^h : \{0,1\}^M \rightarrow \{0,1\}^N$ be a polynomial-sized stateless classical circuit that makes oracle queries to h.

Definition 2. *Let $H : \{0,1\}^M \rightarrow \{0,1\}^N$ be a random function. A stateful quantum polynomial-time simulator* $\mathsf{Sim}^H : \{0,1\}^m \rightarrow \{0,1\}^n$ *is indifferentiable for C if, for any polynomial-time distinguisher $\mathcal{D}$ making queries to h, H,*

$$|\Pr[\mathcal{D}^{h,C^h}() = 1] - \Pr[\mathcal{D}^{\mathsf{Sim}^H,H}() = 1]| < \mathsf{negl}$$

Definition 3. *C^h is quantum indifferentiable from a random oracle if there exists an indifferentiable simulator* Sim *for C.*

Intuitively, in the "real" world, h is a random function and H is set to be C^h. C^h is indifferentiable if this real world is indistinguishable from an "ideal" world, where H is a random function, and h is set to be Sim^h for some efficient simulator Sim.

In order to help us prove indifferentiability of a simulator Sim, we introduce two weaker requirements. The first is *indistinguishability*, a weakened version of indifferentiability where the distinguisher is not allowed any queries to H:

Definition 4. *A simulator* Sim *is* indistinguishable *if, for any polynomial-time distinguisher* $\mathcal{D}$ *making queries to* h,

$$|\Pr[\mathcal{D}^h() = 1] - \Pr[\mathcal{D}^{\mathsf{Sim}^H}() = 1]| < \mathsf{negl}$$

Next, we introduce the notion of *consistency*. Here, we set h to be simulated by Sim^H, and we ask the adversary to distinguish honest evaluations of H from evaluations of C^h (where again h is still simulated by Sim^H).

Definition 5. *A simulator* Sim *is* consistent *if, for any polynomial-time distinguisher* $\mathcal{D}$ *making queries to* h, H, *if* H *is simulated by* Sim^H, *then*

$$|\Pr[\mathcal{D}^{\mathsf{Sim}^H, H}() = 1] - \Pr[\mathcal{D}^{\mathsf{Sim}^H, C^{\mathsf{Sim}^H}}() = 1]| < \mathsf{negl}$$

Lemma 6. *Any consistent and indistinguishable simulator is indifferentiable.*

The proof of Lemma 6 is straightforward, and proved in the full version [Zha18].

Finally, it is straightforward to adapt the definitions and Lemma 6 to handle the case of many random compression functions $h_1, \ldots, h_\ell$. In this case, C makes queries to $h_1, \ldots, h_\ell$, $\mathcal{D}$ has quantum oracle access to $h_1, \ldots, h_\ell$ and H, while S makes quantum queries to H and simulates $h_1, \ldots, h_\ell$.

5.2   A Simple Domain Extender

We now consider a simple domain extender. Let $h_1 : \{0,1\}^m \to \{0,1\}^n, h_2 : \{0,1\}^n \times \{0,1\}^\ell \to \{0,1\}^n$ be two functions. Let $C^{h_1, h_2}(x_1, x_2) = h_2(h_1(x_1), x_2)$.

Theorem 4. *If* h_1, h_2 *are random oracles, the simple domain extender* C *is indifferentiable from a random oracle.*

Coron et al. [CDMP05] show that the indifferentiability of C is sufficient to prove the indifferentiability of Merkle-Damgård for a particular choice of prefix-free encoding (see paper for details). That part of the paper translates immediately to the quantum setting, so Theorem 4 then shows quantum indifferentiability for the same prefix free encoding. In the full version [Zha18], we show more generally that Merkle-Damgård is indifferentiable for *any* choice of prefix-free encoding. All the main ideas for the full proof are already contained in the proof of Theorem 4 below, just the details get a bit more complicated in the more general setting.

5.3   Our Simulator

Before describing our simulator, we need some terminology. For a database D of input/output pairs, a *collision* is two pairs $(x_1, y_1), (x_2, y_2) \in D, x_1 \neq x_2$ such that $y_1 = y_2$. For an input $(y, x_2) \in \{0, 1\}^n \times \{0, 1\}^\ell$, a *completion* in D is a pair $(x_1, y) \in D$. For such a completion, we will call $w = (x_1, x_2)$ the associated input.

We define a classical procedure FindInput. FindInput takes as input $x \in \{0, 1\}^n \times \{0, 1\}^\ell$, and a database D. It parses x as $(y, x_2) \in \{0, 1\}^n \times \{0, 1\}^\ell$. Then, it looks for a completion $(x_1, y) \in D$. If found, it will take, say, the completion with the smallest x_1 value, and output $(b = 1, w = (x_1, x_2))$. If no completion is found, it will output $(b = 0, w = 0^{m+\ell})$. Note that for the output values in D, FindInput only needs to apply an equality check on those values, testing if they contain y. By applying such an equality check to each output register, it can compute b and w. Looking forward, when we implement FindInput in superposition, this means FindInput only touches the output registers of D by making a computational basis test.

We are now ready to describe our simulator. Sim will keep a (superposition over) database D_a, which represents the simulation of the random oracle h_a that it will update according to the CStO update procedure. D_a is originally empty. It will also have a private random oracle h_b. For concreteness, h_b will be implemented using another instance of CStO, but it will be notationally convenient to treat h_b as being a uniformly random function.

On h_1 queries, Sim makes a query to h_a, performing the appropriate CStO update procedure to D_a. On h_2 queries, Sim performs a unitary operation with the following action on basis states:

$$|x, y\rangle \otimes |D_a\rangle \mapsto \begin{cases} |x, y \oplus h_b(x)\rangle \otimes |D_a\rangle & \text{if FindInput}(x, D_a) = (0, 0^{m+\ell}) \\ |x, y \oplus H(w)\rangle \otimes |D_a\rangle & \text{if FindInput}(x, D_a) = (1, w) \end{cases}$$

This unitary is straightforward to implement with a single query to each of h_b and H, and is detailed in the full version [Zha18].

In the next three subsections, we prove that our simulator is indifferentiable. In Sect. 5.4, we prove a useful commutativity lemma. Then in Sects. 5.5 and 5.6, we prove the indistinguishability and consistency, respectively, of Sim. By Lemma 6, this proves that Sim is indifferentiable, proving Theorem 4.

5.4   The Almost Commutativity of StdDecomp and FindInput

Lemma 7. *Consider a quantum system over x, D, x', z. The following two unitaries $O(1/\sqrt{2^n})$-almost commute:*

– StdDecomp, *acting on the x, D registers.*
– FindInput, *taking as input the D, x' registers and XORing the output into z.*

The intuition is that, for StdDecomp to have any effect, either (1) $D(x) = \bot$ or (2) $D(x)$ is in uniform superposition; StdDecomp will simply toggle between the two cases. Now, a uniform superposition puts a weight of $1/\sqrt{2^n}$ on each possible y value. Since there is only a single possible y value for $D(x)$ that matches x', it is exponentially unlikely that FindInput will find a match at input x in Case (2). On the other hand, it will *never* find a match at input x in Case (1). Hence, there is an exponentially small error between the action of FindInput on these two cases. We prove the lemma formally in the full version [Zha18].

5.5 Indistinguishability

Lemma 8. Sim *is indistinguishable. In particular, for any distinguisher $\mathcal{D}$ making at most q queries to h_1, h_2,*

$$|\Pr[\mathcal{D}^{h_1,h_2}() = 1] - \Pr[\mathcal{D}^{\mathsf{Sim}^H}() = 1]| < O(q^2/\sqrt{2^n})$$

Proof. Recall that in the ideal world where h_1, h_2 are simulated by Sim^H, h_1 is implemented by a CStO oracle on database D_a. By applying Lemma 4, we can think of the simulator's other oracle h_b as another instance of CStO for a database D_b. Additionally, H can be simulated with yet another instance of CStO for a database E. Similarly, in the real world, h_1, h_2 will be implemented by independent instances of CStO with databases D_a, D_b. Note that, in either case, h_1 is implemented by a CStO oracle on database D_a. Therefore, the only difference between the two cases is how h_2 is implemented.

We define a classical encoding procedure Encode for pairs D_a, D_b of databases. Intuitively, Encode will scan the values $((z, x_2), y)$ in D_b, seeing if any of the (z, x_2) values correspond to a completion in D_a. If so, such a completion will have an associated input w. Encode will reasonably guess that such a completion corresponds to an evaluation of $H(w) = C^{h_1,h_2}(w)$. Therefore, Encode will remove the value $((z, x_2), y)$ in D_b, and add the pair (w, y) to a new database E, intuitively representing the oracle H. In more detail, Encode does the following:

- For each pair $((z, x_2), y) \in D_b$, run FindInput$((z, x_2), D_a) = (b, w)$. If $b = 1$, re-label the pair to (w, y)
- Remove all re-labeled pairs D_b (which are easily identifiable since the input will be larger) and place them in a new database E.

We define the following Decode procedure, which operates on triples D_a, D_b, E:

- Merge the databases D_b, E
- For each pair (w, y) that was previously in E, where $w = (x_1, x_2)$, evaluate $z = D_a(x_1)$. Re-label (w, y) to $((z, x_2), y)$. If $z = \perp$ or if the input (z, x_2) was already in the database, output $\perp$ and abort.

Note that Encode, Decode are independent of the order elements are processed. It also follows from the descriptions above that Decode(Encode(D_a, D_b)) $= (D_a, D_b)$. Therefore, Encode can be implemented in superposition, giving the unitary that maps $|D_a, D_b\rangle$ to $|\mathsf{Encode}(D_a, D_b)\rangle$. Also note that Encode$(\emptyset, \emptyset) = (\emptyset, \emptyset, \emptyset)$.

With this notation in hand, we are now ready to prove security: consider a potential distinguisher $\mathcal{D}$. We prove security through a sequence of hybrids.

Hybrid 0. This is the real world, where h_1, h_2 are random oracles. Let p_0 be the probability $\mathcal{D}$ outputs 1 in this case.

Hybrid 1. This is still the real world, but we add an abort condition. Namely, after any query to h_1, we measure if the database h_a contains a collision; if so, we immediately abort and stop the simulation. Let p_1 be the probability $\mathcal{D}$ outputs 1 in Hybrid 1.

Lemma 9. $|p_1 - p_0| \leq O(\sqrt{q^3/2^n})$.

Proof. First, suppose that before the ith query to h_1, the superposition over h_a has support only on databases containing no collisions. Let $|\psi\rangle$ be the joint state of the adversary and simulator just after the query to h_1. Then write $|\psi\rangle = |\psi_0\rangle + |\psi_1\rangle$ where $|\psi_0\rangle$ is the projection onto states where h_a has no collisions, and $|\psi_1\rangle$ is the projection onto states where h_a contains at least one collision. Following the proof of Theorem 2, we know that $\||\psi_1\rangle\| \leq \sqrt{i/2^n}$.

Therefore, if we let $|\psi_q\rangle$ be the joint state after the qth query in **Hybrid 0** and $|\phi_q\rangle$ the joint state in **Hybrid 2**, we would have that $\||\psi_q\rangle - |\phi_q\rangle\| \leq \sum_{i=0}^{q} \sqrt{i/2^n} \leq O(\sqrt{q^3/2^n})$. By Lemma 1, this means that $|p_1 - p_0| \leq O(\sqrt{q^3/2^n})$ as desired. $\qquad\square$

Hybrid 2. In this hybrid, there are three databases D_a, D_b, E, initialized to $|\emptyset, \emptyset, \emptyset\rangle$. Each query is answered in the following way:

- Apply Decode to the D_a, D_b, E registers. Measure if Decode gives $\perp$, in which case abort. Otherwise, there are now just two database registers D_a, D_b.
- Answer an h_1 (resp. h_2) query by applying the CStO update procedure to D_a (resp. D_b).
- Apply Encode to D_a, D_b.
- Apply the collision check to the database D_a.

Let p_2 be the probability $\mathcal{D}$ outputs 1 in Hybrid 2.

Lemma 10. $p_1 = p_0$.

Proof. We start with **Hybrid 1**. First, by Lemma 4, we can implement D_a, D_b in Hybrid 1 as independent instances of CStO. Now, between all the queries insert Encode followed by Decode. Also insert the two procedures before the first query. Now each query is preceded by a Decode and followed by a collision check and an Encode. Note that Encode, Decode do not affect the database D_a, and so commute with the collision check. Therefore, we can swap the order of the collision check and Encode that follow each query.

By merging the Decode, query, Encode and collision check operations together, we get exactly the update procedure of Hybrid 2. All that's left is an initial Encode procedure at the very beginning, which produces $|\emptyset, \emptyset, \emptyset\rangle$ as the database state, just as in Hybrid 2. $\qquad\square$

Hybrid 3. This hybrid is the ideal world, where h_1, h_2 queries are answered by Sim, except that we will have the abort condition if a collision in h_a is ever found. In other words, instead of decoding, applying the query, and then encoding, in Hybrid 3 we act directly on the encoded state using the algorithms specified by Sim. For h_1 queries, the difference from Hybrid 2 is just that the queries are made directly to h_a, instead of Decode, then h_a query, then Encode. For h_2 queries, the differences appear more substantial. h_2 queries, on superpositions over x, y, D_a, D_b, E, can be summarized as follows:

1. Compute the unitary mapping $|x, y, D_a, D_b, E\rangle \mapsto |x, y, D_a, D_b, E, (b, w) = \mathsf{FindInput}(x, D_a)\rangle$
2. In superposition, apply the following conditional procedures:
3. Conditioned on $b = 0$,
   (a) Apply StdDecomp to uncompress D_b at x.
   (b) Apply in superposition the map

   $$|x, y, D_a, D_b, E, b, w\rangle \mapsto |x, y \oplus D_b(x), D_a, D_b, E, b, w\rangle$$

   (c) Apply StdDecomp to re-compress D_b at x.
4. Conditioned on $b = 1$,
   (a) Apply StdDecomp to uncompress E at w.
   (b) Apply in superposition the map

   $$|x, y, D_a, D_b, E, b, w\rangle \mapsto |x, y \oplus E(w), D_a, D_b, E, b, w\rangle$$

   (c) Apply StdDecomp to re-compress E at w.
5. Uncompute (b, w) by running $\mathsf{FindInput}(x, D_a)$ in superposition again.

Let p_3 be the probability $\mathcal{D}$ outputs 1 in this hybrid.

Lemma 11. $|p_3 - p_2| \leq O(q^2/\sqrt{2^n})$.

Proof. We start with the very last query, and gradually change the queries one-by-one from how they were answered in Hybrid 2 to Hybrid 3.

For h_1 queries, we observe that it suffices to swap the order of Encode and CStO. Indeed, suppose we move the final Encode to come before CStO. The previous query ended with an Encode, and now the current query begins with Decode then Encode. Since Decode ∘ Encode is the identity, all thee of these operations collapse into a single Encode, which we keep at the end of the previous query. The result is that the current query is just a direct call to CStO, as in Hybrid 3. Then it remains to show that we can swap the order of Encode and CStO. For this, notice that Encode only interacts with D_a through FindInput. As such, all steps in Encode, CStO commute except for the two StdDecomp operations in CStO and the FindInput operation in Encode for each entry in D_b (plus another FindInput operation when un-computing the scratch-space of Encode in order to implement in superposition). By Lemma 7, these $\leq 4q$ operations each $O(1/\sqrt{2^n})$-almost commute, meaning Encode and CStO $O(q/\sqrt{2^n})$-almost commute.

For h_2 queries, fix an x, D_a and suppose D_a contains no collisions as guaranteed. There are two cases:

– FindInput$(x, D_a) = (0, 0^{m+\ell})$. Then in Hybrid 2, decoding/encoding does not affect the labeling for an (x, z) pair in D_b. As such, Hybrid 2 will uncompress D_b at x, apply the map $|x, y, D_a, D_b, E\rangle \mapsto |x, y \oplus D_b(x), D_a, D_b, E\rangle$ and then re-compress D_b at x, for these x, D_a.

– FindInput$(x, D_a) = (1, w)$. Then in Hybrid 2, by the collision-freeness of D_a, decoding will re-label a $(w, z) \in E$ (if present) to $(x, z) \in D_b$. The effect of Hybrid 2 in this case will be to uncompress E at w, apply the map $|x, y, D_a, D_b, E\rangle \mapsto |x, y \oplus E(x), D_a, D_b, E\rangle$, and then re-compress E at w.

In either case, answering h_2 queries in Hybrid 2 and 3 act identically. Therefore, this change introduces no error.

After q h_1 or h_2 queries, the total error between Hybrid 1 and Hybrid 2 is at most $O(q^2/\sqrt{2^n})$. $\square$

Hybrid 4. This is the ideal world, where we remove the abort condition from Hybrid 3. Let p_4 be the probability $\mathcal{D}$ outputs 1 in Hybrid 4. By an almost identical proof to that of Lemma 9, we have:

Lemma 12. $|p_4 - p_3| \leq O(\sqrt{q^3/2^n})$

Summing up, we have that $|p_0 - p_4| < O(q^2/\sqrt{2^n})$, proving Lemma 8. $\square$

5.6   Consistency

Lemma 13. Sim *is consistent. In particular, for any distinguisher $\mathcal{D}$ making at most q quantum queries to h_1, h_2, H,*

$$|\Pr[\mathcal{D}^{\mathsf{Sim}^H, H}() = 1] - \Pr[\mathcal{D}^{\mathsf{Sim}^H, C^{\mathsf{Sim}^H}}() = 1]| < O(\sqrt{q^3/2^n})$$

In other words, h_1, h_2 are simulated as Sim^H, and the adversary cannot distinguish between H and C^{h_1, h_2}.

Proof. We first work out how H queries are answered using C^{h_1, h_2}, when we simulate h_1, h_2 using Sim^H. The input registers will be labeled with $x = (x_1, x_2)$, and the output registers labeled with y.

1. First, make an h_1 query on the x_1 registers, writing the output to some new registers initialized to $z = 0^n$. Since we are implementing h_1 using CStO, this is accomplished using the following steps:
   (a) Apply StdDecomp to un-compress D_a at x_1
   (b) Evaluate the map $|x_1, z, x_2, y\rangle \otimes |D_a\rangle \mapsto |x_1, z \oplus D_a(x_1), x_2, y\rangle \otimes |D_a\rangle$, where z is the new register that was initialized to 0.
   (c) Re-compress D_a at x_1 by applying StdDecomp again.
2. Next, make an h_2 query on input (z, x_2) (where z where the registers created previously) with output registers y. This has the effect of mapping to:

$$|x_1, z, x_2, y \oplus h_b(x)\rangle \otimes |D_a\rangle \text{ if FindInput}((z, x_2), D_a) = (0, 0^{m+\ell})$$
$$|x_1, z, x_2, y \oplus H(w)\rangle \otimes |D_a\rangle \text{ if FindInput}(z, x_2), D_a) = (1, w)$$

3. Finally, make another h_1 query to un-compute the value of z. This is accomplished in the following steps:
   (a) Apply StdDecomp to un-compress D_a at x_1
   (b) Evaluate the map $|x_1, z, x_2, y\rangle \otimes |D_a\rangle \mapsto |x_1, z \oplus D_a(x_1), x_2, y\rangle \otimes |D_a\rangle$.
   (c) Re-compress D_a at x_1 by applying StdDecomp again.
   (d) Then discard the z registers.

Let $\mathcal{D}$ be a potential distinguisher. We consider the following hybrids:

Hybrid 0. In this hybrid, H queries are answered using C^{h_1, h_2}, as worked out above. Let p_0 be the probability $\mathcal{D}$ outputs 1.

Hybrid 1. This hybrid is identical to Hybrid 0, except that Steps 1c and 3a are removed. Let p_1 be the probability $\mathcal{D}$ outputs 1 in this hybrid.

Lemma 14. $|p_1 - p_0| < O(q/\sqrt{2^n})$.

Proof. Since Steps 1c and 3a are inverses of each other, Hybrid 1 is equivalent to moving Step 3a up to occur just after Step 1c. Note that Step 2 only interacts with D_a through two applications of FindInput (one for computing, one for un-computing), which in turn $O(1/\sqrt{2^n})$-almost commutes with Step 1c. By Lemma 7, each query to H therefore creates an error $O(1/\sqrt{2^n})$, yielding a total error of $O(q/\sqrt{2^n})$.   □

Hybrid 2. This hybrid is identical to Hybrid 2, except that after each query we measure if the database D_a contains a collision. If so, we abort and stop the simulation. Let p_2 be the probability $\mathcal{D}$ outputs 1 in this hybrid. By an almost identical proof to that of Lemma 9, we have:

Lemma 15. $|p_2 - p_1| < O(\sqrt{q^3/2^n})$.

Hybrid 3. This hybrid is identical to Hybrid 2 as outlined above, except that:

- Steps 1c and 3a are removed (as in Hybrid 1 and 2)
- The operation in Step 2 is replaced with

$$|x_1, z, x_2, y\rangle \otimes |D_a\rangle \mapsto |x_1, z, x_2, y \oplus H(x_1, x_2)\rangle \otimes |D_a\rangle$$

In other words Hybrid 3 is identical to Hybrid 2, except that we change Step 2. Let p_3 be the probability $\mathcal{D}$ outputs 1 in this hybrid.

Lemma 16. $p_3 = p_2$.

Proof. In either hybrid, since we do not apply the Steps 1c and 3a, D_a is guaranteed to contain the pair (x_1, z), where z is the same as in Step 2. Therefore, in Hybrid 2, FindInput$((z, x_2), D_a)$ is guaranteed to find a completion. Moreover, for D_a that contain no collisions, FindInput$((z, x_2), D_a)$ will find exactly the completion (x_1, z). In this case, $w = (x_1, x_2)$, and Hybrid 2 will make a query to H on (x_1, x_2). The end result is that for D_a containing no collisions, Step 2 is identical in both Hybrids. Since the collision check guarantees no collisions in D_a, this shows that the two hybrids are identical.   □

Hybrid 4. In this hybrid, H queries are made directly to H, but we still have the abort condition. Let p_4 be the probability $\mathcal{D}$ outputs 1 in this hybrid.

Lemma 17. $p_4 = p_3$.

Proof. In Hybrid 3, what remains of Steps 1 and 3 are exact inverses of each other and moreover commute with the new Step 2 from Hybrid 3. Therefore, we can remove Steps 1 and 3 altogether without affecting how oracle queries are answered. The result is identical to Hybrid 4. $\square$

Hybrid 5. This hybrid has H queries made directly to H, but without the abort condition. Let p_5 be the probability $\mathcal{D}$ outputs 1 in this hybrid. By an almost identical proof to that of Lemma 9, we have:

Lemma 18. $|p_5 - p_4| < O(\sqrt{q^3/2^n})$.

Overall then $|p_0 - p_5| < O(\sqrt{q^3/2^n})$, finishing the proof of Lemma 13. $\square$

6 Fujisaki Okamoto CCA-Secure Encryption

Here, we summarize our results on the Fujisaki-Okamoto transformation [FO99]. The transformation starts with a symmetric key encryption scheme $(\mathsf{Enc}_S, \mathsf{Dec}_S)$ and a public key encryption scheme $(\mathsf{Gen}_P, \mathsf{Enc}_P, \mathsf{Dec}_P)$. Assuming only mild security properties of these two schemes (which are much easier to obtain than strong CCA security), the conversion produces a new public key scheme $(\mathsf{Gen}, \mathsf{Enc}, \mathsf{Dec})$ which is secure against chosen ciphertext attacks. Let G, H are two random oracles, where G outputs keys for Enc_S and H outputs the random coins used by Enc_P. The scheme is as follows:

- $\mathsf{Gen} = \mathsf{Gen}_P$.
- $\mathsf{Enc}(\mathsf{pk}, m)$ chooses a random $\delta \in \{0,1\}^n$, and computes $d \leftarrow \mathsf{Enc}_S(H(\delta), m)$. Then it computes $c \leftarrow \mathsf{Enc}_P(\mathsf{pk}, \delta; G(\delta, d))$, and outputs (c, d)
- $\mathsf{Dec}(\mathsf{sk}, (c, d))$ first computes $\delta' \leftarrow \mathsf{Dec}_P(\mathsf{sk}, c)$. Then it checks that $c = \mathsf{Enc}_P(\mathsf{pk}, \delta'; G(\delta', d))$; if not, output $\bot$. Finally it computes and outputs $m' \leftarrow \mathsf{Dec}_S(H(\delta'), d)$

The main difficulty in the classical proof of security is allowing the reduction to answer decryption queries. The key idea is that, in order for the adversary to generate a valid ciphertext, it must have queried the oracles on δ. The reduction will simulate G, H on the fly by keeping track of tables of input/output pairs. When a chosen ciphertext query comes in, it will scan the tables looking for a δ that "explains" the ciphertext.

In the quantum setting, we run into a similar recording barrier as in the indifferentiability setting. Our key observation is that the output values of the G, H tables are only used for set membership tests. Just like equality tests used in our indifferentiability simulator, set membership tests in the primal and Fourier domain very nearly commute. As such, we can use our compressed oracles to mimic the classical proof following our techniques. Our reduction can even handle chosen ciphertext queries on quantum superpositions of ciphertexts. In the full version [Zha18], we prove the following theorem:

Theorem 5. *If* $(\mathsf{Enc}_S, \mathsf{Dec}_S)$ *is one-time secure and* $(\mathsf{Gen}, \mathsf{Enc}_P, \mathsf{Dec}_P)$ *is well-spread and one-way secure, then* $(\mathsf{Gen}, \mathsf{Enc}, \mathsf{Dec})$ *is quantum CCA secure in the quantum random oracle model.*

Acknowledgements. This work is supported in part by NSF and DARPA. Opinions, findings and conclusions or recommendations expressed in this material are those of the author(s) and do not necessarily reflect the views of NSF or DARPA.

References

[AS04] Aaronson, S., Shi, Y.: Quantum lower bounds for the collision and the element distinctness problems. J. ACM **51**(4), 595–605 (2004)

[ATTU16] Anand, M.V., Targhi, E.E., Tabia, G.N., Unruh, D.: Post-quantum security of the CBC, CFB, OFB, CTR, and XTS modes of operation. Cryptology ePrint Archive, Report 2016/197 (2016). http://eprint.iacr.org/2016/197

[BBBV97] Bennett, C.H., Bernstein, E., Brassard, G., Vazirani, U.: Strengths and weaknesses of quantum computing. SIAM J. Comput. **26**(5), 1510–1523 (1997)

[BDF+11] Boneh, D., Dagdelen, Ö., Fischlin, M., Lehmann, A., Schaffner, C., Zhandry, M.: Random oracles in a quantum world. In: Lee, D.H., Wang, X. (eds.) ASIACRYPT 2011. LNCS, vol. 7073, pp. 41–69. Springer, Heidelberg (2011). https://doi.org/10.1007/978-3-642-25385-0_3

[BHT98] Brassard, G., Høyer, P., Tapp, A.: Quantum cryptanalysis of hash and claw-free functions. In: Lucchesi, C.L., Moura, A.V. (eds.) LATIN 1998. LNCS, vol. 1380, pp. 163–169. Springer, Heidelberg (1998). https://doi.org/10.1007/BFb0054319

[BR93] Bellare, M., Rogaway, P.: Random oracles are practical: a paradigm for designing efficient protocols. In: Denning, D.E., Pyle, R., Ganesan, R., Sandhu, R.S., Ashby, V. (eds.) ACM CCS 93, pp. 62–73. ACM Press, November 1993

[BZ13] Boneh, D., Zhandry, M.: Secure signatures and chosen ciphertext security in a quantum computing world. In: Canetti, R., Garay, J.A. (eds.) CRYPTO 2013, Part II. LNCS, vol. 8043, pp. 361–379. Springer, Heidelberg (2013). https://doi.org/10.1007/978-3-642-40084-1_21

[CBH+17] Czajkowski, J., Bruinderink, L.G., Hülsing, A., Schaffner, C., Unruh, D.: Post-quantum security of the sponge construction. Cryptology ePrint Archive, Report 2017/771 (2017). http://eprint.iacr.org/2017/771

[CDG+15] Cabarcas, D., Demirel, D., Göpfert, F., Lancrenon, J., Wunderer, T.: An unconditionally hiding and long-term binding post-quantum commitment scheme. Cryptology ePrint Archive, Report 2015/628 (2015). http://eprint.iacr.org/2015/628

[CDG+17] Chase, M., et al.: Post-quantum zero-knowledge and signatures from symmetric-key primitives. Cryptology ePrint Archive, Report 2017/279 (2017). http://eprint.iacr.org/2017/279

[CDMP05] Coron, J.-S., Dodis, Y., Malinaud, C., Puniya, P.: Merkle-Damgård revisited: how to construct a hash function. In: Shoup, V. (ed.) CRYPTO 2005. LNCS, vol. 3621, pp. 430–448. Springer, Heidelberg (2005). https://doi.org/10.1007/11535218_26

[DFG13] Dagdelen, Ö., Fischlin, M., Gagliardoni, T.: The Fiat–Shamir transformation in a quantum world. In: Sako, K., Sarkar, P. (eds.) ASIACRYPT 2013. LNCS, vol. 8270, pp. 62–81. Springer, Heidelberg (2013). https://doi.org/10.1007/978-3-642-42045-0_4

[Eat17] Eaton, E.: Leighton-Micali hash-based signatures in the quantum random-oracle model. In: Adams, C., Camenisch, J. (eds.) SAC 2017. LNCS, vol. 10719, pp. 263–280. Springer, Cham (2018). https://doi.org/10.1007/978-3-319-72565-9_13

[FO99] Fujisaki, E., Okamoto, T.: Secure integration of asymmetric and symmetric encryption schemes. In: Wiener, M. (ed.) CRYPTO 1999. LNCS, vol. 1666, pp. 537–554. Springer, Heidelberg (1999). https://doi.org/10.1007/3-540-48405-1_34

[Gro96] Grover, L.K.: A fast quantum mechanical algorithm for database search. In: 28th ACM STOC, pp. 212–219. ACM Press, May 1996

[IBM17] IBM: IBM announces advances to IBM quantum systems and ecosystem (2017). https://www-03.ibm.com/press/us/en/pressrelease/53374.wss

[JZC+18] Jiang, H., Zhang, Z., Chen, L., Wang, H., Ma, Z.: IND-CCA-secure key encapsulation mechanism in the quantum random oracle model, revisited. In: Shacham, H., Boldyreva, A. (eds.) CRYPTO 2018. LNCS, vol. 10993, pp. 96–125. Springer, Cham (2018). https://doi.org/10.1007/978-3-319-96878-0_4

[Mit14] Mittelbach, A.: Salvaging indifferentiability in a multi-stage setting. In: Nguyen, P.Q., Oswald, E. (eds.) EUROCRYPT 2014. LNCS, vol. 8441, pp. 603–621. Springer, Heidelberg (2014). https://doi.org/10.1007/978-3-642-55220-5_33

[MRH04] Maurer, U.M., Renner, R., Holenstein, C.: Indifferentiability, impossibility results on reductions, and applications to the random oracle methodology. In: Naor, M. (ed.) TCC 2004. LNCS, vol. 2951, pp. 21–39. Springer, Heidelberg (2004). https://doi.org/10.1007/978-3-540-24638-1_2

[NIS17] NIST: Candidate quantum-resistant cryptographic algorithms publicly available (2017). https://www.nist.gov/news-events/news/2017/12/candidate-quantum-resistant-cryptographic-algorithms-publicly-available

[RSS11] Ristenpart, T., Shacham, H., Shrimpton, T.: Careful with composition: limitations of the indifferentiability framework. In: Paterson, K.G. (ed.) EUROCRYPT 2011. LNCS, vol. 6632, pp. 487–506. Springer, Heidelberg (2011). https://doi.org/10.1007/978-3-642-20465-4_27

[Son14] Song, F.: A note on quantum security for post-quantum cryptography. Cryptology ePrint Archive, Report 2014/709 (2014). http://eprint.iacr.org/2014/709

[TU16] Targhi, E.E., Unruh, D.: Post-quantum security of the Fujisaki-Okamoto and OAEP transforms. In: Hirt, M., Smith, A.D. (eds.) TCC 2016. LNCS, vol. 9986, pp. 192–216. Springer, Heidelberg (2016). https://doi.org/10.1007/978-3-662-53644-5_8

[Unr15] Unruh, D.: Non-interactive zero-knowledge proofs in the quantum random oracle model. In: Oswald, E., Fischlin, M. (eds.) EUROCRYPT 2015. LNCS, vol. 9057, pp. 755–784. Springer, Heidelberg (2015). https://doi.org/10.1007/978-3-662-46803-6_25

[Unr16] Unruh, D.: Collapse-binding quantum commitments without random ora-cles. In: Cheon, J.H., Takagi, T. (eds.) ASIACRYPT 2016. LNCS, vol. 10032, pp. 166–195. Springer, Heidelberg (2016). https://doi.org/10.1007/978-3-662-53890-6_6

[YAJ+17] Yoo, Y., Azarderakhsh, R., Jalali, A., Jao, D., Soukharev, V.: A post-quantum digital signature scheme based on supersingular isogenies. Cryptology ePrint Archive, Report 2017/186 (2017). http://eprint.iacr.org/2017/186

[Zha12a] Zhandry, M.: How to construct quantum random functions. In: 53rd FOCS, pp. 679–687. IEEE Computer Society Press, October 2012

[Zha12b] Zhandry, M.: Secure identity-based encryption in the quantum random oracle model. In: Safavi-Naini, R., Canetti, R. (eds.) CRYPTO 2012. LNCS, vol. 7417, pp. 758–775. Springer, Heidelberg (2012). https://doi.org/10.1007/978-3-642-32009-5_44

[Zha15] Zhandry, M.: A note on the quantum collision and set equality problems. Quant. Inf. Comput. 15(7 & 8) (2015)

[Zha18] Zhandry, M.: How to record quantum queries, and applications to quantum indifferentiability. Cryptology ePrint Archive, Report 2018/276 (2018). https://eprint.iacr.org/2018/276

Quantum Security Proofs
Using Semi-classical Oracles

Andris Ambainis[1]([⊠]), Mike Hamburg[2]([⊠]), and Dominique Unruh[3]

[1] University of Latvia, Riga, Latvia
andris.ambainis@lu.lv
[2] Rambus Security Division, San Francisco, USA
mike@shiftleft.org
[3] University of Tartu, Tartu, Estonia

Abstract. We present an improved version of the one-way to hiding (O2H) Theorem by Unruh, J ACM 2015. Our new O2H Theorem gives higher flexibility (arbitrary joint distributions of oracles and inputs, multiple reprogrammed points) as well as tighter bounds (removing square-root factors, taking parallelism into account). The improved O2H Theorem makes use of a new variant of quantum oracles, semi-classical oracles, where queries are partially measured. The new O2H Theorem allows us to get better security bounds in several public-key encryption schemes.

Keywords: Post-quantum cryptography ·
Quantum random oracle model · One-way to hiding ·
Public-key encryption · Provable security

1 Introduction

Ever since it was first introduced in [6] as a proof technique for cryptographic proofs, the random oracle model has been widely used to analyze cryptographic schemes, especially when highly efficient, practical solutions are desired. In the post-quantum setting, however, we need to be careful how the random oracle is modeled. When the adversary makes a query, the input to the random oracle should not be measured [8]. That is, queries should be possible in superposition between different inputs (we then speak of a "quantum random oracle"). Otherwise, the random oracle model would be a very unrealistic idealization of the real world since a quantum adversary can evaluate, say, a hash function in superposition.

Unfortunately, proving the security in the quantum random oracle model is considerably more difficult than in the classical random oracle model. One example of a classical proof technique that is not easy to mimic is programming of the random oracle. In this technique, we run the adversary with access to a random oracle but we change the answer to certain queries during the execution. In a nutshell, as long as we can show that the probability of changing a value that the adversary has already queried is negligible, the adversary will not notice

© International Association for Cryptologic Research 2019
A. Boldyreva and D. Micciancio (Eds.): CRYPTO 2019, LNCS 11693, pp. 269–295, 2019.
https://doi.org/10.1007/978-3-030-26951-7_10

the programming, and the proof goes through. In the quantum setting, this does not make sense. The adversary could query the superposition of all inputs in its first query. Then any programming would change a value that has already been queried.

A technique that can solve this problem (at least in certain situations) is the One-Way to Hiding (O2H) Theorem from [33]. The O2H Theorem solves the reprogramming problem by showing, roughly speaking, that we can bound the probability that the adversary distinguishes between two oracles G and H (the original and the reprogrammed oracle) in terms of the probability that the adversary can guess the location where the oracle is reprogrammed (we speak of the "guessing game"). This conceptually simple theorem has proven powerful in a number of security proofs for post-quantum secure encryption schemes and other constructions (see our overview in Sect. 1.2). However, the O2H Theorem has a number of limitations that limit its applicability, or give bad bounds in concrete security proofs.

In this work, we present a new version of the O2H Theorem that improves on the state of the art in a number of aspects:

- **Non-uniform random oracles.** The random oracle that is reprogrammed does not have to be a uniformly random function. We allow any distribution of oracles, e.g., invertible permutations, ideal ciphers, etc.
- **Multiple reprogrammed points.** We can reprogram the oracle in more than a single point. That is, we can reprogram the random oracle at a set of positions S and then bound the probability that the adversary detects this reprogramming with a single application of the O2H Theorem.
- **Arbitrary joint distributions.** We allow the distribution of reprogrammed locations and of the adversary's input to be arbitrarily correlated with the distribution of the random oracle. This is especially important if the reprogrammed location depends on the random oracle (e.g., reprogramming $H(x)$ where $x := H(r)$ for random r).
- **Tighter bounds for guessing games.** Our O2H Theorem bounds the difference of the square-roots of the adversary probabilities between two games. In many cases involving guessing games (i.e., where we intend to show that the probability of a certain event is negligible) this leads to bounds that are quadratically better.
- **Tighter bounds using semi-classical oracles.** We introduce a new technique, called semi-classical oracles. By applying the O2H Theorem to games involving semi-classical oracles, we can again get better bounds in some cases. (Whether some advantage is gained depends very much on the specific proof in which the O2H Theorem is used.)
- **Query depth.** Our O2H Theorem distinguishes query number q and query depth d. Thus, for cases in which the adversary has a high parallelism, we get better bounds (and for sequential adversaries nothing is lost by setting $d := q$).

One crucial novelty in our O2H Theorem is the use of "semi-classical oracles". In a nutshell, a semi-classical oracle is an oracle that only measures whether the adversary queried a given "forbidden" input, but does not measure anything beyond that. (In contrast, a quantum oracle does not measure anything, and a classical oracle measures everything.) So, for example, if the adversary queries a superposition of non-measured inputs, nothing is measured.

Our O2H Theorem bounds the distinguishing probability between two oracles G and H again in terms of the success probability in a "guessing game" where the adversary has to query an oracle on one of the forbidden inputs on which G and H differ. But in contrast to the original O2H Theorem, the adversary is given a semi-classical oracle in the guessing game! (In the original O2H Theorem, the adversary is given a quantum oracle.) Using a semi-classical oracle, the guessing game can be expressed more simply since it is well-defined whether the forbidden input has been queried or not. (In the original O2H Theorem, we instead have to stop at a random query and measure whether that particular query queries the forbidden input. This makes the description of the game more complex, and the random selection of a single query is the reason why the original O2H Theorem gives worse bounds.)

We stress that the semi-classical oracles are purely a proof technique and occur in intermediate games in proofs involving the new O2H Theorem. The final security results still hold in the quantum random oracle model, not in some "semi-classical random oracle model".

In this work, we introduce semi-classical oracles, state and prove the new O2H Theorem (together with a query complexity result about searching in semi-classical oracles), and demonstrate its usefulness by elementary examples and by exploring the impact on the security bounds of existing encryption schemes.

Organization. In Sect. 1.1 we shortly discuss some related work, and in Sect. 1.2 we discuss the impact of our result on existing cryptographic schemes. Section 2 presents basic notation. Our notion of semi-classical oracles is introduced in Sect. 3. We also state our main theorems in Sect. 3, the proofs are deferred to Sect. 5 (after the examples). We present examples how to use the new technique in Sect. 4.

1.1   Related Work

Variants of the O2H Theorem. Variants of the O2H Theorem were introduced in [14,22,31–33], see the beginning of Sect. 1.2 for more details.

Other Proof Techniques for the Quantum Random Oracle Model. [10] showed that Grover search is optimal with respect to worst-case complexity ([36] when parallelism is considered). [21,32] generalized this to the average-case which implies that finding preimages of the random oracle is hard. [8] introduced "history-free reductions" which basically amounts to replacing the random oracle by a different function right from the start. [38] showed that random oracles can be simulated using $2q$-wise independent functions. Based on this, [32] introduces a technique for extracting preimages of the random oracle. [38] introduces the "semi-constant distributions" technique that allows us to program the random oracle in many random locations with a challenge value without the adversary noticing. [37] improves on this with the "small-range distribution" technique that allows us to simulate random oracles using random looking functions with a small range. [39] shows that random oracles are indistinguishable from random permutations, and as a consequence that random oracles are collision resistant (this is generalized by [4,15,29] to the case of non-uniformly distributed functions). Collision-resistance of the random oracle is generalized to the "collapsing property" which allows us to show that measuring the output of the random oracle effectively measures the input. More general methods for problems in quantum query complexity (not limited to random oracles) include the polynomial method [5] and the adversary method [1]. [3] shows that the difficulties of using the quantum random oracle are not just a matter of missing proof techniques, but that in certain cases classically secure schemes are not secure in the quantum random oracle model.

Cryptosystems Whose Security Proof is Based on O2H Theorems. See Sect. 1.2.

1.2 Impact on Existing Cryptosystems

Above, we explained why our new O2H Theorem can lead to better bounds. We will also illustrate that point with a few simple examples in Sect. 4. However, to better judge the impact on realistic cryptosystems, we need to ask the question how the bounds achieved by existing security proofs improve.

We are aware of the following results in the quantum random oracle model that employ some variant of the original O2H Theorem from [33]: [33] introduced the O2H Theorem to build revocable timed-release encryption schemes, [31] introduced an "adaptive" version of the O2H Theorem[1] to analyze a quantum position verification protocol, [32] made the O2H Theorem even more adaptive and used this for the design of non-interactive zero-knowledge proof systems and signature schemes (and this in turn is the basis for various follow-up schemes such as [9,11–13,18,35]). [34] uses the O2H variant from [32] to prove security of Fiat-Shamir [16], both as a proof system and as a signature scheme. [14] uses a variant of the O2H Theorem for proving security of Leighton-Micali signatures [25] (their variant generalizes [33] in some aspects but only works when the position where the oracle is programmed is information-theoretically hidden). [28] uses the O2H Theorem for constructing PRFs and MACs. [30] was the first paper to employ the O2H Theorem for designing public key encryption schemes: it proved the security of variants of the Fujisaki-Okamoto transform [17] and the OAEP transform [7] (introducing one extra hash value in the ciphertext for "key confirmation"). [19] modularized and improved the Fujisaki-Okamoto variant from [30], also using key confirmation. [27] proved security of a construction without key confirmation, still using the O2H Theorem. [22] introduced a variant of the O2H Theorem that allows some of the oracles and inputs given

---

[1] Which allows to reprogram the random oracle at a location that is influenced by the adversary.

to the adversary to be non-uniformly distributed, subject to the independence and uniformity of certain random variables, and uses it to prove the security of further public-key encryption schemes. (Since our O2H Theorem can also handle non-uniform inputs, it might be that it can serve as a drop-in replacement in the proofs in [22] removing the necessity to check the independence conditions.) [24] proves security of public-key encryption schemes with explicit rejection; an earlier version [23] of [24] used the O2H Theorem from [22], the current version uses our new O2H Theorems. [20] analyzes public-key encryption and authenticated key exchange schemes, using the original O2H Theorem from [33] in the first revision, but improving the bounds using our new O2H Theorem.

Thus, O2H Theorems might be one of the most widely used proof technique for cryptosystems involving quantum random oracles. We expect that our improvement of the O2H Theorem allows us to derive better security bounds for most of the above schemes. To give some evidence to this hypothesis, we report on the advantages gained by using our improvement in three of the works above, namely Targhi-Unruh [30], Hövelmanns-Kiltz-Schäge-Unruh [20], and Jiang-Zhang-Ma [24].

In case of [24], an earlier draft [23] used the O2H variant from [22], while the current version [24] already uses our new O2H Theorem. Since the O2H variant from [22] was introduced to handle the case where not all oracles and adversary inputs are independent, this demonstrates that our O2H Theorem can handle this case, too. (Besides giving tighter bounds.) Similarly, the first eprint version of [20] used the original O2H Theorem from [33], while the second version was updated to use our new O2H Theorem.

The old and new bounds are summarized in Fig. 1. The figure lists the advantages against IND-CCA security for different settings. Since it is difficult to compare the various formulas, in the column "queries", we summarize the relationship between query number and attack probability: Assuming that the terms involving ε, the advantage against the underlying public-key encryption scheme, dominate all other terms, how many queries does one have to make to break the scheme (with constant probability)? E.g., given an advantage $q\sqrt{\varepsilon}$, we need $q \approx \varepsilon^{-1/2}$ queries for a successful attack, so we write $q^2 \approx 1/\varepsilon$ in that case.

Furthermore, in the full version [2], we reprove the security of the Fujisaki-Okamoto variant from [30] using our O2H Theorem. That result is particularly interesting because of its heavy use of the O2H Theorem. This allows us to make use of several of the new features of our O2H Theorem.

– It uses "nested invocations" of the O2H Theorem. That is, first the O2H Theorem is applied as usual to a pair of games, leading to a guessing game in which we need to show that the guessing probability P_{guess} of the adversary is negligible. But then the O2H Theorem is applied again to prove this. Since the bound obtained by the O2H Theorem contains a square root over P_{guess}, the nested application of the O2H Theorem introduces nested square roots, i.e., a forth root. This leads to a particularly bad bound in [30].

In contrast, our new O2H Theorem allows us to directly bound the difference of the square roots of the success probabilities of the adversary in two

Setting	Bound	Queries
Targhi-Unruh [30]		
old O2H, one-way	$\varepsilon_{sym} + q^{9/5}2^{-\gamma/5} + q^{3/2}\varepsilon^{1/4} + q^{3/2}2^{-n_1/4}$	$q^6 \approx 1/\varepsilon$
new O2H, IND-CPA	$\varepsilon_{sym} + q^{9/5}2^{-\gamma/5} + qq_{dec}^{1/2}\varepsilon^{1/2} + q^{3/2}q_{dec}2^{-n/2}$	$q^2 q_{dec} \approx 1/\varepsilon$
new O2H, one-way	$\varepsilon_{sym} + q^{9/5}2^{-\gamma/5} + q^{3/2}q_{dec}\varepsilon^{1/2}$	$q^3 q_{dec}^2 \approx 1/\varepsilon$
Hövelmanns-Kiltz-Schäge-Unruh [20]		
old O2H, IND-CPA	$q\varepsilon^{1/2} + q2^{-n/2}$	$q^2 \approx 1/\varepsilon$
new O2H, IND-CPA	$q^{1/2}\varepsilon^{1/2} + q2^{-n/2}$	$q \approx 1/\varepsilon$
Jiang-Zhang-Ma [24]		
old O2H, one-way	$q\varepsilon^{1/2}$	$q^2 \approx 1/\varepsilon$
new O2H, one-way	$q\varepsilon^{1/2}$	$q^2 \approx 1/\varepsilon$
new O2H, IND-CPA	$q^{1/2}\varepsilon^{1/2} + q2^{-n/2} + q2^{-n'}$	$q \approx 1/\varepsilon$

The "setting" column says whether the proof uses the old/new O2H and whether it is based on one-wayness or IND-CPA security of the underlying public-key encryption scheme.

The "bound" column gives the bound on the advantage of the adversary against IND-CCA security, up to constant factor. (In the case of [30] a hybrid public-key encryption scheme is constructed, in the other cases a KEM.) ε is the advantage of the reduced adversary against the one-wayness or IND-CPA security of the underlying public-key scheme, respectively. (A complete description would contain the runtime of that adversary. For this overview this is not relevant since in all cases, that runtime did not change when switching to the new O2H Theorem.) ε_{sym} is the advantage against the underlying symmetric encryption scheme. q is the number of queries (random oracle + decryption queries), q_{dec} only the decryption queries. γ is the min-entropy of ciphertexts, n the plaintext length of the underlying public-key scheme, and n' is the length of the additional hash appended to the ciphertext in [24].

The "queries" column summarizes the effect of queries compared to the security of the underlying public-key scheme (see the explanation in the text, higher exponent is worse).

For simplicity, we give the bounds for the case where no decryption errors occur.

Fig. 1. Security bounds of different Fujisaki-Okamoto variants with new and old O2H Theorems.

games. This means that in a nested invocation, when we analyze P_{guess}, the O2H Theorem directly tells us how $\sqrt{P_{\text{guess}}}$ changes (instead of how P_{guess} changes). This avoids the nested square root.

- It uses the adaptive version of the O2H Theorem (from [31]). While our O2H Theorem is not adaptive (in the sense that the input where the oracle is reprogrammed has to be fixed at the beginning of the game), it turns out that in the present case our new O2H Theorem can replace the adaptive one. This is because our new O2H Theorem allows us to reprogram the oracle at a large number of inputs (not just a single one). It turns out we do not need to adaptively choose the one input to reprogram, we just reprogram all potential inputs. At least in the proof from [30], this works without problems.

We restate (in [2]) the proof from [30] both under the assumption that the underlying public-key encryption scheme is one-way and under the assumption that it is IND-CPA secure. While in the original proof, we get essentially the same bound no matter which of the two assumptions we use, with the new O2H Theorem, the resulting bounds are much better when using IND-CPA security (but there is also an improvement in the one-way case).

The resulting bounds are given in Fig. 1 as well. We see that the biggest improvement is in the case of IND-CPA security, where the dependence on the query number changed from the sixth power to cubic.

We also noticed a mistake in the proof,[2] which we fixed in our proof. (We do not know if the fix carries over to the original proof.)

But our analysis also shows some potential for future research on the O2H Theorem. The proof from [30] constructs a plaintext extractor Dec^{**} that is relatively inefficient because it iterates through a large number of possible candidate keys. Thus the number of oracle queries performed by Dec^{**} (namely, $O(qq_{dec})$) by far outweighs the number of oracle queries performed by the adversary (namely, $O(q)$). This large number of queries negatively influences the bounds obtained when applying the new O2H Theorem. However, the $O(qq_{dec})$ queries performed by Dec^{**} are all classical, only $O(q)$ quantum queries are made. Our O2H Theorem treats classical and quantum queries the same. A variant of the O2H Theorem that gives better bounds when only a small fraction of the queries are quantum would lead to improvements in the bounds obtained here. We leave this as a problem for future work.

2   Preliminaries

For basics of quantum computing, we refer to a standard textbook such as [26].

Given a function $f : X \to Y$, we model a quantum-accessible oracle $\mathcal{O}$ for f as a unitary transformation U_f operating on two registers Q, R with spaces $\mathbb{C}^X$ and $\mathbb{C}^Y$, respectively, where $U_f : |q, r\rangle \mapsto |q, r \oplus f(x)\rangle$, where $\oplus$ is some involutive group operation (e.g., XOR if Y is a set of bitstrings).

A quantum oracle algorithm is an algorithm that can perform classical and quantum computations, and that can query classical and/or quantum-accessible oracles. We allow an oracle algorithm A to perform oracle queries in parallel. We say A is a q-query algorithm if it performs at most q oracle queries (counting parallel queries as separate queries), and has query depth d if it invokes the oracle at most d times (counting parallel queries as one query). For example, if A performs 5 parallel queries followed by 7 parallel queries, we have $q = 12$ and $d = 2$.

The distinction between query number and query depth is important because realistic brute-force attacks are highly parallel. It's easy to do 2^{64} hash queries

---

[2] In Game 7 in [30], a secret δ^* is encrypted using a one-time secure encryption scheme, and the final step in the proof concludes that therefore δ^* cannot be guessed. However, Game 7 contains an oracle Dec^{**} that in turn accesses δ^* directly, invalidating that argument.

on parallel machines—the Bitcoin network does this several times a minute—but it would take millennia to do them sequentially. Query depth is also important because early quantum computers are likely to lose coherency quickly, limiting them to shallow circuits. Our model does not capture this limitation because it does not differentiate between a deep quantum computation and several shallow ones with measurements between. But we hope that future work can account for coherency using a notion of query depth.

We will make use of the well-known fact that any quantum oracle algorithm $A^{\mathcal{O}}(z)$ can be transformed into a *unitary* quantum oracle algorithm with constant factor computational overhead and the same query number and query depth. Such an algorithm has registers Q_A (for its state), and $Q_1, \ldots, Q_n$ and $R_1, \ldots, R_n$ for query inputs and outputs, respectively. It starts with an initial state $|\Psi\rangle$ (that may depend on the input z). Then, A alternatingly applies a fixed unitary U on all registers (independent of z and $\mathcal{O}$), and performs parallel queries. Parallel queries apply the oracle $\mathcal{O}$ to Q_i, R_i for each $i = 1, \ldots, n$. (I.e., if $\mathcal{O}$ is implemented by U_f, we apply $U_f \otimes \cdots \otimes U_f$ between U-applications.) Finally, the classical output of $A^{\mathcal{O}}(z)$ is the result of a projective measurement on the final state of A. This implies that in many situations, we can assume our algorithms to be unitary without loss of generality.

3   Semi-classical Oracles

Classical oracles measure both their input and their output, whereas quantum-accessible oracles measure neither. We define semi-classical oracles, which measure their output but not their input. Formally, a semi-classical oracle $\mathcal{O}_f^{SC}$ for a function f with domain X and codomain Y is queried with two registers: an input register Q with space $\mathbb{C}^X$ and an output register R with space $\mathbb{C}^Y$.

When queried with a value $|x\rangle$ in Q, the oracle performs a measurement of $f(x)$. Formally, it performs the measurements corresponding to the projectors $M_y : y \in Y$ where $M_y := \sum_{x \in S : f(x) = y} |x\rangle\langle x|$. The oracle then initializes the R register to $|y\rangle$ for the measured y.

In this paper, the function f is always the indicator function f_S for a set S, where $f_S(x) = 1$ if $x \in S$ and 0 otherwise. For brevity, we overload the notation $\mathcal{O}_S^{SC}$ to be the semiclassical oracle for this index function.

To illustrate this, let us see what happens if the adversary performs the same query with a quantum oracle, a classical oracle, and a semi-classical oracle implementing the indicator function for S, respectively: Say the adversary sends the query $\sum_x 2^{-n/2}|x\rangle|0\rangle$, and say $S = \{x_0\}$. When querying a quantum oracle, the oracle returns the state $\sum_x 2^{-n/2}|x\rangle|f_S(x)\rangle = 2^{-n/2}|x\rangle|1\rangle + \sum_{x \neq x_0} 2^{-n/2}|x\rangle|0\rangle$. When querying a classical oracle, the resulting state will be $|x\rangle|f_S(x)\rangle$ for a uniformly random x. But when querying a semi-classical oracle, with probability $1 - 2^{-n}$, the resulting state is $\sum_{x \neq x_0} \frac{1}{\sqrt{2^n - 1}}|x\rangle|0\rangle$, and with probability 2^{-n}, the resulting state is $|x_0\rangle|1\rangle$. In particular, the superposition between all $|x\rangle$ that are not in S is preserved!

In the execution of a quantum algorithm $A^{\mathcal{O}_S^{SC}}$, let Find be the event that $\mathcal{O}_S^{SC}$ ever returns $|1\rangle$. This is a well-defined classical event because $\mathcal{O}_S^{SC}$ measures its output. This event is called Find because if it occurs, the simulator could immediately stop execution and measure the input register Q to obtain a value $x \in S$. If H is some other quantum-accessible oracle with domain X and codomain Y, we define $H \setminus S$ ("H punctured on S") as an oracle which, on input x, first queries $\mathcal{O}_S^{SC}(x)$ and then $H(x)$. We call this "puncturing" for the following reason: when Find does not occur, the outcome of $A^{H \setminus S}$ is independent of $H(x)$ for all $x \in S$. Those values are effectively removed from H's domain. The following lemma makes this fact formal.

Lemma 1. *Let $S \subseteq X$ be random. Let $G, H : X \to Y$ be random functions satisfying $\forall x \notin S$. $G(x) = H(x)$. Let z be a random bitstring. $(S, G, H, z$ may have arbitrary joint distribution.)*
Let A be a quantum oracle algorithm (not necessarily unitary).
Let E be an arbitrary (classical) event.
Then $\Pr[E \wedge \neg\mathsf{Find} : x \leftarrow A^{H \setminus S}(z)] = \Pr[E \wedge \neg\mathsf{Find} : x \leftarrow A^{G \setminus S}(z)]$.

Unruh's "one-way to hiding" (O2H) Theorem [33] is a key ingredient in most post-quantum security analyses. This theorem bounds how much a quantum adversary's behavior can change when the random oracle changes on a set S, based on the probability that measuring a random query would give a result in S, which we call the "guessing probability". Semi-classical oracles allow us to split the O2H Theorem into two parts. The first part bounds how much a quantum adversary's behavior changes when a random oracle is punctured on S based on $\Pr[\mathsf{Find}]$:

Theorem 1 (Semi-classical O2H). *Let $S \subseteq X$ be random. Let $G, H : X \to Y$ be random functions satisfying $\forall x \notin S$. $G(x) = H(x)$. Let z be a random bitstring. $(S, G, H, z$ may have arbitrary joint distribution.)*
Let A be an oracle algorithm of query depth d (not necessarily unitary).
Let

$$P_{\text{left}} := \Pr[b = 1 : b \leftarrow A^H(z)]$$

$$P_{\text{right}} := \Pr[b = 1 : b \leftarrow A^G(z)] \tag{1}$$

$$P_{\text{find}} := \Pr[\mathsf{Find} : A^{G \setminus S}(z)] \overset{Lem.\ 1}{=} \Pr[\mathsf{Find} : A^{H \setminus S}(z)]$$

Then

$$|P_{\text{left}} - P_{\text{right}}| \leq 2\sqrt{(d+1) \cdot P_{\text{find}}} \quad and \quad \left|\sqrt{P_{\text{left}}} - \sqrt{P_{\text{right}}}\right| \leq 2\sqrt{(d+1) \cdot P_{\text{find}}}$$

The theorem also holds with bound $\sqrt{(d+1)P_{\text{find}}}$ for the following alternative definitions of P_{right}:

$$P_{\text{right}} := \Pr[b = 1 : b \leftarrow A^{H \setminus S}(z)], \tag{2}$$

$$P_{\text{right}} := \Pr[b = 1 \wedge \neg\text{Find} : b \leftarrow A^{H \backslash S}(z)], \tag{3}$$

$$P_{\text{right}} := \Pr[b = 1 \wedge \neg\text{Find} : b \leftarrow A^{G \backslash S}(z)], \tag{4}$$

$$P_{\text{right}} := \Pr[b = 1 \vee \text{Find} : b \leftarrow A^{H \backslash S}(z)], \tag{5}$$

$$P_{\text{right}} := \Pr[b = 1 \vee \text{Find} : b \leftarrow A^{G \backslash S}(z)]. \tag{6}$$

In this theorem, we give A only access to a single oracle (G or H). In many settings, there may be additional oracles that A has access to. It may not be obvious at the first glance, but Theorem 1 applies in that case, too. Since there is no assumption on the runtime of A, or on the size of z, nor on the number of queries made to the additional oracles, additional oracles can simply be encoded as part of z. That is, if we want to consider an adversary $A^{H,F}()$, we can instead write $A^H(F)$ where F is a complete (exponential size) description of F.

The proof of Theorem 1 is given in Sect. 5.2.

The second part relates $\Pr[\text{Find}]$ to the guessing probability:

Theorem 2 (Search in semi-classical oracle). *Let A be any quantum oracle algorithm making some number of queries at depth at most d to a semi-classical oracle with domain X. Let $S \subseteq X$ and $z \in \{0,1\}^*$. (S, z may have arbitrary joint distribution.)*

Let B be an algorithm that on input z chooses $i \xleftarrow{\$} \{1, \dots, d\}$; runs $A^{\mathcal{O}_z^{SC}}(z)$ until (just before) the i-th query; then measures all query input registers in the computational basis and outputs the set T of measurement outcomes.

Then

$$\Pr[\text{Find} : A^{\mathcal{O}_S^{SC}}(z)] \leq 4d \cdot \Pr[S \cap T \neq \varnothing : T \leftarrow B(z)] \tag{7}$$

The proof is given in Sect. 5.3.

In the simple but common case that the input of A is independent of S, we get the following corollary:

Corollary 1. *Suppose that S and z are independent, and that A is a q-query algorithm. Let $P_{\max} := \max_{x \in X} \Pr[x \in S]$. Then*

$$\Pr[\text{Find} : A^{\mathcal{O}_S^{SC}}(z)] \leq 4q \cdot P_{\max}. \tag{8}$$

For example, for uniform $x \in \{1, \dots, N\}$, $A^{\mathcal{O}_{\{x\}}^{SC}}$ finds x with probability $\leq 4q/N$.

Proof. Since the query depth of A does not occur in the lemma, we can assume that A does not perform parallel queries. Then the output T of B in Theorem 2 has $|T| \leq 1$, and $d = q$. Thus $\Pr[S \cap T \neq \varnothing : T \leftarrow B(z)]$ is simply the probability that $B(z)$ outputs an element of S. Hence $\Pr[S \cap T \neq \varnothing : T \leftarrow B(z)] \leq P_{\max}$. Then by Theorem 2, $\Pr[\text{Find} : A^{\mathcal{O}_S^{SC}}(z)] \leq 4q \cdot P_{\max}$. $\square$

Note that Corollary 1 is essentially optimal (we cannot improve on the factor 4, see Appendix A). Thus, searching in a semi-classical oracle is still slightly easier than in a classical one.

4   Examples How to Use the O2H Theorems

To illustrate the use of the theorems from the previous section, we give two illustrative examples: hardness of searching in a sparse random function, and hardness of inverting a random oracle with leakage (in the sense that an only computationally secret encryption of the preimage is given to the adversary).

4.1   Hardness of Searching in a Sparse Random Function

Consider the following setting: $H : X \rightarrow \{0, 1\}$ is a random function where for each x, $H(x) = 1$ with probability $\leq \lambda$ (not necessarily independently). What is the probability to find x with $H(x) = 1$ in q queries? We will prove an upper bound.

We solve this problem using the semi-classical O2H technique introduced by Theorem 1. Let A be a q-query algorithm with depth d. We want to bound $\Pr[H(x) = 1 : x \leftarrow A^H()]$. We do this by a series of games.

Game 1. $x \leftarrow A^H()$. *Measure* x. *Then* A *wins if* $H(x) = 1$.

We would like to apply Theorem 1 to this game. But it doesn't work well to apply it to A^H because H is also used outside of A. Therefore, we use a different but obviously equivalent game:

Game 2. *Define* $\hat{A}^H()$ *to run* $x \leftarrow A^H()$; *measure* x; *and return* $b := H(x)$. *Game 2 runs* $b \leftarrow \hat{A}^H()$. *Then* A *wins if* $b = 1$.

Note that $\hat{A}$ is a $(q + 1)$-query algorithm with depth $d + 1$.

We can apply the semi-classical O2H Theorem (Theorem 1), variant (4)[3] to this game, where $G := 0$ (the constant zero function) and $S :- \{x : H(x) - 1\}$. This gives us:

$$\left| \underbrace{\sqrt{\Pr[b = 1 : \text{Game 2}]}}_{P_{\text{left}}} - \underbrace{\sqrt{\Pr[b = 1 \wedge \neg\text{Find} : \text{Game 3}]}}_{P_{\text{right}}} \right|$$

$$\leq \sqrt{(d + 2) \underbrace{\Pr[\text{Find} : \text{Game 3}]}_{P_{\text{find}}}} \quad (9)$$

with

Game 3. *Run* $b \leftarrow \hat{A}^{G \backslash S}()$. *Then* A *wins if* $b = 1$ *and not* Find.

---

[3] Theorem 1 gives us different options how to define the right game. Conceptually simplest is variant (1) (it does not involve a semi-classical oracle in the right game), but it does not apply in all situations. The basic idea behind all variants is the same, namely that the adversary gets access to an oracle G that behaves differently on the set S of marked elements.

In the present proof, we use specifically variant (4) because then Game 4 will be of a form that is particularly easy to analyze (the adversary has winning probability 0 there).

which is equivalent to

Game 4. $x \leftarrow A^{G \setminus S}()$; set $b \leftarrow (G \setminus S)(x)$. Then A wins if $b = 1$ and not Find.

What has happened so far? We have used the O2H Theorem to rewrite a game with access to an oracle H (Game 1) into the same game with a different oracle $G = 0$ (Game 4) ("right game"). The new oracle is considerably simpler: in this specific case, it is all zero. The difference between the two games is bounded by (9) in terms of how hard it is to find an element in the set S (the "marked elements"), i.e., a position where G and H differ (the "finding game"). This is the typical way of applying an O2H Theorem: Replace the oracle H by something simpler, continue the game-based proof from the right game, and additionally perform a second game-based proof to bound the probability of finding a marked element in the finding game.

However, there are several crucial differences to the use of prior O2H lemmas (e.g., [33]). First, prior O2H Theorems required G and H to be uniformly random functions, and to differ only at a single location x. But here H is not assumed to be uniform, and it differs from G at more than a single input (i.e. at the entire set S). This allows us to analyze search problems with multiple targets.

Second, (9) has square roots on the left-hand side. This is optional: Theorem 1 also gives a bound without square roots. In our example, since P_{right} is very small, the square-root variant gives smaller bounds for P_{left}.

Third, the finding game is expressed using semi-classical oracles. This is never a limitation because we can always replace the semi-classical oracles by quantum-accessible ones using Theorem 2 (which then gives bounds comparable to the O2H from [33]). However, as we will see in the next section, in some cases semi-classical oracles give better bounds.

In our case, we trivially have $\Pr[G(x) = 1 \land \neg \text{Find} : \text{Game 4}] = 0$ since $G = 0$.

However, analyzing $\Pr[\text{Find} : \text{Game 3}]$ is less trivial. At the first glance, it seems that having access to the oracle $G = 0$ yields no information about S, and thus finding an element of S is down to pure luck, and cannot succeed with probability greater than $(q+1)\lambda$. But in fact, computing $G \setminus S$ requires measuring whether each query is in S. The measurement process can leak information about S. Section A shows that at least in some cases, it is possible to find elements of S with greater probability than $(q + 1)\lambda$. Fortunately, we have a result for this situation, namely Corollary 1, which shows that $\Pr[\text{Find} : \text{Game 4}] \leq 4(q+1)\lambda$.

Plugging this into (9), we get

$$\Pr[H(x) = 1 : \text{Game 1}] \leq 4(d + 2)(q + 1)\lambda.$$

Without the square roots on the left-hand side of (9), we would get only the bound $\sqrt{4(d + 2)(q + 1)\lambda}$.

We summarize what we have proven in the following lemma:

Lemma 2 (Search in unstructured function). Let H be a random function, drawn from a distribution such that $\Pr[H(x) = 1] \leq \lambda$ for all x. Let A be a q-query adversary with query depth d. Then $\Pr[H(x) = 1 : b \leftarrow A^H()] \leq 4(d + 2)(q + 1)\lambda$.

While this is a simple consequence of our O2H technique, we are not aware that this bound was already presented in the literature. While [36] already showed a trade-off between parallelism and query number in unstructured quantum search. However, our result gives an explicit (and tight) success probability and applies even to functions whose outputs are not i.i.d. For the special case of no-parallelism $(d = q)$ and i.i.d. functions, the best known bound was [21, Theorem 1] which we improve upon by a factor of 2. Additionally, our lemma allows the different outputs of H to be correlated while prior results require them to be independent.

4.2   Hardness of Inverting a Random Oracle with Leakage

The previous example considered a pure query-complexity problem, searching in a random function. It can easily be solved with other techniques (giving slightly different bounds). Where O2H Theorems shine is the combination of computational hardness and random oracles. The following example illustrates this.

Let E be a randomized algorithm taking input from a space X, such that it is difficult to distinguish the distributions

$$\mathcal{D}_1 := \{(x, E(x)) : x \xleftarrow{\$} X\} \text{ and } \mathcal{D}_0 := \{(x_1, E(x_2)) : x_1, x_2 \xleftarrow{\$} X\}$$

For a quantum algorithm B, define its E-distinguishing advantage as

$$\text{Adv}_{\text{IND}-E}(B) := \left| \begin{array}{c} \Pr\left[1 \leftarrow B(x, e) : (x, e) \leftarrow \mathcal{D}_1\right] \\ - \Pr\left[1 \leftarrow B(x, e) : (x, e) \leftarrow \mathcal{D}_0\right] \end{array} \right|$$

For example, E could be IND-CPA-secure encryption. Let $H : X \to Y$ be a random oracle which is independent of E. How hard is it to invert H with a leakage of E? That is, given a quantum oracle algorithm A, we want to bound

$$\text{Adv}_{\text{OW-LEAK}-E}(A) := \Pr\left[A^H(H(x), E(x)) = x : x \xleftarrow{\$} X\right]$$

We can do this using a series of games. For brevity, we will go into slightly less detail than in Sect. 4.1. Let w_i be the probability that the adversary wins Game i.

Game 0 (Original). $x \xleftarrow{\$} X; x' \leftarrow A^H(H(x), E(x))$. *The adversary wins if* $x' = x$.

Now choose a random $y \xleftarrow{\$} Y$, and set a different random oracle $G := H(x := y)$ which is the same as H on every input except $S := \{x\}$. We can define a new game where the adversary has access to $G \setminus S$:

Game 1 (Punctured, first try). $x \xleftarrow{\$} X; x' \leftarrow A^{G\setminus\{x\}}(H(x), E(x))$. *The adversary wins if* $x' = x$ *and not* Find.

Applying Theorem 1 variant (4),[4] we find that

$$\left| \underbrace{\sqrt{\Pr[x' = x : \text{Game } 0]}}_{P_{\text{left}} = w_0} - \underbrace{\sqrt{\Pr[x' = x \wedge \neg\text{Find} : \text{Game } 1]}}_{P_{\text{right}} = w_1} \right|$$
$$\leq \underbrace{\sqrt{(d+1)\Pr\left[\text{Find} : \text{Game } 1\right]}}_{P_{\text{find}}}$$

Unlike in Sect. 4.1, this time we do not have a trivial bound for w_1. We could bound it in terms of distinguishing advantage against E. But let's instead try to make this game more like the ones in Sect. 4.1: we can cause the adversary to Find instead of winning. To do this, we just apply an extra hash operation. Let $\hat{A}^H(y, e)$ be the algorithm which runs $x' \leftarrow A^H(y, e)$; computes $H(x')$ and ignores the result; and then returns x'. Then $\hat{A}$ performs $q + 1$ queries at depth $d + 1$. This gives us a new game:

Game 2 (Original with extra hash). $x \xleftarrow{\$} X; x' \leftarrow \hat{A}^H(H(x), E(x))$. *The adversary wins if $x' = x$.*

Clearly $w_2 = w_0$. The new punctured game is also similar:

Game 3 (Punctured, extra hash). $x \xleftarrow{\$} X; x' \leftarrow \hat{A}^{G\backslash\{x\}}(H(x), E(x))$. *The adversary wins if $x' = x$ and not* Find.

Applying Theorem 1 variant (4)[5] as before gives

$$|\sqrt{w_3} - \sqrt{w_2}| \leq \sqrt{(d+2)\Pr\left[\text{Find} : \text{Game } 3\right]} \tag{10}$$

But the adversary cannot win Game 3: the extra hash query triggers Find if $x' = x$, and the adversary does not win if Find. Therefore $w_3 = 0$. Plugging this into (10) and squaring both sides gives:

$$w_0 = w_2 \leq (d+2)\Pr\left[\text{Find} : \text{Game } 3\right] \tag{11}$$

It remains to bound the right-hand side. We first note that in Game 3, the value $H(x)$ is only used once, since the adversary does not have access to $H(x)$: it only has access to G, which is the same as H everywhere except x. So Game 3 is the same as if $H(x)$ is replaced by a random value:

Game 4 (No $H(x)$). Set $x \xleftarrow{\$} X; y \xleftarrow{\$} Y; \hat{A}^{G\backslash\{x\}}(y, E(x))$. *We do not care about the output of $\hat{A}$, but only whether it* Find*s.*

Clearly $\Pr\left[\text{Find} : \text{Game } 4\right] = \Pr\left[\text{Find} : \text{Game } 3\right]$. Finally, we apply the indistinguishability assumption by comparing to the following game:

---

[4] Choosing a different variant here would slightly change the formula below but lead to the same problems.

[5] The reason for choosing this particular variant is that same as in footnote 3.

Game 5 (IND-E challenge). $(x_1, x_2) \overset{\$}{\leftarrow} X; y \overset{\$}{\leftarrow} Y; \hat{A}^{G \setminus \{x_1\}}(y, E(x_2))$.

Let $B(x, e)$ be an algorithm which chooses $y \overset{\$}{\leftarrow} Y$; runs $\hat{A}^{G \setminus \{x\}}(y, e)$; and returns 1 if Find and 0 otherwise. Then B runs in about the same time as A plus $(q + 1)$ comparisons. If (y, e) are drawn from $\mathcal{D}_1$, then this experiment is equivalent to Game 4, and it they are drawn from $\mathcal{D}_0$ then it is equivalent to Game 5. Therefore B is a distinguisher for E with advantage exactly

$$\text{Adv}_{\text{IND}-E}(B) = |\Pr[\text{Find} : \text{Game 5}] - \Pr[\text{Find} : \text{Game 4}]| \qquad (12)$$

Furthermore, in Game 5, the oracle G is punctured at x_1, which is uniformly random and independent of everything else in the game. So by Theorem 2,

$$\Pr[\text{Find} : \text{Game 5}] \leq 4(q + 1)/\text{card}(X)$$

Combining this with (11) and (12), we have

$$\text{Adv}_{\text{OW-LEAK}-E}(A) \leq (d + 2)\text{Adv}_{\text{IND}-E}(B) + \frac{4(d + 2)(q + 1)}{\text{card}(X)}$$

This is a much better bound than we would have gotten without using semi-classical oracles (i.e., the O2H Theorem from [33]). In front of $\text{Adv}_{\text{IND}-E}(B)$, we only have the factor $d + 2$. In contrast, if we had applied Theorem 2 directly after using Theorem 1, then we would have gotten a factor of $O(qd)$ in front of $\text{Adv}_{\text{IND}-E}(B)$. If we had used the O2H from [33], then we would have gotten an even greater bound of $O(q\sqrt{\text{Adv}_{\text{IND}-E}(B) + 1/\text{card}(X)})$. However, this bound with semi-classical oracles assumes indistinguishability, whereas an analysis with the original O2H Theorem would only require E to be one-way.

5 Proofs

5.1 Auxiliary Lemmas

The fidelity $F(\sigma, \tau)$ between two density operators is $\text{tr}\sqrt{\sqrt{\sigma}\tau\sqrt{\sigma}}$, the trace distance $\text{TD}(\sigma, \tau)$ is defined as $\frac{1}{2}\text{tr}|\sigma - \tau|$, and the Bures distance $B(\tau, \sigma)$ is $\sqrt{2 - 2F(\tau, \sigma)}$.

Lemma 3. *For states* $|\Psi\rangle, |\Phi\rangle$ *with* $\||\Psi\rangle\| = \||\Phi\rangle\| = 1$, *we have*

$$F(|\Psi\rangle\langle\Psi|, |\Phi\rangle\langle\Phi|) \geq 1 - \frac{1}{2}\||\Psi\rangle - |\Phi\rangle\|^2$$

so that

$$B(|\Psi\rangle\langle\Psi|, |\Phi\rangle\langle\Phi|) \leq \||\Psi\rangle - |\Phi\rangle\|$$

Proof. We have

$$\||\Psi\rangle - |\Phi\rangle\|^2 = ((\langle\Psi| - \langle\Phi|)(|\Psi\rangle - |\Phi\rangle)) = \||\Psi\rangle\|^2 + \||\Phi\rangle\|^2 - \langle\Psi|\Phi\rangle - \langle\Phi|\Psi\rangle$$

$$= 2 - 2\Re(\langle\Psi|\Phi\rangle) \geq 2 - 2|\langle\Psi|\Phi\rangle| \overset{(*)}{=} 2 - 2F(|\Psi\rangle\langle\Psi|, |\Phi\rangle\langle\Phi|)$$

where $\Re$ denotes the real part, and $(*)$ is by definition of the fidelity F (for pure states). Thus $F(|\Psi\rangle\langle\Psi|, |\Phi\rangle\langle\Phi|) \geq 1 - \frac{1}{2}\||\Psi\rangle - |\Phi\rangle\|^2$ as claimed. The second inequality follows from the definition of Bures distance. $\qquad\square$

Lemma 4 (Distance measures vs. measurement probabilities). *Let* ρ_1, ρ_2 *be density operators (with* $\operatorname{tr} \rho_i = 1$*). Let* M *be a binary measurement (e.g., represented as a POVM). Let* P_i *be the probability that* M *returns* 1 *when measuring* ρ_i.
Then

$$\sqrt{P_1 P_2} + \sqrt{(1 - P_1)(1 - P_2)} \geq F(\rho_1, \rho_2) \tag{13}$$

Also,

$$\left| \sqrt{P_1} - \sqrt{P_2} \right| \leq B(\rho_1, \rho_2). \tag{14}$$

Furthermore,

$$|P_1 - P_2| \leq \operatorname{TD}(\rho_1, \rho_2) \leq B(\rho_1, \rho_2). \tag{15}$$

Proof. In this proof, given a probability P, let $\bar{P} := 1 - P$. Let $\mathcal{E}$ be the super-operator that maps ρ to the classical bit that contains the result of measuring ρ using M. That is, for every density operator ρ with $\operatorname{tr} \rho = 1$, $\mathcal{E}(\rho) = \begin{pmatrix} p & 0 \\ 0 & \bar{p} \end{pmatrix}$ where p is the probability that M returns 1 when measuring ρ.

Then $\rho_i' := \mathcal{E}(\rho_i) = \begin{pmatrix} P_i & 0 \\ 0 & \bar{P}_i \end{pmatrix}$ for $i = 1, 2$. We then have

$$F(\rho_1, \rho_2) \overset{(*)}{\leq} F(\rho_1', \rho_2') \overset{(**)}{=} \left\| \sqrt{\rho_1'} \sqrt{\rho_2'} \right\|_{\operatorname{tr}}$$

$$= \operatorname{tr} \begin{pmatrix} \sqrt{P_1 P_2} & 0 \\ 0 & \sqrt{\bar{P}_1 \bar{P}_2} \end{pmatrix} = \sqrt{P_1 P_2} + \sqrt{\bar{P}_1 \bar{P}_2}$$

where $(*)$ is due to the monotonicity of the fidelity [26, Thm. 9.6], and $(**)$ is the definition of fidelity. This shows (13). To prove (14), we compute:

$$\left(\sqrt{P_1} - \sqrt{P_2} \right)^2 = P_1 + P_2 - 2\sqrt{P_1 P_2}$$

$$\leq P_1 + P_2 - 2\sqrt{P_1 P_2} + \left(\sqrt{\bar{P}_1} - \sqrt{\bar{P}_2} \right)^2$$

$$= 2 - 2\sqrt{P_1 P_2} - 2\sqrt{\bar{P}_1 \bar{P}_2} \overset{(13)}{\leq} 2 - 2F(\rho_1, \rho_2) \overset{(*)}{=} B(\rho_1, \rho_2)^2$$

where $(*)$ is by definition of the Bures distance. This implies (14).

The first inequality in (15) is well-known (e.g., [26, Thm. 9.1]). For the second part, we calculate

$$\operatorname{TD}(\rho, \tau) \overset{(*)}{\leq} \sqrt{1 - F(\rho, \tau)^2} = \sqrt{\frac{1 + F(\rho, \tau)}{2}} \cdot \sqrt{2 - 2F(\rho, \tau)}$$

$$= \sqrt{\frac{1 + F(\rho, \tau)}{2}} \cdot B(\rho, \tau) \overset{(**)}{\leq} B(\rho, \tau)$$

Here the inequality marked $(*)$ is shown in [26, (9.101)], and $(**)$ is because $0 \leq F(\rho, \tau) \leq 1$. $\square$

5.2   Proof of Theorem 1

In the following, let $H : X \to Y$, $S \subseteq X$, $z \in \{0,1\}^*$.

Lemma 5 (O2H in terms of pure states). *Fix H, S, z. Let $A^H(z)$ be a unitary quantum oracle algorithm of query depth d. Let Q_A denote the register containing all of A's state.*

Let L be a quantum register with space $\mathbb{C}^{2^d}$ (for the "query log").

Let $B^{H,S}(z)$ be the unitary algorithm on registers Q_A, L that operates like $A^H(z)$, except:

- *It initializes the register L with $|0 \ldots 0\rangle$.*
- *When A performs its i-th set of parallel oracle queries on input/output registers $(Q_1, R_1), \ldots, (Q_n, R_n)$ that are part of Q_A, B instead first applies U_S on $(Q_1, \ldots, Q_n, L)$ and then performs the oracle queries. Here U_S is defined by:*

$$U_S |x_1, \ldots, x_n\rangle |l\rangle := \begin{cases} |x_1, \ldots, x_n\rangle |l\rangle & (\text{every } x_j \notin S), \\ |x_1, \ldots, x_n\rangle |\text{flip}_i(l)\rangle & (\text{any } x_j \in S) \end{cases}$$

Let $|\Psi_{\text{left}}\rangle$ denote the final state of $A^H(z)$, and $|\Psi_{\text{right}}\rangle$ the final state of $B^{H,S}(z)$.

Let $\tilde{P}_{\text{find}}$ be the probability that a measurement of L in the state $|\Psi_{\text{right}}\rangle$ returns $\neq 0$. (Formally, $\left\| (I \otimes (I - |0\rangle\langle0|)) |\Psi_{\text{right}}\rangle \right\|^2$.)

Then

$$\left\| |\Psi_{\text{left}}\rangle \otimes |0\rangle - |\Psi_{\text{right}}\rangle \right\|^2 \le (d+1)\tilde{P}_{\text{find}}.$$

Proof. We first define a variant B_{count} of the algorithm B that, instead of keeping a log of the successful oracle queries (as B does in L), just counts the number of successful oracle queries (in a register C). Specifically:

Let C be a quantum register with space $\mathbb{C}^{\{0,\ldots,d\}}$, i.e., C can store states $|0\rangle, \ldots, |d\rangle$. Let $B^{H,S}_{\text{count}}(z)$ be the unitary algorithm on registers Q_A, S that operates like $A^H(z)$, except:

- *It initializes the register C with $|0\rangle$.*
- *When A performs its i-th set of parallel oracle queries on input/output registers $((Q_1, R_1), \ldots)$ that are part of Q_A, B instead first applies U'_S on $(Q_1, \ldots, Q_n), C$ and then performs the oracle queries. Here U'_S is defined by:*

$$U'_S |x_1, \ldots, x_n\rangle |c\rangle := \begin{cases} |x_1, \ldots, x_n\rangle |c\rangle & (\text{every } x_j \notin S), \\ |x_1, \ldots, x_n\rangle |c+1 \bmod d+1\rangle & (\text{any } x_j \in S) \end{cases}$$

Note that the mod $d+1$ part of the definition of U'_S has no effect on the behavior of $\tilde{B}$ because U_S is applies only d times. However, the mod $d+1$ is required so that U_S is unitary.

Consider the state $|\Psi_{\text{count}}\rangle$ at the end of the execution $B_{\text{count}}^{H,S}(z)$. This may be written

$$|\Psi_{\text{count}}\rangle = \sum_{i=0}^{d} |\Psi_i'\rangle |i\rangle_C. \tag{16}$$

for some (non-normalized) states $|\Psi_i'\rangle$ on Q_A.

Consider the linear (but not unitary) map $N' : |x\rangle|y\rangle \mapsto |x\rangle|0\rangle$. Obviously, N' commutes with the oracle queries and with the unitary applied by A between queries (since those unitaries do not operate on C.) Furthermore $N'U_S' = N'$, and the initial state of B_{count} is invariant under N'. Thus $N'|\Psi_{\text{count}}\rangle$ is the same as the state we get if we execute B_{count} without the applications of U_S'. But that state is $|\Psi_{\text{left}}\rangle|0\rangle_C$ because the only difference between B_{count} and A is that B_{count} initializes C with $|0\rangle$ and applies U_S' to it.

So we have

$$\sum_{i=0}^{d} |\Psi_i'\rangle |0\rangle_C = N'|\Psi_{\text{count}}\rangle = |\Psi_{\text{left}}\rangle|0\rangle_C$$

and hence

$$|\Psi_{\text{left}}\rangle = \sum_{i=0}^{d} |\Psi_i'\rangle. \tag{17}$$

The state $|\Psi_{\text{right}}\rangle$ is a state on Q_A, L and thus can be written as

$$|\Psi_{\text{right}}\rangle = \sum_{l \in \{0,1\}^q} |\Psi_l\rangle|l\rangle_L \tag{18}$$

for some (non-normalized) states $|\Psi_l\rangle$ on Q_A.

Furthermore, both $|\Psi_{\text{count}}\rangle$ and $|\Psi_{\text{right}}\rangle$, when projected onto $|0\rangle$ in register C/L, respectively, result in the same state, namely the state corresponding to no query to $\mathcal{O}_S^{SC}$ succeeding. By (16) and (18), the result of that projection is $|\Psi_0\rangle|0\rangle_L$ and $|\Psi_0'\rangle|0\rangle_C$, respectively. Hence

$$|\Psi_0\rangle = |\Psi_0'\rangle. \tag{19}$$

Furthermore, the probability that no query succeeds is the square of the norm of that state. Hence

$$\left\| |\Psi_0\rangle \right\|^2 = 1 - \tilde{P}_{\text{find}}. \tag{20}$$

We have

$$\sum_{i=0}^{d} \left\| |\Psi_i'\rangle \right\|^2 = \sum_{i=0}^{d} \left\| |\Psi_i'\rangle|i\rangle_C \right\|^2 = \left\| \sum_{i=0}^{d} |\Psi_i'\rangle|i\rangle_C \right\|^2 \overset{(16)}{=} \left\| |\Psi_{\text{count}}\rangle \right\|^2 = 1.$$

$$\sum_{l \in \{0,1\}^d} \left\| |\Psi_l\rangle \right\|^2 = \sum_{l \in \{0,1\}^d} \left\| |\Psi_l\rangle|l\rangle_L \right\|^2 = \left\| \sum_{l \in \{0,1\}^d} |\Psi_l\rangle|l\rangle_L \right\|^2 \overset{(18)}{=} \left\| |\Psi_{\text{right}}\rangle \right\|^2 = 1.$$

Thus

$$\sum_{i=1}^{d}\left\|\,|\Psi_i'\rangle\right\|^2 = 1 - \left\|\,|\Psi_0'\rangle\right\|^2 \overset{(20)}{=} \tilde{P}_{\text{find}}, \qquad \sum_{\substack{l\in\{0,1\}^d \\ l\neq 0}}\left\|\,|\Psi_l\rangle\right\|^2 = 1 - \left\|\,|\Psi_0\rangle\right\|^2 \overset{(20)}{=} \tilde{P}_{\text{find}}. \quad (21)$$

Therefore

$$\left\|\,|\Psi_{\text{right}}\rangle - |\Psi_{\text{left}}\rangle|0\rangle_L\right\|^2 \overset{(18)}{=} \left\|(|\Psi_0\rangle - |\Psi_{\text{left}}\rangle)|0\rangle + \sum_{\substack{l\in\{0,1\}^d \\ l\neq 0}}|\Psi_l\rangle|l\rangle\right\|^2$$

$$= \left\|\,|\Psi_0\rangle - |\Psi_{\text{left}}\rangle\right\|^2 + \sum_{\substack{l\in\{0,1\}^d \\ l\neq 0}}\left\|\,|\Psi_l\rangle\right\|^2 \overset{(21)}{=} \left\|\,|\Psi_0\rangle - |\Psi_{\text{left}}\rangle\right\|^2 + \tilde{P}_{\text{find}}$$

$$\overset{(19),(17)}{=} \left\|\sum_{i=1}^{d}|\Psi_i'\rangle\right\|^2 + \tilde{P}_{\text{find}} \overset{(*)}{\leq} \left(\sum_{i=1}^{d}\left\|\,|\Psi_i'\rangle\right\|\right)^2 + \tilde{P}_{\text{find}} \overset{(**)}{\leq} d\cdot\sum_{i=1}^{d}\left\|\,|\Psi_i'\rangle\right\|^2 + \tilde{P}_{\text{find}}$$

$$\overset{(21)}{=} d\tilde{P}_{\text{find}} + \tilde{P}_{\text{find}} = (d+1)\tilde{P}_{\text{find}}.$$

Here $(*)$ uses the triangle inequality, and $(**)$ the AM-QM (or Jensen's) inequality. This is the inequality claimed in the lemma.   □

Theorem 1 follows mechanically from Lemma 5 by applying Lemmas 4 and 3 to each case.

Lemma 6 (O2H in terms of mixed states). *Let X, Y be sets, and let $H : X \to Y, S \subset X, z \in \{0,1\}^*$ be random. (With some joint distribution.)*

Let A be an algorithm which queries H at depth d. Let P_{find} be as in Theorem 1.

Let ρ_{left} denote the final state of $A^H(z)$.

Let ρ_{right} denote the final state of $A^{H\setminus S}$. This is the state of the registers Q_A and L, where Q_A is the state of A itself, and L is a register that contains the log of the responses of $\mathcal{O}_S^{SC}$. If the i-th query to $\mathcal{O}_S^{SC}$ returns ℓ_i, then L contains $|\ell_1 \dots \ell_q\rangle$ at the end of the execution of B.

Then $F(\rho_{\text{left}} \otimes |0\rangle\langle0|, \rho_{\text{right}}) \geq 1 - \frac{1}{2}(d+1)P_{\text{find}}$ and $B(\rho_{\text{left}} \otimes |0\rangle\langle0|, \rho_{\text{right}}) \leq \sqrt{(d+1)P_{\text{find}}}$.

Proof. Without loss of generality, we can assume that A is unitary: If A is not unitary, we can construct a unitary variant of A that uses an extra auxiliary register Z, and later trace out that register again from the states ρ_{left} and ρ_{right}.

Let $|\Psi_{\text{left}}^{HSz}\rangle$ be the state $|\Psi_{\text{left}}\rangle$ from Lemma 5 for specific values of H, S, z. And analogously for $|\Psi_{\text{right}}^{HSz}\rangle$ and $\tilde{P}_{\text{find}}^{HSz}$.

Then $\rho_{\text{left}} = \text{Exp}_{HSz}[|\Psi_{\text{left}}^{HSz}\rangle\langle\Psi_{\text{left}}^{HSz}|]$.

Furthermore, if we define $\rho'_{\text{right}} := \text{Exp}_{HSz}[|\Psi_{\text{right}}^{HSz}\rangle\langle\Psi_{\text{right}}^{HSz}|]$, then $\rho_{\text{right}} = \mathcal{E}_L(\rho'_{\text{right}})$ where $\mathcal{E}_L$ is the quantum operation that performs a measurement in the computational basis on the register L.

And $P_{\text{find}} = \text{Exp}_{HSz}[\tilde{P}_{\text{find}}^{HSz}]$.
Then

$$
\begin{aligned}
F(\rho_{\text{left}} &\otimes |0\rangle\langle 0|, \rho_{\text{right}}) \\
&= F\big(\mathcal{E}_L(\rho_{\text{left}} \otimes |0\rangle\langle 0|), \mathcal{E}_L(\rho'_{\text{right}})\big) \\
&\overset{(*)}{\geq} F\big(\rho_{\text{left}} \otimes |0\rangle\langle 0|, \rho'_{\text{right}}\big) \\
&= F\left(\underset{HSz}{\text{Exp}}\Big[|\Psi_{\text{left}}^{HSz}\rangle\langle\Psi_{\text{left}}^{HSz}| \otimes |0\rangle\langle 0|\Big], \underset{HSz}{\text{Exp}}\Big[|\Psi_{\text{right}}^{HSz}\rangle\langle\Psi_{\text{right}}^{HSz}|\Big]\right) \\
&\overset{(**)}{\geq} \underset{HSz}{\text{Exp}}\Big[F\big(|\Psi_{\text{left}}^{HSz}\rangle\langle\Psi_{\text{left}}^{HSz}| \otimes |0\rangle\langle 0|, |\Psi_{\text{right}}^{HSz}\rangle\langle\Psi_{\text{right}}^{HSz}|\big)\Big] \\
&\overset{\text{Lem. 3}}{\geq} 1 - \tfrac{1}{2}\underset{HSz}{\text{Exp}}\Big[\big\||\Psi_{\text{left}}^{HSz}\rangle \otimes |0\rangle - |\Psi_{\text{right}}^{HSz}\rangle\big\|^2\Big] \\
&\overset{\text{Lem. 5}}{\geq} 1 - \frac{1}{2}\underset{HSz}{\text{Exp}}\Big[(d+1)\tilde{P}_{\text{find}}^{HSz}\Big] = 1 - \tfrac{1}{2}(d+1)P_{\text{find}}.
\end{aligned}
$$

Here $(*)$ follows from the monotonicity of the fidelity [26, Thm. 9.6], and $(**)$ follows from the joint concavity of the fidelity [26, (9.95)]. This shows the first bound from the lemma.

The Bures distance B is defined as $B(\rho, \tau)^2 = 2(1 - F(\rho, \tau))$. Thus

$$
\begin{aligned}
B(\rho_{\text{left}} \otimes |0\rangle\langle 0|, \rho_{\text{right}})^2 &= 2(1 - F(\rho_{\text{left}} \otimes |0\rangle\langle 0|, \rho_{\text{right}})) \\
&\leq 2(1 - (1 - \tfrac{1}{2}(d+1)P_{\text{find}})) = (d+1)P_{\text{find}},
\end{aligned}
$$

hence $B(\rho_{\text{left}} \otimes |0\rangle\langle 0|, \rho_{\text{right}}) \leq \sqrt{(d+1)P_{\text{find}}}$. $\square$

Theorem 1 (Semi-classical O2H – restated). *Let $S \subseteq X$ be random. Let $G, H : X \to Y$ be random functions satisfying $\forall x \notin S.\ G(x) = H(x)$. Let z be a random bitstring. $(S, G, H, z$ may have arbitrary joint distribution.)*

Let A be an oracle algorithm of query depth d (not necessarily unitary). Let

$$
\begin{aligned}
P_{\text{left}} &:= \Pr[b = 1 : b \leftarrow A^H(z)] \\
P_{\text{right}} &:= \Pr[b = 1 : b \leftarrow A^G(z)] \\
P_{\text{find}} &:= \Pr[\text{Find} : A^{G\backslash S}(z)] \overset{\text{Lem. 1}}{=} \Pr[\text{Find} : A^{H\backslash S}(z)]
\end{aligned}
\tag{1}
$$

Then

$$
|P_{\text{left}} - P_{\text{right}}| \leq 2\sqrt{(d+1)\cdot P_{\text{find}}} \quad \text{and} \quad \left|\sqrt{P_{\text{left}}} - \sqrt{P_{\text{right}}}\right| \leq 2\sqrt{(d+1)\cdot P_{\text{find}}}
$$

The theorem also holds with bound $\sqrt{(d+1)P_{\text{find}}}$ for the following alternative definitions of P_{right}:

$$
P_{\text{right}} := \Pr[b = 1 : b \leftarrow A^{H\backslash S}(z)],
\tag{2}
$$

$$P_{\text{right}} := \Pr[b = 1 \wedge \neg\mathsf{Find} : b \leftarrow A^{H \backslash S}(z)], \tag{3}$$

$$P_{\text{right}} := \Pr[b = 1 \wedge \neg\mathsf{Find} : b \leftarrow A^{G \backslash S}(z)], \tag{4}$$

$$P_{\text{right}} := \Pr[b = 1 \vee \mathsf{Find} : b \leftarrow A^{H \backslash S}(z)], \tag{5}$$

$$P_{\text{right}} := \Pr[b = 1 \vee \mathsf{Find} : b \leftarrow A^{G \backslash S}(z)]. \tag{6}$$

Proof. We first prove the theorem using the definition of P_{right} from (2).

Let M be the measurement that measures, given the the register Q_A, L, what the output b of A is. Here Q_A is the state space of A, and L is the additional register introduced in Lemma 6. (Since A obtains b by measuring Q_A, such a measurement M exists.)

Let $P_M(\rho)$ denote the probability that M returns 1 when measuring a state ρ. Then $P_{\text{left}} = P_M(\rho_{\text{left}} \otimes |0\rangle\langle 0|)$ and $P_{\text{right}} = P_M(\rho_{\text{right}})$ where ρ_{left} and ρ_{right} are defined in Lemma 6.

Then

$$
\begin{aligned}
\left| P_{\text{left}} - P_{\text{right}} \right| &= \left| P_M(\rho_{\text{left}} \otimes |0\rangle\langle 0|) - P_M(\rho_{\text{right}}) \right| \\
&\overset{\text{Lem. 4}}{\leq} B(\rho_{\text{left}} \otimes |0\rangle\langle 0|, \rho_{\text{right}}) \\
&\overset{\text{Lem. 6}}{\leq} \sqrt{(d+1)P_{\text{find}}} \\
\left| \sqrt{P_{\text{left}}} - \sqrt{P_{\text{right}}} \right| &= \left| \sqrt{P_M(\rho_{\text{left}} \otimes |0\rangle\langle 0|)} - \sqrt{P_M(\rho_{\text{right}})} \right| \\
&\overset{\text{Lem. 4}}{\leq} B(\rho_{\text{left}} \otimes |0\rangle\langle 0|, \rho_{\text{right}}) \\
&\overset{\text{Lem. 6}}{\leq} \sqrt{(d+1)P_{\text{find}}}.
\end{aligned}
$$

This shows the theorem with the definition of P_{right} from (2).

Now we show the theorem using the definition of P_{right} from (3). Let M instead be the measurement that measures whether $b = 1$ and L contains $|0\rangle$ (this means Find did not happen). Then $P_{\text{left}} = P_M(\rho_{\text{left}} \otimes |0\rangle\langle 0|)$ and $P_{\text{right}} = P_M(\rho_{\text{right}})$, and the rest of the proof is as in the case of (2).

Now we show the theorem using the definition of P_{right} from (5). Let M instead be the measurement that measures whether $b = 1$ or L contains $|x\rangle$ for $x \neq 0$ (this means Find did happen). Then $P_{\text{left}} = P_M(\rho_{\text{left}} \otimes |0\rangle\langle 0|)$ and $P_{\text{right}} = P_M(\rho_{\text{right}})$, and the rest of the proof is as in the case of (2).

Now we show the theorem using the definition of P_{right} from (4). This follows immediately by case (3), and the fact that $\Pr[b = 1 \wedge \neg\mathsf{Find} : b \leftarrow A^{H \backslash S}(z)] = \Pr[b = 1 \wedge \neg\mathsf{Find} : b \leftarrow A^{G \backslash S}(z)]$ by Lemma 1.

Now we show the theorem using the definition of P_{right} from (6). By Lemma 1,

$$\Pr[b = 1 \wedge \neg\mathsf{Find} : b \leftarrow A^{H \backslash S}(z)] = \Pr[b = 1 \wedge \neg\mathsf{Find} : b \leftarrow A^{G \backslash S}(z)] \tag{22}$$

$$\Pr[\text{true} \wedge \neg\text{Find} : b \leftarrow A^{H \backslash S}(z)] = \Pr[\text{true} \wedge \neg\text{Find} : b \leftarrow A^{G \backslash S}(z)]. \qquad (23)$$

From (23), we get (by considering the complementary event):

$$\Pr[\text{Find} : b \leftarrow A^{H \backslash S}(z)] = \Pr[\text{Find} : b \leftarrow A^{G \backslash S}(z)]. \qquad (24)$$

Adding (22) and (24), we get

$$\Pr[b = 1 \vee \text{Find} : b \leftarrow A^{H \backslash S}(z)] = \Pr[b = 1 \vee \text{Find} : b \leftarrow A^{G \backslash S}(z)]. \qquad (25)$$

Then case (6) follows from case (5) and the fact (25).

Now we show the theorem using the definition of P_{right} from (1). Let

$$P_{\text{mid}} := \Pr[b = 1 \wedge \neg\text{Find} : b \leftarrow A^{H \backslash S}(z)],$$
$$P'_{\text{mid}} := \Pr[b = 1 \wedge \neg\text{Find} : b \leftarrow A^{G \backslash S}(z)],$$
$$P'_{\text{find}} := \Pr[\text{Find} : A^{G \backslash S}(z)].$$

By the current lemma, case (3) (which we already proved), we have

$$|P_{\text{left}} - P_{\text{mid}}| \le \sqrt{(d+1)P_{\text{find}}}, \qquad |P_{\text{left}} - P_{\text{mid}}| \le \sqrt{(d+1)P_{\text{find}}},$$

and by case (4), we also get

$$|P_{\text{right}} - P'_{\text{mid}}| \le \sqrt{(d+1)P'_{\text{find}}}, \qquad |P_{\text{right}} - P'_{\text{mid}}| \le \sqrt{(d+1)P'_{\text{find}}},$$

Note that in the second case, we invoke the current lemma with G and H exchanged, and our P_{right} is their P_{left}.

By Lemma 1, $P_{\text{mid}} = P'_{\text{mid}}$ and by (24), $P_{\text{find}} = P'_{\text{find}}$. With this and the triangle inequality, we get

$$|P_{\text{left}} - P_{\text{right}}| \le 2\sqrt{(d+1)P_{\text{find}}}, \qquad |P_{\text{left}} - P_{\text{right}}| \le 2\sqrt{(d+1)P_{\text{find}}}.$$

as required.   □

5.3   Proof of Theorem 2

In the following, let $S \subseteq X$, $z \in \{0,1\}^*$.

Lemma 7. *Fix S, z (S, z are not randomized in this lemma.) Let $A^H(z)$ be a unitary oracle algorithm with query depth d.*

Let B be an oracle algorithm that on input z does the following: pick $i \xleftarrow{\$} \{1, \dots, d\}$, runs $A^{\mathcal{O}^{SC}_\varnothing}(z)$ until (just before) the i-th query, measure all query input registers in the computational basis, output the set T of measurement outcomes.

Then

$$\Pr[\text{Find} : A^{\mathcal{O}^{SC}_S}(z)] \le 4d \cdot \Pr[S \cap T \ne \varnothing : T \leftarrow B(z)].$$

Proof. Let $|\Psi_i\rangle$ be the (non-normalized) state of $A^{\mathcal{O}_S^{SC}}(z)$ right after the i-th query in the case that the first i queries return 0. That is, $\||\Psi_i\rangle\|^2$ is the probability that the first i queries return 0, and $|\Psi_i\rangle/\||\Psi_i\rangle\|$ is the state conditioned on that outcome. Let $|\Psi_i'\rangle$ be the corresponding state of $A^{\mathcal{O}_\varnothing^{SC}}(z)$, that is, $|\Psi_i'\rangle$ is the state just after the ith query (or before, since queries to $\mathcal{O}_\varnothing^{SC}$ do not affect the state). Note that $|\Psi_0\rangle = |\Psi_0'\rangle$ is the initial state of $A(z)$ (independent of the oracle).

From the state $|\Psi_i\rangle$, the algorithm A first applies a fixed unitary U that depends only on A. Then it queries the semi-classical oracle $\mathcal{O}_S^{SC}$.

Let P_S be the orthogonal projector projecting the query input registers $Q_1, \ldots, Q_n$ onto states $|T\rangle$ with $S \cap T \neq \varnothing$, formally $P_S := \sum_{T \text{ s.t. } S \cap T \neq \varnothing} |T\rangle\langle T|$. Thus $\|P_S U|\Psi_i\rangle\|^2$ is the probability of measuring T with $S \cap T \neq \varnothing$ in registers $Q_1, \ldots, Q_n$ given the state $U|\Psi_i\rangle$.

Then the i-th query to $\mathcal{O}_S^{SC}$ applies $I - P_S$ to $|\Psi_i\rangle$. Therefore $|\Psi_{i+1}\rangle = (I - P_S)U|\Psi_i\rangle$.

Let $p_i = 1 - \||\Psi_i\rangle\|^2$ be the probability that one of the first i queries returns 1, and let

$$r_i := p_i + 2\||\Psi_i\rangle - |\Psi_i'\rangle\|^2 = 1 - \||\Psi_i\rangle\|^2 + 2\||\Psi_i\rangle\|^2 - 4\Re\langle\Psi_i'|\Psi_i\rangle + 2\underbrace{\||\Psi_i'\rangle\|^2}_{=1}$$

$$= 3 - 4\Re\langle\Psi_i'|\Psi_i\rangle + \||\Psi_i\rangle\|^2. \tag{26}$$

Notice that $r_0 = 0$ since $|\Psi_0\rangle = |\Psi_0'\rangle$ and $\||\Psi_0\rangle\| = 1$. During the $(i+1)$-st query, $U|\Psi_i\rangle$ is changed to $U|\Psi_i\rangle - P_S U|\Psi_i\rangle$, and $U|\Psi_i'\rangle$ stays the same, so that

$$|\Psi_{i+1}\rangle = U|\Psi_i\rangle - P_S U|\Psi_i\rangle$$
$$|\Psi_{i+1}'\rangle = U|\Psi_i'\rangle$$

Therefore,

$$\||\Psi_{i+1}\rangle\|^2 = \|U|\Psi_i\rangle\|^2 - \langle\Psi_i|U^\dagger P_S U|\Psi_i\rangle - \langle\Psi_i|U^\dagger P_S^\dagger U|\Psi_i\rangle + \langle\Psi_i|U^\dagger P_S^\dagger P_S U|\Psi_i\rangle$$
$$= \||\Psi_i\rangle\|^2 - \langle\Psi_i|U^\dagger P_S U|\Psi_i\rangle \tag{27}$$

because P_S is a projector and thus $P_S^\dagger P_S = P_S^\dagger = P_S$. Likewise,

$$\langle\Psi_{i+1}'|\Psi_{i+1}\rangle = \langle\Psi_i'|U^\dagger U|\Psi_i\rangle - \langle\Psi_i'|U^\dagger P_S U|\Psi_i\rangle$$
$$= \langle\Psi_i'|\Psi_i\rangle - \langle\Psi_i'|U^\dagger P_S U|\Psi_i\rangle \tag{28}$$

Let

$$g_i := \langle\Psi_{i-1}'|U^\dagger P_S U|\Psi_{i-1}'\rangle = \|P_S U|\Psi_{i-1}'\rangle\|^2.$$

Then g_i is the probability that the algorithm B returns T with $S \cap T \neq \varnothing$ when measured at the i-th query.

We calculate

$$r_{i+1} - r_i \stackrel{(26)}{=} -4\Re\langle\Psi'_{i+1}|\Psi_{i+1}\rangle + \||\Psi_{i+1}\rangle\|^2 + 4\Re\langle\Psi'_i|\Psi_i\rangle - \||\Psi_i\rangle\|^2$$

$$\stackrel{(27),(28)}{=} 4\Re\langle\Psi'_i|U^\dagger P_S U|\Psi_i\rangle - \langle\Psi_i|U^\dagger P_S U|\Psi_i\rangle$$

$$= 4\langle\Psi'_i|U^\dagger P_S U|\Psi'_i\rangle - \underbrace{\langle 2\Psi'_i - \Psi|U^\dagger P_S U|2\Psi'_i - \Psi_i\rangle}_{\geq 0}$$

$$\leq 4\langle\Psi'_i|U^\dagger P_S U|\Psi'_i\rangle = 4g_{i+1}$$

Since $r_0 = 0$, by induction we have

$$\Pr[\text{Find} : A^{\mathcal{O}_S^{SC}}(z)] = p_d \leq r_d \leq 4\sum_{i=1}^{d} g_i = 4d \cdot \Pr[S \cap T \neq \varnothing : T \leftarrow B(z)]$$

as claimed.   □

Theorem 2 (Search in semi-classical oracle – restated). *Let A be any quantum oracle algorithm making some number of queries at depth at most d to a semi-classical oracle with domain X. Let $S \subseteq X$ and $z \in \{0,1\}^*$. (S, z may have arbitrary joint distribution.)*

Let B be an algorithm that on input z chooses $i \stackrel{\$}{\leftarrow} \{1, \ldots, d\}$; runs $A^{\mathcal{O}_\varnothing^{SC}}(z)$ until (just before) the i-th query; then measures all query input registers in the computational basis and outputs the set T of measurement outcomes.

Then

$$\Pr[\text{Find} : A^{\mathcal{O}_S^{SC}}(z)] \leq 4d \cdot \Pr[S \cap T \neq \varnothing : T \leftarrow B(z)] \tag{7}$$

Proof. Immediate from Lemma 7 by using the fact that A can always be transformed into a unitary oracle algorithm, and by averaging.   □

Acknowledgements. Thanks to Daniel Kane, Eike Kiltz, and Kathrin Hövelmanns for valuable discussions. Ambainis was supported by the ERDF project 1.1.1.5/18/A/020. Unruh was supported by institutional research funding IUT2-1 of the Estonian Ministry of Education and Research, the United States Air Force Office of Scientific Research (AFOSR) via AOARD Grant "Verification of Quantum Cryptography" (FA2386-17-1-4022), the Mobilitas Plus grant MOBERC12 of the Estonian Research Council, and the Estonian Centre of Exellence in IT (EXCITE) funded by ERDF.

A   Optimality of Corollary 1

Lemma 8. *If $S = \{x\}$ where $x \stackrel{\$}{\leftarrow} \{1, \ldots, N\}$, then there is a q-query algorithm $A^{\mathcal{O}_S^{SC}}$ such that*

$$\Pr[\text{Find} : A^{\mathcal{O}_S^{SC}}()] \geq \frac{4q - 3}{N} - \frac{8q(q-1)}{N^2}$$

Proof. The algorithm is as follows:

- Make the first query with amplitude $1/\sqrt{N}$ in all positions.
- Between queries, transform the state by the unitary $U := 2E/N - I$ where E is the matrix containing 1 everywhere. That U is unitary follows since $U^\dagger U = 4E^2/N^2 - 4E/N + I = I$ using $E^2 = NE$.

One may calculate by induction that the final non-normalized state has amplitude

$$\left(1 - \frac{2}{N}\right)^{q-1} \cdot \frac{1}{\sqrt{N}}$$

in all positions except for the xth one (where the amplitude is 0), so its squared norm is

$$1 - \Pr[\mathsf{Find}] = \left(1 - \frac{2}{N}\right)^{2q-2} \cdot \frac{1}{N} \cdot (N - 1) = \left(1 - \frac{2}{N}\right)^{2q-2} \cdot \left(1 - \frac{1}{N}\right)$$

As a function of $1/N$, this expression's derivatives alternate on $[0, 1/2]$, so it is below its second-order Taylor expansion:

$$1 - \Pr[\mathsf{Find}] \leq 1 - \frac{4q - 3}{N} + \frac{8q(q-1)}{N^2}$$

This completes the proof.   □

References

1. Ambainis, A.: Quantum lower bounds by quantum arguments. J. Comput. Syst. Sci. **64**(4), 750–767 (2002). https://doi.org/10.1006/jcss.2002.1826
2. Ambainis, A., Hamburg, M., Unruh, D.: Quantum security proofs using semi-classical oracles. IACR ePrint2018/904 (2019). Full version of this paper
3. Ambainis, A., Rosmanis, A., Unruh, D.: Quantum attacks on classical proof systems: the hardness of quantum rewinding. In: 55th FOCS, pp. 474–483. IEEE Computer Society Press, October 2014
4. Balogh, M., Eaton, E., Song, F.: Quantum collision-finding in non-uniform random functions. In: Lange, T., Steinwandt, R. (eds.) PQCrypto 2018. LNCS, vol. 10786, pp. 467–486. Springer, Cham (2018). https://doi.org/10.1007/978-3-319-79063-3_22
5. Beals, R., Buhrman, H., Cleve, R., Mosca, M., de Wolf, R.: Quantum lower bounds by polynomials. J. ACM **48**(4), 778–797 (2001). https://doi.org/10.1145/502090.502097
6. Bellare, M., Rogaway, P.: Random oracles are practical: a paradigm for designing efficient protocols. In: Ashby, V. (ed.) ACM CCS 1993, pp. 62–73. ACM Press, November 1993
7. Bellare, M., Rogaway, P.: Optimal asymmetric encryption. In: De Santis, A. (ed.) EUROCRYPT 1994. LNCS, vol. 950, pp. 92–111. Springer, Heidelberg (1995). https://doi.org/10.1007/BFb0053428
8. Boneh, D., Dagdelen, Ö., Fischlin, M., Lehmann, A., Schaffner, C., Zhandry, M.: Random oracles in a quantum world. In: Lee, D.H., Wang, X. (eds.) ASIACRYPT 2011. LNCS, vol. 7073, pp. 41–69. Springer, Heidelberg (2011). https://doi.org/10.1007/978-3-642-25385-0_3

9. Boneh, D., Eskandarian, S., Fisch, B.: Post-quantum EPID group signatures from symmetric primitives. Cryptology ePrint Archive, Report 2018/261 (2018). https://eprint.iacr.org/2018/261

10. Boyer, M., Brassard, G., Høyer, P., Tapp, A.: Tight bounds on quantum searching. Fortschritte der Physik **46**(4–5), 493–505 (1998)

11. Chase, M., et al.: Post-quantum zero-knowledge and signatures from symmetric-key primitives. In: Thuraisingham, B.M., Evans, D., Malkin, T., Xu, D. (eds.) ACM CCS 2017, pp. 1825–1842. ACM Press, October/November 2017

12. Chen, M.S., Hülsing, A., Rijneveld, J., Samardjiska, S., Schwabe, P.: SOFIA: $\mathcal{MQ}$-based signatures in the QROM. In: Abdalla, M., Dahab, R. (eds.) PKC 2018, Part II. LNCS, vol. 10770, pp. 3–33. Springer, Heidelberg (Mar (2018). https://doi.org/10.1007/978-3-319-76581-5_1

13. Derler, D., Ramacher, S., Slamanig, D.: Post-quantum zero-knowledge proofs for accumulators with applications to ring signatures from symmetric-key primitives. In: Lange, T., Steinwandt, R. (eds.) PQCrypto 2018. LNCS, vol. 10786, pp. 419–440. Springer, Cham (2018). https://doi.org/10.1007/978-3-319-79063-3_20

14. Eaton, E.: Leighton-Micali hash-based signatures in the quantum random-oracle model. In: Adams, C., Camenisch, J. (eds.) SAC 2017. LNCS, vol. 10719, pp. 263–280. Springer, Cham (2018). https://doi.org/10.1007/978-3-319-72565-9_13

15. Ebrahimi, E.E., Unruh, D.: Quantum collision-resistance of non-uniformly distributed functions: upper and lower bounds. Quantum Inf. Comput. **18**(15&16), 1332–1349 (2018). http://www.rintonpress.com/xxqic18/qic-18-1516/1332-1349.pdf

16. Fiat, A., Shamir, A.: How to prove yourself: practical solutions to identification and signature problems. In: Odlyzko, A.M. (ed.) CRYPTO 1986. LNCS, vol. 263, pp. 186–194. Springer, Heidelberg (1987). https://doi.org/10.1007/3-540-47721-7_12

17. Fujisaki, E., Okamoto, T.: Secure integration of asymmetric and symmetric encryption schemes. J. Cryptol. **26**(1), 80–101 (2013)

18. Galbraith, S.D., Petit, C., Silva, J.: Identification protocols and signature schemes based on supersingular isogeny problems. In: Takagi, T., Peyrin, T. (eds.) ASIACRYPT 2017. LNCS, vol. 10624, pp. 3–33. Springer, Cham (2017). https://doi.org/10.1007/978-3-319-70694-8_1

19. Hofheinz, D., Hövelmanns, K., Kiltz, E.: A modular analysis of the Fujisaki-Okamoto transformation. In: Kalai, Y., Reyzin, L. (eds.) TCC 2017. LNCS, vol. 10677, pp. 341–371. Springer, Cham (2017). https://doi.org/10.1007/978-3-319-70500-2_12

20. Hövelmanns, K., Kiltz, E., Schäge, S., Unruh, D.: Generic authenticated key exchange in the quantum random oracle model. Cryptology ePrint Archive, Report 2018/928 (2018). https://eprint.iacr.org/2018/928

21. Hülsing, A., Rijneveld, J., Song, F.: Mitigating multi-target attacks in hash-based signatures. In: Cheng, C.-M., Chung, K.-M., Persiano, G., Yang, B.-Y. (eds.) PKC 2016. LNCS, vol. 9614, pp. 387–416. Springer, Heidelberg (2016). https://doi.org/10.1007/978-3-662-49384-7_15

22. Jiang, H., Zhang, Z., Chen, L., Wang, H., Ma, Z.: IND-CCA-secure key encapsulation mechanism in the quantum random oracle model, revisited. In: Shacham, H., Boldyreva, A. (eds.) CRYPTO 2018. LNCS, vol. 10993, pp. 96–125. Springer, Cham (2018). https://doi.org/10.1007/978-3-319-96878-0_4

23. Jiang, H., Zhang, Z., Ma, Z.: Key encapsulation mechanism with explicit rejection in the quantum random oracle model. In: Lin, D., Sako, K. (eds.) PKC 2019. LNCS, vol. 11443, pp. 618–645. Springer, Cham (2019). https://doi.org/10.1007/978-3-030-17259-6_21

24. Jiang, H., Zhang, Z., Ma, Z.: Key encapsulation mechanism with explicit rejection in the quantum random oracle model. Cryptology ePrint Archive, Report 2019/052 (2019). https://eprint.iacr.org/2019/052

25. Leighton, F.T., Micali, S.: Large provably fast and secure digital signature schemes based on secure hash functions. US Patent 5,432,852 (1995)

26. Nielsen, M., Chuang, I.: Quantum Computation and Quantum Information, 1st edn. Cambridge University Press, Cambridge (2000)

27. Saito, T., Xagawa, K., Yamakawa, T.: Tightly-secure key-encapsulation mechanism in the quantum random oracle model. In: Nielsen, J.B., Rijmen, V. (eds.) EURO-CRYPT 2018. LNCS, vol. 10822, pp. 520–551. Springer, Cham (2018). https://doi.org/10.1007/978-3-319-78372-7_17

28. Song, F., Yun, A.: Quantum security of NMAC and related constructions. In: Katz, J., Shacham, H. (eds.) CRYPTO 2017. LNCS, vol. 10402, pp. 283–309. Springer, Cham (2017). https://doi.org/10.1007/978-3-319-63715-0_10

29. Targhi, E.E., Tabia, G.N., Unruh, D.: Quantum collision-resistance of non-uniformly distributed functions. In: Takagi, T. (ed.) PQCrypto 2016. LNCS, vol. 9606, pp. 79–85. Springer, Cham (2016). https://doi.org/10.1007/978-3-319-29360-8_6

30. Targhi, E.E., Unruh, D.: Post-quantum security of the Fujisaki-Okamoto and OAEP transforms. In: Hirt, M., Smith, A. (eds.) TCC 2016. LNCS, vol. 9986, pp. 192–216. Springer, Heidelberg (2016). https://doi.org/10.1007/978-3-662-53644-5_8

31. Unruh, D.: Quantum position verification in the random oracle model. In: Garay, J.A., Gennaro, R. (eds.) CRYPTO 2014. LNCS, vol. 8617, pp. 1–18. Springer, Heidelberg (2014). https://doi.org/10.1007/978-3-662-44381-1_1

32. Unruh, D.: Non-interactive zero-knowledge proofs in the quantum random oracle model. In: Oswald, E., Fischlin, M. (eds.) EUROCRYPT 2015. LNCS, vol. 9057, pp. 755–784. Springer, Heidelberg (2015). https://doi.org/10.1007/978-3-662-46803-6_25

33. Unruh, D.: Revocable quantum timed-release encryption. J. ACM **62**(6), 49:1–49:76 (2015). Preprint on IACR ePrint 2013/606

34. Unruh, D.: Post-quantum security of Fiat-Shamir. In: Takagi, T., Peyrin, T. (eds.) ASIACRYPT 2017. LNCS, vol. 10624, pp. 65–95. Springer, Cham (2017). https://doi.org/10.1007/978-3-319-70694-8_3

35. Yoo, Y., Azarderakhsh, R., Jalali, A., Jao, D., Soukharev, V.: A post-quantum digital signature scheme based on supersingular isogenies. In: Kiayias, A. (ed.) FC 2017. LNCS, vol. 10322, pp. 163–181. Springer, Cham (2017). https://doi.org/10.1007/978-3-319-70972-7_9

36. Zalka, C.: Grover's quantum searching algorithm is optimal. Phys. Rev. A **60**, 2746–2751 (1999). https://arxiv.org/abs/quant-ph/9711070

37. Zhandry, M.: How to construct quantum random functions. In: 53rd FOCS, pp. 679–687. IEEE Computer Society Press, October 2012

38. Zhandry, M.: Secure identity-based encryption in the quantum random oracle model. In: Safavi-Naini, R., Canetti, R. (eds.) CRYPTO 2012. LNCS, vol. 7417, pp. 758–775. Springer, Heidelberg (2012). https://doi.org/10.1007/978-3-642-32009-5_44

39. Zhandry, M.: A note on the quantum collision and set equality problems. Quantum Inf. Comput. **15**(7&8) (2015)

Quantum Indistinguishability of Random Sponges

Jan Czajkowski[1]($\boxtimes$) (iD), Andreas Hülsing[2]($\boxtimes$) (iD), and Christian Schaffner[1]($\boxtimes$) (iD)

[1] QuSoft, University of Amsterdam, Amsterdam, The Netherlands
{j.czajkowski,c.schaffner}@uva.nl
[2] TU Eindhoven, Eindhoven, The Netherlands
andreas@huelsing.net

Abstract. In this work we show that the sponge construction can be used to construct quantum-secure pseudorandom functions. As our main result we prove that random sponges are quantum indistinguishable from random functions. In this setting the adversary is given superposition access to the input-output behavior of the construction but not to the internal function. Our proofs hold under the assumption that the internal function is a random function or permutation. We then use this result to obtain a quantum-security version of a result by Andreeva, Daemen, Mennink, and Van Assche (FSE'15) which shows that a sponge that uses a secure PRP or PRF as internal function is a secure PRF. This result also proves that the recent attacks against CBC-MAC in the quantum-access model by Kaplan, Leurent, Leverrier, and Naya-Plasencia (Crypto'16) and Santoli, and Schaffner (QIC'16) can be prevented by introducing a state with a non-trivial inner part.

The proof of our main result is derived by analyzing the joint distribution of any q input-output pairs. Our method analyzes the statistical behavior of the considered construction in great detail. The used techniques might prove useful in future analysis of different cryptographic primitives considering quantum adversaries. Using Zhandry's PRF/PRP switching lemma we then obtain that quantum indistinguishability also holds if the internal block function is a random permutation.

Keywords: Symmetric cryptography · Keyed sponges ·
Indistinguishability · Quantum security · Message-authentication codes

1 Introduction

Originally introduced in the context of cryptographic hash functions, the sponge construction [2] became one of the most widely used constructions in symmetric cryptography. Consequently, sponges get used in keyed constructions, including message authentication codes (MAC), stream ciphers, and authenticated encryption (AE), see e.g. [1,4,5,7,13,17,20]. For all these applications it is either necessary or at least sufficient for security if a secretly keyed sponge is indistinguishable from a random function. That this is indeed the case was already shown in

© International Association for Cryptologic Research 2019
A. Boldyreva and D. Micciancio (Eds.): CRYPTO 2019, LNCS 11693, pp. 296–325, 2019.
https://doi.org/10.1007/978-3-030-26951-7_11

the original security proof for the sponge construction [3] where cryptographic sponges were shown to be indifferentiable from random functions. This result is widely applicable and consequently was followed up with several improved bounds for specific applications. Recent works [1,13,17] improved the bound for the setting of indistinguishability of secretly keyed sponges.

While these results show the applicability of the sponge construction in today's computing environment, they leave open the question of its applicability in a future post-quantum setting where adversaries have access to quantum computers. Such an attacker can for example run Shor's algorithm [22] to break the security of constructions based on the RSA or discrete-logarithm problem. While such constructions are hardly ever considered for practical symmetric cryptography due to their slow operations, the impact of quantum adversaries goes beyond Shor's algorithm. Conventional security proofs, especially in idealized models, might break down in the light of quantum attackers who are allowed to ask queries in superposition [8]. Going even further, allowing adversaries superposition access to secretly keyed primitives, it was shown that several well known MACs and encryption schemes, including CBC-MAC and the Even-Mansour block cipher become insecure [14,16,21]. While these latter attacks are not applicable in the post-quantum setting, they are indications that secret-key cryptography does not trivially withstand quantum adversaries and that it is necessary to study the security of symmetric cryptography in the post-quantum setting.

In this work we do exactly this: We study the security of secretly keyed sponges against quantum adversaries. Quantum security of sponges was also analyzed in [11], although the authors there focused on different properties then we.

Sponges. The sponge construction [2] is an eXtendable Output Function (XOF) that maps arbitrary-length inputs to outputs of a length specified by an additional input. The construction operates on an $(r + c)$-bit state. The parameter r is called the rate and the parameter c is called the capacity. The first r bits of the state are called the outer part or outer state, the remaining c bits are called the inner part or inner state. The sponge uses an internal function $\mathbf{f}$ mapping $(r + c)$-bit strings to $(r + c)$-bit strings. To process a message consisting of several r-bit blocks, the sponge alternates between mixing a new message block into the outer state and applying $\mathbf{f}$, as shown in Fig. 1. When all message blocks are processed (i.e. absorbed into the internal state) the sponge can be squeezed to produce outputs by alternating between applying $\mathbf{f}$ and outputting the outer state. We write SPONGE$_\mathbf{f}$ for the sponge using $\mathbf{f}$ as internal function.

Sponges can be keyed in several ways. For example, the state can be initialized with the key, referred to as root-keyed sponge in [1]. Another option is to just apply the sponge on the concatenation of key and message. This was called the keyed sponge in [4] and the outer-keyed sponge in [1]. The last and for us most relevant concept is keying the sponge by replacing $\mathbf{f}$ with a keyed function $\mathbf{f}_K$. For the special case of $\mathbf{f}_K$ being a single-key Even-Mansour construction this was called E-M keyed sponge construction in [10] and later the inner-keyed sponge

Input: $\mathbf{M} = M_1\|M_2\|M_3$ Output: $\mathbf{Z} = Z_1\|Z_2$

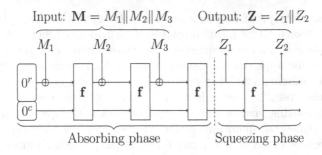

Fig. 1. A scheme illustrating the sponge construction.

in [1]. We refer to the general case for any keyed function $\mathbf{f}_K$ as keyed-internal-function sponge.

Our Results. As main result, we prove that the sponge construction using a random function or permutation is quantumly indistinguishable from a random function (see Theorems 8 and 16). This result can be used to obtain a quantum version of Theorem 1 from [1] (see Theorem 12) which states that the indistinguishability of keyed-internal-function sponges can be derived from the quantum-PRF-security (or quantum-PRP-security in case of a block-cipher) of the keyed internal function. Thereby we not only provide a proof for the security of keyed-internal-function sponges in the post-quantum setting, but even in the stronger quantum settings where the adversary gets full quantum-access to the keyed-internal-function sponge, i.e we prove that keyed-internal-function sponges are quantum PRFs.

Another implication of our result is that the quantum attacks against CBC-MAC mentioned above can be prevented using a state with a non-trivial inner part. The authors of the attack already noted[1] that their attack does not work in this case. More specifically, CBC-MAC can be viewed as full-width sponge (where the state has no inner part, i.e., the capacity is 0). On the other hand, a CBC-MAC where all message blocks are padded with 0^c and the output is truncated to the first r bits can be viewed as an keyed-internal-function sponge. Hence, our result applies and shows that the quantum attacks by Kaplan, Leurent, Leverrier, and Naya-Plasencia [14] and Santoli, and Schaffner [21] using Simon's algorithm are not applicable any longer. Even more, our result proves that this little tweak of CBC-MAC indeed results in a quantum secure MAC.

In the full version of the paper [12] we show a direct proof of indistinguishability for $\mathbf{f}$ being a random permutation. In this proof we state and prove a lemma that generalizes the average case polynomial method to allow for functions that are not necessarily polynomials but are close to one; this result is not necessary to achieve the main goal of the paper but might be useful in other works using similar techniques.

---

[1] See slide 16 (page 26) of their Crypto 2016 presentation available at https://who.rocq.inria.fr/Gaetan.Leurent/files/Simon_CR16_slides.pdf.

A Limitation. The authors of [1] use their Theorem 1 to show security of inner-keyed sponges using the PRP-security of single-key Even-Mansour. Their result does not carry over to the quantum setting as Even-Mansour is vulnerable in the quantum setting [16]. This does not lead an actual attack on inner-keyed sponges in the quantum setting. The attack needs access to the full input to the Even-Mansour cipher, which is never the case for inner-keyed sponges as long as a non-trivial inner state is used. However, the attack on Even-Mansour does render the modular proof strategy not applicable for inner-keyed sponges. We also need to stress that our result so far does not cover the commonly used approaches to secretly key SHA3 for this very reason.

Our Approach. The main technical contribution of our work is a proof that the probability for any given input-output behavior of SPONGE$_f$ is a polynomial in the capacity of the sponge. This observation allows us then to apply the average-case polynomial method of [24] (see Theorem 4 below).

In more detail, recall that the capacity of a SPONGE$_f$ is the size of the inner state (there are 2^c possible inner states for a sponge as in Fig. 1). If the capacity of a sponge increases, it becomes less and less likely that there are collisions in the inner state. Hence for infinite capacity, the inner states are unique and so the internal functions are called on unique inputs and therefore, the sponge behaves like a random function. Our proof formalizes this intuition by carefully analyzing the probabilities for q given input-output values of the sponge in terms of the capacity. We show that these probabilities are in fact polynomials in the inverse of the capacity of degree at most q times the length of the input-output values. We refer to Lemma 9 for the formal statement.

By establishing the capacity as this crucial parameter, we fit directly into the proof technique from [24] that uses approximating polynomials of low degree to show closeness of distributions and in turn small quantum distinguishing advantage. By the PRF/PRP switching lemma from [25], quantum indistinguishability also holds for the case of f being a random permutation. In the appendix, we provide an alternative proof for this case by generalizing the proof technique of [24] to the case of permutations.

Organization. Section 2 introduces the definition of quantum indistinguishability and other notions used throughout this work. In Sect. 3 we extend the above informal discussion of the sponge construction with a more formal description. At the end of the section we show that SPONGE$_f$ is indistinguishable from a random oracle in the conventional-access setting (in contrast to the quantum-access model). In Sect. 4 we state the main result of our paper as well as several derived results. In the full version [12] we also provide an example proof valid for limited distinguishers but giving sufficient details to understand our approach and verify correctness without all the particulars of the full proof. Section 5 contains the proof of Lemma 9, the main technical result of this work. The case of random permutations is covered in Sect. 6. We conclude the paper with Sect. 7 discussing some open problems related to the problem we analyze and related work.

2   Preliminaries and Tools

In this section we introduce the definition of quantum indistinguishability and other notions used throughout this work.

2.1   Quantum Threat Model

The quantum threat model we consider allows the adversary to query oracles in superposition. Oracles are modeled as unitary operators $\mathbf{U_h}$ acting on computational basis states as follows

$$\mathbf{U_h}|X, Y\rangle \mapsto |X, Y \oplus \mathbf{h}(X)\rangle. \tag{1}$$

The adversary is considered to have access to a fault-tolerant (perfect) quantum computer. We do not provide more details on quantum computing as we do not directly require it here, but we refer to [19] instead.

2.2   Distributions

A distribution $\mathfrak{D}$ on a set $\mathcal{X}$ is a function $\mathfrak{D} : \mathcal{X} \to [0,1]$ such that $\sum_{X \in \mathcal{X}} \mathfrak{D}(X) = 1$. We denote sampling X from $\mathcal{X}$ according to $\mathfrak{D}$ by $X \leftarrow \mathfrak{D}$. $\mathcal{Y}^{\mathcal{X}}$ denotes the set of functions $\{\mathbf{f} : \mathcal{X} \to \mathcal{Y}\}$. If $\mathfrak{D}$ is a distribution on $\mathcal{Y}$ then $\mathfrak{D}^{\mathcal{X}}$ denotes a distribution on $\mathcal{Y}^{\mathcal{X}}$ where the output for each input is chosen independently according to $\mathfrak{D}$. By $\xleftarrow{\$} \mathcal{X}$ we denote sampling uniformly at random from the set $\mathcal{X}$.

2.3   Classical and Quantum Indistinguishability

By classical indistinguishability we mean a feature of two distributions that are hard to distinguish if only polynomially many classical queries are allowed. The mentioned polynomial is evaluated on the security parameter. Note however that we have not yet specified it. For now though we leave it implicit, the security parameter will be specified for the particular construction we are going to analyze. In the following we are going to use functions $\mathbb{N} \to \mathbb{R}$ that for big enough argument are smaller than any inverse polynomial, they are called *negligible* functions.

Definition 1 (Classical Indistinguishability). *Two distributions $\mathfrak{D}_1$ and $\mathfrak{D}_2$ over a set $\mathcal{Y}^{\mathcal{X}}$ are computationally classically indistinguishable if no quantum algorithm A can distinguish $\mathfrak{D}_1$ from $\mathfrak{D}_2$ using a polynomial number of classical queries. That is, for all A, there is a negligible function ϵ such that*

$$\left| \Pr_{\mathbf{g} \leftarrow \mathfrak{D}_1} [A^{\mathbf{g}}(.) = 1] - \Pr_{\mathbf{g} \leftarrow \mathfrak{D}_2} [A^{\mathbf{g}}(.) = 1] \right| \leq \epsilon. \tag{2}$$

We write $A^{\mathbf{g}}$ to denote that adversary A has classical oracle access to $\mathbf{g}$. We will use the following generalization of the above definition to specify our goal.

Definition 2 (Quantum Indistinguishability [24]). *Two distributions $\mathfrak{D}_1$ and $\mathfrak{D}_2$ over a set $\mathcal{Y}^{\mathcal{X}}$ are computationally quantumly indistinguishable if no quantum algorithm A can distinguish $\mathfrak{D}_1$ from $\mathfrak{D}_2$ using a polynomial number of quantum queries. That is, for all A, there is a negligible function ϵ such that*

$$\left| \mathop{\mathbb{P}}_{\mathbf{g}\leftarrow\mathfrak{D}_1} \left[A^{|\mathbf{g}\rangle}(.) = 1 \right] - \mathop{\mathbb{P}}_{\mathbf{g}\leftarrow\mathfrak{D}_2} \left[A^{|\mathbf{g}\rangle}(.) = 1 \right] \right| \leq \epsilon. \tag{3}$$

We write $A^{|\mathbf{g}\rangle}$ to denote that adversary A has quantum oracle access to $\mathbf{g}$, i.e. she can query $\mathbf{g}$ on a superposition of inputs.

In what follows the setting that we focus on is indistinguishability from a random oracle. The first distribution is the one analyzed and the other is the uniform distribution over the set of all functions from $\mathcal{X}$ to $\mathcal{Y}$, i.e. $\mathcal{Y}^{\mathcal{X}}$. Sampling a uniformly random function is denoted by $\xleftarrow{\$} \mathcal{Y}^{\mathcal{X}}$.

2.4   Main Tools

In this section we describe the proof technique—based on approximating polynomials—that proves useful when dealing with notions like quantum indistinguishability. In the following $[q] := \{1, 2, \ldots, q\}$.

Theorem 3 (Theorem 3.1 in [26]). *Let A be a quantum algorithm making q quantum queries to an oracle $\mathbf{h} : \mathcal{X} \to \mathcal{Y}$. If we draw $\mathbf{h}$ from some distribution $\mathfrak{D}$, then the quantity $\mathbb{P}_{\mathbf{h}\leftarrow\mathfrak{D}}[A^{|\mathbf{h}\rangle}() = 1]$ is a linear combination of the quantities $\mathbb{P}_{\mathbf{h}\leftarrow\mathfrak{D}}[\forall i \in [2q] : \mathbf{h}(X^i) = Y^i]$, where $\forall i \in [2q] : (X^i, Y^i) \in \mathcal{X} \times \mathcal{Y}$.*

The intuition behind the above theorem is that with q queries the amplitudes of the quantum state of the algorithm depend on at most q input-output pairs. The probability of any outcome is a linear combination of squares of amplitudes, that is why we have $2q$ input-output pairs in the probability function. Finally as the probability of any measurement depends on just $2q$ input-output pairs the same holds for the algorithm's output probability. All the information about $\mathbf{h}$ comes from the queries A made.

We use the above theorem together with statements about approximating polynomials to connect the probability of some input-output behavior of a function from a given distribution with the probability of the adversary distinguishing two distributions.

Theorem 4 (Theorem 7.3 in [24]). *Fix q, and let $\mathfrak{F}_t$ be a family of distributions on $\mathcal{Y}^{\mathcal{X}}$ indexed by $t \in \mathbb{Z}^+ \cup \{\infty\}$. Suppose there is an integer d such that for every $2q$ pairs $\forall i \in [2q] : (X^i, Y^i) \in \mathcal{X} \times \mathcal{Y}$, the function $\mathbf{p}(1/t) = \mathbb{P}_{\mathbf{h}\leftarrow\mathfrak{F}_t}\left[\forall i \in [2q] : \mathbf{h}(X^i) = Y^i\right]$ is a polynomial of degree at most d in $1/t$. Then for any quantum algorithm A making at most q quantum queries, the output distribution under $\mathfrak{F}_t$ and $\mathfrak{F}_\infty$ are $\pi^2 d^3/3t$-close*

$$\left| \mathop{\mathbb{P}}_{\mathbf{h}\leftarrow\mathfrak{F}_t} \left[A^{|\mathbf{h}\rangle}() = 1 \right] - \mathop{\mathbb{P}}_{\mathbf{h}\leftarrow\mathfrak{F}_\infty} \left[A^{|\mathbf{h}\rangle}() = 1 \right] \right| < \frac{\pi^2 d^3}{6t}. \tag{4}$$

This theorem is an average case version of the polynomial method often used in complexity theory. If the polynomial approximating the ideal behavior of $\mathbf{h} \leftarrow \mathfrak{F}_\infty$ is of low degree the distance between polynomials must be small.

3   The Sponge Construction

In this section we give a formal definition of sponges and recall a known result about their indisitinguishability.

3.1   Definition of Sponges

While an informal explanation of sponges was given in the introduction, we now give a more formal definition.

We define a *sponge-compliant* padding as:

Definition 5 (Definition 1 in [6]). *A padding rule is sponge-compliant if it never results in the empty string and if it satisfies the following criterion:*

$$\forall \nu \geq 0 \; \forall \mathbf{M}, \mathbf{M}' \in \{0,1\}^* : \mathbf{M} \neq \mathbf{M}' \Rightarrow \mathbf{M} \| \text{PAD}(|\mathbf{M}|) \neq \mathbf{M}' \| \text{PAD}(|\mathbf{M}'|) \| 0^{\nu r}, \tag{5}$$

where $\|$ denotes concatenation of bit strings.

A formal definition of the construction is provided as Algorithm 1. Note that $\oplus$ denotes the bitwise XOR, $|\mathbf{P}|_r$ denotes the number of blocks of length r in $\mathbf{P}$, $\mathbf{P}_i$ is the i-th block of $\mathbf{P}$ and $\lfloor \mathbf{Z} \rfloor_\ell$ are the first ℓ bits of $\mathbf{Z}$.

Algorithm 1: $\text{SPONGE}_{\mathbf{f}}[\text{PAD}, r]$

Input : $\mathbf{M} \in \{0,1\}^*$, $\ell \geq 0$.
Output: $\mathbf{Z} \in \{0,1\}^\ell$

1 $\mathbf{P} := \mathbf{M} \| \text{PAD}[r](|\mathbf{M}|)$, and $S := 0^{r+c}$.
2 **for** $i = 0$ *to* $|\mathbf{P}|_r - 1$ **do**   // Absorbing phase
3 $\quad \big|\quad S = S \oplus (\mathbf{P}_i \| 0^c)$
4 $\quad \big\lfloor\quad S = \mathbf{f}(S)$
5 $\mathbf{Z} := \lfloor S \rfloor_r$ // Squeezing phase
6 **while** $|\mathbf{Z}| < \ell$ **do**
7 $\quad \big|\quad S = \mathbf{f}(S)$
8 $\quad \big\lfloor\quad \mathbf{Z} = \mathbf{Z} \| \lfloor S \rfloor_r$
9 Output $\lfloor \mathbf{Z} \rfloor_\ell$

3.2   Classical Indistinguishability of Random Sponges

In the following we state the indistinguishability result in the classical domain. We use the following notation for a set of arbitrary finite-length bit strings:

$$\{0,1\}^* := \bigcup_{l \geq 0} \{0,1\}^l, \tag{6}$$

we usually denote this set by $\mathcal{M}$. Before we proceed let us define what we mean by a random oracle.

Definition 6 (Random Oracle). *A random oracle is sampled from a distribution $\mathfrak{R}$ on functions from $\mathcal{M} \times \mathbb{N}$ to $\mathcal{M}$, where $\mathcal{M} := \{0,1\}^*$. We define $\mathbf{h} \leftarrow \mathfrak{R}$ as follows:*

- *Choose $\mathbf{g}$ uniformly at random from $\{\mathbf{g} : \mathcal{M} \rightarrow \{0,1\}^{\infty}\}$, where by $\{0,1\}^{\infty}$ we denote the set of infinitely long bit-strings.*
- *For each $(X, \ell) \in \mathcal{M} \times \mathbb{N}$ set $\mathbf{h}(X, \ell) := \lfloor \mathbf{g}(X) \rfloor_{\ell}$, that is output the first ℓ bits of the output of $\mathbf{g}$.*

Theorem 7 (Classical indistinguishability of SPONGE). *If $\mathbf{f}$ is a random transformation or a random permutation then SPONGE$_{\mathbf{f}}$ defined in Algorithm 1 is classically indistinguishable from a random oracle. Namely for all quantum algorithms A making polynomially many classical queries there is a negligible function ϵ such that*

$$\left| \mathop{\mathbb{P}}_{\mathbf{f} \xleftarrow{\$} \mathcal{S}^{\mathcal{S}}} \left[A^{\text{SPONGE}_{\mathbf{f}}}(.) = 1 \right] - \mathop{\mathbb{P}}_{\mathbf{h} \leftarrow \mathfrak{R}} \left[A^{\mathbf{g}}(.) = 1 \right] \right| \leq \epsilon, \tag{7}$$

where $\mathcal{S} = \{0,1\}^{r+c}$, and $\mathfrak{R}$ is defined according to Definition 6.

Proof. The proof follows closely the proof of Theorem 2 of [2]. Even though we give more power to the adversary giving her access to a quantum computer, the queries are considered to be classical. All arguments in the proof of Bertoni and others depend only on the queries made by the adversary and not her computing power. For that reason we can use the result of [18], which states that a query-based classical result easily translates to the quantum case if we do not change the query model. □

4   Random Sponges Are Quantumly Indistinguishable from Random Oracles

We want to show that the distribution corresponding to random sponges is quantumly indistinguishable from a random oracle. We can define a family of distributions indexed by the security parameter that intuitively gets closer to a random oracle with increasing parameter. For that reason Theorem 4 is a perfect theoretical tool to be used. The relevant tasks that remain are to identify the family of distributions that correspond to our figure of merit, to show that in fact the most secure member of the family with $t = \infty$ is a random oracle, and to prove that the assumptions of Theorem 4 are fulfilled.

The security parameter in SPONGE is the capacity; we parametrize the family of random sponges by the size of the inner state space $t = 2^c$. Intuitively speaking, for $c \to \infty$ each evaluation of the internal function is done with a different inner state. In this case irrespective of the input, the output is a completely random string, which is the definition of a random oracle (RO). Hence we conclude that we identified a family of distributions that is well suited to be used with Theorem 4. If we show that indeed for $t = \infty$ the member of the family is the random oracle we have that:

$$\mathfrak{F}_{2^c} \text{ is quantumly indistinguishable from } \mathfrak{F}_{\infty}$$

$$\Rightarrow \text{ random sponge is quantumly indisitinguishable from RO.} \quad (8)$$

We are left with the task to prove the left-hand side of the above statement. The assumption of Theorem 4 is that the probability of witnessing any input-output behavior on q queries is a polynomial in $1/2^c$. At this point we stumble upon a problem with the set of indices. If we want to use the statement about closeness of polynomials we have to show that $\mathbf{p}$ is a polynomial for any inverse integer and not only for 2^{-c}. This difficulty brings us to the definition of the *generalized sponge construction* SPGEN. The only difference between SPGEN and SPONGE is the space of inner states, we change it from $\{0,1\}^c$ to any finite-size set $\mathcal{C}$. This modification solves the problem of defining distributions for any integer, not only powers of 2. It remains to prove that $\mathbf{p}(|\mathcal{C}|^{-1})$ is in fact a polynomial in $|\mathcal{C}|^{-1}$, where by $|\mathcal{C}|$ we denote cardinality of the set. With that statement proven we fulfill the assumptions of Theorem 4 and show quantum indistinguishability of SPGEN, which implies the same for SPONGE.

In Algorithm 2 we present a generalization of SPONGE. The set of inner states is denoted by $\mathcal{C}$ and can be any finite set, to be specified by the user. The internal function is generalized to any map $\varphi_f : \{0,1\}^r \times \mathcal{C} \to \{0,1\}^r \times \mathcal{C}$. In the following we denote the part of the entire state S in $\{0,1\}^r$ by $\bar{S}$ and call it the *outer* part and the part in $\mathcal{C}$ by $\hat{S}$, we will refer to it as the *inner* part of a state.

Let us now formally state the main claim of this paper. We are going to focus on the internal function being modeled as a random function, in Sect. 6 though, we are going to cover the case of random permutations.

Theorem 8. SPGEN$_{\varphi_f}$ *for random* φ_f *is quantumly indistinguishable from a random oracle. More concretely, for all quantum algorithms* A *making at most* q *quantum queries to* SPGEN*, such that the input length is at most* $m \cdot r$ *bits long and the output length is at most* $z \cdot r$ *bits long,*

$$\left| \mathop{\mathbb{P}}_{\varphi_f \xleftarrow{\$} \mathcal{S}^{\mathcal{S}}} \left[A^{|\text{SPGEN}_{\varphi_f}\rangle}(.) = 1 \right] - \mathop{\mathbb{P}}_{\mathbf{h} \leftarrow \mathfrak{R}} \left[A^{|\mathbf{h}\rangle}(.) = 1 \right] \right| < \frac{\pi^2}{6} \eta^3 |\mathcal{C}|^{-1}, \quad (9)$$

where $\eta := 2q(m+z-2)$ *and* $\mathfrak{R}$ *is defined according to Definition 6. The domain is defined as* $\mathcal{S} = \{0,1\}^r \times \mathcal{C}$ *for some non-empty finite set* $\mathcal{C}$.

Algorithm 2: $\text{SPGEN}_{\varphi_f}[\text{PAD}, r, \mathcal{C}]$

    Input : $\mathbf{M} \in \{0,1\}^*$, $\ell \geq 0$.
    Output: $\mathbf{Z} \in \{0,1\}^\ell$

1 $\mathbf{P} := \text{PAD}(\mathbf{M})$
2 $S := (0^r, I_\mathcal{C}) \in \{0,1\}^r \times \mathcal{C}$.   // $I_\mathcal{C}$-initial value
3 **for** $i = 1$ to $|\mathbf{P}|_r$ **do**   // Absorbing phase
4 | $S := (\bar{S} \oplus \mathbf{P}_i, \hat{S})$
5 | $S := \varphi_f(S)$

6 $\mathbf{Z} := \bar{S}$ // Squeezing phase
7 **while** $|\mathbf{Z}| < \ell$ **do**
8 | $S := \varphi_f(S)$
9 | $\mathbf{Z} := \mathbf{Z} \| \bar{S}$

10 Output $\lfloor \mathbf{Z} \rfloor_\ell$

Before we prove the above theorem we state the main technical lemma.

Lemma 9. *For a fixed q and for every* $(\mathbf{M}, \mathbf{Z}) := \big((\mathbf{M}^i, \mathbf{Z}^i)\big)_{i \in [2q]}$, *where* $\forall i \in [2q] : (\mathbf{M}^i, \mathbf{Z}^i) \in \{0,1\}^* \times \{0,1\}^*$, *such that* $\forall i \in [2q] : |\mathbf{M}^i|_r \leq m, |\mathbf{Z}^i|_r \leq z$, *it holds that*

(i) the probability function is a polynomial in $|\mathcal{C}|^{-1}$ of degree η

$$\mathbb{P}\left[\forall i \subset [2q] : \text{SPGEN}_{\varphi_f}(\mathbf{M}^i, \ell_i) - \mathbf{Z}^i\right] = \sum_{j=0}^{\eta} u_j |\mathcal{C}|^{-j} =: \mathbf{p}(|\mathcal{C}|^{-1}) \qquad (10)$$

(ii) and the coefficient

$$a_0 = \prod_{i=1}^{2q} \delta(\mathbf{M}, \mathbf{Z}, i) 2^{-|\mathbf{Z}^i|}. \qquad (11)$$

All coefficients a_j are real, and the degree of the polynomial equals $\eta := 2q(m + z - 2)$. In the equation describing a_0 we use $\delta(\mathbf{M}, \mathbf{Z}, i)$ to denote a Boolean function that is 0 if $\mathbf{M}^i$ is input more than once and $\mathbf{Z}^i$ is not the longest output of SPGEN on $\mathbf{M}^i$ or is inconsistent with other outputs (inputting the same message for the second time should yield the same output) and is 1 otherwise.

The full proof is presented in Sect. 5.

Proof Idea. Our goal is to explicitly evaluate $\mathbb{P}[\forall i \in [2q] : \text{SPGEN}_{\varphi_f}(\mathbf{M}^i, \ell_i) = \mathbf{Z}^i]$. We base all of our discussion on two facts: SPGEN has a structure that we know and it involves multiple evaluations of the internal function φ_f. φ_f is a random function with well specified probability of yielding some output on a given input. The main idea of our approach is to extract terms like $\mathbb{P}[\varphi_f(S_1) = S_2]$ for some states S_1, S_2 from the overall probability expression and evaluate them.

Let us go through a more detailed plan of the proof. Fix $(\mathbf{M}, \mathbf{Z})$ and set $\ell_i := |\mathbf{Z}^i|$. In the first step we include all intermediate states in the probabilistic event $\left(\forall i \in [2q] : \text{SpGen}_{\varphi_f}(\mathbf{M}^i, \ell_i) = \mathbf{Z}^i\right)$. We write explicitly all inner states and outer states not specified by the input-output pairs $(\mathbf{M}, \mathbf{Z})$. Next we rewrite the full probability expression in the form $\sum \prod \mathbb{P}[\varphi_f(S_1) = S_2 \mid \ldots]$. The sum comes from the fact that there are many possible intermediate states that yield the given input-output behavior. The product is the result of using Bayes' rule to isolate a single evaluation of φ_f in the probability. To correctly evaluate the summands we need to analyze all states in $\mathbb{P}[\varphi_f(S_1) = S_2 \mid \ldots]$ from the perspective of *uniqueness*—we say a state is unique if it is input to φ_f just a single time. Given a specific setup of unique states in all $2q$ evaluations of SpGen we can easily evaluate the probabilities, as the only thing we need to know is that φ_f is random. The final step of the proof is to calculate the number of states in the sum. We sum over all values of states that fulfill the constraints of $\left(\forall i \in [2q] : \text{SpGen}_{\varphi_f}(\mathbf{M}^i, \ell_i) = \mathbf{Z}^i\right)$ and φ_f being a function. The previous analysis of uniqueness of states makes it easier to include the latter constraint; non-unique states have predetermined outputs under φ_f decreasing the number of possible states. After those steps we end up with an explicit expression for $\mathbb{P}\left[\forall i \in [2q] : \text{SpGen}_{\varphi_f}(\mathbf{M}^i, \ell_i) = \mathbf{Z}^i\right]$, which allows us to show that $\mathbf{p}$ is a polynomial of the claimed degree and its limit in $t \to \infty$, i.e. the coefficient a_0 is the probability of uniformly random outputs. □

Proof of Theorem 8. Let us define a family $\mathfrak{F}_t$ indexed by $t \in \mathbb{N} \cup \{\infty\}, t > 0$. $\mathfrak{F}_t$ is a distribution on functions from $\mathcal{M} \times \mathbb{N}$ to $\mathcal{M}$, where $\mathcal{M} := \{0, 1\}^*$. The family is additionally parametrized by the choice of $r \in \mathbb{N}$ and a sponge-compliant padding function PAD. We define $\mathbf{h} \leftarrow \mathfrak{F}_t$ as follows:

- Choose φ_f uniformly at random from $\mathcal{S}^{\mathcal{S}}$, where $\mathcal{S} := \{0, 1\}^r \times \mathcal{C}$ and $\mathcal{C}$ is any finite set of size $t > 0$.
- Use φ_f, $\mathcal{C}$, the fixed r, and PAD to construct $\text{SpGen}_{\varphi_f}[\text{PAD}, r, \mathcal{C}]$.
- For each $(X, \ell) \in \mathcal{M} \times \mathbb{N}$ set $\mathbf{h}(X, \ell) := \text{SpGen}_{\varphi_f}[\text{PAD}, r, \mathcal{C}](X, \ell)$.

To show that we defined $\mathfrak{F}_t$ in the right way, let us analyze Eq. (8) from the point of view of the newly defined distribution. On the one hand from our definition it follows that

$$\underset{\mathbf{h} \leftarrow \mathfrak{F}_t}{\mathbb{P}} \left[A^{|\mathbf{h}\rangle}() = 1\right] = \underset{\mathbf{h} \leftarrow \mathfrak{F}_t}{\mathbb{P}} \left[A^{|\text{SpGen}_{\varphi_f}\rangle}() = 1\right] = \underset{\varphi_f \overset{\$}{\leftarrow} \mathcal{S}^{\mathcal{S}}}{\mathbb{P}} \left[A^{|\text{SpGen}_{\varphi_f}\rangle}() = 1\right],$$

$$(12)$$

where the first equality follows from our definition of $\mathbf{h}$ and the second from the fact that all randomness in $\mathfrak{F}_t$ comes from choosing a random function φ_f. On the other hand if we take $t \to \infty$ the internal function is going to be injective on its inner part. Namely $\hat{\varphi}_f$—the internal function with its output restricted to the inner part—is injective. That implies a different inner state in every evaluation of φ_f in SpGen what in turn implies a random and independent outer part in every step of generating the output, formally

$$\underset{\mathbf{h} \leftarrow \mathfrak{F}_\infty}{\mathbb{P}} \left[A^{|\mathbf{h}\rangle}() = 1\right] = \underset{\mathbf{h} \leftarrow \mathfrak{R}}{\mathbb{P}} \left[A^{|\mathbf{h}\rangle}() = 1\right].$$

$$(13)$$

This intuition is formally captured by Statement (ii) of Lemma 9, where we state that in the limit of $|\mathcal{C}| \to \infty$ the probability of getting particular outputs of SpGen is the same as for a random oracle.

From the above discussion we get that

$$\left| \Pr_{h \leftarrow \mathfrak{F}_t} \left[A^{|h\rangle}() = 1 \right] - \Pr_{h \leftarrow \mathfrak{F}_\infty} \left[A^{|h\rangle}() = 1 \right] \right| =$$

$$\left| \Pr_{\varphi_f \overset{\$}{\leftarrow} \mathcal{SS}} \left[A^{|\text{SpGen}_{\varphi_f}\rangle}() = 1 \right] - \Pr_{h \leftarrow \mathfrak{R}} \left[A^{|h\rangle}() = 1 \right] \right|, \qquad (14)$$

which is the crucial equality for using Theorem 4 to prove our statement. The last element of the proof is the assumption about $\mathbf{p}$ being a polynomial and that is exactly the statement of Lemma 9. □

Quantum indistinguishability of commonly used sponges with binary state follows directly from the general result.

Corollary 10. *If* $\mathbf{f}$ *is a random function or a random permutation, then* SPONGE$_\mathbf{f}$ *is quantumly indistinguishable from a random oracle.*

Proof. For a random function we use Theorem 8 and for a random permutation Theorem 16 and set $\mathcal{C} = \{0, 1\}^c$. □

4.1 Application to Keyed-Internal-Function Sponges

We show that Theorem 8 implies that keyed-internal-function sponges are indistinguishable from a random oracle under quantum access if the used internal function is a quantum-secure PRF (or if the internal function is a permutation, a quantum-secure PRP). This means that in the case $\mathbf{f}$ is a quantum-secure pseudorandom function or permutation the sponge construction is a quantum-secure pseudorandom function. For keyed primitives, indistinguishability from a random oracle/permutation is exactly what we call pseudorandomness.

We first formally define *quantum-secure* pseudorandom functions (PRF) and pseudorandom permutations (PRP).

Definition 11 (Quantum-secure PRF/PRP). *Say* $\mathbf{f} : \mathcal{K} \times \mathcal{S} \to \mathcal{S}$ *is a keyed function (permutation), then we say that* $\mathbf{f}$ *is a quantum-secure pseudorandom function (permutation) if for every quantum algorithm running in polynomial time, there is a negligible function* ϵ^{PR} *such that*

$$\left| \Pr_{K \overset{\$}{\leftarrow} \mathcal{K}} \left[A^{|\mathbf{f}_K\rangle}(.) = 1 \right] - \Pr_{\mathbf{g} \overset{\$}{\leftarrow} \mathcal{SS}} \left[A^{|\mathbf{g}\rangle}(.) = 1 \right] \right| \leq \epsilon^{\text{PR}}(n), \qquad (15)$$

where $n := \lfloor \log |\mathcal{K}| \rfloor$ *and* $\mathbf{g}$ *is sampled uniformly from the set of functions (permutations) from* $\mathcal{S}$ *to* $\mathcal{S}$. *Below, we refer to* ϵ^{PR} *as advantage.*

Now we state and prove a quantum version of Theorem 1 of [1] which formalizes the above statement about quantum security of keyed-internal-function sponges. Note that we state the theorem for the general sponge construction but thanks to Corollary 10 it holds for the regular construction as well.

Theorem 12. *If the internal function $\mathbf{f}$ used in* $\mathrm{SPGEN}_\mathbf{f}$ *is a quantum-secure PRF/PRP with advantage* ϵ^{PR}, *then the resulting keyed-internal-function sponge is a quantum-secure PRF with advantage*

$$\left| \Pr_{K \xleftarrow{\$} \mathcal{K}} \left[A^{|\mathrm{SPGEN}_{\mathbf{f}_K} \rangle}(.) = 1 \right] - \Pr_{\mathbf{g} \leftarrow \mathfrak{R}} \left[A^{|\mathbf{g}\rangle}(.) = 1 \right] \right| \le \epsilon^{\mathrm{PR}} + \frac{\pi^2}{6} \eta^3 |\mathcal{C}|^{-1}, \quad (16)$$

where $\eta := 2q(m + z - 2)$, q *is the number of queries A makes to its oracle, m and z are as defined in the statement of Theorem 8, and $\mathfrak{R}$ is defined according to Definition 6.*

Proof. We give the proof for $\mathbf{f}$ being a keyed function. The proof when $\mathbf{f}$ is a keyed permutation is obtained by using Theorem 16 in place of Theorem 8 and restricting the sets from which $\mathbf{g}$ and $\varphi_\mathbf{f}$ are drawn below to permutations.

We show that the advantage of any quantum adversary in distinguishing the keyed-internal-function sponge from a random oracle is bound by its ability to distinguish $\mathbf{f}$ from a random oracle (permutation, respectively) plus its ability to distinguish a random sponge from a random oracle. In the following calculation we use the triangle inequality and the result of Theorem 8.

$$\left| \Pr_{K \xleftarrow{\$} \mathcal{K}} \left[A^{|\mathrm{SPGEN}_{\mathbf{f}_K}\rangle}(.) = 1 \right] - \Pr_{\mathbf{g} \leftarrow \mathfrak{R}} \left[A^{|\mathbf{g}\rangle}(.) = 1 \right] \right|$$

$$= \left| \Pr_{K \xleftarrow{\$} \mathcal{K}} \left[A^{|\mathrm{SPGEN}_{\mathbf{f}_K}\rangle}(.) = 1 \right] - \Pr_{\varphi_\mathbf{f} \xleftarrow{\$} SS} \left[A^{|\mathrm{SPGEN}_{\varphi_\mathbf{f}}\rangle}(.) = 1 \right] + \right.$$

$$\left. \Pr_{\varphi_\mathbf{f} \xleftarrow{\$} SS} \left[A^{|\mathrm{SPGEN}_{\varphi_\mathbf{f}}\rangle}(.) = 1 \right] - \Pr_{\mathbf{g} \leftarrow \mathfrak{R}} \left[A^{|\mathbf{g}\rangle}(.) = 1 \right] \right| \quad (17)$$

$$\le \underbrace{\left| \Pr_{K \xleftarrow{\$} \mathcal{K}} \left[A^{|\mathrm{SPGEN}_{\mathbf{f}_K}\rangle}(.) = 1 \right] - \Pr_{\varphi_\mathbf{f} \xleftarrow{\$} SS} \left[A^{|\mathrm{SPGEN}_{\varphi_\mathbf{f}}\rangle}(.) = 1 \right] \right|}_{\le \left| \Pr_{K \xleftarrow{\$} \mathcal{K}} [B^{|\mathbf{f}_K\rangle}(.)=1] - \Pr_{\varphi_\mathbf{f} \xleftarrow{\$} SS} [B^{|\varphi_\mathbf{f}\rangle}(.)=1] \right|} +$$

$$\underbrace{\left| \Pr_{\varphi_\mathbf{f} \xleftarrow{\$} SS} \left[A^{|\mathrm{SPGEN}_{\varphi_\mathbf{f}}\rangle}(.) = 1 \right] - \Pr_{\mathbf{g} \leftarrow \mathfrak{R}} \left[A^{|\mathbf{g}\rangle}(.) = 1 \right] \right| \le \epsilon^{\mathrm{PR}} + \frac{\pi^2}{3} \eta^3 |\mathcal{C}|^{-1},}_{\text{Quantum Indistinguishability, Thm. 8 or 16}} \quad (18)$$

where B is an adversary that uses A as a subroutine, simulating A's oracle using its own oracle and the sponge construction. B outputs the same output as A. $\square$

5   Proof of Lemma 9

In this section we give the complete proof of Lemma 9 for the general case of $q \geq 1$ queries the adversary makes and message lengths bounded by some m, not fixed to 2 like in the previous section. In Subsect. 5.1 we expand the probability expression to encompass all intermediate states of $\left(\forall i \in [2q] : \text{SPGEN}_{\varphi_f}(\mathbf{M}^i, \ell_i) = \mathbf{Z}^i\right)$ and individual evaluations of φ_f. In Subsect. 5.2 we introduce the concept of unique states to evaluate the probabilities of $\mathbb{P}[\varphi_f(S_1) = S_2]$. In Subsect. 5.3 we define the algorithm that calculates the cardinality of the set of intermediate states—and equivalently inner functions—consistent with given characteristics. In Subsect. 5.4 we conclude the proof and provide the final expression for the probability of an input-output pair under a random SPGEN_{φ_f}.

We omit the padding function of the sponge construction and assume that the length of all $\mathbf{M}^i$ is a multiple of r. This is done without loss of generality since we can just say that all the considered messages are in fact messages after padding and we do not use any properties of the padding in the proof. Also we focus on q evaluations of SPGEN instead of $2q$ to improve readability.

5.1   Expansion of the Probability Function

In this section we expand the probability function to the point that all intermediate states are accounted for. We consider the event $(\forall i \in [q] : \text{SPGEN}_{\varphi_f}(\mathbf{M}^i, \ell_i) = \mathbf{Z}^i)$ and then include the states that appear between consecutive evaluations of φ_f.

To keep track of the states we introduce the following notation. By the upper-index we denote the number of evaluations of SPGEN, going from 1 to q. The lower index corresponds to the number of evaluations of φ_f in the i-th calculation of SPGEN. A state occurring during the calculation on $\mathbf{M}^i$ that is the input to the j-th evaluation of φ_f is denoted by $S^i_{j\oplus}$. The output of that evaluation is S^i_{j+1}. States traversed in q evaluations of SPGEN can be represented by an array with q rows with $|\mathbf{M}^i|_r + |\mathbf{Z}^i|_r$ columns each. By *array* we mean a 2-dimensional matrix with unequal length of rows.

We call an array like that with values assigned to every state a *nabla configuration* ∇-c. ∇ symbolizes the triangle shape in which we put states between evaluations of φ_f, each corner being an outer or inner part of the state. Now we define ∇-c relative to input-output pairs $(\mathbf{M}, \mathbf{Z})$. The size of the array is determined by the number of blocks in $\mathbf{M}^i$ and $\mathbf{Z}^i$.

Definition 13 (∇-c). *The nabla configuration ∇-c for $(\mathbf{M}, \mathbf{Z})$ is an array of triples $\begin{pmatrix} \bar{S} & \bar{S}_\oplus \\ & \hat{S} \end{pmatrix} \in \{0,1\}^{2r} \times \mathcal{C}$, where $\mathcal{C}$ is an arbitrary non-empty finite set. The array ∇-c consists of q rows, for every i row i has k_i columns and $k_i :=$ $|\mathbf{M}^i|_r + |\mathbf{Z}^i|_r$ ($|\mathbf{M}^i|_r$ denotes the number of r-bit blocks in $\mathbf{M}^i$). Formally we have*

$$\nabla\text{-c} := \left[\begin{pmatrix} \bar{S}^i_j \ \bar{S}^i_{j\oplus} \\ \hat{S}^i_j \end{pmatrix} \right]_{\substack{i\in[q] \\ j\in[k_i]}}. \tag{19}$$

To refer to the element of $\nabla\text{-c}$ *that lies in row* i *and column* j *we write* $\nabla\text{-c}^i_j$. *To refer to parts of the triple that lies in row* i *and column* j *we write*

$$S^i_j \in \nabla\text{-c} \Leftrightarrow \nabla\text{-c}^i_j = \begin{pmatrix} \bar{S} \ \bar{S}_{\oplus} \\ \hat{S} \end{pmatrix} \wedge S^i_j = (\bar{S}, \hat{S})$$

$$S^i_{j\oplus} \in \nabla\text{-c} \Leftrightarrow \nabla\text{-c}^i_j = \begin{pmatrix} \bar{S} \ \bar{S}_{\oplus} \\ \hat{S} \end{pmatrix} \wedge S^i_{j\oplus} = (\bar{S}_{\oplus}, \hat{S}) \tag{20}$$

Let us define the number of evaluations of $\varphi_{\mathbf{f}}$ in $\nabla\text{-c}$ for $(\mathbf{M}, \mathbf{Z})$ as

$$\kappa := \sum_{i=1}^{q} (k_i - 1), \tag{21}$$

note that $|\nabla\text{-c}| = \kappa + q$.

To make good use of the newly introduced concept of nabla configurations $\nabla\text{-c}$ we want to restrict the set of arrays we discuss. We want to put constraints on the set of $\nabla\text{-c}$ to make explicit the requirement that states correspond to a correct input-output behavior of SpGen. The *set of* $\nabla\text{-c}$ *for* $(\mathbf{M}, \mathbf{Z})$ is defined as follows.

Definition 14 ($\nabla\text{-C}(\mathbf{M}, \mathbf{Z})$). *The set of nabla configurations* $\nabla\text{-c}$ *for* $(\mathbf{M}, \mathbf{Z})$ *is a set of arrays of size specified by* $(\mathbf{M}, \mathbf{Z})$, $\nabla\text{-C}(\mathbf{M}, \mathbf{Z}) \subset (\{0,1\}^{2r} \times \mathcal{C})^{\kappa+q}$. *We define* $\nabla\text{-C}(\mathbf{M}, \mathbf{Z})$ *by the following constraints*

$$\forall i \in [q] : \hat{S}^i_1 = I_{\mathcal{C}},$$

$$\forall i \in [q] : \bar{S}^i_1 = 0^r,$$

$$\forall i \in [q], 1 \le j \le |\mathbf{M}^i|_r : \bar{S}^i_{j\oplus} = \bar{S}^i_j \oplus M^i_j,$$

$$\forall i \in [q], |\mathbf{M}^i|_r < j \le k_i : \bar{S}^i_{j\oplus} = \bar{S}^i_j = Z^i_{j-|\mathbf{M}^i|_r}. \tag{22}$$

The formal definition reads

$$\nabla\text{-C}(\mathbf{M}, \mathbf{Z}) := \{\nabla\text{-c} \text{ for } (\mathbf{M}, \mathbf{Z}) : \nabla\text{-c} \text{ fulfills constraints (22)}\}. \tag{23}$$

In the following we assume that rows of all $\nabla\text{-c} \in \nabla\text{-C}(\mathbf{M}, \mathbf{Z})$ are initially sorted according to the following relation. We arrange $(\mathbf{M}^i, \mathbf{Z}^i)$ in non-decreasing order in terms of length, so $\forall i < j : k_i \le k_j$, this also means that rows of $\nabla\text{-c}$ are ordered in this way.

Having established the notation we move on to realizing the goal of this section: rewriting the probability function in a suitable way for further analysis. In the following when we consider $(\varphi_{\mathbf{f}}(S^i_{j\oplus}) = S^i_{j+1})$ for some $\nabla\text{-c}$ we leave implicit that $S^i_{j\oplus}, S^i_{j+1} \in \nabla\text{-c}$. We have that

$$\forall i \in [q] : \text{SpGen}(\mathbf{M}^i) = \mathbf{Z}^i \Leftrightarrow \forall i \in [q] : \bigvee_{\nabla\text{-}c \in \nabla\text{-}C(\mathbf{M},\mathbf{Z})} \left(\varphi_{\mathbf{f}}(S^i_{1\oplus}) = S^i_2\right)$$

$$\wedge \left(\varphi_{\mathbf{f}}(S^i_{2\oplus}) = S^i_3\right) \wedge \cdots \wedge \left(\varphi_{\mathbf{f}}(S^i_{(k_i-1)\oplus}) = S^i_{k_i}\right) \tag{24}$$

$$\Leftrightarrow \bigvee_{\nabla\text{-}c \in \nabla\text{-}C(\mathbf{M},\mathbf{Z})} \bigwedge_{i=1}^{q} \bigwedge_{j=1}^{k_i-1} \left(\varphi_{\mathbf{f}}(S^i_{j\oplus}) = S^i_{j+1}\right). \tag{25}$$

In the above equations we first include the intermediate states and then combine all evaluations of $\varphi_{\mathbf{f}}$. In the following we make use of the fact that the events we take the disjunction of are disjoint and the logical disjunction turns into a sum of the probability.

$$\mathop{\mathbb{P}}_{\varphi_{\mathbf{f}} \xleftarrow{\$} SS} \left[\forall i \in [q] : \text{SpGen}(\mathbf{M}^i) = \mathbf{Z}^i\right] = \mathbb{P}\left[\bigvee_{\nabla\text{-}c} \bigwedge_{i=1}^{q} \bigwedge_{j=1}^{k_i-1} \left(\varphi_{\mathbf{f}}(S^i_{j\oplus}) = S^i_{j+1}\right)\right]$$

$$= \sum_{\nabla\text{-}c \in \nabla\text{-}C(\mathbf{M},\mathbf{Z})} \mathbb{P}\left[\bigwedge_{i=1}^{q} \bigwedge_{j=1}^{k_i-1} \left(\varphi_{\mathbf{f}}(S^i_{j\oplus}) = S^i_{j+1}\right)\right]. \tag{26}$$

To further extract an expression involving the probability of a single $\left(\varphi_{\mathbf{f}}(S^i_{j\oplus}) = S^i_{j+1}\right)$ we use Bayes' rule. By a chain of conditions we want to arrive at a function we can evaluate in the end. At this point we want to choose a particular order of $\left(\varphi_{\mathbf{f}}(S^i_{j\oplus}) = S^i_{j+1}\right)$ events. Let us define the order $\prec$ as

$$(i,j) \prec (i',j') \Leftrightarrow (j < j') \vee (j = j' \wedge i < i'). \tag{27}$$

The above rule imposes an order that begins with the top-left corner of a ∇-c and proceeds downwards to the end of the column to continue from the second column from the left.

$$\mathbf{p}(|\mathcal{C}|^{-1}) = \sum_{\nabla\text{-}c \in \nabla\text{-}C(\mathbf{M},\mathbf{Z})} \mathbb{P}\left[\bigwedge_{i=1}^{q} \bigwedge_{j=1}^{k_i-1} \left(\varphi_{\mathbf{f}}(S^i_{j\oplus}) = S^i_{j+1}\right)\right]$$

$$= \sum_{\nabla\text{-}c} \mathbb{P}\left[\left(\varphi_{\mathbf{f}}(S^q_{(k_q-1)\oplus}) = S^q_{k_q}\right) \mid \bigwedge_{(i,j)\prec(q,k_q-1)} \left(\varphi_{\mathbf{f}}(S^i_{j\oplus}) = S^i_{j+1}\right)\right]$$

$$\cdot \mathbb{P}\left[\bigwedge_{(i,j)\prec(q,k_q-1)} \left(\varphi_{\mathbf{f}}(S^i_{j\oplus}) = S^i_{j+1}\right)\right]$$

$$= \sum_{\nabla\text{-}c \in \nabla\text{-}C(\mathbf{M},\mathbf{Z})} \prod_{(i,j)=(1,1)}^{(q,k_q-1)} \mathbb{P}\left[\left(\varphi_{\mathbf{f}}(S^i_{j\oplus}) = S^i_{j+1}\right) \mid \bigwedge_{(i',j')\prec(i,j)} \left(\varphi_{\mathbf{f}}(S^{i'}_{j'\oplus}) = S^{i'}_{j'+1}\right)\right]. \tag{28}$$

In the case there is no state $(q - 1, k_q - 1)$ we just take the next state preceding $(q, k_q - 1)$ in the order given by Eq. (27).

Up to this point we have performed some transformations of the event $\left(\forall i \in [q] : \text{SPGEN}_{\varphi_f}(\mathbf{M}^i, \ell_i) = \mathbf{Z}^i\right)$, but we did not address the issue of correctness. Is it correct to consider state values in evaluations of SPGEN instead of different φ_f—are we in fact discussing the probability over the random choice of the internal function? The answer to this question is "yes", that is because of the equivalence of every ∇-c with some set of φ_f. We can treat the input-output pairs for φ_f assigned in ∇-c as values in the function table of φ_f. By picking a single ∇-c we fix at most κ rows of this table. As we sample φ_f uniformly at random we are interested in the fraction of functions that are consistent with the input-output pairs $(\mathbf{M}, \mathbf{Z})$ among all functions. Note however, that we only care about κ evaluations of φ_f and all the details of those future evaluations are implicitly simplified in the fraction. This allows us to focus only on the part of the function table corresponding to those few evaluations and that is exactly ∇-c. The summing over nabla configurations ∇-c corresponds to different values of the function table that are still consistent with $(\mathbf{M}, \mathbf{Z})$.

The probability $\mathbb{P}\left[\left(\varphi_f(S_{j\oplus}^i) = S_{j+1}^i\right) \mid \bigwedge_{(i',j') \prec (i,j)} \left(\varphi_f(S_{j'\oplus}^{i'}) = S_{j'+1}^{i'}\right)\right]$ equals either $\frac{1}{2^r \cdot |C|}$ or 1 or 0. If the internal function is queried on a "fresh" input, it outputs any value with uniform probability. If on the other hand it is queried on the same input for the second time, it outputs the value it has output before with probability 1. One might think that the proof is finished, $\mathbf{p}(\lambda) = \sum_i \mathbf{w}_i(\lambda)$, where $\mathbf{w}_i$ are monomials in λ of degree up to $\kappa + q$. There is one problem with that reasoning, namely that the sum limits depend on the variable λ. Up until now we have shown that $\mathbf{p}(\lambda) = \sum_{i=1}^{\mathbf{v}(1/\lambda)} \mathbf{w}_i(\lambda)$, where $\mathbf{v}$ is another polynomial. Even for $\mathbf{v} = \text{id}$ (the identity function) the degree of $\mathbf{p}$ is different than the maximal degree of $\mathbf{w}_i$. This means that we have to analyze the expression derived in Eq. (28) in more detail. To this end, we add more structure to ∇-C$(\mathbf{M}, \mathbf{Z})$ which will make it easier to count the number of values that the intermediate states can assume, i.e. the number of nabla configurations ∇-c in ∇-C$(\mathbf{M}, \mathbf{Z})$.

5.2   Unique and Non-unique States

The goal of this section is to evaluate $\mathbb{P}\left[\left(\varphi_f(S_{j\oplus}^i) = S_{j+1}^i\right) \mid \bigwedge_{(i',j') \prec (i,j)} \left(\varphi_f(S_{j'\oplus}^{i'}) = S_{j'+1}^{i'}\right)\right]$ for any ∇-c and any $(\mathbf{M}, \mathbf{Z})$. We approach this problem by recognizing which states in a particular ∇-c are fed to φ_f once and which are repeated. We define an algorithm that includes the information about *uniqueness* of the intermediate states in ∇-c. The notion of uniqueness is derived relative to the events we condition on in Eq. (28), that is why we took special care of the order in which we use the chain rule.

In this section we introduce two algorithms PREP and FLAG-ASSIGN. The former is an auxiliary algorithm that prepares the array ∇-c for further analysis. The latter algorithm assigns flags to states in ∇-c. Flags signify if a state appears once or more in the array. We use an algorithmic definition to explicitly show every step of the procedure.

Algorithm 3 takes as input an array ∇-c and groups its elements according to the value input to φ_f. An important detail is the sorting rule among states with the same "$\oplus$"-state value; we use the order defined in Eq. 27. The output of Algorithm 3 $\mathrm{PREP}(\nabla$-c$)$ is a vector (1-dimensional matrix), to access its l-th element we write ∇-c$_l$.

Algorithm 3: PREP

    Input : ∇-c for $(\mathbf{M}, \mathbf{Z})$
    Output: $\widetilde{\nabla\text{-c}}$

1 $\widetilde{\nabla\text{-c}} := \nabla$-c, append three work spaces to each element of $\widetilde{\nabla\text{-c}}$
2 **foreach** $1 \leq i \leq q, 1 \leq j \leq k_i - 1$ **do**
3 $\left\lfloor \;\; \widetilde{\nabla\text{-c}}_j^i = (\nabla\text{-c}_j^i, \mathtt{index}, \oplus\text{-}\mathtt{state}, \mathtt{image}) := (\nabla\text{-c}_j^i, (i,j), S_{j\oplus}^i, S_{j+1}^i) \right.$

4 Sort $\widetilde{\nabla\text{-c}}$ primarily according to the third entry and secondarily according to the second entry (using the order defined in Equation (27)).
5 Output $\widetilde{\nabla\text{-c}}$

The main contribution of this subsection is Algorithm 4 which adds to each ∇-c information about the repetitions of the internal states. Running PREP groups the state values. The next step is to assign specific flags to states that are first (according to a specified rule) in each group. To each $S_{j\oplus}^i$ we will assign a flag, $\boxed{\mathrm{u}}$ for unique states, $\boxed{\mathrm{n}}$ for non-unique states, and $\boxed{\mathrm{f}}$ for states that appear twice or more in total but from our perspective it is their first appearance. The output of Algorithm 4 is $\mathrm{FLAG\text{-}ASSIGN}(\nabla$-c$) = \nabla$-cf ("nabla configuration with flags") and $\forall i,j \;:\; \nabla\text{-cf}_j^i = (^{\boxed{\mathrm{F}}}\nabla\text{-c}_j^i, S)$, where the first register is the whole state between evaluations together with the assigned flag of φ_f and S is the corresponding image. To refer to the l-th register of ∇-c$_j^i$ we write ∇-c$_j^i(l)$. Flag $\boxed{\mathrm{f}}$ is important when discussing the relative position of unique flags ($\boxed{\mathrm{u}}$ or $\boxed{\mathrm{f}}$) in the array of ∇-cf. In the end of this section and in the beginning of the next section we are not going to need this distinction but it will become important when analyzing the final probability expression.

Let us define a simple function acting on elements of arrays ∇-cf output by $\mathrm{FLAG\text{-}ASSIGN}$. $\mathrm{FLAG} : \{\boxed{\mathrm{u}}, \boxed{\mathrm{f}}, \boxed{\mathrm{n}}\} \times \{0,1\}^{2r} \times \mathcal{C} \to \{\boxed{\mathrm{u}}, \boxed{\mathrm{f}}, \boxed{\mathrm{n}}\}$,

$$\mathrm{FLAG}(\nabla\text{-cf}_j^i) = \mathrm{FLAG}\left(\begin{pmatrix} \bar{S}_j^i \; \boxed{\mathrm{F}} \; \bar{S}_{j\oplus}^i \\ \boxed{\mathrm{F}} \hat{S}_j^i \end{pmatrix}, S \right) := \boxed{\mathrm{F}}. \tag{29}$$

Algorithm 4: FLAG-ASSIGN

Input : ∇-c for $(\mathbf{M}, \mathbf{Z})$
Output: ∇-cf

1 ∇-cf $= \emptyset$
2 $\widehat{\nabla\text{-c}} := \text{PREP}(\nabla\text{-c})$
3 Set counter $l := 1$
4 **while** $l \leq |\widehat{\nabla\text{-c}}| = \kappa + q$ **do**
5 $\quad$ Set counter $i := 1$ // the number of states with the same value
6 $\quad$ **while** $\widehat{\nabla\text{-c}}_{l+i}(3) = \widehat{\nabla\text{-c}}_l(3)$ **do**
7 $\quad\quad \lfloor \; i := i+1$
8 $\quad$ **if** $i = 1$ **then**
9 $\quad\quad \left(\begin{smallmatrix} \bar{S} & \bar{S}_{\oplus} \\ & \hat{S} \end{smallmatrix}\right) := \widehat{\nabla\text{-c}}_l(1)$, append $\left(\left(\begin{smallmatrix} \bar{S} & \boxed{\text{u}}\bar{S}_{\oplus} \\ & \boxed{\text{u}}\hat{S} \end{smallmatrix}\right), \widehat{\nabla\text{-c}}_l(2), \widehat{\nabla\text{-c}}_l(4)\right)$ to ∇-cf
$\quad\quad$ //
$\quad\quad\quad\quad$ // (state with the same value and a flag, indices, image)
10 $\quad\quad \lfloor \; (i', j') := \widehat{\nabla\text{-c}}_l(2)$
11 $\quad$ **if** $i > 1$ **then**
12 $\quad\quad \left(\begin{smallmatrix} \bar{S} & \bar{S}_{\oplus} \\ & \hat{S} \end{smallmatrix}\right) := \widehat{\nabla\text{-c}}_l(1)$, append $\left(\left(\begin{smallmatrix} \bar{S} & \boxed{\text{f}}\bar{S}_{\oplus} \\ & \boxed{\text{f}}\hat{S} \end{smallmatrix}\right), \widehat{\nabla\text{-c}}_l(2), \widehat{\nabla\text{-c}}_l(4)\right)$ to ∇-cf
13 $\quad\quad$ **for** $j = 1, 2, \ldots, i-1$ **do**
14 $\quad\quad\quad \left(\begin{smallmatrix} \bar{S} & \bar{S}_{\oplus} \\ & \hat{S} \end{smallmatrix}\right) := \widehat{\nabla\text{-c}}_l(1)$, append $\left(\left(\begin{smallmatrix} \bar{S} & \boxed{\text{n}}\bar{S}_{\oplus} \\ & \boxed{\text{n}}\hat{S} \end{smallmatrix}\right), \widehat{\nabla\text{-c}}_l(2), \widehat{\nabla\text{-c}}_l(4)\right)$ to
$\quad\quad\quad \lfloor \; \nabla$-cf
15 $\quad \lfloor \; l := l + i$
16 Make a 2-dimensional array out of ∇-cf according to the second entry in a
$\quad$ standard left-to-right order $((i, j) \prec_{\text{l-r}} (i', j') \Leftrightarrow (i < i') \vee (i = i' \wedge j < j'))$,
$\quad$ delete the second entry of ∇-cf   // ∇-cf^i_j =(state with a flag, image)
17 Output ∇-cf

Transition probabilities in Eq. (28) depend on the flags we assigned to states in ∇-c. We have that

$$\text{FLAG}(\nabla\text{-cf}^i_j) \in \{\boxed{\text{u}}, \boxed{\text{f}}\} \Rightarrow \mathbb{P}\left[\varphi_{\mathbf{f}}(\boxed{\text{u}\vee\text{f}}S^i_{j\oplus}) = S \mid \bigwedge_{(i',j')\prec(i,j)} \left(\varphi_{\mathbf{f}}(S^{i'}_{j'\oplus}) = S^{i'}_{j'+1}\right)\right]$$

$$= \frac{1}{2^r \cdot |\mathcal{C}|},$$

$$\text{FLAG}(\nabla\text{-cf}^i_j) = \boxed{\text{n}} \Rightarrow \mathbb{P}\left[\varphi_{\mathbf{f}}(\boxed{\text{n}}S^i_{j\oplus}) = S \mid \bigwedge_{(i',j')\prec(i,j)} \left(\varphi_{\mathbf{f}}(S^{i'}_{j'\oplus}) = S^{i'}_{j'+1}\right)\right]$$

$$= \begin{cases} 1 & \text{if } S = \nabla\text{-cf}^i_j(2) \\ 0 & \text{otherwise} \end{cases}.$$

$$(30)$$

5.3 Cardinality of ∇-C$(\mathbf{M}, \mathbf{Z})$

In this section we evaluate the number of intermediate states that give $\left(\forall i \in [q] : \text{SPGEN}_{\varphi_f}(\mathbf{M}^i, \ell_i) = \mathbf{Z}^i\right)$. First we impose the constraint of φ_f being a function. Then we want to calculate the product of probabilities in Eq. (28). It depends on the number of unique states in ∇-c so we divide the set of possible states into subsets with the same number of states with the flag $\boxed{\text{u}}$ or $\boxed{\text{f}}$. The next steps involve further divisions of ∇-C$(\mathbf{M}, \mathbf{Z})$.

In the process of calculating the conditional probabilities in Eq. (28) we included in each state in ∇-c the image it should have under φ_f. The set ∇-C$(\mathbf{M}, \mathbf{Z})$ does however contain states that would violate the constraint of φ_f being a function. The first step to calculate the cardinality of ∇-C$(\mathbf{M}, \mathbf{Z})$ is to exclude ∇-c that do not fulfill this requirement. The set of states that should be taken into consideration is defined below, we denote this set by p-∇-CF$(\mathbf{M}, \mathbf{Z})$ (p emphasizes the fact that φ_f is a proper function).

Definition 15 (p-∇-CF$(\mathbf{M}, \mathbf{Z})$). *The set of nabla configurations ∇-c for $(\mathbf{M}, \mathbf{Z})$ with flags and a proper function φ_f is a set of arrays of size specified by* $(\mathbf{M}, \mathbf{Z})$. p-∇-CF$(\mathbf{M}, \mathbf{Z}) \subset \left(\left(\{ \boxed{\text{u}}, \boxed{\text{f}}, \boxed{\text{n}} \} \times \{0,1\}^{2r} \times \mathcal{C} \right) \times \left(\{0,1\}^r \times \mathcal{C} \right) \right)^{\kappa+q}$, *the set is defined in two steps, first we define the set of ∇-cf that are output by* FLAG-ASSIGN,

$$\nabla\text{-CF}(\mathbf{M}, \mathbf{Z}) := \{ \nabla\text{-c} : \exists\, \nabla\text{-c}_0 \in \nabla\text{-C}(\mathbf{M}, \mathbf{Z}), \nabla\text{-c} = \text{FLAG-ASSIGN}(\nabla\text{-c}_0) \}. \tag{31}$$

We define p-∇-CF$(\mathbf{M}, \mathbf{Z})$ *by the following constraints on* ∇-CF$(\mathbf{M}, \mathbf{Z})$:

$$\forall S_j^i \in \nabla\text{-cf}\ \forall j > 1 : S_j^i = \nabla\text{-cf}_{j-1}^i(2). \tag{32}$$

The formal definition reads

$$\mathsf{p}\text{-}\nabla\text{-CF}(\mathbf{M}, \mathbf{Z}) := \{ \nabla\text{-cf} \in \nabla\text{-CF}(\mathbf{M}, \mathbf{Z}) : \nabla\text{-cf fulfills constraints (32)} \}. \tag{33}$$

One may think about p-∇-CF$(\mathbf{M}, \mathbf{Z})$ as follows, first we consider ∇-c: an array of states. The collection of all those arrays—with the exception of those that do not fulfill constraints (22)—is denoted by ∇-C$(\mathbf{M}, \mathbf{Z})$. On each ∇-c $\in \nabla$-C$(\mathbf{M}, \mathbf{Z})$ we run the algorithm FLAG-ASSIGN, getting a collection of ∇-cf—denoted by ∇-CF$(\mathbf{M}, \mathbf{Z})$. Now we discard all those ∇-cf that do no fulfill constraints (32). The collection we are left with is denoted by p-∇-CF$(\mathbf{M}, \mathbf{Z})$. We have the following relations between sets:

$$\nabla\text{-CF}(\mathbf{M}, \mathbf{Z})(1) \overset{\text{omitting the flags}}{\simeq} \nabla\text{-C}(\mathbf{M}, \mathbf{Z}) \tag{34}$$

$$\mathsf{p}\text{-}\nabla\text{-CF}(\mathbf{M}, \mathbf{Z}) \subset \nabla\text{-CF}(\mathbf{M}, \mathbf{Z}). \tag{35}$$

Each p-∇-cf $\in \mathsf{p}$-∇-CF$(\mathbf{M}, \mathbf{Z})$ has some number of unique states: with flag $\boxed{\text{u}}$ or $\boxed{\text{f}}$. Let us denote this number by $\bar{u}$. Equation (30) implies that no matter in what configurations the unique states are, the product of probabilities in

Eq. (28) is the same. Hence the first division of p-∇-CF($\mathbf{M}, \mathbf{Z}$) is in terms of the total number of unique states. We denote the state with a fixed number $\bar{u}$ by p-∇-CF($\mathbf{M}, \mathbf{Z}, \bar{u}$), we have that

$$\text{p-}\nabla\text{-CF}(\mathbf{M}, \mathbf{Z}) = \bigcup_{\bar{u}=1}^{\kappa} \text{p-}\nabla\text{-CF}(\mathbf{M}, \mathbf{Z}, \bar{u}). \tag{36}$$

The product in Eq. (28) for p-∇-cf $\in$ p-∇-CF($\mathbf{M}, \mathbf{Z}, \bar{u}$) evaluates to

$$\prod_{(i,j)=(1,1)}^{(q,k_q-1)} \mathbb{P}\left[\left(\varphi_{\mathbf{f}}(S_{j\oplus}^i) = S_{j+1}^i\right) \mid \bigwedge_{(i',j')\prec(i,j)} \left(\varphi_{\mathbf{f}}(S_{j'\oplus}^{i'}) = S_{j'+1}^{i'}\right)\right] = \left(\frac{1}{2^r \cdot |\mathcal{C}|}\right)^{\bar{u}},$$
$$\tag{37}$$

where all states p-∇-cf are in p-∇-CF($\mathbf{M}, \mathbf{Z}, \bar{u}$).

We have to work a bit more to calculate the total number of states. The number of possibilities in which a single transition event can be realized depends both on the input and the output. For that reason we need to specify the configuration of flags in more detail, not just by the total number of unique states. Let us denote a transition event from a unique state to a unique state by $\left(\varphi_{\mathbf{f}}(\boxed{\mathbf{u} \vee \mathbf{f}} S_{\oplus}) = \boxed{\mathbf{u} \vee \mathbf{f}} S\right)$ and similarly for other flags. The flag of the output is defined by the XORed message block or the output block. Before we go into details of the analysis of the structure of p-∇-CF($\mathbf{M}, \mathbf{Z}$), we list the intuitive principles of counting the output states depending on the input and output states:

(a) $\left(\varphi_{\mathbf{f}}(\boxed{\mathbf{u} \vee \mathbf{f}} S_{\oplus}) = \boxed{\mathbf{u} \vee \mathbf{f}} S\right)$ —the only constraint is that the output cannot be the same as any on the previous unique states, the number of possible output values is at most $2^r \cdot |\mathcal{C}|$ or $|\mathcal{C}|$ and can be smaller by at most κ (the bound is $2^r \cdot |\mathcal{C}|$ if the transition is in the absorbing phase and $|\mathcal{C}|$ if it is in the squeezing phase),

(b) $\left(\varphi_{\mathbf{f}}(\boxed{\mathbf{u} \vee \mathbf{f}} S_{\oplus}) = \boxed{\mathbf{n}} S\right)$ —the output has to be in the set of outputs of states with the flag $\boxed{\mathbf{f}}$, the number of possible output values is at most κ,

(c) $\left(\varphi_{\mathbf{f}}(\boxed{\mathbf{n}} S_{\oplus}) = \boxed{\mathbf{u} \vee \mathbf{f} \vee \mathbf{n}} S\right)$ —the output is defined by the image memorized in the second entry of the state, the number of possible output values $= 1$.

The actual numbers in the above guidelines can be calculated precisely but they depend on the actual case we deal with.

To properly treat the transition events we need to keep track of not only the total number of unique states but also the number of truly unique $\boxed{\mathbf{u}}$ states. We denote the latter by u and the set with those numbers fixed by p-∇-CF($\mathbf{M}, \mathbf{Z}, \bar{u}, u$). In the above paragraph we also noticed that we should include in our considerations the number of unique states in different phases of SpGen. The number of states with the flag $\boxed{\mathbf{u}}$ in the absorbing phase is denoted by u_{abs}. Note that we are addressing all q absorbing phases so we take into account flags of all states with indices $(i, j) \in$

$\{(i', j')\}_{i' \in \{1,\ldots,q\}, j' \in \{1,\ldots,|\mathbf{M}^{i'}|_r\}}$. The number of states with the flag $\boxed{\text{u}}$ in the squeezing phase is denoted by u_{squ} and we take into account states with indices $(i, j) \in \{(i', j')\}_{i' \in \{1,\ldots,q\}, j' \in \{|\mathbf{M}^{i'}|_r+1,\ldots,k_{i'}-1\}}$. Similarly the total number of unique states is denoted by $\bar{u}_{\text{abs}}$ and $\bar{u}_{\text{squ}}$.

Next we fix particular placements of flags in the arrays $\mathsf{p}\text{-}\nabla\text{-cf} \in$ $\mathsf{p}\text{-}\nabla\text{-CF}(\mathbf{M}, \mathbf{Z}, \bar{u}_{\text{abs}}, u_{\text{abs}}, \bar{u}_{\text{squ}}, u_{\text{squ}})$. We no longer need to keep u and $\bar{u}$ explicit as $u = u_{\text{abs}} + u_{\text{squ}}$ and $\bar{u} = \bar{u}_{\text{abs}} + \bar{u}_{\text{squ}}$. Let us define a *placement* P for $(\mathbf{M}, \mathbf{Z})$ as an array of flags $\boxed{\text{F}} \in \{\boxed{\text{u}}, \boxed{\text{f}}, \boxed{\text{n}}\}$ with its dimensions determined by $(\mathbf{M}, \mathbf{Z})$ in the same way as for nabla configurations $\nabla\text{-c}$. The set of placements $\mathcal{P}(\mathbf{M}, \mathbf{Z}, \bar{u}_{\text{abs}}, u_{\text{abs}}, \bar{u}_{\text{squ}}, u_{\text{squ}})$ is defined as the set of all placements P encountered in elements of $\mathsf{p}\text{-}\nabla\text{-CF}(\mathbf{M}, \mathbf{Z}, \bar{u}_{\text{abs}}, u_{\text{abs}}, \bar{u}_{\text{squ}}, u_{\text{squ}})$. We are going to write $\textsc{Flag}(P_j^i)$ to determine the flag in the position (i, j) in placement P. For each P we are able to calculate the size of $\mathsf{p}\text{-}\nabla\text{-CF}(\mathbf{M}, \mathbf{Z}, P)$, we no longer add $\bar{u}_{\text{abs}}$ and other parameters as they are already included in P. Before we define the algorithm performing this calculation we need to bound the number of different placements.

Let us assume for a moment that $(\mathbf{M}, \mathbf{Z})$ restrains only the size of $\mathsf{p}\text{-}\nabla\text{-cf}$ and not the values of the states. If there were no constraints coming from the workings of $\textsc{Flag-Assign}$ then unique states would be distributed in all combinations of picking $\bar{u}_{\text{abs}}$ elements among states in absorbing phases. Additionally, we also want to take into account combinations of u_{abs} elements among the $\bar{u}_{\text{abs}}$ flags. Let us recapitulate: first we distribute $\bar{u}_{\text{abs}}$ flags (without specifying whether they are $\boxed{\text{u}}$ or $\boxed{\text{f}}$) and then assign them concrete values ($\boxed{\text{u}}$ or $\boxed{\text{f}}$). The total number of state-triples in the absorbing phases of $\mathsf{p}\text{-}\nabla\text{-cf}$ is $\mu := \sum_{i=1}^{q} |\mathbf{M}^i|_r$. The number of possibilities for the first step is $\binom{\mu}{\bar{u}_{\text{abs}}}$ and the second step is $\binom{\bar{u}_{\text{abs}}}{u_{\text{abs}}}$. The total number of possibilities of placing the unique flags in absorbing phases is $\binom{\mu}{\bar{u}_{\text{abs}}} \cdot \binom{\bar{u}_{\text{abs}}}{u_{\text{abs}}}$.

The problem of distributing unique states in squeezing phases is the same as in absorbing phases. The total number of state-triples with flags in the squeezing phases of $\mathsf{p}\text{-}\nabla\text{-cf}$ is $\zeta := \sum_{i=1}^{q}(|\mathbf{Z}^i|_r - 1)$. The number of placements is $\binom{\zeta}{\bar{u}_{\text{squ}}}$. We also need to multiply this result by the number of placements of states with flag $\boxed{\text{u}}$ among all unique states.

The two calculations above bring us to the conclusion that our analysis is sufficiently detailed; we have identified and taken into account all parts of $(\forall i \in [q] : \textsc{SpGen}_{\varphi_f}(\mathbf{M}^i, \ell_i) = \mathbf{Z}^i)$ that depend on $|\mathcal{C}|$. In summary we divided $\mathsf{p}\text{-}\nabla\text{-CF}(\mathbf{M}, \mathbf{Z})$ into a small (relatively to $|\mathcal{C}|$) number of subsets whose size we can actually calculate. The last result assures that even though we do not formally describe the structure of the last level of division of $\mathsf{p}\text{-}\nabla\text{-CF}(\mathbf{M}, \mathbf{Z})$, the number of possibilities of next divisions does not depend on $|\mathcal{C}|$. So we have that

$$|\mathcal{P}(\mathbf{M}, \mathbf{Z}, \bar{u}_{\text{abs}}, u_{\text{abs}}, \bar{u}_{\text{squ}}, u_{\text{squ}})| \leq \binom{\mu}{\bar{u}_{\text{abs}}} \binom{\bar{u}_{\text{abs}}}{u_{\text{abs}}} \cdot \binom{\zeta}{\bar{u}_{\text{squ}}} \binom{\bar{u}_{\text{squ}}}{u_{\text{squ}}} \qquad (38)$$

$$\leq \binom{\mu}{\mu/2}^2 \binom{\zeta}{\zeta/2}^2 \leq \binom{\kappa}{\kappa/2}^4 \leq \kappa^{4\kappa}. \qquad (39)$$

Our assumption is that κ is fixed so the number of placements is independent of $|\mathcal{C}|$. Note that we can compute $|\mathcal{P}(\mathbf{M}, \mathbf{Z}, \bar{u}_{\text{abs}}, u_{\text{abs}}, \bar{u}_{\text{squ}}, u_{\text{squ}})|$ for fixed parameters and the above inequality just shows that irrespective of the exact value of the calculation the number of placements does not depend on $|\mathcal{C}|$ and is relatively small.

Let us define a function that helps us accommodate for the fact that some subsets of p-∇-CF$(\mathbf{M}, \mathbf{Z})$ are empty for some specific $(\mathbf{M}, \mathbf{Z})$:

$$\delta(\mathbf{M}, \mathbf{Z}, P) := \begin{cases} 1 \text{ if } \text{p-}\nabla\text{-CF}(\mathbf{M}, \mathbf{Z}, P) \neq \emptyset \\ 0 \text{ otherwise} \end{cases}. \qquad (40)$$

In what follows we leave out the input to δ, as it can be inferred from context. For example δ evaluates to 0 if the input includes $\bar{u}_{\text{abs}} = \mu$ and the first block of the input messages is not always different.

The last division we make is done be characterizing uniqueness of outer and inner parts of states. This step is done to get the precise and correct result, but the high level explanation and an approximation of the output of CALC is already captured by principle (a). We have not captured this situation in detail in our example proof because it becomes important only if longer outputs are present. Here we explain the procedure of including the necessary details.

Main detail we add is assigning flags to outer and inner parts of states individually. We introduce those flags only now to keep the proof as clear as possible; technically to include the additional flags we modify the algorithm FLAG-ASSIGN in such a way that it runs over a configuration ∇-c two additional times but acting solely on outer states and inner states. Those two additional runs assign the same flags as the original one but corresponding to just one of the parts of $S_\oplus$ states. Rest of the discussion after applying FLAG-ASSIGN is unchanged and depends only on flags of the full states.

When discussing placements note that a unique state ($\boxed{u}$ or $\boxed{f}$) can consist of a unique outer state and a unique inner state but also out of a non-unique outer state and a unique inner state or vice versa. After we assign a particular placement $P \in \mathcal{P}(\mathbf{M}, \mathbf{Z}, \bar{u}_{\text{abs}}, u_{\text{abs}}, \bar{u}_{\text{squ}}, u_{\text{squ}})$ there are still many possibilities of arranging outer and inner states flags. There are exactly three possibilities every

unique state can be arranged in: $\begin{pmatrix} \boxed{u} \vee \boxed{f} \\ \boxed{u} \vee \boxed{f} \end{pmatrix}$, $\begin{pmatrix} \boxed{u} \vee \boxed{f} \\ \boxed{n} \end{pmatrix}$, and $\begin{pmatrix} \boxed{n} \\ \boxed{u} \vee \boxed{f} \end{pmatrix}$, where we

symbolize a state $S_\oplus$ by a column vector with flags assigned to its outer state in the first row and inner state in the second row. Hence, for every placement P we have $3^{\bar{u}_{\text{abs}} + \bar{u}_{\text{squ}}}$ placements of the outer and inner states flags. We are going to mark the fact that we have included those additional details into placements by adding a star to the set of placements $P \in \mathcal{P}^*(\mathbf{M}, \mathbf{Z}, \bar{u}_{\mathrm{abs}}, u_{\mathrm{abs}}, \bar{u}_{\mathrm{squ}}, u_{\mathrm{squ}})$. We have that

$$|\mathcal{P}^*(\mathbf{M}, \mathbf{Z}, \bar{u}_{\mathrm{abs}}, u_{\mathrm{abs}}, \bar{u}_{\mathrm{squ}}, u_{\mathrm{squ}})| \leq \kappa^{4\kappa} \cdot 3^{\bar{u}_{\mathrm{abs}} + \bar{u}_{\mathrm{squ}}}. \tag{41}$$

We also write $\mathrm{FLAG}(\bar{P}_j^i)$ and $\mathrm{FLAG}(\hat{P}_j^i)$ to access the flag of the outer and inner part of P_j^i respectively.

Algorithm 5 below shows the algorithm CALC that outputs the number of different p-∇-cf $\in$ p-∇-CF$(\mathbf{M}, \mathbf{Z}, \bar{u}_{\mathrm{abs}}, u_{\mathrm{abs}}, \bar{u}_{\mathrm{squ}}, u_{\mathrm{squ}})$ for some given placement $P \in \mathcal{P}^*(\mathbf{M}, \mathbf{Z}, \bar{u}_{\mathrm{abs}}, u_{\mathrm{abs}}, \bar{u}_{\mathrm{squ}}, u_{\mathrm{squ}})$. To capture the fact that the number of possible values a unique state can have depends on the number of unique states with already assigned values we define the following sets. For unique outer states we have

$$\bar{\mathrm{U}}_{\mathrm{prev}}(P, i, j) := \left| \left\{ P_{j'}^{i'} : (i', j') \prec (i, j) \wedge \mathrm{FLAG}(\bar{P}_{j'}^{i'}) \in \{\mathbf{u}, \mathbf{f}\} \right\} \right|, \tag{42}$$

$$\bar{\mathrm{U}}_{\mathrm{prev}}^{\mathbf{f}}(P, i, j) := \left| \left\{ P_{j'}^{i'} : (i', j') \prec (i, j) \wedge \mathrm{FLAG}(\bar{P}_{j'}^{i'}) = \mathbf{f} \right\} \right|. \tag{43}$$

For unique inner states we have

$$\hat{\mathrm{U}}_{\mathrm{prev}}(P, i, j) := \left| \left\{ P_{j'}^{i'} : (i', j') \prec (i, j) \wedge \mathrm{FLAG}(\hat{P}_{j'}^{i'}) \in \{\mathbf{u}, \mathbf{f}\} \right\} \right|, \tag{44}$$

$$\hat{\mathrm{U}}_{\mathrm{prev}}^{\mathbf{f}}(P, i, j) := \left| \left\{ P_{j'}^{i'} : (i', j') \prec (i, j) \wedge \mathrm{FLAG}(\hat{P}_{j'}^{i'}) = \mathbf{f} \right\} \right|. \tag{45}$$

Note that all of the above quantities (42, 43, 44, 45) are bounded by

$$1 \leq \bar{\mathrm{U}}_{\mathrm{prev}}(P, i, j), \hat{\mathrm{U}}_{\mathrm{prev}}(P, i, j), \bar{\mathrm{U}}_{\mathrm{prev}}^{\mathbf{f}}(P, i, j), \hat{\mathrm{U}}_{\mathrm{prev}}^{\mathbf{f}}(P, i, j) \leq \bar{u}_{\mathrm{abs}} + \bar{u}_{\mathrm{squ}} \leq \kappa. \tag{46}$$

In the algorithm we also use N-POSSIBILITIES is the number of possibilities in which one can assign values to non-unique states in a nabla configuration. N-POSSIBILITIES is bounded by κ^κ. More details on that are provided in the full version [12].

Thanks to the additional details we get the precise form of the expression $\mathbf{p}$.

5.4 Final Expression

In the previous subsections we formalized algorithms that help us analyze the expression in Eq. (28). First we introduced FLAG-ASSIGN that analyzes ∇-c from the perspective of having the same input to $\varphi_{\mathbf{f}}$ multiple times. Then we defined CALC that counts the arrays of states that fulfill a given set of constraints, the number and arrangement of unique states. The final part of the proof of Lemma 9 is to use those algorithms to show that $\mathbf{p}(|\mathcal{C}|^{-1})$ is of the claimed form. We start by formally writing down the expression in terms of divisions of p-∇-CF$(\mathbf{M}, \mathbf{Z})$ we introduced and the outputs of CALC. Next we identify crucial elements of the sum that lead to the claim of the lemma, showing the maximal degree of $|\mathcal{C}|^{-1}$ in the expression $\mathbf{p}(\lambda)$.

Algorithm 5: CALC

Input : $P \in \mathcal{P}^*(\mathbf{M}, \mathbf{Z}, \bar{u}_{\text{abs}}, u_{\text{abs}}, \bar{u}_{\text{squ}}, u_{\text{squ}})$
Output: $\alpha \in \mathbb{N}$, cardinality of the set p-∇-CF$(\mathbf{M}, \mathbf{Z}, P)$

1   $\alpha := 1$
2   **for** $j = 1, \ldots, k_i - 2$, $i = 1, \ldots, q$ **do**
3   **if** $j < |\mathbf{M}^i|_r$ and FLAG$(P_j^i) \in \{\boxed{u}, \boxed{f}\}$ **then**   // Absorbing phases
4   **if** FLAG$(P_{j+1}^i) \in \{\boxed{u}, \boxed{f}\}$ **then** $// \left(\varphi_f(\boxed{u} \vee \boxed{f} S_\oplus) = \boxed{u} \vee \boxed{f} S \right)$
5   **if** FLAG$(\bar{P}_{j+1}^i) \in \{\boxed{u}, \boxed{f}\}$ and FLAG$(\hat{P}_{j+1}^i) \in \{\boxed{u}, \boxed{f}\}$ **then**
        $// \; P_{j+1}^i = \binom{\boxed{u} \vee \boxed{f}}{\boxed{u} \vee \boxed{f}}$
6         $\alpha = \alpha \cdot \left(2^r - \bar{U}_{\text{prev}}(P, i, j+1) \right) \cdot \left(|\mathcal{C}| - \hat{U}_{\text{prev}}(P, i, j+1) \right)$
7   **if** FLAG$(\bar{P}_{j+1}^i) \in \{\boxed{u}, \boxed{f}\}$ and FLAG$(\hat{P}_{j+1}^i) = \boxed{n}$ **then**
        $// \; P_{j+1}^i = \binom{\boxed{u} \vee \boxed{f}}{\boxed{n}}$
8         $\alpha = \alpha \cdot \left(2^r - \bar{U}_{\text{prev}}(P, i, j+1) \right) \cdot \hat{U}_{\text{prev}}^{\boxed{f}}(P, i, j+1)$
9   **if** FLAG$(\bar{P}_{j+1}^i) = \boxed{n}$ and FLAG$(\hat{P}_{j+1}^i) \in \{\boxed{u}, \boxed{f}\}$ **then**
        $// \; P_{j+1}^i = \binom{\boxed{n}}{\boxed{u} \vee \boxed{f}}$
10        $\alpha = \alpha \cdot \hat{U}_{\text{prev}}^{\boxed{f}}(P, i, j+1) \cdot \left(|\mathcal{C}| - \hat{U}_{\text{prev}}(P, i, j+1) \right)$

11   **if** $j \geq |\mathbf{M}^i|_r$ and FLAG$(P_j^i) \in \{\boxed{u}, \boxed{f}\}$ **then**   // Squeezing phases
12   **if** FLAG$(P_{j+1}^i) \in \{\boxed{u}, \boxed{f}\}$ **then** $// \left(\varphi_f(\boxed{u} \vee \boxed{f} S_\oplus) = \boxed{u} \vee \boxed{f} S \right)$
13   **if** FLAG$(\hat{P}_{j+1}^i) \in \{\boxed{u}, \boxed{f}\}$ **then** $// \; P_{j+1}^i \in \{ \binom{\boxed{u} \vee \boxed{f}}{\boxed{u} \vee \boxed{f}}, \binom{\boxed{n}}{\boxed{u} \vee \boxed{f}} \}$
14        $\alpha = \alpha \cdot \left(|\mathcal{C}| - \hat{U}_{\text{prev}}(P, i, j+1) \right)$
15   **if** FLAG$(\hat{P}_{j+1}^i) = \boxed{n}$ **then** $// \; P_{j+1}^i = \binom{\boxed{u} \vee \boxed{f}}{\boxed{n}}$
16        $\alpha = \alpha \cdot \hat{U}_{\text{prev}}^{\boxed{f}}(P, i, j+1)$

17   **for** $i = 1, \ldots, q$, $j = k_i - 1$ **do**
18   **if** FLAG$(P_j^i) \in \{\boxed{u}, \boxed{f}\}$ **then**
19       $\alpha = \alpha \cdot |\mathcal{C}| \cdot 2^{r|\mathbf{Z}^i|_r - \ell_i}$

20   $\alpha = \alpha \cdot \text{N-POSSIBILITIES}(\kappa - \bar{u}_{\text{abs}} - \bar{u}_{\text{squ}}, \bar{u}_{\text{abs}} + \bar{u}_{\text{squ}} - u_{\text{abs}} - u_{\text{squ}}, P)$
21   Output $\alpha \cdot \delta(\mathbf{M}, \mathbf{Z}, P)$

In the previous sections we showed that

$$\mathbf{p}(|\mathcal{C}|^{-1}) = \sum_{\nabla\text{-}c \in \nabla\text{-}C(\mathbf{M},\mathbf{Z})}$$

$$\prod_{(i,j)=(1,1)}^{(q,k_q-1)} \mathbb{P}\left[\left(\varphi_{\mathbf{f}}(S_{j\oplus}^i) = S_{j+1}^i\right) \middle| \bigwedge_{(i',j')\prec(i,j)} \left(\varphi_{\mathbf{f}}(S_{j'\oplus}^{i'}) = S_{j'+1}^{i'}\right)\right] \qquad (47)$$

$$= \underbrace{\sum_{\mathsf{p}\text{-}\nabla\text{-}cf \in \mathsf{p}\text{-}\nabla\text{-}CF(\mathbf{M},\mathbf{Z})}}_{\text{Eq. (49),(50)}}$$

$$\underbrace{\prod_{(i,j)=(1,1)}^{(q,k_q-1)} \mathbb{P}\left[\left(\varphi_{\mathbf{f}}(S_{j\oplus}^i) = S_{j+1}^i\right) \middle| \bigwedge_{(i',j')\prec(i,j)} \left(\varphi_{\mathbf{f}}(S_{j'\oplus}^{i'}) = S_{j'+1}^{i'}\right)\right]}_{\text{Eq. (37)}}, \qquad (48)$$

where the second equality comes from the fact that constraints (32) exclude those ∇-c that have probability 0. Let us also make the division of p-∇-CF($\mathbf{M}, \mathbf{Z}$) explicit

$$\mathsf{p}\text{-}\nabla\text{-}\mathsf{CF}(\mathbf{M}, \mathbf{Z}) =$$

$$\bigcup_{\bar{u}_{\mathrm{abs}}=1}^{\mu} \bigcup_{u_{\mathrm{abs}}=0}^{\mu} \bigcup_{\bar{u}_{\mathrm{squ}}=0}^{\varsigma} \bigcup_{u_{\mathrm{squ}}=0}^{\varsigma} \quad \bigcup_{P \in \mathcal{P}^*(\mathbf{M},\mathbf{Z},\bar{u}_{\mathrm{abs}},u_{\mathrm{abs}},\bar{u}_{\mathrm{squ}},u_{\mathrm{squ}})} \mathsf{p}\text{-}\nabla\text{-}\mathsf{CF}(\mathbf{M}, \mathbf{Z}, P). \qquad (49)$$

Next we use Eq. (37) and the fact that for $P \in \mathcal{P}(\mathbf{M}, \mathbf{Z}, \bar{u}_{\mathrm{abs}}, u_{\mathrm{abs}}, \bar{u}_{\mathrm{squ}}, u_{\mathrm{squ}})$ we have

$$|\mathsf{p}\text{-}\nabla\text{-}\mathsf{CF}(\mathbf{M}, \mathbf{Z}, P)| = \mathrm{CALC}(P) \qquad (50)$$

to expand $\mathbf{p}(|\mathcal{C}|^{-1})$ to

$$\mathbf{p}(|\mathcal{C}|^{-1}) = \sum_{\bar{u}_{\mathrm{abs}},u_{\mathrm{abs}},\bar{u}_{\mathrm{squ}},u_{\mathrm{squ}},P} \mathrm{CALC}(P) \left(\frac{1}{2^r \cdot |\mathcal{C}|}\right)^{\bar{u}_{\mathrm{abs}}+\bar{u}_{\mathrm{squ}}} \qquad (51)$$

To calculate a_0 and the maximal degree of $\mathbf{p}$ let us focus on $\mathbf{p}(|\mathcal{C}|^{-1})$ for all unique (with the flag $\boxed{\mathsf{u}}$ in both outer and inner part) sates:

$$\prod_{i=1}^{q} \prod_{j=1}^{|\mathbf{M}^i|_r-1} (2^r - jq - i)(|\mathcal{C}| - jq - i)$$

$$\prod_{i=1}^{q} \prod_{j=|\mathbf{M}^i|_r}^{k_i-2} (|\mathcal{C}| - jq - i) \prod_{i=1}^{q} \left(2^{r|\mathbf{Z}^i|_r-\ell_i}|\mathcal{C}|\right)(2^r|\mathcal{C}|)^{-\kappa}. \qquad (52)$$

In the above expression if we take all messages of maximal length m and outputs of maximal length z we get a polynomial of degree $\kappa - q = q(m + z - 2)$. This is necessarily the maximal degree as every evaluation of φ_f increases the degree by one, except for the last but this cannot be changed, the last column does not matter at all for the overall probability. Hence the maximal degree of $\mathbf{p}$ is as claimed

$$\eta := q(m + z - 2). \tag{53}$$

In the case all states are unique, i.e. $|\mathcal{C}| \to \infty$, $\mathbf{p}(|\mathcal{C}|^{-1})$ evaluates to $\sim 2^{-\sum_i \ell_i}$. This expression corresponds to the output probability of a random oracle, exactly how expected of a sponge with all different inner states. If we only take the terms $2^r|\mathcal{C}|$ and $|\mathcal{C}|$ and the probability we arrive at $2^{-\sum_i \ell_i}$. This result is only one of the terms in a_0 but note that all other terms will correspond to different placements and will include $\delta(\mathbf{M}, \mathbf{Z}, P)$ with different inputs, being non-zero for different $(\mathbf{M}, \mathbf{Z})$. Hence for any given input-output pairs $(\mathbf{M}, \mathbf{Z})$ for $|\mathcal{C}| \to \infty$ the probability function approaches the probability of a random oracle outputting $\mathbf{Z}$ on $\mathbf{M}$. To get the power of $|\mathcal{C}|$ equal to zero we need to have the same number of unique states (probability terms decreasing the degree by one) as pairs of unique states (increasing the degree by one). Configurations that satisfy those conditions come from inputs and outputs that are either fully unique or exactly the same as at least one other input or output, respectively. One special case occurs if the output is just a single block long then messages can differ by just the last block and still have different outputs.

In our proof we have focused on the case of φ_f being a random transformation. In Sect. 6 we provide the details that should be considered to show that Theorem 8 holds also for random permutations.

6   Internal Permutations

In this section we prove the main result but for the internal function φ_f being a random permutation. We use Zhandry's PRF/PRP switching lemma from [25]. In the full version of the paper [12], we also give a direct proof, resulting in a slightly worse bound.

Theorem 16. SPGEN$_{\varphi_f}$ *for a random permutation φ_f is quantumly indistinguishable from a random oracle. More concretely, for all quantum algorithms A making at most q quantum queries to* SPGEN, *such that the input length is at most $m \cdot r$ bits long and the output length is at most $z \cdot r$ bits long,*

$$\left| \Pr_{\varphi_f \xleftarrow{\$} \mathcal{T}(S)} \left[A^{|\mathrm{SPGEN}_{\varphi_f}\rangle}(.) = 1 \right] - \Pr_{h \leftarrow \Re} \left[A^{|h\rangle}(.) = 1 \right] \right| < \frac{\pi^2}{3} \eta^3 |\mathcal{C}|^{-1}, \tag{54}$$

where the set of permutations is denoted by $\mathcal{T}(S) := \{\varphi_f : S \to S \mid \varphi_f \text{ is a bijection}\}$. The domain is defined as $S = \{0,1\}^r \times \mathcal{C}$ for some non-empty finite set $\mathcal{C}$.

Proof. It was proven in [25] that a random permutation can be distinguished from a random function with probability at most $\pi^2 q^2/6|\mathcal{C}|$ for any adversary making at most q quantum queries. We can use this result in a reduction from distinguishing SPGEN using a random permutation from SPGEN using a random function to distinguishing of a random permutation from a random function. Using this result together with Theorem 8 gives us the resulting bound as follows

$$\left| \Pr_{\varphi_f \xleftarrow{\$} T(\mathcal{S})} \left[A^{|\text{SPGEN}_{\varphi_f}\rangle}(.) = 1 \right] - \Pr_{h \leftarrow \Re} \left[A^{|h\rangle}(.) = 1 \right] \right|$$

$$\leq \left| \Pr_{\varphi_f \xleftarrow{\$} T(\mathcal{S})} \left[A^{|\text{SPGEN}_{\varphi_f}\rangle}(.) = 1 \right] - \Pr_{\varphi_f \xleftarrow{\$} \mathcal{S}^{\mathcal{S}}} \left[A^{|\text{SPGEN}_{\varphi_f}\rangle}(.) = 1 \right] \right| \quad (55)$$

$$+ \left| \Pr_{\varphi_f \xleftarrow{\$} \mathcal{S}^{\mathcal{S}}} \left[A^{|\text{SPGEN}_{\varphi_f}\rangle}(.) = 1 \right] - \Pr_{h \leftarrow \Re} \left[A^{|h\rangle}(.) = 1 \right] \right|$$

$$\leq \left| \Pr_{\varphi_f \xleftarrow{\$} T(\mathcal{S})} \left[B^{|\varphi_f\rangle}(.) = 1 \right] - \Pr_{\phi \xleftarrow{\$} \mathcal{S}^{\mathcal{S}}} \left[B^{|\varphi_f\rangle}(.) = 1 \right] \right| + \frac{\pi^2}{6} \eta^3 |\mathcal{C}|^{-1} \quad (56)$$

$$\leq \frac{\pi^2}{3} \eta^3 |\mathcal{C}|^{-1}. \quad (57)$$

$\square$

7 Open Question

One of the most desirable security notions for hash functions is indifferentiability from a random oracle which is defined with respect to a possible simulator that fools a distinguisher into believing that it interacts with the internal function instead of a simulation of it. Proving indifferentiability is more challenging than indistinguishability. It is not clear whether the natural translation of the classical notion of indidfferentiability to the quantum setting is achievable. Only recently, two articles [9,27] opened the discussion, but so far, the results remain inconclusive.

In our work, we provide a quantum security guarantee more suitable for keyed primitives where an attacker does not have access to the internal building block. On the one hand, we increase the trust that hash functions based on the sponge construction are quantum safe and on the other hand, we formally prove that it is a quantum secure pseudorandom function when used with a keyed internal function—like it is used in the hash-based signatures scheme SPHINCS+ [23] in the instantiation using the Haraka hash function [15].

Acknowledgments. The authors would like to thank Dominique Unruh and Leon Groot Bruiderink for helpful discussions. CS and JC are supported by a NWO VIDI grant (Project No. 639.022.519).

324   J. Czajkowski et al.

References

1. Andreeva, E., Daemen, J., Mennink, B., Van Assche, G.: Security of keyed sponge constructions using a modular proof approach. In: Leander, G. (ed.) FSE 2015. LNCS, vol. 9054, pp. 364–384. Springer, Heidelberg (2015). https://doi.org/10.1007/978-3-662-48116-5_18
2. Bertoni, G., Daemen, J., Peeters, M., van Assche, G.: Sponge functions. In: Ecrypt Hash Workshop, May 2007. http://sponge.noekeon.org/SpongeFunctions.pdf
3. Bertoni, G., Daemen, J., Peeters, M., Van Assche, G.: On the indifferentiability of the sponge construction. In: Smart, N. (ed.) EUROCRYPT 2008. LNCS, vol. 4965, pp. 181–197. Springer, Heidelberg (2008). https://doi.org/10.1007/978-3-540-78967-3_11
4. Bertoni, G., Daemen, J., Peeters, M., Van Assche, G.: On the security of the keyed sponge construction. In: Symmetric Key Encryption Workshop, vol. 2011 (2011)
5. Bertoni, G., Daemen, J., Peeters, M., Van Assche, G.: Sponge-based pseudo-random number generators. In: Mangard, S., Standaert, F.-X. (eds.) CHES 2010. LNCS, vol. 6225, pp. 33–47. Springer, Heidelberg (2010). https://doi.org/10.1007/978-3-642-15031-9_3
6. Bertoni, G., Daemen, J., Peeters, M., Van Assche, G.: Duplexing the sponge: single-pass authenticated encryption and other applications. In: Miri, A., Vaudenay, S. (eds.) SAC 2011. LNCS, vol. 7118, pp. 320–337. Springer, Heidelberg (2012). https://doi.org/10.1007/978-3-642-28496-0_19
7. Bertoni, G., Daemen, J., Peeters, M., Van Assche, G.: Permutation-based encryption, authentication and authenticated encryption. In: Directions in Authenticated Ciphers (2012)
8. Boneh, D., Dagdelen, Ö., Fischlin, M., Lehmann, A., Schaffner, C., Zhandry, M.: Random oracles in a quantum world. In: Lee, D.H., Wang, X. (eds.) ASIACRYPT 2011. LNCS, vol. 7073, pp. 41–69. Springer, Heidelberg (2011). https://doi.org/10.1007/978-3-642-25385-0_3
9. Carstens, T.V., Ebrahimi, E., Tabia, G.N., Unruh, D.: On quantum indifferentiability. Technical report Cryptology ePrint Archive, Report 2018/257 (2018). https://eprint.iacr.org/2018/257
10. Chang, D.H., Dworkin, M.J., Hong, S., Kelsey, J.M., Nandi, M.: A keyed sponge construction with pseudorandomness in the standard model. In: The Third SHA-3 Candidate Conference, NIST (2012)
11. Czajkowski, J., Groot Bruinderink, L., Hülsing, A., Schaffner, C., Unruh, D.: Post-quantum security of the sponge construction. In: Lange, T., Steinwandt, R. (eds.) PQCrypto 2018. LNCS, vol. 10786, pp. 185–204. Springer, Cham (2018). https://doi.org/10.1007/978-3-319-79063-3_9
12. Czajkowski, J., Hülsing, A., Schaffner, C.: Quantum in-distinguishability of random sponges. Cryptology ePrint Archive, Report 2019/069 (2019). https://eprint.iacr.org/2019/069
13. Gaži, P., Pietrzak, K., Tessaro, S.: The exact PRF security of truncation: tight bounds for keyed sponges and truncated CBC. In: Gennaro, R., Robshaw, M. (eds.) CRYPTO 2015. LNCS, vol. 9215, pp. 368–387. Springer, Heidelberg (2015). https://doi.org/10.1007/978-3-662-47989-6_18
14. Kaplan, M., Leurent, G., Leverrier, A., Naya-Plasencia, M.: Breaking symmetric cryptosystems using quantum period finding. In: Robshaw, M., Katz, J. (eds.) CRYPTO 2016. LNCS, vol. 9815, pp. 207–237. Springer, Heidelberg (2016). https://doi.org/10.1007/978-3-662-53008-5_8

15. Kölbl, S., Lauridsen, M.M., Mendel, F., Rechberger, C.: Haraka v2 – efficient short-input hashing for post-quantum applications. IACR Trans. Symmetric Cryptol. **2016**(2), 1–29 (2017). https://doi.org/10.13154/tosc.v2016.i2.1-29
16. Kuwakado, H., Morii, M.: Security on the quantumtype even-mansour cipher. In: 2012 International Symposium on Information Theory and its Applications (ISITA), pp. 312–316. IEEE (2012)
17. Mennink, B., Reyhanitabar, R., Vizár, D.: Security of full-state keyed sponge and duplex: applications to authenticated encryption. In: Iwata, T., Cheon, J.H. (eds.) ASIACRYPT 2015. LNCS, vol. 9453, pp. 465–489. Springer, Heidelberg (2015). https://doi.org/10.1007/978-3-662-48800-3_19
18. Mennink, B., Szepieniec, A.: XOR of PRPs in a quantum world. In: Lange, T., Takagi, T. (eds.) PQCrypto 2017. LNCS, vol. 10346, pp. 367–383. Springer, Cham (2017). https://doi.org/10.1007/978-3-319-59879-6_21
19. Nielsen, M.A., Chuang, I.L.: Quantum computation and quantum information. Cambridge University Press, Cambridge (2010). 10th anniversary
20. Rivest, R.L., Schuldt, J.C.N.: Spritz-a spongy RC4-like stream cipher and hash function (2014). Charles River Crypto Day, 24 October 2014
21. Santoli, T., Schaffner, C.: Using Simon's algorithm to attack symmetric-key cryptographic primitives. In: arXiv preprint arXiv:1603.07856 (2016)
22. Shor, P.W.: Algorithms for quantum computation: discrete logarithms and factoring. In: 1994 Proceedings of 35th Annual Symposium on Foundations of Computer Science, pp. 124–134. IEEE (1994)
23. Sphincs+ Team: SPHINCS+ (2017). https://sphincs.org/
24. Zhandry, M.: How to construct quantum random functions. In: FOCS 2013, pp. 679–687. IEEE Computer Society (2012). https://doi.org/10.1109/FOCS.2012.37
25. Zhandry, M.: A note on the quantum collision and set equality problems. Quantum Inf. Comput. **15**(7&8), 557–567 (2015)
26. Zhandry, M.: Secure identity-based encryption in the quantum random oracle model. Int. J. Quantum Inf. **13**(04), 1550014 (2015)
27. Zhandry, M.: How to record quantum queries, and applications to quantum indifferentiability. Technical report, Cryptology ePrint Archive, Report 2018/276 (2018). https://eprint.iacr.org/2018/276

Revisiting Post-quantum Fiat-Shamir

Qipeng Liu[1(✉)] and Mark Zhandry[2]

[1] Princeton University, Princeton, USA
qipengl@cs.princeton.edu
[2] Princeton University & NTT Research, Princeton, USA

Abstract. The Fiat-Shamir transformation is a useful approach to building non-interactive arguments (of knowledge) in the random oracle model. Unfortunately, existing proof techniques are incapable of proving the security of Fiat-Shamir in the *quantum* setting. The problem stems from (1) the difficulty of quantum rewinding, and (2) the inability of current techniques to adaptively program random oracles in the quantum setting. In this work, we show how to overcome the limitations above in many settings. In particular, we give mild conditions under which Fiat-Shamir is secure in the quantum setting. As an application, we show that existing lattice signatures based on Fiat-Shamir are secure without any modifications.

1 Introduction

The Fiat-Shamir transformation is an approach to remove interaction in a protocol by using a hash function, by setting one party's messages to be hashes of the communication transcript. The transformation has many important applications, from removing interaction from proofs to constructing efficient signatures.

With the growing threat of quantum computers, there is great need for so-called "post quantum" cryptosystems, those secure against quantum attack. In the case of signatures, the most efficient constructions [DKL+18] use the Fiat-Shamir transformation [FS87]. Fiat-Shamir is a general tool to remove interaction from interactive protocols using a hash function.

Classically, the security of the transform is proved in the *classical* random oracle model (ROM) [BR93, PS96]. Here, the hash function is replaced with a truly random function that can only be evaluated by query access. As argued by Boneh et al. [BDF+11], the correct way to model random oracles in the quantum setting is to allow *quantum* queries to the random oracle. While many techniques have been developed to prove security in the quantum ROM [BDF+11, Zha12, BZ13, Unr17, TU15, Unr15, KLS18, Zha18], to date the post-quantum security of general Fiat-Shamir remains unresolved.

In fact, there has been some compelling justification for this state of affiars. Dagdelen, Fischlin, and Gagliardoni [DFG13] demonstrate that there cannot be a reduction with certain natural features (discussed below) which capture many of the existing techniques. What's more, Ambainis, Rosmanis, and Unruh [ARU14]

© International Association for Cryptologic Research 2019
A. Boldyreva and D. Micciancio (Eds.): CRYPTO 2019, LNCS 11693, pp. 326–355, 2019.
https://doi.org/10.1007/978-3-030-26951-7_12

show that many classical results about Fiat-Shamir that rely on rewinding are simply false in the quantum setting. In particular, they show that special soundness is insufficient to prove the security of Fiat-Shamir in the quantum ROM.

As a result, authors have proposed various ways to strengthen the underlying protocol so that post-quantum Fiat-Shamir can be proved (e.g. [DFG13, Unr17, KLS18]) or use an alternative transformation altogether (e.g. [Unr15]). However, in all cases, this leads to a less efficient and less elegant scheme.

1.1 Summary of Results

In this work, we revisit Fiat-Shamir, showing that in many cases Fiat-Shamir can be successfully applied for post-quantum security without modifying the underlying protocols.

Our results come in two parts. The first set of results concerns the Fiat-Shamir transformation itself, resurrecting standard classical results in the quantum ROM:

- If the underlying protocol is an argument (of knowledge), then Fiat-Shamir gives an argument (of knowledge).
- If the underlying protocol is a secure identification scheme, then Fiat-Shamir gives a secure signature scheme.

These results do not require making any additional assumptions on the underlying protocol than what is needed classically (other than, of course, needing security to hold against quantum adversaries).

These results overcome the barrier of Dagdelen, Fischlin, and Gagliardoni [DFG13] by giving a proof that is outside the class of natural reductions they consider. On the other hand, the results side-step the rewinding barrier of Ambainis, Rosmanis, and Unruh [ARU14], as the rewinding barrier already applies to the security of the underlying protocol.

Our second set of results concerns overcoming the rewinding barrier of [ARU14]. Classically, 2-soundness/2-extractability[1] are often used to prove that a protocol is an argument/argument of knowledge. While [ARU14] show that in general these conditions are insufficient in the quantum setting, we show the following:

- We define a notion of *collapsing* for a protocol which is similar to the notion of collapsing for hash functions [Unr16b].
- Abstracting a result of Unruh [Unr16b], we show that the usual classical results carry over to the quantum setting, provided the protocol is collapsing. That is, 2-soundness plus collapsing implies an argument, and 2-extractability plus collapsing implies an argument of knowledge.
- Next, we give two weaker conditions, *either* of which are sufficient for a protocol to be collapsing. The first is that the protocol has an associated lossy function with certain properties. The second is that the protocol is *separable*, a new notion we define.

---

[1] 2-extractability is often called "special soundness" in the literature.

- Finally, we then show that the lattice-based protocol of Lyubashevsky [Lyu12] is separable under the LWE assumption. Piecing together with our other results, we demonstrate that Lyubashevsky's protocol is secure in the quantum random oracle model without any modifications. These results naturally extend to protocols built from this protocol, such as [DKL+18].

A key feature of our results is that they can be used as a black box without requiring the complicated details of quantum computing. In particular, the needed security properties are 2-soundness/2-extractability and associated lossy functions/separability. These properties are essentially classical in nature (except for having to hold with respect to quantum adversaries) and can be proved using classical proof techniques, and trivially porting them into the quantum setting. All of the quantum difficulties are hidden inside our proofs.

1.2   Technical Details

A Quantum ROM Fiat-Shamir Proof. Our first result is to prove the security of Fiat-Shamir in the quantum random oracle model, showing that Fiat-Shamir is an argument (of knowledge) assuming the original protocol is.

Fiat-Shamir operates on a sigma protocol, which is a three-message protocol with a public-coin verifier. The prover has some witness w for a statement x. In the first message, the prover sends a commitment a. Then the verifier chooses a random challenge c which it sends back. Finally, the prover comes up with a response r. The verifier then looks at the transcript (a, c, r), which it accepts or rejects. The protocol is an argument if no (computationally bounded) malicious prover can cause the verifier to output 1 in the case x is false. The protocol is an argument of knowledge if, moreover, from any computationally bounded prover, a valid witness w can be extracted.

Honest verifier zero knowledge means that it is possible to generate valid transcripts (a, c, r) without knowing a witness. Note that this generation procedure typically chooses a based on c and maybe r; as such a generation procedure does not allow one to break the soundness of the argument.

The Fiat-Shamir transformation, using a hash function H, simply replaces the verifier's challenge with $c = H(a)$. Thus the prover can generate the entire interaction for himself. The hope is that the hash function prevents a dishonest prover from using the zero knowledge property to generate the transcript, by forcing c to be determined after a. In fact, in the *classical* random oracle model, this idea can be turned into a proof, showing how to turn any adversary for Fiat-Shamir into an adversary for the original sigma protocol.

In the classical proof, the reduction simulates the random oracle on the fly, keeping track of the points the adversary queries and programming the random oracle to fresh random points with each query. It is straightforward to prove that if the adversary eventually outputs a valid argument $(a, c = H(a), r)$, then one of the random oracle queries must have been on a. If the reduction knew which query this was at the time of that query, it sends a as its commitment to the sigma protocol. When it receives c from the verifier, it programs $H(a) = c$ instead of choosing its own random value. Since the verifier chose c at random anyway, this is undetectable to the adversary. Finally, when the adversary outputs (a, c, r), the reduction simply sends r to the verifier, which will pass. Now, the reduction does not know which query will correspond to the adversary's output when the query is made, so the adversary simply guesses a query at random, and aborts if the guess turned out wrong. The resulting adversary still succeeds with non-negligible probability.

This proof strategy is problematic once we consider quantum queries to the random oracle. The classical on-the-fly simulation strategy of random oracles does not work once quantum queries are allowed. The reason is that the simulation strategy requires recording the adversary's queries; if the queries were quantum, the result is effectively a measurement of the adversary's query. Such a measurement is easily detectable. A mischievous adversary could test for such a measurement, and refuse to keep working if detected.

This is a universal problem in the quantum ROM; as such, the typical solution is to avoid on-the-fly simulation. Instead, the function is set once and for all to be a fixed function chosen from a careful distribution [BDF+11, Zha12, BZ13, Unr17, TU15, Unr15, KLS18]. The reduction then answers the queries with this function, without trying to record anything about the adversary's query. By designing the function to be indistinguishable from a truly random oracle, the adversary cannot tell that it was given a different oracle.

However, while such fixed functions can be made to work in a wide variety of settings, they seem incapable of proving the security of Fiat-Shamir. Indeed, an impossibility of this sort is formalized by [DFG13]. The issue is that a Fiat-Shamir proof needs to extract a from the adversary's queries and feed it into its own verifier. But such an extraction constitutes a detectable measurement. Even worse, it then needs to program the challenge c into the oracle, but this might be happening after many queries to the random oracle. Therefore, it seems crucial for a proof to adaptively program the random oracle.

Compressed Oracles. Toward resolution, we start with a very recent technique that allows for on-the-fly simulation of random oracles in the quantum setting: Zhandry's compressed oracles [Zha18].

Zhandry's key observation is that some sort of on-the-fly simulation analogous to the classical simulation is possible if care is taken to implement the oracle correctly. Concretely, Zhandry simulates the random oracle as a stateful oracle which stores a quantum superposition of databases D, where a database is just a list of input/output pairs (x, y). A database intuitively represents a partial specification of the oracle: if a pair (x, y) is in the database, it means the oracle on input x is set to y, whereas if there is no pair that begins with x, it means the oracle is un-specified at x. Since the oracle actually stores a superposition of databases, a point x can be in superposition of being specified and unspecified. Originally, the database starts out empty.

In the classical setting, on query x, the oracle would look up x in the database and add a pair (x, y) for a random y if x was not found. Afterward (since there is now guaranteed to be a pair (x, y)) it will output y.

In the quantum setting, something similar happens. The following description is slightly inaccurate, but gives the high-level idea. On query x, very roughly, if x is not found in the database, a pair (x, y) is added, where y is in *uniform superposition* over all possible y values. Recall that the query can be quantum, so this addition to the database is happening in superposition. Then once x is guaranteed to be specified, the query is answered (again in superposition).

Now, an important difference from the classical setting is this: in order to maintain perfect indistinguishability from a truly random oracle, a particular test is performed on the database after answering the query. This test determines whether the adversary maintains any knowledge of the oracle at input x. If not, the pair (x, y) is removed from the database.

The above description is informal and slightly inaccurate. But nonetheless by carrying out the operations correctly, Zhandry shows that this approach can be made to correctly simulate a random oracle.

For us, Zhandry's simulation gives a glimmer of hope. Indeed, we notice that the oracle is now recording information about which points the adversary is interested in. Therefore, the database has all the information we need to generate a. Unfortunately though, there is a problem: in order for the reduction to win against the verifier, it must produce a *classical* a. However, in order to produce a classical a, we must measure the adversary's database. But such a measurement will affect the state of the oracle, and can be detected by the adversary. Indeed, it is straightforward to devise adversaries that can catch such a measurement and refuse to keep running.

Our New Extraction Technique. First, we observe that when the adversary outputs (a, c, r), the first thing the verifier does is to check that $c = H(a)$. If the adversary succeeds, it means that the adversary knows about the value of H at a. But a lemma of Zhandry [Zha18] shows that in the compressed oracle simulation, the pair (a, c) must be in the oracle's database (whp). By the end of the experiment, a has been measured (since the adversary produces a classical output) which roughly has the effect of measuring a in the oracle's database. Since the oracle's database starts out empty, this must mean that (a, c) was added at some query. One may hope that this means it is possible to measure a random query to get a.

Unfortunately, things are not so straightforward. The problem is that a might not have been added to the database at a well-defined point in time. It could be that each of the adversary's queries is on a superposition that contains a, and only after making several queries does the adversary have enough information to determine $H(a)$.

Now, as a thought experiment, consider running the adversary, and after each query measuring the database in the compressed oracle. We will define the adversary's *history* as the vector of resulting databases $(D_1, \ldots, D_q)$. Suppose the adversary still was able to output (a, c, r) that passed verification. Then we know that $(a, c) \in D_q$, and so there must be some point i at which a first enters D_i. But this means the adversary actually queries on input a for query i. This means we could use the classical strategy for extracting a.

Unfortunately, measuring all the queries would of course destroy the adversary's state, making it potentially unlikely the adversary would still pass verification. The good news is that we can show the probability of passing verification is at least non-zero. Indeed, Boneh and Zhandry [BZ13] give a measurement lemma which says that if a measurement has T possibilities, it can only reduce the adversary's success probability by at most a multiplicative factor of T. Therefore, the adversary still passes with probability at least the reciprocal of the number of database histories. Of course, the number of histories is exponentially large, so this is not useful yet. We note that the measurement lemma is tight in general.

However, we can use this notion of a history to help us achieve an extraction technique with a higher success probability. For a history h, let $|\phi_h\rangle$ be the final state (where the queries were measured as above) of the algorithm conditioned on observing the history h. Recall that quantum states are complex vectors of unit norm. In contrast, $|\phi_h\rangle$ will not be normalized, but instead have norm whose square is equal to the probability of observing h.

Our key idea is to group histories in together, and apply a generalization of the measurement lemma to the groups of histories. We show that a polynomial number of groups of histories are possible, leading to a non-negligible chance of success.

In more detail, we observe that the adversary's final state, if we did not measure the history, is exactly $\sum_h |\phi_h\rangle$ where the sum is over all possible histories. This is similar to the classical case, where the adversary's probability distribution is the sum of the conditional probability distributions for each history, weighted by the probability of that history. The key difference is that in the quantum setting, the relation between states and probabilities distributions requires squaring the amplitudes.

Next, we partition the histories into a polynomial number of sets $S_1, \ldots, S_q$. Set S_i consists of all histories $(D_1, \ldots, D_q)$ for which:

- D_{i-1} does not contain a
- D_i through D_q all contain a

For the clarity of exposition, we assume that the adversary always outputs a successful tuple (a, c, r), meaning we know that a is in D_q. Therefore, D_q will contain a in all histories. As such, the sets S_i in fact do partition the space of all possible histories. In the more general case where the adversary may fail, we would include a set $S_\perp$ of histories where D_q does not contain q.

Now we consider the states $|\phi_{S_i}\rangle = \sum_{h \in S_i} |\phi_h\rangle$. We note that $\sum_i |\phi_{S_i}\rangle$ is exactly the adversary's final state, since the S_i form a partition. By generalizing the Boneh-Zhandry measurement lemma, we can show that the $|\phi_{S_i}\rangle$ must result in (a, c, r) which pass verification with non-negligible probability.

Therefore, our goal is to extract a from the adversary's query, and then hope that the resulting state is $|\phi_{S_i}\rangle$ for some i. First, we choose a random i. For that query, we measure two things:

- Whether that query resulted in a value being added to the database
- And if so, we measure that value to get a guess a' for a

If successful, this corresponds to the requirement that histories have D_{i-1} which did not contain a and D_i contained a. If unsuccessful, we abort. Then, for each subsequent query, we measure if a' is still in the database, corresponding to the requirement that $a \in D_j$ for all subsequent databases; if not we abort. At the end, we test that the value a' we measured happens to match the a in the adversary's output (a, c, r). If $a' = a$, the end result is exactly the state $|\phi_{S_i}\rangle$, since our measurements remove all histories except those in S_i.

We show that this procedure succeeds with non-negligible probability, and then by applying the generalized measurement lemma we get that (a, c, r) passes verification with non-negligible probability. The result is that we can actually extract the a at query time, and still have the adversary succeed in producing a valid (a, c, r), just as in the classical setting.

Our New Programming Technique. Unfortunately, the above is not quite sufficient for a reduction. After all, while we can now query the verifier on a, it is unclear what it should do with the response c. It could program $H(a) = c$ by adding the pair (a, c) to the database (recall that H was previously unprogrammed at a since $a \notin D_{i-1}$). However, this is different from what the compressed oracle would have done: the compressed oracle would have added a uniform superposition over c of (a, c) pairs.

In particular, the information the compressed oracle uses to determine if a pair should be removed is stored in the phase information of the output registers in the database. By inserting a classical value c into the output, there is no phase information for the compressed oracle to use. Actually, this will cause the compressed oracle to almost always decide to keep the value in the database, even if it should have been removed.

A natural solution is: in query i once we have extracted a, switch the oracle database for input a to be permanently "uncompressed". On all other inputs, the database will behave as before, but on the special input a, it will no longer run the check to remove a from the database.

Such a modification can indeed be made to Zhandry's compressed oracle, allowing for programming a random c. However, it does not quite work for us. Remember that our extraction technique above required testing whether a was in the database after query i. But this test needed to be applied to the original compressed oracle, not the new oracle which doesn't compress a. In particular, the new compressed oracle will always report that a is in the database. Roughly this means our extraction captures all histories where a was added to the database at query i, even those where it was subsequently removed and added again.

Let T_i be the set of histories of this form. Notice that the T_i's do not partition all histories: the multi-set obtained by unioning the T_i contains each history multiple times. In fact, the number of times each history is included is equal to the number of times a is added to the database in that history. Some histories will add a many times.

In order to overcome this issue, we need a way to partition the set of histories such that the set of histories for query i is independent of the history after the query. This corresponds to, after query i, no longer testing whether a is in the database. If we do not need such a test, we can switch the oracle at a to be uncompressed and then program a random c.

One thought is to reverse the sets S_i. That is, let S_i' be the set of histories where a is *not* in the history at any query up until i, and then is added at query i; we do not care after i if a is added or removed from the database. These S_i' certainly partition the set of all histories, but unfortunately they cannot be sampled efficiently. The problem is that a is not known until it is added to the database in query i; yet, sampling histories in S_i' requires knowing a at the very beginning in order to test for a's presence from the start.

Our solution is to try to combine the features of S_i and S_i' so that we do not need to know a at the beginning, but also do not need to test for a's presence at the end. Toward that end, we define sets $T_{i,j,k}$. A history is in set $T_{i,j,k}$ if:

- a is added to the database at query i
- a remains in the database until query j, at which point it is removed
- a remains absent from the database until query k, at which point it is added a second time.

These sets can be easily sampled: at query i, we measure to learn a guess a' for a. Then we keep testing to make sure that a' is in the database until query j, at which point we make sure that a' is removed. Then we keep testing that a' is absent until query k, when it is added back in. Once we get to query k, the database is now programmed at point a', and we will never need to check for the presence of a' in the database again. Therefore we can change the compressed oracle to be uncompressed at a', and simply program it's value to c. When the adversary finally outputs (a, c, r), we test if $a' = a$; if so, the adversary's state is exactly the collection of histories in $T_{i,j,k}$.

The problem, of course, is that these $T_{i,j,k}$ also do not partition the space of all histories. In fact, if a history adds a a total of ℓ times, it will appear in $\ell - 1$ histories. Therefore the multi-set obtained by unioning the $T_{i,j,k}$ contains each history equal to the number of times a is added, minus 1.

Our final idea is to observe that if we take the multiset derived from the T_i's, and *subtract* the multiset derived from the $T_{i,j,k}$'s, we will get every history exactly once. That means if we define $|\phi_T\rangle = \sum_{h \in T} |\phi_h\rangle$, we have that

$$|\phi\rangle = \left(\sum_i |\phi_{T_i}\rangle \right) - \left(\sum_{i,j,k} |\phi_{T_{i,j,k}}\rangle \right)$$

Analogous to the case of the S_i's this allows us to sample a $|\phi_{T_i}\rangle$ or $|\phi_{T_{i,j,k}}\rangle$—which let us extract a and program c—and then have the adversary give us a valid (a, c, r) with non-negligible probability. The reduction then simply sends r and convinces the verifier. The end result is any adversary for Fiat-Shamir can be turned into an adversary for the original interactive protocol, completing the proof of security.

How to Rewind an Argument. For our next set of results, we show how to rewind a sigma protocol to allow for proving that the protocol is an argument (of knowledge). We note that [ARU14] show that 2-soundness/2-extractability is insufficient. Therefore, we aim to identify some mild extra conditions that will allow for the proof to go through.

The difficulty in proving soundness comes from the difficulty of quantum rewinding, which was first observed by Watrous [Wat06]. In a classical rewinding proof, the adversary commits to a, gets a challenge c_1 from the verifier, and responds with r_1. Then, the adversary is rewound to just after a is produced. The adversary is then run on a different challenge c_2, which causes it to give a different response r_2. Then the tuple (a, c_1, r_1, c_2, r_2) either breaks 2-soundness, or in the case of 2-extractability can be used to generate a witness. 2-soundness/2-extractability are typically easy to prove using standard tools.

In the quantum setting, a problem arises. Namely, while the adversary is quantum, the r_1 it produces during the first run is classical. This means that r_1 must be measured. But this measurement in general cannot be undone. As such, it is in general impossible to rewind back to the first message to try again. [ARU14] formalizes this observation by showing (relative to an oracle) that there are schemes for which 2-soundness/2-extractability are not enough to prove security.

The natural solution, and the approach we take in this work, is to show that for some schemes rewinding is possible. Basically, in the absence of measurements quantum computation *is* reversible. Therefore we know that if r_1 is not measured, then the adversary can be rewound and it will succeed in producing r_2. What we need to show is that measuring r_1 does not significantly impact the probability that the adversary will successfully produce r_2.

Unruh [Unr12] shows that if a sigma protocol additionally satisfies the notion of *strict* soundness—meaning that for every a, c there is *unique* valid r—then rewinding is possible. The idea is that you can leave r_1 in superposition and not measure it. Then, just the fact that (a, c_1, r_1) passed verification means that the superposition over r_1 collapses to the unique valid r_1. Therefore, measuring r_1 has no additional affect over measuring whether verification succeeded. Of course, measuring whether verification succeeded will also affect the probability r_2 passes, but Unruh shows that the probability is not too low.

Collapsing Protocols. Unfortunately, strict soundness is undesirable in practice, as it leads to inefficient schemes. Instead, Unruh [Unr16b] shows that for a particular protocol built from an object known as a collapse-binding commitment, rewinding is possible even though there are multiple valid r. Collapse-binding commitments can in turn be built from a so-called a collapsing hash function.

We abstract Unruh's ideas, defining a general notion of *collapsing* for sigma protocols. Roughly, a collapsing sigma protocol is one where there may be many valid r's for a given (a, c), but the adversary cannot tell whether a superposition of valid r's is measured or not. This is exactly what Unruh's protocol guarantees, and is exactly what is needed to be able to rewind in the setting of many r's.

By following Unruh's techniques, we show that collapsing is a sufficient extra condition to get the classical results to carry though to the quantum setting.

But now we face another challenge: how do we construct a collapsing sigma protocol? We can look for techniques for building collapsing hash functions or commitments and see if they apply. However, the techniques are sparse. [Unr16b] only shows that a random oracle is collapsing, and a more recent work of Unruh's [Unr16a] gives a construction using lossy trapdoor functions (LTDFs). However, trying to embed a LTDF in the sigma protocol construction will result a less efficient scheme, which will be important for the application to signatures. In particular, Lyubashevsky's scheme is inherently lossy, and moving to a regime where there is an injective mode will significantly increase parameter sizes.

Associated Lossy Functionss. Our resolution is to devise a new technique for proving that a sigma protocol (or hash function) is collapsing. They key idea is that the protocol itself does not need to be lossy, just that there is an associated lossy function (not necessarily trapdoored) with a useful relationship to the protocol.

In more detail, an associated lossy function for a sigma protocol consists of two sampling procedures $\mathsf{Gen}_L, \mathsf{Gen}_I$. $\mathsf{Gen}_I(a, c)$ takes as input the first two messages of the protocol, and outputs a function f. It guarantees that over the space of valid r, f is injective. In contrast, $\mathsf{Gen}_L(a, c)$ samples a lossy mode f, which is guaranteed to be constant over the space of valid r. In either case, no guarantees are made on invalid r. Lastly, we require that for any a, c, the two modes are computationally indistinguishable (even if the attacker knows a, c).

Any scheme with an associated lossy function is collapsing. Indeed, given a, c and a superposition over valid r, sample a lossy mode f. Then measuring $f(r)$ has no effect on the state (since f is constant over the set of valid r). Then we switch f to an injective mode and still measure $f(r)$. By the computational indistinguishability of the modes, this change is undetectable. Finally, in the injective mode, $f(r)$ information-theoretically contains all information about r, so measuring $f(r)$ is equivalent to measuring r. This means we can measure r without detection.

Next, we observe that typical lattice-based sigma protocols have associated lossy functions. For example, Lyubashevsky's signature scheme [Lyu12] uses a sigma protocol where the set of valid responses r are short vectors such that $A \cdot r = u \bmod q$ where A is a short wide matrix that is part of the public key and u depends on a, c. We will define our associated lossy function to be the natural lossy function built from the Learning With Errors (LWE) problem [AKPW13]. A lossy mode f is sampled by choosing a tall skinny matrix C, a matrix E with short entries, and computing $B = C \cdot A + E \bmod q$. The function $f_B(r)$ is then $\lfloor B \cdot r \bmod q \rceil$, where $\lfloor \cdot \rceil$ represents a suitably course rounding. Since r is short and E has short entries, we will have that $B \cdot r \bmod q \approx C \cdot A \cdot r \bmod q = C \cdot u \bmod q$, which is independent of which valid r is used.

For the injective mode, we simply choose B at random mod q. By choosing parameters correctly, one can ensure that $f_B(r)$ is injective.

One problem with the above is that, in order for the lossy mode to be constant, we need that q is super-polynomial. Otherwise, rounding errors will cause $f_B(r)$ in the lossy mode to not quite equal $\lfloor C \cdot u \rceil$, and the errors will depend on r. As such, for polynomial modulus, $f_B(r)$ is not constant on valid r. Using a super-polynomial modulus will negatively impact the efficiency of the scheme, and requires a stronger computational assumption.

Our first observation is that we do not actually need full indistinguishability of the measured vs not measured r. For our application to sigma protocols, we just need that anything that happens when r is unmeasured will also happen *with reasonable probability* when r is measured. But the two cases could be distinguishable in the strict sense. This gives a weak notion of collapsing which is sufficient for rewinding.

What this allows us to do is shrink q to be small, and we will have that the lossy mode in constant with non-negligible probability, which we show is sufficient. However, we still need q to be somewhat larger than what is required classically. This is because when we prove that the lossy mode is constant, we need to union bound over each row of C. Decreasing the height of C improves the probability of success, but we need to keep C a certain height so that the injective mode is actually injective.

Separable Sigma Protocols. In order circumvent the above difficulties and get an optimally-small q, we show that we can get by using a single row of C.

In more detail, we will say that a sigma protocol is *separable* if there is an associated family of functions with particular properties. Like associated lossy functions, the family of functions has two modes: a *preserving* mode (which can be seen as the analog of the lossy mode) and a *separating* mode (the analog of the injective mode). Unlike the lossy functions, the family of functions here will output only a single bit. In this case, there clearly can not be an injective mode.

Instead, we will use the following requirements. A preserving mode f is still constant on valid r. On the other hand, the separating mode has the property that, for any valid $r \neq r'$, $f(r) = f(r')$ with probability, say, $1/2$.

We show that such separating functions can be used to show collapsing. What's more, for lattice-based schemes, the separating functions can be seen as instances of the lossy functions where C is just a single row. As before, we will need to allow for some weak indistinguishability between preserving and separating modes, leading to weak collapsing. We will also need to handle separating modes where the probability is not necessarily exactly $1/2$. We show how to do all of this, demonstrating that Lyubashevsky's sigma protocol [Lyu12] is weakly collapsing.

Putting It All Together. Piecing our results from the previous sections together, we show that Lyubashevsky's signature scheme [Lyu12] is secure under standard lattice assumptions. Namely, 2-soundness follows from the SIS assumption, under the same asymptotic parameters needed to prove security classically. The separating function we need in the quantum setting follows from the LWE

assumption; recall that LWE implies SIS. The result is that the sigma protocol underlying Lyubashevsky's signatures is sound under the LWE assumption.
Then we apply our Fiat-Shamir proof, obtaining existentially unforgeable signatures. Our techniques readily extend to schemes based on Lyubashevsky's, such
as the efficient signature scheme of [DKL+18].

Other Results. Our techniques for showing lattice-based sigma protocols are
collapsing can also be applied to hash functions. In particular, our techniques
show that the SIS hash function is collapsing. Recall that the SIS hash function
is specified by a short wide matrix A, takes as inputs short vectors r, and outputs
$A \cdot r \mod q$.

If q is super-polynomial, then SIS will have an associated lossy function
with strong indistinguishability, namely the same function constructed for the
sigma protocols. As such, SIS with super-polynomial q is collapsing. On the
other hand, for polynomial q, SIS is weakly separable using the same functions
as above, showing that SIS is weakly collapsing. This gives the to-date most
efficient standard-model collapsing hash function.

Limitations. The obvious limitation of our work is the tightness of our reductions. Our Fiat-Shmir proof is quite loose, losing a factor of q^9 where q is the
number of random oracle queries; we leave tightening our proof as an important
open problem.

This looseness makes our results all but useless for guiding parameter choices
in practice. However, we note that in practice parameter choices typically are
chosen to block the best attacks rather than the bounds obtained by reductions.
Of course, getting a tight bound that matches the parameters used in practice is
the ideal outcome, but this is often not attainable. Indeed, even the classical Fiat-
Shamir proof is somewhat loose. This has lead to some authors (e.g. [DKL+18])
to make new assumptions that incorporate the hash function which can be tightly
connected to the security of their scheme. These new assumptions can then be
justified (with a loss!) using the classical Fiat-Shamir proof.

We therefore view our results as at least showing asymptotically that Lyubashevsky's and related signature schemes are secure, meaning there are no fundamental weaknesses incurred by using the Fiat-Shamir heuristic in the quantum
world. Alternatively, our proof can be used to give a quantum justification for
assumptions which can then be tightly connected to the security of schemes.

2   Weakly Collapsing Sigma Protocol

2.1   Sigma Protocol

First, let us recall the definition of sigma protocol. The full definition can be
found in the full version [LZ19].

For every λ, there is a relation $\mathcal{R}_\lambda = \{(x, w) : x \in L_\lambda, w \in W(x)\}$ such
that the length of x and w is bounded by a polynomial of λ, x is a statement

in an NP language L_λ and $W(x)$ is the set of witness for proving $x \in L_\lambda$. In other words, there is an polynomial time algorithm runs in $\mathsf{poly}(\lambda)$ that decides whether $(x, w) \in \mathcal{R}_\lambda$.

A **sigma protocol** for $\mathcal{R}_\lambda$ consists two polynomial time algorithms, prover $\mathcal{P}$ and verifier $\mathcal{V}$. The sigma protocol procedure looks like the follows:

- $\mathcal{P}$ is given both x, w and generates $(a, st) \leftarrow \mathcal{P}.\mathsf{Commit}(1^\lambda, x, w)$. st is its own state and it sends the commitment a to $\mathcal{V}$;
- $\mathcal{V}$ given x and a, generates a challenge c uniformly at random in $\{0, 1\}^\lambda$ where wlog λ is the security parameter of this protocol;
- $\mathcal{P}$ given the challenge c, generates a response $r \leftarrow \mathcal{P}.\mathsf{Prove}(1^\lambda, x, w, st, c)$;
- $\mathcal{V}.\mathsf{Ver}(1^\lambda, x, a, c, r)$ returns $0/1$ meaning the transcript is valid or not.

When it is clear in the context, we omit 1^λ for convenience.

Sometimes, we will need to consider a distribution over instances. In these cases, we associate a $\mathsf{Gen}(\cdot)$ algorithm to a sigma protocol. $\mathsf{Gen}(1^\lambda)$ outputs a pair of $(x, w) \in \mathcal{R}_\lambda$. $\mathsf{Gen}(\cdot)$ defines a distribution over $\mathcal{R}_\lambda$. In this setting, we use pk to denote x and sk to denote (x, w). Moreover, we have $\mathcal{P}.\mathsf{Commit}(\mathsf{sk}) = \mathcal{P}.\mathsf{Commit}(x, w)$, $\mathcal{P}.\mathsf{Prove}(\mathsf{sk}, st, c) = \mathcal{P}.\mathsf{Prove}(x, w, st, c)$ and $\mathcal{V}.\mathsf{Ver}(\mathsf{pk}, a, c, r) = \mathcal{V}.\mathsf{Ver}(x, a, c, r)$. This notation will be useful when we build an ID protocol or a signature scheme from a sigma protocol. In this case, some definitions are average-case definitions: for example, correctness is defined as probability that the above procedure outputs 1 taken the randomness of challenge c, $\mathcal{P}, \mathcal{V}$ and also the distribution over $\mathcal{R}_\lambda$ induced by $\mathsf{Gen}(\cdot)$.

2.2   Collapsing

In addition to the usual properties considered classically, we define a new notion of security for sigma protocols, inspired by Unruh's notion of collapsing for hash functions and commitments [Unr16b]:

Definition 1 (Collapsing Sigma Protocol). *For any λ, for any $\mathsf{Gen}(1^\lambda)$ and any polynomial time quantum distinguisher $\mathcal{D}$, define the following game* $\mathsf{CollapsingGame}^b_{\mathcal{D}, \mathsf{pk}, \mathsf{sk}}$:

- *$(\mathsf{pk}, \mathsf{sk}) \leftarrow \mathsf{Gen}(1^\lambda)$, $\mathcal{D}$ is given pk and generates and sends a to the challenger; it then gets a uniformly random c from the challenger Ch; then it generates a superposition $|\phi\rangle$ over all r (may not be a valid r) together with its own quantum states and sends the part $|\phi\rangle$ to the challenger Ch;*
- *Upon receiving $|\phi\rangle$, Ch verifies in superposition that $|a, c\rangle|\phi\rangle$ is a superposition over valid transcripts. If the verification fails, Ch outputs a random bit and aborts. Otherwise, let $|\phi'\rangle$ be the superposition after the measurement, which is the projection of $|\phi\rangle$ onto r such that $|a, c, r\rangle$ is valid.*
  Then Ch flips a coin b, if $b = 0$, it does nothing; if $b = 1$, it measures $|\phi'\rangle$ in computational basis. Finally it sends the superposition back to $\mathcal{D}$.
- *The experiment's output is what $\mathcal{D}$ outputs.*

We say a quantum sigma protocol associated with Gen$(\cdot)$ *is collapsing if for every polynomial time quantum distinguisher* $\mathcal{D}$, *the probability* $\mathcal{D}$ *distinguishes is negligible, in other words, there is a negligible function* negl, *such that*

$$\left| \Pr\left[\mathsf{CollapsingGame}^0_{\mathcal{D},\mathsf{pk},\mathsf{sk}} = 0\right] - \Pr\left[\mathsf{CollapsingGame}^1_{\mathcal{D},\mathsf{pk},\mathsf{sk}} = 0\right] \right| \leq \mathsf{negl}(\lambda)$$

Where probabilities are taken over the randomness of $(\mathsf{pk},\mathsf{sk}) \leftarrow \mathsf{Gen}(1^\lambda)$ *and the randomness of* $\mathcal{D}$.

We can similarly define weakly collapsing property which is used in the rest of the paper.

Definition 2 ((γ-)Weakly Collapsing). *We say a quantum secure sigma protocol associated with* Gen(1^λ) *is weakly collapsing, if there exists a non-negligible* $\gamma(\cdot)$, *such that for any polynomial time quantum distinguisher* $\mathcal{D}$,

$$\Pr\left[\mathsf{CollapsingGame}^1_{\mathcal{D},\mathsf{pk},\mathsf{sk}} = 0\right] \geq \gamma(\lambda) \cdot \Pr\left[\mathsf{CollapsingGame}^0_{\mathcal{D},\mathsf{pk},\mathsf{sk}} = 0\right] - \mathsf{negl}(\lambda)$$

Weak collapsing captures the setting where measuring the adversary's response causes a noticeable change in outcome in contrast to not measuring, but any event that occurs in the un-measured setting also occurs in the measured setting. We can similarly define a *worst case* version of weak collapsing where that holds *for any* choice of $(x,w) \in R$, rather than for a random $(\mathsf{pk},\mathsf{sk})$ chosen from Gen.

In the next subsections, we give sufficient conditions for demonstrating the collapsing property. Our definitions are given for sigma protocols, but can easily be extended to hash functions. A key feature of our definitions is that they are essentially classical definitions, as opposed to collapsing which is inherently quantum. As such, we believe our weaker definitions will be easier to instantiate, as we demonstrate in Sect. 4.

2.3 Compatible Lossy Function

A compatible lossy function can be thought as a function generator CLF.Gen$(\cdot)$. It takes all the parameters λ, pk, sk, a, c and mode $\in \{\mathsf{constant},\mathsf{injective}\}$, outputs a constant or small range (polynomial size) function over all valid r. Here valid r means $\mathcal{V}.\mathsf{Ver}(\mathsf{pk}, a, c, r) = 1$. Also, no efficient quantum algorithm can distinguish whether it is given a function description from constant mode or injective mode. In the full version [LZ19], we give the full definition, and show that it implies collapsing. For the remainder of this section, we will instead focus on an even weaker notion.

2.4 Compatible Separable Function

Definition 3 ((τ, β)-Compatible Separable Function). *A compatible separable function for a sigma protocol is an efficient procedure* CSF.Gen$(\lambda, \mathsf{pk}, \mathsf{sk}, a, c, \mathsf{mode})$ *which takes a security parameter* λ, pk, sk, *a commitment* a, *a challenge* c *and* mode $\in \{\mathsf{preserving},\mathsf{separating}\}$, *it outputs a description of an efficiently computable function* f *that outputs* $0, 1$ *such that*

1. preserving *mode: over the set* $V_{a,c}$ *of valid* r, *with non-negligible probability* f *is a constant function. Formally, there exists a non-negligible function* $\tau(\cdot)$, *such that for all* $\lambda, \mathsf{pk}, \mathsf{sk}$, *for all* a, c, *let* $\mathcal{F}_{\mathsf{p}}$ *be the distribution sampled by* $\mathsf{CSF.Gen}(\lambda, \mathsf{pk}, \mathsf{sk}, a, c, \mathsf{preserving})$,

$$\Pr_{f \leftarrow \mathcal{F}_{\mathsf{p}}} [|Im(f)| = 1] \geq \tau(\lambda)$$

where $Im(f)$ *is the image of* f *over all valid* r *satisfying* (a, c, r) *is a valid transcript.*

2. separating *mode: there exists an* α *such that, for all valid* $r \neq r'$, *the probability of* $f(r) = f(r')$ *is **exactly*** $\frac{1+\alpha}{2}$ *where the randomness is taken over the choice of* f.
   Formally, there exists $\beta(\lambda) < \tau(\lambda)$ *such that* $\tau(\lambda) - \beta(\lambda)$ *is non-negligible, for all* $\lambda, \mathsf{pk}, \mathsf{sk}$, *for all* a, c, *let* $\mathcal{F}_{\mathsf{s}}$ *be the distribution of functions that sampled by* $\mathsf{CSF.Gen}(\lambda, \mathsf{pk}, \mathsf{sk}, a, c, \mathsf{injective})$, *there exists an* $\alpha(\cdot)$ *which is upper bounded by* $\beta(\cdot)$ *(but which is potentially negative), for every pair of valid* $r \neq r'$,

$$\Pr_{f \leftarrow \mathcal{F}_{\mathsf{s}}} [f(r) = f(r')] = \frac{1 + \alpha(\lambda)}{2}$$

3. ***Indistinguishability:*** *Let us first define* $\mathsf{SFGame}^b_{\mathcal{D},\mathsf{pk},\mathsf{sk}}$:
   - $\mathcal{D}$ *is given* pk *and interacts with the challenger* Ch *which has* pk, sk,
   - $\mathcal{D}$ *sends a pair of valid* a, c *to the challenger,*
   - Ch *chooses a random function* f *from* $\mathcal{F}_p$ *if* $b = 0$ *or from* $\mathcal{F}_s$ *if* $b = 1$, *where* $\mathcal{F}_p$ *or* $\mathcal{F}_s$ *is determined by* $\mathsf{pk}, \mathsf{sk}, a, c$,
   - $\mathcal{D}$ *is given the description of* f, *the result of the game is* $\mathcal{D}$'s *output.*
   We require that for every λ, *for every polynomial time quantum distinguisher* $\mathcal{D}$, *taken the randomness of* $(\mathsf{pk}, \mathsf{sk}) \leftarrow \mathsf{Gen}(1^\lambda)$,

$$\left| \Pr\left[\mathsf{SFGame}^0_{\mathcal{D},\mathsf{pk},\mathsf{sk}} = 0 \right] - \Pr\left[\mathsf{SFGame}^1_{\mathcal{D},\mathsf{pk},\mathsf{sk}} = 0 \right] \right| \leq \mathsf{negl}(\lambda)$$

Lemma 1. *If a sigma protocol associated with* $\mathsf{Gen}(\cdot)$ *has* (τ, β)-*compatible separable functions, it is* $\frac{\tau - \beta}{2}$-*weakly collapsing.*

Proof. Assume there is a non-negligible function $\epsilon(\cdot)$ and a polynomial time quantum distinguisher $\mathcal{D}$ that breaks the $\frac{\tau - \beta}{2}$-weakly collapsing property of this sigma protocol. From the definition, taken the randomness of pk, sk, we have,

$$\Pr\left[\mathsf{CGame}^1_{\mathcal{D},\mathsf{pk},\mathsf{sk}} = 0 \right] < \frac{\tau(\lambda) - \beta(\lambda)}{2} \cdot \Pr\left[\mathsf{CGame}^0_{\mathcal{D},\mathsf{pk},\mathsf{sk}} = 0 \right] - \epsilon(\lambda)$$

where CGame stands for $\mathsf{CollapsingGame}$.

Let us assume there exist a (τ, β)-compatible separable function. We will build an adversary $\mathcal{A}$ that uses $\mathcal{D}$ as a subroutine and breaks the compatible separable function. Here is what $\mathcal{A}$ does:

- $\mathcal{A}$ given pk, it runs $\mathcal{D}$ (which taks pk as input) and gets a,
- $\mathcal{A}$ samples $c \xleftarrow{\$} \{0, 1\}^\lambda$, and gives c to $\mathcal{D}$ and a, c to the challenger Ch,

– $\mathcal{A}$ gets $|\phi\rangle$ from $\mathcal{D}$ and a function f from Ch. It first checks $|\phi\rangle$ contains valid r on superposition. If the measurement does not pass, $\mathcal{A}$ randomly guesses a bit. Otherwise, let $|\phi'\rangle = \sum_r \alpha_r |r\rangle$ be the superposition after the measurement. It applies f to $|\phi'\rangle$,

$$|\phi''\rangle = U_f |\phi'\rangle = \sum_{\text{valid } r} \alpha_r \cdot (-1)^{f(r)} |r\rangle$$

– It gives $|\phi''\rangle$ to $\mathcal{D}$ and outputs what $\mathcal{D}$ outputs.

For any $\mathsf{pk}, \mathsf{sk}, a, c$, any possible $|\phi'\rangle = \sum_{\text{valid } r} \alpha_r |r\rangle$ in the above game, what is the density matrix of $|\phi'\rangle$ or $|\phi'\rangle$ measured in computational basis? If the state is not measured (which corresponds to the density matrix in $\mathsf{CGame}^0_{\mathcal{D},\mathsf{pk},\mathsf{sk}}$), we have the density matrix is

$$\rho_0 = \sum_{\text{valid } r,r'} \bar{\alpha}_r \alpha_{r'} |r\rangle\langle r'|$$

and if $|\phi'\rangle$ is measured (which corresponds to the density matrix in $\mathsf{CGame}^1_{\mathcal{D},\mathsf{pk},\mathsf{sk}}$), the density matrix is $\rho_1 = \sum_{\text{valid } r} |\alpha_r|^2 \cdot |r\rangle\langle r|$.

If we take a function $f \leftarrow \mathcal{F}_p$, let U_f be a unitary $U_f |r\rangle = (-1)^{f(r)} |r\rangle$. Apply U_f to ρ_0, we have

$$\rho_p = \sum_{f \leftarrow \mathcal{F}_p} \frac{1}{|\mathcal{F}_p|} \cdot U_f \rho_0 U_f^\dagger = \Pr_{f \leftarrow \mathcal{F}_p}[|Im(f)| = 1] \cdot \rho_0 + \sum_{\substack{f \leftarrow \mathcal{F}_p \\ f \text{ is not constant}}} \frac{1}{|\mathcal{F}_p|} \cdot U_f \rho_0 U_f^\dagger$$

which is easy to see that ρ_p is a convex combination of ρ_0 and $U_f \rho_0 U_f^\dagger$ for f is not constant. The above equality holds because when f is a constant function, U_f is an identity. It says if a distinguisher outputs 0 when ρ_0 is given, the same distinguisher outputs 0 with probability at least $\Pr[|Im(f)| = 1] \geq \tau(\lambda)$ when ρ_p is given. In other words, we have

$$\Pr[\mathsf{SFGame}^0_{\mathcal{A},\mathsf{pk},\mathsf{sk}} = 0] \geq \tau(\lambda) \cdot \Pr[\mathsf{CGame}^0_{\mathcal{D},\mathsf{pk},\mathsf{sk}} = 0]$$

Next if we apply U_f where $f \leftarrow \mathcal{F}_s$ to the density matrix ρ_0, we have

$$\rho_s = \sum_{f \leftarrow \mathcal{F}_s} \frac{1}{|\mathcal{F}_s|} \cdot U_f \rho_0 U_f^\dagger = \sum_{\text{valid } r,r'} \sum_{f \leftarrow \mathcal{F}_s} \frac{1}{|\mathcal{F}_s|} \cdot \bar{\alpha}_r \alpha_{r'} \cdot U_f |r\rangle\langle r'| U_f^\dagger$$

$$= \sum_{\text{valid } r} |\alpha_r|^2 \cdot |r\rangle\langle r| + \sum_{\text{valid } r \neq r'} \bar{\alpha}_r \alpha_{r'} \cdot |r\rangle\langle r'| \cdot \left\{ \sum_{f \leftarrow \mathcal{F}_s} \frac{1}{|\mathcal{F}_s|} (-1)^{f(r) + f(r')} \right\}$$

$$= (1 - \alpha(\lambda)) \cdot \rho_1 + \alpha(\lambda) \cdot \rho_0$$

If $\alpha(\lambda) \leq 0$, we have $\rho_1 = \frac{1}{1 - \alpha(\lambda)} \cdot \rho_s + \frac{-\alpha(\lambda)}{1 - \alpha(\lambda)} \cdot \rho_0$. If a distinguisher outputs 0 when ρ_s is given, the same distinguisher outputs 0 with probability at least $\frac{1}{2}$ when ρ_1 is given. In other words, for any distinguisher $\mathcal{D}'$,

$$\Pr[\mathcal{D}'(\rho_s) = 0] \leq 2 \cdot \Pr[\mathcal{D}'(\rho_1) = 0]$$

If $\alpha(\lambda)$ is positive, we have $\rho_s = (1 - \alpha(\lambda)) \cdot \rho_1 + \alpha(\lambda) \cdot \rho_0$. In other words, for any distinguisher $\mathcal{D}'$, because $\alpha(\lambda) < \beta(\lambda)$,

$$\Pr[\mathcal{D}'(\rho_s) = 0] = (1 - \alpha(\lambda)) \cdot \Pr[\mathcal{D}'(\rho_1) = 0] + \alpha(\lambda) \cdot \Pr[\mathcal{D}'(\rho_0) = 0]$$
$$\leq \Pr[\mathcal{D}'(\rho_1) = 0] + \beta(\lambda) \cdot \Pr[\mathcal{D}'(\rho_0) = 0]$$

Combining the two above equations, taken over the randomness of $\mathsf{pk}, \mathsf{sk}, a, c$,

$$\Pr[\mathsf{SFGame}^1_{\mathcal{A},\mathsf{pk},\mathsf{sk}} = 0] \leq 2 \cdot \Pr[\mathsf{CGame}^1_{\mathcal{D},\mathsf{pk},\mathsf{sk}} = 0] + \\ \beta(\lambda) \cdot \Pr[\mathsf{CGame}^0_{\mathcal{D},\mathsf{pk},\mathsf{sk}} = 0]$$

Finally, we show that $\mathcal{A}$ breaks the compatible separable function,

$$\Pr[\mathsf{SFGame}^0_{\mathcal{A},\mathsf{pk},\mathsf{sk}} = 0] - \Pr[\mathsf{SFGame}^1_{\mathcal{A},\mathsf{pk},\mathsf{sk}} = 0]$$
$$> \tau(\lambda) \cdot \Pr[\mathsf{CGame}^0_{\mathcal{D},\mathsf{pk},\mathsf{sk}} = 0] - $$
$$\left(2 \cdot \Pr[\mathsf{CGame}^1_{\mathcal{D},\mathsf{pk},\mathsf{sk}} = 0] + \beta(\lambda) \cdot \Pr[\mathsf{CGame}^0_{\mathcal{D},\mathsf{pk},\mathsf{sk}} = 0]\right)$$
$$= (\tau(\lambda) - \beta(\lambda)) \cdot \Pr[\mathsf{CGame}^0_{\mathcal{D},\mathsf{pk},\mathsf{sk}} = 0] - 2 \cdot \Pr[\mathsf{CGame}^1_{\mathcal{D},\mathsf{pk},\mathsf{sk}} = 0]$$
$$> 2 \cdot \epsilon(\lambda)$$

□

3   Quantum ID Protocol and Quantum HVZKPoK

In this section, we will see that given a quantum secure sigma protocol with weakly collapsing property, we can overcome the difficulty of doing quantum rewinding and build a quantum secure identification protocol. The same technique can be applied to HVZKPoK.

3.1   Quantum ID Protocol

Theorem 1. *Assume we have a quantum secure sigma protocol with associated* $\mathsf{Gen}(\cdot)$ *which satisfies the weakly collapsing property (with perfect/weak completeness). Then it is a quantum secure identification protocol (with perfect/weak completeness).*

In other words, if a sigma protocol has (1) perfect/weak completeness, (2) post-quantum 2-soundness, (3) statistical/post-quantum computational HVZK and (4) weakly collapsing property, it is a sigma protocol with (1) perfect/weak completeness, (2) post-quantum ID soundness.

Proof. We recall the definitions of the various properties in the full version [LZ19]. The full proof of Theorem 1 is in the full version [LZ19]. Here, we briefly sketch the proof.

Assume there is an algorithm $\mathcal{A}$ breaks the soundness of the sigma protocol as an ID protocol. We can use $\mathcal{A}$ and output one valid tuple (a, c, r). If we can then rewind the algorithm to just after a was produced, we can run it again and will find two valid tuples (a, c, r) and (a, c', r'). Notice that c, c' are distinct with overwhelming probability.

However, when $\mathcal{A}$ generates (a, c, r), it will in general be a superposition over r. By measuring this superposition, $\mathcal{A}$ has a non-negligible change to output a valid r. Measurement will destroy superposition and we can not roll-back the quantum machine and restart the whole algorithm.

Suppose we just measure whether (a, c, r) is a valid transcript, but not the entire superposition over r. Even though this will alter the adversary's state, Unruh [Unr12] demonstrates that (a, c', r') from the second run will still be a valid transcript with non-negligible probability. However, by not measuring the first transcript, we still do not have a classical (a, c, r) that we can output along with (a, c', r').

Fortunately, weak collapsing tells us that even if $\mathcal{A}$ measures the superposition over r, (a, c', r') will still be a valid transcript with non-negligible probability. So we will obtain two pairs $(a, c, r), (a, c', r')$ with non-negligible probability. $\square$

3.2 Quantum HVZKPoK

Theorem 2. *If a sigma protocol has (1) perfect completeness, (2) statistical/ post-quantum computational HVZK, (3) worst case weakly collapsing property and (4) 2-extractability, it is a quantum HVZKPoK. In other words, it is a sigma protocol with (1) perfect completeness, (2) statistical/post-quantum computational HVZK and (3) $(c, p, \kappa, \mathsf{negl}) - validity$ form $c = 3$, polynomial p and negligible functions $\kappa = 0, \mathsf{negl}$.*

The proof idea can also be found in the full version [LZ19].

4   Construction of Collapsing Sigma Protocol

The following protocol is from [Lyu12]. Although in the paper, Lyubashevsky only shows a digital signature scheme, it follows the framework of Fiat-Shamir. We extract the following sigma protocol from the digital signature. We will reprove it is a quantum secure sigma protocol (which is already shown to be secure as a signature scheme in [Lyu12]) and then show it has compatible lossy/separable functions. We will have parameters, most of the proofs (already shown in [Lyu12]) and the proof of compatible lossy functions in the full version [LZ19] and only show the proof of compatible separable functions in this section.

- Gen(1^λ): $\mathbf{A} \xleftarrow{\$} \mathbb{Z}_q^{n \times m}$ and $\mathbf{S} \xleftarrow{\$} \{-d, \cdots, d\}^{m \times k}$ and let $\mathsf{pk} = (\mathbf{A}, \mathbf{T} = \mathbf{AS})$ and $\mathsf{sk} = (\mathbf{A}, \mathbf{S})$.
- **Commitment Stage:** $\mathcal{P}$ given sk, $\mathbf{y} \xleftarrow{\$} D_\sigma^m$ and $\mathbf{a} = \mathbf{Ay}$. It sends $\mathbf{a}$ to $\mathcal{V}$.
- **Challenge Stage:** $\mathcal{V}$ randomly samples $\mathbf{c} \xleftarrow{\$} \{-1, 0, 1\}^k$ satisfying $\|\mathbf{c}\|_1 \leq \kappa$ and sends $\mathbf{c}$ to $\mathcal{P}$.

– **Response Stage:** $\mathcal{P}$ after getting $\mathbf{c}$, $\mathbf{r} = \mathbf{Sc} + \mathbf{y}$ and sends $\mathbf{y}$ with probability $pr(\mathbf{c}, \mathbf{r})$. Otherwise, it sends $\bot$.

$$pr(\mathbf{c}, \mathbf{r}) = \min\left\{\frac{D_\sigma^m(\mathbf{r})}{M \cdot D_{\mathbf{Sc}, \sigma}^m(\mathbf{r})}, 1\right\}$$

– **Verification Stage:** $\mathcal{V}$ outputs 1 if $\mathbf{Ar} = \mathbf{Tc} + \mathbf{a}$ and $\|\mathbf{r}\|_2 \leq \eta\sigma\sqrt{m}$.

Remark: The definition of discrete Normal D_σ^m and $D_{\mathbf{v}, \varsigma}^m$ can be found in the full version [LZ19]. We note that the protocol only satisfies a *weak completeness* requirement, where the honest prover succeeds with non-negligible probability.

The challenge stage looks different from a challenge stage defined by a sigma protocol. But indeed, we can think of it as choosing a random bit string and mapping it to a vector $\mathbf{c}$ that $\mathbf{c} \in \{-1, 0, 1\}^k$ and $\|\mathbf{c}\|_1 \leq \kappa$.

We reprove this scheme is a secure quantum sigma protocol in the full version [LZ19]. Next let us prove it is weakly collapsing. Theorem 3 directly follows from Theorem 4.

Theorem 3. *The sigma protocol constructed above is weakly collapsing.*

Compatible Separable Functions.

Theorem 4. *There exists (τ, β)-compatible separable function* CSF.Gen *where* $\tau(\lambda) = 0.499$ *and* $\beta(\lambda) = 1/q(\lambda)^2$, *for any* λ, $\mathsf{pk} = (\mathbf{A}, \mathbf{T})$, $\mathsf{sk} = (\mathbf{A}, \mathbf{S})$, a, c,

$$\mathcal{F}_p = \left\{f : f(\mathbf{r}) = [(\mathbf{uA} + \mathbf{e}) \cdot \mathbf{r} + z]_{[q/2]}, \mathbf{u} \xleftarrow{\$} \mathbb{Z}_q^n, \mathbf{e} \xleftarrow{\$} D_{q, \alpha q}^m, z \xleftarrow{\$} \mathbb{Z}_q\right\}$$

$$\mathcal{F}_s = \left\{f : f(\mathbf{r}) = [\mathbf{v} \cdot \mathbf{r} + z]_{[q/2]}, \mathbf{v} \xleftarrow{\$} \mathbb{Z}_q^m, z \xleftarrow{\$} \mathbb{Z}_q\right\}$$

where $[x]_{[q/2]}$ rounds $x/[q/2]$ to the nearest integer (0 or 1), $\alpha q > 2\sqrt{n}$, $\Delta = (\eta\sigma\sqrt{m}) \cdot (\alpha q) \cdot 2\sqrt{m} = q/8$. In which case, $q - 32\eta\sigma m\sqrt{n}$ is a polynomial of λ.

Proof. **Preserving:** First, let us show that for any λ, pk, sk, a, c, the corresponding $\mathcal{F}_p$ has many constant functions.

Because we say $\mathbf{r}$ is valid if and only if $\mathbf{Ar} = \mathbf{Tc} + \mathbf{a}$ and $\mathbf{r}$ is short. For any function $f \xleftarrow{\$} \mathcal{F}_p$, we have

$$f(\mathbf{r}) = [(\mathbf{uA} + \mathbf{e}) \cdot \mathbf{r} + z]_{[q/2]} = [\mathbf{uAr} + \mathbf{er} + z]_{[q/2]}$$

where $\mathbf{uAr} + z = \mathbf{uA}(\mathbf{Tc} + \mathbf{a}) + z$ is constant regardless of the input $\mathbf{r}$ and with the random choice of z, its value is uniformly at random in $\mathbb{Z}_q$.

We have the following corollary that bounds the inner product of $\mathbf{e}$ and $\mathbf{r}$,

Corollary 1. *For any $\mathbf{r} \in \mathbb{R}^m$, $\|\mathbf{r}\| \leq \eta\sigma\sqrt{m}$, we have*

$$\Pr\left[|\langle \mathbf{e}, \mathbf{r}\rangle| > \Delta \, ; \mathbf{e} \leftarrow D_{q, \alpha q}^m\right] \leq 2e^{-\frac{\Delta^2}{2(\eta\sigma\sqrt{m})^2(\alpha q)^2}}$$

By letting $\Delta = (\eta\sigma\sqrt{m})(\alpha q) \cdot 2\sqrt{m}$, we have the above probability is bounded by $2e^{-m}$.

By setting $\Delta = q/8$, in which case $\alpha q = \frac{q}{16 \cdot \eta \sigma m}$, we know that

1. $\mathbf{uAr} + z$ falls into $[\Delta, [q/2] - \Delta]$ or $[[q/2] + \Delta, q - \Delta]$ with probability $\geq 1/2$,
2. Draw $\mathbf{e} \xleftarrow{\$} D_{q,\alpha q}^m$, for all valid $\mathbf{r}$, with overwhelming probability, $|\langle \mathbf{e}, \mathbf{r} \rangle| \leq \Delta$.

So $\tau(\lambda) = \Pr_{f \leftarrow \mathcal{F}_p}[|Im(f)| = 1] > \frac{1}{2} - \mathsf{negl}(\lambda) > 0.499$.

   0 **Separating:** Second, let us show that there exists a $\beta(\cdot)$ such that for any λ, pk, sk, $\mathbf{a}, \mathbf{c}$, for any pair of valid $\mathbf{r} \neq \mathbf{r}'$, $f(\mathbf{r})$ and $f(\mathbf{r}')$ will be mapped to the same bits with the same probability $\frac{1+\alpha(\lambda)}{2}$ where $\beta(\lambda) = \alpha(\lambda) = \frac{1}{q^2}$.

   Fixing $\mathbf{r} \neq \mathbf{r}'$, let us consider the distribution of $(\mathbf{vr} + z, \mathbf{vr}' + z)$ for random chosen $\mathbf{v}, z$. Given a random chosen $\mathbf{v}$, the difference $\mathbf{vr} - \mathbf{vr}'$ is uniformly at random. And given the random choice of z, $(\mathbf{vr} + z, \mathbf{vr}' + z)$ is a uniformly random element in $\mathbb{Z}_q \times \mathbb{Z}_q$. Therefore we have

$$\Pr_{f \leftarrow \mathcal{F}_s}[f(\mathbf{r}) = f(\mathbf{r}')] = 1 - \frac{2 \cdot ([q/2] + 1) \cdot [q/2]}{q^2} = \frac{1 + \alpha(\lambda)}{2} \quad \text{where } \alpha(\lambda) = \frac{1}{q^2}$$

It also satisfies that $\tau - \beta$ is non-negligible.

Indistinguishability: A distinguisher is given either $(\mathbf{uA} + \mathbf{e}, z)$ or $(\mathbf{v}, z)$. It corresponds to an instance of DLWE. Based on the quantum security of DLWE, indistinguishability holds.   □

Compatible Lossy Functions. It also has a compatible lossy function. The full theorem statement is in the full version [LZ19].

5   Compressed Oracles

In [Zha18], Zhandry showed a new proof technique to analyze random oracles $[2^N] \rightarrow [2^N]$ under quantum query access. The technique allows a simulator, given a random oracle machine making polynomial number of queries, to simulate a quantum random oracle efficiently. The full details can be found in the full version [LZ19], and we sketch the details here:

1. **Compressed Fourier Oracles:** Assume a simulator $\mathcal{B}$ is simulating a quantum random oracle for $\mathcal{A}$. The simulator $\mathcal{B}$ maintains a superposition over databases of pairs $D = \{(x_i, u_i)\}$ (here we always assume a database is sorted according to x_i). At the beginning, $\mathcal{B}$ only has $|D_0\rangle$ which is a pure state over an empty database D_0. We will think of the database as being the specification for a function, where $(x_i, u_i) \in D$ means $x_i \mapsto u_i$, whereas if x is not present in the database, then $x \mapsto 0$.
   Define $D(x) = \bot$ if x is not in the database and $D(x) = u_i$ if there is a pair (x_i, u_i) such that $x = x_i$. We then define the following operation $\oplus$ for a database D and a pair (x, u). Intuitively, thinking of D as the encoding of a function, it will XOR u into the image of x. More precisely, (1) if $u = 0$, $D \oplus (x, u) = D$, (2) else if $D(x) = \bot$, $D \oplus (x, u) = D \cup \{(x, u)\}$, (3) else if

$D(x) = u_i$ and $u + u_i \equiv 0 \pmod{2^N}$, $D \oplus (x, u) = D \setminus \{(x, u_i)\}$ and (4) otherwise, $D \oplus (x, u) = (D \setminus \{(x, u_i)\}) \cup \{(x, u_i + u)\}$.

So we start with $\sum_{x,u} a_{x,u}^0 |x, u\rangle \otimes |D_0\rangle$ where D_0 is empty. After making the i-th query, we have

$$\text{CFourierO} \sum_{x,u,D} a_{x,u,D}^{i-1} |x, u\rangle \otimes |D\rangle \Rightarrow \sum_{x,u,D} a_{x,u,D}^{i-1} |x, u\rangle \otimes |D \oplus (x, u)\rangle$$

One observation is when the algorithm $\mathcal{A}$ only makes q queries, any database in the superposition contains at most q non-zero entries. So $\mathcal{B}$ can efficiently simulate quantum random oracle. And Zhandry shows the density matrices of $\mathcal{A}$ given $\mathcal{B}$ or a true quantum random oracle are identical.

2. **Compressed Phase Oracles:** By applying the QFT on the database of a compressed Fourier oracle, we get a compressed phase oracle.

   In this model, a database contains all the pairs (x_i, u_i) which means the oracle outputs u_i on x_i and uniformly at random on other inputs. We can also define $D(x) = \bot$ if x is not in the database and $D(x) = u_i$ if there is a pair (x_i, u_i) such that $x = x_i$. When making a query on $|x, u, D\rangle$,

   – If (x, u') is in the database D for some u', a phase $\omega_N^{uu'}$ (where $\omega_N = e^{2\pi i/2^N}$) will be added to the state; it corresponds to update u' to $u' + u$ in the compressed Fourier oracle model;

   – Otherwise a superposition is appended to the state $|x\rangle \otimes \sum_{u'} \omega_N^{uu'} |u'\rangle$; it corresponds to put a new pair (x, u') in the list in the compressed Fourier oracle model;

   – Also make sure that the list will never have a $(x, 0)$ pair in the compressed Fourier oracle model (by doing a QFT and see if the register is 0); if there is one, delete that pair;

   – all the 'append' and 'delete' operations above means doing QFT on $|0\rangle$ or a uniform superposition.

   Intuitively, it is identical to a compressed Fourier oracle. You can image QFT is automatically applied to every entry of the compressed Fourier database and converts it to a compressed phase oracle.

   In this paper, we introduce two more quantum oracle variations. These variations can be based on both compressed Fourier oracles and compressed phase oracles. Here we only introduce the first case. The second one is straightforward.

– The first variation is **almost compressed Fourier oracles**, which is based on compressed Fourier oracles. For most points, we simulate using the compressed Fourier oracle. However, for a small set of points, we just keep them as a (uncompressed) phase oracle. Formally, let x^* be an element in the domain of the random oracle $O : X \to Y$. The database D contains only the (x, u) pairs for $x \neq x^*$, the whole system can be written as the following, at the beginning of the computation, D_0 is an empty list:

$$\sum_{x,u} \alpha_{x,u} |x, u\rangle \otimes \left(|D_0\rangle \otimes \sum_r |r\rangle \right)$$

By making a quantum query, the simulator does the follows:

- If the query is (x, u) and $x \neq x^*$, the simulator updates D as what it does in the compressed Fourier oracle setting;
- If the query is on the special point (x^*, u), the second part of the oracle is updated as a phase oracle:

$$\alpha_{x^*,u,D,u'}|x^*, u\rangle \otimes |D\rangle \otimes \sum_r \omega_N^{u'r}|r\rangle$$

$$\Rightarrow \alpha_{x^*,u,D,u'}|x^*, u\rangle \otimes |D\rangle \otimes \sum_r \omega_N^{(u'+u)r}|r\rangle$$

In other words, we only apply QFT on most of the domain but x^*. This random oracle model can be extended to the case where we exclude a polynomial numbe of special points from D. As long as the number is polynomial, it can be efficiently simulated.

- The second one is inspired from our technique of extracting information from quantum oracle queries in the next section. Assume before the i-th query, the database does not have x^*, in other words, for any D containing x^* and arbitrary x, u, z, $\alpha_{x,u,z,D} = 0$. The superposition is

$$\sum_{\substack{x,u,z,D \\ D(x^*)=\perp}} \alpha_{x,u,z,D}|x, u, z, D\rangle$$

Then we can **switch random oracle models** between the i-th query: before the i-th query, we simulate a random oracle as a compressed Fourier oracle, and right before the i-th query, we switch to almost compressed Fourier random oracle. We call i is the switch stage. Because before the i-th query, every database D with non-zero weight does not contain x^*, we can simply append $\sum_r |r\rangle$ to the superposition. So the superposition now becomes

$$\sum_{\substack{x,u,z,D \\ D(x^*)=\perp}} \alpha_{x,u,z,D}|x, u, z, D\rangle \otimes \sum_r |r\rangle$$

6   Extracting Information from Quantum Oracle Queries

We first describe a technique for extracting the adversary's query, without perturbing its behavior too much. The setting is the following. The adversary makes some number of oracle queries (let us say q) to a random oracle, implemented as a compressed Fourier oracle. At the end of the interaction, we measure the entire state of the adversary and oracle, obtaining (w, D), where w is some string that we will call a witness. We will only be interested in the case where D is non-empty. Let $\gamma_{w,D}$ denote the probability of obtaining w, D.

We now consider the following experiment on the adversary. We run the adversary as above, but we pick a random query $i \in [q]$ or a random triple $i < j < k \in [q]$ with equal probability. That is, we pick a random i with probability $1/(q + \binom{q}{3})$ or pick a random triple i, j, k with probability $1/(q + \binom{q}{3})$. Then we do Exp_i or $\mathsf{Exp}_{i,j,k}$ as follows:

1. Exp_i: Before making the i-th query, we measure the query register to get x^* and check if the database D does not have x^* before the i-th query and has x^* right after the i-th query.

In other words, before measuring query register, let us assume the state is

$$\sum_{x,u,z,D} \alpha_{x,u,z,D} |x,u,z,D\rangle$$

Conditioned on the measurement gives x^*, the state becomes

$$\sum_{u,z,D} \alpha_{x^*,u,z,D} |x^*,u,z,D\rangle$$

If the database D does not have x^* before the i-th query and has x^* right after the i-th query, it means (1) all D does not contain x^*, (2) $u \neq 0$ so that after the i-th query, all D will contain x^*. So if the check passes, the state becomes

$$\sum_{u \neq 0,z,D:D(x^*)=\perp} \alpha_{x^*,u,z,D} |x^*,u,z,D\rangle$$

And then we do not care whether D contains x^* for all the remaining oracle queries and computation. If it does not satisfy any condition, we abort.

We know that after the measurement, the superposition contains all D that does not contain x^*. We can switch to almost compressed Fourier oracle with the special point x^*.

2. $\mathsf{Exp}_{i,j,k}$: We measure the query register to get x^* before making the i-th query. And we check the following (on superposition) that
   - D does not have x^* before the i-th query,
   - D always has x^* after the i-th query and before the j-th query,
   - D does not have x^* after the j-th query and before the k-th query,
   - D has x^* right after the k-th query. (But we do not care whether D contains x^* for the remaining oracle queries and computation.)

If the check does not pass, we abort. Just right before the k-th query, we switch to almost compressed Fourier oracles with the special point x^*.

Let $\gamma_{i,x^*,w,D}$ be the probability that conditioned on we are in Exp_i, the measurement gives x^* and the final output is w, D. Let $\gamma_{i,j,k,x^*,w,D}$ be the probability that conditioned on we are in $\mathsf{Exp}_{i,j,k}$, the measurement gives x^* and the final output is w, D. We have the following lemma:

Theorem 5. *For any w, D, for any x such that $D(x) \neq \perp$, there are at least one i or one tuple $i < j < k$ such that $\gamma_{i,x,w,D} \geq \gamma_{w,D}/(q+\binom{q}{3})^2$ or $\gamma_{i,j,k,x,w,D} \geq \gamma_{w,D}/(q+\binom{q}{3})^2$.*

Proof. Let $\sum_{x,y,z} \alpha_{x,y,z} |x,y,z\rangle$ be the state of the adversary just before the first query, and let $U^{(i)}_{x,y,z,x',y',z'}$ be the transition function after the i-th query. For vectors $\boldsymbol{x}, \boldsymbol{y}, \boldsymbol{z}$ and w, let

$$\alpha_{\boldsymbol{x},\boldsymbol{y},\boldsymbol{z},w} = \alpha_{x_1,y_1,z_1} U^{(1)}_{x_1,y_1,z_1,x_2,y_2,z_2} \cdots U^{(q)}_{x_q,y_q,z_q,w}$$

Then we can write the final joint state of the adversary and oracle as:

$$\sum_{x,y,z,w} \alpha_{x,y,z,w} |w\rangle \otimes \left| \bigoplus_{i=1}^{q} (x_i, y_i) \right\rangle$$

For any D, define the following sets S_D: it contains all the vector x, y pairs such that $\bigoplus_{i=1}^{q}(x_i, y_i) = D$. Thus we have $\gamma_{w,D} = |\gamma'_{w,D}|^2$ where

$$\gamma'_{w,D} = \sum_{(x,y) \in S_D, z} \alpha_{x,y,z,w}$$

Next consider any x such that $D(x) \neq \perp$, we can define the following sets:

- $S_{D,i}$: it contains all the vector x, y such that
  1. The fixed x is not in the database defined by $\oplus_{j=1}^{i-1}(x_i, y_i)$,
  2. $x_i = x$ and $y_i \neq 0$.
  In other words, x is not in the database before the i-th query and appears in the database right after i-th query. We can define $\gamma'_{i,x,w,D} = \sum_{(x,y) \in S_{D,i},z} \alpha_{x,y,z,w}$. Similarly we have $\gamma_{i,x,w,D} = |\gamma'_{i,x,w,D}|^2$.
- $S_{D,i,j,k}$: it contains all the vector x, y such that
  1. x is not in the database before the i-th query,
  2. x is in the database after the i-th query and before the j-th query,
  3. x is not in the database after the j-th query and before the k-th query,
  4. x appears in the database right after the k-th query.
  We can define $\gamma'_{i,j,k,x,w,D} = \sum_{(x,y) \in S_{D,i,j,k},z} \alpha_{x,y,z,w}$. Similarly we have $\gamma_{i,j,k,x,w,D} = |\gamma'_{i,j,k,x,w,D}|^2$.

Then we have the following lemma:

Lemma 2. *For any w, D and any x such that $D(x) \neq \perp$, we have*

$$\sum_{i} \gamma'_{i,x,w,D} - \sum_{i<j<k} \gamma'_{i,j,k,x,w,D} = \gamma'_{w,D}$$

Given the lemma above, we can argue that there exists some i or some triple $i < j < k$ such that either $|\gamma'_{i,x,w,D}| \geq |\gamma_{w,D}|/(q + \binom{q}{3})$ or $|\gamma'_{i,j,k,x,w,D}| \geq |\gamma_{w,D}|/(q + \binom{q}{3})$ by triangle inequality. Combining with $\gamma_{i,x,w,D} = |\gamma'_{i,x,w,D}|^2$ and $\gamma_{i,j,k,x,w,D} = |\gamma'_{i,j,k,x,w,D}|^2$, we complete the proof of our theorem. The only thing we need to prove is Lemma 2.

Proof. Consider every $(x, y) \in S_D$ and z, consider the database defined by these vectors. Assume x is inserted t times into the database. On the left side, $\alpha_{x,y,z,w,D}$ will appear in $\sum_i \gamma'_{i,x,w,D}$ exactly t times and appear in the second term $\sum_{i<j<k} \gamma'_{i,j,k,x,w,D}$ exactly $t - 1$ times. On the right side, it appears only once. Every $\alpha_{x,y,z,w,D}$ appears exactly once on both side. So the left side is equal to the right side. $\qquad\square$

We finish our proof for the Theorem 5.   □

And we notice that if $\mathcal{A}$ makes measurement during computation, the theorem also holds. And all the theorems and corollary below apply to the case where the algorithm can make measurement during computation. This proof and all proofs for the theorems below are in the full version [LZ19].

Theorem 6. *For any w, compressed Fourier database D and any x such that $D(x) \neq \perp$, let $\tau_{x,w,D}$ be the probability that in the above extracting experiment (that is to randomly pick Exp_i or $\mathsf{Exp}_{i,j,k}$), the measurement gives x and the output is w, D, we have $\tau_{x,w,D} \geq \frac{1}{(q+\binom{q}{3})^3} \cdot \gamma_{w,D}$.*

Proof. It follows directly from Theorem 5. Because we have probability $\frac{1}{q+\binom{q}{3}}$ to stay in the experiment that maximize the probability of getting x and outputting w, D, the total probability is at least $\tau_{x,w,D} \geq \frac{1}{(q+\binom{q}{3})^3} \cdot \gamma_{w,D}$.   □

Theorem 6 can be generalized to the setting where D is a compressed phase database, i.e, applying QFT on compressed Fourier database.

Corollary 2. *Define a set S contains pairs of w and compressed phase database D. Define a measurement, $P_0 = \sum_{(w,D) \in S} |w, D\rangle\langle w, D|$, $P_1 = I - P_0$.*

Let τ be the probability that in the extracting experiment, the extraction gives some $x_{w,D}$ in the database D for a given pair (w, D) and the final measurement is 0. Let γ be the probability that in the normal game, the final measurement is 0. q is the total number of oracle queries made. We have $\tau \geq \frac{1}{(q+\binom{q}{3})^3} \cdot \gamma$.

7   Programming Quantum Random Oracles

Lemma 3. *Assume an adversary $\mathcal{A}$ is interacting with an almost compressed phase oracle whose the switch stage is i and the special point is x^*. Wlog, assume the random oracle maps $\{0,1\}^N \to \{0,1\}^N$. Instead of appending $\sum_r |r\rangle$ before the i-th query, the simulator chooses a random r and appends $|r\rangle$ to the whole superposition. Then the adversary and the simulator keeps running. Finally the simulator measures the output registers.*

Let $\gamma_{r,w,D}$ be the probability that the output is $w, D \cup \{(x^*, r)\}$ in the normal game (where D does not contain x^*) and $\gamma'_{r,w,D}$ be the probability that the output is $w, D \cup \{(x^*, r)\}$ in the modified game with $|r\rangle$ is appended. We have

$$\frac{1}{2^N} \gamma'_{r,w,D} = \gamma_{r,w,D}$$

where D is a compressed phase database.

In other words, if we choose r uniformly at random, the probability of getting certain output does not change at all even if we program the oracle at x^* to output r. The lemma also holds if the almost compressed phase oracle has several special points and applies the technique to all the special points. The proof directly follows the proof for a single special point.

Proof. The proof is in the full version [LZ19]. Intuitively, when $1/\sqrt{2^N} \cdot \sum_r |r\rangle$ is appended, from $\mathcal{A}$'s view, the density matrix remains the same as the case where a random $|r\rangle$ is appended. $\qquad\square$

Corollary 3. *Assume an adversary $\mathcal{A}$ is interacting with an almost compressed phase oracle whose the switch stage is i and the special point is x^*. Wlog, assume the random oracle maps $\{0,1\}^N \to \{0,1\}^N$. Instead of appending $\sum_r |r\rangle$ before the i-th query, the simulator chooses a random r and appends $|r\rangle$ to the whole superposition. Then the adversary and the simulator keeps running. Finally the simulator measures the output registers.*

Let S be a set of w and compressed phase database $D \cup \{(x^*, r)\}$. Define a measurement P_0, P_1,

$$P_0 = \sum_{(w, D \cup \{(x^*, r)\}) \in S} |w, D \cup \{(x^*, r)\}\rangle\langle w, D \cup \{(x^*, r)\}| \quad P_1 = I - P_0$$

Let γ be the probability that the measurement gives 0 in the normal game and γ' the probability that the measurement gives 0 in the extracting game where $|r\rangle$ is randomly chosen. We have $\gamma = \gamma'$.

The lemma also holds if the almost compressed phase oracle has several special points and applies the technique to all the special points.

8 Fiat-Shamir in the QROM

8.1 Post-quantum Signature

Consider a (weakly complete) quantum secure identification protocol $\mathcal{P}, \mathcal{V}$, Fiat-Shamir approach gives a post-quantum digital signature as follows:

- It generates a pair of valid keys for identification protocol, say $(\mathsf{pk}, \mathsf{sk})$. pk is the verification key and sk is the signing key.
- $\mathsf{Sign}^H(\mathsf{sk}, m)$: it generates $(a, st) \leftarrow \mathcal{P}.\mathsf{Commit}(\mathsf{sk})$, and $c \leftarrow H(a\|m)$; and it generates $r \leftarrow \mathcal{P}.\mathsf{Prove}(\mathsf{sk}, st, c)$. If r is not valid, it runs another round. It keeps running until r is valid. Finally it returns $\sigma = (a, c, r)$.
- $\mathsf{Ver}^H(\mathsf{pk}, m, \sigma = (a', c', r'))$: given pk, m and a', c', r', it first verifies whether c' is generated honestly, in other words, $c' = H(a'\|m)$. Then it checks (a', c', r') is a valid transcript by checking whether $\mathcal{V}.\mathsf{Ver}(\mathsf{pk}, a', c', r') = 1$.

Theorem 7. *For a (weakly complete) secure quantum identification protocol with unpredictable commitment, Fiat-Shamir heuristic gives a secure post-quantum digital signature in the quantum random oracle model.*

First, let us look at completeness. By definition, there exist sets Good_λ, such that for all $(\mathsf{pk}, \mathsf{sk}) \in \mathsf{Good}_\lambda$, a honest generated transcript (a, c, r) is valid with some non-negligible probability at least $\eta(\lambda)$. It is easy to see when Sign^H runs the sigma protocol $\lambda \cdot \frac{1}{\eta(\lambda)}$ rounds, it generates a valid transcript with probability $\geq 1 - O(e^{-\lambda})$. Besides, if $(\mathsf{pk}, \mathsf{sk})$ is sampled by $\mathsf{Gen}(1^\lambda)$, with overwhelming probability $(\mathsf{pk}, \mathsf{sk}) \in \mathsf{Good}_\lambda$. Completeness follows. Next, let us look at security (existential unforgeability).

Proof. Assume we have quantum polynomial time $\mathcal{A}$ that makes q classical signing queries and p quantum oracle queries breaks the digital signature with advantage ϵ where ϵ is non-negligible.

Hyb 0: Let $\mathsf{Ch_{Sign}}$ be the challenger in $\mathcal{A}$'s game. The game is defined as the following:

---

1. $\mathcal{A}$ makes p quantum oracle queries to the random oracle which is simulated by $\mathcal{B}$;
2. $\mathcal{A}$ makes q classical signing queries to the challenger $\mathsf{Ch_{Sign}}$. Every time $\mathcal{A}$ wants to make a classical signing query, it measures the query register (to make sure the signing query is classical).
   To answer signing queries m_i, the challenger draws $(a_i, st) \leftarrow \mathcal{P}.\mathsf{Commit(sk)}$, makes a classical oracle query to the random oracle to get $c_i = H(a_i \| m_i)$ and gets $r_i = \mathcal{P}.\mathsf{Prove(sk}, st, c_i)$. $\mathsf{Ch_{Sign}}$ sends $\sigma_i = (a_i, c_i, r_i)$ to $\mathcal{A}$.

Wlog, the final superposition will have three parts. The first part is $\mathcal{A}$'s registers containing a new signature, the second part is $\mathsf{Ch_{Sign}}$'s registers which contain all the signing queries made by $\mathcal{A}$ and the third part is the oracle's registers (which $\mathcal{B}$ simulates it by using a compressed phase oracle).

Define the following measurement that checks if $\mathcal{A}$ succeeds in forgery:

$$P_0 = \sum_{\substack{\text{valid } m, \sigma, s \\ \{(m_i, \sigma_i)\}, D}} |m, \sigma, s\rangle | \{(m_i, \sigma_i)\}\rangle |D\rangle \langle m, \sigma, s| \langle \{(m_i, \sigma_i)\}| \langle D|$$

and $P_1 = I - P_0$. In P_0, we require that the output satisfies

1. $\sigma = (a, c, r)$ and $\sigma_i = (a_i, c_i, r_i)$.
2. It contains a valid new signature m, σ and all signing queries m_i, σ_i.
3. m, σ is new relative to $\{(m_i, \sigma_i)\}_{i=1}^q$, i.e, $(m, \sigma) \notin \{(m_i, \sigma_i)\}_{i=1}^q$.
4. All the signatures (including the newly forged one) are valid. First, for all i, $\mathcal{V}.\mathsf{Ver(sk}, a_i, c_i, r_i) = 1$ and $\mathcal{V}.\mathsf{Ver(sk}, a, c, r) = 1$. And second, for all i, $D(a_i \| m_i) = c_i$ and $D(a \| m) = c$.

Because D is a compressed phase oracle. It is possible that $D(a_i \| m_i) = \bot$ but still we have $H(a_i \| m_i) = c_i$. But in this case, $H(a_i \| m_i)$ is completely random. From Lemma 5 in [Zha18], there is only negligible loss (as long as q is polynomial). So we have in the above game, the final measurement gives 0 with probability at least $\epsilon_0 = \epsilon - \mathsf{negl}(\lambda)$ which is non-negligible.

Next we are going to modify the above game step by step until we get a $\mathcal{B}$ which simulates signing queries and breaks the underlying identification protocol. The difference of each hybrid is marked and the detailed algorithms in each hybrid are in the full version [LZ19].

Hyb 1: Here for each classical query $a_i||m_i$**made by** $\mathsf{Ch_{Sign}}$**,** $\mathcal{B}$ **checks the current compressed phase database does not have** $a_i||m_i$**.** In other words, $\mathcal{B}$ applies the measurement $\sum_{w,D:D(a_i||m_i)=\perp} |w,D\rangle\langle w,D|$.

Because the sigma protocol has unpredictable commitments, the probability the measurement does not pass is negligible in λ. And every time $\mathcal{B}$ checks $a_i||m_i$ is not in any database, it puts $a_i||m_i$ into the set of the special points, i.e, append $\sum_{c_i} |c_i\rangle$ to the oracle superposition denoting $D(a_i||m_i) = c_i$.

Let ϵ_1 be the probability that in the above game, all the intermediate measurements pass and the final measurement gives 0. We have $\epsilon_1 \geq \epsilon_0 - \mathsf{negl}(\lambda)$ which is non-negligible.

Hyb 2: The algorithm $\mathcal{A}$ is interacting with a simulated random oracle (simulated by $\mathcal{B}$) and $\mathsf{Ch_{Sign}}$. $\mathcal{B}$ **applies our extracting technique in Sect. 6:** it randomly picks i or $i, j, k \in [p]$, and does one of the experiments.

We care about the probability the all that measurements/checks pass, the extracted $x = a||m$ contains the same thing (the same a, m) as the message of the forged signature $x, \sigma = (a, c, r)$ and the final measurement gives 0 which tells a valid new signature is generated correctly.

From Corollary 2, given $w = ((m, \sigma), s, \{(m_i, \sigma_i)\}_{i=1}^q)$ and D that passes the measurement P_0, define $x_{w,D} = a||m$. Then we have the probability that the above experiment passes all the checks, the extracted query is $a||m$ and the final output measured over P_0, P_1 is 0 is at least $\epsilon_2 \geq \frac{1}{(q+\binom{q}{3})^3} \cdot \epsilon_1$.

Hyb 3: At the time of appending $\sum_c |c\rangle$ or $\sum_{c_i} |c_i\rangle$ to the superposition, $\mathcal{B}$ **randomly picks** c **and** c_i **and appends** $|c\rangle$ **and** $|c_i\rangle$. From Corollary 3, the probability that the experiment passes all the checks, the extracted query is $a||m$ and the final output measured over P_0, P_1 is 0 remains the same, i.e, $\epsilon_3 = \epsilon_2$.

Hyb 4: Now each c_i is chosen uniformly at random. $\mathcal{B}$ **can simulate** $\mathsf{Ch_{Sign}}$ **using the honest generated transcripts.** Every time $\mathcal{A}$ makes a signing query m_i, $\mathcal{B}$ picks the next generated transcript (a_i, c_i, r_i). Let $H(a_i||m_i) = c_i$ and $\sigma_i = (a_i, c_i, r_i)$.

The distribution of transcripts does not change. So the overall probability that the experiment passes all the checks, the extracted query is $a||m$ and the final output measured over P_0, P_1 is 0 remains the same, i.e, $\epsilon_4 = \epsilon_3$.

Hyb 5: In the final hybrid, $|c\rangle$ **is not longer chosen uniformly at random.** $\mathcal{B}$ is now in the game of breaking the quantum computational soundness of an identification protocol with the challenger $\mathsf{Ch_{id}}$.

$\mathcal{B}$ gives a to $\mathsf{Ch_{id}}$ where the extracted query is $x = a||m$, and receives c from $\mathsf{Ch_{id}}$. It then **uses the given** $|c\rangle$ **instead of the randomly chosen one.** The distribution does not change because c is also uniformly chosen by $\mathsf{Ch_{id}}$. The overall probability that the experiment passes all the checks, the extracted query is $a\|m$ and the final output measured over P_0, P_1 is 0 remains the same, i.e, $\epsilon_5 = \epsilon_4$ is non-negligible.

And because the extracted query is $x = a\|m$ and the newly forged signature is $m, \sigma = (a, c, r)$. We know that a, c, r is valid. So $\mathcal{B}$ can use an adversary $\mathcal{A}$ for breaking the signature scheme with advantage ϵ, to break the underlying identification protocol with advantage at least $\Omega(\epsilon/p^9) - \mathsf{negl}(\lambda)$.   □

8.2   Quantum NIZKPoK

We have the following theorem (The proof is in the full version [LZ19].):

Theorem 8. *If a sigma protocol has (1) perfect completeness, (2) post-quantum computational HVZK, (3) quantum proof of knowledge, (4) unpredictable commitments, the Fiat-Shamir heuristic gives a quantum NIZKPoK.*

Acknowledgements. This work is supported in part by NSF and DARPA. Opinions, findings and conclusions or recommendations expressed in this material are those of the author(s) and do not necessarily reflect the views of NSF or DARPA.

References

[AKPW13] Alwen, J., Krenn, S., Pietrzak, K., Wichs, D.: Learning with rounding, revisited. In: Canetti, R., Garay, J.A. (eds.) CRYPTO 2013. LNCS, vol. 8042, pp. 57–74. Springer, Heidelberg (2013). https://doi.org/10.1007/978-3-642-40041-4_4

[ARU14] Ambainis, A., Rosmanis, A., Unruh, D.: Quantum attacks on classical proof systems: the hardness of quantum rewinding. In: 55th FOCS, pp. 474–483. IEEE Computer Society Press, October 2014

[BDF+11] Boneh, D., Dagdelen, Ö., Fischlin, M., Lehmann, A., Schaffner, C., Zhandry, M.: Random oracles in a quantum world. In: Lee, D.H., Wang, X. (eds.) ASIACRYPT 2011. LNCS, vol. 7073, pp. 41–69. Springer, Heidelberg (2011). https://doi.org/10.1007/978-3-642-25385-0_3

[BR93] Bellare, M., Rogaway, P.: Random oracles are practical: a paradigm for designing efficient protocols. In: Denning, D.E., Pyle, R., Ganesan, R., Sandhu, R.S., Ashby, V. (eds.) ACM CCS 93, pp. 62–73. ACM Press, November 1993

[BZ13] Boneh, D., Zhandry, M.: Secure signatures and chosen ciphertext security in a quantum computing world. In: Canetti, R., Garay, J.A. (eds.) CRYPTO 2013. LNCS, vol. 8043, pp. 361–379. Springer, Heidelberg (2013). https://doi.org/10.1007/978-3-642-40084-1_21

[DFG13] Dagdelen, Ö., Fischlin, M., Gagliardoni, T.: The Fiat-Shamir transformation in a quantum world. Cryptology ePrint Archive, Report 2013/245 (2013). http://eprint.iacr.org/2013/245

[DKL+18] Ducas, L., et al.: Crystals-dilithium: a lattice-based digital signature scheme. IACR Trans. Cryptographic Hardware Embed. Syst. **2018**(1), 238–268 (2018)

[FS87]   Fiat, A., Shamir, A.: How to prove yourself: practical solutions to identi-
         fication and signature problems. In: Odlyzko, A.M. (ed.) CRYPTO 1986.
         LNCS, vol. 263, pp. 186–194. Springer, Heidelberg (1987). https://doi.org/
         10.1007/3-540-47721-7_12

[KLS18] Kiltz, E., Lyubashevsky, V., Schaffner, C.: A concrete treatment of Fiat-
         Shamir signatures in the quantum random-oracle model. In: Nielsen, J.B.,
         Rijmen, V. (eds.) EUROCRYPT 2018. LNCS, vol. 10822, pp. 552–586.
         Springer, Cham (2018). https://doi.org/10.1007/978-3-319-78372-7_18

[Lyu12] Lyubashevsky, V.: Lattice signatures without trapdoors. In: Pointcheval,
         D., Johansson, T. (eds.) EUROCRYPT 2012. LNCS, vol. 7237, pp.
         738–755. Springer, Heidelberg (2012). https://doi.org/10.1007/978-3-642-
         29011-4_43

[LZ19]   Liu, Q., Zhandry, M.: Revisiting post-quantum Fiat-Shamir. Cryptology
         ePrint Archive, Report 2019/262 (2019). https://eprint.iacr.org/2019/262

[PS96]   Pointcheval, D., Stern, J.: Provably secure blind signature schemes.
         In: Kim, K., Matsumoto, T. (eds.) ASIACRYPT 1996. LNCS, vol.
         1163, pp. 252–265. Springer, Heidelberg (1996). https://doi.org/10.1007/
         BFb0034852

[TU15]   Targhi, E.E., Unruh, D.: Quantum security of the Fujisaki-Okamoto and
         OAEP transforms. Cryptology ePrint Archive, Report 2015/1210 (2015).
         http://eprint.iacr.org/2015/1210

[Unr12] Unruh, D.: Quantum proofs of knowledge. In: Pointcheval, D., Johansson,
         T. (eds.) EUROCRYPT 2012. LNCS, vol. 7237, pp. 135–152. Springer,
         Heidelberg (2012). https://doi.org/10.1007/978-3-642-29011-4_10

[Unr15] Unruh, D.: Non-interactive zero-knowledge proofs in the quantum ran-
         dom oracle model. In: Oswald, E., Fischlin, M. (eds.) EUROCRYPT 2015.
         LNCS, vol. 9057, pp. 755–784. Springer, Heidelberg (2015). https://doi.
         org/10.1007/978-3-662-46803-6_25

[Unr16a] Unruh, D.: Collapse-binding quantum commitments without random ora-
         cles. In: Cheon, J.H., Takagi, T. (eds.) ASIACRYPT 2016. LNCS, vol.
         10032, pp. 166–195. Springer, Heidelberg (2016). https://doi.org/10.1007/
         978-3-662-53890-6_6

[Unr16b] Unruh, D.: Computationally binding quantum commitments. In: Fis-
         chlin, M., Coron, J.-S. (eds.) EUROCRYPT 2016. LNCS, vol. 9666, pp.
         497–527. Springer, Heidelberg (2016). https://doi.org/10.1007/978-3-662-
         49896-5_18

[Unr17] Unruh, D.: Post-quantum security of Fiat-Shamir. In: Takagi, T., Peyrin,
         T. (eds.) ASIACRYPT 2017. LNCS, vol. 10624, pp. 65–95. Springer, Cham
         (2017). https://doi.org/10.1007/978-3-319-70694-8_3

[Wat06] Watrous, J.: Zero-knowledge against quantum attacks. In: Kleinberg, J.M.
         (eds.) 38th ACM STOC, pp. 296–305. ACM Press, May 2006

[Zha12] Zhandry, M.: Secure identity-based encryption in the quantum random ora-
         cle model. In: Safavi-Naini, R., Canetti, R. (eds.) CRYPTO 2012. LNCS,
         vol. 7417, pp. 758–775. Springer, Heidelberg (2012). https://doi.org/10.
         1007/978-3-642-32009-5_44

[Zha18] Zhandry, M.: How to record quantum queries, and applications to quantum
         indifferentiability. Cryptology ePrint Archive, Report 2018/276 (2018).
         https://eprint.iacr.org/2018/276

Security of the Fiat-Shamir Transformation in the Quantum Random-Oracle Model

Jelle Don[1,2], Serge Fehr[1,3,4], Christian Majenz[2,4](✉),
and Christian Schaffner[2,4](✉)

[1] Centrum Wiskunde & Informatica (CWI), Amsterdam, Netherlands
{jelle.don,serge.fehr}@cwi.nl
[2] Institute for Logic, Language and Computation, University of Amsterdam,
Amsterdam, Netherlands
{c.majenz,c.schaffner}@uva.nl
[3] Mathematical Institute, Leiden University, Leiden, Netherlands
[4] QuSoft, Amsterdam, Netherlands

Abstract. The famous Fiat-Shamir transformation turns any public-coin three-round interactive proof, i.e., any so-called Σ-protocol, into a non-interactive proof in the random-oracle model. We study this transformation in the setting of a *quantum adversary* that in particular may query the random oracle in quantum superposition.

Our main result is a generic reduction that transforms any quantum dishonest prover attacking the Fiat-Shamir transformation in the quantum random-oracle model into a similarly successful quantum dishonest prover attacking the underlying Σ-protocol (in the standard model). Applied to the standard soundness and proof-of-knowledge definitions, our reduction implies that both these security properties, in both the computational and the statistical variant, are preserved under the Fiat-Shamir transformation even when allowing quantum attacks. Our result improves and completes the partial results that have been known so far, but it also proves wrong certain claims made in the literature.

In the context of post-quantum secure signature schemes, our results imply that for any Σ-protocol that is a proof-of-knowledge against quantum dishonest provers (and that satisfies some additional natural properties), the corresponding Fiat-Shamir signature scheme is secure in the quantum random-oracle model. For example, we can conclude that the non-optimized version of Fish, which is the bare Fiat-Shamir variant of the NIST candidate Picnic, is secure in the quantum random-oracle model.

1 Introduction

The (Quantum) Random-Oracle Model. The *random-oracle model* (ROM) is a means to treat a cryptographic hash function H as an ideal primitive. In the ROM, the only way to "compute" the hash $H(x)$ of any value x is by making a *query* to an imaginary entity, the *random oracle* (RO), which has chosen H

© International Association for Cryptologic Research 2019
A. Boldyreva and D. Micciancio (Eds.): CRYPTO 2019, LNCS 11693, pp. 356–383, 2019.
https://doi.org/10.1007/978-3-030-26951-7_13

uniformly at random from the set of *all* functions with the considered domain and range.

The hope is that if a cryptographic scheme is secure in the ROM then it is also secure in the standard model, as long as H is instantiated with a "good enough" cryptographic hash function. Even though in general we cannot hope to obtain provable security in the standard model in this way, (since there exist artificial counter examples [CGH04]), this approach works extremely well in practice, leading to very efficient schemes that tend to resist all known attacks.

What makes the ROM particularly convenient is that in the security proof of a cryptographic scheme, we can control the RO. For instance, simply by recording the queries that the adversary makes to the RO, we know exactly which hash values he knows, and the hash value $H(x)$ is random to him for any x that he has not queried. Furthermore, we can *reprogram* the RO, meaning that we can let $H(x)$ be some particular value y for some specific x, as long as it is random from the adversary's perspective.

When considering a *quantum* adversary, the picture changes a bit. In order to model that such an adversary can evaluate any hash function *in superposition* on different inputs, we must allow such a quantum adversary in the ROM to make superposition queries to the RO: for any superposition $\sum_x \alpha_x |x\rangle$ it may learn $\sum_x \alpha_x |x\rangle |H(x)\rangle$ by making a single query to the RO. This is referred to as the *quantum random-oracle model* (QROM) [BDF+11].

Unfortunately, these superposition queries obstruct the above mentioned advantages of the ROM. By basic properties of quantum mechanics one cannot observe or locally copy such superposition queries made by the adversary without disturbing them. Also, reprogramming is usually done for an x that is queried by the adversary at a certain point, so also here we are stuck with the problem that we cannot look at the queries without disturbing them.

As a consequence, security proofs in the ROM almost always do not carry over to the QROM. This lack of proof does not mean that the schemes become insecure; on the contrary, unless there is some failure because of some other reason[1], we actually expect typical schemes to remain secure. However, it is often not obvious how to find a security proof in the QROM. Some examples where security in the QROM has been established are [Unr14, Zha15, ES15, Unr15, KLS18, ABB+17, Zha18, SXY18, BDK+18].

Main Technical Result. Our main technical result (Theorem 2) can be understood as a particular way to overcome—to some extent—the above described limitation in the QROM of not being able to "read out" any query to the RO and to then reprogram the corresponding hash value. Concretely, we achieve the following.

We consider an arbitrary quantum algorithm $\mathcal{A}$ that makes queries to the RO and in the end outputs a pair (x, z), where z is supposed to satisfy some relation with respect to $H(x)$, e.g., $z = H(x)$. We then show how to *extract* early

---

[1] E.g., the underlying computational hardness assumption does not hold anymore in the context of a quantum adversary.

on, by measuring one of the queries that $\mathcal{A}$ makes, the very x that $\mathcal{A}$ will output, and to *reprogram* the RO at the point x with a fresh random value Θ, with the effect that the pair (x, z) that $\mathcal{A}$ then outputs now satisfies the given relation with respect to Θ, with a not too large loss in probability.

The way this works is surprisingly simple. We choose the query that we measure uniformly at random among all the queries that $\mathcal{A}$ makes (also counting $\mathcal{A}$'s output), in order to (hopefully) obtain x. Subsequently we reprogram the RO, so as to answer x with Θ, *either* from this point on *or* from the following query on, where this binary choice is made at random. This last random decision seems counter-intuitive, but it makes our proof work. Indeed, we prove that the probability that (x, z) satisfies the required relation drops by no more than a factor $O(q^2)$, where q is the number of oracle queries $\mathcal{A}$ makes.

Application to the Fiat-Shamir Transformation. The Fiat-Shamir transformation [FS87] turns any public-coin three-round interactive proof, i.e., any so-called Σ-protocol, into a non-interactive proof in the (Q)ROM. In the classical case it is well known that the security properties of the Σ-protocol are inherited by the Fiat-Shamir transformation [BR93, FKMV12]. In the quantum setting, when considering the security of the Fiat-Shamir transformation against quantum dishonest provers in the QROM, mainly negative results are known—see below for a more detailed exposition of previous results and how they compare to ours.

It is quite easy to see that the above result on the reprogrammability of the RO is exactly what is needed to turn a quantum prover that attacks the Fiat-Shamir transformation into a quantum prover that attacks the underlying Σ protocol. Indeed, from any Fiat-Shamir dishonest prover $\mathcal{A}$ that tries to produce a proof $\pi = (a, z)$ for a statement x, we obtain an interactive dishonest prover for the Σ protocol that extracts a from $\mathcal{A}$ and sends it to the verifier, and then uses the received challenge c to reprogram the RO, so that the z output by $\mathcal{A}$ will be a correct reply with respect to c with a probability not much smaller than the probability that $\mathcal{A}$ succeeds in forging π in the QROM.

This gives us a very generic transformation (stated in Theorem 8 below) from a Fiat-Shamir dishonest prover to a Σ-protocol dishonest prover that is similarly successful, up to a loss in probability of order $O(q^2)$. Applied to the standard notions of soundness and proof-of-knowledge, we prove that both these security properties, in both the computational and the statistical variant, are preserved under the Fiat-Shamir transformation in the QROM (Corollaries 13 and 16).

Comparison with Prior Results. Mainly negative results are known about the security of the Fiat-Shamir transformation against quantum attacks. Figure 1 shows a table copied from [ARU14], which outlines the different negative results on the security of Σ-protocols against quantum attackers that carry over to the Fiat-Shamir transformation. All the potential positive claims on the security of the Fiat-Shamir transformation were left unanswered (see Fig. 1).

Currently, the only known positive result on the security of the Fiat-Shamir transformation against quantum attacks is the result by Unruh [Unr17], which shows that *statistical* soundness of the Σ-protocol implies *computational*

Properties of Σ-protocol		Σ-protocol directly		Fiat-Shamir transf.	
special soundness	strict soundness	PoK	proof	PoK	proof
perf	comp	attack	stat	attack	**stat**
comp	comp	attack	attack	attack	attack
perf	perf	stat	stat	**stat**	**stat**

Fig. 1. Table adapted from [ARU14], showing which versions of *special soundness* and *strict soundness*, which we call *unique responses*, imply that the Σ-protocol is a *proof of knowledge (PoK)* or a *proof* (in the sense of ordinary soundness). The values comp, stat and perf mean that the considered property holds respectively computationally, statistically and perfectly, and attack means that there exist example schemes that allow an attack. Gray values are copied from [ARU14]. The last column shows that the negative results carry over to the Fiat-Shamir transformation, while our results (in **bold face**) complete the table by showing that also the positive results carry over. Previously, the lower right corner entry was only known to be comp, and the other two entries were unknown. If the computational version of the unique responses, or strict soundness, property is replaced by our quantum strengthening (Definition 24), all instances of attack can be replaced by **comp**.

soundness of the Fiat-Shamir transformation. This means, the lower right **stat** in the Fiat-Shamir column in Fig. 1 was known to be 'comp'.

Our generic transformation from a Fiat-Shamir dishonest prover to a Σ-protocol dishonest prover implies that *all* the (considered) security properties of the Σ-protocol carry over *unchanged* to the Fiat-Shamir transformation, i.e., without degradation from 'stat' to 'comp'. Hence, we show that all the three open settings from [ARU14] are statistically secure, as shown in Fig. 1.[2]

We point out that [DFG13] claims an impossibility result about the soundness of the Fiat-Shamir transformation as a quantum proof of knowledge, which contradicts one of our implications above. However, their result only applies to a restricted notion of proof of knowledge where the extractor is not allowed to measure any of the adversary's queries to the random oracle. The rational for this restriction was that such a measurement would disturb the adversary's quantum state beyond control; however, our technical result shows that it actually is possible to measure one of the adversary's queries and still have sufficient control over the adversary's behavior.

Relativizing Prior Negative Results. At first glance, the negative results from [ARU14] together with our new positive results, as shown in the Fiat-Shamir column in Fig. 1, seem to give a complete answer to the question of the security of the Fiat-Shamir transformation against quantum attacks. However, there is actually more to it.

We consider a *stronger* but still meaningful notion of *computational unique responses*, which is in the spirit of the *collapsing property* as introduced by Unruh

---

[2] In the (quantum) random-oracle model, *statistical* security considers a computationally unbounded attacker with a polynomially bounded number of oracle queries.

[Unr16]. We call the new notion *quantum computationally unique responses* and define it in Definition 24. Adapting a proof from [Unr12], it is not hard to see that a Σ-protocol with (perfect or computational) special soundness and quantum computational unique responses is a computational proof of knowledge. Therefore, our result then implies that its Fiat-Shamir transformation is a computational proof of knowledge as well.

Finally, our result also implies that if the Σ-protocol is *computationally sound* (as a 'proof'), then its Fiat-Shamir transformation is computationally sound as well. Interestingly, Unruh seems to suggest in [Unr17] (right after Theorem 21) that this is not true in general, due to a counterexample from [ARU14]. The counter example is, however, a Σ-protocol that is computationally *special* sound but not computationally sound (the issue being that in the quantum setting, special soundness does not imply ordinary soundness).

Thus, with the right adjustments of the considered *computational* soundness properties, the three negative answers in the Fiat-Shamir column in Fig. 1 may actually be turned into positive answers. One caveat here is that we expect proving quantum computationally unique responses to be much harder than computational unique responses.

Application to Signatures. Our positive results on the Fiat-Shamir transformation have direct applications to the security of Fiat-Shamir signatures. From the proof-of-knowledge property of the Fiat-Shamir transformation we immediately obtain the security of the Fiat-Shamir signature scheme under a *no-message attack*, assuming that the public key is a hard instance (Theorem 21). Furthermore, [Unr17] and [KLS18] have shown that for Fiat-Shamir signatures, up to some loss in the security parameter and under some additional mild assumptions on the underlying Σ-protocol, one can also derive security under *chosen-message attack*.

In conclusion, Fiat-Shamir signatures offer security against quantum attacks (in the QROM) if the underlying Σ-protocol is a proof of knowledge against quantum attacks and satisfies a few additional natural assumptions (Theorem 22).

As a concrete application, using Unruh's result on the collapsing property of the RO [Unr16] to argue the collapsing version of computational unique responses (which we call *quantum* computational unique responses) for the underlying Σ-protocol, we can conclude that the non-optimized version of Fish, which is the Fiat-Shamir variant of Picnic, is secure in the QROM.

Comparison with Concurrent Results. In concurrent and independent work [LZ19][3], Liu and Zhandry show results that are very similar to ours: they also show the security of the Fiat-Shamir transformation in the QROM, and they introduce a similar stronger version of the computational unique responses property in order to argue that a Σ-protocol is a (computational) proof of knowledge

---

[3] The paper [LZ19] was put on eprint (ia.cr/2019/262) a few days after our eprint version (ia.cr/2019/190).

against a quantum adversary. In short, [LZ19] differs from the work here in the following aspects. In [LZ19], the result on the Fiat-Shamir transformation is obtained using a very different approach, resulting in a greater loss in the reduction: $O(q^9)$ compared to the $O(q^2)$ loss that we obtain. On the other hand, on the quantum proof of knowledge front, Liu and Zhandry introduce some additional techniques that, for instance, allow them to prove that the Σ-protocol underlying Dilithium satisfies (their variant) of the newly introduced strong version of the computational unique responses property, while we phrase this as a conjecture in order to conclude the security of (some variant of) the Dilithium signature scheme.

2   Reprogramming the Quantum Random Oracle

We show and analyze a particular way to reprogram a random oracle in the quantum setting, where the oracle can be queried in superposition.

2.1   Notation

We consider a quantum oracle algorithm $\mathcal{A}$ that makes q queries to an *oracle*, i.e., an unspecified function $H : \mathcal{X} \to \mathcal{Y}$ with finite non-empty sets $\mathcal{X}, \mathcal{Y}$. We may assume without loss of generality that $\mathcal{A}$ makes no intermediary measurements. Formally, $\mathcal{A}$ is then described by a sequence of unitaries $A_1, \ldots, A_q$ and an initial state $|\phi_0\rangle$.[4] The unitaries A_i act on registers X, Y, Z, E, where X and Y have respective $|\mathcal{X}|$- and $|\mathcal{Y}|$-dimensional state spaces, while Z and E is arbitrary. As will become clear, X and Y are the quantum registers for the queries to H as well as for the final output x, Z is for the output z, and E is internal memory. For any concrete choice of $H : \mathcal{X} \to \mathcal{Y}$, we can write

$$\mathcal{A}^H |\phi_0\rangle := A_q \mathcal{O}^H \cdots A_1 \mathcal{O}^H |\phi_0\rangle,$$

for the execution of $\mathcal{A}$ with the oracle instantiated by H, where $\mathcal{O}^H$ is the unitary $\mathcal{O}^H : |x\rangle|y\rangle \mapsto |x\rangle|y \oplus H(x)\rangle$ that acts on registers X and Y.

It will be convenient to introduce the following notation. For $0 \le i, j \le q$ we set

$$\mathcal{A}^H_{i \to j} := A_j \mathcal{O}^H \cdots A_{i+1} \mathcal{O}^H$$

with the convention that $\mathcal{A}^H_{i \to j} := \mathbb{1}$ for $j \le i$. Furthermore, we set

$$|\phi_i^H\rangle := \left(\mathcal{A}^H_{0 \to i} \right) |\phi_0\rangle$$

to be the state of $\mathcal{A}$ after the i-th step but right before the $(i+1)$-st query, and so that $|\phi_q^H\rangle$ equals $\left(\mathcal{A}^H_{0 \to q} \right) |\phi_0\rangle = \mathcal{A}^H |\phi_0\rangle$, the output state produced by $\mathcal{A}$.

Finally, for a given function $H : \mathcal{X} \to \mathcal{Y}$ and for fixed $x \in \mathcal{X}$ and $\Theta \in \mathcal{Y}$, we define the *reprogrammed* function $H*\Theta x : \mathcal{X} \to \mathcal{Y}$ that coincides with H on $\mathcal{X} \setminus \{x\}$ but maps x to Θ. With this notation at hand, we can then write

$$\left(\mathcal{A}^{H*\Theta x}_{i \to q} \right) \left(\mathcal{A}^H_{0 \to i} \right) |\phi_0\rangle = \left(\mathcal{A}^{H*\Theta x}_{i \to q} \right) |\phi_i^H\rangle$$

---

[4] Alternatively, we may understand $|\phi_0\rangle$ as an auxiliary input given to $\mathcal{A}$.

for an execution of $\mathcal{A}$ where the oracle is reprogrammed at a given point x after the i-th query.

We are interested in the probability that after the execution of $\mathcal{A}^H$ and upon measuring register X in the computational basis to obtain $x \in \mathcal{X}$, the state of register Z is of a certain form dependent on x and $H(x)$. This relation is captured by a projection G_x^H, where, more generally, for $x, x' \in \mathcal{X}$ and $\Theta \in \mathcal{Y}$ we set

$$G_{x,x'}^\Theta = |x'\rangle\langle x'| \otimes \mathbb{1} \otimes \Pi_{x,\Theta} \otimes \mathbb{1},$$

where $\{\Pi_{x,\Theta}\}_{x \in \mathcal{X}, \Theta \in \mathcal{Y}}$ is a family of projections acting on Z, which we refer to as a *quantum predicate*. We use the short hands G_x^Θ for $G_{x,x}^\Theta$ and G_x^H for $G_x^{H(x)}$, i.e.,

$$G_x^H = |x\rangle\langle x| \otimes \mathbb{1} \otimes \Pi_{x,H(x)} \otimes \mathbb{1}.$$

For an arbitrary but fixed $x_\circ \in \mathcal{X}$, we then consider the probability

$$\|G_{x_\circ}^H |\phi_q^H\rangle\|_2^2 .$$

Understanding $\mathcal{A}^H$ as an algorithm that outputs the measured x together with the state z in register Z, we will denote this probability also by

$$\Pr\left[x = x_\circ \wedge V(x, H(x), z) : (x, z) \leftarrow \mathcal{A}^H\right],$$

understanding V to be a quantum predicate specified by the projections $\Pi_{x,H(x)}$.

2.2   Main Technical Result

We consider a quantum oracle algorithm $\mathcal{A}$ as formalized above, and we define a two-stage algorithm $\mathcal{S}$ with black-box access to $\mathcal{A}$ as follows. In the first stage, $\mathcal{S}$ tries to predict $\mathcal{A}$'s future output x, and then, upon input a (random) Θ, in the second stage tries to output what $\mathcal{A}$ is supposed to output, but now with respect to Θ instead of $H(x)$.

$\mathcal{S}$ works by running $\mathcal{A}$, but with the following modifications. First, one of the $q + 1$ queries of $\mathcal{A}$ (also counting the final output in register X) is selected uniformly at random and this query is measured, and the measurement outcome x is output by (the first stage of) $\mathcal{S}$. Then, this very query of $\mathcal{A}$ is answered either using the original H *or* using the reprogrammed oracle $H * \Theta x$, with the choice being made at random, while all the remaining queries of $\mathcal{A}$ are answered using oracle $H * \Theta x$.[5] Finally, (the second stage of) $\mathcal{S}$ outputs whatever $\mathcal{A}$ outputs.

Here, the figure of merit is the probability that for a fixed x, both the intermediate measurement and a measurement of the register X return x *and* that the register Z contains a state that satisfies the considered quantum predicate with respect to x and its (now reprogrammed) hash value Θ. Formally, this probability is captured by

$$\mathop{\mathbb{E}}_{\Theta, i, b}\left[\left\|G_x^\Theta \left(\mathcal{A}_{i+b \to q}^{H*\Theta x}\right)\left(\mathcal{A}_{i \to i+b}^H\right) X |\phi_i^H\rangle\right\|_2^2\right]$$

---

[5] If it is the final output that is measured then there is nothing left to reprogram.

where here and from now on, we use X as a short hand for the projection $|x\rangle\langle x|$ acting on X. The expectation is taken over $\Theta \in \mathcal{Y}$, $i \in \{0, ..., q\}$ and $b \in \{0, 1\}$ uniformly random. Note that the random bit $b \in \{0, 1\}$ determines whether the measured query is answered with H or with $H*\Theta x$.

We write $\mathcal{S}^{\mathcal{A}}[H]$ to emphasize that $\mathcal{S}$ only makes black-box access to $\mathcal{A}$ and that it depends on H. Our main technical lemma below then ensures that for any H and for a random $\Theta \in \mathcal{Y}$, the success probability of $\mathcal{S}^{\mathcal{A}}[H]$ is up to an order-q^2 loss not much smaller than that of $\mathcal{A}^{H*\Theta x}$, and therefore not much smaller than that of $\mathcal{A}^H$ in case of a random H.

Lemma 1. *For any $H : \mathcal{X} \to \mathcal{Y}$ and $x \in \mathcal{X}$, it holds that*

$$\mathop{\mathbb{E}}_{\Theta,i,b}\left[\left\|G_x^{\Theta}\left(\mathcal{A}_{i+b \to q}^{H*\Theta x}\right)\left(\mathcal{A}_{i \to i+b}^H\right)X|\phi_i^H\rangle\right\|_2^2\right] \geq \frac{\mathbb{E}_{\Theta}\left[\left\|G_x^{\Theta}|\phi_q^{H*\Theta x}\rangle\right\|_2^2\right]}{2(q+1)(2q+3)} - \frac{\left\||X|\phi_q^H\rangle\right\|_2^2}{2(q+1)|\mathcal{Y}|}.$$

where the expectation is over random $\Theta \in \mathcal{Y}$, $i \in \{0, \dots, q\}$ and $b \in \{0, 1\}$.[6]

Proof. We assume that the Y-register of $|\phi_q^H\rangle = \left(\mathcal{A}_{0 \to q}^H\right)|\phi_0\rangle$ is $|0\rangle$ no matter what H is; this is without loss of generality since it can always be achieved by an insignificant modification to $\mathcal{A}$, i.e., by swapping Y with a default register within E. For the purpose of the proof, we introduce an additional step $\mathcal{A}_{q \to q+1}^H$ that simply applies $\mathcal{O}^H$, and we expand the notions of $|\phi_j^H\rangle$ and $\mathcal{A}_{i \to j}^H$ to allow $j = q + 1$. Finally, we "enhance" G_x^{Θ} to[7]

$$\tilde{G}_x^{\Theta} := G_x^{\Theta}(\mathbb{1} \otimes |0\rangle\langle 0| \otimes \mathbb{1} \otimes \mathbb{1}) - X \otimes |0\rangle\langle 0| \otimes \Pi_{x,\Theta} \otimes \mathbb{1}.$$

For any $0 \leq i \leq q$, inserting a resolution of the identity and exploiting that

$$\left(\mathcal{A}_{i+1 \to q+1}^{H*\Theta x}\right)\left(\mathcal{A}_{i \to i+1}^H\right)\left(\mathbb{1} - X\right)|\phi_i^H\rangle = \left(\mathcal{A}_{i \to q+1}^{H*\Theta x}\right)\left(\mathbb{1} - X\right)|\phi_i^H\rangle,$$

we can write

$$\begin{aligned}
\left(\mathcal{A}_{i+1 \to q+1}^{H*\Theta x}\right)&|\phi_{i+1}^H\rangle \\
&= \left(\mathcal{A}_{i+1 \to q+1}^{H*\Theta x}\right)\left(\mathcal{A}_{i \to i+1}^H\right)\left(\mathbb{1} - X\right)|\phi_i^H\rangle + \left(\mathcal{A}_{i+1 \to q+1}^{H*\Theta x}\right)\left(\mathcal{A}_{i \to i+1}^H\right)X|\phi_i^H\rangle \\
&= \left(\mathcal{A}_{i \to q+1}^{H*\Theta x}\right)\left(\mathbb{1} - X\right)|\phi_i^H\rangle + \left(\mathcal{A}_{i+1 \to q+1}^{H*\Theta x}\right)\left(\mathcal{A}_{i \to i+1}^H\right)X|\phi_i^H\rangle \\
&= \left(\mathcal{A}_{i \to q+1}^{H*\Theta x}\right)|\phi_i^H\rangle - \left(\mathcal{A}_{i \to q+1}^{H*\Theta x}\right)X|\phi_i^H\rangle + \left(\mathcal{A}_{i+1 \to q+1}^{H*\Theta x}\right)\left(\mathcal{A}_{i \to i+1}^H\right)X|\phi_i^H\rangle
\end{aligned}$$

---

[6] We consider $|\mathcal{Y}|$ to be superpolynomial in the security parameter, so that $\frac{1}{2(q+1)|\mathcal{Y}|}$ is negligible and can be neglected. In cases where $|\mathcal{Y}|$ is polynomial, the presented bound is not optimal, but an improved bound can be derived with the same kind of techniques.

[7] Informally, these modifications mean that we let $\mathcal{A}$ make one more query to get $H(x)$ into register Y, and $\tilde{G}_x^{H(x)}$ would then check that Y indeed contains $H(x)$.

Rearranging terms, applying $\tilde{G}_x^\Theta$ and using the triangle equality, we can thus bound

$$\left\| \tilde{G}_x^\Theta (\mathcal{A}_{i \to q+1}^{H*\Theta x}) |\phi_i^H\rangle \right\|_2 \leq \left\| \tilde{G}_x^\Theta (\mathcal{A}_{i+1 \to q+1}^{H*\Theta x}) |\phi_{i+1}^H\rangle \right\|_2$$
$$+ \left\| \tilde{G}_x^\Theta (\mathcal{A}_{i \to q+1}^{H*\Theta x}) X |\phi_i^H\rangle \right\|_2$$
$$+ \left\| \tilde{G}_x^\Theta (\mathcal{A}_{i+1 \to q+1}^{H*\Theta x}) (\mathcal{A}_{i \to i+1}^{H}) X |\phi_i^H\rangle \right\|_2.$$

Summing up the respective sides of the inequality over $i = 0, \ldots, q$, we get

$$\left\| \tilde{G}_x^\Theta |\phi_{q+1}^{H*\Theta x}\rangle \right\|_2 \leq \left\| \tilde{G}_x^\Theta |\phi_{q+1}^H\rangle \right\|_2 + \sum_{\substack{0 \leq i \leq q \\ b \in \{0,1\}}} \left\| \tilde{G}_x^\Theta (\mathcal{A}_{i+b \to q+1}^{H*\Theta x}) (\mathcal{A}_{i \to i+b}^{H}) X |\phi_i^H\rangle \right\|_2.$$

By squaring both sides, dividing by $2q+3$ (i.e., the number of terms on the right hand side), and using Jensen's inequality on the right hand side, we obtain

$$\frac{\left\| \tilde{G}_x^\Theta |\phi_{q+1}^{H*\Theta x}\rangle \right\|_2^2}{2q+3} \leq \left\| \tilde{G}_x^\Theta |\phi_{q+1}^H\rangle \right\|_2^2 + \sum_{\substack{0 \leq i \leq q \\ b \in \{0,1\}}} \left\| \tilde{G}_x^\Theta (\mathcal{A}_{i+b \to q+1}^{H*\Theta x}) (\mathcal{A}_{i \to i+b}^{H}) X |\phi_i^H\rangle \right\|_2^2$$

and thus

$$\mathop{\mathbb{E}}_{i,b} \left[\left\| \tilde{G}_x^\Theta (\mathcal{A}_{i+b \to q+1}^{H*\Theta x}) (\mathcal{A}_{i \to i+b}^{H}) X |\phi_i^H\rangle \right\|_2^2 \right] \geq \frac{\left\| \tilde{G}_x^\Theta |\phi_{q+1}^{H*\Theta x}\rangle \right\|_2^2}{2(q+1)(2q+3)} - \frac{\left\| \tilde{G}_x^\Theta |\phi_{q+1}^H\rangle \right\|_2^2}{2(q+1)}. \tag{1}$$

Since both $|\Theta\rangle\langle\Theta|$ and $\mathcal{A}_{q \to q+1}^{H*\Theta x} = \mathcal{O}^{H*\Theta x}$ commute with G_x^Θ, we get

$$\left\| \tilde{G}_x^\Theta (\mathcal{A}_{i+b \to q+1}^{H*\Theta x}) (\mathcal{A}_{i \to i+b}^{H}) X |\phi_i^H\rangle \right\|_2^2 \leq \left\| G_x^\Theta (\mathcal{A}_{i+b \to q+1}^{H*\Theta x}) (\mathcal{A}_{i \to i+b}^{H}) X |\phi_i^H\rangle \right\|_2^2$$
$$= \left\| G_x^\Theta (\mathcal{A}_{i+b \to q}^{H*\Theta x}) (\mathcal{A}_{i \to i+b}^{H}) X |\phi_i^H\rangle \right\|_2^2. \tag{2}$$

Also, because $(X \otimes |\Theta\rangle\langle\Theta|)\mathcal{O}^{H*\Theta x} = (X \otimes \mathbb{1})\mathcal{O}^{H*\Theta x}$, and $\mathcal{O}^{H*\Theta x}$ commutes with G_x^Θ, we get

$$\left\| \tilde{G}_x^\Theta |\phi_{q+1}^{H*\Theta x}\rangle \right\|_2^2 = \left\| G_x^\Theta |\phi_q^{H*\Theta x}\rangle \right\|_2^2. \tag{3}$$

Finally,

$$\mathop{\mathbb{E}}_{\Theta} \left[\left\| \tilde{G}_x^\Theta |\phi_{q+1}^H\rangle \right\|_2^2 \right] \leq \mathop{\mathbb{E}}_{\Theta} \left[\left\| (X \otimes |\Theta\rangle\langle\Theta|)\mathcal{O}^H |\phi_q^H\rangle \right\|_2^2 \right] \leq \frac{1}{|\mathcal{Y}|} \left\| X |\phi_q^H\rangle \right\|_2^2. \tag{4}$$

Inserting (2), (3) and (4) into (1) yields the claimed result.   □

2.3   Switching Notation, and Simulating the Random Oracle

Introducing more algorithmic-probabilistic notation, we write

$$(x, x', z) \leftarrow \langle \mathcal{S}^\mathcal{A}[H], \Theta \rangle$$

to specify the probability space determined as follows, relying on the above construction of the two-stage algorithm $\mathcal{S}$ when given $\mathcal{A}$. In the first stage $\mathcal{S}^{\mathcal{A}}[H]$ produces x, and then in the second stage, upon receiving Θ, it produces x' and z, where z may be quantum. Our figure of merit above, i.e., the left hand side of the bound in Lemma 1 (with x replaced by $x_\circ$), is then denoted by

$$\Pr_{\Theta}\left[x=x_\circ \wedge x'=x_\circ \wedge V(x,\Theta,z) : (x,x',z) \leftarrow \langle \mathcal{S}^{\mathcal{A}}[H],\Theta \rangle\right],$$

where the subscript Θ in $\Pr_\Theta$ denotes that the probability is averaged over a random choice of Θ.

Using this notation, but also weakening the bound slightly by not requiring $x' = x_\circ$, for any H and $x_\circ$ the bound from Lemma 1 then becomes

$$\Pr_{\Theta}\left[x=x_\circ \wedge V(x,\Theta,z) : (x,z) \leftarrow \langle \mathcal{S}^{\mathcal{A}}[H],\Theta \rangle\right]$$

$$\gtrsim \frac{1}{O(q^2)}\Pr_{\Theta}\left[x=x_\circ \wedge V(x,H(x),z) : (x,z) \leftarrow \mathcal{A}^{H*\Theta x}\right]$$

where the approximate inequality $\gtrsim$ hides the term

$$\frac{1}{2(q+1)|\mathcal{Y}|}\Pr_{H}\left[x=x_\circ : (x,z) \leftarrow \mathcal{A}^{H}\right].$$

Recall that the output z may be a quantum state, in which case the predicate V is given by a measurement that depends on x, and $H(x)$ or Θ, respectively.

We fix a family $\mathcal{H}$ of $2(q + 1)$-wise independent hash functions and average the above inequality over a random choice of $H \in \mathcal{H}$ from this family. We simply write $\mathcal{S}$ for $\mathcal{S}[H]$ with H chosen like that. Furthermore, we observe that, for any fixed x, the family $\{H * \Theta x \mid H \in \mathcal{H}, \Theta \in \{0,1\}^n\}$ is a family of $2(q + 1)$-wise independent hash functions as well. Finally, we use that $\mathcal{A}$ (together with the check $V(x, H(x), z)$) cannot distinguish a random function $H*\Theta x$ in that family from a fully random function H [Zha12]. This gives us the following variation of Lemma 1, which we state as our main technical theorem:

Theorem 2 (Measure-and-Reprogram). *Let $\mathcal{X}, \mathcal{Y}$ be finite non-empty sets. There exists a black-box polynomial-time two-stage quantum algorithm $\mathcal{S}$ with the following property. Let $\mathcal{A}$ be an arbitrary oracle quantum algorithm that makes q queries to a uniformly random $H : \mathcal{X} \to \mathcal{Y}$ and that outputs some $x \in \mathcal{X}$ and a (possibly quantum) output z. Then, the two-stage algorithm $\mathcal{S}^{\mathcal{A}}$ outputs some $x \in \mathcal{X}$ in the first stage and, upon a random $\Theta \in \mathcal{Y}$ as input to the second stage, a (possibly quantum) output z, so that for any $x_\circ \in \mathcal{X}$ and any predicate[8] V:*

$$\Pr_{\Theta}\left[x=x_\circ \wedge V(x,\Theta,z) : (x,z) \leftarrow \langle \mathcal{S}^{\mathcal{A}},\Theta \rangle\right]$$

$$\gtrsim \frac{1}{O(q^2)}\Pr_{H}\left[x=x_\circ \wedge V(x,H(x),z) : (x,z) \leftarrow \mathcal{A}^{H}\right],$$

where the $\gtrsim$ hides a term that is bounded by $\frac{1}{2q|\mathcal{Y}|}$ when summed over all $x_\circ$.

---

[8] We recall that in case z is a quantum state, V is given by means of a measurement.

Remark 3. We do not spell out in detail what it means for a quantum algorithm like S to be *black-box*; see e.g. [Unr17] for a rigorous definition. What we obviously need here is that S^A has access to A's initial state $|\phi_0\rangle$ and to q, and is given black-box access to the unitaries A_i. Furthermore, for later purposes, we need the following composition property: if S is a black-box algorithm with access to A, and K is a black-box algorithm with access to S^A, then there exists a black-box algorithm K^S with access to A so that $(K^S)^A = K^{(S^A)}$.

3   Security of the Fiat-Shamir Transformation

In this section, we show how to reduce security of the Fiat-Shamir transformation to the security of the underlying Σ-protocol: any dishonest prover attacking the Fiat-Shamir transformation can be turned into a dishonest prover that succeeds to break the underlying Σ-protocol with the same probability up to a polynomial loss. This reduction is obtained by a straightforward application of Theorem 2. Our security reduction holds very generically and is not strongly tight to the considered notion of security, as long as the respective security definitions for the Σ-protocol and the Fiat-Shamir transformation "match up".

3.1 Σ-protocols

We recall the definition of a Σ-protocol.

Definition 4 (Σ−protocol). *A Σ-protocol $\Sigma = (\mathcal{P}, \mathcal{V})$ for a relation $R \subseteq \mathcal{X} \times \mathcal{W}$ is a three-round two-party interactive protocol of the form:*

$\underline{Prover\ \mathcal{P}(x, w)}$	$\underline{Verifier\ \mathcal{V}(x)}$
$\xrightarrow{\quad a \quad}$	
$\xleftarrow{\quad c \quad}$	$c \xleftarrow{\ \$\ } C$
$\xrightarrow{\quad z \quad}$	Accept iff $V(x, a, c, z) = 1$

Using our terminology and notation from above, $\mathcal{P}$ is a two-stage algorithm and we can write

$$(a, z) \leftarrow \langle \mathcal{P}(x, w), c \rangle$$

for the generation of the first message a in the first stage and the reply z in the second stage once given the challenge c.

Remark 5. We allow the set of *instances* $\mathcal{X}$, the set of *witnesses* $\mathcal{W}$ and the relation R to depend on a security parameter η. Similarly, the interactive algorithms $\mathcal{P}$ and $\mathcal{V}$ may depend on η (or have η as part of their input). However, for ease of notation, we suppress these dependencies on η unless they are crucial.

Remark 6. We do not necessarily require a Σ-protocol to be perfectly or statistically correct. This allows us to include protocols that use *rejection sampling*, where with a constant probability, the value z would leak too much information on the witness w and so the prover sends $\perp$ instead. On the other hand, by default we consider the soundness/knowledge error to be negligible, i.e., a dishonest prover succeeds only with negligible probability to make the verifier accept if x is not a valid instance or the prover has no witness for it (depending on the considered soundness notion). Negligible soundness/knowledge error can always be achieved by parallel repetition (see e.g. [Dam10]).

3.2 The Fiat-Shamir Transformation

The *Fiat-Shamir transformation* turns a Σ-protocol Σ into a non-interactive proof system, denoted $\mathsf{FS}[\Sigma]$, by replacing the verifier's random choice of $c \in \mathcal{C}$ with $c := H(x, a)$, where $H : \mathcal{X}' \to \mathcal{C}$ is a hash function with a domain $\mathcal{X}'$ that contains all pairs $x' = (x, a)$ with $x \in \mathcal{X}$ and a produced by $\mathcal{P}$. In other words, upon input x and w, the honest FS-prover produces $\pi = (a, z)$ by running the two-stage Σ-protocol prover $\mathcal{P}$ but using $c = H(x, a)$ as challenge (i.e., as input to the second stage). In case Σ is not statistically correct, the above process of producing $\pi = (a, z)$ is repeated sufficiently many times until $V(x, a, H(x, a), z)$ is satisfied (or some bound is reached). In either case, we will write this as

$$\pi = (a, z) \leftarrow P_{FS}^H(x, w).$$

We may write as $V_{FS}^H(x, \pi)$ the FS verifier's check whether $V(x, a, H(x, a), z)$ is satisfied or not. In the security analysis, the hash function H is modeled by a random oracle, i.e. by oracle access to a uniformly random $H : \mathcal{X}' \to \mathcal{C}$.

When considering an *adversary* $\mathcal{A}$ that tries to *forge* a proof for some instance $x \in \mathcal{X}$, one can distinguish between an *arbitrary but fixed* x, and an x that is *chosen* by $\mathcal{A}$ and output along with a in case of Σ-protocols, respectively along with π in case of the Fiat-Shamir transformation. If x is fixed then the adversary is called *static*, otherwise it is called *adaptive*. For the typical security definitions for Σ-protocols this distinction between a static and an adaptive $\mathcal{A}$ makes no difference (see Lemmas 12 and 15 below), but for the Fiat-Shamir transformation it (potentially) does.

3.3 The Generic Security Reduction

Since an adaptive adversary is clearly not less powerful than a static adversary, we restrict our attention for the moment to the adaptive case. Recall that such an adaptive FS-adversary $\mathcal{A}$ outputs the instance $x \in \mathcal{X}$ along with the proof $\pi = (a, z)$, and the figure of merit is the probability that x, a, z satisfies $V(x, a, H(x, a), z)$. Thus, we can simply apply Theorem 2, with (x, a) playing the role of what is referred to as x in the theorem statement, to obtain the existence of an adaptive Σ-adversary $\mathcal{S}^{\mathcal{A}}$ that produces (x, a) in a first stage, and upon receiving a random challenge c produces z, such that for any $x_\circ \in \mathcal{X}$

$$\Pr_c\left[x = x_\circ \wedge V(x, a, c, z) : (x, a, z) \leftarrow \langle \mathcal{S}^{\mathcal{A}}, c \rangle\right]$$

$$\gtrsim \frac{1}{O(q^2)} \Pr_H\left[x = x_\circ \wedge V(x, a, H(x, a), z), z) : (x, a, z) \leftarrow \mathcal{A}^H\right],$$

where the approximate inequality hides a term that is bounded by $\frac{1}{2q|\mathcal{C}|}$ when summed over all $x_\circ \in \mathcal{X}$. Understanding that x is given to $\mathcal{V}$ along with the first message a but also treating it as an output of $\mathcal{S}^{\mathcal{A}}$, while $\mathcal{V}$'s output v is its decision to accept or not, we write this as

$$\Pr\left[x = x_\circ \wedge v = accept : (x, v) \leftarrow \langle \mathcal{S}^{\mathcal{A}}, \mathcal{V} \rangle\right]$$

$$\gtrsim \frac{1}{O(q^2)} \Pr_H\left[x = x_\circ \wedge V_{FS}^H(x, \pi) : (x, \pi) \leftarrow \mathcal{A}^H\right].$$

Summed over all $x_\circ \in \mathcal{X}$, this in particular implies that

$$\Pr\left[\langle \mathcal{S}^{\mathcal{A}}, \mathcal{V} \rangle = accept\right] \geq \frac{1}{O(q^2)} \Pr_H\left[V_{FS}^H(x, \pi) : (x, \pi) \leftarrow \mathcal{A}^H\right] - \frac{1}{2q|\mathcal{C}|}.$$

Remark 7. We point out that the above arguments extend to a FS-adversary $\mathcal{A}$ that, besides the instance x and the proof $\pi = (a, z)$, also produces some local (possibly quantum) output satisfying some (quantum) predicate that may depend on x, a, z. The resulting Σ-adversary $\mathcal{S}^{\mathcal{A}}$ is then ensured to produce a local output that satisfies the considered predicate as well, up to the given loss in the probability. Indeed, we can simply include this local output in z and extend the predicate V accordingly.

In a very broad sense, the above means that for *any* FS-adversary $\mathcal{A}$ there exists a Σ-adversary $\mathcal{S}^{\mathcal{A}}$ that *"achieves the same thing"* up to a $O(q^2)$ loss in success probability. Hence, for matching corresponding security definitions, security of a Σ-protocol (against a dishonest prover) implies security of its Fiat-Shamir transform.

We summarize here the above basic transformation from an adaptive FS-adversary $\mathcal{A}$ to an adaptive Σ-adversary $\mathcal{S}^{\mathcal{A}}$.

Theorem 8. *There exists a black-box quantum polynomial-time two-stage quantum algorithm S such that for any adaptive Fiat-Shamir adversary $\mathcal{A}$, making q queries to a uniformly random function H with appropriate domain and range, and for any $x_\circ \in \mathcal{X}$:*

$$\Pr\left[x = x_\circ \wedge v = accept : (x, v) \leftarrow \langle \mathcal{S}^{\mathcal{A}}, \mathcal{V} \rangle\right]$$

$$\gtrsim \frac{1}{O(q^2)} \Pr_H\left[x = x_\circ \wedge V_{FS}^H(x, \pi) : (x, \pi) \leftarrow \mathcal{A}^H\right],$$

where the $\gtrsim$ hides a term that is bounded by $\frac{1}{2q|\mathcal{C}|}$ when summed over all $x_\circ$.

Below, we apply the above general reduction to the respective standard definitions for *soundness* and *proof of knowledge*. Each property comes in the variants *computational* and *statistical*, for guarantees against computationally bounded or unbounded adversaries respectively, and one may consider the static or the adaptive case.

3.4   Preservation of Soundness

Let $\Sigma = (\mathcal{P}, \mathcal{V})$ be a Σ-protocol for a relation R, and let $\mathsf{FS}[\Sigma]$ be its Fiat-Shamir transformation. We set $\mathcal{L} := \{x \in \mathcal{X} \mid \exists w \in \mathcal{W} : R(x, w)\}$. It is understood that $\mathcal{P}$ and $\mathcal{V}$, as well as R and thus $\mathcal{L}$, may depend on a security parameter η. We note that in the following definition, we overload notation a bit by writing $\mathcal{A}$ for both for the ordinary static and for the adaptive adversary (even though a given $\mathcal{A}$ is usually either static or adaptive).

Definition 9. Σ *is (computationally/statistically) sound if there exists a negligible function $\mu(\eta)$ such that for any (quantum polynomial-time/unbounded) adversary $\mathcal{A}$ and any $\eta \in \mathbb{N}$:*

$$\Pr\left[\langle \mathcal{A}, \mathcal{V}(x)\rangle = accept\right] \le \mu(\eta)$$

for all $x \notin \mathcal{L}$; respectively, in case of an **adaptive** *$\mathcal{A}$:*

$$\Pr\left[x \notin \mathcal{L} \wedge v = accept : (x, v) \leftarrow \langle \mathcal{A}, \mathcal{V}\rangle\right] \le \mu(\eta).$$

$\mathsf{FS}[\Sigma]$ *is (computationally/statistically) sound if there exists a negligible function $\mu(\eta)$ and a constant e such that for any (quantum polynomial-time/unbounded) adversary $\mathcal{A}$ and any $\eta \in \mathbb{N}$:*

$$\Pr_{H}\left[V_{FS}^{H}(x, \pi) : \pi \leftarrow \mathcal{A}^{H}\right] \le q^{e} \mu(\eta)$$

for all $x \notin \mathcal{L}$; respectively, in case of an **adaptive** *$\mathcal{A}$:*

$$\Pr_{H}\left[V_{FS}^{H}(x, \pi) \wedge x \notin \mathcal{L} : (x, \pi) \leftarrow \mathcal{A}^{H}\right] \le q^{e} \mu(\eta).$$

Remark 10. Note that for the soundness of $\mathsf{FS}[\Sigma]$, the adversary $\mathcal{A}$'s success probability may unavoidably grow with the number q of oracle queries, but we require that it grows only polynomially in q.

Remark 11. In line with Sect. 2, the description of a quantum algorithm $\mathcal{A}$ is understood to include the initial state $|\phi_0\rangle$. As such, when quantifying over all $\mathcal{A}$ it is understood that this includes a quantification over all $|\phi_0\rangle$ as well. This stays true when considering $\mathcal{A}$ to be quantum polynomial-time, which means that the unitaries A_i can be computed by polynomial-time quantum circuits, and q is polynomial in size, but does not put any restriction on $|\phi_0\rangle$.[9] This is in line with [Unr12, Def. 1], which explicitly spells out this quantification.

---

[9] In other words, $\mathcal{A}$ is then *non-uniform* quantum polynomial-time with *quantum* advice.

We consider the following to be folklore knowledge; for completeness, we still give a proof in Appendix A.

Lemma 12. *If Σ is computationally/statistically sound for* static *adversaries then it is also computationally/statistically sound for* adaptive *adversaries.*

The following is now an immediate application of Theorem 8 and the above observation regarding static and adaptive security for Σ-protocols.

Corollary 13. *Let Σ be a Σ-protocol with superpolynomially sized challenge space $\mathcal{C}$. If Σ is computationally/statistically sound against a static adversary then $\mathsf{FS}[\Sigma]$ is computationally/statistically sound against an adaptive adversary.*

Proof. Applying Theorem 8, we find that for any adaptive FS-adversary $\mathcal{A}$, polynomially bounded in the computational setting, there exists an adaptive Σ-protocol adversary $\mathcal{S}^{\mathcal{A}}$, polynomially bounded if $\mathcal{A}$ is, so that

$$\Pr\left[x \notin \mathcal{L} \wedge V_{FS}^{H}(x,\pi) : (x,\pi) \leftarrow \mathcal{A}^{H}\right]$$

$$= \sum_{x_\circ \notin \mathcal{L}} \Pr\left[x = x_\circ \wedge V_{FS}^{H}(x,\pi) : (x,\pi) \leftarrow \mathcal{A}^{H}\right]$$

$$\leq O(q^2) \cdot \left(\left(\sum_{x_\circ \notin \mathcal{L}} \Pr\left[x = x_\circ \wedge v = accept : (x,v) \leftarrow \langle \mathcal{S}^{\mathcal{A}}, \mathcal{V}\rangle\right]\right) + \frac{1}{2q|\mathcal{C}|}\right)$$

$$= O(q^2) \cdot \left(\Pr\left[x \notin \mathcal{L} \wedge v = accept : (x,v) \leftarrow \langle \mathcal{S}^{\mathcal{A}}, \mathcal{V}\rangle\right]\right) + \frac{O(q)}{|\mathcal{C}|}$$

$$\leq O(q^2) \cdot \mu(\eta) + \frac{O(q)}{|\mathcal{C}|}$$

where the last inequality holds for some negligible function $\mu(\eta)$ if Σ is sound against an adaptive adversary. The latter is ensured by the assumed soundness against a static adversary and Lemma 12. This bound can obviously be written as $q^2\mu'(\eta)$ for another negligible function $\mu'(\eta)$, showing the claimed soundness of $\mathsf{FS}[\Sigma]$. $\square$

3.5   Preservation as a Proof of Knowledge

We now recall the definition of a proof of knowledge, sometimes also referred to as (witness) extractability, tailored to the case of a negligible "knowledge error". Informally, the requirement is that if $\mathcal{A}$ succeeds in proving an instance x, then by using $\mathcal{A}$ as a black-box only it is possible to extract a witness for x. In case of an arbitrary but fixed x, this property is formalized in a rather straightforward way; however, in case of an adaptive $\mathcal{A}$, the formalization is somewhat subtle, because one can then not refer to *the* x for which $\mathcal{A}$ manages to produce a proof. We adopt the approach (though not the precise formalization) from [Unr17], which requires x to satisfy an arbitrary but fixed predicate.

Definition 14. Σ *is a (computational/statistical) proof of knowledge if there exists a quantum polynomial-time black-box 'knowledge extractor'* $\mathcal{K}$, *a polynomial* $p(\eta)$, *a constant* $d \geq 0$, *and a negligible function* $\kappa(\eta)$ *such that for any (quantum polynomial-time/unbounded) adversary* $\mathcal{A}$, *any* $\eta \in \mathbb{N}$ *and any* $x \in \mathcal{X}$:

$$\Pr\left[(x,w) \in R : w \leftarrow \mathcal{K}^{\mathcal{A}}(x)\right] \geq \frac{1}{p(\eta)} \cdot \Pr\left[\langle \mathcal{A}, \mathcal{V}(x)\rangle = accept\right]^d - \kappa(\eta);$$

respectively, in case of an **adaptive** $\mathcal{A}$:

$$\Pr\left[x \in X \wedge (x,w) \in R : (x,w) \leftarrow \mathcal{K}^{\mathcal{A}}\right]$$

$$\geq \frac{1}{p(\eta)} \cdot \Pr\left[x \in X \wedge v = accept : (x,v) \leftarrow \langle \mathcal{A}, \mathcal{V}\rangle\right]^d - \kappa(\eta)$$

for any subset $X \subseteq \mathcal{X}$.

FS[Σ] *is a (computational/statistical) proof of knowledge if there exists a polynomial-time black-box 'knowledge extractor'* $\mathcal{E}$, *a polynomial* $p(\eta)$, *constants* $d, e \geq 0$, *and a negligible function* $\mu(\eta)$, *such that for any (quantum polynomial-time/unbounded) algorithm* $\mathcal{A}$, *any* $\eta \in \mathbb{N}$ *and any* $x \in \mathcal{X}$:

$$\Pr\left[(x,w) \in R : (x,w) \leftarrow \mathcal{E}^{\mathcal{A}}\right] \geq \frac{1}{q^e p(\eta)} \cdot \Pr_H\left[V_{FS}^H(x,\pi) : \pi \leftarrow \mathcal{A}^H\right]^d - \mu(\eta);$$

respectively, in case of an **adaptive** $\mathcal{A}$:

$$\Pr\left[x \in X \wedge (x,w) \in R : (x,w) \leftarrow \mathcal{E}^{\mathcal{A}}\right]$$

$$\geq \frac{1}{q^e p(\eta)} \cdot \Pr_H\left[x \in X \wedge V_{FS}^H(x,\pi) : (x,\pi) \leftarrow \mathcal{A}^H\right]^d - \mu(\eta)$$

for any subset $X \subseteq \mathcal{X}$, *where* q *is the number of queries* $\mathcal{A}$ *makes.*

Also here, for Σ-protocols static security implies adaptive security.

Lemma 15. *If* Σ *is a computational/statistical proof of knowledge for static* $\mathcal{A}$ *then it is also a computational/statistical proof of knowledge for adaptive* $\mathcal{A}$.

Again, the following is now an immediate application of Theorem 8 and the above observation regarding static and adaptive security for Σ-protocols.

Corollary 16. *Let* Σ *be a* Σ-protocol with superpolynomially sized $\mathcal{C}$. *If* Σ *is a computational/statistical proof of knowledge for static adversaries then* FS[Σ] *is a computational/statistical proof of knowledge for adaptive adversaries.*

Proof. First, we observe that by Lemma 15, we may assume Σ to be a computational/statistical proof of knowledge for *adaptive* adversaries. Let $\mathcal{K}$ be the black-box knowledge extractor. Let $\mathcal{A}$ be an (quantum polynomial-time/unbounded) adaptive FS-adversary $\mathcal{A}$. We define a black-box knowledge extractor $\mathcal{E}$ for FS[Σ] as follows. $\mathcal{E}^{\mathcal{A}}$ simply works by running $\mathcal{K}^{\mathcal{S}^{\mathcal{A}}}$, where $\mathcal{S}^{\mathcal{A}}$ the adaptive Σ-protocol adversary obtained by invoking Theorem 8. For any subset $X \subseteq \mathcal{X}$, invoking the proof-of-knowledge property of Σ and using Theorem 8, we see that

$$\Pr\left[x \in X \wedge (x, w) \in R : (x, w) \leftarrow \mathcal{E}^{\mathcal{A}}\right]$$

$$= \Pr\left[x \in X \wedge (x, w) \in R : (x, w) \leftarrow \mathcal{K}^{\mathcal{S}^{\mathcal{A}}}\right]$$

$$= \frac{1}{p(\eta)} \cdot \Pr\left[x \in X \wedge v = accept(x, v) \leftarrow \langle \mathcal{S}^{\mathcal{A}}, \mathcal{V} \rangle\right]^d - \kappa(\eta)$$

$$= \frac{1}{p(\eta)} \cdot \left(\sum_{x_\circ \in X} \Pr\left[x = x_\circ \wedge v = accept(x, v) \leftarrow \langle \mathcal{S}^{\mathcal{A}}, \mathcal{V} \rangle\right] \right)^d - \kappa(\eta)$$

$$\geq \frac{1}{p(\eta)} \left(\frac{1}{O(q^2)} \sum_{x_\circ \in X} \Pr_H\left[x = x_\circ \wedge V_{FS}^H(x, \pi) : (x, \pi) \leftarrow \mathcal{A}^H\right] - \frac{1}{2q|\mathcal{C}|} \right)^d - \kappa(\eta)$$

$$\geq \frac{1}{p(\eta) \cdot O(q^{2d})} \cdot \Pr_H\left[x \in X \wedge V_{FS}^H(x, \pi) : (x, \pi) \leftarrow \mathcal{A}^H\right]^d - \mu(\eta)$$

for some negligible function $\mu(\eta)$.   □

Remark 17. We point out that in [Unr17] Unruh considers a stronger notion of extractability than our Definition 14, where it is required that, in some sense, the extractor also recovers any local (possibly quantum) output of the adversary $\mathcal{A}$. In the light of Remark 7, we expect that our result also applies to this stronger notion of extractability.

4   Application to Fiat-Shamir Signatures

Any Fiat-Shamir non-interactive proof system can easily be transformed into a public-key signature scheme.[10] The signer simply proves knowledge of a witness (the secret key) for a composite statement $x^* := x\|m$, which includes the public key x as well as the message m. The signature σ then consists of a proof for x^*.

Definition 18. *A binary relation R with instance generator G is said to be* **hard** *if for any quantum polynomial-time algorithm $\mathcal{A}$ we have*

$$\Pr\left[(x, w') \in R : (x, w) \leftarrow G, w' \leftarrow \mathcal{A}(x)\right] \leq \mu(\eta)$$

for some negligible function $\mu(\eta)$, where G is such that it always outputs a pair $(x, w) \in R$.

Definition 19. *A Fiat-Shamir signature scheme* **based on a Σ-protocol** $\Sigma = (\mathcal{P}, \mathcal{V})$ *for a hard relation R with instance generator G, denoted by* $\mathsf{Sig}[\Sigma]$ *is defined by the triple (Gen, Sign, Verify), with*

---

[10] In fact, that is how the Fiat-Shamir transform was originally conceived in [FS87]. Only later [BG93] adapted the idea to construct a non-interactive zero-knowledge proof system.

- Gen: *Pick* $(x, w) \leftarrow G$, *set* $sk := (x, w)$ *and* $pk := x$.
- Sign$^H(sk, m)$: *Return* (m, σ) *where* $\sigma \leftarrow P_{FS}^H(x\|m, w)$.
- Verify$^H(pk, m, \sigma)$: *Return* $V_{FS}^H(x\|m, \sigma)$.

Here $(P_{FS}^H, V_{FS}^H) = \mathsf{FS}[\Sigma^*]$, *where* $\Sigma^* = (\mathcal{P}^*, \mathcal{V}^*)$ *is the* Σ-*protocol obtained from* Σ *by setting* $\mathcal{P}^*(x\|m) = \mathcal{P}(x)$ *and* $\mathcal{V}^*(x\|m) = \mathcal{V}(x)$ *for any* m.

Note that by definition of FS in Sect. 3.2, we use $V_{FS}^H(x\|m, \sigma)$ as shortcut for $V(x\|m, a, H(x\|m, a), z)$.

We investigate the following standard security notions for signature schemes.

Definition 20 (sEUF − CMA/EUF − NMA). *A signature scheme fulfills* strong existential unforgeability under chosen-message attack (sEUF − CMA) *if for all quantum polynomial-time algorithms* $\mathcal{A}$ *and for uniformly random* $H : \mathcal{X}' \rightarrow \mathcal{C}$ *it holds that*

$$\Pr\left[\mathsf{Verify}^H(pk, m, \sigma) \wedge (m, \sigma) \notin \mathbf{Sig}\text{-}\mathbf{q} : (pk, sk) \leftarrow \mathsf{Gen}, (m, \sigma) \leftarrow \mathcal{A}^{H, \mathbf{Sig}}(pk)\right]$$

is negligible. Here $\mathbf{Sig}$ *is classical oracle which upon classical input* m *returns* Sign$^H(m, sk)$, *and* $\mathbf{Sig}\text{-}\mathbf{q}$ *is the list of all queries made to* $\mathbf{Sig}$.

Analogously, a signature scheme fulfills existential unforgeability under no-message attack (EUF − NMA) *if for all quantum polynomial-time algorithms* $\mathcal{A}$ *and for uniformly random* $H : \mathcal{X}' \rightarrow \mathcal{C}$ *it holds that*

$$\Pr\left[\mathsf{Verify}^H(pk, m, \sigma) : (pk, sk) \leftarrow \mathsf{Gen}, (m, \sigma) \leftarrow \mathcal{A}^H(pk)\right]$$

is negligible.

The unforgeability (against no-message attacks) of a Fiat-Shamir signature scheme is shown below to follow from the proof-of-knowledge property of the underlying proof system (hence, as we now know, of the underlying Σ-protocol), under the assumption that the relation is hard, i.e. it is infeasible to compute sk from pk.

Theorem 21. *Let* Σ *be* Σ-*protocol for some hard relation* R, *with superpolynomially sized challenge space* $\mathcal{C}$ *and the proof-of-knowledge property according to Definition 14. Then, the Fiat-Shamir signature scheme* $\mathsf{Sig}[\Sigma]$ *fulfills* EUF − NMA *security.*

Proof. Let $\mathcal{A}$ be an adversary against EUF − NMA, issuing at most q quantum queries to H. We show that

$$\mathsf{Adv}_{\mathsf{Sig}[\Sigma]}^{\mathsf{EUF-NMA}}(\mathcal{A}) := \Pr\left[\mathsf{Verify}^H(pk, m, \sigma) : (pk, sk) \leftarrow \mathsf{Gen}, (m, \sigma) \leftarrow \mathcal{A}^H(pk)\right]$$

is negligible.

Recall from Definition 19 of Fiat-Shamir signatures that the Σ-protocol Σ^* is the Σ-protocol Σ where the prover and verifier ignore the message part m of the instance $x\|m$. A successful forgery (m, σ) is such that $V_{FS}^H(x\|m, \sigma)$ accepts the proof σ. Therefore,

$$\text{Adv}_{\text{Sig}[\Sigma]}^{\text{EUF--NMA}}(\mathcal{A}) = \underset{(x,w)\leftarrow G}{\mathbb{E}} \left[\underset{H}{\text{Pr}} \left[V_{FS}^H(x\|m, \sigma) : (m, \sigma) \leftarrow \mathcal{A}^H(x) \right] \right]. \quad (5)$$

Note that if Σ is a proof of knowledge, so is Σ^*. Our Corollary 16 assures that if Σ^* is a proof of knowledge, then also $\text{FS}[\Sigma^*]$ is a proof of knowledge.

For fixed instance x, let X be the set of instance/message strings $x'\|m$ where $x' = x$. We apply the knowledge extractor from Definition 14 to the adaptive FS-attacker $\mathcal{A}^H(x)$ that has x hard-wired and outputs it along with a message m and the proof/signature σ: There exists a knowledge extractor $\mathcal{E}$, constants d, e and a polynomial p (all independent of x) such that

$$\underset{H}{\text{Pr}} \left[x'\|m \in X \wedge V_{FS}^H(x'\|m, \sigma) : (x'\|m, \sigma) \leftarrow \mathcal{A}^H(x) \right]$$
$$\leq \left(\text{Pr} \left[x'\|m \in X \wedge (x', w) \in R : (x'\|m, w) \leftarrow \mathcal{E}^{\mathcal{A}} \right] q^e p(\eta) + \mu(\eta) \right)^{1/d} \quad (6)$$

Finally, taking the expected value of (6) over the choice of the instance x according to the hard-instance generator G, we obtain that the left hand side equals $\text{Adv}_{\text{Sig}[\Sigma]}^{\text{EUF--NMA}}(\mathcal{A})$. For the right-hand side, we can use the concavity of $(\cdot)^{1/d}$ (note that we can assume without loss of generality that $d > 1$) and apply Jensen's inequality to obtain

$$\underset{x\leftarrow G}{\mathbb{E}} \left[\left(\text{Pr} \left[x'\|m \in X \wedge (x', w) \in R : (x'\|m, w) \leftarrow \mathcal{E}^{\mathcal{A}} \right] q^e p(\eta) + \mu(\eta) \right)^{1/d} \right]$$
$$\leq \left(\underset{x\leftarrow G}{\mathbb{E}} \text{Pr} \left[x'\|m \in X \wedge (x', w) \in R : (x'\|m, w) \leftarrow \mathcal{E}^{\mathcal{A}} \right] q^e p(\eta) + \mu(\eta) \right)^{1/d}.$$

Note that the expected probability is the success probability of the extractor to produce a witness w matching the instance x. As long as the relation R is hard according to Definition 18, this success probability is negligible, proving our claim. □

If we wish for unforgeability *under chosen-message attack*, zero-knowledge is required as well. [Unr17] and [KLS18] contain partial results that formalize this intuition, but they were unable to derive the extractability of the non-interactive proof system. Instead, they modify the Σ-protocol to have a *lossy mode* [AFLT12], i.e. a special key-generation procedure that produces key pairs whose public keys are computationally indistinguishable from the real ones, but under which it is impossible for any (even unbounded) quantum adversary to answer correctly.

Our new result above completes these previous analyses, so that we can now state precise conditions under which a Σ-protocol gives rise to a (strongly) unforgeable Fiat-Shamir signature scheme, without the need for lossy keys.

Theorem 22. *Let Σ be Σ-protocol for some hard relation R, with superpolynomially sized challenge space $\mathcal{C}$ and the proof-of-knowledge property according to Definition 14. Assume further that Σ is ε-perfect (non-abort) honest-verifier zero-knowledge (naHVZK), has α bits of min entropy and computationally unique responses as defined in [KLS18]. Then, $\mathsf{Sig}[\Sigma]$ fulfills $\mathsf{sEUF-CMA}$ security.*

Proof. By Theorem 3.3 of [KLS18], we can use the naHVZK, min-entropy and computationally-unique-response properties of Σ to reduce an $\mathsf{sEUF-CMA}$ adversary to an $\mathsf{EUF-NMA}$ adversary[11]. The conclusion then follows immediately from our Theorem 21 above. $\qquad\square$

5   Extractable Σ-protocols from Quantum Computationally Unique Responses

In the last section, we have seen that the proof-of-knowledge property of the underlying Σ-protocol is crucial for a Fiat-Shamir signature scheme to be unforgeable. In [Unr12], Unruh proved that special soundness (a witness can be constructed efficiently from two different accepting transcripts) and perfect unique responses are sufficient conditions for a Σ-protocol to achieve this property in the context of quantum adversaries. The perfect-unique-responses property is used to show that the final measurement of the Σ-protocol adversary that produces the response is nondestructive conditioned on acceptance. This property ensures that the extractor can measure the response, and then rewind "as if nothing had happened".

A natural question is therefore which other property except the arguably quite strict condition of perfect unique responses is sufficient to imply extractability together with special soundness. In [ARU14], the authors show that computationally unique responses is insufficient to replace perfect unique responses. A Σ-protocol has computationally unique responses if the verification relation V is collision-resistant from responses to commitment-challenge pairs in the sense that it is computationally hard to find two valid responses for the same commitment-challenge pair.

In [Unr16], Unruh introduced the notion of collapsingness, a quantum generalization of the collision-resistance property for hash functions. It is straightforward to generalize this notion to apply to binary relations instead of just functions.

Definition 23 (generalized from [Unr16]). *Let $R : \mathcal{X} \times \mathcal{Y} \to \{0,1\}$ be a relation with $|X|$ and $|Y|$ superpolynomial in the security parameter η, and define the following two games for polynomial-time two-stage adversaries $\mathcal{A} = (\mathcal{A}_1, \mathcal{A}_2)$,*

Game 1 :
$(S, X, Y) \leftarrow \mathcal{A}_1, \ r \leftarrow R(X, Y), \ X \leftarrow \mathcal{M}(X), \ Y \leftarrow \mathcal{M}(Y), \ b \leftarrow \mathcal{A}_2(S, X, Y)$

Game 2 :
$(S, X, Y) \leftarrow \mathcal{A}_1, \ r \leftarrow R(X, Y), \qquad\qquad Y \leftarrow \mathcal{M}(Y), \ b \leftarrow \mathcal{A}_2(S, X, Y).$

---

[11] See also Theorem 25 in [Unr17] for a different proof technique.

Here, X and Y are registers of dimension $|X|$ and $|Y|$, respectively, $\mathcal{M}$ denotes a measurement in the computational basis, and applying R to quantum registers is done by computing the relation coherently and measuring it. R is called collapsing *from $\mathcal{X}$ to $\mathcal{Y}$, if an adversary cannot distinguish the two experiments if the relation holds, i.e. if for all adversaries $\mathcal{A}$ it holds that*

$$\left| \Pr_{\mathcal{A},\ \text{Game 1}} [r = b = 1] - \Pr_{\mathcal{A},\ \text{Game 2}} [r = b = 1] \right| \leq \text{negl}(\eta). \tag{7}$$

Note that this definition is equivalent to Definition 23 in [Unr16] for functions, i.e. if $R(x, y) = 1$ if and only if $f(x) = y$ for some function f.

Via the relation that is computed by the second stage of the verifier, the collapsingness property can be naturally defined for Σ-protocols.

Definition 24 (Quantum computationally unique responses). *A Σ-protocol has* quantum computationally unique responses, *if the verification predicate $V(x, \cdot, \cdot, \cdot) : \mathcal{Y} \times \mathcal{C} \times \mathcal{Z} \rightarrow \{0,1\}$ seen as a relation between $\mathcal{Y} \times \mathcal{C}$ and $\mathcal{Z}$ is collapsing from $\mathcal{Z}$ to $\mathcal{Y} \times \mathcal{C}$, where $\mathcal{Y}$, $\mathcal{C}$ and $\mathcal{Z}$ are the commitment, challenge and response spaces of the protocol, respectively.*

Intuitively, for fixed commitment-challenge pairs, no adversary should be able to determine whether a superposition over successful responses z has been measured or not. As in the case of hash functions (where collapsingness is a natural stronger quantum requirement than collision-resistance), quantum computationally unique responses is a natural stronger quantum requirement than computationally unique responses.

The following is a generalization of Theorem 9 in [Unr12] where the assumption of perfect unique responses is replaced by the above quantum computational version. Additionally, we relax the special soundness requirement to t-*soundness*, which requires that for any first message a, for uniformly random chosen challenges $c_1, \ldots, c_t$, and for any responses $z_1, \ldots, z_t$ with $V(x, a_i, c_i, z_i)$ for all $i \in \{1, \ldots, t\}$, a witness w for x can be efficiently computed except with negligible probability (over the choices of the c_i).

Theorem 25 (Generalization of Theorem 9 from [Unr12]). *Let Π be a Σ-protocol with t-soundness for some constant t and with quantum computationally unique responses. Then Π is a computational proof of knowledge as in Definition 14.*

The proof follows very much the proof of Theorem 9 in [Unr12], up to some small extensions; thus, we only give a proof sketch here.

Proof (sketch). We consider the following extractor $\mathcal{K}$. It runs $\mathcal{A}$ to the point where it outputs a. Then, it chooses a random challenge c_1 and sends it to $\mathcal{A}$, and obtains a response z_1 by measuring $\mathcal{A}$'s corresponding register. $\mathcal{K}$ then rewinds $\mathcal{A}$ (on the measured state!) and chooses and sends to $\mathcal{A}$ a fresh random challenge c_2, resulting in a response z_2, etc., up to obtaining response z_t. If $V(x, a_i, c_i, z_i)$ for all $i \in \{1, \ldots, t\}$ then $\mathcal{K}$ can compute w except with negligible probability by the t-soundness property; otherwise, it aborts.

It remains to analyze the probability, denoted by F below, that $V(x, a_i, c_i, z_i)$ for all i. If the Σ-protocol has *perfect* unique responses then measuring the response z is *equivalent* to measuring whether the response satisfies the verification predicate V (with respect to x, a, c). Lemma 29 in Appendix B, which generalizes Lemma 7 in [Unr12], allows us then to control the probability F by means of the probability V that $\mathcal{A}$ succeeds in convincing the verifier in an ordinary run (this holds for an arbitrary but fixed a, and on average over a by means of Jensen's inequality). If the Σ-protocol has *quantum computationally* unique responses instead, then measuring the response z is *computationally indistinguishable* from measuring whether the response satisfies the verification predicate, and so there can only be a negligible loss in the success probability of $\mathcal{K}$ compared to above. $\square$

We expect the above theorem to be very useful in practice, for the following reason. Usually, Σ-protocols deployed in Fiat-Shamir signature schemes have computationally unique responses to ensure strong unforgeability via Theorem 22 or similar reductions. On the other hand, only very artificial separations between the notions of collision resistance and collapsingness for hash functions are known (e.g. the one presented in [Zha17]). It is therefore plausible that many Σ-protocols deployed in strongly unforgeable Fiat-Shamir signature schemes have quantum computationally unique responses as well. In the next section we take a look at a couple of examples that form the basis of some signature schemes submitted to the NIST competition for the standardization of post-quantum cryptographic schemes.

6   Application to NIST Submissions

In the previous sections we gave sufficient conditions for a Fiat-Shamir signature scheme to be existentially unforgeable in the QROM. Several schemes of the Fiat-Shamir kind have made it into the second round of the NIST postquantum standardization process. In this section we outline how our result might be applied to some of these schemes, and under which additional assumptions. We leave the problems of applying our techniques to the actual (highly optimized) signature schemes and of working out the concrete security bounds for future work.

6.1   Picnic

In order to obtain QROM-security, Picnic uses the *Unruh transform* [Unr15] instead of the Fiat-Shamir transformation, incurring a 1.6x loss in efficiency (according to [CDG+17]) compared to Fish, which is the same scheme under plain Fiat-Shamir.

The underlying sigma-protocol for these schemes is ZKB++ [CDG+17], an optimized version of ZKBoo [GMO16], which uses an arbitrary one-way function ϕ, a commitment scheme COM and a multi-party computation protocol to prove knowledge of a secret key. Roughly, a prover runs the multi-party protocol 'in its head' (i.e. simulates the three agents from the protocol, see [IKOS07]) to compute $pk := \phi(sk)$. Only a prover who knows the secret key can produce the correct view of all three agents, but the public key suffices to verify the correctness of two of the views. In the first round, the prover uses COM to commit to all three views separately, and sends these commitments to the verifier. The verifier replies with a random challenge $i \in \{1, 2, 3\}$, to which the prover in turn responds by opening the i-th and $i+1$-th commitment.

ZKBoo does not specify a concrete commitment scheme for COM. A natural option is to commit by hashing the input together with some random bits.

Corollary 26. Sig[ZKBoo] *is strongly existentially unforgeable in the QROM when* COM *is instantiated with a hash function H.*

Proof. If we treat H as a quantum-accessible random oracle, then H is collapsing by [Unr16]. Since the response of the prover in the third round consists only of openings to the commitments c_i, c_{i+1}, i.e. preimages of c_i and c_{i+1} under H, and since collapsingness is closed under concurrent composition [Feh18], the collapsingness of H implies that ZKBoo has quantum computational unique responses. ZKBoo further has 3-soundness, and thus the claim follows using Theorems 25 and 22.   □

ZKB++ improves on ZKBoo by introducing optimizations specific to the signature context, which complicate the analysis of the overall scheme. We therefore leave the adaption of Corollary 26 to ZKB++ and Fish for future work.

6.2 Lattice-Based Fiat-Shamir Signature Schemes – CRYSTALS-Dilithium and qTesla

In [Lyu09] and [Lyu12], Lyubashevsky developed a Fiat-Shamir signature scheme based on (ring) lattice assumptions. In the following, we explain the lattice case and mention ring-based lattice terms in parentheses. The underlying sigma protocol, which forms the basis of the NIST submissions CRYSTALS-Dilithium and qTesla, can be roughly described as follows. The instance is given by a key pair $((A, T), S)$, with $T = AS$. Here, A and S are matrices of appropriate dimensions over a finite field (polynomials of appropriate degree), and S is *small*. For the first message to the verifier, the prover selects a random short vector (small polynomial) y, and sends over Ay. The second message, from the verifier to the prover, is a random vector (polynomial) c with entries (coefficients) in $\{-1, 0, 1\}$ and a small Hamming weight. The third message, i.e. the response of the prover, is $z = Sc + y$, which is short (small) as well. The prover actually sends z only with a particular probability, which is chosen so as to make the distribution of (sent) z independent of S. Otherwise, it aborts and tries again. Verification is done by checking whether z is indeed short (small), and whether $Az - Ay = Tc$. Let us denote this protocol by LatticeΣ. In the following we restrict our attention to the lattice case, but we expect that one can do a similar analysis for the ring-based schemes.

The security of the scheme is, in the lattice case, based on the SHORT INTE-GER SOLUTION (SIS) problem, which essentially guarantees that it is hard to find an integral solution to a linear system that has a small norm. The computationally unique responses property for the simple Σ-protocol described above, in fact, follows directly from SIS: If one can find a vector c and two short vectors x_i, $i = 1, 2$ such that $Ax_0 = c = Ax_1$, then the difference $x = x_1 - x_0$ is a short solution to the linear system $Ax = 0$.

Another way to formulate the computationally unique responses property for the above Σ-protocol is as follows. Let $S \subset \mathbb{F}_q^n$ be the set of short vectors. Let $f_A : S \to \mathbb{F}_q^m$ be the restriction to S of the linear map given by the matrix $A \in \mathbb{F}_q^{m \times n}$. The Σ-protocol above has computationally unique responses if and only if f_A is collision resistant. As pointed out at the end of Sect. 5, the known examples that separate the collision resistance and collapsingness properties are fairly artificial. Hence it is a natural to assume that f_A is collapsing as well.

Assumption 27. *For m, n and q polynomial in the security parameter η, the function family f_A keyed by a uniformly random matrix $A \in \mathbb{F}_q^{m \times n}$ is collapsing.*

Under Assumption 27, LatticeΣ has quantum computational unique responses, and hence gives rise to an unforgeable Fiat-Shamir signature scheme.

Corollary 28. *Under Assumption 27, Sig[LatticeΣ] is strongly existentially unforgeable in the QROM.*

As mentioned at the end of the introduction, in their concurrent and independent work [LZ19], Lie and Zhandry show that f_A satisfies their notion of *weak-collapsingness* (assuming hardness of LWE), which roughly says that there is some non-negligible probability that the adversary *does not* notice a measurement. Weak-collapsingness implies a similarly weakened variant of our property 'quantum computational responses', which is still sufficient to let the proof of Theorem 25 go through, albeit with a worse but still non-negligible success probability for the knowledge-extractor.

Acknowledgement. We thank Tommaso Gagliardoni and Dominique Unruh for comments on early basic ideas of our approach, and Andreas Hülsing, Eike Kiltz and Greg Zaverucha for helpful discussions. We thank Thomas Vidick for helpful remarks on an earlier version of this article.

JD and SF were partly supported by the EU Horizon 2020 Research and Innovation Program Grant 780701 (PROMETHEUS). JD, CM, and CS were supported by a NWO VIDI grant (Project No. 639.022.519).

A   Proof of Lemmas 12 and 15

Proof (of Lemma 12). Let $\mathcal{A}$ be an adaptive Σ-protocol adversary, producing x and a in the first stage, and z in the second stage. We then consider the following algorithms. $\mathcal{A}_{init}$ runs the first stage of $\mathcal{A}$ (using the same initial state), outputting x and a. Let $|\psi_{x,a}\rangle$ be the corresponding internal state at this point.

Furthermore, for any possible x and a, $\mathcal{A}_{x,a}$ is the following static Σ-protocol adversary. Its initial state is $|\psi_{x,a}\rangle|a\rangle$ and in the first stage it simply outputs a, and in the second stage, after having received the verifier's challenge, it runs the second stage of $\mathcal{A}$. We then see that

$$\Pr\left[x \notin \mathcal{L} \wedge v = accept : (x,v) \leftarrow \langle \mathcal{A}, \mathcal{V}\rangle\right]$$

$$= \sum_{x_\circ \notin \mathcal{L}} \Pr\left[x = x_\circ \wedge v = accept : (x,v) \leftarrow \langle \mathcal{A}, \mathcal{V}\rangle\right]$$

$$= \sum_{x_\circ \notin \mathcal{L}} \sum_a \Pr\left[\mathcal{A}_{init} = (x_\circ, a)\right] \Pr\left[\langle \mathcal{A}_{x_\circ,a}, \mathcal{V}(x_\circ)\rangle = accept\right].$$

Since $\Pr\left[\langle \mathcal{A}_{x_\circ,a}, \mathcal{V}(x_\circ)\rangle = accept\right]$ is bounded by a negligible function, given that $\mathcal{A}_{x,a}$ is a (quantum polynomial-time/unbounded) static adversary, the claim follows. □

Proof (of Lemma 15). Let $\mathcal{A}$ be an adaptive Σ-protocol adversary, producing x and a in the first stage, and z in the second stage. We construct a black-box knowledge extractor $\mathcal{K}_{ad}$ that works for any such $\mathcal{A}$. In a first step, $\mathcal{K}_{ad}^{\mathcal{A}}$ runs the first stage of $\mathcal{A}$ using the black-box access to $\mathcal{A}$ (and having access to the initial state of $\mathcal{A}$). Below, we call this first stage of $\mathcal{A}$ as $\mathcal{A}_{init}$. This produces x and a, and we write $|\psi_{x,a}\rangle$ for the corresponding internal state. Then, it runs $\mathcal{K}_{na}^{\mathcal{A}^{x,a}}$, where $\mathcal{K}_{na}$ is the knowledge extractor guaranteed to exist for static adversaries, and $\mathcal{A}^{x,a}$ is the static adversary that works as follows. It's initial state is $|\psi_{x,a}\rangle|a\rangle$ and in the first stage it simply outputs a, and in the second stage it runs the second stage of $\mathcal{A}$ on the state $|\psi_{x,a}\rangle$. Note that having obtained x and a and the state $|\psi_{x,a}\rangle$ as first step of $\mathcal{K}_{ad}^{\mathcal{A}}$, $\mathcal{K}_{na}^{\mathcal{A}^{x,a}}$ can then be executed with black box access to (the second stage of) $\mathcal{A}$. For any subset $X \subseteq \mathcal{X}$, we now see that

$$\Pr\left[x \in X \wedge (x,w) \in R : (x,w) \leftarrow \mathcal{K}_{ad}^{\mathcal{A}}\right]$$

$$= \sum_{x \in X} \sum_a \Pr\left[\mathcal{A}_{init} = (x,a)\right] \Pr\left[(x,w) \in R : w \leftarrow \mathcal{K}_{na}^{\mathcal{A}^{x,a}}\right]$$

$$\geq \sum_{x \in X} \sum_a \Pr\left[\mathcal{A}_{init} = (x,a)\right] \cdot \frac{1}{p(\eta)} \cdot \Pr\left[\langle \mathcal{A}^{x,a}, \mathcal{V}(x)\rangle = accept\right]^d - \kappa(\eta)$$

$$\geq \frac{1}{p(\eta)} \left(\sum_{x \in X} \sum_a \Pr\left[\mathcal{A}_{init} = (x,a)\right] \Pr\left[\langle \mathcal{A}^{x,a}, \mathcal{V}(x)\rangle = accept\right]\right)^d - \kappa(\eta)$$

$$= \frac{1}{p(\eta)} \Pr\left[x \in X \wedge v = 1 : (x,v) \leftarrow \langle \mathcal{A}^{x,a}, \mathcal{V}(x)\rangle\right]^d - \kappa(\eta),$$

where the first inequality is because of the static proof-of-knowledge property, and the second is Jensen's inequality, noting that we may assume without loss of generality that $d \geq 1$. □

B   Generalization of Lemma 7 from [Unr12]

Lemma 29. *Let $P_1, \ldots, P_n$ be projections and $|\psi\rangle$ a state vector, and set*

$$V := \frac{1}{n} \sum_i \langle \psi | P_i | \psi \rangle = \frac{1}{n} \sum_i \| P_i | \psi \rangle \|^2 \quad and \quad F := \frac{1}{n^t} \sum_{i_1 \cdots i_t} \| P_{i_t} \cdots P_{i_1} | \psi \rangle \|^2.$$

Then $F \geq V^{2t-1}$.

The case $t = 2$ was proven in [Unr12, Lemma 7]. We show here how to extend the proof to $t = 3$; the general case works along the same lines.

Proof (of the case $t = 3$). For convenience, set $A := \frac{1}{n} \sum_i P_i$ and $|\psi_{ijk}\rangle := P_k P_j P_i |\psi\rangle$. Then, using convexity of the function $x \mapsto x^5$ to argue the first inequality, we get

$$V^5 = (\langle \psi | A | \psi \rangle)^5 = \langle \psi | A^5 | \psi \rangle = \frac{1}{n^5} \sum_{ijk\ell m} \langle \psi | P_i P_j P_k P_\ell P_m | \psi \rangle$$

$$= \frac{1}{n^5} \sum_{ijk\ell m} \langle \psi_{ijk} | \psi_{m\ell k} \rangle = \frac{1}{n} \sum_k \left(\frac{1}{n^2} \sum_{ij} \langle \psi_{ijk} | \right) \left(\frac{1}{n^2} \sum_{\ell m} |\psi_{m\ell k}\rangle \right)$$

$$= \frac{1}{n} \sum_k \left\| \frac{1}{n^2} \sum_{ij} |\psi_{ijk}\rangle \right\|^2 \leq \frac{1}{n^3} \sum_{ijk} \| |\psi_{ijk}\rangle \|^2 = F,$$

where the last inequality is Claim 2 in the proof of Lemma 7 in [Unr12]   □

References

[ABB+17] Alkim, E., et al.: Revisiting TESLA in the quantum random oracle model. In: Lange, T., Takagi, T. (eds.) PQCrypto 2017. LNCS, vol. 10346, pp. 143–162. Springer, Cham (2017). https://doi.org/10.1007/978-3-319-59879-6_9

[AFLT12] Abdalla, M., Fouque, P.-A., Lyubashevsky, V., Tibouchi, M.: Tightly-secure signatures from lossy identification schemes. In: Pointcheval, D., Johansson, T. (eds.) EUROCRYPT 2012. LNCS, vol. 7237, pp. 572–590. Springer, Heidelberg (2012). https://doi.org/10.1007/978-3-642-29011-4_34

[ARU14] Ambainis, A., Rosmanis, A., Unruh, D.: Quantum attacks on classical proof systems: the hardness of quantum rewinding. In: 2014 IEEE 55th Annual Symposium on Foundations of Computer Science, pp. 474–483, October 2014

[BDF+11] Boneh, D., Dagdelen, Ö., Fischlin, M., Lehmann, A., Schaffner, C., Zhandry, M.: Random oracles in a quantum world. In: Lee, D.H., Wang, X. (eds.) ASIACRYPT 2011. LNCS, vol. 7073, pp. 41–69. Springer, Heidelberg (2011). https://doi.org/10.1007/978-3-642-25385-0_3

[BDK+18] Bos, J., et al.: CRYSTALS - Kyber: a CCA-secure module-lattice-based KEM. In: 2018 IEEE European Symposium on Security and Privacy (EuroS P), pp. 353–367, April 2018

[BG93]   Bellare, M., Goldreich, O.: On defining proofs of knowledge. In: Brickell, E.F. (ed.) CRYPTO 1992. LNCS, vol. 740, pp. 390–420. Springer, Heidelberg (1993). https://doi.org/10.1007/3-540-48071-4_28

[BR93]   Bellare, M., Rogaway, P.: Random oracles are practical: a paradigm for designing efficient protocols. In: Proceedings of the 1st ACM Conference on Computer and Communications Security, pp. 62–73. ACM (1993)

[CDG+17] Chase, M., et al. Post-quantum zero-knowledge and signatures from symmetric-key primitives. In: Proceedings of the 2017 ACM SIGSAC Conference on Computer and Communications Security, CCS 2017, pp. 1825–1842. ACM, New York (2017)

[CGH04]   Canetti, R., Goldreich, O., Halevi, S.: The random oracle methodology, revisited. J. ACM **51**(4), 557–594 (2004)

[Dam10]   Damgard, I.: On sigma-protocols, Lecture Notes, Faculty of Science Aarhus University, Department of Computer Science (2010)

[DFG13]   Dagdelen, Ö., Fischlin, M., Gagliardoni, T.: The Fiat–Shamir transformation in a quantum world. In: Sako, K., Sarkar, P. (eds.) ASIACRYPT 2013. LNCS, vol. 8270, pp. 62–81. Springer, Heidelberg (2013). https://doi.org/10.1007/978-3-642-42045-0_4

[ES15]   Eaton, E., Song, F.: Making existential-unforgeable signatures strongly unforgeable in the quantum random-oracle model. In: 10th Conference on the Theory of Quantum Computation, Communication and Cryptography, pp. 147 (2015)

[Feh18]   Fehr, S.: Classical proofs for the quantum collapsing property of classical hash functions. In: Beimel, A., Dziembowski, S. (eds.) TCC 2018. LNCS, vol. 11240, pp. 315–338. Springer, Cham (2018). https://doi.org/10.1007/978-3-030-03810-6_12

[FKMV12] Faust, S., Kohlweiss, M., Marson, G.A., Venturi, D.: On the non-malleability of the Fiat-Shamir transform. In: Galbraith, S., Nandi, M. (eds.) INDOCRYPT 2012. LNCS, vol. 7668, pp. 60–79. Springer, Heidelberg (2012). https://doi.org/10.1007/978-3-642-34931-7_5

[FS87]   Fiat, A., Shamir, A.: How to prove yourself: practical solutions to identification and signature problems. In: Odlyzko, A.M. (ed.) CRYPTO 1986. LNCS, vol. 263, pp. 186–194. Springer, Heidelberg (1987). https://doi.org/10.1007/3-540-47721-7_12

[GMO16]   Giacomelli, I., Madsen, J., Orlandi, C.: ZKBoo: faster zero-knowledge for Boolean circuits. In: 25th USENIX Security Symposium (USENIX Security 16), Austin, TX, pp. 1069–1083. USENIX Association (2016)

[IKOS07] Ishai, Y., Kushilevitz, E., Ostrovsky, R., Sahai, A.: Zero-knowledge from secure multiparty computation. In: Proceedings of the Thirty-ninth Annual ACM Symposium on Theory of Computing - STOC 2007, p. 21 (2007)

[KLS18]   Kiltz, E., Lyubashevsky, V., Schaffner, C.: A concrete treatment of Fiat-Shamir signatures in the quantum random-oracle model. In: Nielsen, J.B., Rijmen, V. (eds.) EUROCRYPT 2018. LNCS, vol. 10822, pp. 552–586. Springer, Cham (2018). https://doi.org/10.1007/978-3-319-78372-7_18

[Lyu09]   Lyubashevsky, V.: Fiat-Shamir with aborts: applications to lattice and factoring-based signatures. In: Matsui, M. (ed.) ASIACRYPT 2009. LNCS, vol. 5912, pp. 598–616. Springer, Heidelberg (2009). https://doi.org/10.1007/978-3-642-10366-7_35

[Lyu12] Lyubashevsky, V.: Lattice signatures without trapdoors. In: Pointcheval, D., Johansson, T. (eds.) EUROCRYPT 2012. LNCS, vol. 7237, pp. 738–755. Springer, Heidelberg (2012). https://doi.org/10.1007/978-3-642-29011-4_43

[LZ19] Liu, Q., Zhandry, M.: Revisiting post-quantum Fiat-Shamir. Cryptology ePrint Archive, Report 2019/262 (2019). https://eprint.iacr.org/2019/262

[SXY18] Saito, T., Xagawa, K., Yamakawa, T.: Tightly-secure key-encapsulation mechanism in the quantum random oracle model. In: Nielsen, J.B., Rijmen, V. (eds.) EUROCRYPT 2018. LNCS, vol. 10822, pp. 520–551. Springer, Cham (2018). https://doi.org/10.1007/978-3-319-78372-7_17

[Unr12] Unruh, D.: Quantum proofs of knowledge. In: Pointcheval, D., Johansson, T. (eds.) EUROCRYPT 2012. LNCS, vol. 7237, pp. 135–152. Springer, Heidelberg (2012). https://doi.org/10.1007/978-3-642-29011-4_10

[Unr14] Unruh, D.: Quantum position verification in the random oracle model. In: Garay, J.A., Gennaro, R. (eds.) CRYPTO 2014. LNCS, vol. 8617, pp. 1–18. Springer, Heidelberg (2014). https://doi.org/10.1007/978-3-662-44381-1_1

[Unr15] Unruh, D.: Non-interactive zero-knowledge proofs in the quantum random oracle model. In: Oswald, E., Fischlin, M. (eds.) EUROCRYPT 2015. LNCS, vol. 9057, pp. 755–784. Springer, Heidelberg (2015). https://doi.org/10.1007/978-3-662-46803-6_25

[Unr16] Unruh, D.: Computationally binding quantum commitments. In: Fischlin, M., Coron, J.-S. (eds.) EUROCRYPT 2016. LNCS, vol. 9666, pp. 497–527. Springer, Heidelberg (2016). https://doi.org/10.1007/978-3-662-49896-5_18

[Unr17] Unruh, D.: Post-quantum security of Fiat-Shamir. In: Takagi, T., Peyrin, T. (eds.) ASIACRYPT 2017. LNCS, vol. 10624, pp. 65–95. Springer, Cham (2017). https://doi.org/10.1007/978-3-319-70694-8_3

[Zha12] Zhandry, M.: How to construct quantum random functions. In: 2012 IEEE 53rd Annual Symposium on Foundations of Computer Science, pp. 679–687. IEEE, October 2012

[Zha15] Zhandry, M.: Secure identity-based encryption in the quantum random oracle model. Int. J. Quantum Inf. 13(04), 1550014 (2015)

[Zha17] Zhandry, M.: Quantum lightning never strikes the same state twice. http://arxiv.org/abs/1711.02276 (2017)

[Zha18] Zhandry, M.: How to record quantum queries, and applications to quantum indifferentiability. Cryptology ePrint Archive, Report 2018/276 (2018). https://eprint.iacr.org/2018/276

Leakage Resilience

Unconditionally Secure Computation Against Low-Complexity Leakage

Andrej Bogdanov[1]([✉]), Yuval Ishai[2]([✉]), and Akshayaram Srinivasan[3]

[1] Chinese University of Hong Kong, Shatin, Hong Kong
andrejb@gmail.com
[2] Technion, Haifa, Israel
yuvali@cs.technion.ac.il
[3] University of California, Berkeley, USA
akshayaram@berkeley.edu

Abstract. We consider the problem of constructing leakage-resilient circuit compilers that are secure against global leakage functions with bounded output length. By global, we mean that the leakage can depend on all circuit wires and output a low-complexity function (represented as a multi-output Boolean circuit) applied on these wires. In this work, we design compilers both in the stateless (a.k.a. single-shot leakage) setting and the stateful (a.k.a. continuous leakage) setting that are *unconditionally* secure against AC^0 leakage and similar low-complexity classes.

In the stateless case, we show that the original private circuits construction of Ishai, Sahai, and Wagner (Crypto 2003) is actually secure against AC^0 leakage. In the stateful case, we modify the construction of Rothblum (Crypto 2012), obtaining a simple construction with unconditional security. Prior works that designed leakage-resilient circuit compilers against AC^0 leakage had to rely either on secure hardware components (Faust et al., Eurocrypt 2010, Miles-Viola, STOC 2013) or on (unproven) complexity-theoretic assumptions (Rothblum, Crypto 2012).

1 Introduction

There is a rich body of work on protecting computations that involve sensitive data against partial information leakage. This line of work is motivated by practical side-channel attacks that use physical measurements such as running time [36] or power consumption [37] to compromise secret keys embedded in cryptographic hardware or software. The recent high-profile Meltdown, Spectre, and Foreshadow attacks [13,35,38] demonstrated the vulnerability of most modern computer systems to this kind of attacks.

A clean theoretical model that captures the goal of protecting general computations against leakage is that of a *leakage resilient circuit compiler* (LRCC). Here the computation is modeled as a logical circuit, and the leakage as a function applying to the internal wires of the circuit. The goal of a LRCC is to randomize the computation of a given circuit in a way that resists broad classes of leakage

© International Association for Cryptologic Research 2019
A. Boldyreva and D. Micciancio (Eds.): CRYPTO 2019, LNCS 11693, pp. 387–416, 2019.
https://doi.org/10.1007/978-3-030-26951-7_14

while at the same time respecting the input-output relation of the original circuit. The problem of LRCC has many flavors, depending on the computational model and the type of leakage.

A crude form of LRCC was already given in the 1980s by the seminal works on secure multiparty computation [6,15,27,44]. Such protocols distribute computations across multiple parties in a way that resists leakage from a bounded number of parties. The work of Ishai, Sahai, and Wagner (ISW) [32] initiated a more explicit and refined study of LRCC at the circuit level, but still focused on the case of localized "probing attack" leakage that applies to a bounded number of circuit wires. In spite of its restricted nature, this leakage model turned out to be quite relevant to practical defenses against side-channel attacks. This is due in part to the simplicity of the constructions and the ability of the same leakage model to accommodate more realistic *noisy* leakage [19,23] that obtains an independent noisy measurement of every wire in the circuit. LRCCs in this model have been the subject of a large body of theoretical and applied work (see, e.g., [1,3–5,16,17,21,22,42] and references therein).

Originating from the works of Micali and Reyzin [39] and Faust et al. [23,24], another line of work went in the direction of accommodating more general types of leakage classes that apply restricted types of functions to *all* wires in the circuit. In particular, Faust et al. [23] presented a variant of the ISW compiler that employs small leak-free hardware components to protect against any class of "computationally simple" leakage functions for which strong average-case lower bounds are known. The most prominent example is that of AC^0 *leakage*, computed by constant-depth polynomial-size circuits with unbounded fan-in AND/OR/NOT gates and a bounded number of outputs. Subsequent works along this line studied LRCCs for different classes of global leakage under a variety of trusted hardware or setups and computational intractability assumptions [7–9,11,12,18,20,25,26,28–30,34,40,41,43].

Constant-Depth Leakage. The focus of this work is mainly on the class of AC^0 leakage and related constant-depth complexity classes, such as AC^0 augmented with additional mod-p gates. This type of leakage strictly generalizes the ISW leakage model, which as discussed above is relevant to many realistic scenarios. Moreover, while the class AC^0 does not capture some natural leakage functions, such as ones that take weighted sums of many wire values, it does apply to a wide variety of natural attacks. For instance, suppose that a system crashes if a secret value represented by a wire bundle is in a certain forbidden range, and there are many such wire bundles that may lead to the system crashing. Then, whether the system crashes at a given moment is a single bit of depth-3 AC^0 leakage that can be observed by the outside world. One can similarly cast in this class other types of natural leakage functions that take the conjunction, disjunction, maximum, or minimum of values that can themselves be computed by low-depth circuits.

Stateless vs. Stateful LRCC. Before describing our contributions, it is instructive to present the current state of the art in a more precise way. The ISW paper introduced two variants of the LRCC problem: a simpler *stateless* variant and a more complex *stateful* variant. The stateless variant captures standard computations that map a secret input to a secret or public output, where the computation is subject to a single round of *one-shot leakage*. For instance, this scenario can apply to zero-knowledge authentication by a hardware device, or computations performed by payment terminals and access control readers (see [26] for further discussion). In a more theoretical context, stateless LRCCs have also been applied towards constructing different zero-knowledge flavors of probabilistically checkable proofs [33]. The *stateful* variant of LRCCs captures a system (such as a personal computer or an IoT device) with persistent memory that may store secrets. Users interacting with this system can feed it with a sequence of inputs and observe the resulting outputs. For instance, think of an encryption device that stores a secret encryption key, takes a plaintext as input and produces a ciphertext as output. Stateful LRCCs may be subject to *continuous leakage* that applies a different leakage function in each round. To help defend against this kind of leakage, they are allowed to refresh their internal state.

More formally, in the *stateless* variant of LRCC, the goal is to compile a (deterministic, stateless) circuit C into a randomized circuit $\widehat{C}$, such that together with leak-free randomized input encoder Enc and output decoder Dec we get the following correctness and security guarantees: (1) For any input x, we have $\mathsf{Dec}(\widehat{C}(\mathsf{Enc}(x))) = C(x)$; (2) For any admissible leakage function $\ell \in \mathcal{L}$, applying ℓ to the internal wires of the computation $\widehat{C}(\mathsf{Enc}(x))$ reveals essentially nothing about x. To rule out a trivial solution in which the entire computation is carried out by the leak-free components Enc and Dec, these components are required to be *universal* in the sense that they depend only on the input and output size of C and not on C itself. The ISW construction protects computations against leakage that involves a bounded number of wire-probes. That is, the leakage ℓ can output the values of t wires in $\widehat{C}$. Here we are interested in a bigger class $\mathcal{L}$ that includes constant-depth circuits with t bits of output.

The *stateful* variant of LRCC considers the more challenging goal of protecting computations against *continual leakage*. Here the ideal functionality is specified by a deterministic, *stateful* circuit C, mapping the current input and state to the current output and the next state. The input and output are considered to be public whereas the state is secret. The goal, as before, is to transform C into a leakage-resilient randomized circuit $\widehat{C}$. The circuit $\widehat{C}$ is initialized with some randomized encoding $\hat{s}_0$ of the initial secret state s_0 of C. The computation can then proceed in a virtually unlimited number of rounds, where in each round $\widehat{C}$ receives an input, produces an output, and replaces the old encoding of the secret state by a fresh encoding of a new state. The correctness goal is to ensure that $\widehat{C}[\hat{s}_0]$ has the same input-output functionality as $C[s_0]$. The security goal is defined again with respect to a class $\mathcal{L}$ of leakage functions, where the adversary may adaptively choose a different function $\ell \in \mathcal{L}$ in each round. The security goal is to ensure that whatever the adversary learns by interacting with $\widehat{C}[\hat{s}_0]$ and by additionally observing the leakage, it can simulate by interacting with $C[s_0]$ without obtaining any leakage.

State of the Art. Existing results of LRCCs for AC^0 and similar constant-depth leakage classes leave a number of basic questions open. In the stateful case, the works of Faust et al. [23] and Miles and Viola [41] yield constructions that require small but leak-free trusted hardware components, whose number is linear in the size of C and whose size grows with a statistical security parameter. Alternatively, Rothblum [43] showed how to eliminate the trusted hardware components, but at the cost of further complicating the construction and relying on an unproven complexity theoretic conjecture (the so-called "IPPP conjecture") that remains open to date. In the stateless case, the trusted hardware components in the constructions of [23,41] can be replaced by correlated random input bits that are fed directly into the stateless circuit in addition to the input x [10,26,41]. However, this requires the user of the leakage-resilient circuit $\widehat{C}$ to work at least as hard as computing C rather than simply feed $\widehat{C}$ with its input.

We note that unlike the case of security against *noisy* leakage, which is implied by security against probing attacks [19], this is *not* the case for security against AC^0 leakage. Indeed, there are pairs of distributions over $\{0,1\}^N$ that cannot be distinguished by probing any $N^{0.99}$ of their bits, and yet they *can* be distinguished by AC^0 circuits with one bit of output [10,14]. In the stateful case, an additional difficulty stems from the need to prove simulation-based security rather than mere indistinguishability by AC^0 circuits. The efficient simulation requirement poses a major challenge in some related contexts [33].

1.1   Our Contribution

In this work, we improve the above state of the art in both the stateless and stateful case by proving two main unconditional results.

In the *stateless* case (with one-shot leakage), we show that the original ISW construction [32], which is quite simple and concretely efficient, is actually unconditionally secure against a much wider class of low-complexity leakage functions that includes AC^0. We also show similar results for leakage computed by AC^0 circuits with mod-p gates, for a prime modulus $p > 2$, though in this case our security only follows from standard complexity-theoretic conjectures. In contrast to previous constructions from [10,26,41], here the circuit $\widehat{C}$ directly computes on the input x and does not require additional correlated random inputs or trusted leak-free hardware. This construction is also simpler and more efficient than the (conditional) construction from [43].

In the *stateful* case (with continuous leakage), we modify the previous construction of Rothblum [43], obtaining the first construction that *unconditionally* resists AC^0 leakage without relying on trusted leak-free hardware.

At a higher level of generality, both of our constructions satisfy a composition theorem of the following form (Theorems 4 and 5): For any given class of leakage functions $\mathcal{L}$, if parity has low correlation with $\mathcal{L}$ composed with NC^0 (namely, functions where each output depends on a constant number of inputs), then our constructions are secure against leakage from $\mathcal{L}$. For $\mathcal{L} = NC^0$ we recover the ISW result, for $\mathcal{L} = AC^0$ we obtain our main result, and for $\mathcal{L} = AC^0[\mathrm{mod}\,p]$

we get the extension to constant-depth circuits with mod p gates, assuming this class has low correlation with parities.

Here is a formal statement of the results in these cases of interest. For the relevant definitions see Sect. 3. The corresponding constructions are described in Sects. 4 and 5.

Corollary 1. *The ISW compiler when applied to circuits of size S and input length k is a $k\epsilon$-leakage resilient stateless circuit compiler against the following classes, where n is the security parameter:*

1. *Functions that depend on the values of at most $(n-1)/2$ wires, with $\epsilon = 0$,*
2. *Unbounded fan-in AND/OR/NOT circuits of size $s - O(n^2 S)$, depth d, and $c_d n/(\log s)^d$ outputs, with $\epsilon = 2^{-c_d n/(\log s)^d}$,*
3. *Unbounded fan-in AND/OR/NOT/MOD$_p$ circuits of size $s - O(n^2 S)$, depth d, and m outputs, assuming n-bit random parity-0 and parity-1 strings are $2 \cdot 3^{-m}\epsilon$-indistinguishable by such circuits of size s and depth $d+1$ (and one output).*

Here c_d is a constant that depends on d only. Part 1 recovers the stateless security result of Ishai, Sahai, and Wagner. Parts 2 and 3 are new.

Corollary 2. *There exists a construction of LRCC for a class of stateful circuits of size S that is $O(\epsilon T(S+n))$-leakage resilient stateful circuit compiler against the following leakage classes, where T, S, and n are the number of rounds of the leakage experiment, the circuit size, and the security parameter, respectively:*

1. *Unbounded fan-in AND/OR/NOT circuits of size $2^{n^{O(1/d)}} - O(n^3 S)$, depth d, and $n^{O(1/d)}$ outputs, with $\epsilon = 2^{-n^{O(1/d)}}$.*
2. *Unbounded fan-in AND/OR/NOT/MOD$_p$ circuits of size $s - O(n^3 S)$, depth d, and m outputs, assuming n-bit random parity-0 and parity-1 strings are $2 \cdot 3^{-m}\epsilon$-indistinguishable by such circuits of size $O(2^m s)$ and depth $d+1$ (and one output).*

2 Our Techniques

In this section, we give a high-level overview of our techniques for constructing a leakage resilient compiler that is unconditionally secure against AC^0 leakage. We start with a brief overview of the prior approaches and highlight the limitations of these approaches in obtaining an unconditional result. Next, in Sect. 2.1, we give an overview of the proof that the original private circuit construction of Ishai, Sahai and Wagner [32] is secure against AC^0 leakage in the stateless a.k.a. single-shot leakage setting. Finally, in Sect. 2.2, we discuss our construction of a leakage resilient circuit compiler in the stateful a.k.a. continuous leakage setting.

Prior Approaches. All the prior works [23,32,40,41,43] (including ours) follow the same high-level blue print in constructing a leakage resilient circuit compiler. Each wire in the original circuit C is transformed into a "bundle" of n-wires in the compiled circuit $\widehat{C}$ such that the bundle encodes the bit carried by the wire (using a suitable encoding procedure). Few examples of the encoding procedures used in the prior work are the (i) parity encoding [23,32,43] i.e., the parity of the wire bundle is equal to the value carried by the wire and (ii) group encoding [40,41] i.e., each element in the bundle is represented as an element of an alternating group and the product of the group elements encodes the bit carried by the wire. For concreteness, let us assume that the wires are encoded using the parity encoding. The next step in these constructions is to implement the addition and the multiplication gates over the wire bundles. That is, every gate $g \in \{+,*\}$ in the original circuit C, is transformed into a gadget $\widehat{g}$ that takes in 2 wire bundles, say $\mathbf{a}, \mathbf{b} \in \{0,1\}^n$ and outputs a wire bundle $\mathbf{c}$ such that parity of $\mathbf{c}$ is equal to $g(\oplus\mathbf{a}, \oplus\mathbf{b})$. Thus, evaluating these gate gadgets in $\widehat{C}$ will eventually lead us to the output wire bundles which are finally decoded by computing their parity. This construction ensures correctness i.e., the compiled circuit computes the same function as that of the original circuit. However, to prove security, these works required an additional refreshing gadget (denoted as Refresh). The refreshing gadget takes in a wire bundle $\mathbf{x}$ and outputs a random bundle $\mathbf{y}$ conditioned on $\oplus\mathbf{y} = \oplus\mathbf{x}$. In other words, this gadget refreshes the randomness used in the encoding. To get a secure construction, the implementation of each gate gadget $\widehat{g}$ were augmented in such a way that the output wire bundle, say $\mathbf{c}$ is sent through the Refresh gadget and the resultant wire bundle is the new output. At an intuitive level, this leads to a secure construction as the Refresh gadget ensures that the randomness used in encoding the output of each gate is refreshed and hence, the leakage that has been accumulated as a result of the $\widehat{g}$ computation does not propagate to the higher layers. This allowed the prior works to argue security against specific leakage classes such as AC^0 circuits. However, the task of implementing this refreshing gadget is highly challenging and this is the primary reason that the prior works had to rely on secure hardware components [23,40,41] or computational assumptions [43]. Specifically, Faust et al. used a secure hardware component to generate a random vector $\mathbf{z}$ whose parity is 0 and implemented the Refresh gadget as $\mathbf{y} = \mathbf{x} + \mathbf{z}$. This ensures that $\mathbf{y}$ has the same parity as that of $\mathbf{x}$ and additionally, it is distributed randomly conditioned on its parity being fixed. Rothblum removed the need of secure hardware components by generating random encodings of 0 using a more involved procedure (that will be explained later) but had to rely on a computational assumption in the proof of security. In the next two subsections, we discuss our approach of dealing with the problem of generating a random encoding of 0, first in the stateless setting and then in the more complicated stateful setting.

2.1   Unconditional Result in the Stateless Setting

The key insight behind our unconditional result in the stateless setting is that refreshing the output of every gate gadget is actually an overkill and a far weaker property called as "local sampleability" is sufficient. Before we go into the details, let us first give the definition of a local sampler. A circuit $\mathsf{Samp}(\mathbf{x}; r)$ ($\mathbf{x} \in \{0, 1\}^n$ is the regular input and r is the randomness) is said to be a 2-local sampler if each output bit of the circuit depends at most two bits of the regular input $\mathbf{x}$. It can be easily seen that for every r, $\mathsf{Samp}(\mathsf{PAR}(n, 0); r)$ is indistinguishable to $\mathsf{Samp}(\mathsf{PAR}(n, 1); r)$ by AC^0 circuits where $\mathsf{PAR}(n, b)$ is an uniform distribution over n-bit strings whose parity is b.

The main technical lemma which allows us to prove security in the stateless setting is the following. Fix the encodings of all input bits except one, say $\mathbf{x}$ and let $\widehat{C}$ be the compiled circuit in the construction of Ishai, Sahai and Wagner [32]. Then, the distribution of the wires in $\widehat{C}$ is identical to the output of a 2-local sampler $\mathsf{Samp}(\mathbf{x}; r)$ for an uniformly chosen r. This allows us to prove an unconditional result as we can go over a sequence of hybrids such that in each hybrid, we fix the encodings of all bits except one (say, $\mathbf{x}$), use $\mathsf{Samp}(\mathbf{x}; r)$ to generate the distribution of all the wires in $\widehat{C}$ and then conclude that the wire distribution is indistinguishable to AC^0 circuits when $\mathbf{x}$ encodes the bit 0 or 1. We stress that unlike the prior unconditional results in the stateless setting [23,41], our construction does not require a source of correlated randomness generated in a leak-free manner. We also remark that in the prior results, the number of bits of this correlated randomness string is very large and in the worst case, could be as large as the circuit itself.

Before we delve into the details of the proof of the main lemma, let us first recall the construction of Ishai, Sahai and Wagner [32]. As mentioned before, in this construction, each wire in the original circuit is transformed into a bundle of n wires such that the parity of this wire bundle is equal to the value carried by the wire. Given this encoding, implementing the addition gadget is simple. It takes in two wire bundles, $\mathbf{a}, \mathbf{b} \in \{0, 1\}^n$ and outputs $\mathbf{c} = \mathbf{a} + \mathbf{b}$. We give the details of the multiplication gadget below.

Construction 1. *On input two wire bundles $\mathbf{a}$ and $\mathbf{b}$, the multiplication gadget does the following:*

1. *Define the matrix $\mathbf{M} \in \{0, 1\}^{n \times n}$ such that $M_{i,j} = a_i b_j$.*
2. *For every $1 \leq i, j \leq n$ and $i < j$, choose a random bit $z_{i,j}$.*
3. *For every $1 \leq i, j \leq n$ and $i < j$, set $z_{j,i} = z_{i,j} \oplus (M_{j,i} \oplus M_{i,j})$.*
4. *For every $1 \leq i \leq n$, set $c_i = (\oplus_{j \neq i} z_{i,j}) \oplus M_{i,i}$.*
5. *Output $\mathbf{c} = (c_1, \ldots, c_n)$.*

Correctness of both the gadgets is straightforward to verify. Let us fix the encodings of all the input bits except one, say $\mathbf{x}$. To prove the main lemma, we need to show that the wire distribution in the compiled circuit conditioned on this fixing is identical to the output of a 2-local sampler.

Proof Overview. We prove this lemma via an inductive argument. We first prove that the distribution of the internal wires in an addition and a multiplication gate is identical to a locally sampleable distribution. We then use induction to prove that the wire assignment in the entire circuit is locally sampleable.

Local sampleability of addition gadget is trivial and the main challenge is to show local sampleability of multiplication gadget. For simplicity, let us consider a multiplication gate at the first layer of the circuit where one input is $\mathbf{x}$ (which is the non-fixed encoding) and the other input is $\mathbf{b}$ (for some fixed $\mathbf{b}$). The other cases are dealt in Sect. 4 of our paper. We need to show that for any $\mathbf{b}$, there exists a 2-local sampler $\mathsf{Samp}_{\mathsf{mult}}(\mathbf{x}; z')$ such that the output of the sampler (for an uniform z') is identical to the distribution of the internal wire assignments of a multiplication gate on input $\mathbf{x}, \mathbf{b}$.

At first inspection, it appears that the internal wire assignments of the multiplication gadget are "non-local." Specifically, consider the wires in the computation of c_n; it depends on every bit of $\mathbf{x}$. So the main question is how do we prove that the wires are 2-locally sampleable? The key insight is that while the internal wires of the multiplication gadget could be non-local, it is distributed identically to a 2-locally sampleable distribution. So, we need to demonstrate a 2-locally sampleable distribution (which is the output of a $\mathsf{Samp}_{\mathsf{mult}}$) and argue that this distribution is identical to the distribution of the internal wires of the multiplication gadget. We now give details of such a sampler $\mathsf{Samp}_{\mathsf{mult}}$. On input $\mathbf{x}$ and uniform randomness z', $\mathsf{Samp}_{\mathsf{mult}}$ (that depends on $\mathbf{b}$) does the following:

1. Define the matrix $\mathbf{M} \in \{0,1\}^{n \times n}$ where the (i,j)-th element $M_{i,j} = x_i \cdot b_j$.
2. For every $1 \leq i \leq n, 1 \leq j \leq n$ and $i < j$, choose a random bit $z'_{i,j}$ and define $z_{i,j} = z'_{i,j} \oplus M_{i,j}$.
3. For every $1 \leq i \leq n, 1 \leq j \leq n$ and $i < j$, set $z_{j,i} = z_{i,j} \oplus (M_{j,i} \oplus M_{i,j})$.
4. For every $1 \leq i \leq n$, set $c'_i = (\oplus_{j \neq i} z_{i,j}) \oplus M_{i,i}$.
5. Output $\mathbf{M}$, $\{z_{i,j}\}_{i<j}$, all the wires in the computation of $\{z_{i,j}\}_{i>j}$ and the computation of $\{c'_i\}_{i \in [n]}$ along with the vector $\mathbf{c}' = (c'_1, \ldots, c'_n)$ (which are the output wires).

The only difference between the wire assignments output by $\mathsf{Samp}_{\mathsf{mult}}$ and the actual wire assignments in multiplication gate is how $\{z_{i,j}\}_{i<j}$ is set. Note that if z' is chosen uniformly at random then the distribution of $\{z_{i,j}\}_{i<j}$ is identical to the uniform distribution. Thus, the wire assignment output by $\mathsf{Samp}_{\mathsf{mult}}$ is identical to the actual wire assignment in the implementation of the multiplication gate for a randomly chosen z. To see the 2-local sampleability of $\mathsf{Samp}_{\mathsf{mult}}$, observe that for any $i < j$, $z_{i,j}$ depends only on x_i. Furthermore, for any $i > j$, it can be observed that $z_{i,j} = z'_{j,i} \oplus M_{i,j}$ depends on only x_i and wires used in computing $z_{i,j}$ is a 2-local function in $\mathbf{x}$. These two observations imply that for every $i \in [n]$, computing c'_i depends only on x_i and hence the wires in this computation are locally sampleable. This shows that the output of $\mathsf{Samp}_{\mathsf{mult}}$ is a 2-local distribution. Combining this with the inductive argument allows us to obtain an unconditional result in the stateless setting.

2.2   Unconditional Result in the Stateful Setting

In this subsection, we give a high level overview of our construction of a leakage-resilient circuit compiler against AC^0 circuits in the stateful setting that has unconditional security. As mentioned before, the prior results in this setting either relied on secure hardware components or on computational assumptions.

Main Challenges. In the stateful setting, there are two key challenges that we need to overcome. The first challenge is dealing with absence of a trusted decoder. In the stateless setting, a trusted decoder was available and this allowed the simulator to "cheat" by hardwiring the correct output in the trusted decoder such that even when the circuit is run on some junk inputs, the output obtained is consistent with the actual output. However, in the stateful case, no such trusted decoder is available and this makes the task of simulation much harder. In this case, the simulator must somehow incorporate the correct output (without knowing the actual input) in the wire distribution such that a leakage function cannot distinguish this from the real word distribution. When considering leakage classes such as AC^0 functions, this task is even more challenging as these functions can check local consistency of the gates. The second challenge in the stateful setting is the necessity to refresh the randomness. Unlike the stateless setting where we observed that local sampleability is sufficient, in the stateful case, we need to additionally refresh the randomness used in the encoding procedure. To see why this is the case, consider a stateful circuit that has a PRF key k as its state and computes $PRF(k, x)$ on a regular input x. If the randomness of the key k is not refreshed across multiple queries, then in $O(n|k|)$ leakage queries, the entire key can be successfully retrieved by leakage functions that output a single bit. Thus, we need to refresh the randomness of the state bundles across queries and for technical reasons, we also need to refresh the randomness of the output of every gate.

Rothblum's Construction. The starting point of our construction is the work of Rothblum [43] who showed that under a complexity theoretic assumption referred to as "Inner Products with Pre-Processing" (IPPP)[1], there exists a construction of a leakage resilient circuit compiler against AC^0 in the stateful setting. Unfortunately, this assumption is unproven and even the state of highly restricted versions of the assumption such as allowing only linear functions in the pre-processing phase [2] is far from being resolved. In the rest of this subsection, we first give a high level overview of the construction of Rothblum, indicate why the IPPP assumption is needed, and then discuss our approach of removing the need for the assumption.

Recall that in the stateful setting, the output of every gate is refreshed and thus, the first step is to implement the **Refresh** gadget. This **Refresh** gadget in fact helps in overcoming both the challenges that we discussed earlier. Firstly, it helps in refreshing the randomness and thus, helps in overcoming the second challenge. To overcome the first challenge, we additionally send the wire bundles coming

---

[1] Let D'_0, D'_1 be uniform distributions over $2n$-bit strings such that for every $(\mathbf{x}, \mathbf{y}) \in D'_b$, $<\mathbf{x}, \mathbf{y}> = b$. IPPP states that it is hard for AC^0 circuits to distinguish between D'_0 and D'_1 even when given $f(\mathbf{x})$ and $g(\mathbf{y})$ for arbitrary polynomial-time computable functions f, g.

out of the output gate through the Refresh gadget and compute the parity of the resultant output. In the ideal world distribution, the simulator will change the internal workings of the Refresh gadget such that instead of only refreshing the randomness, this gadget could also switch the parity when needed. This helps the simulator to hardcode the correct output of the circuit even when it is run with some junk input.

Now, to implement the Refresh gadget, it is sufficient to generate a random encoding of the bit 0. The main technical contribution in Rothblum's work is a method to securely generate a random encoding of 0 without the use of hardware components. This is done as follows. A generator matrix $\mathbf{G} \in \{0,1\}^{n \times 2n}$ is chosen uniformly at random subject to the parity of each column of $\mathbf{G}$ being 0. This generator matrix is part of the state of the compiled circuit $\widehat{C}$. Whenever a random encoding of 0 is required, choose $\mathbf{r}$ uniformly at random from $\{0,1\}^{2n}$ and compute $\mathbf{G} \cdot \mathbf{r}$. It is straightforward to see that the resultant vector is statistically close to a random vector whose parity is 0. This vector is then used in the Refresh gadget. In Rothblum's work, the circuit for computing the matrix-vector product $\mathbf{G} \cdot \mathbf{r}$ is the trivial $O(n^2)$ sized circuit (denoted by C_{MV}).

While the above idea may seem extremely simple at first sight, the proof that this is indeed secure in the presence of AC^0 leakage is highly involved and requires the use of the (unproven) IPPP assumption. Intuitively, the IPPP assumption is used in the proof to generate the assignment to every wire in C_{MV} by an AC^0 circuit. To see this, consider the following two hybrids in the proof of security from Rothblum's work. In the first hybrid, $\mathbf{G}, \mathbf{r}$ are sampled as in the construction i.e., $\mathbf{G}$ is chosen randomly subject to its column parity being 0 and $\mathbf{r}$ is chosen uniformly at random. In the second hybrid, $\mathbf{G}, \mathbf{r}$ are both chosen uniformly at random from their respective domains. Just given $(\mathbf{G}, \mathbf{r})$, these two distributions are clearly indistinguishable to an AC^0 function. However, to make sure that these hybrids are indistinguishable to an AC^0 leakage function, one needs to additionally generate, in constant depth, all the intermediate wire values in C_{MV} when given $\mathbf{G}$ and $\mathbf{r}$ as inputs. Rothblum showed that this is indeed possible with polynomial time, independent pre-processing on $\mathbf{G}$ and $\mathbf{r}$ and that is why IPPP assumption is needed.

Our Approach. In this work, we remove the need for the IPPP assumption by designing a new gadget called "RandZero" that generates a random encoding of 0. Crucially, unlike the circuit C_{MV}, it has a special property that its wire assignments are locally sampleable. This allows us to get rid of the pre-processing phase in Rothblum's paper and obtain an unconditionally secure construction. We now give more details of our approach.

Like in Rothblum's construction, we choose a generator matrix $\mathbf{G} \leftarrow \{0,1\}^{n \times n}$ uniformly at random subject to its column parity being 0 and make it part of the state. When we have to generate a random encoding of 0, we choose $\mathbf{r}$ uniformly at random and compute $\mathsf{RandZero}(\mathbf{G}, \mathbf{r})$. Below, we give the description of this gadget.

Construction 2. *Given a matrix* $\mathbf{G} \in \{0,1\}^{n \times n}$ *and a vector* $\mathbf{r} \in \{0,1\}^n$, RandZero *does the following:*

1. *Define the matrix* $\mathbf{M} \in \{0,1\}^{n \times n}$ *where the* (i,j)-*th element* $M_{i,j} = G_{i,j} r_j$.
2. *For every* $1 \leq i \leq n, 1 \leq j \leq n$ *and* $i < j$, *choose a random bit* $z_{i,j}$.
3. *For every* $1 \leq i \leq n, 1 \leq j \leq n$ *and* $i < j$, *set* $z_{j,i} = (z_{i,j} \oplus M_{j,i}) \oplus M_{i,j}$.
4. *For every* $1 \leq i \leq n$, *compute* $c_i = (\oplus_{j \neq i} z_{i,j}) \oplus M_{i,i}$.
5. *Output* $\mathbf{c} = (c_1, \ldots, c_n)$.

We first make a couple of simple observations. The first observation is that the parity of the output $\mathbf{c}$ is same as that of the vector $\mathbf{G} \cdot \mathbf{r}$. The second observation is that the distribution of $\mathbf{c}$ is uniformly random subject to its parity being equal to parity of the vector $\mathbf{G} \cdot \mathbf{r}$. Thus, when the column parity of $\mathbf{G}$ is 0, we can use the output of this gadget to refresh the randomness.

Notice that the above gadget has a lot of similarities with the multiplication gadget in the work of Ishai, Sahai and Wagner [32] (described in Construction 1). In fact, the only difference is how the matrix $\mathbf{M}$ is defined. We thus, extend the local sampleability property that we proved for Construction 1 to this construction. In the actual proof of security, we go over a sequence of hybrids (similar to the hybrid sequence used in Rothblum's work) and show that each neighboring hybrids in the sequence are indistinguishable to AC^0 leakage using the local sampleability property of our RandZero gadget. This allows us to prove an unconditional result. See Sect. 5 for the details.

3   Preliminaries

Notation We will denote vectors by bold lowercase letters (e.g., $\mathbf{x}$) and matrices with bold uppercase letters (e.g., $\mathbf{M}$). We will denote the i-th entry of a vector $\mathbf{x}$ by x_i and the (i,j)-th entry of the matrix $\mathbf{M}$ by $M_{i,j}$. We use $\mathbf{e}_k \in \{0,1\}^n$ for the unit vector whose k-th coordinate is 1 and the rest of the coordinates to be 0.

We use the notation $\mathsf{W}[C]$ for the vector of wire values of a circuit C (under a canonical ordering consistent with the direction of evaluation), and $\mathsf{PAR}(n, b)$ for the distribution on n-bit strings that is chosen uniformly at random subject to having parity b.

3.1   Indistinguishability

Definition 1 (Statistical distance). *Let D_1 and D_2 be two distributions on a set S. The statistical distance between D_1 and D_2 is defined to be:*

$$\Delta(D_1, D_2) = \max_{T \subseteq S} |D_1(T) - D_2(T)| = \frac{1}{2} \sum_{s \in S} |\Pr[D_1 = s] - \Pr[D_2 = s]|$$

We say that D_1 is ϵ-close to D_2 if $\Delta(D_1, D_2) \leq \epsilon$, and ϵ-far otherwise.

Definition 2 (ϵ-indistinguishability). *Let X and Y be two distribution over the same domain. We say that (X, Y) is ϵ-indistinguishable by a class of functions $\mathcal{C}$ if for every $C \in \mathcal{C}$, $\Delta(C(X), C(Y)) \leq \epsilon$.*

3.2   Circuit Complexity

A class of functions $\mathcal{C}$ is *closed under restriction* (resp., *negation*) if for every f in $\mathcal{C}$, the function obtained by fixing the value of any input (resp., negating it) is also in $\mathcal{C}$.

The composition $\mathcal{C} \circ \mathcal{C}'$ consists of all functions $(f \circ f')(x) = f(f'(x))$, where $f \in \mathcal{C}$ and $f' \in \mathcal{C}'$.

We use $\mathsf{NC}^0[c]$ for the class of all multi-input, multi-output Boolean functions in which every output depends on at most c inputs, $\mathsf{AC}^0(d,s,m)$ for the class of circuits that use unbounded fan-in AND-OR-NOT gates, have depth d, size at most s and m output bits, and $\mathsf{AC}^0[B](d,s,m)$ for circuits that may have other types of basis gates B that are closed under negation. If the input or output length is unrestricted or clear from context it is left out of the notation. The following claim follows directly from the definition.

Claim 1. $\mathsf{NC}^0[c] \circ \mathsf{NC}^0[c'] \subseteq \mathsf{NC}^0[cc']$, $\mathsf{AC}^0(d,s,m) \circ \mathsf{NC}^0[c] \subseteq \mathsf{AC}^0(d+1, s+n \cdot 2^c)$, and $\mathsf{AC}^0[B](d,s,m) \circ \mathsf{NC}^0[c] \subseteq \mathsf{AC}^0[B](d+2, s+n \cdot 2^c)$ where n is the output length of the $\mathsf{NC}^0[c]$ circuit.

A 2-adaptive circuit over $\mathcal{C}$ is a collection of functions (A, B_y), where y ranges over all possible output values of C. The value of the circuit on input x is $(A(x), B_{A(x)}(x))$.

Claim 2. If (D_1, D_2) is ϵ-indistinguishable by $\mathsf{AC}^0(2d+1, (2^m+1)(s+O(1)), 2m)$ (resp., $\mathsf{AC}^0[B](2d+1, (2^m+1)(s+O(1)), 2m))$, then it is ϵ-indistinguishable by all 2-adaptive circuits over $\mathsf{AC}^0(d,s,m)$ (resp., $\mathsf{AC}^0[B](d,s)$).

Claim 3. If (D_0, D_1) is ϵ-indistinguishable by $\mathsf{AC}^0(d,s,1)$ (resp., $AC^0[B](d,s,1)$) then it is $3^m\epsilon/2$-indistinguishable by $\mathsf{AC}^0(d,2s,m)$ (resp., $AC^0[B](d+1,s,m)$).

We give the proof of the above two claims in the full version.

We conclude with Håstad's unconditional result on indistinguishability of parity by constant-depth circuits.

Theorem 3 ([31]). *For any $d,s \in \mathbb{N}$ there exists a constant c_d that depends only on d such that $(\mathsf{PAR}(n,0), \mathsf{PAR}(n,1))$ is $2^{-c_d n/(\log s)^{d-1}}$-indistinguishable by $\mathsf{AC}^0(d,s,1)$*

Corollary 3. *There exists a constant c_d such that $(\mathsf{PAR}(n,0), \mathsf{PAR}(n,1))$ are $2^{-c_d n/(\log s)^{d-1}}$-indistinguishable by $\mathsf{AC}^0(d, s/2, c_d n/(\log s)^{d-1})$ and $2^{-n^{O(1/d)}}$-indistinguishable by 2-adaptive circuits over $\mathsf{AC}^0(d/2-1, 2^{n^{O(1/d)}}, n^{O(1/d)})$.*

3.3   Leakage Resilient Circuit Compilers

In this subsection, we give the definitions of leakage resilient circuit compiler (abbreviated as LRCC) for stateful and stateless circuits.

LRCC for Stateful Circuits. We first recall the notion of stateful circuits. This description is taken verbatim from [32]. A stateful circuit is a circuit augmented with *memory cells.* A memory cell is a stateful gate with fan-in 1: on any invocation of the circuit, it outputs the previous input to the gate, and stores the current input for the next invocation. Thus, memory cells act as delay elements. We extend the usual definition of a circuit by allowing stateful circuits to possibly contain cycles, so long as every cycle traverses at least one memory cell. When specifying a stateful circuit, we must also specify an initial state for the memory cells. When C denotes a circuit with memory cells and s_0 an initial state for the memory cells, we write $C[s_0]$ for the circuit C with memory cells initially filled with s_0. Stateful circuits can also have external input and output wires. For instance, in an AES circuit the internal memory cells contain the secret key, the input wires a plaintext, and the output wires produce the corresponding ciphertext. The computation of $C[s]$ on an input x results in a wire assignment W (a wire assignment is a string that is obtained by concatenating the values carried by all the wires in C), the output y and an updated state s_1.

Definition 3 (($\mathcal{L}, \tau, \epsilon$)-**leakage resilient implementation**). *Let C be a deterministic stateful circuit, $\mathcal{L}$ be a leakage class, τ be a round parameter and ϵ be an error parameter. We say that $(\widehat{C}, \mathsf{Setup})$ is an $(\mathcal{L}, \tau, \epsilon)$-leakage resilient implementation of C if:*

- *$\widehat{C}$ is a randomized, stateful circuit.*
- Setup *is a randomized mapping from the initial state s_0 of C to an initial state $\widehat{s}_0$ of $\widehat{C}$.*
- ***Correctness.*** *For every $k \in \mathbb{N}$ and every sequence of inputs $x_1, \ldots, x_k$, we require that probability (over the random coins of Setup and $\widehat{C}$) that the same outputs are obtained by (stateful) invocations of $C[s_0]$ and $\widehat{C}[\widehat{s}_0]$ on this input sequence is 1.*
- ***Security.*** *For every (possibly unbounded) stateful adversary $\mathcal{A}$, there exists a (stateful) simulator $\mathcal{S}$ such that for every initial state s_0 :*

$$\left| \Pr[\mathsf{Real}_{\mathcal{A}, \widehat{C}, \mathsf{Setup}, \mathcal{L}}(s_0, \tau) = 1] - \Pr[\mathsf{Ideal}_{\mathcal{A}, \widehat{C}, \mathsf{Setup}, \mathcal{S}, \mathcal{L}}(s_0, \tau) = 1] \right| \leq \epsilon$$

where Real *and* Ideal *experiments are defined in Fig. 1.*

Definition 4 (LRCC for Stateful Circuits). *Let n be the security parameter. A leakage resilient stateful circuit compiler for the (stateful) circuit class $\mathcal{C}$ is a pair of polynomial-time algorithms $(\mathsf{Tr}, \mathsf{St})$ such that:*

- Tr *is a deterministic algorithm that maps a deterministic stateful circuit in $C \in \mathcal{C}$ and the security parameter 1^n to another stateful, randomized circuit $\widehat{C}$.*
- St *is a randomized algorithm that maps an initial state s_0 of C and the security parameter 1^n to an initial state $\widehat{s}_0$ of $\widehat{C}$.*

For a leakage class $\mathcal{L}(n)$, round parameter $\tau(n)$ and error parameter $\epsilon(n)$, we say that $(\mathsf{Tr}, \mathsf{St})$ is a $(\mathcal{L}(n), \tau(n), \epsilon(n))$-leakage resilient circuit compiler for $\mathcal{C}$, if for every stateful circuit $C \in \mathcal{C}$, $(\mathsf{Tr}(C, 1^n), \mathsf{St}(\star, 1^n))$ is a $(\mathcal{L}(n), \tau(n), \epsilon(n))$-leakage resilient implementation of C.

$$\mathsf{Real}_{\mathcal{A},\widehat{C},\mathsf{Setup},\mathcal{L}}(s_0,\tau)$$

1. $\widehat{s}_0 \leftarrow \mathsf{Setup}(s_0)$.
2. Set $y_0, z_0 = \perp$.
3. **for** every round t from 1 to τ:
   - $x_t, \ell_t \leftarrow \mathcal{A}(\widehat{C}, y_{t-1}, z_{t-1})$ where $\ell_t \in \mathcal{L}$.
   - $(\widehat{\mathsf{W}}_t, y_t, \widehat{s}_t) \Leftarrow \widehat{C}[\widehat{s}_{t-1}](x_t)$.
   - $z_t = \ell_t(\widehat{\mathsf{W}}_t)$.
4. Output whatever $\mathcal{A}$ outputs.

$$\mathsf{Ideal}_{\mathcal{A},\widehat{C},\mathsf{Setup},\mathcal{S},\mathcal{L}}(s_0,\tau)$$

1. Set $y_0, z_0 = \perp$.
2. **for** every round t from 1 to τ:
   - $x_t, \ell_t \leftarrow \mathcal{A}(\widehat{C}, y_{t-1}, z_{t-1})$ where $\ell_t \in \mathcal{L}$.
   - $(\mathsf{W}_t, y_t, s_t) \Leftarrow C[s_{t-1}](x_t)$
   - $z_t = \ell_t(\mathcal{S}(C, x_t, y_t))$.
3. Output whatever $\mathcal{A}$ outputs.

Fig. 1. Real and Ideal experiments

LRCC for Stateless Circuits. We now define a leakage-resilient circuit compiler for stateless circuits.

Definition 5 ($(\mathcal{L}, \epsilon)$-leakage resilient implementation). *Let $C : \{0,1\}^k \to \{0,1\}^m$ be a deterministic stateless circuit, $\mathcal{L}$ be a leakage class, and ϵ be an error parameter. We say that $(I, \widehat{C}, O)$ is a $(\mathcal{L}, \epsilon)$-leakage resilient implementation of C if:*

- $I : \{0,1\}^k \to \{0,1\}^{\widehat{k}}$ *is a randomized input encoder which maps an input x to an encoded input $\widehat{x}$.*
- $\widehat{C}$ *is a randomized circuit that maps an encoded input $\widehat{x}$ to an encoded output $\widehat{y} \in \{0,1\}^{\widehat{m}}$.*
- $O : \{0,1\}^{\widehat{m}} \to \{0,1\}^m$ *is the deterministic output decoder that maps an encoded output $\widehat{y}$ to y.*
- **Correctness:** *For every input $x \in \{0,1\}^k$, $\Pr[O(\widehat{C}(I(x))) = f(x)] = 1$ where the probability is over the random coins of I and $\widehat{C}$.*
- **Security:** *For any two inputs $x_0, x_1 \in \{0,1\}^k$, let $(\mathsf{W}_0, \widehat{y}_0) \Leftarrow \widehat{C}[I(x_0)]$ and $(\mathsf{W}_1, \widehat{y}_1) \Leftarrow \widehat{C}[I(x_1)]$ where W_0 (resp. W_1) represents the assignment to every wire of $\widehat{C}$ on input $I(x_0)$ (resp. $I(x_1)$). For any leakage function $\ell \in \mathcal{L}$, the statistical distance between $\ell(\mathsf{W}_0)$ and $\ell(\mathsf{W}_1)$ is at most ϵ.*

Definition 6 (LRCC for Stateless Circuits). *Let n be the security parameter and let $\mathcal{C}$ be a class of stateless circuits taking k input bits and having m output bits. A leakage resilient stateless circuit compiler for the class $\mathcal{C}$ is a tuple of polynomial-time algorithms $(\mathsf{Enc}, \mathsf{Tr}, \mathsf{Dec})$ where*

- Enc *is a randomized input encoder which maps an input $x \in \{0,1\}^k$ and the security parameter 1^n to an encoded input $\widehat{x}$.*
- Tr *is a deterministic algorithm that maps a deterministic stateless circuit in $C \in \mathcal{C}$ and the security parameter 1^n to another stateful, randomized circuit $\widehat{C}$. $\widehat{C}$ maps an encoded input $\widehat{x}$ to an encoded output $\widehat{y}$.*
- Dec *is the deterministic output decoder that maps an encoded output $\widehat{y}$ to $y \in \{0,1\}^m$.*

For a leakage class $\mathcal{L}(n)$ and the error parameter $\epsilon(n)$, we say that $(\mathsf{Enc}, \mathsf{Tr}, \mathsf{Dec})$ is a $(\mathcal{L}(n), \epsilon(n))$-leakage resilient circuit compiler for $\mathcal{C}$ if for every $C \in \mathcal{C}$, $(\mathsf{Enc}(\star, 1^n), \mathsf{Tr}(C, 1^n), \mathsf{Dec})$ is a $(\mathcal{L}(n), \epsilon(n))$-leakage resilient implementation of C.

4   Improved Analysis of the ISW Construction

The leakage-resilient circuit transformer of Ishai, Sahai, and Wagner [32] is shown in Fig. 2. Ishai et al. proved it is correct and perfectly secure against leakage functions that depend on at most $n/2 - 1$ wires.

The input encoder $\mathsf{Enc}(1^n, x)$: Every input bit $x_i \in \{0, 1\}$ is encoded independently by $\mathbf{x}_i \in \{0, 1\}^n$ which is random conditioned on its parity being equal to x_i.

The transformer $\mathsf{Tr}(1^n, C)$:

Every wire $w \in \{0, 1\}$ of C is replaced by a wire bundle $\mathbf{w} \in \{0, 1\}^n$.

Every addition gate $a + b$ in C is implemented by $\mathbf{a} + \mathbf{b}$, where $\mathbf{a}, \mathbf{b}$ are the wire bundles representing a, b, respectively.

Every multiplication gate $a \times b$ is implemented as follows. Compute the matrix $\mathbf{Z} \in \{0, 1\}^{n \times n}$ given by

$$Z_{ij} = \begin{cases} \text{a random bit,} & \text{if } i < j \\ a_i b_j, & \text{if } i = j \\ Z_{ji} + a_i b_j + a_j b_i, & \text{if } i > j \end{cases}$$

and output the matrix-vector product $\mathbf{Z} \cdot \mathbf{1}$ computed from left to right.

The output decoder $\mathsf{Dec}(1^n, \mathbf{y}_1 \cdots \mathbf{y}_m)$: Replace every encoded output wire bundle $\mathbf{y}_j$ by its parity $y_{j1} + \cdots + y_{jn}$.

Fig. 2. The Ishai-Sahai-Wagner circuit compiler [32].

The transformer maintains the invariant that every wire w of C is represented by a wire bundle $\mathbf{w}$ that XORs to the bit value w, ensuring correctness; for details of the correctness proof see [32].

Theorem 4. *Let $\mathcal{C}$ be any class of functions that is closed under restriction and negation of inputs. Assume $(\mathsf{PAR}(n, 0), \mathsf{PAR}(n, 1))$ is ϵ-indistinguishable by $\mathcal{C} \circ \mathsf{NC}^0[2]$. Then the ISW circuit compiler is $(\mathcal{C}, k\epsilon)$-leakage resilient stateless compiler where k is the input size of the circuit.*

Let $\widehat{C}(\mathbf{x}_1, \ldots, \mathbf{x}_k)$ represent the transformed circuit when it is given wire bundles $\mathbf{x}_1, \ldots, \mathbf{x}_k$ as its inputs. The following lemma is key to the proof of Theorem 4.

Lemma 1. *For every circuit C of size S on k inputs, every k strings* $\mathbf{w}_1, \ldots, \mathbf{w}_k \in \{0,1\}^n$, *and every k bits $c_1, \ldots, c_k$, the wire distributions of* $\widehat{C}(\mathbf{w}_1 + c_1 \cdot \mathbf{x}, \ldots, \mathbf{w}_k + c_k \cdot \mathbf{x})$ *in the cases $\mathbf{x} \sim \mathsf{PAR}(n,0)$ and $\mathbf{x} \sim \mathsf{PAR}(n,1)$ are* ϵ-*indistinguishable by C under the assumption in Theorem 4.*

Proof of Theorem 4: Fix a leakage function $\ell \in \mathcal{C}$. We need to show that $\ell(\mathsf{W})$ is statistically close to $\ell(\mathsf{W}')$ where W and W' are the wires of $\widehat{C}(\mathsf{Enc}(x))$ and $\widehat{C}(\mathsf{Enc}(x'))$ for any $x, x' \in \{0,1\}^k$. First consider the case when x and x' differ in a single bit, say the i-th bit. Hardwiring all encoded inputs except for $\mathbf{x}_i$ into $\widehat{C}$ and applying Lemma 1 with $\mathbf{w}_j = \mathbf{x}_j, c_j = 0$ for $j \neq i$, and $\mathbf{w}_i = \mathbf{0}, c_i = 1, \mathbf{x} = \mathbf{x}_i$, it follows that $\widehat{C}(\mathsf{Enc}(x))$ and $\widehat{C}(\mathsf{Enc}(x'))$ are ϵ-indistinguishable by $\mathcal{C}$.

For the general case, consider the hybrid wire distributions $\widehat{C}(\mathsf{Enc}(x^i))$, where $x^0 = x$, $x^k = x'$, and x^{i-1}, x^i differ in at most one bit. By what was just proved $\widehat{C}(\mathsf{Enc}(x^{i-1}))$ and $\widehat{C}(\mathsf{Enc}(x^i))$ are ϵ-indistnguishable, so by the triangle inequality $\widehat{C}(\mathsf{Enc}(x))$ and $\widehat{C}(\mathsf{Enc}(x'))$ must be $k\epsilon$-indistinguishable.   □

The main idea in the proof of Lemma 1 is the following claim, which states that the wire distribution of any single gate in the transformed circuit can be described locally, and moreover the output of the gate obeys the same type of distribution as its inputs.

Claim 4. For all $g \in \{+, \times\}$ and $\mathbf{w}, \mathbf{w}', c, c'$ there exists a simulator Sim such that

1. The wires of $\mathsf{Sim}(\mathbf{w} + c \cdot \mathbf{x}, \mathbf{w}' + c' \cdot \mathbf{x})$ and $\hat{g}(\mathbf{w} + c \cdot \mathbf{x}, \mathbf{w}' + c' \cdot \mathbf{x})$ are identically distributed even conditioned on $\mathbf{x}$.
2. The value $\mathbf{y}$ assigned to the output bundle by $\mathsf{Sim}(\mathbf{w} + c \cdot \mathbf{x}, \mathbf{w}' + c' \cdot \mathbf{x})$ equals $\mathbf{w}'' + c'' \cdot \mathbf{x}$ for some $\mathbf{w}''$ and c'' that depend on the internal randomness of Sim only.
3. Every wire of $\mathsf{Sim}(\mathbf{w} + c \cdot \mathbf{x}, \mathbf{w}' + c' \cdot \mathbf{x})$ depends on at most two bits of $\mathbf{x}$.

Proof of Lemma 1: We consider the following slightly stronger formulation of the lemma as it enables a proof by induction: Under the same assumptions, the joint distribution

$$\left(\mathbf{x}, \mathsf{W}[\widehat{C}(\mathbf{w}_1 + c_1 \cdot \mathbf{x}, \ldots, \mathbf{w}_k + c_k \cdot \mathbf{x})] \right)$$

in the cases $\mathbf{x} \sim \mathsf{PAR}(n,0)$ and $\mathbf{x} \sim \mathsf{PAR}(n,1)$ are ϵ-indistinguishable by circuits that are $\mathcal{C} \circ \mathsf{NC}^0[2]$ functions in the first input $\mathbf{x}$ and $\mathcal{C}$ functions in the second input $\mathsf{W}[\cdots]$.

The proof is by induction on S. When $S = 0$, there are no internal gates so the leakage function ℓ observes $\mathbf{x}$ together with the input wires $(\mathbf{w}_1 + c_1 \cdot \mathbf{x}, \ldots, \mathbf{w}_k + c_k \cdot \mathbf{x})$ and attempts to distinguish $\mathbf{x} \sim \mathsf{PAR}(n,0)$ from $\mathbf{x} \sim \mathsf{PAR}(n,1)$. As each input wire bundle is either a constant or a shift of $\mathbf{x}$, the second input can be emulated from the first one by the closure properties of $\mathcal{C}$. Therefore the distributions $\mathsf{PAR}(n,0)$ and $\mathsf{PAR}(n,1)$ can be distinguished by $\mathcal{C}$, and therefore by $\mathcal{C} \circ \mathsf{NC}^0[2]$, with the same advantage ϵ.

Now suppose the lemma holds for all circuits of size $S-1$. Given a circuit C of size S, let g be a bottom gate of C and x_i, x_j its (possibly identical) inputs. The leakage function ℓ of interest observes $\mathbf{x}$, the wires of $\widehat{g}(\mathbf{w}_i + c_i \cdot \mathbf{x}, \mathbf{w}_j + c_j \cdot \mathbf{x})$, and the wires of $\widehat{C^-}(\mathbf{w}_1 + c_1 \cdot \mathbf{x}, \ldots, \mathbf{w}_k + c_k \cdot \mathbf{x}, \mathbf{y})$, where C^- is the circuit obtained by removing gate g from C and replacing its output by y.

By part 1 of Claim 4, the wires of $\widehat{g}(\mathbf{w}_i + c_i \cdot \mathbf{x}, \mathbf{w}_j + c_j \cdot \mathbf{x})$ can be replaced by those of $\mathsf{Sim}(\mathbf{w}_i + c_i \cdot \mathbf{x}, \mathbf{w}_j + c_j \cdot \mathbf{x})$ without affecting the distinguisher's advantage. By part 3 they are 2-local functions of $\mathbf{x}$. Therefore they are a $\mathcal{C} \circ \mathsf{NC}^0[2]$ function of $\mathbf{x}$, so can be omitted from the input to ℓ. The Lemma now follows from part 2 of Claim 4 and the inductive hypothesis applied to the circuit C^-.   □

Proof of Claim 4: If g is an addition gate, set $\mathsf{Sim} = \widehat{+}$: The output is the sum of its two inputs confirming part 2, and there are no wires other than the output wires, from where part 3 follows.

Let $\mathbf{a} = \mathbf{w} + c\mathbf{x}$ and $\mathbf{b} = \mathbf{w}' + c'\mathbf{x}$. If g is a multiplication gate, the simulator $\mathsf{Sim}(\mathbf{a}, \mathbf{b})$ works like $\widehat{\times}$, but uses the following alternative implementation of the matrix $\mathbf{Z}$:

$$Z_{ij} = \begin{cases} \text{a random bit} + a_i w'_j + b_i w_j, & \text{if } i < j \\ a_i b_j, & \text{if } i = j \\ Z_{ji} + a_i b_j + a_j b_i, & \text{if } i > j \end{cases}$$

This alternative implementation of $\mathbf{Z}$ does not affect the distribution of the entries of $\mathbf{Z}$ and therefore of the wires of the transformed circuit. We now argue properties 2 and 3 of Claim 4.

When $i = j$ and $i < j$, Z_{ij} only depends on the i-th bit of $\mathbf{a}$ and $\mathbf{b}$, which are independent of all but possibly the i-th bit of $\mathbf{x}$. When $i > j$, $Z_{ij} = Z_{ji} + a_i b_j + a_j b_i$ and this equals randomness plus the bit

$$(a_j w'_i + b_j w_i) + (a_i b_j + a_j b_i).$$

The first bracketed term equals $c x_j w'_i + c' x_j w_i$ plus a term that only depends on $\mathbf{w}$. The second one equals

$$(w_i + c x_i)(w'_j + c' x_j) + (w'_i + c' x_i)(w_j + c x_j)$$
$$= (c x_i w'_j + c' x_i w_j) + (c x_j w'_i + c' x_j w_i) + (w_i w'_j + w_j w_i).$$

Therefore the sum of the two equals $c x_i w'_j + c' x_i w_j$ plus a term that only depends on $\mathbf{w}$. It follows that for any i, j, Z_{ij} can only depend on the i-th bit of $\mathbf{x}$ and the wires in the computation of $Z_{i,j}$ for $i > j$ is a 2-local function of $\mathbf{x}$. We thus conclude that the wires in the computation of $\mathbf{Z} \cdot \mathbf{1}$ is a 1-local function in $\mathbf{x}$ and the output is of the form $\mathbf{w}'' + c'' \cdot \mathbf{x}$.   □

Corollary 1 follows directly from Theorem 4, Claim 1 and Corollary 3.

5   LRCC for Stateful Circuits

In this section, we give a construction of leakage resilient circuit compiler and prove its security against leakage classes that have low correlation with parity.

The class $\mathcal{C} \circ \mathsf{NC}^0[c]$ consists of all composed functions $f \circ g$ where $f \in \mathcal{C}$ and every output of g depends on at most c inputs.

Theorem 5. *Let c be a universal constant and $\mathcal{C}$ be any class of functions that is closed under restriction. If $(\mathsf{PAR}(n, 0), \mathsf{PAR}(n, 1))$ is ϵ-indistinguishable by 2-adaptive functions in $\mathcal{C} \circ \mathsf{NC}^0[c]$, then the construction in Fig. 3 is a $(\mathcal{C}, T, O(\epsilon T(S + n)))$-leakage resilient stateful circuit compiler for the class of stateful circuits of size S and T is the number of rounds.*

Organization. In Sect. 5.1, we will describe a building block that generates a random encoding of 0 and prove some useful properties. In Sect. 5.2, we give the description of the transformer $(\mathsf{Tr}, \mathsf{St})$. In Sects. 5.3–5.5, we prove the security of the construction.

5.1   The Zero-Encoder

In this subsection, we describe and analyze a circuit $\mathsf{RandZero}$ that produces random encodings of the bit zero.

Construction 6. $\mathsf{RandZero}$: *On input matrix $\mathbf{G} \in \{0, 1\}^{n \times n}$ and vector $\mathbf{r} \in \{0, 1\}^n$, calculate*

$$
Z_{ij} = \begin{cases} a \ random \ bit, & if \ i < j, \\ G_{ii}r_i, & if \ i = j, \\ Z_{ji} + G_{ij}r_j + G_{ji}r_i, & if \ i > j, \end{cases}
$$

and output the matrix-vector product $\mathbf{Z} \cdot \mathbf{1}$ computed from left to right.

We denote by $\mathsf{W}[\mathsf{RandZero}(\mathbf{G}, \mathbf{r}; \mathbf{z})]$ the wire assignment of the circuit on input $\mathbf{G}, \mathbf{r}$ and internal randomness $\mathbf{z}$. The dependence on internal randomness is hidden when irrelevant.

For an n-by-m matrix $\mathbf{R}$ with columns $\mathbf{r}_1, \dots, \mathbf{r}_m$, we write $\mathsf{RandZero}(\mathbf{G}, \mathbf{R})$ for the multi-output circuit $(\mathsf{RandZero}(\mathbf{G}, \mathbf{r}_1; \mathbf{z}_1), \dots, \mathsf{RandZero}(\mathbf{G}, \mathbf{r}_m; \mathbf{z}_m))$, where $\mathbf{z}_i$ is chosen uniformly and independently.

Basic Properties. The following facts can be inferred directly from the construction.

Fact 7 (Output distribution). *For every $\mathbf{G}$ and $\mathbf{r}$, $\mathbf{c} = \mathsf{RandZero}(\mathbf{G}, \mathbf{r})$ is uniformly random conditioned on $\mathbf{1}^T \cdot \mathbf{c} = \mathbf{1}^T \cdot \mathbf{G} \cdot \mathbf{r}$.*

In particular, when the columns of $\mathbf{G}$ have parity zero then $\mathsf{RandZero}(\mathbf{G}, \mathbf{r})$ is a random string of parity zero. On the other hand, when the columns of $\mathbf{G}$ have parity one and $\mathbf{r}$ is random, then the $\mathsf{RandZero}(\mathbf{G}, \mathbf{r})$ is a uniformly random string.

Proof. The equation is satisfied as both the left and right-hand sides are equal to the sum of the entries of $\mathbf{Z}$. On the other hand $\mathbf{c}$ is $(n-1)$-wise independent as any $n-1$ of its outputs depend on distinct random bits.

Fact 8 (Linearity). $\mathsf{W}[\mathsf{RandZero}(\mathbf{G}, \mathbf{r}_1 + \mathbf{r}_2)]$ *is identically distributed to* W $[\mathsf{RandZero}(\mathbf{G}, \mathbf{r}_1; \mathbf{z}_1)] + \mathsf{W}[\mathsf{RandZero}(\mathbf{G}, \mathbf{r}_2; \mathbf{z}_2)]$ *provided at least one of* $\mathbf{z}_1$, $\mathbf{z}_2$ *is uniformly random.*

Proof. $\mathsf{W}[\mathsf{RandZero}(\mathbf{G}, \mathbf{r}; \mathbf{z})]$ is a linear function of $\mathbf{r}$ and $\mathbf{z}$, so even when say $\mathbf{z}_1$ is fixed, $\mathbf{z} = \mathbf{z}_1 + \mathbf{z}_2$ is uniform.

Simulation. The following claims provide simulations of the $\mathsf{RandZero}$ that are in a suitable sense "indepenent" of its respective inputs $\mathbf{G}$ and $\mathbf{r}$.

Claim 5. There exists a simulator circuit Simr such that

1. For every $\mathbf{G}$ and $\mathbf{r}$, $\mathsf{W}[\mathsf{Simr}(\mathbf{G}, \mathbf{r})]$ and $\mathsf{W}[\mathsf{RandZero}(\mathbf{G}, \mathbf{r})]$ are identically distributed.[2]
2. The output of $\mathsf{Simr}(\mathbf{G}, \mathbf{r}; \mathbf{z})$ equals $\mathsf{Diagonal}(r_1, \ldots, r_n)\mathbf{G}^T\mathbf{1}$ plus some function that depends only on $\mathbf{z}$.
3. For fixed $\mathbf{G}$ and $\mathbf{z}$, $\mathsf{W}[\mathsf{Simr}(\mathbf{G}, \mathbf{r}; \mathbf{z})]$ is an NC^0 function of $\mathbf{r}$.

Claim 6. There exists a simulator Simv such that

1. For every $\mathbf{G}$, $\mathbf{r}$, and $\mathbf{v} \in \{0,1\}^n$, $\mathsf{W}[\mathsf{Simv}(\mathbf{G}, \mathbf{v}, \mathbf{r})]$ and $\mathsf{W}[\mathsf{RandZero}(\mathbf{G} + \mathbf{v} \cdot \mathbf{1}^T, \mathbf{r})]$ are identically distributed.
2. $\mathsf{Simv}(\mathbf{G}, \mathbf{v}, \mathbf{r})$ equals $\mathbf{v}\mathbf{r}^T\mathbf{1}$ plus some function that does not depend on $\mathbf{v}$.
3. For fixed $\mathbf{G}, \mathbf{r}, \mathbf{z}$, $\mathsf{W}[\mathsf{Simr}(\mathbf{G}, \mathbf{v}, \mathbf{r}; \mathbf{z})]$ is an NC^0 function of $\mathbf{v}$.

We defer the proofs of these claims to the full version.

5.2   Construction

We give the description of our leakage resilient circuit compiler $(\mathsf{Tr}, \mathsf{St})$ in Fig. 3.

Correctness. The invariant maintained by the implementation is that the value of each wire w of C equals the parity of the wire bundle $\mathbf{w}$ in $\widehat{C}$ representing it. By construction this is true for the input wires and the state wires. In all applications of $\mathsf{RandZero}$, the parity of the output of $\mathsf{RandZero}$ equals zero by Fact 7. It follows that the output of addition has parity $\mathbf{1}^T\mathbf{a} + \mathbf{1}^T\mathbf{b} = \sum(a_i + b_i)$, the output of multiplication has parity $\mathbf{1}^T\mathbf{a}^T\mathbf{b}\mathbf{1} = (\sum a_i)(\sum b_i)$, and the state wire updates, including those to $\mathbf{G}$, preserve parity. Finally, the output gates equal the parity of the corresponding wires, establishing correctness.

---

[2] The simulator circuit Simr is the composition of $\mathsf{RandZero}$ and a preprocessing circuit. The irrelevant wires from preprocessing are discounted when comparing the two distributions.

The construction. Given a security parameter 1^n, a circuit C, and an initial state $s \in \{0,1\}^k$:

Initialization:

The encoded state consists of k wire bundles $\mathbf{s}$, where the i-th one is a random n-bit string of parity s_i. In addition the state contains an $n \times n$ matrix $\mathbf{G}$ that is random conditioned on $\mathbf{1}^T\mathbf{G} = \mathbf{0}^T$.

Every wire w of C is represented by an n-wire bundle $\mathbf{w}$ in the transformed circuit $\widehat{C} = \mathsf{Tr}[C]$.

Computation:

Every input gate x in C is implemented by the wire bundle $x \cdot \mathbf{e}_1$, where $\mathbf{e}_1 = (1, 0, \dots, 0)$.

Every addition gate $a + b$ in C is implemented as $\mathbf{a} + \mathbf{b} + \mathsf{RandZero}(\mathbf{G}, \mathbf{r})$, where $\mathbf{a}, \mathbf{b}$ are the bundles representing a, b and $\mathbf{r}$ is a random string.

Every multiplication gate $a \times b$ in C is implemented as $(\mathbf{a} \cdot \mathbf{b}^T + \mathsf{RandZero}(\mathbf{G}, \mathbf{R})) \cdot \mathbf{1}$, where where $\mathbf{a}, \mathbf{b}$ are the bundles representing a, b, $\mathbf{R}$ is a random $n \times n$ matrix, and matrix-vector multiplication is implemented left-to-right.

For every output gate in C represented by wire bundle $\mathbf{out}$, compute $\mathbf{out}' = (\mathbf{out} + \mathsf{RandZero}(\mathbf{G}, \mathbf{r}))$ for a random $\mathbf{r}$ and decode the output as $\mathbf{1}^T \cdot \mathbf{out}'$.

State update:

Replace every bundle $\mathbf{s}_i$ of the state by $\mathbf{s}_i + \mathsf{RandZero}(\mathbf{G}, \mathbf{r}_i)$ for a random $\mathbf{r}_i$.
Replace $\mathbf{G}$ by $\mathsf{RandZero}(\mathbf{G}, \mathbf{R})$ for a random n by n matrix $\mathbf{R}$.

Fig. 3. LRCC $(\mathsf{Tr}, \mathsf{St})$ for stateful circuits.

Security. We now prove the security part of Theorem 5. We will show that for every (possibly unbounded) stateful adversary $\mathcal{A}$, there exists a (stateful) simulator $\mathcal{S}$ such that for every initial state, the adversary's view in the real and ideal experiment described in Fig. 1 are statistically close.

In Sect. 5.3, we give the description of our simulator. The security proof consists of two steps, following the structure in the works of Faust et al. [23] and Rothblum [43] (a pictorial representation of the structure of the proof is given in Fig. 4). First, in Sect. 5.4, we describe a local *internal reconstruction procedure* that represents the adversary's view as a local (NC^0) function of an *external wire distribution*. This distribution contains explicit descriptions for all the wires in all evaluation rounds of $\widehat{C}$, as well as some additional information for the multiplication gates and state updates.

Then in Sect. 5.5, we gradually modify the components of the external wire distribution until the wire values in $\widehat{C}$ observed by the adversary become independent of the wires of C and so the adversary's view can be simulated, unless various circuits obtained by restricting inputs in the composition of the leakage and the internal reconstruction procedure can compute parity.

Computation tableau of C Hybrid Data

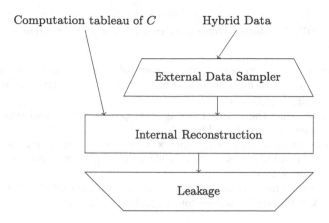

Fig. 4. Components of the security proof. When the external sampler is given the input data for Hybrid_0, the adversary's view is identical to the output of the transformed circuit as in the real world. In Hybrid_3, the adversary's view is identical to the output of the simulator as in the ideal world. Indistinguishability of consecutive hybrids is argued by analyzing the view of the the leakage function composed with Internal Reconstruction.

5.3 Description of the Simulator

We give the description of the simulator $\mathcal{S}$ in Fig. 5.

5.4 External Data Sampler

The external data associated to a circuit wire (of C in a given round) consists of the wires of a copy of the circuit RandZero. The external data associated to a gate consists of the external data of all its incident wires, plus some auxiliary data specific to the gate. We give the description of the external data sampler in Fig. 6.

The external wire distribution denotes the induced distribution on the output of the external data sampler when it run by sampling $\mathbf{G}_1$ (which is the generator matrix of the first round) and for every round, sampling $\{\mathbf{r}_i\}, \mathbf{R}$ from some distribution.

Internal Reconstruction Procedures. We now prove the following lemmas.

Lemma 2 (Addition Reconstruction Procedure). *Fix a round and let $\mathbf{G}$ be the generator matrix for this round. There exists an NC^0 circuit IR_+ that, given inputs $a, b \in \{0, 1\}$ and the external gate data $\mathsf{W}_a = \mathsf{W}[\mathsf{RandZero}(\mathbf{G}, \mathbf{r}_a; \mathbf{z}_a)]$, $\mathsf{W}_b = \mathsf{W}[\mathsf{RandZero}(\mathbf{G}, \mathbf{r}_b; \mathbf{z}_b)]$, $\mathsf{W}_c = \mathsf{W}[\mathsf{RandZero}(\mathbf{G}, \mathbf{r}_c; \mathbf{z}_c)]$ outputs an assignment to the wires of a transformed addition gate $\widehat{+}$ such that if $\mathbf{r}_c$ and $\mathbf{z}_c$ are uniformly random, the output of IR_+ is identically distributed to the wires of $\widehat{+}((a\mathbf{e}_1 + \mathbf{o}_a), (b\mathbf{e}_1 + \mathbf{o}_b))$, where $\mathbf{o}_a$, $\mathbf{o}_b$ are the outputs of W_a, W_b, respectively.*

The (stateful) simulator. Given a security parameter 1^n, a circuit C, inputs x, and outputs y:

Initialization. The encoded state consists of k wire bundles $\mathbf{s}$, where the i-th one is <u>uniformly random</u> n-bit string. The matrix $\mathbf{G}$ is random <u>conditioned on $\mathbf{1}^T\mathbf{G} = \mathbf{1}^T$</u>.

The simulator runs the circuit $\widehat{C}$ using the input, addition, and multiplication gates implementation from Figure 3.

For every output gate of $\widehat{C}$ with input $\mathbf{x}$ whose value in y is *out*, the output of the gate $\widehat{C}$ is simulated as $\mathbf{1}^T(\mathbf{x} + \mathsf{RandZero}(\mathbf{G}, \mathbf{r}))$, where $\mathbf{r}$ is a random string of parity *out* $+ \mathbf{1}^T\mathbf{x}$.

State update: The state update is the same as in 3, except that the matrix $\mathbf{R}$ used in $\mathbf{G}$'s update is random <u>conditioned on $\mathbf{1}^T\mathbf{R} = \mathbf{1}^T$</u>.

Fig. 5. The simulator $\mathcal{S}$.

The External Data Sampler. The input to the Sampler consists of the round number t, a generator matrix for this round $\mathbf{G}_t$, a wire update seed $\mathbf{r}_{wt}$ for each wire bundle w, and a state update seed matrix $\mathbf{R}_t$.

To sample the external wires for the round number t do the following:

1. For every input wire, sample the external data as $\mathsf{W}[\mathsf{RandZero}(\mathbf{G}_t, \mathbf{0}; 0)]$.
2. For all other wires w, sample the external data $\mathsf{W}[\mathsf{RandZero}(\mathbf{G}_t, \mathbf{r}_{wt})]$.
3. For every multiplication gate, sample the auxiliary data $\mathsf{W}[\mathsf{RandZero}(\mathbf{G}_t, \mathbf{F})]$, where $\mathbf{F}$ is a uniformly random $n \times (n-1)$ matrix.
4. For the state update, sample $\mathsf{W}[\mathsf{RandZero}(\mathbf{G}_t, \mathbf{R}_t)]$ and update $\mathbf{G}_{t+1}$ to equal the output of this circuit.

Fig. 6. External data sampler

Proof. The circuit IR_+ outputs the values $(a\mathbf{e}_1 + \mathbf{o}_a)$ and $(b\mathbf{e}_1 + \mathbf{o}_b)$ for the input wires $\mathbf{a}$ and $\mathbf{b}$ and $\mathsf{W}_a + \mathsf{W}_b + \mathsf{W}_c$ for the wires of the $\mathsf{RandZero}(\mathbf{G}, \mathbf{r})$ circuit used in the implementation of $\widehat{+}$, and obtains the output by adding the values assigned to the top gate of $\widehat{+}$.

By Fact 8, $\mathsf{W}_a + \mathsf{W}_b + \mathsf{W}_c$ is identically distributed to $\mathsf{W}[\mathsf{RandZero}(\mathbf{G}, \mathbf{r})]$ for a random $\mathbf{r}$, from where the identical distribution of the wires follows.

Note that updating the state can be expressed as special case of the addition circuit (i.e., setting one of the input vectors as $\mathbf{0}$). Hence, we get the following corollary.

Corollary 4 (State Update Reconstruction Procedure). *Fix a round and let $\mathbf{G}$ be the generator matrix for this round. There exists an NC^0 circuit IR_{st} that, given inputs $a \in \{0,1\}$ and the external gate data $\mathsf{W}_a =$*

$W[\text{RandZero}(\mathbf{G}, \mathbf{r}_a; \mathbf{z}_a)]$, $W_c = W[\text{RandZero}(\mathbf{G}, \mathbf{r}_c; \mathbf{z}_c)]$, *outputs an assignment to all the wires in the transformed state update gate* $\widehat{st}$ *such that if* $\mathbf{r}_c$ *and* $\mathbf{z}_c$ *are uniformly random, the output of* IR_{st} *is identically distributed to the wires of* $\widehat{st}(a\mathbf{e}_1 + \mathbf{o}_a)$, *where* $\mathbf{o}_a$ *is the output in* W_a.

Lemma 3 (Output Reconstruction Procedure). *Fix a round and let* $\mathbf{G}$ *be the generator matrix for this round. There exists an* NC^0 *circuit* IR_{out} *that, given inputs* $a \in \{0,1\}$ *and the external gate data* $W_a = W[\text{RandZero}(\mathbf{G}, \mathbf{r}_a; \mathbf{z}_a)]$, $W_c = W[\text{RandZero}(\mathbf{G}, \mathbf{r}_c; \mathbf{z}_c)]$, *outputs an assignment to all the wires except those in the final decoding step of a transformed output gate* $\widehat{out}$ *such that:*

1. *If* $\mathbf{1}^T \cdot \mathbf{G} = \mathbf{0}^T$ *and* $\mathbf{r}_c$ *and* $\mathbf{z}_c$ *are uniformly random, the output of* IR_{out} *is identically distributed to these wires in* $\widehat{out}(a\mathbf{e}_1 + \mathbf{o}_a)$, *where* $\mathbf{o}_a$ *is the output in* W_a.
2. *If* $\mathbf{1}^T \cdot \mathbf{G} = \mathbf{1}^T$ *and* $\mathbf{r}_c \sim \text{PAR}(n, 0)$, $\mathbf{z}_c$ *is chosen uniformly random, the output of* IR_{out} *is identically distributed to these wires in the simulated distribution.*

Proof. Consider the NC^0 circuit from Lemma 2 where we set $b = 0$ and $\mathbf{o}_b, \mathbf{r}_b$ and W_b to be all zeroes string. The first part of the corollary is a direct consequence of Lemma 2. To see the second part, note that the NC^0 circuit from Lemma 2 implicitly sets the randomness used in the gadget as $\mathbf{r} = \mathbf{r}_a + \mathbf{r}_c$. Thus, parity of $\mathbf{r}$ is equal to the parity of $\mathbf{G} \cdot (\mathbf{r}_a + \mathbf{r}_c)$ (since column parity of $\mathbf{G}$ is 1). This is equal to parity of $\mathbf{o}_a + \mathbf{o}_c$ (follows from Fact 7) which is in turn equal to the parity of $(a\mathbf{e}_1 + \mathbf{o}_a) + (a\mathbf{e}_1 + \mathbf{o}_c)$. Since $\mathbf{r}_c$ is chosen uniformly subject to its parity being 0, $\mathbf{r}$ is distributed uniformly subject to its parity being equal to the parity of $(a\mathbf{e}_1 + \mathbf{o}_a) + (a\mathbf{c}_1 + \mathbf{o}_c)$. This is precisely the simulated distribution.

Lemma 4 (Multiplication Reconstruction Procedure). *Fix a round and let* $\mathbf{G}$ *be the generator matrix for this round. There exists an* NC^0 *circuit* $IR_{\times}$ *that, given inputs* $a, b \in \{0,1\}$ *and the external gate data* $W_a = W[\text{RandZero}(\mathbf{G}, \mathbf{r}_a; \mathbf{z}_a)]$, $W_b = W[\text{RandZero}(\mathbf{G}, \mathbf{r}_b; \mathbf{z}_b)]$, $W_c = W[\text{RandZero}(\mathbf{G}, \mathbf{r}_c; \mathbf{z}_c)]$, $W_F = W[\text{RandZero}(\mathbf{G}, \mathbf{F}; z_F)]$ *outputs an assignment to the wires of a transformed multiplication gate* $\widehat{\times}$ *such that if* $\mathbf{r}_c, \mathbf{z}_c, \mathbf{F}, z_F$ *are uniformly random, the output of* $IR_{\times}$ *is identically distributed to the wires of* $\widehat{\times}((a\mathbf{e}_1 + \mathbf{o}_a), (b\mathbf{e}_1 + \mathbf{o}_b))$, *where* $\mathbf{o}_a$, $\mathbf{o}_b$ *are the outputs of* W_a, W_b, *respectively.*

We give the proof of this lemma in the full version.

Lemma 5 (Composition). *There exists a circuit* IR *such that for every round, given the tableau of* C *and the external data for that round, outputs an assignment to all the wires of the transformed circuit except for those wires involved in the final output decoding such that:*

1. *(Locality)* IR *is in* NC^0, *and moreover every gate in the output of* IR *only depends the tableau of the gate and on external data for its incident wires and the gate.*
2. *(Real world distribution) If* $\mathbf{G}$ *for the first round is sampled randomly such that* $\mathbf{1}^T \cdot \mathbf{G} = \mathbf{0}^T$ *and for every round, if the external data is generated by giving the sampler* $\{\mathbf{r}_i\}, \mathbf{R}$ *that are chosen uniformly at random, the concatenated outputs of* IR *in every round is identical to the real distribution of these wires.*

3. *(Ideal world distribution) If* $\mathbf{G}$ *for the first round is sampled randomly such that* $\mathbf{1}^T \cdot \mathbf{G} = \mathbf{1}^T$ *and for every round, if the external data is generated by giving the sampler* $\mathbf{r}_i \xleftarrow{\$} \{0,1\}^n$ *for every wire* i *that is not an output wire and for every output wire* i, $\mathbf{r}_i \sim \mathsf{PAR}(n, 0)$ *and* $\mathbf{R} \xleftarrow{\$} \{0,1\}^{n \times n}$ *subject to* $\mathbf{1}^T \mathbf{R} = \mathbf{1}^T$ *then the concatenated outputs of* IR *for every round is identical to the simulated distribution of these wires.*

We give the proof of this lemma in the full version.

5.5   Proof of Indistinguishability

In this subsection, we complete the proof of security. For this purpose we describe describe four hybrid distributions $\mathsf{Hybrid}_0, \mathsf{Hybrid}_1, \mathsf{Hybrid}_2, \mathsf{Hybrid}_3$ observed by the leakage. We argue that Hybrid_0 and Hybrid_3 are identically distributed to the wires of the transformed circuit and the simulator's output, respectively, and that all pairs of consecutive distributions are computationally indistinguishable by the leakage.

The four distributions are sampled by instantiating the external data sampler with different inputs, and then applying the internal reconstruction in Lemma 5 to the output. The inputs used to instantiate the external data sampler are:

Hybrid_0: Initial $\mathbf{G}$ is random conditioned on having zero column-parity ($\mathbf{1}^T \mathbf{G} = \mathbf{0}^T$). all wire update seeds $\mathbf{r}_{wt}$ and all state update seeds $\mathbf{R}_t$ are uniformly random.

Hybrid_1: $\mathbf{G}$ is sampled as in Hybrid_0. All wire update seeds $\mathbf{r}_{wt}$ and all state update seeds $\mathbf{R}_t$ are random conditioned on having column-parity 0 ($\mathbf{1}^T \mathbf{r}_{wt} = 0, \mathbf{1}^T \mathbf{R}_t = \mathbf{0}^T$).

Hybrid_2: $\mathbf{r}_{wt}$ are sampled as in Hybrid_1. $\mathbf{G}$ and $\mathbf{R}_t$ are random conditioned on having column-parity 1 ($\mathbf{1}^T \mathbf{G} = \mathbf{1}^T, \mathbf{1}^T \mathbf{R}_t = \mathbf{1}^T$).

Hybrid_3: $\mathbf{G}$ and $\mathbf{R}_t$ are sampled as in Hybrid_2. $\mathbf{r}_{wt}$ are uniformly random except for the output wires, which remain unchanged.

We note that the assignment to the final output decoding wires is a deterministic function of the external data. Thus, it follows from part 2 of Lemma 5, the view of the leakage function in Hybrid_0 is identical to the real distribution of the transformed circuit's wires, and by part 3, its view in Hybrid_3 is identical to the output of the simulator. To finish the proof, we establish the following three claims.

Claim 7. Under the assumptions of Theorem 5, the adversary's outputs on Hybrid_0 and Hybrid_1 are $O(\epsilon T(S + n))$-statistically close.

Proof. We fix $\mathbf{G} = \mathbf{G}_1$ and modify the distribution of the relevant seeds $\mathbf{r}_{wt}$ and the columns of $\mathbf{R}_t$ one by one, in increasing order of the round t. As the effect of both types of seeds is the same, without loss of generality, we analyze the effect of changing a seed of type $\mathbf{r}_{wt}$ from being uniformly random to having parity zero, assuming all the other seeds are fixed to maximize the adversary's distinguishing advantage.

We can simulate the first $(t-1)$ rounds of the leakage experiment using the fixed seeds. In the t-th round, we can generate all the external data for this round non-uniformly except $\mathsf{W}[\mathsf{RandZero}(\mathbf{G}_t, \mathbf{r}_{wt})]$. As all random seeds from the previous rounds have been fixed, by Fact 7 $\mathbf{G}_t$ is a fixed matrix with column-parity zero. By part 1 of Claim 5, this external data item can therefore be replaced by $\mathsf{W}[\mathsf{Simr}(\mathbf{G}_t, \mathbf{r}_{wt})]$ without affecting the adversary's advantage. By part 3 of Claim 5, we infer that $\mathsf{W}[\mathsf{Simr}(\mathbf{G}_t, \mathbf{r}_{wt})]$ is NC^0 computable from $\mathbf{r}_{wt}$ and therefore, we can generate all the external data for the t-th round by an NC^0 circuit. Now, running the internal reconstruction procedure IR (which is again an NC^0 circuit) on this external data outputs an assignment to every wire of $\widehat{C}$ in the t-th round except those in the final output decoding step. Since $\mathbf{G}_t^T \mathbf{1} = \mathbf{0}$, by part 2 of Claim 5, the output of $\mathsf{Simr}(\mathbf{G}_t, \mathbf{r}_{wt})$ is statistically independent of $\mathbf{r}_{wt}$. Therefore, the wires of all the gates in the computation (including the final output decoding in case that w is an output wire) that are evaluated after w are independent of $\mathbf{r}_{wt}$ and can be fixed to maximize the adversary's advantage. Thus, we can generate the wire assignment to every wire of $\widehat{C}$ in the t-th round using an NC^0 circuit. The subsequent rounds of the leakage experiment can be simulated from the fixed seeds since even if w is an updated state wire, the output of $\mathsf{Simr}(\mathbf{G}_t, \mathbf{r}_{wt})$ is statistically independent of $\mathbf{r}_{wt}$ and hence the bundles which feed into the subsequent rounds are independent of $\mathbf{r}_{wt}$ and depend only on the fixed seeds.

By the above argument, we deduced that (i) the first $(t-1)$ rounds of the leakage experiment can be simulated independent of $\mathbf{r}_{wt}$, (ii) the wire assignment in t-th round are NC^0 computable from $\mathbf{r}_{wt}$, and (iii) the subsequent rounds of the experiment are independent of $\mathbf{r}_{wt}$. Therefore the adversary's advantage cannot exceed the ability of $\mathcal{C} \circ \mathsf{NC}^0$ in distinguishing a uniform random string from a parity-zero string. This is at most twice the advantage in distinguishing random parity-zero and parity-one strings, which is assumed to be ϵ.

By the triangle inequality, the adversary's advantage accumulated by all $O(T(S+n))$ changes is at most $O(\epsilon T(S+n))$.

Claim 8. Under the assumptions of Theorem 5, the adversary's outputs on Hybrid_1 and Hybrid_2 are $O(\epsilon T)$-statistically close.

Proof. We modify the distribution on the matrices $\mathbf{G} = \mathbf{G}_1, \mathbf{R}_1, \ldots, \mathbf{R}_n$ one by one such that they are random subject to their column parity being 1.

The change in the distribution of $\mathbf{G}$ can be implemented by setting $\mathbf{G} = \mathbf{G}' + \mathbf{v} \cdot \mathbf{1}^T$, where $\mathbf{G}'$ is a random column-parity zero matrix and $\mathbf{v}$ changes from a random parity-0 to a random parity-1 vector.

To analyze the effect of this change, we apply part 1 Claim 6 and replace all items of type $\mathsf{W}[\mathsf{RandZero}(\mathbf{G}, \mathbf{r}_{w1})]$, $\mathsf{W}[\mathsf{RandZero}(\mathbf{G}, \mathbf{F})]$, and $\mathsf{W}[\mathsf{RandZero}(\mathbf{G}, \mathbf{R}_1)]$ in the external data for the first round by $\mathsf{W}[\mathsf{Simv}(\mathbf{G}', \mathbf{v}, \mathbf{r}_{w1})]$, $\mathsf{W}[\mathsf{Simv}(\mathbf{G}', \mathbf{v}, \mathbf{F})]$, and $\mathsf{W}[\mathsf{Simv}(\mathbf{G}', \mathbf{v}, \mathbf{R}_1)]$ without affecting the adversary's advantage. This defines the external data for the first round and by part 3 of Claim 6, we can generate this by an NC^0 circuit. Now, applying the internal reconstructing procedure, IR (which is again an NC^0 circuit) from Lemma 5 on this external data allows us to generate all the wires in the computation of $\widehat{C}$ in the first round, except the assignment to the final output decoding wires. By part 2 of Claim 6, the output of $\mathsf{Simv}(\mathbf{G'}, \mathbf{v}, \mathbf{r})$ is independent of $\mathbf{v}$ provided $\mathbf{r}$ has parity zero, which is true in all instantiations. Therefore all the wires in the final output decoding step of the first round are independent of $\mathbf{v}$ and can be non-uniformly computed. Thus, we have generated the assignment to every wire of $\widehat{C}$ in the first round by an NC^0 circuit. The subsequent rounds are independent of $\mathbf{v}$ as a direct consequence of part 2 of Claim 6. Thus, the assumption that random strings of parity zero and one are indistinguishable by $C \circ NC^0$, we obtain that the adversary's outputs when $\mathbf{G}$ is modified are ϵ-close.

We now analyze the change in advantage when $\mathbf{R}_{t-1}$ is modified from having column-parity zero to one. We represent $\mathbf{R}_{t-1}$ as $\mathbf{R'} + \mathbf{v} \cdot \mathbf{1}^T$, where $\mathbf{R'}$ s a random column-parity zero matrix and $\mathbf{v}$ changes from a random parity-0 to a random parity-1 vector. We fix all the random seeds given as input the external data sampler except for $\mathbf{v}$ such that adversary's distinguishing advantage is maximized conditioned on this fixing. This allows us to simulate the first $(t-2)$ rounds of the leakage experiment.

Recall that $\mathbf{G}_t = \mathsf{RandZero}(\mathbf{G}_{t-1}, \mathbf{R}_{t-1})$. By part 1 of Claim 5, we may replace $W[\mathsf{RandZero}(\mathbf{G}_{t-1}, \mathbf{R}_{t-1})]$ in external data of the $(t-1)$-th round with $W[\mathsf{Simr}(\mathbf{G}_{t-1}, \mathbf{R}_{t-1})]$ without affecting the adversary's advantage. This defines the external data for the $(t-1)$-th round as well as the assignment to the final output decoding wires which are independent of $\mathbf{v}$ and hence can be non-uniformly fixed. As a consequence of part 3 of Claim 5 and part 1 of Lemma 5, we deduce that the assignment to all the wires of $\widehat{C}$ in the $(t-1)$-th round can be generated by an NC^0 circuit. Since the column parity of $\mathbf{G}_{t-1}$ is 1, by part 2 of Claim 5 $\mathbf{G}_t = \mathsf{RandZero}(\mathbf{G}_{t-1}, \mathbf{R}_{t-1})$ can be expressed as $\mathbf{G'} + \mathbf{v} \cdot \mathbf{1}^T$ where $\mathbf{G'}$ is independent of $\mathbf{v}$. We may now use Claim 6 and Lemma 5 in an analogous manner to the first part of the proof to deduce that the assignment to all the wires of $\widehat{C}$ in the t-th round can be generated by an NC^0 circuit. Again, it follows from the part 2 of Claim 6, the subsequent rounds of the leakage experiment can be simulated independent of $\mathbf{v}$.

We thus, conclude that the advantage of the adversary cannot exceed that of a 2-adaptive circuit in the class $C \circ NC^0$ in distinguishing random strings $\mathbf{v}$ of parity zero and one. By assumption, this advantage is at most ϵ.

By the triangle inequality, the adversary's advantage accumulated by all T changes is at most ϵT.

Claim 9. Under the assumptions of Theorem 5, the adversary's outputs on Hybrid_2 and Hybrid_3 are $O(\epsilon T S)$-statistically close.

We give the proof of this Claim in the full version.

From the above claims, we deduce that the real distribution is $O((S + n) \cdot \tau \cdot \epsilon)$-close to the simulated distribution. This completes the proof of Theorem 5. Corollary 2 follows directly from Theorem 5, Claim 1 and Corollary 3.

Acknowledgements. The first author's research is supported by Hong Kong RGC GRF CUHK14208215 and CUHK14207618. The second author's research is supported by ERC Project NTSC (742754), ISF grant 1709/14, NSF-BSF grant 2015782, and a grant from the Ministry of Science and Technology, Israel and Department of Science and Technology, Government of India. The third author's research is supported in part from DARPA/ARL SAFEWARE Award W911NF15C0210, AFOSR Award FA9550-15-1-0274, AFOSR YIP Award, a Hellman Award and research grants by the Okawa Foundation, Visa Inc., and Center for LongTerm Cybersecurity (CLTC, UC Berkeley).

References

1. Ajtai, M.: Secure computation with information leaking to an adversary. In: Proceedings of the 43rd ACM Symposium on Theory of Computing, STOC 2011, San Jose, CA, USA, 6–8 June 2011, pp. 715–724 (2011). https://doi.org/10.1145/1993636.1993731

2. Akavia, A., Bogdanov, A., Guo, S., Kamath, A., Rosen, A.: Candidate weak pseudorandom functions in AC^0 o MOD_2. In: Naor, M. (ed.) ITCS 2014, pp. 251–260. ACM, January 2014

3. Ananth, P., Ishai, Y., Sahai, A.: Private circuits: a modular approach. In: Shacham, H., Boldyreva, A. (eds.) CRYPTO 2018. LNCS, vol. 10993, pp. 427–455. Springer, Cham (2018). https://doi.org/10.1007/978-3-319-96878-0_15

4. Battistello, A., Coron, J.-S., Prouff, E., Zeitoun, R.: Horizontal side-channel attacks and countermeasures on the ISW masking scheme. In: Gierlichs, B., Poschmann, A.Y. (eds.) CHES 2016. LNCS, vol. 9813, pp. 23–39. Springer, Heidelberg (2016). https://doi.org/10.1007/978-3-662-53140-2_2

5. Belaïd, S., Benhamouda, F., Passelègue, A., Prouff, E., Thillard, A., Vergnaud, D.: Randomness complexity of private circuits for multiplication. In: Fischlin, M., Coron, J.-S. (eds.) EUROCRYPT 2016. LNCS, vol. 9666, pp. 616–648. Springer, Heidelberg (2016). https://doi.org/10.1007/978-3-662-49896-5_22

6. Ben-Or, M., Goldwasser, S., Wigderson, A.: Completeness theorems for non-cryptographic fault-tolerant distributed computation (extended abstract). In: STOC, pp. 1–10 (1988)

7. Benhamouda, F., Degwekar, A., Ishai, Y., Rabin, T.: On the local leakage resilience of linear secret sharing schemes. In: Shacham, H., Boldyreva, A. (eds.) CRYPTO 2018. LNCS, vol. 10991, pp. 531–561. Springer, Cham (2018). https://doi.org/10.1007/978-3-319-96884-1_18

8. Bitansky, N., Canetti, R., Halevi, S.: Leakage-tolerant interactive protocols. In: Cramer, R. (ed.) TCC 2012. LNCS, vol. 7194, pp. 266–284. Springer, Heidelberg (2012). https://doi.org/10.1007/978-3-642-28914-9_15

9. Bitansky, N., Dachman-Soled, D., Lin, H.: Leakage-tolerant computation with input-independent preprocessing. In: Garay, J.A., Gennaro, R. (eds.) CRYPTO 2014. LNCS, vol. 8617, pp. 146–163. Springer, Heidelberg (2014). https://doi.org/10.1007/978-3-662-44381-1_9

10. Bogdanov, A., Ishai, Y., Viola, E., Williamson, C.: Bounded indistinguishability and the complexity of recovering secrets. In: Robshaw, M., Katz, J. (eds.) CRYPTO 2016. LNCS, vol. 9816, pp. 593–618. Springer, Heidelberg (2016). https://doi.org/10.1007/978-3-662-53015-3_21

11. Boyle, E., Garg, S., Jain, A., Kalai, Y.T., Sahai, A.: Secure computation against adaptive auxiliary information. In: Canetti, R., Garay, J.A. (eds.) CRYPTO 2013. LNCS, vol. 8042, pp. 316–334. Springer, Heidelberg (2013). https://doi.org/10.1007/978-3-642-40041-4_18

12. Boyle, E., Goldwasser, S., Jain, A., Kalai, Y.T.: Multiparty computation secure against continual memory leakage. In: Proceedings of the 44th Symposium on Theory of Computing Conference, STOC 2012, New York, NY, USA, 19–22 May 2012, pp. 1235–1254 (2012). https://doi.org/10.1145/2213977.2214087

13. Bulck, J.V., et al.: Foreshadow: extracting the keys to the intel SGX kingdom with transient out-of-order execution. In: 27th USENIX Security Symposium, USENIX Security 2018, Baltimore, MD, USA, 15–17 August 2018, pp. 991–1008 (2018). https://www.usenix.org/conference/usenixsecurity18/presentation/bulck

14. Bun, M., Kothari, R., Thaler, J.: Quantum algorithms and approximating polynomials for composed functions with shared inputs. In: Proceedings of the Thirtieth Annual ACM-SIAM Symposium on Discrete Algorithms, SODA 2019, San Diego, California, USA, 6–9 January 2019, pp. 662–678 (2019)

15. Chaum, D., Crépeau, C., Damgård, I.: Multiparty unconditionally secure protocols (extended abstract). In: STOC, pp. 11–19 (1988)

16. Coron, J.-S.: Higher order masking of look-up tables. In: Nguyen, P.Q., Oswald, E. (eds.) EUROCRYPT 2014. LNCS, vol. 8441, pp. 441–458. Springer, Heidelberg (2014). https://doi.org/10.1007/978-3-642-55220-5_25

17. Coron, J.-S., Prouff, E., Rivain, M., Roche, T.: Higher-order side channel security and mask refreshing. In: Moriai, S. (ed.) FSE 2013. LNCS, vol. 8424, pp. 410–424. Springer, Heidelberg (2014). https://doi.org/10.1007/978-3-662-43933-3_21

18. Dachman-Soled, D., Liu, F.-H., Zhou, H.-S.: Leakage-resilient circuits revisited – optimal number of computing components without leak-free hardware. In: Oswald, E., Fischlin, M. (eds.) EUROCRYPT 2015. LNCS, vol. 9057, pp. 131–158. Springer, Heidelberg (2015). https://doi.org/10.1007/978-3-662-46803-6_5

19. Duc, A., Dziembowski, S., Faust, S.: Unifying leakage models: from probing attacks to noisy leakage. In: Nguyen, P.Q., Oswald, E. (eds.) EUROCRYPT 2014. LNCS, vol. 8441, pp. 423–440. Springer, Heidelberg (2014). https://doi.org/10.1007/978-3-642-55220-5_24

20. Dziembowski, S., Faust, S.: Leakage-resilient circuits without computational assumptions. In: Cramer, R. (ed.) TCC 2012. LNCS, vol. 7194, pp. 230–247. Springer, Heidelberg (2012). https://doi.org/10.1007/978-3-642-28914-9_13

21. Dziembowski, S., Faust, S., Skorski, M.: Noisy leakage revisited. In: Oswald, E., Fischlin, M. (eds.) EUROCRYPT 2015. LNCS, vol. 9057, pp. 159–188. Springer, Heidelberg (2015). https://doi.org/10.1007/978-3-662-46803-6_6

22. Faust, S., Paglialonga, C., Schneider, T.: Amortizing randomness complexity in private circuits. In: Takagi, T., Peyrin, T. (eds.) ASIACRYPT 2017. LNCS, vol. 10624, pp. 781–810. Springer, Cham (2017). https://doi.org/10.1007/978-3-319-70694-8_27

23. Faust, S., Rabin, T., Reyzin, L., Tromer, E., Vaikuntanathan, V.: Protecting circuits from leakage: the computationally-bounded and noisy cases. In: Gilbert, H. (ed.) EUROCRYPT 2010. LNCS, vol. 6110, pp. 135–156. Springer, Heidelberg (2010). https://doi.org/10.1007/978-3-642-13190-5_7

24. Faust, S., Rabin, T., Reyzin, L., Tromer, E., Vaikuntanathan, V.: Protecting circuits from computationally bounded and noisy leakage. SIAM J. Comput. **43**(5), 1564–1614 (2014). extended abstract in Eurocrypt 2010

25. Garg, S., Jain, A., Sahai, A.: Leakage-resilient zero knowledge. In: Rogaway, P. (ed.) CRYPTO 2011. LNCS, vol. 6841, pp. 297–315. Springer, Heidelberg (2011). https://doi.org/10.1007/978-3-642-22792-9_17

26. Genkin, D., Ishai, Y., Weiss, M.: How to construct a leakage-resilient (stateless) trusted party. In: Kalai, Y., Reyzin, L. (eds.) TCC 2017. LNCS, vol. 10678, pp. 209–244. Springer, Cham (2017). https://doi.org/10.1007/978-3-319-70503-3_7

27. Goldreich, O., Micali, S., Wigderson, A.: How to play any mental game or a completeness theorem for protocols with honest majority. In: Aho, A. (ed.) 19th ACM STOC, pp. 218–229. ACM Press, May 1987

28. Goldwasser, S., Rothblum, G.N.: Securing computation against continuous leakage. In: Rabin, T. (ed.) CRYPTO 2010. LNCS, vol. 6223, pp. 59–79. Springer, Heidelberg (2010). https://doi.org/10.1007/978-3-642-14623-7_4

29. Goldwasser, S., Rothblum, G.N.: How to compute in the presence of leakage. In: 53rd Annual IEEE Symposium on Foundations of Computer Science, FOCS 2012, New Brunswick, NJ, USA, 20–23 October 2012, pp. 31–40 (2012). https://doi.org/10.1109/FOCS.2012.34

30. Goyal, V., Ishai, Y., Maji, H.K., Sahai, A., Sherstov, A.A.: Bounded-communication leakage resilience via parity-resilient circuits. In: FOCS 2016, pp. 1–10 (2016)

31. Håstad, J.: On the correlation of parity and small-depth circuits. SIAM J. Comput. 43(5), 1699–1708 (2014). https://doi.org/10.1137/120897432

32. Ishai, Y., Sahai, A., Wagner, D.: Private circuits: securing hardware against probing attacks. In: Boneh, D. (ed.) CRYPTO 2003. LNCS, vol. 2729, pp. 463–481. Springer, Heidelberg (2003). https://doi.org/10.1007/978-3-540-45146-4_27

33. Ishai, Y., Weiss, M., Yang, G.: Making the best of a leaky situation: zero-knowledge PCPs from leakage-resilient circuits. In: Kushilevitz, E., Malkin, T. (eds.) TCC 2016. LNCS, vol. 9563, pp. 3–32. Springer, Heidelberg (2016). https://doi.org/10.1007/978-3-662-49099-0_1

34. Juma, A., Vahlis, Y.: Protecting cryptographic keys against continual leakage. In: Rabin, T. (ed.) CRYPTO 2010. LNCS, vol. 6223, pp. 41–58. Springer, Heidelberg (2010). https://doi.org/10.1007/978-3-642-14623-7_3

35. Kocher, P., et al.: Spectre attacks: exploiting speculative execution. CoRR abs/1801.01203 (2018). http://arxiv.org/abs/1801.01203

36. Kocher, P.C.: Timing attacks on implementations of Diffie-Hellman, RSA, DSS, and other systems. In: Koblitz, N. (ed.) CRYPTO 1996. LNCS, vol. 1109, pp. 104–113. Springer, Heidelberg (1996). https://doi.org/10.1007/3-540-68697-5_9

37. Kocher, P., Jaffe, J., Jun, B.: Differential power analysis. In: Wiener, M.J. (ed.) CRYPTO 1999. LNCS, vol. 1666, pp. 388–397. Springer, Heidelberg (1999). https://doi.org/10.1007/3-540-48405-1_25

38. Lipp, M., et al.: Meltdown: reading kernel memory from user space. In: 27th USENIX Security Symposium, USENIX Security 2018, Baltimore, MD, USA, 15–17 August 2018, pp. 973–990 (2018). https://www.usenix.org/conference/usenixsecurity18/presentation/lipp

39. Micali, S., Reyzin, L.: Physically observable cryptography. In: Naor, M. (ed.) TCC 2004. LNCS, vol. 2951, pp. 278–296. Springer, Heidelberg (2004). https://doi.org/10.1007/978-3-540-24638-1_16

40. Miles, E.: Iterated group products and leakage resilience against NC1. In: Naor, M. (ed.) ITCS 2014, pp. 261–268. ACM, January 2014

41. Miles, E., Viola, E.: Shielding circuits with groups. In: Boneh, D., Roughgarden, T., Feigenbaum, J. (eds.) 45th ACM STOC, pp. 251–260. ACM Press, June 2013

42. Rivain, M., Prouff, E.: Provably secure higher-order masking of AES. In: Mangard, S., Standaert, F.-X. (eds.) CHES 2010. LNCS, vol. 6225, pp. 413–427. Springer, Heidelberg (2010). https://doi.org/10.1007/978-3-642-15031-9_28
43. Rothblum, G.N.: How to compute under AC^0 leakage without secure hardware. In: Safavi-Naini, R., Canetti, R. (eds.) CRYPTO 2012. LNCS, vol. 7417, pp. 552–569. Springer, Heidelberg (2012). https://doi.org/10.1007/978-3-642-32009-5_32
44. Yao, A.C.C.: How to generate and exchange secrets (extended abstract). In: 27th FOCS, pp. 162–167. IEEE Computer Society Press, October 1986

Tight Leakage-Resilient CCA-Security from Quasi-Adaptive Hash Proof System

Shuai Han[1,4], Shengli Liu[1,2,3(✉)], Lin Lyu[1], and Dawu Gu[1]

[1] School of Electronic Information and Electrical Engineering,
Shanghai Jiao Tong University, Shanghai 200240, China
{dalen17,slliu,lvlin,dwgu}@sjtu.edu.cn
[2] State Key Laboratory of Cryptology, P.O. Box 5159, Beijing 100878, China
[3] Westone Cryptologic Research Center, Beijing 100070, China
[4] Ant Financial, Hangzhou 310012, China

Abstract. We propose the concept of quasi-adaptive hash proof system (QAHPS), where the projection key is allowed to depend on the specific language for which hash values are computed. We formalize leakage-resilient(LR)-ardency for QAHPS by defining two statistical properties, including LR-$\langle \mathscr{L}_0, \mathscr{L}_1 \rangle$-universal and LR-$\langle \mathscr{L}_0, \mathscr{L}_1 \rangle$-key-switching.

We provide a generic approach to tightly leakage-resilient CCA (LR-CCA) secure public-key encryption (PKE) from LR-ardent QAHPS. Our approach is reminiscent of the seminal work of Cramer and Shoup (Eurocrypt'02), and employ three QAHPS schemes, one for generating a uniform string to hide the plaintext, and the other two for proving the well-formedness of the ciphertext. The LR-ardency of QAHPS makes possible the tight LR-CCA security. We give instantiations based on the standard k-Linear (k-LIN) assumptions over asymmetric and symmetric pairing groups, respectively, and obtain fully compact PKE with tight LR-CCA security. The security loss is $O(\log Q_e)$ where Q_e denotes the number of encryption queries. Specifically, our tightly LR-CCA secure PKE instantiation from SXDH has only 4 group elements in the public key and 7 group elements in the ciphertext, thus is the most efficient one.

1 Introduction

Tightly Secure Public-Key Encryption. Usually, the security proof of a public-key encryption (PKE) scheme is accomplished through a security reduction. In a security reduction, any probabilistic polynomial-time (PPT) adversary $\mathcal{A}$ successfully attacking the PKE scheme with advantage $\epsilon_\mathcal{A}$ is converted to another PPT algorithm $\mathcal{B}$ that solves a specific problem with advantage $\epsilon_\mathcal{B}$, such that $\epsilon_\mathcal{A} \leq \ell \cdot \epsilon_\mathcal{B}$. Here ℓ is called the security loss factor. If ℓ is a polynomial in the number of encryption queries Q_e and/or the number of decryption queries Q_d, the security reduction is called a loose one. To achieve a target security level, one has to augment the security parameter λ to compensate for the security loss ℓ. If Q_e (Q_d) is large, say 2^{30}, a loose reduction will pay the price of inefficiency,

© International Association for Cryptologic Research 2019
A. Boldyreva and D. Micciancio (Eds.): CRYPTO 2019, LNCS 11693, pp. 417–447, 2019.
https://doi.org/10.1007/978-3-030-26951-7_15

since the compensation will slow the algorithms of PKE and enlarge the sizes of public/secret key and ciphertexts. Therefore, it is desirable that ℓ is a constant or only linear in the security parameter λ. Such a security reduction is called a tight one or an almost tight one.

Starting from the work of Bellare et al. [8], brilliant works have been done in the construction of tightly (multi-challenge) IND-CCA secure PKE. Hofheinz and Jager [25] designed the first tightly IND-CCA secure PKE from a standard assumption. More efficient constructions follow in [7,9,17,18,20,23,24,30,31].

Leakage-Resilient Security. The traditional security requirements for PKE are indistinguishability under chosen-plaintext attacks (IND-CPA) and chosen-ciphertext attacks (IND-CCA), which implicitly assume that the secret key of PKE is completely hidden from adversaries. In practice, however, various kinds of side-channel attacks on the physical implementation of the PKE algorithms [21] demonstrated that partial information about the secret key might be leaked to the attackers, thus threaten the security of PKE. To deal with key leakage, Akavia et al. [5] and Naor and Segev [32] formalized the leakage-resilient (LR) security model and defined LR-CPA/CCA securities, which stipulate the PKE remain IND-CPA/CCA secure even if an adversary has access to a leakage oracle and obtains additional information about the secret key. In this work, we focus on the bounded leakage-resilient model [5], where the total amount of key leakage is bounded.

Generally, there are two approaches for designing PKE with LR-CCA security. The first is an adaption of the Naor-Yung double encryption paradigm [33] to the LR setting. Through this approach, an LR-CPA secure PKE can be upgraded to an LR-CCA secure one, with the help of a simulation-sound non-interactive zero-knowledge proof system (SS-NIZK) [28,32] or a true-simulation extractable NIZK (tSE-NIZK) [11]. However, the resulting PKE may not be efficient due to the usage of SS-NIZK/tSE-NIZK. The second approach utilizes the more efficient Cramer-Shoup hash proof system (HPS) paradigm [10] based on the fact that HPS is intrinsically leakage-resilient [32]. Through this approach, many efficient LR-CCA secure PKE schemes were designed [15,16,34].

Efficient PKE with Tight LR-CCA Security. Although great progress was made on tight IND-CCA security, only Abe et al. [2] ever considered LR-CCA secure PKE with a tight security reduction. They followed the Naor-Yung paradigm and employed a tightly secure tSE-NIZK. Due to the tightness-preserving of the Naor-Yung paradigm, the resulting PKE is tightly LR-CCA secure. However, their PKE is highly impractical. The ciphertext of their PKE contains more than 800 group elements. Even plugging in the recent efficient and tightly secure SS-NIZKs/tSE-NIZKs [17,19][1], the resulting LR-CCA secure

---

[1] Gay et al. [19] constructed the state-of-the-art tightly secure (structure-preserving) signature schemes, where the signature is comprised of 14 group elements. By applying the framework in [2,25], this signature scheme can be transformed to a tightly secure SS-NIZK/tSE-NIZK whose proof contains around 40 group elements.

PKE still contains over 100 group elements in the public key or around 40 group elements in the ciphertext, thus is far from practical. A most recent work by Abe et al. [3] presented a construction of quasi-adaptive NIZK (QA-NIZK) with tight unbounded simulation-soundness (USS) based on the MDDH assumptions and tried to use it to obtain a tightly CCA-secure PKE via the paradigm of CPA-PKE + USS-QA-NIZK. It is also possible to achieve tight LR-CCA security if the underlying PKE building block is LR-CPA secure. Unfortunately, their USS-QA-NIZK suffers from an attack, as shown in their full-version paper [4] (in which the QA-NIZK was updated to a new one but its USS security remains to be justified).

For the sake of efficiency, one might like to try the second approach to LR-CCA security. However, the Cramer-Shoup HPS paradigm [10, 32] does not work well in the face of multi-challenge ciphertexts (cf. Subsect. 1.1 for a detailed explanation). To pursue tight security reduction, great effort has been devoted to new designs of PKE from variants of HPS [17, 18]. Gay et al. [17] used combinations of multiple HPSs to construct PKE and proved its tight IND-CCA security (not LR-CCA), but at the price of more than 100 group elements in the public key. Gay et al. [18] evolved HPS to a so-called "qualified proof system" (QPS) to obtain tightly IND-CCA secure PKE with full compactness (compact ciphertext and compact public key). However, their PKE is unlikely to be LR-CCA secure.[2] Up to now, there is no available approach to efficient PKE with tight LR-CCA security.

Our Contribution. In this paper, we propose a novel approach to the design of tightly LR-CCA secure PKE. More precisely,

- We propose the concept of quasi-adaptive HPS (QAHPS), and formalize LR-ardency for QAHPS by defining two statistical properties, including LR-$\langle \mathscr{L}_0, \mathscr{L}_1 \rangle$-universal and LR-$\langle \mathscr{L}_0, \mathscr{L}_1 \rangle$-key-switching. Our LR-ardent QAHPS generalizes the well-known universal$_1$, universal$_2$ [10] and extracting [12] HPSs.
- We provide a generic approach to tightly LR-CCA secure PKE from LR-ardent QAHPS, inheriting the spirit of the Cramer-Shoup HPS paradigm to LR-CCA security [10, 32], but in the multi-challenge setting. Ignoring leakage resilience, our construction provides a new approach to tightly IND-CCA secure PKE with full compactness, which may be of independent interest.
- We give efficient instantiations based on the matrix DDH (MDDH) assumptions [14] (which include the standard k-linear (k-LIN) and SXDH assumptions) over asymmetric and symmetric pairing groups, respectively. This results in the most efficient PKE schemes with tight LR-CCA security.

---

[2] The properties of "constrained soundness" and "extensibility" of QPS are needed for the tight IND-CCA security proof of the PKE proposed by Gay et al. [18]. We note that these two properties of their QPS are unlikely to hold when partial information about the secret key of QPS is leaked to adversary. See our full version [22] for more details. Thus it is reasonable to conjecture that their PKE is not LR-CCA secure.

Table 1. Comparison among tightly (LR-)CCA secure PKE schemes. Here λ denotes the security parameter and $Q_e = \mathsf{poly}(\lambda)$ the number of challenge ciphertexts. $|PK|$ and $|C| - |M|$ show the size of public key and ciphertext overhead, where size means the number of group elements in the underlying groups. "k-LIN" is short for the k-Linear assumption. For pairing-free groups, 1-LIN = DDH; for asymmetric pairing groups, 1-LIN = SXDH, which requires the DDH assumption hold in both $\mathbb{G}_1$ and $\mathbb{G}_2$. "sym" stands for symmetric pairing groups and "asym" asymmetric pairing groups. "LR?" asks whether the security is proved in the leakage-resilient setting. The analysis of $\mathsf{PKE}^{\mathsf{lr}}_{\mathsf{sym}}$ is given in our full version [22]. We note that the security loss $O(\log Q_e) = O(\log \lambda)$ is lower than $O(\lambda)$.

Scheme	$|PK|$	$|C| - |M|$	Sec. loss	Assumption	Pairing	LR?
LPJY15 [30, 31]	$O(\lambda)$	47	$O(\lambda)$	2-LIN	yes (sym)	—
AHY15 [7]	$O(\lambda)$	12	$O(\lambda)$	2-LIN	yes (sym)	—
GCDCT16 [20]	$O(\lambda)$	$6k$	$O(\lambda)$	k-LIN ($k \geq 1$)	yes (asym)	—
GHKW16 [17]	$O(\lambda)$	$3k$	$O(\lambda)$	k-LIN ($k \geq 1$)	no	—
Hof16 [23]	2	60	$O(\lambda)$	1-LIN = SXDH	yes (asym)	—
Hof17 [24]	28 (resp. $2k^2 + 10k$)	6 (resp. $k + 4$)	$O(\lambda)$	2-LIN (resp. k-LIN)	yes (sym)	—
Hof17 [24]	20	28	$O(\lambda)$	DCR	—	—
GHK17 [18]	6	3	$O(\lambda)$	1-LIN = DDH	no	—
GHK17 [18]	20 (resp. $k^3 + k^2 + 4k$)	8 (resp. $k^2 + 2k$)	$O(\lambda)$	2-LIN (resp. k-LIN)	no	—
ADKNO13 [2]	≥ 40	861	$O(1)$	2-LIN	yes (sym)	$\checkmark$
Ours: $\mathsf{PKE}^{\mathsf{lr}}_{\mathsf{asym}}$	4 (resp. $k^2 + 3k$)	7 (resp. $4k + 3$)	$O(\log Q_e) = O(\log \lambda)$	1-LIN = SXDH (resp. k-LIN)	yes (asym)	$\checkmark$
Ours: $\mathsf{PKE}^{\mathsf{lr}}_{\mathsf{sym}}$	10 (resp. $k^2 + 3k$)	6 (resp. $2k + 2$)	$O(\log Q_e) = O(\log \lambda)$	2-LIN (resp. k-LIN)	yes (sym)	$\checkmark$

Specifically, our tightly LR-CCA secure PKE instantiation from SXDH over asymmetric pairing groups has only 4 group elements in the public key and 7 group elements in the ciphertext, hence a couple of hundred times smaller than that of [2] (which has to be over symmetric pairing groups)[3]. The security loss of LR-CCA security is $O(\log Q_e) = O(\log \lambda)$, where $Q_e = \mathsf{poly}(\lambda)$ denotes the number of encryption queries and λ the security parameter.

In Table 1, we compare our tightly (LR-)CCA secure PKE with existing ones.

1.1 Technical Overview

We firstly recall the Cramer-Shoup paradigm for constructing (LR-)CCA secure PKE [10,32], explain the difficulty of extending it to the multi-challenge setting, then detail our new approach for designing tightly LR-CCA secure PKE.

The Cramer-Shoup Paradigm: (LR-)CCA Secure PKE from HPS. Hash Proof System (HPS) was originated in [10] and can be instantiated from a collection of assumptions. The power of HPS was firstly shown by Cramer and Shoup [10], who proposed a paradigm for constructing IND-CCA secure PKE from a smooth-HPS and a universal$_2$ tag-based (labeled) HPS. Naor and Segev [32] showed that HPS is a natural candidate for LR-CCA secure PKE, and

---

[3] To the best of our knowledge, the PKE scheme in [2] is the only tightly LR-CCA secure one prior to our work.

proved a variant of the Cramer-Shoup PKE scheme to be LR-CCA secure. Over the years, HPS and its variants have demonstrated their charm with a variety of applications in public-key cryptosystem [6,15,29,34,36], to name a few.

Roughly speaking, an HPS is associated with an NP-language $\mathcal{L} \subseteq \mathcal{X}$ and has two evaluation modes. In the private evaluation mode, the hash value $\Lambda_{sk}(x)$ of an arbitrary $x \in \mathcal{X}$ can be efficiently computed from the hashing key sk and x, i.e., $\mathsf{Priv}(sk, x) = \Lambda_{sk}(x)$; in the public evaluation mode, the hash value $\Lambda_{sk}(x)$ of an instance $x \in \mathcal{L}$ is completely determined by the projection key $pk = \alpha(sk)$, and can be efficiently computed from pk with the help of any witness w for $x \in \mathcal{L}$, i.e., $\mathsf{Pub}(pk, x, w) = \Lambda_{sk}(x)$. The notion of HPS can be generalized to tag-based HPS, where a tag τ serves as an auxiliary input for Λ_{sk}, Pub and Priv.

A typical construction of CCA-secure PKE from a smooth HPS $= (\Lambda_{(\cdot)}, \alpha,$ Pub, Priv) and a universal$_2$ tag-based $\widetilde{\mathsf{HPS}} = (\widetilde{\Lambda}_{(\cdot)}, \widetilde{\alpha}, \widetilde{\mathsf{Pub}}, \widetilde{\mathsf{Priv}})$ works as follows [10]. The public key contains $pk = \alpha(sk)$ and $\widetilde{pk} = \widetilde{\alpha}(\widetilde{sk})$. The ciphertext is

$$C = (x, \quad d = \mathsf{Pub}(pk, x, w) + M, \quad \pi = \widetilde{\mathsf{Pub}}(\widetilde{pk}, x, w, \tau)),$$

where M is a plaintext, $x \leftarrow_\$ \mathcal{L}$ with witness w and $\tau = \mathsf{H}(x, d)$ with H a collision-resistant hash function. The CCA-security with a single challenge ciphertext $C^* = (x^*, d^*, \pi^*)$ is justified by the following arguments.

(1) By the hardness of the subset membership problem (SMP) related to HPS and $\widetilde{\mathsf{HPS}}$, we can replace $x^* \leftarrow_\$ \mathcal{L}$ in the challenge ciphertext with $x^* \leftarrow_\$ \mathcal{X} \setminus \mathcal{L}$, and compute $C^* = (x^*, \ d^* = \Lambda_{sk}(x^*) + M, \ \pi^* = \widetilde{\Lambda}_{\widetilde{sk}}(x^*, \tau^*))$.

(2) By the (perfectly) universal$_2$ property of tag-based $\widetilde{\mathsf{HPS}}$, any ill-formed ciphertext $C = (x \in \mathcal{X} \setminus \mathcal{L}, \ d, \pi')$ results in a uniformly distributed $\pi = \widetilde{\Lambda}_{\widetilde{sk}}(x, \tau)$, even conditioned on $\widetilde{pk} = \widetilde{\alpha}(\widetilde{sk})$ and $\pi^* = \widetilde{\Lambda}_{\widetilde{sk}}(x^*, \tau^*)$. Thus any decryption query on ill-formed ciphertexts will be rejected (due to the fact that $\pi' = \pi$ holds with a negligible probability).

(3) Now the information that the decryption oracle leaks about sk is limited to $pk = \alpha(sk)$. By the smoothness of HPS, $\Lambda_{sk}(x^*)$ involved in the challenge ciphertext is uniformly random conditioned on $pk = \alpha(sk)$, thus it perfectly hides M and the IND-CCA security follows.

LR-CCA security is also easy to achieve since the universal$_2$ property of $\widetilde{\mathsf{HPS}}$ is intrinsically leakage-resilient, and the smoothness of HPS guarantees that $\Lambda_{sk}(x^*)$ still has enough entropy in case of key leakage, then an extractor can be applied to $\Lambda_{sk}(x^*)$ to distill a uniform string to hide M.

Note that the above arguments only apply to the single-challenge setting. In the more realistic setting of multiple challenge ciphertexts, the universal$_2$ property of $\widetilde{\mathsf{HPS}}$ and the smoothness of HPS are too weak to support arguments (2) and (3). More precisely, argument (2) fails since multiple $\{\pi^* = \widetilde{\Lambda}_{\widetilde{sk}}(x^*, \tau^*)\}$ involved in the challenge ciphertexts might leak too much information about $\widetilde{sk}$, and argument (3) fails since the limited entropy contained in sk is not enough to randomize multiple $\{\Lambda_{sk}(x^*)\}$ involved in the challenge ciphertexts. Consequently, one has to resort to a hybrid argument to prove (multi-challenge) (LR-)CCA security, which inevitably introduces a security loss of factor Q_e [8].

Quasi-Adaptive HPS. We provide a novel approach to tightly (LR)-CCA secure PKE in the multi-challenge setting. The core building block in our approach is a new technical tool named *quasi-adaptive HPS (QAHPS)*, which generalizes HPS in a quasi-adaptive setting [26]. Different from (traditional) HPS [10], QAHPS is associated with a collection $\mathscr{L} = \{\mathcal{L}_\rho\}_\rho$ of NP-languages, and the projection key pk_ρ is allowed to depend on the language $\mathcal{L}_\rho$. In particular, QAHPS possesses a family of projection functions $\alpha_{(.)}$ indexed by a language parameter ρ, so that the action of $\Lambda_{sk}(\cdot)$ on $\mathcal{L}_\rho$ is completely determined by $pk_\rho = \alpha_\rho(sk)$. Intuitively, this allows us to distribute different projection keys for computing hash values of instances from different languages. Tag-based QAHPS can be similarly defined by allowing Λ_{sk}, Pub and Priv to take a tag τ as an auxiliary input.

Our Approach: Tightly LR-CCA Secure PKE from QAHPS. We need three QAHPS schemes for our PKE construction, QAHPS $= (\Lambda_{(.)}, \alpha_{(.)}$, Pub, Priv), $\widehat{\text{QAHPS}} = (\widehat{\Lambda}_{(.)}, \widehat{\alpha}_{(.)}, \widehat{\text{Pub}}, \widehat{\text{Priv}})$ and a tag-based $\widetilde{\text{QAHPS}} = (\widetilde{\Lambda}_{(.)}, \widetilde{\alpha}_{(.)}$, $\widetilde{\text{Pub}}, \widetilde{\text{Priv}})$. The public key is comprised of $pk_\rho = \alpha_\rho(sk)$, $\widehat{pk}_\rho = \widehat{\alpha}_\rho(\widehat{sk})$ and $\widetilde{pk}_\rho = \widetilde{\alpha}_\rho(\widetilde{sk})$. The ciphertext is

$$C = (\; x,\; d = \text{Pub}(pk_\rho, x, w) + M,\; \pi = \widehat{\text{Pub}}(\widehat{pk}_\rho, x, w) + \widetilde{\text{Pub}}(\widetilde{pk}_\rho, x, w, \tau)\;)$$
$$= (\; x,\; d = \Lambda_{sk}(x) + M,\; \pi = \widehat{\pi} + \widetilde{\pi} = \widehat{\Lambda}_{\widehat{sk}}(x) + \widetilde{\Lambda}_{\widetilde{sk}}(x, \tau)\;),$$

where M is a plaintext, $x \leftarrow_{\$} \mathcal{L}_\rho$ with witness w and $\tau = \mathsf{H}(x, d)$ with H a collision-resistant hash function.

For a simple exposition, we first briefly explain why our approach works in the multi-challenge setting and provide a high-level proof of its tight IND-CCA security. Then we show how to extend our approach to the leakage-resilient setting.

Intuition of Tight CCA-Security Proof. Similar to the single-challenge (LR-)CCA security proof of the PKE from HPS, our proof goes with three steps.

(1) Replace all $\{x^* \leftarrow_{\$} \mathcal{L}_\rho\}$ in the challenge ciphertexts with $\{x^* \leftarrow_{\$} \mathcal{L}_{\rho_0}\}$.[4]
    This step is computationally indistinguishable due to the hardness of SMP.
(2) Reject any decryption query on ill-formed ciphertext $C = (x \in \mathcal{X} \setminus \mathcal{L}_\rho, d, \pi')$.
(3) Replace all $\{\Lambda_{sk}(x^*)\}$ involved in the challenge ciphertexts with uniform strings. Then CCA-security follows.

As shown before, the universal$_2$ and smooth properties are insufficient to support (2) and (3) to achieve tight CCA-security. Thus, stronger properties are needed from QAHPS.

---

[4] Here $\mathcal{L}_{\rho_0}$ is from another language collection $\mathscr{L}_0$ and only appears in the security proof. The same is true for $\mathcal{L}_{\rho_1}$ and $\mathscr{L}_1$, as shown later.

Technical Tool for(2): Ardent QAHPS. We define two statistical properties for QAHPS. Let $\mathscr{L}_0 = \{\mathcal{L}_{\rho_0}\}_{\rho_0}$ and $\mathscr{L}_1 = \{\mathcal{L}_{\rho_1}\}_{\rho_1}$ be two language collections.

- **(Perfectly $\langle \mathscr{L}_0, \mathscr{L}_1 \rangle$-Universal).** It demands the uniformity of $\Lambda_{sk}(x)$ conditioned on $\alpha_{\rho_0}(sk)$ and $\alpha_{\rho_1}(sk)$ for any $x \in \mathcal{X} \setminus (\mathcal{L}_{\rho_0} \cup \mathcal{L}_{\rho_1})$, i.e.,

$$\left(\alpha_{\rho_0}(sk), \ \alpha_{\rho_1}(sk), \ \boxed{\Lambda_{sk}(x)} \right) \quad \equiv \quad \left(\alpha_{\rho_0}(sk), \ \alpha_{\rho_1}(sk), \ \boxed{\pi} \leftarrow_{\$} \Pi \right). \quad (1)$$

- **(Perfectly $\langle \mathscr{L}_0, \mathscr{L}_1 \rangle$-Key-Switching).** It requires that $\alpha_{\rho_1}(sk)$ can be switched to $\alpha_{\rho_1}(sk')$ for an independent sk' in the presence of $\alpha_{\rho_0}(sk)$, i.e.,

$$\left(\alpha_{\rho_0}(sk), \ \boxed{\alpha_{\rho_1}(sk)} \right) \quad \equiv \quad \left(\alpha_{\rho_0}(sk), \ \boxed{\alpha_{\rho_1}(sk')} \right). \quad (2)$$

It is also reasonable to define $\langle \mathscr{L}, \mathscr{L}_0 \rangle$-universal and $\langle \mathscr{L}, \mathscr{L}_0 \rangle$-key-switching. We call QAHPS enjoying these two kinds of properties a perfectly *ardent QAHPS*. Ardency of QAHPS can be naturally adapted for tag-based $\widehat{\text{QAHPS}}$.

With ardent QAHPS, $\widehat{\text{QAHPS}}$ and tag-based $\widehat{\text{QAHPS}}$, we describe the high-level idea of justifying (2). By modifying and adapting the latest techniques for proving tight security [19] (which in turn built upon [17,18,24]), we partition the ciphertext space economically according to a counter $ctr \in \{1, \cdots, Q_e\}$, which records the serial number of each encryption query issued by the adversary. Taking ctr as a binary string of length $n := \lceil \log Q_e \rceil$, our proof proceeds with n hybrids. In the i-th hybrid, $i \in \{0, 1, \cdots, n\}$, a random function $\mathsf{RF}_i(ctr_{|i})$ on the first i bits of ctr (instead of $\widehat{sk}$) is employed to compute $\widetilde{\pi}^* = \widetilde{\Lambda}_{\mathsf{RF}_i(ctr_{|i})}(x^*, \tau^*)$ for the challenge ciphertexts; meanwhile, it is also used to compute $\widetilde{\pi} - \widetilde{\Lambda}_{\mathsf{RF}_i(ctr_{|i})}(x, \tau)$ for the decryption of ciphertexts with $x \notin \mathcal{L}_\rho$. In order to go from the i-th hybrid to the $(i+1)$-th hybrid, firstly we replace all $\{x^* \leftarrow_{\$} \mathcal{L}_{\rho_0}\}$ in the challenge ciphertexts with $\{x^* \leftarrow_{\$} \mathcal{L}_{\rho_0} \cup \mathcal{L}_{\rho_1}$ s.t. $x^* \in \mathcal{L}_{\rho_0}$ if $ctr_{i+1} = 0$ and $x^* \in \mathcal{L}_{\rho_1}$ if $ctr_{i+1} = 1\}$; next we employ the ardency of $\widehat{\text{QAHPS}}$ and $\widehat{\text{QAHPS}}$ to add a dependency of $\mathsf{RF}_i(ctr_{|i})$ on the $(i+1)$-th bit ctr_{i+1} so that $\mathsf{RF}_i(ctr_{|i})$ moves to $\mathsf{RF}_{i+1}(ctr_{|i+1})$, as shown below.

- **($\langle \mathscr{L}_0, \mathscr{L}_1 \rangle$-universal forces the instances in decryption queries to fall in $\mathcal{L}_{\rho_0} \cup \mathcal{L}_{\rho_1}$).** By the $\langle \mathscr{L}_0, \mathscr{L}_1 \rangle$-universal property of $\widehat{\text{QAHPS}}$, any decryption query on ciphertext with $x \notin \mathcal{L}_{\rho_0} \cup \mathcal{L}_{\rho_1}$ is rejected. The reason is that, the information of $\widehat{sk}$ leaked by the challenge ciphertexts and by the decryption of ciphertexts with $x \in \mathcal{L}_{\rho_0} \cup \mathcal{L}_{\rho_1}$ is limited to $\widehat{\alpha}_{\rho_0}(\widehat{sk})$ and $\widehat{\alpha}_{\rho_1}(\widehat{sk})$.
- **($\langle \mathscr{L}_0, \mathscr{L}_1 \rangle$-key-switching allows the usage of two independent keys for $\mathcal{L}_{\rho_0}$ and $\mathcal{L}_{\rho_1}$).** Note that for $x \in \mathcal{L}_{\rho_0}$, $\widetilde{\pi} = \widetilde{\Lambda}_{\mathsf{RF}_i(ctr_{|i})}(x, \tau)$ is completely determined by $\widetilde{\alpha}_{\rho_0}(\mathsf{RF}_i(ctr_{|i}))$, while for $x \in \mathcal{L}_{\rho_1}$, it is completely determined by $\widetilde{\alpha}_{\rho_1}(\mathsf{RF}_i(ctr_{|i}))$. By the $\langle \mathscr{L}_0, \mathscr{L}_1 \rangle$-key-switching property of $\widehat{\text{QAHPS}}$,

$$\left(\widetilde{\alpha}_{\rho_0}(\mathsf{RF}_i(ctr_{|i})), \ \widetilde{\alpha}_{\rho_1}(\mathsf{RF}_i(ctr_{|i})) \right) \quad \equiv \quad \left(\widetilde{\alpha}_{\rho_0}(\mathsf{RF}_i(ctr_{|i})), \ \widetilde{\alpha}_{\rho_1}(\overline{\mathsf{RF}}_i(ctr_{|i})) \right),$$

where $\overline{\mathsf{RF}}_i$ is an independent random function. Consequently, we can use $\overline{\mathsf{RF}}_i(ctr_{|i})$ to compute $\widetilde{\pi}^*$ for challenge ciphertexts with $x^* \in \mathcal{L}_{\rho_1}$, and to compute $\widetilde{\pi}$ for the decryption of ciphertexts with $x \in \mathcal{L}_{\rho_1}$.

Now we successfully double the entropy in $\mathsf{RF}_i(ctr_{|i})$ to get $\mathsf{RF}_{i+1}(ctr_{|i+1})$ (which equals $\mathsf{RF}_i(ctr_{|i})$ if $ctr_{i+1} = 0$ and $\overline{\mathsf{RF}}_i(ctr_{|i})$ if $ctr_{i+1} = 1$)[5] and this leads us to the $(i+1)$-th hybrid. After n hybrids, for any ill-formed ciphertext with $x \notin \mathcal{L}_\rho$, $\widetilde{\pi} = \widetilde{\Lambda}_{\mathsf{RF}_n(ctr)}(x, \tau)$ is fully randomized by $\mathsf{RF}_n(ctr)$, thus the decryption on such ciphertexts will be rejected.

Technical Tool for (3): Multi-Extracting. We define a computational property for QAHPS so that it can amplify the (limited) entropy of a uniform sk to randomize multiple $\{\Lambda_{sk}(x^*)\}$.

- **($\mathcal{L}_0$-Multi-Extracting).** It demands the pseudorandomness of $\Lambda_{sk}(x_j)$ for multiple instances x_j uniformly chosen from $\mathcal{L}_{\rho_0}$, i.e.,

$$\{x_j \leftarrow_\$ \mathcal{L}_{\rho_0}, \boxed{\Lambda_{sk}(x_j)}\}_{j \in [Q_e]} \stackrel{c}{\approx} \{x_j \leftarrow_\$ \mathcal{L}_{\rho_0}, \boxed{\pi_j} \leftarrow_\$ \Pi\}_{j \in [Q_e]}.$$

By requiring ardent QAHPS to be $\mathcal{L}_0$-multi-extracting, we are able to justify (3). Note that after the change in (2), the decryption oracle might leak $pk_\rho = \alpha_\rho(sk)$ about sk, therefore, the $\mathcal{L}_0$-multi-extracting property is not applicable immediately. We solve this problem by first applying the $\langle \mathcal{L}, \mathcal{L}_0 \rangle$-key-switching property of QAHPS to switch sk to an independent sk' in the computation of $\{\Lambda_{sk'}(x^*)\}$. Under uniform sk', the $\mathcal{L}_0$-multi-extracting property applies and the $\{\Lambda_{sk'}(x^*)\}$ involved in the challenge ciphertexts can be replaced with uniform strings $\{\mathsf{rand}\}$. Then CCA-security follows.

Extension to Tight LR-CCA Security. Like the leakage-resilient PKE [6, 32,34] from HPS, it is easy to upgrade the tight CCA-security of our PKE construction to tight LR-CCA, as long as the $\langle \mathcal{L}_0, \mathcal{L}_1 \rangle$-universal and $\langle \mathcal{L}_0, \mathcal{L}_1 \rangle$-key-switching properties of QAHPS holds even if some information $L(sk)$ about sk is leaked. The LR-CCA security proof almost verbatim follows the proof of IND-CCA security. We refer to the main body for more details.

By instantiating leakage-resilient ardent QAHPS over pairing-friendly groups, our approach yields the most efficient tightly LR-CCA secure PKE from the MDDH assumptions, with security loss $O(\log Q_e)$.

1.2 Relation to Existing Techniques for Tight Security

To obtain tight (LR-)CCA security, it is inevitable to implement "consistency check", explicitly or implicitly, to reject decryption queries on ill-formed ciphertexts. In [2,23,25,30,31], a NIZK proof is added in the ciphertext as an explicit

---

[5] Note that for the instance $x^* \in \mathcal{L}_{\rho_0} \cup \mathcal{L}_{\rho_1}$ in challenge ciphertext, the bit indicating whether $x^* \in \mathcal{L}_{\rho_0}$ or $x^* \in \mathcal{L}_{\rho_1}$ is consistent with the $(i+1)$-th bit of ctr, i.e., $x^* \in \mathcal{L}_{\rho_0}$ if $ctr_{i+1} = 0$ and $x^* \in \mathcal{L}_{\rho_1}$ if $ctr_{i+1} = 1$. But this might not be true for the instances $x \in \mathcal{L}_{\rho_0} \cup \mathcal{L}_{\rho_1}$ in the decryption queries. This problem is circumvented by borrowing the trick from [18,24]. We refer to the main body for details.

consistency check, where NIZK is required to have tight unbounded simulation-soundness (SS) or true-simulation extractability (tSE). Efficient NIZK with tight SS/tSE is very hard to construct, thus leading to large public keys or ciphertexts in these schemes. Gay et al. [17] implicitly employed a designated-verifier NIZK (DV-NIZK) with tight SS in their construction, which results in large public keys (of over 100 group elements).

In order to get more efficient constructions, Hofheinz [24] used *benign proof system* (BPS) as a main technical tool, which is essentially a DV-NIZK with strong soundness, but not as strong as SS. Gay et al. [18] proposed *qualified proof system* (QPS), which is a combination of a DV-NIZK and an HPS. The weak (computational) soundness requirement for QPS enables efficient instantiations, hence resulting in the most compact PKE with tight CCA-security from the DDH assumption over non-pairing groups.

Our construction of PKE employs LR-ardent QAHPS, with LR-$\langle \mathscr{L}_0, \mathscr{L}_1 \rangle$-universal and LR-$\langle \mathscr{L}_0, \mathscr{L}_1 \rangle$-key-switching properties. QAHPS can be regarded as a (deterministic) DV-NIZK, and the LR-$\langle \mathscr{L}_0, \mathscr{L}_1 \rangle$-universal property corresponds to (statistical) soundness which is weaker than BPS but stronger than QPS. Our LR-ardent QAHPS can be instantiated over pairing-friendly groups.

The key-leakage resilience of (QA)HPS enables us to obtain tight LR-CCA security. However, this feature does not apply to the PKE constructions [18,24] from BPS or QPS. For example, the soundness of QPS is a computational notion and might not be justified in the LR setting (cf. our full version [22] for the reasons). Thus, the PKE in [18] is unlikely to be tightly LR-CCA secure but is pairing-free, while ours are over pairing-groups but achieve tight LR-CCA security.

2 Preliminaries

Let $\lambda \in \mathbb{N}$ denote the security parameter. For $i, j \in \mathbb{N}$ with $i < j$, define $[i, j] := \{i, i+1, \cdots, j\}$ and $[j] := \{1, 2, \cdots, j\}$. Denote by $x \leftarrow_s \mathcal{X}$ the operation of picking an element x according to a distribution $\mathcal{X}$. If $\mathcal{X}$ is a set, then this denotes that x is sampled uniformly at random from $\mathcal{X}$. For an algorithm $\mathcal{A}$, denote by $y \leftarrow_s \mathcal{A}(x; r)$, or simply $y \leftarrow_s \mathcal{A}(x)$, the operation of running $\mathcal{A}$ with input x and randomness r and assigning the output to y, and by $\mathbf{T}(\mathcal{A})$ the running time of $\mathcal{A}$. "PPT" is short for probabilistic polynomial-time. Denote by poly some polynomial function, and negl some negligible function. For a primitive XX and a security notion YY, we typically denote the advantage of a PPT adversary $\mathcal{A}$ by $\mathsf{Adv}_{\mathrm{XX}, \mathcal{A}}^{\mathrm{YY}}(\lambda)$ and define $\mathsf{Adv}_{\mathrm{XX}}^{\mathrm{YY}}(\lambda) := \max_{\mathrm{PPT} \mathcal{A}} \mathsf{Adv}_{\mathrm{XX}, \mathcal{A}}^{\mathrm{YY}}(\lambda)$. For an $\ell \times k$ matrix $\mathbf{A}$ with $\ell > k$, denote the upper k rows of $\mathbf{A}$ by $\overline{\mathbf{A}}$ and the lower $\ell - k$ rows of $\mathbf{A}$ by $\underline{\mathbf{A}}$. For a string $\tau \in \{0, 1\}^\lambda$ and an integer $i \in [0, \lambda]$, denote by $\tau_i \in \{0, 1\}$ the i-th bit of τ and $\tau_{|i} \in \{0, 1\}^i$ the first i bits of τ. Let ε denote an empty string. For random variables X, Y, Z, let $\Delta(X, Y)$ denote the statistical distance between X and Y, $\Delta(X, Y \mid Z)$ a shorthand for $\Delta((X, Z), (Y, Z))$, and $\widetilde{\mathbf{H}}_\infty(X \mid Y)$ the average min-entropy of X conditioned on Y, where the formal definitions appear in the full version [22].

Games. Our security proof will consist of game-based security reductions. A game G starts with an INITIALIZE procedure and ends with a FINALIZE procedure. There are also some optional procedures $\text{PROC}_1, \cdots, \text{PROC}_n$ performing as oracles. All procedures are described using pseudo-code, where initially all variables are empty strings ε and all sets are empty. That an adversary $\mathcal{A}$ is executed in G implies the following procedure: $\mathcal{A}$ first calls INITIALIZE, obtaining the corresponding output; then it may make arbitrary oracle-queries to PROC_i according to their specifications, and obtain their outputs; finally it makes one single call to FINALIZE. The output of FINALIZE is called the output of the game G. The symbol "$\Rightarrow$" stands for "Return" in the description of algorithms and procedures. By $\mathsf{G}^{\mathcal{A}} \Rightarrow b$ we mean that G outputs b after interacting with $\mathcal{A}$. By $\Pr_i[\cdot]$ we denote the probability of a particular event occurring in game G_i.

2.1 Public-Key Encryption

A public-key encryption (PKE) scheme $\mathsf{PKE} = (\mathsf{Param}, \mathsf{Gen}, \mathsf{Enc}, \mathsf{Dec})$ with message space $\mathcal{M}$ consists of a tuple of PPT algorithms: the parameter generation algorithm $\mathsf{PP} \leftarrow_s \mathsf{Param}(1^\lambda)$ outputs a public parameter PP, and we require PP to be an implicit input of other algorithms; the key generation algorithm $(\mathsf{PK}, \mathsf{SK}) \leftarrow_s \mathsf{Gen}(\mathsf{PP})$ outputs a pair of public key PK and secret key SK; the encryption algorithm $C \leftarrow_s \mathsf{Enc}(\mathsf{PK}, M)$ takes as input a public key PK and a message $M \in \mathcal{M}$, and outputs a ciphertext C; the decryption algorithm $M / \bot \leftarrow \mathsf{Dec}(\mathsf{SK}, C)$ takes as input a secret key SK and a ciphertext C, and outputs either a message M or a failure symbol $\bot$. *Perfect correctness* of PKE requires that, for all $\mathsf{PP} \leftarrow_s \mathsf{Param}(1^\lambda)$ and $(\mathsf{PK}, \mathsf{SK}) \leftarrow_s \mathsf{Gen}(\mathsf{PP})$, all messages $M \in \mathcal{M}$, it holds that $\mathsf{Dec}(\mathsf{SK}, \mathsf{Enc}(\mathsf{PK}, M)) = M$.

LR-CCA Security for PKE. Naor and Segev [32] defined the leakage-resilient CCA (LR-CCA) security for PKE. In contrast to IND-CCA, the LR-CCA security also allows the adversary $\mathcal{A}$ to make LEAK (key leakage) queries adaptively and obtain additional information $L(\mathsf{SK})$ about the secret key SK, where $L : \mathcal{SK} \longrightarrow \{0,1\}^* \backslash \{\varepsilon\}$ is the leakage function submitted by $\mathcal{A}$. According to [32], two restrictions are necessary: *(i)* the total amount of leakage bits is *bounded* by some positive integer κ; *(ii)* $\mathcal{A}$ can only access the LEAK oracle *before* it obtains a challenge ciphertext (otherwise $\mathcal{A}$ could trivially win by querying the first few bits of $\mathsf{Dec}(\cdot, C^*)$ after receiving a challenge ciphertext C^*).

We present the definition of the κ-leakage-resilient CCA security in its multi-ciphertext version. The leakage-rate of the LR-CCA security is defined as the ratio of κ to the bit-length of secret key, i.e., $\kappa/\mathsf{BitLength}(\mathsf{SK})$.

Definition 1 (Multi-Ciphertext κ-Leakage-Resilient CCA Security). *Let $\kappa = \kappa(\lambda)$. A PKE scheme PKE is κ-LR-CCA secure, if for any PPT adversary $\mathcal{A}$, it holds that $\mathsf{Adv}_{\mathsf{PKE}, \mathcal{A}}^{\kappa - lr - cca}(\lambda) := \big| \Pr[\kappa\text{-lr-cca}^{\mathcal{A}} \Rightarrow 1] - \frac{1}{2} \big| \leq \mathsf{negl}(\lambda)$, where game κ-lr-cca is specified in Fig. 1.*

If $\kappa = 0$, κ-LR-CCA security is reduced to the traditional IND-CCA security.

Proc. INITIALIZE:	Proc. LEAK(L):	Proc. ENC(M_0, M_1):	Proc. DEC(C):
$PP \leftarrow_s \text{Param}(1^\lambda)$.	If (chal = true)	chal := true.	If $C \in \mathcal{Q}_{\mathcal{ENC}}$,
$(PK, SK) \leftarrow_s \text{Gen}(PP)$.	$\lor (l + \|L(SK)\| > \kappa)$,	If $\|M_0\| \neq \|M_1\|$, Return $\perp$.	Return $\perp$.
$\beta \leftarrow_s \{0,1\}$. // challenge bit	Return $\perp$.	$C^* \leftarrow_s \text{Enc}(PK, M_\beta)$.	Return Dec(SK, C).
$l := 0$. // bit length of leakage	$l := l + \|L(SK)\|$.	$\mathcal{Q}_{\mathcal{ENC}} := \mathcal{Q}_{\mathcal{ENC}} \cup \{C^*\}$.	
chal := false.	Return $L(SK)$.	Return C^*.	Proc. FINALIZE(β'):
Return (PP, PK).			Return $(\beta' = \beta)$.

Fig. 1. κ-lr-cca security game for PKE, where $\|L(SK)\|$ denotes the bit length of $L(SK)$.

2.2 Pairing Groups

Let $\text{PGGen}(1^\lambda)$ be a PPT algorithm outputting a description of pairing group $\mathcal{PG} = (\mathbb{G}_1, \mathbb{G}_2, \mathbb{G}_T, p, e, P_1, P_2, P_T)$, where $\mathbb{G}_1$, $\mathbb{G}_2$ and $\mathbb{G}_T$ are additive cyclic groups of order p, p is a prime number of bit-length at least λ, $e : \mathbb{G}_1 \times \mathbb{G}_2 \longrightarrow \mathbb{G}_T$ is a non-degenerated bilinear pairing, and P_1, P_2, P_T are generators of $\mathbb{G}_1, \mathbb{G}_2, \mathbb{G}_T$, respectively, with $P_T := e(P_1, P_2)$. We assume that the operations in $\mathbb{G}_1$, $\mathbb{G}_2$, $\mathbb{G}_T$ and the pairing e are efficiently computable. We require the pairing group $\mathcal{PG}$ to be an implicit input of other algorithms.

We use the implicit representation of group elements following [14]. For a matrix $\mathbf{A} = (a_{i,j})$ over $\mathbb{Z}_p$, denote by $[\mathbf{A}]_s := (a_{i,j} \cdot P_s)$ the implicit representation of $\mathbf{A}$ in $\mathbb{G}_s$ (which may be $\mathbb{G}_1$, $\mathbb{G}_2$, or $\mathbb{G}_T$). Clearly, given $\mathbf{A}$, $[\mathbf{B}]_s$, $[\mathbf{C}]_s$ and $\mathbf{D}$ with composable dimensions, one can efficiently compute $[\mathbf{AB}]_s$, $[\mathbf{B}+\mathbf{C}]_s$, $[\mathbf{CD}]_s$; given $[\mathbf{A}]_1$ and $[\mathbf{B}]_2$, one can efficiently compute $[\mathbf{AB}]_T$ with the pairing e.

Let $\ell, k \geq 1$ be integers with $\ell > k$. A probabilistic distribution $\mathcal{D}_{\ell,k}$ is called a *matrix distribution*, if it outputs matrices in $\mathbb{Z}_p^{\ell \times k}$ of full rank k in polynomial time. Without loss of generality, we assume that the first k rows of $\mathbf{A} \leftarrow_s \mathcal{D}_{\ell,k}$ are linearly independent. Let $\mathcal{D}_k := \mathcal{D}_{k+1,k}$. Denote by $\mathcal{U}_{\ell,k}$ the *uniform distribution* over all matrices in $\mathbb{Z}_p^{\ell \times k}$. Let $\mathcal{U}_k := \mathcal{U}_{k+1,k}$. We review the Matrix DDH (MDDH) and Q-fold MDDH assumptions relative to PGGen, as well as the random self-reducibility of the MDDH assumptions, in the full version [22].

2.3 Collision-Resistant Hashing

Definition 2 (Collision-Resistant Hashing). *A family of functions* $\mathcal{H} = \{H : \mathcal{X} \longrightarrow \mathcal{Y}\}$ *is collision-resistant, if for any PPT adversary $\mathcal{A}$, it holds that*

$$\text{Adv}_{\mathcal{H},\mathcal{A}}^{cr}(\lambda) := \Pr\left[H \leftarrow_s \mathcal{H}, (x, x') \leftarrow_s \mathcal{A}(H) : H(x) = H(x') \land x \neq x'\right] \leq \text{negl}(\lambda).$$

3   Quasi-Adaptive HPS: Ardency and Leakage Resilience

For hash proof system (HPS) defined in [10], the associated NP-language $\mathcal{L}$ is generated in the setup phase once and for all, and the projection key pk is used for computing hash values of instances in this fixed $\mathcal{L}$.

In this section, we formalize the notion of *quasi-adaptive HPS (QAHPS)*,[6] which is associated with a collection $\mathscr{L} = \{\mathcal{L}_\rho\}_\rho$ of NP-languages. Different from

---

[6] Quasi-adaptiveness of HPS was discussed in [27]. Here we give a formal definition of QAHPS and build our novel LR-ardency notion over it.

HPS, the projection key pk_ρ of QAHPS is allowed to depend on the specific language $\mathcal{L}_\rho$ for which hash values are computed.

As the main technical novelty, we propose two new statistical properties for QAHPS, including κ-LR-$\langle \mathcal{L}_0, \mathcal{L}_1 \rangle$-*universal* and κ-LR-$\langle \mathcal{L}_0, \mathcal{L}_1 \rangle$-*key-switching*. This type of QAHPS is termed as *LR-ardent QAHPS*. We also define the tag-based version of QAHPS and adapt the notion of LR-ardency for it. LR-ardent QAHPS and tag-based one will serve as our core technical tools.

3.1   Language Distribution

In this subsection, we formalize the collection of NP-languages, with which a QAHPS is associated, as a language distribution.

Definition 3 (Language Distribution). *A language distribution $\mathcal{L}$ is a probability distribution that outputs a language parameter ρ as well as a trapdoor td in polynomial time. The language parameter ρ publicly defines an NP-language $\mathcal{L}_\rho \subseteq \mathcal{X}_\rho$. For simplicity, we assume that the universe $\mathcal{X}_\rho$ is the same for all languages $\mathcal{L}_\rho$, denoted by $\mathcal{X}$. The trapdoor td is required to contain enough information for deciding whether or not an instance $x \in \mathcal{X}$ is in $\mathcal{L}_\rho$. We require that there are PPT algorithms for sampling $x \leftarrow_s \mathcal{L}_\rho$ uniformly together with a witness w and sampling $x \leftarrow_s \mathcal{X}$ uniformly.*

We define a subset membership problem (SMP) for a language distribution $\mathcal{L}$, which asks whether an element is uniformly chosen from $\mathcal{L}_\rho$ or $\mathcal{X}$.

Definition 4 (Subset Membership Problem). *The subset membership problem (SMP) related to a language distribution $\mathcal{L}$ is hard, if for any PPT adversary $\mathcal{A}$, it holds that $\mathsf{Adv}^{smp}_{\mathcal{L},\mathcal{A}}(\lambda) := |\Pr[\mathcal{A}(\rho, x) = 1] - \Pr[\mathcal{A}(\rho, x') = 1]| \leq \mathsf{negl}(\lambda)$, where $(\rho, td) \leftarrow_s \mathcal{L}$, $x \leftarrow_s \mathcal{L}_\rho$ and $x' \leftarrow_s \mathcal{X}$.*

We also define a multi-fold version of SMP, which is to distinguish multiple instances, all of which are uniformly chosen either from $\mathcal{L}_\rho$ or from $\mathcal{X}$.

Definition 5 (Multi-fold SMP). *The multi-fold SMP related to a language distribution $\mathcal{L}$ is hard, if for any PPT adversary $\mathcal{A}$, any polynomial $Q = \mathsf{poly}(\lambda)$,*

$$\mathsf{Adv}^{Q\text{-}msmp}_{\mathcal{L},\mathcal{A}}(\lambda) := \left| \Pr\left[\mathcal{A}(\rho, \{x_j\}_{j \in [Q]}) = 1\right] - \Pr\left[\mathcal{A}(\rho, \{x'_j\}_{j \in [Q]}) = 1\right] \right| \leq \mathsf{negl}(\lambda)$$

holds, where $(\rho, td) \leftarrow_s \mathcal{L}$, $x_1, \cdots, x_Q \leftarrow_s \mathcal{L}_\rho$ and $x'_1, \cdots, x'_Q \leftarrow_s \mathcal{X}$.

By a standard hybrid argument, SMP and multi-fold SMP are equivalent. For some language distributions, such as those for linear subspaces (cf. Subsect. 5.2), the hardness of multi-fold SMP can be tightly reduced to that of SMP.

3.2   Quasi-Adaptive HPS

Definition 6 (Quasi-Adaptive Hash Proof System). *A quasi-adaptive hash proof system (QAHPS) QAHPS = (Setup, $\alpha_{(\cdot)}$, Pub, Priv) for a language distribution $\mathcal{L}$ consists of a tuple of PPT algorithms:*

– $pp \leftarrow_s \mathsf{Setup}(1^\lambda)$: *The setup algorithm outputs a public parameter pp, which implicitly defines* $(\mathcal{SK}, \Pi, \Lambda_{(\cdot)})$, *where*
  • $\mathcal{SK}$ *is the hashing key space and* Π *is the hash value space;*
  • $\Lambda_{(\cdot)} : \mathcal{X} \longrightarrow \Pi$ *is a family of hash functions indexed by a hashing key* $sk \in \mathcal{SK}$, *where* $\mathcal{X}$ *is the universe for languages output by* $\mathscr{L}$.
  We assume that $\Lambda_{(\cdot)}$ *is efficiently computable and there are PPT algorithms for sampling* $sk \leftarrow_s \mathcal{SK}$ *uniformly and sampling* $\pi \leftarrow_s \Pi$ *uniformly. We require pp to be an implicit input of other algorithms.*
– $pk_\rho \leftarrow \alpha_\rho(sk)$: *The projection algorithm outputs a projection key* pk_ρ *of hashing key* $sk \in \mathcal{SK}$ *w.r.t. the language parameter* ρ.
– $\pi \leftarrow \mathsf{Pub}(pk_\rho, x, w)$: *The public evaluation algorithm outputs the hash value* $\pi = \Lambda_{sk}(x) \in \Pi$ *of* $x \in \mathcal{L}_\rho$, *with the help of the projection key* $pk_\rho = \alpha_\rho(sk)$ *specified by* ρ *and a witness* w *for* $x \in \mathcal{L}_\rho$.
– $\pi \leftarrow \mathsf{Priv}(sk, x)$: *The private evaluation algorithm outputs the hash value* $\pi = \Lambda_{sk}(x) \in \Pi$ *of* $x \in \mathcal{X}$, *directly using the hashing key* sk.

Perfect correctness (a.k.a. projectiveness) of QAHPS *requires that, for all possible* $pp \leftarrow_s \mathsf{Setup}(1^\lambda)$ *and* $(\rho, td) \leftarrow_s \mathscr{L}$, *all hashing keys* $sk \in \mathcal{SK}$ *with* $pk_\rho = \alpha_\rho(sk)$ *the corresponding projection key w.r.t.* ρ, *all* $x \in \mathcal{L}_\rho$ *with all possible witnesses* w, *it holds that* $\mathsf{Pub}(pk_\rho, x, w) = \Lambda_{sk}(x) = \mathsf{Priv}(sk, x)$.

Remark 1 (Relation to HPS). In contrast to the HPS defined by Cramer and Shoup [10], there are two main differences:

• Instead of a single language, QAHPS is associated with a collection of languages $\mathscr{L} = \{\mathcal{L}_\rho\}_\rho$ characterized by a language distribution. In particular, the specific language $\mathcal{L}_\rho$ is no longer generated in the setup phase Setup.

• Instead of a single projection function, QAHPS possesses a family of projection functions $\alpha_{(\cdot)} : \mathcal{SK} \longrightarrow \mathcal{PK}_{(\cdot)}$ indexed by a language parameter ρ, so that the action of $\Lambda_{sk}(\cdot)$ on $\mathcal{L}_\rho$ is completely determined by $pk_\rho := \alpha_\rho(sk)$.

In a nutshell, the relation between HPS and QAHPS is analogous to the relation between NIZK and QA-NIZK [26].

Remark 2 (Relation to DV-QA-NIZK). An HPS is essentially a (deterministic) designated-verifier non-interactive zero-knowledge (DV-NIZK) proof system [17]. Similarly, our QAHPS can be viewed as a (deterministic) DV-QA-NIZK.

Dodis et al. [12] defined an extracting property for (traditional) HPS, which requires the hash value $\Lambda_{sk}(x)$ to be uniformly distributed over Π for any $x \in \mathcal{X}$, as long as sk is uniformly chosen from $\mathcal{SK}$. Intuitively, $\Lambda_{(\cdot)}(x)$ acts as an extractor and extracts the entropy from sk. Here, we introduce a *computational* analogue of the extracting property in a *multi-fold* version for QAHPS, called *multi-extracting property*, which demands the pseudorandomness of $\Lambda_{sk}(x_j)$ for multiple instances x_j, $j \in [Q]$.

Definition 7 ($\mathscr{L}_0$-Multi-Extracting QAHPS). *Let* $\mathscr{L}_0$ *be a language distribution (which might be different from* $\mathscr{L}$). QAHPS *for* $\mathscr{L}$ *is called* $\mathscr{L}_0$-*multi-extracting, if for any PPT adversary* $\mathcal{A}$, *any* $Q = \mathsf{poly}(\lambda)$, $\mathsf{Adv}_{\mathsf{QAHPS},\mathcal{A}}^{Q-\mathscr{L}_0-mext}(\lambda) :=$

$$| \operatorname{Pr}\left[\mathcal{A}(pp, \rho_0, \{x_j, \boxed{\Lambda_{sk}(x_j)}\}_{j \in [Q]}) = 1\right] - \operatorname{Pr}\left[\mathcal{A}(pp, \rho_0, \{x_j, \boxed{\pi_j}\}_{j \in [Q]}) = 1\right] |$$

is negligible, where $pp \leftarrow_\$ \mathsf{Setup}(1^\lambda)$, $(\rho_0, td_0) \leftarrow_\$ \mathscr{L}_0$, $sk \leftarrow_\$ \mathcal{SK}$, $x_1, \cdots, x_Q \leftarrow_\$ \mathcal{L}_{\rho_0}$, *and* $\pi_1, \cdots, \pi_Q \leftarrow_\$ \Pi$.

We note that the $\mathscr{L}_0$-multi-extracting property is defined in an *average-case* flavor, i.e., the instances x_j, $j \in [Q]$, are uniformly chosen from $\mathcal{L}_{\rho_0}$.

3.3   Ardent QAHPS with Leakage Resilience

In this subsection, we introduce two statistical properties for QAHPS, including κ-LR-$\langle \mathscr{L}_0, \mathscr{L}_1 \rangle$-universal and κ-LR-$\langle \mathscr{L}_0, \mathscr{L}_1 \rangle$-key-switching. These two properties are formalized in a general manner and are parameterized by $\kappa \in \mathbb{N}$ and two language distributions $\langle \mathscr{L}_0, \mathscr{L}_1 \rangle$. We name QAHPS enjoying these properties as *LR-ardent* QAHPS. We highlight the leakage $L(sk)$ with gray boxes, in order to show the difference from the perfectly ardent QAHPS as stated in Subsect. 1.1.

Definition 8 (Leakage-Resilient Ardent QAHPS). *Let* $\kappa = \kappa(\lambda) \in \mathbb{N}$, *and let* $\mathscr{L}_0, \mathscr{L}_1$ *be a pair of language distributions. A QAHPS scheme* QAHPS *for a language distribution* $\mathscr{L}$ *is called* κ-*leakage-resilient* $\langle \mathscr{L}_0, \mathscr{L}_1 \rangle$-*ardent* ($\kappa$-LR-$\langle \mathscr{L}_0, \mathscr{L}_1 \rangle$-*ardent*), *if the following two properties hold:*

- (κ-**LR**-$\langle \mathscr{L}_0, \mathscr{L}_1 \rangle$-**Universal**). *With overwhelming probability* $1 - 2^{-\Omega(\lambda)}$ *over* $pp \leftarrow_\$ \mathsf{Setup}(1^\lambda)$, $(\rho_0, td_0) \leftarrow_\$ \mathscr{L}_0$ *and* $(\rho_1, td_1) \leftarrow_\$ \mathscr{L}_1$, *for all* $x \in \mathcal{X} \setminus (\mathcal{L}_{\rho_0} \cup \mathcal{L}_{\rho_1})$ *and all leakage functions* $L : \mathcal{SK} \longrightarrow \{0,1\}^\kappa$, *if* $sk \leftarrow_\$ \mathcal{SK}$, *then*

$$\widetilde{\mathbf{H}}_\infty\big(\Lambda_{sk}(x) \mid \alpha_{\rho_0}(sk), \alpha_{\rho_1}(sk), \boxed{L(sk)}\big) \geq \Omega(\lambda). \tag{3}$$

We require the inequality to hold for adaptive choices of x *and* L, *where* x *and* L *can arbitrarily depend on* ρ_0, ρ_1, $\alpha_{\rho_0}(sk)$, $\alpha_{\rho_1}(sk)$.

- (κ-**LR**-$\langle \mathscr{L}_0, \mathscr{L}_1 \rangle$-**Key-Switching**). *With overwhelming probability* $1 - 2^{-\Omega(\lambda)}$ *over* $pp \leftarrow_\$ \mathsf{Setup}(1^\lambda)$ *and* $(\rho_0, td_0) \leftarrow_\$ \mathscr{L}_0$, *for all leakage functions* $L : \mathcal{SK} \longrightarrow \{0,1\}^\kappa$, *it holds that:*

$$\Delta\big((\rho_1, \boxed{\alpha_{\rho_1}(sk)}), (\rho_1, \boxed{\alpha_{\rho_1}(sk')}) \mid \alpha_{\rho_0}(sk), \boxed{L(sk)}\big) \leq 2^{-\Omega(\lambda)}, \tag{4}$$

where the probability is over $sk, sk' \leftarrow_\$ \mathcal{SK}$ *and* $(\rho_1, td_1) \leftarrow_\$ \mathscr{L}_1$. *We require the inequality to hold for* L *that is arbitrarily dependent on* ρ_0, $\alpha_{\rho_0}(sk)$. *However,* L *is required to be independent of* ρ_1.

When $\kappa = 0$, the term "κ-LR" is omitted from these properties. The parameter $\langle \mathscr{L}_0, \mathscr{L}_1 \rangle$ is also omitted when it is clear from context.

Definition 9 (Ardent QAHPS). QAHPS *is called* $\langle \mathscr{L}_0, \mathscr{L}_1 \rangle$-*ardent if it is 0-leakage-resilient* $\langle \mathscr{L}_0, \mathscr{L}_1 \rangle$-*ardent.*

Furthermore, if (3) and (4) are replaced by (1) and (2), then it is **perfectly** $\langle \mathscr{L}_0, \mathscr{L}_1 \rangle$-**universal** and **key-switching** which is obviously

(0-LR-)$\langle \mathcal{L}_0, \mathcal{L}_1 \rangle$-universal and key-switching. Observe that, perfectly universal property itself carries leakage resilience to some extent as shown in Lemma 1. (See the full version [22] for the proof.)

Lemma 1 (Perfectly $\langle \mathcal{L}_0, \mathcal{L}_1 \rangle$-Universal $\Rightarrow$ LR-$\langle \mathcal{L}_0, \mathcal{L}_1 \rangle$-Universal). *If a QAHPS scheme is perfectly $\langle \mathcal{L}_0, \mathcal{L}_1 \rangle$-universal, then it is κ-LR-$\langle \mathcal{L}_0, \mathcal{L}_1 \rangle$-universal for any $\kappa \leq \log |\Pi| - \Omega(\lambda)$, where Π is the hash value space of QAHPS.*

Remark 3 (On the Independence Between $L(\cdot)$ and ρ_1). We stress that, in the definition of κ-LR-$\langle \mathcal{L}_0, \mathcal{L}_1 \rangle$-key-switching, the independence between the leakage function $L(\cdot)$ and the language parameter ρ_1 is necessary. Otherwise, this property is unsatisfiable by simply taking $L(\cdot)$ as the first κ bits of $\alpha_{\rho_1}(\cdot)$.

Remark 4 (On the Choices of $\langle \mathcal{L}_0, \mathcal{L}_1 \rangle$). We stress that, in the above definition, $\mathcal{L}_0$ or $\mathcal{L}_1$ is allowed to be $\mathcal{L}$ itself. In particular, it is reasonable to define κ-LR-$\langle \mathcal{L}, \mathcal{L}_0 \rangle$-ardency for a QAHPS scheme QAHPS for $\mathcal{L}$. Besides, we note that κ-LR-$\langle \mathcal{L}_0, \mathcal{L}_1 \rangle$-universal is identical to κ-LR-$\langle \mathcal{L}_1, \mathcal{L}_0 \rangle$-universal.

Remark 5 (Relation to the Universal$_1$, Universal$_2$ and Extracting Properties). The $\langle \mathcal{L}_0, \mathcal{L}_1 \rangle$-universal property of QAHPS generalizes the currently available universal and extracting properties of (traditional) HPS. With different choices of $\mathcal{L}_0$ and $\mathcal{L}_1$, it will turn into the universal$_1$, the universal$_2$ and the extracting properties of HPS defined in [10,12], respectively.

More precisely, let $\mathcal{L}_\perp$ (or simply $\perp$) denote a special *empty* language distribution, which always outputs $\rho_\perp$ defining the empty language $\mathcal{L}_{\rho_\perp} = \{\}$, and let $\mathcal{L}_{\text{sing}}$ denote a special *singleton* language distribution, which samples $x \leftarrow_s \mathcal{X}$ uniformly and outputs ρ_x defining a singleton language $\mathcal{L}_{\rho_x} = \{x\}$. We assume that $\alpha_{\rho_\perp}(sk) = \perp$ and $\alpha_{\rho_x}(sk) = \Lambda_{sk}(x)$ hold for any $sk \in \mathcal{SK}$ and $x \in \mathcal{X}$, both of which are very natural and are satisfied by our instantiations in Sect. 5. Then: *(i)* $\langle \mathcal{L}, \perp \rangle$-universal corresponds to the average-case universal$_1$ property; *(ii)* $\langle \mathcal{L}, \mathcal{L}_{\text{sing}} \rangle$-universal corresponds to the average-case universal$_2$ property; *(iii)* Perfectly $\langle \perp, \perp \rangle$-universal corresponds to the extracting property.

The leakage-resilient ardency of QAHPS can be adapted to a weak version.

Definition 10 (Leakage-Resilient Weak-Ardent QAHPS). *Let $\kappa = \kappa(\lambda) \in \mathbb{N}$, and let $\mathcal{L}_0, \mathcal{L}_1$ be a pair of language distributions. A QAHPS scheme QAHPS for a language distribution $\mathcal{L}$ is called κ-leakage-resilient $\langle \mathcal{L}_0, \mathcal{L}_1 \rangle$-weak-ardent ($\kappa$-LR-$\langle \mathcal{L}_0, \mathcal{L}_1 \rangle$-weak-ardent), if QAHPS is $\langle \perp, \perp \rangle$-universal and supports κ-LR-$\langle \mathcal{L}_0, \mathcal{L}_1 \rangle$-key-switching. Similarly, $\kappa = 0$ leads to* **weak-ardent QAHPS**.

3.4 Extension to the Tag-Based Setting

The notion of (traditional) HPS was generalized to extended HPS (a.k.a. labeled HPS) in [10] and tag-based HPS in [35], respectively, by allowing the hash functions $\Lambda_{(\cdot)}$ to have an additional element called label/tag as input.

Similarly, in a tag-based QAHPS, the public parameter pp also implicitly defines a tag space $\mathcal{T}$. Meanwhile, the hash functions $\Lambda_{(\cdot)}$, the public evaluation algorithm Pub and the private evaluation algorithm Priv also take a tag $\tau \in \mathcal{T}$ as input. Accordingly, perfect correctness requires $\mathsf{Pub}(pk_\rho, x, w, \tau) = \Lambda_{sk}(x, \tau) = \mathsf{Priv}(sk, x, \tau)$ for all tags $\tau \in \mathcal{T}$. The formal definition of tag-based QAHPS can be found in our full version [22].

The notion of LR-ardency is naturally adapted for tag-based QAHPS. A tag-based QAHPS is κ-leakage-resilient $\langle \mathcal{L}_0, \mathcal{L}_1 \rangle$-ardent ($\kappa$-LR-$\langle \mathcal{L}_0, \mathcal{L}_1 \rangle$-ardent), if it is both κ-LR-$\langle \mathcal{L}_0, \mathcal{L}_1 \rangle$-universal and κ-LR-$\langle \mathcal{L}_0, \mathcal{L}_1 \rangle$-key-switching.

- (κ-LR-$\langle \mathcal{L}_0, \mathcal{L}_1 \rangle$-**Universal for Tag-Based QAHPS**). It takes tags into account and considers two hash values with different tags. With overwhelming probability $1 - 2^{-\Omega(\lambda)}$ over $pp \leftarrow_\$ \mathsf{Setup}(1^\lambda)$, $(\rho_0, td_0) \leftarrow_\$ \mathcal{L}_0$ and $(\rho_1, td_1) \leftarrow_\$ \mathcal{L}_1$, for all $x \in \mathcal{X} \setminus (\mathcal{L}_{\rho_0} \cup \mathcal{L}_{\rho_1})$, all $x' \in \mathcal{X}$, all $\tau, \tau' \in \mathcal{T}$ with $\tau \neq \tau'$ and all leakage functions $L : \mathcal{SK} \longrightarrow \{0, 1\}^\kappa$, if $sk \leftarrow_\$ \mathcal{SK}$, then

$$\widetilde{\mathbf{H}}_\infty\big(\Lambda_{sk}(x, \tau) \mid \alpha_{\rho_0}(sk), \ \alpha_{\rho_1}(sk), \ \Lambda_{sk}(x', \tau'), \ \boxed{L(sk)} \ \big) \ \geq \ \Omega(\lambda).$$

We require the inequality to hold for adaptive choices of x, x', τ, τ' and L, where they can arbitrarily depend on $\rho_0, \rho_1, \alpha_{\rho_0}(sk), \alpha_{\rho_1}(sk)$.

- (κ-LR-$\langle \mathcal{L}_0, \mathcal{L}_1 \rangle$-**Key-Switching for Tag-Based QAHPS**). This property remains the same as (4) for the non-tag-based QAHPS, since no tag is involved in the projection algorithm $\alpha_{(\cdot)}$.

Similarly, the κ-LR-$\langle \mathcal{L}_0, \mathcal{L}_1 \rangle$-weak-ardency of tag-based QAHPS asks for both $\langle \bot, \bot \rangle$-universal and κ-LR-$\langle \mathcal{L}_0, \mathcal{L}_1 \rangle$-key-switching properties.

- ($\langle \bot, \bot \rangle$-**Universal for Tag-Based QAHPS**). With overwhelming probability $1 - 2^{-\Omega(\lambda)}$ over $pp \leftarrow_\$ \mathsf{Setup}(1^\lambda)$, for all $x, x' \in \mathcal{X}$ and all $\tau, \tau' \in \mathcal{T}$ with $\tau \neq \tau'$, it holds that:

$$\widetilde{\mathbf{H}}_\infty\big(\Lambda_{sk}(x, \tau) \mid \Lambda_{sk}(x', \tau') \big) \ \geq \ \Omega(\lambda),$$

where the probability is over $sk \leftarrow_\$ \mathcal{SK}$ and x, τ can arbitrarily depend on $\Lambda_{sk}(x', \tau')$.

We also give (equivalent) game-based definitions for κ-LR-ardency of QAHPS and tag-based QAHPS in the full version [22].

4   LR-CCA-Secure PKE via LR-Ardent QAHPS

We present a modular approach to tightly LR-CCA secure PKE from LR-ardent QAHPS. Our approach employs an LR-weak-ardent QAHPS, an LR-ardent $\widehat{\text{QAHPS}}$ and an LR-weak-ardent tag-based $\widehat{\text{QAHPS}}$, all of which are associated with the same language distribution $\mathcal{L}$.

4.1   The Generic Construction of PKE

Our PKE construction makes use of the following building blocks.

- Three language distributions $\mathcal{L}, \mathcal{L}_0$ and $\mathcal{L}_1$, all of which have hard subset membership problems.

- An LR-weak-ardent QAHPS = $(\mathsf{Setup}, \alpha_{(\cdot)}, \mathsf{Pub}, \mathsf{Priv})$ for $\mathscr{L}$, whose hash value space Π is an (additive) group.
- An LR-ardent $\widehat{\mathsf{QAHPS}} = (\widehat{\mathsf{Setup}}, \widehat{\alpha}_{(\cdot)}, \widehat{\mathsf{Pub}}, \widehat{\mathsf{Priv}})$ for $\mathscr{L}$.
- An LR-weak-ardent tag-based $\widetilde{\mathsf{QAHPS}} = (\widetilde{\mathsf{Setup}}, \widetilde{\alpha}_{(\cdot)}, \widetilde{\mathsf{Pub}}, \widetilde{\mathsf{Priv}})$ for $\mathscr{L}$, whose tag space is $\widetilde{\mathcal{T}}$.
- A collision-resistant function family $\mathcal{H} = \{\mathsf{H} : \mathcal{X} \times \Pi \longrightarrow \widetilde{\mathcal{T}}\}$.

The LR-ardency requirements for the QAHPS schemes are listed in Table 2.

Table 2. Requirements on QAHPS, $\widehat{\mathsf{QAHPS}}$ and tag-based $\widetilde{\mathsf{QAHPS}}$ for κ-LR-CCA security of PKE. Here $\langle \mathscr{L}_0, \mathscr{L}_1 \rangle$-key-switching for $\widehat{\mathsf{QAHPS}}$ is not listed, since it is not necessary in the κ-LR-CCA security proof. We stress that the $\langle \bot, \bot \rangle$-universal property of QAHPS, the $\langle \mathscr{L}_0, \mathscr{L}_1 \rangle$-universal property of $\widehat{\mathsf{QAHPS}}$, and the $\langle \bot, \bot \rangle$-universal and $\langle \mathscr{L}_0, \mathscr{L}_1 \rangle$-key-switching properties of $\widetilde{\mathsf{QAHPS}}$ do not have to be leakage-resilient.

	LR-weak-ardency of QAHPS	LR-ardency of $\widehat{\mathsf{QAHPS}}$	LR-weak-ardency of $\widetilde{\mathsf{QAHPS}}$
universal	$\langle \bot, \bot \rangle$	κ-LR-$\langle \mathscr{L}, \mathscr{L}_0 \rangle$, $\langle \mathscr{L}_0, \mathscr{L}_1 \rangle$	$\langle \bot, \bot \rangle$
key-switching	κ-LR-$\langle \mathscr{L}, \mathscr{L}_0 \rangle$	κ-LR-$\langle \mathscr{L}, \mathscr{L}_0 \rangle$	κ-LR-$\langle \mathscr{L}, \mathscr{L}_0 \rangle$, $\langle \mathscr{L}_0, \mathscr{L}_1 \rangle$

The proposed scheme PKE = (Param, Gen, Enc, Dec) with message space $\mathcal{M} = \Pi$ is presented in Fig. 2. The perfect correctness of PKE follows from the perfect correctness of QAHPS, $\widehat{\mathsf{QAHPS}}$ and $\widetilde{\mathsf{QAHPS}}$ directly.

$PP \leftarrow_{\!s} \mathsf{Param}(1^\lambda):$

$pp \leftarrow_{\!s} \mathsf{Setup}(1^\lambda)$, which defines $(\mathcal{SK}, \Pi, \Lambda_{(\cdot)})$.

$\widehat{pp} \leftarrow_{\!s} \widehat{\mathsf{Setup}}(1^\lambda)$, which defines $(\widehat{\mathcal{SK}}, \widehat{\Pi}, \widehat{\Lambda}_{(\cdot)})$.

$\widetilde{pp} \leftarrow_{\!s} \widetilde{\mathsf{Setup}}(1^\lambda)$, which defines $(\widetilde{\mathcal{SK}}, \widetilde{\mathcal{T}}, \widetilde{\Pi}, \widetilde{\Lambda}_{(\cdot)})$.

$(\rho, td) \leftarrow_{\!s} \mathscr{L}$. $\mathsf{H} \leftarrow_{\!s} \mathcal{H}$.

$\Rightarrow PP := (pp, \widehat{pp}, \widetilde{pp}, \rho, \mathsf{H})$.

$(PK, SK) \leftarrow_{\!s} \mathsf{Gen}(PP):$

$sk \leftarrow_{\!s} \mathcal{SK}.\quad pk_\rho := \alpha_\rho(sk)$.

$\widehat{sk} \leftarrow_{\!s} \widehat{\mathcal{SK}}.\quad \widehat{pk}_\rho := \widehat{\alpha}_\rho(\widehat{sk})$.

$\widetilde{sk} \leftarrow_{\!s} \widetilde{\mathcal{SK}}.\quad \widetilde{pk}_\rho := \widetilde{\alpha}_\rho(\widetilde{sk})$.

$\Rightarrow PK := (pk_\rho, \widehat{pk}_\rho, \widetilde{pk}_\rho)$,

$\quad SK := (sk, \widehat{sk}, \widetilde{sk})$.

$C \leftarrow_{\!s} \mathsf{Enc}(PK, M):$

$x \leftarrow_{\!s} \mathcal{L}_\rho$ with witness w.

$d := \mathsf{Pub}(pk_\rho, x, w) + M \in \Pi$.

$\tau := \mathsf{H}(x, d) \in \widetilde{\mathcal{T}}$.

$\widehat{\pi} := \widehat{\mathsf{Pub}}(\widehat{pk}_\rho, x, w) \in \widehat{\Pi}$.

$\widetilde{\pi} := \widetilde{\mathsf{Pub}}(\widetilde{pk}_\rho, x, w, \tau) \in \widetilde{\Pi}$.

$\Rightarrow C := (x, d, \widehat{\pi}, \widetilde{\pi})$.

$M / \bot \leftarrow \mathsf{Dec}(SK, C):$

Parse $C = (x, d, \widehat{\pi}', \widetilde{\pi}')$.

$M := d - \mathsf{Priv}(sk, x) \in \Pi$.

$\tau := \mathsf{H}(x, d) \in \widetilde{\mathcal{T}}$.

$\widehat{\pi} := \widehat{\mathsf{Priv}}(\widehat{sk}, x) \in \widehat{\Pi}$.

$\widetilde{\pi} := \widetilde{\mathsf{Priv}}(\widetilde{sk}, x, \tau) \in \widetilde{\Pi}$.

$\Rightarrow$ If $\widehat{\pi}' = \widehat{\pi}$ and $\widetilde{\pi}' = \widetilde{\pi}$, Return M;

Else,   Return $\bot$.

Fig. 2. Generic construction of PKE from QAHPS, $\widehat{\mathsf{QAHPS}}$ and tag-based $\widetilde{\mathsf{QAHPS}}$.

Remark 6 (A More Efficient Variant). If $\widehat{\mathsf{QAHPS}}$ and tag-based $\widehat{\mathsf{QAHPS}}$ share the same hash value space (i.e., $\widehat{\Pi} = \widetilde{\Pi}$) and $\widehat{\Pi}$ $(= \widetilde{\Pi})$ is an (additive) group[7], the hash values $\widehat{\pi}$ and $\widetilde{\pi}$ can be combined into $\widehat{\pi} + \widetilde{\pi}$, thus saving one element from the ciphertext.

4.2 LR-CCA Security of PKE

In this subsection, we prove the LR-CCA security of our generic PKE construction in Fig. 2. The security proof and the concrete security bound also apply to the more efficient variant PKE as shown in Remark 6.

Theorem 1 (LR-CCA Security of PKE). *If (i) $\mathscr{L}$, $\mathscr{L}_0$ and $\mathscr{L}_1$ have hard subset membership problems, (ii) QAHPS is a κ-LR-weak-ardent QAHPS scheme for $\mathscr{L}$, $\widehat{\mathsf{QAHPS}}$ is a κ-LR-ardent QAHPS scheme for $\mathscr{L}$ and $\widetilde{\mathsf{QAHPS}}$ is a κ-LR-weak-ardent tag-based QAHPS scheme for $\mathscr{L}$, which satisfy the properties listed in Table 2, (iii) QAHPS is $\mathscr{L}_0$-multi-extracting, (iv) $\mathcal{H}$ is a collision-resistant function family, then the proposed PKE scheme in Fig. 2 is κ-LR-CCA secure.*

Concretely, for any adversary $\mathcal{A}$ who makes at most Q_e times of ENC queries and Q_d times of DEC queries, there exist adversaries $\mathcal{B}_1, \cdots, \mathcal{B}_5$, such that $\mathbf{T}(\mathcal{B}_1) \approx \mathbf{T}(\mathcal{B}_4) \approx \mathbf{T}(\mathcal{B}_5) \approx \mathbf{T}(\mathcal{A}) + (Q_e + Q_d) \cdot \mathsf{poly}(\lambda)$, $\mathbf{T}(\mathcal{B}_2) \approx \mathbf{T}(\mathcal{B}_3) \approx \mathbf{T}(\mathcal{A}) + (Q_e + Q_e \cdot Q_d) \cdot \mathsf{poly}(\lambda)$, with $\mathsf{poly}(\lambda)$ independent of $\mathbf{T}(\mathcal{A})$, and

$$\mathsf{Adv}_{\mathsf{PKE},\mathcal{A}}^{\kappa\text{-}lr\text{-}cca}(\lambda) \le \mathsf{Adv}_{\mathscr{L},\mathcal{B}_1}^{Q_e\text{-}msmp}(\lambda) + (2n+1) \cdot \mathsf{Adv}_{\mathscr{L}_0,\mathcal{B}_2}^{Q_e\text{-}msmp}(\lambda) + 2n \cdot \mathsf{Adv}_{\mathscr{L}_1,\mathcal{B}_3}^{Q_e\text{-}msmp}(\lambda)$$
$$+ \mathsf{Adv}_{\mathcal{H},\mathcal{B}_4}^{cr}(\lambda) + \mathsf{Adv}_{\mathsf{QAHPS},\mathcal{B}_5}^{Q_e\text{-}\mathscr{L}_0\text{-}mext}(\lambda)$$
$$+ (3 + Q_d + Q_d Q_e + n(Q_d + Q_e + Q_d Q_e)) \cdot 2^{-\Omega(\lambda)}, \text{ for } n = \lceil \log Q_e \rceil.$$

Remark 7. The last term $(\ldots) \cdot 2^{-\Omega(\lambda)}$ in the above security bound encompasses the statistical differences introduced by the LR-universal and LR-key-switching properties of the three QAHPS schemes. We stress that only factors of computational reductions matter to the tightness of a security reduction.

Proof of Theorem 1. We prove the theorem by defining a sequence of games $\mathsf{G}_0 - \mathsf{G}_6$ and showing adjacent games indistinguishable. A brief description of differences between adjacent games is summarized in Table 3.

Game G_0: This is the κ-lr-cca security game (cf. Fig. 1). Let Win denote the event that $\beta' = \beta$. By definition, $\mathsf{Adv}_{\mathsf{PKE},\mathcal{A}}^{\kappa\text{-}lr\text{-}cca}(\lambda) = \left| \mathrm{Pr}_0[\mathsf{Win}] - \frac{1}{2} \right|$.

In this game, when answering an ENC query (M_0, M_1), the challenger samples $x^* \leftarrow_{\$} \mathcal{L}_\rho$ with witness w^*, computes $d^* := \mathsf{Pub}(pk_\rho, x^*, w^*) + M_\beta \in \Pi$, $\tau^* := \mathsf{H}(x^*, d^*) \in \widetilde{\mathcal{T}}$, $\widehat{\pi}^* := \widehat{\mathsf{Pub}}(\widehat{pk}_\rho, x^*, w^*) \in \widehat{\Pi}$ and $\widetilde{\pi}^* := \widetilde{\mathsf{Pub}}(\widetilde{pk}_\rho, x^*, w^*, \tau^*) \in \widetilde{\Pi}$. Then, the challenger returns the challenge ciphertext $C^* = (x^*, d^*, \widehat{\pi}^*, \widetilde{\pi}^*)$ to the adversary $\mathcal{A}$ and puts C^* to a set $\mathcal{Q}_{\mathcal{ENC}}$. Upon a DEC query $C = (x, d, \widehat{\pi}', \widetilde{\pi}')$,

---

[7] In fact, this condition can be weakened by only requiring $\widehat{\Pi}$ and $\widetilde{\Pi}$ to be subsets of an (additive) group.

Table 3. Brief Description of Games $G_0 - G_6$ for the κ-LR-CCA security proof of PKE. Here column "ENC" suggests how the challenge ciphertext $C^* = (x^*, d^*, \widehat{\pi}^*, \widetilde{\pi}^*)$ is generated: sub-column "x^* from" refers to the language from which x^* is chosen; sub-column "d^* using" (resp. "$\widehat{\pi}^*$ using", "$\widetilde{\pi}^*$ using") indicates the keys that are used in the computation of d^* (resp. $\widehat{\pi}^*$, $\widetilde{\pi}^*$). Column "DEC checks" describes the additional check made by DEC upon a decryption query $C = (x, d, \widehat{\pi}', \widetilde{\pi}')$, besides the routine check $C \notin \mathcal{Q}_{\mathcal{ENC}} \wedge \widehat{\pi}' = \widehat{\pi} \wedge \widetilde{\pi}' = \widetilde{\pi}$; DEC outputs $\perp$ if the check fails.

	ENC			DEC checks	Remark/Assumption
	x^* from	d^* using	$\widehat{\pi}^*$ using	$\widetilde{\pi}^*$ using		
G_0	$\mathcal{L}_\rho$	pk_ρ	$\widehat{pk}_\rho$	$\widetilde{pk}_\rho$		κ-LR-CCA game
G_1	$\mathcal{L}_\rho$	sk	$\widehat{sk}$	$\widetilde{sk}$		perfect correctness of QAHPS, $\widehat{\text{QAHPS}}$, $\widetilde{\text{QAHPS}}$
G_2	$\mathcal{L}_\rho$	sk	$\widehat{sk}$	$\widetilde{sk}$	$\tau \notin \mathcal{Q}_{\mathcal{TAG}}$	collision-resistance of $\mathcal{H}$
G_3	$\mathcal{L}_{\rho 0}$	sk	$\widehat{sk}$	$\widetilde{sk}$	$\tau \notin \mathcal{Q}_{\mathcal{TAG}}$	multi-fold SMP of $\mathcal{L}$ and $\mathcal{L}_0$
G_4	$\mathcal{L}_{\rho 0}$	sk	$\widehat{sk}$	$\widetilde{sk}$	$\tau \notin \mathcal{Q}_{\mathcal{TAG}}, x \in \mathcal{L}_\rho$	Lemma 2 (Rejection Lemma)
G_5	$\mathcal{L}_{\rho 0}$	sk'	$\widehat{sk}$	$\widetilde{sk}$	$\tau \notin \mathcal{Q}_{\mathcal{TAG}}, x \in \mathcal{L}_\rho$	LR-$\langle \mathcal{L}, \mathcal{L}_0 \rangle$-key-switching of QAHPS
G_6	$\mathcal{L}_{\rho 0}$	$=$ rand	$\widehat{sk}$	$\widetilde{sk}$	$\tau \notin \mathcal{Q}_{\mathcal{TAG}}, x \in \mathcal{L}_\rho$	$\mathcal{L}_0$-multi-extracting of QAHPS

the challenger answers $\mathcal{A}$ as follows. Compute $M := d - \mathsf{Priv}(sk, x) \in \Pi$, $\tau := \mathsf{H}(x, d) \in \mathcal{T}$, $\widehat{\pi} := \widehat{\mathsf{Priv}}(\widehat{sk}, x) \in \widehat{\Pi}$ and $\widetilde{\pi} := \widetilde{\mathsf{Priv}}(\widetilde{sk}, x, \tau) \in \widetilde{\Pi}$. If $C \notin \mathcal{Q}_{\mathcal{ENC}} \wedge \widehat{\pi}' = \widehat{\pi} \wedge \widetilde{\pi}' = \widetilde{\pi}$, return M; otherwise return $\perp$.

Game G_1: It is the same as G_0, except that, when answering $\mathsf{ENC}(M_0, M_1)$, the challenger computes d^*, $\widehat{\pi}^*$ and $\widetilde{\pi}^*$ directly using the secret key $\mathsf{SK} = (sk, \widehat{sk}, \widetilde{sk})$:

- $d^* := \mathsf{Priv}(sk, x^*) + M_\beta \in \Pi$,
- $\widehat{\pi}^* := \widehat{\mathsf{Priv}}(\widehat{sk}, x^*) \in \widehat{\Pi}$ and $\widetilde{\pi}^* := \widetilde{\mathsf{Priv}}(\widetilde{sk}, x^*, \tau^*) \in \widetilde{\Pi}$.

Since $x^* \in \mathcal{L}_\rho$ with witness w^*, by the perfect correctness of QAHPS, $\widehat{\text{QAHPS}}$ and $\widetilde{\text{QAHPS}}$, the changes are just conceptual. Consequently, $\Pr_0[\mathsf{Win}] = \Pr_1[\mathsf{Win}]$.

Game G_2: It is the same as G_1, except that, when answering $\mathsf{ENC}(M_0, M_1)$, the challenger also puts τ^* to a set $\mathcal{Q}_{\mathcal{TAG}}$, and when answering $\mathsf{DEC}\big(C = (x, d, \widehat{\pi}', \widetilde{\pi}')\big)$, the challenger adds the following new rejection rule:

- If $\tau \in \mathcal{Q}_{\mathcal{TAG}}$, return $\perp$ directly.

Claim 1. $\big| \Pr_1[\mathsf{Win}] - \Pr_2[\mathsf{Win}] \big| \leq \mathsf{Adv}_{\mathcal{H}}^{cr}(\lambda)$.

Proof. By Coll denote the event that $\mathcal{A}$ ever queries $\mathsf{DEC}\big(C = (x, d, \widehat{\pi}', \widetilde{\pi}')\big)$ s.t.

$$\exists\, C^* = (x^*, d^*, \widehat{\pi}^*, \widetilde{\pi}^*) \in \mathcal{Q}_{\mathcal{ENC}}, \text{ s.t. } C = (x, d, \widehat{\pi}', \widetilde{\pi}') \neq (x^*, d^*, \widehat{\pi}^*, \widetilde{\pi}^*) = C^*$$
$$\wedge\ \widehat{\pi}' = \widehat{\pi} \wedge \widetilde{\pi}' = \widetilde{\pi} \wedge \tau = \mathsf{H}(x, d) = \mathsf{H}(x^*, d^*) = \tau^* \in \mathcal{Q}_{\mathcal{TAG}}.$$

Clearly, G_1 and G_2 are the same until Coll occurs, therefore $\big| \Pr_1[\mathsf{Win}] - \Pr_2[\mathsf{Win}] \big| \leq \Pr_2[\mathsf{Coll}]$. Note that $(x, d) = (x^*, d^*)$ implies $(\widehat{\pi}, \widetilde{\pi}) = (\widehat{\pi}^*, \widetilde{\pi}^*)$. Hence Coll happens if and only if $(x, d) \neq (x^*, d^*)$, which suggests a collision.

Thus, $\big| \Pr_1[\mathsf{Win}] - \Pr_2[\mathsf{Win}] \big| \leq \Pr_2[\mathsf{Coll}] \leq \mathsf{Adv}_{\mathcal{H}}^{cr}(\lambda)$, and Claim 1 follows. ∎

Game G_3: This game is the same as game G_2, except that, in INITIALIZE, the challenger picks $(\rho_0, td_0) \leftarrow_\$ \mathscr{L}_0$ as well, and for all the ENC queries, the challenger samples $x^* \leftarrow_\$ \mathcal{L}_{\rho_0}$ instead of $x^* \leftarrow_\$ \mathcal{L}_\rho$.

Claim 2. $\left| \Pr_2[\text{Win}] - \Pr_3[\text{Win}] \right| \leq \text{Adv}_{\mathscr{L}}^{Q_e\text{-}msmp}(\lambda) + \text{Adv}_{\mathscr{L}_0}^{Q_e\text{-}msmp}(\lambda).$

Proof. We introduce an intermediate game $G_{2.5}$ between G_2 and G_3:

- **Game** $G_{2.5}$: It is the same as game G_2, except that $x^* \leftarrow_\$ \mathcal{X}$ in ENC.

Since witness w^* for x^* is not used at all in games G_2, $G_{2.5}$ and G_3, we can directly construct two adversaries $\mathcal{B}$ and $\mathcal{B}'$ for solving the multi-fold SMP related to $\mathscr{L}$ and the multi-fold SMP related to $\mathscr{L}_0$ respectively, so that $\left| \Pr_2[\text{Win}] - \Pr_{2.5}[\text{Win}] \right| \leq \text{Adv}_{\mathscr{L},\mathcal{B}}^{Q_e\text{-}msmp}(\lambda)$ and $\left| \Pr_{2.5}[\text{Win}] - \Pr_3[\text{Win}] \right| \leq \text{Adv}_{\mathscr{L}_0,\mathcal{B}'}^{Q_e\text{-}msmp}(\lambda)$. ∎

Game G_4: This game is the same as game G_3, except that, when answering $\text{DEC}\big(C = (x, d, \widehat{\pi}', \widetilde{\pi}')\big)$, the challenger adds another new rejection rule:

- If $x \notin \mathcal{L}_\rho$, return $\bot$ directly.

Lemma 2 (Rejection Lemma). *For $n = \lceil \log Q_e \rceil$,* $\left| \Pr_3[\text{Win}] - \Pr_4[\text{Win}] \right| \leq 2n \cdot \big(\text{Adv}_{\mathscr{L}_0}^{Q_e\text{-}msmp}(\lambda) + \text{Adv}_{\mathscr{L}_1}^{Q_e\text{-}msmp}(\lambda) \big) + (2 + Q_d + Q_d Q_e + n \cdot (Q_d + Q_e + Q_d Q_e)) \cdot 2^{-\Omega(\lambda)}.$

The proof of Lemma 2 appears in our full version [22] due to lack of space. We stress that this proof is very modular and relies on the LR-ardency of the three QAHPS schemes. Technically speaking, we modified and adapted the latest partitioning techniques in [19] (which in turn built upon [17,18,24]) for our strategy, so that the hash values $\widetilde{\pi} = \widetilde{\Lambda}_{\widetilde{sk}}(x, \tau)$ for $x \notin \mathcal{L}_\rho$ are fully randomized to $\widetilde{\pi} = \widetilde{\Lambda}_{\mathsf{RF}(ctr)}(x, \tau)$ by $\mathsf{RF}(ctr)$, where RF is a random function. This is accomplished in only $O(\log Q_e) = O(\log \lambda)$ steps. Each step is moved forward from $\mathsf{RF}_i(ctr_{|i})$ to $\mathsf{RF}_{i+1}(ctr_{|i+1})$, making use of the LR-universal and LR-key-switching properties of $\mathsf{QAHPS}, \widehat{\mathsf{QAHPS}}$ and $\widetilde{\mathsf{QAHPS}}$, together with language switching among $\mathcal{L}_\rho$, $\mathcal{L}_{\rho_0}$ and $\mathcal{L}_{\rho_1}$ (cf. Subsect. 1.1).

Game G_5: It is the same as G_4, except that, in INITIALIZE, the challenger picks another $sk' \leftarrow_\$ \mathcal{SK}$ besides sk, and when answering $\text{ENC}(M_0, M_1)$, the challenger computes d^* using sk' rather than sk:

- $d^* := \mathsf{Priv}(sk', x^*) + M_\beta \in \Pi.$

The challenger still uses sk to compute the public key in INITIALIZE and to answer DEC queries.

Claim 3. $|\Pr_4[\text{Win}] - \Pr_5[\text{Win}]| \leq 2^{-\Omega(\lambda)}.$

Proof. We analyze the information about sk (resp. sk and sk') that $\mathcal{A}$ may obtain in G_4 (resp. G_5).

- In INITIALIZE, $\mathcal{A}$ obtains $pk_\rho = \alpha_\rho(sk)$ from the public key PK.
- In ENC, since $x^* \leftarrow_\$ \mathcal{L}_{\rho_0}$, the behavior of ENC is completely determined by $\alpha_{\rho_0}(sk)$ (resp. $\boxed{\alpha_{\rho_0}(sk')}$).
- In DEC, the challenger will not output M unless $x \in \mathcal{L}_\rho$ (due to the new rejection rule added in G_4), thus the behavior of DEC is completely determined by $\alpha_\rho(sk)$.
- From oracle LEAK(L), $\mathcal{A}$ obtains at most κ-bit information of sk.

Note that, L is indeed independent of ρ_0. The reason is as follows: (1) ρ_0 is used only in ENC; (2) $\mathcal{A}$ is not allowed to query LEAK as long as it has queried ENC.

By the κ-LR-$\langle \mathcal{L}, \mathcal{L}_0 \rangle$-key-switching property of QAHPS (cf. (4)), we have

$$\Delta\big((\rho_0, \boxed{\alpha_{\rho_0}(sk)}) , (\rho_0, \boxed{\alpha_{\rho_0}(sk')}) \mid \alpha_\rho(sk), L(sk) \big) \ \leq \ 2^{-\Omega(\lambda)}.$$

Thus, $|\mathrm{Pr}_4[\mathsf{Win}] - \mathrm{Pr}_5[\mathsf{Win}]| \leq 2^{-\Omega(\lambda)}$, and Claim 3 follows. $\blacksquare$

Game G_6: This game is the same as game G_5, except that, for all the ENC queries, the challenger samples $d^* \leftarrow_\$ \Pi$ uniformly at random.

Claim 4. $\big| \mathrm{Pr}_5[\mathsf{Win}] - \mathrm{Pr}_6[\mathsf{Win}] \big| \leq \mathsf{Adv}_{\mathsf{QAHPS}}^{Q_e - \mathcal{L}_0 - mext}(\lambda)$.

Proof. The difference between G_5 and G_6 lies in ENC and can be characterized by the following two distributions:

- G_5: $\big(x_j^* \leftarrow_\$ \mathcal{L}_{\rho_0}, \ d_j^* := \boxed{\mathsf{Priv}(sk', x_j^*)} + M_{\beta,j} \in \Pi \big)_{j \in [Q_e]}$,
- G_6: $\big(x_j^* \leftarrow_\$ \mathcal{L}_{\rho_0}, \ d_j^* \leftarrow_\$ \Pi \big)_{j \in [Q_e]}$,

where x_j^*, d_j^*, $M_{\beta,j}$ denote the x^*, d^*, M_β in the j-th ENC query, respectively.

We note that sk' is used only in the computations of d^* in ENC. By the $\mathcal{L}_0$-multi-extracting property of QAHPS, the above two distributions are computationally indistinguishable. Consequently, Claim 4 follows. $\blacksquare$

Finally in game G_6, d^* is uniformly chosen from Π regardless of the value of β, thus the challenge bit β is completely hidden to $\mathcal{A}$. Then $\mathrm{Pr}_6[\mathsf{Win}] = \frac{1}{2}$. Taking all things together, Theorem 1 follows. $\square$

5   Instantiations over Asymmetric Pairing Groups

Now we instantiate our generic PKE construction in Sect. 4 based on the matrix DDH assumptions over asymmetric pairing groups. Specifically, we present the instantiations of the language distributions $\mathscr{L}, \mathscr{L}_0, \mathscr{L}_1$, the LR-weak-ardent QAHPS, the LR-ardent $\widehat{\mathsf{QAHPS}}$, the LR-weak-ardent tag-based $\widetilde{\mathsf{QAHPS}}$ and the resulting scheme $\mathsf{PKE}_{\mathsf{asym}}^{\mathsf{lr}}$, in Subsects. 5.2, 5.3, 5.4, 5.5, and 5.6, respectively.

In the full version [22], we also show instantiations of $\mathscr{L}, \mathscr{L}_0, \mathscr{L}_1$, QAHPS, $\widehat{\mathsf{QAHPS}}, \widetilde{\mathsf{QAHPS}}$ and $\mathsf{PKE}_{\mathsf{sym}}^{\mathsf{lr}}$ over symmetric pairing groups.

5.1   The Language Distribution for Linear Subspaces

Let $\mathcal{PG} = (\mathbb{G}_1, \mathbb{G}_2, \mathbb{G}_T, p, e, P_1, P_2, P_T)$ be an asymmetric pairing group. For any matrix distribution $\mathcal{D}_{\ell,k}$, which outputs matrices in $\mathbb{Z}_p^{\ell \times k}$, it naturally gives rise to a language distribution $\mathscr{L}_{\mathcal{D}_{\ell,k}}$ for linear subspaces over groups $\mathbb{G}_1$ and $\mathbb{G}_2$:

- $\mathscr{L}_{\mathcal{D}_{\ell,k}}$ invokes $\mathbf{A}_1, \mathbf{A}_2 \leftarrow_{\$} \mathcal{D}_{\ell,k}$, and outputs a language parameter $\rho = ([\mathbf{A}_1]_1, [\mathbf{A}_2]_2) \in \mathbb{G}_1^{\ell \times k} \times \mathbb{G}_2^{\ell \times k}$ together with a trapdoor $td = (\mathbf{A}_1, \mathbf{A}_2)$.

The matrix ρ defines a linear subspace language $\mathcal{L}_\rho$ on $\mathbb{G}_1^\ell \times \mathbb{G}_2^\ell$:[8]

$$\mathcal{L}_\rho = \left\{ ([\mathbf{c}_1]_1, [\mathbf{c}_2]_2) \mid \exists\, \mathbf{w}_1, \mathbf{w}_2 \in \mathbb{Z}_p^k \setminus \{\mathbf{0}\}, \text{ s.t. } [\mathbf{c}_1]_1 = [\mathbf{A}_1 \mathbf{w}_1]_1 \wedge [\mathbf{c}_2]_2 = [\mathbf{A}_2 \mathbf{w}_2]_2 \right\}$$
$$= \mathsf{span}([\mathbf{A}_1]_1) \times \mathsf{span}([\mathbf{A}_2]_2) \subseteq \mathcal{X} = \left(\mathbb{G}_1^\ell \setminus \{[\mathbf{0}]_1\} \right) \times \left(\mathbb{G}_2^\ell \setminus \{[\mathbf{0}]_2\} \right).$$

The trapdoor td can be used to decide whether or not an instance $([\mathbf{c}_1]_1, [\mathbf{c}_2]_2)$ is in $\mathcal{L}_\rho$ efficiently: with $td = (\mathbf{A}_1, \mathbf{A}_2)$, one can first compute a basis of the kernel space of $\mathbf{A}_1^\top$ (resp. $\mathbf{A}_2^\top$), namely $\mathbf{A}_1^\perp \in \mathbb{Z}_p^{\ell \times (\ell-k)}$ satisfying $\mathbf{A}_1^\top \cdot \mathbf{A}_1^\perp = \mathbf{0}$ (resp. $\mathbf{A}_2^\perp \in \mathbb{Z}_p^{\ell \times (\ell-k)}$ satisfying $\mathbf{A}_2^\top \cdot \mathbf{A}_2^\perp = \mathbf{0}$), then check whether $[\mathbf{c}_1^\top]_1 \cdot \mathbf{A}_1^\perp = [\mathbf{0}]_1 \wedge [\mathbf{c}_2^\top]_2 \cdot \mathbf{A}_2^\perp = [\mathbf{0}]_2$ holds.

Clearly, the SMP related to $\mathscr{L}_{\mathcal{D}_{\ell,k}}$ corresponds to a hybrid of the $\mathcal{D}_{\ell,k}$-MDDH assumptions over $\mathbb{G}_1$ and $\mathbb{G}_2$, and the multi-fold SMP related to $\mathscr{L}_{\mathcal{D}_{\ell,k}}$ corresponds to a hybrid of the Q-fold $\mathcal{D}_{\ell,k}$-MDDH assumptions over $\mathbb{G}_1$ and $\mathbb{G}_2$ for any $Q = \mathsf{poly}(\lambda)$. The same also holds for the uniform distribution $\mathcal{U}_{\ell,k}$. Formally, we have the following lemma, which is a corollary of the random self-reducibility of $\mathcal{D}_{\ell,k}$-MDDH and $\mathcal{U}_{\ell,k}$-MDDH.

Lemma 3 ($\mathcal{D}_{\ell,k}/\mathcal{U}_{\ell,k}$-**MDDH** $\Rightarrow$ **Multi-fold SMP related to** $\mathscr{L}_{\mathcal{D}_{\ell,k}}/\mathscr{L}_{\mathcal{U}_{\ell,k}}$). *Let $Q > \ell - k$. For any adversary $\mathcal{A}$, there exist adversaries $\mathcal{B}_1$ and $\mathcal{B}_2$ such that $\mathbf{T}(\mathcal{B}_1) \approx \mathbf{T}(\mathcal{B}_2) \approx \mathbf{T}(\mathcal{A}) + Q \cdot \mathsf{poly}(\lambda)$ with $\mathsf{poly}(\lambda)$ independent of $\mathbf{T}(\mathcal{A})$, and $\mathsf{Adv}_{\mathscr{L}_{\mathcal{D}_{\ell,k}}, \mathcal{A}}^{Q\text{-}msmp}(\lambda) \leq (\ell-k) \cdot \mathsf{Adv}_{\mathcal{D}_{\ell,k}, \mathbb{G}_1, \mathcal{B}_1}^{mddh}(\lambda) + (\ell-k) \cdot \mathsf{Adv}_{\mathcal{D}_{\ell,k}, \mathbb{G}_2, \mathcal{B}_2}^{mddh}(\lambda) + 2/(p-1)$.*

For any adversary $\mathcal{A}$, there exist adversaries $\mathcal{B}_1$ and $\mathcal{B}_2$ such that $\mathbf{T}(\mathcal{B}_1) \approx \mathbf{T}(\mathcal{B}_2) \approx \mathbf{T}(\mathcal{A}) + Q \cdot \mathsf{poly}(\lambda)$ with $\mathsf{poly}(\lambda)$ independent of $\mathbf{T}(\mathcal{A})$, and

$$\mathsf{Adv}_{\mathscr{L}_{\mathcal{U}_{\ell,k}}, \mathcal{A}}^{Q\text{-}msmp}(\lambda) \leq \mathsf{Adv}_{\mathcal{U}_{\ell,k}, \mathbb{G}_1, \mathcal{B}_1}^{mddh}(\lambda) + \mathsf{Adv}_{\mathcal{U}_{\ell,k}, \mathbb{G}_2, \mathcal{B}_2}^{mddh}(\lambda) + 2/(p-1).$$

5.2   The Instantiation of Language Distributions

To instantiate the generic PKE construction in Sect. 4, the first thing we need to do is to determine three language distributions $\mathscr{L}$, $\mathscr{L}_0$ and $\mathscr{L}_1$ carefully.

Let $\ell \geq 2k+1$. Let $\mathcal{D}_{\ell,k}$ be an (arbitrary) matrix distribution, and $\mathcal{U}_{\ell,k}, \mathcal{U}'_{\ell,k}$ independent copies of the uniform distribution, all of which output matrices in $\mathbb{Z}_p^{\ell \times k}$. Based on the previous subsection, we designate the language distributions $\mathscr{L}$, $\mathscr{L}_0$ and $\mathscr{L}_1$ as follows.

---

[8] For technical reasons, the zero vector $[\mathbf{0}]_1$ (resp. $[\mathbf{0}]_2$) must be excluded from $\mathsf{span}([\mathbf{A}_1]_1)$ and $\mathbb{G}_1^\ell$ (resp. $\mathsf{span}([\mathbf{A}_2]_2)$ and $\mathbb{G}_2^\ell$). For the sake of simplicity, we forgo making this explicit in the sequel.

- $\mathscr{L} := \mathscr{L}_{\mathcal{D}_{\ell,k}}$, which invokes $\mathbf{A}_1, \mathbf{A}_2 \leftarrow_s \mathcal{D}_{\ell,k}$ and outputs $(\rho = ([\mathbf{A}_1]_1, [\mathbf{A}_2]_2),$ $td = (\mathbf{A}_1, \mathbf{A}_2))$;
- $\mathscr{L}_0 := \mathscr{L}_{\mathcal{U}_{\ell,k}}$, which invokes $\mathbf{A}_{0,1}, \mathbf{A}_{0,2} \leftarrow_s \mathcal{U}_{\ell,k}$ and outputs $(\rho_0 = ([\mathbf{A}_{0,1}]_1,$ $[\mathbf{A}_{0,2}]_2), td_0 = (\mathbf{A}_{0,1}, \mathbf{A}_{0,2}))$;
- $\mathscr{L}_1 := \mathscr{L}_{\mathcal{U}'_{\ell,k}}$, which invokes $\mathbf{A}_{1,1}, \mathbf{A}_{1,2} \leftarrow_s \mathcal{U}'_{\ell,k}$ and outputs $(\rho_1 = ([\mathbf{A}_{1,1}]_1,$ $[\mathbf{A}_{1,2}]_2), td_1 = (\mathbf{A}_{1,1}, \mathbf{A}_{1,2}))$.

5.3   The Instantiation of LR-Weak-Ardent QAHPS

We present the construction of $\mathsf{QAHPS} = (\mathsf{Setup}, \alpha_{(.)}, \mathsf{Pub}, \mathsf{Priv})$ for the language distribution $\mathscr{L}$ $(= \mathscr{L}_{\mathcal{D}_{\ell,k}})$ in Fig. 3. It is straightforward to check the perfect correctness of QAHPS.

$\underline{pp \leftarrow_s \mathsf{Setup}(1^\lambda)}:$	$pk_\rho \leftarrow \alpha_\rho(sk),$
$\mathcal{PG} = (\mathbb{G}_1, \mathbb{G}_2, \mathbb{G}_T, p, e, P_1, P_2, P_T) \leftarrow_s \mathsf{PGGen}(1^\lambda).$	where $\rho = ([\mathbf{A}_1]_1, [\mathbf{A}_2]_2) \in \mathbb{G}_1^{\ell \times k} \times \mathbb{G}_2^{\ell \times k}:$
$\Rightarrow pp := \mathcal{PG}$, which implicitly defines	Parse $sk = \mathbf{k} \in \mathbb{Z}_p^\ell.$
$(\mathcal{SK} := \mathbb{Z}_p^\ell, \ \Pi := \mathbb{G}_2, \ \Lambda_{(.)}),$	$[\mathbf{p}^\top]_2 := \mathbf{k}^\top \cdot [\mathbf{A}_2]_2 \in \mathbb{G}_2^{1 \times k}.$
where $\Lambda_{sk}([\mathbf{c}_1]_1, [\mathbf{c}_2]_2) := \mathbf{k}^\top \cdot [\mathbf{c}_2]_2 \in \mathbb{G}_2$ for	$\Rightarrow pk_\rho := [\mathbf{p}^\top]_2.$
any $sk = \mathbf{k} \in \mathbb{Z}_p^\ell$ and $([\mathbf{c}_1]_1, [\mathbf{c}_2]_2) \in \mathcal{X} = \mathbb{G}_1^\ell \times \mathbb{G}_2^\ell.$	
$[\pi]_2 \leftarrow \mathsf{Pub}(pk_\rho, ([\mathbf{c}_1]_1, [\mathbf{c}_2]_2), (\mathbf{w}_1, \mathbf{w}_2) \in \mathbb{Z}_p^k \times \mathbb{Z}_p^k),$	$[\pi]_2 \leftarrow \mathsf{Priv}(sk, ([\mathbf{c}_1]_1, [\mathbf{c}_2]_2) \in \mathcal{X}):$
where $([\mathbf{c}_1]_1, [\mathbf{c}_2]_2) \in \mathcal{L}_\rho$ for $\rho = ([\mathbf{A}_1]_1, [\mathbf{A}_2]_2):$	Parse $sk = \mathbf{k} \in \mathbb{Z}_p^\ell.$
Parse $pk_\rho = [\mathbf{p}^\top]_2 \in \mathbb{G}_2^{1 \times k}.$	$\Rightarrow [\pi]_2 := \mathbf{k}^\top \cdot [\mathbf{c}_2]_2 \in \mathbb{G}_2.$
$\Rightarrow [\pi]_2 := [\mathbf{p}^\top]_2 \cdot \mathbf{w}_2 \in \mathbb{G}_2.$	

Fig. 3. Construction of LR-weak-ardent QAHPS over asymmetric pairing groups.

Theorem 2 ($\mathscr{L}_0$-Multi-Extracting of QAHPS). *If the $\mathcal{U}_{k+1,k}$-MDDH assumption holds over $\mathbb{G}_2$, then the proposed QAHPS in Fig. 3 is $\mathscr{L}_0$-multi-extracting, where the language distribution $\mathscr{L}_0$ $(= \mathscr{L}_{\mathcal{U}_{\ell,k}})$ is specified in Subsect. 5.2.*

Concretely, for any adversary $\mathcal{A}$, any polynomial $Q = \mathsf{poly}(\lambda)$, there exists an adversary $\mathcal{B}$, such that $\mathbf{T}(\mathcal{B}) \approx \mathbf{T}(\mathcal{A}) + Q \cdot \mathsf{poly}(\lambda)$ with $\mathsf{poly}(\lambda)$ independent of $\mathbf{T}(\mathcal{A})$, and $\mathsf{Adv}_{\mathsf{QAHPS}, \mathcal{A}}^{Q-\mathscr{L}_0-mext}(\lambda) \leq \mathsf{Adv}_{\mathcal{U}_{k+1,k}, \mathbb{G}_2, \mathcal{B}}^{mddh}(\lambda) + 1/(p-1).$

The proof of Theorem 2 is in the full version [22] due to the space limitation.

The LR-weak-ardency of QAHPS follows from the theorem below. The proof of the theorem is quite similar to that for Theorem 4 (to be described later), thus we omit it here and put it in the full version [22].

Theorem 3 (LR-weak-ardency of QAHPS). *Let $\ell \geq 2k + 1$ and $\kappa \leq \log p - \Omega(\lambda)$. The proposed QAHPS for $\mathscr{L}$ in Fig. 3 satisfies the properties listed in Table 2, i.e., (1) it is perfectly $\langle \perp, \perp \rangle$-universal and (2) it supports κ-LR-$\langle \mathscr{L}, \mathscr{L}_0 \rangle$-key-switching, where the language distributions $\mathscr{L} = \mathscr{L}_{\mathcal{D}_{\ell,k}}$ and $\mathscr{L}_0 = \mathscr{L}_{\mathcal{U}_{\ell,k}}$ are specified in Subsect. 5.2.*

5.4   The Instantiation of LR-Ardent QAHPS

We present the construction of $\widehat{\mathsf{QAHPS}} = (\widehat{\mathsf{Setup}}, \widehat{\alpha}_{(\cdot)}, \widehat{\mathsf{Pub}}, \widehat{\mathsf{Priv}})$ for $\mathscr{L}\ (= \mathscr{L}_{\mathcal{D}_{\ell,k}})$ in Fig. 4. It is straightforward to check the perfect correctness of $\widehat{\mathsf{QAHPS}}$. The construction is inspired by the "OR-proof" proposed in [1] and the QA-NIZK for linear subspaces proposed in [28].

$\widehat{pp} \leftarrow_{\$} \widehat{\mathsf{Setup}}(1^\lambda)$:

$\mathcal{PG} = (\mathbb{G}_1, \mathbb{G}_2, \mathbb{G}_T, p, e, P_1, P_2, P_T) \leftarrow_{\$} \mathsf{PGGen}(1^\lambda)$.

$\Rightarrow \widehat{pp} := \mathcal{PG}$, which implicitly defines

$\qquad (\widehat{\mathcal{SK}} := \mathbb{Z}_p^{\ell \times \ell}, \ \widehat{\Pi} := \mathbb{G}_T, \ \widehat{\Lambda}_{(\cdot)})$,

where $\widehat{\Lambda}_{\widehat{sk}}([\mathbf{c}_1]_1, [\mathbf{c}_2]_2) := [\mathbf{c}_2]_2^\top \cdot \widehat{\mathbf{K}} \cdot [\mathbf{c}_1]_1 \in \mathbb{G}_T$ for

any $\widehat{sk} = \widehat{\mathbf{K}} \in \mathbb{Z}_p^{\ell \times \ell}$ and $([\mathbf{c}_1]_1, [\mathbf{c}_2]_2) \in \mathcal{X} = \mathbb{G}_1^\ell \times \mathbb{G}_2^\ell$.

$\widehat{pk}_\rho \leftarrow \widehat{\alpha}_\rho(\widehat{sk})$,

where $\rho = ([\mathbf{A}_1]_1, [\mathbf{A}_2]_2) \in \mathbb{G}_1^{\ell \times k} \times \mathbb{G}_2^{\ell \times k}$:

Parse $\widehat{sk} = \widehat{\mathbf{K}} \in \mathbb{Z}_p^{\ell \times \ell}$.

$[\widehat{\mathbf{P}}]_T := [\mathbf{A}_2]_2^\top \cdot \widehat{\mathbf{K}} \cdot [\mathbf{A}_1]_1 \in \mathbb{G}_T^{k \times k}$.

$\Rightarrow \widehat{pk}_\rho := [\widehat{\mathbf{P}}]_T$.

$[\widehat{\pi}]_T \leftarrow \widehat{\mathsf{Pub}}(\widehat{pk}_\rho, ([\mathbf{c}_1]_1, [\mathbf{c}_2]_2), (\mathbf{w}_1, \mathbf{w}_2) \in \mathbb{Z}_p^k \times \mathbb{Z}_p^k)$,

where $([\mathbf{c}_1]_1, [\mathbf{c}_2]_2) \in \mathcal{L}_\rho$ for $\rho = ([\mathbf{A}_1]_1, [\mathbf{A}_2]_2)$:

Parse $\widehat{pk}_\rho = [\widehat{\mathbf{P}}]_T \in \mathbb{G}_T^{k \times k}$.

$\Rightarrow [\widehat{\pi}]_T := \mathbf{w}_2^\top \cdot [\widehat{\mathbf{P}}]_T \cdot \mathbf{w}_1 \in \mathbb{G}_T$.

$[\widehat{\pi}]_T \leftarrow \widehat{\mathsf{Priv}}(\widehat{sk}, ([\mathbf{c}_1]_1, [\mathbf{c}_2]_2) \subset \mathcal{X})$:

Parse $\widehat{sk} = \widehat{\mathbf{K}} \in \mathbb{Z}_p^{\ell \times \ell}$.

$\Rightarrow [\widehat{\pi}]_T := [\mathbf{c}_2]_2^\top \cdot \widehat{\mathbf{K}} \cdot [\mathbf{c}_1]_1 \in \mathbb{G}_T$.

Fig. 4. Construction of LR-ardent $\widehat{\mathsf{QAHPS}}$ over asymmetric pairing groups.

The hash function $\widehat{\Lambda}_{\widehat{sk}}([\mathbf{c}_1]_1, [\mathbf{c}_2]_2)$ multiplies $\widehat{\mathbf{K}}$ with $[\mathbf{c}_1]_1$ and $[\mathbf{c}_2]_2$.

Theorem 4 (LR-ardency of $\widehat{\mathsf{QAHPS}}$). *Let $\ell \geq 2k + 1$ and $\kappa \leq \log p - \Omega(\lambda)$. The proposed $\widehat{\mathsf{QAHPS}}$ scheme for $\mathscr{L}$ in Fig. 4 satisfies the properties listed in Table 2, more precisely, (1) it is κ-LR-$\langle \mathscr{L}, \mathscr{L}_0 \rangle$- and perfectly $\langle \mathscr{L}_0, \mathscr{L}_1 \rangle$-universal and (2) it supports κ-LR-$\langle \mathscr{L}, \mathscr{L}_0 \rangle$-key-switching, where the language distributions $\mathscr{L} = \mathscr{L}_{\mathcal{D}_{\ell,k}}$, $\mathscr{L}_0 = \mathscr{L}_{\mathcal{U}_{\ell,k}}$ and $\mathscr{L}_1 = \mathscr{L}_{\mathcal{U}'_{\ell,k}}$ are specified in Subsect. 5.2.*

Proof of Theorem 4.

[Perfectly $\langle \mathscr{L}, \mathscr{L}_0 \rangle$-Universal.] Let $(\rho = ([\mathbf{A}_1]_1, [\mathbf{A}_2]_2) \in \mathbb{G}_1^{\ell \times k} \times \mathbb{G}_2^{\ell \times k}, td) \leftarrow_{\$} \mathscr{L}$ and $(\rho_0 = ([\mathbf{A}_{0,1}]_1, [\mathbf{A}_{0,2}]_2) \in \mathbb{G}_1^{\ell \times k} \times \mathbb{G}_2^{\ell \times k}, td_0) \leftarrow_{\$} \mathscr{L}_0$. With overwhelming probability $1 - 2^{-\Omega(\lambda)}$, both $(\mathbf{A}_1, \mathbf{A}_{0,1}) \in \mathbb{Z}_p^{\ell \times 2k}$ and $(\mathbf{A}_2, \mathbf{A}_{0,2}) \in \mathbb{Z}_p^{\ell \times 2k}$ are of full column rank. For $\widehat{sk} = \widehat{\mathbf{K}} \leftarrow_{\$} \mathbb{Z}_p^{\ell \times \ell}$ and any $([\mathbf{c}_1]_1, [\mathbf{c}_2]_2) \in \mathcal{X} \setminus (\mathcal{L}_\rho \cup \mathcal{L}_{\rho_0})$, we consider the distribution of $\widehat{\Lambda}_{\widehat{sk}}([\mathbf{c}_1]_1, [\mathbf{c}_2]_2)$ conditioned on $\widehat{pk}_\rho = \widehat{\alpha}_\rho(\widehat{sk})$ and $\widehat{pk}_{\rho_0} = \widehat{\alpha}_{\rho_0}(\widehat{sk})$.

Let $\mathbf{a}_1^\perp \in \mathbb{Z}_p^\ell$ (resp. $\mathbf{a}_2^\perp \in \mathbb{Z}_p^\ell$, $\mathbf{a}_{0,1}^\perp \in \mathbb{Z}_p^\ell$, $\mathbf{a}_{0,2}^\perp \in \mathbb{Z}_p^\ell$) be an arbitrary non-zero vector in the kernel space of $\mathbf{A}_1^\top$ (resp. $\mathbf{A}_2^\top$, $\mathbf{A}_{0,1}^\top$, $\mathbf{A}_{0,2}^\top$) such that $\mathbf{A}_1^\top \cdot \mathbf{a}_1^\perp = \mathbf{0}$ (resp. $\mathbf{A}_2^\top \cdot \mathbf{a}_2^\perp = \mathbf{0}$, $\mathbf{A}_{0,1}^\top \cdot \mathbf{a}_{0,1}^\perp = \mathbf{0}$, $\mathbf{A}_{0,2}^\top \cdot \mathbf{a}_{0,2}^\perp = \mathbf{0}$) holds. For the convenience of our analysis, we sample $\widehat{sk} = \widehat{\mathbf{K}} \leftarrow_{\$} \mathbb{Z}_p^{\ell \times \ell}$ equivalently via $\widehat{sk} = \widehat{\mathbf{K}} := \widetilde{\mathbf{K}} + \mu_1 \cdot \mathbf{a}_{0,2}^\perp \cdot (\mathbf{a}_1^\perp)^\top + \mu_2 \cdot \mathbf{a}_2^\perp \cdot (\mathbf{a}_{0,1}^\perp)^\top \in \mathbb{Z}_p^{\ell \times \ell}$, where $\widetilde{\mathbf{K}} \leftarrow_{\$} \mathbb{Z}_p^{\ell \times \ell}$ and $\mu_1, \mu_2 \leftarrow_{\$} \mathbb{Z}_p$. Consequently, we have $\widehat{pk}_\rho = \widehat{\alpha}_\rho(\widehat{sk}) = [\mathbf{A}_2]_2^\top \cdot \widehat{\mathbf{K}} \cdot [\mathbf{A}_1]_1 = [\mathbf{A}_2]_2^\top \cdot \widetilde{\mathbf{K}} \cdot [\mathbf{A}_1]_1$, $\widehat{pk}_{\rho_0} = \widehat{\alpha}_{\rho_0}(\widehat{sk}) = [\mathbf{A}_{0,2}]_2^\top \cdot \widehat{\mathbf{K}} \cdot [\mathbf{A}_{0,1}]_1 = [\mathbf{A}_{0,2}]_2^\top \cdot \widetilde{\mathbf{K}} \cdot [\mathbf{A}_{0,1}]_1$, which may leak $\widetilde{\mathbf{K}}$, but μ_1 and μ_2 are completely hidden. Besides,

$$\widehat{\Lambda}_{\widehat{sk}}([\mathbf{c}_1]_1, [\mathbf{c}_2]_2) = [\mathbf{c}_2]_2^\top \cdot \widehat{\mathbf{K}} \cdot [\mathbf{c}_1]_1$$
$$= [\mathbf{c}_2]_2^\top \cdot \widetilde{\mathbf{K}} \cdot [\mathbf{c}_1]_1 + \boxed{\mu_1 \cdot [\mathbf{c}_2^\top \mathbf{a}_{0,2}^\perp]_2 \cdot [\mathbf{c}_1^\top \mathbf{a}_1^\perp]_1^\top} + \boxed{\mu_2 \cdot [\mathbf{c}_2^\top \mathbf{a}_2^\perp]_2 \cdot [\mathbf{c}_1^\top \mathbf{a}_{0,1}^\perp]_1^\top}.$$

We divide the condition $([\mathbf{c}_1]_1, [\mathbf{c}_2]_2) \in \mathcal{X} \setminus (\mathcal{L}_\rho \cup \mathcal{L}_{\rho_0})$ into three cases:

- Case I: $[\mathbf{c}_1]_1 \in \mathsf{span}([\mathbf{A}_1]_1)$.
  It must hold that $[\mathbf{c}_1]_1 \notin \mathsf{span}([\mathbf{A}_{0,1}]_1)$ and $[\mathbf{c}_2]_2 \notin \mathsf{span}([\mathbf{A}_2]_2)$: the former holds since $\mathsf{span}([\mathbf{A}_1]_1) \cap \mathsf{span}([\mathbf{A}_{0,1}]_1) = \emptyset$ (recall that the zero vector $[\mathbf{0}]_1$ is excluded from span spaces) and the latter is due to the fact that $([\mathbf{c}_1]_1, [\mathbf{c}_2]_2) \notin \mathcal{L}_\rho = \mathsf{span}([\mathbf{A}_1]_1) \times \mathsf{span}([\mathbf{A}_2]_2)$.
  Thus, we can always find an $\mathbf{a}_2^\perp \in \mathbb{Z}_p^\ell$ such that $[\mathbf{c}_2^\top \mathbf{a}_2^\perp]_2 \neq [\mathbf{0}]_2$ holds and find an $\mathbf{a}_{0,1}^\perp \in \mathbb{Z}_p^\ell$ such that $[\mathbf{c}_1^\top \mathbf{a}_{0,1}^\perp]_1 \neq [\mathbf{0}]_1$ holds. Then, conditioned on $\widehat{pk}_\rho$ and $\widehat{pk}_{\rho_0}$, $\mu_2 \cdot [\mathbf{c}_2^\top \mathbf{a}_2^\perp]_2 \cdot [\mathbf{c}_1^\top \mathbf{a}_{0,1}^\perp]_1^\top$ is uniformly distributed over $\mathbb{G}_T$ due to the randomness of μ_2, so is $\widehat{\Lambda}_{\widehat{sk}}([\mathbf{c}_1]_1, [\mathbf{c}_2]_2)$

- Case II: $[\mathbf{c}_2]_2 \in \mathsf{span}([\mathbf{A}_{0,2}]_2)$.
  It must hold that $[\mathbf{c}_1]_1 \notin \mathsf{span}([\mathbf{A}_{0,1}]_1)$ and $[\mathbf{c}_2]_2 \notin \mathsf{span}([\mathbf{A}_2]_2)$: the former is due to the fact that $([\mathbf{c}_1]_1, [\mathbf{c}_2]_2) \notin \mathcal{L}_{\rho_0} = \mathsf{span}([\mathbf{A}_{0,1}]_1) \times \mathsf{span}([\mathbf{A}_{0,2}]_2)$ and the latter holds since $\mathsf{span}([\mathbf{A}_2]_2) \cap \mathsf{span}([\mathbf{A}_{0,2}]_2) = \emptyset$ (recall that the zero vector $[\mathbf{0}]_2$ is excluded from span spaces).
  Similar to the analysis of Case I, conditioned on $\widehat{pk}_\rho$ and $\widehat{pk}_{\rho_0}$, $\widehat{\Lambda}_{\widehat{sk}}([\mathbf{c}_1]_1, [\mathbf{c}_2]_2)$ is uniformly distributed over $\mathbb{G}_T$.

- Case III: $[\mathbf{c}_1]_1 \notin \mathsf{span}([\mathbf{A}_1]_1) \wedge [\mathbf{c}_2]_2 \notin \mathsf{span}([\mathbf{A}_{0,2}]_2)$.
  In this case, we can always find an $\mathbf{a}_1^\perp \in \mathbb{Z}_p^\ell$ such that $[\mathbf{c}_1^\top \mathbf{a}_1^\perp]_1 \neq [\mathbf{0}]_1$ holds and find an $\mathbf{a}_{0,2}^\perp \in \mathbb{Z}_p^\ell$ such that $[\mathbf{c}_2^\top \mathbf{a}_{0,2}^\perp]_2 \neq [\mathbf{0}]_2$ holds. Then, conditioned on $\widehat{pk}_\rho$ and $\widehat{pk}_{\rho_0}$, $\mu_1 \cdot [\mathbf{c}_2^\top \mathbf{a}_{0,2}^\perp]_2 \cdot [\mathbf{c}_1^\top \mathbf{a}_1^\perp]_1^\top$ is uniformly distributed over $\mathbb{G}_T$ due to the randomness of μ_1, so is $\widehat{\Lambda}_{\widehat{sk}}([\mathbf{c}_1]_1, [\mathbf{c}_2]_2)$.

In summary, $\widehat{\Lambda}_{\widehat{sk}}([\mathbf{c}_1]_1, [\mathbf{c}_2]_2)$ is uniformly distributed over $\mathbb{G}_T$ conditioned on $\widehat{pk}_\rho$ and $\widehat{pk}_{\rho_0}$ no matter which case it is.

This implies that $\widehat{\mathsf{QAHPS}}$ is perfectly $\langle \mathscr{L}, \mathscr{L}_0 \rangle$-universal.

[Perfectly $\langle \mathscr{L}_0, \mathscr{L}_1 \rangle$-Universal.] It can be proved in a similar way as above.

[κ-LR-$\langle \mathscr{L}, \mathscr{L}_0 \rangle$-Universal. It follows from Lemma 1.

[κ-**LR-$\langle\mathscr{L},\mathscr{L}_0\rangle$-Key-Switching.**] Let $(\rho = ([\mathbf{A}_1]_1, [\mathbf{A}_2]_2),\ td) \leftarrow_{\$} \mathscr{L}$ and let $L : \widetilde{\mathcal{SK}} \longrightarrow \{0,1\}^{\kappa}$ be an arbitrary leakage function. For $\widehat{sk} = \widehat{\mathbf{K}} \leftarrow_{\$} \mathbb{Z}_p^{\ell \times \ell}$, $\widehat{sk'} = \widehat{\mathbf{K}'} \leftarrow_{\$} \mathbb{Z}_p^{\ell \times \ell}$ and $(\rho_0 = ([\mathbf{A}_{0,1}]_1, [\mathbf{A}_{0,2}]_2), td_0) \leftarrow_{\$} \mathscr{L}_0$, we aim to prove

$$\Delta\Big(\ (\rho_0, \underbrace{\boxed{[\mathbf{A}_{0,2}]_2^\top \widehat{\mathbf{K}}[\mathbf{A}_{0,1}]_1}}_{\widehat{\alpha}_{\rho_0}(\widehat{sk})}\ ), (\rho_0, \underbrace{\boxed{[\mathbf{A}_{0,2}]_2^\top \widehat{\mathbf{K}'}[\mathbf{A}_{0,1}]_1}}_{\widehat{\alpha}_{\rho_0}(\widehat{sk'})}\ )\ \Big|\ \underbrace{[\mathbf{A}_2]_2^\top \widehat{\mathbf{K}}[\mathbf{A}_1]_1}_{\widehat{\alpha}_{\rho}(\widehat{sk})},\ \boxed{L(\widehat{\mathbf{K}})}\ \Big) \le 2^{-\Omega(\lambda)}.$$

$$(5)$$

Taking $[\mathbf{A}_{0,1}]_1$ as a universal hash function and the ℓ rows of $\widehat{\mathbf{K}}$ as ℓ independent inputs, we have that

$$\Delta\Big(\ ([\mathbf{A}_{0,1}]_1, \boxed{\widehat{\mathbf{K}}[\mathbf{A}_{0,1}]_1}), ([\mathbf{A}_{0,1}]_1, \boxed{[\mathbf{U}]_1})\ \Big|\ \widehat{\mathbf{K}}[\mathbf{A}_1]_1,\ \boxed{L(\widehat{\mathbf{K}})}\ \Big) \le 2^{-\Omega(\lambda)}, \quad (6)$$

where $\mathbf{U} \leftarrow_{\$} \mathbb{Z}_p^{\ell \times k}$, by the multi-fold generalized leftover hash lemma (see [13] and our full version [22]). Meanwhile, $\widehat{\mathbf{K}'}$ is uniform and independent of $\mathbf{A}_{0,1}, \mathbf{A}_1$ and $\widehat{\mathbf{K}}$. So,

$$([\mathbf{A}_{0,1}]_1, \boxed{[\mathbf{U}]_1}, \widehat{\mathbf{K}}[\mathbf{A}_1]_1,\ \boxed{L(\widehat{\mathbf{K}})}\ ) \equiv ([\mathbf{A}_{0,1}]_1, \boxed{\widehat{\mathbf{K}'}[\mathbf{A}_{0,1}]_1}, \widehat{\mathbf{K}}[\mathbf{A}_1]_1,\ \boxed{L(\widehat{\mathbf{K}})}\ ). \quad (7)$$

(6) and (7) implies

$$\Delta\Big(\ ([\mathbf{A}_{0,1}]_1, \boxed{\widehat{\mathbf{K}}[\mathbf{A}_{0,1}]_1}), ([\mathbf{A}_{0,1}]_1, \boxed{\widehat{\mathbf{K}'}[\mathbf{A}_{0,1}]_1})\ \Big|\ \widehat{\mathbf{K}}[\mathbf{A}_1]_1,\ \boxed{L(\widehat{\mathbf{K}})}\ \Big) \le 2^{-\Omega(\lambda)}. \quad (8)$$

Note that the variables in $\Delta()$ of (5) can be regarded as outputs of certain randomized function of the variables in $\Delta()$ of (8), therefore (5) holds.

This completes the proof of κ-LR-$\langle\mathscr{L},\mathscr{L}_0\rangle$-key-switching. $\qquad\square$

5.5 The Instantiation of LR-Weak-Ardent Tag-Based QAHPS

We present the construction of tag-based $\widehat{\mathsf{QAHPS}} = (\widehat{\mathsf{Setup}}, \widetilde{\alpha}_{(.)}, \widetilde{\mathsf{Pub}}, \widetilde{\mathsf{Priv}})$ for the language distribution $\mathscr{L}\ (= \mathscr{L}_{\mathcal{D}_{\ell,k}})$ in Fig. 5. It is straightforward to check the perfect correctness of $\widetilde{\mathsf{QAHPS}}$.

$\widetilde{pp} \leftarrow_{\$} \widetilde{\mathsf{Setup}}(1^\lambda)$:	$\widetilde{pk}_\rho \leftarrow \widetilde{\alpha}_\rho(\widetilde{sk})$,
$\mathcal{PG} = (\mathbb{G}_1, \mathbb{G}_2, \mathbb{G}_T, p, e, P_1, P_2, P_T) \leftarrow_{\$} \mathsf{PGGen}(1^\lambda)$.	where $\rho = ([\mathbf{A}_1]_1, [\mathbf{A}_2]_2) \in \mathbb{G}_1^{\ell \times k} \times \mathbb{G}_2^{\ell \times k}$:
$\Rightarrow \widetilde{pp} := \mathcal{PG}$, which implicitly defines	Parse $\widetilde{sk} = \widetilde{\mathbf{K}} \in \mathbb{Z}_p^{2 \times \ell}$.
$\quad (\widetilde{\mathcal{SK}} := \mathbb{Z}_p^{2 \times \ell},\ \widetilde{\mathcal{T}} := \mathbb{G}_2,\ \widetilde{\Pi} := \mathbb{G}_T,\ \widetilde{\Lambda}_{(.)})$,	$[\widetilde{\mathbf{P}}]_1 := \widetilde{\mathbf{K}} \cdot [\mathbf{A}_1]_1 \in \mathbb{G}_1^{2 \times k}$.
where $\widetilde{\Lambda}_{\widetilde{sk}}(([\mathbf{c}_1]_1, [\mathbf{c}_2]_2), [\tau]_2) := [1, \tau]_2 \cdot \widetilde{\mathbf{K}} \cdot [\mathbf{c}_1]_1 \in \mathbb{G}_T$	$\Rightarrow \widetilde{pk}_\rho := [\widetilde{\mathbf{P}}]_1$.
for any $\widetilde{sk} = \widetilde{\mathbf{K}} \in \mathbb{Z}_p^{2 \times \ell}$, $([\mathbf{c}_1]_1, [\mathbf{c}_2]_2) \in \mathcal{X} = \mathbb{G}_1^\ell \times \mathbb{G}_2^\ell$ and $[\tau]_2 \in \mathbb{G}_2$.	
$[\widetilde{\pi}]_T \leftarrow \widetilde{\mathsf{Pub}}(\widetilde{pk}_\rho, ([\mathbf{c}_1]_1, [\mathbf{c}_2]_2), (\mathbf{w}_1, \mathbf{w}_2) \in \mathbb{Z}_p^k \times \mathbb{Z}_p^k, [\tau]_2 \in \mathbb{G}_2)$,	
where $([\mathbf{c}_1]_1, [\mathbf{c}_2]_2) \in \mathcal{L}_\rho$ for $\rho = ([\mathbf{A}_1]_1, [\mathbf{A}_2]_2)$:	$[\widetilde{\pi}]_T \leftarrow \widetilde{\mathsf{Priv}}(\widetilde{sk}, ([\mathbf{c}_1]_1, [\mathbf{c}_2]_2) \in \mathcal{X}, [\tau]_2)$:
Parse $\widetilde{pk}_\rho = [\widetilde{\mathbf{P}}]_1 \in \mathbb{G}_1^{2 \times k}$.	Parse $\widetilde{sk} = \widetilde{\mathbf{K}} \in \mathbb{Z}_p^{2 \times \ell}$.
$\Rightarrow [\widetilde{\pi}]_T := [1, \tau]_2 \cdot [\widetilde{\mathbf{P}}]_1 \cdot \mathbf{w}_1 \in \mathbb{G}_T$.	$\Rightarrow [\widetilde{\pi}]_T := [1, \tau]_2 \cdot \widetilde{\mathbf{K}} \cdot [\mathbf{c}_1]_1 \in \mathbb{G}_T$.

Fig. 5. Construction of LR-weak-ardent tag-based $\widetilde{\mathsf{QAHPS}}$ over asym. pairing groups.

Theorem 5 (LR-weak-ardency of Tag-Based $\widehat{\mathsf{QAHPS}}$). *Let $\ell \geq 2k+1$ and $\kappa \leq \log p - \Omega(\lambda)$. The proposed tag-based $\widehat{\mathsf{QAHPS}}$ scheme for $\mathscr{L}$ in Fig. 5 satisfies the properties listed in Table 2, i.e., (1) it is $\langle \perp, \perp \rangle$-universal and (2) it supports κ-LR-$\langle \mathscr{L}, \mathscr{L}_0 \rangle$- and $\langle \mathscr{L}_0, \mathscr{L}_1 \rangle$-key-switching, where $\mathscr{L} = \mathscr{L}_{\mathcal{D}_{\ell,k}}$, $\mathscr{L}_0 = \mathscr{L}_{\mathcal{U}_{\ell,k}}$ and $\mathscr{L}_1 = \mathscr{L}_{\mathcal{U}'_{\ell,k}}$ are specified in Subsect. 5.2.*

The proof of the theorem is quite similar to that of Theorem 4, thus we omit it here and put it in the full version [22].

5.6   Tightly LR-CCA-Secure PKE over Asymmetric Pairing Groups

We are able to instantiate (the more efficient variant of) our generic construction of LR-CCA secure PKE in Sect. 4 (cf. Remark 6) with the LR-weak-ardent $\widehat{\mathsf{QAHPS}}$ (cf. Fig. 3), the LR-ardent $\widehat{\mathsf{QAHPS}}$ (cf. Fig. 4) and the LR-weak-ardent tag-based $\widehat{\mathsf{QAHPS}}$ (cf. Fig. 5) over asymmetric pairing groups $\mathcal{PG} = (\mathbb{G}_1, \mathbb{G}_2, \mathbb{G}_T, p, e, P_1, P_2, P_T)$. Let $\mathcal{H} = \{H : \mathbb{G}_1^\ell \times \mathbb{G}_2^{\ell+1} \longrightarrow \mathbb{G}_2\}$ be a collision-resistant function family. We present the instantiation $\mathsf{PKE}^{\mathsf{lr}}_{\mathsf{asym}}$ with message space $\mathcal{M} = \mathbb{G}_2$ in Fig. 6. The scheme can be easily extended to encrypt vectors over $\mathbb{G}_2$, by replacing the vector $\mathbf{k}$ in the secret key with a matrix.

$\mathsf{PP} \leftarrow_\$ \mathsf{Param}(1^\lambda)$:	$(\mathsf{PK}, \mathsf{SK}) \leftarrow_\$ \mathsf{Gen}(\mathsf{PP})$:
$\mathcal{PG} = (\mathbb{G}_1, \mathbb{G}_2, \mathbb{G}_T, p, e, P_1, P_2, P_T) \leftarrow_\$ \mathsf{PGGen}(1^\lambda)$.	$\mathbf{k} \leftarrow_\$ \mathbb{Z}_p^\ell$. $\quad [\mathbf{p}^\top]_2 := \mathbf{k}^\top \cdot [\mathbf{A}_2]_2 \in \mathbb{G}_2^{1 \times k}$.
$\mathbf{A}_1, \mathbf{A}_2 \leftarrow_\$ \mathcal{D}_{\ell,k}$. $\quad \mathsf{H} \leftarrow_\$ \mathcal{H}$,	$\widehat{\mathbf{K}} \leftarrow_\$ \mathbb{Z}_p^{\ell \times \ell}$, $\quad [\widehat{\mathbf{P}}]_T := [\mathbf{A}_2]_2^\top \cdot \widehat{\mathbf{K}} \cdot [\mathbf{A}_1]_1 \in \mathbb{G}_T^{k \times k}$.
$\Rightarrow \mathsf{PP} := (\mathcal{PG}, [\mathbf{A}_1]_1, [\mathbf{A}_2]_2, \mathsf{H})$.	$\widetilde{\mathbf{K}} \leftarrow_\$ \mathbb{Z}_p^{2 \times \ell}$. $\quad [\widetilde{\mathbf{P}}]_1 := \widetilde{\mathbf{K}} \cdot [\mathbf{A}_1]_1 \in \mathbb{G}_1^{2 \times k}$.
	$\Rightarrow \mathsf{PK} := ([\mathbf{p}]_2, [\widehat{\mathbf{P}}]_T, [\widetilde{\mathbf{P}}]_1)$, $\quad \mathsf{SK} := (\mathbf{k}, \widehat{\mathbf{K}}, \widetilde{\mathbf{K}})$.
$C \leftarrow_\$ \mathsf{Enc}(\mathsf{PK}, [M]_2 \subset \mathbb{G}_2)$:	$[M]_2 / \perp \leftarrow \mathsf{Dec}(\mathsf{SK}, C)$:
$\mathbf{w}_1 \leftarrow_\$ \mathbb{Z}_p^k$. $\quad [\mathbf{c}_1]_1 := [\mathbf{A}_1]_1 \cdot \mathbf{w}_1 \in \mathbb{G}_1^\ell$.	Parse $C = ([\mathbf{c}_1]_1, [\mathbf{c}_2]_2, [d]_2, [\pi']_T)$.
$\mathbf{w}_2 \leftarrow_\$ \mathbb{Z}_p^k$. $\quad [\mathbf{c}_2]_2 := [\mathbf{A}_2]_2 \cdot \mathbf{w}_2 \in \mathbb{G}_2^\ell$.	$[M]_2 := [d]_2 - \mathbf{k}^\top \cdot [\mathbf{c}_2]_2 \in \mathbb{G}_2$.
$[d]_2 := [\mathbf{p}^\top]_2 \cdot \mathbf{w}_2 + [M]_2 \in \mathbb{G}_2$.	$[\tau]_2 := \mathsf{H}([\mathbf{c}_1]_1, [\mathbf{c}_2]_2, [d]_2) \in \mathbb{G}_2$.
$[\tau]_2 := \mathsf{H}([\mathbf{c}_1]_1, [\mathbf{c}_2]_2, [d]_2) \in \mathbb{G}_2$.	$[\pi]_T := \underbrace{[\mathbf{c}_2]_2^\top \cdot \widehat{\mathbf{K}} \cdot [\mathbf{c}_1]_1}_{[\widehat{\pi}]_T} + \underbrace{[1, \tau]_2 \cdot \widetilde{\mathbf{K}} \cdot [\mathbf{c}_1]_1}_{[\widetilde{\pi}]_T} \in \mathbb{G}_T$.
$[\pi]_T := \underbrace{\mathbf{w}_2^\top \cdot [\widehat{\mathbf{P}}]_T \cdot \mathbf{w}_1}_{[\widehat{\pi}]_T} + \underbrace{[1, \tau]_2 \cdot [\widetilde{\mathbf{P}}]_1 \cdot \mathbf{w}_1}_{[\widetilde{\pi}]_T} \in \mathbb{G}_T$.	$\Rightarrow$ If $[\pi']_T = [\pi]_T$, Return $[M]_2 \in \mathbb{G}_2$;
$\Rightarrow C := ([\mathbf{c}_1]_1, [\mathbf{c}_2]_2, [d]_2, [\pi]_T) \in \mathbb{G}_1^\ell \times \mathbb{G}_2^{\ell+1} \times \mathbb{G}_T$.	Else, $\qquad\qquad$ Return $\perp$.

Fig. 6. The instantiation $\mathsf{PKE}^{\mathsf{lr}}_{\mathsf{asym}}$ over asymmetric pairing groups. The message space is $\mathcal{M} = \mathbb{G}_2$. Here $\mathcal{H} = \{H : \mathbb{G}_1^\ell \times \mathbb{G}_2^{\ell+1} \longrightarrow \mathbb{G}_2\}$ is a collision-resistant function family.

For $\ell \geq 2k+1$ and $\kappa \leq \log p - \Omega(\lambda)$, by combining Theorem 1, Lemma 3 and Theorems 2, 3, 4, 5 together, we obtain the following corollary regarding the LR-CCA security of our instantiation $\mathsf{PKE}^{\mathsf{lr}}_{\mathsf{asym}}$.

Corollary 1 (LR-CCA Security of $\mathsf{PKE}^{\mathsf{lr}}_{\mathsf{asym}}$). *Let $\ell \geq 2k+1$ and $\kappa \leq \log p - \Omega(\lambda)$. If (i) the $\mathcal{D}_{\ell,k}$-MDDH assumption holds over both $\mathbb{G}_1$ and $\mathbb{G}_2$,* *(ii)* $\mathcal{H}$ *is a collision-resistant function family, then the instantiation* PKE^{lr}_{asym} *in Fig. 6 is* κ*-LR-CCA secure. Concretely, for any adversary* $\mathcal{A}$ *who makes at most* Q_e *times of* ENC *queries and* Q_d *times of* DEC *queries, there exist adversaries* $\mathcal{B}_1$, $\mathcal{B}_2$ *and* $\mathcal{B}_3$, *such that* $\mathbf{T}(\mathcal{B}_3) \approx \mathbf{T}(\mathcal{A}) + (Q_e + Q_d) \cdot \mathsf{poly}(\lambda)$, $\mathbf{T}(\mathcal{B}_1) \approx \mathbf{T}(\mathcal{B}_2) \approx \mathbf{T}(\mathcal{A}) + (Q_e + Q_e \cdot Q_d) \cdot \mathsf{poly}(\lambda)$, *with* $\mathsf{poly}(\lambda)$ *independent of* $\mathbf{T}(\mathcal{A})$, *and*

$$\mathsf{Adv}^{\kappa\text{-}lr\text{-}cca}_{\mathsf{PKE}^{lr}_{asym},\mathcal{A}}(\lambda) \leq (4\lceil \log Q_e \rceil + \ell - k + 2) \cdot \left(\mathsf{Adv}^{mddh}_{\mathcal{D}_{\ell,k},\mathbb{G}_1,\mathcal{B}_1}(\lambda) + \mathsf{Adv}^{mddh}_{\mathcal{D}_{\ell,k},\mathbb{G}_2,\mathcal{B}_2}(\lambda)\right)$$
$$+ \mathsf{Adv}^{cr}_{\mathcal{H},\mathcal{B}_3}(\lambda) + (4 + Q_d + Q_d Q_e + \lceil \log Q_e \rceil (Q_d + Q_e + Q_d Q_e)) \cdot 2^{-\Omega(\lambda)}.$$

Tight LR-CCA Security, Efficiency and Leakage-Rate of PKE^{lr}_{asym}**.** When $\mathcal{D}_{\ell,k} := \mathcal{U}_{\ell,k}$, the LR-CCA security of PKE^{lr}_{asym} is tightly reduced to the standard k-LIN assumption since k-LIN implies $\mathcal{U}_{\ell,k}$-MDDH. Let $k\mathbb{G}$ denote k elements in $\mathbb{G}$. By taking $\ell = 2k + 1$, we have PP : $(2k^2 + k)\mathbb{G}_1 + (2k^2 + k)\mathbb{G}_2$, PK : $2k\mathbb{G}_1 + k\mathbb{G}_2 + k^2\mathbb{G}_T$, SK : $(4k^2 + 10k + 4)\mathbb{Z}_p$, and C : $(2k+1)\mathbb{G}_1 + (2k+2)\mathbb{G}_2 + 1\mathbb{G}_T$. See Table 1 for details. Furthermore, if we choose $\kappa = \log p - \Omega(\lambda)$, then the leakage-rate of the LR-CCA security is $\kappa/\mathsf{BitLength}(\mathsf{SK}) = \frac{1}{4k^2+10k+4} \cdot (1 - \frac{\Omega(\lambda)}{\log p})$, which is arbitrarily close to $1/(4k^2 + 10k + 4)$ if we choose a sufficiently large p. Particularly, in case $k = 1$, the tight LR-CCA security of PKE^{lr}_{asym} is based on the SXDH assumption and it has PK : $2\mathbb{G}_1 + 1\mathbb{G}_2 + 1\mathbb{G}_T$, C : $3\mathbb{G}_1 + 4\mathbb{G}_2 + 1\mathbb{G}_T$ and leakage-rate $= 1/18 - o(1)$.

Remark 8 (Tight LR-CCA Security in the Multi-User Setting). For better readability, we merely considered the LR-CCA security in the single-user setting so far. Our results extend naturally to the multi-user setting. (The definition of LR-CCA security in the multi-user setting is presented in the full version [22].) In our single-user LR-CCA security proof (i.e., the proof of Theorem 1), most steps are statistical arguments (e.g., using the LR-universal or LR-key-switching properties of the underlying QAHPS schemes), thus could be easily carried over to the multi-user setting. The only points that are not statistical and hence need to be adapted is the use of the SMP assumptions (e.g., the game transition $\mathsf{G}_2 \rightarrow \mathsf{G}_3$ in the proof of Theorem 1) and the multi-extracting property (the game transition $\mathsf{G}_5 \rightarrow \mathsf{G}_6$). The adaptions are straightforward: the former is essentially unchanged, since the language parameter ρ that the SMP is w.r.t. is part of the public parameters PP, shared by all users; the latter could be tightly reduced to the MDDH assumptions for multiple users, by the random self-reducibility of MDDH.

Acknowledgments. We would like to thank the anonymous reviewers for their comments and suggestions. We are grateful to Dennis Hofheinz and Jiaxin Pan for helpful discussions and advices. Shuai Han, Shengli Liu and Lin Lyu are supported by the National Natural Science Foundation of China Grant (No. 61672346). Dawu Gu is supported by the National Natural Science Foundation of China Grant (No. U1636217) together with Program of Shanghai Academic Research Leader (16XD1401300). Shuai Han is also supported by the National Natural Science Foundation of China Grant (No. 61802255).

References

1. Abdalla, M., Benhamouda, F., Pointcheval, D.: Disjunctions for hash proof systems: new constructions and applications. In: Oswald, E., Fischlin, M. (eds.) EUROCRYPT 2015, Part II. LNCS, vol. 9057, pp. 69–100. Springer, Heidelberg (2015). https://doi.org/10.1007/978-3-662-46803-6_3

2. Abe, M., David, B., Kohlweiss, M., Nishimaki, R., Ohkubo, M.: Tagged one-time signatures: tight security and optimal tag size. In: Kurosawa, K., Hanaoka, G. (eds.) PKC 2013. LNCS, vol. 7778, pp. 312–331. Springer, Heidelberg (2013). https://doi.org/10.1007/978-3-642-36362-7_20

3. Abe, M., Jutla, C.S., Ohkubo, M., Roy, A.: Improved (almost) tightly-secure simulation-sound QA-NIZK with applications. In: Peyrin, T., Galbraith, S.D. (eds.) ASIACRYPT 2018, Part I. LNCS, vol. 11272, pp. 627–656. Springer, Cham (2018). https://doi.org/10.1007/978-3-030-03326-2_21

4. Abe, M., Jutla, C.S., Ohkubo, M., Roy, A.: Improved (almost) tightly-secure simulation-sound QA-NIZK with applications. IACR Cryptology ePrint Archive, Report 2018/849 (2018). http://eprint.iacr.org/2018/849/20190207:025738

5. Akavia, A., Goldwasser, S., Vaikuntanathan, V.: Simultaneous hardcore bits and cryptography against memory attacks. In: Reingold, O. (ed.) TCC 2009. LNCS, vol. 5444, pp. 474–495. Springer, Heidelberg (2009). https://doi.org/10.1007/978-3-642-00457-5_28

6. Alwen, J., Dodis, Y., Naor, M., Segev, G., Walfish, S., Wichs, D.: Public-key encryption in the bounded-retrieval model. In: Gilbert, H. (ed.) EUROCRYPT 2010. LNCS, vol. 6110, pp. 113–134. Springer, Heidelberg (2010). https://doi.org/10.1007/978-3-642-13190-5_6

7. Attrapadung, N., Hanaoka, G., Yamada, S.: A framework for identity-based encryption with almost tight security. In: Iwata, T., Cheon, J.H. (eds.) ASIACRYPT 2015, Part I. LNCS, vol. 9452, pp. 521–549. Springer, Heidelberg (2015). https://doi.org/10.1007/978-3-662-48797-6_22

8. Bellare, M., Boldyreva, A., Micali, S.: Public-key encryption in a multi-user setting: security proofs and improvements. In: Preneel, B. (ed.) EUROCRYPT 2000. LNCS, vol. 1807, pp. 259–274. Springer, Heidelberg (2000). https://doi.org/10.1007/3-540-45539-6_18

9. Chen, J., Wee, H.: Fully, (almost) tightly secure IBE and dual system groups. In: Canetti, R., Garay, J.A. (eds.) CRYPTO 2013, Part II. LNCS, vol. 8043, pp. 435–460. Springer, Heidelberg (2013). https://doi.org/10.1007/978-3-642-40084-1_25

10. Cramer, R., Shoup, V.: Universal hash proofs and a paradigm for adaptive chosen ciphertext secure public-key encryption. In: Knudsen, L.R. (ed.) EUROCRYPT 2002. LNCS, vol. 2332, pp. 45–64. Springer, Heidelberg (2002). https://doi.org/10.1007/3-540-46035-7_4

11. Dodis, Y., Haralambiev, K., López-Alt, A., Wichs, D.: Efficient public-key cryptography in the presence of key leakage. In: Abe, M. (ed.) ASIACRYPT 2010. LNCS, vol. 6477, pp. 613–631. Springer, Heidelberg (2010). https://doi.org/10.1007/978-3-642-17373-8_35

12. Dodis, Y., Kiltz, E., Pietrzak, K., Wichs, D.: Message authentication, revisited. In: Pointcheval, D., Johansson, T. (eds.) EUROCRYPT 2012. LNCS, vol. 7237, pp. 355–374. Springer, Heidelberg (2012). https://doi.org/10.1007/978-3-642-29011-4_22

13. Dodis, Y., Ostrovsky, R., Reyzin, L., Smith, A.: Fuzzy extractors: how to generate strong keys from biometrics and other noisy data. SIAM J. Comput. **38**(1), 97–139 (2008)

14. Escala, A., Herold, G., Kiltz, E., Ràfols, C., Villar, J.L.: An algebraic framework for Diffie-Hellman assumptions. In: Canetti, R., Garay, J.A. (eds.) CRYPTO 2013, Part II. LNCS, vol. 8043, pp. 129–147. Springer, Heidelberg (2013). https://doi.org/10.1007/978-3-642-40084-1_8

15. Faonio, A., Venturi, D.: Efficient public-key cryptography with bounded leakage and tamper resilience. In: Cheon, J.H., Takagi, T. (eds.) ASIACRYPT 2016, Part I. LNCS, vol. 10031, pp. 877–907. Springer, Heidelberg (2016). https://doi.org/10.1007/978-3-662-53887-6_32

16. Fujisaki, E., Xagawa, K.: Public-key cryptosystems resilient to continuous tampering and leakage of arbitrary functions. In: Cheon, J.H., Takagi, T. (eds.) ASIACRYPT 2016, Part I. LNCS, vol. 10031, pp. 908–938. Springer, Heidelberg (2016). https://doi.org/10.1007/978-3-662-53887-6_33

17. Gay, R., Hofheinz, D., Kiltz, E., Wee, H.: Tightly CCA-secure encryption without pairings. In: Fischlin, M., Coron, J.-S. (eds.) EUROCRYPT 2016. LNCS, vol. 9665, pp. 1–27. Springer, Heidelberg (2016). https://doi.org/10.1007/978-3-662-49890-3_1

18. Gay, R., Hofheinz, D., Kohl, L.: Kurosawa-Desmedt meets tight security. In: Katz, J., Shacham, H. (eds.) CRYPTO 2017. LNCS, vol. 10403, pp. 133–160. Springer, Cham (2017). https://doi.org/10.1007/978-3-319-63697-9_5

19. Gay, R., Hofheinz, D., Kohl, L., Pan, J.: More efficient (almost) tightly secure structure-preserving signatures. In: Nielsen, J.B., Rijmen, V. (eds.) EUROCRYPT 2018, Part II. LNCS, vol. 10821, pp. 230–258. Springer, Cham (2018). https://doi.org/10.1007/978-3-319-78375-8_8

20. Gong, J., Chen, J., Dong, X., Cao, Z., Tang, S.: Extended nested dual system groups, revisited. In: Cheng, C.-M., Chung, K.-M., Persiano, G., Yang, B.-Y. (eds.) PKC 2016, Part I. LNCS, vol. 9614, pp. 133–163. Springer, Heidelberg (2016). https://doi.org/10.1007/978-3-662-49384-7_6

21. Halderman, J.A., et al.: Lest we remember: cold boot attacks on encryption keys. In: van Oorschot, P.C. (ed.) USENIX Security Symposium 2008, pp. 45–60. USENIX Association (2008)

22. Han, S., Liu, S., Lyu, L., Gu, D.: Tight leakage-resilient CCA-security from quasi-adaptive hash proof system. IACR Cryptology ePrint Archive, Report 2019/512 (2019). http://eprint.iacr.org/2019/512

23. Hofheinz, D.: Algebraic partitioning: fully compact and (almost) tightly secure cryptography. In: Kushilevitz, E., Malkin, T. (eds.) TCC 2016, Part I. LNCS, vol. 9562, pp. 251–281. Springer, Heidelberg (2016). https://doi.org/10.1007/978-3-662-49096-9_11

24. Hofheinz, D.: Adaptive partitioning. In: Coron, J.-S., Nielsen, J.B. (eds.) EUROCRYPT 2017, Part III. LNCS, vol. 10212, pp. 489–518. Springer, Cham (2017). https://doi.org/10.1007/978-3-319-56617-7_17

25. Hofheinz, D., Jager, T.: Tightly secure signatures and public-key encryption. In: Safavi-Naini, R., Canetti, R. (eds.) CRYPTO 2012. LNCS, vol. 7417, pp. 590–607. Springer, Heidelberg (2012). https://doi.org/10.1007/978-3-642-32009-5_35

26. Jutla, C.S., Roy, A.: Shorter quasi-adaptive NIZK proofs for linear subspaces. In: Sako, K., Sarkar, P. (eds.) ASIACRYPT 2013. LNCS, vol. 8269, pp. 1–20. Springer, Heidelberg (2013). https://doi.org/10.1007/978-3-642-42033-7_1

27. Jutla, C.S., Roy, A.: Dual-system simulation-soundness with applications to UC-PAKE and more. In: Iwata, T., Cheon, J.H. (eds.) ASIACRYPT 2015, Part I. LNCS, vol. 9452, pp. 630–655. Springer, Heidelberg (2015). https://doi.org/10.1007/978-3-662-48797-6_26

28. Kiltz, E., Wee, H.: Quasi-adaptive NIZK for linear subspaces revisited. In: Oswald, E., Fischlin, M. (eds.) EUROCRYPT 2015. LNCS, vol. 9057, pp. 101–128. Springer, Heidelberg (2015). https://doi.org/10.1007/978-3-662-46803-6_4

29. Kurosawa, K., Desmedt, Y.: A new paradigm of hybrid encryption scheme. In: Franklin, M.K. (ed.) CRYPTO 2004. LNCS, vol. 3152, pp. 426–442. Springer, Heidelberg (2004). https://doi.org/10.1007/978-3-540-28628-8_26

30. Libert, B., Peters, T., Joye, M., Yung, M.: Non-malleability from malleability: simulation-sound quasi-adaptive NIZK proofs and CCA2-secure encryption from homomorphic signatures. In: Nguyen, P.Q., Oswald, E. (eds.) EUROCRYPT 2014. LNCS, vol. 8441, pp. 514–532. Springer, Heidelberg (2014). https://doi.org/10.1007/978-3-642-55220-5_29

31. Libert, B., Peters, T., Joye, M., Yung, M.: Compactly hiding linear spans. In: Iwata, T., Cheon, J.H. (eds.) ASIACRYPT 2015, Part I. LNCS, vol. 9452, pp. 681–707. Springer, Heidelberg (2015). https://doi.org/10.1007/978-3-662-48797-6_28

32. Naor, M., Segev, G.: Public-key cryptosystems resilient to key leakage. In: Halevi, S. (ed.) CRYPTO 2009. LNCS, vol. 5677, pp. 18–35. Springer, Heidelberg (2009). https://doi.org/10.1007/978-3-642-03356-8_2

33. Naor, M., Yung, M.: Public-key cryptosystems provably secure against chosen ciphertext attacks. In: Ortiz, H. (ed.) STOC 1990, pp. 427–437. ACM (1990)

34. Qin, B., Liu, S.: Leakage-resilient chosen-ciphertext secure public-key encryption from hash proof system and one-time lossy filter. In: Sako, K., Sarkar, P. (eds.) ASIACRYPT 2013, Part II. LNCS, vol. 8270, pp. 381–400. Springer, Heidelberg (2013). https://doi.org/10.1007/978-3-642-42045-0_20

35. Qin, B., Liu, S., Chen, K.: Efficient chosen-ciphertext secure public-key encryption scheme with high leakage-resilience. IET Inf. Secur. 9(1), 32–42 (2015)

36. Wee, H.: Dual projective hashing and its applications — lossy trapdoor functions and more. In: Pointcheval, D., Johansson, T. (eds.) EUROCRYPT 2012. LNCS, vol. 7237, pp. 246–262. Springer, Heidelberg (2012). https://doi.org/10.1007/978-3-642-29011-4_16

Non-malleable Secret Sharing in the Computational Setting: Adaptive Tampering, Noisy-Leakage Resilience, and Improved Rate

Antonio Faonio[1](✉) and Daniele Venturi[2](✉)

[1] IMDEA Software Institute, Madrid, Spain
antonio.faonio@imdea.org
[2] Department of Computer Science, Sapienza University of Rome, Rome, Italy
venturi@di.uniroma1.it

Abstract. We revisit the concept of *non-malleable* secret sharing (Goyal and Kumar, STOC 2018) in the computational setting. In particular, under the assumption of one-to-one one-way functions, we exhibit a *computationally* private, *threshold* secret sharing scheme satisfying all of the following properties.

- **Continuous non-malleability:** No computationally-bounded adversary tampering independently with all the shares can produce mauled shares that reconstruct to a value related to the original secret. This holds even in case the adversary can tamper *continuously*, for an *unbounded* polynomial number of times, with the same target secret sharing, where the next sequence of tampering functions, as well as the subset of shares used for reconstruction, can be chosen *adaptively* based on the outcome of previous reconstructions.
- **Resilience to noisy leakage:** Non-malleability holds even if the adversary can additionally leak information independently from all the shares. There is no bound on the length of leaked information, as long as the overall leakage does not decrease the min-entropy of each share by too much.
- **Improved rate:** The information rate of our final scheme, defined as the ratio between the size of the message and the maximal size of a share, asymptotically approaches 1 when the message length goes to infinity.

Previous constructions achieved information-theoretic security, sometimes even for arbitrary access structures, at the price of *at least one* of the following limitations: (i) Non-malleability only holds against one-time tampering attacks; (ii) Non-malleability holds against a bounded number of tampering attacks, but both the choice of the tampering functions and of the sets used for reconstruction is non-adaptive; (iii) Information rate asymptotically approaching zero; (iv) No security guarantee in the presence of leakage.

A. Faonio—Supported by the Spanish Government through the projects Datamantium (ref. RTC-2016-4930-7), SCUM (RTI2018-102043-B-I00), and ERC2018-092822, and by the Madrid Regional Government under project BLOQUES (ref. S2018/TCS-4339).

A. Boldyreva and D. Micciancio (Eds.): CRYPTO 2019, LNCS 11693, pp. 448–479, 2019.
https://doi.org/10.1007/978-3-030-26951-7_16

Keywords: Secret sharing · Non-malleability · Leakage resilience ·
Computational security

1   Introduction

In a secret sharing (SS) scheme, a trusted dealer divides a secret message m into
shares that are distributed to n parties, in such a way that any authorized subset
of parties can efficiently determine the secret, whereas unauthorized subsets of
parties have (statistically) no information about the message. In this paper, we
focus on *threshold* secret sharing (TSS), where the unauthorized subsets are those
with at most $\tau - 1$ players, for a parameter $\tau \leq n$.

The above type of SS is also known as τ-out-of-n TSS, and was originally
introduced by Shamir [56] and Blakey [14]. SS has found many applications to
cryptography, ranging from data storage [45] and threshold cryptography [28],
to secure message transmission [31], multi-party computation [12,20,40], and
private circuits [9,38,46].

An important parameter of an SS scheme is its *information rate*, defined as
the ratio between the size of the message and the maximal size of a share. It is
well-known that the best possible information rate for TSS satisfying statistical
privacy is 1, meaning that the size of each share must at least be equal to that
of the message being shared [11].

1.1   Non-malleable Secret Sharing

Classical SS offers no guarantee in the presence of a *tampering adversary* modifying (possibly all!) the shares. Motivated by this shortcoming, Goyal and
Kumar [42] introduced *one-time non-malleable* secret sharing (NMSS), which
intuitively guarantees that even if all of the shares are tampered once, the reconstructed message is either equal to the original shared value or independent of
it. The only limitation is that the adversary is restricted to change the shares
independently, a model sometimes known under the name of *individual tampering*. As usual, in order to reconstruct the secret, only $\varrho \leq n$ shares are required,
and typically the reconstruction threshold ϱ equals the privacy threshold τ.

Recently, the topic of NMSS has received a lot of attention. We summarize
the state of the art below, and in Table 1.

– In their original paper, Goyal and Kumar [42] gave a construction of NMSS
   with 1-time non-malleability against individual tampering. The rate of this
   construction is $\Theta(\frac{1}{n \log \mu})$, where μ is the size of the message. In the same
   paper, the authors also propose a more complex construction that satisfies
   1-time non-malleability in a stronger model where the adversary is allowed
   to jointly tamper subsets of up to $\tau - 1$ shares.
   In [43], the same authors construct NMSS satisfying 1-time non-malleability
   against individual and joint tampering, and further supporting arbitrary
   monotone access structures. The rate of these constructions asymptotically
   approaches zero when the length of the message goes to infinity.

Table 1. Comparison of state-of-the-art NMSS schemes. The value n denotes the number of parties, μ denotes the size of the message, ℓ denotes the leakage parameter, λ denotes the security parameter, and τ (resp. ϱ) is the privacy (resp. reconstruction) threshold in case of TSS, where $\varrho = \tau$ unless stated otherwise. In case of general access structures, τ_{max} is the maximum size of a minimal authorized subset. IT stands for "individual tampering", JT for "joint tampering", NAT for "non-adaptive tampering", NACR for "non-adaptive concurrent reconstruction", and ACR for "adaptive concurrent reconstruction".

Reference	Access Structure	Non-Malleability	Leakage Resilience	Rate	Assumption	Notes
[42]	Threshold ($\tau \geq 2$)	1-time	✗	$\Theta\left(\frac{1}{n \log \mu}\right)$	—	IT
[43]	Threshold ($\tau \geq 2$)	1-time	✗	$\Theta(\mu^{-9})$	—	JT
	Arbitrary (monotone)	1-time	✗	$\Theta\left(\frac{1}{n \log \mu}\right)$	—	IT
	Threshold ($\tau = n$)	1-time	✗	$\Theta(\mu^{-6})$	—	JT
[10]	Threshold ($\tau \geq 4$)	p-time	✗	$\Theta\left(\frac{1}{p^3 \cdot \tau \cdot \log^2 n}\right)$	—	IT, NAT
	Arbitrary (4-monotone)	p-time	✗	$\Theta\left(\frac{1}{p^3 \cdot \tau_{max} \cdot \log^2 n}\right)$	—	IT, NAT
[2]	Arbitrary (3-monotone)	p-time	✗	$\Theta\left(\frac{1}{n \log \mu}\right)$	—	IT, NAT, NACR
[58]	Arbitrary (4-monotone)	1-time	✗	$\Theta(1)$	—	IT
[49]	Arbitrary (monotone)	1-time	ℓ-Bounded	$\Theta\left(\frac{1}{\ell n \log n \log \mu}\right)$	—	IT
This paper	Threshold ($\tau \leq \varrho - 1$)	poly-time	Noisy	$\Omega\left(\frac{\mu}{\mu + n^2 \lambda^8}\right)$	1-to-1 OWFs	IT, ACR

– Badrinarayanan and Srinivasan [10] construct NMSS with improved rate. In particular, they put forward a stronger security model called p-time non-malleability, in which the adversary can tamper with the same target secret sharing $s = (s_1, \ldots, s_n)$ for $p \geq 1$ times, by *non-adaptively* specifying sequences of tampering functions

$$(f_1^{(1)}, \ldots, f_n^{(1)}), \ldots, (f_1^{(p)}, \ldots, f_n^{(p)}) \tag{1}$$

yielding mauled shares $\tilde{s}^{(q)} = (\tilde{s}_1^{(q)}, \ldots, \tilde{s}_n^{(q)})$, for each $q \in [p]$. Non-malleability here means that for every reconstruction set $\mathcal{T}$ with size at least τ, fixed *before* tampering takes place, the secrets reconstructed out of $\tilde{s}_{\mathcal{T}}^{(1)}, \ldots, \tilde{s}_{\mathcal{T}}^{(p)}$ are independent of the original message.
The main result of [10] are NMSS schemes with p-time non-malleability, both for threshold access structures (with $\varrho = \tau \geq 4$), and for arbitrary 4-monotone access structures, with rates, respectively, $\Theta\left(\frac{1}{p^3 \cdot \tau \cdot \log^2 n}\right)$ and $\Theta\left(\frac{1}{p^3 \cdot \tau_{\max} \cdot \log^2 n}\right)$ (where $\tau_{\max}$ is the maximum size of a minimal authorized subset). Importantly, the maximal value of p is a priori fixed and, in fact, the shares' size can depend on it. Moreover, they proved that, in the information-theoretic setting, it is impossible to construct NMSS achieving non-malleability against an unbounded polynomial number of tampering attempts.

– Aggarwal *et al.* [2] consider a strengthening of p-time non-malleability, in which the adversary tampers non-adaptively p times, as in Eq. (1), but additionally specifies p different sets $\mathcal{T}_1, \ldots, \mathcal{T}_p$ for the reconstruction of each mauled shares $\tilde{s}^{(1)}, \ldots, \tilde{s}^{(p)}$. In other words, the requirement is now that $\tilde{s}_{\mathcal{T}_1}^{(1)}, \ldots, \tilde{s}_{\mathcal{T}_p}^{(p)}$ are independent of the original message. They dub their model p-time non-malleability under *non-adaptive concurrent reconstruction*, since the sets $\mathcal{T}_1, \ldots, \mathcal{T}_p$ are specified in a non-adaptive fashion.
The main result of [2] is a construction of NMSS with rate $\Theta(\frac{1}{n \log \mu})$, satisfying p-time non-malleability under non-adaptive concurrent reconstruction.

– Srinivasan and Vasudevan [58] construct the first NMSS for 4-monotone access structures, and satisfying 1-time non-malleability with rate $\Theta(1)$.

– Finally, Kumar, Meka, and Sahai [49] construct NMSS with 1-time non-malleability, but where the adversary is additionally allowed to adaptively leak information on the shares independently, i.e. they considered for the first time *leakage-resilient* NMSS (LR-NMSS). Note that here, the choice of the tampering functions can adaptively depend on the leakage. The rate of this scheme asymptotically approaches zero.

1.2   Our Contributions

All the above mentioned works construct NMSS, with different characteristics, in the *information-theoretic* setting, where both the privacy and the non-malleability of the scheme holds even against unbounded adversaries. A natural question is whether one can improve the state of the art in the *computational* setting, where the adversary for privacy and non-malleability is computationally bounded. Note that this is particularly appealing, in view of the fact that fully-fledged *continuous* non-malleability is impossible to achieve in the information-theoretic setting [10]. Hence, the following question is open:

> *Can we construct NMSS where a* computationally-bounded *adversary can tamper adaptively, with the* same *target shares, for an* unbounded polynomial *number of times, and under* adaptive concurrent reconstruction?

In this work, we answer the above question affirmatively for the case of threshold access structures and individual tampering, assuming 1-to-1 one-way functions (OWFs). Our final scheme has rate asymptotically approaching 1, and furthermore satisfies leakage resilience.

Theorem 1 (Main Theorem, Informal). *Let* $\tau, \varrho, n \in \mathbb{N}$ *be such that* $\tau, \varrho \leq n$ *and* $\tau \leq \varrho - 1$. *Assuming 1-to-1 OWFs, there exists* noisy-leakage-resilient, continuously non-malleable τ-out-of-n *secret sharing (LR-CNMSS) under* adaptive concurrent reconstruction *(where at least* ϱ *parties are needed to reconstruct the secret), with information rate (asymptotically) one.*

We observe that leakage resilience holds in the so-called *noisy*-leakage model, where the actual amount of information that can be leaked independently from each share is unbounded, as long as the uncertainty of each share does not decrease by too much. Also, notice that there is a minimal gap[1] between the reconstruction threshold ϱ and the privacy threshold τ (i.e., $\tau \leq \varrho - 1$). Interestingly, as we explain in Sect. 4.2, CNMSS cannot exist unconditionally for the optimal parameters $\tau = \varrho$, and thus our work leaves open the question of constructing TSS where both privacy and continuous non-malleability hold statistically, as long as $\tau < \varrho$.

A final remark is that the definition of continuous non-malleability uses a special self-destruct feature, in which after the first *invalid* mauled secret sharing is found (i.e., a collection of shares $\tilde{s}_{\mathcal{T}_q}^{(q)}$ whose reconstruction equals an error symbol $\perp$), the answer to all *future* tampering queries is by default set to be $\perp$. As we show in Sect. 4.3, such a feature is necessary, in the sense that without it no CNMSS exists (even without considering leakage and concurrent reconstruction).

1.3 Tamper-Resilient Threshold Signatures

As an application, we consider a generalization of the classical transformation from standard security to tamper-proof security via non-malleable codes [33], in the setting of threshold cryptography. For concreteness, we focus on threshold signatures, which allow to secret share a signing key among n servers, in such a way that any subset of at least ϱ servers can interact in order to produce the signature of a message. The standard security guarantee here is that an adversary

---

[1] Secret sharing scheme with a gap between reconstruction and privacy are known in literature as *ramp* secret sharing scheme.

corrupting up to $\tau - 1$ servers cannot forge a valid signature, even after observing several transcripts of the signing protocol with the honest servers.

Given any CNMSS, we show how to compile a non-interactive threshold signature into an interactive (2-round) threshold signature that additionally is secure in the presence of *continuous* tampering attacks. More precisely, we imagine an external forger corrupting the memory of (possibly all!) the servers independently (say via a malware installed on each of the servers), and observing several signatures produced using arbitrarily modified secret-key shares.

A similar application was recently considered in [2]. The main advantage of our model is that the attacker is allowed to tamper continuously with the memory of the servers, and further can adaptively choose the subset of servers participating in each invocation of the signature protocol; on the negative side, our adversary is not allowed to fully corrupt any of the servers, whereas in the model of [2] the forger, after tampering once, obtains the secret-key shares of $\tau - 1$ servers. In our perspective, this difference stems from the fact that [2] makes a non-black-box usage of the underlying NMSS, which allows to exploit a slightly stronger form of non-malleability which, although not formalized by the authors, seems to be met by their specific construction. (I.e., non-malleability still holds even if the attacker learns a subset of the original shares, after tampering is over; such a property is sometimes known as *augmented* non-malleability in the non-malleable codes literature [1, 25].) In contrast, our compiler only makes black-box calls to the underlying primitives.

1.4   Further Related Works

Robust Secret Sharing. In *robust* SS (see, e.g. [13, 16, 54, 55]), a monolithic adversary can (non-adaptively) corrupt up to τ players, and thus jointly tamper their shares. Robustness guarantees that given all the $\varrho = n$ shares, the reconstructed message is identical to the original shared value.

While robustness is a strong form of non-malleability, it is clearly impossible when more than $n/2$ shares are corrupted (even in the computational setting).

Non-malleable Codes. The concept of NMSS is intimately related to the notion of non-malleable codes (NMCs) [33]. Intuitively, a NMC allows to encode a message in such a way that tampering with the resulting codeword via a function $f \in \mathcal{F}$, where $\mathcal{F}$ is a set of allowed tampering functions that is a parameter in the definition, yields a modified codeword that either decodes to the original message or to an unrelated value. Several constructions of NMCs exist in the literature, for different families $\mathcal{F}$; one of the most popular choices is to think of the tampering function as a sequence of n functions $f = (f_1, \ldots, f_n)$, where each function f_i modifies a different chunk of the codeword arbitrarily, yet independently. This is often known as the n-split-state model [3, 4, 6, 7, 17–19, 21, 22, 32, 33, 47, 50, 51], the most general case being the case $n = 2$.

As shown by Aggarwal *et al.* [7], every NMC in the 2-split-state model is a 2-out-of-2 NMSS in disguise. Similarly, it is easy to see that any (leakage-resilient) *continuously* NMC (LR-CNMC) in the 2-split-state model [25,34,37,53] is a 2-out-of-2 LR-CNMSS as per our definition.

Leakage-Resilient Codes. When no tampering is considered, our definition of LR-CNMSS collapses to that of leakage-resilient secret sharing, as originally introduced by Davì, Dziembowski, and Venturi, for the case $n = \tau = \varrho = 2$ [27]. This topic recently received renewed attention, see, in particular, [2,49,58].

2 Technical Highlights

Intuitively, the proof of Theorem 1 proceeds in two steps. In the first step, we show how to obtain LR-CNMSS with information rate asymptotically approaching 0, assuming 1-to-1 OWFs. In the second step, we show how to boost the asymptotic rate generically, from 0 to 1, under the same assumption. Below, we explain these two steps with some details, after presenting our security model informally.

2.1 Security Model

Let Σ be an n-party TSS, with reconstruction threshold ϱ (i.e., given at least ϱ shares we can efficiently reconstruct the message) and privacy threshold τ (i.e., $\tau - 1$ shares reveal no information on the message to the eyes of a computationally-bounded adversary). In order to define continuous non-malleability for TSS, we consider an efficient adversary interacting with a target secret sharing $s = (s_1, \ldots, s_n)$ of some message $m \in \mathcal{M}$, via the following queries.

- **Tampering:** The attacker can specify a sequence of efficiently-computable functions $(f_1^{(q)}, \ldots, f_n^{(q)})$, yielding mauled shares

$$\tilde{s}^{(q)} = (\tilde{s}_1^{(q)}, \ldots, \tilde{s}_n^{(q)}) = (f_1^{(q)}(s_1), \ldots, f_n^{(q)}(s_n)),$$

along with a set $\mathcal{T}_q \subseteq [n]$, with size $\tilde{\varrho} \geq \varrho$. The answer to such a query is the message $\tilde{m}^{(q)}$ which is reconstructed using the shares $\tilde{s}_{\mathcal{T}_q}^{(q)}$. The above queries can be chosen in a fully-adaptive fashion for all $q \in [p]$, where p is an *arbitrary polynomial* in the security parameter; however, after the first tampering query generating an invalid message $\bot$ during reconstruction, the system switches to a *"self-destruct mode"* in which the answer to future tampering queries is automatically set to $\bot$.
- **Leakage:** The attacker can specify an efficiently-computable function g, and an index $i \in [n]$, upon which it obtains $g(s_i)$. These queries can be chosen in a fully-adaptive fashion, as long as the uncertainty of each share conditioned on the leakage (measured via conditional average min-entropy [30]) is reduced at most by a value $\ell \in \mathbb{N}$ that is a parameter of the scheme.

The formal definition of leakage-resilient continuous non-malleability essentially says that for each pair of messages $m_0, m_1 \in \mathcal{M}$, the adversary's view in the above experiment is computationally indistinguishable in the two cases where $m = m_0$ and $m = m_1$. Note that when $n = \tau = \varrho = 2$, and further when ℓ is an upper bound on the total amount of leakage, our definition collapses to the standard notion of a LR-CNMC in the split-state model [7,51].

One might observe that our definition is game based, whereas all previous definitions of non-malleable secret sharing are simulation based. While it would be possible to give a simulation-based definition for LR-CNMSS, it is not hard to show that the two formulations are equivalent, as long as the length of the shared value is super-logarithmic in the security parameter. The same equivalence, in fact, holds true for the case of LR-CNMCs [33,53].

We also remark that the limitations of computational security and self-destruct are somewhat inherent. First, as shown by [10], no TSS scheme with $\varrho = \tau$, and satisfying statistical privacy, can achieve information-theoretic continuous non-malleability w.r.t. an arbitrary polynomial number of tampering queries; as we explain in Sect. 4.2, however, the latter might still be possible with a non-zero gap $\tau < \varrho$. Second, as we formally prove in Sect. 4.3, it is also impossible to achieve continuous non-malleability without a self-destruct capability. The latter is reminiscent of similar impossibility results in the settings of tamper-resilient cryptography and non-malleable codes [37,39]. Note that both these impossibility results hold even without considering leakage and concurrent reconstruction.

2.2   First Step: Achieving Continuous Non-malleability (Poor Rate)

A Scheme with Low Privacy. Consider the following simple idea, inspired by [42], how to construct a 2-out-of-n CNMSS by leveraging any CNMC in the split-state model (i.e., any 2-out-of-2 CNMSS). To share a message $m \in \mathcal{M}$, we enumerate over all the possible pairs of distinct indices smaller than n, and for each such pair we compute a 2-out-of-2 CNMSS of the message. In other words, for each subset $\mathcal{H} = \{h_1, h_2\} \in \binom{[n]}{2}$, we consider a non-malleable split-state encoding $s_{\mathcal{H}} := (s_{\mathcal{H},h_1}, s_{\mathcal{H},h_2})$ of the message m, which we assign to the indices h_1 and h_2. The final share s_i^* for party $i \in [n]$ is then defined to be the collection of all the shares $s_{\mathcal{H},i}$, where $\mathcal{H}$ is such that $i \in \mathcal{H}$. Reconstruction is defined in the natural way, i.e. given an authorized set $\mathcal{H}' = \{h_1', h_2'\}$, we simply ignore all the shares but $s_{\mathcal{H}'}$, and use $(s_{\mathcal{H}',h_1'}, s_{\mathcal{H}',h_2'})$ to reconstruct the message.

Intuitively, the above scheme is secure because the $\binom{n}{2}$ shares of the message m are independently sampled, and furthermore the reconstruction for an authorized set $\mathcal{H}$ is independent of all the shares but one. In particular, the 2-threshold privacy property follows easily by privacy of the underlying CNMC. As for continuous non-malleability, consider a sequence of hybrid experiments, one hybrid for each subset $\mathcal{H}$ in $\binom{[n]}{2}$ in lexicographic order: In each hybrid step, we change the distribution of the target secret sharing $s^* = (s_1^*, \ldots, s_n^*)$ by letting $(s_{\mathcal{H},h_1}, s_{\mathcal{H},h_2})$ be a 2-out-of-2 CNMSS of m_0 for all sets in $\binom{[n]}{2}$ up to $\mathcal{H}$, whereas we use m_1 to define the remaining shares.

For the proof, we can build a reduction to the continuous non-malleability of the underlying split-state encoding. In particular, the simulation of a generic tampering query of the form $(\mathcal{T}, (f_1, \ldots, f_n))$, proceeds as follows:

- If $\mathcal{T}$ and $\mathcal{H}$ do not share any index, then they cannot possibly interfere with each other. In particular, the reduction knows all the shares for the positions in $\mathcal{T}$, and therefore it can simulate the answer without even querying the underlying tampering oracle for the split-state CNMC.
- If $\mathcal{T}$ and $\mathcal{H}$ share (at least) an index, then we can use the target tampering oracle to compute the mauled shares corresponding to $\mathcal{T}$ using the tampering oracle corresponding to $\mathcal{H}$. However, there is a catch. Let, e.g., be $\mathcal{T} = \{t_1, t_2\}$ and $\mathcal{H} = \{h_1, h_2\}$, and suppose $t_2 = h_1$. To compute the tampered share $\tilde{s}_{\mathcal{T}, t_2}$, we need to know the value $s_{\mathcal{H}, h_1}$, which is only accessible through the tampering oracle; as a consequence, the reduction would only be able to obtain the reconstructed message corresponding to $(\tilde{s}_{\mathcal{T}, t_2}, \tilde{s}_{\mathcal{T}, t_1})$, which is possibly different from the reconstructed message corresponding to $(\tilde{s}_{\mathcal{T}, t_1}, \tilde{s}_{\mathcal{T}, t_2})$. We bypass this problem by assuming that the underlying split-state CNMC has *symmetric decoding*, namely the decoding output is invariant w.r.t. the order of the two shares. As we explain later, this property is satisfied by known schemes.

Amplifying the Privacy. Intuitively, the transformation above is based on the fact that by composing a secret sharing for an access structure $\mathcal{A}$ with a secret sharing for an access structure $\mathcal{A}'$, we obtain a new secret sharing for access structure $\mathcal{A} \cup \mathcal{A}'$. Unfortunately, we cannot generalize this idea to go from ϱ-out-of-ϱ to ϱ-out-of-n secret sharing for any $\varrho \leq n$, as for efficiency we need $\binom{n}{\varrho} \approx n^\varrho$ to be polynomial in n.

The key idea behind our main construction of CNMSS is to compose together $\binom{n}{2}$ secret sharing schemes with different access structures, such that their union gives the desired ϱ-threshold access structure. Specifically, consider the following construction of a ϱ-out-of-n TSS based on a split-state CNMC, on an authenticated secret-key encryption (AE) scheme, and on an auxiliary $(\varrho - 3)$-out-of-$(n - 2)$ TSS.

For a fixed pair of indices $\mathcal{H} = \{h_1, h_2\} \in \binom{[n]}{2}$, pick a uniformly random key $\kappa_{\mathcal{H}}$ for the AE scheme, compute a split-state encoding of $\kappa_{\mathcal{H}}$, and call the resulting shares $(s_{\mathcal{H}, h_1}, s_{\mathcal{H}, h_2})$; hence, encrypt the message m under the key $\kappa_{\mathcal{H}}$ obtaining a ciphertext $c_{\mathcal{H}}$, and secret share $c_{\mathcal{H}}$ using the auxiliary TSS, yielding shares $(s_{\mathcal{H}, h_3}, \ldots, s_{\mathcal{H}, h_n})$ where $\{h_3, \ldots, h_n\} = [n] \setminus \mathcal{H}$. Notice that this scheme has access structure $\mathcal{A}_{\mathcal{H}} = \{\mathcal{S} \subseteq [n] : |\mathcal{S}| \geq \varrho, \mathcal{H} \subset \mathcal{S}\}$. By repeating the above procedure for each set $\mathcal{H} \in \binom{[n]}{2}$, we obtain that the final share s_i^* for party $i \in [n]$ is the collection of all the shares $s_{\mathcal{H}, i}$, so that $\bigcup_{\mathcal{H} \in \binom{[n]}{2}} \mathcal{A}_{\mathcal{H}}$ yields the ϱ-threshold access structure, as desired. Moreover, the size of each share is still polynomial in the number of parties.

The proof of threshold privacy is rather straightforward, at least if we set the privacy threshold for the final scheme to be $\tau \leq \varrho - 2$. However, in the computational setting, we can even show privacy $\tau \leq \varrho - 1$. The key idea is that either the adversary has enough shares to reconstruct the underlying ciphertext (but in this case it does not have access to the secret key, and therefore it learns nothing by semantic security of the encryption scheme), or, the adversary knows at most $\varrho - 3$ shares of the ciphertext (which by perfect privacy of the auxiliary TSS reveal nothing about the ciphertext).

Proving Continuous Non-malleability. The intuition for non-malleability of the secret sharing scheme with access structure $\mathcal{A}_{\mathcal{H}}$ is that by tampering the shares corresponding to indices h_1, h_2, the adversary either obtains the original key or a completely unrelated value: In the former case, by the authenticity of the AE scheme, the adversary cannot produce a new ciphertext that decrypts correctly; in the latter case, by the semantic security of the AE scheme, the adversary cannot produce a ciphertext that decrypts to a related message (under the unrelated key generated via tampering).

Next, we analyze how continuous non-malleability is preserved when we compose together the different secret sharing schemes with access structure $\mathcal{A}_{\mathcal{H}}$ (for $\mathcal{H} \in \binom{[n]}{2}$). In contrast to the simple composition for the 2-out-of-n CNMSS construction hinted above, in the new composed scheme the share of party i consists of both the shares of a split-state encoding of a key, and the shares of a ciphertext under an auxiliary standard TSS. Hence, in a tampering query, the adversary could swap these two kinds of shares, with the consequence that the reconstruction procedure of the underlying $(\varrho - 3)$-out-of-$(n - 2)$ TSS would depend on one of the two shares of the split-state CNMC. To resolve this problem we rely on two different ideas: First, we additionally assume that the split-state CNMC is resilient to *noisy leakage*; second, we make sure that the reconstruction procedure of the auxiliary TSS does not leak information about single shares.

The second idea is the most important one. In fact, by simply assuming leakage resilience we could at most tolerate an a priori bounded number of tampering queries. The reason for this is that, even if each reconstruction leaks just a single bit of a share $s_{\mathcal{H},i}$ under the split-state CNMC, after $|s_{\mathcal{H},i}|$ consecutive tampering queries this share could be leaked without provoking a self-destruct. The latter is better understood by looking at Shamir's TSS, where to share $m \in \mathcal{M}$ we pick a random polynomial of degree ϱ that evaluates to m at point 0, and distribute to the i-th party the share s_i obtained by evaluating the polynomial at point $i \in [n]$. The reconstruction algorithm, given any set of ϱ shares s_i, interpolates the corresponding points, thus obtaining a polynomial that is evaluated on the origin. It is easy to see that such a reconstruction procedure, under tampering attacks, potentially leaks a lot of information about the single points (without the risk of self-destruct). In particular, the reconstruction algorithm is a linear function of the shares, and thus perturbing one point by a multiplicative factor, allows to recover the value of a share in full via a single tampering query.

We now show how to avoid the above leakage. Fix some index $i \in [n]$ for the i-th share. Given an authorized set of size ϱ, we let our reconstruction procedure select two different subsets[2] of size $\varrho - 3$, such that one subset includes the index i, whereas the second subset excludes it. Thus, we run the standard reconstruction procedure twice, one for each subset, and we accept the reconstructed message if and only if the two runs yield the same value, otherwise we return an error message (which triggers a self-destruct). The main observation is that the second run of the reconstruction algorithm is independent of $s_{\mathcal{H},i}$, and thus, conditioned on the returned message not being $\perp$, the output of the reconstruction is independent of $s_{\mathcal{H},i}$. On the other hand, when the returned message is equal to $\perp$, the output of the reconstruction could indeed leak information about the share with index i, but notice that this situation triggers a self-destruct, and thus such leakage happens only once.

More in details, for the proof we perform a hybrid argument over all sets $\mathcal{H} = \{h_1, h_2\} \in \binom{[n]}{2}$, where at each step we change the shared value of the secret sharing relative to the access structure $\mathcal{A}_{\mathcal{H}}$. To show that each pair of adjacent hybrids are computationally indistinguishable, we consider a reduction to the continuous non-malleability of the underlying split-state CNMC. Denote by $(s_{\mathcal{H},h_1}, s_{\mathcal{H},h_2})$ the target codeword. Note that the reduction can sample all the randomness necessary to create the shares $s_1^*, \ldots, s_n^*$, except for the shares $s_{h_1}^*, s_{h_2}^*$ for which the values $s_{\mathcal{H},h_1}, s_{\mathcal{H},h_2}$ are missing and will be defined through the target tampering oracle. Now, suppose the adversary sends a tampering query $(\mathcal{T} = \{t_1, \ldots, t_\varrho\}, (f_1, \ldots, f_n))$, and suppose that $t_1 = h_1$ and $t_3 = h_2$.[3] While the reduction cannot simulate the tampered shares $\tilde{s}_{h_1}^*$ and $\tilde{s}_{h_2}^*$ locally, it can use the tampering oracle to obtain the decoding relative to the split-state codeword $(\tilde{s}_{\mathcal{T},t_1}, \tilde{s}_{\mathcal{T},t_2})$; in fact, $\tilde{s}_{\mathcal{T},t_2}$ can be computed by the reduction itself—as it knows the share $s_{t_2}^*$ in full—and hard-wired into the description of the right tampering function, whereas the value $\tilde{s}_{\mathcal{T},t_1}$ can be perfectly emulated inside the tampering oracle by hard-wiring into the left tampering function all the information known about $s_{h_1}^*$.

In order to complete the simulation, the reduction still needs to run twice the reconstruction process of the underlying TSS, given the tampered shares $\tilde{s}_{\mathcal{T},t_3}, \ldots, \tilde{s}_{\mathcal{T},t_\varrho}$. Note that since the values $\tilde{s}_{\mathcal{T},t_4}, \ldots, \tilde{s}_{\mathcal{T},t_\varrho}$ can be computed locally, the reduction can perform one reconstruction (yielding a first reconstructed ciphertext c_1). However, in order to run the second reconstruction, it needs the value $\tilde{s}_{\mathcal{T},t_3}$ which is not directly available, as it might depend on $s_{\mathcal{H},t_3} = s_{\mathcal{H},h_2}$. The idea is then to get the second ciphertext c_2 via a leakage query. We claim that, as long as $c_1 = c_2$, such leakage does not decrease the min-entropy of $s_{\mathcal{H},h_2}$; roughly speaking, the reason is that $c_2 = c_1$ can be also computed as a function of $\tilde{s}_{\mathcal{H},t_4}, \ldots, \tilde{s}_{\mathcal{H},t_\varrho}$, which are known by the reduction and independent of $s_{\mathcal{H},t_3}$.

---

[2] In retrospect, this is the reason why we set the reconstruction/privacy threshold of the underlying TSS to $\varrho - 3$ (i.e., 2 shares for decoding the non-malleable encoding and $\varrho - 3 + 1 = \varrho - 2$ shares to run the reconstruction procedure of the TSS twice).

[3] Clearly, the reduction needs to handle many other cases; however, this particular case is enough to illustrate our technique.

Notice that the double-reconstruction trick—i.e., running the reconstruction procedure twice, in the above example one with t_3 and one without—is sufficient to prove that the reconstruction does not leak information about one specific share. However, we need to ensure that no information about any of the shares is leaked. One simple idea would be to lift the previous argument by repeating the reconstruction for all subsets of size $\varrho - 3$. Nicely, in the case of, e.g. Shamir's TSS this is not necessary. In fact, we can have a more efficient reconstruction procedure that only checks two subsets. This is because if two different subsets of size $\varrho - 3$ yield polynomials with identical evaluation in the origin, then they must encode the same polynomial, and since these two subsets cover an entire authorized set, then we are ensured that using any other subset would yield the same reconstructed message.

Instantiating the Construction. All that remains is to construct a split-state CNMC with the special symmetric decoding feature, and for which the non-malleability property still holds even in the presence of noisy (independent) leakage from the left and right shares.

We do this by revisiting the recent construction of Ostrovsky *et al.* [53], which gives a split-state CNMC assuming non-interactive, perfectly binding commitments (which in turn can be based on 1-to-1 OWFs). In their scheme, a split-state encoding of a message m is a pair of values $(L, R) = ((com, L'), (com, R'))$, where com is a non-interactive commitment to the message m using randomness δ, and (L', R') is a split-state encoding of the string $m \| \delta$ obtained by running an auxiliary code satisfying leakage-resilient one-time non-malleability, in the information-theoretic setting and in the bounded-leakage model. The decoding algorithm first checks that the left and right share contain the same commitment. If not, it returns $\perp$. Else, it decodes (L', R') obtaining a string $m' = m \| \delta$, and returns m if and only if δ is a valid opening of com w.r.t. m.

Our first observation is that the above code satisfies symmetric decoding, as long as the inner encoding (L', R') does. Additionally, we extend the security proof of [53] to show that if the auxiliary split-state code is secure in the noisy-leakage model, so is the final encoding. As a side result, and thanks to the power of noisy leakage, we even obtain a simpler proof.

The missing piece of the puzzle is then to exhibit a split-state code satisfying leakage-resilient one-time non-malleability, in the information-theoretic setting and in the noisy-leakage model, and with symmetric decoding. Luckily, it turns out that the coding scheme by Aggarwal *et al.* [7], based on the inner-product extractor [23], already satisfies all these requirements. We refer the interested reader to the full version of this paper [36] for the details.

2.3   Second Step: Amplifying the Rate

Next, we describe another generic transformation yielding LR-CNMSS with information rate asymptotically approaching 1, starting from a LR-CNMSS with asymptotic rate 0, and an AE scheme. Such transformations, in the setting of non-malleable codes, are sometimes known as rate compilers [1, 8, 25].

Our rate compiler generalizes a construction by Agrawal *et al.* [1] in the setting of split-state NMCs, which has been very recently analyzed also in the case of continuous tampering [25]. In order to secret share the message $m \in \mathcal{M}$, we first sample a uniformly random key κ for the AE scheme, and then we encrypt the message m under this key, yielding a ciphertext c. Hence, we secret share the key κ using the underlying rate-0 secret sharing scheme, yielding n shares $(\kappa_1, \ldots, \kappa_n)$. Finally, we set the share of party $i \in [n]$ to be $s_i = (\kappa_i, c)$. The reconstruction procedure, given ϱ shares, first checks that all shares contain the same ciphertext c. If not, an error is triggered. Else, the secret key is reconstructed from the shares and used to decrypt the unique ciphertext c.

Note that the length of the secret key is independent of the size of the message, and thus the above construction achieves information rate asymptotically approaching 1. As for security, it is not hard to show that the compiled scheme inherits the threshold privacy property from the underlying rate-0 secret sharing. Here, we additionally need to rely on the semantic security of the AE scheme to argue that the ciphertext c reveals nothing about the message.

Proving Continuous Non-malleability. Turning to continuous non-malleability, the main step of the proof is a game hop in which the values $(\kappa_1, \ldots, \kappa_n)$ result from a secret sharing of an unrelated key $\kappa' \neq \kappa$. In order to establish the indistinguishability between this modified experiment and the original experiment, we consider a reduction to the continuous non-malleability of the underlying LR-CNMSS. Such a reduction can interact with a target secret sharing $(\kappa_1, \ldots, \kappa_n)$ that is either a secret sharing of κ or of κ'. The main obstacle, here, comes from the simulation of tampering queries. In fact, although the reduction can perfectly emulate the distribution of the individual shares $s_i = (\kappa_i, c)$ inside the tampering oracle, as the ciphertext c can be sampled locally, the difficulty is that to emulate the output of the reconstruction w.r.t. a given subset $\mathcal{T} = \{t_1, \ldots, t_{\tilde{\varrho}}\}$ we need to: (i) ensure that all of the mauled shares $\tilde{s}_{t_j} = (\tilde{\kappa}_{t_j}, \tilde{c}_{t_j})$ actually contain the same ciphertext, i.e. $\tilde{c}_{t_1} = \ldots = \tilde{c}_{t_{\tilde{\varrho}}} = \tilde{c}$, and (ii) use the mauled secret key $\tilde{\kappa}$ received by the reduction in response to a tampering query in order to obtain the decryption of the unique ciphertext $\tilde{c}$ (if such a ciphertext exists).

We overcome both of the above obstacles by exploiting the fact that the starting CNMSS is resilient to noisy leakage. This is crucial in our setting, since the size of the ciphertext might very well exceed the maximal length of a share of the secret key. Hence, generalizing a trick from [25,34], we proceed to check equality of all the ciphertexts in a block-wise fashion, by leaking blocks of λ bits from each share, where λ is the security parameter. This leakage routine continues until eventually we obtain the entire ciphertext $\tilde{c}$, unless some of the blocks leaked from each share differ, in which case we answer the tampering query by $\bot$ and trigger a self-destruct.

It remains to show that the above methodology does not result in too much leakage. Intuitively, this holds because up to the point where the leaked blocks of the ciphertexts are all the same, the leakage on each share can be thought of as a function of the other shares, so that this leakage does not decrease the min-entropy of each share more than conditioning on the other shares, which is fine since in known constructions the mutual information between the shares is very low. On the other hand, when a self-destruct is triggered, we reveal only λ bits of information; by a standard argument, this causes a min-entropy drop of roughly λ bits, which again is tolerated by the underlying scheme.

3   Preliminaries

3.1   Standard Cryptographic Primitives

Threshold Secret Sharing. An n-party secret sharing scheme Σ consists of a pair of polynomial-time algorithms (Share, Rec) specified as follows: (i) The randomized sharing algorithm Share takes as input a message $m \in \mathcal{M}$, and outputs n shares $s_1, \ldots, s_n$ where each $s_i \in \mathcal{S}_i$; (ii) The deterministic algorithm Rec takes as input a certain number of candidate shares and outputs a value in $\mathcal{M} \cup \{\bot\}$. Given $s = (s_1, \ldots, s_n)$ and a subset $\mathcal{I} \subseteq [n]$, we often write $s_{\mathcal{I}}$ to denote the shares $(s_i)_{i \in \mathcal{I}}$.

Definition 1 (Threshold secret sharing). *Let $n, \tau, \varrho \in \mathbb{N}$, with $\tau \leq \varrho \leq n$. We say that $\Sigma = $ (Share, Rec) is an (n, τ, ϱ)-threshold secret sharing scheme ((n, τ, ϱ)-TSS for short) over message space $\mathcal{M}$ and share space $\mathcal{S} = \mathcal{S}_1 \times \cdots \times \mathcal{S}_n$ if it is an n-party secret sharing with the following properties.*

(i) ϱ-Threshold Reconstruction: For all messages $m \in \mathcal{M}$, and for all subsets $\mathcal{I} \subseteq [n]$ such that $|\mathcal{I}| \geq \varrho$, we have that $\mathsf{Rec}((\mathsf{Share}(m))_{\mathcal{I}}) = m$, with overwhelming probability over the randomness of the sharing algorithm.

(ii) τ-Threshold Privacy: For all pairs of messages $m_0, m_1 \in \mathcal{M}$, and for all unqualified subsets $\mathcal{U} \subseteq [n]$ such that $|\mathcal{U}| < \tau$, we have that

$$\{(\mathsf{Share}(1^\lambda, m_0))_{\mathcal{U}}\}_{\lambda \in \mathbb{N}} \approx_c \{(\mathsf{Share}(1^\lambda, m_1))_{\mathcal{U}}\}_{\lambda \in \mathbb{N}}.$$

If the ensembles $\{(\mathsf{Share}(1^\lambda, m_0))_{\mathcal{U}}\}_{\lambda \in \mathbb{N}}$ and $\{(\mathsf{Share}(1^\lambda, m_1))_{\mathcal{U}}\}_{\lambda \in \mathbb{N}}$ are statistically close (resp. identically distributed), we speak of statistical *(resp.* perfect*) τ-threshold privacy.*

Typical TSS schemes achieve the optimal parameters $\varrho = \tau$. However, having a small gap between the privacy and reconstruction threshold makes sense too, and looking ahead our constructions will have minimal gap $\varrho - \tau \geq 1$.

Special Reconstruction. We will need TSS schemes meeting an additional reconstruction property, called *special reconstruction*. This means that for any subset $\mathcal{I} \subset [n]$ of size at least $\varrho + 1$, and for any $m \in \mathcal{M}$ which is secret shared as in $(s_1, \ldots, s_n) \leftarrow_\$ \mathsf{Share}(m)$, if there are two subsets $\mathcal{I}_1, \mathcal{I}_2 \subset \mathcal{I}$ of size ϱ such that

$$\mathsf{Rec}((s_i)_{i \in \mathcal{I}_1}) = \mathsf{Rec}((s_i)_{i \in \mathcal{I}_2}),$$

then the above equation holds for all subsets $\mathcal{I}_1, \mathcal{I}_2 \subset \mathcal{I}$ of size ϱ.

$$
\begin{array}{ll}
\underline{\mathbf{G}_{\Pi,\mathsf{A}}^{\mathsf{sem}}(\lambda, b):} & \underline{\mathbf{G}_{\Pi,\mathsf{A}}^{\mathsf{auth}}(\lambda):} \\
\kappa \leftarrow\!\!\text{\$}\ \mathcal{K} & \kappa \leftarrow\!\!\text{\$}\ \mathcal{K} \\
(m_0, m_1, \alpha) \leftarrow\!\!\text{\$}\ \mathsf{A}_0(1^\lambda) & (m, \alpha) \leftarrow\!\!\text{\$}\ \mathsf{A}_0(1^\lambda) \\
c \leftarrow\!\!\text{\$}\ \mathsf{AEnc}(\kappa, m_b) & c \leftarrow\!\!\text{\$}\ \mathsf{AEnc}(\kappa, m) \\
\text{Return } \mathsf{A}_1(c, \alpha) & c' \leftarrow\!\!\text{\$}\ \mathsf{A}_1(c, \alpha) \\
& \text{Return 1 iff:} \\
& \quad \text{(i) } c' \neq c; \text{ and} \\
& \quad \text{(ii) } \mathsf{ADec}(\kappa, c') \neq \bot
\end{array}
$$

Fig. 1. Experiments defining security of authenticated encryption.

Authenticated Encryption. A (secret-key) authenticated encryption (AE) scheme is a tuple of polynomial-time algorithms $\Pi = (\mathsf{KGen}, \mathsf{AEnc}, \mathsf{ADec})$ specified as follows: (i) The randomized algorithm KGen takes as input the security parameter $\lambda \in \mathbb{N}$, and outputs a uniform key $\kappa \leftarrow\!\!\text{\$}\ \mathcal{K}$; (ii) The randomized algorithm AEnc takes as input a key $\kappa \in \mathcal{K}$ and a message $m \in \mathcal{M}$, and outputs a ciphertext $c \in \mathcal{C}$; (iii) The deterministic algorithm ADec takes as input a key $\kappa \in \mathcal{K}$ and a ciphertext $c \in \{0, 1\}^*$, and outputs a value $m \in \mathcal{M} \cup \{\bot\}$, where $\bot$ denotes an invalid ciphertext. We call $\mathcal{K}, \mathcal{M}, \mathcal{C}$, respectively, the key, message, and ciphertext space of Π.[4]

We say that Π meets correctness if for all $\kappa \in \mathcal{K}$, and all messages $m \in \mathcal{M}$, we have that $\mathbb{P}[\mathsf{ADec}(\kappa, \mathsf{AEnc}(\kappa, m)) = m] = 1$ (where the probability is taken over the randomness of AEnc). As for security, we will need AE schemes that satisfy two properties (see below for formal definitions). The first property, usually known as *semantic security*, says that it is hard to distinguish the encryption of any two (adversarially chosen) messages. The second property, usually called *authenticity*, says that, without knowing the secret key, it is hard to produce a valid ciphertext (i.e., a ciphertext that does not decrypt to $\bot$).

Definition 2 (Security of AE). *Let* $\Pi = (\mathsf{KGen}, \mathsf{AEnc}, \mathsf{ADec})$ *be an AE scheme. We say that* Π *is secure if the following holds for the games defined in Fig. 1.*

$$\forall\ PPT\ \mathsf{A}: \left\{\mathbf{G}_{\Pi,\mathsf{A}}^{\mathsf{sem}}(\lambda, 0)\right\}_{\lambda \in \mathbb{N}} \approx_c \left\{\mathbf{G}_{\Pi,\mathsf{A}}^{\mathsf{sem}}(\lambda, 1)\right\}_{\lambda \in \mathbb{N}},$$

$$\mathbb{P}\left[\mathbf{G}_{\Pi,\mathsf{A}}^{\mathsf{auth}}(\lambda) = 1\right] \in \mathtt{negl}(\lambda).$$

Note that since both authenticity and semantic security are one-time guarantees, in principle, information-theoretic constructions with such properties are possible when $|\mathcal{K}| \geq |\mathcal{M}|$. However, we are interested in constructions where $|\mathcal{M}| \gg |\mathcal{K}|$, for which the existence of one-way functions is necessary.

---

[4] These sets typically depend on the security parameter, but we drop this dependency to simplify notation.

3.2   Non-malleable Codes

A split-state code $\Gamma = (\mathsf{Enc}, \mathsf{Dec})$ consists of a pair of polynomial-time algorithms specified as follows: (i) The randomized encoding algorithm Enc takes as input a message $m \in \mathcal{M}$ and returns a split-state codeword $(L, R) \in \mathcal{L} \times \mathcal{R}$; (ii) The (deterministic) decoding algorithm Dec takes as input a codeword $(L, R) \in (\{0, 1\}^*)^2$ and outputs a value in $\mathcal{M} \cup \{\bot\}$, where $\bot$ denotes an *invalid* codeword. A codeword (L, R) such that $\mathsf{Dec}(L, R) \neq \bot$ is called a *valid* codeword; we call $\mathcal{M}$ the message space, and $\mathcal{L}, \mathcal{R}$ the left and right codeword space.

We say that Γ satisfies *correctness* if, for all $m \in \mathcal{M}$, we have that $\mathsf{Dec}(\mathsf{Enc}(m)) = m$ with overwhelming probability over the randomness of the encoding.

Noisy Leakage. We will leverage codes where non-malleability (as defined below) is satisfied even in the presence of adversaries that can obtain *independent leakage* on the two shares of a target encoding (L, R).

Following a long tradition in leakage-resilient cryptography [29,35,52], we model the leakage as an arbitrary function of its input. The only restriction is that the overall leakage on L does not decrease the min-entropy of L more than a fixed amount $\ell \in \mathbb{N}$ (that is a parameter of the scheme). Of course, an analogous condition must be satisfied for the leakage on the right side R. We formalize this restriction via a notion of *admissibility*, as defined below.

Definition 3 (Admissible adversaries for split-state codes). *Let $\Gamma = (\mathsf{Enc}, \mathsf{Dec})$ be a split-state code. We say that a PPT adversary A is ℓ-admissible if it outputs a sequences of leakage queries (chosen adaptively) $(g_{\mathsf{left}}^{(q)}, g_{\mathsf{right}}^{(q)})_{q \in [p]}$, with $p(\lambda) \in \mathsf{poly}(\lambda)$, such that for all messages $m \in \mathcal{M}$:*

$$\widetilde{\mathbb{H}}_\infty \left(\mathbf{L}|\mathbf{R}, g_{\mathsf{left}}^{(1)}(\mathbf{L}), \cdots, g_{\mathsf{left}}^{(p)}(\mathbf{L}) \right) \geq \widetilde{\mathbb{H}}_\infty(\mathbf{L}|\mathbf{R}) - \ell$$

$$\widetilde{\mathbb{H}}_\infty \left(\mathbf{R}|\mathbf{L}, g_{\mathsf{right}}^{(1)}(\mathbf{R}), \cdots, g_{\mathsf{right}}^{(p)}(\mathbf{R}) \right) \geq \widetilde{\mathbb{H}}_\infty(\mathbf{R}|\mathbf{L}) - \ell,$$

where $(\mathbf{L}, \mathbf{R})$ is the joint random variable corresponding to $\mathsf{Enc}(1^\lambda, m)$.

Note that we measure the min-entropy drop due to the leakage w.r.t. the conditional average min-entropy of $L|R$ and $R|L$. We find this meaningful as it allows to capture automatically the correlation between L and R. Alternatively, we could define admissibility by conditioning only on the leakage (without further considering the other share in the equations above); we observe, however, that these two notions of admissibility are equivalent up to a small loss in the leakage parameter. This is due to the fact that, in known instantiations [7,50], the mutual information between L and R is small, a property sometimes known as conditional independence [25,34,53].

Continuous Non-malleability. Intuitively, a split-state code is non-malleable [33, 51] if no adversary tampering *independently* (yet arbitrarily) with the two sides

$\text{CNMC}_{\Gamma,\text{A}}(\lambda, m_0, m_1, b)$:

$(L, R) \leftarrow_\$ \text{Enc}(m_b)$

$\text{stop} \leftarrow \text{false}$

$\text{Return A}^{\mathcal{O}_{\text{nmc}}((L,R),\cdot,\cdot),\mathcal{O}_{\text{leak}}((L,R),\cdot,\cdot)}(1^\lambda)$

$\mathcal{O}_{\text{leak}}((L, R), \text{side}, g)$:

If $\text{side} = \text{left}$

  Return $g(L)$

If $\text{side} = \text{right}$

  Return $g(R)$

Oracle $\mathcal{O}_{\text{nmc}}((L, R), f_{\text{left}}, f_{\text{right}})$:

If $\text{stop} = \text{true}$

  Return $\bot$

Else

  $(\tilde{L}, \tilde{R}) = (f_{\text{left}}(L), f_{\text{right}}(R))$

  $\tilde{m} = \text{Dec}(\tilde{L}, \tilde{R})$

  If $\tilde{m} \in \{m_0, m_1\}$

    Return ♥

  If $\tilde{m} = \bot$

    Return $\bot$, and $\text{stop} \leftarrow \text{true}$

  Else

    Return $\tilde{m}$

Fig. 2. Experiment defining continuously non-malleable codes in the split-state model. The tampering oracle $\mathcal{O}_{\text{nmc}}$ is implicitly parameterized by the flag stop.

of a given target encoding (L, R) of some value m, can generate a modified codeword $(\tilde{L}, \tilde{R})$ that decodes to a value related to m. Continuous non-malleability [37] is a strengthening of this guarantee, where the attacker is allowed to tamper continuously, and adaptively, with (L, R), until a decoding error occurs, after which the system "self-destructs" and stops answering tampering queries. Such a self-destruct capability, that in practice might be implemented via a public write-once flag, is well known to be necessary for achieving continuous non-malleability, as otherwise simple attacks are possible [39].

We formalize continuous non-malleability for split-state non-malleable codes using a game-based definition. Simulation-based definitions also exist, but the two formulations are known to be equivalent as long as the messages to be encoded have super-logarithmic length in the security parameter [33,53]. In order to model (split-state) tampering attacks, we use a stateless leakage oracle $\mathcal{O}_{\text{leak}}$ and a stateful oracle $\mathcal{O}_{\text{nmc}}$ that are initialized with a target encoding (L, R) of either of two messages $m_0, m_1 \in \mathcal{M}$. The goal of the attacker is to distinguish which message was encoded, while performing both leakage and tampering attacks: The leakage oracle allows the adversary to obtain information from L and R, while the tampering oracle allows the adversary to tamper with L and R independently. In case the decoded message corresponding to a modified codeword $(\tilde{L}, \tilde{R})$ is equal to one of the original messages m_0, m_1, the oracle returns a special symbol ♥, as otherwise it would be trivial to distinguish which message was encoded by querying the oracle with, e.g., the identity function.

Definition 4 (Split-state continuously non-malleable codes). *Let $\Gamma = (\text{Enc}, \text{Dec})$ be a split-state code. We say that Γ is an ℓ-noisy leakage-resilient split-state* continuously non-malleable *code (ℓ-LR-CNMC for short) if for all $m_0, m_1 \in \mathcal{M}$ and for all PPT ℓ-admissible adversaries A as per Definition 3, we have that*

$$\{\text{CNMC}_{\Gamma,\text{A}}(\lambda, m_0, m_1, 0)\}_{\lambda \in \mathbb{N}} \approx_c \{\text{CNMC}_{\Gamma,\text{A}}(\lambda, m_0, m_1, 1)\}_{\lambda \in \mathbb{N}}, \quad (2)$$

where, for $b \in \{0, 1\}$, experiment $\text{CNMC}_{\Gamma,\text{A}}(\lambda, m_0, m_1, b)$ is depicted in Fig. 2.

Message Uniqueness. An important property that must be satisfied by any split-state continuously non-malleable code is that of *message uniqueness* (MU) [37, 53]. Informally, this means that if we fix the left side L of an encoding, there are no[5] two right sides R_1, R_2, such that both (L, R_1) and (L, R_2) are *valid* codewords that decode to *different* messages $m_1 \neq m_2$. (An analogous guarantee must hold if we fix the right side.)

A simple observation, due to [53], is that both the left side L and the right side R of a split-state non-malleable encoding constitute a perfectly binding commitment to the message.

Lemma 1 ([53]). *Let Γ be a split-state code satisfying MU. Then, for any string $L \in \{0, 1\}^*$ (resp. $R \in \{0, 1\}^*$), there exists at most a single value $m \in \mathcal{M}$ such that $\mathsf{Dec}(L, R) = m \neq \perp$ for some $R \in \{0, 1\}^*$ (resp. for some $L \in \{0, 1\}^*$).*

Additional Properties. For our main construction, we will need CNMCs satisfying two additional properties as defined below. The first property, called symmetric decoding, says that for all possible inputs L, R, decoding (L, R) yields the same as decoding (R, L). Note that this implies some (very weak) form of resilience against tampering via permutations, in that any split-state continuously non-malleable code with symmetric decoding is still secure w.r.t. attackers that first tamper the two states (L, R) independently, and later swap L and R.

Definition 5 (Symmetric decoding). *We say that a split-state code $\Gamma = (\mathsf{Enc}, \mathsf{Dec})$ has symmetric decoding if for all $L, R \in (\{0, 1\}^*)^2$, we have that $\mathsf{Dec}(L, R) = \mathsf{Dec}(R, L)$.*

The second property, called codewords uniformity, requires that, for any message, the encoder outputs codewords that are uniform over the set of all possible encodings of the message.

Definition 6 (Codewords uniformity). *We say that a split-state code $\Gamma = (\mathsf{Enc}, \mathsf{Dec})$ has codewords uniformity if for all $m \in \mathcal{M}$, we have that $\mathsf{Enc}(1^\lambda, m)$ is distributed uniformly over the set of all possible pairs (L, R) s.t. $\mathsf{Dec}(L, R) = m$.*

4 Continuously Non-malleable Secret Sharing

4.1 Non-malleability Under Adaptive Concurrent Reconstruction

We now give the definition of leakage-resilient continuously non-malleable secret sharing (LR-CNMSS) under adaptive concurrent reconstruction. We focus on the case of threshold secret sharing, where the adversary is allowed to tamper (possibly all!) the shares arbitrarily, but independently. Non-malleability intuitively guarantees that the reconstructed message, where the indices $\mathcal{T}$ (with $|\mathcal{T}| = \tilde{\varrho} \geq \varrho$) used for reconstruction are also chosen by the adversary, is independent of the original message.

---

[5] Observe that "perfect" MU, as opposed to "computational" MU is wlog. in the plain model.

Importantly, in our model, the adversary is allowed to tamper continuously, and adaptively, with the same target secret sharing; the set used for reconstruction in each tampering attempt is also adversarial, and moreover can be chosen adaptively based on the outcome of previous queries. This feature, known as *concurrent reconstruction*, was already considered in previous work [2], although in a non-adaptive setting. There are only two limitations: (i) The adversary is computationally bounded; (ii) After the first tampering query yielding a mauled secret sharing that reconstructs to $\bot$, the answer to all future tampering queries will be $\bot$ by default. The second limitation is sometimes known as "self-destruct feature" in the literature of non-malleable codes [37]. Both of these limitations are somewhat *necessary* (see below).

In order to make our model even stronger, we further allow the adversary to leak information independently from all the shares. The only restriction here is that the leakage does not decrease the amount of uncertainty contained in each of the shares by too much. This leads to the notion of admissible adversary, which is similar in spirit to the notion of admissible adversaries for codes (cf. Sect. 3.2), as defined below.

Definition 7 (Admissible adversaries for secret sharing). *Let $\Sigma = (\mathsf{Share}, \mathsf{Rec})$ be an n-party secret sharing scheme. We say that a PPT adversary A is ℓ-admissible if it outputs a sequence of leakage queries (chosen adaptively) $(i, g_i^{(q)})_{i \in [n], q \in [p]}$, with $p(\lambda) \in \mathtt{poly}(\lambda)$, such that for all $i \in [n]$, and for all $m \in \mathcal{M}$:*

$$\widetilde{\mathbb{H}}_\infty \left(\mathbf{S}_i | (\mathbf{S}_j)_{j \neq i}, g_i^{(1)}(\mathbf{S}_i), \cdots, g_i^{(p)}(\mathbf{S}_i) \right) \geq \widetilde{\mathbb{H}}_\infty (\mathbf{S}_i | (\mathbf{S}_j)_{j \neq i}) - \ell,$$

where $(\mathbf{S}_1, \ldots, \mathbf{S}_n)$ is the random variable corresponding to $\mathsf{Share}(1^\lambda, m)$.

$\underline{\mathbf{CNMSS}_{\Sigma, \mathsf{A}}(\lambda, m_0, m_1, b)\text{:}}$
$s := (s_1, \ldots, s_n) \leftarrow_\$ \mathsf{Share}(m_b)$
$\mathbf{stop} \leftarrow \mathbf{false}$
Return $\mathsf{A}^{\mathcal{O}_{\mathsf{nmss}}(s, \cdot, \cdot), \mathcal{O}_{\mathsf{leak}}(s, \cdot, \cdot)}(1^\lambda)$

$\underline{\text{Oracle } \mathcal{O}_{\mathsf{leak}}(s, i \in [n], g)\text{:}}$
Return $g(s_i)$

$\underline{\text{Oracle } \mathcal{O}_{\mathsf{nmss}}(s, \mathcal{T}, (f_1, \ldots, f_n))\text{:}}$
If $\mathbf{stop} = \mathbf{true}$
    Return $\bot$
Else
    $\mathcal{T} := \{t_1, \ldots, t_{\tilde{\varrho}}\}$
    $\tilde{s} := (\tilde{s}_1, \ldots, \tilde{s}_n) = (f_1(s_1), \ldots, f_n(s_n))$
    $\tilde{m} = \mathsf{Rec}(\tilde{s}_{t_1}, \ldots, \tilde{s}_{t_{\tilde{\varrho}}})$
    If $\tilde{m} \in \{m_0, m_1\}$
        Return $\heartsuit$
    If $\tilde{m} = \bot$ return $\bot$, and $\mathbf{stop} \leftarrow \mathbf{true}$
    Else return $\tilde{m}$

Fig. 3. Experiment defining leakage-resilient continuously non-malleable secret sharing against individual tampering, under adaptive concurrent reconstruction. Note that the oracle $\mathcal{O}_{\mathsf{nmss}}$ is implicitly parameterized by the flag $\mathbf{stop}$.

Definition 8 (Continuously non-malleable threshold secret sharing).
Let $n, \tau, \varrho, \ell \in \mathbb{N}$. Let $\Sigma = (\mathsf{Share}, \mathsf{Rec})$ be an n-party secret sharing over message space $\mathcal{M}$ and share space $\mathcal{S} = \mathcal{S}_1 \times \cdots \times \mathcal{S}_n$. We say that Σ is an ℓ-noisy leakage-resilient continuously non-malleable (n, τ, ϱ)-threshold secret sharing scheme under adaptive concurrent reconstruction $((n, \tau, \varrho, \ell)$-LR-CNMSS for short) if it is an (n, τ, ϱ)-TSS as per Definition 1, and additionally for all pairs of messages $m_0, m_1 \in \mathcal{M}$, and all PPT ℓ-admissible adversaries A as per Definition 7, we have:

$$\{\mathbf{CNMSS}_{\Sigma, \mathsf{A}}(\lambda, m_0, m_1, 0)\}_{\lambda \in \mathbb{N}} \approx_c \{\mathbf{CNMSS}_{\Sigma, \mathsf{A}}(\lambda, m_0, m_1, 1)\}_{\lambda \in \mathbb{N}},$$

where, for $b \in \{0, 1\}$, experiment $\mathbf{CNMSS}_{\Sigma, \mathsf{A}}(\lambda, m_0, m_1, b)$ is depicted in Fig. 3.

Remark 1 (On game-based security). Note that Definition 8 is game based in spirit. This is in contrast with all previous definitions of non-malleable secret sharing, which instead are simulation based. While, one could also formulate a simulation-based definition for LR-CNMSS, it is not hard to show that the two formulations are equivalent as long as the shared value has super-logarithmic length in the security parameter. A similar equivalence holds for the case of (continuously) non-malleable codes [33, 53].

Remark 2 (On the relation with CNMCs). When $\ell = 0$, $n = 2$, and $\tau = \varrho = 2$, one obtains the definition of split-state CNMCs as a special case. In fact, similar to [7], one can show that any split-state CNMC satisfies 2-threshold privacy.

In the following subsections, we show that both limitations of computational security and self-destruct are somewhat inherent in our model (even when no leakage is allowed, i.e. $\ell = 0$). This is immediate for the case $n = 2 = \tau = \varrho = 2$, as the same limitations hold for the case of split-state CNMCs [37]. The theorems below[6] generalize the impossibility results of [37] for certain values of n, τ, ϱ.

4.2   Shared-Value Uniqueness

Consider the following natural generalization of the MU property for continuously non-malleable codes (cf. Sect. 3.2) to the case of TSS schemes.[7]

Definition 9 (Shared-value uniqueness). *Let $\Sigma = (\mathsf{Share}, \mathsf{Rec})$ be an n-party TSS with reconstruction threshold $\varrho \leq n$. We say that Σ satisfies shared-value uniqueness (SVU) if for all subsets $\mathcal{I} = \{i_1, \ldots, i_\varrho\} \subseteq [n]$, there exists $j^* \in [\varrho]$ such that for all shares $s_{i_1}, \ldots, s_{i_{j^*-1}}, s_{i_{j^*+1}}, \ldots, s_{i_\varrho}$, and for all $s_{i_{j^*}}, s'_{i_{j^*}}$, we have that either*

$$m = \mathsf{Rec}(s_{i_1}, \ldots, s_{i_{j^*}}, \ldots, s_{i_\varrho}) = \mathsf{Rec}(s_{i_1}, \ldots, s'_{i_{j^*}}, \ldots, s_{i_\varrho}) = m', \qquad (3)$$

where $m, m' \in \mathcal{M}$, or at least one of m, m' equals $\perp$.

---

[6] We stress that the attacks described in the proof of Theorems 2 and 3 do not require to change the reconstruction set $\mathcal{T}$ among different queries, and thus even hold without considering concurrent reconstruction.

[7] As for MU, "perfect" SVU, rather than "computational" SVU, is wlog. in the plain model.

Intuitively, the above property says that for every possible choice of an authorized set $\mathcal{I}$, there exists at least one index $i_{j^*} \in \mathcal{I}$, such that if we fix arbitrarily all the shares but the one in position i_{j^*}, the reconstruction process can possibly output a single outcome within the space of all valid messages. The theorem below (whose proof appears in the full version [36]) says that SVU is necessary for achieving continuous non-malleability (without leakage) for threshold secret sharing, in the computational setting.

Theorem 2. *For any $n, \tau, \varrho \in \mathbb{N}$, with $\tau \leq \varrho \leq n$, every $(n, \tau, \varrho, 0)$-LR-CNMSS must also satisfy SVU.*

Notice that in the information-theoretic setting, when the privacy threshold τ equals the reconstruction threshold ϱ, and when considering the authorized set $\mathcal{I} = [\varrho]$, statistical privacy implies that for each $i^* \in [\varrho]$ there always exist shares $(s_1, \ldots, s_{i^*-1}, s_{i^*}, s_{i^*+1}, \ldots, s_\varrho)$ and $(s_1, \ldots, s_{i^*-1}, s'_{i^*}, s_{i^*+1}, \ldots, s_\varrho)$ that violate SVU. Hence, CNMSS with the optimal parameters $\tau = \varrho$ is impossible in the information-theoretic setting, a fact recently established in [10].

Corollary 1 ([10]). *For any $n, \tau, \varrho \in \mathbb{N}$, with $\tau = \varrho \leq n$, there is no $(n, \tau, \varrho, 0)$-LR-CNMSS in the information-theoretic setting.*

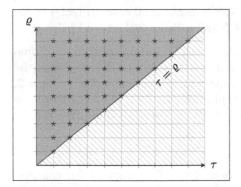

Fig. 4. Possible parameters ϱ, τ of CNMSS. Values on the red line require computational assumptions.

Mind the Gap. What if there is a small gap between the reconstruction threshold ϱ and the privacy threshold τ (e.g., $\tau \leq \varrho - 1$)? In this case, the above impossibility result does not apply. For concreteness, let Σ be an $(n, \varrho - 1, \varrho)$-TSS and consider the reconstruction set $\mathcal{I} = [\varrho]$. By perfect privacy, since any collection of $\varrho - 2$ shares reveals no information on the shared value, for every sequence of shares $s_1, \ldots, s_{\varrho-2}$, and for every message $\hat{m} \in \mathcal{M}$, there exist at least two shares $\hat{s}_{\varrho-1}, \hat{s}_\varrho$ such that running the reconstruction algorithm upon $(s_1, \ldots, s_{\varrho-2}, \hat{s}_{\varrho-1}, \hat{s}_\varrho)$ yields $\hat{m}$

as output. However, there is no guarantee that a pair of shares $(\hat{s}'_{\varrho-1}, \hat{s}'_\varrho)$ yielding another message $\hat{m}' \neq \hat{m}$, and such that, e.g., $\hat{s}'_{\varrho-1} = \hat{s}_{\varrho-1}$, actually exists. This circumvents the attack described above. Put differently, whenever $\tau = \varrho - 1$, given any collection of $\varrho - 1$ shares, we can consider two cases (cf. also Fig. 4):

– There are at least two possible *valid* outcomes for the reconstruction procedure. In this case, a computationally unbounded attacker can still find a sequence of shares violating SVU, and thus continuous non-malleability requires computational assumptions.

– The shared value is information-theoretically determined, i.e. there exists an inefficient algorithm which can reconstruct the message. In this case, SVU is not violated, and thus it is plausible that TSS with perfect privacy and statistical continuous non-malleability exists.

4.3   Necessity of Self-destruct

Finally, in the full version [36], we show that continuous non-malleability as per Definition 8 is impossible without assuming self-destruct. This fact is reminiscent of a similar impossibility result for continuously non-malleable codes [37], and tamper-resilient cryptography [39].

Theorem 3. *For any $n, \tau, \varrho \in \mathbb{N}$, with $\tau \leq \varrho \leq n$, there is no $(n, \tau, \varrho, 0)$-LR-CNMSS without assuming the self-destruct capability.*

5   A Scheme with Poor Rate

Before describing our scheme, we introduce some useful notation. The shares will be of the form $s_i^* = (s_{\mathcal{H},i})_{\mathcal{H} \in \binom{[n]}{2}}$ (see Fig. 5), where $i \in [n]$. Given a set $\mathcal{A} \subseteq [n]$, we identify with $\hat{\mathcal{A}}$ the first two indices (according to the natural order) of $\mathcal{A}$.

Basic Construction of LR-CNMSS

Let $\Pi = (\mathsf{AEnc}, \mathsf{ADec})$, $\Sigma = (\mathsf{Share}, \mathsf{Rec})$, and $\Gamma = (\mathsf{Enc}, \mathsf{Dec})$ be as described in the text. Consider the following construction of an n-party secret sharing $\Sigma^* = (\mathsf{Share}^*, \mathsf{Rec}^*)$ with reconstruction threshold $\varrho < n$, and message space $\mathcal{M}^* = \mathcal{M}$.

Sharing function $\mathsf{Share}^*(m)$: The secret sharing of a message $m \in \mathcal{M}^*$ is a collection of shares $s^* = (s_1^*, \ldots, s_n^*)$, where $s_i^* = (s_{\mathcal{H},i})_{\mathcal{H} \in \binom{[n]}{2}}$ and for any $\mathcal{H} = \{h_1, h_2\} \in \binom{[n]}{2}$ the share $s_{\mathcal{H},i}$ is computed following the steps below:
1. Let $\bar{\mathcal{H}} = [n] \setminus \mathcal{H} = \{h_3, \ldots, h_n\}$;
2. Sample $\kappa_{\mathcal{H}} \leftarrow\!\!{\scriptstyle\$}\, \mathcal{K}$ and run $c_{\mathcal{H}} \leftarrow\!\!{\scriptstyle\$}\, \mathsf{AEnc}(\kappa_{\mathcal{H}}, m)$;
3. Compute $(s_{\mathcal{H},h_1}, s_{\mathcal{H},h_2}) \leftarrow\!\!{\scriptstyle\$}\, \mathsf{Enc}(\kappa_{\mathcal{H}})$ and $(s_{\mathcal{H},h_3}, \ldots, s_{\mathcal{H},h_n}) \leftarrow\!\!{\scriptstyle\$}\, \mathsf{Share}(c_{\mathcal{H}})$.

Reconstruction function $\mathsf{Rec}^*(s_{\mathcal{I}}^*)$: Let $\mathcal{I} = \{i_1, \ldots, i_\varrho\}$. Wlog. we assume that the set $\mathcal{I}$ is ordered and that is made of exactly ϱ indices. (If not, we can just order it and use only the first ϱ indices.)
1. Let $\hat{\mathcal{I}} = \{i_1, i_2\}$, and parse $s_{\mathcal{I}}^* = (s_{i_1}^*, \ldots, s_{i_\varrho}^*)$, where for each $j \in [\varrho]$ we have $s_{i_j}^* = (s_{\mathcal{H}, i_j})_{\mathcal{H} \in \binom{[n]}{2}}$;
2. Compute $\kappa = \mathsf{Dec}(s_{\hat{\mathcal{I}}, i_1}, s_{\hat{\mathcal{I}}, i_2})$, and for sets $\mathcal{A}_1 = \{i_3, \ldots, i_{\varrho-1}\}$ and $\mathcal{A}_2 = \{i_4, \ldots, i_\varrho\}$ let $c_1 = \mathsf{Rec}((s_{\hat{\mathcal{I}}, a})_{a \in \mathcal{A}_1})$ and $c_2 = \mathsf{Rec}((s_{\hat{\mathcal{I}}, a})_{a \in \mathcal{A}_2})$;
3. If $c_1 \neq c_2$ output $\perp$, else let $c = c_1 = c_2$ and return $m = \mathsf{ADec}(\kappa, c)$.

Fig. 5. A construction of leakage-resilient continuously non-malleable secret sharing for threshold access structures, in the computational setting.

Our threshold secret sharing $\Sigma^* = (\mathsf{Share}^*, \mathsf{Rec}^*)$, which is formally depicted in Fig. 5, is based upon the following ingredients:

- An authenticated secret-key encryption (AE) scheme $\Pi = (\mathsf{AEnc}, \mathsf{ADec})$ (cf. Sect. 3.1), with message space $\mathcal{M}$, ciphertext space $\mathcal{C}$, and key space $\mathcal{K} = \{0, 1\}^{\lambda}$.
- An $(n-2)$-party secret sharing scheme $\Sigma = (\mathsf{Share}, \mathsf{Rec})$, with reconstruction threshold equal to $\varrho - 3$, message space $\mathcal{C}$, and share space $\mathcal{S}^{n-2}$ (cf. Sect. 3.1).
- A split-state encoding $\Gamma = (\mathsf{Enc}, \mathsf{Dec})$, with message space $\mathcal{K}$ and codeword space $\mathcal{L} \times \mathcal{R}$ (cf. Sect. 3.2).

The main intuition behind the construction has been already discussed in Sect. 2. The formal proof of the theorem below can be found in the full version [36].

Theorem 4. *Let* $n, \varrho, \ell, \ell^* \in \mathbb{N}$ *be such that* $n \geq \varrho > 2$. *Assuming that* Π *is a secure AE scheme, that* Σ *is a* $(n-2, \varrho-3, \varrho-3)$-*TSS with perfect threshold privacy and with the special reconstruction property, and that* Γ *is an* ℓ-*LR-CNMC with symmetric decoding and with codewords uniformity, the secret sharing scheme* Σ^* *of Fig. 3 is an* $(n, \varrho-1, \varrho, \ell^*)$-*LR-CNMSS, as long as* $\ell = \ell^* + 2\gamma + O(\log \lambda)$ *where* $\gamma = \log |\mathcal{C}|$ *is the size of a ciphertext under* Π.

Instantiating the Construction. In the full version of this paper [36], we show how to instantiate Theorem 4, under the assumption of 1-to-1 OWFs. It is well-known that authenticated encryption can be constructed in a black-box way from any OWF, whereas we can use the classical Shamir's construction [56] for the underlying TSS scheme. The latter is easily seen to meet the special reconstruction property.

It remains to exhibit a split-state CNMC with the required properties, which we do by revisiting the construction (and security analysis) of [53].

6   Boosting the Rate

6.1   Information Rate of Secret Sharing

An important measure of the efficiency of a secret sharing scheme is its information rate, defined as the ratio between the size of the message and the maximum size of a share as function of the size of the message and the number of shares.[8]

---

[8] One can also define a more general notion of information rate for secret sharing schemes [15], which depends on the entropy of the distribution $\mathbf{M}$ of the input message. The above definition is obtained as a special case, by considering the uniform distribution.

Rate-Optimizing Compiler for LR-CNMSS

Let $\Sigma' = (\mathsf{Share}', \mathsf{Rec}')$ be an n-party TSS over message space $\mathcal{M}' := \mathcal{K}$ and share space $\mathcal{S}'^n$. Let $\Pi = (\mathsf{AEnc}, \mathsf{ADec})$ be an authenticated secret-key encryption scheme with key space $\mathcal{K}$, message space $\mathcal{M}$, and ciphertext space $\mathcal{C}$. Consider the following construction of a derived n-party TSS over message space $\mathcal{M}$ and share space $\mathcal{S} := (\mathcal{S}' \times \mathcal{C})^n$.

Sharing function $\mathsf{Share}(m)$: Sample $\kappa \leftarrow_\$ \mathcal{K}$, and compute $c \leftarrow_\$ \mathsf{AEnc}(\kappa, m)$. Let $(\kappa_1, \ldots, \kappa_n) \leftarrow_\$ \mathsf{Share}'(\kappa)$. Output $s = (s_1, \ldots, s_n)$, where $s_i := (\kappa_i, c)$ for all $i \in [n]$.

Reconstruction function $\mathsf{Rec}(s_\mathcal{I})$: Parse $s_\mathcal{I} = (s_{i_1}, \ldots, s_{i_\varrho})$, where $s_{i_j} = (\kappa_{i_j}, c_{i_j})$ for all $j \in [\varrho]$. Let $\kappa = \mathsf{Rec}'(\kappa_{i_1}, \ldots, \kappa_{i_\varrho})$; if $\kappa = \bot$, return $\bot$. Else, if $c_{i_1} = \ldots = c_{i_\varrho} := c$, output $\mathsf{ADec}(\kappa, c)$, and otherwise output $\bot$.

Fig. 6. Boosting the rate of any leakage-resilient continuously non-malleable secret sharing (in the computational setting).

Definition 10 (Rate of secret sharing). *Let $\Sigma = (\mathsf{Share}, \mathsf{Rec})$ be an n-party secret sharing over message space $\mathcal{M}$ and share space $\mathcal{S} = \mathcal{S}_1 \times \cdots \times \mathcal{S}_n$. We define the information rate of Σ to be the ratio*

$$\rho(\mu, n, \lambda) := \min_{i \in [n]} \frac{\mu}{\sigma_i(\mu, n, \lambda)}$$

where $\mu = \log|\mathcal{M}|$ and $\sigma_i(\mu, n, \lambda) = \log|\mathcal{S}_i|$ denote, respectively, the bit-length of the message and of the i-th share under Σ. Moreover, we say that Σ has asymptotic rate 0 (resp. 1) if $\inf_{\lambda \in \mathbb{N}} \lim_{\mu \to \infty} \rho(\mu, n, \lambda)$ is 0 (resp. 1).

In the full version [36], we show an instantiation of the TSS scheme from Sect. 5 with shares of length $O(n^2 \cdot \max\{\lambda^8, \mu + \lambda\})$. Hence, we have obtained:

Corollary 2. *Let $\lambda \in \mathbb{N}$ be the security parameter. Under the assumption of 1-to-1 OWFs, there exists a noisy-leakage-resilient continuously non-malleable n-party threshold secret sharing for μ-bit messages, with rate $\Omega\left(\frac{\mu}{n^2 \cdot (\lambda^8 + \mu)}\right)$.*

6.2 A Rate-Optimizing Compiler

In this section, we show how to optimize the rate of any LR-CNMSS, under computational assumptions. We will achieve this through a so-called rate compiler, i.e. a black-box transformation that takes any LR-CNMSS with asymptotic rate 0 and returns a LR-CNMSS with asymptotic rate 1.

Our compiler is formally described in Fig. 6, and is inspired by a beautiful idea of Aggarwal *et al.* [1], who considered a similar question for the case of (one-time) non-malleable codes against split-state tampering; recently, their approach was also analyzed in the case of continuous tampering [25]. Intuitively, the construction works as follows. The sharing function samples a uniformly random key κ for a symmetric encryption scheme, and secret shares κ using the underlying rate-0 threshold secret sharing, obtaining shares $\kappa_1, \ldots, \kappa_n$. Next, the input message m is encrypted under the key κ, yielding a ciphertext c, and the final share of each player is defined to be $s_i = (\kappa_i, c)$. Importantly, the reconstruction function, before obtaining the key κ and decrypting the ciphertext c, checks that the ciphertext contained in every given share is the same.

Note that when the initial secret sharing scheme is a 2-out-of-2 TSS, i.e. Σ' is actually a split-state LR-CNMC, we obtain as a special case one of the rate compilers analyzed in [25]. A notable advantage of our result, however, is that we can instantiate the construction in the plain model (whereas Coretti $et\ al.$ assume a CRS). In the full version [36], we establish the following result.

Theorem 5. *Let* $n, \tau, \varrho \in \mathbb{N}$, *with* $\tau \leq \varrho \leq n$. *Assuming that* Σ' *is an* $(n, \tau, \varrho, \ell')$-*LR-CNMSS, and that* Π *is a secure AE scheme, the secret sharing scheme* Σ *of Fig. 6 is an* (n, τ, ϱ, ℓ)-*LR-CNMSS as long as* $\ell' = \ell + \lambda + O(\log \lambda)$.

Note that since the key size is independent of the message size, the length of a share is $\mu + \texttt{poly}(n, \lambda)$, thus yielding a rate of $\frac{\mu}{\mu + \texttt{poly}(n, \lambda)}$. This asymptotically approaches 1 when the message size goes to infinity.

Corollary 3. *Under the assumption of 1-to-1 OWFs, there exists a noisy-leakage-resilient continuously non-malleable threshold secret sharing with asymptotic information rate 1.*

7 Threshold Signatures Under Adaptive Memory Corruptions

7.1 Syntax

An n-party threshold signature is a tuple $\Pi = (\mathsf{KGen}, \Xi, \mathsf{Vrfy})$ specified as follows. (i) The PPT algorithm KGen takes as input the security parameter, and outputs a verification key $vk \in \mathcal{VK}$, and n secret keys $sk_1, \ldots, sk_n \in \mathcal{SK}$; (ii) $\Xi = (\mathsf{P}_1, \ldots, \mathsf{P}_n)$ specifies a set of protocols which can be run by a subset $\mathcal{I}$ of n interactive PPT Turing machines $\mathsf{P}_1, \ldots, \mathsf{P}_n$, where each P_i takes as input a message $m \in \mathcal{M}$ and secret key sk_i, and where we denote by $(\sigma, \xi) \xleftarrow{\Xi}_{\$} \langle \mathsf{P}_i(sk_i, m) \rangle_{i \in \mathcal{I}}$ a run of Ξ by the parties $(\mathsf{P}_i)_{i \in \mathcal{I}}$, yielding a signature σ and transcript ξ. (iii) The deterministic polynomial-time algorithm Vrfy takes as input the verification key vk, and a pair (m, σ), and returns a bit.

For a parameter $\varrho \leq n$, we say that an n-party threshold signature is ϱ-correct if for all $\lambda \in \mathbb{N}$, all $(vk, sk_1, \ldots, sk_n)$ output by $\mathsf{KGen}(1^\lambda)$, all messages $m \in \mathcal{M}$, and all subsets $\mathcal{I}$ such that $|\mathcal{I}| \geq \varrho$, the following holds:

$$\mathbb{P}\left[\mathsf{Vrfy}(vk, (m, \sigma)) = 1 : \ (\sigma, \xi) \xleftarrow{\Xi}_{\$} \langle \mathsf{P}_i(sk_i, m) \rangle_{i \in \mathcal{I}}\right] = 1.$$

We also consider *non-interactive* threshold signature schemes. Such schemes are fully specified by a tuple of polynomial-time algorithms $(\mathsf{KGen}, \mathsf{TSign}, \mathsf{Combine}, \mathsf{Vrfy})$, such that $\mathsf{KGen}, \mathsf{Vrfy}$ are as in the interactive case, whereas the protocol Ξ, run by a subset $\mathcal{I}$ of the parties, has the following simple structure:

$$
\begin{array}{|ll|}
\hline
\mathbf{G}^{\mathsf{hbc}}_{\Pi,\mathsf{A},\mathcal{U}}(\lambda)\colon \quad \mathbf{G}^{\mathsf{nm\text{-}tsig}}_{\Pi,\mathsf{A}}(\lambda)\colon & \\
\hline
\end{array}
$$

$\mathbf{G}^{\mathsf{hbc}}_{\Pi,\mathsf{A},\mathcal{U}}(\lambda)\colon$ $\mathbf{G}^{\mathsf{nm\text{-}tsig}}_{\Pi,\mathsf{A}}(\lambda)\colon$	Oracle $\mathcal{O}_{\mathsf{sign}}(\vec{sk}, \mathcal{T}, (f_1, \dots, f_n), m)\colon$
$(vk, sk_1, \dots, sk_n) \leftarrow\!\!{\scriptstyle\$}\ \mathsf{KGen}(1^\lambda)$	If $\mathtt{stop} = \mathtt{true}$
$\mathcal{U} := \emptyset;\ \ \mathtt{stop} \leftarrow \mathtt{false}$	$\quad$ Return $\bot$
$(m^*, \sigma^*) \leftarrow\!\!{\scriptstyle\$}\ \mathsf{A}^{\mathcal{O}_{\mathsf{sign}}(\vec{sk},\cdot,\vec{\mathsf{id}},\cdot)}(vk, (sk_u)_{u \in \mathcal{U}})$	Else
$(m^*, \sigma^*) \leftarrow\!\!{\scriptstyle\$}\ \mathsf{A}^{\mathcal{O}_{\mathsf{sign}}(\vec{sk},\cdot,\cdot,\cdot)}(vk)$	$\quad (\tilde{sk}_1, \dots, \tilde{sk}_n) = (f_1(sk_1), \dots, f_n(sk_n))$
Return 1 iff:	$\quad (\xi, \sigma) \xleftarrow{\Xi}{\scriptstyle\$} \langle \mathsf{P}_t(\tilde{sk}_t, m)\rangle_{t \in \mathcal{T}}$
$\quad$ (a) $m^* \notin \mathcal{Q}$,	$\quad \mathcal{Q} := \mathcal{Q} \cup \{m\}$
$\quad$ (b) $\mathsf{Vrfy}(vk, (m^*, \sigma^*)) = 1$	$\quad$ If $\sigma = \bot$ set $\mathtt{stop} \leftarrow \mathtt{true}$
	$\quad$ Return $(\xi_{\mathcal{U} \cap \mathcal{T}}, \sigma)$

Fig. 7. Experiments defining privacy and continuous non-malleability for threshold signatures. The vector $\vec{\mathsf{id}}$ contains the identity function (repeated n times).

- For each $i \in \mathcal{I}$, party P_i computes locally $\sigma_i \leftarrow\!\!{\scriptstyle\$}\ \mathsf{TSign}(sk_i, m)$ and broadcasts the resulting signature share σ_i;
- For each $i \in \mathcal{I}$, party P_i locally computes $\sigma \leftarrow\!\!{\scriptstyle\$}\ \mathsf{Combine}(vk, (\sigma_i)_{i \in \mathcal{I}})$; most notably, algorithm $\mathsf{Combine}$ only uses public information.

7.2 Security Model

We assume authenticated and private channels between each pair of parties. The standard security notion for threshold signatures deals with an adversary A statically corrupting a subset $\mathcal{U}$ of the players, with size below the reconstruction threshold of the scheme. The guarantee is that the attacker should not be able to forge a valid signature on a fresh message, even after seeing a polynomial number of executions of the signature protocol on several messages and involving different subsets of the players; note that, for each such subset $\mathcal{I}$, the attacker learns the transcript of the signature protocol relative to the players in $\mathcal{U} \cap \mathcal{I}$. Below, we formalize this guarantee in the honest-but-curious case.

Definition 11 (Privacy for threshold signatures). *Let $\Pi = (\mathsf{KGen}, \Xi, \mathsf{Vrfy})$ be an n-party threshold signature scheme. We say that Π is τ-private against honest-but-curious adversaries if for all PPT attackers A, and all subsets $\mathcal{U} \subset [n]$ such that $|\mathcal{U}| < \tau$:*

$$\mathbb{P}\left[\mathbf{G}^{\mathsf{hbc}}_{\Pi,\mathsf{A},\mathcal{U}}(\lambda) = 1\right] \in \mathsf{negl}(\lambda).$$

where the game $\mathbf{G}^{\mathsf{hbc}}_{\Pi,\mathsf{A},\mathcal{U}}(\lambda)$ is described in Fig. 7.

Non-malleability. Next, we consider an adversary able to corrupt the memory of each party independently. The security guarantee is still that of existential unforgeability, except that the attacker can now see a polynomial number of executions of the signature protocol under related secret-key shares, where both the modified shares and the subset of parties used for each signature computation, can be chosen adaptively. However, since in this case no player is actually corrupted and the protocol's messages are sent via private channels, for each run of the signature protocol the attacker only learns the signature (but not the transcript).

Definition 12 (Tamper-resilient threshold signatures). *Let $\Pi = (\mathsf{KGen}, \Xi, \mathsf{Vrfy})$ be an n-party threshold signature scheme. We say that Π is secure under continuous memory tampering if for all PPT adversaries A:*

$$\mathbb{P}\left[\mathbf{G}_{\Pi,\mathsf{A}}^{\mathsf{nm\text{-}tsig}}(\lambda) = 1\right] \in \mathtt{negl}(\lambda),$$

where the game $\mathbf{G}_{\Pi,\mathsf{A}}^{\mathsf{nm\text{-}tsig}}(\lambda)$ is described in Fig. 7.

7.3 The Compiler

Given an n-party threshold signature $\Pi = (\mathsf{KGen}, \Xi, \mathsf{Vrfy})$, and an n-party TSS $\Sigma = (\mathsf{Share}, \mathsf{Rec})$, consider the following modified n-party threshold signature $\Pi^* = (\mathsf{KGen}^*, \Xi^*, \mathsf{Vrfy}^*)$.

- **Key generation** $\mathsf{KGen}^*(1^\lambda)$: Upon input the security parameter, run $(vk, sk_1, \ldots, sk_n) \leftarrow_{\$} \mathsf{KGen}(1^\lambda)$, compute $(sk_{i,1}, \ldots, sk_{i,n}) \leftarrow_{\$} \mathsf{Share}(sk_i)$ for each $i \in [n]$, set $sk_i^* = (sk_{i',i})_{i' \in [n]}$, and output $(vk, sk_1^*, \ldots, sk_n^*)$.
- **Signature protocol** $\Xi^* = (\mathsf{P}_1^*, \ldots, \mathsf{P}_n^*)$: For any subset $\mathcal{I} \subset [n]$, and any message $m \in \mathcal{M}$, the protocol $\langle \mathsf{P}_i^*(sk_i^*, m) \rangle_{i \in \mathcal{I}}$ proceeds as follows:
  - Party P_i^* parses $sk_i^* = (sk_{i',i})_{i' \in [n]}$ and sends $sk_{i',i}$ to the i'-th party, for every $i' \in \mathcal{I} \setminus \{i\}$.
  - Party P_i^* waits to receive the messages $sk_{i,i''}$ for every $i'' \in \mathcal{I} \setminus \{i\}$, and afterwards it computes $sk_i = \mathsf{Rec}((sk_{i,i''})_{i'' \in \mathcal{I}})$.
  - The players run $(\xi, \sigma) \xleftarrow{\Xi}_{\$} \langle \mathsf{P}_i(sk_i, m) \rangle_{i \in \mathcal{I}}$.
- **Verification algorithm** Vrfy^*: Return the same as $\mathsf{Vrfy}(vk, (m, \sigma))$.

Intuitively, in the above protocol we first create a verification key vk and secret-key shares $(sk_1, \ldots, sk_n)$ under Π; hence, each value sk_i is further divided into n shares $(sk_{i,1}, \ldots, sk_{i,n})$ via the secret sharing Σ. The final secret-key share sk_i^* for the i-th party consists of the shares $(sk_{1,i}, \ldots, sk_{n,i})$, i.e. the collection of all the i-th shares under Σ. In order to sign a message, each player first sends to each other player the corresponding share. This way, party P_i can reconstruct sk_i, and the involved players can then run the original signature protocol Ξ. The proof of the theorem below appears in the full version [36].

Theorem 6. *For any $n, \varrho, \tau \in \mathbb{N}$ such that $n \geq \varrho \geq \tau$, assuming that Π is non-interactive, ϱ-correct, and τ-private against honest-but-curious adversaries, and that Σ is an $(n, \tau, \varrho, 0)$-LR-CNMSS, then the above defined threshold signature Π^* is ϱ-correct, τ-private against honest-but-curious adversaries, and secure under continuous memory tampering.*

We give a sketch for the proof of Theorem 6. We focus on showing security against continuous tampering, as honest-but-curious security readily follows from the privacy of the CNMSS Σ and the honest-but-curious security of Π.

The proof is a classical hybrid argument where we switch step by step from the real distribution to a distribution where all the tampering queries are applied to shares which encode dummy secret keys. In this last experiment, the reduction can simulate the tampering oracle $\mathcal{O}_{\mathsf{sign}}(\vec{sk}, \cdot, \cdot, \cdot)$ as a function of the dummy shares only, and therefore the simulation is independent of the real secret keys. Thus, we can rely on the unforgeability of the non-interactive threshold signature scheme to conclude the proof.

However, there is a subtlety. In particular, in one of the intermediate hybrid steps, the adversary might, for example, overwrite the shares relative to a secret key sk_i with shares that reconstruct to an unrelated secret key $\tilde{sk}_i$, while keeping all the other shares untouched. If the starting threshold signature scheme would be interactive, we would need to be able to simulate a run of the signature protocol where all the inputs are the same but the i-th input, which lies out of the capability of an honest-but-curious adversary. On the other hand, if the threshold signature scheme is non-interactive as we assume, this problem disappears, as we can first run the signature protocol using the original secret-key shares, and later simulate the (single) message of the i-th server thanks to the knowledge of the mauled secret-key share $\tilde{sk}_i$.

8   Conclusions and Open Problems

We have initiated the study of *non-malleable, threshold* secret sharing withstanding a powerful adversary that can obtain both *noisy leakage* from each of the shares *independently*, and an *arbitrary polynomial* number of reconstructed messages corresponding to shares which can be *arbitrarily* related to the original ones (as long as the shares are modified *independently*). Importantly, in our model, both the tampering functions (mauling the original target secret sharing) and the reconstruction subsets (specifying which shares contribute to the reconstructed message) can be chosen *adaptively* by the attacker. Our main result establishes the existence of such schemes in the *computational setting*, under the minimal assumption of 1-to-1 OWFs, and with information rate asymptotically approaching 1 (as the message length goes to infinity).

Our work leaves several interesting open problems. We mention some of them below.

- **Mind the gap:** As we show, continuous non-malleability is impossible to achieve in the information-theoretic setting whenever the reconstruction threshold ϱ (i.e., the minimal number of shares required to reconstruct the message) is equal to the privacy threshold τ (i.e., any collection of $\tau - 1$ shares computationally hides the message). Our schemes, however, have a minimal gap $\varrho - \tau \geq 1$. It remains open to construct CNMSS for the optimal parameters $\varrho = \tau$, possibly with information-theoretic security (even without considering leakage and adaptive concurrent reconstruction).
- **Optimal rate:** It is well known that, in the computational setting, there exist robust threshold secret sharing schemes with optimal information rate n [48] (i.e., the size of each share is μ/n where μ is the message size). It remains

open whether continuously non-malleable threshold secret sharing schemes with such rate exist, and under which assumptions.

- **Arbitrary access structures:** Can we construct continuously non-malleable secret sharing beyond the threshold access structure, e.g. where the sets of authorized players can be represented by an arbitrary polynomial-size monotone span program, as in [43]?
- **Joint tampering:** Can we construct continuously non-malleable secret sharing where the non-malleability property holds even if joint tampering with the shares is allowed, as in [42,43]?
- **Applications:** Finally, it would be interesting to explore other applications of continuously non-malleable secret sharing besides tamper resistance, e.g. in the spirit of non-malleable cryptography, as in [24,26,41,42,44].

References

1. Aggarwal, D., Agrawal, S., Gupta, D., Maji, H.K., Pandey, O., Prabhakaran, M.: Optimal computational split-state non-malleable codes. In: Kushilevitz, E., Malkin, T. (eds.) TCC 2016. LNCS, vol. 9563, pp. 393–417. Springer, Heidelberg (2016). https://doi.org/10.1007/978-3-662-49099-0_15
2. Aggarwal, D., et al.: Stronger leakage-resilient and non-malleable secret-sharing schemes for general access structures. Cryptology ePrint Archive, Report 2018/1147 (2018). https://ia.cr/2018/1147
3. Aggarwal, D., Dodis, Y., Kazana, T., Obremski, M.: Non-malleable reductions and applications. In: STOC, pp. 459–468 (2015)
4. Aggarwal, D., Dodis, Y., Lovett, S.: Non-malleable codes from additive combinatorics. In: STOC, pp. 774–783 (2014)
5. Aggarwal, D., Dodis, Y., Lovett, S.: Non-malleable codes from additive combinatorics. SIAM J. Comput. **47**(2), 524–546 (2018)
6. Aggarwal, D., Döttling, N., Nielsen, J.B., Obremski, M., Purwanto, E.: Continuous non-malleable codes in the 8-split-state model. Cryptology ePrint Archive, Report 2017/357 (2017). https://ia.cr/2017/357
7. Aggarwal, D., Dziembowski, S., Kazana, T., Obremski, M.: Leakage-resilient non-malleable codes. In: Dodis, Y., Nielsen, J.B. (eds.) TCC 2015. LNCS, vol. 9014, pp. 398–426. Springer, Heidelberg (2015). https://doi.org/10.1007/978-3-662-46494-6_17
8. Agrawal, S., Gupta, D., Maji, H.K., Pandey, O., Prabhakaran, M.: A rate-optimizing compiler for non-malleable codes against bit-wise tampering and permutations. In: Dodis, Y., Nielsen, J.B. (eds.) TCC 2015. LNCS, vol. 9014, pp. 375–397. Springer, Heidelberg (2015). https://doi.org/10.1007/978-3-662-46494-6_16
9. Ananth, P., Ishai, Y., Sahai, A.: Private circuits: a modular approach. In: Shacham, H., Boldyreva, A. (eds.) CRYPTO 2018. LNCS, vol. 10993, pp. 427–455. Springer, Cham (2018). https://doi.org/10.1007/978-3-319-96878-0_15
10. Badrinarayanan, S., Srinivasan, A.: Revisiting non-malleable secret sharing. Cryptology ePrint Archive, Report 2018/1144 (2018). https://ia.cr/2018/1144
11. Beimel, A.: Secret-sharing schemes: a survey. In: Chee, Y.M., et al. (eds.) IWCC 2011. LNCS, vol. 6639, pp. 11–46. Springer, Heidelberg (2011). https://doi.org/10.1007/978-3-642-20901-7_2

12. Ben-Or, M., Goldwasser, S., Wigderson, A.: Completeness theorems for non-cryptographic fault-tolerant distributed computation (extended abstract). In: STOC, pp. 1–10 (1988)
13. Bishop, A., Pastro, V., Rajaraman, R., Wichs, D.: Essentially optimal robust secret sharing with maximal corruptions. In: Fischlin, M., Coron, J.-S. (eds.) EUROCRYPT 2016. LNCS, vol. 9665, pp. 58–86. Springer, Heidelberg (2016). https://doi.org/10.1007/978-3-662-49890-3_3
14. Blakley, G.R.: Safeguarding cryptographic keys. In: Proceedings of AFIPS 1979 National Computer Conference, vol. 48, pp. 313–317 (1979)
15. Blundo, C., Santis, A.D., Gargano, L., Vaccaro, U.: On the information rate of secret sharing schemes. Theoret. Comput. Sci. **154**(2), 283–306 (1996)
16. Carpentieri, M., De Santis, A., Vaccaro, U.: Size of shares and probability of cheating in threshold schemes. In: Helleseth, T. (ed.) EUROCRYPT 1993. LNCS, vol. 765, pp. 118–125. Springer, Heidelberg (1994). https://doi.org/10.1007/3-540-48285-7_10
17. Chandran, N., Kanukurthi, B., Raghuraman, S.: Information-theoretic local non-malleable codes and their applications. In: Kushilevitz, E., Malkin, T. (eds.) TCC 2016. LNCS, vol. 9563, pp. 367–392. Springer, Heidelberg (2016). https://doi.org/10.1007/978-3-662-49099-0_14
18. Chattopadhyay, E., Goyal, V., Li, X.: Non-malleable extractors and codes, with their many tampered extensions. In: STOC, pp. 285–298 (2016)
19. Chattopadhyay, E., Zuckerman, D.: Non-malleable codes against constant split-state tampering. In: FOCS, pp. 306–315 (2014)
20. Chaum, D., Crépeau, C., Damgård, I.: Multiparty unconditionally secure protocols (extended abstract). In: STOC, pp. 11–19 (1988)
21. Cheraghchi, M., Guruswami, V.: Capacity of non-malleable codes. In: Innovations in Theoretical Computer Science, pp. 155–168 (2014)
22. Cheraghchi, M., Guruswami, V.: Non-malleable coding against bit-wise and split-state tampering. In: Lindell, Y. (ed.) TCC 2014. LNCS, vol. 8349, pp. 440–464. Springer, Heidelberg (2014). https://doi.org/10.1007/978-3-642-54242-8_19
23. Chor, B., Goldreich, O.: Unbiased bits from sources of weak randomness and probabilistic communication complexity. SIAM J. Comput. **17**(2), 230–261 (1988)
24. Coretti, S., Dodis, Y., Tackmann, B., Venturi, D.: Non-malleable encryption: simpler, shorter, stronger. In: Kushilevitz, E., Malkin, T. (eds.) TCC 2016. LNCS, vol. 9562, pp. 306–335. Springer, Heidelberg (2016). https://doi.org/10.1007/978-3-662-49096-9_13
25. Coretti, S., Faonio, A., Venturi, D.: Rate-optimizing compilers for continuously non-malleable codes. Cryptology ePrint Archive, Report 2019/055 (2019). https://ia.cr/2019/055
26. Coretti, S., Maurer, U., Tackmann, B., Venturi, D.: From single-bit to multi-bit public-key encryption via non-malleable codes. In: Dodis, Y., Nielsen, J.B. (eds.) TCC 2015. LNCS, vol. 9014, pp. 532–560. Springer, Heidelberg (2015). https://doi.org/10.1007/978-3-662-46494-6_22
27. Davì, F., Dziembowski, S., Venturi, D.: Leakage-resilient storage. In: Garay, J.A., De Prisco, R. (eds.) SCN 2010. LNCS, vol. 6280, pp. 121–137. Springer, Heidelberg (2010). https://doi.org/10.1007/978-3-642-15317-4_9
28. Desmedt, Y., Frankel, Y.: Shared generation of authenticators and signatures. In: Feigenbaum, J. (ed.) CRYPTO 1991. LNCS, vol. 576, pp. 457–469. Springer, Heidelberg (1992). https://doi.org/10.1007/3-540-46766-1_37
29. Dodis, Y., Haralambiev, K., López-Alt, A., Wichs, D.: Cryptography against continuous memory attacks. In: FOCS, pp. 511–520 (2010)

30. Dodis, Y., Ostrovsky, R., Reyzin, L., Smith, A.D.: Fuzzy extractors: how to generate strong keys from biometrics and other noisy data. SIAM J. Comput. **38**(1), 97–139 (2008)
31. Dolev, D., Dwork, C., Waarts, O., Yung, M.: Perfectly secure message transmission. J. ACM **40**(1), 17–47 (1993)
32. Dziembowski, S., Kazana, T., Obremski, M.: Non-malleable codes from two-source extractors. In: Canetti, R., Garay, J.A. (eds.) CRYPTO 2013. LNCS, vol. 8043, pp. 239–257. Springer, Heidelberg (2013). https://doi.org/10.1007/978-3-642-40084-1_14
33. Dziembowski, S., Pietrzak, K., Wichs, D.: Non-malleable codes. In: Innovations in Computer Science, pp. 434–452 (2010)
34. Faonio, A., Nielsen, J.B., Simkin, M., Venturi, D.: Continuously non-malleable codes with split-state refresh. In: ACNS, pp. 1–19 (2018)
35. Faonio, A., Nielsen, J.B., Venturi, D.: Fully leakage-resilient signatures revisited: graceful degradation, noisy leakage, and construction in the bounded-retrieval model. Theoret. Comput. Sci. **660**, 23–56 (2017)
36. Faonio, A., Venturi, D.: Non-malleable secret sharing in the computational setting: adaptive tampering, noisy-leakage resilience, and improved rate. Cryptology ePrint Archive, Report 2019/105 (2019). https://ia.cr/2019/105
37. Faust, S., Mukherjee, P., Nielsen, J.B., Venturi, D.: Continuous non-malleable codes. In: Lindell, Y. (ed.) TCC 2014. LNCS, vol. 8349, pp. 465–488. Springer, Heidelberg (2014). https://doi.org/10.1007/978-3-642-54242-8_20
38. Faust, S., Rabin, T., Reyzin, L., Tromer, E., Vaikuntanathan, V.: Protecting circuits from leakage: the computationally-bounded and noisy cases. In: Gilbert, H. (ed.) EUROCRYPT 2010. LNCS, vol. 6110, pp. 135–156. Springer, Heidelberg (2010). https://doi.org/10.1007/978-3-642-13190-5_7
39. Gennaro, R., Lysyanskaya, A., Malkin, T., Micali, S., Rabin, T.: Algorithmic Tamper-proof (ATP) security: theoretical foundations for security against hardware tampering. In: Naor, M. (ed.) TCC 2004. LNCS, vol. 2951, pp. 258–277. Springer, Heidelberg (2004). https://doi.org/10.1007/978-3-540-24638-1_15
40. Goldreich, O., Micali, S., Wigderson, A.: How to play any mental game or A completeness theorem for protocols with honest majority. In: STOC, pp. 218–229 (1987)
41. Goyal, V., Jain, A., Khurana, D.: Witness signatures and non-malleable multi-prover zero-knowledge proofs. Cryptology ePrint Archive, Report 2015/1095 (2015). http://ia.cr/2015/1095
42. Goyal, V., Kumar, A.: Non-malleable secret sharing. In: STOC, pp. 685–698 (2018)
43. Goyal, V., Kumar, A.: Non-malleable secret sharing for general access structures. In: Shacham, H., Boldyreva, A. (eds.) CRYPTO 2018. LNCS, vol. 10991, pp. 501–530. Springer, Cham (2018). https://doi.org/10.1007/978-3-319-96884-1_17
44. Goyal, V., Pandey, O., Richelson, S.: Textbook non-malleable commitments. In: STOC, pp. 1128–1141 (2016)
45. HashiCorp: The Vault project. https://www.vaultproject.io/. Accessed 22 Dec 2018
46. Ishai, Y., Sahai, A., Wagner, D.: Private circuits: securing hardware against probing attacks. In: Boneh, D. (ed.) CRYPTO 2003. LNCS, vol. 2729, pp. 463–481. Springer, Heidelberg (2003). https://doi.org/10.1007/978-3-540-45146-4_27
47. Kanukurthi, B., Obbattu, S.L.B., Sekar, S.: Four-state non-malleable codes with explicit constant rate. In: Kalai, Y., Reyzin, L. (eds.) TCC 2017. LNCS, vol. 10678, pp. 344–375. Springer, Cham (2017). https://doi.org/10.1007/978-3-319-70503-3_11

48. Krawczyk, H.: Secret sharing made short. In: Stinson, D.R. (ed.) CRYPTO 1993. LNCS, vol. 773, pp. 136–146. Springer, Heidelberg (1994). https://doi.org/10.1007/3-540-48329-2_12

49. Kumar, A., Meka, R., Sahai, A.: Leakage-resilient secret sharing. Cryptology ePrint Archive, Report 2018/1138 (2018). https://ia.cr/2018/1138

50. Li, X.: Improved non-malleable extractors, non-malleable codes and independent source extractors. In: STOC, pp. 1144–1156 (2017)

51. Liu, F.-H., Lysyanskaya, A.: Tamper and leakage resilience in the split-state model. In: Safavi-Naini, R., Canetti, R. (eds.) CRYPTO 2012. LNCS, vol. 7417, pp. 517–532. Springer, Heidelberg (2012). https://doi.org/10.1007/978-3-642-32009-5_30

52. Naor, M., Segev, G.: Public-key cryptosystems resilient to key leakage. SIAM J. Comput. **41**(4), 772–814 (2012)

53. Ostrovsky, R., Persiano, G., Venturi, D., Visconti, I.: Continuously non-malleable codes in the split-state model from minimal assumptions. In: Shacham, H., Boldyreva, A. (eds.) CRYPTO 2018. LNCS, vol. 10993, pp. 608–639. Springer, Cham (2018). https://doi.org/10.1007/978-3-319-96878-0_21

54. Rabin, T., Ben-Or, M.: Verifiable secret sharing and multiparty protocols with honest majority (extended abstract). In: STOC, pp. 73–85 (1989)

55. Rogaway, P., Bellare, M.: Robust computational secret sharing and a unified account of classical secret-sharing goals. In: CCS, pp. 172–184 (2007)

56. Shamir, A.: How to share a secret. Commun. ACM **22**(11), 612–613 (1979)

57. Shoup, V.: Sequences of games: a tool for taming complexity in security proofs. Cryptology ePrint Archive, Report 2004/332 (2004). http://ia.cr/2004/332

58. Srinivasan, A., Vasudevan, P.N.: Leakage resilient secret sharing and applications. Cryptology ePrint Archive, Report 2018/1154 (2018). https://ia.cr/2018/1154

Leakage Resilient Secret Sharing and Applications

Akshayaram Srinivasan[(✉)] and Prashant Nalini Vasudevan[(✉)]

University of California, Berkeley, USA
{akshayaram,prashvas}@berkeley.edu

Abstract. A secret sharing scheme allows a dealer to share a secret among a set of n parties such that any authorized subset of the parties can recover the secret, while any unauthorized subset learns no information about the secret. A *leakage-resilient* secret sharing scheme (introduced in independent works by Goyal and Kumar, STOC '18 and Benhamouda, Degwekar, Ishai and Rabin, CRYPTO '18) additionally requires the secrecy to hold against every unauthorized set of parties even if they obtain some bounded leakage from every other share. The leakage is said to be *local* if it is computed independently for each share. So far, the only known constructions of local leakage resilient secret sharing schemes are for threshold access structures for very low ($O(1)$) or very high ($n - o(\log n)$) thresholds.

In this work, we give a compiler that takes a secret sharing scheme for any monotone access structure and produces a local leakage resilient secret sharing scheme for the same access structure, with only a constant-factor asymptotic blow-up in the sizes of the shares. Furthermore, the resultant secret sharing scheme has optimal leakage-resilience rate, i.e., the ratio between the leakage tolerated and the size of each share can be made arbitrarily close to 1. Using this secret sharing scheme as the main building block, we obtain the following results:

- **Rate Preserving Non-Malleable Secret Sharing.** We give a compiler that takes any secret sharing scheme for a 4-monotone access structure (A 4-monotone access structure has the property that any authorized set has size at least 4.) with rate R and converts it into a non-malleable secret sharing scheme for the same access structure with rate $\Omega(R)$. The previous such non-zero rate construction (Badrinarayanan and Srinivasan, EUROCRYPT '19) achieved a rate of $\Theta(R/t_{\max} \log^2 n)$, where $t_{\max}$ is the maximum size of any minimal set in the access structure. As a special case, for any threshold $t \geq 4$ and an arbitrary $n \geq t$, we get the first constant-rate construction of t-out-of-n non-malleable secret sharing.

- **Leakage-Tolerant Multiparty Computation for General Interaction Patterns.** For any function f, we give a reduction

Research supported in part from DARPA/ARL SAFEWARE Award W911NF15C0210, AFOSR Award FA9550-15-1-0274, AFOSR YIP Award, a Hellman Award and research grants by the Okawa Foundation, Visa Inc., and Center for LongTerm Cybersecurity (CLTC, UC Berkeley).

A. Boldyreva and D. Micciancio (Eds.): CRYPTO 2019, LNCS 11693, pp. 480–509, 2019.
https://doi.org/10.1007/978-3-030-26951-7_17

from constructing a leakage-tolerant secure multi-party computation protocol for computing f that obeys any given interaction pattern to constructing a secure (but not necessarily leakage-tolerant) protocol for a related function that obeys the star interaction pattern. Together with the known results for the star interaction pattern, this gives leakage tolerant MPC for any interaction pattern with statistical/computational security. This improves upon the result of (Halevi et al., ITCS 2016), who presented such a reduction in a leak-free environment.

1 Introduction

Secret sharing [Sha79, Bla79] is a fundamental cryptographic primitive that allows a secret to be shared among a set of parties in such a way that only certain authorized subsets of parties can recover the secret by pooling their shares together; while any subset of parties that is not authorized do not learn anything about the secret from their shares. Secret sharing has had widespread applications across cryptography, ranging from secure multiparty computation [GMW87, BGW88, CCD88] and threshold cryptographic systems [DF90, Fra90, DDFY94] to leakage resilient circuit compilers [ISW03, FRR+10, Rot12]

While sufficient in idealized settings, in several practically relevant scenarios (as illustrated by the recent Meltdown and Spectre attacks [LSG+18, KGG+18], for instance), it is not satisfactory to assume that the set of unauthorized parties have no information at all about the remaining shares. They could, for instance, have access to some side-channel on the devices storing the other shares that leaks some information about them, and we would like for the secret to still remain hidden in this case. Such *leakage-resilience* has been widely studied in the past as a desirable property in various settings and cryptographic primitives [MR04, DP08, AGV09, NS09, . . .]. In this paper, we study leakage-resilience in secret sharing – we ask that the secret remain hidden from unauthorized subsets of parties even if they have access to some small amount of information about the shares of the remaining parties.

The Leakage Model. A secret sharing scheme consist of a sharing algorithm, which takes a secret and shares it into a set of shares, and a reconstruction algorithm, which takes some subset of these shares and reconstructs the secret from it. In this work, we do not deal with the leakage from the machines that run these procedures. Instead, the leakage that we care about is that which could happen from the machines that these shares are stored on after they have been generated, and the sharing and reconstruction are assumed to be leak-free.

More specifically, we are interested in *local* leakage resilience, which means that secrets are hidden from an adversary that works as follows. First, it specifies an unauthorized subset of parties, and for each of the remaining parties, it specifies a leakage function that takes its share as input, performs an arbitrary (possibly inefficient) computation and outputs a small pre-determined number of bits. Once the shares are generated, the adversary is given all the shares of the unauthorized subset, and the output of the corresponding leakage function applied to each of the remaining shares. This form of leakage-resilience for secret sharing was formalized in recent work by Goyal and Kumar [GK18a], and Benhamouda, Degwekar, Ishai and Rabin [BDIR18].

This leakage model may be seen as an adaptation of the "memory attacks" model introduced by Akavia, Goldwasser, and Vaikuntanathan [AGV09] to the context of secret sharing. In this model, the basic axiom is that everything that is stored in the memory is subject to leakage, and the only restriction is that the leakage function must be shrinking. This model was introduced as an alternative to the well-studied "Only Computational Leaks" (OCL) model [MR04] (which we do not consider in this work) in order to capture known real-world attacks that were not captured by the OCL model. A notable example of such an attack is the cold-boot attack by Halderman et al. [HSH+09], which showed measures to leak a significant fraction of the bits of a secret if it was ever stored in a part of memory which could be accessed by an adversary (e.g. DRAM). The definition of leakage-resilience for secret sharing that we work with is intended (as was the memory attacks model) to protect against such attacks on the machines that store the shares after they have been generated.

Goyal and Kumar, and Benhamouda et al., showed constructions of leakage-resilient threshold secret sharing schemes (where subsets above a certain size are authorized) for certain thresholds. They then showed how such schemes could be used to construct leakage-resilient multi-party computation protocols and non-malleable secret sharing schemes. Given the prevalence of secret-sharing in cryptographic constructions and the importance of resilience to leakage, one may reasonably expect many more applications of leakage-resilient secret sharing to be discovered in the future.

In this work, we are interested in constructing local leakage resilient secret sharing schemes for a larger class of access structures[1] (and in particular for all thresholds). Beyond showing feasibility, our focus is on optimizing the following parameters of our schemes:

- the *rate*, which is the ratio of the size of the secret to the size of a share, and,
- the *leakage-resilience rate*, which is the ratio of the number of bits of leakage tolerated per share to the size of a share.

We present a construction of leakage-resilient secret sharing that is near-optimal in terms of the above parameters, and show applications of our construction to constructing constant-rate non-malleable secret sharing schemes and leakage-tolerant multi-party computation protocols.

1.1   Our Results and Techniques

Our primary result is a transformation that converts a secret sharing scheme for any access structure $\mathcal{A}$ into a local leakage resilient secret sharing scheme for $\mathcal{A}$

---

[1] The access structure of a secret sharing scheme is what we call the set of authorized subsets of parties.

whose rate is only a small constant factor less than that of the original scheme, and which has an optimal leakage-resilience rate of 1.

Informal Theorem 1. *There is a compiler that, given a secret sharing scheme for a monotone access structure $\mathcal{A}$ with rate R, produces a secret sharing scheme for $\mathcal{A}$ that has rate $R/3.01$ and is local leakage resilient with leakage-resilience rate tending to 1.*

In particular, for any $t \leq n$, starting from t-out-of-n Shamir secret sharing [Sha79] gives us a t-out-of-n threshold secret sharing scheme with rate $1/3.01$ and leakage-resilience rate 1. The only constructions of local leakage resilient secret sharing known before our work were for threshold access structures with either very small or very large thresholds. Goyal and Kumar [GK18a] presented a construction for $t = 2$, which had both rate and leakage-resilience rate $\Theta(1/n)$. This was extended to any constant t by Badrinarayanan and Srinivasan [BS19], with rate $\Theta(1/\log(n))$ and leakage-resilience rate $\Theta(1/n\log(n))$. Benhamouda et al. [BDIR18] showed that t-out-of-n Shamir secret sharing over certain fields is local leakage-resilient if $t = n - o(n)$, and this has rate 1 and leakage-resilience rate roughly $1/4$.

Outline of Our Compiler. We will now briefly describe the functioning of our compiler for the case of a t-out-of-n threshold secret sharing scheme, for simplicity. It makes use of a strong seeded randomness extractor Ext, which is an algorithm that takes two inputs – a seed s and a source w – and whose output $\mathrm{Ext}(s, w)$ is close to being uniformly random if s is chosen at random and w has sufficient min-entropy. The extractor being "strong" means that the output remains close to uniform even if the seed is given.

We take any threshold secret sharing scheme (such as Shamir's [Sha79]), and share our secret m with it to obtain the set of shares $(\mathsf{Sh}_1, \ldots, \mathsf{Sh}_n)$. We first choose a uniform seed s, and for each $i \in [n]$, we choose a uniformly random "source" w_i (all of appropriate lengths), and mask Sh_i using $\mathrm{Ext}(s, w_i)$. That is, we compute $\mathsf{Sh}'_i = \mathsf{Sh}_i \oplus \mathrm{Ext}(s, w_i)$. We then secret share s using a 2-out-of-n secret sharing scheme to get the set of shares $S_1, \ldots, S_n$. The share corresponding to party i in our scheme is now set to $(w_i, \mathsf{Sh}'_i, S_i)$.

Given t such shares, to recover the secret, we first reconstruct the seed from any two S_i's and then unmask Sh'_i by XORing with $\mathrm{Ext}(s, w_i)$ to obtain Sh_i. We then use the reconstruction procedure of the underlying secret sharing to recover the message.

The correctness and privacy of the constructed scheme are straightforward to check. To argue the local leakage resilience of this construction, we go over a set of $n - t + 1$ hybrids where in each hybrid, we will replace one Sh_i with the all 0's string. Once we have replaced $n - t + 1$ such shares with the 0's string, we can then rely on the secrecy of the underlying secret sharing scheme to show that the message is perfectly hidden. Thus, it is now sufficient to show that any two adjacent hybrids in the above argument are statistically close. To argue that the adjacent hybrids, say Hyb_i and Hyb_{i+1}, are statistically close, we rely on the randomness property of the extractor. The key here is that as long as the leakage from the source w_i is much smaller than its length, it still has enough entropy for the output of the extractor on w_i to be statistically close to random. This allows us to argue that $\text{Ext}(s, w_i)$ acts as a one-time pad and thus, we can replace Sh_i with the all 0's string without an adversary being able to tell.

However, in order to make the argument work, we must ensure that the leakage from the source is independent of the seed (which is required for the extractor to work). This is where we will be using the fact that the seed is secret shared using a 2-out-of-n secret sharing scheme. Intuitively, this ensures that a local leakage function has no idea what the seed is, and so cannot leak anything about w_i that depends on the seed. In our reduction, we fix the share S_i to be independent of the seed and then leak from the source w_i. Once the seed is known[2], we can sample the other shares $(S_1, \ldots, S_{i-1}, S_{i+1}, \ldots, S_n)$ as a valid 2-out-of-n secret sharing of s that is consistent with the fixed share S_i. This allows us to argue that the leakage on w_i is independent of the seed. There is a small caveat here that the masked value Sh_i' is dependent on the seed and hence we cannot argue independence of the leakage on the source and the seed. However, we use a simple trick of masking Sh_i' by another one-time pad and then secret share the one-time pad key along with the seed s and use this argue that this masked value is independent of the seed.

This construction described above has several useful properties. The most significant one is that the transformation is rather simple and only incurs a very small overhead when compared to the original secret sharing scheme. In particular, the rate of the resultant leakage resilient secret sharing has only a small constant factor loss when compared to the initial secret sharing scheme. Also, we can sample the seed s of the extractor once and use it for sharing multiple secrets.[3] The second advantage is that it easily generalizes to all monotone access structures, basically, the only difference is that we use a secret sharing scheme for this access structure to obtain the set of shares $(\text{Sh}_1, \ldots, \text{Sh}_n)$, and the rest of the steps are exactly the same as before. The third advantage is that the resultant secret sharing scheme has optimal leakage-resilience rate, i.e., the ratio between the number of bits of leakage tolerated and size of the share tends to 1 as the amount of leakage that the scheme is designed to handle increases. Finally, if we use the inner product two-source extractor of Chor and Goldreich [CG88] as the underlying extractor and the Shamir secret sharing scheme, then the sharing procedure is a linear function of the secret and a quadratic function of the randomness, and this can be implemented very efficiently.

Stronger Leakage-Resilience. We also extend our construction to satisfy a stronger notion of leakage resilience, which we describe next. In the earlier definition of local leakage, the leakage functions that are applied on the shares of

---

[2] As the extractor is a strong seeded extractor, $\text{Ext}(s, w_i)$ is statistically close to uniform even given the seed.

[3] For the security of this modification to go through, we need the adversary to specify all the secrets and leakage functions upfront – it cannot adaptively choose the secrets and leakage functions depending on the previous leakage.

honest parties are required to be specified independently of the shares that are completely revealed to the adversary. In our stronger definition, these leakage functions are allowed to depend on some number of the adversary's shares.

In particular, we construct t-out-of-n threshold secret sharing schemes that are resilient to such stronger leakage where the adversary is given $(t-1)$ shares, and the leakage functions applied on the honest party's shares are allowed to depend on $(t-2)$ of these shares. This construction, which is in fact a simple modification of our earlier one, has worse rate, but still has optimal leakage-resilience rate. Referring temporarily to the above as $(t-2, t-1)$-strong local leakage, we have the following.

Informal Theorem 2. *For any $t \leq n$, there is a t-out-of-n threshold secret sharing scheme that is resilient against $(t-2, t-1)$-strong local leakage, has rate $\Omega(1/n)$, and leakage-resilience rate tending to 1.*

It is easy to check that this definition is impossible to achieve for a t-out-of-n threshold secret sharing scheme if we allow the leakage functions to depend on all $(t-1)$ of the adversary's shares, as the leakage function on any honest party's share can use the $(t-1)$ shares along with this share to reconstruct the secret and leak a few bits of the secret. Later in this section, we will describe an application of this strong leakage resilient secret sharing scheme in constructing leakage tolerant MPC for general interaction patterns.

Application 1: Rate-Preserving Non-Malleable Secret Sharing. Non-malleable secret sharing schemes, introduced by Goyal and Kumar [GK18a], are secret sharing schemes where it is not possible to tamper with the shares of a secret s (in certain limited ways) so as to convert them to shares corresponding to a different secret $\tilde{s}$ that is related to s (such as $s+1$ or s with the first bit flipped). We are interested in security against an adversary that tampers each share independent of the others (called individual tampering). Such an adversary works as follows. Initially, it specifies n "tampering functions" $f_1, \ldots, f_n$ and an authorized set. A secret s is then shared into $(\mathsf{Sh}_1, \ldots, \mathsf{Sh}_n)$ and the shares are tampered to get $\widetilde{\mathsf{Sh}}_i \leftarrow f_i(\mathsf{Sh}_i)$. The requirement now is that if the above specified authorized set of parties try to reconstruct the secret using the shares $\{\widetilde{\mathsf{Sh}}_i\}$, the resulting secret $\tilde{s}$ is either the same as s or something completely independent.

In this setting, Goyal and Kumar presented a construction of a non-malleable t-out-of-n threshold secret sharing scheme, and in a later paper [GK18b] extended this to general access structures. Their constructions, however, had an asymptotic rate of zero.

Badrinarayanan and Srinivasan [BS19] gave a rate-efficient compiler that takes any secret sharing scheme for a 4-monotone[4] access structure and outputs a non-malleable secret sharing scheme for the same access structure. The main tool used in their compiler was a local leakage resilient threshold secret sharing

---

[4] k-monotone means that all authorized sets in the access structure are of size at least k.

scheme. The loss in the rate of the resulting non-malleable secret sharing scheme depended on the parameters of the underlying local leakage resilient secret sharing. In particular, to have only a constant loss in the rate, it was important to have a local leakage resilient threshold secret sharing scheme that had a constant rate and a constant leakage-resilience rate. We plug in our leakage resilient secret sharing scheme that has both these features with the compiler of Badrinarayanan and Srinivasan to obtain a rate-preserving compiler for non-malleable secret sharing.

Informal Theorem 3. *There is a compiler that, given a secret sharing scheme for a 4-monotone access structure $\mathcal{A}$ with rate R, produces a secret sharing scheme for $\mathcal{A}$ that has rate $\Omega(R)$ and is non-malleable against individual tampering.*

Application 2: Leakage-Tolerant MPC for General Interaction Patterns. Next, we provide an application of our constructions to secure multiparty computation (MPC), an area where secret sharing is rather pervasive. In particular, we study MPC protocols obeying a specified interaction pattern.

Background. An interaction pattern (introduced by Halevi et al. [HIJ+16]) generalizes the communication graph of a standard MPC protocol. It is defined as a directed graph which specifies the sequence of messages that have to be sent during the execution of a MPC protocol – its vertices correspond to the messages, and edges indicate dependencies between messages. We illustrate by example with the ring interaction pattern. Here, the first message is sent by the party P_1 to the party P_2 and depending on this message, P_2 sends a message to P_3 and so on. Finally, the party P_n sends a message to P_1 who computes the output based on this message. The directed graph corresponding to this has $(n + 1)$ nodes, one corresponding to each message and one for the output, and the graph is a single directed path that goes from the first message to the last and then to the output node. To give another example, a standard 2-round MPC protocol with n parties can be represented by an interaction pattern graph with two sets of $\binom{n}{2}$ nodes, representing the messages sent by each party to every other party in the two rounds. The edges then go from the nodes corresponding to first-round messages to second-round messages, according to the protocol.

Given an interaction pattern specified by such a directed graph, the main goal is to understand which functions can be computed securely by a protocol following this pattern. It is known that without any form of correlated randomness setup, even simple functions such as majority cannot be computed with any meaningful form of security for certain interaction patterns [BGI+14]. It is also known from a sequence of works [HLP11, GGG+14, BGI+14] that standard notions of security in MPC that guarantee that only the output is leaked are impossible to achieve for certain interaction patterns. To see this, consider the star interaction pattern [FKN94] where there is a special party called the evaluator and every other party sends a single message to the evaluator who then computes the output. In this interaction pattern, if the evaluator colludes with some subset of the parties, then it is easy to see that the colluding parties can learn the entire residual function resulting from fixing the honest parties' inputs to the function being computed.

In other interaction patterns, the residual function that the colluding parties are able to learn may be different. In general, Halevi et al. [HIJ+16] classify the parties' inputs into *fixed* and *free* – every honest party's input is fixed, and so is a corrupted party's input if there exists a path from a message sent by the corrupted party to the output that passes through at least one honest party's message. The inputs of the remaining corrupted parties are free. To capture the inherent security loss in certain interaction patterns, Halevi et al. allow the adversary to learn the residual function with the above set of fixed inputs, and say a protocol that is compliant with an interaction pattern is secure if it hides everything other than this residual function.

Defining Leakage Tolerance. We extend the above definition of security to also account for possible leakage from the states of honest parties. Specifically, we define the notion of leakage tolerance for an MPC protocol that is compliant with an interaction pattern along the same lines as that of leakage tolerant MPC [GJS11,BCH12]. In the setting of leakage tolerance, as in the standard setting, we consider an adversary who corrupts an arbitrary subset of parties and can see their entire views. But in addition to this, the adversary also obtains bounded leakage on the complete internal state – that includes the correlated randomness, the input, the secret randomness, and the entire view of the protocol – of every honest party. The only process that we assume happens in a leak-free manner is the correlated randomness generation phase which is anyway independent of the actual inputs of the parties. After this leak-free randomness generation, every bit of an honest party's secret state including its input is subject to leakage. Here, the adversary can potentially learn bounded information about the honest party's input since it has access to all of the honest parties' secret state. We would like to guarantee that nothing beyond such bounded information about the inputs and the residual function is actually leaked to the adversary – note that this is the best possible security we can hope for in this setting. Technically, we account for this leakage by allowing the simulator to learn the same amount of information about the honest parties' inputs.

What makes the task of providing such security non-trivial is that, unlike a standard MPC simulator who is allowed to cheat in generating the protocol messages, a simulator in the leakage tolerance setting cannot deviate from the protocol specification. This is because any deviation can be caught by the adversary by leveraging the leakage on the secret state of the honest party. At first sight, the task of designing such a simulator seems impossible as we require the simulator to generate the correct protocol messages based only the output (or more generally, based on the residual function). However, notice that the leakage functions are local to the honest party's view. Hence, the simulator must follow the protocol correctly at the local level but must somehow cheat at the global level, i.e., in generating the joint distribution of the protocol messages. To make this task even more demanding, we do not wish to use any computational assumptions and only make use of information theoretic tools to achieve leakage tolerance.

Our Results. In this setting, we upgrade one of the results of Halevi et al. [HIJ+16] to have the additional guarantee of leakage tolerance. They showed that the star interaction pattern described earlier is complete for obtaining MPC for general interaction patterns – given a secure protocol for a function f that is compliant with the star interaction pattern, they showed how to construct a secure protocol for f compliant with any other interaction pattern. In this work, we show that star interaction pattern is complete for obtaining leakage-tolerant MPC for general interaction patterns. Specifically, we obtain the following.

Informal Theorem 4. *There is a compiler that, given a function $f : \{0,1\}^n \to \{0,1\}$, an interaction pattern $\mathcal{I}$, and a secure protocol for f compliant with the star interaction pattern, produces a secure protocol (with a leak-free setup phase producing correlated randomness) for f compliant with $\mathcal{I}$ that is leakage tolerant.*

Using the known protocols for the star interaction pattern [BGI+14, BKR17, GGG+14], we obtain the following corollaries for any interaction pattern $\mathcal{I}$ and function $f : \{0,1\}^n \to \{0,1\}$:

- An $\mathcal{I}$-compliant protocol for f with statistical leakage tolerance against upto $(n-1)$ passive corruptions, with communication exponential in n.
- An efficient $\mathcal{I}$-compliant protocol for $f \in \mathsf{NC}^1$ with statistical leakage tolerance against a constant number of passive corruptions.
- Assuming the existence of one-way functions, and that f is computable by a polynomial-sized circuit, an efficient $\mathcal{I}$-compliant protocol for f with computational leakage tolerance against a constant number of passive corruptions.
- Assuming the existence of indistinguishability obfuscation and one-way functions, and that f is computable by a polynomial-sized circuit, an efficient $\mathcal{I}$-compliant protocol for f with computational leakage tolerance against upto $(n-1)$ passive corruptions.

Our actual construction also covers functions where each party has multiple bits as input and the function can output multiple bits (see Theorem 9). The compiler we use is the same as that of Halevi et al., except for using a leakage-resilient secret sharing scheme where theirs uses additive secret sharing. However, the proof of leakage tolerance is quite involved and, in fact, it turns out that standard local leakage resilience is insufficient for this purpose and we require strong leakage resilience. We now provide some intuition on why this is the case. In the Halevi et al.'s construction, some set of secrets are shared among all the parties in the correlated randomness generation phase. The messages sent during the execution of the protocol comprise of a subset of a party's shares. So, a party's secret state not only includes its own shares, but also the shares received from the other parties. Thus, the leakage function on an honest party's internal state is not local as it gets to see a subset of the other parties' shares.

Thus, we need a secret sharing scheme satisfying the stronger notion of leakage resilience, where the leakage on the honest party's share can potentially depend on the shares of corrupted parties. For this purpose, we make use of the secret sharing scheme described in Informal Theorem 2.

1.2 Related Work

In a concurrent and independent work, Aggarwal et al. [ADN+18] also construct leakage-resilient secret sharing schemes for any access structure from any secret sharing scheme for that access structure. Their transformation incurs a $O(1/n)$-factor loss in the rate and achieves a leakage-resilience rate of $(1 - c)$ for a small constant c. In comparison, our transformation has a constant-factor loss in the rate and achieves a leakage-resilience rate of 1. They use their techniques and results to construct non-malleable secret sharing for 3-monotone access structures with an asymptotic rate of 0, and threshold signatures that are resilient to leakage and mauling attacks. In comparison, our compiler for non-malleable secret sharing is rate-preserving, but works only for 4-monotone access structures. Their work also considers the stronger model of concurrent tampering and gives positive results in this model as well.

In another concurrent and independent work, Kumar et al. [KMS18] also consider the problem of obtaining leakage-resilient secret sharing schemes in a stronger leakage model. In particular, they consider a leakage model where every bit of the leakage can depend on an adaptively chosen set of $O(\log n)$ shares. They give constructions of such secret sharing schemes for general access structures via a connection to problems that have large communication complexity. The rate and the leakage-resilience rate of the construction are both $\Theta(1/\text{poly}(n))$. As an application, they construct a leakage-resilient non-malleable secret sharing scheme where the tampering function can obtain bounded, adaptive leakage from each share. In comparison, our strong leakage-resilient secret sharing scheme works against local leakage with a single level of adaptivity, where the leakage on each honest party's share could depend on at most $(t - 2)$ shares in a t-out-of-n threshold scheme; our scheme has rate $\Omega(1/n)$ and a leakage-resilience rate of 1.

Apart from these, most closely related to our work are the papers by Goyal and Kumar on non-malleable secret sharing [GK18a, GK18b], Benhamouda et al. on leakage-resilient secret sharing and MPC [BDIR18], and Badrinarayanan and Srinivasan on non-malleable secret sharing with non-zero rate [BS19].

Local leakage resilient secret sharing (in the sense in which we use this term) was first studied by Goyal and Kumar [GK18a] and Benhamouda et al. [BDIR18] (independently of each other). [GK18a] constructed a local leakage resilient 2-out-of-n threshold secret sharing scheme with rate and leakage-resilience rate both $\Theta(1/n)$. They used this as a building block to construct non-malleable threshold secret sharing schemes secure against individual and joint tampering (where the adversary is allowed to jointly tamper sets of shares). A later paper also by Goyal and Kumar [GK18b] extended this to a compiler that adds non-malleability to a secret sharing scheme for any access structure. The non-malleable schemes resulting from both of these works, however, had rate tending to 0. Badrinarayanan and Srinivasan [BS19] later presented a compiler that converts any rate R secret sharing scheme to a non-malleable one for the same access structure with rate $\Theta(R/t_{max} \log^2 n)$, where t_{max} is the maximum size of any minimal set in the access structure. In the process, they constructed local leakage resilient t-out-of-n secret sharing schemes for a constant t that had rate $\Theta(1/\log(n))$ and leakage-resilience rate $\Theta(1/n\log(n))$.

Benhamouda et al. [BDIR18] were interested in studying the leakage-resilience of existing secret sharing schemes and MPC protocols. Inspired by the results of Guruswami and Wootters [GW16] that implied the possibility of recovering the secret from single-bit local leakage of Shamir shares over small characteristic fields, they investigated the leakage resilience of Shamir secret sharing over larger characteristic fields. They showed that, for large enough characteristic and large enough number of parties n, this scheme is leakage-resilient (with leakage-resilience rate close to $1/4$) as long as the threshold is large (at least $n - o(\log(n))$). They used this fact to show leakage-resilience of the GMW protocol [GMW87] (using Beaver's triples), and to show an impossibility result for multi-party share conversion.

Boyle et al. [BGK14] define and construct leakage-resilient verifiable secret sharing schemes where the sharing and reconstruction are performed by interactive protocols (as opposed to just algorithms). They also show that a modification of the Shamir secret sharing scheme satisfies a weaker notion of leakage-resilience than the one we consider here, where it is only required that a random secret retain sufficient entropy given the leakage on the shares.

Dziembowski and Pietrzak [DP07] construct secret sharing schemes (that they call intrusion-resilient) that are resilient to adaptive leakage where the adversary is allowed to iteratively ask for leakage from different shares. Their reconstruction procedure is also interactive, however, requiring as many rounds of interaction as the adaptivity of the leakage tolerated.

Leakage-resilience of secure multiparty computation has been studied in the past in various settings [BGJK12, GIM+16, DHP11]. More broadly, leakage-resilience of various cryptographic primitives have been quite widely studied – we refer the reader to the survey by Alwen et al. [ADW09] and the references therein. The notion of leakage tolerance was introduced by Garg et al. [GJS11] and Bitansky et al. [BCH12], and has been the subject of many papers since [BCG+11, BGJ+13, BDL14].

Secure multiparty computation with general interaction patterns was first studied by Halevi et al. [HIJ+16], who showed a reduction from general interaction patterns to the star pattern (which is what we base our reduction on). For any interaction pattern, they then showed an inefficient information-theoretically secure protocol for general functions, and an efficient one for symmetric functions; they also showed a computationally secure protocol for general functions assuming the existence of indistinguishability obfuscation and one-way functions, and for symmetric functions under an assumption about multilinear maps.

Subsequent Work. Subsequent to our work, Nielsen and Simkin [NS19] showed a lower bound on the share size of leakage resilient secret sharing schemes that satisfies the property that $\hat{t}$ shares completely determine the other $n-\hat{t}$ shares. In particular, they showed that the size of the shares of such schemes for threshold access structures with threshold t must be at least $\ell(n-t)/\hat{t}$ where ℓ is the size of the leakage tolerated. This in particular, shows that Shamir secret sharing cannot be leakage resilient for thresholds $o(n)$ when leaking, say, $1/4$-th of the share size. On the other hand, it does not apply to schemes like ours where each share contains some randomness independent of the other shares and is not determined even given all the other shares.

2 Preliminaries

Notation. We use capital letters to denote distributions and their support, and corresponding lowercase letters to denote a sample from the same. Let $[n]$ denote the set $\{1, 2, \ldots, n\}$ and U_r denote the uniform distribution over $\{0,1\}^r$. For a finite set S, we denote $x \xleftarrow{\$} S$ as sampling x uniformly at random from the set S. For any $i \in [n]$, let x_i denote the symbol at the i-th co-ordinate of x, and for any $T \subseteq [n]$, let $x_T \in \{0,1\}^{|T|}$ denote the projection of x to the co-ordinates indexed by T. We write $\circ$ to denote concatenation. We assume the reader's familiarity with the standard definitions of min-entropy, statistical distance and seeded extractors and for completeness give the definition in the full version.

We first give the definition of a k-monotone access structure, then define a sharing function and finally define a secret sharing scheme.

Definition 1 (k-Monotone Access Structure). *An access structure $\mathcal{A}$ is said to be monotone if for any set $S \in \mathcal{A}$, any superset of S is also in $\mathcal{A}$. We will call a monotone access structure $\mathcal{A}$ as k-monotone if for any $S \in \mathcal{A}$, $|S| \geq k$.*

Definition 2 (Sharing Function [Bei11]). *Let $[n] = \{1, 2, \ldots, n\}$ be a set of identities of n parties. Let $\mathcal{M}$ be the domain of secrets. A sharing function Share is a randomized mapping from $\mathcal{M}$ to $\mathcal{S}_1 \times \mathcal{S}_2 \times \ldots \times \mathcal{S}_n$, where $\mathcal{S}_i$ is called the domain of shares of party with identity i. A dealer distributes a secret $m \in \mathcal{M}$ by computing the vector Share$(m) = (\mathsf{S}_1, \ldots, \mathsf{S}_n)$, and privately communicating each share S_i to the party i. For a set $T \subseteq [n]$, we denote Share$(m)_T$ to be a restriction of Share(m) to its T entries.*

Definition 3 (($\mathcal{A}, n, \epsilon_c, \epsilon_s$)-Secret Sharing Scheme [Bei11]). *Let $\mathcal{M}$ be a finite set of secrets, where $|\mathcal{M}| \geq 2$. Let $[n] = \{1, 2, \ldots, n\}$ be a set of identities (indices) of n parties. A sharing function Share with domain of secrets $\mathcal{M}$ is a $(\mathcal{A}, n, \epsilon_c, \epsilon_s)$-secret sharing scheme with respect to monotone access structure $\mathcal{A}$ if the following two properties hold:*

- *Correctness: The secret can be reconstructed by any set of parties that are part of the access structure $\mathcal{A}$. That is, for any set $T \in \mathcal{A}$, there exists a*

deterministic reconstruction function $\mathsf{Rec} : \otimes_{i \in T} \mathcal{S}_i \to \mathcal{M}$ *such that for every* $m \in \mathcal{M}$,
$$\Pr[\mathsf{Rec}(\mathsf{Share}(m)_T) = m] = 1 - \epsilon_c$$
where the probability is over the randomness of the Share *function. We will slightly abuse the notation and denote* Rec *as the reconstruction procedure that takes in* $T \in \mathcal{A}$ *and* $\mathsf{Share}(m)_T$ *as input and outputs the secret.*

- **Statistical Privacy:** *Any collusion of parties not part of the access structure should have "almost" no information about the underlying secret. More formally, for any unauthorized set* $U \subseteq [n]$ *such that* $U \notin \mathcal{A}$, *and for every pair of secrets* $m_0, m_1 \in M$, *for any distinguisher* D *with output in* $\{0, 1\}$, *the following holds:*

$$|\Pr[D(\mathsf{Share}(m_0)_U) = 1] - \Pr[D(\mathsf{Share}(m_1)_U) = 1]| \leq \epsilon_s$$

We define the rate of the secret sharing scheme as $\lim_{|m| \to \infty} \frac{|m|}{\max_{i \in [n]} |\mathsf{Share}(m)_i|}$.

Remark 1 (Threshold Secret Sharing Scheme). For ease of notation, we will denote a t-out-of-n threshold secret sharing scheme as $(t, n, \epsilon_c, \epsilon_s)$-secret sharing scheme.

3   Leakage Resilient Secret Sharing Scheme

In this section, we will define and construct a leakage resilient secret sharing scheme against a class of local leakage functions. We first recall the definition of a leakage resilient secret sharing scheme from [GK18a].

Definition 4 (Leakage Resilient Secret Sharing [GK18a]). *An* $(\mathcal{A}, n, \epsilon_c, \epsilon_s)$ *secret sharing scheme* $(\mathsf{Share}, \mathsf{Rec})$ *for message space* $\mathcal{M}$ *is said to be* ϵ-*leakage resilient against a leakage family* $\mathcal{F}$ *if for all functions* $f \in \mathcal{F}$ *and for any two messages* $m_0, m_1 \in \mathcal{M}$:

$$|f(\mathsf{Share}(m_0)) - f(\mathsf{Share}(m_1))| \leq \epsilon$$

3.1   Local Leakage Resilience

In this subsection, we will transform any secret sharing scheme to a leakage resilient secret sharing scheme against the local leakage function family. We first recall the definition of this function family.

Local Leakage Function Family. Let $(\mathcal{S}_1 \times \mathcal{S}_2 \ldots \times \mathcal{S}_n)$ be the domain of shares for some secret sharing scheme, and $\mathcal{A}$ be an access structure. The corresponding local leakage function family is given by $\mathcal{F}_{\mathcal{A}, \mu} = \{f_{K, \vec{\tau}} : K \subseteq [n], K \notin \mathcal{A}, \tau_i : \mathcal{S}_i \to \{0, 1\}^\mu\}$ where $f_{K, \vec{\tau}}$ on input $(\mathsf{share}_1, \ldots, \mathsf{share}_n)$ outputs share_i for each $i \in K$ in the clear and outputs $\tau_i(\mathsf{share}_i)$ for every $i \in [n] \setminus K$.

Following [BDIR18], we will call secret sharing schemes resilient to $\mathcal{F}_{\mathcal{A},\vec{\tau}}$ as *local leakage resilient secret sharing*. We will define the *leakage-resilience rate* of such a secret sharing scheme to be $\lim_{\mu \to \infty} \frac{\mu}{\max_{i \in [n]} \log |\mathcal{S}_i|}$.

Remark 2. We remark that Definition 4 is satisfiable against the leakage function class $\mathcal{F}_{\mathcal{A},\mu}$ (for any $\mu > 0$) only if the access structure is 2-monotone (see Definition 1). Hence, in the rest of the paper, we will concentrate on 2-monotone access structures.

Description of the Compiler. We will give a compiler that takes any $(\mathcal{A}, n, \epsilon_c, \epsilon_s)$ secret sharing scheme for any 2-monotone $\mathcal{A}$ and outputs a local leakage resilient secret sharing scheme for $\mathcal{A}$. We give the description of the compiler in Fig. 1.

Let (Share, Rec) be a $(\mathcal{A}, n, \epsilon_c, \epsilon_s)$ secret sharing scheme for sharing secrets from $\mathcal{M}$ with share size equal to ρ bits. Let $(\text{Share}_{(2,n)}, \text{Rec}_{(2,n)})$ be a 2-out-of-n Shamir Secret sharing. Let $\text{Ext} : \{0,1\}^\eta \times \{0,1\}^d \to \{0,1\}^\rho$ be a $(\eta - \mu, \epsilon)$-average-case, strong seeded extractor.

LRShare : To share a secret $m \in \mathcal{M}$:
1. Run Share(m) to obtain the shares $(\text{Sh}_1, \dots, \text{Sh}_n)$.
2. Choose a uniform seed $s \xleftarrow{\$} \{0,1\}^d$ and a masking string $r \xleftarrow{\$} \{0,1\}^\rho$.
3. For each $i \in [n]$ do:
    - (a) Choose $w_i \xleftarrow{\$} \{0,1\}^\eta$.
    - (b) Set $\text{Sh}'_i = \text{Sh}_i \oplus \text{Ext}(w_i, s)$.
4. Run $\text{Share}_{(2,n)}(s, r)$ to obtain $S_1, \dots, S_n$.
5. Output share$_i$ as $(w_i, \text{Sh}'_i \oplus r, S_i)$.

LRRec : Given the shares $\text{share}_{j_1}, \text{share}_{j_2}, \dots, \text{share}_{j_\ell}$ where $K = \{j_1, \dots, j_k\} \in \mathcal{A}$ do:
1. For each $i \in K$, parse share$_i$ as (w_i, S'_i, S_i).
2. Run $\text{Rec}_{(2,n)}(S_{j_1}, S_{j_2})$ to recover (s, r).
3. For each $i \in K$ do:
    - (a) Compute $\text{Sh}'_i = S'_i \oplus r$.
    - (b) Recover Sh_i by computing $\text{Sh}'_i \oplus \text{Ext}(w_i, s)$.
4. Run $\text{Rec}(\text{Sh}_{j_1}, \dots, \text{Sh}_{j_k})$ to recover the secret m.

Fig. 1. Local leakage-resilient secret sharing

Theorem 5. *Consider any 2-monotone access structure $\mathcal{A}$ and $\mu \in \mathbb{N}$ and a secret domain $\mathcal{M}$ with secrets of length m. Suppose for some $\eta, d, \rho \in \mathbb{N}$ and $\epsilon_c, \epsilon_s, \epsilon \in [0, 1)$, the following exist:*

- *A $(\mathcal{A}, n, \epsilon_c, \epsilon_s)$ secret sharing scheme for the secret domain $\mathcal{M}$ with share length ρ.*

- A $(\eta - \mu, \varepsilon)$-average-case strong seeded extractor Ext : $\{0,1\}^\eta \times \{0,1\}^d \to \{0,1\}^\rho$.

Then, the construction in Fig. 1, when instantiated with these, is a $(\mathcal{A}, n, \epsilon_c, \epsilon_s)$ secret sharing scheme for $\mathcal{M}$ that is $2(\epsilon_s + n \cdot \epsilon)$-leakage resilient against $\mathcal{F}_{\mathcal{A},\mu}$. It has share size $(\eta + 2\rho + d)$.

We give the proof of this theorem in the full version of the paper.

Instantiation. Next we demonstrate an instantiation of Theorem 5 with the state-of-the-art explicit construction of strong seeded extractors from the work of Guruswami, Umans and Vadhan [GUV09].

Theorem 6 ([GUV09]). *For any constant $\alpha > 0$, and all integers $n, k > 0$ there exists a polynomial time computable (k, ϵ)-strong seeded extractor Ext : $\{0,1\}^n \times \{0,1\}^d \to \{0,1\}^m$ with $d = O(\log n + \log(\frac{1}{\epsilon}))$ and $m = (1 - \alpha)k$.*

We now instantiate our scheme with the following building blocks:

- Let (Share, Rec) be a secret sharing scheme for a 2-monotone access structure $\mathcal{A}$ for sharing m-bit messages with rate R.
- We use the Guruswami, Umans and Vadhan [GUV09] strong seeded extractor (refer Theorem 6). We set $n = 1.01m/R + \log(1/\epsilon) + \mu$ and $d = O(\log n + \log(1/\epsilon))$ and from Theorem 6 and from [DORS08], it follows that Ext is a $(1.01m/R + \log(1/\epsilon), 2\epsilon)$ average-case, strong seeded extractor.

Thus, (using terminology from Fig. 1) we get $|\mathsf{share}_i| = |w_i| + |\mathsf{Sh}_i| + |S_i| = n + m/R + (m/R + d) = 3.01m/R + \mu + O(\log m + \log \mu + \log 1/\epsilon)$.

Corollary 1. *If there exists a secret sharing scheme for a 2-monotone access structure with rate R, then there exists an ϵ-local leakage resilient secret sharing for $\mathcal{A}$ against $\mathcal{F}_{\mathcal{A},\mu}$ for some negligible ϵ with rate $R/3.01$ and leakage-resilience rate 1.*

For the special case of threshold secret sharing scheme for which we know constructions with rate 1 [Sha79], we obtain the following corollary, where $\mathcal{F}_{(t,n),\mu}$ denotes the local leakage function family corresponding to the t-out-of-n threshold access structure.

Corollary 2. *For any $n, t, \mu \in \mathbb{N}$ such that $t \leq n$, and $\varepsilon \in (0,1)$, there is a t-out-of-n threshold secret sharing scheme that is $(2n\varepsilon)$-leakage resilient against $\mathcal{F}_{(t,n),\mu}$, and has rate $\Omega(1)$, and leakage-resilience rate 1.*

3.2   Strong Local Leakage Resilience

In this subsection, we consider a stronger notion of leakage resilience for secret sharing, in which the leakage on the "honest" shares is allowed to depend arbitrarily on the "corrupted" shares – this is meant to capture a scenario where an adversary first learns the shares of t of the n parties, and then specifies leakage functions that are applied to the remaining $(n - t)$ shares, the outputs of which are then given to the adversary. This corresponds to leakage resilience against the function family described below.

Our motivation for studying this specific strengthening of local leakage resilience is an application to constructing leakage-tolerant MPC protocols where local leakage resilience turns out to be insufficient (see Sect. 5). For simplicity, we will describe our results (and definitions) in this subsection only for threshold access structures (which suffices for our MPC construction), but they can be generalized to all access structures in a straightforward manner.

Semi-local Leakage Function Family. Let $(\mathcal{S}_1 \times \cdots \times \mathcal{S}_n)$ be the domain of shares for some secret sharing scheme, and $t, t' \in [n]$ and μ be natural numbers. A semi-local leakage function family is parametrized by three numbers t (the adaptivity threshold), t' (the corruption threshold), and μ (the amount of leakage), such that $t \leq t'$. The family $\mathcal{H}_{t,t',\mu}$ consists of functions $\{h_{T,T',\vec{\tau}}\}$, where the subsets $T \subseteq T' \subseteq [n]$ are such that $|T| = t$ and $|T'| = t'$; and for $i \in [n] \setminus T'$, the function τ_i takes inputs from $(\mathcal{S}_{i_1} \times \cdots \times \mathcal{S}_{i_t}) \times \mathcal{S}_i$ (where $T = \{i_1, \ldots, i_t\}$), and outputs μ bits. The function $h_{T,T',\vec{\tau}}$, when given input $(\mathsf{share}_1, \ldots, \mathsf{share}_n)$, outputs share_i for each $i \in T'$, and $\tau_i((\mathsf{share}_{i_1}, \ldots, \mathsf{share}_{i_t}), \mathsf{share}_i)$ for $i \notin T'$.

A secret sharing scheme resilient to leakage by such function families is said to be *strongly local leakage resilient.*

Game-Based Definition. Strong local leakage resilience of a secret sharing scheme $(\mathsf{LRShare}, \mathsf{LRRec})$ may alternatively, and perhaps more naturally, be defined as the inability of the adversary to guess the bit b correctly in the following game:

1. The adversary selects the sets $T \subseteq T' \subseteq [n]$ such that $|T| = t$ and $|T'| = t'$. It then picks messages $m_0, m_1 \in \mathcal{M}$, and sends all of these to the challenger.
2. The challenger picks a random bit b and computes $(\mathsf{share}_1, \ldots, \mathsf{share}_n) \leftarrow \mathsf{LRShare}(m_b)$. It sends share_T to the adversary.
3. The adversary now chooses a local leakage function $f_{(T' \setminus T), \mu}$ that operates on the $(n - t)$ shares $(\mathsf{share}_i)_{i \notin T}$. It sends this to the challenger.
4. The challenger sends the leakage $f_{(T' \setminus T), \mu}((\mathsf{share}_i)_{i \notin T})$.
5. The adversary outputs a guess b' for b.

We require that $\Pr[b = b'] = 1/2 + \mathrm{negl}(m)$. To see that these two definitions are equivalent, note that the task of the adversary in the game is essentially to specify a function from $\mathcal{H}_{t,t',\mu}$ – any function $h_{T,T',\vec{\tau}}$ in this class is specified by sets $T \subseteq T'$, outputs the shares in T' in the clear and also leaks some information about the honest parties' shares depending on the shares in T. And what the adversary gets from the challenger is precisely the output of this function applied to the shares.

We show that a modification of the construction from Sect. 3.1 can achieve strong local leakage resilience. This is presented in Fig. 2.

Let $(\mathsf{Share}_{(t,n)}, \mathsf{Rec}_{(t,n)})$ represent a t-out-of-n threshold secret sharing scheme for secrets in an unspecified domain; let ρ be the bit-length of each share under this scheme when the secret is from the secret domain $\mathcal{M}$. Let η and d be such that there is a (k, ε)-average-case strong seeded extractor $\mathsf{Ext} : \{0,1\}^\eta \times \{0,1\}^d \to \{0,1\}^\rho$ that outputs ρ bits, where $k = (\eta - \mu)$.

$\mathsf{LRShare}$: To share a secret $m \in \mathcal{M}$:
    1. Run $\mathsf{Share}_{(t,n)}(m)$ to obtain the shares $(\mathsf{Sh}_1, \ldots, \mathsf{Sh}_n)$.
    2. Choose a uniform seed $s \xleftarrow{\$} \{0,1\}^d$.
    3. For each $i \in [n]$ do:
       (a) Choose $w_i \xleftarrow{\$} \{0,1\}^\eta$.
       (b) Choose a masking string $r_i \xleftarrow{\$} \{0,1\}^\rho$.
       (c) Set $\mathsf{Sh}'_i = \mathsf{Sh}_i \oplus \mathsf{Ext}(w_i, s) \oplus r_i$.
       (d) Run $\mathsf{Share}_{(t,n)}(r_i)$ to obtain $r_{(i,1)}, \ldots, r_{(i,n)}$.
    4. Run $\mathsf{Share}_{(t,n)}(s)$ to obtain $S_1, \ldots, S_n$.
    5. Output share_i as $(w_i, \mathsf{Sh}'_i, S_i, (r_{(1,i)}, \ldots, r_{(n,i)}))$.
LRRec : Given any set of t shares $\mathsf{share}_{i_1}, \mathsf{share}_{i_2}, \ldots, \mathsf{share}_{i_t}$, do:
    1. For each i_j, parse share_{i_j} as $(w_{i_j}, S'_{i_j}, S_{i_j}, (r_{(1,i_j)}, \ldots, r_{(n,i_j)}))$.
    2. Run $\mathsf{Rec}_{(t,n)}(S_{i_1}, \ldots, S_{i_t})$ to recover s.
    3. For each i_j, do:
       (a) Run $\mathsf{Rec}_{(t,n)}(r_{(i_j,i_1)}, \ldots, r_{(i_j,i_t)})$ to recover r_{i_j}.
       (b) Recover Sh_{i_j} by computing $S'_{i_j} \oplus \mathsf{Ext}(w_{i_j}, s) \oplus r_{i_j}$.
    4. Run $\mathsf{Rec}(\mathsf{Sh}_{i_1}, \ldots, \mathsf{Sh}_{i_t})$ to recover the secret m.

Fig. 2. Strongly local leakage-resilient secret sharing

Theorem 7. *Consider any $n, t, \mu \in \mathbb{N}$ such that $t \le n$ and a secret domain $\mathcal{M}$. Suppose for some $\eta, d, R \in \mathbb{N}$ and $\epsilon \in [0, 1)$, the following exist:*

- *A perfect t-out-of-n threshold secret sharing scheme with share size ρ for secrets in $\mathcal{M}$.*
- *A $(\eta - \mu, \varepsilon)$-average-case strong seeded extractor $\mathsf{Ext} : \{0,1\}^\eta \times \{0,1\}^d \to \{0,1\}^\rho$.*

Then, the construction in Fig. 2, when instantiated with these, is a t-out-of-n threshold secret sharing scheme for $\mathcal{M}$ that is $(2n\varepsilon)$-leakage resilient against $\mathcal{H}_{(t-2),(t-1),\mu}$. It has share size $(\eta + \rho + d + n\rho)$.

Using the same instantiations as in Sect. 3.1, we get the following.

Corollary 3. *For any $n, t, \mu \in \mathbb{N}$ such that $t \le n$, and $\varepsilon \in [0, 1]$, there is a t-out-of-n threshold secret sharing scheme that is $(2n\varepsilon)$-leakage resilient against $\mathcal{H}_{(t-2),(t-1),\mu}$, and has rate $\Omega(1/n)$, and leakage-resilience rate 1.*

We prove Theorem 7 along the same lines as Theorem 5, and we give the details in the full version.

4 Rate Preserving Non-Malleable Secret Sharing

In this section, we will use the leakage resilient secret sharing scheme in Sect. 3 to construct a non-malleable secret sharing scheme. Specifically, we give a compiler that takes any secret sharing scheme for a 4-monotone access structure (see Definition 1) with rate R and converts it into a non-malleable secret sharing scheme for the same access structure with rate $\Omega(R)$.

In the full version, we give some background on non-malleable codes and below we recall the definition of non-malleable secret sharing for a monotone access structure $\mathcal{A}$.

Definition 5 (Non-Malleable Secret Sharing for General Access Structures [GK18b]). *Let* (Share, Rec) *be a* $(\mathcal{A}, n, \epsilon_c, \epsilon_s)$*-secret sharing scheme for message space* $\mathcal{M}$ *and access structure* $\mathcal{A}$. *Let* $\mathcal{F}$ *be a family of tampering functions. For each* $f \in \mathcal{F}$, $m \in \mathcal{M}$ *and authorized set* $T \in \mathcal{A}$, *define the tampered distribution* $\mathsf{Tamper}_m^{f,T}$ *as* $\mathsf{Rec}(f(\mathsf{Share}(m))_T)$ *where the randomness is over the sharing function* Share. *We say that the* $(\mathcal{A}, n, \epsilon_c, \epsilon_s)$*-secret sharing scheme,* (Share, Rec) *is* ϵ'*-non-malleable w.r.t.* $\mathcal{F}$ *if for each* $f \in \mathcal{F}$ *and any authorized set* $T \in \mathcal{A}$, *there exists a distribution* $D^{f,T}$ *over* $\mathcal{M} \cup \{\mathsf{same}^\star\}$ *such that for any* m,

$$|\mathsf{Tamper}_m^{f,T} - \mathrm{copy}(D^{f,T}, m)| \leq \epsilon'$$

where copy *is defined by* $\mathrm{copy}(x, y) = \begin{cases} x & \text{if } x \neq \mathsf{same}^\star \\ y & \text{if } x = \mathsf{same}^\star \end{cases}$. *We call* ϵ' *as the simulation error.*

4.1 Construction

We give a construction of a non-malleable secret sharing scheme for a 4-monotone access structures against the individual tampering function family $\mathcal{F}_{\mathsf{ind}}$ (see below).

Individual Tampering Family $\mathcal{F}_{\mathsf{ind}}$. Let Share be the sharing function of the secret sharing scheme that outputs n-shares in $\mathcal{S}_1 \times \mathcal{S}_2 \ldots \times \mathcal{S}_n$. The function family $\mathcal{F}_{\mathsf{ind}}$ is composed of tuples of functions $(f_1, \ldots, f_n)$ where each $f_i : \mathcal{S}_i \rightarrow \mathcal{S}_i$.

Construction. The construction is same as the one given in [BS19] but we instantiate the leakage-resilient secret sharing scheme with the one constructed in the previous section. We now give the description of the building blocks and then give the construction. In the following, we will denote a t-out-of-n monotone access structure as (t, n).

Building Blocks. The construction uses the following building blocks. We instantiate them with concrete schemes later:

- A 3-split-state non-malleable code (Enc, Dec) where Enc : $\mathcal{M} \to \mathcal{L} \times \mathcal{C} \times \mathcal{R}$ and the simulation error of the scheme is ϵ_1. Furthermore, we assume that for any two messages $m, m' \in \mathcal{M}$, $(C, R) \approx_{\epsilon_2} (C', R')$ where $(L, C, R) \leftarrow \mathsf{Enc}(m)$ and $(L', C', R') \leftarrow \mathsf{Enc}(m')$.
- A $(\mathcal{A}, n, \epsilon_c, \epsilon_s)$ (where $\mathcal{A}$ is 4-monotone) secret sharing scheme $(\mathsf{SecShare}_{(\mathcal{A},n)}, \mathsf{SecRec}_{(\mathcal{A},n)})$ with statistical privacy (with error ϵ_s) for message space $\mathcal{L}$. We will assume that the size of each share is m_1.
- A $(3, n, 0, 0)$ secret sharing scheme $(\mathsf{LRShare}_{(3,n)}, \mathsf{LRRec}_{(3,n)})$ that is ϵ_3-leakage resilient against leakage functions $\mathcal{F}_{(3,n),m_1}$ for message space $\mathcal{C}$. We assume that the size of each share is m_2.
- A $(2, n, 0, 0)$ secret sharing scheme $(\mathsf{LRShare}_{(2,n)}, \mathsf{LRRec}_{(2,n)})$ for message space $\mathcal{R}$ that is ϵ_4-leakage resilient against leakage functions $\mathcal{F}_{(2,n),\mu}$ where $\mu = m_1 + m_2$. We assume that the size of each share is m_3.

We give the formal description of the construction in Fig. 3 (taken verbatim from [BS19]).

Imported Theorem 8 ([BS19]). *For any arbitrary $n \in \mathbb{N}$ and any 4-monotone access structure $\mathcal{A}$, the construction given in Fig. 3 is a $(\mathcal{A}, n, \epsilon_c, \epsilon_s + \epsilon_2)$ secret sharing scheme. Furthermore, it is $(\epsilon_1 + \epsilon_3 + \epsilon_4)$-non-malleable against $\mathcal{F}_{\mathsf{ind}}$.*

We defer the rate analysis to the full version of the paper and only state the corollary below.

Corollary 4. *For any $n \in \mathbb{N}$, $\rho > 0$ and 4-monotone access structure $\mathcal{A}$, if there exists a statistically private (with privacy error ϵ) secret sharing scheme for $\mathcal{A}$ that can share m-bit secrets with rate R, there exists a non-malleable secret sharing scheme for sharing m-bit secrets for the same access structure $\mathcal{A}$ against $\mathcal{F}_{ind}$ with rate $\Omega(R)$ and simulation error $\epsilon + 2^{-\Omega(m/\log^{1+\rho}(m))}$.*

5   Leakage Tolerant MPC for General Interaction Patterns

In this section, we will construct a leakage tolerant secure multiparty computation protocol for any interaction pattern (defined below). We will first recall some basic definitions from [HIJ+16].

Let $(\mathsf{SecShare}_{(\mathcal{A},n)}, \mathsf{SecRec}_{(\mathcal{A},n)})$ be a $(\mathcal{A}, n, \epsilon_c, \epsilon_s)$ (where $\mathcal{A}$ is 4-monotone) secret sharing scheme. Let $(\mathsf{Enc}, \mathsf{Dec})$ be a 3-split state non-malleable code and $(\mathsf{LRShare}_{(t,n)}, \mathsf{LRRec}_{(t,n)})$ be leakage resilient threshold secret sharing schemes with threshold t.

$\mathsf{Share}(m)$: To share a secret $s \in \mathcal{M}$ do:
1. Encode the secret s as $(\mathsf{L}, \mathsf{C}, \mathsf{R}) \leftarrow \mathsf{Enc}(s)$.
2. Compute the shares

$$(\mathsf{SL}_1, \ldots, \mathsf{SL}_n) \leftarrow \mathsf{SecShare}_{(\mathcal{A},n)}(\mathsf{L})$$

$$(\mathsf{SC}_1, \ldots, \mathsf{SC}_n) \leftarrow \mathsf{LRShare}_{(3,n)}(\mathsf{C})$$

$$(\mathsf{SR}_1, \ldots, \mathsf{SR}_n) \leftarrow \mathsf{LRShare}_{(2,n)}(\mathsf{R})$$

3. For each $i \in [n]$, set share_i as $(\mathsf{SL}_i, \mathsf{SC}_i, \mathsf{SR}_i)$ and output $(\mathsf{share}_1, \ldots, \mathsf{share}_n)$ as the set of shares.

$\mathsf{Rec}(\mathsf{Share}(m)_T)$: Given a set of shares in an authorized set $T' \in \mathcal{A}$, let $T \subseteq T'$ denote a minimal authorized set. To reconstruct the secret from the shares in set T (of size at most t), do:
1. Let the shares corresponding to the set T be $(\mathsf{share}_{i_1}, \ldots, \mathsf{share}_{i_t})$.
2. For each $j \in \{i_1, \ldots, i_t\}$, parse share_j as $(\mathsf{SL}_j, \mathsf{SC}_j, \mathsf{SR}_j)$.
3. Reconstruct

$$\mathsf{L} := \mathsf{SecRec}_{(\mathcal{A},n)}(\mathsf{SL}_{i_1}, \ldots, \mathsf{SL}_{i_t})$$

$$\mathsf{C} := \mathsf{LRRec}_{(3,n)}(\mathsf{SC}_{i_1}, \mathsf{SC}_{i_2}, \mathsf{SC}_{i_3})$$

$$\mathsf{R} := \mathsf{LRRec}_{(2,n)}(\mathsf{SR}_{i_1}, \mathsf{SR}_{i_2})$$

4. Output the secret s as $\mathsf{Dec}(\mathsf{L}, \mathsf{C}, \mathsf{R})$.

Fig. 3. Construction of non-malleable secret sharing scheme for 4-monotone access structure taken verbatim from [BS19]

5.1   Basic Definitions

This subsection consists of definitions and some associated exposition, all taken verbatim from [HIJ+16].

We begin by defining the syntax for specifying a communication pattern $\mathcal{I}$ and a protocol Π that complies with it. In all the definitions below, we let $\mathcal{P} = \{P_1, \ldots, P_n\}$ denote a fixed set of parties who would participate in the protocol. When we want to stress the difference between a protocol message as an entity by itself (e.g., "the 3rd message of party P_1") and the content of that message in a specific run of the protocol, we sometime refer to the former as a "message slot" and the latter as the "message content." To define an N-message interaction pattern for the parties in $\mathcal{P}$, we assign a unique identifier to each message slot. Without loss of generality, the identifiers are the indices 1 through N. An interaction pattern is then defined via a set of constraints on these message slots, specifying the sender and receiver of each message, as well as the other messages that it depends on. These constraints are specified by a message dependency graph, where the vertices are the message slots and the edges specify the dependencies.

Definition 6 (Interaction pattern [HIJ+16]). *An N-message interaction pattern for the set of parties $\mathcal{P}$ is specified by a message dependency directed acyclic labeled graph,*

$$\mathcal{I} = ([N], D, L : V \to \mathcal{P} \times (\mathcal{P} \cup \mathsf{Out}))$$

The vertices are the message indices $[N]$, each vertex $i \in [N]$ is labeled by a sender-receiver pair $L(i) = (S_i, R_i)$, with $R_i = \mathsf{Out}$ meaning that this message is output by party S_i rather than sent to another party. The directed edges in D specify message dependencies, where an edge $i \to j$ means that message j in the protocol may depend on message i. The message-dependency graph must satisfy two requirements:

- *$\mathcal{I}$ is acyclic. We assume without loss of generality that the message indices are given in topological order, so $i < j$ for every $(i \to j) \in D$.*
- *If message j depends on message i, then the sender of message j is the receiver of message i. That is, for every $(i \to j) \in D$, we have $S_j = R_i$ (where $L(i) = (S_i, R_i)$ and $L(j) = (S_j, R_j)$).*

We assume without loss of generality that each party $P \in \mathcal{P}$ has at most one output, namely at most one $i \in [N]$ such that $L(i) = (P, \mathsf{Out})$. For a message $j \in [N]$, we denote its incoming neighborhood, i.e. all the messages that it depends on, by $\mathsf{DepOn}(j) := \{i : (i \to j) \in D\}$.

An n-party, N-message interaction pattern, is an N-message pattern for $\mathcal{P} = [n]$. We will interchangeably denote the i-th party as either using i or P_i.

A well known example of an interaction pattern is the star pattern which we define below.

Star Interaction Pattern. A $n + 1$-party, $n + 1$-message interaction pattern is called a star interaction pattern, if for each $i \in [n]$, $L(i) = (P_i, P_{n+1})$, $(i \to n + 1) \in D$ and $L(n + 1) = (P_{n+1}, \mathsf{Out})$. In other words, for every $i \in [n]$, P_i sends a single message to P_{n+1} who computes the output from all the messages received.

$\mathcal{I}$-compliant MPC. We next define the syntax of an MPC protocol complying with a restricted fixed interaction pattern. Importantly, our model includes general correlated randomness set-up, making protocols with limited interaction much more powerful.

Definition 7 ($\mathcal{I}$ compliant protocol [HIJ+16]). *Let $\mathcal{I} = ([N], D, L)$ be an n-party N-message interaction pattern. An n-party protocol complying with $\mathcal{I}$ is specified by a pair of algorithms $\Pi = (\mathsf{Gen}, \mathsf{Msg})$ of the following syntax:*

- Gen *is a randomized sampling algorithm that outputs an n-tuple of correlated random strings $(r_1, \ldots, r_n)$.*

- Msg *is a deterministic algorithm specifying how each message is computed from the messages on which it depends. Concretely, the input of Msg consists of the index $i \in [N]$ of a vertex in the dependency graph, the randomness r_{S_i} and input x_{S_i} for the sender S_i corresponding to that vertex, and an assignment of message-content to all the messages that message i depends on, $M : \text{DepOn}(i) \rightarrow \{0,1\}^*$. The output of* Msg *is an outgoing message in $\{0,1\}^*$, namely the string that the sender S_i should send to the receiver R_i.*

The execution of such a protocol Π with pattern $\mathcal{I}$ proceeds as follows. During an offline set-up phase, before the inputs are known, Gen is used to generate the correlated randomness $(r_1, ..., r_n)$ and distribute r_i to party P_i. In the online phase, on inputs $(x_1, ..., x_n)$, the parties repeatedly invoke Msg on vertices (message-slots) in $\mathcal{I}$ to compute the message-content they should send. The execution of Π goes over the message slots in a topological order, where each message is sent after all messages on which it depends have been received. We do not impose any restriction on the order in which messages are sent, other than complying with the depend-on relation as specified by $\mathcal{I}$. Once all messages (including outputs) are computed, the parties have local outputs $(y_1, ..., y_n)$, where we use $y_i = \perp$ to indicate that P_i does not have an output.

For a set $T \subset [n]$ of corrupted parties, let view_T denote the entire view of T during the protocol execution. This view includes the inputs x_T, correlated randomness r_T, and messages received by T. (Sent messages and outputs are determined by this information.) The view does not include messages exchanged between honest parties. Security of a protocol with communication pattern $\mathcal{I}$ requires that for any subset of corrupted parties $T \subset \mathcal{P}$, the view view_T reveals as little about the inputs $x_{\overline{T}}$ of honest parties as is possible with the interaction pattern $\mathcal{I}$. We formulate this notion of "as little as possible" via the notion of fixed vs. free inputs: If parties P_i, P_j are corrupted and no path of messages from P_i to P_j passes through any honest party, then the adversary can learn the output of P_j on every possible value of x_i. However, if there is some honest party on some communication path from P_i to P_j, then having to send a message through that party may be used to "fix" the input of P_i that was used to generate that message, so the adversary can only learn the value of the function on that one input.

Definition 8 (Fixed vs. free inputs). *For an interaction pattern $\mathcal{I}$, parties $P_i, P_j \in \mathcal{P}$ (input and output parties), and a set $T \subset P$ of corrupted parties, we say that P_i has fixed input with respect to $\mathcal{I}, T$ and P_j if either*

- $P_i \notin T$ *(the input party is honest), or*
- *there is a directed path in $\mathcal{I}$ starting with some message sent by P_i, ending with some message received by P_j, and containing at least one message sent by some honest party $P_h \notin T$.*

We say that P_i has free input (with respect to $\mathcal{I}, T, P_j$) if $P_i \in T$ and its input is not fixed. We let $\text{Free}(\mathcal{I}, T, P_j) \subseteq T$ denote the set of parties with free inputs, and $\text{Fixed}(\mathcal{I}, T, P_j) = P \backslash \text{Free}(\mathcal{I}, T, P_j)$ is the complement set of parties with fixed input (all with respect to $\mathcal{I}, T$ and P_j).

Using the notion of fixed inputs, we can now capture the minimum information available to the adversary by defining a suitable restriction of the function f that the protocol needs to compute.

Definition 9. *For an n-party functionality f, interaction pattern $\mathcal{I}$, corrupted set $T \subset P$, input $x = (x_1, \ldots, x_n)$ and output party $P_j \in P$, the residual function $f_{\mathcal{I},T,x,P_j}$ is the function obtained from f_j by restricting the input variables indexed by $F = \mathsf{Fixed}(\mathcal{I}, T, P_j)$ to their values in x. That is, for input variables $x'_{\overline{F}} = \{x'_i\}_{i \notin F}$, we define $f_{\mathcal{I},T,x,P_j}(x'_{\overline{F}}) = f_j(x'_1, \ldots, x'_n)$, where $x'_i = x_i$ for all $i \in F$.*

We formalize our notion of security in the semi-honest model below. To get around general impossibility results for security with polynomial-time simulation [HLP11, GGG+14, BGI+14], we will allow by default simulators to be unbounded (but will also consider bounded simulation variants). We start by considering perfectly/statistically/computationally secure protocols.

Definition 10 *(Security with semi-honest adversaries). Let f be a deterministic n-party functionality, $\mathcal{I}$ be an n-party, N-message interaction pattern, and $\Pi = (\mathsf{Gen}, \mathsf{Msg})$ be an n-party protocol complying with $\mathcal{I}$. We say that Π is a perfectly T-secure protocol for f in the semi-honest model for a fixed set $T \subset P$ of corrupted parties if the following requirements are met:*

- *$Correctness$: For every input $x = (x_1, \ldots, x_n)$, the outputs at the end of the protocol execution are always equal to $f(x)$ (namely, with probability 1 over the randomness of Gen).*
- *$Semi$-$honest$ $security$: There is an unbounded simulator S that for any input x is given x_T and the truth tables of the residual functions $f_{\mathcal{I},T,x,P_j}$ for all $P_j \in T$, and its output is distributed identically/statistically close/computationally indistinguishable to $\mathsf{view}_T(x)$.*

Remark 3 (Efficient Simulation). For the case where we require the simulator to be efficient, we provide the simulator with oracle access to the residual function $f_{\mathcal{I},T,x,P_j}$.

5.2   Definition: Leakage Tolerant MPC for an Interaction Pattern

We now define what it means for an MPC protocol compliant with an interaction pattern $\mathcal{I}$ to be *leakage-tolerant*.

We consider an $(n + 1)$-party $\mathcal{P} = \{P_1, \ldots, P_n, P_{n+1}\}$ protocol $\Pi = (\mathsf{Gen}, \mathsf{Msg})$ that is compliant with an interaction pattern $\mathcal{I}$ with a single output party, namely, P_{n+1} (that does not have any inputs)[5] that computes a function $f : (\{0,1\}^m)^n \rightarrow \{0,1\}^*$, where the party P_i gets input $x_i \in \{0,1\}^m$ for each $i \in [n]$. The execution of Π proceeds along an identical fashion as in the standard

---

[5] The case of multiple output parties reduces to the case of single output party by considering each output party computing a specific function of the other parties input.

MPC for general interaction pattern (see Definition 7) and we recall this once again. In the offline phase before the parties get to know their actual inputs, the algorithm Gen is run and this outputs the correlated randomness $(r_1, \ldots, r_{n+1})$ where r_i is given to party P_i. In the online phase, on inputs $(x_1, \ldots, x_n)$, the parties repeatedly invoke Msg on vertices (message-slots) in $\mathcal{I}$ to compute the message-content they should send. The execution of Π goes over the message slots in a topological order, where each message is sent after all messages on which it depends have been received. Once all messages are sent, the output party P_{n+1} computes the output.

Let us say that at the end of a protocol Π, the party P_i's view $view_i$ is from a domain $\mathcal{V}_i$. Recall that $view_i$ includes the correlated randomness output by Gen, party P_i's input x_i as well as the messages that it has received during the execution of the protocol. Let us denote $\Pi(x)$ as the joint distribution of the views of every party during the execution of the protocol. We are interested in adversaries that statically corrupt t $(<n)$ of the parties, obtaining their entire states, and also obtain some leakage on the states of the other uncorrupted parties. More formally, we represent the view of such adversaries as families of functions of the form $\mathcal{G}_{t,\mu} = \{g_{T,\vec{\tau}} : T \subseteq [n], |T| \leq t, \tau_i : \mathcal{V}_i \to \{0,1\}^{\mu}\}$; where $g_{T,\vec{\tau}}(\Pi(x))$ outputs $view_i$ for every $i \in T$, and $\tau_i(view_i)$ for $i \notin T$, when the protocol Π is run with input x – we refer to such a function as a (T, μ)-leakage function. Informally, we assume that the algorithm Gen runs in a leak-free manner and from then on, the honest party's entire secret state is subject to leakage.

Definition 11 (Leakage Tolerance against Semi-honest Adversaries).
Let f be a deterministic n-party functionality, $\mathcal{I}$ be an n-party, N-message interaction pattern, and $\Pi = (\text{Gen}, \text{Msg})$ be an n-party protocol complying with $\mathcal{I}$. We say that Π is a (T, μ)-leakage tolerant protocol for f in the semi-honest model for a set $T \subseteq \mathcal{P}$ if it satisfies the following properties:

- **Correctness:** *The protocol Π computes $f(x)$ correctly for any input $x = (x_1, \ldots, x_n)$.*
- **Leakage Tolerance:** *For any (T, μ)-leakage function $g_{T,\vec{\tau}}$, there is an unbounded simulator $\mathcal{S}$ satisfying the following.*
  - *For any input $x = (x_1, \ldots, x_n)$, the simulator $\mathcal{S}$ is given the inputs of the corrupted parties x_T and the truth tables of the residual functions $f_{\mathcal{I},T,x,P_j}$ for all $P_j \in T$ as input. It is allowed a single query to an oracle $\mathcal{O}[x_{\overline{T}}]$, which takes as input a tuple of functions $(\sigma_i)_{i \in \overline{T}}$, where each function is of the form $\sigma_i : \{0,1\}^m \to \{0,1\}^{\mu}$, and outputs $(\sigma_i(x_i))_{i \in \overline{T}}$.*
  - *We require that:*

  $$g_{T,\vec{\tau}}(\Pi(x)) \approx \mathcal{S}^{\mathcal{O}[x_{\overline{T}}]}(f_{\mathcal{I},T,x,P_j}, x_T)$$

  where $\approx$ might indicate identical/statistically close/computationally indistinguishable.

We say that Π is a (t, μ)-leakage tolerant protocol for f if it is (T, μ)-leakage tolerant for all $T \subseteq \mathcal{P}$ and $|T| \leq t$.

5.3   Construction

In this subsection, we give a construction of a leakage-tolerant semi-honest MPC for any interaction pattern $\mathcal{I}$. Specifically, we give a reduction from a leakage-tolerant semi-honest MPC for any interaction pattern $\mathcal{I}$ to constructing a (possible leakage intolerant) MPC protocol for the star interaction pattern. The construction we give is the same as the one given in [HIJ+16] with the only change being that we use our strong local leakage-resilient scheme instead of any secret sharing scheme.

Before we describe the construction, we introduce the following notation. For a function $f : (\{0,1\}^m)^n \to \{0,1\}^*$, we denote by $f^{bit} : \{0,1\}^{mn} \to \{0,1\}^*$ the function that takes mn bits as inputs, groups them together in order into n strings of length m each, and applies f on them.

Building Blocks. The construction uses the following building blocks:

- A star compliant, semi-honest protocol $\Pi^* = (\mathsf{Gen}^*, \mathsf{Msg}^*, \mathsf{Eval}^*)$ that securely (either perfect/statistical/computational) computes the function f^{bit}. Here, Msg^* denotes the next message function of the parties $P_1, \ldots, P_{mn}$ and Eval^* is the function computed by the evaluator (or in other words, party P_{mn+1}).
- A $(n+1, n+1, 0, 0)$ threshold secret sharing scheme $(\mathsf{LRShare}, \mathsf{LRRec})$ that is ϵ-strong leakage resilient for some negligible ϵ against the function family $\mathcal{H}_{n-1,n,\mu}$ (where $\mathcal{H}$ function class is defined in Sect. 3.2).

Construction. Let $f : (\{0,1\}^m)^n \to \{0,1\}^*$ be a n-party functionality that depends on all its inputs and $\mathcal{I}$ be an interaction pattern with a single sink. Let $\mathcal{P} = \{P_1, \ldots, P_{n+1}\}$ be the set of parties with P_{n+1} being the evaluator who does not have any inputs. We give the construction of an $\mathcal{I}$ compliant protocol in Fig. 4.

Theorem 9. *If Π^* computes f^{bit} with statistical/computational security and $(\mathsf{LRShare}, \mathsf{LRRec})$ is an ϵ-strong leakage resilient secret sharing scheme against $\mathcal{H}_{n-1,n,\mu}$ for some negligible ϵ, then the construction in Fig. 4 is a semi-honest, $\mathcal{I}$-compliant protocol for f that is (n, μ)-leakage tolerant with statistical/computational security. Furthermore, if each party uses R bits of correlated randomness and sends M bits in the protocol Π^*, then each party in the protocol in Fig. 4 uses $O(m(R + n^2M + n\mu))$ bits of correlated randomness and sends $O((n^2M + n\mu)m)$ bits.*

We give the proof of this theorem in the full version. Using the known protocols for the star interaction pattern from the works of [BGI+14, BKR17, GGG+14], we obtain the following corollary.

Corollary 5 ([BGI+14, BKR17, GGG+14]). *Let $\mathcal{I}$ be a n-party interaction pattern with a single sink and let be $f : (\{0,1\}^m)^n \to \{0,1\}^*$ be a function which depends on all its inputs. Then,*

Gen : To generate the correlated randomness, do:

1. Run Gen* to obtain the correlated randomness $(r_1, \ldots, r_{mn+1})$.
2. For each $i \in [mn]$ and $\sigma \in \{0,1\}$, compute $m_i^\sigma := \mathsf{Msg}^*(\sigma, r_i)$.
3. For each $i \in [mn]$ and $\sigma \in \{0,1\}$, compute $(m_{i,1}^\sigma, \ldots, m_{i,n+1}^\sigma) \leftarrow \mathsf{LRShare}(m_i^\sigma)$.
4. Choose random permutation strings $b_1, \ldots, b_n \leftarrow \{0,1\}^m$, one for each party P_i, $i \leq n$.
5. Let $c = b_1 \circ b_2 \circ \ldots \circ b_n$. For each $i \in [mn]$, let c_i denote the i-th bit of c.
6. For each $j \in [n]$, the correlated randomness for party j is $(\{m_{i,j}^{c_i}, m_{i,j}^{1-c_i}\}_{i \in [mn]}, b_j)$. The correlated randomness of the evaluator P_{n+1} is $(r_{mn+1}, \{m_{i,n+1}^{c_i}, m_{i,n+1}^{1-c_i}\}_{i \in [mn]})$

Msg : On input $x_j \in \{0,1\}^m$ and the correlated randomness, party P_j does the following:

1. Parses the correlated randomness as $(\{M_{i,j}^0, M_{i,j}^1\}_{i \in [mn], \sigma \in \{0,1\}}, b_j)$.
2. Computes $s_j = x_j \oplus b_j$ and sends s_j on every path to the evaluator in $\mathcal{I}$.
3. Then, for every P_k such that some path from P_k to the evaluator goes through P_j, party P_j waits until it receives the string s_k and then sends $\{M_{(k-1)m+\ell,j}^{s_{k,\ell}}\}_{\ell \in [m]} = \{m_{(k-1)m+\ell,j}^{x_{k,\ell}}\}_{\ell \in [m]}$ on every path to the evaluator.
4. For every P_k such that no path from P_k to the evaluator goes through P_j, party P_j sends both shares $\{M_{(k-1)m+\ell,j}^0, M_{(k-1)m+\ell,j}^1\}_{\ell \in [m]}$ on every path to the evaluator.
5. In addition, P_j forwards every message that it receives from other parties on some $\mathcal{I}$-path to the evaluator.

Eval: The evaluator uses its correlated randomness to reconstruct $M_{(k-1)m+\ell}^{s_{k,\ell}}$ for every $k \in [n]$ and $\ell \in [m]$. It then uses the function Eval* on these reconstructed values to learn the output.

Fig. 4. A $\mathcal{I}$ compliant protocol computing f. The construction is same as the one in [HIJ+16] except that we use our leakage resilient secret sharing.

- There is a statistical $\mathcal{I}$-compliant leakage tolerant protocol that securely computes f against upto $n-1$ passive corruptions. The communication complexity is exponential in n, m.
- If f is computable by a circuit in NC^1 and $m = O(\log n)$, then there exists an efficient $\mathcal{I}$-compliant leakage tolerant protocol that computes f with statistical security upto a constant number of corruptions. Assuming one-way functions, every f that is computable by polynomial-sized circuits has a computationally secure, efficient, $\mathcal{I}$-compliant leakage tolerant protocol upto a constant number of corruptions.
- Assuming indistinguishability obfuscation and one-way functions, every function computable by polynomial-sized circuits has a computationally secure, efficient, $\mathcal{I}$-compliant leakage tolerant protocol against upto $n-1$ passive corruptions.

References

[ADN+18] Aggarwal, D., et al.: Stronger leakage-resilient and non-malleable secret-sharing schemes for general access structures. Cryptology ePrint Archive, Report 2018/1147 (2018). https://eprint.iacr.org/2018/1147

[ADW09] Alwen, J., Dodis, Y., Wichs, D.: Survey: leakage resilience and the bounded retrieval model. In: Kurosawa, K. (ed.) ICITS 2009. LNCS, vol. 5973, pp. 1–18. Springer, Heidelberg (2010). https://doi.org/10.1007/978-3-642-14496-7_1

[AGV09] Akavia, A., Goldwasser, S., Vaikuntanathan, V.: Simultaneous hardcore bits and cryptography against memory attacks. In: Reingold, O. (ed.) TCC 2009. LNCS, vol. 5444, pp. 474–495. Springer, Heidelberg (2009). https://doi.org/10.1007/978-3-642-00457-5_28

[BCG+11] Bitansky, N., Canetti, R., Goldwasser, S., Halevi, S., Kalai, Y.T., Rothblum, G.N.: Program obfuscation with leaky hardware. In: Lee, D.H., Wang, X. (eds.) ASIACRYPT 2011. LNCS, vol. 7073, pp. 722–739. Springer, Heidelberg (2011). https://doi.org/10.1007/978-3-642-25385-0_39

[BCH12] Bitansky, N., Canetti, R., Halevi, S.: Leakage-tolerant interactive protocols. In: Cramer, R. (ed.) TCC 2012. LNCS, vol. 7194, pp. 266–284. Springer, Heidelberg (2012). https://doi.org/10.1007/978-3-642-28914-9_15

[BDIR18] Benhamouda, F., Degwekar, A., Ishai, Y., Rabin, T.: On the local leakage resilience of linear secret sharing schemes. In: Shacham, H., Boldyreva, A. (eds.) CRYPTO 2018, Part I. LNCS, vol. 10991, pp. 531–561. Springer, Cham (2018). https://doi.org/10.1007/978-3-319-96884-1_18

[BDL14] Bitansky, N., Dachman-Soled, D., Lin, H.: Leakage-tolerant computation with input-independent preprocessing. In: Garay, J.A., Gennaro, R. (eds.) CRYPTO 2014, Part II. LNCS, vol. 8617, pp. 146–163. Springer, Heidelberg (2014). https://doi.org/10.1007/978-3-662-44381-1_9

[Bei11] Beimel, A.: Secret-sharing schemes: a survey. In: Chee, Y.M., et al. (eds.) IWCC 2011. LNCS, vol. 6639, pp. 11–46. Springer, Heidelberg (2011). https://doi.org/10.1007/978-3-642-20901-7_2

[BGI+14] Beimel, A., Gabizon, A., Ishai, Y., Kushilevitz, E., Meldgaard, S., Paskin-Cherniavsky, A.: Non-interactive secure multiparty computation. In: Garay, J.A., Gennaro, R. (eds.) CRYPTO 2014, Part II. LNCS, vol. 8617, pp. 387–404. Springer, Heidelberg (2014). https://doi.org/10.1007/978-3-662-44381-1_22

[BGJ+13] Boyle, E., Garg, S., Jain, A., Kalai, Y.T., Sahai, A.: Secure computation against adaptive auxiliary information. In: Canetti, R., Garay, J.A. (eds.) CRYPTO 2013, Part I. LNCS, vol. 8042, pp. 316–334. Springer, Heidelberg (2013). https://doi.org/10.1007/978-3-642-40041-4_18

[BGJK12] Boyle, E., Goldwasser, S., Jain, A., Kalai, Y.T.: Multiparty computation secure against continual memory leakage. In: Karloff, H.J., Pitassi, T. (eds.), 44th Annual ACM Symposium on Theory of Computing, pp. 1235–1254. ACM Press, May 2012

[BGK14] Boyle, E., Goldwasser, S., Kalai, Y.T.: Leakage-resilient coin tossing. Distrib. Comput. **27**(3), 147–164 (2014)

[BGW88] Ben-Or, M., Goldwasser, S., Wigderson, A.: Completeness theorems for non-cryptographic fault-tolerant distributed computation (extended abstract). In: Proceedings of the 20th Annual ACM Symposium on Theory of Computing, Chicago, Illinois, USA, 2–4 May 1988, pp. 1–10 (1988)

[BKR17] Benhamouda, F., Krawczyk, H., Rabin, T.: Robust non-interactive multi-party computation against constant-size collusion. In: Katz, J., Shacham, H. (eds.) CRYPTO 2017, Part I. LNCS, vol. 10401, pp. 391–419. Springer, Cham (2017). https://doi.org/10.1007/978-3-319-63688-7_13

[Bla79] Blakley, G.R.: Safeguarding cryptographic keys. In: Proceedings of AFIPS 1979 National Computer Conference, vol. 48, pp. 313–317 (1979)

[BS19] Badrinarayanan, S., Srinivasan, A.: Revisiting non-malleable secret sharing. In: Ishai, Y., Rijmen, V. (eds.) EUROCRYPT 2019, Part I. LNCS, vol. 11476, pp. 593–622. Springer, Cham (2019). https://doi.org/10.1007/978-3-030-17653-2_20

[CCD88] Chaum, D., Crepeau, C., Damgaard, I.: Multiparty unconditionally secure protocols (extended abstract). In: Proceedings of the 20th Annual ACM Symposium on Theory of Computing, Chicago, Illinois, USA, 2–4 May 1988, pp. 11–19. ACM (1988)

[CG88] Chor, B., Goldreich, O.: Unbiased bits from sources of weak randomness and probabilistic communication complexity. SIAM J. Comput. 17(2), 230–261 (1988)

[DDFY94] De Santis, A., Desmedt, Y., Frankel, Y., Yung, M.: How to share a function securely. In: 26th Annual ACM Symposium on Theory of Computing, pp. 522–533. ACM Press, May 1994

[DF90] Desmedt, Y., Frankel, Y.: Threshold cryptosystems. In: Brassard, G. (ed.) CRYPTO 1989. LNCS, vol. 435, pp. 307–315. Springer, New York (1990). https://doi.org/10.1007/0-387-34805-0_28

[DHP11] Damgard, I., Hazay, C., Patra, A.: Leakage resilient secure two-party computation. Cryptology ePrint Archive, Report 2011/256 (2011). http://eprint.iacr.org/2011/256

[DORS08] Dodis, Y., Ostrovsky, R., Reyzin, L., Smith, A.: Fuzzy extractors: how to generate strong keys from biometrics and other noisy data. SIAM J. Comput. 38, 97–139 (2008)

[DP07] Dziembowski, S., Pietrzak, K.: Intrusion-resilient secret sharing. In: 48th Annual Symposium on Foundations of Computer Science, pp. 227–237. IEEE Computer Society Press, October 2007

[DP08] Dziembowski, S., Pietrzak, K.: Leakage-resilient cryptography. In: 49th Annual Symposium on Foundations of Computer Science, pp. 293–302. IEEE Computer Society Press, October 2008

[FKN94] Feige, U., Kilian, J., Naor, M.: A minimal model for secure computation (extended abstract). In: 26th Annual ACM Symposium on Theory of Computing, pp. 554–563. ACM Press, May 1994

[Fra90] Frankel, Y.: A practical protocol for large group oriented networks. In: Quisquater, J.-J., Vandewalle, J. (eds.) EUROCRYPT 1989. LNCS, vol. 434, pp. 56–61. Springer, Heidelberg (1990). https://doi.org/10.1007/3-540-46885-4_8

[FRR+10] Faust, S., Rabin, T., Reyzin, L., Tromer, E., Vaikuntanathan, V.: Protecting circuits from leakage: the computationally-bounded and noisy cases. In: Gilbert, H. (ed.) EUROCRYPT 2010. LNCS, vol. 6110, pp. 135–156. Springer, Heidelberg (2010). https://doi.org/10.1007/978-3-642-13190-5_7

[GGG+14] Goldwasser, S., et al.: Multi-input functional encryption. In: Nguyen, P.Q., Oswald, E. (eds.) EUROCRYPT 2014. LNCS, vol. 8441, pp. 578–602. Springer, Heidelberg (2014). https://doi.org/10.1007/978-3-642-55220-5_32

[GIM+16] Goyal, V., Ishai, Y., Maji, H.K., Sahai, A., Sherstov, A.A.: Bounded-communication leakage resilience via parity-resilient circuits. In: Dinur, I. (ed.), 57th Annual Symposium on Foundations of Computer Science, pp. 1–10. IEEE Computer Society Press, October 2016

[GJS11] Garg, S., Jain, A., Sahai, A.: Leakage-resilient zero knowledge. In: Rogaway, P. (ed.) CRYPTO 2011. LNCS, vol. 6841, pp. 297–315. Springer, Heidelberg (2011). https://doi.org/10.1007/978-3-642-22792-9_17

[GK18a] Goyal, V., Kumar, A.: Non-malleable secret sharing. In: Proceedings of the 50th Annual ACM SIGACT Symposium on Theory of Computing, STOC 2018, Los Angeles, CA, USA, 25–29 June 2018, pp. 685–698 (2018)

[GK18b] Goyal, V., Kumar, A.: Non-malleable secret sharing for general access structures. In: Shacham, H., Boldyreva, A. (eds.) CRYPTO 2018, Part I. LNCS, vol. 10991, pp. 501–530. Springer, Cham (2018). https://doi.org/10.1007/978-3-319-96884-1_17

[GMW87] Goldreich, O., Micali, S., Wigderson, A.: How to play any mental game or a completeness theorem for protocols with honest majority. In: Aho, A. (ed.), 19th Annual ACM Symposium on Theory of Computing, pp. 218–229. ACM Press, May 1987

[GMW17] Gupta, D., Maji, H.K., Wang, M.: Constant-rate non-malleable codes in the split-state model. Cryptology ePrint Archive, Report 2017/1048 (2017). http://eprint.iacr.org/2017/1048

[GUV09] Guruswami, V., Umans, C., Vadhan, S.P.: Unbalanced expanders and randomness extractors from Parvaresh-Vardy codes. J. ACM 56(4), 20 (2009)

[GW16] Guruswami, V., Wootters, M.: Repairing Reed-Solomon codes. In: Wichs, D., Mansour, Y. (eds.), 48th Annual ACM Symposium on Theory of Computing, pp. 216–226. ACM Press, June 2016

[HIJ+16] Halevi, S., Ishai, Y., Jain, A., Kushilevitz, E., Rabin, T.: Secure multiparty computation with general interaction patterns. In: Sudan, M. (ed.), ITCS 2016: 7th Conference on Innovations in Theoretical Computer Science, pp. 157–168. Association for Computing Machinery, January 2016

[HLP11] Halevi, S., Lindell, Y., Pinkas, B.: Secure computation on the web: computing without simultaneous interaction. In: Rogaway, P. (ed.) CRYPTO 2011. LNCS, vol. 6841, pp. 132–150. Springer, Heidelberg (2011). https://doi.org/10.1007/978-3-642-22792-9_8

[HSH+09] Halderman, J.A., et al.: Lest we remember: cold-boot attacks on encryption keys. Commun. ACM 52(5), 91–98 (2009)

[ISW03] Ishai, Y., Sahai, A., Wagner, D.: Private circuits: securing hardware against probing attacks. In: Boneh, D. (ed.) CRYPTO 2003. LNCS, vol. 2729, pp. 463–481. Springer, Heidelberg (2003). https://doi.org/10.1007/978-3-540-45146-4_27

[KGG+18] Kocher, P., et al.: Spectre attacks: exploiting speculative execution. CoRR, abs/1801.01203 (2018)

[KMS18] Kumar, A., Meka, R., Sahai, A.: Leakage-resilient secret sharing. IACR Cryptology ePrint Archive, 2018:1138 (2018)

[KOS18] Kanukurthi, B., Obbattu, S.L.B., Sekar, S.: Non-malleable randomness encoders and their applications. In: Nielsen, J.B., Rijmen, V. (eds.) EURO-CRYPT 2018, Part III. LNCS, vol. 10822, pp. 589–617. Springer, Cham (2018). https://doi.org/10.1007/978-3-319-78372-7_19

[LSG+18] Lipp, M., et al.: Meltdown. CoRR, abs/1801.01207 (2018)

[MR04] Micali, S., Reyzin, L.: Physically observable cryptography (extended abstract). In: Naor, M. (ed.) TCC 2004. LNCS, vol. 2951, pp. 278–296. Springer, Heidelberg (2004). https://doi.org/10.1007/978-3-540-24638-1_16

[NS09] Naor, M., Segev, G.: Public-key cryptosystems resilient to key leakage. In: Halevi, S. (ed.) CRYPTO 2009. LNCS, vol. 5677, pp. 18–35. Springer, Heidelberg (2009). https://doi.org/10.1007/978-3-642-03356-8_2

[NS19] Nielsen, J.B., Simkin, M.: Lower bounds for leakage-resilient secret sharing. IACR Cryptology ePrint Archive, 2019:181 (2019)

[Rot12] Rothblum, G.N.: How to compute under $\mathcal{AC}^0$ leakage without secure hardware. In: Safavi-Naini, R., Canetti, R. (eds.) CRYPTO 2012. LNCS, vol. 7417, pp. 552–569. Springer, Heidelberg (2012). https://doi.org/10.1007/978-3-642-32009-5_32

[Sha79] Shamir, A.: How to share a secret. Commun. Assoc. Comput. Mach. **22**(11), 612–613 (1979)

Stronger Leakage-Resilient and Non-Malleable Secret Sharing Schemes for General Access Structures

Divesh Aggarwal[3]([✉]), Ivan Damgård[1]([✉]), Jesper Buus Nielsen[1],
Maciej Obremski[3], Erick Purwanto[3], João Ribeiro[2], and Mark Simkin[1]

[1] Aarhus University, Aarhus, Denmark
{ivan,jbn,simkin}@cs.au.dk
[2] Imperial College London, London, UK
j.lourenco-ribeiro17@imperial.ac.uk
[3] National University of Singapore, Singapore, Singapore
{divesh,erickp}@comp.nus.edu.sg, obremski.math@gmail.com

Abstract. In this work we present a collection of compilers that take secret sharing schemes for an arbitrary access structure as input and produce either leakage-resilient or non-malleable secret sharing schemes for the same access structure. A leakage-resilient secret sharing scheme hides the secret from an adversary, who has access to an unqualified set of shares, even if the adversary additionally obtains some size-bounded leakage from *all* other secret shares. A non-malleable secret sharing scheme guarantees that a secret that is reconstructed from a set of tampered shares is either equal to the original secret or completely unrelated. To the best of our knowledge we present the first generic compiler for leakage-resilient secret sharing for general access structures. In the case of non-malleable secret sharing, we strengthen previous definitions, provide separations between them, and construct a non-malleable secret sharing scheme for general access structures that fulfills the strongest definition with respect to independent share tampering functions. More precisely, our scheme is secure against *concurrent tampering*: The adversary is allowed to (non-adaptively) tamper the shares multiple times, and in each tampering attempt can freely choose the qualified set of shares to be used by the reconstruction algorithm to reconstruct the tampered secret. This is a strong analogue of the multiple-tampering setting for split-state non-malleable codes and extractors.

We show how to use leakage-resilient and non-malleable secret sharing schemes to construct leakage-resilient and non-malleable threshold signatures. Classical threshold signatures allow to distribute the secret key of a signature scheme among a set of parties, such that certain qualified subsets can sign messages. We construct threshold signature schemes that remain secure even if an adversary leaks from or tampers with all secret shares.

© International Association for Cryptologic Research 2019
A. Boldyreva and D. Micciancio (Eds.): CRYPTO 2019, LNCS 11693, pp. 510–539, 2019.
https://doi.org/10.1007/978-3-030-26951-7_18

1   Introduction

In a *secret sharing scheme*, a dealer who holds a secret s chosen from a domain $\mathcal{M}$ can compute a set of *shares* by evaluating a randomized function on s which we write as $\mathbf{Share}(s) = (s_1, \ldots, s_n)$.

A secret sharing comes with an *access structure* $\mathcal{A}$, which is a family of subsets of the indices $1, \ldots, n$, such that if one is given a subset of the shares of s corresponding to a set $A \in \mathcal{A}$ (a *qualified* set), then one can compute s efficiently, whereas any subset of shares corresponding to a set not in $\mathcal{A}$ (an *unqualified* set) contains no, or almost no information about the secret. An important special case is *threshold* secret sharing, where the access structure contains all set of size at least some threshold value.

Secret-sharing is one of the most basic and oldest primitives in cryptography, introduced by Blakley and Shamir in the late seventies [6, 22]. It allows to strike a meaningful balance between availability and confidentiality of secret information. Namely, we can store the n shares in n different servers and ensure that (i) as long as a qualified set of servers is alive, the secret is available, and (ii) even if an unqualified set of shares is stolen, the secret remains confidential.

After its introduction, several variants of secret sharing have been suggested that address the problem of authenticity of the secret: we want to guarantee that we reconstruct the original value, even if not all players are honest. One such variant is *robust* secret sharing, where the dealer is honest but some unqualified set of share holders are malicious and may return incorrect shares. It is required that the secret is still correctly reconstructed from the set of all shares in such a case. In *verifiable secret sharing*, the dealer may be dishonest as well, but via interaction in the sharing phase we can enforce that a unique secret is still determined and that this is the value that will be reconstructed later.

In all these older settings, the adversary is of the classic type that completely corrupts a certain subset of the players in the protocol, either to steal information or to corrupt data, whereas the players who are not corrupted are "completely honest". In many scenarios, however, this may not be the most realistic model of attacks. Instead, it may make more sense to assume that the adversary will try to attack all share holders, and will have some partial success in all or most of the cases.

For the case of attacks against confidentiality, we can model this as *leakage resilient* secret sharing, where the adversary is allowed to specify a leakage function Leak and will be told the value $\mathsf{Leak}(s_1, \ldots, s_n)$. Then, under certain restrictions on Leak, we want that the adversary learns essentially nothing about s. Typically, so called *local leakage* is considered, where $\mathsf{Leak}(s_1, \ldots, s_n) = (\mathsf{Leak}_1(s_1), \ldots, \mathsf{Leak}_n(s_n))$ for local leakage functions Leak_i with bounded output size. This makes sense in a scenario where shares are stored in physically separated locations. It is known that some secret sharing schemes are naturally leakage-resilient against local leakage whereas others are not [5]. Boyle et al. [8] showed how to construct (locally) leakage-resilient verifiable secret sharing for threshold access structures. Goyal and Kumar [16] construct a specific type of leakage-resilient 2-out-of-n secret sharing as part of non-malleable secret sharing construction. To the best of our knowledge, it is not known how to construct leakage-resilient schemes from regular secret sharing schemes in general.

The case of attacks that try to corrupt the secret has been considered only recently, and for this purpose the notion of *non-malleable secret sharing* was introduced by Goyal and Kumar [16]. In this model, the adversary specifies a tampering function f which acts on the shares, and then the reconstruction algorithm is applied to a qualified subset of $f(s_1, ..., s_n)$. The demand, simplistically speaking, is that either the original secret is reconstructed or it is destroyed, i.e., the reconstruction result is unrelated to the original secret. Note that since f is allowed to touch all shares, we cannot avoid the case where an unrelated secret is reconstructed, as f could always replace all shares by shares of a different secret. In line with all previous works, we consider local tampering functions, which individually tamper with each share. This is a sensible assumption if, for example, each share is stored in a different server. Of course, such a tampering is closely related to the earlier notion of non-malleable codes against split-state tampering [14]. The main difference between non-malleable codes and secret sharing schemes is that, in addition to non-malleability, we also insist that the correctness and privacy properties of the secret sharing scheme are satisfied. Interestingly, some non-malleable codes can also be seen as primitive versions of general non-malleable secret sharing schemes. In fact, non-malleable codes in the 2-split-state model (where each codeword is split into two halves which are tampered independently) are 2-out-of-2 non-malleable secret sharing schemes [2].

The first non-malleable secret sharing schemes were constructed in [16] for threshold access structures, and, in a follow-up work [17], for general access structures, where an adversary is allowed to independently tamper with each share in a minimal reconstruction set. In the latter work, a general compiler was given that builds a non-malleable secret sharing scheme from a regular secret sharing scheme.

An application of non-malleable secret sharing to secure message transmission was given in [16], but another very natural application, which does not seem to have been considered before, is to threshold cryptography. Let us consider, for instance, a threshold signature scheme. In such an application, the secret key is secret-shared among n servers, who then collaborate to generate a signature such that the signature itself is the only new information released.

Some threshold signature schemes have "built-in" protection against tampering. Namely, they establish a public commitment to each share of the secret key, and when a server contributes to a new signature, it must prove in zero-knowledge that it is behaving consistently with the commitment. If the commitment cannot be tampered, this will imply that tampered shares cannot contribute to a signature. However, in many protocols for signature generation, one can avoid zero-knowledge proofs by optimistically generating a signature assuming that all players behave correctly. The observation is that one can always verify the signature in the end and take some alternative action if it fails. This will be very efficient if players behave honestly almost always. Such a protocol is not secure if executed on tampered shares, and adding zero-knowledge proofs does not make sense in this case.

It therefore seems natural to try to use a non-malleable secret sharing scheme instead. This of course raises the question of how we can generate signatures efficiently and securely – existing threshold signatures assume regular secret sharing, and it is not clear how we can use existing non-malleable schemes without resorting to generic multiparty computation.

However, suppose for a moment that we could solve this issue. Now, if the shares have in fact been tampered with, this tampering will become clear once it is found out that the signature does not verify, and one can then take action (e.g., stop the system and restore the secret key from a back-up). The intuition is that we have managed to make the tampering harmless, because non-malleability implies that the faulty signature is generated from an unrelated secret.

Unfortunately, however, the original definition is unlikely to be sufficient to prove this intuition for a realistic system. The problem is that a real-life system will most likely have to serve many different signature requests that arrive in an uncoordinated fashion over an asynchronous network like the Internet. Therefore, once the first faulty signature has been detected and action has been taken, we should assume that in the mean time several other signature requests have already been served, possibly by different qualified sets of servers.

The standard definition of non-malleable secret sharing [16,17] is not sufficient to prove security in this case because it only talks about one invocation of the reconstruction algorithm. What we need is a stronger definition, namely *non-malleability with concurrent reconstruction*. In this model, we consider an experiment where, after the tamperings have been done, the reconstruction algorithm is run (in parallel) on *several qualified subsets*. We require that all the instances of the reconstruction return either the original secret or something unrelated. It is not known how to construct secret sharing schemes with this stronger property.

1.1 Our Contributions

In this paper, we resolve all of the above open questions:

- We present a general compiler that transforms any secret sharing scheme into a *leakage-resilient* one for the same access structure and preserves the efficiency of the original scheme. The compiled scheme withstands bounded size local leakage from all shares. The result extends to attacks that are strictly stronger than previously considered: the adversary can be told complete information on an unqualified set of shares and can in addition be given local leakage from all the other shares, and still will not learn the secret. To the best of our knowledge, this is the first result of its kind.
  If the share length of the underlying secret sharing scheme is ℓ, then the compiler can yield a leakage-resilient scheme with shares of length $O(\ell)$ and leakage rate $1 - c$ for an arbitrarily small constant $c > 0$. Moreover, if we allow a blow-up of the share length in the compiled scheme from ℓ to $\omega(\ell)$, then we can achieve a leakage rate of $1 - o(1)$.

- We present another compiler that transforms any secret sharing scheme realizing an access structure $\mathcal{A}$ where every qualified set T has size at least 3 into a scheme for the same access structure that is *non-malleable with concurrent reconstruction* with respect to individual share tampering. More precisely, the adversary chooses a polynomial (in the number of parties) number of qualified sets $T_1, T_2, \ldots$, where it may be the case that $T_i = T_j$ for some i and j, along with associated tampering functions $f^{(1)}, f^{(2)}, \ldots$, where $f^{(i)}$ tampers each share independently. We may think of this setting as a strong analogue of the multiple-tampering paradigm for non-malleable codes and extractors: The adversary is allowed to (non-adaptively) tamper the shares multiple times, and in each tampering attempt is further allowed to freely choose the qualified set to be used by the reconstruction algorithm in the tampering experiment.
- We present a compiler that turns any threshold signature scheme into one that is secure against tampering, assuming the original scheme is secure in the standard sense. In particular, the compiled scheme is secure even if faulty signatures are constructed from several qualified sets after tampering. We allow the adversary to either tamper with all shares of the secret key, or to maliciously corrupt an unqualified subset of the signature servers. The compiler adds two rounds to the signing protocol of the original scheme. The computational complexity is essentially that of the original signature protocol plus that of the reconstruction in a non-malleable secret sharing scheme. The overhead is actually only necessary each time the system is initialized from storage that may have been tampered, and therefore its cost amortizes over all signatures generated while the system is on-line.
- We present a compiler that turns any threshold signature scheme into one that is secure in the standard sense even if the adversary, additionally, obtains size-bounded leakage from *all* secret key shares. The compiler follows the same blueprint and is as efficient as our compiler for non-malleable threshold signatures.

1.2   Independent Work

In the late stages of this work, it came to our knowledge that other independent, concurrent works obtained results similar to ours. Srinivasan and Vasudevan [24] give a compiler that transforms a secret sharing scheme for any access structure into a leakage-resilient secret sharing scheme for the same access structure. Their compiler is rate-preserving and has leakage rate approaching 1. In comparison, if the underlying secret sharing scheme has constant rate, our leakage-resilient secret sharing compiler achieves rate $\Omega(1/n)$ and leakage rate $1 - c$ for an arbitrarily small constant $c > 0$, and must have rate 0 if we require leakage rate $1 - o(1)$. They also construct leakage resilient schemes in a stronger leakage model, where leakage functions may be chosen adaptively.

Srinivasan and Vasudevan use the results obtained to construct positive rate non-malleable threshold secret sharing schemes against a single tampering that modifies each share independently for 4-monotone access structures[1]. In comparison, the non-malleable secret sharing compiler that we obtain for a single tampering works for all 3-monotone access structures but has rate $\Theta(\frac{1}{n \log m})$ in the same setting, where m denotes the length of the secret and n denotes the number of parties, and so converges to 0. Finally, they consider applications to leakage-resilient secure multiparty computation.

Badrinarayanan and Srinivasan [3] construct non-malleable secret sharing schemes with respect to independent share tampering, both against a single tampering and against multiple tamperings. They are able to realize all 4-monotone access structures. Moreover, they optimize the rates of their constructions to obtain schemes with positive rate and a concretely efficient scheme. However, their tampering model is weaker than ours: While in our model, named *concurrent reconstruction*, the adversary is allowed to (non-adaptively) tamper the shares multiple times and in each tampering can choose a potentially different reconstruction set for the tampering experiment, the model studied in [3] forces the adversary to always choose the same reconstruction set for all tamperings. Their schemes are not secure in the stronger concurrent reconstruction model, and the authors explicitly mention the concurrent reconstruction model as a natural strengthening of their tampering model. In contrast, our compiler transforms any secret sharing scheme realizing a 3-monotone access structure into a (rate-0) non-malleable secret sharing scheme secure against multiple tamperings in the concurrent reconstruction model.

Kumar, Meka, and Sahai [20] also study leakage-resilient and non-malleable secret sharing. They consider a stronger leakage model than ours, where each leaked bit may depend on up to p shares which can be chosen adaptively by the adversary. They give a compiler that transforms a standard secret sharing scheme into a leakage-resilient one in the model just described, for p logarithmic in the number of parties. It is also shown that noticeably improving the dependence of the share length on p obtained there would lead to non-trivial progress on important open questions related to communication complexity. Finally, they consider the notion of *leakage-resilient non-malleable* secret sharing with respect to independent share tampering. Here, the adversary has access to leakage from the shares, which he can then make use of to choose tampering functions. They construct schemes in this model for the case of a single tampering. For comparison, our non-malleable secret sharing schemes cannot withstand leakage, but, as already mentioned in the previous paragraph, allow the adversary to tamper the shares multiple times, each time with a potentially different reconstruction set in the associated tampering experiment.

1.3   Technical Overview

In this section, we give a high-level overview of the proof ideas and techniques used to construct each one of our compilers.

---

[1] An access structure $\mathcal{A}$ is said to be *k-monotone* if $|T| \geq k$ for all $T \in \mathcal{A}$.

All of our secret sharing scheme compilers are based on the same key idea: Let $s_1, \ldots, s_n$ denote the shares obtained via the underlying secret sharing scheme. We encode each share s_i using some (randomized) coding scheme $(\mathbf{Enc}, \mathbf{Dec})$ to obtain two values L_i and R_i. Then, the new compiled shares are obtained by, for each $i = 1, \ldots, n$, giving L_i to the i-th party, and R_i to every other party. At the end of this procedure, the i-th party has a compiled share, denoted S_i, of the form $S_i = (R_1, \ldots, R_{i-1}, L_i, R_{i+1}, \ldots, R_n)$.

Reconstruction of the underlying secret is possible from any qualified set of parties, as they will learn the corresponding pairs (L_i, R_i), and hence the underlying share s_i. The different compilers arise by instantiating the idea above with coding schemes satisfying different properties. One basic property that is required from all coding schemes is that one half of the codeword (L_i, R_i) reveals almost nothing about s_i.

Leakage-Resilient Secret-Sharing Scheme. In order to obtain a leakage-resilient secret-sharing scheme via the idea above, we instantiate the coding scheme $(\mathbf{Enc}, \mathbf{Dec})$ as follows: Let Ext be a strong seeded extractor. Roughly speaking, a strong seeded extractor is a deterministic function that produces a close-to-uniform output when given a sample from a source with high min-entropy along with a short, independent, and uniform seed, *even when the seed is known to the distinguisher*. Then, $\mathbf{Enc}(m)$ samples (L, R) from the preimage $\mathsf{Ext}^{-1}(m)$ close to uniformly at random. Here, L corresponds to the weak source, while R corresponds to the uniform, independent seed. To recover m from a codeword c, we simply set $\mathbf{Dec}(L, R) := \mathsf{Ext}(L, R)$. This coding scheme is efficient if Ext is itself efficient, and furthermore Ext supports *efficient close-to-uniform preimage sampling*. More precisely, this means that, given m, there exists an efficient algorithm that samples an element of $\mathsf{Ext}^{-1}(m)$ close to uniformly at random. The idea behind this coding scheme is the same as the one used by Cheraghchi and Guruswami [11] in order to obtain split-state non-malleable codes from non-malleable extractors (variations of these objects are defined in Sect. 2, but are not important for this discussion).

We instantiate our compiler with linear strong seeded extractors coupled with a careful choice of parameters in order to obtain a leakage-resilient scheme with good leakage rate. A result of [9] ensures that we can efficiently sample close to uniformly from the preimage of any linear strong seeded extractor, provided the error of the extractor is small enough.

We now discuss why this construction is leakage-resilient. For simplicity, assume that L_i and R_i are independent and uniform for $i = 1, \ldots, n$. This is not true in practice, and a little more care is needed to show that leakage-resilience holds in Sect. 4. However, it lets us present the main idea behind the proof in a clearer way.

Suppose the adversary holds shares from a set of unqualified parties T. Without loss of generality, let $T = \{1, \ldots, t\}$. Furthermore, we also assume the adversary learns some limited information about all shares, i.e., he learns $\mathsf{Leak}_i(S_i)$ for some function Leak_i and all $i = 1, \ldots, n$. Note that the adversary knows the pairs (L_i, R_i) for $i = 1, \ldots, t$, and hence the shares $s_1, \ldots, s_t$ obtained via the underlying secret sharing scheme. Furthermore, he knows R_i (the seeds of the extractor) for $i = t + 1, \ldots, n$. The goal of the adversary is now to obtain extra knowledge about $L_{t+1}, \ldots, L_n$ from the leaked information. Since, by hypothesis, the leaked information about L_i is only a small linear fraction of its length, and is independent of R_i, we can condition L_i on the output of $\mathsf{Leak}_i(S_i)$. As a result, L_i conditioned on $\mathsf{Leak}_i(S_i)$ is still independent of R_i, and still has high min-entropy. This means that the output of $\mathsf{Ext}(L_i, R_i)$ still looks close-to-uniform to the adversary, even when R_i is given (recall that we use a strong extractor). It follows that the leaked information gives almost no information about the shares outside T, and hence we can use the statistical privacy of the underlying secret sharing scheme to conclude the proof.

Non-Malleable Secret-Sharing Scheme with Concurrent Reconstruction. In order to obtain a non-malleable scheme, we use the same basic idea as before, but with a few modifications. To begin, we require the following primitives:

- A secret sharing scheme (**Share, Rec**) for an access structure in which every qualified set has size at least 3;
- A strong two-source non-malleable extractor **nmExt** secure against multiple tamperings which supports *efficient preimage sampling*, in the sense that we can sample uniformly from its preimages $\mathbf{nmExt}^{-1}(z)$.

A non-malleable extractor is a stronger notion of an extractor introduced in [11]. More precisely, its output must still be close to uniform even conditioned on the output of the extractor on a tampered version of the original input. Similarly as before, such an extractor is said to be *strong* if the property above still holds when the distinguisher is also given the value of one of the input sources. Since their introduction, non-malleable extractors have received a lot of attention due to their connection to split-state non-malleable codes [9–11,21]. We note that constructions of such strong non-malleable extractors handling a sublinear (in the input length) number of tamperings and supporting efficient preimage sampling are known [9,18].

The coding scheme (**Enc, Dec**) is obtained from **nmExt** analogously to the leakage-resilient scheme. Namely, $\mathbf{Enc}(m)$ samples (L, R) uniformly at random from $\mathbf{nmExt}^{-1}(m)$, and we set $\mathbf{Dec}(L', R') := \mathbf{nmExt}(L', R')$.

To encode the shares $(s_1, \ldots, s_n)$ into $(S_1, \ldots, S_n)$, we proceed as follows:

1. Sample $P \leftarrow \{0, 1\}^p$;
2. Set $(L_i, R_i) \leftarrow \mathbf{Enc}(P \| s_i)$ for $i = 1, \ldots, n$, where $\|$ denotes string concatenation;
3. Set $S_i = (R_1, \ldots, R_{i-1}, L_i, R_{i+1}, \ldots, R_n)$ for $i = 1, \ldots, n$.

We will now briefly walk through the proof of statistical privacy and non-malleability for a single reconstruction set. Statistical privacy follows from the statistical privacy properties of the underlying secret sharing scheme and the fact that (**Enc**, **Dec**) as defined above can be seen as a 2-out-of-2 secret sharing scheme.

In order to show statistical privacy, fix an unqualified set of parties T, which we may assume is $T = \{1, \ldots, t\}$. First, the fact that a split-state non-malleable code is also a 2-out-of-2 secret sharing scheme implies that we can replace the values $R_{t+1}, \ldots, R_n$ in all shares by independent and uniformly random values. Second, the pairs $(L_1, R_1), \ldots, (L_t, R_t)$ encode shares $s_1, \ldots, s_t$, respectively, belonging to an unqualified set of the underlying secret sharing scheme. As a result, the statistical privacy of that scheme implies we can replace these encodings by those induced by a different secret.

In order to show non-malleability, fix a qualified set of parties T, with $t = |T| \geq 3$. For simplicity, assume again $T = \{1, \ldots, t\}$. An adversary that wishes to tamper the shares in T chooses tampering functions $f_1, \ldots, f_t$, one per share. Write a tampered share $S_i' = f_i(S_i)$ as $S_i' = (R_1'^{(i)}, \ldots, R_{i-1}'^{(i)}, L_i', R_{i+1}'^{(i)}, \ldots, R_n'^{(i)})$ for $i = 1, \ldots, t$. We now have the following reconstruction procedure, which may output a special symbol $\perp$ if it detects tampering:

1. For each $i = 1, \ldots, n$, check that $R_i'^{(j_1)} = R_i'^{(j_2)}$ for all $j_1, j_2 \neq i$. If this is not the case, then output $\perp$;
2. If the check holds, set $R_1' = R_1'^{(2)}$ and $R_i' = R_i'^{(1)}$ for $i = 2, \ldots, t$. Then, decode and parse $P_i' \| s_i' \leftarrow \mathbf{Dec}(L_i', R_i')$ for $i = 1, \ldots, t$;
3. If $P_i' \neq P_j'$ for some $i, j \leq t$, output $\perp$. Else, output $\mathbf{Rec}^T(s_1', \ldots, s_t')$.

Note that the consistency checks in Steps 1 and 3 correspond to properties that must be satisfied if $(S_1', \ldots, S_t')$ is a valid set of shares. Roughly speaking, in order to show non-malleability we must be able to simulate the reconstruction of tampered shares without knowledge of the encoded secret m (except if the adversary does not modify any share, in which case we may output m).

We prove non-malleability in two steps. First, we consider the following *intermediate* tampering experiment on $(S_1, \ldots, S_t)$:

- For each $i = 1, \ldots, n$, check that $R_i'^{(j_1)} = R_i'^{(j_2)}$ for all $j_1, j_2 \neq i$. If this is not the case, then output $\perp$;
- If the check holds, set $R_1' = R_1'^{(2)}$ and $R_i' = R_i'^{(1)}$ for $i = 2, \ldots, t$. For each $i = 1, \ldots, t$, set $\mathsf{output}_i = \mathsf{same}^*$ if $L_i' = L_i$ and $R_i' = R_i$. Otherwise, set $\mathsf{output}_i \leftarrow \mathbf{Dec}(L_i', R_i')$;
- If $\mathsf{output}_i = \mathsf{same}^*$ for all $i = 1, \ldots, t$, output same^*. Else, output $(\mathsf{output}_1, \ldots, \mathsf{output}_t)$.

This is an intermediate tampering experiment in the sense that it corresponds to a stage of the reconstruction procedure on the tampered shares where the values of the shares that remain the same have not yet been revealed. A key result we show is that the output of the intermediate tampering experiment described above has almost no correlation with the initial values $P \| s_i$ for $i = 1, \ldots, n$. In particular, we can replace each such value by an independent and uniformly random one, and hence by a set of uniform values independent of the secret m

encoded by the shares $s_1, \ldots, s_n$. We leverage a novel property of strong non-malleable extractors (Lemmas 24 and 28) to prove this result, which may be of independent interest.

By the result just described, we now know how to simulate the intermediate tampering experiment for any secret m without any knowledge of m itself. However, to be able to simulate the behavior of the real reconstruction procedure on the tampered shares, we must know what the simulator must output when $\mathsf{output}_i = \mathsf{same}^*$ and $\mathsf{output}_j \neq \mathsf{same}^*$ for some $i, j \leq t$. In the second step, we show that the reconstruction procedure will output $\bot$ (i.e., tampering is detected, and hence the procedure is aborted) with high probability in this situation. This is because, with high probability, the decoded prefixes will not match among all parties in this case. As a result, we can simply have our simulator output $\bot$ in such a case, and it will coincide with the output of the real reconstruction procedure with high probability.

The argument above implies that our secret sharing scheme is non-malleable against a single tampering of a reconstruction set. This result extends to the concurrent reconstruction setting, where the adversary is allowed to tamper the shares multiple times with different tampering functions and qualified sets. We refer to the later sections for details on the proof for the general case.

Threshold Signature Scheme Secure Against Tampering. Finally, our threshold signature compiler starts from the assumption that the secret key is to be secret-shared among a set of servers. We assume that we have protocols for generating n signature shares as well as a protocol for computing the final signature from these shares. Further, we assume that these protocols are secure even if an adversary maliciously corrupts an unqualified subset of size t of the $n \geq 2t + 1$ servers.

To construct the compiled protocol, we first apply our second compiler from above, such that we now share the secret key using non-malleable secret sharing. Recall that this scheme involves encoding the original share s_i to get a pair (L_i, R_i) where the i-th server holds L_i and all other servers hold R_i. If now the i-th server wants to generate a signature share, it requests R_i from all other servers and waits until it gets back $n - t$ responses. If all received R_i are the same, it accepts the value and decodes (L_i, R_i) to obtain key share s_i. Note that since $n \geq 2t + 1$ and the server gets $n - t$ responses, we ensure that it gets back at least one honest response. At this point the server generates a signature share as it would do in the original protocol.

A rough intuition on why this is secure follows: Recall that our model says that the adversary can either tamper with the shares, or corrupt t of servers. If he tampers, he is not allowed to corrupt anyone, and this means that the servers are executing the non-malleable reconstruction protocol securely, and will either get the correct original shares (and thus create correct signatures) or will get something unrelated, in which case the output cannot compromise any secret key share. In the other case, the adversary has chosen to corrupt a set of servers. However, then we know that the shares we start from are correct. This means that sending the required R_i's in the clear to i-th server does not leak any extra information than it should. In fact, it merely enables the server to get his original share. The checks we enforce ensure that an honest player get its correct original share, and hence security follows from the threshold signature scheme we started with.

1.4 Open Questions

Several exciting questions remain open. The first natural direction is to improve the rates of our constructions. This can be achieved indirectly by coming up with better explicit constructions of strong seeded extractors and strong seedless non-malleable extractors. Another possibility is to improve the relationship between the share length of the compiled scheme and the number of parties. All of our constructions, as well as the constructions of Goyal and Kumar [16,17], have share sizes which are at least linear in the number of parties, and it would be interesting to see whether one can obtain a weaker dependence.

Our work introduces stronger definitions for non-malleable secret sharing schemes. However, our new notions, as well as the previous ones, are fundamentally non-adaptive in the sense that the tampering functions and reconstruction sets have to be chosen without seeing any of the shares a priori. We believe it would be more in the spirit of secret sharing if the tampering functions and reconstruction sets could be chosen *after* seeing some unqualified set of shares. On a similar note, a logical next step would be to define and attempt to construct continuous non-malleable secret sharing schemes (in the spirit of [15]), where the adversary is allowed to choose the tampering function and qualified set to be reconstructed adaptively.

Our definition of leakage-resilient secret sharing schemes is also non-adaptive. It would be interesting to construct schemes which remain leakage resilient even if the adversary has access to an unqualified set of shares prior to choosing the leakage functions. Moreover, we obtain leakage rate $1 - c$ for an arbitrarily small constant $c > 0$ while preserving the share length (up to a multiplicative constant). However, our share length suffers a polynomial blow-up if we want to achieve leakage rate $1 - o(1)$. It would be interesting to give constructions of leakage-resilient schemes (even in the non-adaptive setting) with an improved tradeoff between leakage rate and share length.

1.5 Organization

The rest of the paper is organized as follows: We present notation, relevant definitions, and known lemmas that we use throughout the paper in Sect. 2. We present and study our compiler for non-malleable secret sharing in Sect. 3. In Sect. 4, we present our compiler for leakage-resilient secret sharing. Finally, in Sect. 5, we discuss our compiler for non-malleable and leakage-resilient threshold signatures. Most detailed arguments have been deferred to the full version of this work [1].

2   Preliminaries

We denote the set $\{1, \ldots, n\}$ by $[n]$. Random variables are usually denoted by uppercase letters such as X, Y, and Z. We denote sets by calligraphic letters such as $\mathcal{A}$ and $\mathcal{M}$. We may denote the probability that a random variable X belongs to a set $\mathcal{S}$ by $X(\mathcal{S})$. We use the notation $z \leftarrow Z$ to denote that z is sampled according to distribution Z. If instead we write, say, $s \leftarrow \mathcal{S}$, this means that s is sampled uniformly at random from the set $\mathcal{S}$. Given an n-tuple x and a set $\mathcal{S} \subseteq [n]$ with $\mathcal{S} = \{i_1, \ldots, i_s\}$ and $i_j < i_{j+1}$ for $j = 1, \ldots, s-1$, we define $x_{\mathcal{S}} = (x_{i_1}, \ldots, x_{i_s})$. By an efficient algorithm, we mean an algorithm that runs in time polynomial in the length of the input.

2.1   Statistical Distance and Min-Entropy

In this section, we introduce statistical distance and min-entropy, along with related results.

Definition 1 (Statistical Distance). *Let X and Y be two distributions over a set S. The* statistical distance *between X and Y, denoted by $\Delta(X;Y)$, is given by*

$$\Delta(X;Y) := \max_{T \subseteq S}(|X(T) - Y(T)|) = \frac{1}{2}\sum_{s \in S}|X(s) - Y(s)|.$$

We say X is ε-close to Y, denoted $X \approx_{\varepsilon} Y$, if $\Delta(X;Y) \le \varepsilon$, and we write $\Delta(X;Y|Z)$ as shorthand for $\Delta((X,Z);(Y,Z))$.

The following known properties of the statistical distance are useful throughout the paper.

Lemma 2. *For any two random variables X and Y, and any randomized function f, we have that*

$$\Delta(f(X); f(Y)) \le \Delta(X;Y).$$

Lemma 3 ([11]). *Fix random variables X and Y such that*

$$X \approx_{\varepsilon} Y.$$

Let X' and Y' denote X and Y conditioned on an event E, respectively. If $X(E) = p$ (i.e., the probability of event E under X is p), then

$$X' \approx_{\varepsilon/p} Y'.$$

Definition 4 (Min-Entropy and Conditional Min-Entropy). *Fix a distribution X over $\mathcal{X}$. The* min-entropy *of X, denoted by $\mathbf{H}_{\infty}(X)$, is given by*

$$\mathbf{H}_{\infty}(X) := -\log\left(\max_{x \in \mathcal{X}} X(x)\right).$$

Moreover, the conditional min-entropy of X given Z, *denoted by* $\mathbf{H}_\infty(X|Z)$, *is given by*

$$\mathbf{H}_\infty(X|Z) := -\log\left(\mathbb{E}_{z \leftarrow Z}\left[2^{-\mathbf{H}_\infty(X|Z=z)}\right]\right),$$

where $\mathbb{E}_{z \leftarrow Z}$ *denotes the expected value over* Z.

The following property of the conditional min-entropy is also fundamental.

Lemma 5 ([13]). *Let* (X, Z) *be some joint probability distribution. Then, if* Z *is supported on at most* 2^ℓ *values, we have*

$$\mathbf{H}_\infty(X|Z) \geq \mathbf{H}_\infty(X) - \ell.$$

2.2 Non-Malleable Codes and Extractors

In order to design our compilers, we will need to use some variants of extractors and non-malleable codes. We present the relevant definitions and results in this section.

Non-malleable codes are coding schemes with strong robustness guarantees against adversarial errors. We begin by defining coding schemes.

Definition 6 (Coding Scheme). *A tuple of functions* $(\mathbf{Enc}, \mathbf{Dec})$ *where* $\mathbf{Enc} : \mathcal{M} \to \mathcal{C}$ *may be randomized but* $\mathbf{Dec} : \mathcal{C} \to \mathcal{M} \cup \{\bot\}$ *is deterministic is said to be a* coding scheme *if the correctness property*

$$\Pr(\mathbf{Dec}(\mathbf{Enc}(m)) = m) = 1$$

holds for every $m \in \mathcal{M}$, *where the probability is taken over the randomness of the encoder* $\mathbf{Enc}$.

Definition 7 (Non-Malleable Code [14]). *We say that a coding scheme* $(\mathbf{Enc} : \mathcal{M} \to \mathcal{X} \times \mathcal{X}, \mathbf{Dec} : \mathcal{X} \times \mathcal{X} \to \mathcal{M} \cup \{\bot\})$ *is* ε-non-malleable in the split-state model *if for all functions* $F, G : \mathcal{X} \to \mathcal{X}$ *there exists a distribution* $SD^{F,G}$ *over* $\mathcal{M} \cup \{\mathsf{same}^*, \bot\}$ *such that*

$$\mathsf{Tamper}_m^{F,G} \approx_\varepsilon \mathsf{Sim}_m^{F,G}$$

for all $m \in \mathcal{M}$, *where*

$$\mathsf{Tamper}_m^{F,G} = \left\{ \begin{array}{l} (L, R) \leftarrow \mathbf{Enc}(m) \\ Output\ \mathbf{Dec}(F(L), G(R)) \end{array} \right\},$$

and

$$\mathsf{Sim}_m^{F,G} = \left\{ \begin{array}{l} d \leftarrow SD^{F,G} \\ If\ d = \mathsf{same}^*,\ output\ m \\ Else,\ output\ d \end{array} \right\}.$$

Additionally, $SD^{F,G}$ *should be efficiently samplable given oracle access to* $F(\cdot)$ *and* $G(\cdot)$.

We will also require a few variants of randomness extractors. We begin with the basic definition.

Definition 8 (Extractor). *An efficient function* $\mathsf{Ext} : \mathcal{X} \times \{0,1\}^d \to \mathcal{Z}$ *is a strong* (k, ε)-*extractor if for all* X, W *such that* X *is distributed over* $\mathcal{X}$ *and* $\mathbf{H}_\infty(X|W) \geq k$ *we have*

$$\mathsf{Ext}(X, U_d), W, U_d \approx_\varepsilon U_{\mathcal{Z}}, W, U_d.$$

Moreover, we say Ext *supports* efficient preimage sampling *if, given* $z \in \mathcal{Z}$, *there exists an efficient algorithm that samples an element of* $\mathsf{Ext}^{-1}(z)$ *uniformly at random.*

We describe some known explicit constructions of linear strong extractors that we will need to instantiate our leakage-resilient secret sharing compiler of Sect. 4 in [1]. We will also need a stronger notion of an (independent-source) extractor, for which the output still looks uniform even conditioned on the output of the extractor on a tampered version of the original input.

Definition 9 (Strong Two-Source Non-Malleable Extractor). *A function* $\mathbf{nmExt} : \mathcal{X}^2 \to \mathcal{Z}$ *is said to be a* (k, ε, τ) *strong two-source non-malleable extractor if the following property holds: For independent distributions* X, Y *over* $\mathcal{X}$ *and* W *independent of* Y *such that* $\mathbf{H}_\infty(X|W), \mathbf{H}_\infty(Y) \geq k$, *and for all tampering functions* $(f_1, g_1), \ldots, (f_\tau, g_\tau)$ *it holds that*

$$\mathbf{nmExt}(X, Y), W, Y, \{\mathcal{D}_{f_i, g_i}(X, Y)\}_{i \in [\tau]} \approx_c U_{\mathcal{Z}}, W, Y, \{\mathcal{D}_{f_i, g_i}(X, Y)\}_{i \in [\tau]},$$

where $\mathcal{D}_{f,g}(X, Y)$ *is defined as*

$$\mathcal{D}_{f,g}(X, Y) := \begin{cases} \mathsf{same}^*, & \text{if } f(X) = X \text{ and } g(Y) = Y, \\ \mathbf{nmExt}(f(X), g(Y)), & \text{otherwise.} \end{cases}$$

The function $\mathbf{nmExt}$ *is said to support* efficient preimage sampling *if, given* $z \in \mathcal{Z}$, *there is an efficient algorithm that samples an element of the preimage* $\mathbf{nmExt}^{-1}(z)$ *uniformly at random.*

There exist explicit constructions of strong two-source non-malleable extractors with good parameters, supporting efficient preimage sampling, both against single and multiple tamperings [9,21]. Although it is not stated in [9] that the extractor found there is strong, it is known that this property holds [19]. A statement and proof of this result appears in [18]. We will use the following two explicit non-malleable extractors.

Lemma 10 ([21]). *For any field* $\mathbb{F}$ *of cardinality* 2^N, *there exists a constant* $\delta \in (0, 1)$ *and a function* $\mathbf{nmExt} : \mathbb{F}^2 \to \{0,1\}^\ell$ *such that* $\mathbf{nmExt}$ *is an efficient* $((1 - \delta)N, \varepsilon, 1)$ *strong two-source non-malleable extractor with* $\ell = \Omega(N)$ *and* $\varepsilon = 2^{-\Omega(N/\log N)}$. *Moreover,* $\mathbf{nmExt}$ *supports efficient preimage sampling and it is a balanced function, i.e., the preimage sets* $\mathbf{nmExt}^{-1}(z)$ *have the same size for all* $z \in \{0,1\}^\ell$.

Lemma 11 ([9,18]). *For any field $\mathbb{F}$ of cardinality 2^N, there exists a constant $\delta \in (0,1)$ and a function $\mathbf{nmExt} : \mathbb{F}^2 \to \{0,1\}^\ell$ such that $\mathbf{nmExt}$ is an efficient $(N - N^\delta, \varepsilon, \tau)$ strong two-source non-malleable extractor with $\ell = N^{\Omega(1)}$, $\tau = N^{\Omega(1)}$, and $\varepsilon = 2^{-N^{\Omega(1)}}$. Moreover, $\mathbf{nmExt}$ supports efficient preimage sampling and it is a balanced function, i.e., the preimage sets $\mathbf{nmExt}^{-1}(z)$ have the same size for all $z \in \{0,1\}^\ell$.*

The connection between non-malleable extractors with efficient preimage sampling and split-state non-malleable codes is made clear by the following result.

Lemma 12 ([11]). *Fix an explicit two-source $(n, \varepsilon, 1)$-non-malleable extractor $\mathbf{nmExt} : \mathbb{F}^2 \to \{0,1\}^\ell$ that supports efficient preimage sampling. The coding scheme $(\mathbf{NMEnc}, \mathbf{NMDec})$ is defined as follows:*

– $\mathbf{NMEnc}(m)$: *Sample* $(L, R) \leftarrow \mathbf{nmExt}^{-1}(m)$, *and output* (L, R);
– $\mathbf{NMDec}(L', R')$: *Output* $\mathbf{nmExt}(L', R')$.

Then, $(\mathbf{NMEnc}, \mathbf{NMDec})$ is an efficient split-state ε'-non-malleable code for $\varepsilon' = \varepsilon(2^\ell + 1)$.

Combining Li's non-malleable extractor [21] and Lemma 12 immediately leads to the following result, also found in [21].

Corollary 13 ([21]). *For any field $\mathbb{F}$ of cardinality 2^N, there exists an efficient split-state ε-non-malleable code $(\mathbf{NMEnc}, \mathbf{NMDec})$ with $\mathbf{NMEnc} : \{0,1\}^\ell \to \mathbb{F}^2$, $\mathbf{NMDec} : \mathbb{F}^2 \to \{0,1\}^\ell \cup \{\bot\}$, $\ell = \Theta(N/\log N)$, and $\varepsilon = 2^{-\Omega(N/\log N)}$.*

2.3   Secret-Sharing Schemes

In this section, we introduce our definitions of leakage-resilient and non-malleable secret sharing schemes. We begin by defining basic secret sharing concepts.

Definition 14 (Access Structure). *We say $\mathcal{A}$ is an* access structure *for n parties if $\mathcal{A}$ is a monotone class of subsets of $[n]$, i.e., if $A \in \mathcal{A}$ and $A \subseteq B$, then $B \in \mathcal{A}$. We call sets $T \in \mathcal{A}$* authorized *or* qualified, *and* unauthorized *or* unqualified *otherwise.*

Definition 15 (Secret Sharing Scheme [4]). *Let $\mathcal{M}$ be a finite set of secrets, where $|\mathcal{M}| \geq 2$. A (randomized) sharing function $\mathbf{Share} : \mathcal{M} \to \mathcal{S}_1 \times \cdots \times \mathcal{S}_n$ is an (n, ε)-Secret Sharing Scheme for secret space $\mathcal{M}$ realizing access structure $\mathcal{A}$ if the following two properties hold:*

1. *$\mathbf{Correctness.}$ The secret can be reconstructed by any authorized set of parties. That is, for any set $T \in \mathcal{A}$, where $T = \{i_1, \ldots, i_t\}$, there exists a deterministic reconstruction function $\mathbf{Rec}^T : \otimes_{i \in T} \mathcal{S}_i \to \mathcal{M}$ such that for every $m \in \mathcal{M}$,*

$$\Pr[\mathbf{Rec}^T(\mathbf{Share}(m)_T) = m] = 1,$$

where the probability is taken over the randomness of $\mathbf{Share}$.

2. **Statistical Privacy.** *Any collusion of unauthorized parties should have "almost" no information about the underlying secret. More formally, for all unauthorized sets $T \notin \mathcal{A}$ and for every pair of secrets $a, b \in \mathcal{M}$, we have*

$$\mathbf{Share}(a)_T \approx_\varepsilon \mathbf{Share}(b)_T.$$

Besides the usual secret sharing properties, we can additionally require that the unauthorized parties do not learn anything about the underlying secret, even if given some leakage from all the shares. This leads to the notion of *leakage-resilient* secret sharing.

Definition 16 (Leakage-Resilient Secret-Sharing Scheme). *A secret sharing scheme* (**Share, Rec**) *realizing access structure $\mathcal{A}$ is said to be an (n, ε, ρ)-leakage-resilient secret sharing scheme if the following property additionally holds:*

- **Leakage-Resilient Statistical Privacy.** *For all unauthorized sets $T \notin \mathcal{A}$, functions $\mathsf{Leak}_i : \mathcal{S}_i \to \{0,1\}^{\lfloor \rho \log |\mathcal{S}_i| \rfloor}$ for $i = 1, \ldots, n$, and for every pair of secrets $a, b \in \mathcal{M}$, we have*

$$\mathbf{Share}(a)_T, \{\mathsf{Leak}_i(\mathbf{Share}(a)_i)\}_{i \in [n]} \approx_\varepsilon \mathbf{Share}(b)_T, \{\mathsf{Leak}_i(\mathbf{Share}(b)_i)\}_{i \in [n]}.$$

Alternatively, we can require some security against tampering attacks on the shares produced by the secret sharing scheme: Either the secret reconstructed from the tampered shares is the same as the original secret, or it is almost independent of it. The notion of *non-malleable* secret sharing was first considered in [16,17], but only with respect to tampering attacks on qualified sets belonging to the minimal access structure.

Definition 17 (Non-Malleable Secret Sharing Scheme). *Let* (**Share, Rec**) *be an (n, ε)-secret sharing scheme for secret space $\mathcal{M}$ realizing access structure $\mathcal{A}$. Let $\mathcal{F}$ be some family of tampering functions. For each $f \in \mathcal{F}$, $m \in \mathcal{M}$ and authorized set $T \in \mathcal{A}$, define the tampering experiment*

$$\mathsf{STamper}_m^{f,T} = \begin{Bmatrix} \mathbf{s} \leftarrow \mathbf{Share}(m) \\ \widetilde{\mathbf{s}} \leftarrow f(\mathbf{s}) \\ \widetilde{m} \leftarrow \mathbf{Rec}(\widetilde{\mathbf{s}}_T) \\ Output~\widetilde{m} \end{Bmatrix},$$

which is a random variable over the randomness of the sharing function **Share**. *We say that* (**Share, Rec**) *is ε'-non-malleable with respect to $\mathcal{F}$ if for each $f \in \mathcal{F}$ and authorized set $T \in \mathcal{A}$, there exists a distribution $SD^{f,T}$ (corresponding to the simulator) over $\mathcal{M} \cup \{\mathsf{same}^*, \bot\}$ such that we have*

$$\mathsf{STamper}_m^{f,T} \approx_{\varepsilon'} \mathsf{SSim}_m^{f,T},$$

for all $m \in \mathcal{M}$ and authorized sets $T \in \mathcal{A}$, where

$$\mathsf{SSim}_m^{f,T} = \begin{Bmatrix} \widetilde{m} \leftarrow SD^{f,T} \\ If~\widetilde{m} = \mathsf{same}^*,~output~m \\ Else,~output~\widetilde{m} \end{Bmatrix}.$$

Additionally, $SD^{f,T}$ should be efficiently samplable given oracle access to $f(\cdot)$.

We also consider a stronger notion of non-malleable secret sharing, where the adversary is allowed to tamper the shares multiple times, and in each tampering attempt is free to choose the qualified set to be used by the reconstruction algorithm in the tampering experiment.

Definition 18 (Non-Malleability with Concurrent Reconstruction).
Let (**Share, Rec**) *be an* (n, ε)-*secret sharing scheme for secret space* $\mathcal{M}$ *realizing access structure* $\mathcal{A}$. *Let* τ *be a fixed constant. Let* $\mathcal{F}$ *be some family of tampering functions. For* $m \in \mathcal{M}$, $\mathbf{f} = (f^{(1)}, \ldots, f^{(\tau)}) \in \mathcal{F}^\tau$, *and* $\mathbf{T} = (T_1, \ldots, T_\tau) \in \mathcal{A}^\tau$, *define the tampering experiment*

$$\mathbf{SCRTamper}_m^{\mathbf{f},\mathbf{T}} = \left(\mathbf{STamper}_m^{f^{(1)},T_1}, \mathbf{STamper}_m^{f^{(2)},T_2}, \ldots, \mathbf{STamper}_m^{f^{(\tau)},T_\tau}\right),$$

where each $\mathbf{STamper}_m^{f^{(i)},T_i}$ *is defined as in Definition 17. We say that* (**Share, Rec**) *is* (ε', τ)-*concurrent-reconstruction-non-malleable with respect to* $\mathcal{F}$ *if for each tuple* $\mathbf{f} \in \mathcal{F}^\tau$ *and tuple of authorized sets* $\mathbf{T} \in \mathcal{A}^\tau$, *there exists a distribution* $SD^{\mathbf{f},\mathbf{T}}$ *over* $(\mathcal{M} \cup \{\bot, \mathsf{same}^*\})^\tau$ *such that*

$$\mathbf{SCRTamper}_m^{\mathbf{f},\mathbf{T}} \approx_{\varepsilon'} \mathbf{SCRSim}_m^{\mathbf{f},\mathbf{T}}$$

for all $m \in \mathcal{M}$, *where*

$$\mathbf{SCRSim}_m^{\mathbf{f},\mathbf{T}} = \left\{ \begin{array}{l} (\tilde{m}_1, \ldots, \tilde{m}_\tau) \leftarrow SD^{\mathbf{f},\mathbf{T}} \\ \textit{Output } (\tilde{m}_1', \ldots, \tilde{m}_\tau'), \textit{ where } \tilde{m}_i' = m \textit{ if } \tilde{m}_i = \mathsf{same}^*, \\ \textit{and } \tilde{m}_i' = \tilde{m}_i \textit{ otherwise} \end{array} \right\}.$$

Additionally, $SD^{\mathbf{f},\mathbf{T}}$ *should be efficiently samplable given oracle access to* $f^{(i)}(\cdot)$ *for* $i = 1, \ldots, \tau$.

In this work, we will focus on the case where each share is tampered independently. With this in mind, we define the family of so-called t-split-state tampering functions, which we denote by $\mathcal{F}_t^{\mathrm{split}}$.

Definition 19 (t-Split-State Tampering Functions). *The family of* t-*split-state tampering functions over a domain* $\mathcal{X}$, *denoted by* $\mathcal{F}_t^{split}$ *(the domain is omitted for brevity), consists of all functions* $f : \mathcal{X}^t \to \mathcal{X}^t$ *for which there exist functions* $f_i : \mathcal{X} \to \mathcal{X}$ *with* $i \in [t]$ *such that* $f(x) = (f_1(x_1), \ldots, f_t(x_t))$, *where* $x = (x_1, \ldots, x_t)$ *and* $x_i \in \mathcal{X}$ *for* $i \in [t]$.

We show separations between Definitions 17, 18, and the definition of non-malleable secret sharing from [17] under split-state tampering in [1].

Observe that split-state tampering of non-malleable codes and extractors as in Definitions 7 and 9 corresponds to considering the family of tampering functions $\mathcal{F}_2^{\mathrm{split}}$.

The following result states that split-state non-malleable codes are 2-out-of-2 non-malleable secret sharing schemes.

Lemma 20 ([2]). *Suppose* (**NMEnc, NMDec**) *is an* ε-*non-malleable code in the split-state model. Fix messages* m *and* m', *and let* $(L, R) \leftarrow \mathbf{NMEnc}(m)$ *and* $(L', R') \leftarrow \mathbf{NMEnc}(m')$. *Then, we have*

$$L \approx_{2\varepsilon} L' \quad \textit{and} \quad R \approx_{2\varepsilon} R'.$$

3 Non-Malleable Secret-Sharing

3.1 Non-Malleable Secret-Sharing Scheme Against Individual Tamperings

Before proceeding to the more general case of non-malleability with concurrent reconstruction, we describe our candidate secret sharing scheme and prove it is non-malleable against a single tampering with respect to functions which tamper the shares independently.

Theorem 21. *Fix a number of parties n and an integer p. Furthermore, assume we have access to the following primitives:*

1. *For $\varepsilon_1 \geq 0$, let $(\mathbf{AShare}, \mathbf{ARec})$ be an (n, ε_1)-secret sharing scheme realizing an access structure $\mathcal{A}$ such that $|T| \geq 3$ holds whenever $T \in \mathcal{A}$. Suppose the corresponding shares lie in $\{0,1\}^r$ and the secrets in some set $\mathcal{M}$;*
2. *Let $\mathbf{nmExt} : \{0,1\}^N \times \{0,1\}^N \to \{0,1\}^\ell$ be the $((1 - \delta)N, \varepsilon_2, 1)$ strong two-source non-malleable extractor from Lemma 10, where $\ell = r + p$. Hence, $\ell \leq \Omega(N)$ and $\varepsilon_2 = 2^{-\Omega(N/\log N)}$.*

Then, there exists an $(n, \varepsilon_1 + 4n\varepsilon_2(2^\ell + 1))$-secret sharing scheme realizing access structure $\mathcal{A}$ that is $n(2^{\ell+1}(\varepsilon_2 + 2^{-\delta N/2 + 1}) + 2^{-p})$-non-malleable w.r.t. $\mathcal{F}_n^{split}$. The resulting scheme $(\mathbf{NMShare}, \mathbf{NMRec})$ shares an element of $\mathcal{M}$ into n shares, where each share contains n elements of $\{0,1\}^N$. Finally, if the two primitives are efficient and the access structure $\mathcal{A}$ supports efficient membership queries, then the constructed scheme $(\mathbf{NMShare}, \mathbf{NMRec})$ is also efficient.

We describe our construction of the non-malleable secret sharing scheme $(\mathbf{NMShare}, \mathbf{NMRec})$.

NMShare: Our sharing function takes as input a secret $m \in \mathcal{M}$ and proceeds as follows:
1. Share m using $\mathbf{AShare}$ to obtain $s_1, \ldots, s_n \leftarrow \mathbf{AShare}(m)$;
2. Pick $P \leftarrow \{0,1\}^p$;
3. For each $i \in [n]$, encode the share s_i to obtain

$$(L_i, R_i) \leftarrow \mathbf{nmExt}^{-1}(P \| s_i);$$

4. For each $i \in [n]$, construct $share_i = (R_1, \ldots, R_{i-1}, L_i, R_{i+1}, \ldots, R_n)$;
5. Output $(share_1, \ldots, share_n)$.

NMRec: Our reconstruction function takes as input shares $\{share_i : i \in T\}$ corresponding to an authorized set $T \in \mathcal{A}$ and proceeds as follows:
1. Sort T so that $T = \{i_1, \ldots, i_t\}$, where $t = |T|$, and $i_j < i_{j+1}$;
2. For each $j \in [t]$, parse the shares in T to obtain

$$(R_1^{(i_j)}, \ldots, R_{i_j-1}^{(i_j)}, L_{i_j}, R_{i_j+1}^{(i_j)}, \ldots, R_n^{(i_j)}) \leftarrow share_{i_j};$$

3. For every $\ell \in [n]$, check that the $R_\ell^{(i_j)}$ have the same value for all j such that $i_j \neq \ell$. If this is not the case, output $\perp$;
4. For every $j \in [t]$, decode and parse $P_{i_j} \| s_{i_j} \leftarrow \mathbf{nmExt}(L_{i_j}, R_{i_j}^{(i_k)})$, where i_k is the smallest element of $T - \{i_j\}$;
5. If there exist $j, j' \in [t]$ such that $P_{i_j} \neq P_{i_{j'}}$, output $\perp$;
6. Else, reconstruct $m \leftarrow \mathbf{ARec}(s_{i_1}, \ldots, s_{i_t})$, and output m.

Correctness and Efficiency: Follows in a straightforward manner from the construction.

Statistical Privacy: Fix two secrets a and b, and let T be an unauthorized set of size t. Without loss of generality, we may assume that $T = \{1, 2, \ldots, t\}$. Set

$$aS_T \leftarrow \textbf{NMShare}(a)_T,$$
$$bS_T \leftarrow \textbf{NMShare}(b)_T.$$

Furthermore, let $as_1, \ldots, as_n$ and $bs_1, \ldots, bs_n$ be the shares obtained from **AShare**(a) and **AShare**(b), respectively, in Step 1 of the **NMShare** procedure.

Our goal is to show that the distributions of these two sets of shares, aS_T and bS_T, are close in statistical distance. More precisely, we will show that

$$aS_T \approx_{\varepsilon_1 + 4n\varepsilon_2(2^\ell + 1)} bS_T$$

for all unauthorized sets T and secrets a, b.

We have $aS_T = (aS_1, \ldots, aS_t)$ and $bS_T = (bS_1, \ldots, bS_t)$, with

$$aS_i = (aR_1, \ldots, aR_{i-1}, aL_i, aR_{i+1}, \ldots, aR_n),$$
$$bS_i = (bR_1, \ldots, bR_{i-1}, bL_i, bR_{i+1}, \ldots, bR_n).$$

As a result, we can write

$$aS_T = [(aL_i, aR_i)_{i \leq t}, aR_{t+1}, \ldots, aR_n],$$
$$bS_T = [(bL_i, bR_i)_{i \leq t}, bR_{t+1}, \ldots, bR_n].$$

Our first claim is that we can replace $aR_{t+1}, \ldots, aR_n$ by encodings of independent, uniformly random messages with small penalty in statistical distance by invoking Lemma 20.

Lemma 22. *Let $R^*_{t+1}, \ldots, R^*_n \in \mathbb{F}$ be sampled as follows: For each $j = t + 1, \ldots, n$, independently sample a uniformly random message m^*, encode and parse $(L^*, R^*) \leftarrow \textbf{nmExt}^{-1}(m^*)$, and set $R^*_j = R^*$. Then,*

$$(aL_i, aR_i)_{i \leq t}, aR_{t+1}, \ldots, aR_n \approx_{2n\varepsilon_2(2^\ell + 1)} (aL_i, aR_i)_{i \leq t}, R^*_{t+1}, \ldots, R^*_n.$$

Proof. The proof can be found in [1]. □

Observe that, by the statistical privacy of the underlying secret sharing scheme, we have

$$\Delta((aL_i, aR_i)_{i \leq t}; (bL_i, bR_i)_{i \leq t})$$
$$\leq \Delta((aL_i, aR_i)_{i \leq t}; (bL_i, bR_i)_{i \leq t} | P)$$
$$\leq \varepsilon_1, \tag{1}$$

where P is the prefix used when encoding the shares with $\mathbf{nmExt}^{-1}$. This is because T is an unauthorized set, and each (aL_i, aR_i) (resp. (bL_i, bR_i)) depends on (aL_j, aR_j) (resp. (bL_j, bR_j)) for $j \neq i$ only through the share as_i or bs_i it encodes, when the prefix P is fixed. Combining Lemma 22 with (1) and a repeated application of the triangle inequality yields

$$\Delta(aS_T; bS_T)$$
$$= \Delta([(aL_i, aR_i)_{i \leq t}, aR_{t+1}, \ldots, aR_n]; [(bL_i, bR_i)_{i \leq t}, bR_{t+1}, \ldots, bR_n])$$
$$\leq \Delta([(aL_i, aR_i)_{i \leq t}, aR_{t+1}, \ldots, aR_n]; [(aL_i, aR_i)_{i \leq t}, R^*_{t+1}, \ldots, R^*_n])$$
$$+ \Delta([(aL_i, aR_i)_{i \leq t}, R^*_{t+1}, \ldots, R^*_n]; [(bL_i, bR_i)_{i \leq t}, R^*_{t+1}, \ldots, R^*_n])$$
$$+ \Delta([(bL_i, bR_i)_{i \leq t}, R^*_{t+1}, \ldots, R^*_n]; [(bL_i, bR_i)_{i \leq t}, bR_{t+1}, \ldots, bR_n])$$
$$\leq 2n\varepsilon_2(2^\ell + 1) + \varepsilon_1 + 2n\varepsilon_2(2^\ell + 1)$$
$$= \varepsilon_1 + 4n\varepsilon_2(2^\ell + 1),$$

which concludes the proof of statistical privacy.

Statistical Non-Malleability: Let T be an authorized set of size $t \geq 3$. Without loss of generality, we may assume that $T = \{1, 2, \ldots, t\}$. Let $f_1, \ldots, f_t$ be the corresponding tampering functions. Let $s_1, \ldots, s_n \in \{0, 1\}^{k+p}$ be arbitrary strings, and let $\mathbf{s} = (s_1, \ldots, s_n)$.

Definition 23. *We define the following partial tampering experiment* $\mathsf{IntTamp}_{\mathbf{s}}^{T,f}$.

1. *For each $i \in [n]$, $(L_i, R_i) \leftarrow \mathbf{nmExt}^{-1}(s_i)$.*
2. *For each $i \in [n]$, let $S_i = (R_1, \ldots, R_{i-1}, L_i, R_{i+1}, \ldots, R_n)$.*
3. *For each $j \in [t]$, let f_j be a function that maps S_j to*

$$\widetilde{R}_1^{(j)}, \ldots, \widetilde{R}_{j-1}^{(j)}, \widetilde{L}_j^{(j)}, \widetilde{R}_{j+1}^{(j)}, \ldots, \widetilde{R}_n^{(j)}.$$

4. *Check whether $\widetilde{R}_i^{(j_1)} = \widetilde{R}_i^{(j_2)}$ for all distinct i, j_1, j_2 where $i \in [n]$, and $j_1, j_2 \in T$. If any of them is not true, then $\mathsf{IntTamp}_{\mathbf{s}}^{T,f} = \perp$.*
5. *For each $i \geq 2$, let $\widetilde{R}_i = \widetilde{R}_i^{(1)}$, and let $\widetilde{R}_1 = \widetilde{R}_1^{(2)}$.*
6. *For each $i \in [t]$, if $L_i = \widetilde{L}_i$ and $R_i = \widetilde{R}_i$, then $\mathsf{output}_i = \mathsf{same}^*$, else $\mathsf{output}_i = \mathbf{nmExt}(\widetilde{L}_i, \widetilde{R}_i)$.*
7. *$\mathsf{IntTamp}_{\mathbf{s}}^{T,f} = (\mathsf{output}_1, \mathsf{output}_2, \ldots, \mathsf{output}_t)$.*

We require the following auxiliary lemma.

Lemma 24. *Let $\mathbf{nmExt} : \{0,1\}^N \times \{0,1\}^N \to \{0,1\}^\ell$ be a (k, ε, τ) strong non-malleable two-source extractor. Also, let $h_1 : \{0,1\}^N \to \mathcal{Z}$, $h_2 : \{0,1\}^N \to \mathcal{Z}$, and $h_3 : \{0,1\}^N \to \{0,1\}$ be functions for some set $\mathcal{Z}$. For functions $F, G : \{0,1\}^N \to \{0,1\}^N$, let $\mathcal{A}_{F,G}$ be an algorithm that takes as input $x, y \in \{0,1\}^N$, and does the following: If $h_1(x) \neq h_2(y)$, or if $h_3(y) = 1$, then output $\perp$, else if $F(x) = x$, and $G_j(y) = y$, output same^*, else output $\mathbf{nmExt}(F(x), G(y))$. For X, Y uniform and independent in $\{0,1\}^N$, we have that*

$$\Delta := \Delta(\mathbf{nmExt}(X, Y) ; U_\ell \mid Y, \mathcal{A}_{F,G}(X, Y)) \leq \varepsilon + 2^{-\frac{N-k}{2}+1}.$$

Proof. The proof can be found in [1].   □

Lemma 24 can be used to prove the following key component of our non-malleability proof.

Lemma 25. *For any* $\mathbf{s}, \mathbf{s}' \in \{0,1\}^{n\ell}$ *we have that*

$$\mathsf{IntTamp}_{\mathbf{s}}^{T,f} \approx_{n2^{\ell+1}\gamma} \mathsf{IntTamp}_{\mathbf{s}'}^{T,f},$$

where $\gamma = \varepsilon + 2^{-\delta N/2+1}$.

Proof. We show that, for $\mathbf{s} = (s_1, s_2 \ldots, s_n)$, and $\mathbf{s}' = (s_1', s_2, \ldots, s_n)$, we have

$$\mathsf{IntTamp}_{\mathbf{s}}^{T,f} \approx_{2^{\ell+1}\gamma} \mathsf{IntTamp}_{\mathbf{s}'}^{T,f}.$$

The general result then follows by a hybrid argument using an analogous reasoning.

For $i = 2, \ldots, n$, let $(L_i, R_i) \leftarrow \mathbf{nmExt}^{-1}(s_i)$, and let L_1^*, R_1^* be chosen independently and uniformly at random from $\{0,1\}^N$. Fix $L_2, \ldots, L_n, R_2, \ldots, R_n$. Assume that we run Steps 3 to 7 of the $\mathsf{IntTamp}_{\mathbf{s}}^{T,f}$ experiment described above, with L_1, R_1 replaced by L_1^*, R_1^*. We replace Step 5 by the following:

– For each $i \neq 2$, let $\widetilde{R}_i = \widetilde{R}_i^{(2)}$, and let $\widetilde{R}_2 = \widetilde{R}_2^{(3)}$,

i.e., we ensure that $\widetilde{R}_2, \ldots, \widetilde{R}_n$ are not a function of L_1^*. Notice that due to the consistency check in Step 4, the output of the tampering experiment remains the same. Then, recalling the variables we have fixed, it follows that $\widetilde{L}_1$ is a deterministic functions of L_1^*, and $\widetilde{R}_1, \ldots, \widetilde{R}_n, \widetilde{L}_2, \ldots, \widetilde{L}_n$ are deterministic functions of R_1^*. Define

$$h_1(L_1^*) := (\widetilde{R}_2^{(1)}, \ldots, \widetilde{R}_n^{(1)}),$$
$$h_2(R_1^*) := (\widetilde{R}_2^{(3)}, \widetilde{R}_3^{(2)}, \ldots, \widetilde{R}_n^{(2)}),$$
$$F(L_1^*) := \widetilde{L}_1,$$
$$G(R_1^*) := \widetilde{R}_1^{(2)}.$$

Also, let $h_3(R_1^*) = 1$ if and only if any of the checks in Step 4 with $j_1, j_2 \neq 1$ (i.e., the checks that are not dependent on L_1^*) fail. We can now instantiate Lemma 24 with h_1, h_2, h_3, F, G and the strong two-source non-malleable extractor from Lemma 10 to obtain

$$\Delta(\mathbf{nmExt}(L_1^*, R_1^*); U_\ell \mid \mathcal{A}_{F,G}(L_1^*, R_1^*), L_2, \ldots, L_n, R_2, \ldots, R_n, R_1^*) \leq \gamma. \quad (2)$$

Let $(L_1', R_1') \leftarrow \mathbf{nmExt}^{-1}(s_1')$, and observe that $\Pr[U_\ell = s] = 2^{-\ell}$ for all s.

We now apply Lemma 3 to (2) by conditioning the right hand side of the statistical distance term in (2) on $U_\ell = s_1$. Since the remaining random variables on the right hand side are independent of U_ℓ, they are unaffected by this conditioning. The corresponding conditioning on the left hand side of the statistical distance term in (2) is $\mathbf{nmExt}(L_1^*, R_1^*) = s_1$. Under this fixing, the tuple

$$(L_1^*, R_1^*), (L_2, R_2), \ldots, (L_n, R_n)$$

is jointly distributed exactly as $(L_i, R_i)_{i=1,\ldots,n}$. Therefore, we can replace all occurrences of L_1^* and R_1^* by L_1 and R_1, respectively, on the left hand side of the statistical distance term in (2). Combining these observations with (2), Lemma 3, and the fact that $\Pr[U_\ell = s_1] = 2^{-\ell}$, we conclude that

$$\Delta(\mathcal{A}_{F,G}(L_1, R_1), R_1; \mathcal{A}_{F,G}(L_1^*, R_1^*), R_1^* | L_2, \ldots, L_n, R_2, \ldots, R_n) \leq 2^\ell \gamma.$$

Letting $(L_1', R_1') \leftarrow \mathbf{nmExt}^{-1}(s_1')$, the same reasoning with s_1' in place of s_1 and (L_1', R_1') in place of (L_1, R_1) leads to

$$\Delta(\mathcal{A}_{F,G}(L_1^*, R_1^*), R_1^*; \mathcal{A}_{F,G}(L_1', R_1'), R_1' | L_2, \ldots, L_n, R_2, \ldots, R_n) \leq 2^\ell \gamma.$$

Applying the triangle inequality yields

$$\Delta(\mathcal{A}_{F,G}(L_1, R_1), R_1; \mathcal{A}_{F,G}(L_1', R_1'), R_1' | L_2, \ldots, L_n, R_2, \ldots, R_n) \leq 2^{\ell+1} \gamma, \quad (3)$$

Observe that $\mathsf{IntTamp}_{\mathbf{s}}^{T,f}$ and $\mathsf{IntTamp}_{\mathbf{s}'}^{T,f}$ are deterministic functions of the left hand side and right hand side of (3), respectively. As a result, we conclude that

$$\mathsf{IntTamp}_{\mathbf{s}}^{T,f} \approx_{2^{\ell+1}\gamma} \mathsf{IntTamp}_{\mathbf{s}'}^{T,f},$$

as desired.   □

We prove statistical non-malleability of our proposed construction with recourse to Lemma 25.

Theorem 26. *The secret sharing scheme* (**NMShare, NMRec**) *defined above is ε-non-malleable with respect to $\mathcal{F}_n^{split}$ for $\varepsilon = n(2^{\ell+1}\gamma + 2^{-p})$, where $\gamma = \varepsilon_2 + 2^{-\delta N/2 + 1}$.*

Proof. The proof can be found in [1].   □

To conclude this section, we remark that we can instantiate Theorem 26 with concrete parameters to obtain a compiler that transforms regular secret sharing schemes into non-malleable ones. The blowup in the share length is logarithmic in the original share length and at most quasilinear in the number of parties n. The error for statistical privacy suffers an exponentially small additive blowup, while the error for non-malleability is exponentially small. Concrete instantiations can be found in [1].

3.2   Non-Malleability with Concurrent Reconstruction

In this section, we show that the secret sharing scheme described in Sect. 3.1 also satisfies the stronger notion of non-malleability with concurrent reconstruction as in Definition 18. Recall that in the concurrent reconstruction setting, the adversary is allowed to choose qualified sets $T_1, \ldots, T_\tau$ along with associated tampering functions $f^{(1)}, \ldots, f^{(\tau)}$, and can observe the outcomes of the experiments $\mathsf{STamper}_m^{f^{(i)}, T_i}$ for $i \in [\tau]$. We have the following result.

Theorem 27. *Fix a number of parties n and an integer p. Furthermore, assume we have access to the following primitives:*

1. *For $\varepsilon_1 \geq 0$, let $(\mathbf{AShare}, \mathbf{ARec})$ be an (n, ε_1)-secret sharing scheme realizing an access structure $\mathcal{A}$ such that $|T| \geq 3$ holds whenever $T \in \mathcal{A}$. Suppose the corresponding shares lie in $\{0,1\}^r$ and the secrets in some set $\mathcal{M}$;*
2. *Let $\mathbf{nmExt} : \{0,1\}^N \times \{0,1\}^N \to \{0,1\}^\ell$ be the $(N - N^\delta, \varepsilon_2, \tau)$ strong two-source non-malleable extractor from Lemma 11, where $\ell = r + p$. Hence, $\tau = N^\delta$, $\ell \leq N^{\Omega(1)}$, and $\varepsilon_2 = 2^{-N^{\Omega(1)}}$.*

Then, there exists an $(n, \varepsilon_1 + 4n\varepsilon_2(2^\ell + 1))$-secret sharing scheme realizing access structure $\mathcal{A}$ that is (ε, τ)-concurrent-reconstruction-non-malleable w.r.t. $\mathcal{F}_n^{split}$, where

$$\varepsilon = n(2^{\ell+1}(\varepsilon_2 + 4\tau 2^\tau 2^{-N^\delta/4\tau}) + \tau \cdot 2^{-p}).$$

The resulting scheme $(\mathbf{NMShare}, \mathbf{NMRec})$ shares an element of $\mathcal{M}$ into n shares, where each share contains n elements of $\{0,1\}^N$. Finally, if the two primitives are efficient and the access structure $\mathcal{A}$ supports efficient membership queries, then the constructed scheme $(\mathbf{NMShare}, \mathbf{NMRec})$ is also efficient.

The candidate scheme for Theorem 27 has been defined in Sect. 3.1, and statistical privacy is already proved there. We now present the proof of non-malleability, beginning with an auxiliary lemma which generalizes Lemma 24 to the case of multiple tamperings.

Lemma 28. *Let $\mathbf{nmExt} : \{0,1\}^N \times \{0,1\}^N \to \{0,1\}^\ell$ be an $(N - N^\delta, \varepsilon, \tau)$ strong non-malleable two-source extractor. Also, let $h_{1j} : \{0,1\}^N \to \mathcal{Z}$, $h_{2j} : \{0,1\}^N \to \mathcal{Z}$, and $h_{3j} : \{0,1\}^N \to \{0,1\}$ for $1 \leq j \leq \tau$ be functions mapping to some set $\mathcal{Z}$. For functions $F_1, \ldots, F_\tau, G_1, \ldots, G_\tau : \{0,1\}^N \to \{0,1\}^N$, let $\mathcal{A}_{F_j, G_j}$ be an algorithm that takes as input $x, y \in \{0,1\}^N$ and does the following: If $h_{1j}(x) \neq h_{2j}(y)$, or if $h_{3j}(y) = 1$, then output $\perp$, else if $F_j(x) = x$, and $G_j(y) = y$, output same^*, else output $\mathbf{nmExt}(F_j(x), G_j(y))$. For X, Y uniform and independent in $\{0,1\}^N$, we have that*

$$\Delta := \Delta(\mathbf{nmExt}(X, Y) \; ; \; U_\ell \mid Y, \mathcal{A}_{F_1, G_1}(X, Y), \ldots, \mathcal{A}_{F_\tau, G_\tau}(X, Y))$$
$$\leq \varepsilon + 4\tau 2^\tau 2^{-N^\delta/4\tau}.$$

Proof. The proof can be found in [1]. □

Given a tuple of qualified sets $\mathbf{T} = (T_1, \ldots, T_\tau)$ and a tuple of associated tampering functions $\mathbf{f} = (f^{(1)}, \ldots, f^{(\tau)})$, we define the intermediate tampering experiment for $\mathbf{T}$ as follows:

$$\mathsf{IntTamp}_\mathbf{s}^{\mathbf{T},\mathbf{f}} := \mathsf{IntTamp}_\mathbf{s}^{T_1, f^{(1)}}, \ldots, \mathsf{IntTamp}_\mathbf{s}^{T_\tau, f^{(\tau)}}.$$

We may also denote the tampering function f associated to a reconstruction set $T \in \mathbf{T}$ by $f^{(T)}$. The following lemma is the main component of our proof of non-malleability with concurrent reconstruction. Its proof follows similarly to that of Lemma 25, but using Lemma 28 instead of Lemma 24.

Lemma 29. *For any* $\mathbf{s}, \mathbf{s}' \in \{0,1\}^{n\ell}$ *we have that*

$$\mathit{IntTamp}_\mathbf{s}^{\mathbf{T},\mathbf{f}} \approx_{n2^{\ell+1}\gamma} \mathit{IntTamp}_{\mathbf{s}'}^{\mathbf{T},\mathbf{f}},$$

where $\gamma = \varepsilon_2 + 4\tau 2^\tau 2^{-N^\delta/4\tau}$.

Proof. The proof can be found in [1].   □

The following result states that statistical non-malleability holds for our proposed construction. The proof is similar to that of Theorem 26.

Theorem 30. *The secret sharing scheme* (**NMShare, NMRec**) *is* (ε, τ) *concurrent reconstruction non-malleable with respect to* $\mathcal{F}_n^{split}$ *for* $\varepsilon = n(2^{\ell+1}\gamma + \tau 2^{-p})$, *where* $\gamma = \varepsilon_2 + 4\tau 2^\tau 2^{-N^\delta/4\tau}$.

Proof. The proof can be found in [1].   □

Similarly to Sect. 3.1, we can instantiate Theorem 27 with concrete parameters to obtain a compiler that transforms regular secret sharing schemes into ones satisfying non-malleability with concurrent reconstruction. The blowup in the share length is now polynomial in the original share length and the number of parties n. As before, the error for statistical privacy suffers an exponentially small additive blowup, while the error for non-malleability is exponentially small. Concrete instantiations can be found in [1].

4   Leakage-Resilient Secret-Sharing Scheme

In this section, we give a construction of a compiler that turns any secret sharing scheme into a leakage-resilient one. More precisely, we have the following result.

Theorem 31. *Fix a number of parties* n *and* $\rho \in (0,1)$. *Furthermore, suppose we have access to the following primitives:*

1. *For any* $\varepsilon_1 \geq 0$, *let* (**AShare, ARec**) *be any* (n, ε_1)-*secret sharing scheme which shares an element of the set* $\mathcal{M}$ *into* n *shares of length* ℓ, *and*

2. Let $\mathsf{Ext} : \{0,1\}^N \times \{0,1\}^d \to \{0,1\}^\ell$ be a strong (k, ε_2)-extractor such that

$$\rho \leq \frac{N-k}{(n-1)d+N}. \tag{4}$$

Moreover, assume that Ext supports close-to-uniform preimage sampling, i.e., there is an efficient algorithm $\mathcal{S}$ such that the output of $\mathcal{S}$ on input z, denoted $\mathcal{S}(z)$, satisfies

$$\mathcal{S}(z) \approx_{\varepsilon_3} D_z \tag{5}$$

for every $z \in \{0,1\}^\ell$, where D_z is uniformly distributed over $\mathsf{Ext}^{-1}(z)$.

Then, there exists an $(n, \varepsilon_1 + 2\varepsilon_2 \cdot n \cdot 2^{\ell n} + 2n \cdot \varepsilon_3, \rho)$-leakage resilient secret sharing scheme realizing access structure $\mathcal{A}$.

Remark 1. Note that, in general, the preimage sampling algorithm $\mathcal{S}$ considered in Theorem 31 may fail to return an element of $\mathsf{Ext}^{-1}(z)$. In such a case, we say that $\mathcal{S}$ fails.

We describe our construction of the non-malleable secret sharing scheme (**LRShare, LRRec**).

LRShare: Our sharing function takes as input a secret $m \in \mathcal{M}$ and proceeds as follows:
1. Share m using **AShare** to obtain $s_1, \ldots, s_n \leftarrow \mathbf{AShare}(m)$;
2. For each $i \in [n]$, sample $(L_i, R_i) \leftarrow \mathcal{S}(s_i)$;
3. If $\mathcal{S}(s_i)$ fails for some i, set $share_i = (\bot, s_i)$ for all $i \in [n]$;
4. Else, for each $i \in [n]$ construct $share_i = (R_1, \ldots, R_{i-1}, L_i, R_{i+1}, \ldots, R_n)$;
5. Output $(share_1, \ldots, share_n)$.

LRRec: Our reconstruction function takes as input shares $\{share_i : i \in T\}$ corresponding to an authorized set $T \in \mathcal{A}$ and proceeds as follows:
1. Sort T so that $T = \{i_1, \ldots, i_t\}$, where $t = |T|$, and $i_j < i_{j+1}$;
2. If $share_i$ contains $\bot$, then recover $s_{i_1}, \ldots, s_{i_t}$ directly from $share_{i_1}, \ldots, share_{i_t}$ and reconstruct $m \leftarrow \mathbf{ARec}(s_{i_1}, \ldots, s_{i_t})$;
3. Else, for each $j \in [t]$ obtain L_j from $share_j$ and R_j from $share_k$ for some $k \in T \setminus \{j\}$, and compute $s_j = \mathsf{Ext}(L_j, R_j)$. Reconstruct $m \leftarrow \mathbf{ARec}(s_{i_1}, \ldots, s_{i_t})$;
4. Output m.

The proof of Theorem 31 has a similar structure to the proof of statistical privacy in Sect. 3.1, but some additional care must be taken to deal with the leakage. It can be found in [1]. We also study the tradeoff between share-length and leakage rate we can achieve via the compiler using linear strong extractors in [1].

5   Threshold Signatures

(n,t)-Threshold signatures, introduced by Desmedt [12], allow to distribute the secret key of a signature scheme among n players such that any subset of t players can sign messages. Threshold signatures exist based on the RSA [23] and discrete logarithm [7] problems.

Definition 32. (Threshold Signature Scheme [23]**).** *An (n,t)-threshold signatures scheme is defined by a tuple of algorithms* (**TGen, TSign, TRec, TVerify**). *The key generation algorithm* **TGen** *takes the security parameter 1^λ as input and outputs a verification key vk and secret keys $sk_1, \ldots, sk_n$. The (possibly interactive) signing algorithm* **TSign** *takes a secret key sk_i and a message $m \in \mathcal{M}$ as input and after potentially interacting with the other parties it outputs a signature share σ_i. The reconstruction algorithm* **TRec** *takes the verification key vk, any t signature shares, and outputs a signature σ. The verification algorithm* **TVerify** *takes a signature σ, a message m, and a verification key vk as input and outputs a bit $b \in \{0,1\}$. We call a threshold signature scheme secure if the following holds:*

1. **Correctness.** *Any authorized set of parties can generate a valid signature. That is, for any set $T = \{i_1, \ldots, i_t\}$ of size at least t and for any $m \in \mathcal{M}$, it holds that*

$$\Pr[\mathbf{TVerify}(vk, \mathbf{TRec}(vk, \sigma_{i_1}, \ldots, \sigma_{i_t}), m) = 1] = 1,$$

   where $\sigma_i \leftarrow \mathbf{TSign}(sk_i, m)$ and $(vk, sk_1, \ldots, sk_n) \leftarrow \mathbf{TGen}(1^\lambda)$.
2. **Unforgeability.** *No collusion of unauthorized parties can forge a signature. More formally, we consider a probabilistic polynomial time adversary A, who can corrupt up to $t-1$ parties to learn their secret keys. The adversary may, on behalf of the corrupt parties, engage in a polynomial number of (possibly interactive) signature share generations with the honest parties for messages of its choice. Let Q be the set of messages that the adversary signs in this fashion. We require that the probability of A outputting a valid message signature pair (m^*, σ^*) with $m^* \notin Q$ is negligible in λ.*

In this work we extend the notion of threshold signatures in two directions. We propose non-malleable as well as leakage-resilient threshold signatures. These two separate notions require that a threshold signature scheme remains secure even if tampering or leakage on the secret keys of each player occurs. Throughout this section we assume a asynchronous communication network with eventual delivery. In such a network each message can be delayed arbitrarily, but it is guaranteed that any sent message eventually arrives at its destination. We also assume that any pair of parties is connected by a secure point-to-point channel.

5.1   Non-Malleable Threshold Signatures

A non-malleable threshold signature scheme requires that even an adversary, who obtains a polynomial number of signature shares under tampered keys for

messages of its choice, may not produce a valid forgery. We model this security
guarantee as follows:

Definition 33 (Non-Malleable Threshold Signature Scheme). *Let*

$$\mathcal{S} = (\mathbf{NMTGen}, \mathbf{NMTSign}, \mathbf{NMTRec}, \mathbf{NMTVerify})$$

*be a secure threshold signature scheme according to Definition 32. Let $\mathcal{F}$ be some
family of tampering functions. For each $f \in \mathcal{F}$, and any probabilistic polynomial
time adversary A, define the tampering experiment*

$$\mathsf{SigTamper}_\lambda^f = \left\{ \begin{array}{l} (vk, sk_1, \ldots, sk_n) \leftarrow \mathbf{NMTGen}(1^\lambda) \\ (\widetilde{sk}_1, \ldots, \widetilde{sk}_n) \leftarrow f(sk_1, \ldots, sk_n) \\ (i_1, \ldots, i_{t-1}) \leftarrow A(1^\lambda) \\ (m^*, \sigma^*) \leftarrow A^{\widetilde{\mathcal{O}}}(vk, \widetilde{sk}_{i_1}, \ldots, \widetilde{sk}_{i_{t-1}}) \\ \mathit{Output}\ (m^*, \sigma^*) \end{array} \right\},$$

*where the oracle $\widetilde{\mathcal{O}}(\cdot) = (\mathbf{NMTSign}(\widetilde{sk}_1, \cdot), \ldots, \mathbf{NMTSign}(\widetilde{sk}_n, \cdot))$ allows the
adversary to obtain a polynomial number of (honestly generated) signature shares
generation for messages of its choice. Let Q be the set of messages that A queries
to $\widetilde{\mathcal{O}}$. We say $\mathcal{S}$ is non-malleable w.r.t. $\mathcal{F}$ if for all $f \in \mathcal{F}$*

$$\Pr[\mathbf{NMTVerify}(vk, \mathbf{TRec}(vk, \sigma^*, m^*) = 1 \ \wedge \ m^* \notin Q] \leq \mathsf{negl}(\lambda).$$

Our construction follows the same blueprint as our non-malleable secret sharing schemes.

Theorem 34. *For any number of parties $n \geq 2t+1$ and threshold t, if we have
the following primitives:*

1. *A non-interactive[2] secure (n,t)-threshold signatures scheme (**TGen**, **TSign**,
   TRec, **TVerify**).*
2. *A coding scheme (**NMEnc**, **NMDec**) that is ε-non-malleable w.r.t $\mathcal{F}_2^{split}$,
   where $\varepsilon \leq \mathsf{negl}(\lambda)$.*

then there exists a non-malleable threshold signature scheme w.r.t. $\mathcal{F}_n^{split}$.

We construct a non-malleable threshold signature scheme $\mathcal{S} = (\mathbf{NMTGen},
\mathbf{NMTSign}, \mathbf{NMTRec}, \mathbf{NMTVerify})$ as follows.

NMTGen: Our key generation function takes the security parameter 1^λ as its
   input and proceeds as follows:
   1. $(vk, sk_1', \ldots, sk_n') \leftarrow \mathbf{TGen}(1^\lambda)$
   2. For each $i \in [n]$, encode the key sk_i' to obtain $(L_i, R_i) \leftarrow \mathbf{NMEnc}(sk_i')$;

---

[2] We call a threshold signature scheme non-interactive if every party can generate a
   signature share without interacting with the other parties. Many existing schemes
   are of this form, see for example [7,23].

3. For each $i \in [n]$, construct $sk_i = (R_1, \ldots, R_{i-1}, L_i, R_{i+1}, \ldots, R_n)$;
4. Output $(vk, sk_1, \ldots, sk_n)$.

NMTSign: Party i with secret $sk_i = (R_1, \ldots, R_{i-1}, L_i, R_{i+1}, \ldots, R_n)$ constructs its signature share as follows:

1. Request R_i from all other parties and wait for the first $n - t$ responses $(R_i^1, \ldots, R_i^{n-t})$.
2. Check whether $R_i^1 = \cdots = R_i^{n-t}$ and output $\bot$ if not.
3. Reconstruct the secret key $sk' \leftarrow \mathbf{NMDec}(L_i, R_i^1)$ and output $\bot$ if $sk' = \bot$.
4. Compute signature share $\sigma_i \leftarrow \mathbf{TSign}(sk_i', m)$.
5. Output σ_i.

NMTRec: Given verification key vk and signature shares $\sigma_{i_1}, \ldots, \sigma_{i_t}$, we construct a signature as follows:

1. $\sigma \leftarrow \mathbf{TRec}(vk, \sigma_{i_1}, \ldots, \sigma_{i_t})$.
2. Output σ.

NMTVerify: Given verification key vk, signature σ, and message m, we do the following:

1. $b \leftarrow \mathbf{TVerify}(vk, \sigma, m)$.
2. Output b.

Notice that the way **NMTSign** is formulated now, a single tampered share can make the protocol output $\bot$. If this is undesirable, the two first steps in **NMTSign:** can be replaced by

1. Request R_i from all other parties and collect responses $R_i^1, R_i^2, \ldots$.
2. If and when a subset of the responses of size $n - t$ are all identical to some R_i, use this R_i in the following steps.

In an asynchronous network with eventual delivery, all $n - t$ honest parties will eventually get the request for R_i and send their value. Therefore party i eventually receive all these $n - t$ shares (and possibly some corrupted shares too). Therefore, if there is no tampering, then party i will eventually receive $n - t$ copies of the correct share. In all cases party i will hear from at least one honest party as in the original scheme, so security follows along the lines of the security for the original scheme. We present the analysis for the original scheme in [1], which yields Theorem 34.

5.2 Leakage-Resilient Threshold Signatures

In a leakage-resilient threshold signature scheme, the adversary may obtain an unqualified subset of secret keys and a bounded amount of leakage from *all* other secret keys. Even given this information, we require that the adversary may not be able to output a valid forgery.

Definition 35 (Leakage-Resilient Threshold Signature Scheme). *Let* $\mathcal{S} = (\mathbf{LTGen}, \mathbf{LTSign}, \mathbf{LTRec}, \mathbf{LTVerify})$ *be a tuple of probabilistic polynomial time algorithms. Let $\mathcal{F}$ be a family of leakage functions. For each $f \in \mathcal{F}$, and any probabilistic polynomial time adversary A, define the following experiment*

$$\mathbf{SigLeak}_\lambda^f = \left\{ \begin{array}{l} (vk, sk_1, \ldots, sk_n) \leftarrow \mathbf{LTGen}(1^\lambda) \\ (i_1, \ldots, i_{t-1}) \leftarrow A(1^\lambda) \\ (\ell_1, \ldots, \ell_n) \leftarrow f(sk_1, \ldots, sk_n) \\ (m^*, \sigma^*) \leftarrow A^{\mathcal{O}}(vk, (sk_{i_1}, \ldots, sk_{i_{t-1}}), (\ell_1, \ldots, \ell_n)) \\ Output\ (m^*, \sigma^*) \end{array} \right\},$$

where the oracle $\mathcal{O}(\cdot)$ allows the adversary, on behalf of the corrupted parties, to engage in a polynomial number of (possibly interactive) signature shares generation for messages of its choice. Let Q be the set of messages that A queries to $\mathcal{O}$. We say $\mathcal{S}$ is leakage-resilient w.r.t. $\mathcal{F}$ if for all $f \in \mathcal{F}$

$$\Pr[\mathbf{NMTVerify}(vk, \mathbf{TRec}(vk, \sigma^*, m^*) = 1 \ \wedge \ m^* \notin Q] \leq \mathsf{negl}(\lambda).$$

Building upon our previous results, we construct a leakage-resilient threshold signature scheme.

Theorem 36. *For any number of parties $n \geq 2t+1$ and threshold t, if we have the following primitives:*

1. *A non-interactive secure (n, t)-threshold signatures scheme (**TGen**, **TSign**, **TRec**, **TVerify**).*
2. *A two-source $(n - \ell - \log 1/\varepsilon, 2\varepsilon)$-extractor **nmExt** with efficient preimage sampling from the space $\mathcal{X} = \{0,1\}^n$, where $\varepsilon \leq \mathsf{negl}(\lambda)$.*

*then the construction from Theorem 34, where we replace each call to **NMEnc** with **nmExt**$^{-1}$ and each call to **NMDec** with **nmExt**, is a leakage-resilient threshold signature scheme w.r.t. $\mathcal{F}_{\ell,n}^{split}$, where $\mathcal{F}_{\ell,n}^{split}$ is the set of leakage functions that tamper with each share independently and the output of each tampering function is bounded in size by ℓ bits.*

Proof. The proof can be found in [1]. □

References

1. Aggarwal, D., et al.: Stronger leakage-resilient and non-malleable secret-sharing schemes for general access structures. Cryptology ePrint Archive, Report 2018/1147 (2018). https://eprint.iacr.org/2018/1147
2. Aggarwal, D., Dziembowski, S., Kazana, T., Obremski, M.: Leakage-resilient non-malleable codes. In: Dodis, Y., Nielsen, J.B. (eds.) TCC 2015. LNCS, vol. 9014, pp. 398–426. Springer, Heidelberg (2015). https://doi.org/10.1007/978-3-662-46494-6_17
3. Badrinarayanan, S., Srinivasan, A.: Revisiting non-malleable secret sharing. Cryptology ePrint Archive, Report 2018/1144 (2018). https://eprint.iacr.org/2018/1144
4. Beimel, A.: Secret-sharing schemes: a survey. In: Chee, Y.M., et al. (eds.) IWCC 2011. LNCS, vol. 6639, pp. 11–46. Springer, Heidelberg (2011). https://doi.org/10.1007/978-3-642-20901-7_2

5. Benhamouda, F., Degwekar, A., Ishai, Y., Rabin, T.: On the local leakage resilience of linear secret sharing schemes. In: Shacham, H., Boldyreva, A. (eds.) CRYPTO 2018. LNCS, vol. 10991, pp. 531–561. Springer, Cham (2018). https://doi.org/10.1007/978-3-319-96884-1_18
6. Blakley, G.R.: Safeguarding cryptographic keys. In: Proceedings of AFIPS 1979 National Computer Conference, vol. 48, pp. 313–317 (1979)
7. Boldyreva, A.: Threshold signatures, multisignatures and blind signatures based on the gap-Diffie-Hellman-group signature scheme. In: Desmedt, Y.G. (ed.) PKC 2003. LNCS, vol. 2567, pp. 31–46. Springer, Heidelberg (2003). https://doi.org/10.1007/3-540-36288-6_3
8. Boyle, E., Goldwasser, S., Kalai, Y.T.: Leakage-resilient coin tossing. Distrib. Comput. **27**(3), 147–164 (2014)
9. Chattopadhyay, E., Goyal, V., Li, X.: Non-malleable extractors and codes, with their many tampered extensions. In: Proceedings of the Forty-Eighth Annual ACM Symposium on Theory of Computing, pp. 285–298. ACM (2016)
10. Chattopadhyay, E., Zuckerman, D.: Non-malleable codes in the constant split-state model. In: FOCS (2014)
11. Cheraghchi, M., Guruswami, V.: Non-malleable coding against bit-wise and split-state tampering. In: Lindell, Y. (ed.) TCC 2014. LNCS, vol. 8349, pp. 440–464. Springer, Heidelberg (2014). https://doi.org/10.1007/978-3-642-54242-8_19
12. Desmedt, Y.: Society and group oriented cryptography: a new concept. In: Pomerance, C. (ed.) CRYPTO 1987. LNCS, vol. 293, pp. 120–127. Springer, Heidelberg (1988). https://doi.org/10.1007/3-540-48184-2_8
13. Dodis, Y., Ostrovsky, R., Reyzin, L., Smith, A.: Fuzzy extractors: how to generate strong keys from biometrics and other noisy data. SIAM J. Comput. **38**(1), 97–139 (2008)
14. Dziembowski, S., Pietrzak, K., Wichs, D.: Non-malleable codes. In: ICS, pp. 434–452. Tsinghua University Press (2010)
15. Faust, S., Mukherjee, P., Nielsen, J.B., Venturi, D.: Continuous non-malleable codes. In: Lindell, Y. (ed.) TCC 2014. LNCS, vol. 8349, pp. 465–488. Springer, Heidelberg (2014). https://doi.org/10.1007/978-3-642-54242-8_20
16. Goyal, V., Kumar, A.: Non-malleable secret sharing. In: Proceedings of the 50th Annual ACM SIGACT Symposium on Theory of Computing, pp. 685–698. ACM (2018)
17. Goyal, V., Kumar, A.: Non-malleable secret sharing for general access structures. In: Shacham, H., Boldyreva, A. (eds.) CRYPTO 2018. LNCS, vol. 10991, pp. 501–530. Springer, Cham (2018). https://doi.org/10.1007/978-3-319-96884-1_17
18. Goyal, V., Kumar, A., Park, S., Richelson, S., Srinivasan, A.: Non-malleable commitments from non-malleable extractors (2018 unpublished)
19. Kumar, A.: Personal communication (2018)
20. Kumar, A., Meka, R., Sahai, A.: Leakage-resilient secret sharing. Cryptology ePrint Archive, Report 2018/1138 (2018). https://eprint.iacr.org/2018/1138
21. Li, X.: Improved non-malleable extractors, non-malleable codes and independent source extractors. In: Proceedings of the 49th Annual ACM SIGACT Symposium on Theory of Computing, pp. 1144–1156. ACM (2017)
22. Shamir, A.: How to share a secret. Commun. ACM **22**(11), 612–613 (1979)
23. Shoup, V.: Practical threshold signatures. In: Preneel, B. (ed.) EUROCRYPT 2000. LNCS, vol. 1807, pp. 207–220. Springer, Heidelberg (2000). https://doi.org/10.1007/3-540-45539-6_15
24. Srinivasan, A., Vasudevan, P.N.: Leakage resilient secret sharing and applications. Cryptology ePrint Archive, Report 2018/1154 (2018). https://eprint.iacr.org/2018/1154

Memory Hard Functions and Privacy Amplification

Memory-Hard Functions
from Cryptographic Primitives

Binyi Chen[1($\boxtimes$)] and Stefano Tessaro[2($\boxtimes$)]

[1] UC Santa Barbara, Santa Barbara, USA
binyichen@cs.ucsb.edu
[2] University of Washington, Seattle, USA
tessaro@cs.washington.edu

Abstract. Memory-hard functions (MHFs) are moderately-hard functions which enforce evaluation costs both in terms of time and memory (often, in form of a trade-off). They are used e.g. for password protection, password-based key-derivation, and within cryptocurrencies, and have received a considerable amount of theoretical scrutiny over the last few years. However, analyses see MHFs as modes of operation of some underlying hash function $\mathcal{H}$, modeled as a monolithic random oracle. This is however a very strong assumption, as such hash functions are built from much simpler primitives, following somewhat ad-hoc design paradigms.

This paper initiates the study of how to securely instantiate $\mathcal{H}$ within MHF designs using common cryptographic primitives like block ciphers, compression functions, and permutations. Security here will be in a model in which the adversary has parallel access to an idealized version of the underlying primitive. We will provide provably memory-hard constructions from all the aforementioned primitives. Our results are generic, in that we will rely on hard-to-pebble graphs designed in prior works to obtain our constructions.

One particular challenge we encounter is that $\mathcal{H}$ is usually required to have large outputs (to increase memory hardness without changing the description size of MHFs), whereas the underlying primitives generally have small output sizes.

Keywords: Memory-hard functions · Provable security · Ideal models

1 Introduction

Memory-hard functions (MHFs) are functions which are moderately hard to compute both in terms of *time* and *memory*, in the sense that their computation is subject to a time-memory trade-off – relatively fast computation requires memory, whereas low-memory implies slow (or even very slow) computation. This ensures for example that the area-time complexity of custom-made hardware (e.g., ASICs) needed to evaluate MHFs is large (and thus, the dollar cost of this

© International Association for Cryptologic Research 2019
A. Boldyreva and D. Micciancio (Eds.): CRYPTO 2019, LNCS 11693, pp. 543–572, 2019.
https://doi.org/10.1007/978-3-030-26951-7_19

hardware), and this fact makes them suitable for password hashing, password-based key derivation, and proof of work in cryptocurrencies, where attackers may leverage such hardware. The first practical MHF, Scrypt, was proposed by Percival [19,20]. Starting with Alwen and Serbinenko [7], several works have been devoted to the theoretical analysis of MHFs (cf. e.g. [1–8,12–14]), also exposing weaknesses in practical designs like Argon2 [10] (the winner of the password-hashing competition), Catena [17], and Balloon hashing [13].

The starting point of our work is the observation that theoretical works describe MHFs as modes of operation of an underlying primitive, usually a (hash) function $\mathcal{H} : \{0,1\}^M \rightarrow \{0,1\}^W$ (where $M \geq W$), modeled as a *random oracle* [9] within security proofs. However, this completely ignores the implementation details behind $\mathcal{H}$ which may make it far from an ideal random oracle – often, such designs are completely ad-hoc and based on much simpler objects (e.g., Scrypt's resembles a permutation-based stream-cipher design), in particular because W is much larger than for conventional hash functions (e.g., a few thousand bits).

Therefore, we would like to study MHFs at a finer level of granularity that considers the inner structure of $\mathcal{H}$, and we would like to understand *how* such an $\mathcal{H}$ is meant to be built in a sound way. We stress that it is not enough for $\mathcal{H}$ to be a random oracle in the sense of *indifferentiability* [18], since memory-hardness definitions are multi-stage games to which indifferentiability does not apply [22]. Therefore, such analyses would call for completely new theory.

We also note that the primitive on which an MHF is based matters – Ren and Devadas [21] pointed out the advantages of building MHFs from AES, as the availability of on-chip hardware implementations (AES-NI) significantly reduces the efficiency speed-up of dedicated hardware by ensuring a conventional CPU can evaluate the function *already* at a cost similar to that of dedicated hardware.

OUR CONTRIBUTIONS – A HIGH-LEVEL VIEW. This paper initiates the study of provably-secure MHFs built from basic symmetric primitives, which we model as ideal – we consider *block ciphers*, *permutations* and *compression functions*. We prove general results that will enable us to obtain MHFs based on them, in a model where these primitives are ideal and the adversary is allowed to make multiple calls *in parallel*. (This naturally adapts the parallel random-oracle model from previous MHF analyses to primitives.)

As our first contribution, we provide one-call efficient instantiations of $\mathcal{H}$ from such primitives. We will adapt previous lemmas based on "ex-post-facto arguments" (dating back to [15]) to reduce the security of a large class of MHFs based on directed acyclic graphs (DAGs) to the pebbling complexity of the underlying DAG. (These are usually called data-independent MHFs, or iMHFs for short, and are favored designs due to their resilience to side-channel attacks.)

This will already give us iMHFs from all aforementioned primitives. However, a DAG $\mathbb{G}$ of N vertice yields a function whose computation operates on N memory blocks of size L bits, where L is the output length of the primitive (e.g., $L = 128$ bits for AES). In this case, a good choice of $\mathbb{G}$ would ensure that product of time and memory[1] to evaluate the function is (nearly) $\Omega(N^2 L)$ – increasing memory hardness means increasing N, which leads to a larger function description. A better option (consistent with practice) is to keep the same graph, but operate on *larger* blocks of size $W \gg L$, to ensure the time-memory product is now $\Omega(N^2 W)$.

To do this, we will provide a generic construction of an $\mathcal{H}$ with W-bit output using an underlying primitive with a shorter output. We will refer to $\mathcal{H}$ as a *wide-block labeling function* (as opposed to a *small-block* one like those we gave above), and the resulting MHF will be called a *wide-block MHF*. (Our design will have the added benefit of allowing for a variable W.) Our construction will guarantee the final MHF is memory hard as long as the graph $\mathbb{G}$ is sufficiently *depth-robust*, a notion we review below.

We stress that all practical constructions implicitly design wide-block labeling functions, for which existing analyses provide no guarantees, as they abstract them away as random oracles, which they are not. While we failed to provide either proofs or attacks on practical designs, initiating the study of provably secure constructions in the more realistic primitive-based setting is an important step.

The remainder of this section will provide a more in-detail overview of our results, as well as a concise introduction to the formalism.

1.1   Overview of Our Results

Before highlighting our result in more detail, we briefly review some notions at an informal level.

GRAPH-BASED IMHFS. This paper deals with *graph-based data-independent* MHFs (which we refer to as iMHFs, for short), defined by a DAG $\mathbb{G} = (\mathbb{V}, \mathbb{E})$ on N vertices. For simplicity, we assume $\mathbb{V} = \{v_1, \ldots, v_N\}$, and each edge has the form (v_i, v_j) where $i < j$, i.e., vertices are topologically order – vertex v_1 is the *source*, v_N is the (unique) *sink*. Previous works [3,7] use $\mathbb{G}$ and a *labeling* function $\mathcal{H} : \{0,1\}^{\leq \delta W + \log N} \to \{0,1\}^W$ (we refer to W as the *block length* of the MHF and δ the maximal indegree of $\mathbb{G}$) to instantiate an MHF $\mathcal{F}_{\mathbb{G},\mathcal{H}}$. On input M, we first assign the label $\ell_1 = \mathcal{H}(\langle 1 \rangle \| M)$ to the source, where $\langle i \rangle$ is a $O(\log N)$-bit encoding of i, and then each vertex v_i is assigned a label

$$\ell_i = \mathcal{H}(\langle i \rangle \| \ell_{j_1} \| \ldots \| \ell_{j_d}) \,,$$

where $v_{j_1}, \ldots, v_{j_d}$ are the predecessor vertices of v_i. Finally, we output ℓ_N.

CMC AND PEBBLING. To capture the evaluation costs for $\mathcal{F}_{\mathbb{G},\mathcal{H}}$, following [7] we adopt the *cumulative memory complexity* (CMC). We model the labeling function $\mathcal{H}$ as a random oracle, and assume the adversary proceeds in steps. In

---

[1] We will use the more fine-grained metric of cumulative memory complexity (CMC), but for now the product of time and memory will suffice for an informal understanding.

each step i, the adversary holds state σ_{i-1} (where $\sigma_0 = M$), and can compute a *vector* of queries to $\mathcal{H}$, as well as next state σ_i, which it will receive in the next step, together with the outputs of the evaluations of $\mathcal{H}$ on the query vector. The CMC of the adversary is defined as the sum of the sizes of states, and $\mathsf{CMC}(\mathcal{F}_{G,\mathcal{H}})$ denotes the best-possible (expected) CMC of an adversary to evaluate $\mathcal{F}_{G,\mathcal{H}}$.

The evaluation of $\mathcal{F}_{G,\mathcal{H}}$ is tightly related to a *(parallel) pebbling game* for the graph $\mathbb{G}$. Initially, the graph has no pebble on it, but in each step i, the player can (i) remove any subset of the pebbles, and (ii) put a pebble on a vertex $v \in \mathbb{V}$ if all parents of v have been pebbled at the previous step. (This is vacuously true for the source.) Multiple legal moves can be taken in one single step. (This differs from traditional black pebbling games, where each step allows one single legal move.) The player wins the game if the sink node has been pebbled. The *cumulative complexity* (CC) of the pebbling is defined as the cumulative sum of the number of pebbles on the graph in each step, and the CC of the graph $\mathsf{cc}(\mathbb{G})$ is the minimal CC over all pebbling strategies.

Intuitively, a pebbling strategy is equivalent to an evaluation strategy for $\mathcal{F}_{G,\mathcal{H}}$ which only remembers labels in its memory. In [7] it was shown that such strategies are essentially optimal, i.e., $\mathsf{CMC}(\mathcal{F}_{G,\mathcal{H}}) \approx \mathsf{cc}(\mathbb{G}) \cdot W$.

DEPTH-ROBUST GRAPHS. *Depth-robust graphs* are class of graphs with high CC: Specifically, we say a graph $\mathbb{G} = (\mathbb{V}, \mathbb{E})$ is (e, d)-depth-robust if, after removing any nodes set $S \subseteq \mathbb{V}$ where $|S| \leq e$, the subgraph $\mathbb{G} - S$ still has a path with length d. Previous work [3] proved that any (e, d)-depth-robust graph $\mathbb{G}$ has cumulative complexity $\mathsf{cc}(\mathbb{G}) \geq e \cdot d$. Also, they show that constructions of (constant indegree) depth-robust graphs with $de = \Omega(N^2/\log(N))$ exist, which gives best-possible CC [1]. Later on, Alwen, Blocki, and Harsha [2] gave a procedure that samples with high probability a graph with the same depth-robustness guarantees, with a much simpler description.

OUR CONTRIBUTIONS. Our two main contributions provide generic methods to devise constructions of MHFs from a simple primitive, like a block cipher, a permutation (that can be instantiated from a *fixed-key* block cipher), or a compression function. We consider a natural extension of the above model where the adversary queries an ideal version of the primitive.

1. We first define a simple class of so-called *small-block* labeling functions $\mathcal{H}_{\mathsf{fix}}$ which make one call to an underlying primitive. They transform a hard-to-pebble graph $\mathbb{G}$ (with maximal indegree 2) into a memory hard function $\mathcal{F}_{G,\mathcal{H}_{\mathsf{fix}}}$ as described above, but where $\mathcal{H}$ is now instantiated from the underlying primitive via $\mathcal{H}_{\mathsf{fix}}$, and the resulting block length is L, the output length of the primitive. (E.g., if we used AES, then $L = 128$ bits.) Moreover, we prove that the CMC of $\mathcal{F}_{G,\mathcal{H}_{\mathsf{fix}}}$ is approximately $\mathsf{cc}(\mathbb{G}) \cdot L$.

2. We then consider the problem of extending the block length of an iMHF to *increase memory hardness without changing* the underlying graph $\mathbb{G}$. To this end, from $\mathcal{H}_{\mathsf{fix}}$ with output length L, we define and construct a class of *wide-block* labeling functions, which in fact support *variable* block length. For any tunable parameters $\delta, W = 2^w \in \mathbb{N}$, the wide-block hash function

$\mathcal{H}_{\delta,w} : \{0,1\}^{\delta W} \to \{0,1\}^W$ turns any depth-robust graph $\mathbb{G}$ (with maximal indegree δ) into a memory hard function $\mathcal{F}_{\mathbb{G},\mathcal{H}_{\delta,w}}$ via graph labeling. The CMC of $\mathcal{F}_{\mathbb{G},\mathcal{H}_{\delta,w}}$ is approximately

$$\mathsf{CMC}(\mathcal{F}_{\mathbb{G},\mathcal{H}_{\delta,w}}) \approx \mathsf{cc}(\mathbb{G}) \cdot \delta W^3/L^2 \ .$$

Note that this is larger than $\mathsf{cc}(\mathbb{G}) \cdot W$ because, intuitively, we need to make multiple calls to the primitive to evaluate H, and use extra memory. In particular, we prove that the evaluation of $\mathcal{F}_{\mathbb{G},\mathcal{H}_{\delta,w}}$ can be done sequentially with time $N\delta(W/L)^2$ and memory $N \cdot W$, i.e., the resulting CMC is $N^2 \delta W^3/L^2$, via a naive strategy which runs N times the best-possible algorithm to evaluate $\mathcal{H}$, and keeps all W-bit labels in memory, in addition to internal states. Hence, if $\mathsf{cc}(\mathbb{G}) = \Theta(N^2/\log N)$ and $\delta = O(1)$, this means that the best possible CMC can have a gain of a factor at most $O(\log N)$ over the "naive" sequential strategy. This is the same upper bound on the speed-up we could establish for iMHFs from monolithic random oracles.[2]

We stress that because these results are generic, constructions can be obtained by using any graph $\mathbb{G}$ (or distribution over graphs) with sufficient depth-robustness guarantees.[3] We give some more details about these results next.

SMALL-BLOCK LABELING FUNCTION: CONSTRUCTIONS AND INTUITION. The small-block labeling functions $\mathcal{H}_{\mathsf{fix}}$ takes an input[4] $x \in \{0,1\}^L \cup \{0,1\}^{2L}$ and outputs an L-bit label. For a compression function cf, the resulting output is $\mathsf{cf}(x)$; for an ideal cipher ic, we split the input into a key part $k \in \{0,1\}^L \cup \{\bot\}$ (where $\bot$ is a designated key separate from the L-bit strings, which as with compression functions, will be necessary to implement variable input length) and an input part $x \in \{0,1\}^L$, the resulting output is $\mathsf{ic}(k,x) \oplus x$; for a random permutation rp, we denote as x^* the exclusive-or sum of L-bit input blocks and the output is $\mathsf{rp}(x^*) \oplus x^*$.

For any graph $\mathbb{G} = (\mathbb{V}, \mathbb{E})$, the memory hardness of $\mathcal{F}_{\mathbb{G},\mathcal{H}_{\mathsf{fix}}}$ is argued similarly as in previous work [7]. The high level idea is to transform the execution of any algorithm A that computes the MHF into an *ex-post-facto* pebbling for the graph $\mathbb{G}$, and argue that the cumulative memory complexity of A is proportional to the cumulative complexity of the pebbling. Here we generalize the technique of [7] – which relies on a compression argument – so that it works even if:

1. The ideal-primitive input contains no explicit information of the node v. (This was not the case in prior work.)

---

[2] Actually for certain graphs, we prove that the efficiency gap can be reduced to the optimal bound $O(1)$, by giving a more memory-efficient *sequential* algorithm.

[3] Our first result in fact only requires a lower bound on $\mathsf{cc}(\mathbb{G})$. It is an interesting open question to provide a wide-block labeling function which only relies on a lower bound for $\mathsf{cc}(\mathbb{G})$, rather than the (stronger) depth-robustness requirement.

[4] We assume the compression function allows both L- and $2L$-bit inputs, though most compression functions do not allow this by design. This could however be easily achieved by reserving one bit of the input to implement domain separation, and then padding short inputs.

2. The adversary can make *inverse* queries to the ideal primitive (as we also consider block ciphers now).
3. The input length of the primitive is fixed, and usually shorter than the actual input length of the labeling function.

Remark 1. Note that Blocki et al. [11] independently proposed a proof that addressed the first and the third challenge. But to the best of our knowledge, our technique is the only one that works even if the adversary makes *inverse* queries.

SUCCINCT MHFS FROM WIDE-BLOCK LABELING FUNCTIONS. Given a small-block labeling function $\mathcal{H}_{\text{fix}}$ and tunable parameters $\delta, W = 2^w \in \mathbb{N}$, the wide-block labeling function $\mathcal{H}_{\delta,w} : \{0,1\}^{\delta W} \to \{0,1\}^W$ is essentially a graph labeling function built upon $\mathcal{H}_{\text{fix}}$ and a gadget graph $\mathbb{G}_{\delta,W}$. $\mathbb{G}_{\delta,W}$ is the *composition* of two subgraphs, namely, a MIX graph $\mathbb{G}_{\text{mix}}$, and a *source-to-sink depth robust graph* $\mathbb{G}_{\text{ssdr}} = (\mathbb{V}', \mathbb{E}')$ that satisfies for any subset $S \subseteq \mathbb{V}'$ (with bounded size), $\mathbb{G}_{\text{ssdr}} - S$ has a long path starting from a source node of $\mathbb{G}_{\text{ssdr}}$ and ending at a sink node of $\mathbb{G}_{\text{ssdr}}$.

For any (e,d)-depth-robust graph $\mathbb{G} = (\mathbb{V}, \mathbb{E})$, the CMC of $\mathcal{F}_{\mathbb{G}, \mathcal{H}_{\delta,w}}$ is argued by opening the graph structure underlying $\mathcal{H}_{\delta,w}$, and consider $\mathcal{F}_{\mathbb{G}, \mathcal{H}_{\delta,w}}$ as a graph function built upon $\mathcal{H}_{\text{fix}}$ and *a bootstrapped graph* $\text{Ext}_{\delta,W}(\mathbb{G})$. We show that the graph $\text{Ext}_{\delta,W}(\mathbb{G})$ is extremely depth-robust and thus has pebbling complexity $\Omega(\delta W^3 / L^3) \cdot ed$. Then by the property of $\mathcal{H}_{\text{fix}}$, we can build the connection between the CMC of $\mathcal{F}_{\mathbb{G}, \mathcal{H}_{\delta,w}}$ and the CC of $\text{Ext}_{\delta,W}(\mathbb{G})$.

DEPTH-ROBUSTNESS OF $\text{Ext}_{\delta,W}(\mathbb{G})$. Given any (bounded-size) nodes subset S of $\text{Ext}_{\delta,W}(\mathbb{G})$, we show the existence of an extremely long path in $\text{Ext}_{\delta,W}(\mathbb{G}) - S$ in three steps: First, S is transformed into a small set S' in $\mathbb{G}$, and we obtain a long path P in $\mathbb{G} - S'$ by depth-robustness of $\mathbb{G}$; second, by *source-to-sink depth-robustness* of the SSDR graph, each vertex v in P is transformed into a path P_v^* in $\text{Ext}_{\delta,W}(\mathbb{G}) - S$; finally, the structure of the MIX graph helps to elegantly connect the paths in $\{P_v^*\}_{v \in P}$ into an extremely long path in $\text{Ext}_{\delta,W}(\mathbb{G}) - S$.

Remark 2. Note that our wide-block labeling functions can only turn *depth-robust graphs* (instead of arbitrary graphs with high CC) into memory hard functions. It is hard to link CMC and $\text{cc}(\mathbb{G})$ directly using our extension framework. The hardness lies in linking $\text{cc}(\text{Ext}_{\delta,W}(\mathbb{G}))$ and $\text{cc}(\mathbb{G})$. In particular, even if the gadget graph $\mathbb{G}_{\delta,W}$ has high CC, we do not know how to prove that $\text{cc}(\text{Ext}_{\delta,W}(\mathbb{G})) \geq \text{cc}(\mathbb{G}) \cdot \text{cc}(\mathbb{G}_{\delta,W})$. This is because we do not know how to transform a pebbling P_1 (of $\text{Ext}_{\delta,W}(\mathbb{G})$) into a *legal* pebbling P_2 (of $\mathbb{G}$), and argue that $\text{cc}(\mathsf{P}_1)$ is *at least* $\text{cc}(\mathsf{P}_2)$ times $\text{cc}(\mathbb{G}_{\delta,W})$.

2 Preliminaries

NOTATION. Let $\mathbb{N}$ and $\mathbb{R}$ denote the sets of natural numbers and real numbers respectively. Denote by $[n]$ the set of integers $\{1, \ldots, n\}$. By $\log(\cdot)$ we always refer to binary logarithm. For strings x and y, $|x|$ is the length of x and we use $x\|y$ or (x, y) to denote the concatenation of x and y. For a set $\mathbb{X}$, $x \xleftarrow{\$} \mathbb{X}$ is the process of assigning to x an element picked uniformly from $\mathbb{X}$, and $|\mathbb{X}|$ denotes the number of elements in $\mathbb{X}$. For a distribution $\mathcal{D}$, we use $x \leftarrow \mathcal{D}$ to denote the sampling of x from distribution $\mathcal{D}$. For an algorithm A, we use $\mathsf{A}(x; r)$ to denote the output of the algorithm on input x and random coins r.

2.1 Memory-Hard Functions in the Parallel Ideal Primitive Model

IDEAL PRIMITIVES. In this paper, we consider three ideal primitives, namely, *compression functions*, *ideal ciphers*, and *random permutations*. All primitives will have an understood block length $L = 2^{\ell}$, which is assumed to be a power of two. In the following context, we will omit L in the ideal-primitive notation if there is no ambiguity.

Denote by $\mathbb{CF}$ the set of functions[5] with domain $\{0, 1\}^L \cup \{0, 1\}^{2L}$ and image $\{0, 1\}^L$. Denote by $\mathbb{IC}$ the set of keyed permutations with domain $\mathcal{K} \times \{0, 1\}^L$ and image $\{0, 1\}^L$. For simplicity, the key space is set as $\mathcal{K} := \{\bot\} \cup \{0, 1\}^L$ in the following context. Finally, we let $\mathbb{RP}$ be the set of permutations with input/output length L.

PARALLEL IDEAL PRIMITIVE MODEL. Towards modeling the computation of memory-hard functions, we generalize the *Parallel Random Oracle Model* defined by Alwen and Serbinenko [7] to *Parallel Ideal Primitive Model*. Let $\mathbb{IP} = \mathbb{CF}/\mathbb{IC}/\mathbb{RP}$ be a type of ideal primitive set. For any oracle-aided algorithm A, input x and internal randomness r, the execution $\mathsf{A}(x; r)$ works as follows. First, a function ip (with block length L) is uniformly chosen from the set $\mathbb{IP}$. The oracle-aided algorithm A can make oracle query to ip as follows: If $\mathsf{ip} = \mathsf{cf}$ is a randomly sampled compression function, the algorithm can make queries with form ("$\mathbb{CF}$", x) and receive value $\mathsf{cf}(x)$. If $\mathsf{ip} = \mathsf{ic}$ is a randomly sampled ideal cipher, the algorithm can make *forward* queries with form ("$\mathbb{IC}$", $+, k, x$) and receive value $\mathsf{ic}(k, x)$, or make *inverse* queries with form ("$\mathbb{IC}$", $-, k, y$) and receive value $\mathsf{ic}^{-1}(k, y)$. Similarly, if $\mathsf{ip} = \mathsf{rp}$ is a randomly sampled permutation, the algorithm can make *forward* queries with form ("$\mathbb{RP}$", $+, x$) and receive value $\mathsf{rp}(x)$, or make *inverse* queries with form ("$\mathbb{RP}$", $-, y$) and receive value $\mathsf{rp}^{-1}(y)$.

Let $\sigma_0 = (x, \emptyset)$ denote the initial input state. For each round $i \in \mathbb{N}$, $\mathsf{A}(x; r)$ takes input state σ_{i-1}, performs *unbounded* computation, and generates an output state $\bar{\sigma}_i = (\delta_i, \mathbf{q}_i, \mathbf{out}_i)$, where δ_i is a binary string, $\mathbf{q}_i$ is a vector of queries to the ideal primitive ip, and each element of $\mathbf{out}_i$ is with form (v, ℓ_v) where v and ℓ_v are L-bit output labels. We define $\sigma_i = (\delta_i, \mathbf{ans}(\mathbf{q}_i))$ to be the input state for round $i + 1$, where $\mathbf{ans}(\mathbf{q}_i)$ is the vector of ideal primitive answers to $\mathbf{q}_i$. The execution terminates after round $T \in \mathbb{N}$ if $|\mathbf{q}_T| = 0$. We use $\mathsf{A}^{\mathsf{ip}}(x; r)$

---

[5] We assume the compression function allows both L- and $2L$-bit inputs, though most compression functions do not allow this by design. This could however be easily achieved by reserving one bit of the input to implement domain separation, and then padding short inputs.

to indicate both the execution output (i.e., the concatenation of output labels) and the execution *trace* (i.e., all of the input and output states $(\sigma_0, \bar{\sigma}_1, \sigma_1, \dots)$). We also assume an upper bound q on the total number of output labels/ideal primitive queries that an algorithm makes, i.e., $\sum_{i \geq 1} |\mathbf{q}_i| + |\mathbf{out}_i| \leq q$. We call A a *sequential* algorithm if $|\mathbf{q}_i| = 1$ for every $1 \leq i < T$, otherwise A is a *parallel* algorithm.

<u>COMPLEXITY MEASURES.</u> Given the trace $A^{ip}(x; r)$ on input x, randomness r and ideal primitive ip, we define as time complexity $\mathsf{Tm}(A^{ip}(x; r))$ the number of rounds ran by A, and space complexity $\mathsf{Spc}(A^{ip}(x; r))$ the size of the maximal input state. Moreover, we define $\mathsf{Tm}(A)$ (and $\mathsf{Spc}(A)$) to be the maximal time (and space) complexity of A over all choices of x, r and ip.[6] We define cumulative memory complexity (CMC) [7] in the parallel ideal primitive model.

Definition 1 (Cumulative Memory Complexity). *Given trace $A^{ip}(x; r)$ (with input states $(\sigma_0, \sigma_1, \dots)$). we define cumulative memory complexity*

$$\mathsf{CMC}(A^{ip}(x; r)) := \sum_{i=0}^{\mathsf{Tm}(A^{ip}(x;r))} |\sigma_i|$$

to be the sum of input states' size over time. For a real value $\epsilon \in [0, 1]$, and a family of functions $\mathcal{F} = \{f^{ip} : \mathcal{X} \to \mathcal{Y}\}_{ip \in \mathbb{IP}}$, we define the ϵ-cumulative memory complexity of $\mathcal{F}$ to be

$$\mathsf{CMC}_\epsilon(\mathcal{F}) := \min_{x \in \mathcal{X}, A \in \mathcal{A}_{x,\epsilon}} \mathbb{E}[\mathsf{CMC}(A^{ip}(x; r))],$$

where the expectation is taken over the uniform choices of ip and r. $\mathcal{A}_{x,\epsilon}$ is the set of parallel algorithms[7] that satisfy the following: with probability at least ϵ (over the uniform choices of ip and r), the algorithm on input x and oracle ip outputs $f^{ip}(x)$.

<u>MEMORY-HARD FUNCTIONS.</u> We now define memory hard functions in the parallel ideal primitive model. Intuitively, there exists a relatively efficient *sequential* algorithm that computes the MHFs, and any *parallel* algorithm that evaluates the functions incurs high CMC cost.

Definition 2 (Memory Hard Functions). *For an ideal primitive set $\mathbb{IP} = \mathbb{CF}/\mathbb{IC}/\mathbb{RP}$, a family of functions $\mathcal{F} = \{f^{ip} : \mathcal{X} \to \mathcal{Y}\}_{ip \in \mathbb{IP}}$ is $(C_\mathcal{F}^\parallel, \Delta_\mathcal{F}, T_\mathcal{F})$- memory hard if and only if the following properties hold. ($C_\mathcal{F}^\parallel, \Delta_\mathcal{F}$ are functions that take as input a real value in $(0, 1]$ and output a real value, $T_\mathcal{F}$ is an integer.)*

---

[6] $\mathsf{Tm}(A)$ (and $\mathsf{Spc}(A)$) measure *worst-case sequential efficiency* by providing *upper bounds* on time/memory.

[7] Recall that the total number of output labels/ideal primitive queries that the algorithm makes is at most q.

Memory-hardness: *For any $\epsilon \in (0,1]$, we have* $\mathsf{CMC}_\epsilon(\mathcal{F}) \geq \mathsf{C}_{\mathcal{F}}^{\|}(\epsilon)$.

Efficiency-gap: *For any $\epsilon \in (0,1]$, it holds that*

$$\frac{\min_{A \in \mathcal{A}_{\mathcal{F}, T_{\mathcal{F}}}} (\epsilon \cdot \mathsf{Tm}(A) \cdot \mathsf{Spc}(A))}{\mathsf{CMC}_\epsilon(\mathcal{F})} \leq \Delta_{\mathcal{F}}(\epsilon),$$

where $\mathcal{A}_{\mathcal{F}, T_{\mathcal{F}}}$ is the set of deterministic sequential algorithms that run in at most $T_{\mathcal{F}}$ steps and correctly output $f^{\mathsf{ip}}(x)$ for any ip and x.

2.2   Graphs and Pebbling Models

GRAPH NOTATIONS. We use $\mathbb{G} = (\mathbb{V}, \mathbb{E})$ to denote a directed acyclic graph (DAG) with $N = 2^n$ nodes, where $\mathbb{V} = \{1, \ldots, N\}$. Let $\mathsf{src}(\mathbb{G}) \subseteq \mathbb{V}$ be the set of source nodes and $\mathsf{sink}(\mathbb{G}) \subseteq \mathbb{V}$ be the set of sink nodes. For a node $v \in \mathbb{V}$, $\mathsf{pred}(v) := \{u : (u, v) \in \mathbb{E}\}$ are the predecessor nodes of v, $\mathsf{succ}(v) := \{w : (v, w) \in \mathbb{E}\}$ is the set of v's successors. We use $\mathsf{indeg}(v) := |\mathsf{pred}(v)|$ to denote the indegree of v, and $\mathsf{indeg}(\mathbb{G}) := \max_{v \in \mathbb{V}} \mathsf{indeg}(v)$ is the indegree of $\mathbb{G}$. For a directed acyclic path P, the length of P is the number of nodes it traverses. $\mathsf{depth}(\mathbb{G})$ is the length of the longest path in $\mathbb{G}$. For a nodes set $S \subseteq \mathbb{V}$, $\mathbb{G} - S$ is the DAG obtained from $\mathbb{G}$ by removing S and incident edges. Next, we review a useful graph-theoretic property called depth-robustness.

Definition 3 (Depth-Robustness [3]). *A DAG $\mathbb{G} = (\mathbb{V}, \mathbb{E})$ is (e, d)-depth-robust if and only if $\mathsf{depth}(\mathbb{G} - S) \geq d$ for any $S \subseteq \mathbb{V}$ where $|S| \leq e$.*

Next, we define a stronger notion of depth-robustness called *source-to-sink-depth-robustness*. Intuitively, it means that after removing any nodes set with certain size, there still exists a long path from a source node to a sink node.

Definition 4 (Source-to-Sink-Depth-Robustness). *A DAG $\mathbb{G} = (\mathbb{V}, \mathbb{E})$ is (e, d)-source-to-sink-depth-robust if and only if for any $S \subseteq \mathbb{V}$ where $|S| \leq e$, $\mathbb{G} - S$ has a path (with length at least d) that starts from a source node of $\mathbb{G}$ and ends up in a sink node of $\mathbb{G}$.*

GRAPH PEBBLING. We consider a pebbling game played on a DAG $(\mathbb{G} = \mathbb{V}, \mathbb{E})$ [7]. We denote by a *parallel* pebbling on $\mathbb{G}$ as a sequence of pebbling configurations $\mathsf{P} = (\mathsf{P}_0, \ldots, \mathsf{P}_{t_{\mathsf{peb}}})$ where $\mathsf{P}_0 = \emptyset$ and $\mathsf{P}_i \subseteq \mathbb{V}$ ($1 \leq i \leq t_{\mathsf{peb}}$). We define two properties for P.

- *Legality:* We say P is legal if it satisfies follows: A pebble can be put on a node $v \in \mathbb{V}$ only if v is a *source* node or v's predecessors were all pebbled at the end of the previous step, that is, for any $i \in [t_{\mathsf{peb}}]$ and any $v \in \mathsf{P}_i \setminus \mathsf{P}_{i-1}$, it holds that $\mathsf{pred}(v) \subseteq \mathsf{P}_{i-1}$.[8]
- *Successfulness:* We say P is successful if it satisfies follows: Every sink node has been pebbled at least once, that is, for any $v \in \mathsf{sink}(\mathbb{G})$, there exists $i \in [t_{\mathsf{peb}}]$ such that $v \in \mathsf{P}_i$.

---

[8] $\mathsf{pred}(v) = \emptyset$ for $v \in \mathsf{src}(\mathbb{G})$.

We say P is a *sequential* pebbling if it further satisfies that $|P_i \setminus P_{i-1}| = 1$ for every $i \in [t_{peb}]$. Next we define pebbling complexities of graphs.

Definition 5 (Complexity Measures [7]). *For a pebbling strategy* $P = (P_0 = \emptyset, \ldots, P_{t_{peb}})$, *we define the cumulative complexity (and ST-complexity) of* P *to be*

$$cc(P) := \sum_{i=0}^{t_{peb}} |P_i|, \qquad st(P) := t_{peb} \cdot \max_{i \in [t_{peb}]} (|P_i|).$$

For a DAG $\mathbb{G} = (\mathbb{V}, \mathbb{E})$, *let* $\mathcal{P}^{\parallel}(\mathbb{G})$ *be the set of parallel pebblings of* $\mathbb{G}$ *(that are legal and successful); for any* $t \in \mathbb{N}$, *let* $\mathcal{P}_t(\mathbb{G})$ *be the set of sequential pebblings of* $\mathbb{G}$ *that (are legal and successful) and takes at most* t *steps. We define the cumulative complexity (and ST-complexity) of* $\mathbb{G}$ *to be*

$$cc(\mathbb{G}) := \min_{P \in \mathcal{P}^{\parallel}(\mathbb{G})} cc(P), \qquad st(\mathbb{G}, t) := \min_{P \in \mathcal{P}_t(\mathbb{G})} st(P).$$

There is a tight relation between depth-robustness and cumulative complexity.

Lemma 1 ([3]). *Let* $\mathbb{G}$ *be an* (e, d)-*depth-robust DAG, then* $cc(\mathbb{G}) \geq e \cdot d$.

2.3 Graph-Based iMHFs from Labeling Functions

For a DAG $\mathbb{G} = (\mathbb{V}, \mathbb{E})$ with $N = 2^n$ nodes, we index the nodes set $\mathbb{V} = \{1, \ldots, N\}$ by a topological order so that $src(\mathbb{G}) = \{1, \ldots, n_s\}$ and $sink(\mathbb{G}) = \{N - n_t + 1, \ldots, N\}$. Fix $W = 2^w$, $\delta := indeg(\mathbb{G})$ and let $\mathbb{IP} = \mathbb{CF}/\mathbb{IC}/\mathbb{RP}$ be the set of ideal primitives. Denote by

$$\mathcal{H} = \mathcal{H}_{\delta,w} = \left\{ lab_\gamma^{ip} : \{0,1\}^{\gamma W} \to \{0,1\}^W \right\}_{\gamma \in [\delta], ip \in \mathbb{IP}}$$

a family of labeling functions. We define a family of *graph functions* $\mathcal{F}_{\mathbb{G},\mathcal{H}} = \{F_{\mathbb{G},\mathcal{H}}^{ip} : \{0,1\}^{n_s W} \to \{0,1\}^{n_t W}\}_{ip \in \mathbb{IP}}$ based on $\mathbb{G}$ and $\mathcal{H}$: For an input $\mathbf{x} = (x_1, \ldots, x_{n_s}) \in \{0,1\}^{n_s W}$, denote $\ell_i := lab_1^{ip}(x_i)$ as the label of the ith source ($1 \leq i \leq n_s$), we recursively define the label of $v \in [N]$ as

$$\ell_v := lab_\gamma^{ip}(\ell_{v_1}, \ldots, \ell_{v_\gamma})$$

where $(v_1, \ldots, v_\gamma)$ are the predecessors of v. The output $F_{\mathbb{G},\mathcal{H}}^{ip}(x)$ is defined as the concatenation of sinks' labels, that is, $(\ell_{N-n_t+1} \| \ldots \| \ell_N)$.

PREPROCESSING THE INPUTS. If $n_s = |src(\mathbb{G})| > 1$, we implicitly assume that the input vector $\mathbf{x} = (x_1, \ldots, x_{n_s})$ has no overlapping blocks (and we call it a *non-colliding* input vector), that is, for any $i, j \in \mathbb{N}$ such that $i \neq j$, we have $x_i \neq x_j$. This constraint is necessary for preventing the adversary from easily saving memory. For example, if the blocks in the input vector are identical, the adversary only needs to store a single block instead of the entire input vector. The constraint/assumption is also reasonable as we can re-randomize the original input using a random oracle $RO : \{0,1\}^{n_s W} \to \{0,1\}^{n_s W}$, and the output blocks will be distinct with overwhelming probability when $n_s \ll 2^{W/2}$.

Remark 3 (Graph constraint). In the following context, the graphs we are concerned with should satisfy certain properties. In particular, each 2-indegree DAG $\mathbb{G} = (\mathbb{V}, \mathbb{E})$ considered in Sect. 3 should be *predecessors-distinct*, that is, for any two distinct vertices $u, v \in \mathbb{V} \setminus \mathsf{src}(\mathbb{G})$, we have $\mathsf{pred}(u) \neq \mathsf{pred}(v)$. Looking ahead, this constraint is used to prevent non-source nodes label collisions. Additionally, each δ-indegree DAG $\mathbb{G} = (\mathbb{V}, \mathbb{E})$ considered in Sect. 4 satisfies a property called *first-predecessor-distinctness*, that is, there exists a map from each non-source node $v \in \mathbb{V} \setminus \mathsf{src}(\mathbb{G})$ to a single node $\mathsf{fpre}(v) \in \mathsf{pred}(v)$, so that for any two distinct vertices $u, v \in \mathbb{V} \setminus \mathsf{src}(\mathbb{G})$, we have $\mathsf{fpre}(u) \neq \mathsf{fpre}(v)$. Looking ahead, this constraint is used to guarantee that the 2-indegree bootstrapped graph $\mathsf{Ext}_{\delta, W}(\mathbb{G})$ built upon $\mathbb{G}$ is *predecessors-distinct*. We stress that practical DAG constructions usually contain a subpath that traverses all of the vertices, and thus are both first-predecessor-distinct and predecessors-distinct.[9]

3   MHFs from Small-Block Labeling Functions

In this section, we construct a family of graph-based iMHFs based on what we refer to as a *small-block labeling function*, i.e., a simple hash function based on an ideal primitive, which preserves its block length. (Note that this notion is introduced for modularity reason – we could define our designs directly as depending on a primitive.) In Sect. 3.1, we define and construct of *efficient* small-block labeling functions from primitives, and in Sect. 3.2, we prove that the constructions satisfies the required properties. Finally, in Sect. 3.3, we construct iMHFs from small-block labeling functions.

3.1   Small-Block Labeling Functions: Definition and Construction

Definition 6 (Small-Block Labeling Functions).   *For an ideal primitive* $\mathbb{IP} = \mathbb{CF}/\mathbb{IC}/\mathbb{RP}$ *with block length* $L = 2^{\ell}$, *we say*

$$\mathcal{H}_{\mathsf{fix}} = \left\{ \mathsf{flab}^{\mathsf{ip}} : \left\{ \{0,1\}^{L} \cup \{0,1\}^{2L} \right\} \to \{0,1\}^{L} \right\}_{\mathsf{ip} \in \mathbb{IP}}$$

is a family of β-small-block labeling functions if it has the following property.

   $\beta(\cdot, \cdot)$**-pebbling reducibility:** *For any* $\epsilon \in (0, 1]$ *and 2-indegree (predecessors-distinct[10]) DAG* $\mathbb{G} = (\mathbb{V}, \mathbb{E})$,[11] *let* $\mathcal{F}_{\mathbb{G}, \mathcal{H}_{\mathsf{fix}}}$ *be the graph function built upon* $\mathbb{G}$ *and* $\mathcal{H}_{\mathsf{fix}}$. *We have*

$$\mathsf{CMC}_{\epsilon}(\mathcal{F}_{\mathbb{G}, \mathcal{H}_{\mathsf{fix}}}) \geq \beta(\epsilon, \log |\mathbb{V}|) \cdot \mathsf{cc}(\mathbb{G}),$$

where $\mathsf{cc}(\mathbb{G})$ *is the cumulative complexity of* $\mathbb{G}$ *(Definition 5).*

---

[9] First-predecessor-distinctness holds as each non-source node v can pick her previous node in the subpath (that traverses all of the vertices) as their *first predecessor*; predecessors-distinctness holds as otherwise a cycle would exist.

[10] See Remark 3 for definition of predecessors-distinct graphs.

[11] $\mathbb{G}$ can have multiple source/sink nodes.

CONSTRUCTION. Next, we show how to construct small-block labeling functions from ideal primitives. Our main contribution is a construction from a random permutation, which can be instantiated from fixed-key AES. For completeness, we also present constructions from ideal ciphers and compression functions. We fix the input domain to be $\{0,1\}^L \cup \{0,1\}^{2L}$ and the output space to be $\{0,1\}^L$, and denote as $\mathbb{RP}$, $\mathbb{IC}$, $\mathbb{CF}$ the random permutations, ideal ciphers, and compression functions, respectively.

1. Given any $\mathsf{rp} \in \mathbb{RP}$, we define the labeling function $\mathsf{flab}^{\mathsf{rp}}(\cdot)$ as follows: For any input $x \in \{0,1\}^L$, the output is $\mathsf{flab}^{\mathsf{rp}}(x) := \mathsf{rp}(x) \oplus x$; for any input $(x_1, x_2) \in \{0,1\}^{2L}$, denote as $x^* := x_1 \oplus x_2 \in \{0,1\}^L$, the output is $\mathsf{flab}^{\mathsf{rp}}(x_1, x_2) := \mathsf{rp}(x^*) \oplus x^*$.
2. Given any $\mathsf{ic} \in \mathbb{IC}$, we define the labeling function $\mathsf{flab}^{\mathsf{ic}}(\cdot)$ as follows: For any input $x \in \{0,1\}^L$, the output is $\mathsf{flab}^{\mathsf{ic}}(x) := \mathsf{ic}(\bot, x) \oplus x$; for any input $(k, x) \in \{0,1\}^{2L}$, the output is $\mathsf{flab}^{\mathsf{ic}}(k, x) := \mathsf{ic}(k, x) \oplus x$.
3. Given any $\mathsf{cf} \in \mathbb{CF}$, we define the labeling function $\mathsf{flab}^{\mathsf{cf}}(\cdot)$ as follows: For any input $x \in \{0,1\}^L \cup \{0,1\}^{2L}$, the output is $\mathsf{flab}^{\mathsf{cf}}(x) := \mathsf{cf}(x)$.

Note that all of the above constructions are highly efficient as they call the ideal-primitive only once. Next we show that the constructions are pebbling reducible.

Remark 4. The construction for compression functions is interesting, even in view of prior work, because of the fact that prior work included the node identity into the hash-function input, thus effectively requiring $2L + \log N$-bit inputs, whereas here we can get away with $2L$.

3.2 Small-Block Labeling Functions: Pebbling Reducibility

In this section, we show that the labeling functions constructed in Sect. 3.1 satisfy pebbling reducibility, via the following three theorems.

Theorem 1. *Assume an adversary can make no more than q_1 oracle calls and q_2 output calls such that $\mathsf{q}_1 + \mathsf{q}_2 = \mathsf{q} = 2^{L/4}$. $\mathcal{H}_{\mathsf{fix}} = \{\mathsf{flab}^{\mathsf{cf}}\}_{\mathsf{cf} \in \mathbb{CF}}$ built upon compression function $\mathbb{CF}$ is $\beta(\cdot, \cdot)$-pebbling reducible, where for all $\epsilon \geq 3 \cdot 2^{-L/8}$ and $N \leq 2^{L/8}$, it holds that $\beta(\epsilon, \log N) \geq \frac{\epsilon L}{8}$.*

Theorem 2. *Assume an adversary can make no more than q_1 oracle calls and q_2 output calls such that $\mathsf{q}_1 + \mathsf{q}_2 = \mathsf{q} = 2^{L/4}$. $\mathcal{H}_{\mathsf{fix}} = \{\mathsf{flab}^{\mathsf{ic}}\}_{\mathsf{ic} \in \mathbb{IC}}$ built upon ideal cipher $\mathbb{IC}$ is $\beta(\cdot, \cdot)$-pebbling reducible, where for all $\epsilon \geq 3 \cdot 2^{-L/8}$ and $N \leq 2^{L/8}$, it holds that $\beta(\epsilon, \log N) \geq \frac{\epsilon L}{8}$.*

Theorem 3. *Assume an adversary can make no more than q_1 oracle calls and q_2 output calls such that $\mathsf{q}_1 + \mathsf{q}_2 = \mathsf{q} = 2^{L/8}$. $\mathcal{H}_{\mathsf{fix}} = \{\mathsf{flab}^{\mathsf{rp}}\}_{\mathsf{rp} \in \mathbb{RP}}$ built upon random permutation $\mathbb{RP}$ is $\beta(\cdot, \cdot)$-pebbling reducible, where for all $\epsilon \geq 3 \cdot 2^{-L/10}$ and $N \leq 2^{L/10}$, it holds that $\beta(\epsilon, \log N) \geq \frac{\epsilon L}{40}$.*

Next we present the proofs for Theorems 1, 2 and 3. First, we introduce some notation for graph labeling, then we highlight the proof techniques and introduce the notion of ex-post-facto pebbling in the ideal primitive model. Finally, we provide the formal proof.

GRAPH LABEL NOTATIONS. Fix ideal primitive $\mathbb{IP} = \mathbb{CF}/\mathbb{IC}/\mathbb{RP}$,[12] input vector $\mathbf{x}$ and any graph $\mathbb{G} = (\mathbb{V}, \mathbb{E})$. For a primitive $\mathsf{ip} \in \mathbb{IP}$ and any node $v \in \mathbb{V}$, we denote as ℓ_v the graph label of v. If v is a source, $\mathsf{prelab}(v)$ is the corresponding input label x_v. If v is a non-source node, we define $\mathsf{prelab}(v)$ based on the type of the ideal primitive:

- If $\mathbb{IP} = \mathbb{RP}$, we define $\mathsf{prelab}(v)$ as the exclusive-or sum of v's parents' ℓ-labels.
- If $\mathbb{IP} = \mathbb{IC}/\mathbb{CF}$, we define $\mathsf{prelab}(v)$ as the concatenation of v's parents' ℓ-labels.

Similarly, for every node $v \in \mathbb{V}$, we define $\mathsf{aftlab}(v)$ based on the type of the ideal primitive:

- If $\mathbb{IP} = \mathbb{RP}/\mathbb{CF}$, we define $\mathsf{aftlab}(v) = \mathsf{ip}(\mathsf{prelab}(v))$.
- If $\mathbb{IP} = \mathbb{IC}$ and v has only one parent, we define $\mathsf{aftlab}(v) = \mathsf{ip}(\bot, \mathsf{prelab}(v))$. Otherwise if v has two parents, denote as $\mathsf{prelab}(v) = (y_1, y_2)$ (where $y_1, y_2 \in \{0,1\}^L$ are ℓ-labels of v's parents), we define $\mathsf{aftlab}(v)$ as $(y_1, \mathsf{ip}(y_1, y_2))$.

In the following context, we abuse the notation a bit in that if $\mathsf{prelab}(v)$ (or $\mathsf{aftlab}(v)$) is an L-bit string and ip is an ideal cipher, we use $\mathsf{ip}(\mathsf{prelab}(v))$ (or $\mathsf{ip}^{-1}(\mathsf{aftlab}(v))$) to denote $\mathsf{ip}(\bot, \mathsf{prelab}(v))$ (or $\mathsf{ip}^{-1}(\bot, \mathsf{aftlab}(v))$). Moreover, for an ideal cipher query with input $x_c = (\bot, x)$, we say $x_c = \mathsf{prelab}(v)$ (or $x_c = \mathsf{aftlab}(v)$) if and only if $x = \mathsf{prelab}(v)$ (or $x = \mathsf{aftlab}(v)$), respectively.

We remark that $\mathsf{prelab}(v)$ (and $\mathsf{aftlab}(v)$) are more than just single labels, they are used to identify the node from a query input to the ideal primitive.

PROOF HIGHLIGHT. Similar as in [7], the proof idea is to transform any algorithm execution A into an *ex-post-facto* pebbling, and argue that the cumulative memory complexity of A is proportional to the cumulative complexity of the pebbling. This is proved by mapping each node $v \in \mathbb{V}$ to an ideal-primitive entry $(\mathsf{prelab}(v), \mathsf{ip}(\mathsf{prelab}(v)))$, and argue that for each round $i \in \mathbb{N}$, the input state σ_i should have large size as it is an encoding for many ideal-primitive entries. In particular, for every node v in the ith pebbling configuration, $\mathsf{ip}(\mathsf{prelab}(v))$ (and ℓ_v) can be decoded from an oracle-call input in the partial execution $\mathsf{A}(\sigma_i)$. Here we generalize the technique of [7] so that it works even if:

1. The ideal-primitive input $\mathsf{prelab}(v)$ contains no explicit information of the node index v. (Note that in previous work [7], $\mathsf{prelab}(v)$ has v as a prefix.)
2. The adversary can make *inverse* queries to the ideal primitive.
3. The input length of the primitive is much shorter than the actual input length of the labeling function.

---

[12] $\mathbb{CF}$ denotes the compression function, $\mathbb{IC}$ denotes the ideal cipher, and $\mathbb{RP}$ denotes the random permutation.

EX-POST-FACTO PEBBLING. Similar as in [7], we define a notion called *ex-post-facto pebbling in the ideal primitive model*. Fix ideal primitive $\mathbb{IP} = \mathbb{CF}/\mathbb{IC}/\mathbb{RP}$, input vector $\mathbf{x}$, DAG $\mathbb{G} = (\mathbb{V}, \mathbb{E})$. For any $\mathsf{ip} \in \mathbb{IP}$, randomness r, and the execution trace $\mathsf{A}^{\mathsf{ip}}(\mathbf{x}; r)$ (that runs for $t_{\mathsf{peb}} + 1$ rounds), we turn the trace into an *ex-post-facto pebbling*

$$\mathcal{P}(\mathsf{A}^{\mathsf{ip}}(\mathbf{x}, r)) = (\mathsf{P}_0 = \emptyset, \ldots, \mathsf{P}_{t_{\mathsf{peb}}}).$$

For each oracle call/query that asks for the ideal-primitive value on input x_c, we say that the call is a *correct* call for a node $v \in \mathbb{V}$ if and only if x_c matches $\mathsf{prelab}(v)$ and the call is forward, or x_c matches $\mathsf{aftlab}(v)$ and the call is an inverse call. We define the ex-post-facto pebbling configurations in reverse order. For i from t_{peb} to 1, denote as σ_i the input state of round $i + 1$ and $\mathsf{A}(\sigma_i)$ the partial execution of $\mathsf{A}^{\mathsf{ip}}(\mathbf{x}; r)$ after round i, the pebbling configuration P_i is defined as follows. (In the following context, by round γ, we always mean the γ-th round in the execution $\mathsf{A}^{\mathsf{ip}}(\mathbf{x}, r)$.)

1. *Critical Calls:* We sort the output/ideal primitive calls of $\mathsf{A}(\sigma_i)$ in chronological order[13] and determine whether they are *critical* calls.
   - An output call (in round $\gamma > i$) with label (v, ℓ_v) is a *critical* call for $v \in \mathbb{V}$ if and only if v is a sink and in the trace $\mathsf{A}(\sigma_i)$, no correct call for v appeared before round γ.
   - An ideal-primitive call (in round $\gamma > i$) is a *critical* call for a node $u \in \mathbb{V}$ if and only if the following conditions both hold: (i) the ideal-primitive call is a correct call for a successor node $v \in \mathsf{succ}(u)$ and in the trace $\mathsf{A}(\sigma_i)$, no correct call for u appeared before round γ; (ii) v is in P_γ.
2. *Pebbling Configuration:* A node $v \in \mathbb{V}$ is included into the pebbling configuration P_i if and only if *both* of the following conditions hold:
   - There is at least one critical call for v in the trace $\mathsf{A}(\sigma_i)$.
   - There is at least one correct call for v between round 1 and round i (inclusively).[14]

In a critical call, the algorithm provides the information of a graph label without recomputing, hence the call is useful in extracting ideal-primitive entries. On a side note, by definition of critical call and ex-post-facto pebbling, for any round i, we might possibly put a node u into P_i only if u is a sink or one of its successor $v \in \mathsf{succ}(u)$ is in P_γ for some $\gamma > i$.

Proof (of Theorems 1, 2 and 3). Fix ideal primitive type $\mathbb{IP} = \mathbb{CF}/\mathbb{IC}/\mathbb{RP}$, input vector $\mathbf{x}$, adversary A, and any graph $\mathbb{G} = (\mathbb{V}, \mathbb{E})$, the proof consists of the following four steps.

LABEL COLLISIONS. First, we show that with probability at least $1 - \epsilon_{\mathsf{coll}}(\mathbb{IP})$ (over the choice of the ideal primitive), the pre-labels $\{\mathsf{prelab}(v)\}_{v \in \mathbb{V}}$ are all distinct.[15]

---

[13] We assume an implicit order for the calls in the same round.

[14] Note that the existence of a correct call for v in round i does not imply $v \in \mathsf{P}_i$, because v may not have a critical call in the future.

[15] If $\mathbb{IP} = \mathbb{IC}/\mathbb{RP}$, this also implies that $\{\mathsf{aftlab}(v)\}_{v \in \mathbb{V}}$ are distinct.

Lemma 2. *Fix ideal primitive* $\mathbb{IP} = \mathbb{CF}/\mathbb{IC}/\mathbb{RP}$ *(with block length L), predecessors-distinct DAG* $\mathbb{G} = (\mathbb{V}, \mathbb{E})$ *(with n_s source nodes), non-colliding input vector* $\mathbf{x} \in \{0,1\}^{n_s L}$,[16] *and* $\mathcal{H}_{\mathsf{fix}} = \{\mathsf{flab}^{\mathsf{ip}}\}_{\mathsf{ip} \in \mathbb{IP}}$ *constructed in Sect. 3. With probability at least* $1 - \epsilon_{\mathsf{coll}}(\mathbb{IP})$ *(over the uniformly random choice of* ip*), the graph labeling satisfies that the pre-labels* $\{\mathsf{prelab}(v)\}_{v \in \mathbb{V}}$ *are all distinct. Here* $\epsilon_{\mathsf{coll}}(\mathbb{CF}) = |\mathbb{V}|^2 / 2^{L+1}$ *and* $\epsilon_{\mathsf{coll}}(\mathbb{IC}) = \epsilon_{\mathsf{coll}}(\mathbb{RP}) = |\mathbb{V}|^2 / 2^L$.

Proof. The proof is deferred to full version. □

The property in Lemma 2 is useful in determining the node index v when one sees an ideal-primitive query related to v. Moreover, it guarantees that each node v maps to a unique ideal-primitive input entry $\mathsf{prelab}(v)$.

PEBBLING LEGALITY. Next, we show that with high probability (over the uniform choices of the ideal primitive ip and random coins r), the *ex-post-facto* pebbling $\mathcal{P}(\mathsf{A}^{\mathsf{ip}}(\mathbf{x}, r)) = (\mathsf{P}_0 = \emptyset, \ldots, \mathsf{P}_{t_{\mathsf{peb}}})$ for $\mathsf{A}^{\mathsf{ip}}(\mathbf{x}; r)$ is *legal*, and thus

$$\sum_{i=0}^{t_{\mathsf{peb}}} |\mathsf{P}_i| \geq \mathsf{cc}(\mathbb{G})$$

as long as the pebbling is *successful*.

Before presenting the lemma, we prove a claim that will be useful in many places.

Claim 1. *Fix any execution* $\mathsf{A}^{\mathsf{ip}}(\mathbf{x}; r)$ *(with input states $\sigma_0, \sigma_1, \ldots$) whose ex-post-facto pebbling is* $\mathcal{P}(\mathsf{A}) = (\mathsf{P}_0, \ldots, \mathsf{P}_{t_{\mathsf{peb}}})$. *For any $i \in [t_{\mathsf{peb}}]$ and any vertex $v \in \mathsf{P}_i \setminus \mathsf{P}_{i-1}$, it holds that there is a correct call for v in round i.*

Proof. The proof is deferred to full version. □

Lemma 3. *Fix* $\mathbb{IP} = \mathbb{CF}/\mathbb{IC}/\mathbb{RP}$ *(with block length L), predecessors-distinct DAG* $\mathbb{G} = (\mathbb{V}, \mathbb{E})$ *(with n_s source nodes), non-colliding input vector* $\mathbf{x} \in \{0,1\}^{n_s L}$, *algorithm* A, *and* $\mathcal{H}_{\mathsf{fix}} = \{\mathsf{flab}^{\mathsf{ip}}\}_{\mathsf{ip} \in \mathbb{IP}}$ *constructed in Sect. 3. With probability at least* $1 - \epsilon_{\mathsf{coll}}(\mathbb{IP}) - \epsilon_{\mathsf{legal}}(\mathbb{IP})$ *(over the uniformly random choices of* ip *and* A*'s internal coins r), the pre-labels are distinct and the ex-post-facto pebbling for* $\mathsf{A}^{\mathsf{ip}}(\mathbf{x}; r)$ *is legal. Here* $\epsilon_{\mathsf{coll}}(\mathbb{IP})$ *is the same as in Lemma 2 and* $\epsilon_{\mathsf{legal}}(\mathbb{CF}) = \mathsf{q} \cdot |\mathbb{V}| / 2^{L-1}$, $\epsilon_{\mathsf{legal}}(\mathbb{IC}) = \epsilon_{\mathsf{legal}}(\mathbb{RP}) = \mathsf{q} \cdot |\mathbb{V}| / 2^{L-2}$, *where* q *is an upper bound on the number of calls made by* A.

Proof. The proof is deferred to full version. □

PEBBLING REDUCTION. Next, we build the connection between the state size and the size of the pebbling configuration. In particular, we show that with high probability, the input state size $|\sigma_i|$ is proportional to $|\mathsf{P}_i|$ for all $i \in \mathbb{N}$.

---

[16] By non-colliding, we mean $\mathbf{x} = (x_1, \ldots, x_{n_s})$ where $x_i \neq x_j$ for every $i \neq j$.

Lemma 4. *Fix $L = 2^\ell$, predecessors-distinct DAG $\mathbb{G} = (\mathbb{V}, \mathbb{E})$ (with n_s source nodes), non-colliding input vector $\mathbf{x} \in \{0,1\}^{n_s L}$, algorithm A (that makes at most $q - 1$ calls), and $\mathcal{H}_{\mathsf{fix}} = \{\mathsf{flab}^{\mathsf{ip}}\}_{\mathsf{ip} \in \mathbb{IP}}$ constructed in Sect. 3. Set values $\beta_{\mathrm{CF}} := \lfloor L - 2\log q - \log |\mathbb{V}| - \log 3 \rfloor$, $\beta_{\mathrm{IC}} := \lfloor L - 1 - 2\log q - \log |\mathbb{V}| - \log 3 \rfloor$, and $\beta_{\mathrm{RP}} := \lfloor \frac{L}{2} - 1 - 2\log q - \log |\mathbb{V}| - \log 3 \rfloor$. For any $\mathbb{IP} = \mathrm{CF}/\mathrm{IC}/\mathrm{RP}$ and $\lambda \in \mathbb{N}$, define $\mathrm{E}_{\mathsf{pred}}^{\lambda, \mathbb{IP}}$ as the event where the following three conditions all hold:*

1. *The pre-labels are distinct from each other.*
2. *The ex-post-facto pebbling $(\mathsf{P}_0, \mathsf{P}_1, \ldots, \mathsf{P}_{t_{\mathsf{peb}}})$ for $\mathsf{A}^{\mathsf{ip}}(\mathbf{x}; r)$ is legal.*
3. *There exists $i \in \mathbb{N}$ such that $|\sigma_i| < |\mathsf{P}_i| \cdot \beta_{\mathbb{IP}} - \lambda$, where σ_i denotes the input state for round $i + 1$ and P_i denotes the pebbling configuration in round i.*

It holds that $\Pr[\mathrm{E}_{\mathsf{pred}}^{\lambda, \mathbb{IP}}] \leq 2^{-\lambda}$ for all $\lambda \in \mathbb{N}$, where the probability is taken over the choice of $\mathsf{ip} \xleftarrow{\$} \mathbb{IP}$ and random coins of A.

Proof. Without loss of generality we fix r to be the optimal random coins of A that maximizes $\Pr[\mathrm{E}_{\mathsf{pred}}^{\lambda, \mathbb{IP}}]$. We will show a predictor P (that hardwires r and has oracle access to ip), such that if $\mathrm{E}_{\mathsf{pred}}^{\lambda, \mathbb{IP}}$ happens (which implies $|\sigma_i| < |\mathsf{P}_i| \cdot \beta_{\mathbb{IP}} - \lambda$ for some $i \in \mathbb{N}$), there will be a hint h with no more than $|\mathsf{P}_i| \cdot L - \lambda$ (and $|\mathsf{P}_i| \cdot (L - 1) - \lambda$ when $\mathbb{IP} = \mathrm{IC}/\mathrm{RP}$) bits, where $P(h)$ can predict $|\mathsf{P}_i|$ ideal primitive entries correctly. Thus by the compression arguments that ideal primitives cannot be compressed (i.e., Lemmas 9 and 10), $\mathrm{E}_{\mathsf{pred}}^{\lambda, \mathbb{IP}}$ happens with probability no more than $2^{-\lambda}$ and the lemma holds. Next we describe the hint h and the predictor P.

THE HINT. For any choice of $\mathsf{ip} \in \mathbb{IP}$, if event $\mathrm{E}_{\mathsf{pred}}^{\lambda, \mathbb{IP}}$ happens, there exists a round $i \in \mathbb{N}$ such that $|\sigma_i| < |\mathsf{P}_i| \cdot \beta_{\mathbb{IP}} - \lambda$, where σ_i is the input state of round $i + 1$ and $\mathsf{P}_i = (v_1, v_2, \ldots, v_{|\mathsf{P}_i|})$ is the ex-post-facto pebbling configuration. The hint consists of the state σ_i and the following helper information. (In the following context, if not describe explicitly, by critical call, we always mean a critical call in the trace $\mathsf{A}(\sigma_i)$.)

- A sequence $Q_i = (\mathsf{id}_1, \mathsf{id}_2, \ldots, \mathsf{id}_{|\mathsf{P}_i|}) \in [q - 1]^{|\mathsf{P}_i|}$, where id_j $(1 \leq j \leq |\mathsf{P}_i|)$ is the index of the *first* critical call for $v_j \in \mathsf{P}_i$ in the trace $\mathsf{A}(\sigma_i)$. (Recall that we sort the calls in chronological order, and assume an implicit order for the calls in the same round.)
- A nodes sequence $W_i = (w_1, w_2, \ldots, w_{|\mathsf{P}_i|})$, where $w_j = v_j$ $(1 \leq j \leq |\mathsf{P}_i|)$ if the id_j-th call is an output call; otherwise, if the id_j-th call is a correct call for some successor of v_j, then w_j is assigned as the corresponding successor node.
- A sequence $B_i = (b_1, b_2, \ldots, b_{|\mathsf{P}_i|})$, where $b_j \in \{0, 1, 2\}$ is used to indicate the relation between w_j and v_j. In particular, $w_j = v_j$ if $b_j = 0$, otherwise v_j is the b_j-th predecessor of w_j.
- A sequence $C_i = (\mathsf{cid}_1, \mathsf{cid}_2, \ldots, \mathsf{cid}_{|\mathsf{P}_i|})$, where $\mathsf{cid}_j = 0$ $(1 \leq j \leq |\mathsf{P}_i|)$ if there is no correct call for $v_j \in \mathsf{P}_i$ in the trace $\mathsf{A}(\sigma_i)$, otherwise cid_j is the query index of the *first* correct call for v_j.

– If $\mathbb{IP} = \mathbb{RP}$, the hint includes an extra sequence $H_i = (h_1, h_2, \ldots, h_{|\mathsf{P}_i|})$, where h_j $(1 \leq j \leq |\mathsf{P}_i|)$ is the label ℓ_{v_j} if there exists some $k > j$ such that $\mathsf{id}_j = \mathsf{id}_k$ (i.e., another node $v_k \in \mathsf{P}_i$ has the same *first* critical call), otherwise h_j is set as empty[17]. We see that there are at most $\lfloor |\mathsf{P}_i|/2 \rfloor$ non-empty values in the sequence, as any ideal-primitive call can be a critical call for at most two vertices.

Note that we can easily recover the configuration P_i from the hint W_i and B_i. The size of the hint is no more than $\mathsf{len}_{\mathbb{IP}} := |\mathsf{P}_i| \cdot L - \lambda$ (and $\mathsf{len}_{\mathbb{IP}} := |\mathsf{P}_i| \cdot (L-1) - \lambda$ when $\mathbb{IP} = \mathbb{IC}/\mathbb{RP}$) bits given the setting of $\beta_{\mathbb{IP}}$.

THE PREDICTOR P. Given any input the predictor P parses the input into σ_i, Q_i, W_i, B_i, C_i and H_i as mentioned before[18], and recovers the pebbling configuration P_i. Then P runs the partial execution $\mathsf{A}(\sigma_i)$ and attempts to predict $(\mathsf{prelab}(v), \mathsf{ip}(\mathsf{prelab}(v)))$ for every $v \in \mathsf{P}_i$ *without querying* $\mathsf{ip}(\mathsf{prelab}(v))$. In the following context, if not describe explicitly, by critical call, we always mean a critical call in the trace $\mathsf{A}(\sigma_i)$.

When simulating $\mathsf{A}(\sigma_i)$, the predictor uses the following approach to determine if an ideal-primitive call is a correct call for a node v: The predictor keeps track of the labels $\mathsf{prelab}(v)$, $\mathsf{aftlab}(v)$ and ℓ_v for every $v \in \mathbb{V}$. Moreover, after knowing the labels of v's predecessors, the predictor updates $\mathsf{prelab}(v)$ accordingly. Given an ideal-primitive call from A, P determines call correctness by checking the following cases *sequentially*:

– If P knows from hint Q_i that the call is the *first* critical call for some node $v \in \mathsf{P}_i$, then the predictor knows that it is also a correct call for some node w, where w can be extracted from the hint W_i.
– If the call is the first correct call[19] for some node $v \in \mathsf{P}_i$, then P will know it from the hint C_i.
– The call is a *forward* call. Then the predictor checks if there exists a node $v \in \mathbb{V}$ where $\mathsf{prelab}(v)$ was updated and $\mathsf{prelab}(v)$ matches the call input x_c. If so, P asserts that it is a correct call for v.
– $\mathbb{IP} = \mathbb{IC}/\mathbb{RP}$ and the call is an *inverse call*. Then the predictor first checks if there is a node $v \in \mathbb{V}$ where $\mathsf{aftlab}(v)$ was updated and $\mathsf{aftlab}(v)$ matches the call input x_c. If no such v exists, P queries the oracle, and checks if the answer is consistent with some updated $\mathsf{prelab}(v)$ $(v \in \mathbb{V})$.
– If one of the above checks succeed, then after recognizing the correct call for v, P updates $\mathsf{prelab}(v)$, $\mathsf{aftlab}(v)$ and ℓ_v accordingly.

Claim 2. *Fix execution $\mathsf{A}^{\mathsf{ip}}(\mathbf{x}; r)$ and round i, suppose the pre-labels are distinct, and the ex-post-facto pebbling $(\mathsf{P}_0, \ldots, \mathsf{P}_{t_{\mathsf{peb}}})$ is legal. For any round $\gamma > i$, assume the predictor successfully extracted ℓ-labels for all (first) critical calls (in $\mathsf{A}(\sigma_i)$) between round i and round γ. Then for any vertex $v \in \mathsf{P}_i \cup \cdots \cup \mathsf{P}_\gamma$, and any*

---

[17] Note that we don't need an indicator (e.g., $h_j = \bot$) to tell if h_j is empty or not, as we can know it from the sequence Q_i. This enables us to have a shorter H_i.
[18] We assume that the encoding of the hint is unambiguous.
[19] Recall that there is an implicit chronological order for the calls.

correct call for v in round γ (denote the call as $C(v)$), the predictor will correctly recognize the call $C(v)$ when simulating $\mathsf{A}(\sigma_i)$.

Proof. The proof is deferred to full version.   □

Next we show how to simulate $\mathsf{A}(\sigma_i)$ and predict ideal-primitive entries.

The predictor simulates $\mathsf{A}(\sigma_i)$ (which corresponds to the partial execution of A after round i) and keeps track of the labels $\mathsf{prelab}(v)$, $\mathsf{aftlab}(v)$ and ℓ_v for every $v \in \mathbb{V}$. For each round $\gamma > i$, after receiving the calls from A, the predictor P does follows *sequentially*.

1. *Handling critical calls:* P first enumerates node $v_j \in \mathsf{P}_i$ according to *reverse topological order*[20] and checks the following: If the id_j-th call (i.e. v_j's *first* critical call) is in round γ and ℓ_{v_j} is unknown yet, the predictor uses the hint to extract the label ℓ_{v_j}. The extraction from a critical output call is trivial, thus we assume that the call is an ideal-primitive call. From the hint, the predictor knows that it is a correct ideal primitive call for a node $w_j \in \mathsf{succ}(v_j)$ where w_j can be extracted from the hint W_i. (Note that $w_j \in \mathsf{P}_\gamma$ by definition of critical calls.) The predictor first extracts $\mathsf{prelab}(w_j)$ from the call input/output:
   - If the call is forward, $\mathsf{prelab}(w_j)$ can be identified from the call input.
   - If $w_j \in \mathsf{P}_i$ and the call is an inverse call, since P chooses nodes in P_i according to reverse topological order, and in $\mathsf{A}(\sigma_i)$ the first critical call for w_j appears no later than any correct call for w_j, P must have already extracted ℓ_{w_j}, and thus the predictor can extract $\mathsf{prelab}(w_j)$ from ℓ_{w_j} and the call input without querying the oracle.
   - If $w_j \notin \mathsf{P}_i$ and the call is an inverse call, P can query the oracle and extract the information of $\mathsf{prelab}(w_j)$ from the oracle answer.
   Given w_j and $\mathsf{prelab}(w_j)$, if $\mathbb{IP} = \mathbb{CF}$ or $\mathbb{IP} = \mathbb{IC}$, P can directly extract the label ℓ_{v_j} from $\mathsf{prelab}(w_j)$ and b_j; if $\mathbb{IP} = \mathbb{RP}$ and v_j is the only predecessor of w_j, P can extract $\ell_{v_j} = \mathsf{prelab}(w_j)$; if $\mathbb{IP} = \mathbb{RP}$ and w_j has another predecessor u, we argue that ℓ_u was already known and thus the predictor can obtain the label $\ell_{v_j} = \mathsf{prelab}(w_j) \oplus \ell_u$.
   - If $u \notin \mathsf{P}_i$, since the ex-post-facto pebbling is legal and $w_j \in \mathsf{P}_\gamma$, there exists a round γ' ($i < \gamma' < r$) such that $u \in \mathsf{P}_{\gamma'} \setminus \mathsf{P}_{\gamma'-1}$. By Claim 1, there is a correct call $C(u)$ for u in round γ'. Then by Claim 2, P will recognize the call $C(u)$ and update the label ℓ_u.
   - If u is in P_i but the first critical call for u is before round γ (but after round i), then ℓ_u was already known before round γ.
   - If u equals some node $v_k \in \mathsf{P}_i$ such that v_k and v_j have the same *first* critical call, since ℓ_{v_j} was unknown, it must be the case that $k < j$ and $h_k = \ell_{v_k}$, hence the predictors knew ℓ_u initially from the hint H_i.
2. *Handling correct calls for P_i:* For each node $v_j \in \mathsf{P}_i$ and each correct ideal-primitive call for v_j (note that by Claim 2, P correctly recognizes the call, as the ℓ-labels of (first) critical calls upto round γ were correctly extracted),

---

[20] $v_{|\mathsf{P}_i|}$ is picked first, then $v_{|\mathsf{P}_i|-1},...,$ and finally v_1.

since the predictor already knew ℓ_{v_j} after handling the first critical call for v_j,[21] she can answer the call *without* querying the ideal primitive:

- If $\mathbb{IP} = \mathbb{CF}$, then ℓ_{v_j} is the query answer.
- If $\mathbb{IP} = \mathbb{IC}$ and the call input has the value (k, x) where $k \in \{0,1\}^L \cup \{\bot\}$ and $x \in \{0,1\}^L$, the answer is $\ell_{v_j} \oplus x$ because $\ell_{v_j} = x \oplus \mathsf{ip}(k, x)$ for a forward call and $\ell_{v_j} = x \oplus \mathsf{ip}^{-1}(k, x)$ for an inverse call.
- If $\mathbb{IP} = \mathbb{RP}$ and the call input has the value x, the answer is $\ell_{v_j} \oplus x$ because $\ell_{v_j} = x \oplus \mathsf{ip}(x)$ for a forward call and $\ell_{v_j} = x \oplus \mathsf{ip}^{-1}(x)$ for an inverse call.

For each round $\gamma > i$, after checking correct/critical calls for all nodes in P_i, the predictor answers the other unanswered calls by making queries to the ideal primitive. Note that in round γ, for every node $v \in \mathsf{P}_i \cup \cdots \cup \mathsf{P}_\gamma$, if there is a correct ideal-primitive call for v, since P already extracted ℓ-labels for all (first) critical calls upto round γ, by Claim 2, P will recognize the call, get the call answer, then update the labels $\mathsf{prelab}(v)$, $\mathsf{aftlab}(v)$, ℓ_v and the pre-labels of v's successors.

After executing $\mathsf{A}(\sigma_i)$, the predictor will compute $\mathsf{prelab}(v)$ for every $v \in \mathbb{V}$ according to topological order, and predict $\mathsf{ip}(\mathsf{prelab}(v))$ for every $v \in \mathsf{P}_i$. In particular, if $\mathbb{IP} = \mathbb{CF}$, $\mathsf{ip}(\mathsf{prelab}(v)) = \ell_v$; if $\mathbb{IP} = \mathbb{IC}$, let x be the last L-bit string of $\mathsf{prelab}(v)$, then $\mathsf{ip}(\mathsf{prelab}(v)) = x \oplus \ell_v$; if $\mathbb{IP} = \mathbb{RP}$, then $\mathsf{ip}(\mathsf{prelab}(v)) = \mathsf{prelab}(v) \oplus \ell_v$. Note that if $\mathrm{E}_{\mathsf{pred}}^{\lambda, \mathbb{IP}}$ happens and the input is the hint h mentioned above, the predictor does not need to query $\mathsf{ip}(\mathsf{prelab}(v))$ for any $v \in \mathsf{P}_i$ as the answer can be computed from $\mathsf{prelab}(v)$ and the extracted label ℓ_v.

<u>CORRECTNESS OF THE PREDICTOR.</u> If $\mathrm{E}_{\mathsf{pred}}^{\lambda, \mathbb{IP}}$ happens and P's input is the hint mentioned above, the predictor will correctly predict $(\mathsf{prelab}(v), \mathsf{ip}(\mathsf{prelab}(v)))$ for every $v \in \mathsf{P}_i$ without querying $\mathsf{ip}(\mathsf{prelab}(v))$. Recall that $\{\mathsf{prelab}(v)\}$ are distinct so that P also predicts $|\mathsf{P}_i|$ ideal-primitive entries.

First, we note that the labels being updated (including $\mathsf{prelab}(v)$, $\mathsf{aftlab}(v)$ and ℓ_v for $v \in \mathbb{V}$) are correct by induction on the time order of updating. Initially, only the pre-labels of source vertices were updated which are correct. Assume all the labels being updated are correct up to now. A new label $\mathsf{prelab}(v)$ (or $\mathsf{aftlab}(v)$) will be updated because one of the following possibilities:

1. P recognizes the *first* correct call for $v \in \mathsf{P}_i$ from the hint C_i (and thus correct by the hint).
2. P recognizes a correct call for v by finding out that the call input/output matches the previously updated $\mathsf{aftlab}(v)$ (or $\mathsf{prelab}(v)$) which is correct by inductive hypothesis.
3. P computes the label according to topological order (at the end).
4. $\mathsf{prelab}(v)$ is updated because the ℓ-labels of v's predecessors were all updated previously (which are correct by inductive hypothesis).

Similarly, a new label ℓ_v will be updated either because the possibility 2 as above, or because P extracts ℓ_v from the *first* critical call for v (and thus correct by

---

[21] Recall that in $\mathsf{A}(\sigma_i)$, there was no correct call for v before the round of the first critical call for v.

the hint). Note that the argument above also implies that P will not output an incorrect prediction.

It remains to prove that P will never query $\mathsf{ip}(\mathsf{prelab}(v))$ for any $v \in \mathsf{P}_i$. First, when simulating $\mathsf{A}(\sigma_{\sigma_i})$, P will recognize the first correct call of v from the hint C_i and answer the call using the extracted label ℓ_v. Then $\mathsf{prelab}(v)$, $\mathsf{aftlab}(v)$ and ℓ_v will all be updated. For the following correct calls, since $\mathsf{prelab}(v)$, $\mathsf{aftlab}(v)$ and ℓ_v have been updated, P will recognize and answer the call without querying ip. Lastly, when computing $\mathsf{prelab}(v)$ for $v \in \mathbb{V}$ according to topological order, P will not query $\mathsf{ip}(\mathsf{prelab}(v))$ for any $v \in \mathsf{P}_i$ as the answer will be computed from $\mathsf{prelab}(v)$ and the extracted label ℓ_v.

In summary, with probability at least $\Pr[\mathrm{E}_{\mathsf{pred}}^{\lambda,\mathbb{IP}}]$, there exists a short hint h where $P(h)$ correctly guesses $|\mathsf{P}_i|$ ideal-primitive entries, thus by Lemmas 9 and 10, we have $\Pr[\mathrm{E}_{\mathsf{pred}}^{\lambda,\mathbb{IP}}] \leq 2^{-\lambda}$ and the lemma holds.   □

PUTTING ALL THINGS TOGETHER. For an execution $\mathsf{A}^{\mathsf{ip}}(\mathbf{x}, r)$, we say $\mathsf{A}^{\mathsf{ip}}(\mathbf{x}, r)$ is correct if the algorithm generates the correct graph function output at the end; we say $\mathsf{A}^{\mathsf{ip}}(\mathbf{x}, r)$ is lucky if it is correct but there is a vertex $v \in \mathsf{sink}$ where A did not make any correct call for v before outputting the label ℓ_v. Note that if $\mathsf{A}^{\mathsf{ip}}(\mathbf{x}, r)$ is correct but not lucky, the ex-post-facto pebbling will be successful. Moreover, with similar compression argument as in Lemmas 2 and 3, the probability (over the uniform choice of ip and A's internal coins) that A is lucky is no more than $\epsilon_{\mathsf{luck}}(\mathbb{IP})$, where $\epsilon_{\mathsf{luck}}(\mathbb{CF}) = |\mathbb{V}|/2^L$ and $\epsilon_{\mathsf{luck}}(\mathbb{IC}) = \epsilon_{\mathsf{luck}}(\mathbb{RP}) = |\mathbb{V}|/2^{L-1}$.

In summary, for any algorithm A that correctly computes the graph function with probability $\epsilon_{\mathsf{A}} > 2 \cdot (\epsilon_{\mathsf{coll}}(\mathbb{IP}) + \epsilon_{\mathsf{legal}}(\mathbb{IP}) + \epsilon_{\mathsf{luck}}(\mathbb{IP}))$, we set $\lambda \in \mathbb{N}$ as the minimal integer such that $\epsilon(\lambda) = \epsilon_{\mathsf{coll}}(\mathbb{IP}) + \epsilon_{\mathsf{legal}}(\mathbb{IP}) + \epsilon_{\mathsf{luck}}(\mathbb{IP}) + 2^{-\lambda} \leq \epsilon_{\mathsf{A}}/2$. Then the following conditions hold with probability more than $\epsilon_{\mathsf{A}} - \epsilon(\lambda) \geq \epsilon_{\mathsf{A}}/2$:

1. The pre-labels are distinct from each other.
2. The ex-post-facto pebbling is legal and successful, hence

$$\sum_{i=1}^{t_{\mathsf{peb}}} |\mathsf{P}_i| \geq \mathsf{cc}(\mathbb{G}).$$

3. For every $i \in [t_{\mathsf{peb}}]$, it holds that $|\sigma_i| \geq |\mathsf{P}_i| \cdot \beta_{\mathbb{IP}} - \lambda$. Here $\mathsf{A}^{\mathsf{ip}}(\mathbf{x}; r)$ terminates at round $t_{\mathsf{peb}} + 1$, σ_i is the input state for round $i + 1$, and P_i is the pebbling configuration in round i.
   Thus we have

$$\mathsf{CMC}(\mathsf{A}^{\mathsf{ip}}(\mathbf{x}; r)) \geq \sum_{i=1}^{t_{\mathsf{peb}}} |\sigma_i| \geq \sum_{i=1}^{t_{\mathsf{peb}}} (|\mathsf{P}_i| \cdot \beta_{\mathbb{IP}} - \lambda)$$

$$\geq \left(\sum_{i=1}^{t_{\mathsf{peb}}} |\mathsf{P}_i| \right) \cdot \beta_{\mathbb{IP}} - t_{\mathsf{peb}} \cdot \lambda$$

$$\geq \mathsf{cc}(\mathbb{G}) \cdot \beta_{\mathbb{IP}} - t_{\mathsf{peb}} \cdot \lambda \geq \mathsf{cc}(\mathbb{G}) \cdot \beta_{\mathbb{IP},\lambda},$$

where $\beta_{\mathbb{IP},\lambda} = \beta_{\mathbb{IP}} - \lambda$ as $\mathsf{cc}(\mathbb{G}) \geq t_{\mathsf{peb}}$.

Therefore we have

$$\mathbb{E}[\mathsf{CMC}(\mathsf{A}^{\mathsf{ip}}(\mathbf{x};r))] \geq \frac{\epsilon_{\mathsf{A}}}{2} \cdot \beta_{\mathbb{IP},\lambda} \cdot \mathsf{cc}(\mathbb{G}).$$

By plugging in the corresponding $\epsilon_{\mathsf{coll}}(\mathbb{IP})$, $\epsilon_{\mathsf{legal}}(\mathbb{IP})$, $\epsilon_{\mathsf{luck}}(\mathbb{IP})$ and $\beta_{\mathbb{IP}}$ for the ideal primitive $\mathbb{IP}$, we can find the optimal parameter $\lambda_{\mathbb{IP}}$, and compute

$$\beta(\epsilon_{\mathsf{A}}, \log |\mathbb{V}|) = \frac{\epsilon_{\mathsf{A}}}{2} \cdot (\beta_{\mathbb{IP}} - \lambda_{\mathbb{IP}}),$$

which leads to Theorems 1, 2 and 3.

$\square$

3.3 iMHFs from Small-Block Labeling Functions

In this section, from any graph, we construct graph-based iMHFs from the small-block labeling functions built in Sect. 3.1.

Proposition 1. *Fix $L = 2^{\ell}$ and let $\mathcal{H}_{\mathsf{fix}}$ be the β-small-block labeling function built in Sect. 3.1. For any 2-indegree (predecessors-distinct) DAG $\mathbb{G} = (\mathbb{V}, \mathbb{E})$ with $N = 2^n$ vertices and single source/sink, the graph labeling functions $\mathcal{F}_{\mathbb{G}, \mathcal{H}_{\mathsf{fix}}}$ is $(\mathsf{C}_{\mathcal{F}}^{\|}, \Delta_{\mathcal{F}}, N)$-memory hard, where for all $\epsilon \in [3 \cdot 2^{-L/10}, 1]$, it holds that*

$$\mathsf{C}_{\mathcal{F}}^{\|}(\epsilon) \geq \Omega(\epsilon \cdot \mathsf{cc}(\mathbb{G}) \cdot L), \qquad \Delta_{\mathcal{F}}(\epsilon) \leq O\left(\frac{\mathsf{st}(\mathbb{G}, N)}{\mathsf{cc}(\mathbb{G})}\right).$$

Proof. The proof is deferred to full version. $\square$

The graph $\mathbb{G}$ in [3] has pebbling complexities $\mathsf{cc}(\mathbb{G}) = \Omega(N^2/\log N)$ and $\mathsf{st}(\mathbb{G}, N) = O(N^2/\log N)$, thus we obtain the following corollary.

Corollary 1. *Fix $L = 2^{\ell}$ and let $\mathcal{H}_{\mathsf{fix}}$ be the β-small-block labeling function built in Sect. 3.1. Let $\mathbb{G} = (\mathbb{V}, \mathbb{E})$ be the 2-indegree (predecessors-distinct) DAG in [3] (with $N = 2^n$ vertices). The graph labeling functions $\mathcal{F}_{\mathbb{G}, \mathcal{H}_{\mathsf{fix}}}$ is $(\mathsf{C}_{\mathcal{F}}^{\|}, \Delta_{\mathcal{F}}, N)$-memory hard, where for all $\epsilon \in [3 \cdot 2^{-L/10}, 1]$, it holds that*

$$\mathsf{C}_{\mathcal{F}}^{\|}(\epsilon) \geq \Omega\left(\frac{\epsilon \cdot N^2 \cdot L}{\log N}\right), \qquad \Delta_{\mathcal{F}}(\epsilon) \leq O(1).$$

4 MHFs from Wide-Block Labeling Functions

Ideally, we target a CMC which is as high as possible, while keeping the evaluation of the function within a feasible margin for the legitimate users. An option is to use a bigger graph with high CC and small-block labeling functions. However, this can lead to large description size. A way out here is to choose a graph family that has succinct description. Unfortunately, as far as we know, practical hard-to-pebble graphs are randomly sampled and do not have a succinct description of the actual graph, only of the sampling process. To reduce description complexity of MHFs, in this section, we construct a family of graph-based iMHFs based on an abstraction called *wide-block labeling functions*. In Sect. 4.1, we define and construct a family of wide-block labeling functions from small-block labeling functions. In Sect. 4.2, we prove that the construction satisfies pebbling reducibility with respect to depth-robust graphs. Finally in Sect. 4.3, we construct succinct iMHFs from wide-block labeling functions.

4.1   Wide-Block Labeling Functions: Definition and Construction

Definition 7 (Wide-Block Labeling Functions). *For any ideal primitive* $\mathbb{IP} = \mathbb{CF}/\mathbb{IC}/\mathbb{RP}$, $\delta \in \mathbb{N}$ *and* $W = 2^w$, *we say*

$$\mathcal{H}_{\delta,w} = \left\{ \mathsf{vlab}^{\mathsf{ip}}_{\gamma,w} : \{0,1\}^{\gamma W} \to \{0,1\}^W \right\}_{\mathsf{ip}\in\mathbb{IP},1\leq\gamma\leq\delta}$$

is a family of $\beta_{\delta,w}$*-wide-block labeling functions if it satisfies the following property.*

$\beta_{\delta,w}$**-pebbling reducibility w.r.t. depth-robust graphs:** *For any* $\epsilon \in [0,1]$ *and any* δ*-indegree* (e,d)*-depth robust (first-predecessor-distinct) DAG* $\mathbb{G} = (\mathbb{V}, \mathbb{E})^{22}$, *the graph functions* $\mathcal{F}_{\mathbb{G},\mathcal{H}_{\delta,w}}$ *satisfies*

$$\mathsf{CMC}_\epsilon(\mathcal{F}_{\mathbb{G},\mathcal{H}_{\delta,w}}) \geq e \cdot (d-1) \cdot \beta_{\delta,w}(\epsilon, \log|\mathbb{V}|),$$

where $\mathsf{CMC}_\epsilon(\cdot)$ *is* ϵ*-cumulative-memory-complexity (Definition 1).*

CONSTRUCTION. Next we show how to construct wide-block labeling functions from small-block labeling functions. The construction is the composition of two graph functions MIX and SSDR, which can be built from any small-block labeling functions.

Remark 5. There are tailored-made variable-length hash functions available in the real-world, for example within Scrypt [19,20] and Argon2 [10]. However, even by modeling the underlying block/stream cipher as an ideal primitive, we do not know how to prove the pebbling-reducibility of the hash functions. Hence we seek another construction of labeling functions.

In the following context, we fix the indegree parameter $\delta \in \mathbb{N}$, ideal primitive length $L = 2^\ell$, output length $W = 2^w$ of the wide-block labeling functions, and denote as $K = 2^k := W/L$ the ratio between W and L. We will omit these variables in notation when it is clear in the context.

We show how to construct the family of labeling functions $\mathcal{H}_{\delta,w}$. For any $1 \leq \gamma \leq \delta$, and any ideal primitive $\mathsf{ip} \in \mathbb{IP}$, we define the labeling function $\mathsf{vlab}^{\mathsf{ip}}_{\gamma,w} : \{0,1\}^{\gamma W} \to \{0,1\}^W$ as the composition of two functions, namely,

---

^{22} $\mathbb{G}$ has a single source/sink vertex.

$\mathsf{mix}_\gamma^{\mathsf{ip}} : \{0,1\}^{\gamma W} \to \{0,1\}^W$ and $\mathsf{ssdr}_\delta^{\mathsf{ip}} : \{0,1\}^W \to \{0,1\}^W$. More precisely, for an input vector $\mathbf{x} \in \{0,1\}^{\gamma W}$, we define the W-bit function output as

$$\mathsf{vlab}_{\gamma,w}^{\mathsf{ip}}(\mathbf{x}) := \mathsf{ssdr}_\delta^{\mathsf{ip}}(\mathsf{mix}_\gamma^{\mathsf{ip}}(\mathbf{x})).$$

Next, we specify the functions $\mathsf{mix}_\gamma^{\mathsf{ip}}$ and $\mathsf{ssdr}_\delta^{\mathsf{ip}}$.

COMPONENT: MIX FUNCTIONS. Denote as $\mathsf{flab}^{\mathsf{ip}} : \{0,1\}^L \cup \{0,1\}^{2L} \to \{0,1\}^L$ a small-block labeling function (Definition 6), and let $K := W/L$ be the ratio between W and L. We define

$$\mathsf{mix}_\gamma^{\mathsf{ip}} := \mathsf{F}_{\mathbb{G}_{\mathsf{mix}}^{\gamma,K}}^{\mathsf{ip}} : \{0,1\}^{\gamma W} \to \{0,1\}^{W=KL}$$

as the graph function (Sect. 2.3) built upon a DAG $\mathbb{G}_{\mathsf{mix}}^{\gamma,K}$ and the labeling function $\mathsf{flab}^{\mathsf{ip}}$. (Note that we can use $\mathsf{flab}^{\mathsf{ip}}$ as the labeling function since the maximal indegree of $\mathbb{G}_{\mathsf{mix}}^{\gamma,K}$ is 2.) The graph $\mathbb{G}_{\mathsf{mix}}^{\gamma,K} = (\mathbb{V}_{\mathsf{mix}}^{\gamma,K}, \mathbb{E}_{\mathsf{mix}}^{\gamma,K})$ is defined as follows.

Nodes set: The set $\mathbb{V}_{\mathsf{mix}}^{\gamma,K}$ has γK source nodes (which represent the γK input blocks), and we use $\langle 0, j \rangle$ ($1 \le j \le \gamma K$) to denote the jth source node. Besides, there are γK columns each with K nodes. We use $\langle i, j \rangle$ ($1 \le i \le \gamma K$, $1 \le j \le K$) to denote the node at the ith column and jth row. The K nodes at the last column are the sink nodes (which represent the K output blocks).

Edges set: The set $\mathbb{E}_{\mathsf{mix}}^{\gamma,K}$ has $\gamma K^2 + \gamma(K-1)K + K - 1$ edges. Each source node $\langle 0, i \rangle$ ($1 \le i \le \gamma K$) has K outgoing edges to the K nodes of column i, namely, $\{\langle i, j \rangle\}_{j \in [K]}$. For each column i ($1 \le i < \gamma K$) and each row j ($1 \le j \le K$), the node $\langle i, j \rangle$ has an outgoing edge to $\langle i+1, j \rangle$ at the next column. Finally, each source node $\langle 0, j \rangle$ ($2 \le j \le K$) has an outgoing edge to $\langle 1, j \rangle$[23] (Fig. 1).

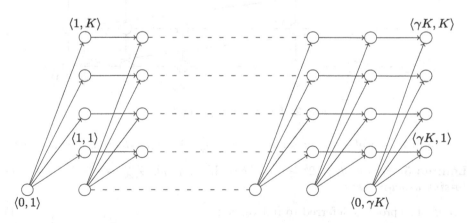

Fig. 1. The graph $\mathbb{G}_{\mathsf{mix}}^{\gamma,K}$ for $K = 4$. We omitted the edges from $\langle 0, j \rangle$ to $\langle 1, j \rangle$ ($2 \le j \le K$) for clarity of the figure.

---

[23] The last $K - 1$ edges make sure that the K nodes at column 1 have distinct sets of predecessors (Sect. 2.3).

COMPONENT: SSDR FUNCTIONS. Denote as $\mathsf{flab}^{\mathsf{ip}} : \{0,1\}^L \cup \{0,1\}^{2L} \to \{0,1\}^L$ a small-block labeling function (Definition 6), and let $K := W/L$ be the ratio between W and L. Fix $\delta \in \mathbb{N}$, we define

$$\mathsf{ssdr}_\delta^{\mathsf{ip}} := \mathsf{F}_{\mathbb{G}_{\mathsf{ssdr}}^{\delta,K}}^{\mathsf{ip}} : \{0,1\}^W \to \{0,1\}^W$$

as the graph function built upon the labeling function $\mathsf{flab}^{\mathsf{ip}}$ and a DAG $\mathbb{G}_{\mathsf{ssdr}}^{\delta,K}$. (Note that we can use $\mathsf{flab}^{\mathsf{ip}}$ as the labeling function since the maximal indegree of $\mathbb{G}_{\mathsf{ssdr}}^{\delta,K}$ is 2.) $\mathbb{G}_{\mathsf{ssdr}}^{\delta,K} = (\mathbb{V}_{\mathsf{ssdr}}^{\delta,K}, \mathbb{E}_{\mathsf{ssdr}}^{\delta,K})$ is a *source-to-sink-depth-robust* graph (Definition 4) defined as follows.

Nodes set: The set $\mathbb{V}_{\mathsf{ssdr}}^{\delta,K}$ has $K(1 + \delta K)$ vertices distributing across $1 + \delta K$ columns and K rows. For every $i \in \{0, \ldots, \delta K\}$ and every $j \in \{1, \ldots, K\}$, we use $\langle i, j \rangle$ to denote the node at column i and row j. The K nodes at column 0 are the source nodes and the K nodes at column δK are the sink nodes.

Edges set: The set $\mathbb{E}_{\mathsf{ssdr}}^{\delta,K}$ consists of 3 types of edges. The first type is called *horizontal edges*: For every i ($0 \leq i < \delta K$) and every j ($1 \leq j \leq K$), there is an edge from node $\langle i, j \rangle$ to node $\langle i + 1, j \rangle$. The second type is called *vertical edges*: For every i ($2 \leq i \leq \delta K$) and every j ($1 \leq j < K$), there is an edge from node $\langle i, j \rangle$ to node $\langle i, j + 1 \rangle$. The third type is called *backward edges*: For every j ($1 \leq j < K$), there is an edge from node $\langle \delta K, j \rangle$ to node $\langle 1, j + 1 \rangle$. In total, there are $\delta K^2 + \delta K \cdot (K - 1) < 2\delta K^2$ edges (Fig. 2).

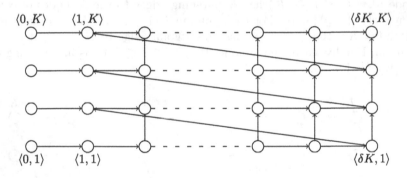

Fig. 2. The graph $\mathbb{G}_{\mathsf{ssdr}}^{\delta,K}$ for $K = 4$

We prove a useful lemma showing that $\mathbb{G}_{\mathsf{ssdr}}^{\delta,K}$ is *source-to-sink-depth-robust*.

Lemma 5. *Fix any $K = 2^k \geq 4$ and $\delta \in \mathbb{N}$, the graph $\mathbb{G}_{\mathsf{ssdr}}^{\delta,K}$ is $(\frac{K}{4}, \frac{\delta K^2}{2})$-source-to-sink-depth-robust.*

Proof. The proof is deferred to full version.   □

4.2   Wide-Block Labeling Functions: Pebbling Reducibility

In this section, we show that the labeling functions constructed in Sect. 4.1 satisfy pebbling reducibility with respect to (first-predecessor-distinct) depth-robust graphs. We will make use of the following notation.

<u>GRAPH COMPOSITION:</u> Given a graph $\mathbb{G}_1$ (with n_1 source nodes and n_2 sink nodes), and a graph $\mathbb{G}_2$ (with n_2 source nodes and n_3 sink nodes), we define $\mathbb{G}_1 \circ \mathbb{G}_2$ as the composition of $\mathbb{G}_1$ and $\mathbb{G}_2$, namely, we merge the ith sink node of $\mathbb{G}_1$ with the ith source node of $\mathbb{G}_2$ for each $i \in [n_2]$[24], and take the union of the rest parts of the graphs.

Theorem 4. *Fix $L = 2^\ell$, $W = 2^w \geq L$, and set $K := W/L$. Let $\mathcal{H}_{\text{fix}}$ be any β_{fix}-small-block labeling functions. For any $\delta \in \mathbb{N}$, the labeling functions $\mathcal{H}_{\delta,w}$ constructed in Sect. 4.1 is $\beta_{\delta,w}$-pebbling-reducible w.r.t. (first-predecessor-distinct[25]) depth-robust graphs (with single source/sink) where*

$$\beta_{\delta,w}(\epsilon, \log |\mathbb{V}|) \geq \frac{\delta K^3}{8} \cdot \beta_{\text{fix}}(\epsilon, \log |\mathbb{V}|).$$

Here $\epsilon \in (0,1]$ and $|\mathbb{V}|$ is the number of vertices in the graph.

Remark 6 (Generalization). For the wide-block labeling functions constructed in Sect. 4.1, we make use of a specific graph $\mathbb{G}_{\text{ssdr}}^{\delta,K}$ that is source-to-sink depth robust. We emphasize, however, that any source-to-sink depth robust graphs suffice. In particular, by replacing $\mathbb{G}_{\text{ssdr}}^{\delta,K}$ with any 2-indegree DAG $\mathbb{G}^*$ where i) $\mathbb{G}^*$ has K source/sink nodes and ii) $\mathbb{G}^*$ is (e^*, d^*)-source-to-sink depth robust, the corresponding wide-block labeling functions is still β-pebbling-reducible, where

$$\beta(\epsilon, \log |\mathbb{V}|) \geq e^* \cdot d^* \cdot \beta_{\text{fix}}(\epsilon, \log |\mathbb{V}|).$$

We leave finding new source-to-sink depth-robust graphs as an interesting direction for future work.

Remark 7. Note that in Theorem 4, the pebbling reducibility only holds for depth-robust graphs. It is hard to directly link CMC and $\text{cc}(\mathbb{G})$. More discussions can be found at Remark 2.

Proof (of Theorem 4). Let $\mathbb{G} = (\mathbb{V}, \mathbb{E})$ be any (first-predecessor-distinct) (e,d)-depth-robust DAG with δ-indegree and single source/sink, let $\mathcal{F}_{\mathbb{G},\mathcal{H}_{\delta,w}}$ be the graph functions built upon $\mathbb{G}$ and $\mathcal{H}_{\delta,w}$. It is sufficient to show that for every $\epsilon \in (0,1]$,

$$\text{CMC}_\epsilon(\mathcal{F}_{\mathbb{G},\mathcal{H}_{\delta,w}}) \geq \beta_{\text{fix}}(\epsilon, \log |\mathbb{V}|) \cdot \frac{\delta K^3}{8} \cdot e \cdot (d-1).$$

By opening the underlying graph structure of $\mathcal{H}_{\delta,w}$, we see that $\mathcal{F}_{\mathbb{G},\mathcal{H}_{\delta,w}}$ is also a graph function built upon functions $\mathcal{H}_{\text{fix}}$ and an extension graph $\text{Ext}_{\delta,K}(\mathbb{G})$ that has the following properties.

- **Nodes Expansion:** Every node $v \in \mathbb{V}$ in the original graph $\mathbb{G} = (\mathbb{V}, \mathbb{E})$ is expanded into K nodes, that is,

$$\text{copy}(v) := \left(v^{(1)}, \ldots, v^{(K)} \right).$$

---

[24] We assume an implicit order for nodes in $\mathbb{G}_1$ and $\mathbb{G}_2$.
[25] See Remark 3 for definition of first-predecessor-distinctness.

– **Neighborhood Connection:** For every *non-source* node $v \in \mathbb{V} - \mathsf{src}(\mathbb{G})$, denote as $\mathsf{pred}(v) := (u_1, \ldots, u_\gamma)$ the predecessors of v in $\mathbb{G}$. In $\mathsf{Ext}_{\delta,K}(\mathbb{G})$, there is a subgraph $\mathbb{G}_{\mathsf{mix}}^{\gamma,K}(v) \circ \mathbb{G}_{\mathsf{ssdr}}^{\delta,K}(v)$ that connects

$$\mathsf{neighbor}(v) := \{\mathsf{copy}(u_1), \ldots, \mathsf{copy}(u_\gamma)\}$$

to the set $\mathsf{copy}(v)$, where $\mathsf{neighbor}(v)$ (and $\mathsf{copy}(v)$) are the source nodes (and the sink nodes) of $\mathbb{G}_{\mathsf{mix}}^{\gamma,K}(v) \circ \mathbb{G}_{\mathsf{ssdr}}^{\delta,K}(v)$, respectively. Note $\mathbb{G}_{\mathsf{mix}}^{\gamma,K}(v) \circ \mathbb{G}_{\mathsf{ssdr}}^{\delta,K}(v)$ has the identical graph structure with the composition of $\mathbb{G}_{\mathsf{mix}}^{\gamma,K}$ and $\mathbb{G}_{\mathsf{ssdr}}^{\delta,K}$.

By first-predecessor-distinctness of $\mathbb{G}$ and by the graph structure of the MIX graph, it holds that $\mathsf{Ext}_{\delta,K}(\mathbb{G})$ is a predecessors-distinct graph with 2-indegree. Next, we will show that the extension graph $\mathsf{Ext}_{\delta,K}(\mathbb{G})$ is $(e, (d-1) \cdot \delta K)$-depth-robust for $K \in \{1,2\}$ and $(eK/4, (d-1) \cdot \delta K^2/2)$-depth-robust for $K \geq 4$. By Lemma 1, for any $K = 2^k \geq 1$, we have

$$\mathsf{cc}(\mathsf{Ext}_{\delta,K}(\mathbb{G})) \geq \frac{\delta K^3}{8} \cdot e \cdot (d-1).$$

Thus by β_{fix}-pebbling reducibility of $\mathcal{H}_{\mathsf{fix}}$[26], we obtain Theorem 4.

Before proving the depth-robustness of the extension graph, we introduce a useful notation called *meta-node* [3]. Intuitively, meta-node maps each vertex of the original graph $\mathbb{G}$ to a set of vertices in $\mathsf{Ext}_{\delta,K}(\mathbb{G})$.

META-NODE: We define meta-node $\mathsf{nodes}(v)$ for every node $v \in \mathbb{V}$: For every *non-source* node $v \in \mathbb{V} - \mathsf{src}(\mathbb{G})$, we define $\mathsf{nodes}(v)$ as the set of vertices in the graph $\mathbb{G}_{\mathsf{mix}}^{\gamma,K}(v) \circ \mathbb{G}_{\mathsf{ssdr}}^{\delta,K}(v) - \mathsf{neighbor}(v)$; for every *source* node $v \in \mathsf{src}(\mathbb{G})$, we define $\mathsf{nodes}(v) := \mathsf{copy}(v)$. Note that for any $u, v \in \mathbb{V}$ such that $u \neq v$, the sets $\mathsf{nodes}(u)$ and $\mathsf{nodes}(v)$ are disjoint.

DEPTH-ROBUSTNESS OF THE EXTENSION GRAPH: Next we show the depth robustness of the extension graph. We first consider the simpler case where $K \in \{1,2\}$. (In the following context, for a graph $\mathbb{G} = (\mathbb{V}, \mathbb{E})$, we sometimes think $\mathbb{G} = \mathbb{V} \cup \mathbb{E}$ as the union of set $\mathbb{V}$ and $\mathbb{E}$ if there is no ambiguity.)

Lemma 6. *For any $K = 2^k \in \{1,2\}$ and (e,d)-depth robust DAG $\mathbb{G} = (\mathbb{V}, \mathbb{E})$ that has maximal indegree $\delta \in \mathbb{N}$, the corresponding extension graph $\mathsf{Ext}_{\delta,K}(\mathbb{G})$ is $(e, (d-1) \cdot \delta K)$-depth-robust.*

Proof. The proof is deferred to full version. □

Next, we consider the more general case where $K \geq 4$.

Lemma 7. *For any $K = 2^k \geq 4$ and any (e,d)-depth robust DAG $\mathbb{G} = (\mathbb{V}, \mathbb{E})$ with maximal indegree $\delta \in \mathbb{N}$, the corresponding extension graph $\mathsf{Ext}_{\delta,K}(\mathbb{G})$ is $(\frac{K}{4} \cdot e, \frac{\delta K^2}{2} \cdot (d-1))$-depth-robust.*

---

[26] Note that β_{fix}-pebbling reducibility holds for multi-sources graphs.

Proof. For any nodes subset $S_{ext} \subseteq \text{Ext}_{\delta,K}(\mathbb{G})$ such that $|S_{ext}| \leq \frac{K}{4} \cdot e$, we show that $\text{depth}(\text{Ext}_{\delta,K}(\mathbb{G}) - S_{ext}) \geq \frac{\delta K^2}{2} \cdot (d-1)$, which finishes the proof.

<u>STEP 1:</u> From S_{ext}, we first derive a set of nodes $S \subseteq \mathbb{V}$ in the graph $\mathbb{G}$, and find a long path in $\mathbb{G} - S$.

Claim 3. *Define a set*

$$S := \left\{ v \in \mathbb{V} : |\text{nodes}(v) \cap S_{ext}| \geq \frac{K}{4} \right\},$$

there exists a d-path[27] $P = (v_1, \ldots, v_d)$ in the graph $\mathbb{G} - S$.

Proof. The proof is deferred to full version. □

<u>STEP 2:</u> Given the path $P = (v_1, \ldots, v_d) \subseteq \mathbb{G} - S$, next in Lemma 8 we show that for every $i \in [d-1]$, there exists a long path from $\text{copy}(v_i)$ to $\text{copy}(v_{i+1})$ in the graph $\text{Ext}_{\delta,K}(\mathbb{G}) - S_{ext}$, then by connecting the $d-1$ paths, we obtain a path with length at least $\frac{\delta K^2}{2} \cdot (d-1)$, hence finish the proof of Lemma 7. Note that the path extraction from $\text{copy}(v_i)$ to $\text{copy}(v_{i+1})$ consists of two steps: First we exploit the structure of SSDR graphs and obtain a long path ending at a node in $\text{copy}(v_{i+1})$, then we exploit the structure of MIX graphs and connect $\text{copy}(v_i)$ to the source node of the obtained path.

Lemma 8. *Given the path $P = (v_1, \ldots, v_d) \subseteq \mathbb{G} - S$ (obtained in Claim 3) and the graph $\text{Ext}_{\delta,K}(\mathbb{G}) - S_{ext}$, there exists a nodes sequence $(u_1, \ldots, u_d)$ (where $u_i \in \text{copy}(v_i) - S_{ext}$ for every $i \in [d]$), such that for every $i \in [d-1]$, there is a path (with length at least $\frac{\delta K^2}{2}$) that connects u_i and u_{i+1} in $\text{Ext}_{\delta,K}(\mathbb{G}) - S_{ext}$.*

Proof. We first show that there exists a path (with length at least $\frac{\delta K^2}{2}$) from some node $u_1 \in \text{copy}(v_1) - S_{ext}$ to some node $u_2 \in \text{copy}(v_2) - S_{ext}$. (The arguments for $u_2, \ldots, u_d$ will be similar.) The idea consists of two steps: First, we find a *long* source-to-sink path in $\mathbb{G}_{ssdr}^{\delta,K}(v_2)$; second, we connect u_1 to the starting node of the source-to-sink path. We stress that the path we obtain has no intersection with S_{ext}.

<u>FINDING THE SOURCE-TO-SINK PATH:</u> We first define a set S_{ssdr} and find a source-to-sink path in $\mathbb{G}_{ssdr}^{\delta,K}(v_2) - S_{ssdr}$.

Claim 4. *Define* row $\subseteq [K]$ *as the set of row indices where j is in* row *if and only if the jth row of $\mathbb{G}_{mix}^{\gamma,K}(v_2) - \text{neighbor}(v_2)$ has intersection with S_{ext}. Define a set*

$$S_{ssdr} := \{\langle 0, j \rangle_{ssdr}\}_{j \in \text{row}} \cup (S_{ext} \cap \mathbb{G}_{ssdr}^{\delta,K}(v_2)),$$

where $\langle 0, j \rangle_{ssdr}$ is the source node of $\mathbb{G}_{ssdr}^{\delta,K}(v_2)$ at row j. The graph $\mathbb{G}_{ssdr}^{\delta,K}(v_2) - S_{ssdr}$ has a source-to-sink path of $\mathbb{G}_{ssdr}^{\delta,K}(v_2)$ with length at least $\frac{\delta K^2}{2}$.

---

[27] A d-path is a path with d vertices.

Proof. The proof is deferred to full version. □

<u>PATHS CONNECTION:</u> Next, we show how to connect $\mathsf{copy}(v_1) - S_{\mathsf{ext}}$ to the starting node of the source-to-sink path. Here we exploit the structure of MIX graphs.

Claim 5. *Denote as u_1 an arbitrary node in the non-empty set[28] $\mathsf{copy}(v_1) - S_{\mathsf{ext}}$ and $P_{\mathsf{ssdr}}(v_2)$ the source-to-sink path obtained in Claim 4. The graph $\mathbb{G}_{\mathsf{mix}}^{\gamma,K}(v_2) - S_{\mathsf{ext}}$ has a path from u_1 to the starting node of $P_{\mathsf{ssdr}}(v_2)$.*

Proof. The proof is deferred to full version. □

Finally, using identical arguments, we can show that for every $i \in \{2, \dots, d-1\}$, there exists a path (with length at least $\frac{\delta K^2}{2}$) from the node $u_i \in \mathsf{copy}(v_i) - S_{\mathsf{ext}}$ to some node $u_{i+1} \in \mathsf{copy}(v_{i+1}) - S_{\mathsf{ext}}$. Hence we finish the proof of Lemma 8. □

From Lemma 8, we obtain Lemma 7. □

From Lemmas 6 and 7, we obtain Theorem 4. □

4.3 iMHFs from Wide-Block Labeling Functions

In this section, from a relatively *small* depth-robust graph, we construct a graph-based iMHF with *strong* memory hardness based on the wide-block labeling functions built in Sect. 4.1.

Theorem 5. *Fix $L = 2^\ell$, $W = 2^w$ and set $K := W/L$. Let $\mathcal{H}_{\delta,w}$ be the wide-block labeling functions built in Sect. 4.1. For any (first-predecessor-distinct[29]) (e,d)-depth-robust DAG $\mathbb{G} = (\mathbb{V}, \mathbb{E})$[30] with δ-indegree and $N = 2^n$ vertices, the graph-based iMHFs family $\mathcal{F}_{\mathbb{G}, \mathcal{H}_{\delta,w}}$ is $(\mathsf{C}_\mathcal{F}^\parallel, \Delta_\mathcal{F}, 2\delta N K^2)$-memory hard, where for sufficiently large $\epsilon \leq 1$, it holds that*

$$\mathsf{C}_\mathcal{F}^\parallel(\epsilon) \geq \Omega(\epsilon \cdot e \cdot d \cdot \delta \cdot K^2 \cdot W), \qquad \Delta_\mathcal{F}(\epsilon) \leq O\left(\frac{\mathsf{st}(\mathbb{G}, N)}{e \cdot d}\right).$$

The graph $\mathbb{G}$ in [3] is $(\Omega(N/\log N), \Omega(N))$-depth-robust and satisfies $\mathsf{st}(\mathbb{G}, N) = O(N^2/\log N)$, thus we obtain the following corollary.

Corollary 2. *Fix $L = 2^\ell$, $W = 2^w$ and set $K := W/L$. Let $\mathcal{H}_{2,w}$ be the labeling functions built in Sect. 4.1 and $\mathbb{G} = (\mathbb{V}, \mathbb{E})$ be the 2-indegree DAG in [3] (with $N = 2^n$ vertices). The graph labeling functions $\mathcal{F}_{\mathbb{G}, \mathcal{H}_{2,w}}$ is $(\mathsf{C}_\mathcal{F}^\parallel, \Delta_\mathcal{F}, O(N K^2))$-memory hard, where for sufficiently large $\epsilon \leq 1$, it holds that*

$$\mathsf{C}_\mathcal{F}^\parallel(\epsilon) \geq \Omega\left(\frac{\epsilon \cdot N^2 \cdot K^2 \cdot W}{\log N}\right), \qquad \Delta_\mathcal{F}(\epsilon) \leq O(1).$$

Proof (of Theorem 5). The proof is deferred to full version. □

---

[28] Note that $\mathsf{copy}(v_1) - S_{\mathsf{ext}}$ is non-empty because $|\mathsf{copy}(v_1) \cap S_{\mathsf{ext}}| \leq |\mathsf{nodes}(v_1) \cap S_{\mathsf{ext}}| < \frac{K}{4} < K = |\mathsf{copy}(v_1)|$. The first inequality holds as $\mathsf{copy}(v_1) \subseteq \mathsf{nodes}(v_1)$, the second inequality holds because $v_1 \notin S$.

[29] See Remark 3 for definition of first-predecessor-distinctness.

[30] $\mathbb{G}$ has single source/sink.

5   Instantiations and Open Problems

We defer instantiations and discussions of future work in full version.

Acknowledgments. The authors were partially supported by NSF grants CNS-1553758 (CAREER), CNS-1719146, CNS-1528178, and IIS-1528041, and by a Sloan Research Fellowship.

A   Compression Arguments

Lemma 9 ([16]). *Fix an algorithm* A, *let* $\mathcal{B}$ *be a sequence of random bits.* A *on input a hint* $h \in \mathcal{H}$ *adaptively queries specific bits of* $\mathcal{B}$ *and outputs* p *indices of* $\mathcal{B}$ *that were not queried before, along with guesses for each of the bits. The probability (over the choice of* $\mathcal{B}$ *and randomness of* A*) that there exists an* $h \in \mathcal{H}$ *where* A(h) *guesses all bits correctly is at most* $|\mathcal{H}|/2^p$.

Lemma 10. *Fix* $L \in \mathbb{N}$ *and an algorithm* A *that can make no more than* $\mathsf{q} = 2^{L-2}$ *oracle queries. Let* ic *be an ideal cipher uniformly chosen from the set* $\mathbb{IC}$ *with domain* $\mathcal{K} \times \{0,1\}^L$ *and image* $\{0,1\}^L$.[31] A *on input a hint* $h \in \mathcal{H}$ *adaptively makes forward/inverse queries to* ic, *and outputs* $p \leq 2^{L-2}$ *ideal primitive entries (as well as guesses for each of the entry values) that were not queried before. The probability (over the choice of* ic *and randomness of* A*) that there exists an* $h \in \mathcal{H}$ *where* A(h) *guesses all permutation entries correctly is at most* $|\mathcal{H}|/2^{p(L-1)}$.

Proof. The proof is deferred to full version.   □

References

1. Alwen, J., Blocki, J.: Efficiently computing data-independent memory-hard functions. In: Robshaw, M., Katz, J. (eds.) CRYPTO 2016, Part II. LNCS, vol. 9815, pp. 241–271. Springer, Heidelberg (2016). https://doi.org/10.1007/978-3-662-53008-5_9
2. Alwen, J., Blocki, J., Harsha, B.: Practical graphs for optimal side-channel resistant memory-hard functions. In: Thuraisingham, B.M., Evans, D., Malkin, T., Xu, D. (eds.), ACM CCS 17, pp. 1001–1017. ACM Press, October/November 2017
3. Alwen, J., Blocki, J., Pietrzak, K.: Depth-robust graphs and their cumulative memory complexity. In: Coron, J.-S., Nielsen, J.B. (eds.) EUROCRYPT 2017, Part III. LNCS, vol. 10212, pp. 3–32. Springer, Cham (2017). https://doi.org/10.1007/978-3-319-56617-7_1
4. Alwen, J., Blocki, J., Pietrzak, K.: Sustained space complexity. In: Nielsen, J.B., Rijmen, V. (eds.) EUROCRYPT 2018, Part II. LNCS, vol. 10821, pp. 99–130. Springer, Cham (2018). https://doi.org/10.1007/978-3-319-78375-8_4
5. Alwen, J., Chen, B., Kamath, C., Kolmogorov, V., Pietrzak, K., Tessaro, S.: On the complexity of scrypt and proofs of space in the parallel random oracle model. In: Fischlin, M., Coron, J.-S. (eds.) EUROCRYPT 2016, Part II. LNCS, vol. 9666, pp. 358–387. Springer, Heidelberg (2016). https://doi.org/10.1007/978-3-662-49896-5_13

---

[31] A random permutation can be viewed as an ideal cipher with a fixed key.

6. Alwen, J., Chen, B., Pietrzak, K., Reyzin, L., Tessaro, S.: Scrypt is maximally memory-hard. In: Coron, J.-S., Nielsen, J.B. (eds.) EUROCRYPT 2017, Part III. LNCS, vol. 10212, pp. 33–62. Springer, Cham (2017). https://doi.org/10.1007/978-3-319-56617-7_2

7. Alwen, J., Serbinenko, V.: High parallel complexity graphs and memory-hard functions. In: Servedio, R.A. Rubinfeld, R. (eds.), 47th ACM STOC, pp. 595–603. ACM Press, June 2015

8. Alwen, J., Tackmann, B.: Moderately hard functions: definition, instantiations, and applications. In: Kalai, Y., Reyzin, L. (eds.) TCC 2017, Part I. LNCS, vol. 10677, pp. 493–526. Springer, Cham (2017). https://doi.org/10.1007/978-3-319-70500-2_17

9. Bellare, M., Rogaway, P.: Random oracles are practical: a paradigm for designing efficient protocols. In: Ashby, V. (ed.), ACM CCS 93, pp. 62–73. ACM Press, November 1993

10. Biryukov, A., Dinu, D., Khovratovich, D.: Argon2 password hash. Version 1.3 (2016). https://www.cryptolux.org/images/0/0d/Argon2.pdf

11. Blocki, J., Harsha, B., Kang, S., Lee, S., Xing, L., Zhou, S.: Data-independent memory hard functions: new attacks and stronger constructions. Cryptology ePrint Archive, Report 2018/944 (2018). http://eprint.iacr.org/2018/944

12. Blocki, J., Zhou, S.: On the depth-robustness and cumulative pebbling cost of Argon2i. In: Kalai, Y., Reyzin, L. (eds.) TCC 2017, Part I. LNCS, vol. 10677, pp. 445–465. Springer, Cham (2017). https://doi.org/10.1007/978-3-319-70500-2_15

13. Boneh, D., Corrigan-Gibbs, H., Schechter, S.: Balloon hashing: a memory-hard function providing provable protection against sequential attacks. In: Cheon, J.H., Takagi, T. (eds.) ASIACRYPT 2016, Part I. LNCS, vol. 10031, pp. 220–248. Springer, Heidelberg (2016). https://doi.org/10.1007/978-3-662-53887-6_8

14. Dryja, T., Liu, Q.C., Park, S.: Static-memory-hard functions, and modeling the cost of space vs. time. In: Beimel, A., Dziembowski, S. (eds.) TCC 2018, Part I. LNCS, vol. 11239, pp. 33–66. Springer, Cham (2018). https://doi.org/10.1007/978-3-030-03807-6_2

15. Dwork, C., Naor, M., Wee, H.: Pebbling and proofs of work. In: Shoup, V. (ed.) CRYPTO 2005. LNCS, vol. 3621, pp. 37–54. Springer, Heidelberg (2005). https://doi.org/10.1007/11535218_3

16. Dziembowski, S., Kazana, T., Wichs, D.: One-time computable self-erasing functions. In: Ishai, Y. (ed.) TCC 2011. LNCS, vol. 6597, pp. 125–143. Springer, Heidelberg (2011). https://doi.org/10.1007/978-3-642-19571-6_9

17. Forler, C., Lucks, S., Wenzel, J.: Catena: a memory-consuming password scrambler. IACR Cryptology ePrint Archive 2013/525 (2013)

18. Maurer, U., Renner, R., Holenstein, C.: Indifferentiability, impossibility results on reductions, and applications to the random oracle methodology. In: Naor, M. (ed.) TCC 2004. LNCS, vol. 2951, pp. 21–39. Springer, Heidelberg (2004). https://doi.org/10.1007/978-3-540-24638-1_2

19. Percival, C.: Stronger key derivation via sequential memory-hard functions. In: BSDCan 2009 (2009)

20. Percival, C., Josefsson, S.: The scrypt password-based key derivation function (2012)

21. Ren, L., Devadas, S.: Bandwidth hard functions for ASIC resistance. In: Kalai, Y., Reyzin, L. (eds.) TCC 2017, Part I. LNCS, vol. 10677, pp. 466–492. Springer, Cham (2017). https://doi.org/10.1007/978-3-319-70500-2_16

22. Ristenpart, T., Shacham, H., Shrimpton, T.: Careful with composition: limitations of the indifferentiability framework. In: Paterson, K.G. (ed.) EUROCRYPT 2011. LNCS, vol. 6632, pp. 487–506. Springer, Heidelberg (2011). https://doi.org/10.1007/978-3-642-20465-4_27

Data-Independent Memory Hard Functions: New Attacks and Stronger Constructions

Jeremiah Blocki[1]($\boxtimes$), Ben Harsha[1], Siteng Kang[2],
Seunghoon Lee[1], Lu Xing[1], and Samson Zhou[3]

[1] Purdue University, West Lafayette, USA
jblocki@purdue.edu
[2] Penn State University, State College, USA
[3] Indiana University, Bloomington, USA

Abstract. Memory-hard functions (MHFs) are a key cryptographic primitive underlying the design of moderately expensive password hashing algorithms and egalitarian proofs of work. Over the past few years several increasingly stringent goals for an MHF have been proposed including the requirement that the MHF have high sequential space-time (ST) complexity, parallel space-time complexity, amortized area-time (aAT) complexity and sustained space complexity. Data-Independent Memory Hard Functions (iMHFs) are of special interest in the context of password hashing as they naturally resist side-channel attacks. iMHFs can be specified using a directed acyclic graph (DAG) G with $N = 2^n$ nodes and low indegree and the complexity of the iMHF can be analyzed using a pebbling game. Recently, Alwen et al. [ABH17] constructed a DAG called DRSample that has aAT complexity at least $\Omega(N^2/\log N)$. Asymptotically DRSample outperformed all prior iMHF constructions including Argon2i, winner of the password hashing competition (aAT cost $\mathcal{O}(N^{1.767})$), though the constants in these bounds are poorly understood. We show that the greedy pebbling strategy of Boneh et al. [BCS16] is particularly effective against DRSample e.g., the aAT cost is $\mathcal{O}(N^2/\log N)$. In fact, our empirical analysis *reverses* the prior conclusion of Alwen et al. that DRSample provides stronger resistance to known pebbling attacks for practical values of $N \leq 2^{24}$. We construct a new iMHF candidate (DRSample+BRG) by using the bit-reversal graph to extend DRSample. We then prove that the construction is asymptotically optimal under every MHF criteria, and we empirically demonstrate that our iMHF provides the best resistance to *known* pebbling attacks. For example, we show that any parallel pebbling attack either has aAT cost $\omega(N^2)$ or requires at least $\Omega(N)$ steps with $\Omega(N/\log N)$ pebbles on the DAG. This makes our construction the first practical iMHF with a strong sustained space-complexity guarantee and immediately implies that any parallel pebbling has aAT complexity $\Omega(N^2/\log N)$. We also prove that any sequential pebbling (including the greedy pebbling attack) has aAT cost $\Omega(N^2)$ and, if a plausible conjecture holds, any parallel pebbling has aAT cost $\Omega(N^2 \log \log N/\log N)$—the best possible bound for an iMHF. We implement our new iMHF and

© International Association for Cryptologic Research 2019
A. Boldyreva and D. Micciancio (Eds.): CRYPTO 2019, LNCS 11693, pp. 573–607, 2019.
https://doi.org/10.1007/978-3-030-26951-7_20

demonstrate that it is just as fast as Argon2. Along the way we propose a simple modification to the Argon2 round function that increases an attacker's aAT cost by nearly an order of magnitude without increasing running time on a CPU. Finally, we give a pebbling reduction that proves that in the parallel random oracle model (PROM) the cost of evaluating an iMHF like Argon2i or DRSample+BRG is given by the pebbling cost of the underlying DAG. Prior pebbling reductions assumed that the iMHF round function concatenates input labels before hashing and did not apply to practical iMHFs such as Argon2i, DRSample or DRSample+BRG where input labels are instead XORed together.

1   Introduction

Memory Hard Functions (MHFs) are a key cryptographic primitive in the design of password hashing, algorithms and egalitarian proof of work puzzles [Lee11]. In the context of password hashing we want to ensure that the function can be computed reasonably quickly on standard hardware, but that it is prohibitively expensive to evaluate the function millions or billions of times. The first property ensures that legitimate users can authenticate reasonably quickly, while the purpose of the latter goal is to protect low-entropy secrets (e.g., passwords, PINs, biometrics) against brute-force offline guessing attacks. One of the challenges is that the attacker might attempt to reduce computation costs by employing customized hardware such as a Field Programmable Gate Array (FPGA) or an Application Specific Integrated Circuit (ASIC). MHFs were of particular interest in the 2015 Password Hashing Competition [PHC16], where the winner, Argon2 [BDK16], and all but one finalists [FLW14,SAA+15,Pes14] claimed some form of memory hardness.

Wiener [Wie04] defined the full cost of an algorithm's execution to be the number of hardware components multiplied by the duration of their usage e.g., if the algorithm needs to allocate $\Omega(N)$ blocks of memory for $\Omega(N)$ time steps then full evaluation costs would scale quadratically. At an intuitive level, a strong MHF $f(\cdot)$ should have the property that the *full cost* [Wie04] of evaluation grows as fast as possible in the running time parameter N. Towards this end, a number of increasingly stringent security criteria have been proposed for a MHF including sequential space-time complexity, parallel space-time complexity, amortized area-time complexity (aAT) and sustained space-complexity. The sequential (resp. parallel) space-time complexity of a function $f(\cdot)$ measures the space-time cost of the best sequential (resp. parallel) algorithm evaluating $f(\cdot)$ i.e., if a computation runs in time t and requires space s then the space-time cost is given by the product st. The requirement that a hash function has high space-time complexity rules out traditional hash iteration based key-derivation functions like PBKDF2 and bcrypt as both of these functions be computed in linear time $\mathcal{O}(N)$ and constant space $\mathcal{O}(1)$. Blocki et al. [BHZ18] recently presented an economic argument that algorithms with low space-time complexity such as bcrypt and PBKDF2 are no longer suitable to protect low-entropy secrets like passwords i.e., one cannot provide meaningful protection against a rational attacker with customized hardware (FPGA, ASIC) without introducing an unacceptably long authentication delay. By contrast, they argued that MHFs with true cost $\Omega(N^2)$ can ensure that a rational attacker will quickly give up since marginal guessing costs are substantially higher.

The Catena-Bit Reversal MHF [FLW14] has provably optimal sequential space-time complexity $\Omega(N^2)$—the space-time complexity of any sequential algorithm running in time N is at most $\mathcal{O}(N^2)$ since at most N blocks of memory can be allocated in time N. However, Alwen and Serbinenko [AS15] showed that the *parallel space-time* complexity of this MHF is just $\mathcal{O}(N^{1.5})$. Even parallel space-time complexity has limitations in that it does not amortize nicely. The stronger notion of Amortized Area-Time (aAT) complexity (and the asymptotically equivalent notion of cumulative memory complexity (cmc)) measures the amortized cost of any parallel algorithm evaluating the function $f(\cdot)$ on m distinct inputs. Alwen and Serbinenko [AS15] gave a theoretical example of a function $f(\cdot)$ with the property that the amortized space-time cost of evaluating the function on $m = \sqrt{N}$ distinct inputs is approximately m times cheaper than the parallel space-time cost i.e., evaluating the function on the last $m - 1$ inputs is essentially free. This is problematic in the context of password hashing where the attacker wants to compute the function $f(\cdot)$ multiple times i.e., on each password in a cracking dictionary. The amortization issue is not merely theoretical. Indeed, the aAT complexity of many MHF candidates is significantly lower than $\mathcal{O}(N^2)$ e.g., the aAT complexity of Balloon Hash [BCS16] is just $\mathcal{O}(N^{5/3})$ [AB16, ABP17] and for password hashing competition winner Argon2i [BDK16] the aAT cost is at most $\mathcal{O}(N^{1.767})$ [AB16, AB17, ABP17, BZ17].

The scrypt MHF, introduced by Percival in 2009 [Per09], was proven to have cmc/aAT complexity $\Omega(N^2)$ in the random oracle model [ACP+17]. However, it is possible for an scrypt attacker to achieve any space-time trade-off subject to the constraint that $st = \Omega(N^2)$ without penalty e.g., an attacker could evaluate scrypt in time $t = \Omega(N^2)$ with space $s = \mathcal{O}(1)$. Alwen et al. [ABP18] argued that this flexibility potentially makes it easier to develop ASICs for scrypt, and proposed the even stricter MHF requirement of *sustained space complexity*, which demands that any (parallel) algorithm evaluating the function $f(\cdot)$ requires at least t time steps in which the space usage is $\geq s$—this implies that aAT $\geq st$. Alwen et al. [ABP18] provided a theoretical construction of a MHF with maximal sustained space complexity i.e., evaluation requires space $s = \Omega(N/\log N)$ for time $t = \Omega(N)$. However, there are no practical constructions of MHFs that provide strong guarantees with respect to sustained space complexity.

Data-Independent vs Data-Dependent Memory Hard Functions. Memory Hard Functions can be divided into two categories: Data-Independent Memory Hard Functions (iMHFs) and Data-Dependent Memory Hard Functions (dMHFs). Examples of dMHFs include scrypt [Per09], Argon2d [BDK16] and Boyen's halting puzzles [Boy07]. Examples of iMHFs include Password Hashing Competition (PHC) [PHC16] winner Argon2i [BDK16], Balloon Hashing [BCS16] and DRSample [ABH17]. In this work we primarily focus on the design and analysis of secure iMHFs. iMHFs are designed to resist certain side-channel attacks e.g., cache timing [Ber05] by requiring that the induced memory access pattern does not depend on the (sensitive) input e.g., the user's password. By contrast, the induced memory access for a dMHFs is allowed to depend on the function input.

Alwen and Blocki [AB16] proved that *any* iMHF has aAT complexity at most $\mathcal{O}(N^2 \log\log N/\log N)$, while the dMHF scrypt provably has aAT complexity $\Omega(N^2)$ in the random oracle model—a result which cannot be matched by any iMHF. However, the aAT complexity of a dMHF may be greatly reduced after a side-channel attack. If a brute-force attacker is trying to find $x \leq m$ s.t. $f(x) = y$ and the attacker also has learned the correct memory access pattern induced by the real input x^* (e.g., via a side-channel attack) then the attacker can quit evaluation $f(x)$ immediately once it is clear that the induced memory access pattern on input $x \neq x^*$ is different. For example, the aAT complexity of scrypt (resp. [Boy07]) after a side-channel attack is just $\mathcal{O}(N)$ (resp. $\mathcal{O}(1)$).

Hybrid Modes. Alwen and Blocki [AB16, AB17] showed that the aAT complexity of most iMHFs was significantly lower than one would hope, but their techniques do not extend to MHFs. In response, the Argon2 spec [KDBJ17] was updated to list Argon2id as the recommended mode of operation for password hashing instead of the purely data-independent mode Argon2i. Hybrid independent-dependent (id) modes, such as Argon2id [KDBJ17], balance side-channel resistance with high aAT complexity by running the MHF in data-independent mode for $N/2$ steps before switching to data-dependent mode for the final $N/2$ steps. If there is a side-channel attack then security reduces to that of the underlying iMHF (e.g., Argon2i), and if there is no side-channel attack then the function is expected to have optimal aAT complexity $\Omega(N^2)$. We remark that, even for a hybrid mode, it is important to ensure that the underlying iMHF is as strong as possible a side-channel attack on a hybrid "id" mode of operation will reduce security to that of the underlying iMHF.

1.1   Related Work

MHF Goals. Dwork et al. and Abadi et al. [DGN03, ABMW05] introduced the notion of a memory-bound function where we require that *any* evaluation algorithm results in a large number of cache-misses. Ren and Devadas recently introduced a refinement to this notion called bandwidth-hardness [RD17]. To the best of our knowledge Percival was the first to propose the goal that a MHF should have high space-time complexity [Per09] though Boyen's dMHF construction appears to achieve this goal [Boy07] and the notion of space-time complexity is closely related to the notion of "full cost" proposed by Wiener [Wie04]. Metrics like space-time complexity and Amortized Area-Time Complexity [AS15, ABH17] aim to capture the cost of the hardware (e.g., DRAM chips) the attacker must purchase to compute an MHF—amortized by the number of MHF instances computed over the lifetime of the hardware components.

By contrast, bandwidth hardness [RD17] aims to capture the *energy cost* of the electricity required to compute the MHF once. If the attacker uses an ASIC to compute the function then the *energy* expended during computation will typically be small in comparison with the energy expended during a cache-miss. Thus, a bandwidth hard function aims to ensure that *any* evaluation strategy either results in $\Omega(N)$ cache-misses or $\omega(N)$ evaluations of the hash function.

In the full version [BHK+18] we argue that, in the context of password hashing, aAT complexity is more relevant than bandwidth hardness because the "full cost" [Wie04] can scale quadratically in the running time parameter N. However, one would ideally want to design a MHF that has high aAT complexity and is also maximally bandwidth hard. Blocki et al. [BRZ18] recently showed that any MHF with high aAT complexity is at least somewhat bandwidth hard. Furthermore, all practical iMHFs (including Catena-Bit Reversal [FLW14], Argon2i and DRSample) are maximally bandwidth hard [RD17, BRZ18], including our new construction DRS+BRG.

Graph Pebbling and iMHFs. An iMHF $f_{G,H}$ can be viewed as a mode of operation over a directed acyclic graph (DAG) $G = (V = [N], E)$ that encodes data-dependencies (because the DAG is static the memory access pattern will be identical for all inputs) and a compression function $H(\cdot)$. Alwen and Serbinenko [AS15] defined $f_{G,H}(x) = \mathsf{lab}_{G,H,x}(N)$ to be the label of the last node in the graph G on input x. Here, the label of the first node $\mathsf{lab}_{G,H,x}(1) = H(1, x)$ is computed using the input x and for each internal node v with $\mathsf{parents}(v) = v_1, \ldots, v_\delta$ we have

$$\mathsf{lab}_{G,H,x}(v) = H(v, \mathsf{lab}_{G,H,x}(v_1), \ldots, \mathsf{lab}_{G,H,x}(v_\delta)).$$

In practice, one requires that the maximum indegree is constant $\delta = \mathcal{O}(1)$ so that the function $f_{G,H}$ can be evaluated in sequential time $\mathcal{O}(N)$. Alwen and Serbinenko [AS15] proved that the cmc complexity (asymptotically equivalent to aAT complexity) of the function $f_{G,H}$ can be fully described in terms of the black pebbling game—defined later in Sect. 2.2. The result is significant in that it reduces the complex task of building an iMHF with high aAT complexity to the (potentially easier) task of constructing a DAG with maximum pebbling cost. In particular, Alwen and Serbinenko showed that any algorithm evaluating the function $f_{G,H}$ in the parallel random oracle model *must* have cumulative memory cost at least $\Omega\left(w \times \Pi_{cc}^{\parallel}(G)\right)$, where $\Pi_{cc}^{\parallel}(G)$ is the cumulative pebbling cost of G (defined in Sect. 2.2), $H : \{0, 1\}^* \to \{0, 1\}^w$ is modeled as a random oracle and $w = |H(z)|$ is the number of output bits in a single hash value. Similar, pebbling reductions have been given for bandwidth hardness [BRZ18] and sustained space complexity [ABP18] using the same labeling rule.

While these pebbling reductions are useful in theory, *practical* iMHF implementations do not use the labeling rule proposed in [AS15]. In particular, Argon2i, DRSample and our own iMHF implementation (DRSample+BRG) all use the following labeling rule

$$\mathsf{lab}_{G,H,x}(v) = H(\mathsf{lab}_{G,H,x}(v_1) \oplus \ldots \oplus \mathsf{lab}_{G,H,x}(v_\delta)),$$

where $v_1, \ldots, v_\delta = \mathsf{parents}(v)$ and the DAGs have indegree $\delta = 2$. The XOR labeling rule allows one to work with a faster round function $H : \{0,1\}^w \to \{0,1\}^w$ e.g., Argon2i builds $H : \{0,1\}^{8192} \to \{0,1\}^{8192}$ using the Blake2b permutation function and DRSample(+BRG) uses the same labeling rule as Argon2i. When we define $f_{G,H}$ using the above, the pebbling reduction of [AS15] no longer applies. Thus, while we know that the pebbling cost of DRSample (resp. Argon2i) is $\Omega(N^2/\log N)$ [ABH17] (resp. $\tilde{\Omega}(N^{1.75})$ [BZ17]), technically it had never been proven that DRSample (resp. Argon2i) has aAT complexity $\Omega(wN^2/\log N)$ (resp. $\tilde{\Omega}(wN^{1.75})$) in the parallel random oracle model.

Argon2i and DRSample. Arguably, two of the most significant iMHFs candidates are Argon2i [BDK16] and DRSample [ABH17]. Argon2i was the winner of the recently completed password hashing competition [PHC16] and DRSample [ABH17] was the first *practical* construction of an iMHF with aAT complexity proven to be *at least* $\Omega(N^2/\log N)$ in the random oracle model. In an asymptotic sense this upper bound almost matches the general upper bound $\mathcal{O}(N^2 \log\log N/\log N)$ on the aAT cost of any iMHF established by Alwen and Blocki [AB16]. A recent line of research [AB16, AB17, ABP17, BZ17] has developed theoretical depth-reducing attacks on Argon2i showing that the iMHF has aAT complexity *at most* $\mathcal{O}(N^{1.767})$[1]. The DRSample [ABH17] iMHF modifies the edge distribution of the Argon2i graph to ensure that the underlying directed acyclic graph (DAG) satisfies a combinatorial property called depth-robustness, which is known to be *necessary* [AB16] and *sufficient* [ABP17] for developing an MHF with high aAT complexity.

While the aAT complexity of DRSample is at least $c_1 N^2/\log N$ for some constant c_1, the *constant c* in this lower bound is poorly understood—Alwen et al. [ABH17] only proved the lower bound when $c_1 \approx 7 \times 10^{-6}$. Similarly, Argon2i has aAT complexity at least $c_2 N^{1.75}/\log N$ [BZ17] though the constants from this lower bound are also poorly understood[2]. On the negative side the asymptotic lower bounds do not *absolutely* rule out the possibility of an attack that reduces aAT complexity by several orders of magnitude. Alwen et al. [ABH17] also presented an empirical analysis of the aAT cost of DRSample and Argon2i by measuring the aAT cost of these functions against a wide battery of pebbling attacks [AB16, ABP17, ABH17]. The results of this empirical analysis were quite positive for DRSample and indicated that DRSample was not only stronger in an asymptotic sense, but that it also provided greater resistance to other pebbling attacks than other iMHF candidates like Argon2i in practice.

Boneh et al. [BCS16] previously presented a greedy pebbling attack that reduced the pebbling cost of Argon2i by a moderate constant factor of 4 to 5. The greedy pebbling attack does not appear to have been included in the empirical analysis of Alwen et al. [ABH17]. In a strict asymptotic sense the depth-reducing

---

[1] This latest attack almost matches the *lower bound* of $\tilde{\Omega}\left(N^{1.75}\right)$ on the aAT complexity of Argon2i.

[2] Blocki and Zhou did not explicitly work out the constants in their lower bound, but it appears that $c_2 \approx 5 \times 10^{-7}$ [ABH17].

attacks of Alwen and Blocki [AB16, AB17] achieved more substantial $\Omega(N^{0.2+})$-factor reductions in pebbling cost, which may help to explain the omission of the greedy algorithm in [ABH17]. Nevertheless, it is worth noting that the greedy pebbling strategy is a simple sequential pebbling strategy that would be easy to implement in practice. By contrast, there has been debate about the *practical feasibility* of implementing the more complicated pebbling attacks of Alwen and Blocki [AB16] (Alwen and Blocki [AB17] argued that the attacks do not require unrealistic parallelism or memory bandwidth, but to the best of our knowledge the attacks have yet to be implemented on an ASIC).

1.2   Contributions

Stronger Attacks. We present a theoretical and empirical analysis of the greedy pebbling attack [BCS16] finding that DRSample has aAT complexity at most $\lesssim N^2/\log N$. The greedy pebbling attack that achieves this bound is *sequential*, easy to implement and achieves high attack quality even for practical values of N. In fact, for *practical* values of $N \leq 2^{24}$ we show that DRSample is *more* vulnerable to *known pebbling attacks* than Argon2i, which *reverses* previous conclusions about the *practical* security of Argon2i and DRSample [ABH17]. We next consider a defense proposed by Biryukov et al. [BDK16] against the greedy pebbling attack, which we call the XOR-extension gadget. While this defense defeats the *original* greedy pebbling attack [BCS16], we found a simple generalization of the greedy pebbling attack that thwarts this defense. We also use the greedy pebbling attack to prove that *any* DAG with indegree two has a sequential pebbling with aAT cost $\lesssim \frac{N^2}{4}$.

We also develop a *novel* greedy algorithm for constructing depth-reducing sets, which is the critical first step in the parallel pebbling attacks of Alwen and Blocki [AB16, AB17]. Empirical analysis demonstrates that this greedy algorithm constructs *significantly smaller* depth-reducing sets than previous state of the art techniques [AB16, AB17, ABH17], which leads to higher quality attacks [AB16] and leaving us in an uncomfortable situation where there high quality pebbling attacks against all iMHF candidates e.g., DRSample is susceptible to the greedy pebbling attack while Argon2i is susceptible to depth-reducing attacks [AB16, AB17, ABH17].

New iMHF Candidate with Optimal Security. We next develop a new iMHF candidate DRSample+BRG by overlaying a bit-reversal graph [LT82, FLW14] on top of DRSample, and analyze the new DAG empirically and theoretically. Interestingly, while *neither* DAG (DRSample or BRG) is known to have strong sustained space complexity guarantees, we can prove that *any* parallel pebbling either has maximal sustained space complexity (meaning that there are at least $\Omega(N)$ steps with $\Omega(N/\log N)$ pebbles on the DAG) or has aAT cost at least $\omega(N^2)$. This makes our construction the first practical construction with strong guarantees on the sustained space-complexity—prior constructions of Alwen et al. [ABP18] were theoretical. DRSample+BRG is asymptotically optimal with respect to all proposed MHF metrics including bandwidth hardness (*both* BRG and DRSample are bandwidth hard [RD17,BRZ18]) and aAT complexity (inherited from DRSample [ABH17]). We also show that our construction optimally resists the greedy attack and *any* extensions. In particular, we prove sequential pebbling of the bit-reversal graph has cumulative memory cost (cmc) and aAT cost at least $\Omega(N^2)$. This result generalizes a well-known result that the bit-reversal graph has sequential space-time cost $\Omega(N^2)$ and may be of independent interest e.g., it demonstrates that Password Hashing Competition Finalist Catena-BRG [FLW14] is secure against *all* sequential attacks.

Our empirical analysis indicates that DRSample+BRG offers strong resistance to *all known* attacks, including the greedy pebbling attack, depth-reducing attacks and several other novel attacks introduced in this paper. In particular, even for very large $N = 2^{24}$ (2^{24} 1 KB blocks = 16 GB) the *best* attack had aAT cost over $\frac{N^2}{11}$—for comparison *any* DAG with indegree two has aAT cost $\lesssim \frac{N^2}{4}$.

We also show that the aAT/cmc of DRSample+BRG is *at least* $\Omega(N^2 \log \log N / \log N)$ under a plausible conjecture about the depth-robustness of DRSample. As evidence for our conjecture we analyze three state-of-the-art approaches for constructing a depth-reducing set, including the layered attack [AB16], Valiant's Lemma [AB16, Val77] and the reduction of Alwen et al. [ABP17], which can transform any pebbling with low aAT cost (e.g., the Greedy Pebbling Attack) into a depth-reducing set. We show that each attack fails to refute our conjecture. Thus, even if the conjecture is false we would require significant improvements to state-of-the art to refute it.

Black Pebbling Reduction for XOR Labeling Rule. While Alwen and Serbinenko showed that any algorithm evaluating the graph labeling function $f_{G,H}$ in the parallel random oracle model *must* have cumulative memory cost at least $\Omega\left(w \times \Pi_{cc}^{\|}(G)\right)$, their proof made the restrictive assumption that labels are computed using the concatenation rule $\mathsf{lab}_{G,H,x}(v) = H(v, \mathsf{lab}_{G,H,x}(v_1), \ldots, \mathsf{lab}_{G,H,x}(v_\delta))$. However, most *practical* iMHF implementations (e.g., Argon2i and DRSample(+BRG)) all follow the more efficient XOR labeling rule $\mathsf{lab}_{G,H,x}(v) = H(\mathsf{lab}_{G,H,x}(v_1) \oplus \ldots \oplus \mathsf{lab}_{G,H,x}(v_\delta))$ where $v_1, \ldots, v_\delta = \mathsf{parents}(v)$ and the DAGs have indegree $\delta = \mathcal{O}(1)$. The XOR labeling rule allows one to work with a faster round function $H : \{0,1\}^w \to \{0,1\}^w$, e.g., Argon2i builds $H : \{0,1\}^{8192} \to \{0,1\}^{8192}$, to speed up computation so that we fill more memory.

We extend the results of Alwen and Serbinenko to show that, for suitable DAGs, $f_{G,H}$ has cumulative memory cost at least $\Omega\left(w \times \Pi_{cc}^{\|}(G)/\delta\right)$ when using the XOR labeling rule. The loss of δ is necessary as the pebbling complexity of the complete DAG K_N is $\Pi_{cc}^{\|}(K_n) = \Omega(N^2)$, but $f_{K_N,H}$ has cmc/aAT cost at most $\mathcal{O}(N)$ when defined using the XOR labeling rule. In practice, all of the graphs we consider have $\delta = \mathcal{O}(1)$ so this loss is not significant.

One challenge we face in the reduction is that it is more difficult to extract labels from the random oracle query $\mathsf{lab}_{G,H,x}(v_1) \oplus \ldots \oplus \mathsf{lab}_{G,H,x}(v_\delta)$ than from the query $\mathsf{lab}_{G,H,x}(v_1), \ldots, \mathsf{lab}_{G,H,x}(v_\delta)$. Another challenge we face is that the labeling function $H'(x,y) = H(x \oplus y)$ is not even collision resistant e.g., $H'(y,x) = H'(x,y)$. In fact, one can exploit this property to find graphs G on N nodes where the function $f_{G,H}$ is a constant function: Suppose we start with a DAG $G' = (V' = [N - 3], E')$ on $N - 3$ nodes that has high pebbling cost $\Pi_{cc}^{\parallel}(G')$ and define $G = (V = [N], E = E' \cup \{(N - 3, N - 2), (N - 3, N - 1), (N - 4, N - 2), (N - 4, N - 1), (N - 2, N), (N - 1, N)\})$ by adding directed edges from node $N - 3$ and $N - 4$ to nodes $N - 2, N - 1$ and then adding directed edges from $N - 2$ and $N - 1$ to node N. Note that for any input x we have $\mathsf{lab}_{G,H,x}(N - 2) = H(\mathsf{lab}_{G,H,x}(N - 3) \oplus \mathsf{lab}_{G,H,x}(N - 3)) = \mathsf{lab}_{G,H,x}(N - 1)$. It follows that

$$f_{G,H}(x) = \mathsf{lab}_{G,H,x}(N) = H(\mathsf{lab}_{G,H,x}(N - 2) \oplus \mathsf{lab}_{G,H,x}(N - 1)) = H(0^w)$$

is a constant function. Thus, the claim that $f_{G,H}$ has cumulative memory cost at least $\Omega\left(w \times \Pi_{cc}^{\parallel}(G)/\delta\right)$ cannot hold for arbitrary graphs.

The above example exploited the absence of the explicit term v in $\mathsf{lab}_{G,H,x}(v)$ to produce two nodes that always have the same label. However, we can prove that if the DAG $G = (V = [N], E)$ contains all edges of the form $(i, i + 1)$ for $i < N$ then *any* algorithm evaluating the function $f_{G,H}$ in the parallel random oracle model *must* have cumulative memory cost at least $\Omega\left(w \times \Pi_{cc}^{\parallel}(G)/\delta\right)$. Furthermore, the cumulative memory cost of an algorithm computing $f_{G,H}$ on m distinct inputs must be at least $\Omega\left(mw \times \Pi_{cc}^{\parallel}(G)\right)$. We stress that all of the practical iMHFs we consider, including Argon2i and DRSample(+BRG), satisfy this condition.

Sequential Round Function. We show how a parallel attacker could reduce aAT costs by nearly an order of magnitude by computation of the Argon2i round function in parallel. For example, the first step to evaluate the Argon2 round function $H(X, Y)$ is to divide the input $R = X \oplus Y \in \{0,1\}^{8192}$ into 64 groups of 16-byte values $R_0, \ldots, R_{63} \in \{0,1\}^{128}$ and then compute $(Q_0, Q_1, \ldots, Q_7) \leftarrow \mathcal{BP}(R_0, \ldots, R_7), \ldots, (Q_{56}, Q_{56}, \ldots, Q_{63}) \leftarrow \mathcal{BP}(R_{56}, \ldots, R_{63})$. Each call to the Blake2b permutation $\mathcal{BP}$ can be trivially evaluated in parallel, which means that the attacker can easily reduce the depth of the circuit evaluating Argon2 by a factor of 8 *without* increasing the area of the circuit i.e., memory usage remains constant. The issue affects *all* Argon2 modes of operation (including data-dependent modes like Argon2d and Argon2id) and could potentially be used in combination with other pebbling attacks [AB16, AB17] for an even more dramatic decrease in aAT complexity. We also stress that this gain is independent of any other optimizations that an ASIC attacker might make to speed up computation of $\mathcal{BP}$ e.g., if the attacker can evaluate $\mathcal{BP}$ four-times faster than the honest party then the attacker will be able to evaluate the round function H $8 \times 4 = 32$-times faster than the honest party. We propose a simple modification to the Argon2 round function by injecting a few additional data-dependencies to ensure that evaluation is inherently sequential. While the modification is simple we show it increases a parallel attacker's aAT costs by nearly an order of magnitude. Furthermore, empirical analysis indicates that our modifications have *negligible* impact on the running time on a CPU.

Implementation of Our iMHF. We develop an implementation of our new iMHF candidate DRSample+BRG, which also uses the improved sequential Argon2 round function. The source code is available on Github at https://github.com/antiparallel-drsbrg-argon/Antiparallel-DRS-BRG. Empirical tests indicate that the running time of DRSample+BRG is equivalent to that of Argon2 for the honest party, while our prior analysis indicates the aAT costs, energy costs and sustained space complexity are all higher for DRSample+BRG.

2   Preliminaries

In this section we will lay out notation and important definitions required for the following sections.

2.1   Graph Notation and Definitions

We use $G = (V, E)$ to denote a directed acyclic graph and we use $N = 2^n$ to denote the number of nodes in $V = \{1, \ldots, N\}$. Given a node $v \in V$, we use $\mathsf{parents}(v) = \{u : (u, v) \in E\}$ to denote the *immediate parents* of node v in G. In general, we use $\mathsf{ancestors}_G(v) = \bigcup_{i \geq 1} \mathsf{parents}_G^i(v)$ to denote the set of all ancestors of v—here, $\mathsf{parents}_G^2(v) = \mathsf{parents}_G(\mathsf{parents}_G(v))$ denotes the grandparents of v and $\mathsf{parents}_G^{i+1}(v) = \mathsf{parents}_G(\mathsf{parents}_G^i(v))$. When G is clear from context we will simply write $\mathsf{parents}$ ($\mathsf{ancestors}$). We use $\mathsf{indeg}(G) = \max_v |\mathsf{parents}(v)|$ to denote the maximum indegree of any node in G. All of the practical graphs we consider will contain each of the edges $(i, i+1)$ for $i < N$. Thus, there is a single source node 1 and a single sink node N. Most of the graphs we consider will have $\mathsf{indeg}(G) = 2$ and in this case we will use $r(i) < i$ to denote the *other* parent of node i besides $i - 1$. Given a subset of nodes $S \subseteq V$ we use $G - S$ to refer to the graph with all nodes in S deleted and we use $G[S] = G - (V \setminus S)$ to refer to the graph obtained by deleting all nodes except S. Finally, we use $G_{\leq k} = G[\{1, \ldots, k\}]$ to refer to the graph induced by the first k nodes.

Block Depth-Robustness: Block depth-robustness is a stronger variant of depth-robustness. First, we define $N(v, b) = \{v - b + 1, v - b + 2, \ldots, v\}$ to be the set of b contiguous nodes ending at node v. For a set of vertices $S \subseteq V$, we also define $N(S, b) = \bigcup_{v \in S} N(v, b)$. We say that a graph is (e, d, b) block depth-robust if, for every set $S \subseteq V$ of size $|S| \leq e$, $\mathsf{depth}(G - N(S, b)) \geq d$. When $b = 1$ we simply say that the graph is (e, d) depth-robust. It is known that highly depth-robust DAGs G have high pebbling complexity, and can be used to construct strong iMHFs with high aAT complexity in the random oracle model [ABP17].

In certain cases, block depth-robustness can be used to establish even *stronger* lower bounds on the pebbling complexity of a graph [ABH17, BZ17]. Alwen et al. gave an algorithm DRSample that (whp) outputs a DAG G that is (e, d, b) block depth-robust with $e = \Omega(N/\log N)$, $d = \Omega(N)$ and $b = \Omega(\log N)$ [ABH17].

Graph Labeling Functions. As mentioned in the introduction, an iMHF $f_{G,H}$ can be described as a mode of operation over a directed acyclic graph using a round function H. Intuitively, the graph represents data dependencies between the memory blocks that are generated as computation progresses and each vertex represents a value being computed based on some dependencies. The function $f_{G,H}(x)$ can typically be defined as a labeling function i.e., given a set of vertices $V = [N] = \{1, 2, 3, \ldots, N\}$, a compression function $H = \{0,1\}^* \to \{0,1\}^m$ (often modeled as a Random Oracle in security analysis), and an input x, we "label" the nodes in V as follows. All source vertices (those with no parents) are labeled as $\ell_v(x) = H(v, x)$ and all other nodes with parents $v_1, v_2, \ldots, v_\delta$ are labeled $\ell_v(x) = F_{v,H}(\ell_{v_1}(x), \ell_{v_2}(x), \ldots, \ell_{v_\delta}(x))$ for a function $F_{v,H}(\cdot)$ that depends on $H(\cdot)$. The output $f_{G,H}(x)$ is then defined to be the label(s) of the sink node(s) in G.

In theoretical constructions (e.g., [AS15]) we often have $F_{v,H}(\ell_{v_1}(x), \ell_{v_2}(x), \ldots, \ell_{v_\delta}(x)) = H(v, \ell_{v_1}(x), \ell_{v_2}(x), \ldots, \ell_{v_\delta}(x))$ while in most real world constructions (e.g., Argon2i [BDK16]) we have $F_{v,H}(\ell_{v_1}(x), \ell_{v_2}(x), \ldots, \ell_{v_\delta}(x)) = H(\ell_{v_1}(x) \oplus \ell_{v_2}(x) \ldots \oplus \ell_{v_\delta}(x))$. To ensure that the function $f_{G,H}$ can be computed in $\mathcal{O}(N)$ steps, we require that G is an N-node DAG with constant indegree δ.

2.2 iMHFs and the Parallel Black Pebbling Game

Alwen and Serbinenko [AS15] and Alwen and Tackmann [AT17] provided reductions proving that in the parallel random oracle model (PROM) the amortized area time complexity of the function $f_{G,H}$ is completely captured by the (parallel) black pebbling game on the DAG G when we instantiate the round function as $F_{v,H}(\ell_{v_1}(x), \ell_{v_2}(x), \ldots, \ell_{v_\delta}(x)) = H(v, \ell_{v_1}(x), \ell_{v_2}(x), \ldots, \ell_{v_\delta}(x))$. However, *practical constructions* such as Argon2i use a different round function $F^{\oplus}_{v,H}(\ell_{v_1}(x), \ell_{v_2}(x), \ldots, \ell_{v_\delta}(x)) = H\left(\bigoplus_{j=1}^{\delta} \ell_{v_j}(x)\right)$. In Sect. 6 we extend prior pebbling reductions to handle the round function $F^{\oplus}_{v,H}$, which justifies the use of pebbling games to analyze *practical constructions* of iMHFs such as Argon2i or DRSample.

Intuitively, placing a pebble on a node represents computing the corresponding memory block and storing it in memory. The rules of the black pebbling game state that we cannot place a pebble on a node v until we have pebbles on the parents of node v i.e., we cannot compute a new memory block until we have access to all of the memory blocks on which the computation depends. More formally, in the black pebbling game on a directed graph $G = (V, E)$, we place pebbles on certain vertices of G over a series of t rounds. A valid pebbling P is a sequence $P_0, P_1, \ldots, P_t$ of sets of vertices satisfying the following properties: (1) $P_0 = \emptyset$, (2) $\forall v \in P_i \setminus P_{i-1}$ we have parents$(v) \subseteq P_{i-1}$, and (3) $\forall v \in V, \exists i$ s.t. $v \in P_i$.

Intuitively, P_i denotes the *subset* of data-labels stored in memory at time i and $P_i \setminus P_{i-1}$ denotes the new data-labels that are computed during round i— the second constraint states that we can only compute these new data-labels if all of the necessary dependent data values were already in memory. The final constraint says that we must eventually pebble all nodes (otherwise we would never compute the output labels for $f_{G,H}$). We say that a pebbling is *sequential* if $\forall i > 0$ we have $|P_i \setminus P_{i-1}| \leq 1$ i.e., in every round at most *one* new pebble is placed on the graph. We use $\mathcal{P}^{\|}(G)$ (resp. $\mathcal{P}(G)$) to denote the set of all valid parallel (resp. sequential) black pebblings of the DAG G. We define the space-time cost of a pebbling $P = (P_1, \ldots, P_t) \in \mathcal{P}_G^{\|}$ to be $\mathsf{st}(P) = t \times \max_{1 \leq i \leq t} |P_i|$ and the sequential space-time pebbling cost, denoted $\Pi_{st}(G) = \min_{P \in \mathcal{P}_G} \mathsf{st}(P)$, to be the space-time cost of the best legal pebbling of G.

There are many other pebbling games one can define on a DAG including the red-blue pebbling game [JWK81] and the black-white pebbling game [Len81]. Red-blue pebbling games can be used to analyze the bandwidth-hardness of an iMHF [RD17, BRZ18]. In this work, we primarily focus on the (parallel) black pebbling game to analyze the amortized Area-Time complexity and the sustained space complexity of a memory-hard function.

Definition 1 (Time/Space/Cumulative Pebbling Complexity). *The time, space, space-time and cumulative complexity of a pebbling* $P = \{P_0, \ldots, P_t\}$ $\in \mathcal{P}_G^{\|}$ *are defined to be:*

$$\Pi_t(P) = t \qquad \Pi_s(P) = \max_{i \in [t]} |P_i| \qquad \Pi_{st}(P) = \Pi_t(P) \cdot \Pi_s(P) \qquad \Pi_{cc}(P) = \sum_{i \in [t]} |P_i|.$$

For $\alpha \in \{s, t, st, cc\}$ *the sequential and parallel pebbling complexities of G are defined as*

$$\Pi_\alpha(G) = \min_{P \in \mathcal{P}_G} \Pi_\alpha(P) \qquad and \qquad \Pi_\alpha^{\|}(G) = \min_{P \in \mathcal{P}_G^{\|}} \Pi_\alpha(P).$$

It follows from the definition that for $\alpha \in \{s, t, st, cc\}$ and any G, the parallel pebbling complexity is always at most as high as the sequential, i.e., $\Pi_\alpha(G) \geq \Pi_\alpha^{\|}(G)$, and cumulative complexity is at most as high as space-time complexity, i.e., $\Pi_{st}(G) \geq \Pi_{cc}(G)$ and $\Pi_{st}^{\|}(G) \geq \Pi_{cc}^{\|}(G)$. Thus, we have $\Pi_{st}(G) \geq \Pi_{cc}(G) \geq \Pi_{cc}^{\|}(G)$ and $\Pi_{st}(G) \geq \Pi_{st}^{\|}(G) \geq \Pi_{cc}^{\|}(G)$. However, the relationship between $\Pi_{st}^{\|}(G)$ and $\Pi_{cc}(G)$ is less clear. It is easy to provide examples of graphs for which $\Pi_{cc}(G) \ll \Pi_{st}^{\|}(G)$ [3]. Alwen and Serbinenko showed that for the

---

[3] One such graph G would be to start with the pyramid graph $\triangle_k$, which has $\mathcal{O}(k^2)$ nodes, a single sink node t and append a path W of length k^3 starting at this sink node t. The pyramid graph requires $\Pi_s^{\|}(\triangle_k) = \Theta(k)$ space to pebble and has $\Pi_{cc}(\triangle_k) \leq \Pi_{st}(\triangle_k) \leq k^3$. Similarly, the path W requires at least $\Pi_t^{\|}(W) = \Pi_t(W)$ $= k^3$ steps to pebble the path (even in parallel). Thus, $\Pi_{st}^{\|}(G) \geq k^4$. By contrast, we have $\Pi_{cc}(G) \leq \Pi_{cc}(\triangle_k) + k^3 \leq k^3 + k^3 \ll k^4$ since we can place a pebble on node t with cost $\Pi_{cc}(\triangle_k)$, discard all other pebbles from the graph, and then walk this pebble across the path.

bit-reversal graph $G = \mathsf{BRG}_n$ with $\mathcal{O}(N = 2^n)$ nodes we have $\Pi_{st}^{\|}(G) = \mathcal{O}(n\sqrt{n})$. In Sect. 4.2 we show that $\Pi_{cc}(G) = \Omega(N^2)$. Thus, for some DAGs we have $\Pi_{cc}(G) \gg \Pi_{st}^{\|}(G)$.

Definition 2 (Sustained Space Complexity [ABP18]). *For $s \in \mathbb{N}$ the s-sustained-space (s-ss) complexity of a pebbling $P = \{P_0, \ldots, P_t\} \in \mathcal{P}_G^{\|}$ is: $\Pi_{ss}(P, s) = |\{i \in [t] : |P_i| \geq s\}|$. More generally, the sequential and parallel s-sustained space complexities of G are defined as*

$$\Pi_{ss}(G, s) = \min_{P \in \mathcal{P}_G} \Pi_{ss}(P, s) \quad and \quad \Pi_{ss}^{\|}(G, s) = \min_{P \in \mathcal{P}_G^{\|}} \Pi_{ss}(P, s) \ .$$

We remark that for any s we have $\Pi_{cc}(G) \geq \Pi_{ss}(G, s) \times s$ and $\Pi_{cc}^{\|}(G) \geq \Pi_{ss}^{\|}(G, s) \times s$.

2.3   Amortized Area-Time Cost (aAT)

Amortized Area-Time (aAT) cost is a way of viewing the cost to compute an iMHF, and it is closely related to the cost of pebbling a graph. Essentially, aAT cost represents the cost to keep pebbles in memory and adds in a factor representing the cost to compute the pebble. Here we require an additional factor, the core-memory ratio R, a multiplicative factor representing the ratio between computation cost vs memory cost. In this paper we are mainly focused on analysis of Argon2, which has previous calculations showing $R = 3000$ [BK15]. It can be assumed that this value is being used for R unless otherwise specified. The formal definition of the aAT complexity of a pebbling $P = (P_0, \ldots, P_T)$ of the graph G is as follows:

$$\mathsf{aAT}_R(P) = \sum_{i=1}^{T} |P_i| + R \sum_{i=1}^{T} |P_i \setminus P_{i-1}|$$

The (sequential) aAT complexity of a graph G is defined to be the aAT complexity of the optimal (sequential) pebbling strategy. Formally,

$$\mathsf{aAT}_R(G) = \min_{P \in \mathcal{P}(G)} \mathsf{aAT}_R(G), \quad and \quad \mathsf{aAT}^{\|}_R(G) = \min_{P \in \mathcal{P}^{\|}(G)} \mathsf{aAT}_R(P).$$

One of the nice properties of $\mathsf{aAT}^{\|}$ and $\Pi_{cc}^{\|}$ complexity is that both cost metrics amortize nicely i.e., if G^m consists of m independent copies of the DAG G then $\mathsf{aAT}^{\|}_R(G^m) = m \times \mathsf{aAT}^{\|}_R(G)$. We remark that $\mathsf{aAT}^{\|}_R(G) \geq \Pi_{cc}^{\|}(G)$, but that in most cases we will have $\mathsf{aAT}^{\|}_R(G) \approx \Pi_{cc}^{\|}(G)$ since the number of queries to the random oracle is typically $o\left(\Pi_{cc}^{\|}(G)\right)$. We will work with $\Pi_{cc}^{\|}(G)$ when conducting theoretical analysis and we will use $\mathsf{aAT}^{\|}_R(G)$ when conducting empirical experiments, as the constant factor R is important in practice. This also makes it easier to compare our empirical results with prior work [AB17, ABH17].

2.4   Attack Quality

In many cases we will care about how efficient certain pebbling strategies are compared to others. When we work with an iMHF, we have a naïve sequential algorithm $\mathcal{N}$ for evaluation e.g., the algorithm described in the Argon2 specifications [BDK16]. Typically, the naïve algorithm $\mathcal{N}$ is relatively expensive e.g., $\mathsf{aAT}_R(\mathcal{N}) = N^2/2 + RN$. We say that an attacker $\mathcal{A}$ is *successful* at reducing evaluation costs if $\mathsf{aAT}_R(\mathcal{A}) < \mathsf{aAT}_R(\mathcal{N})$. Following [AB16] we define the quality of the attack as

$$\text{AT-quality}(\mathcal{A}) = \frac{\mathsf{aAT}_R(\mathcal{N})}{\mathsf{aAT}_R(\mathcal{A})},$$

which describes how much more efficiently $\mathcal{A}$ evaluates the function compared to $\mathcal{N}$.

3   Analysis of the Greedy Pebbling Algorithm

In this section we present a theoretical and empirical analysis of the greedy pebbling attack [BCS16] that *reverses* previous conclusions about the *practical* security of Argon2i vs DRSample [ABH17]. We prove two main results using the greedy algorithm. First, we show that for any N node DAG G with indegree 2 and a unique topological ordering, we have $\mathsf{aAT}_R(G) \leq \frac{N^2 + 2N}{4} + RN$—see Theorem 1. Second, we prove that for any constant $\eta > 0$ and a random DRSample DAG G on N nodes, we have $\Pi_{st}(G) \leq (1 + \eta)2N^2/\log N$ with high probability—see Theorem 2. We stress that in both cases the bounds are *explicit* not *asymptotic*, and that the pebbling attacks are simple and sequential.

Alwen and Blocki [AB16] previously had shown that any DAG G with constant indegree has $\mathsf{aAT}^{\parallel}_R(G) \in \mathcal{O}(N^2 \log \log N/\log N)$, but the constants from this bound were not well understood and did not rule out the existence of an N node DAG G with $\mathsf{aAT}^{\parallel}_R(G) \geq N^2/2 + RN$ for *practical* values of N e.g., unless we use more than 16 GB of RAM we have $N \leq 2^{24}$ for Argon2i or DRSample[4]. By contrast, Theorem 1 immediately implies that $\mathsf{aAT}^{\parallel}_R(G) \leq \frac{N^2 + 2N}{4} + RN$. Similarly, Alwen et al. [ABH17] previously showed that with high probability a DRSample DAG G has $\mathsf{aAT}^{\parallel}_R(G) \in \Omega(N^2/\log N)$, but the constants in this lower bound were not well understood. On a theoretical side, our analysis shows that this bound is tight i.e., $\mathsf{aAT}^{\parallel}_R(G) \in \Theta(N^2/\log N)$. It also proves that DRSample does not quite match the generic upper bound of Alwen and Blocki [AB16].

Extension of the Greedy Pebbling Attack. Our analysis leaves us in an uncomfortable position where *every practical* iMHF candidate has high-quality pebbling attacks i.e., greedy pebble for DRSample and depth-reducing attacks for Argon2i. We would like to develop a practical iMHF candidate that provides

---

[4] In Argon2, the block-size is $1KB$ so when we use $N = 2^{24}$ nodes the honest party would require 16 GB $(= N \times$ KB$)$ of RAM to evaluate the MHF. Thus, we view 2^{24} as a reasonable upper bound on the number of blocks that would be used in practical applications.

strong resistance against all known pebbling attacks for all practical values of $N \leq 2^{24}$. We first consider a defense proposed by Biryukov et al. [BDK16] against the greedy pebbling attack. While this defense provides optimal protection against the greedy pebbling attack, we introduce an extension of the greedy pebbling attack that we call the *staggered* greedy pebbling attack and show that the trick of Biryukov et al. [BDK16] fails to protect against the extended attack.

3.1 The Greedy Pebbling Algorithm

We first review the greedy pebbling algorithm. We first introduce some notation.

gc(v): For each node $v < N$ we let gc(v) $= \max\{w| \ (v,w) \in E\}$ denote the maximum child of node v—if $v < N$ then the set $\{w| \ (v,w) \in E\}$ is non-empty as it contains the node $v + 1$. If node v has no children then set gc(v) := v.

$\chi(i)$: This represents what we call the crossing set of the ith node. It is defined as $\chi(i) = \{v|v \leq i \ \wedge \ \text{gc}(v) > i\}$. Intuitively this represents the set of nodes $v \leq i$ incident to a directed edge (v,u) that "crosses over" node i i.e. $u > i$.

Greedy Pebbling Strategy: Set GP(G) $= P = (P_1, \ldots, P_N)$ where $P_i = \chi(i)$ for each $i \leq N$. Intuitively, the pebbling strategy can be described follows: In round i we place a pebble on node i and we then discard *any* pebbles on nodes v that are no longer needed in any future round i.e., for all future nodes $w > i$ we have $v \notin$ parents(w) (equivalently, the greatest-child of node v is gc(v) $\leq i$). We refer the reader to the full version [BHK+18] for a formal algorithmic description.

We first prove the following *general* lower bound for *any* N node DAG with indeg(G) ≤ 2 that has a unique topological ordering i.e., G contains each of the edges $(i, i+1)$. In particular, Theorem 1 shows that for any such DAG G we have $\Pi_{st}(G) \lesssim \frac{N^2}{2}$ and $\Pi_{cc}(G) \lesssim N^2/4$. We stress that this is *twice* as efficient as the naive pebbling algorithm $\mathcal{N}$, which set $P_i = \{1, \ldots, i\}$ for each $i \leq N$ and has cumulative cost $\Pi^{\|}_{cc}(\mathcal{N}) = \frac{N^2}{2}$. Previously, the gold standard was to find constructions of DAGs G with N nodes such that $\Pi^{\|}_{cc}(G) \gtrsim \frac{N^2}{2}$ for *practical* values of N—asymptotic results did not rule out this possibility even for $N \leq 2^{40}$. Theorem 1 demonstrates that the best we could hope for is to ensure $\Pi^{\|}_{cc}(G) \gtrsim \frac{N^2}{4}$ for *practical* values of N.

Theorem 1. *Let $r : \mathbb{N}_{>0} \rightarrow \mathbb{N}$ be any function with the property that $r(i) < i-1$ for all $i \in \mathbb{N}_{>0}$. Then the DAG $G = (V, E)$ with N nodes $V = \{1, \ldots, N\}$ and edges $E = \{(i-1, i) \ : \ 1 < i \leq N\} \cup \{(r(i), i) \ : \ 2 < i \leq N\}$ has $\Pi_{st}(G) \leq \frac{N^2 + 2N}{2}$ and $\Pi_{cc}(G) \leq \frac{N^2 + 2N}{4}$ and aAT$_R(G) \leq \frac{N^2 + 2N}{4} + RN$.*

The full proof of Theorem 1 is in the full version [BHK+18] of this paper. Intuitively, Theorem 1 follows from the observation that in any pebbling we have $|P_i| \leq i$, and in the greedy pebbling we also have $|P_i| \leq N - i$ since there can be at most $N - i$ nodes w such that $w = r(v)$ for some $v > i$ and other pebbles on any other node would have been discarded by the greedy pebbling algorithm.

3.2   Analysis of the Greedy Pebble Attack on DRSample

We now turn our attention to the specific case of the iMHF DRSample. A DAG G sampled from this distribution has edges of the form $(i, i+1)$ and $(r(i), i)$ where each $r(i) < i$ is independently selected from some distribution. It is not necessary to understand all of the details of this distribution to follow our analysis in this section as the crucial property that we require is given in Claim 1. The proof of Claim 1 (along with a description of DRSample [ABH17]) is found in the full version [BHK+18] of this paper. Intuitively, Claim 1 follows because we have $\Pr[r(j) = i] \sim \frac{1}{\log j} \times \frac{1}{|j-i|}$ for each node $i < j$ in DRSample.

Claim 1. *Let G be a randomly sampled DRSample DAG with N nodes and let $Y_{i,j}$ be an indicator random variable for the event that $r(j) < i$ for nodes $i < j \leq N$. Then we have $\mathbf{E}[Y_{i,j}] = \Pr[r(j) < i] \leq 1 - \frac{\log(j-i-1)}{\log j}$.*

If $P = (P_1, \ldots, P_N) = \mathsf{GP}(G)$, then we remark that $\chi(i)$ can be viewed as an alternate characterization of the set $P_i = \chi(i)$ of pebbles on the graph at time i. Lemma 1 now implies that with high probability, we will have $|P_i| \leq (1+\delta)N/n$ during *all pebbling rounds*.

Lemma 1. *Given a DAG G on $N = 2^n$ nodes sampled using the randomized DRSample algorithm for any $\eta > 0$, we have*

$$\Pr\left[\max_i |\chi(i)| > (1+\eta)\left(\frac{2N}{n}\right)\right] \leq \exp\left(\frac{-2\eta^2 N}{3n} + n\ln 2\right).$$

Lemma 1, which bounds the size of $\max_i |\chi(i)|$, is proved in the full version [BHK+18]. Intuitively, the proof uses the observation that $|\chi(i)| \leq \sum_{j=i+1}^N Y_{i,j}$ where $Y_{i,j}$ is an indicator random variable for the event that $r(j) \leq i$. This is because $|\chi(i)|$ is upper bounded by the number of edges that "cross" over the node i. We can then use Claim 1 and standard concentration bounds to obtain Lemma 1.

Theorem 2, our main result in this section, now follows immediately from Lemma 1. Theorem 2 states that, except with negligibly small probability, the sequential pebbling cost of a DRSample DAG is at most $(1+\eta)\left(\frac{2N^2}{n}\right) + RN$.

Theorem 2. *Let G be a randomly sampled DRSample DAG with $N = 2^n$ nodes. Then for all $\eta > 0$ we have*

$$\Pr\left[\Pi_{st}(\mathsf{GP}(G)) > (1+\eta)\left(\frac{2N^2}{n}\right)\right] \leq \exp\left(\frac{-2\eta^2 N}{3n} + n\ln 2\right).$$

Proof. Fix $\eta > 0$ and consider a randomly sampled N-node DRSample DAG G. Recall that $|P_i| = \chi(i)$ where $P = \mathsf{GP}(G)$. It follows that $\Pi_{st}(\mathsf{GP}(G)) \leq N \max_{i \in [N]} |\chi(i)|$. By Lemma 1, except with probability $\exp\left(\frac{-\eta^2 N/n}{3} + n\ln 2\right)$, we have

$$\Pi_{st}(\mathsf{GP}(G)) \leq N \times \max_{i \in [N]} |\chi(i)| \leq (1+\eta)\left(\frac{2N^2}{n}\right).$$

$\square$

Discussion. Theorem 2 implies that the (sequential) aAT complexity of DRSample is $\mathsf{aAT}_R(G) \lesssim 2N^2/\log N \in \mathcal{O}(N^2/\log N)$, which asymptotically matches the lower bound of $\Omega(N^2/\log N)$ [ABH17]. More significant from a practical standpoint is that the constant factors in the upper bound are given explicitly. Theorem 2 implies attack quality at least $\gtrsim \frac{\log N}{4}$ since the cost of the naïve pebbling algorithm is $N^2/2$. Thus, for *practical* values of $N \leq 2^{24}$ we will get high-quality attacks and our empirical analysis suggests that attack quality actually scales with $\log N$. On a positive note, the pebbling attack is *sequential*, which means that we could adjust the naïve (honest) evaluation algorithm to simply use $\mathcal{N}$ to use $\mathsf{GP}(G)$ instead because the greedy pebbling strategy is *sequential*. While this would lead to an *egalitarian* function, the outcome is still undesirable from the standpoint of password hashing where we want to ensure that the attacker's absolute aAT costs are as high as possible given a fixed running time N.

3.3 Empirical Analysis of the GP Attack

We ran the greedy pebbling attack against several iMHF DAGs including Argon2i, DRSample and our new construction DRSample+BRG (see Sect. 4) and compare the attack quality of the greedy pebbling attack with prior depth-reducing attacks. The results, seen in Fig. 2 (left), show that the GP attack was especially effective against the DRSample DAG, improving attack quality by a factor of up to 7 (at $n = 24$) when compared to previous state-of-the-art depth-reducing attacks (Valiant, Layered, and various hybrid approaches) [Val77, AB16, ABH17].

The most important observation about Fig. 2 (left) is simply how effective the greedy pebbling attack is against DRSample. We remark that attack quality for DRSample with $N = 2^n$ nodes seems to be approximately n—slightly better than the theoretical guarantees from Theorem 2. While DRSample may have the strongest asymptotic guarantees (i.e. $\mathsf{aAT}^{\|}(G) = \Omega(N^2/\log N)$ for DRSample vs. $\mathsf{aAT}^{\|}(G) = \mathcal{O}(N^{1.767})$ for Argon2i) Argon2i seems to provide better resistance to known pebbling attacks for *practical* parameter ranges.

Our tests found that while the Greedy Pebbling attack does sometimes outperform depth-reducing attacks at smaller values of n, the depth-reducing attacks appear to be superior once we reach graph sizes that would likely be used in practice. As an example, when $n = 20$ we find that the attack quality of the greedy pebbling attack is just 2.99, while the best depth-reducing attack achieved attack quality 6.25 [ABH17].

3.4 Defense Against Greedy Pebbling Attack: Attempt 1 XOR Extension

Biryukov et al. [BDK16] introduced a simple defense against the greedy pebbling attack of Boneh et al. [BCS16] for iMHFs that make two passes over memory. Normally during computation the block $B_{i+N/2}$ would be stored at memory location i overwriting block B_i. The idea of the defense is to XOR the two blocks $B_{i+N/2}$ and B_i before overwriting block B_i in memory. Biryukov et al. [BDK16] observed that this defense does not *significantly* slow down computation because block B_i would have been loaded into cache before it is overwritten in either case. The effect of performing this extra computation is effectively to add each edge of the form $(i - \frac{N}{2}, i)$ to the DAG G. In particular, this means that the greedy pebbling algorithm will not discard the pebble on node $i - \frac{N}{2}$ until round i, which is when the honest pebbling algorithm would have discarded the pebble anyway. Given a graph $G = (V, E)$ we use $G^{\oplus} = (V, E^{\oplus})$ to denote the XOR-extension graph of G where $E^{\oplus} = E \cup \{(i - \frac{N}{2}, i) \mid i > \frac{N}{2}\}$. It is easy to see that $\Pi_{cc}^{\parallel}(\mathsf{GP}(G^{\oplus})) \geq \frac{N^2 + 2N}{4}$, which would make it tempting to conclude that the XOR-extension defeats the greedy pebbling attack.

Greedy Pebble Extension: Given a graph G on N nodes, let $P = (P_1, \ldots, P_N) = \mathsf{GP}(G)$ and let $Q = (Q_1, \ldots, Q_{N/2}) = \mathsf{GP}(G_{\leq N/2})$. Define $\mathsf{GPE}(G^{\oplus}) = (P_1^{\oplus}, \ldots, P_N^{\oplus})$ where $P_{i+N/2-1}^{\oplus} = Q_i \cup P_{i+N/2-1}$ and $P_i^{\oplus} = P_i$ for $i < N/2$. Intuitively, the attack exploits the fact that we *always* ensure that we have a pebble on the extra node $v \in \mathsf{parents}(N/2 + v)$ at time $N/2 + v - 1$ by using the greedy pebble algorithm to synchronously re-pebble the nodes $1, \ldots, N/2$ a second time.

Theorem 3 demonstrates that the new generalized greedy pebble algorithm is effective against the XOR-extension gadget. In particular, Corollary 2 states that we still obtain high-quality attacks against $\mathsf{DRSample}^{\oplus}$ so the XOR-gadget does not significantly improve the aAT cost of DRSample.

Theorem 3. *Let $r : \mathbb{N}_{>0} \to \mathbb{N}$ be any function with the property that $r(i) < i$ for all $i \in \mathbb{N}_{>0}$ and let $G = (V, E)$ be a graph with N nodes $V = \{1, \ldots, N\}$ and directed edges $E = \{(i, i+1) \mid i < N\} \cup \{r(i), i \mid 1 < i \leq N\}$. If $P = \mathsf{GP}(G) \in \mathcal{P}(G)$ and $Q \in \mathcal{P}(G_{\leq N/2})$ then the XOR-extension graph $G^{\oplus}$ of G has amortized Area-Time complexity at most*

$$\mathsf{aAT}^{\parallel}{}_R(G^{\oplus}) \leq \sum_{i=1}^{N/2} |P_i| + \sum_{i=1}^{N} |Q_i| + \frac{3RN}{2}.$$

Corollary 1. *Let $r : \mathbb{N}_{>0} \to \mathbb{N}$ be any function with the property that $r(i) < i$ for all $i \in \mathbb{N}_{>0}$ and let $G = (V, E)$ be a graph with N nodes $V = \{1, \ldots, N\}$ and directed edges $E = \{(i, i+1) \mid i < N\} \cup \{r(i), i \mid 1 < i \leq N\}$. Then for the XOR-extension graph $G^{\oplus}$ we have $\mathsf{aAT}^{\parallel}{}_R(G^{\oplus}) \leq \frac{5N^2 + 12N}{16} + \frac{3RN}{2}$.*

The proof of Theorem 3 can be found in the full version [BHK+18]. One consequence of Theorem 3 is that the XOR-extension gadget does not rescue DRSample from the greedy pebble attack—see Corollary 2.

Corollary 2. *Fix $\eta > 0$ be a fixed constant and let $G = (V, E)$ be a randomly sampled DRSample DAG with $N = 2^n$ nodes $V = \{1, \ldots, N\}$ and directed edges $E = \{(i, i+1) \mid i < N\} \cup \{r(i), i \mid 1 < i \leq N\}$. Then*

$$\Pr\left[\mathsf{aAT}^{\parallel}{}_R(G^{\oplus}) > (1+\eta)\left(\frac{3N^2}{n} - \frac{N^2}{n(n-1)}\right) + \frac{3RN}{2}\right] \leq \exp\left(\frac{-\eta^2 N}{3(n-1)} + 1 + n\ln 2\right).$$

Proof. Fix $\eta > 0$ and let $P = \mathsf{GP}(G)$ where G is a randomly sampled DRSample DAG. By Lemma 1, except with probability $\exp\left(\frac{-2\eta^2 N}{3n} + n\ln 2\right)$, we have $\max_i |P_i| = \max_i |\chi(i)| \leq (1+\eta)\frac{2N}{n}$, which means that $\sum_{i=1}^{N} |P_i| \leq (1+\eta)\frac{2N^2}{n}$. Similarly, let $Q = \mathsf{GP}(G_{\leq N/2})$ be a greedy pebbling of the subgraph formed by the first $N/2$ nodes in G. We remark that $G_{\leq N/2}$ can be viewed as a randomly DRSample DAG with $N/2 = 2^{n-1}$ nodes. Thus except with probability $\exp\left(\frac{-\eta^2 N}{3(n-1)} + (n-1)\ln 2\right)$, we have $\max_{i \leq N/2} |Q_i| = \max_i |\chi(i)| \leq (1+\eta)\frac{N}{n-1}$ since the first $N/2$ nodes of G form a random DRSample DAG with $N/2 = 2^{n-1}$ nodes. This would imply that $\sum_{i=1}^{N/2} |Q_i| \leq (1+\eta)\frac{N}{n-1}$. Putting both bounds together Theorem 3 implies that $\mathsf{aAT}^{\|}(G^{\oplus}) \leq (1+\eta)\left(\frac{3N^2}{n} - \frac{N^2}{n(n-1)}\right) + \frac{3RN}{2}$. $\square$

4 New iMHF Construction with Optimal Security

In this section, we introduce a new iMHF construction called DRSample+BRG. The new construction is obtained by overlaying a bit-reversal graph BRG_n [LT82] on top of a random DRSample DAG. If G denotes a random DRSample DAG with $N/2$ nodes then we will use $\mathsf{BRG}(G)$ to denote the bit-reversal overlay with N nodes. Intuitively, the result is a graph that resists both the greedy pebble attack (which is effective against DRSample alone) and depth-reducing attacks (which DRSample was designed to resist). An even more exciting result is that we can show that DRSample+BRG is the first practical construction to provide strong sustained space complexity guarantees. Interestingly, neither graph (DRSample or BRG) is individually known to provide strong sustained space guarantees. Instead, several of our proofs exploit the synergistic properties of both graphs. We elaborate on the desirable properties of DRSample+BRG below.

First, our new construction inherits desirable properties from *both* the bit-reversal graph and DRSample. For example, $\Pi_{cc}^{\|}(\mathsf{BRG}(G)) \geq \Pi_{cc}^{\|}(G) = \Omega(N^2/\log N)$. Similarly, it immediately follows that $\mathsf{BRG}(G)$ is maximally bandwidth hard. In particular, Ren and Devadas [RD17] showed that BRG_n is maximally bandwidth hard, and Blocki et al. [BRZ18] showed that DRSample is maximally bandwidth hard.

Second, $\mathsf{BRG}(G)$ provides optimal resistance to the greedy pebbling attack—$\Pi_{cc}^{\|}(\mathsf{GP}(\mathsf{BRG}(G))) \approx N^2/4$. Furthermore, we can show that *any* c-parallel pebbling attack $P = (P_1, \ldots, P_t)$ in which $|P_{i+1} \setminus P_i| \leq c$ has cost $\Pi_{cc}(P) = \Omega(N^2)$. This rules out any *extension* of the greedy pebble attack e.g., GPE is 2-parallel. In fact, we prove that this property already holds for any c-parallel pebbling of the bit reversal graph BRG_n. Our proof that $\Pi_{cc}(\mathsf{BRG}_n) = \Omega(N^2)$ generalizes the well-known result that $\Pi_{st}(\mathsf{BRG}_n) = \Omega(N^2)$ and may be of independent interest.

Third, we can show that *any* parallel pebbling P of $\mathsf{BRG}(G)$ *either* has $\Pi_{cc}(P) = \Omega(N^2)$ or has maximal sustained space complexity $\Pi_{ss}(P, s) = \Omega(N)$ for space $s = \Omega(N/\log N)$ i.e., there are at least $\Omega(N)$ steps with at least

$\Omega(N/\log N)$ pebbles on the graph. To prove this last property we must rely on properties of *both* graphs G and BRG_n i.e., the fact that DRSample is highly block depth-robust and the fact that edges BRG_n are evenly distributed over every interval. This makes $\mathsf{BRG}(G)$ the first *practical* construction of a DAG with provably strong sustained space complexity guarantees.

Finally, we can show that $\Pi_{cc}^{\parallel}(G) = \Omega(N^2 \log\log N/\log N)$, matching the general upper bound of Alwen and Blocki [AB16], under a plausible conjecture about the block-depth-robustness of G. In particular, we conjecture that G is (e, d, b)-block depth-robust for $e = \Omega\left(\frac{N\log\log N}{\log N}\right)$, $d = \Omega\left(\frac{N\log\log N}{\log N}\right)$ and $b = \Omega\left(\frac{\log N}{\log\log N}\right)$. In the full version   [BHK+18], we also show how to construct a constant indegree DAG G' with $\Pi_{cc}^{\parallel}(G') = \Omega(N^2 \log\log N/\log N)$ from *any* (e, d)-depth robust graph by overlaying a superconcentrator on top of G [Pip77]. However, the resulting construction is not *practically efficient*. Thus we show the bit reversal overlay $G' = \mathsf{BRG}(G)$ satisfies the same complexity bounds under the slightly stronger assumption that G is *block*-depth-robust. As evidence for the conjecture we show that *known* attacks require the removal of a set S of $e = \Omega\left(\frac{N\log\log N}{\log N}\right)$ to achieve $\mathsf{depth}(G - S) \leq \frac{N}{\sqrt{\log N}}$. Thus, we would need to find *substantially* improved depth-reducing attacks to refute the conjectures.

Bit-Reversal Graph Background. The bit reversal graph was originally proposed by Lenguer and Tarjan [LT82] who showed that any sequential pebbling has maximal space-time complexity. Forler et al. [FLW14] previously incorporated this graph into the design of their iMHF candidate Catena, which received special recognition at the password hashing competition [PHC16]. While we are not focused on sequential space-time complexity, the bit reversal graph has several other useful properties that we exploit in our analysis (see Lemma 2).

Local Samplable. We note that one benefit of DRS+BRG is that it is locally samplable, a notion mentioned as desirable in [ABH17]. Specifically, we want to be able to compute the parent blocks with time and space $\mathcal{O}(\log|V|)$ with small constants. DRS+BRG meets this requirement. Edges sampled from DRSample were shown to be locally navigable in [ABH17], and each bit-reversal edge a simple operation called requires one bit reversal operation, which can easily be computed in time $\mathcal{O}(\log|V|)$. The formal description of the bit-reversal overlay graph $\mathsf{BRG}(G)$ is presented in Definition 4.

The Bit-Reversal DAG. Given a sequence of bits $X = x_1 \circ x_2 \circ \cdots x_n$, let $\mathsf{ReverseBits}(X) = x_n \circ x_{n-1} \circ \cdots \circ x_1$. Let $\mathsf{integer}(X)$ be the integer representation of bit-string X starting at 1 so that $\mathsf{integer}(\{0,1\}^n) = [2^n]$ i.e., $\mathsf{integer}(0^n) = 1$ and $\mathsf{integer}(1^n) = 2^n$. Similarly, let $\mathsf{bits}(v, n)$ be the length n binary encoding of $(v - 1) \mod 2^n$ e.g., $\mathsf{bits}(1, n) = 0^n$ and $\mathsf{bits}(2^n, n) = 1^n$ so that for all $v \in [2^n]$ we have $\mathsf{integer}(\mathsf{bits}(v, n)) = v$.

Definition 3. *We use the notation* BRG_n *to denote the bit reversal graph with* 2^{n+1} *nodes. In particular,* $\mathsf{BRG}_n = (V = [2^{n+1}], E = E_1 \cup E_2)$ *where* $E_1 := \{(i, i+1) : 1 \leq i < 2^{n+1}\}$ *and* $E_2 := \{(x, 2^n + y) : x = \mathsf{integer}(\mathsf{ReverseBits}(\mathsf{bits}(y, n)))\}$. *That is,* E_2 *contains an edge from node* $x \leq 2^n$ *to node* $2^n + y$ *in* BRG_n *if and only if* $x = \mathsf{integer}(\mathsf{ReverseBits}(\mathsf{bits}(y, n)))$.

Claim 2 states that the cumulative memory cost of the greedy pebbling strategy $\mathsf{GP}(\mathsf{BRG}_n)$ is at least $N^2 + N$.

Claim 2. $\Pi_{cc}(\mathsf{GP}(\mathsf{BRG}_n)) \geq N^2 + N$

Proof. Let $P = (P_1, \ldots, P_{2N}) = \mathsf{GP}(\mathsf{BRG}_n)$. We first note that for all $i \leq N$ we have $P_i = \{1, \ldots, i\}$ since $\mathsf{gc}(i) > N$—every node on the bottom layer $[N]$ has an edge to some node on the top layer $[N + 1, 2N]$. Second, observe that for any round $i > N$ we have $|(P_i \setminus P_{i+1}) \cap [N]| \leq 1$ since the only pebble in $[N]$ that might be discarded is the (unique) parent of node i. Thus,

$$\sum_{i=1}^{2N} |P_i| \geq \sum_{i=1}^{N} i + \sum_{i=1}^{N} (N - i + 1) = N(N + 1).$$

$\square$

Thus, we now define the bit-reversal overlay of the bit reversal graph on a graph G_1. If the graph G_1 has N nodes then $\mathsf{BRG}(G_1)$ has $2N$ nodes, and the subgraph induced by the first N nodes of $\mathsf{BRG}(G_1)$ is simply G_1.

Definition 4. *Let* $G_1 = (V_1 = [N], E_1)$ *be a fixed DAG with* $N = 2^n$ *nodes and* $\mathsf{BRG}_n = (V = [2N], E)$ *denote the bit-reversal graph. Then we use* $\mathsf{BRG}(G_1) = (V, E \cup E_1)$ *to denote the bit-reversal overlay of* G_1.

In our analysis, we will rely heavily on the following key-property of the bit-reversal graph from Lemma 2.

Lemma 2. *Let* $G = \mathsf{BRG}_n$ *and* $N = 2^n$ *so that* G *has* $2N$ *nodes. For a given* b, *partition* $[N]$ *into* $\frac{N}{2^{n-b}} = 2^b$ *intervals* $I_k = [(k-1)2^{n-b}, k2^{n-b} - 1]$, *each having length* 2^{n-b}, *for* $1 \leq k \leq 2^b$. *Then for any interval* I *of length* 2^{b+1}, *with* $I \subseteq [N + 1, 2N]$, *there exists an edge from each* I_k *to* I, *for* $1 \leq k \leq 2^b$.

Proof of Lemma 2. Let I be any interval of length 2^b, with $I \subseteq [N + 1, 2N]$. Note that every 2^b length bitstring appears as a suffix in I. Thus, there exists an edge from each interval containing a unique 2^b length bitstring as a prefix. It follows that there exists an edge from each I_k to I, for $1 \leq k \leq 2^b$. $\square$

As we will see, the consequences of Lemma 2 will have powerful implications for the pebbling complexity of $G = \mathsf{BRG}(G_1)$ whenever the underlying DAG G_1 is (e, d, b)-block-depth-robust. In particular, Lemma 3 states that if we start with pebbles on a set $|P_i| < e/2$ then for *any initially empty* interval I of $\mathcal{O}(N/b)$ consecutive nodes in the top-half of G we have the property that $H := G - \bigcup_{x \in P_i} [x - b + 1, x]$ is an $(e/2, d, b)$-block-depth-robust graph that will need to be *completely re-pebbled* (at cost *at least* $\Pi_{cc}^{\|}(H) \geq ed/2$) just to advance a pebble across the interval I. See the full version [BHK+18] for the proof of Lemma 3.

Lemma 3. *Let $G_1 = (V_1 = [N], E)$ be a (e, d, b)-block depth-robust graph with $N = 2^n$ nodes and let $G = \mathsf{BRG}(G_1)$ denote the bit-reversal extension of G_1 with $2N$ nodes $V(G) = [2N]$. For any interval $I = \left[N + i + 1, N + i + 1 + \frac{4N}{b}\right] \subseteq [2N]$ and any $S \subseteq [1, N + i]$ with $|S| < \frac{e}{2}$, ancestors$_{G-S}(I)$ is $\left(\frac{e}{2}, d, b\right)$-block depth-robust.*

Lemma 4. *Let G be a (e, d, b)-block depth-robust DAG with $N = 2^n$ and let $G' = \mathsf{BRG}(G)$ be the bit reversal overlay of G. Let $P \in \mathcal{P}^{\|}(G')$ be a legal pebbling of G' and let t_v be the first time where $v \in P_{t_v}$. Then for all $v \geq 1$ such that $e' := |P_{t_{v+N}}| \leq \frac{e}{4}$ and $v \leq N - \frac{32Ne'}{be}$, we have*

$$\sum_{j=t_{v+N}}^{t_{v+N+\frac{32Ne'}{be'}}-1} |P_j| \geq \frac{ed}{2}.$$

Proof of Lemma 4. Let $v \leq N - \frac{32Ne}{be'}$ be given such that the set $S = P_{t_{N+v}}$ has size at most $e' = |S| \leq e/4$ and set $b' = \frac{eb}{4e'}$. Consider the ancestors of the interval $I = [N + v + 1, N + v + \frac{8N}{b'}]$ in the graph $G' - S$. Note that $I \cap S = \emptyset$ since v is the maximum node that has been pebbled at time t_{N+v}. We have

$$H := G - \bigcup_{x \in S} [x - b' + 1, x] \subseteq \mathsf{ancestor}_{G'-S}(I)$$

because for any node $u \in V(G)$ if $u \notin \bigcup_{x \in S}[x - b' + 1, x]$ then $[u, u + b' - 1] \cap S = \emptyset$ which implies that there exists an "S-free path" from u to I by Lemma 2. Thus, H will have to be repebbled completely at some point during the time interval $\left[t_{v+N}, t_{v+N+\frac{32Ne'}{be}-1}\right]$ since $\frac{32Ne'}{be} \geq \frac{8N}{b}$.

Since $b' = \frac{eb}{4e'} \geq b$ we note that the e' intervals of length b' we are removing can be covered by at most $\lceil b'/b \rceil e' = \lceil e/(4e') \rceil e' \leq (e/4) + e' \leq e/2$ intervals of length e. Hence, Lemma 3 implies that H is still $(e/2, d, b)$-block depth-robust and, consequently, we have that $\Pi_{cc}^{\|}(H) \geq ed/2$ by [ABP17]. We can conclude that

$$\sum_{j=t_{v+N}}^{t_{v+N+\frac{32Ne'}{be}-1}} |P_j| \geq \Pi_{cc}^{\|}(H) \geq ed/2.$$

$\square$

4.1   Sustained Space Complexity (Tradeoff Theorem)

We prove that for any parameter $e = \mathcal{O}\left(\frac{N}{\log N}\right)$, either the cumulative pebbling cost of any parallel (legal) pebbling P is at least $\Pi(P) = \Omega(N^3/(e \log N))$, or there are at least $\Omega(N)$ steps with at least e pebbles on the graph i.e., $\Pi_{ss,e}(P) = \Omega(N)$. Note that the cumulative pebbling cost rapidly increases as e decreases e.g., if $e = \sqrt{N}/\log N$ then any pebbling P for which $\Pi_{ss}(P, e) = o(N)$ must have $\Pi(P) = \Omega(N^{2.5})$.

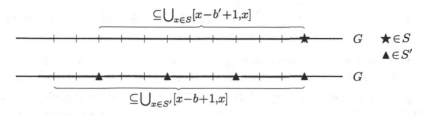

Fig. 1. Intervals $\bigcup_{x \in S}[x - b' + 1, x]$ and $\bigcup_{x \in S'}[x - b + 1, x]$ when $b' = 10$ and $b = 3$. Observe that $\bigcup_{x \in S'}[x - b + 1, x] \supset \bigcup_{x \in S}[x - b' + 1, x]$ over the integers.

To begin we start with the known result that (with high probability) a randomly sampled DRSample DAG G is (e, d, b)-block depth-robust with $e = \Omega(N/\log N)$, $b = \Omega(\log N)$, and $d = \Omega(N)$ [ABH17]. Lemma 5 now implies that the DAG is also (e', d, b')-block depth-robust for any suitable parameters e' and b'. Intuitively, if we delete e' intervals of length $b' > b$ then we can cover these deleted intervals with *at most* $e'\left(\frac{b'}{b} + 1\right)$ intervals of length b, as illustrated in Fig. 1. The formal proof of Lemma 5 is in the full version [BHK+18].

Lemma 5. *Suppose that a DAG G is (e, d, b)-block depth-robust and that parameters e' and b' satisfy the condition that $e'\left(\frac{b'}{b}\right) + e' \leq \frac{e}{2}$. Then G is (e', d, b')-block depth-robust, and for all S with size $|S| \leq e'$ the graph $H = G - \bigcup_{x \in S}[x - b' + 1, x]$ is $\left(\frac{e}{2}, d, b\right)$-block depth-robust.*

Together Lemmas 4 and 5 imply that we must incur pebbling cost $\Omega(ed)$ to pebble *any* interval of $\Omega\left(\frac{Ne'}{be}\right)$ consecutive nodes in the top half of $\mathsf{BRG}(G)$, starting from *any* configuration with at most $e' \leq e/4$ pebbles on the graph.

Theorem 4, our main result in this subsection, now follows because for any pebbling $P \in \Pi^{\|}(\mathsf{BRG}(G))$ and any interval I of $\Omega\left(\frac{Ne'}{be}\right)$ nodes in the top-half of G we must either (1) keep at least e' pebbles on the graph while we walk a pebble across the first half of the interval I, or (2) pay cost $\Omega(ed)$ to re-pebble a depth-robust graph. Since there are $\Omega\left(\frac{eb}{e'}\right)$ such disjoint intervals we must either keep $|P_i| \geq e'$ pebbles on the graph for $\Omega(N)$ rounds, or pay cost $\Pi_{cc}^{\|}(P) \geq \frac{e^2 db}{64 e'}$.

Theorem 4. *Let G be any (e, d, b)-block depth-robust DAG on $N = 2^n$ nodes, and $G' = \mathsf{BRG}(G)$ be the bit reversal overlay of G. Then for any pebbling $P \in \Pi^{\|}(G)$ and all $e' \leq \frac{e}{4}$, we have either $\Pi_{cc}^{\|}(P) \geq \frac{e^2 db}{64 e'}$, or $\Pi_{ss}(P, e') \geq \frac{N}{4} - o(N)$ i.e., at least $\frac{N}{4} - o(N)$ rounds i in which $|P_i| \geq e'$.*

Corollary 3 follows immediately from Theorem 4.

Corollary 3. *Let G be any $\left(\frac{c_1 N}{\log N}, c_2 N, c_3 \log N\right)$-block depth-robust DAG on $N = 2^n$ nodes for some constants $c_1, c_2, c_3 > 0$ and let $G' = \mathsf{BRG}(G)$ be the bit reversal overlay of G. Then for any $e' < \frac{c_1 N}{4 \log N}$ and any pebbling $P \in \mathcal{P}^{\|}(G')$*

we have either $\Pi_{cc}^{\parallel}(P) \geq \frac{c_1^2 c_2 c_3 N^3}{64e' \log N}$, or $\Pi_{ss}(P, e') \geq \frac{N}{4} - o(N)$ i.e., there are at least $\frac{N}{4} - o(N)$ rounds j in which $|P_j| \geq e'$.

Remark 1. Alwen et al. previously proved that for constants $c_1 = 2.4 \times 10^{-4}$, $c_2 = 0.03$ and $c_3 = 160$, a randomly sampled DAG G from DRSample will be $\left(\frac{c_1 N}{\log N}, c_2 N, c_3 \log N \right)$-block depth-robust except with negligible probability [ABH17]. Thus, with high probability Corollary 3 can be applied to the bit reversal overlay $\mathsf{BRG}(G)$. Notice also that as e' decreases, the lower bound on $\Pi_{cc}^{\parallel}(P)$ increases rapidly e.g., if a pebbling does not have at least $\Omega(N)$ steps with at least $e' = \Omega\left(\sqrt{N}\right)$ pebbles on the graph, then $\Pi_{cc}^{\parallel}(P) = \tilde{\Omega}(N^{2.5})$.

A Conjectured (Tight) Lower Bound on $\Pi_{cc}^{\parallel}(\mathsf{BRG}(G))$. The idea behind the proof of Theorem 5 in the full version [BHK+18] is very similar to the proof of Theorem 4—an attacker must either keep $e/2$ pebbles on the graph most of the time or the attacker must pay $\Omega(edb)$ to repebble an (e, d)-depth $\Omega(b)$ times. In fact, a slightly weaker version (worse constants) of Theorem 5 follows as a corollary of Theorem 4 since $\Pi_{cc}^{\parallel}(P) \geq e' \times \Pi_{ss}(P, e')$. Under our conjecture that DRSample DAGs are $(c_1 N \log \log N / \log N, c_2 N \log \log N / \log N, c_3 \log N / \log \log N)$-block depth-robust graph, Theorem 5 implies that $\Pi_{cc}^{\parallel}(\mathsf{BRG}(G)) = \Omega(N^2 \log \log N / \log N)$. In fact, any pebbling must either keep $\Omega(N \log \log N / \log N)$ pebbles on the graph for $\approx N/4$ steps or the pebbling has cost $\Omega(N^2 \log \log N)$.

Theorem 5. *Let G_1 be an (e, d, b)-block depth-robust graph with $N = 2^n$ nodes. Then $\Pi_{cc}^{\parallel}(\mathsf{BRG}(G_1)) \geq \min\left(\frac{eN}{2}, \frac{edb}{32}\right)$.*

Evidence for Conjecture. In the full version [BHK+18] we present evidence for our conjecture on the (block) depth-robustness of DRSample. We show that *all* known techniques for constructing depth-reducing sets *fail* to refute our conjecture. Along the way we introduce a general technique for bounding the size of a set S produced by Valiant's Lemma[5]. In this attack we partition the

---

[5] In the full version [BHK+18] we also analyze the performance of Valiant's Lemma attack against Argon2i. Previously, the best known upper bound was that Valiant's Lemma yields a depth-reducing set of size $e = \mathcal{O}\left(\frac{N \log(N/d)}{\log N}\right)$ for any DAG G with constant indegree. For the specific case of Argon2i this upper bound on e was significantly larger than the upper bound—$e = \tilde{\mathcal{O}}\left(\frac{N}{d^{1/3}}\right)$—obtained by running the layered attack [AB17,BZ17]. Nevertheless, empirical analysis of both attacks surprisingly indicated that Valiant's Lemma yields *smaller* depth-reducing sets than the layered attack for Argon2i. We show how to customize the analysis of Valiant's Lemma attack to a *specific* DAG such as DRSample or Argon2i. Our theoretical analysis of Valiant's Lemma explains these surprising empirical results. By focusing on Argon2i specifically we can show that, for a target depth d, the attacker yields a depth-reducing set of size $e = \tilde{\mathcal{O}}\left(\frac{N}{d^{1/3}}\right) \ll \mathcal{O}\left(\frac{N \log(N/d)}{\log N}\right)$, which is optimal and *matches* the performance of the layered attack [BZ17].

edges into sets $E_1, \ldots, E_n$ where E_i contains the set of all edges (u, v) such that the most significant different bit of (the binary encoding of) u and v is i. By deleting j of these edge sets (e.g., by removing one node incident to each edge) we can reduce the depth of the graph to $N/2^j$. In the full version [BHK+18] we show that for any edge distribution function $r(v) < v$ we have

$$\mathbb{E}[|E_i|] = \frac{N}{2^i} + \sum_{j=0}^{\frac{N}{2^i}-1} \sum_{m=0}^{2^{i-1}-1} \Pr\left[2^{i-1} + m \geq v - r(v) > m\right]$$

where the value of the random variable $|E_i|$ will be tightly concentrated around its mean since for each node v the edge distribution function $r(v)$ is independent.

4.2   (Nearly) Sequential Pebblings of BRG_n Have Maximum Cost

In this section, we show that for *any* constant $c \geq 1$ *any* c-parallel pebbling P of BRG_n must have cost $\Pi_{cc}(P) = \Omega(N^2)$. A pebbling $P = (P_1, \ldots, P_t)$ is said to be c-parallel if we have $|P_{i+1} \setminus P_i| \leq c$ for all round $i < t$. We remark that this rules out *any* natural extension of the greedy pebbling attack e.g., the extension from the previous section that defeated the XOR extension graph $G^\oplus$ was a $c = 2$-parallel pebbling. We also remark that our proof generalizes a well-known result of [LT82] that implied that $\Pi_{st}(\mathsf{BRG}_n) = \Omega(N^2)$ for *any* sequential pebbling. For parallel pebblings it is known that $\Pi_{st}^\| = \mathcal{O}(N^{1.5})$ [AS15] though this pebbling attack requires parallelism $c = \sqrt{N}$.

It is easy to show (e.g., from Lemma 2) that starting from a configuration with $|\Gamma_i| \leq e$ pebbles on the graph, it will take $\Omega(N)$ steps to advance a pebble $\mathcal{O}(e)$ steps on the top of the graph. It follows that $\Pi_{st}(\mathsf{BRG}_n) = \Omega(N^2)$. The challenge in lower bounding $\Pi_{cc}(G)$ as in Theorem 6 is that space usage might not remain constant throughout the pebbling. Once we have proved that $\Pi_{cc}(G) = \Omega(N^2)$ we then note that any c-parallel pebbling P can be transformed into a sequential pebbling Q s.t. $\Pi_{cc}(Q) \leq c \times \Pi_{cc}(P)$ by dividing each transition $P_i \rightarrow P_{i+1}$ into c transitions to ensure that $|Q_j \setminus Q_{j-1}| \leq 1$. Thus, it follows that $\Pi_{cc}(P) = \Omega(N^2)$ for any c-parallel pebbling.

Theorem 6. *Let* $G = \mathsf{BRG}_n$ *and* $N = 2^n$. *Then* $\Pi_{cc}(G) = \Omega(N^2)$.

The full proof of Theorem 6 can be found in the full version [BHK+18]. Briefly, we introduce a potential function Φ and then argue that, beginning with a configuration with at most $\mathcal{O}(e)$ pebbles on the graph, advancing the pebble e steps on the top of the graph either costs $\Omega(Ne)$ (i.e., we keep $\Omega(e)$ pebbles on the graph for the $\Omega(N)$ steps required to advance the pebble e steps) or increases the potential function by $\Omega(Ne)$ i.e., we *significantly* reduce the number of pebbles on the graph during the interval. Note that the cost $\Omega(Ne)$ to advance a pebble e steps on the top of the graph corresponds to an average cost of $\Omega(N)$ per node on the top of the graph. Thus, the total cost is $\Omega(N^2)$. Lemma 6, which states that it is expensive to transition from a configuration with *few* pebbles on the graph to a configuration with *many* well-spread pebbles on the graph, is a core piece of the potential function argument.

Lemma 6. *Let $G = \mathsf{BRG}_n$ for some integer $n > 0$ and $N = 2^n$. Let $P = (P_1, \ldots, P_t) \in \mathcal{P}(G)$ be some legal sequential pebbling of G. For a given b, partition $[N]$ into $\frac{N}{2^b} = 2^{n-b}$ intervals $I_x = \left[(x-1)2^b + 1, x \times 2^b\right]$, each having length 2^b, for $1 \le x \le 2^{n-b}$. Suppose that at time i, at most $\frac{N}{2^{b'+3}}$ of the intervals contain a pebble with $b' \ge b$ and at time j, at least $\frac{N}{2^{b'+1}}$ of the intervals contain a pebble. Then $|P_i| + \ldots + |P_j| \ge \frac{N^2}{2^{b'+5}}$ and $(j - i) \ge \frac{2^{b-b'}N}{4}$.*

5   Empirical Analysis

We empirically analyze the quality of DRS+BRG by subjecting it to a variety of known depth-reducing pebbling attacks [AB16, AB17] as well as the "new" greedy pebbling attack. We additionally present a *new heuristic* algorithm for constructing *smaller* depth-reducing sets, which we call greedy depth reduce. We extend the pebbling attack library of Alwen et al. [ABH17] to include the greedy pebbling algorithm [BCS16] as well as our new heuristic algorithm. The source code is available on Github at https://github.com/NewAttacksAndStrongerConstructions/PebblingAndDepthReductionAttacks.

5.1   Greedy Depth Reduce

We introduce a novel greedy algorithm for constructing a depth-reducing set S such that $\mathsf{depth}(G - S) \le d_{tgt}$. Intuitively, the idea is to repeatedly find the node $v \in V(G) \setminus S$ that is incident to the largest number of paths of length d_{tgt} in $G - S$ and add v to S until $\mathsf{depth}(G - S) \le d_{tgt}$. While we can compute $\mathsf{incident}(v, d_{tgt})$, the number of length d_{tgt} paths incident to v, in polynomial time using dynamic programming, it will take $\mathcal{O}(Nd_{tgt})$ time and space to fill in the dynamic programming table. Thus, a naïve implementation would run in total time $\mathcal{O}(Nd_{tgt}e)$ since we would need to recompute the array after each iteration. This proves not to be feasible in many instances we encountered e.g. $N = 2^{24}$, $d_{tgt} = 2^{16}$ and $e \approx 6.4 \times 10^5$ and we would need to run the algorithm multiple times in our experiments. Thus, we adopt two key heuristics to reduce the running time. The first heuristic is to fix some parameter $d' \le d_{tgt}$ (we used $d' = 16$ whenever $d_{tgt} \ge 16$) and repeatedly delete nodes incident to the largest number of paths of length d' *until* $\mathsf{depth}(G - S) \le d_{tgt}$. The second heuristic is to select a larger set $T \subseteq V(G) \setminus S$ of k nodes (we set $k = 400 \times 2^{(18-n)/2}$ in our experiments) to delete in each round so that we can reduce the number of times we need to re-compute $\mathsf{incident}(v, d_{tgt})$. We select T in a greedy fashion: repeatedly select a node v (with maximum value $\mathsf{incident}(v, d')$) subject to the constraint $\mathbf{dist}(v, T) \le r$ for some radius r (we used $r = 8$ in our experiments) until $|T| \ge k$ or there are no nodes left to add—here $\mathbf{dist}(v, T)$ denotes the length of the *shortest directed path* connecting v to T in $G - S$. In our experiments we also minimized the number of times we need to run the greedy heuristic algorithm for each DAG G by *first* identifying the target depth value $d_{tgt}^* = 2^j$ with $j \in [n]$ which resulted in the highest quality attack against G when using *other* algorithms (Valiant's Lemma/Layered Attack) to build the depth-reducing set S. For each DAG G we then ran our heuristic algorithm with target depths $d_{tgt} = 2^j \times d^*_{tgt}$ for each $j \in \{-1, 0, 1\}$. A more formal description of the *heuristic algorithm* can be found in the full version [BHK+18].

Figure 3 explicitly compares the performance of our greedy heuristic algorithm with prior state-of-the-art algorithms for constructing depth-reducing sets. Given a DAG G (either Argon2i, DRSample or DRS+BRG) on $N = 2^n$ nodes and a target depth d_{tgt} we run each algorithm to find a (small) set S such that $\mathsf{depth}(G - S) \le d_{tgt}$. The figure on the left (resp. right) plots the size of the depth-reducing set $e = |S|$ vs. the size of the graph N (logscale) when the target depth $d_{tgt} = 8$ (resp. $d_{tgt} = 16$). Our analysis indicates that our greedy heuristic algorithm outperforms all prior state-of-the-art algorithms for constructing depth-reducing sets including Valiant's Lemma [Val77] and the layered attack [AB16]. In particular, the greedy algorithm consistently outputs a depth-reducing that is 2.5 to 5 times smaller than the best depth-reducing set found by any other approach—the improvement is strongest for the DRSample graph.

5.2 Comparing Attack Quality

We ran each DAG G (either Argon2i, DRSample or DRS+BRG) with $N = 2^n$ nodes against a battery of pebbling attacks including both depth-reducing attacks [AB16, AB17] and the greedy pebble attack. In our analysis we focused on graphs of size $N = 2^n$ with n ranging from $n \in [14, 24]$, representing memory ranging from 16 MB to 16 GB. Our results are shown in Fig. 2. While DRSample provided strong resistance to depth-reducing attacks (right), the greedy pebbling attack (left) yields *a very* high-quality attack (for $n \ge 20$ the attack quality is $\approx n$) against DRSample. Similarly, as we can see in Fig. 2, Argon2i provides reasonably strong resistance to the *greedy pebble* attack (left), but is vulnerable to depth-reducing attacks (right). DRS+BRG strikes a *healthy* middle ground as it provides good resistance to both attacks. In particular, even if we use our new greedy heuristic algorithm to construct the depth-reducing sets (right), the attack quality never exceeds 6 for DRS+BRG. In summary, DRS+BRG provides the strongest resistance to *known* pebbling attacks for *practical* parameter ranges $n \in [14, 24]$.

As Fig. 2 (right) demonstrates attack quality almost always improves when we use the new greedy algorithm to construct depth-reducing sets. The one exception was that for larger Argon2i DAGs prior techniques (i.e., Valiant's Lemma) outperform greedy. We conjecture that this is because we had to select the parameter $d' \ll d^*_{tgt}$ for efficiency reasons. For DRSample and DRS+BRG the value d^*_{tgt} was reasonably small i.e., for DRSample we always had $d^*_{tgt} \le 16$ allowing us to set $d' = d^*_{tgt}$. We believe that the greedy heuristic algorithm would outperform prior techniques if we were able to set $d' \sim d^*_{tgt}$ and that this would lead to even higher quality attacks against Argon2i. However, the time to pre-compute the depth-reducing set will increase linearly with d'.

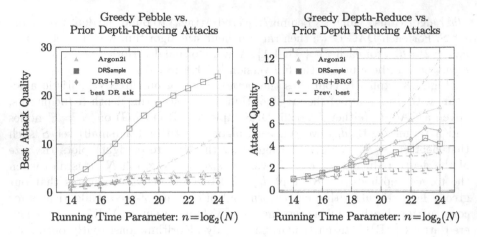

Fig. 2. Attack quality for greedy pebble and greedy depth reduce

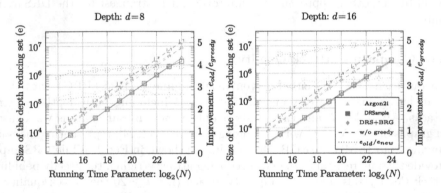

Fig. 3. Greedy depth-reduce vs prior state of the art

6 Pebbling Reduction

Alwen and Serbinenko [AS15] previously showed that, in the parallel random oracle model, the cumulative memory complexity (cmc) of an iMHFs $f_{G,H}$ can be characterized by the black pebbling cost $\Pi_{cc}^{\parallel}(G)$ of the underlying DAG. However, their reduction assumed that the output of $f_{G,H}(x) := \mathsf{lab}_{G,H,x}(N)$ is the label of the last node N of G where labels are defined recursively using the concatenation rule $\mathsf{lab}_{G,H,x}(v) := H(v, \mathsf{lab}_{G,H,x}(v_1), \ldots, \mathsf{lab}_{G,H,x}(v_\delta))$ where $v_1, \ldots, v_\delta = \mathsf{parents}_G(v)$. I To improve performance, real world implementations of iMHFs such as Argon2i, DRSample and our own implementation of BRG(DRSample) use the XOR labeling rule $\mathsf{lab}_{G,H,x}(v) := H(\mathsf{lab}_{G,H,x}(v_1) \oplus \mathsf{lab}_{G,H,x}(v_2) \oplus \ldots \oplus \mathsf{lab}_{G,H,x}(v_\delta))$ so that we can avoid Merkle-Damgard and work with a *faster* round function $H : \{0,1\}^w \rightarrow \{0,1\}^w$ instead of requiring $H : \{0,1\}^{(\delta+1)w} \rightarrow \{0,1\}^w$.

We prove that in the parallel random oracle model, the cumulative memory complexity of $f_{G,H}$ is still captured by $\Pi_{cc}^{\|}(G)$ when using the XOR labeling rule (under certain restrictions discussed below that will hold for all of the iMHF constructions we consider in this paper). We postpone a fully formal definition of cumulative memory complexity cmc to the full version [BHK+18] as it is identical to [AS15]. Intuitively, one can consider the *execution trace* $\mathsf{Trace}_{\mathcal{A},R,H}(x) = \{(\sigma_i, Q_i)\}_{i=1}^{t}$ of an attacker $\mathcal{A}^{H(\cdot)}(x; R)$ on input value x with internal randomness R. Here, Q_i denotes the set of random oracle queries made in *parallel* during round i and σ_i denotes the state of the attacker immediately before the queries Q_i are answered. In this case, $\mathsf{cmc}(\mathsf{Trace}_{\mathcal{A},R,H}(x)) := \sum_i |\sigma_i|$ sums the memory required during each round in the parallel random oracle model[6]. For a list of distinct inputs $X = (x_1, x_2, \ldots, x_m)$, let $f_{G,H}^{\times m}(X)$ be the ordered tuple $f_{G,H}^{\times m}(X) = (f_{G,H}(x_1), f_{G,H}(x_2), \ldots, f_{G,H}(x_m))$. Then the memory cost of a $f_{G,H}^{\times m}$ is defined by

$$\mathsf{cmc}_{q,\epsilon}(f_{G,H}^{\times m}) = \min_{\mathcal{A},x} \mathbb{E}\left[\mathsf{cmc}(\mathsf{Trace}_{\mathcal{A},R,H}(x))\right],$$

where the expectation is taken over the selection of the random oracle $H(\cdot)$ as well as the internal randomness R of the algorithm $\mathcal{A}$. The minimum is taken over all valid inputs $X = (x_1, x_2, \ldots, x_m)$ with $x_i \neq x_j$ for $i < j$ and all algorithms $\mathcal{A}^{H(\cdot)}$ that compute $f_{G,H}^{\times m}(X)$ correctly with probability at least ϵ and make at most q queries for each computation of $f_{G,H}(x_i)$. Let $G^{\times m}$ be a DAG with mN nodes, including m sources and m sinks.

Theorem 7, our main result, states that $\mathsf{cmc}_{q,\epsilon}(f_{G,H}^{\times m}) \geq \frac{\epsilon w m}{8\delta} \cdot \Pi_{cc}^{\|}(G)$. Thus, the cost of computing $f_{G,H}$ on m distinct inputs and constant indegree graphs G is at least $\Omega\left(m \times w \times \Pi_{cc}^{\|}(G)\right)$—here, we assume that $H : \{0,1\}^w \to \{0,1\}^w$. We remark that for practical iMHF constructions we will have indegree $\delta \in \{2, 3\}$ so that $\mathsf{cmc}_{q,\epsilon}(f_{G,H}^{\times m}) = \Omega\left(\Pi_{cc}^{\|}(G)\right)$. The δ-factor loss is necessary. For example, the complete DAG K_N has maximum pebbling cost $\Pi_{cc}^{\|}(K_N) \geq N(N-1)/2$, but $\mathsf{cmc}_{q,\epsilon}(f_{K_N,H}^{\times m}) = \mathcal{O}(Nw)$ when we use the XOR labeling rule[7].

Theorem 7. *Let G be a DAG with N nodes, indegree $\delta \geq 2$, and* $\mathsf{parents}(u) \neq \mathsf{parents}(v)$ *for all pairs $u \neq v \in V$, and let $f_{G,H}$ be a function that follows the XOR labeling rule, with label size w. Let $\mathcal{H}$ be a family of random oracle functions with outputs of label length w and $H = (H_1, H_2)$, where $H_1, H_2 \in \mathcal{H}$.*

---

[6] Given a constant R that represents the core/memory area ratio we can define $\mathsf{aAT}^{\|}_R(\mathsf{Trace}_{\mathcal{A},R,H}(x)) = \mathsf{cmc}(\mathsf{Trace}_{\mathcal{A},R,H}(x)) + R\sum_i |Q_i|$. We will focus on lower bounds on cmc since the notions are asymptotically equivalent and lower bounds on aAT complexity.

[7] In particular, if we let $L_v = \mathsf{lab}_{K_N,H,x}(v) = H(L_{v-1} \oplus \ldots \oplus L_1)$ denotes the label of node v given input x then the prelabel of node v is $Y_v = \mathsf{prelab}_{K_N,H,x}(v) = L_{i-1} \oplus \ldots \oplus L_1$. Given only Y_v we can obtain $L_v = H(Y_v)$ and $Y_{v+1} = Y_v \oplus L_v$. Thus, $\mathsf{cmc}_{q,\epsilon}(f_{K_N,H}) = \mathcal{O}(Nw)$ since we can compute $f_{K_N,H}(x) = L_N$ in linear time with space $\mathcal{O}(w)$.

Let m be a number of parallel instances such that $mN < 2^{w/32}$, $q < 2^{w/32}$ be the maximum number of queries to a random oracle, and let $\frac{\epsilon}{4} > 2^{-w/2+2} > \frac{qmN+1}{2^w - m^2N^2 - mN} + \frac{2m^2N^2}{2^w - mN}$. Then $\mathsf{cmc}_{q,\epsilon}(f_{G,H}^{\times m}) \geq \frac{\epsilon m w}{8\delta} \cdot \Pi_{cc}^{\|}(G)$.

As in [AS15] the pebbling reduction relies on an extractor argument to show that we can find a black pebbling $P = (P_1, \ldots, P_t)$ s.t. $|P_i| = \mathcal{O}(|\sigma_i|/w)$. The extractor takes a hint h of length $|h| = |\sigma_i| + h_2$ and then extracts ℓ distinct random oracle pairs $(x_1, H(x_1)), \ldots, (x_\ell, H(x_\ell))$ by simulating the attacker. Here, one can show that $\ell \geq h_2/w + \Omega(|P_i|)$, which implies that $|\sigma_i| = \Omega(w|P_i|)$ since a random oracle cannot be compressed.

There are several additional challenges we must handle when using the XOR labeling rule. First, in [AS15] we effectively use an *independent* random oracle $H_v(\cdot) = H(v, \cdot)$ to compute the label of each node v—a property that does not hold for the XOR labeling rule we consider. Second, when we use the XOR labeling it is more challenging for the extractor to extract the value of labels from random oracle queries made by the (simulated) attacker. For example, the random oracle query the attacker must submit to compute $\mathsf{lab}_{G,H,x}(v)$ is now $\bigoplus_{i=1}^{\delta} \mathsf{lab}_{G,H,x}(v_i)$ instead of $(v, \mathsf{lab}_{G,H,x}(v_1), \ldots, \mathsf{lab}_{G,H,x}(v_\delta))$—in the latter case it is trivial to read each of the labels for nodes $v_1, \ldots, v_\delta$. Third, even if H is a random oracle the XOR labeling rule uses a round function $F(x, y) = H(x \oplus y)$ that is not even collision resistant e.g., $F(x, y) = F(y, x)$. Because of this, we will not be able to prove a pebbling reduction for *arbitrary* DAGs G.

In fact, one can easily find examples of DAGs G where $\mathsf{cmc}(f_{G,H}) \ll \Pi_{cc}^{\|}(G)$ i.e., the cumulative memory complexity is much less than the cumulative pebbling cost by exploiting the fact that $\mathsf{lab}_{G,H,x}(u) = \mathsf{lab}_{G,H,x}(v)$ whenever $\mathsf{parents}(u) = \mathsf{parents}(v)$. For example, observe that if $\mathsf{parents}(N) = \{u, v\}$ and $\mathsf{parents}(u) = \mathsf{parents}(v)$ then

$$f_{G,H}(x) = \mathsf{lab}_{G,H,x}(N) = H(\mathsf{lab}_{G,H,x}(u) \oplus \mathsf{lab}_{G,H,x}(v)) = H(0^w),$$

so that $f_{G,H}(x)$ becomes a constant function and any attempt to extract a pebbling from an execution trace computing $f_{G,H}$ would be a fruitless exercise!

For this reason, we only prove that $\mathsf{cmc}(f_{G,H}) = \Omega\left(\Pi_{cc}^{\|}(G) \times w\right)$ when $G = (V = [N], E)$ satisfies the *unique parents* property i.e., for any pair of vertices $u \neq v$ we have $\mathsf{parents}(v) \neq \mathsf{parents}(u)$. We remark that any DAG that contains all edges of the form $(i, i+1)$ with $i < N$ will satisfy this property since $v - 1 \notin \mathsf{parents}(u)$. Thus, Argon2i, DRSample and DRSample+BRG all satisfy the unique parents property.

Extractor: We argue that, except with negligible probability, a successful execution trace must have the property that $|\sigma_i| = \Omega(w|P_i|)$ for each round of some legal pebbling P. Our extractor takes a hint, which include σ_i (to simulate the attacker), the set P_i and some (short) additional information e.g., to identify the index of the next random oracle query q_v where the label for node v will appear as input. To address the challenge that the query $q_v = \mathsf{lab}_{G,H,x}(v) \oplus \mathsf{lab}_{G,H,x}(u)$ we increase both the size of the hint and the number of labels being extracted e.g., our hint might additionally include the pair $(u, \mathsf{lab}_{G,H,x}(u))$, which allows us to extract both $\mathsf{lab}_{G,H,x}(v)$ and $\mathsf{lab}_{G,H,x}(u)$ from q_v. Our extractor will attempt to extract labels for each node $v \in P_i$ as well as for a few extra sibling nodes such as u, which means that we must take care to ensure that we never ruin the extracted label $\mathsf{lab}_{G,H,x}(u)$ by submitting the random oracle query $\bigoplus_{i=1}^{\delta} u_i$ to $H(\cdot)$. If G satisfies the *unique parents* property then we can prove that with high probability our *extractor* will be successful. It follows that $|\sigma_i| = \Omega(w|P_i|)$ since the hint must be long enough to encode all of the labels that we extract.

7   An Improved Argon2 Round Function

In this section we show how a parallel attacker could reduce aAT costs by nearly an order of magnitude by computing the Argon2i round function in parallel. We then present a tweaked round function to ensure that the function must be computed *sequentially*. Empirical analysis indicates that our modifications have *negligible* impact on the running time performance of Argon2 for the honest party (sequential), while the modifications will *increase* the attackers aAT costs by nearly an order of magnitude.

Review of the Argon2 Compression Function. We begin by briefly reviewing the Argon2 round function $\mathcal{G} : \{0,1\}^{8192} \to \{0,1\}^{8192}$, which takes two $1\,\mathrm{KB}$ blocks X and Y as input and outputs the next block $\mathcal{G}(X,Y)$. $\mathcal{G}$ builds upon a second function $\mathcal{BP} : \{0,1\}^{1024} \to \{0,1\}^{1024}$, which is the Blake2b round function [SAA+15]. In our analysis we treat $\mathcal{BP}$ as a blackbox. For a more detailed explanation including the specific definition of $\mathcal{BP}$, we refer the readers to the Argon2 specification [BDK16].

To begin, $\mathcal{G}$ takes the intermediate block $R = X \oplus Y$ (which is being treated as an 8×8 array of 16-byte values $R_0, \ldots, R_{63}$), and runs $\mathcal{BP}$ on each row to create a second intermediate stage Q. We then apply $\mathcal{BP}$ to Q column-wise to obtain one more intermediate value Z: Specifically:

$$(Q_0, Q_1, \ldots, Q_7) \leftarrow \mathcal{BP}(R_0, R_1, \ldots, R_7) \qquad (Z_0, Z_8, \ldots, Z_{56}) \leftarrow \mathcal{BP}(Q_0, Q_8, \ldots, Q_{56})$$
$$(Q_8, Q_9, \ldots, Q_{15}) \leftarrow \mathcal{BP}(R_8, R_9, \ldots, R_{15}) \qquad (Z_1, Z_9, \ldots, Z_{57}) \leftarrow \mathcal{BP}(Q_1, Q_9, \ldots, Q_{57})$$
$$\cdots$$
$$(Q_{56}, Q_{57}, \ldots, Q_{63}) \leftarrow \mathcal{BP}(R_{56}, R_{57}, \ldots, R_{63}) \qquad (Z_7, Z_{15}, \ldots, Z_{63}) \leftarrow \mathcal{BP}(Q_7, Q_{15}, \ldots, Q_{63})$$

To finish, we have one last XOR, giving the result $\mathcal{G}(X,Y) = R \oplus Z$.

ASIC vs CPU AT Cost. From the above description, it is clear that computation of the round function can be parallelized. In particular, the first (resp. last) eight calls to the permutation $\mathcal{BP}$ are all independent and could easily be evaluated in parallel i.e., compute $\mathcal{BP}(R_0, R_1, \ldots, R_7), \ldots, \mathcal{BP}(R_{56}, R_{57}, \ldots, R_{64})$

then compute $\mathcal{BP}(Q_0, Q_8, \ldots, Q_{56}), \ldots, \mathcal{BP}(Q_7, Q_{15}, \ldots, Q_{63})$ in parallel. Similarly, XORing the $1\,\text{KB}$ blocks in the first $(R = X \oplus Y)$ and last $(\mathcal{G}(X, Y) = R \oplus Z)$ steps can be done in parallel. Thus if we let $t_{\mathcal{BP}}^{ASIC}$ (resp. $t_{\mathcal{BP}}^{CPU}$) denote the time to compute $\mathcal{BP}$ on an ASIC (resp. CPU) we have $t_{\mathcal{G}}^{ASIC} \approx 2t_{\mathcal{BP}}^{ASIC}$ whereas $t_{\mathcal{G}}^{CPU} \approx 16 \times t_{\mathcal{BP}}^{CPU}$ since the honest party (CPU) must evaluate each call to $\mathcal{BP}$ sequentially. Suppose that the MHF uses the round function $\mathcal{G}$ to fill N blocks of size $1\,\text{KB}$ e.g., $N = 2^{20}$ is $1\,\text{GB}$. Then the total area-time product on an ASIC (resp. CPU) would approximately be $\left(A_{mem}^{ASIC} N\right) \times \left(t_{\mathcal{G}}^{ASIC} N\right) \approx 2N^2 \times A_{mem}^{ASIC} t_{\mathcal{BP}}^{ASIC}$ (resp. $\left(A_{mem}^{CPU} N\right) \times \left(16 t_{\mathcal{BP}}^{CP} N\right)$ where A_{mem}^{ASIC} (resp. A_{mem}^{ASIC}) is the area required to store a $1\,\text{KB}$ block in memory on an ASIC (resp. CPU). Since memory is egalitarian we have $A_{mem}^{ASIC} \approx A_{mem}^{CPU}$ whereas we may have $t_{\mathcal{G}}^{ASIC} \ll t_{\mathcal{G}}^{CPU}$. If we can make $\mathcal{G}$ inherently sequential then we have $t_{\mathcal{G}}^{ASIC} \approx 16 t_{\mathcal{BP}}^{ASIC}$, which means that the new AT cost on an ASIC is $16 N^2 \times A_{mem}^{ASIC} t_{\mathcal{BP}}^{ASIC}$ which is eight times higher than before. We remark that the change would not necessarily increase the running time $N \times t_{\mathcal{G}}^{CPU}$ on a CPU since evaluation is already sequential. We stress that the improvement (resp. attack) applies to *all* modes of Argon2 both data-dependent (Argon2d, Argon2id) and data-independent (Argon2i), and that the attack could potentially be combined with other pebbling attacks [AB16, BCS16].

Remark 2. We remark that the implementation of $\mathcal{BP}$ in Argon2 is heavily optimized using SIMD instructions so that the function $\mathcal{BP}$ would be computed in parallel on *most* computer architectures. Thus, we avoid trying to make $\mathcal{BP}$ sequential as this would slow down *both* the attacker *and* the honest party i.e., both $t_{\mathcal{BP}}^{CPU}$ and $t_{\mathcal{BP}}^{ASIC}$ would increase.

Inherently Sequential Round Function. We present a small modification to the Argon2 compression function that prevents the above attack. The idea is simply to inject extra data-dependencies between calls to $\mathcal{BP}$ to ensure that an attacker must evaluate each call to $\mathcal{BP}$ sequentially just like the honest party would. In short, we require the first output byte from the $i - 1^{th}$ call to $\mathcal{BP}$ to be XORed with the ith input byte for the current (i^{th}) call.

In particular, we now compute $\mathcal{G}(X, Y)$ as:

$(Q_0, Q_1, \ldots, Q_7) \leftarrow \mathcal{BP}(R_0, R_1, \ldots, R_7)$ $(Z_0, Z_8, \ldots, Z_{56}) \leftarrow \mathcal{BP}(Q_0, Q_8, \ldots, Q_{56})$

$(Q_8, Q_9, \ldots, Q_{15}) \leftarrow \mathcal{BP}(R_8, R_9 \oplus Q_0, \ldots, R_{15})$ $(Z_1, Z_9, \ldots, Z_{57}) \leftarrow \mathcal{BP}(Q_1, Q_9 \oplus Z_0, \ldots, Q_{57})$

$\cdots$ $\cdots$

$(Q_{56}, Q_{57}, \ldots, Q_{63}) \leftarrow \mathcal{BP}(R_{56}, R_{57}, \ldots, R_{64} \oplus Q_{48})$ $(Z_7, Z_{15}, \ldots, Z_{63}) \leftarrow \mathcal{BP}(Q_7, Q_{15}, \ldots, Q_{63} \oplus Z_6)$

where, as before, $R = X \oplus Y$ and the output is $\mathcal{G}(X, Y) = Z \oplus R$.

We welcome cryptanalysis of both this round function and the original Argon2 round function. We stress that the primary threat to passwords is brute-force attacks (not hash inversions/collisions etc.) so increasing evaluation costs is arguably the primary goal.

Implementation and Empirical Evaluation. To determine the performance impact this would have on Argon2, we modified the publicly available code to include this new compression function. The source code is available on Github at https://github.com/antiparallel-drsbrg-argon/Antiparallel-DRS-BRG. We then ran experiments using both the Argon2 and DRS+BRG edge distributions, and further split these groupings to include/exclude the new round function for a total of four conditions. For each condition, we evaluated 1000 instances of the memory hard function in single-pass mode with memory parameter $N = 2^{20}$ blocks (i.e., $1\,GB = N \times 1\,KB$). In our experiments, we interleave instances from different conditions to ensure that any incidental interference from system processes affects each condition equally. The experiments were run on a desktop with an Intel Core 15-6600K CPU capable of running at 3.5 GHz with 4 cores. After 1000 runs of each instance, we observed only small differences in runtimes, (3%) at most. The exact results can be seen in Table 1 along with 99% confidence intervals. The evidence suggests that there is no large difference between any of these versions and that the anti-parallel modification would not cause a large increase in running time for legitimate users.

Table 1. Anti-parallel runtimes with 99% confidence

	Argon2i	DRS+BRG
Current	1405.541 ± 1.036 ms	1445.275 ± 1.076 ms
Anti-parallel	1405.278 ± 1.121 ms	1445.017 ± 0.895 ms

Acknowledgments. Seunghoon Lee was supported in part by NSF award CNS #1755708. Ben Harsha was supported by a Rolls-Royce Doctoral Fellowship. The views expressed in this paper are those of the authors and do not necessarily reflect the views of National Science Foundation or Rolls-Royce.

References

[AB16]   Alwen, J., Blocki, J.: Efficiently computing data-independent memory-hard functions. In: Robshaw, M., Katz, J. (eds.) CRYPTO 2016, Part II. LNCS, vol. 9815, pp. 241–271. Springer, Heidelberg (2016). https://doi.org/10.1007/978-3-662-53008-5_9

[AB17]   Alwen, J., Blocki, J.: Towards practical attacks on Argon2i and balloon hashing. In: 2017 IEEE European Symposium on Security and Privacy (EuroS&P), pp. 142–157. IEEE (2017)

[ABH17] Alwen, J., Blocki, J., Harsha, B.: Practical graphs for optimal side-channel resistant memory-hard functions. In: Thuraisingham, B.M., Evans, D., Malkin, T., Xu, D. (eds.), ACM CCS 2017, pp. 1001–1017. ACM Press, October/November 2017

[ABMW05] Abadi, M., Burrows, M., Manasse, M., Wobber, T.: Moderately hard, memory-bound functions. ACM Trans. Internet Technol. 5(2), 299–327 (2005)

[ABP17] Alwen, J., Blocki, J., Pietrzak, K.: Depth-robust graphs and their cumulative memory complexity. In: Coron, J.-S., Nielsen, J.B. (eds.) EUROCRYPT 2017, Part III. LNCS, vol. 10212, pp. 3–32. Springer, Cham (2017). https://doi.org/10.1007/978-3-319-56617-7_1

[ABP18] Alwen, J., Blocki, J., Pietrzak, K.: Sustained space complexity. In: Nielsen, J.B., Rijmen, V. (eds.) EUROCRYPT 2018, Part II. LNCS, vol. 10821, pp. 99–130. Springer, Cham (2018). https://doi.org/10.1007/978-3-319-78375-8_4

[ACP+17] Alwen, J., Chen, B., Pietrzak, K., Reyzin, L., Tessaro, S.: Scrypt is maximally memory-hard. In: Coron, J.-S., Nielsen, J.B. (eds.) EUROCRYPT 2017, Part III. LNCS, vol. 10212, pp. 33–62. Springer, Cham (2017). https://doi.org/10.1007/978-3-319-56617-7_2

[AS15] Alwen, J., Serbinenko, V.: High parallel complexity graphs and memory-hard functions. In: Servedio, R.A., Rubinfeld, R. (eds.), 47th ACM STOC, pp. 595–603. ACM Press, June 2015

[AT17] Alwen, J., Tackmann, B.: Moderately hard functions: definition, instantiations, and applications. In: Kalai, Y., Reyzin, L. (eds.) TCC 2017, Part I. LNCS, vol. 10677, pp. 493–526. Springer, Cham (2017). https://doi.org/10.1007/978-3-319-70500-2_17

[BCS16] Boneh, D., Corrigan-Gibbs, H., Schechter, S.: Balloon hashing: a memory-hard function providing provable protection against sequential attacks. In: Cheon, J.H., Takagi, T. (eds.) ASIACRYPT 2016, Part I. LNCS, vol. 10031, pp. 220–248. Springer, Heidelberg (2016). https://doi.org/10.1007/978-3-662-53887-6_8

[BDK16] Biryukov, A., Dinu, D., Khovratovich, D.: Argon2: new generation of memory-hard functions for password hashing and other applications. In: 2016 IEEE European Symposium on Security and Privacy (EuroS&P), pp. 292–302. IEEE (2016)

[Ber05] Bernstein, D.J.: Cache-timing attacks on AES (2005)

[BHK+18] Blocki, J., Harsha, B., Kang, S., Lee, S., Xing, L., Zhou, S.: Data-independent memory hard functions: new attacks and stronger constructions (full version). Cryptology ePrint Archive, Report 2018/944 (2018). https://eprint.iacr.org/2018/944

[BHZ18] Blocki, J., Harsha, B., Zhou, S.: On the economics of offline password cracking. In: 2018 IEEE Symposium on Security and Privacy, pp. 853–871. IEEE Computer Society Press, May 2018

[BK15] Biryukov, A., Khovratovich, D.: Tradeoff cryptanalysis of memory-hard functions. In: Iwata, T., Cheon, J.H. (eds.) ASIACRYPT 2015, Part II. LNCS, vol. 9453, pp. 633–657. Springer, Heidelberg (2015). https://doi.org/10.1007/978-3-662-48800-3_26

[Boy07] Boyen, X.: Halting password puzzles - hard-to-break encryption from human-memorable keys. In: 16th USENIX Security Symposium–SECURITY 2007, pp. 119–134. The USENIX Association, Berkeley (2007). http://www.cs.stanford.edu/~xb/security07/

[BRZ18] Blocki, J., Ren, L., Zhou, S.: Bandwidth-hard functions: reductions and lower bounds. In: Lie, D., Mannan, M., Backes, M., Wang, X. (eds.) ACM CCS 2018, pp. 1820–1836. ACM Press, October 2018

[BZ17] Blocki, J., Zhou, S.: On the depth-robustness and cumulative pebbling cost of Argon2i. In: Kalai, Y., Reyzin, L. (eds.) TCC 2017, Part I. LNCS, vol. 10677, pp. 445–465. Springer, Cham (2017). https://doi.org/10.1007/978-3-319-70500-2_15

[DGN03] Dwork, C., Goldberg, A., Naor, M.: On memory-bound functions for fighting spam. In: Boneh, D. (ed.) CRYPTO 2003. LNCS, vol. 2729, pp. 426–444. Springer, Heidelberg (2003). https://doi.org/10.1007/978-3-540-45146-4_25

[FLW14] Forler, C., Lucks, S., Wenzel, J.: Memory-demanding password scrambling. In: Sarkar, P., Iwata, T. (eds.) ASIACRYPT 2014, Part II. LNCS, vol. 8874, pp. 289–305. Springer, Heidelberg (2014). https://doi.org/10.1007/978-3-662-45608-8_16

[JWK81] Hong, J.-W., Kung, H.T.: I/o complexity: the red-blue pebble game. In: Proceedings of the Thirteenth Annual ACM Symposium on Theory of Computing, STOC 1981, pp. 326–333. ACM, New York, NY, USA (1981)

[KDBJ17] Khovratovich, D., Dinu, D., Biryukov, A., Josefsson, S.: The memory-hard Argon2 password hash and proof-of-work function. Memory (2017)

[Lee11] Lee, C.: Litecoin (2011)

[Len81] Lengauer, T.: Black-white pebbles and graph separation. Acta Informatica 16(4), 465–475 (1981)

[LT82] Lengauer, T., Tarjan, R.E.: Asymptotically tight bounds on time-space trade-offs in a pebble game. J. ACM 29(4), 1087–1130 (1982)

[Per09] Percival, C.: Stronger key derivation via sequential memory-hard functions (2009)

[Pes14] Peslyak, A.: yescrypt: password hashing scalable beyond bcrypt and scrypt (2014)

[PHC16] Password hashing competition. (2016). https://password-hashing.net/

[Pip77] Pippenger, N.: Superconcentrators. SIAM J. Comput. 6(2), 298–304 (1977)

[RD17] Ren, L., Devadas, S.: Bandwidth hard functions for ASIC resistance. In: Kalai, Y., Reyzin, L. (eds.) TCC 2017, Part I. LNCS, vol. 10677, pp. 466–492. Springer, Cham (2017). https://doi.org/10.1007/978-3-319-70500-2_16

[SAA+15] Simplício Jr., M.A., Almeida, L.C., Andrade, E.R., dos Santos, P.C.F., Barreto, P.S.L.M.: Lyra2: password hashing scheme with improved security against time-memory trade-offs. Cryptology ePrint Archive, Report 2015/136 (2015). http://eprint.iacr.org/2015/136

[Val77] Valiant, L.G.: Graph-theoretic arguments in low-level complexity. In: Gruska, J. (ed.) MFCS 1977. LNCS, vol. 53, pp. 162–176. Springer, Heidelberg (1977). https://doi.org/10.1007/3-540-08353-7_135

[Wie04] Wiener, M.J.: The full cost of cryptanalytic attacks. J. Cryptol. 17(2), 105–124 (2004)

Simultaneous Amplification: The Case of Non-interactive Zero-Knowledge

Vipul Goyal[1], Aayush Jain[2(✉)], and Amit Sahai[2]

[1] CMU, Pittsburgh, USA
vipul@cmu.edu
[2] UCLA, Los Angeles, USA
{aayushjain,sahai}@cs.ucla.edu

Abstract. In this work, we explore the question of simultaneous privacy and soundness amplification for non-interactive zero-knowledge *argument* systems (NIZK). We show that any δ_s−sound and δ_z−zero-knowledge NIZK candidate satisfying $\delta_s + \delta_z = 1 - \epsilon$, for any constant $\epsilon > 0$, can be turned into a computationally sound and zero-knowledge candidate with the only extra assumption of a subexponentially secure public-key encryption.

We develop novel techniques to leverage the use of leakage simulation lemma (Jetchev-Peitzrak TCC 2014) to argue amplification. A crucial component of our result is a new notion for secret sharing NP instances. We believe that this may be of independent interest.

To achieve this result we analyze following two transformations:
- **Parallel Repetition:** We show that using parallel repetition any δ_s−sound and δ_z−zero-knowledge NIZK candidate can be turned into (roughly) δ_s^n−sound and $1 - (1 - \delta_z)^n$−zero-knowledge candidate. Here n is the repetition parameter.
- **MPC based Repetition:** We propose a new transformation that amplifies zero-knowledge in the same way that parallel repetition amplifies soundness. We show that using this any δ_s−sound and δ_z−zero-knowledge NIZK candidate can be turned into (roughly) $1 - (1 - \delta_s)^n$−sound and $2 \cdot \delta_z^n$−zero-knowledge candidate.

Then we show that using these transformations in a zig-zag fashion we can obtain our result. Finally, we also present a simple transformation which directly turns any NIZK candidate satisfying $\delta_s, \delta_z < 1/3 - 1/\mathsf{poly}(\lambda)$ to a secure one.

1 Introduction

Amplification techniques are central to cryptography and complexity theory. The basic approach is to first obtain a construction which achieves the desired property but "with some error". In the next step, the initial construction is compiled into a final one which achieves a much smaller error parameter. This is often done by having the final construction invoke the initial construction several times. Thus, we say that the compiler is used to "amplify" the desired security property by reducing or eliminating the error.

© International Association for Cryptologic Research 2019
A. Boldyreva and D. Micciancio (Eds.): CRYPTO 2019, LNCS 11693, pp. 608–637, 2019.
https://doi.org/10.1007/978-3-030-26951-7_21

Amplification techniques have served as a gateway towards significant progress in cryptography (as well as complexity theory). As an example, all the initial constructions of zero-knowledge proofs were obtained via soundness amplification. First a zero-knowledge proof with a significant soundness error was obtained, and then, either sequential or parallel repetition was used to reduce the soundness error to negligible. Within the area of complexity theory, soundness amplification of interactive protocols has played a central role in various important advances such as in probabilistically checkable proofs (PCPs) and hardness of approximation. Another rich line of research studies hardness amplifications and its various connections to coding theory [23]. Not only does amplification help us develop our understanding of the assumptions that the primitives can be based upon, it is an invaluable tool to construct complex primitives. A notable recent success is that of [1], where, a security amplification theorem for functional encryption was pivotal to constructing first obfuscation scheme from succinctly stated and instance-independent assumptions.

Simultaneous Amplification. The problem of amplification is known to be especially challenging if one tries to amplify multiple properties simultaneously. A well-known example of this concerns oblivious transfer (OT). Weak oblivious transfer considers a situation where the security of both the sender and the receiver is prone to failure: a malicious sender might have advantage ϵ_1 in guessing the choice bit of the receiver, while, a malicious receiver might have advantage ϵ_2 in guessing the input bit of the sender which it did not select. A rich body of literature has studied amplification techniques to obtain a full-fledged OT given a weak OT [11,36,37]. These amplification techniques have proven to be useful in a variety of problem including cryptography from noisy channels [10,24], and, multi-party differentially private protocols [16].

Our Focus: Amplification for Non-interactive Zero-Knowledge Arguments. In this work, we study simultaneous amplification of soundness and zero-knowledge. As discussed before, a number of works have studied amplifying soundness for interactive proofs (and arguments), and as such, some of these results apply even to zero-knowledge protocols. However what if the zero-knowledge property had an error to start with?[1] More concretely, we are interested in the following question.

Suppose one is given a non-interactive zero-knowledge (NIZK) argument with soundness error δ_s and zero-knowledge error δ_z, is it possible to compile it into a full-fledged secure non-interactive zero-knowledge argument system?

In more detail, consider $(\delta_s, \delta_z) - $ NIZK, where δ_s is the probability with which any efficient adversary can win in the soundness experiment. Similarly δ_z is the advantage with which any efficient adversary can distinguish between simulated and honest proofs. (Please see next Section for more formal definitions.)

---

[1] The most important reason to consider this is that it may be easier to construct NIZK with relaxed soundness and zero knowledge requirements. Indeed, in the past, even slight relaxations of zero knowledge, such as ϵ-zero knowledge [12], have led to simpler protocols.

We first observe that it is trivial to construct a NIZK candidate where $\delta_s + \delta_z = 1$. This can be constructed by sampling a crs as a bit which is set to 1 with probability δ_s and 0 otherwise. If crs $= 1$, the verification algorithm is supposed to verify the string $\perp$ as a valid proof, and otherwise it should only verify a valid NP witness of the given instance as a valid proof. This system is trivially δ_s-sound, and a simulator that just outputs $\perp$ achieves $(1 - \delta_s) = \delta_z$-zero knowledge. Of course, we cannot expect this trivial system to be amplifiable.

Thus the above question can be rewritten as:

Is it possible to amplify (δ_s, δ_z)−non-interactive zero-knowledge, where $\delta_s + \delta_z = 1 - \epsilon$ for any constant $\epsilon > 0$, to full-fledged non-interactive zero-knowledge under standard cryptographic assumptions?

To our knowledge, this question has not been studied before. We believe the question of amplifying soundness and zero-knowledge simultaneously is a basic one which is interesting in its own right.

We answer this in the affirmative, by giving such a transformation assuming that subexponentially secure public-key encryption exists. Formally, we prove the following theorem:

Theorem 1. *Assume a subexponentially secure* PKE *scheme, and a* NIZK *candidate Π with δ_s−soundness and δ_z−zero-knowledge where δ_z, δ_s are in $(0, 1)$ with $\delta_s + \delta_z < 1$ for all polynomial time adversaries, then there exists a fully secure* NIZK *candidate against all polynomial time adversaries.*

NIZK is a basic primitive in cryptography which is widely used to obtain the constructions of other basic and advanced primitives. Yet, despite much effort, NIZK is unfortunately known from very few assumptions: [5,6,8,13,17–19,32, 35]. E.g., we do not yet know a NIZK system that is proven secure under the assumption of (even subexponentially secure) DDH or LWE. Given this state of the art our work gives an alternative easier path to construct NIZKs since now one only needs to obtain constructions satisfying $\delta_s + \delta_z < 1$ (as opposed to constructions achieving the standard notion where δ_s and δ_z are negligible).

We develop several novel techniques to prove our result. An interesting primitive we introduce is the notion of *secret sharing NP instances*.

Secret Sharing of NP Instances. Towards constructing a NIZK amplification theorem, our main technical tool is what we call *secret sharing of NP Instances*. Very roughly, this allows breaking a (statement, witness) pair into n different (statement, witness) pairs such that each pair can then be verified individually while no single pair (or upto a threshold t of pairs) reveals any information about the original witness. Additionally it allows that if more than some other threshold t' of instances are satisfiable then x itself should be satisfiable. We believe secret sharing of NP instances to be a novel conceptual tool which is of independent interest. Please see Sect. 2 for more details and a technical overview. Inspired by [1], to prove our result, we use and build upon the ideas used to prove the dense model theorem [33].

Related Works. We are not aware of any prior works on amplifying zero-knowledge and soundness simultaneously. However there have been a number of prior works on amplification in general. Soundness amplification of interactive proofs has been studied in a rich line of works [3,7,21,31]. As mentioned before, another line of research studies amplification and combiners for oblivious transfer [20,30]. Another related result concerns "polarization" (which is a type of simultaneous amplification) of complete problems for SZK [34].

2   Technical Overview

Suppose we have been given a NIZK candidate where $\delta_s + \delta_z = 1 - \epsilon$ for any constant $\epsilon > 0$, how do we construct one where $\delta_s + \delta_z < \mathsf{negl}$?
We study three basic transformations and analyze their effects on the parameters (δ_s, δ_z).

- **Parallel Repetition:** We show that this transformation converts a NIZK candidate with parameters (δ_s, δ_z) to roughly $(\delta_s^n, 1 - (1 - \delta_z)^n)$, where n is some parameter which can be set to be any polynomial in λ. Thus, this transformation boosts soundness but worsens zero-knowledge property.
- **MPC-based Repetition:** We show that this transformation converts a NIZK candidate with parameters (δ_s, δ_z) to roughly $(1 - (1 - \delta_s)^n, 2 \cdot \delta_z^n)$, where n is some parameter which can be set to be any polynomial in λ. Thus, this transformation boosts zero-knowledge but worsens soundness property.
- **MPC-based Amplification:** This transformation converts a NIZK candidate with parameters (δ_s, δ_z) satisfying $\delta_s, \delta_z < 1/3 - 1/\mathsf{poly}(\lambda)$ to a fully secure NIZK candidate.

Then, we show using these three transformation how to take any (δ_S, δ_z) NIZK satisfying $\delta_s + \delta_z = 1 - \epsilon$ for any constant $\epsilon > 0$, and output a fully secure NIZK candidate.

2.1   Parallel Repetition

As a warm up that is useful to introduce some of the ideas we will use, let us first consider the standard parallel repetition transformation. The construction is as follows. Let Π be the underlying candidate. The setup algorithm of the transformed candidate $\Pi_{\|}$ does the following. It computes $\Pi.\mathsf{Setup}(1^\lambda) \to \mathsf{crs}_i$ for $i \in [n]$, where n is some repetition parameter. It sets $\mathsf{crs} = (\mathsf{crs}_1, ..., \mathsf{crs}_n)$. The prover then proves $x \in L$ using the given witness w, employing each crs_i independently to form n proofs $\pi = (\pi_1, ..., \pi_n)$. Finally, the verification succeeds if each π_i verifies with respect to crs_i. We discuss at a high level various properties associated with this scheme.

$(\delta_s^n + \mathsf{negl})$ *-Soundness:* This is already known from many of the previous works (such as [7]) that soundness is amplified this way for any non-interactive argument system upon parallel repetition. The (overly simplified) intuition is the following. If the soundness error is δ_s, then there exists a hardcore set S of size $(1 - \delta_s) \cdot |\mathcal{R}|$ where $\mathcal{R}$ is the space of randomness for the coins of Π.Setup. This hardcore set has the property that if crs is generated using randomness from this set, then any adversary $\mathcal{A}$ of some large bounded size, will only break soundness with a small probability ϵ_s. Then, if we have n parallel systems, the probability that no crs_i is sampled using randomness from this set S falls as δ_s^n. In order to prove this formally, in spirit of [7], we prove the following lemma. The details can be found in the full version.

Lemma 1. *Let $F : \{0,1\}^\lambda \to \{0,1\}^l$ be a function where $l = \mathsf{poly}(\lambda)$ and $E : \{0,1\}^{\lambda+l+r(\lambda)} \to \{0,1\}$ be a circuit of size e. Let $\delta \geq \epsilon \in (0,1)$ and $s, s' > 0$ be functions of λ. If for all circuits $C : \{0,1\}^{l(\lambda)} \to \{0,1\}^{r(\lambda)}$ of size s we have*

$$\Pr_{u \xleftarrow{\$} \{0,1\}^\lambda} [E(u, F(u), C(F(u))) = 1] \leq \delta$$

Then there exists a set S of size $|S| = (1 - \delta)2^\lambda$ and a polynomial $s_{overhead}(\lambda)$ (independent of s, s' and e) such that: For all circuits $C' : \{0,1\}^{l(\lambda)} \to \{0,1\}^{r(\lambda)}$ of size less than $s' = \frac{s\epsilon(1-\delta)}{\delta} - e - s_{overhead}$

$$\Pr_{u \xleftarrow{\$} S} [E(u, F(u), C'(F(u))) = 1] \leq \epsilon$$

Roughly F is the algorithm Π.Setup, C is the adversary and E is the algorithm that tests if soundness is broken. Since the size of E is a factor that determines the size of the adversary that can be handled, we want to keep it small. Thus, we work with a NIZK argument of knowledge candidate instead of a NIZK candidate. This is done by using a public key of a public key encryption scheme (generated at setup) to encrypt the witness, and the NIZK system is used to prove that this encrypted witness is valid. Then, it becomes possible to check if the soundness of Π was broken by simply decrypting the witness and testing its validity for the instance x. This ensures that size of E is polynomially bounded.

$1 - (1 - \delta_z)^n - Zero\text{-}Knowledge$: Since parameters are very crucial to achieve our result, we also have to show that zero-knowledge is not completely destroyed by parallel repetition. This is so that we can tolerate some amount of degradation. To achieve this theorem, we prove and rely on the following lemma:

Theorem 2. *Fix $1^\lambda, x \in \mathsf{SAT}$ with $|x| = \mathsf{poly}(\lambda)$ and corresponding witness u. Define two functions E_b for $b \in \{0,1\}$, that takes as input $\{0,1\}^{\ell_b}$. Here ℓ_b is the length of randomness required to compute the following.*
Consider the following process:

1. *Sample $r_1, r_2 \leftarrow \{0,1\}^{\ell_0}$.*
2. *Run Π.Setup$(1^\lambda; r_1) \to$ crs.*
3. *Run Π.Prove(crs, x, u) $\to \pi$.*
4. *Sample $\tilde{r} \leftarrow \{0,1\}^{\ell_1}$*
5. *Compute $(\widetilde{crs}, \tilde{\pi}) \leftarrow \Pi$.Sim$(1^\lambda, x; \tilde{r})$.*

6. E_0 on input $(r_1, r_2) \in \{0,1\}^{\ell_0}$ outputs (crs, π).

7. E_1 on input $\tilde{r} \in \{0,1\}^{\ell_1}$ outputs $(\widetilde{\text{crs}}, \tilde{\pi})$.

If Π satisfies $\delta-$zero knowledge for all adversaries of size s, then, there exists two computable (not necessarily efficient) measures $\mathcal{M}_0$ and $\mathcal{M}_1$ ($\mathcal{M}_b$ defined over $\{0,1\}^{\ell_b}$ for $b \in \{0,1\}$) of density exactly $1 - \delta$ such that, for all circuits $\mathcal{A}$ of size $s' < s\epsilon^2/128(\ell_0 + \ell_1 + 1)$,

$$\left| \Pr_{(r_1,r_2) \leftarrow \mathcal{D}_{\mathcal{M}_0}} [\mathcal{A}(E_0(r_1,r_2)) = 1] - \Pr_{\tilde{r} \leftarrow \mathcal{D}_{\mathcal{M}_1}} [\mathcal{A}(E_1(\tilde{r})) = 1] \right| < \epsilon$$

Here both measures may depend on (x, u)

This theorem roughly says that there exists two measures $\mathcal{S}_0$ and $\mathcal{S}_1$ of density exactly $1 - \delta_z$ such that the when the proof and setup is done using randomness from $\mathcal{S}_0$ then for a bounded adversary it is computationally indistinguishable from the case when the crs and the proof is simulated using randomness from $\mathcal{S}_1$. Thus, using this one can show that if randomness from for all n parallel systems is generated from this measure $\mathcal{S}_0$, then it is computationally close to the case when the proofs for all n systems are simulated using randomness from $\mathcal{S}_1$. Since the densities of $\mathcal{S}_0$ and $\mathcal{S}_1$ is exactly equal to $1 - \delta_z$, this allows to (informally) argue that the zero-knowledge parameter of the resulting candidate is (very roughly) bounded by $1 - (1 - \delta_z)^n + \text{negl}$. Here is the formal theorem statement:

Theorem 3. *Assuming Π is δ_z-zero-knowledge against adversaries of size s, $\Pi_\parallel$ is $(1 - (1 - \delta_z)^n) + O(n \cdot \epsilon)-$zero-knowledge against adversaries of size $s' = s \cdot \epsilon^2/\text{poly}(\lambda)$ for some fixed polynomial poly.*

The details can be found in the full version. Given that we have a way to reduce soundness error while not letting zero-knowledge degrade too much, we turn to the next question:

> *Is there a natural transformation that amplifies zero-knowledge, while not degrading soundness too much?*

We consider this question and propose a very natural transformation to achieve this. We call it MPC-based repetition because it achieves parameters similar to parallel repetition where the roles of zero-knowledge error and soundness error are switched, but it is based on secure multi-party computation (MPC) protocols instead of simple parallel invocation of the NIZK candidate. In another words, it is a natural dual of the construction above.

2.2   MPC-Based Repetition

A First Idea: Before we describe our approach, we first describe a seemingly more natural approach that we do not know how to analyze: Specifically, consider the new candidate which runs $\Pi.\text{Setup} \rightarrow \text{crs}_i$ for $i \in [2]$. The prover first computes π_1 with respect to crs_1 for the given NP relation. The prover then considers the NP relation that is satisfied with a "witness" that is any valid proof with respect to the verification procedure of the NIZK candidate. Then, the prover can use π_1 as a witness to satisfy this new relation, and thus compute π_2 with respect to crs_2. The output is then set as π_2. For this construction it may seem reasonable to expect that soundness should fall as $1 - (1 - \delta_s)^2$, because if both $\mathsf{crs}_1, \mathsf{crs}_2$ are sampled using randomness from the hardcore set, then the soundness should hold. It may also seem reasonable to expect that zero-knowledge should be amplified as δ_z^2 as it appears that zero-knowledge should be retained as long as either π_1 or π_2 is computed from the hardcore set. We do not know how to formally convert this intuition into a proof. In fact, as far as we know, this intuition may be false, and we leave it as an interesting open problem to analyse this construction. We now summarize the difficulties in turning the intuition above into a proof:

- Arguing soundness is hard because the NIZK candidate is only required to have computational soundness. Therefore, with respect to crs_2 there may always exist a valid witness π_1 for an instance x, crs_1 even when $x \notin L$. As a result, we do not know how to analyze how soundness is affected by this construction.
- Arguing zero-knowledge is also hard for important technical reasons related to hard core sets, that we also have to keep in mind when we try to repair this state of affairs. When randomness is sampled from the hardcore measure to prove instance x, crs_1, it may already leak information about the witness for x, as the hardcore measure now can depend on w.

For the reasons above we consider a completely different approach. Crucial to our approach is the following primitive, which we call verifiable sharing scheme for NP statements (denoted by NPSS). We believe this notion may be of independent interest to other interesting applications.

Secret Sharing NP Instances: Informally speaking[2], an NPSS scheme consists of three algorithms Share, Verify, and Sim. Given any instance $x \in$ SAT and its witness w, we have that Share(n, x, w) outputs n instances along with witnesses $\{x_i, w_i\}_{i \in [n]}$ such that the following guarantees are met. The scheme is parameterized by two thresholds t_1, t_2.

1. If $x \in$ SAT with w being a valid witness, then the output of Share(n, x, w) will have the property that w_i is a valid witness of the statement $x_i \in$ SAT for all $i \in [n]$.
2. **Robustness for threshold t_1.** There exists a verification algorithm Verify such that if Verify$(n, x, x_1, ..., x_n) = 1$, then if there is a set $S \subset [n]$ of size greater than or equal to t_1 such that $x_i \in$ SAT for $i \in S$, then we have that $x \in$ SAT. Furthermore there is an efficient algorithm that recovers the witness to x given witnesses for the statements x_i where $i \in S$.

---

[2] Formal details can be found in Sect. 5.

3. **Simulatability for threshold** t_2. Consider any set $Z \subset [n]$ of size less than or equal to t_2. Then, informally, we want that the instances $x_1, .., x_n$ and witnesses $\{w_i\}_{i \in Z}$ should not "reveal any knowledge" about membership of x in SAT. That is, the output of $\mathsf{Sim}(n, x, Z)$ is computationally indistinguishable from the output of $\mathsf{Share}(n, x, w)$ restricted to all instances $x_1, \ldots, x_n$ and witnesses $\{w_i\}_{i \in Z}$.

Our actual notion of NPSS also includes a setup algorithm $\mathsf{Setup}(1^\lambda)$ that outputs public parameters pp, that is also input to constituent NPSS algorithms. We will describe how to construct such a sharing scheme for various choices of t_1, t_2 later. Assuming we have such a notion, we now describe how to achieve our goal. The following is our construction of $\Pi_\perp$ with repetition parameter n. Here is our construction. In the following set $t_1 = n$ and $t_2 = n - 1$ for the NPSS scheme.

– $\Pi_\perp.\mathsf{Setup}(1^\lambda)$:
  - Run $\Pi.\mathsf{Setup}(1^\lambda) \to \mathsf{crs}_i$ for $i \in [n]$.
  - Run $\mathsf{NPSS}.\mathsf{Setup}(1^\lambda) \to \mathsf{pp}$.
  - Output $\mathsf{crs} = (\mathsf{pp}, \mathsf{crs}_1, \ldots, \mathsf{crs}_n)$.
– $\Pi_\perp.\mathsf{Prove}(\mathsf{crs}, x, w)$:
  - Run $\mathsf{NPSS}.\mathsf{Share}(\mathsf{pp}, n, x, w) \to (x_1, \ldots, x_n, w_1, \ldots, w_n)$
  - Run $\Pi.\mathsf{Prove}(\mathsf{crs}_i, x_i, w_i) \to \pi_i$ for $i \in [n]$.
  - Output $\pi = (x_1, \ldots, x_n, \pi_1, \ldots, \pi_n)$.
– $\Pi_\perp.\mathsf{Verify}(\mathsf{crs}, x, \pi)$:
  - Parse $\pi = (x_1, \ldots, x_n, \pi_1, \ldots, \pi_n)$.
  - Run $\mathsf{NPSS}.\mathsf{Verify}(\mathsf{pp}, n, x, x_1, \ldots, x_n)$.
  - Run $\Pi.\mathsf{Verify}(x_i, w_i)$ for $i \in [n]$.
  - Output 1 if all these steps pass. Output 0 otherwise.

We now revisit both the soundness and zero-knowledge property to observe the change in the parameters.

$(1 - (1 - \delta_s))^n - Soundness$: The idea here is that since the size of the hardcore measure is $(1 - \delta_s)|\mathcal{R}|$, where $\mathcal{R}$ is the set from which the randomness for $\Pi.\mathsf{Setup}$ is chosen, with probability $(1 - \delta_s)^n$ all crs_i for $i \in [n]$ will behave nicely. In such a case, if crs_i is used to prove $x_i \in \mathsf{SAT}$, then any efficient adversary can produce a false proof only with some tiny probability ϵ_s. Thus, by the robustness property and the lemmas described above we can argue soundness. A PKE scheme plays an important role because the associated secret key is used by our reduction to verify in polynomial time if the adversary has indeed succeeded in breaking soundness. Note that this is a highly simplified description and the proof requires a very careful analysis of the structure of the adversary. This proof can be found in Sect. 8. Here is the formal theorem:

Theorem 4. *Assuming PKE is perfectly correct and Π is δ_s-sound against adversaries of size s, then for every $1 > \epsilon > 0$, $\Pi_\perp$ is $(1-(1-\delta_s)^n)+O(\epsilon)-sound$ against adversaries of size $s' = O(s \cdot \epsilon \cdot \delta_s/(1-\delta_s))-\mathsf{poly}(\lambda)$ for a fixed polynomial poly.*

$2 \cdot \delta_z^n - zero\text{-}knowledge$: Proving zero-knowledge for this construction turns out to be highly nontrivial. Let us understand why is this the case. Consider an honest sharing of instance x and witness y, denoted by $x_1, ..., x_n$ with corresponding witnesses $w_1, ..., w_n$. As noted above, Theorem 2 says that there exist two hard-core measures $\mathcal{S}_{0,i}$ and $\mathcal{S}_{1,i}$ of density $1 - \delta_z$ such that the distribution of honestly generated pair (crs_i, π_i) for x_i generated using randomness from $\mathcal{S}_{0,i}$ is computationally close to the simulated distribution generated by choosing randomness from $\mathcal{S}_{1,i}$. Thus it seems that with probability at least $1 - \delta_z^n$, we should have at least one index $i \in [n]$, where we can shift to simulating proofs for one index i^*. Then, it seems plausible that we can use the security of NPSS scheme to simulate sharing $x_1, ..., x_n, \{w_i\}_{i \neq i^*}$. But unfortunately, this intuition fails to materialize as these measures $\mathcal{S}_{0,i}, \mathcal{S}_{1,i}$ are inefficient and may depend on w_i itself. In fact, this has been a major hurdle in various amplification scenarios, and that is why amplifying security for complex cryptographic primitives is considered a hard problem.

In order to fix this issue, we rely on the techniques building the dense model theorem. We overcome this issue by using the following idea, which can be made formal via the work on simulating auxiliary input [9,27]. Because the hardcore measure has reasonable probability mass $1 - \delta_z$, it cannot *verifiably* contain useful information to the adversary. For example, even if the hardcore distribution revealed the first few bits of the w_i, the adversary could not *know* for sure that these bits were in fact the correct bits. Indeed, we use the works of [9,27] to make this idea precise, and show that the hardcore measures can be simulated in a way that fools all efficient adversaries, with a simulation that runs in subexponential time. This allows us to argue witness indistinguishability. Finally, as witness indistinguishability is enough to get zero-knowledge the result holds. Similar techniques were also used in [1], to give an amplification theorem for any functional encryption scheme. Let us now go over the steps of the argument carefully. We will prove witness indistinguishability first. Consider an instance x and two witnesses (y_0, y_1). For all indices $i \in [n]$ let us output $\mathsf{crs} = (\mathsf{pp}, \mathsf{crs}_1, ..., \mathsf{crs}_n)$, instance $x_1, ..., x_n$ and proofs $\pi_1, ..., \pi_n$. We construct a series of hybrids from $\mathbf{Hybrid}_0$ to $\mathbf{Hybrid}_m$ where $\mathbf{Hybrid}_0$ is the hybrid where witness y_b for a random $b \in \{0, 1\}$ is used to prove honestly and $\mathbf{Hybrid}_m$ is independent of the witness. We prove that $|\Pr[\mathcal{A}(\mathbf{Hybrid}_0) = 1] - \Pr[\mathcal{A}(\mathbf{Hybrid}_m) = 1]| \leq \delta_z^n + \mathsf{negl}$ for any efficient adversary $\mathcal{A}$. Thus, this gives us the required result. Before delving slightly in the details, we recall the following two theorems. First theorem describes how sampling an element from measures of high density is computationally indistinguishable to sampling an element uniformly from a large set constructed using the measure.

Theorem 5 (Imported Theorem [22]). *Let $\mathcal{M}$ be any measure on $\{0, 1\}^n$ of density $\mu(\mathcal{M}) \geq 1 - \rho(n)$ Let $\gamma(n) \in (0, 1/2)$ be any function. Then, for a random set $\mathcal{S}$ chosen according to the measure $\mathcal{M}$ the following two holds with probability at least $1 - 2(2^{-2^n \gamma^2 (1-\rho)^4/64})$:*

$$- (1 - \tfrac{\gamma(1-\rho)}{4})(1 - \rho)2^n \leq |\mathcal{S}| \leq (1 + \tfrac{\gamma(1-\rho)}{4})(1 - \rho)2^n$$

– For such a random set S, for any distinguisher $\mathcal{A}$ with size $|\mathcal{A}| \le 2^n(\frac{\gamma^2(1-\rho)^4}{64n})$ satisfying

$$| \Pr_{x \leftarrow S}[\mathcal{A}(x) = 1] - \Pr_{x \leftarrow \mathcal{D}_{\mathcal{M}}}[\mathcal{A}(x) = 1]| \le \gamma$$

The following theorem from [9] says that for every distribution X and every potentially inefficient function $g : X \rightarrow \{0,1\}^{\ell_X}$, there exists a relatively efficient function h such that $(X, g(X))$ is computationally close to $(X, h(X))$. The complexity of h is roughly $O(s\epsilon^{-2}2^{\ell_X})$. Here s is the size of adversaries that h wants to fool and ϵ is the maximum distinguishing advantage against adversaries of size s.

We also import a theorem from [9] that will be used by our security proofs.

Theorem 6 (Imported Theorem [9]). *Let $n, \ell \in \mathbb{N}$, $\epsilon > 0$ and $\mathcal{C}_{leak}$ be a family of distinguisher circuits from $\{0,1\}^n \times \{0,1\}^\ell \rightarrow \{0,1\}$ of size $s(n)$. Then, for every distribution (X, Z) over $\{0,1\}^n \times \{0,1\}^\ell$, there exists a simulator $h : \{0,1\}^n \rightarrow \{0,1\}^\ell$ such that:*

– h has size bounded by $s' = O(s2^\ell \epsilon^{-2})$.
– (X, Z) and $(X, h(X))$ are indistinguishable by $\mathcal{C}_{leak}$. That is for every $C \in \mathcal{C}_{leak}$,

$$| \Pr_{(x,z) \leftarrow (X,Z)}[C(x, z) = 1] - \Pr_{x \leftarrow X, h}[C(x, h(x)) = 1]| \le \epsilon$$

Now we define our hybrids:

1. We define the first hybrid as the hybrid where each index $i \in [n]$ uses hardcore measure $S_{0,i}$ to generate π_i with probability $1-\delta_z$, and its complement $1-S_{0,i}$ otherwise. This is done by maintaining a string $z \in \{0,1\}^n$ which sets $z_i = 1$ with probability $1 - \delta_z$ and $z_i = 0$ otherwise. This string describes how randomness for various indices are chosen. Note that this hybrid is identical to **Hybrid$_0$**.
2. Next we define **Hybrid$_2$** where we abort if $z = 0^n$. This occurs with probability bounded by δ_z^n. Thus $| \Pr[\mathcal{A}(\textbf{Hybrid}_1) = 1] - \Pr[\mathcal{A}(\textbf{Hybrid}_2) = 1]| \le \delta_z^n$
3. Next, for all indices where $z_i = 1$, generate π_i using Π.Sim algorithm where the randomness is sampled from $S_{1,i}$ whose density is also equal to $1-\delta_z$. This hybrid is computationally close for an efficient adversary due to Theorem 2.
4. Now we consider the following inefficient machine Machine that takes as input $(z, x, x_1, ..., x_n, \{w_i\}_{i|z_i=0})$ and outputs $(R_1, .., R_n)$ where R_i is the randomness sampled to generate proof for the index i. This may involve the machine to potentially brute force break $x_1, .., x_n$ and sample from various measures involved. This hybrid is identical to the previous hybrid as its just a representation change. At this point, ideally we would like to use Theorem 6 from [9,27], recalled above. We would like to "fake" the output of Machine using an efficient simulator h constructed using Theorem 6. However since the size of h grows exponentially with the length of the randomness used to prove, there is no hope to argue any security.

5. To fix this, we observe that the density of hardcore measure as well as its complement is quite large. In other words, suppose, $\delta_z, 1 - \delta_z > 2^{-\lambda/10}$. Thus we can rely on Theorem 5 and have Machine to sample a large enough sets Set_i for $i \in [n]$ from the measures and use that set to generate the proofs. This hybrid is indistinguishable because of Theorem 5. By large enough, we mean that they will at least have about $2^{-\lambda/10} \cdot |R|$ elements.

6. Now for each index $i \in [n]$, sample uniformly a set SetR_i from the space of randomness of Π by choosing $q = \lambda 2^{\lambda/10}$ inputs. Thus the probability of $\text{SetR}_i \cap \text{Set}_i = \phi$ is bounded by $e^{-\lambda}$. Then, change Machine to take as input $z, \text{SetR}_1, .., \text{SetR}_n, x_1, ..., x_n$ and output indices $(j_1, ..., j_n)$. Each index j_i denotes the index of the randomness in SetR_i used for generating (crs_i, π_i) pair for system i. This is picked by sampling randomness uniformly from $\text{Set}_i \cap \text{SetR}_i$. These hybrids are statistically close with the statistical distance being bounded by the probability that the intersection of SetR_i and Set_i is empty.

7. Now since Machine always outputs indices of length bounded by λ^2, we can use theorem 6 to simulate it. This ensure that size of h grows as $s' \cdot 2^{n\lambda^2} \cdot \epsilon'^{-2}$. Here ϵ' is the advantage with which we want to fool the adversary of size s'.

8. Finally we use complexity leveraging and a super-strong PKE to instantiate NPSS to argue that even for adversaries of the same size as that of h, cannot distinguish the case when $x_1, ..., x_n, \{w_i\}_{i|z_i=0}$ are generated using y_b, or they are simulated. This makes the hybrid independent of b.

This leaves us with the following question:

How to Construct NPSS? Our constructions of NPSS are inspired by the MPC-in-the-head paradigm [25]. The idea is to visualise n parties $P_1, .., P_n$ in an MPC protocol where each party P_i has an additive secret sharing y_i of the witness w. What they do is, they run MPC protocol to compute the relation function $R(x, \Sigma_i y_i)$. In an honest behavior this should output 1. Thus when the MPC protocol, such as [4], is run each party P_i receives an output out_i and it has its view view_i (which contains its randomness, input y_i and messages sent and received by it). Then there is also a transcript T which is the collection of messages sent and received by each party. We define x_i to be the circuit that has a PKE encryption of the commitment of T, inputs y_i and party's randomness hardwired and it takes as input a set of corresponding commitment openings and checks:

1. view_i is a valid view for this MPC protocol corresponding to the transcript T. That is each message in the view is computed correctly using incoming messages and a fixed valid input and randomness. This step only takes as input the openings corresponding to commitments of view_i.

2. The output in the view_i is 1.

This allows us to secret share instances. We can prove security we rely on properties of underlying MPC protocol. For example, [4] has two properties (other than correctness):

1. Upto $n/3$ semi-honest views are simulatable.
2. Even if at most $n/3$ parties behave arbitrarily, they can't force honest parties to receive an incorrect output. This property is called perfect robustness.

This allows us to give an instantiation for $t_1 = \lfloor n/3 \rfloor$ and $t_2 = \lfloor n/3 \rfloor$. We rely on the protocol of [14] in the OT-hybrid model [26] to get an instantiation for $t_1 = n$ and $t_2 = n - 1$. The details can be found in Sect. 6.3 and the full version. Thus, this is the formal theorem:

Theorem 7. *Assume that there exists a subexponentially secure public key encryption and a NIZK candidate Π satisfying δ_z-zero-knowledge against adversaries of size Size_Π where $\delta_z, 1 - \delta_z > 2^{-\lambda/5}$. If $\mathsf{Size}_\Pi > \mathsf{Size}_1 \epsilon^{-2} \mathsf{poly}(\lambda)$ for any $1 > \epsilon > 0$ and $0 < \mathsf{Size}_1 < 2^{\lambda/5}$ then the construction $\Pi_\perp$ satisfies $2\delta_z^n + O(n\epsilon + 2^{-\lambda^c})$-witness indistinguishability against adversaries of size Size_1. Here poly is some fixed polynomial. $c > 0$ is a fixed constant.*

2.3   The General Case: $\delta_s + \delta_z < 1$

This is perhaps best understood using an example. Consider $\delta_s = 0.3$ and $\delta_z = 0.60$. Consider the following steps:

- Run parallel repetition using the repetition parameter $n_1 = \log_2 \lambda$. Thus the new parameters are (upto negligible additive factors) $\delta'_s = 0.3^{n_1}$ and $\delta'_z = 1 - 0.4^{n_1}$. Observe that $\delta'_s = \lambda^{-\log_2 10/3}$ and $\delta'_z = 1 - \lambda^{-\log_2 10/4}$.
- On the resulting candidate, perform sequential repetition with parameter $n_2 = \lambda^{\log_2 10/3}$. Thus, we observe that the soundness parameter changes as $\delta''_s = 1 - (1 - \delta'_s)^{n_2}$. Note that this is roughly $1 - e^{-1}$ (e is the base of natural logarithm). As for the zero-knowledge, $\delta''_z = 2 \cdot (1 - \lambda^{=\log_2 10/4})^{n_2}$. As $\log_2 10/3 > \log_2 10/4 > 0$, we have that $\delta''_z = \mathsf{negl}$ for some negligible. Thus, finally we made progress.
- Apply parallel repetition with parameter λ to get a fully secure NIZK!

The idea above can be used to handle any parameters satisfying $\delta_s + \delta_z = 1 - \epsilon$ for any constant $\epsilon > 0$. Details can be found in Sect. 9.

Simultaneous Amplification: We observe that the transformation described above is highly inefficient as we have to compose one transformation on top of other. When $\delta_s, \delta_z \leq 1/3 - 1/\mathsf{poly}$ then one can provide a single transformation which yields a fully secure NIZK. The details can be found in the full version.

2.4   Reader's Guide

In Sect. 3, we recall some preliminaries useful for the rest of the paper. In Sect. 4 we define the notion of a NIZK candidate. In Sect. 5 we define the notion of NPSS. In full version [15], we construct the notion of NPSS. In Sect. 7 we prove a lemma useful for arguing soundness amplification. In Sect. 8, we analyse our MPC based repetition transformation. We analyse the parallel repetition construction in the full version. In Sect. 9 we show how to convert a candidate satisfying $\delta_s + \delta_z = 1 - \epsilon$ for any constant $\epsilon > 0$ to a fully secure candidate. Finally, in full version, we present our direct transformation that transforms any candidate with $\delta_s, \delta_z < 1/3 - 1/\text{poly}(\lambda)$ to a fully secure one.

3   Preliminaries

We denote by λ the security parameter. We say that a function $\epsilon(\lambda)$ is negligible in λ if $\epsilon(\lambda) = o(1/\lambda^c)$ for every $c \in \mathbb{N}$, and we write $\text{negl}(\lambda)$ to denote a negligible function in λ. For a distribution X, we denote by $x \leftarrow X$ the process of sampling a value of x from the distribution X. For a set S, we denote by $s \xleftarrow{\$} S$ the process of sampling uniformly from S.

For two sequence of random variable $X = \{X_\lambda\}_{\lambda \in \mathbb{N}}$ and $Y = \{Y_\lambda\}_{\lambda \in \mathbb{N}}$, we say that X and Y are computationally indistinguishable if for any probabilistic polynomial time distinguisher D,

$$\left| \Pr[D(1^\lambda, x \leftarrow X_\lambda) = 1] - \Pr[D(1^\lambda, y \leftarrow Y_\lambda) = 1] \right| \leq \text{negl}(\lambda)$$

for any sufficiently large $\lambda \in \mathbb{N}$. We say that the distributions are subexponentially indistinguishable if this negl is $2^{-\lambda^\varepsilon}$ for some constant $\varepsilon > 0$. We now define the notion of statistical distance.

Definition 1 (Statistical Distance). *Let E be a finite set, Ω a probability space, and $X, Y : \Omega \to E$ random variables. We define the statistical distance between X and Y to be the function Dist defined by $\text{Dist}(X, Y) = \frac{1}{2}\Sigma_{e \in E} |\Pr_X(X = e) - \Pr_Y(Y = e)|$.*

3.1   Amplification Preliminaries

Now we recall some notions and theorems that will be useful for the rest of the paper.

Definition 2 (Distinguishing Gap). *For any adversary $\mathcal{A}$ and two distributions $\mathcal{X} = \{\mathcal{X}_\lambda\}_{\lambda \in \mathbb{N}}$ and $\mathcal{Y} = \{\mathcal{Y}_\lambda\}_{\lambda \in \mathbb{N}}$, define $\mathcal{A}$'s distinguishing gap in distinguishing these distributions to be $|\Pr_{x \leftarrow \mathcal{X}_\lambda}[\mathcal{A}(1^\lambda, x) = 1] - \Pr_{y \leftarrow \mathcal{Y}_\lambda}[\mathcal{A}(1^\lambda, y) = 1]|$.*

Now we recall the definition of a measure.

Definition 3. *A measure is a function $\mathcal{M} : \{0,1\}^k \to [0,1]$. The size of a measure is $|\mathcal{M}| = \Sigma_{x \in \{0,1\}^k} \mathcal{M}(x)$. The density of a measure, $\mu(\mathcal{M}) = |\mathcal{M}|2^{-k}$.*

Each measure $\mathcal{M}$ induces a probability distribution $\mathcal{D}_\mathcal{M}$.

Definition 4. *Let $\mathcal{M} : \{0,1\}^k \to [0,1]$ be a measure. The distribution defined by measure $\mathcal{M}$ (denoted by $\mathcal{D}_\mathcal{M}$) is a distribution over $\{0,1\}^k$, where for every $x \in \{0,1\}^k$, $\Pr_{X \leftarrow \mathcal{D}_\mathcal{M}}[X = x] = \mathcal{M}(x)/|\mathcal{M}|$.*

We will consider a scaled version $\mathcal{M}_c$ of a measure $\mathcal{M}$ for a constant $0 < c < 1$ defined as $\mathcal{M}_c = c\mathcal{M}$. Note that $\mathcal{M}_c$ induces the same distribution as $\mathcal{M}$.

3.2   Useful Lemmas

We first import the following theorem from [29].

Theorem 8 (Imported Theorem [29]**).** *Let* $E : \{0,1\}^n \rightarrow \mathcal{X}$ *and* $F : \{0,1\}^m \rightarrow \mathcal{X}$ *be two functions, and let* $\epsilon, \gamma \in (0,1)$ *and* $s > 0$ *be given. If for all distinguishers* $\mathcal{A}$ *with size* s *we have*

$$| \Pr_{x \leftarrow \{0,1\}^n}[\mathcal{A}(E(x)) = 1] - \Pr_{y \leftarrow \{0,1\}^m}[\mathcal{A}(F(y)) = 1]| \leq \epsilon$$

Then there exist two measures $\mathcal{M}_0$ *(on* $\{0,1\}^n$*) and* $\mathcal{M}_1$ *(on* $\{0,1\}^n$*) that depend on* γ, s *such that:*

- $\mu(\mathcal{M}_b) \geq 1 - \epsilon$ *for* $b \in \{0,1\}$
- *For all distinguishers* $\mathcal{A}'$ *of size* $s' = \frac{s\gamma^2}{128(m+n+1)}$

$$| \Pr_{x \leftarrow \mathcal{D}_{\mathcal{M}_0}}[\mathcal{A}(E(x)) = 1] - \Pr_{y \leftarrow \mathcal{D}_{\mathcal{M}_1}}[\mathcal{A}(F(y)) = 1]| \leq \gamma$$

Now we describe a lemma from [22], that shows that if we sample a set S from any measure $\mathcal{M}$ by choosing each element i in the support with probability $\mathcal{M}(i)$, then no circuit of (some) bounded size can distinguish a sample x chosen randomly from the set S from an element sampled from distribution given by $\mathcal{M}$. Formally,

Theorem 9 (Imported Theorem [22]**).** *Let* $\mathcal{M}$ *be any measure on* $\{0,1\}^n$ *of density* $\mu(\mathcal{M}) \geq 1 - \rho(n)$*. Let* $\gamma(n) \in (0,1/2)$ *be any function. Then, for a random set* S *chosen according to the measure* $\mathcal{M}$ *the following two holds with probability at least* $1 - 2(2^{-2^n \gamma^2 (1-\rho)^4/64})$:

- $(1 - \frac{\gamma(1-\rho)}{4})(1-\rho)2^n \leq |S| \leq (1 + \frac{\gamma(1-\rho)}{4})(1-\rho)2^n$
- *For such a random set* S*, for any distinguisher* $\mathcal{A}$ *with size* $|\mathcal{A}| \leq 2^n(\frac{\gamma^2(1-\rho)^4}{64n})$ *satisfying*

$$| \Pr_{x \leftarrow S}[\mathcal{A}(x) = 1] - \Pr_{x \leftarrow \mathcal{D}_{\mathcal{M}}}[\mathcal{A}(x) = 1]| \leq \gamma$$

We also import a theorem from [9] that will be used by our security proofs. This lemma would be useful to simulate the randomness used to encrypt in an inefficient hybrid.

Theorem 10 (Imported Theorem [9]**).** *Let* $n, \ell \in \mathbb{N}$*,* $\epsilon > 0$ *and* $\mathcal{C}_{leak}$ *be a family of distinguisher circuits from* $\{0,1\}^n \times \{0,1\}^\ell \rightarrow \{0,1\}$ *of size* $s(n)$*. Then, for every distribution* (X, Z) *over* $\{0,1\}^n \times \{0,1\}^\ell$*, there exists a simulator* $h : \{0,1\}^n \rightarrow \{0,1\}^\ell$ *such that:*

- *h has size bounded by* $s' = O(s2^\ell \epsilon^{-2})$*.*
- (X, Z) *and* $(X, h(X))$ *are indistinguishable by* $\mathcal{C}_{leak}$*. That is for every* $C \in \mathcal{C}_{leak}$,

$$| \Pr_{(x,z) \leftarrow (X,Z)}[C(x,z) = 1] - \Pr_{x \leftarrow X, h}[C(x, h(x)) = 1]| \leq \epsilon$$

4   Definitions

Let SAT denote the language of satisfiable circuits. Let R denote the corresponding relation for SAT. For any instance x in SAT such that w is a witness of x, we write $R(x, w) = 1$ and $x(w) = 1$ to mean the same thing. Any candidate for an NP-complete language can be used to build a candidate for SAT (via NP reductions) and that is why we focus on that.

4.1   Non-interactive Zero-Knowledge Candidates

A NIZK candidate $\Pi =$ (Setup, Prove, Verify, Sim) is composed of the following p.p.t. algorithms:

- Setup(1^λ) $\to$ crs: The setup algorithm is a randomized algorithm that takes as input the security parameter and outputs a common reference string crs.
- Prove(crs, x, w) $\to \pi$: The proving algorithm is a randomized algorithm that takes as input a common reference string crs, an instance x in the language SAT and a witness w such that $R(x, w) = 1$. The algorithm outputs a proof string π.
- Verify(crs, x, π) $\to \{0, 1\}$: The deterministic verification algorithm takes as input a common reference string crs, an instance x and a string π and it outputs from the set $\{0, 1\}$.
- Sim($1^\lambda, x$) $\to (\widetilde{\text{crs}}, \widetilde{\pi})$: The randomized Sim algorithm (short for simulator) takes as an input an instance x and outputs a common reference string $\widetilde{\text{crs}}$ along with a simulated proof string $\widetilde{\pi}$.

Remark 1. Wherever unspecified, the strings such as crs, π e.t.c. lie in $\{0, 1\}^*$.

Completeness. We say that a NIZK candidate Π is complete if the following property is satisfied. For any instance x in SAT and its witness w such that $R(x, w) = 1$ it holds that:

$$Pr[\text{crs} \leftarrow \text{Setup}(1^\lambda), \pi \leftarrow \text{Prove}(\text{crs}, x, w), \text{Verify}(\text{crs}, x, \pi) = 1] \geq 1 - \text{negl}(\lambda)$$

Here the probability is taken over coins of the algorithms of Π

δ_s–**Soundness.** We define two notion of soundness:

Adaptive Soundness: For any non-uniform p.p.t adversary $\mathcal{A}$ consider the following experiment:

1. Run crs $\leftarrow$ Setup(1^λ).
2. Adversary outputs $(x, \pi) \leftarrow \mathcal{A}(1^\lambda, \text{crs})$.
3. Output 1 if $x \notin$ SAT and Verify(crs, x, π) = 1.

We say that the candidate Π is (adaptive) δ_s–sound if the probability that the above experiment (over coins of all algorithms of the candidate and the adversary) outputs 1 is at most δ_s.

Non-adaptive Soundness: For any non uniform p.p.t adversary $\mathcal{A}$ and any instance $x \notin \mathsf{SAT}$ with $|x| = \mathsf{poly}(\lambda)$, consider the following experiment:

1. Run $\mathsf{crs} \leftarrow \mathsf{Setup}(1^\lambda)$.
2. Adversary outputs $\pi \leftarrow \mathcal{A}(1^\lambda, \mathsf{crs})$.
3. Output 1 if $\mathsf{Verify}(\mathsf{crs}, x, \pi) = 1$.

We say that the candidate Π is (non-adaptive)-δ_s sound if the probability that the above experiment (over coins of all algorithms of the candidate and the adversary) outputs 1 is at most δ_s.

Remark 2. Wherever unspecified we will refer to the adaptive soundness of any candidate.

δ_z–**Zero Knowledge.** We say that a NIZK candidate Π is δ_z–zero knowledge if the following property is satisfied. For any instance x and a witness w such that $R(x, w) = 1$, and all p.p.t adversaries $\mathcal{A}$

$$|Pr[\mathsf{crs} \leftarrow \mathsf{Setup}(1^\lambda), \mathcal{A}(\mathsf{crs}, x, \pi \leftarrow \mathsf{Prove}(\mathsf{crs}, x, w)) = 1]-$$

$$Pr[(\mathsf{crs}, \pi) \leftarrow \mathsf{Sim}(1^\lambda, x), \mathcal{A}(\mathsf{crs}, x, \pi) = 1]| \leq \delta_z(\lambda)$$

Here the probability is taken over coins of the algorithms of Π and the adversary $\mathcal{A}$.

Remark 3. In general, a NIZK candidate is not required to satisfy soundness or zero knowledge. So, for example a candidate that outputs the witness in the clear is also a valid candidate. We will specify soundness and zero-knowledge properties when referring to them.

Remark 4. We say that a NIZK candidate is secure if it is $\mathsf{negl}(\lambda)$–sound and $\mathsf{negl}(\lambda)$–zero knowledge for some negligible function negl.

Remark 5. (Length of Instance). We could also consider a definition where length of instance is given as input to the Setup algorithm so that the argument system can only be used for statements of that fixed length. In particular, it can also be set as the security parameter. Our analysis can be easily extended for such a definition. We omit introducing this parameter for simplicity.

NIWI *Candidate.* A non-interactive witness indistinguishable argument (NIWI) candidate Π consists of three algorithms Setup, Prove and Verify with the same syntax as for a NIZK candidate. It has same completeness and δ_s–soundness property. Instead of δ_z–zero-knowledge property it has δ_w–witness indistinguishability requirement which is defined below.

δ_w–**Witness Indistinguishability.** We say that a NIWI candidate Π is δ_w–witness indistinguishability if the following property is satisfied. For any instance x and any valid witness w_0, w_1 such that $R(x, w_b) = 1$ for $b \in \{0, 1\}$, and all (non-uniform) p.p.t adversaries $\mathcal{A}$

$$|Pr[\text{crs} \leftarrow \text{Setup}(1^\lambda), \mathcal{A}(\text{crs}, x, \pi \leftarrow \text{Prove}(\text{crs}, x, w_0), w_0, w_1) = 1]-$$

$$Pr[\text{crs} \leftarrow \text{Setup}(1^\lambda), \mathcal{A}(\text{crs}, x, \pi \leftarrow \text{Prove}(\text{crs}, x, w_1), w_0, w_1) = 1]| \leq \delta_w(\lambda)$$

Here the probability is taken over coins of the algorithms of Π and the adversary $\mathcal{A}$.

5 Verifiable Sharing for Statements

In this section, we define a new notion of sharing for SAT statements. We will denote it with NPSS. A verifiable sharing scheme for statements NPSS consists of the following p.p.t. algorithms:

- Setup$(1^\lambda) \rightarrow$ pp: The setup algorithm takes as input the security parameter and outputs public parameters pp.
- Share$(\text{pp}, n, x, w) \rightarrow (x_1, ..., x_n, w_1, .., w_n)$: The sharing algorithm takes as input an instance x and a witness w such that $R(x, w) = 1$ along with number of parties n and the public parameter pp. It outputs n instances $(x_1, .., x_n)$ along with valid corresponding witnesses $\{w_i\}_{i \in [n]}$.
- Verify$(\text{pp}, n, x, x_1, .., x_n) :\rightarrow \{1, 0\}$: The Verify algorithm is a deterministic algorithm that takes as input public parameter pp, any instance x, a number n and a set of n instances x_i for $i \in [n]$. It outputs from $\{0, 1\}$.

We require that a NPSS satisfy the following properties.

Correctness: We say a verifiable sharing scheme for statements in SAT is correct if it happens for any satisfiable instance x in SAT having a witness w and $n \in \mathbb{N}$,

$$Pr\left[\begin{array}{c} \text{Setup}(1^\lambda) \rightarrow \text{pp} \\ \text{Share}(\text{pp}, n, x, w) \rightarrow (x_1, ..., x_n, w_1, .., w_n) \\ R(x_i, w_i) = 1 \forall i \in [n] \\ \text{Verify}(\text{pp}, n, x, x_1, ..., x_n) = 1 \end{array}\right] \geq 1 - 2^{-\lambda} \qquad (1)$$

Here the probability is only over the coins of Setup.

Next important property is of robustness for a threshold $t_{\text{NPSS}, r}$. This property says that if $(x_1, .., x_n)$ be shared instances associated with x. Then if there exists any set T of size $t_{\text{NPSS}, r}$ such that x_i is in SAT for all $i \in T$, this implies that x itself is satisfiable.

Robustness: This property says that for any instance x, number $n \in \mathbb{N}$, any sharing $(x_1, .., x_n)$ and any $T \subseteq [n]$ of size at least $t_{\text{NPSS}, r}$: If $\exists \{w_i\}_{i \in T}$ such that Verify$(\text{pp}, x, n, x_1, .., x_n) = 1$ and $R(x_i, w_i) = 1$ for all $i \in T$, then there exists w such that w is a witness of x. Formally, for any (even unbounded adversary $\mathcal{A}$), the following holds:

$$Pr\left[\begin{array}{c} \text{Setup}(1^\lambda) \rightarrow \text{pp} \\ \mathcal{A}(\text{pp}) \rightarrow (x, x_1, ..., x_n) \\ \text{Verify}(\text{pp}, n, x, x_1, ..., x_n) = 1 \\ \exists w_i, R(x_i, w_i) = 1 \forall i \in [T] \\ \nexists w, R(x, w) = 1 \end{array}\right] \leq 2^{-\lambda} \qquad (2)$$

Here the probability is over the coins of the Setup.

Finally, last property is that of simulatability for a threshold $t_{\mathsf{NPSS},sim}$. In layman terms it says that for any instance x, a set of $t_{\mathsf{NPSS},sim}$ witnesses do not reveal anything about membership of x in the language SAT.

Simulatability: This property says that there exists a polynomial time simulator Sim that takes as input any $x \in \mathsf{SAT}$, n, and a set $T \subseteq [n]$ of size less than or equal to $t_{\mathsf{NPSS},sim}$. It outputs simulated instance-shares $\mathsf{Sim}(\mathsf{pp}, n, x, T) \rightarrow (x_1, .., x_n, \{w_i\}_{i \in T})$. Then consider the following distributions:

Distribution 1.

- Run $\mathsf{Setup}(1^\lambda) \rightarrow \mathsf{pp}$
- Compute $\mathsf{Share}(\mathsf{pp}, n, x, w) \rightarrow (x_1, ..., x_n, w_1, ..., x_n)$
- Output $\{\mathsf{pp}, x, x_1, ..., x_n, \{w_i\}_{i \in [T]}\}$

Distribution 2.

- Run $\mathsf{Setup}(1^\lambda) \rightarrow \mathsf{pp}$
- Compute $\mathsf{Sim}(\mathsf{pp}, n, x, T) \rightarrow (x_1, ..., x_n, \{w_i\}_{i \in T})$
- Output $\{\mathsf{pp}, x, x_1, ..., x_n, \{w_i\}_{i \in [T]}\}$

Then it holds that for any polynomial time adversary $\mathcal{A}$, the distinguishing gap between these two distributions is $\mathsf{negl}(\lambda)$ for some negligible function negl.

Remark: In general, we ask Robustness and Simulatability property to hold with respect to thresholds $t_{\mathsf{NPSS},r}$ and $t_{\mathsf{NPSS},sim}$. Whenever required, we will instantiate these values once and omit explicitly mentioning them for simplicity.

6   Instantiating Verifiable Sharing of Statements

This section is organized as follows. In Sect. 6.1 we describe an MPC Framework that will be used to construct verifiable sharing scheme. In Sect. 6.2 we describe how to instantiate the framework. Then in Sect. 6.3 we describe the construction.

6.1 Σ-Pre-processing MPC

In this section we define an MPC framework associated with a protocol Σ, which we call $\Sigma-$pre-processing MPC. This framework will be used to instantiate verifiable sharing of statements. Let $\mathcal{F} = \{\mathcal{F}_\lambda\}_{\lambda \in \mathbb{N}}$ be a class of polynomial sized circuits. Here the security parameter λ is the length of inputs to this family. Our MPC framework consists of the following algorithms

- $\underline{\mathsf{Preproc}(y, n, 1^\ell)} \rightarrow (y_1, r_1, ..., y_n, r_n)$: This randomized algorithm takes as input the number of parties n, size of the function ℓ and the input y. It outputs pre-processed inputs and randomness $y_1, r_1, ..., y_n, r_n$. Here y_i, r_i is viewed as input and randomness of the party P_i participating in the protocol Σ.

- Eval$(f, y_1, r_1, ..., y_n, r_n) \to T$: The deterministic Eval algorithm takes as input the function $f \in \mathcal{F}_{|y|}$ and n input-randomness pairs (y_i, r_i) for $i \in [n]$. It outputs the entire emulated transcript of the protocol Σ (run by n parties $P_1, .., P_n$) to compute f using the inputs $(y_1, .., y_n)$ and the randomness $(r_1, .., r_n)$. Let us represent the transcript as $T = \{(i, j, k, T_{i,j,k}), \mathsf{Out}_i\}_{i \in [n], j \in [n], k \in \phi_{|f|}}$. Here $T_{i,j,k}$ represents the message sent by party P_i to P_j in round k. Here $\phi_{|f|}$ denotes the number of rounds in Σ and Out_i denotes the output of P_i.

Notation: We now give some notation. Let T denote the transcript of the protocol Σ run between n parties to compute any function f on the inputs $\{y_i\}_{i \in [n]}$ using randomness $\{r_i\}_{i \in [n]}$. We define by view_i the set containing the input y_i, randomness r_i and messages sent and received by the party i along with its output Out_i. More formally, we let $\mathsf{view}_i = \{y_i, r_i, \{T_{i,j,k}\}_{j \in [n], k \in \phi_{|f|}}, \mathsf{Out}_i, \{T_{j,i,k}\}_{j \in [n], k \in \phi_{|f|}}\}$. Further, we say that for any party i, view_i is consistent with the transcript T if the messages sent and received by party i are exactly equal to ones described in the transcript T and Out_i is also the output that occurs in the transcript. Second, by $V_{\Sigma, f, n}()$ we denote a circuit that takes as input (i, view_i) for $i \in [n]$ and checks if the view_i is consistent with the protocol Σ computing f. If the check passes it outputs 1 and 0 otherwise. That is, it internally emulates the next message function and checks if all the outgoing messages of P_i are correctly computed using the input and previous messages. We say that view_i is consistent if $V_{\Sigma, f, n}(i, \mathsf{view}_i) = 1$.

Now we require the following properties from this framework.

Perfect Correctness:

Definition 5 *(Perfect Correctness). For any input $y \in \{0,1\}^*$, $n \in \mathbb{N}$ and function $f \in \mathcal{F}_{|y|}$, consider the following experiment:*

- *Run* Preproc$(y, n, 1^{|f|}) \to (y_1, r_1, ..., y_n, r_n)$.
- *Run* Eval$(f, y_1, r_1, ..., y_n, r_n) \to T$.
- *Output 1 if* $\mathsf{Out}_i = f(y)$ *for all $i \in [n]$ and 0 otherwise.*

We say that a Σ−preprocessing MPC is perfectly correct if $Pr[\mathsf{Expt}(y, n, f) = 1] = 1$. Here the probability is taken over the coins of all the algorithms.

Perfect Privacy:

Definition 6 *(Privacy for a threshold $t_{\Sigma, sim}$). We say that the a Σ−preprocessing MPC satisfies perfect privacy for a threshold $t_{\Sigma, sim}$ if there exists a simulator Sim such that for any $y \in \{0,1\}^*$, any $f \in \mathcal{F}_{|y|}$ and any set S of size less than or equal to $t_{\Sigma, sim}$ the following two experiments are computationally close.*

Expt_1

- *Run* Preproc$(y, n, 1^{|y|}) \to (y_1, r_1, ..., y_n, r_n)$

– *Run* Eval$(f, y_1, r_1, .., y_n, r_n) \to T$
– *Output* $\{\text{view}_i\}_{i \in S}$

Expt_2

– *Output* Sim$(1^{|y|}, f(y), n, S) \to \{\text{view}_i\}_{i \in S}$

Robustness:

Definition 7 *(Robustness for a threshold $t_{\Sigma,r}$). We say that a $\Sigma-$preprocessing MPC is robust if the following happens: Let $f \in \mathcal{F}_\lambda$ for any $\lambda \in \mathbb{N}$ be a function such that $f(y) \neq 1$ for all $y \in \{0,1\}^\lambda$. Then, given any number of parties n, candidate transcript T and its consistent views $\{\text{view}_i\}_{i \in S}$ corresponding to some set $S \subseteq [n]$ of size $t_{\Sigma,r}$, it holds that if $V_{\Sigma,f,n}(i, \text{view}_i) = 1$ for all $i \in S$ then,*

$$\text{Out}_i \neq 1$$

for some $i \in S$

This intuitively means that a collusion of at most $n - t_{\Sigma,r}$ parties can't force an incorrect output onto honest parties.

6.2 Instantiating MPC Framework for $t_{\Sigma,sim} = \lfloor n/3 \rfloor$ and $t_{\Sigma,r} = \lceil 2n/3 \rceil$

We cite [4] as the protocol. This protocol satisfies these three properties [2]:

1. Perfect correctness for 0 corruptions.
2. Perfect security for up to $n/3$ semi-honest corruptions.
3. Perfect robustness for up to $n/3$ corruptions.

The framework then works as follows. The Preproc algorithm takes as input the witness w and secret shares it using additive secret sharing scheme to get shares $y_1, .., y_n$. It also samples randomness for the parties $(r_1, .., r_n)$ to participate in a protocol computing $f(\Sigma_i y_i)$. The Eval algorithm emulates the protocol and outputs the transcript.

Thus using [4] we can achieve robustness and perfect privacy properties.

6.3 Construction of Verifiable Sharing Scheme for Statements

In this section we construct Verifiable Sharing Scheme for Statements from a $\Sigma-$pre-processing MPC Δ_Σ with thresholds $t_{\Sigma,r}, t_{\Sigma,sim}$ and a statistically binding non-interactive commitment scheme Com. We describe the construction below.

– Setup(1^λ) : Run the setup of the commitment scheme Com.Setup$(1^\lambda) \to$ pp.
– Share(pp, n, x, w) : The algorithm takes as input the number of parties n, instance x and witness w along with commitment parameters pp. It runs the algorithm described in Fig. 1 to output $(x_1, ..., x_n, w_1, .., w_n)$.

Inputs: Commitment parameter pp, Number of parties n, instance $x \in \mathsf{SAT}$ and a valid witness w.

Notation: Let $f = R(x, \cdot)$ be the circuit denoting the corresponding NP relation R hardwired with the instance x.

1. Run the pre-process algorithm of the MPC framework on input w. That is $\Delta.\mathsf{Preproc}(w, n, 1^{|f|}) \rightarrow (y_1, r_1, ..., y_n, r_n)$
2. Run the evaluation algorithm of the framework to get a transcript. $\Delta_\Sigma.\mathsf{Eval}(f, y_1, r_1, ..., y_n, r_n) \rightarrow T$
3. Parse the transcript as $\{i, j, k, T_{i,j,k}, \mathsf{Out}_i\}_{i \in [n], j \in [n], k \in \phi_{|f|}}$. Here $T_{i,j,k}$ refers to the message sent by party P_i to party P_j in round k, and Out_i refers to the output of party P_i.
4. Let view_i denote the set $\{y_i, r_i, T_{i,j,k}, T_{j,i,k}, \mathsf{Out}_i\}_{j \in [n], k \in \phi_{|f|}}$.
5. Compute commitments $Z_{i,j,k} = \mathsf{Com}(\mathsf{pp}, T_{i,j,k}; s_{i,j,k})$ for $i, j \in [n]$ and $k \in \phi_{|f|}$.
6. Compute commitments $Z_{\mathsf{Out},i} = \mathsf{Com}(\mathsf{pp}, \mathsf{Out}_i, s_{i,\mathsf{Out}})$ and $Z_i = \mathsf{Com}(\mathsf{pp}, y_i, r_i; s_i)$ for $i \in [n]$.
7. Define by $Z_{\mathsf{view},i} = \{Z_i, Z_{\mathsf{Out},i}, Z_{i,j,k}, Z_{j,i,k}\}_{j \in [n], k \in \phi_{|f|}}$. Output the circuit $x_i[Z_{\mathsf{view},i}, f]$ (defined in Figure 2) as the ith share.
8. For every $i \in [n]$ witness are given out as the set of associated commitment openings and the views,. That is output $w_i = \{\{s_i, s_{\mathsf{Out},i}, s_{i,j,k}, s_{j,i,k}\}_{j \in [n], k \in \phi_{|f|}}, \mathsf{view}_i\}$.

Fig. 1. Description of Share algorithm

Inputs: Commitment openings $\{s_i, s_{\mathsf{Out},i}, s_{i,j,k}, s_{j,i,k}\}_{j \in [n], k \in \phi_{|f|}}$, view of the party P_i $\mathsf{view}_i = \{y_i, r_i, T_{i,j,k}, T_{j,i,k}, \mathsf{Out}_i\}$

Hardwired: pp, $Z_{\mathsf{view},i} = \{Z_i, Z_{\mathsf{Out},i}, Z_{i,j,k}, Z_{j,i,k}\}_{j \in [n], k \in [\phi_{|f|}]}$ and function f.

1. Check that the commitment openings are valid.
   - $Z_i = \mathsf{Com}(\mathsf{pp}, y_i, r_i; s_i)$.
   - $Z_{\mathsf{Out},i} = \mathsf{Com}(\mathsf{pp}, \mathsf{Out}_i, s_{\mathsf{Out},i})$.
   - $Z_{i,j,k} = \mathsf{Com}(\mathsf{pp}, T_{i,j,k}; s_{i,j,k})$ for all $j \in [n]$ and $k \in [\phi_{|f|}]$
   - $Z_{j,i,k} = \mathsf{Com}(\mathsf{pp}, T_{j,i,k}; s_{j,i,k})$ for all $j \in [n]$ and $k \in [\phi_{|f|}]$
2. Check that $V_{\Sigma,f,n}(i, \mathsf{view}_i) = 1$.
3. If all the above checks output 1, output 1 otherwise output 0.

Fig. 2. Description of circuit x_i

- <u>Verify</u>$(\mathsf{pp}, n, x, x_1, ..., x_n)$: The Verify algorithm takes as input the instance x and shares $x_1, .., x_n$ and does the following (Fig. 2):
  - Let $f = R(x, \cdot)$ be the relation function hardwired with x. Check that there exists strings $Z_T = \{Z_i, Z_{\mathsf{Out},i}, Z_{i,j,k}, Z_{j,i,k}\}_{i \in [n], j \in [n], k \in [\phi_{|f|}]}$ in the circuit descriptions.

- Check that these commitments to the views $Z_{\text{view},i}$ for $i \in [n]$ are consistent to a single commitment to a transcript $Z_T = \{Z_i, Z_{\text{Out},i},$ $Z_{i,j,k}, Z_{j,i,k}\}_{i\in[n],j\in[n],k\in[\phi_{|f|}]}$. Here each $Z_{\text{view},i} = \{Z_i, Z_{\text{Out},i}, Z_{i,j,k},$ $Z_{j,i,k}\}_{j\in[n],k\in[\phi_{|f|}]}$ for all $i \in [n]$.
- If all the above checks pass output 1 otherwise output 0.

We prove the associated properties in the full version.

7 Technical Lemmas

Now we prove some technical lemmas useful for the rest of the paper.

We now present a hardcore set lemma that represents the soundness experiment.

Lemma 2. *Let* $F : \{0,1\}^\lambda \to \{0,1\}^l$ *be a function where* $l = \mathsf{poly}(\lambda)$ *and* $E : \{0,1\}^{\lambda+l+r(\lambda)} \to \{0,1\}$ *be a circuit of size* e. *Let* $\delta \geq \epsilon \in (0,1)$ *and* $s, s' > 0$ *be functions of* λ. *If for all circuits* $C : \{0,1\}^{l(\lambda)} \to \{0,1\}^{r(\lambda)}$ *of size* s *we have*

$$\Pr_{u \xleftarrow{\$} \{0,1\}^\lambda} [E(u, F(u), C(F(u))) = 1] \leq \delta$$

Then there exists a set S *of size* $|S| = (1-\delta)2^\lambda$ *and a polynomial* $s_{overhead}(\lambda)$ *(independent of* s, s' *and* e*) such that: For all circuits* $C' : \{0,1\}^{l(\lambda)} \to \{0,1\}^{r(\lambda)}$ *of size less than* $s' = \frac{s\epsilon(1-\delta)}{\delta} - e - s_{overhead}$

$$\Pr_{u \xleftarrow{\$} S} [E(u, F(u), C'(F(u))) = 1] \leq \epsilon$$

Proof. The proof strategy can be described as follows: we assume that there does not exist a hardcore set of size $(1-\delta)2^\lambda$ for circuits of size less than s'. We use this fact to construct a circuit of size s which contradicts the assumption made in the theorem statement.

Formally, let us assume that the following happens: for every set $S \subset \{0,1\}^\lambda$ such that $|S| = (1-\delta)2^\lambda$ there exists a circuit C_S of size s',

$$\Pr_{u \xleftarrow{\$} S} [E(u, F(u), C_S(F(u))) = 1] \geq \epsilon$$

We now define two collections:

1. Collection of inputs $\mathbb{X} \subseteq \{0,1\}^\lambda$. This collection is initialised to be empty and stores the list of "solved inputs". Here, we say that $x \in \{0,1\}^\lambda$ is solved by C, if $E(F(x), C(F(x))) = 1$.
2. Collection of circuits $\mathbb{C}$ which stores circuits of size s'. This collection is also initialised to be empty and stores circuits that "solve" at least $\delta(1-\epsilon)$ fraction of input points.

This collection $\mathbb{C}$ will later be used to build a circuit $C[\mathbb{C}]$ of size s such that it will solve at least $\mathbb{X}$. Contradiction will come from the fact $|\mathbb{X}|$ is greater than $2^\lambda \delta$.

Both $\mathbb{X}$ and $\mathbb{C}$ are build iteratively as follows. Pick any set S_1 of size $(1-\delta) \cdot 2^\lambda$. There exists a circuit C_1 of size s' such that $\Pr_{u \xleftarrow{\$} S_1}[E(u, F(u), C_1(F(u))) = 1] \geq \epsilon$ as per the hypothesis. Let X_1 be the maximal subset of S_1 of size at least $(1-\delta)\epsilon 2^\lambda$ such that $\Pr_{u \xleftarrow{\$} X_1}[E(u, F(u), C_1(F(u))) = 1] = 1$. The size $|X_1| \geq \epsilon(1-\delta)2^\lambda$.

We now update $\mathbb{X} = \mathbb{X} \cup X_1$ and $\mathbb{C} = \mathbb{C} \cup C_1$.

This process is repeated t times (defined later) as follows.

1. Select a set S_i of size at least $(1-\delta)2^\lambda \subseteq \{0,1\}^\lambda \setminus \mathbb{X}$.
2. Let C_i be a circuit of size s' such that $\Pr_{u \xleftarrow{\$} S_i}[E(u, F(u), C_i(F(u))) = 1] \geq \epsilon$.
3. Let X_i be a maximal set of cardinality at least $(1-\delta)\epsilon 2^\lambda$, $\Pr_{u \xleftarrow{\$} X_i}[E(u, F(u), C_i(F(u))) = 1] = 1$.
4. Update $\mathbb{C} = \mathbb{C} \cup C_i$ and $\mathbb{X} = \mathbb{X} \cup X_i$.

Define a circuit $C[\mathbb{C}]$ for $\mathbb{C} = (C_1, .., C_t)$. On any input $F(x) \in \{0,1\}^{l(\lambda)}$, it checks if there exist i such that $E(x, F(x), C_i(F(x))) = 1$. If this is the case it outputs $C_i(F(x))$, otherwise it outputs $C_1(F(x))$. We now claim this process cannot continue indefinitely. Observe the following:

1. $|\mathbb{X}| > t \cdot \epsilon \cdot (1-\delta) \cdot 2^\lambda$
2. $|C[\mathbb{C}]| \leq ts' + t \cdot e + t \cdot s_{overhead}(\lambda)$, for some fixed polynomial $s_{overhead}$ independent of s, s' and e.

Thus we can achieve a contradiction if the following holds simultaneously.

1. $|\mathbb{X}| \geq t \cdot \epsilon \cdot (1-\delta) \cdot 2^\lambda \geq \delta 2^\lambda$.
2. $|C[\mathbb{C}]| \leq t \cdot s' + t \cdot e + t \cdot s_{ovehead}(\lambda) \leq s$.

This is because these conditions ensure that $C[\mathbb{C}]$ is a required circuit that violates the hypothesis. For these conditions to happen we can set any s' and t satisfying, $t \geq \frac{1-\delta}{\delta \cdot \epsilon}$ and $s' \leq \frac{s-p(\lambda)}{t} - e - s_{overhead}$.

8 Sequential Repetition

In this section, we construct $\Pi_\perp$ which is an analogue of parallel repetition. It starts from δ_z-zero knowledge candidate, δ_s sound NIZK candidate and constructs (roughly) δ_z^n-zero knowledge and $1 - (1-\delta_s)^n$ sound NIZK candidate $\Pi_\perp$. Note that these are the parameters for parallel repetition where soundness and zero knowledge errors (parameters) are interchanged and that is why we call it sequential repetition.

Ingredient: We require a verifiable sharing scheme NPSS with the following properties:

- Perfect Correctness.
- Robustness holds if $T = [n]$.
- Computational Simulatability as long as at most $n-1$ witnesses are revealed.

Such a scheme can be constructed by instantiating Σ-preprocessing MPC framework with perfectly correct, information theoretically secure GMW protocol [14] in the OT hybrid model [28]. This protocol satisfies information theoretic security for $n-1$ corruptions. More details can be found in the full version. We also assume that the commitment scheme used in constructing NPSS uses perfectly correct a public key encryption scheme PKE. We now describe our construction.

- $\Pi_\perp$.Setup(1^λ) :
  - Run Π.Setup(1^λ) $\rightarrow$ crs$_i$ for $i \in [n]$.
  - Run NPSS.Setup(1^λ) $\rightarrow$ pp.
  - Output crs $= ($pp, crs$_1, ...,$ crs$_n)$.
- $\Pi_\perp$.Prove(crs, x, w) :
  - Run NPSS.Share(pp, n, x, w) $\rightarrow (x_1, ..., x_n, w_1, ..., w_n)$
  - Run Π.Prove(crs$_i, x_i, w_i$) $\rightarrow \pi_i$ for $i \in [n]$.
  - Output $\pi = (x_1, ..., x_n, \pi_1, ..., \pi_n)$.
- $\Pi_\perp$.Verify(crs, x, π) :
  - Parse $\pi = (x_1, ..., x_n, \pi_1, ..., \pi_n)$.
  - Run NPSS.Verify(pp, $n, x, x_1, ..., x_n$).
  - Run Π.Verify(x_i, w_i) for $i \in [n]$.
  - Output 1 if all these steps pass. Output 0 otherwise.

Completeness. Completeness follows immediately from the completeness of Π.
$(1 - (1 - \delta_s)^n) - soundness:$

Theorem 11. *Assuming* PKE *is perfectly correct and* Π *is* δ_s*-sound against adversaries of size* s, *then for every* $1 > \epsilon > 0$, $\Pi_\perp$ *is* $(1-(1-\delta_s)^n)+O(\epsilon)-sound$ *against adversaries of size* $s' = O(s \cdot \epsilon \cdot \delta_s/(1-\delta_s)) - poly(\lambda)$ *for a fixed polynomial* poly.

Proof. Let $C = (C_1, ..., C_n)$ be the circuit attacking the soundness experiment. First define a function:
$F(r)$

- Compute Π.Setup($1^\lambda; r$) $\rightarrow$ crs.
- Output crs.

Let pp $\leftarrow$ NPSS.Setup(1^λ). We fix pp, and we claim that soundness holds with overwhelming probability over the coins for generating pp. Now, $C(F(u_1), ..., F(u_n)) = x, x_1, ..., x_n, \pi_1, ..., \pi_n$. Define the output of C_i as x, x_i, π_i.

Denote $c = \delta_s$. Let us recall the soundness experiment in detail.

- The challenger samples $\Pi.\mathsf{Setup}(1^\lambda) \to \mathsf{crs}_i$ for $i \in [t]$. Then it hands over $\mathsf{crs}_\perp = (\mathsf{pp}, \mathsf{crs}_1, .., \mathsf{crs}_t)$
- The adversary on input $\mathsf{crs}_\perp$ comes up with a proof $\pi = (x_1, .., x_n, \pi_1, .., \pi_n)$ and an instance x such that $\mathsf{NPSS.Verify}(\mathsf{pp}, x, x_1, .., x_n) = 1$, $\Pi.\mathsf{Verify}(\mathsf{crs}_i, x_i, \pi_i) = 1$ for $i \in [n]$. The adversary wins if x is unsatisfiable.

We begin by setting some notation for the rest of the proof.

- Define $F(\cdot) = \Pi.\mathsf{Setup}(1^\lambda, \cdot) : \{0,1\}^{\ell_{rand}(\lambda)} \to \{0,1\}^{\ell_{crs}(\lambda)}$. Note that both ℓ_{crs}, ℓ_{rand} are some polynomials.
- Let $C = (C_1, .., C_n)$ be the polynomial sized-circuit attacking the soundness experiment. Each $C_i : \{0,1\}^{n\ell_{crs}} \to \{0,1\}^{\ell_\pi + 2 \cdot \ell_x}$. Each C_i is thought to output x, x_i, π_i. They have pp hardwired.
- Let E denote the circuit that on input $(\mathsf{crs}_i, x_i, \pi_i) \in \{0,1\}^{\ell_{crs} + \ell_{pi}}$ does the following. It checks that $x_i = x_i[Z_{\mathsf{view},i}, R(x, \cdot)]$ (as in the construction of NPSS) and $\Pi.\mathsf{Verify}(\mathsf{crs}_i, x_i, \pi_i) = 1$. Then it opens the commitment $Z_{\mathsf{view},i}$ (using the secret-key corresponding to pp) and checks if the circuit $x_i \notin \mathsf{SAT}$. It outputs 1 if all these checks pass. Since the commitment can be opened in $\mathsf{poly}(\lambda)$ time using the decryption algorithm, size of E is $\mathsf{poly}(n, \lambda)$.

Since Π is c−sound against adversaries of size s, for all circuits D of size s,

$$\Pr_{u \xleftarrow{\$} \{0,1\}^{\ell_{rand}}} [E(u, F(u), D(F(u))) = 1] \le c$$

Thus there exists a hardcore set by Lemma 2 H of size $(1 - c)2^{r(\lambda)}$ such that for any polynomial-sized circuit D' with size $s' \le O(s\epsilon_{s'}(1 - c)/c - s_{overhead} - \mathsf{poly}(\lambda))$,

$$\Pr_{u \xleftarrow{\$} H} [E(u, F(u), D'(F(u))) = 1] \le \epsilon_{s'} \tag{3}$$

for any $0 < \epsilon_{s'} < 1$.

Define V to be the set $\{0,1\}^{r(\lambda)} \times .... \{0,1\}^{r(\lambda)}$ (i.e. the set of randomness used to sample all crs_i for $i \in [n]$). For every set $S \subseteq [n]$, define $V_S = A_1 \times A_2 ... \times A_t$, where $A_i = H$ if $i \in S$ and $A_i = \{0,1\}^r \setminus H$ otherwise. Note that V is a disjoint union of $\{V_S\}_{S \subseteq [n]}$.

For any set W, we define by Break_W the following event that is satisfied if the following conditions are satisfied.

1. $(u_1, .., u_n) \xleftarrow{\$} W$
2. $C_i(F(u_1), ..., F(u_n)) = (x, x_i, \pi_i)$ for all $i \in [n]$.
3. $\Pi.\mathsf{Verify}(F(u_i), x_i, \pi_i) = 1$ for all $i \in [n]$.
4. $\mathsf{NPSS.Verify}(\mathsf{pp}, t, x, x_1, .., x_n) = 1$
5. $x \notin \mathsf{SAT}$

Let,

$$\Pr[\mathsf{Break}_V] = q$$

Then, note that,

$$\Pr[\mathsf{Break}_V] = \Sigma_{S \subseteq [n]} \Pr[\mathsf{Break}_{V_S}]|V_S|/|V|$$

We make the following two claims now.

Claim. $\Sigma_{S \subseteq [n], |S| < n} |V_S| / |V| \leq (1 - (1 - c)^n)$.

Proof. Consider n independent random variables y_i for $i \in [n]$ where $y_i = 0$ with probability c and 1 with probability $1 - c$. The probability that $y \neq 1^n$ is $= 1 - \Pr[y = 1^n]$. Since each bit is independently chosen, the claim follows as $\Pr[y = 1^n] = (1 - c)^n$

Thus, $S^* = [n]$. $\Pr[\mathsf{Break}_V] \leq (1 - c)^n \cdot \Pr[\mathsf{Break}_{V_{S^*}}] + (1 - (1 - c)^n)$ Now we claim that $\Pr[\mathsf{Break}_{V_{S^*}}] \leq n\epsilon_{s'}$
Observe that $\Pr[\mathsf{Break}_V] = q \leq (1 - c)^n \cdot \Pr[\mathsf{Break}_{V_{S^*}}] + (1 - (1 - c)^n)$
Thus $\Pr[\mathsf{Break}_{V_{S^*}}] \geq q - (1 - (1 - c)^n)$ We now define another event Sound_i.

1. $(u_1, .., u_n) \xleftarrow{\$} V_{S^*}$
2. $C_i(F(u_1), ..., F(u_n)) = (x, x_i, \pi_i)$ for all $i \in [n]$.
3. $\Pi.\mathsf{Verify}(F(u_i), x_i, \pi_i) = 1$ for all $i \in [n]$.
4. $\mathsf{NPSS.Verify}(\mathsf{pp}, n, x, x_1, .., x_n) = 1$
5. $x \notin \mathsf{SAT}$
6. $x_i \notin \mathsf{SAT}$

Note that $\Pr[\cup_{i \in S^*} \mathsf{Sound}_i] \geq \Pr[\mathsf{Break}_{V_{S^*}}]$ due to robustness of NPSS scheme. Thus by the union bound,

$$\Sigma_{i \in S^*} \Pr[\mathsf{Sound}_i] \geq q - (1 - (1 - c)^n)$$

as $|S^*| = n$, there exist i^* such that,

$$\Pr[\mathsf{Sound}_{i^*}] \geq \frac{q - (1 - (1 - c)^n)}{n}$$

Finally, define the event Final_{i^*}

1. $(u_1, .., u_n) \xleftarrow{\$} V_{S^*}$
2. $C_i^*(F(u_1), ..., F(u_n)) = (x, x^*, \pi^*)$.
3. $\Pi.\mathsf{Verify}(F(u_{i^*}), x^*, \pi^*) = 1$.
4. Instance x^* is of the form $x^* = x^*[Z_{\mathsf{view}, i^*}, f]$.
5. $x^* \notin \mathsf{SAT}$.

As Final_i is true whenever Sound_i is, $\Pr[\mathsf{Final}_i] \geq (q - (1 - (1 - c)^n))/n$. This translates to the following

$$\Pr_{u_1, .., u_n \xleftarrow{\$} V_{S^*}} [E(u_{i^*}, F(u_{i^*}), C_{i^*}(F(u_1), ..., F(u_n))) = 1] \geq \frac{q - (1 - (1 - c)^n)}{n}$$

This implies that there exists $\{u_i\}_{i \neq i^*}$ such that:

$$\Pr_{u_{i^*} \xleftarrow{\$} V_{S^*}} [E(u_i^*, F(u_{i^*}), C_{i^*}(F(u_1), ..., F(u_n))) = 1] \geq \frac{q - (1 - (1 - c)^n)}{n}$$

The circuit $C_{i^*}(u_1, ..., u_{i^*-1}, \cdot, u_{i^*+1}, .., u_n)$ violates Eq. 3 if $q > n\epsilon_{s'} + 1 - (1-c)^n$.

$2 \cdot \delta_s^n - zero\text{-}knowledge.$

Theorem 12. *Assume that there exists a subexponentially secure public key encryption and a NIZK candidate Π satisfying $\delta_z - zero\text{-}knowledge$ against adversaries of size Size_Π where $\delta_z, 1 - \delta_z > 2^{-\lambda/5}$. If $\mathsf{Size}_\Pi > \mathsf{Size}_1 \epsilon^{-2} \mathrm{poly}(\lambda)$ for any $1 > \epsilon > 0$ and $0 < \mathsf{Size}_1 < 2^{\lambda/5}$ then the construction $\Pi_\perp$ satisfies $2\delta_z^n + O(n\epsilon + 2^{-\lambda^c}) - witness\ indistinguishability$ against adversaries of size Size_1. Here poly is some fixed polynomial. $c > 0$ is a fixed constant.*

We present the proof in the full version.

9   Amplifying Security When $\delta_s + \delta_z < 1$

Now we show the following theorem:

Theorem 13. *Assume a subexponentially secure PKE scheme, and a NIZK candidate Π with $\delta_s - soundness$ and $\delta_z - zero\text{-}knowledge$ where δ_z, δ_s are any constants in $(0, 1)$ with $\delta_s + \delta_z < 1$ for all polynomial time adversaries, then there exists a fully secure NIZK candidate against all polynomial time adversaries.*

We prove this is as follows:

1. First we use parallel repetition with repetition parameter $n_1 = \log \lambda$. Note that in that case, we get $\delta_{s,1} = \delta_s^{n_1} + O(n_1 \epsilon_1)$ soundness and $\delta_{z,1} = 1 - (1 - \delta_z)_1^n + O(n_1 \epsilon_1)$ from the theorems on parallel repetition. This holds for all adversaries of size $\mathsf{Size}_1 = \mathsf{Size} \cdot \epsilon^2 / \mathrm{poly}(\lambda)$ where Size is the size of the adversaries for which Π is secure and ϵ is chosen and poly is fixed.

2. Then we apply sequential repetition on the new parameters. Let $a = \log_2(1/\delta_s)$ and $b = \log_2(1/(1 - \delta_z))$. Note that as $\delta_s + \delta_z < 1$, $b < a$. Then $\delta_{s,1} = 1/\lambda^a + O(\epsilon \log \lambda)$ and $\delta_{z,1} = 1 - 1/\lambda^b + O(\epsilon \log \lambda)$. We now apply sequential repetition with parameter $n_2 = \lambda^a$. Once we do this, following happens.

   - $\delta_{s,2}$, which is the soundness of the resulting candidate, becomes $\delta_{s,2} = 1 - (1 - \delta_{s,1})^{n_2} + O(n_2 \epsilon_2)$. It holds against all adversaries of size $\mathsf{Size}_2 = \mathsf{Size}_1 \cdot \epsilon_2^2 / \mathrm{poly}(\lambda)$, where ϵ_2 is chosen. Thus this is $1 - e^{-1} + O(\mathrm{poly}(\lambda)\epsilon + \epsilon_2)$ if ϵ, ϵ_2 are sufficiently small. Here poly is some fixed polynomial.

   - On the other hand zero-knowledge becomes $\delta_{z,2} = 2 \cdot \delta_{z,1}^{n_2} + O(n_2 \epsilon_2)$. This is equal to $\delta_{z,1}^{n_2} = (1 - 1/\lambda^b + \log \lambda \epsilon)^{\lambda^b}$. This is equal to $e^{-\lambda^{a-b}} + \mathrm{poly}(\lambda)\epsilon$ if ϵ is sufficiently small. Thus this results in $\delta_{z,2} = 2 \cdot e^{-\lambda^{a-b}} + O(\mathrm{poly}(\lambda)\epsilon + \epsilon_3)$. Here poly is some fixed polynomial.

   Finally, we apply parallel repetition once again with parameter $n_3 = \lambda$ to obtain the result.

- $\delta_{s,3}$, which is the soundness of the resulting candidate, becomes $\delta_{s,3} = \delta_{s,2}^{n_3} + O(n_3\epsilon_3)$. It holds against all adversaries of size $\mathsf{Size}_3 = \mathsf{Size}_2 \cdot \epsilon_3^2/\mathsf{poly}(\lambda)$, where ϵ_3 is chosen. This is $2^{-c\lambda} + O(\mathsf{poly}(\lambda)(\epsilon + \epsilon_2 + \epsilon_3))$ if ϵ_2, ϵ is chosen sufficiently small. Here poly is some fixed polynomial and $c > 0$ is some constant.
- On the other hand zero-knowledge becomes $\delta_{z,3} = 1 - (1 - \delta_{z,2})^{\lambda} + O(\lambda\epsilon_3)$. This is bounded by $\lambda \cdot \delta_{z,2} + O(\lambda\epsilon_3) = O(2^{-\lambda_1^c} + \mathsf{poly}(\lambda)\epsilon + \epsilon_2 + \epsilon_3)$ by union bound. Here poly is some fixed polynomial and $c_1 > 0$ is some constant.

This proves the result.

Acknowledgements. Aayush Jain would like to thank Ashutosh Kumar and Alain Passelègue for very insightful discussions about simultaneous amplification and in particular how independent zero-knowledge and soundness amplification theorems imply general simultaneous amplification.

Vipul Goyal is supported in part by a gift from Ripple, a gift from DoS Networks, a grant from Northrop Grumman, a JP Morgan Faculty Fellowship, and, a Cylab seed funding award.

Aayush Jain and Amit Sahai are supported in part from a DARPA/ARL SAFE-WARE award, NSF Frontier Award 1413955, and NSF grant 1619348, BSF grant 2012378, a Xerox Faculty Research Award, a Google Faculty Research Award, an equipment grant from Intel, and an Okawa Foundation Research Grant. Aayush Jain is also supported by a Google PhD fellowship award in Privacy and Security. This material is based upon work supported by the Defense Advanced Research Projects Agency through the ARL under Contract W911NF-15-C- 0205. The views expressed are those of the authors and do not reflect the official policy or position of the Department of Defense, the National Science Foundation, the U.S. Government or Google.

References

1. Ananth, P., Jain, A., Sahai, A.: Indistinguishability obfuscation without multilinear maps: IO from LWE, bilinear maps, and weak pseudorandomness. IACR Cryptology ePrint Archive 2018, 615 (2018)
2. Asharov, G., Lindell, Y.: A full proof of the BGW protocol for perfectly secure multiparty computation. J. Cryptol. **30**(1), 58–151 (2017)
3. Bellare, M., Impagliazzo, R., Naor, M.: Does parallel repetition lower the error in computationally sound protocols? In: FOCS, pp. 374–383 (1997)
4. Ben-Or, M., Goldwasser, S., Wigderson, A.: Completeness theorems for non-cryptographic fault-tolerant distributed computation (extended abstract). In: STOC, pp. 1–10 (1988)
5. Bitansky, N., Canetti, R., Chiesa, A., Tromer, E.: From extractable collision resistance to succinct non-interactive arguments of knowledge, and back again. In: ITCS, pp. 326–349 (2012)
6. Bitansky, N., Paneth, O.: ZAPs and non-interactive witness indistinguishability from indistinguishability obfuscation. In: Dodis, Y., Nielsen, J.B. (eds.) TCC 2015. LNCS, vol. 9015, pp. 401–427. Springer, Heidelberg (2015). https://doi.org/10.1007/978-3-662-46497-7_16
7. Canetti, R., Halevi, S., Steiner, M.: Hardness amplification of weakly verifiable puzzles. In: Kilian, J. (ed.) TCC 2005. LNCS, vol. 3378, pp. 17–33. Springer, Heidelberg (2005). https://doi.org/10.1007/978-3-540-30576-7_2

8. Canetti, R., Lombardi, A., Wichs, D.: Non-interactive zero knowledge and correlation intractability from circular-secure FHE. IACR Cryptology ePrint Archive 2018, 1248 (2018)

9. Chen, Y., Chung, K., Liao, J.: On the complexity of simulating auxiliary input. IACR Cryptology ePrint Archive 2018, 171 (2018)

10. Crépeau, C., Kilian, J.: Achieving oblivious transfer using weakened security assumptions (extended abstract). In: FOCS, pp. 42–52 (1988)

11. Damgård, I., Kilian, J., Salvail, L.: On the (im)possibility of basing oblivious transfer and bit commitment on weakened security assumptions. In: Stern, J. (ed.) EUROCRYPT 1999. LNCS, vol. 1592, pp. 56–73. Springer, Heidelberg (1999). https://doi.org/10.1007/3-540-48910-X_5

12. Dwork, C., Naor, M., Sahai, A.: Concurrent zero-knowledge. In: STOC, pp. 409–418 (1998)

13. Goldreich, O.: Basing non-interactive zero-knowledge on (enhanced) trapdoor permutations: the state of the art. In: Studies in Complexity and Cryptography. Miscellanea on the Interplay Between Randomness and Computation, pp. 406–421 (2011)

14. Goldreich, O., Micali, S., Wigderson, A.: How to play any mental game or a completeness theorem for protocols with honest majority. In: STOC, pp. 218–229 (1987)

15. Goyal, V., Jain, A., Sahai, A.: Simultaneous amplification: the case of non-interactive zero-knowledge. IACR Cryptology ePrint Archive (2019)

16. Goyal, V., Khurana, D., Mironov, I., Pandey, O., Sahai, A.: Do distributed differentially-private protocols require oblivious transfer? In: ICALP, pp. 29:1–29:15 (2016)

17. Groth, J., Ostrovsky, R., Sahai, A.: Non-interactive zaps and new techniques for NIZK. In: Dwork, C. (ed.) CRYPTO 2006. LNCS, vol. 4117, pp. 97–111. Springer, Heidelberg (2006). https://doi.org/10.1007/11818175_6

18. Groth, J., Ostrovsky, R., Sahai, A.: Perfect non-interactive zero knowledge for NP. In: Vaudenay, S. (ed.) EUROCRYPT 2006. LNCS, vol. 4004, pp. 339–358. Springer, Heidelberg (2006). https://doi.org/10.1007/11761679_21

19. Groth, J., Sahai, A.: Efficient non-interactive proof systems for bilinear groups. In: Smart, N. (ed.) EUROCRYPT 2008. LNCS, vol. 4965, pp. 415–432. Springer, Heidelberg (2008). https://doi.org/10.1007/978-3-540-78967-3_24

20. Harnik, D., Ishai, Y., Kushilevitz, E., Nielsen, J.B.: OT-combiners via secure computation. In: Canetti, R. (ed.) TCC 2008. LNCS, vol. 4948, pp. 393–411. Springer, Heidelberg (2008). https://doi.org/10.1007/978-3-540-78524-8_22

21. Håstad, J., Pass, R., Wikström, D., Pietrzak, K.: An efficient parallel repetition theorem. In: Micciancio, D. (ed.) TCC 2010. LNCS, vol. 5978, pp. 1–18. Springer, Heidelberg (2010). https://doi.org/10.1007/978-3-642-11799-2_1

22. Holenstein, T.: Strengthening key agreement using hard-core sets. Ph.D. thesis, ETH Zurich (2006)

23. Impagliazzo, R., Jaiswal, R., Kabanets, V.: Approximate list-decoding of direct product codes and uniform hardness amplification. SIAM J. Comput. 39(2), 564–605 (2009)

24. Ishai, Y., Kushilevitz, E., Ostrovsky, R., Prabhakaran, M., Sahai, A., Wullschleger, J.: Constant-rate oblivious transfer from noisy channels. In: Rogaway, P. (ed.) CRYPTO 2011. LNCS, vol. 6841, pp. 667–684. Springer, Heidelberg (2011). https://doi.org/10.1007/978-3-642-22792-9_38

25. Ishai, Y., Kushilevitz, E., Ostrovsky, R., Sahai, A.: Zero-knowledge from secure multiparty computation. In: STOC, pp. 21–30 (2007)

26. Ishai, Y., Prabhakaran, M., Sahai, A.: Secure arithmetic computation with no honest majority. In: Reingold, O. (ed.) TCC 2009. LNCS, vol. 5444, pp. 294–314. Springer, Heidelberg (2009). https://doi.org/10.1007/978-3-642-00457-5_18

27. Jetchev, D., Pietrzak, K.: How to fake auxiliary input. In: Lindell, Y. (ed.) TCC 2014. LNCS, vol. 8349, pp. 566–590. Springer, Heidelberg (2014). https://doi.org/10.1007/978-3-642-54242-8_24

28. Kilian, J.: Founding cryptography on oblivious transfer. In: STOC, pp. 20–31 (1988)

29. Maurer, U.M., Tessaro, S.: A hardcore lemma for computational indistinguishability: security amplification for arbitrarily weak PRGs with optimal stretch. In: Micciancio, D. (ed.) TCC 2010. LNCS, vol. 5978, pp. 237–254. Springer, Heidelberg (2010). https://doi.org/10.1007/978-3-642-11799-2_15

30. Meier, R., Przydatek, B., Wullschleger, J.: Robuster combiners for oblivious transfer. In: Vadhan, S.P. (ed.) TCC 2007. LNCS, vol. 4392, pp. 404–418. Springer, Heidelberg (2007). https://doi.org/10.1007/978-3-540-70936-7_22

31. Pass, R., Venkitasubramaniam, M.: An efficient parallel repetition theorem for Arthur-Merlin games. In: STOC, pp. 420–429 (2007)

32. Peikert, C., Shiehian, S.: Noninteractive zero knowledge for NP from (plain) learning with errors. IACR Cryptology ePrint Archive 2019, 158 (2019)

33. Reingold, O., Trevisan, L., Tulsiani, M., Vadhan, S.P.: Dense subsets of pseudorandom sets. In: FOCS, pp. 76–85 (2008)

34. Sahai, A., Vadhan, S.P.: A complete problem for statistical zero knowledge. J. ACM 50(2), 196–249 (2003). https://doi.org/10.1145/636865.636868

35. Sahai, A., Waters, B.: How to use indistinguishability obfuscation: deniable encryption, and more. In: Symposium on Theory of Computing, STOC 2014, New York, NY, USA, 31 May–03 June 2014 (2014)

36. Wullschleger, J.: Oblivious-transfer amplification. In: Naor, M. (ed.) EUROCRYPT 2007. LNCS, vol. 4515, pp. 555–572. Springer, Heidelberg (2007). https://doi.org/10.1007/978-3-540-72540-4_32

37. Wullschleger, J.: Oblivious transfer from weak noisy channels. In: Reingold, O. (ed.) TCC 2009. LNCS, vol. 5444, pp. 332–349. Springer, Heidelberg (2009). https://doi.org/10.1007/978-3-642-00457-5_20

The Privacy Blanket of the Shuffle Model

Borja Balle[1,2,3], James Bell[1(✉)], Adrià Gascón[1,2(✉)], and Kobbi Nissim[3]

[1] The Alan Turing Institute, London, UK
jbell@posteo.com, agascon@turing.ac.uk
[2] University of Warwick, Coventry, UK
[3] Georgetown University, Washington, D.C., USA

Abstract. This work studies differential privacy in the context of the recently proposed *shuffle model*. Unlike in the local model, where the server collecting privatized data from users can track back an input to a specific user, in the shuffle model users submit their privatized inputs to a server anonymously. This setup yields a trust model which sits in between the classical curator and local models for differential privacy. The shuffle model is the core idea in the Encode, Shuffle, Analyze (ESA) model introduced by Bittau et al. (SOPS 2017). Recent work by Cheu et al. (EUROCRYPT 2019) analyzes the differential privacy properties of the shuffle model and shows that in some cases shuffled protocols provide strictly better accuracy than local protocols. Additionally, Erlingsson et al. (SODA 2019) provide a privacy amplification bound quantifying the level of curator differential privacy achieved by the shuffle model in terms of the local differential privacy of the randomizer used by each user.

In this context, we make three contributions. First, we provide an optimal single message protocol for summation of real numbers in the shuffle model. Our protocol is very simple and has better accuracy and communication than the protocols for this same problem proposed by Cheu et al. Optimality of this protocol follows from our second contribution, a new lower bound for the accuracy of private protocols for summation of real numbers in the shuffle model. The third contribution is a new amplification bound for analyzing the privacy of protocols in the shuffle model in terms of the privacy provided by the corresponding local randomizer. Our amplification bound generalizes the results by Erlingsson et al. to a wider range of parameters, and provides a whole family of methods to analyze privacy amplification in the shuffle model.

Keywords: Differential privacy · Privacy amplification · Secure shuffling

J. Bell and A. Gascón—Work supported by The Alan Turing Institute under the EPSRC grant EP/N510129/1, and the UK Government's Defence & Security Programme in support of the Alan Turing Institute.

K. Nissim—Work supported by NSF grant no. 1565387, TWC: Large: Collaborative: Computing Over Distributed Sensitive Data. Work partly done while K. N. was visiting the Alan Turing Institute.

A. Boldyreva and D. Micciancio (Eds.): CRYPTO 2019, LNCS 11693, pp. 638–667, 2019.
https://doi.org/10.1007/978-3-030-26951-7_22

1   Introduction

Most of the research in differential privacy focuses on one of two extreme models of distribution. In the curator model, a *trusted* data collector assembles users' sensitive personal information and analyses it while injecting random noise strategically designed to provide both differential privacy and data utility. In the local model, each user i with input x_i applies a local randomizer $\mathcal{R}$ on her data to obtain a message y_i, which is then submitted to an *untrusted* analyzer. Crucially, the randomizer $\mathcal{R}$ guarantees differential privacy independently of the analyzer and the other users, even if they collude. Separation results between the local and curator models are well-known since the early research in differential privacy: certain learning tasks that can be performed in the curator model cannot be performed in the local model [23] and, furthermore, for those tasks that can be performed in the local model there are provable large gaps in accuracy when compared with the curator model. An important example is the summation of binary or (bounded) real-valued inputs among n users, which can be performed with $O(1)$ noise in the curator model [14] whereas in the local model the noise level is $\Omega(\sqrt{n})$ [7,11]. Nevertheless, the local model has been the model of choice for recent implementations of differentially private protocols by Google [16], Apple [25], and Microsoft [13]. Not surprisingly, these implementations require a huge user base to overcome the high error level.

The high level of noise required in the local model has motivated a recent search for alternative models. For example, the Encode, Shuffle, Analyze (ESA) model introduces a trusted shuffler that receives user messages and permutes them before they are handled to an untrusted analyzer [9]. A recent work by Cheu et al. [12] provides a formal analytical model for studying the shuffle model and protocols for summation of binary and real-valued inputs, essentially recovering the accuracy of the trusted curator model. The protocol for real-valued inputs requires users to send multiple messages, with a total of $O(\sqrt{n})$ single bit messages sent by each user. Also of relevance is the work of Ishai et al. [18] showing how to combine secret sharing with secure shuffling to implement distributed summation, as it allows to simulate the Laplace mechanism of the curator model. Instead we focus on the single-message shuffle model.

Another recent work by Erlingsson et al. [15] shows that the shuffling primitive provides privacy amplification, as introducing random shuffling in local model protocols reduces ε to $\varepsilon/\sqrt{n}$.

A word of caution is in place with respect to the shuffle model, as it differs significantly from the local model in terms of the assumed trust. In particular, the privacy guarantee provided by protocols in the shuffle model degrades with the fraction of users who deviate from the protocol. This is because, besides relying on a trusted shuffling step, the shuffle model requires users to provide messages carefully crafted to protect each other's privacy. This is in contrast with the curator model, where this responsibility is entirely held by the trusted curator. Nevertheless, we believe that this model is of interest both for theoretical and practical reasons. On the one hand it allows to explore the space in between the local and curator model, and on the other hand it leads to mechanisms that are easy to explain, verify, and implement; with limited accuracy loss with respect to the curator model.

In this work we do not assume any particular implementation of the shuffling step. Naturally, alternative implementations will lead to different computational trade-offs and trust assumptions. The shuffle model allows to disentangle these aspects from the precise computation at hand, as the result of shuffling the randomized inputs submitted by each user is required to be differentially private, and therefore any subsequent analysis performed by the analyzer will be private due to the postprocessing property of differential privacy.

1.1   Overview of Our Results

In this work we focus on single-message shuffle model protocols. In such protocols (i) each user i applies a local randomizer $\mathcal{R}$ on her input x_i to obtain a single message y_i; (ii) the messages $(y_1, \ldots, y_n)$ are shuffled to obtain $(y_{\sigma(1)}, \ldots, y_{\sigma(n)})$ where σ is a randomly selected permutation; and (iii) an analyzer post-processes $(y_{\sigma(1)}, \ldots, y_{\sigma(n)})$ to produce an outcome. It is required that the mechanism resulting from the combination of the local randomizer $\mathcal{R}$ and the random shuffle should provide differential privacy.

A Protocol for Private Summation. Our first contribution is a single-message shuffle model protocol for private summation of (real) numbers $x_i \in [0, 1]$. The resulting estimator is unbiased and has standard deviation $O_{\varepsilon, \delta}(n^{1/6})$.

To reduce the domain size, our protocol uses a fixed-point representation, where users apply randomized rounding to snap their input x_i to a multiple $\bar{x}_i$ of $1/k$ (where $k = O_{\varepsilon, \delta}(n^{1/3})$). We then apply on $\bar{x}_i$ a local randomizer $\mathcal{R}^{PH}$ for computing private histograms over a finite domain of size $k + 1$. The randomizer $\mathcal{R}^{PH}$ is simply a randomized response mechanism: with (small) probability γ it ignores $\bar{x}_i$ and outputs a uniformly random domain element, otherwise it reports its input $\bar{x}_i$ truthfully. There are hence about γn instances of $\mathcal{R}^{PH}$ whose report is independent to their input, and whose role is to create what we call a *privacy blanket*, which masks the outputs which are reported truthfully. Combining $\mathcal{R}^{PH}$ with a random shuffle, we get the equivalent of a histogram of the sent messages, which, in turn, is the pointwise sum of the histogram of approximately $(1 - \gamma)n$ values $\bar{x}_i$ sent truthfully and the privacy blanket, which is a histogram of approximately γn random values.

To see the benefit of creating a privacy blanket, consider the recent shuffle model summation protocol by Cheu et al. [12]. This protocol also applies randomized rounding. However, for privacy reasons, the rounded value needs to be represented in unary across multiple 1-bit messages, which are then fed into a summation protocol for binary values. The resulting error of this protocol is $O(1)$ (as is achieved in the curator model). However, the use of unary representation requires each user to send $O_{\varepsilon}(\sqrt{n})$ 1-bit messages (whereas in our protocol every user sends a single $O(\log n)$-bit message). We note that Cheu et al. also present a *single message* protocol for real summation with $O(\sqrt{n})$ error.

A Lower Bound for Private Summation. We also provide a matching lower bound showing that any single-message shuffled protocol for summation must exhibit mean squared error of order $\Omega(n^{1/3})$. In our lower bound argument we consider i.i.d. input distributions, for which we show that without loss of generality the local randomizer's image is the interval $[0, 1]$, and the analyzer is a simple summation of messages. With this view, we can contrast the privacy and accuracy of the protocol. On the one hand, the randomizer may need to output $y \in [0, 1]$ on input $x \in [0, 1]$ such that $|x - y|$ is small, to promote accuracy. However, this interferes with privacy as it may enable distinguishing between the input x and a potential input x' for which $|x' - y|$ is large.

Together with our upper bound, this result shows that the single-message shuffle model sits strictly between the curator and the local models of differential privacy. This had been shown by Cheu et al. [12] in a less direct way by showing that (i) the private selection problem can be solved more accurately in the curator model than the shuffle model, and (ii) the private summation problem can be solved more accurately in the shuffle model than in the local model. For (i) they rely on a generic translation from the shuffle to the local model and known lower bounds for private selection in the local model, while our lower bound operates directly in the shuffle model. For (ii) they propose a single-message protocol that is less accurate than ours.

Privacy Amplification by Shuffling. Lastly, we prove a new privacy amplification result for shuffled mechanisms. We show that shuffling n copies of an ε_0-LDP local randomizer with $\varepsilon_0 = O(\log(n/\log(1/\delta)))$ yields an (ε, δ)-DP mechanism with $\varepsilon = O((\varepsilon_0 \wedge 1)e^{\varepsilon_0}\sqrt{\log(1/\delta)/n})$, where $a \wedge b = \min\{a, b\}$. The proof formalizes the notion of a *privacy blanket* that we use informally in the privacy analysis of our summation protocol. In particular, we show that the output distribution of local randomizers (for any local differentially private protocol) can be decomposed as a convex combination of an *input-independent* blanket distribution and an *input-dependent* distribution.

Privacy amplification plays a major role in the design of differentially private mechanisms. These include amplification by subsampling [23] and by iteration [17], and the recent seminal work on amplification via shuffling by Erlingsson et al. [15]. In particular, Erlingsson et al. considered a setting more general than ours which allows for interactive protocols in the shuffle model by first generating a random permutation of the users' inputs and then sequentially applying a (possibly different) local randomizer to each element in the permuted vector. Moreover, each local randomizer is chosen depending on the output of previous local randomizers. To distinguish this setting from ours, we shall call the setting of Erlingsson et al. *shuffle-then-randomize* and ours *randomize-then-shuffle*. We also note that both settings are equivalent when there is a single local randomizer that will be applied to all the inputs. Throughout this paper, unless we explicitly say otherwise, the term *shuffle model* refers to the randomize-then-shuffle setting.

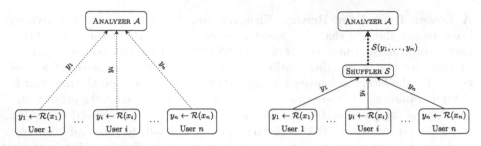

Fig. 1. The local (left) and shuffle (right) models of Differential Privacy. Dotted lines indicate differentially private values with respect to the dataset $\vec{x} = (x_1, \ldots, x_n)$, where user i holds x_i.

In the shuffle-then-randomize setting, Erlingsson et al. provide an amplification bound with $\varepsilon = O(\varepsilon_0\sqrt{\log(1/\delta)/n})$ for $\varepsilon_0 = O(1)$. Our result in the randomize-then-shuffle setting recovers this bound for the case of one randomizer, and extends it to ε_0 which is logarithmic in n. For example, using the new bound, it is possible to shuffle a local randomizer with $\varepsilon_0 = O(\log(\varepsilon^2 n/\log(1/\delta)))$ to obtain a (ε, δ)-DP mechanism with $\varepsilon = \Theta(1)$. Cheu et al. [12] also proved that a level of LDP $\varepsilon_0 = O(\log(\varepsilon^2 n/\log(1/\delta)))$ suffices to achieve (ε, δ)-DP mechanisms through shuffling, though only for binary randomized response in the randomize-then-shuffle setting. Our amplification bound captures the regimes from both [15] and [12], thus providing a unified analysis of privacy amplification by shuffling for arbitrary local randomizers in the randomize-then-shuffle setting. Our proofs are also conceptually simpler than those in [12,15] since we do not rely on privacy amplification by subsampling to obtain our results.

2   Preliminaries

Our notation is standard. We denote domains as $\mathbb{X}$, $\mathbb{Y}$, $\mathbb{Z}$ and randomized mechanism as $\mathcal{M}$, $\mathcal{P}$, $\mathcal{R}$, $\mathcal{S}$. For denoting sets and multisets we will use uppercase letters A, B, etc., and denote their elements as a, b, etc., while we will denote tuples as $\vec{x}$, $\vec{y}$, etc. Random variables, tuples and sets are denoted by X, $\vec{\mathsf{X}}$ and $\mathbf{X}$ respectively. We also use greek letters μ, ν, ω for distributions. Finally, we write $[k] = \{1, \ldots, k\}$, $a \wedge b = \min\{a, b\}$, $[u]_+ = \max\{u, 0\}$ and $\mathbb{N}$ for the natural numbers.

2.1   The Curator and Local Models of Differential Privacy

Differential privacy is a formal approach to privacy-preserving data disclosure that prevents attempts to learn private information about specific to individuals in a data release [14]. The definition of differential privacy requires that the contribution x_i of an individual to a dataset $\vec{x} = (x_1, \ldots, x_n)$ has not much effect on what the adversary sees. This is formalized by considering a dataset $\vec{x}'$ that differs from $\vec{x}$ only in one element, denoted $\vec{x} \simeq \vec{x}'$, and requiring that the views of a potential adversary when running a mechanism on inputs $\vec{x}$ and $\vec{x}'$ are "indistinguishable". Let $\varepsilon \geq 0$ and $\delta \in [0, 1]$. We say that a randomized mechanism $\mathcal{M} : \mathbb{X}^n \to \mathbb{Y}$ is (ε, δ)-DP if

$$\forall \vec{x} \simeq \vec{x}', \forall E \subseteq \mathbb{Y} : \; \mathbb{P}[\mathcal{M}(\vec{x}) \in E] \leq e^\varepsilon \mathbb{P}[\mathcal{M}(\vec{x}') \in E] + \delta.$$

As mentioned above, different models of differential privacy arise depending on whether one can assume the availability of a trusted party (a curator) that has access to the information from all users in a centralized location. This setup is the one considered in the definition above. The other extreme scenario is when each user privatizes their data locally and submits the private values to a (potentially untrusted) server for aggregation. This is the domain of *local differential privacy*[1] (see Fig. 1, left), where a user owns a data record $x \in \mathbb{X}$ and uses a *local randomizer* $\mathcal{R} : \mathbb{X} \to \mathbb{Y}$ to submit the privatized value $\mathcal{R}(x)$. In this case we say that the local randomizer is (ε, δ)-LDP if

$$\forall x, x', \forall E \subseteq \mathbb{Y} : \; \mathbb{P}[\mathcal{R}(x) \in E] \leq e^\varepsilon \mathbb{P}[\mathcal{R}(x') \in E] + \delta.$$

The key difference is that in this case we must protect each user's data, and therefore the definition considers changing a user's value x to another arbitrary value x'.

Moving from curator DP to local DP can be seen as effectively redefining the view that an adversary has on the data during the execution of a mechanism. In particular, if $\mathcal{R}$ is an (ε, δ)-LDP local randomizer, then the mechanism $\mathcal{M} : \mathbb{X}^n \to \mathbb{Y}^n$ given by $\mathcal{M}(x_1, \ldots, x_n) = (\mathcal{R}(x_1), \ldots, \mathcal{R}(x_n))$ is (ε, δ)-DP in the curator sense. The single-message shuffle model sits in between these two settings.

2.2 The Single-Message Shuffle Model

The *single-message shuffle model* of differential privacy considers a data collector that receives one message y_i from each of the n users as in the local model of differential privacy. The crucial difference with the local model is that the shuffle model assumes that a mechanism is in place to provide anonymity to each of the messages, i.e. the data collector is unable to associate messages to users. This is equivalent to assuming that, in the view of the adversary, these messages have been shuffled by a random permutation unknown to the adversary (see Fig. 1, right).

Following the notation in [12], we define a single-message protocol $\mathcal{P}$ in the shuffle model to be a pair of algorithms $\mathcal{P} = (\mathcal{R}, \mathcal{A})$, where $\mathcal{R} : \mathbb{X} \to \mathbb{Y}$, and $\mathcal{A} : \mathbb{Y}^n \to \mathbb{Z}$. We call $\mathcal{R}$ the *local randomizer*, $\mathbb{Y}$ the *message space* of the protocol, $\mathcal{A}$ the *analyzer* of $\mathcal{P}$, and $\mathbb{Z}$ the *output space*. The overall protocol implements a mechanism $\mathcal{P} : \mathbb{X}^n \to \mathbb{Z}$ as follows. Each user i holds a data record x_i, to which she applies the local randomizer to obtain a message $y_i = \mathcal{R}(x_i)$. The messages y_i are then shuffled and submitted to the analyzer. We write $\mathcal{S}(y_1, \ldots, y_n)$ to denote the random shuffling step, where $\mathcal{S} : \mathbb{Y}^n \to \mathbb{Y}^n$ is a *shuffler* that applies

---

[1] Of which, in this paper, we only consider the non-interactive version for simplicity.

a random permutation to its inputs. In summary, the output of $\mathcal{P}(x_1, \ldots, x_n)$ is given by $\mathcal{A} \circ \mathcal{S} \circ \mathcal{R}^n(\vec{x}) = \mathcal{A}(\mathcal{S}(\mathcal{R}(x_1), \ldots, \mathcal{R}(x_n)))$.

From a privacy point of view, our threat model assumes that the analyzer $\mathcal{A}$ is applied to the shuffled messages by an untrusted data collector. Therefore, when analyzing the privacy of a protocol in the shuffle model we are interested in the indistinguishability between the shuffles $\mathcal{S} \circ \mathcal{R}^n(\vec{x})$ and $\mathcal{S} \circ \mathcal{R}^n(\vec{x}')$ for datasets $\vec{x} \simeq \vec{x}'$. In this sense, the analyzer's role is to provide utility for the output of the protocol $\mathcal{P}$, whose privacy guarantees follow from those of the *shuffled mechanism* $\mathcal{M} = \mathcal{S} \circ \mathcal{R}^n : \mathbb{X}^n \to \mathbb{Y}^n$ by the post-processing property of differential privacy. That is, the protocol $\mathcal{P}$ is (ε, δ)-DP whenever the shuffled mechanism $\mathcal{M}$ is (ε, δ)-DP.

When analyzing the privacy of a shuffled mechanism we assume the shuffler $\mathcal{S}$ is a perfectly secure primitive. This implies that a data collector observing the shuffled messages $\mathcal{S}(y_1, \ldots, y_n)$ obtains no information about which user generated each of the messages. An equivalent way to state this fact, which will sometimes be useful in our analysis of shuffled mechanisms, is to say that the output of the shuffler is a multiset instead of a tuple. Formally, this means that we can also think of the shuffler as a deterministic map $\mathcal{S} : \mathbb{Y}^n \to \mathbb{N}_n^{\mathbb{Y}}$ which takes a tuple $\vec{y} = (y_1, \ldots, y_n)$ with n elements from $\mathbb{Y}$ and returns the multiset $Y = \{y_1, \ldots, y_n\}$ of its coordinates, where $\mathbb{N}_n^{\mathbb{Y}}$ denotes the collection of all multisets over $\mathbb{Y}$ with cardinality n. Sometimes we will refer to such multisets $Y \in \mathbb{N}_n^{\mathbb{Y}}$ as *histograms* to emphasize the fact that they can be regarded functions $Y : \mathbb{Y} \to \mathbb{N}$ counting the number of occurrences of each element of $\mathbb{Y}$ in Y.

2.3   Mean Square Error

When analyzing the utility of shuffled protocols for real summation we will use the *mean square error* (MSE) as accuracy measure. The mean squared error of a randomized protocol $\mathcal{P}(\vec{x})$ for approximating a deterministic quantity $f(\vec{x})$ is given by $\mathrm{MSE}(\mathcal{P}, \vec{x}) = \mathbb{E}[(\mathcal{P}(\vec{x}) - f(\vec{x}))^2]$, where the expectation is taken over the randomness of $\mathcal{P}$. Note that when the protocol is unbiased the MSE is equivalent to the variance, since in this case we have $\mathbb{E}[\mathcal{P}(\vec{x})] = f(\vec{x})$ and therefore

$$\mathrm{MSE}(\mathcal{P}, \vec{x}) = \mathbb{E}[(\mathcal{P}(\vec{x}) - \mathbb{E}[\mathcal{P}(\vec{x})])^2] = \mathbb{V}[\mathcal{P}(\vec{x})].$$

In addition to the MSE for a fixed input, we also consider the *worst-case MSE* over all possible inputs $\mathrm{MSE}(\mathcal{P})$, and the *expected MSE* on a distribution over inputs $\mathrm{MSE}(\mathcal{P}, \vec{\mathsf{X}})$. These quantities are defined as follows:

$$\mathrm{MSE}(\mathcal{P}) = \sup_{\vec{x}} \mathrm{MSE}(\mathcal{P}, \vec{x}),$$

$$\mathrm{MSE}(\mathcal{P}, \vec{\mathsf{X}}) = \mathbb{E}_{\vec{x} \sim \vec{\mathsf{X}}}[\mathrm{MSE}(\mathcal{P}, \vec{x})].$$

3   The Privacy of Shuffled Randomized Response

In this section we show a protocol for n parties to compute a private histogram over the domain $[k]$ in the single-message shuffle model. The local randomizer of

---

Algorithm 1. Private Histogram: Local Randomizer $\mathcal{R}^{PH}_{\gamma,k,n}$

Public Parameters: $\gamma \in [0,1]$, domain size k, and number of parties n
Input: $x \in [k]$
Output: $y \in [k]$

Sample $b \leftarrow \text{Ber}(\gamma)$
if $b = 0$ then
| Let $y \leftarrow x$
else
| Sample $y \leftarrow \text{Unif}([k])$
return y

---

our protocol is shown in Algorithm 1, and the analyzer simply builds a histogram of the received messages. The randomizer is parameterized by a probability γ, and consists of a k-ary randomized response mechanism that returns the true value x with probability $1 - \gamma$, and a uniformly random value with probability γ. This randomizer has been studied and used (in the local model) in several previous works [8,21,22]. We discuss how to set γ to satisfy differential privacy next.

3.1   The *Blanket* Intuition

In each execution of Algorithm 1 a subset B of approximately γn parties will submit a random value, while the remaining parties will submit their true value. The values sent by parties in B form a histogram Y_1 of uniformly random values and the values sent by the parties not in B correspond to the true histogram Y_2 of their data. An important observation is that in the shuffle model the information obtained by the server is equivalent to the histogram $Y_1 \cup Y_2$. This observation is a simple generalization of the observation made by Cheu et al. [12] that shuffling of binary data corresponds to secure addition. When $k > 2$, shuffling of categorical data corresponds to a secure histogram computation, and in particular secure addition of histograms. In summary, the information collected by the server in an execution corresponds to a histogram Y with approximately γn random entries and $(1 - \gamma)n$ truthful entries, which as mentioned above we decompose as $Y = Y_1 \cup Y_2$.

To achieve differential privacy we need to set the value γ of Algorithm 1 so that Y changes by an appropriately bounded amount when computed on neighboring datasets where only a certain party's data (say party n) changes. Our privacy argument does not rely on the anonymity of the set B and thus we can assume, for the privacy analysis, that the server knows B. We further assume in the analysis that the server knows the inputs from all parties except the nth one, which gives her the ability to remove from Y the values submitted by any party who responded truthfully among the first $n - 1$.

Now consider two datasets of size n that differ on the input from the nth party. In an execution where party n is in B we trivially get privacy since the value submitted by this party is independent of its input. Otherwise, party n will be submitting their true value x_n, in which case the server can determine Y_2 up to the value x_n using that she knows $(x_1, \ldots, x_{n-1})$. Hence, a server trying to break the privacy of party n observes $Y_1 \cup \{x_n\}$, the union of a random histogram with the input of this party. Intuitively, the privacy of the protocol boils down to setting γ so that Y_1, which we call the random *blanket* of the local randomizer $\mathcal{R}^{PH}_{\gamma,k,n}$, appropriately "hides" x_n.

As we will see in Sect. 5, the intuitive notion of the blanket of a local randomizer can be formally defined for arbitrary local randomizers using a generalization of the notion of total variation distance from pairs to sets of distributions. This will allow us to represent the output distribution of any local randomizer $\mathcal{R}(x)$ as a mixture of the form $(1 - \gamma)\nu_x + \gamma\omega$, for some $0 < \gamma < 1$ and probability distributions ν_x and ω, of which we call ω the *privacy blanket* of the local randomizer $\mathcal{R}$.

3.2 Privacy Analysis of Algorithm 1

Let us now formalize the above intuition, and prove privacy for our protocol for an appropriate choice of γ. In particular, we prove the following theorem, where the assumption $\varepsilon \leq 1$ is only for technical convenience. A more general approach to obtain privacy guarantees for shuffled mechanisms is provided in Sect. 5.

Theorem 1. *The shuffled mechanism* $\mathcal{M} = \mathcal{S} \circ \mathcal{R}^{PH}_{\gamma,k,n}$ *is* (ε, δ)-*DP for any* $k, n \in \mathbb{N}$, $\varepsilon \leq 1$ *and* $\delta \in (0, 1]$ *such that* $\gamma = \max\{\frac{14k\log(2/\delta)}{(n-1)\varepsilon^2}, \frac{27k}{(n-1)\varepsilon}\} < 1$.

Proof. Let $\vec{x}, \vec{x}' \in [k]^n$ be neighboring databases of the form $\vec{x} = (x_1, x_2, \ldots, x_n)$ and $\vec{x}' = (x_1, x_2, \ldots, x_n')$. We assume that the server knows the set B of users who submit random values, which is equivalent to revealing to the server a vector $\vec{b} = (b_1, \ldots, b_n)$ of the bits b sampled in the execution of each of the local randomizers. We also assume the server knows the inputs from the first $n - 1$ parties.

Hence, we define the view $\text{View}_\mathcal{M}$ of the server on a realization of the protocol as the tuple $\text{View}_\mathcal{M}(\vec{x}) = (Y, \vec{x}_\cap, \vec{b})$ containing:

1. A multiset $Y = \mathcal{M}(\vec{x}) = \{y_1, \ldots, y_n\}$ with the outputs y_i of each local randomizer.
2. A tuple $\vec{x}_\cap = (x_1, \ldots, x_{n-1})$ with the inputs from the first $n - 1$ users.
3. The tuple $\vec{b} = (b_1, \ldots, b_n)$ of binary values indicating which users submitted their true values.

Proving that the protocol is (ε, δ)-DP when the server has access to all this information will imply the same level of privacy for the shuffled mechanism $\mathcal{S} \circ \mathcal{R}^{PH}_{\gamma,k,n}$ by the post-processing property of differential privacy.

To show that $\text{View}_\mathcal{M}$ satisfies (ε, δ)-DP it is enough to prove

$$\mathbb{P}_{\mathsf{V} \sim \text{View}_\mathcal{M}(\vec{x})} \left[\frac{\mathbb{P}[\text{View}_\mathcal{M}(\vec{x}) = \mathsf{V}]}{\mathbb{P}[\text{View}_\mathcal{M}(\vec{x}') = \mathsf{V}]} \geq e^\varepsilon \right] \leq \delta.$$

We start by fixing a value V in the range of $\text{View}_\mathcal{M}$ and computing the probability ratio above conditioned on $\mathsf{V} = V$.

Consider first the case where V is such that $b_n = 1$, i.e. party n submits a random value independent of her input. In this case privacy holds trivially since $\mathbb{P}[\text{View}_\mathcal{M}(\vec{x}) = V] = \mathbb{P}[\text{View}_\mathcal{M}(\vec{x}') = V]$. Hence, we focus on the case where party n submits her true value ($b_n = 0$). For $j \in [k]$, let n_j be the number of messages received by the server with value j after removing from Y any truthful answers submitted by the first $n-1$ users. With our notation above, we have $n_j = Y_1(j) + \mathbb{I}[x_n = j]$ and $\sum_{j=1}^k n_j = |B| + 1$ for the execution with input $\vec{x}$. Now assume, without loss of generality, that $x_n = 1$ and $x'_n = 2$. As $x_n = 1$, we have that

$$\mathbb{P}[\text{View}_\mathcal{M}(\vec{x}) = V] = \binom{|B|}{n_1 - 1, n_2, ..., n_k} \frac{\gamma^{|B|}(1-\gamma)^{n-|B|}}{k^{|B|}},$$

corresponding to the probability of a particular pattern $\vec{b}$ of users sampling from the blanket times the probability of obtaining a particular histogram Y_1 when sampling $|B|$ elements uniformly at random from $[k]$. Similarly, using that $x'_n = 2$ we have

$$\mathbb{P}[\text{View}_\mathcal{M}(\vec{x}') = V] = \binom{|B|}{n_1, n_2 - 1, ..., n_k} \frac{\gamma^{|B|}(1-\gamma)^{n-|B|}}{k^{|B|}}.$$

Therefore, taking the ratio between the last two probabilities we find that, in the case $b_n = 0$,

$$\frac{\mathbb{P}[\text{View}_\mathcal{M}(\vec{x}) = V]}{\mathbb{P}[\text{View}_\mathcal{M}(\vec{x}') = V]} = \frac{n_1}{n_2}.$$

Now note that for $\mathsf{V} \sim \text{View}_\mathcal{M}(\vec{x})$ the count $n_2 = n_2(\mathsf{V})$ follows a binomial distribution N_2 with $n-1$ trials and success probability γ/k, and $n_1(\mathsf{V}) - 1 = \mathsf{N}_1 - 1$ follows the same distribution. Thus, we have

$$\mathbb{P}_{\mathsf{V} \sim \text{View}_\mathcal{M}(\vec{x})}\left[\frac{\mathbb{P}[\text{View}_\mathcal{M}(\vec{x}) = V]}{\mathbb{P}[\text{View}_\mathcal{M}(\vec{x}') = V]} \geq e^\varepsilon\right] = \mathbb{P}\left[\frac{\mathsf{N}_1}{\mathsf{N}_2} \geq e^\varepsilon\right],$$

where $\mathsf{N}_1 \sim \text{Bin}\left(n-1, \frac{\gamma}{k}\right) + 1$ and $\mathsf{N}_2 \sim \text{Bin}\left(n-1, \frac{\gamma}{k}\right)$.

We now bound the probability above using a union bound and the multiplicative Chernoff bound. Let $c = \mathbb{E}[\mathsf{N}_2] = \frac{\gamma(n-1)}{k}$. Since $\mathsf{N}_1/\mathsf{N}_2 \geq e^\varepsilon$ implies that either $\mathsf{N}_1 \geq ce^{\varepsilon/2}$ or $\mathsf{N}_2 \leq ce^{-\varepsilon/2}$, we have

$$\mathbb{P}\left[\frac{\mathsf{N}_1}{\mathsf{N}_2} \geq e^\varepsilon\right] \leq \mathbb{P}\left[\mathsf{N}_1 \geq ce^{\varepsilon/2}\right] + \mathbb{P}\left[\mathsf{N}_2 \leq ce^{-\varepsilon/2}\right]$$

$$= \mathbb{P}\left[\mathsf{N}_2 \geq ce^{\varepsilon/2} - 1\right] + \mathbb{P}\left[\mathsf{N}_2 \leq ce^{-\varepsilon/2}\right]$$

$$= \mathbb{P}\left[\mathsf{N}_2 - \mathbb{E}[\mathsf{N}_1] \geq c\left(e^{\varepsilon/2} - 1 - \frac{1}{c}\right)\right]$$

$$+ \mathbb{P}\left[\mathsf{N}_2 - \mathbb{E}[\mathsf{N}_2] \leq c(e^{-\varepsilon/2} - 1)\right].$$

Applying the multiplicative Chernoff bound to each of these probabilities then gives that

$$\mathbb{P}\left[\frac{N_1}{N_2} \geq e^{\varepsilon}\right] \leq \exp\left(-\frac{c}{3}\left(e^{\varepsilon/2} - 1 - \frac{1}{c}\right)^2\right) + \exp\left(-\frac{c}{2}(1 - e^{-\varepsilon/2})^2\right).$$

Assuming $\varepsilon \leq 1$, both of the right hand summands are less than or equal to $\frac{\delta}{2}$ if

$$c = \frac{\gamma(n-1)}{k} \geq \max\left\{\frac{14\log\left(\frac{2}{\delta}\right)}{\varepsilon^2}, \frac{27}{\varepsilon}\right\}.$$

Indeed, for the second term this follows from $1 - e^{-\varepsilon/2} \geq (1 - e^{-1/2})\varepsilon \geq \varepsilon/\sqrt{7}$ for $\varepsilon \leq 1$. For the first term we use that $c \geq \frac{27}{\varepsilon}$ implies $e^{\varepsilon/2} - 1 - \frac{1}{c} \geq \frac{25}{54}\varepsilon$ and $14 \geq \frac{3 \cdot 54^2}{25^2}$. □

Two remarks about this result are in order. First, we should emphasize that the assumption of $\varepsilon \leq 1$ is only required for simplicity when using Chernoff's inequality to bound the probability that the privacy loss random variable is large. Without any restriction on ε, a similar result can be achieved by replacing Chernoff's inequality with Bennett's inequality [10, Theorem 2.9] to account for the variance of the privacy loss random variable in the tail bound. Here we decide not to pursue this route because the ad-hoc privacy analysis of Theorem 1 is superseded by the results in Sect. 5 anyway. The second observation about this result is that, with the choice of γ made above, the local randomizer $\mathcal{R}_{\gamma,k,n}^{PH}$ satisfies ε_0-LDP with

$$\varepsilon_0 = O\left(\log\left(\frac{n\varepsilon^2}{\log(1/\delta)} - k\right)\right) = O\left(\log\left(\frac{n\varepsilon^2}{\log(1/\delta)}\left(1 - \frac{\gamma}{14}\right)\right)\right).$$

This is obtained according to the formula provided by Lemma 6 in Sect. 5.1. Thus, we see that Theorem 1 can be regarded as a privacy amplification statement showing that shuffling n copies of an ε_0-LDP local randomized with $\varepsilon_0 = O_\delta(\log(n\varepsilon^2))$ yields a mechanism satisfying (ε, δ)-DP. In Sect. 5.1 we will show that this is not coincidence, but rather an instance of a general privacy amplification result.

4 Optimal Summation in the Shuffle Model

4.1 Upper Bound

In this section we present a protocol for the problem of computing the sum of real values $x_i \in [0, 1]$ in the single-message shuffle model. Our protocol is parameterized by values c, k, and the number of parties n, and its local randomizer and analyzer are shown in Algorithms 2 and 3, respectively.

Algorithm 2. Local Randomizer $\mathcal{R}_{c,k,n}$

Public Parameters: c, k, and number of parties n
Input: $x \in [0, 1]$
Output: $y \in \{0, 1, \ldots, k\}$

Let $\bar{x} \leftarrow \lfloor xk \rfloor + \text{Ber}(xk - \lfloor xk \rfloor)$ ▷ $\bar{x}$ is the encoding of x with precision k

Sample $b \leftarrow \text{Ber}\left(\frac{c(k+1)}{n}\right)$

if $b = 0$ **then**
  | Let $y \leftarrow \bar{x}$
else
  | Sample $y \leftarrow \text{Unif}(\{0, 1, \ldots, k\})$
return y

Algorithm 3. Analyzer $\mathcal{A}_{c,k,n}$

Public Parameters: c, k, and number of parties n
Input: Multiset $\{y_i\}_{i \in [n]}$, with $y_i \in \{0, 1, \ldots, k\}$
Output: $z \in [0, 1]$

Let $\hat{z} \leftarrow \frac{1}{k} \sum_{i=1}^{n} y_i$

Let $z \leftarrow \text{DeBias}(\hat{z})$, where $\text{DeBias}(w) = \left(w - \frac{c(k+1)}{2}\right) / \left(1 - \frac{c(k+1)}{n}\right)$

return z

The protocol uses the protocol depicted in Algorithm 1 in a black-box manner. To compute a differentially private approximation of $\sum_i x_i$, we fix a value k. Then we operate on the fixed-point encoding of each input x_i, which is an integer $\bar{x}_i \in \{0, \ldots, k\}$. That is, we replace x_i with its fixed-point approximation $\bar{x}_i/k$. The protocol then applies the randomized response mechanism in Algorithm 1 to each $\bar{x}_i$ to submit a value y_i to compute a differentially private histogram of the $(y_1, \ldots, y_n)$ as in the previous section. From these values the server can approximate $\sum_i x_i$ by post processing, which includes a debiasing standard step. The privacy of the protocol described in Algorithms 2 and 3 follows directly from the privacy analysis of Algorithm 1 given in Sect. 3.

Regarding accuracy, a crucial point in this reduction is that the encoding $\bar{x}_i$ of x_i is via randomized rounding and hence unbiased. In more detail, as shown in Algorithm 2, the value x is encoded as $\bar{x} = \lfloor xk \rfloor + \text{Ber}(xk - \lfloor xk \rfloor)$. This ensures that $\mathbb{E}[\bar{x}/k] = \mathbb{E}[x]$ and that the mean squared error due to rounding (which equals the variance) is at most $\frac{1}{4k^2}$. The local randomizer either sends this fixed-point encoding or a random value in $\{0, 1, \ldots, k\}$ with probabilities $1 - \gamma$ and γ, respectively, where (following the analysis in the previous section) we set $\gamma = \frac{k+1}{n}c$. Note that the mean squared error when the local randomizer submits a random value is at most $\frac{1}{2}$. This observations lead to the following accuracy bound.

Theorem 2. *For any $\varepsilon \le 1$, $\delta \in (0,1]$ and $n \in \mathbb{N}$, there exist parameters c, k such that $\mathcal{P}_{c,k,n}$ is (ε, δ)-DP and*

$$\mathrm{MSE}(\mathcal{P}_{c,k,n}) = O\left(n^{1/3} \cdot \frac{\log^{2/3}(1/\delta)}{\varepsilon^{4/3}}\right).$$

Proof. The following bound on $\mathrm{MSE}(\mathcal{P}_{c,k,n})$ follows from the observations above: unbiasedness of the estimator computed by the analyzer and randomized rounding, and the bounds on the variance of our randomized response.

$$
\begin{aligned}
\mathrm{MSE}(\mathcal{P}_{c,k,n}) &= \sup_{\vec{x}} \mathbb{E}[(\mathtt{DeBias}(\hat{z}) - \sum_i x_i)^2] \\
&= \sup_{\vec{x}} \mathbb{E}\left[\left(\sum_i (\mathtt{DeBias}(y_i/k) - x_i)\right)^2\right] \\
&= \sup_{\vec{x}} \sum_i \mathbb{E}\left[(\mathtt{DeBias}(y_i/k) - x_i)^2\right] \\
&= \sup_{\vec{x}} \sum_i \mathbb{V}\left[\mathtt{DeBias}(y_i/k)\right] \\
&= \frac{n}{(1-\gamma)^2} \sup_{x_1} \mathbb{V}[y_1/k] \\
&\le \frac{n}{(1-\gamma)^2} \left(\frac{1-\gamma}{4k^2} + \frac{\gamma}{2}\right) \\
&\le \frac{n}{(1-\gamma)^2} \left(\frac{1}{4k^2} + \frac{c(k+1)}{2n}\right).
\end{aligned}
$$

Choosing the parameter $k = (n/c)^{1/3}$ minimizes the sum in the above expression and provides a bound on the MSE of the form $O(c^{2/3}n^{1/3})$. Plugging in $c = \gamma \frac{n}{k+1} = O\left(\frac{\log(1/\delta)}{\varepsilon^2}\right)$ from our analysis in the previous section (Theorem 1) yields the bound in the statement of the theorem. $\qquad\square$

Note that as our protocol corresponds to an unbiased estimator, the MSE is equal to the variance in this case. Using this observation we immediately obtain the following corollary for estimation of statistical queries in the single-message shuffle model.

Corollary 1. *For every statistical query $q : \mathcal{X} \mapsto [0,1]$, $\varepsilon \le 1, \delta \in (0,1]$ and $n \in \mathbb{N}$, there is an (ε, δ)-DP n-party unbiased protocol for estimating $\frac{1}{n} \sum_i q(x_i)$ in the single-message shuffle model with standard deviation $O\left(\frac{\log^{1/3}(1/\delta)}{n^{5/6}\varepsilon^{2/3}}\right)$.*

4.2   Lower Bound

In this section we show that any differentially private protocol $\mathcal{P}$ for the problem of estimating $\sum_i x_i$ in the single-message shuffle model must have $\mathrm{MSE}(\mathcal{P}) =$

$\Omega(n^{1/3})$ This shows that our protocol from the previous section is optimal, and gives a separation result for the single-message shuffle model, showing that its accuracy lies between the curator and local models of differential privacy.

Reduction in the i.i.d. Setting. We first show that when the inputs to the protocol $\mathcal{P}$ are sampled i.i.d. one can assume, for the purpose of showing a lower bound, that the protocol $\mathcal{P}$ for estimating $\sum_i x_i$ is of a simplified form. Namely, we show that the local randomizer can be taken to have output values in $[0,1]$, and its analyzer simply adds up all received messages.

Lemma 1. *Let $\mathcal{P} = (\mathcal{R}, \mathcal{A})$ be an n-party protocol for real summation in the single-message shuffle model. Let X be a random variable on $[0,1]$ and suppose that users sample their inputs from the distribution $\vec{\mathsf{X}} = (\mathsf{X}_1, \ldots, \mathsf{X}_n)$, where each X_i is an independent copy of X. Then, there exists a protocol $\mathcal{P}' = (\mathcal{R}', \mathcal{A}')$ such that:*

1. *$\mathcal{A}'(y_1, \ldots, y_n) = \sum_{i=1}^n y_i$ and[2] $\mathsf{Im}(\mathcal{R}') \subseteq [0,1]$.*
2. *$MSE(\mathcal{P}', \vec{\mathsf{X}}) \le MSE(\mathcal{P}, \vec{\mathsf{X}})$.*
3. *If the shuffled mechanism $\mathcal{S} \circ \mathcal{R}^n$ is (ε, δ)-DP, then $\mathcal{S} \circ \mathcal{R}'^n$ is also (ε, δ)-DP.*

Proof. Consider the post-processed local randomizer $\mathcal{R}' = f \circ \mathcal{R}$ where $f(y) = \mathbb{E}[\mathsf{X}|\mathcal{R}(\mathsf{X}) = y]$. In Bayesian estimation, f is called the posterior mean estimator, and is known to be a minimum MSE estimator [19]. Since $\mathsf{Im}(\mathcal{R}') \subseteq [0,1]$, we have a protocol $\mathcal{P}'$ satisfying claim 1.

Next we show that $MSE(\mathcal{P}', \vec{\mathsf{X}}) \le MSE(\mathcal{P}, \vec{\mathsf{X}})$. Note that the analyzer $\mathcal{A}$ in protocol $\mathcal{P}$ can be seen as an estimator of $\mathsf{Z} = \sum_i \mathsf{X}_i$ given observations from $\vec{\mathsf{Y}} = (\mathsf{Y}_1, \ldots, \mathsf{Y}_n)$, where $\mathsf{Y}_i = \mathcal{R}(\mathsf{X}_i)$. Now consider an arbitrary estimator h of Z given the observation $\vec{\mathsf{Y}} = \vec{y}$. We have

$$\mathrm{MSE}(h, \vec{y}) = \mathbb{E}[(h(\vec{y}) - \mathsf{Z})^2 | \vec{\mathsf{Y}} = \vec{y}]$$
$$= \mathbb{E}[\mathsf{Z}^2 | \vec{\mathsf{Y}} = \vec{y}] - 2h(\vec{y})\mathbb{E}[\mathsf{Z}|\vec{\mathsf{Y}} = \vec{y}] + h(\vec{y})^2.$$

It follows from minimizing $\mathrm{MSE}(h, \vec{y})$ with respect to h that the minimum MSE estimator of Z given $\vec{\mathsf{Y}}$ is $h(\vec{y}) = \mathbb{E}[\mathsf{Z}|\vec{\mathsf{Y}} = \vec{y}]$. Hence, by linearity of expectation, and the fact that the Y_i are independent,

$$\mathbb{E}[\mathsf{Z}|\vec{\mathsf{Y}} = \vec{y}] = \sum_{i=1}^n \mathbb{E}[\mathsf{X}_i|\vec{\mathsf{Y}} = \vec{y}] = \sum_{i=1}^n \mathbb{E}[\mathsf{X}_i|\mathsf{Y}_i = y_i] = \sum_{i=1}^n f(y_i).$$

Therefore, we have shown that $\mathcal{P}' = (\mathcal{R}', \mathcal{A}')$ implements a minimum MSE estimator for Z given $(\mathcal{R}(\mathsf{X}_1), \ldots, \mathcal{R}(\mathsf{X}_n))$, and in particular $MSE(\mathcal{P}', \vec{\mathsf{X}}) \le MSE(\mathcal{P}, \vec{\mathsf{X}})$.

Part 3 of the lemma follows from the standard post-processing property of differential privacy by observing that the output of $\mathcal{S} \circ \mathcal{R}'^n(\vec{x})$ can be obtained by applying f to each element in the output of $\mathcal{S} \circ \mathcal{R}^n(\vec{x})$. $\qquad\square$

---

[2] Here we use $\mathsf{Im}(\mathcal{R}')$ to denote the image of the local randomizer $\mathcal{R}'$.

Proof of the Lower Bound. It remains to show that, for any protocol $\mathcal{P} = (\mathcal{R}, \mathcal{A})$ satisfying the conditions of Lemma 1, we can find a tuple of i.i.d. random variables $\vec{\mathsf{X}}$ such that $\mathrm{MSE}(\mathcal{P}, \vec{\mathsf{X}}) = \Omega(n^{1/3})$. Recall that by virtue of Lemma 1 we can assume, without loss of generality, that $\mathcal{R}$ is a mapping from $[0, 1]$ into itself, $\mathcal{A}$ sums its inputs, and $\vec{\mathsf{X}} = (\mathsf{X}_1, \ldots, \mathsf{X}_n)$ where the X_i are i.i.d. copies of some random variable X. We first show that under these assumptions we can reduce the search for a lower bound on $\mathrm{MSE}(\mathcal{P}, \vec{\mathsf{X}})$ to consider only the expected square error of an individual run of the local randomizer.

Lemma 2. *Let $\mathcal{P} = (\mathcal{R}, \mathcal{A})$ be an n-party protocol for real summation in the single-message shuffle model such that $\mathcal{R} : [0, 1] \to [0, 1]$ and $\mathcal{A}$ is summation. Suppose $\vec{\mathsf{X}} = (\mathsf{X}_1, \ldots, \mathsf{X}_n)$, where the X_i are i.i.d. copies of some random variable X. Then,*

$$\mathrm{MSE}(\mathcal{P}, \vec{\mathsf{X}}) \geq n\mathbb{E}[(\mathcal{R}(\mathsf{X}) - \mathsf{X})^2].$$

Proof. The result follows from an elementary calculation:

$$
\begin{aligned}
\mathrm{MSE}(\mathcal{P}, \vec{\mathsf{X}}) &= \mathbb{E}\left[\left(\sum_{i \in [n]} \mathcal{R}(\mathsf{X}_i) - \mathsf{X}_i\right)^2\right] \\
&= \sum_i \mathbb{E}[(\mathcal{R}(\mathsf{X}_i) - \mathsf{X}_i)^2] + \sum_{i \neq j} \mathbb{E}[(\mathcal{R}(\mathsf{X}_i) - \mathsf{X}_i)(\mathcal{R}(\mathsf{X}_j) - \mathsf{X}_j)] \\
&= \sum_i \mathbb{E}[(\mathcal{R}(\mathsf{X}_i) - \mathsf{X}_i)^2] + \sum_{i \neq j} \mathbb{E}[\mathcal{R}(\mathsf{X}_i) - \mathsf{X}_i]^2 \\
&\geq n\mathbb{E}[(\mathcal{R}(\mathsf{X}) - \mathsf{X})^2].
\end{aligned}
$$

$\square$

Therefore, to obtain our lower bound it will suffice to find a distribution on $[0, 1]$ such that if $\mathcal{R} : [0, 1] \to [0, 1]$ is a local randomizer for which the protocol $\mathcal{P} = (\mathcal{R}, \mathcal{A})$ is differentially private, then $\mathcal{R}$ has expected square error $\Omega(n^{-2/3})$ under that distribution. We start by constructing such distribution and then show that it satisfies the desired properties.

Consider the partition of the unit interval $[0, 1]$ into k disjoint subintervals of size $1/k$, where $k \in \mathbb{N}$ is a parameter to be determined later. We will take inputs from the set $I = \{m/k - 1/2k \mid m \in [k]\}$ of midpoints of these intervals. For any $a \in I$ we denote by $I(x)$ the subinterval of $[0, 1]$ containing a. Given a local randomizer $\mathcal{R} : [0, 1] \to [0, 1]$ we define the probability $p_{a,b} = \mathbb{P}[\mathcal{R}(a) \in I(b)]$ that the local randomizer maps an input a to the subinterval centered at b for any $a, b \in I$.

Now let $\mathsf{X} \sim \mathtt{Unif}(I)$ be a random variable sampled uniformly from I. The following observations are central to the proof of our lower bound. First observe that $\mathcal{R}$ maps X to a value outside of its interval with probability $\frac{1}{k} \sum_{b \in I}(1 - p_{b,b})$. If this event occurs, then $\mathcal{R}(\mathsf{X})$ incurs a squared error of at least $1/(2k)^2$, as the absolute error will be at least half the width of an interval. Similarly, when $\mathcal{R}$ maps an input a to a point inside an interval $I(b)$ with $a \neq b$, the squared error incurred is at least $(|b - a| - 1/2k)^2$, as the error is at least the distance between the two interval midpoints minus half the width of an interval. The next lemma encapsulates a useful calculation related to this observation.

Lemma 3. *For any $b \in I = \{m/k - 1/2k \mid m \in [k]\}$ we have*

$$\frac{1}{k} \sum_{a \in I \setminus \{b\}} \left(|a - b| - \frac{1}{2k} \right)^2 \geq \frac{1}{48} \left(1 - \frac{1}{k^2} \right).$$

Proof. Let $b = m/k - 1/2k$ for some $m \in [k]$. Then,

$$\frac{1}{k} \sum_{a \in I \setminus \{b\}} \left(|a - b| - \frac{1}{2k} \right)^2 = \frac{1}{k^3} \sum_{i \in [k] \setminus \{m\}} \left(|i - m| - \frac{1}{2} \right)^2$$

$$\geq \frac{1}{4k^3} \sum_{i \in [k] \setminus \{m\}} (i - m)^2 = \frac{1}{4k^3} \sum_{i \in [k]} (i - m)^2,$$

where we used $(u - 1/2)^2 \geq u^2/4$ for $u \geq 1$. Now let $\mathsf{U} \sim \mathtt{Unif}([k])$ and observe that for any $m \in [k]$ we have

$$\sum_{i \in [k]} (i - m)^2 \geq \sum_{i \in [k]} (i - \mathbb{E}[\mathsf{U}])^2 = k \mathbb{V}[\mathsf{U}] = \frac{k^3 - k}{12}.$$

$\square$

Now we can combine the two observations about the error of $\mathcal{R}$ under X into a lower bound for its expected square error. Subsequently we will show how the output probabilities occurring in this bound are related under differential privacy.

Lemma 4. *Let $\mathcal{R} : [0, 1] \to [0, 1]$ be a local randomizer and $\mathsf{X} \sim \mathtt{Unif}(I)$ with $I = \{m/k - 1/2k \mid m \in [k]\}$. Then,*

$$\mathbb{E}[(\mathcal{R}(\mathsf{X}) - \mathsf{X})^2] \geq \sum_{b \in I} \min \left\{ \frac{1 - p_{b,b}}{4k^3}, \frac{1}{48} \left(1 - \frac{1}{k^2} \right) \min_{a \in I} p_{a,b} \right\}.$$

Proof. The bound in obtained by formalizing the two observations made above to obtain two different lower bounds for $\mathbb{E}[(\mathcal{R}(\mathsf{X}) - \mathsf{X})^2]$ and then taking their minimum. Our first bound follows directly from the discussion above:

$$\mathbb{E}[(\mathcal{R}(\mathsf{X}) - \mathsf{X})^2] = \sum_{b \in I} \mathbb{E}[(\mathcal{R}(b) - b)^2] \mathbb{P}[\mathsf{X} = b] = \frac{1}{k} \sum_{b \in I} \mathbb{E}[(\mathcal{R}(b) - b)^2]$$

$$\geq \frac{1}{k} \sum_{b \in I} (1 - p_{b,b}) \cdot \frac{1}{(2k)^2} = \sum_{b \in I} \frac{1 - p_{b,b}}{4k^3}.$$

Our second bound follows from the fact that the squared error is at least $(|b - a| - \frac{1}{2k})^2$ if $X = a$ and $\mathcal{R}(a) \in I(b)$, for $a, b \in I$ such that $a \neq b$:

$$\mathbb{E}[(\mathcal{R}(X) - X)^2] = \frac{1}{k} \sum_{b \in I} \mathbb{E}[(\mathcal{R}(b) - b)^2]$$

$$\geq \frac{1}{k} \sum_{b \in I} \sum_{a \in I \setminus \{b\}} p_{a,b} \left(|b - a| - \frac{1}{2k}\right)^2$$

$$\geq \frac{1}{k} \sum_{b \in I} (\min_{a \in I} p_{a,b}) \sum_{a \in I \setminus \{b\}} \left(|b - a| - \frac{1}{2k}\right)^2$$

$$\geq \sum_{b \in I} (\min_{a \in I} p_{a,b}) \frac{1}{48} \left(1 - \frac{1}{k^2}\right),$$

where the last inequality uses Lemma 3. Finally, we get

$$\mathbb{E}[(\mathcal{R}(X) - X)^2] \geq \min \left\{ \sum_{b \in I} \frac{1 - p_{b,b}}{4k^3}, \sum_{b \in I} (\min_{a \in I} p_{a,b}) \frac{1}{48} \left(1 - \frac{1}{k^2}\right) \right\}$$

$$\geq \sum_{b \in I} \min \left\{ \frac{1 - p_{b,b}}{4k^3}, \frac{1}{48} \left(1 - \frac{1}{k^2}\right) \min_{a \in I} p_{a,b} \right\}.$$

$\square$

Lemma 5. *Let $\mathcal{R} : [0,1] \to [0,1]$ be a local randomizer such that the shuffled protocol $\mathcal{M} = \mathcal{S} \circ \mathcal{R}^n$ is (ε, δ)-DP with $\delta < 1/2$. Then, for any $a, b \in I$, $a \neq b$, either $p_{b,b} < 1 - e^{-\varepsilon}/2$ or $p_{a,b} \geq (1/2 - \delta)/n$.*

Proof. If $p_{b,b} < 1 - e^{-\varepsilon}/2$ then the proof is done. Otherwise, consider the neighboring datasets $\vec{x} = (a, \ldots, a)$ and $\vec{x}' = (b, a, \ldots, a)$. Recall that the output of $\mathcal{M}(\vec{x})$ is the multiset obtained from the coordinates of $(\mathcal{R}(x_1), \ldots, \mathcal{R}(x_n))$. By considering the event that this multiset contains no elements from $I(b)$, the definition of differential privacy gives

$$\mathbb{P}[\mathcal{M}(\vec{x}) \cap I(b) = \emptyset] \leq e^\varepsilon \mathbb{P}[\mathcal{M}(\vec{x}') \cap I(b) = \emptyset] + \delta. \tag{1}$$

As $\mathbb{P}[\mathcal{M}(\vec{x}) \cap I(b) = \emptyset] = (1 - p_{a,b})^n$ and $\mathbb{P}[\mathcal{M}(\vec{x}') \cap I(b) = \emptyset] = (1 - p_{b,b})(1 - p_{a,b})^{n-1} \leq (1 - p_{b,b})$, we get from (1) that

$$(1 - p_{a,b})^n \leq (1 - p_{b,b})e^\varepsilon + \delta.$$

As $p_{b,b} \geq 1 - e^{-\varepsilon}/2$ we get that $p_{a,b} \geq 1 - (1/2 + \delta)^{1/n}$ holds. Finally, $p_{a,b} \geq (1/2 - \delta)/n$ follows from the fact that

$$\left(1 - \frac{1}{n}\left(\frac{1}{2} - \delta\right)\right)^n = 1 - \left(\frac{1}{2} - \delta\right) + \frac{n-1}{2n}\left(\frac{1}{2} - \delta\right)^2 - \cdots$$

$$\geq 1 - \left(\frac{1}{2} - \delta\right) = \frac{1}{2} + \delta,$$

which uses that the terms in the binomial expansion are alternating in sign and decreasing in magnitude.   □

We can now choose $k = \lceil n^{1/3} \rceil$ and combine Lemmas 2, 4 and 5 to obtain our lower bound.

Theorem 3. *Let $\mathcal{P}$ be an (ε, δ)-DP n-party protocol for real summation on $[0,1]$ in the one-message shuffle model with $\delta < 1/2$. Then, $\mathrm{MSE}(\mathcal{P}) = \Omega(n^{1/3})$.*

Proof. By the previous lemmas, taking $\vec{X} = (X_1, \ldots, X_n)$ with independent $X_i \sim \mathrm{Unif}(I)$ we have

$$\mathrm{MSE}(\mathcal{P}, \vec{X}) \geq n \sum_{b \in I} \min \left\{ \frac{1 - p_{b,b}}{4k^3}, \frac{1}{48} \left(1 - \frac{1}{k^2}\right) \min_{a \in I} p_{a,b} \right\}$$

$$\geq n \sum_{b \in I} \min \left\{ \frac{e^{-\varepsilon}}{8k^3}, \frac{1}{48n} \left(1 - \frac{1}{k^2}\right) \left(\frac{1}{2} - \delta\right) \right\}$$

$$= nk \min \left\{ \frac{e^{-\varepsilon}}{8k^3}, \frac{1}{48n} \left(1 - \frac{1}{k^2}\right) \left(\frac{1}{2} - \delta\right) \right\}.$$

Therefore, taking $k = \lceil n^{1/3} \rceil$ yields $\mathrm{MSE}(\mathcal{P}, \vec{X}) = \Omega(n^{1/3})$. Finally, the result follows from observing that a lower bound for the expected MSE implies a lower bound for worst-case MSE:

$$\mathrm{MSE}(\mathcal{P}) = \sup_{\vec{x} \in [0,1]^n} \mathrm{MSE}(\mathcal{P}, \vec{x}) \geq \sup_{\vec{x} \in I^n} \mathrm{MSE}(\mathcal{P}, \vec{x}) \geq \mathrm{MSE}(\mathcal{P}, \vec{X}) = \Omega(n^{1/3}).$$

□

5 Privacy Amplification by Shuffling

In this section we prove a new privacy amplification result for shuffled mechanisms. In particular, we will show that shuffling n copies of an ε_0-LDP local randomizer with $\varepsilon_0 = O(\log(n/\log(1/\delta)))$ yields an (ε, δ)-DP mechanism with $\varepsilon = O((\varepsilon_0 \wedge 1)e^{\varepsilon_0}\sqrt{\log(1/\delta)/n})$, where $a \wedge b = \min\{a, b\}$. For this same problem, the following privacy amplification bound was obtained by Erlingsson et al. in [15], which we state here for the randomize-then-shuffle setting (cf. Sect. 1.1).

Theorem 4 ([15]). *If $\mathcal{R}$ is a ε_0-LDP local randomizer with $\varepsilon_0 < 1/2$, then the shuffled protocol $\mathcal{S} \circ \mathcal{R}^n$ is (ε, δ)-DP with*

$$\varepsilon = 12\varepsilon_0 \sqrt{\frac{\log(1/\delta)}{n}}$$

for any $n \geq 1000$ and $\delta < 1/100$.

Note that our result recovers the same dependencies on ε_0, δ and n in the regime $\varepsilon_0 = O(1)$. However, our bound also shows that privacy amplification can be extended to a wider range of parameters. In particular, this allows us to show that in order to design a shuffled (ε, δ)-DP mechanism with $\varepsilon = \Theta(1)$ it suffices to take any ε_0-LDP local randomizer with $\varepsilon_0 = O(\log(\varepsilon^2 n / \log(1/\delta)))$. For shuffled binary randomized response, a dependence of the type $\varepsilon_0 = O(\log(\varepsilon^2 n / \log(1/\delta)))$ between the local and central privacy parameters was obtained in [12] using an ad-hoc privacy analysis. Our results show that this amplification phenomenon is not intrinsic to binary randomized response, and in fact holds for any pure LDP local randomizer. Thus, our bound captures the privacy amplification regimes from both [15] and [12], thus providing a unified analysis of privacy amplification by shuffling.

To prove our bound, we first generalize the key idea behind the analysis of shuffled randomized response given in Sect. 3. This idea was to ignore any users who respond truthfully, and then show that the responses of users who respond randomly provide privacy for the response submitted by a target individual. To generalize this approach beyond randomized response we introduce the notions of *total variation similarity* $\gamma_{\mathcal{R}}$ and *blanket distribution* $\omega_{\mathcal{R}}$ of a local randomizer $\mathcal{R}$. The similarity $\gamma_{\mathcal{R}}$ measures the probability that the local randomizer will produce an output that is independent of the input data. When this happens, the mechanism submits a sample from the blanket probability distribution $\omega_{\mathcal{R}}$. In the case of Algorithm 1 in Sect. 3, the parameter $\gamma_{\mathcal{R}^{PH}}$ is the probability γ of ignoring the input and submitting a sample from $\omega_{\mathcal{R}^{PH}} = \texttt{Unif}([k])$, the uniform distribution on $[k]$. We define these objects formally in Sect. 5.1, then give further examples and also study the relation between $\gamma_{\mathcal{R}}$ and the privacy guarantees of $\mathcal{R}$.

The second step of the proof is to extend the argument that allows us to ignore the users who submit truthful responses in the privacy analysis of randomized response. In the general case, with probability $1 - \gamma_{\mathcal{R}}$ the local randomizer's outcome depends on the data but is not necessarily deterministic. Analyzing this step in full generality – where the randomizer is arbitrary and the domain might be uncountable – is technically challenging. We address this challenge by leveraging a characterization of differential privacy in terms of hockey-stick divergences that originated in the formal methods community to address the verification for differentially private programs [4–6] and has also been used to prove tight results on privacy amplification by subsampling [1]. As a result of this step we obtain a privacy amplification bound in terms of the expectation of a function of a sum of i.i.d. random variables. Our final bound is obtained by using a concentration inequality to bound this expectation.

The bound we obtain with this method provides a relation of the form $F(\varepsilon, \varepsilon_0, \gamma, n) \le \delta$, where F is a complicated non-linear function. By simplifying this function F further we obtain the asymptotic amplification bounds sketched above, where a bound for γ in terms of ε_0 is used. One can also obtain better mechanism-dependent bounds by computing the exact γ for a given mechanism. In addition, fixing all but one of the parameters of the problem we can numerically solve the inequality $F(\varepsilon, \varepsilon_0, \gamma, n) \leq \delta$ to obtain exact relations between the parameters without having to provide appropriate constants for the asymptotic bounds in closed-form. We experimentally showcase the advantages of this approach to privacy calibration in Sect. 6.

Due to space constraints, mathematical proofs from this section are omitted from the present version of the paper. All missing proofs can be found in the extended technical report [2].

5.1 Blanket Decomposition

The goal of this section is to provide a canonical way of decomposing any local randomizer $\mathcal{R} : \mathbb{X} \to \mathbb{Y}$ as a mixture between an input-dependent and an input-independent mechanism. More specifically, let μ_x denote the output distribution of $\mathcal{R}(x)$. Given a collection of distributions $\{\mu_x\}_{x \in \mathbb{X}}$ we will show how to find a probability γ, a distribution ω and a collection of distribution $\{\nu_x\}_{x \in \mathbb{X}}$ such that for every $x \in \mathbb{X}$ we have the mixture decomposition $\mu_x = (1 - \gamma)\nu_x + \gamma\omega$. Since the component ω does not depend on x, this decomposition shows that $\mathcal{R}(x)$ is input oblivious with probability γ. Furthermore, our construction provides the largest possible γ for which this decomposition can be attained.

To motivate the construction sketched above it will be useful to recall a well-known property of the *total variation distance*. Given probability distributions μ, μ' over $\mathbb{Y}$, this distance is defined as

$$\mathfrak{T}(\mu\|\mu') = \sup_{E \subseteq \mathbb{Y}} (\mu(E) - \mu'(E)) = \frac{1}{2} \int |\mu(y) - \mu'(y)| dy.$$

Note how here we use the notation $\mu(y)$ to denote the "probability" of an individual outcome, which formally is only valid when the space $\mathbb{Y}$ is discrete so that every singleton is an atom. Thus, in the case where $\mathbb{Y}$ is a continuous space we take $\mu(y)$ to denote the density of μ at y, where the density is computed with respect to some base measure on $\mathbb{Y}$. We note that this abuse of notation is introduced for convenience and does not restrict the generality of our results.

The total variation distance admits a number of alternative characterizations. The following one is particularly useful:

$$\mathfrak{T}(\mu\|\mu') = 1 - \int \min\{\mu(y), \mu'(y)\} dy. \tag{2}$$

This shows that $\mathfrak{T}(\mu\|\mu')$ can be computed in terms of the total probability mass that is simultaneously under μ and μ'. Equation 2 can be derived from the interpretation of the total variation distance in terms of couplings [24]. Using this characterization it is easy to construct mixture decompositions of the form $\mu = (1 - \gamma)\nu + \gamma\omega$, $\mu' = (1 - \gamma)\nu' + \gamma\omega$, where $\gamma = 1 - \mathfrak{T}(\mu\|\mu')$ and $\omega(y) = \min\{\mu(y), \mu'(y)\}/\gamma$. These decompositions are optimal in the sense that γ is maximal and ν and ν' have disjoint support.

Extending the ideas above to the case with more than two distributions will provide the desired decomposition for any local randomizer. In particular, we

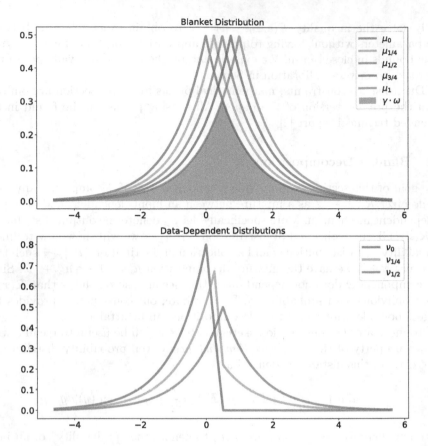

Fig. 2. Illustration of the blanket distribution ω and the data-dependent distributions ν_x corresponding to a 1-LDP Laplace mechanism with inputs on $[0,1]$.

define the *total variation similarity* of a set of distributions $\Lambda = \{\mu_x\}_{x \in \mathbb{X}}$ over $\mathbb{Y}$ as

$$\gamma_\Lambda = \int \inf_x \mu_x(y) dy.$$

We also define the *blanket distribution* of Λ as the distribution given by $\omega_\Lambda(y) = \inf_x \mu_x(y)/\gamma_\Lambda$. In this way, given a set of distributions $\Lambda = \{\mu_x\}_{x \in \mathbb{X}}$ with total variation similarity γ and blanket distribution ω, we obtain a mixture decomposition $\mu_x = (1 - \gamma)\nu_x + \gamma\omega$ for each distribution in Λ, where it is immediate to check that $\nu_x = (\mu_x - \gamma\omega)/(1 - \gamma)$ is indeed a probability distribution. It follows from this construction that γ is maximal since one can show that, by the definition of ω, for each y there exists an x such that $\nu_x(y) = 0$. Thus, it is not possible to increase γ while ensuring that ν_x are probability distributions.

Accordingly, we can identify a local randomizer $\mathcal{R}$ with the set of distributions $\{\mathcal{R}(x)\}_{x \in \mathbb{X}}$ and define the total variation similarity $\gamma_\mathcal{R}$ and the blanket distributions $\omega_\mathcal{R}$ of the mechanism. As usual, we shall just write γ and ω when the randomizer is clear from the context. Figure 2 plots the blanket distribution and the data-dependent distributions corresponding to the local randomizer obtained by the Laplace mechanism with inputs on $[0, 1]$.

The next result provides expressions for the total variation similarity of three important randomizers: k-ary randomized response, the Laplace mechanism on $[0, 1]$ and the Gaussian mechanism on $[0, 1]$. Note that two of these randomizers offer pure LDP while the third one only offers approximate LDP, showing that the notion of total variation similarity and blanket distribution are widely applicable.

Lemma 6. *The following hold:*

1. $\gamma = k/(e^{\varepsilon_0} + k - 1)$ *for ε_0-LDP randomized response on $[k]$,*
2. $\gamma = e^{-\varepsilon_0/2}$ *for ε_0-LDP Laplace on $[0, 1]$,*
3. $\gamma = 2\mathbb{P}[N(0, \sigma^2) \leq -1/2]$ *for a Gaussian mechanism with variance σ^2 on $[0, 1]$.*

This lemma illustrates how the privacy parameters of a local randomizer and its total variation similarity are related in concrete instances. As expected, the probability of sampling from the input-independent blanket grows as the mechanisms become more private. For arbitrary ε_0-LDP local randomizers we are able to show that the probability γ of ignoring the input is at least $e^{-\varepsilon_0}$.

Lemma 7. *The total variation similarity of any ε_0-LDP local randomizer satisfies $\gamma \geq e^{-\varepsilon_0}$.*

5.2   Privacy Amplification Bounds

Now we proceed to prove the amplification bound stated at the beginning of Sect. 5. The key ingredient in this proof is to reduce the analysis of the privacy of a shuffled mechanism to the problem of bounding a function of i.i.d. random variables. This reduction is obtained by leveraging the characterization of differential privacy in terms of hockey-stick divergences.

Let μ, μ' be distributions over $\mathbb{Y}$. The *hockey-stick divergence* of order e^{ε} between μ and μ' is defined as

$$\mathfrak{D}_{e^{\varepsilon}}(\mu \| \mu') = \int [\mu(y) - e^{\varepsilon}\mu'(y)]_+ dy,$$

where $[u]_+ = \max\{0, u\}$. Using these divergences one obtains the following useful characterization of differential privacy.

Theorem 5 ([6]). *A mechanism $\mathcal{M} : \mathbb{X}^n \to \mathbb{Y}$ is (ε, δ)-DP if and only if $\mathfrak{D}_{e^{\varepsilon}}(\mathcal{M}(\vec{x}) \| \mathcal{M}(\vec{x}')) \leq \delta$ for any $\vec{x} \simeq \vec{x}'$.*

This result is straightforward once one observes the identity

$$\int [\mu(y) - e^{\varepsilon}\mu'(y)]_+ dy = \sup_{E \subseteq \mathbb{Y}} (\mu(E) - e^{\varepsilon}\mu'(E)).$$

An important advantage of the integral formulation is that enables one to reason over individual outputs as opposed to sets of outputs for the case of (ε, δ)-DP. This is also the case for the usual sufficient condition for (ε, δ)-DP in terms of a high probability bound for the privacy loss random variable. However, this sufficient condition is not tight for small values of ε [3], so here we prefer to work with the divergence-based characterization.

The first step in our proof of privacy amplification by shuffling is to provide a bound for the divergence $\mathfrak{D}_{e^\varepsilon}(\mathcal{M}(\vec{x}) \| \mathcal{M}(\vec{x}'))$ for a shuffled mechanism $\mathcal{M} = \mathcal{S} \circ \mathcal{R}^n$ in terms of a random variable that depends on the blanket of the local randomizer. Let $\mathcal{R} : \mathbb{X} \to \mathbb{Y}$ be a local randomizer with blanket ω. Suppose $W \sim \omega$ is a $\mathbb{Y}$-valued random variable sampled from the blanket. For any $\varepsilon \geq 0$ and $x, x' \in \mathbb{X}$ we define the *privacy amplification random variable* as

$$L_\varepsilon^{x,x'} = \frac{\mu_x(W) - e^\varepsilon \mu_{x'}(W)}{\omega(W)},$$

where μ_x (resp. $\mu_{x'}$) is the output distribution of $\mathcal{R}(x)$ (resp. $\mathcal{R}(x')$). This definition allows us to obtain the following result.

Lemma 8. *Let $\mathcal{R} : \mathbb{X} \to \mathbb{Y}$ be a local randomizer and let $\mathcal{M} = \mathcal{S} \circ \mathcal{R}^n$ be the shuffling of $\mathcal{R}$. Fix $\varepsilon \geq 0$ and inputs $\vec{x} \simeq \vec{x}'$ with $x_n \neq x_n'$. Suppose $L_1, L_2, \ldots$ are i.i.d. copies of $L_\varepsilon^{x,x'}$ and γ is the total variation similarity of $\mathcal{R}$. Then we have the following:*

$$\mathfrak{D}_{e^\varepsilon}(\mathcal{M}(\vec{x}) \| \mathcal{M}(\vec{x}')) \leq \frac{1}{\gamma n} \sum_{m=1}^{n} \binom{n}{m} \gamma^m (1-\gamma)^{n-m} \mathbb{E}\left[\sum_{i=1}^{m} L_i\right]_+ . \qquad (3)$$

The bound above can also be given a more probabilistic formulation as follows. Let $M \sim \text{Bin}(n, \gamma)$ be the random variable counting the number of users who sample from the blanket of $\mathcal{R}$. Then we can re-write (3) as

$$\mathfrak{D}_{e^\varepsilon}(\mathcal{M}(\vec{x}) \| \mathcal{M}(\vec{x}')) \leq \frac{1}{\gamma n} \mathbb{E}\left[\sum_{i=1}^{M} L_i\right]_+ ,$$

where we use the convention $\sum_{i=1}^{m} L_i = 0$ when $m = 0$.

Leveraging this bound to analyze the privacy of a shuffled mechanism requires some information about the privacy amplification random variables of an arbitrary local randomizer. The main observation here is that $L_\varepsilon^{x,x'}$ has negative expectation. This means we can expect $\mathbb{E}[\sum_{i=1}^{m} L_i]_+$ to decrease with m since adding more variables will shift the expectation of $\sum_{i=1}^{m} L_i$ towards $-\infty$, thus making it less likely to be above 0. Since m represents the number of users who sample from the blanket, this reinforces the intuition that having more users sample from the blanket makes it easier for the data of the nth user to be hidden among these samples. The following lemma will help us make this precise by providing the expectation of $L_\varepsilon^{x,x'}$ as well as its range and second moment.

Lemma 9. *Let* $\mathcal{R} : \mathbb{X} \to \mathbb{Y}$ *be an* ε_0-*LDP local randomizer with total variation similarity* γ. *For any* $\varepsilon \geq 0$ *and* $x, x' \in \mathbb{X}$ *the privacy amplification random variable* $\mathsf{L} = \mathsf{L}_\varepsilon^{x,x'}$ *satisfies:*

1. $\mathbb{E}\mathsf{L} = 1 - e^\varepsilon$,
2. $\gamma e^{-\varepsilon_0}(1 - e^{\varepsilon + 2\varepsilon_0}) \leq \mathsf{L} \leq \gamma e^{\varepsilon_0}(1 - e^{\varepsilon - 2\varepsilon_0})$,
3. $\mathbb{E}\mathsf{L}^2 \leq \gamma e^{\varepsilon_0}(e^{2\varepsilon} + 1) - 2\gamma^2 e^{\varepsilon - 2\varepsilon_0}$.

Now we can use the information about the privacy amplification random variables of an ε_0-LDP local randomizer provided by the previous lemma to give upper bounds for $\mathbb{E}[\sum_{i=1}^m \mathsf{L}_i]_+$. This can be achieved by using concentration inequalities to bound the tails of $\sum_{i=1}^m \mathsf{L}_i$. Based on the information provided by Lemma 9 there are multiple ways to achieve this. In this section we unfold a simple strategy based on Hoeffding's inequality that only uses points (1) and (2) above. In Sect. 5.3 we discuss how to improve these bounds. For now, the following result will suffice to obtain a privacy amplification bound for generic ε_0-LDP local randomizers.

Lemma 10. *Let* $\mathsf{L}_1, \ldots, \mathsf{L}_m$ *be i.i.d. bounded random variables with* $\mathbb{E}\mathsf{L}_i = -a \leq 0$. *Suppose* $b_- \leq \mathsf{L}_i \leq b_+$ *and let* $b = b_+ - b_-$. *Then the following holds:*

$$\mathbb{E}\left[\sum_{i=1}^m \mathsf{L}_i\right]_+ \leq \frac{b^2}{4a}e^{-\frac{2ma^2}{b^2}}.$$

By combining Lemmas 8, 9 and 10 we immediately obtain the main theorem of this section.

Theorem 6. *Let* $\mathcal{R} : \mathbb{X} \to \mathbb{Y}$ *be an* ε_0-*LDP local randomizer and let* $\mathcal{M} = \mathcal{S} \circ \mathcal{R}^n$ *be the corresponding shuffled mechanism. Then* $\mathcal{M}$ *is* (ε, δ)-*DP for any* ε *and* δ *satisfying*

$$\frac{(e^\varepsilon + 1)^2(e^{\varepsilon_0} - e^{-\varepsilon_0})^2}{4n(e^\varepsilon - 1)}e^{-Cn\left(\frac{1}{e^{\varepsilon_0}} \wedge \frac{(e^\varepsilon - 1)^2}{(e^\varepsilon + 1)^2(e^{\varepsilon_0} - e^{-\varepsilon_0})^2}\right)} \leq \delta, \qquad (4)$$

where $C = 1 - e^{-2} \approx 0.86$.

While it is easy to numerically test or solve (4), extracting manageable asymptotics from this bound is less straightforward. The following corollary massages this expression to distill insights about privacy amplification by shuffling for generic ε_0-LDP local randomizers.

Corollary 2. *Let* $\mathcal{R} : \mathbb{X} \to \mathbb{Y}$ *be an* ε_0-*LDP local randomizer and let* $\mathcal{M} = \mathcal{S} \circ \mathcal{R}^n$ *be the corresponding shuffled mechanism. If* $\varepsilon_0 \leq \log(n/\log(1/\delta))/2$, *then* $\mathcal{M}$ *is* (ε, δ)-*DP with* $\varepsilon = O((1 \wedge \varepsilon_0)e^{\varepsilon_0}\sqrt{\log(1/\delta)/n})$.

5.3   Improved Amplification Bounds

There are at least two ways in which we can improve upon the privacy amplification bound in Theorem 6. One is to leverage the moment information about the privacy amplification random variables provided by point (3) in Lemma 9. The other is to compute more precise information about the privacy amplification random variables for specific mechanisms instead of using the generic bounds provided by Lemma 9. In this section we give the necessary tools to obtain these improvements, which we then evaluate numerically in Sect. 6.

Hoeffding's inequality provides concentration for sums of bounded random variables. As such, it is easy to apply because it requires little information on the behavior of the individual random variables. On the other hand, this simplicity can sometimes provide sub-optimal results, especially when the random variables being added have standard deviation which is smaller than their range. In this case one can obtain better results by applying one of the many concentration inequalities that take the variance of the summands into account. The following lemma takes this approach by applying Bennett's inequality to bound the quantity $\mathbb{E}[\sum_{i=1}^{m} L_i]_+$.

Lemma 11. *Let $L_1, \ldots, L_m$ be i.i.d. bounded random variables with $\mathbb{E}L_i = -a \leq 0$. Suppose $L_i \leq b_+$ and $\mathbb{E}L_i^2 \leq c$. Then the following holds:*

$$\mathbb{E}\left[\sum_{i=1}^{m} L_i\right]_+ \leq \frac{b_+}{am \log\left(1 + \frac{ab_+}{c}\right)} e^{-\frac{mc}{b_+^2}\phi\left(\frac{ab_+}{c}\right)},$$

where $\phi(u) = (1 + u)\log(1 + u) - u$.

This results can be combined with Lemmas 7, 8 and 9 to obtain an alternative privacy amplification bound for generic ε_0-LDP local randomizers to the one provided in Theorem 6. However, the resulting bound is cumbersome and does not have a nice closed-form like the one in Theorem 6. Thus, instead of stating the bound explicitly we will evaluate it numerically in the following section.

The other way in which we can provide better privacy bounds is by making them mechanism specific. Lemma 6 already gives exact expression for the total variation similarity γ of three local randomizers. To be able to apply Hoeffding's (Lemma 10) and Bennett's (Lemma 11) inequalities to these local randomizers we need information about the range and the second moment of the corresponding privacy amplification random variables. The following results provide this type of information for randomized response and the Laplace mechanism.

Lemma 12. *Let $\mathcal{R} : [k] \rightarrow [k]$ be the k-ary ε_0-LDP randomized response mechanism. Let $\gamma = k/(e^{\varepsilon_0} + k - 1)$ be the total variation similarity of $\mathcal{R}$ (cf. Lemma 6). For any $\varepsilon \geq 0$ and $x, x' \in \mathbb{X}$, $x \neq x'$, the privacy amplification random variable $L = L_\varepsilon^{x,x'}$ satisfies:*

1. $-(1 - \gamma)ke^\varepsilon \leq L - \gamma(1 - e^\varepsilon) \leq (1 - \gamma)k$,
2. $\mathbb{E}L^2 = \gamma(2 - \gamma)(1 - e^\varepsilon)^2 + (1 - \gamma)^2 k(1 + e^{2\varepsilon})$.

Lemma 13. *Let* $\mathcal{R} : [0,1] \to \mathbb{R}$ *be the* ε_0-*LDP Laplace mechanism* $\mathcal{R}(x) = x + Lap(1/\varepsilon_0)$. *For any* $\varepsilon \geq 0$ *and* $x, x' \in \mathbb{X}$ *the privacy amplification random variable* $\mathsf{L} = \mathsf{L}_\varepsilon^{x,x'}$ *satisfies:*

1. $e^{-\varepsilon_0/2}(1 - e^{\varepsilon + \varepsilon_0}) \leq \mathsf{L} \leq e^{\varepsilon_0/2}(1 - e^{\varepsilon - \varepsilon_0})$,
2. $\mathbb{E}\mathsf{L}^2 \leq \frac{e^{2\varepsilon}+1}{3}(2e^{\varepsilon_0/2} + e^{-\varepsilon_0}) - 2e^\varepsilon(2e^{-\varepsilon_0/2} - e^{-\varepsilon_0})$.

Again, instead of deriving a closed-form expression like (4) specialized to these two mechanisms, we will numerically evaluate the advantage of using mechanism-specific information in the bounds in the next section. Note that we did not provide a version of these results for the Gaussian mechanism for which we showed how to compute γ in Sect. 5.1. The reason for this is that in this case the resulting privacy amplification random variables are not bounded. This precludes us from using the Hoeffding and Bennett bounds to analyze the privacy amplification in this case. Approaches using concentration bounds that do not rely on boundedness will be explored in future work.

6   Experimental Evaluation

In this section we provide a numerical evaluation of the privacy amplification bounds derived in Sect. 5. We also compare the results obtained with our techniques to the privacy amplification bound of Erlingsson et al. [15].

To obtain values of ε and ε_0 from bounds on δ of the form given in Theorem 6 we use a numeric procedure. In particular, we implemented the bounds for δ in Python and then used SciPy's numeric root finding routines to solve for the desired parameter up to a precision of 10^{-12}. This leads to a simple and efficient implementation which can be employed in practical applications for the calibration of privacy parameters of local randomizers in shuffled protocols. The resulting code is available at https://github.com/BorjaBalle/amplification-by-shuffling.

The results of our evaluation are given in Fig. 3. The bounds plotted in this figure are obtained as follows:

1. (EFMRTT'19) is the bound in [15] (see Theorem 4).
2. (Hoeffding, Generic) is the bound from Theorem 6.
3. (Bennett, Generic) is obtained by combining Lemmas 7, 8, 9 and 11.
4. (Hoeffding, RR) is obtained by combining Lemmas 6, 8, 12 and 10.
5. (Bennett, RR) is obtained by combining Lemmas 6, 8, 12 and 11.
6. (Hoeffding, Laplace) is obtained by combining Lemmas 6, 8, 13 and 10.
7. (Bennett, Laplace) is obtained by combining Lemmas 6, 8, 13 and 11.

In panel (i) we observe that our two bounds for generic randomizers give significantly smaller values of ε than the bound from [15] where the constants where not optimized. Additionally, we see that for generic local randomizers, Hoeffding is better for small values of n, while Bennet is better for large values of n. In panel (ii) we observe the advantage of incorporating information in

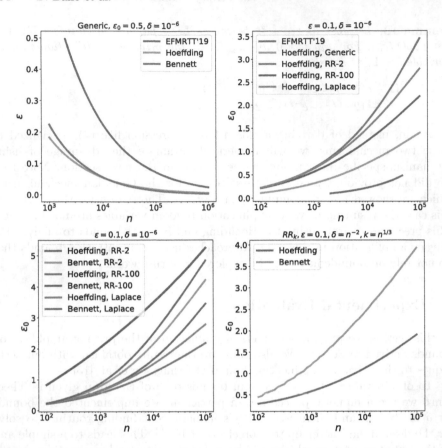

Fig. 3. (i) Comparison of $\varepsilon(n)$ for fixed ε_0 and δ of the bounds obtained for generic ε_0-DP local randomizers using the bound in [15] and our Hoeffding and Bennett bounds. (ii) Comparison of $\varepsilon_0(n)$ for fixed ε and δ for generic and specific local randomizers using the Hoeffding bounds. (iii) Comparison of $\varepsilon_0(n)$ for fixed ε and δ for specific local randomizers using the Hoeffding and Bennett bound. (iv) Comparison of $\varepsilon_0(n)$ for fixed ε and $\delta = n^{-2}$ for a randomized response mechanism with domain size $k = n^{1/3}$ using the Hoeffding and Bennett bounds.

the Hoeffding bound about the specific local randomizer. Additionally, this plot allows us to see that for the same level of local DP, binary randomized response has better amplification properties than Laplace, which in turn is better the randomizer response over a domain of size $k = 100$. In panel (iii) we compare the amplification bounds obtained for specific randomizers with the Hoeffding and Bennett bounds. We observe that for every mechanism the Bennett bound is better than the Hoeffding bound, especially for large values of n. Additionally, the gain of using Bennett instead of Hoeffding is greater for randomized response with $k = 100$ than for other mechanisms. The reason for this is that for fixed ε_0 and large k, the total variation similarity of randomized response is close to

1 (cf. Lemma 6). Finally, in panel (iv) we compare the values of ε_0 obtained for a randomized response with domain size growing with the number of users as $k = n^{1/3}$. This is in line with our optimal protocol for real summation in the single-message shuffle model presented in Sect. 4. We observe that also in this case the Bennett bounds provides a significant advantage over Hoeffding.

To summarize, we showed that our generic bounds outperform the previous amplification bounds developed in [15]. Additionally, we showed that incorporating both information about the variance of the privacy amplification random variable via the use of Bennett's bound, as well as information about the behavior of this random variable for specific mechanisms, leads to significant improvements in the privacy parameters obtained for shuffled protocols. This is important in practice because being able to maximize the ε_0 parameter for the local randomizer – while satisfying a prescribed level of differential privacy in the shuffled protocol – leads to more accurate protocols.

7 Conclusion

We have shown a separation result for the single-message shuffle model, showing that it can not achieve the level of accuracy of the curator model of differential privacy, but that it can yield protocols that are significantly more accurate than the ones from the local model. More specifically, we provided a single message protocol for private n-party summation of real values in $[0, 1]$ with $O(\log n)$-bit communication and $O(n^{1/6})$ standard deviation. We also showed that our protocol is optimal in terms of accuracy by providing a lower bound for this problem. In previous work, Cheu et al. [12] had shown that the selection problem can be solved more accurately in the central model than in the shuffle model, and that the real summation problem can be solved more accurately in the shuffle model than in the local model. For the former, they rely on lower bounds for selection in the local model by means of a generic reduction from the shuffle to the local model, while our lower bound is directly in the shuffle model, offering additional insight. On the other hand, our single-message protocol for summation is more accurate than theirs.

Moreover, we introduced the notion of the privacy blanket of a local randomizer, and show how it allows us to give a generic treatment to the problem of obtaining privacy amplification bounds in the shuffle model that improves on recent work by Erlingsson et al. [15] and Cheu et al. [12]. Crucially, unlike the proofs in [12,15], our proof does not rely on privacy amplification by subsampling. We believe that the notion of the privacy blanket is of interest beyond the shuffle model, as it leads to a canonical decomposition of local randomizers that might be useful also in the study of the local model of differential privacy. For example, Joseph et al. [20] already used a generalization of our blanket decomposition in their study of the role of interactivity in local DP protocols.

References

1. Balle, B., Barthe, G., Gaboardi, M.: Privacy amplification by subsampling: tight analyses via couplings and divergences. In: Advances in Neural Information Processing Systems 31: Annual Conference on Neural Information Processing Systems 2018, NeurIPS 2018, Montréal, Canada, 3–8 December 2018, pp. 6280–6290 (2018)
2. Balle, B., Bell, J., Gascón, A., Nissim, K.: The privacy blanket of the shuffle model. CoRR abs/1903.02837 (2019). http://arxiv.org/abs/1903.02837
3. Balle, B., Wang, Y.X.: Improving the Gaussian mechanism for differential privacy: analytical calibration and optimal denoising. In: Proceedings of the 35th International Conference on Machine Learning, ICML (2018)
4. Barthe, G., Gaboardi, M., Grégoire, B., Hsu, J., Strub, P.: Proving differential privacy via probabilistic couplings. In: Symposium on Logic in Computer Science (LICS), pp. 749–758 (2016)
5. Barthe, G., Köpf, B., Olmedo, F., Béguelin, S.Z.: Probabilistic relational reasoning for differential privacy. In: Symposium on Principles of Programming Languages (POPL), pp. 97–110 (2012)
6. Barthe, G., Olmedo, F.: Beyond differential privacy: composition theorems and relational logic for f-divergences between probabilistic programs. In: Fomin, F.V., Freivalds, R., Kwiatkowska, M., Peleg, D. (eds.) ICALP 2013. LNCS, vol. 7966, pp. 49–60. Springer, Heidelberg (2013). https://doi.org/10.1007/978-3-642-39212-2_8
7. Beimel, A., Nissim, K., Omri, E.: Distributed private data analysis: simultaneously solving how and what. In: Wagner, D.A. (ed.) CRYPTO 2008. LNCS, vol. 5157, pp. 451–468. Springer, Heidelberg (2008). https://doi.org/10.1007/978-3-540-85174-5_25
8. Bhowmick, A., Duchi, J., Freudiger, J., Kapoor, G., Rogers, R.: Protection against reconstruction and its applications in private federated learning. arXiv e-prints arXiv:1812.00984, December 2018
9. Bittau, A., et al.: PROCHLO: strong privacy for analytics in the crowd. In: Proceedings of the 26th Symposium on Operating Systems Principles, Shanghai, China, 28–31 October 2017, pp. 441–459. ACM (2017). https://doi.org/10.1145/3132747.3132769
10. Boucheron, S., Lugosi, G., Massart, P.: Concentration Inequalities: A Nonasymptotic Theory of Independence. Oxford University Press, Oxford (2013)
11. Chan, T.-H.H., Shi, E., Song, D.: Optimal lower bound for differentially private multi-party aggregation. In: Epstein, L., Ferragina, P. (eds.) ESA 2012. LNCS, vol. 7501, pp. 277–288. Springer, Heidelberg (2012). https://doi.org/10.1007/978-3-642-33090-2_25
12. Cheu, A., Smith, A.D., Ullman, J., Zeber, D., Zhilyaev, M.: Distributed differential privacy via shuffling. In: Ishai, Y., Rijmen, V. (eds.) EUROCRYPT 2019. LNCS, vol. 11476, pp. 375–403. Springer, Cham (2019). https://doi.org/10.1007/978-3-030-17653-2_13
13. Ding, B., Kulkarni, J., Yekhanin, S.: Collecting telemetry data privately. In: Guyon, I., et al. (eds.) Advances in Neural Information Processing Systems 30: Annual Conference on Neural Information Processing Systems 2017, Long Beach, CA, USA, 4–9 December 2017, pp. 3574–3583 (2017). http://papers.nips.cc/paper/6948-collecting-telemetry-data-privately
14. Dwork, C., McSherry, F., Nissim, K., Smith, A.D.: Calibrating noise to sensitivity in private data analysis. In: Halevi, S., Rabin, T. (eds.) TCC 2006. LNCS, vol. 3876, pp. 265–284. Springer, Heidelberg (2006). https://doi.org/10.1007/11681878_14

15. Erlingsson, Ú., Feldman, V., Mironov, I., Raghunathan, A., Talwar, K., Thakurta, A.: Amplification by shuffling: from local to central differential privacy via anonymity. In: Proceedings of the Thirtieth Annual ACM-SIAM Symposium on Discrete Algorithms, pp. 2468–2479. SIAM (2019)

16. Erlingsson, Ú., Pihur, V., Korolova, A.: RAPPOR: randomized aggregatable privacy-preserving ordinal response. In: Proceedings of the 2014 ACM SIGSAC Conference on Computer and Communications Security, Scottsdale, AZ, USA, 3–7 November 2014, pp. 1054–1067 (2014)

17. Feldman, V., Mironov, I., Talwar, K., Thakurta, A.: Privacy amplification by iteration. In: 59th IEEE Annual Symposium on Foundations of Computer Science, FOCS 2018, Paris, France, 7–9 October 2018, pp. 521–532 (2018)

18. Ishai, Y., Kushilevitz, E., Ostrovsky, R., Sahai, A.: Cryptography from anonymity. In: FOCS, pp. 239–248. IEEE Computer Society (2006)

19. Jaynes, E.T.: Probability Theory: The Logic of Science. Cambridge University Press, Cambridge (2003)

20. Joseph, M., Mao, J., Neel, S., Roth, A.: The role of interactivity in local differential privacy. CoRR abs/1904.03564 (2019), http://arxiv.org/abs/1904.03564

21. Kairouz, P., Bonawitz, K., Ramage, D.: Discrete distribution estimation under local privacy. In: ICML, JMLR Workshop and Conference Proceedings, vol. 48, pp. 2436–2444 (2016). JMLR.org

22. Kairouz, P., Oh, S., Viswanath, P.: Extremal mechanisms for local differential privacy. J. Mach. Learn. Res. **17**, 17:1–17:51 (2016)

23. Kasiviswanathan, S.P., Lee, H.K., Nissim, K., Raskhodnikova, S., Smith, A.D.: What can we learn privately? In: 49th Annual IEEE Symposium on Foundations of Computer Science, FOCS 2008, Philadelphia, PA, USA, 25–28 October 2008, pp. 531–540. IEEE Computer Society (2008). https://doi.org/10.1109/FOCS.2008.27

24. Lindvall, T.: Lectures on the Coupling Method. Courier Corporation, Chelmsford (2002)

25. Team, A.D.P.: Learning with privacy at scale. Apple Mach. Learn. J. **1**(9) (2017)

Attribute Based Encryption

Realizing Chosen Ciphertext Security Generically in Attribute-Based Encryption and Predicate Encryption

Venkata Koppula[1]($\boxtimes$) and Brent Waters[2]

[1] Weizmann Institute of Science, Rehovot, Israel
venkata.koppula@weizmann.ac.il
[2] University of Texas at Austin and NTT Research, Austin, USA
bwaters@cs.utexas.edu

Abstract. We provide generic and black box transformations from any chosen plaintext secure Attribute-Based Encryption (ABE) or One-sided Predicate Encryption system into a chosen ciphertext secure system. Our transformation requires only the IND-CPA security of the original ABE scheme coupled with a pseudorandom generator (PRG) with a special security property.

In particular, we consider a PRG with an n bit input $s \in \{0,1\}^n$ and $n \cdot \ell$ bit output $y_1, \ldots, y_n$ where each y_i is an ℓ bit string. Then for a randomly chosen s the following two distributions should be computationally indistinguishable. In the first distribution $r_{s_i,i} = y_i$ and $r_{\bar{s}_i,i}$ is chosen randomly for $i \in [n]$. In the second distribution all $r_{b,i}$ are chosen randomly for $i \in [n], b \in \{0,1\}$.

We show that such PRGs can be built from either the computational Diffie-Hellman assumption (in non-bilinear groups) or the Learning with Errors (LWE) assumption (and potentially other assumptions). Thus, one can transform any IND-CPA secure system into a chosen ciphertext secure one by adding either assumption. (Or by simply assuming an existing PRG is hinting secure.) In addition, our work provides a new approach and perspective for obtaining chosen ciphertext security in the basic case of public key encryption.

1 Introduction

In Attribute-Based Encryption [42] (ABE) every ciphertext CT that encrypts a message m is associated with an attribute string x, while each secret, as issued by an authority, will be associated with a predicate function C. A user with a secret key sk that is associated with function C will be able to decrypt a ciphertext associated with x and recover the message if and only if $C(x) = 1$. Additionally, security of ABE systems guarantees that an attacker with access to several keys

B. Waters—Supported by NSF CNS-1908611, CNS-1414082, DARPA SafeWare and Packard Foundation Fellowship.

A. Boldyreva and D. Micciancio (Eds.): CRYPTO 2019, LNCS 11693, pp. 671–700, 2019.
https://doi.org/10.1007/978-3-030-26951-7_23

cannot learn the contents of an encrypted message so long as none of them are so authorized.

Since the introduction of Attribute-Based Encryption and early constructions [26] over a decade ago, there have been many advances in the field ranging from supporting expressive functionality [6,23], to techniques for adaptive security [1,12,30,32,37,44,45], short sized ciphertexts [2], multi-authority [10,11,31] and partially hiding attributes [24,25,46] to name just a few. In almost all of these cases and in most other papers, the treatment of ABE focused on the chosen plaintext (IND-CPA) definition of ABE. This is despite the fact that chosen ciphertext security [13,36,40]—where the attacker can make oracle decryption queries to keys it does not have—is arguably the right definition of security for the same reasons it is the right definition for standard public key cryptography [43]. Likely, most of these works target IND-CPA security since the authors already have their hands full with putting forth new concepts and techniques in manuscripts that often run for many pages. In these circumstances it seems reasonable for such works to initially target chosen plaintext definitions and then for later works to circle back and build toward chosen ciphertext security.

Unfortunately, closing the loop to chosen ciphertext security can be tricky in practice. First, there are a rather large and growing number of ABE constructions. Writing papers to address moving each of these to chosen ciphertext security seems burdensome to authors and program committees alike. One line of work [4,26,34,47] to mediate this problem is to identify features in ABE constructions, which if present mean that CPA security implies chosen ciphertext security. Yamada et al. [47] showed that certain delegability or verifiability properties in ABE systems imply chosen ciphertext security by the Canetti-Halevi-Katz [9] transformation.

Their generality, however, is limited by the need to manually inspect and prove that each construction has such a property. In fact, many schemes might not have these properties. Recent trends for both functionality and proofs techniques might actually work against these properties. For example, an ABE scheme has the verification property roughly if it is possible to inspect a ciphertext and determine if it is well formed and what keys can decrypt it. This property emerged naturally in many of the pairing-based schemes prominent at the time, but is less obvious to prove in LWE-based constructions and actually can run contrary to the predicate encryption goal of hiding an attribute string x from users that cannot decrypt. See for example the one-sided predicate encryption constructions of [24,25,46].

If we desire a truly generic transformation to chosen ciphertext security, then there are essentially two pathways available. The first option is to apply some variant of the Fujisaki-Okamoto [20] transformation (first given for transforming from IND-CPA to IND-CCA security in public key encryption). Roughly, the encryption algorithm will encrypt as its message the true message m appended with a random bitstring r using the random coins $H(r)$ where H is a hash function modeled as a random oracle. The CCA-secure decryption algorithm will apply the original decryption algorithm to a ciphertext CT and recover $m'|r'$.

Next, it re-encrypts the ciphertext under $H(r')$ to get a ciphertext CT' and outputs the message if $CT = CT'$; otherwise it rejects. The upside of this approach is that the added overhead is fairly low as it just adds one additional call to encryption as part of the decryption routine. On the downside the security analysis of this technique appears intrinsically tied to the random oracle model [3].

The second option is to augment encryption by appending a non-interactive zero knowledge proof [5] that a ciphertext was well formed. This approach has been well studied and explored in the context of standard public key encryption [36] and should translate to the ABE context. Additionally, there are standard model NIZK proof assumptions under factoring and pairing-based and lattice based [38] assumptions.[1] A drawback of this approach is that applying any generic gate by gate NIZK to an encryption system will be quite expensive in terms of computational overhead—this will be needed for any generic conversion.

1.1 Our Contribution

In this work we provide a black box transformation for chosen ciphertext security of any ABE or one-sided predicate encryption system.[2]

Our transformation requires only the existence of a IND-CPA secure ABE system as well as a pseudorandom generator (PRG) with a special security property which we call the *hinting property*. This special security property can either be assumed for an "ordinary" (e.g., AES-based) PRG or provably obtained from either the Computational Diffie-Hellman assumption or the Learning with Errors assumption. Our transformation increases ciphertext size by roughly a factor of the security parameter—it requires $2 \cdot n$ sub-ciphertexts for a parameter n. Additionally, it requires about $2n$ additional encryptions of the original system for both the new encryption and decryption routines. While this overhead is an increase over the original CPA system and will likely incur more overhead than hand-tailored CCA systems, it is a significant performance improvement over NIZKs that operate gate by gate over the original encryption circuit.

We also wish to emphasize that our transformation applies to ordinary public key encryption as well as ABE. While chosen ciphertext security for PKE has been known for sometime from the CDH and LWE assumptions, we believe that our work provides new insights into the problem and might lead to furthering the understanding of whether IND-CPA security ultimately implies chosen ciphertext security.

---

[1] The realization of NIZKs from the Learning with Errors assumption is a very recent and exciting development [38] and occured after the initial posting of this work.

[2] The original definition of predicate encryption [7,27] required hiding whether an attribute string of a challenge ciphertext was x_0 or x_1 from an attacker that had a key C where $C(x_0) = C(x_1)$. A weaker form of predicate encryption is where this guarantee is given only if $C(x_0) = C(x_1) = 0$, but not when $C(x_0) = C(x_1) = 1$. This weaker form has been called predicate encryption with one-sided security and anonymous Attribute-Based Encryption. For this paper we will use the term one-sided predicate encryption.

Hinting Property for PRGs: Let PRG be a function that maps n bits to $(n + 1) \cdot n$ bits (output to be parsed as $n + 1$ strings, each of length n). Consider the following experiment between a challenger and an adversary. The challenger chooses an n bit string s, computes $\text{PRG}(s) = z_0 z_1 z_2 \ldots z_n$ (each $z_i \in \{0, 1\}^n$). Next, it chooses n uniformly random strings $v_1, v_2, \ldots, v_n$ each from $\{0, 1\}^n$. It then constructs a $2 \times n$ matrix M as follows: if the ith bit of s is 0, then $M_{0,i} = z_i, M_{1,i} = v_i$, else $M_{0,i} = v_i, M_{1,i} = z_i$.[3] Finally, the challenger either outputs z_0 together with M, or it outputs $2n + 1$ uniformly random strings. A pseudorandom generator is said to satisfy the hinting property if any polynomial time adversary has negligible advantage in this experiment. Note that the seed s is used at two places: first to compute the strings $z_0, z_1, z_2, \ldots, z_n$, and then to decide where to place each z_i in the matrix M. Hence, the second piece of information (i.e. the position of z_i strings serves as an extra *hint* on the PRG). One could simply assume this property of a particular pseudo random generator. Indeed, this seems rather plausible that ordinary types of PRGs would have it. Alternately, we show how to construct PRGs that provably have this property under either the Computational Diffie-Hellman assumption or the LWE assumption. Our constructions of these PRGs use techniques that closely follow previous works [8, 14–16, 22] for a related group of primitives going under a variety of names: Chameleon Encryption, One-Time Signature with Encryption, Batch Encryption, One Way Function with Encryption. We note that while the technical innards for the CDH and LWE realizations of our PRG are similar to the above works, (unlike the above examples) our definition itself does not attach any new functionality requirements to PRG; it simply demands a stronger security property.

Next, we present an overview of our CCA construction. As a warm-up, we will first show how to use any CPA-secure public key encryption (PKE) scheme, together with hinting PRGs to construct a CCA-1 secure PKE scheme. Recall, CCA-1 security is a weaker variant of the CCA security game where the adversary is allowed decryption queries only before sending the challenge messages. After sending the challenge messages, the adversary receives the challenge ciphertext, and must send its guess.

CCA-1 secure PKE from CPA-secure PKE and hinting PRGs. The construction also uses a (standard) pseudorandom generator G with sufficiently long stretch. Let (Setup, Enc, Dec) be any CPA secure scheme, and $H : \{0, 1\}^n \to \{0, 1\}^{(n+1) \cdot n}$ a hinting PRG. We require the CPA scheme to have two properties which can be obtained 'for free'. First, we require that the scheme should have perfect decryption correctness for most public/secret keys. This can be obtained via the transformation of [17]. Next, we require that any ciphertext can be decrypted given the encryption randomness. This is also easily obtained by choosing a random string r during encryption, and appending a one-time pad of the message using r.

---

[3] More compactly, $M_{s_i,i} = z_i$ and $M_{\overline{s_i},i} = v_i$.

The setup of our CCA-1 scheme runs the PKE setup $2n$ times, obtaining $2n$ public key/secret key pairs $\{pk_{b,i}, sk_{b,i}\}_{i \in [n], b \in \{0,1\}}$. It also chooses a uniformly random tag $t = t_1 t_2 \ldots t_n$, where each t_i is a sufficiently long string. The new public key consists of the $2n$ public keys $\{pk_{b,i}\}_{i \in [n], b \in \{0,1\}}$ and tag t, while the new secret key includes only of n out of the $2n$ secret keys, namely $\{sk_{0,i}\}_{i \in [n]}$ (this *secret hiding principle* [18] has been used in many CCA constructions, including the initial CCA systems [13, 36]). To encrypt a message m, the encryption algorithm first chooses a seed $s \leftarrow \{0,1\}^n$ and computes $H(s) = z_0 z_1 \ldots z_n$. It uses z_0 to mask the message m; that is, it computes $c = m \oplus z_0$. The remaining ciphertext will contain n 'signals' that help the decryption algorithm to recover s bit by bit, which in turn will allow it to compute z_0 and hence unmask c.

The ith signal (for each $i \in [n]$) has three components $c_{0,i}, c_{1,i}, c_{2,i}$. If the ith bit of s is 0, then $c_{0,i}$ is an encryption of a random string x_i using the public key $pk_{0,i}$ and randomness z_i, $c_{1,i}$ is an encryption of 0^n using $pk_{1,i}$ (encrypted using true randomness), and $c_{2,i} = G(x_i)$. If the ith bit of s is 1, then $c_{0,i}$ is an encryption of 0^n using public key $pk_{0,i}$ (encrypted using true randomness), $c_{1,i}$ is an encryption of a random string x_i using public key $pk_{1,i}$ and randomness z_i, and $c_{2,i} = G(x_i) + t_i$ (recall t_i is the ith component in the tag). So half the ciphertexts are encryptions of zero, while the remaining are encryptions of random strings (with blocks of the hinting PRG output being used as randomness), and the positioning of the zero/random encryptions reveals the seed s.

The final ciphertext includes the 'main' component c, and n signals $(c_{0,i}, c_{1,i}, c_{2,i})$. A noteworthy point about the ciphertext: first, the components $\{c_{2,i}\}_i$ serve as a perfectly-binding commitment to the seed s.

To decrypt, the decryption algorithm first decrypts each $c_{0,i}$ (recall the secret key is $\{sk_{0,i}\}_{i \in [n]}$) to obtain $y_1 y_2 \ldots y_n$. It then checks if $G(y_i) = c_{2,i}$. If so, it guesses that $s_i = 0$, else it guesses that $s_i = 1$. With this estimate for s, the decryption algorithm can compute $H(s) = z_0 z_1 \ldots z_n$ and then compute $c \oplus z_0$ to learn the message m. While this decryption procedure works correctly, we would like to prevent malicious decryption queries (made during the CCA/CCA-1 experiment), and hence the decryption algorithm needs to enforce additional checks. In particular, the decryption algorithm therefore needs to check that the guess for s is indeed correct. If the ith bit of s is guessed to be 0, then the decryption algorithm checks that $c_{0,i}$ is a valid ciphertext - it simply re-encrypts y_i and checks if this equals $c_{0,i}$. If the ith bit of s is guessed to be 1, then the decryption algorithm first recovers the message underlying ciphertext $c_{1,i}$. Note that $c_{1,i}$ should be encrypted using randomness z_i, hence using z_i, one can recover message $\tilde{y}_i$ from $c_{1,i}$ (using the randomness recovery property of the PKE scheme). It then re-encrypts $\tilde{y}_i$ and checks if it is equal to $c_{1,i}$, and also checks that $c_{2,i} = G(\tilde{y}_i) + t_i$. Finally, if all these checks pass, the decryption algorithm outputs $z_0 \oplus c$.

To summarize, at a very high level, we build a partial trapdoor where the decryption algorithm will recover some of the coins used for encryption. These are then used to partially re-encrypt the ciphertext and test for validity. Influenced by Garg and Hajiabadi [22], we will prove security not by removing the signals for each bit position, but by adding misinformation that drowns out the original signal. Note that to prove security, we need to remove the information of z_0 (and hence information of s) from two places - first, from the commitment $\{c_{2,i}\}_i$; second, from the positions where the z_i values are used for encrypting. For the first one, in the proof, we set the challenge tag t^* such that the signal is ambiguous at each index. More formally, in the challenge ciphertext $c_{0,i}^*$ is an encryption of y_i, $c_{1,i}^*$ is encryption of $\tilde{y}_i$, and $G(y_i) = G(\tilde{y}_i) + t_i^*$. Replacing the encryptions of zeroes with encryptions of these carefully chosen strings involves a delicate argument, which crucially relies on the perfect correctness of our scheme (see discussion in Sect. 4 for more details).

When this is done for all indices, all information about s will be lost from the message space and we are almost done; however, one loose end remains. Each ciphertext at position (s_i, i) will be encrypted under randomness r_i which came from running the pseudorandom generator on s; whereas each ciphertext at position $(\bar{s}_i, i)$ will be encrypted under fresh random coins. To complete the proof we need a computational assumption that will allow us to change all the encryption coins to being chosen freshly at random. Here, we use the security of hinting PRGs, and that completes our proof.

CCA Security. To achieve CCA security, we need to make a few tweaks to the above scheme. The setup algorithm also chooses n pairwise independent hash functions $h_1, h_2, \ldots, h_n$. The encryption algorithm chooses a signing/verification key for a (one-time) signature scheme. Next, instead of using the tag t from the public key, it sets $t_i = h_i(\mathsf{vk})$ (where vk is the verification key). Finally, the encryption algorithm computes a signature on all the ciphertext components, and the final ciphertext consists of all these components together with the signature and the verification key. This idea of using signatures to go from 'tag-based' security to CCA security has been used in several previous CCA constructions, starting with the work of [28]. To prove security, we first ensure that none of the decryption queries correspond to the challenge ciphertext's verification key (this follows from the security of the signature scheme). After this point, the proof follows along the lines of the CCA-1 scheme.

Moving to Attribute Based Encryption/Predicate Encryption - For ABE/PE, the scheme is altered as follows. First, the public key consists of n ABE/PE public keys and n PKE public keys. Let $\mathsf{pk}_{0,i}$ denote the ith ABE/PE public key, and $\mathsf{pk}_{1,i}$ the ith PKE public key. The master secret key only consists of the n ABE/PE master secret keys. The main difference in the encryption algorithm is that the ciphertexts $c_{0,i}$ are now ABE/PE ciphertexts. Suppose we want to encrypt message m for attribute x. Then m is masked using z_0 as before, and the $c_{0,i}$ component is an encryption of zero/random message for attribute x using public key $\mathsf{pk}_{0,i}$ and randomness being truly random/z_i, depending on the ith bit of seed s.

We conclude by remarking that while this work focuses on Attribute-Based Encryption and One-sided Predicate Encryption, we believe our transformation could apply to other specialized forms of encryption. For example, we believe it should immediately translate to any secure broadcast encryption [19] system. As another example, we believe our technique should also apply to ABE systems that are IND-CPA secure under a bounded number of key generation queries. Our technique, however, does not appear to apply to standard predicate encryption as defined in [7, 27] (notions very similar to full blown functional encryption). The core issue is that to test the validity of a ciphertext our decryption algorithm needs to obtain the attribute string x to perform re-encryption. In one-sided predicate encryption, if a user has a secret key for C and $C(x) = 1$ we essentially give up on hiding x and allow this to be recovered; whereas for full hiding we might want to still hide information about x even if $C(x) = 1$.

Finally, we note that even if we cast the notions of ABE aside our work might provide another path to exploring the longstanding open problem of achieving chosen ciphertext security from chosen plaintext security. The primary barrier is in how to achieve a PRG with this hinting security.

1.2   Constructions of Hinting PRGs

Our realizations of hinting PRG largely follow in line with recent works [8, 14–16, 22]. In particular, our CDH realization follows closely to [15] and our LWE realization to [8, 16]. It may have been possible to build our hinting PRG from one of the previous abstractions, but we chose to provide direct number theoretic realizations. We believe that one important distinction is that our hinting PRG is simply a PRG with stronger security properties; unlike the above abstractions our definition in of itself does not ask for expanded functionality. An intriguing open question is if this can be leveraged to obtain further instances with provable security. Below, we provide a high level description of our hinting PRG construction based on the DDH assumption.

In this work, we construct hinting PRG with setup. The setup algorithm outputs public parameters, which are then used for evaluating the PRG. For simplicity, here we assume the PRG maps n bits to n^2 bits. Let p be an n bit prime, and $\mathcal{G}$ a group of order p. The setup algorithm first chooses $2n$ random group elements $\{g_{i,b}\}$ and $2n$ random integers $\{\rho_{i,b}\}$ from $\mathbb{Z}_p$. Next, it uses these group elements and integers to publish $2n$ tables, and each table has $2n$ entries. Let us consider the $(i, b) - th$ table. In this table, the $(i, \bar{b}) - th$ entry is $\perp$; and for all $(k, \beta) \neq (i, \bar{b})$, the $(k, b)th$ entry is $g_{k,\beta}^{\rho_{i,b}}$.

Let us now consider the evaluation procedure. The PRG evaluation on input $x = x_1 x_2 \ldots x_n$ wil output n group elements, where the ith one is derived from the $(i, x_i)th$ table as follows - compute product of elements (in table (i, x_i)) at position (k, x_k). More formally, the ith group element in the output is $(\prod g_{k,x_k})^{\rho_{i,b}}$.

To prove security, we use the DDH assumption to argue that given all the $2n$ tables in the public parameters, it will still be hard to learn $g_{i,b}^{\rho_{i,\bar{b}}}$, for all (i, b). There are a few subtleties though; in particular, we also need a 'lossiness' argument for the proof to work. We refer the reader to the full version of our paper.

1.3 Additional Comparisons

It is instructive to take a closer look at how our work relates to and builds upon the trapdoor function construction of Garg and Hajiabadi [22]. Briefly and in our terminology, Garg and Hajiabadi gave a framework where the evaluation algorithm chooses an input $s \in \{0,1\}^n$ and use this to first produces a value y that produces part of the output. Next, for each position (s_i, i) the evaluation algorithm produces a signal using s and the public parameters of the TDF using a primitive called "one way function with encryption". At the opposite position $(\bar{s}_i, i)$ the evaluation algorithm outputs a random string r_i of sufficient length. With very high probability the random string z_i will not correspond to the valid signal for y at position $(\bar{s}_i, i)$. The inversion algorithm will use knowledge of the TDF secret key plus y to go recover the input s bit by bit. At each position i if a signal is present at $(0, i)$ it records $s_i = 0$ and sets $s_i = 1$ if the signal is at $(1, i)$. If the signal is at both 0 and 1, then recovery fails. One can observe that for almost all choices of public parameters there exist some valid inputs that will cause failure on inversion. To prove security the reduction algorithm at each position change the string z_i from random to a signal under y. The security properties of the one way function with encryption make this undetectable. Once, this is done the only information about s will be contained in y. Since many choices of s will map to y, inverting to the chosen s at this point will be statistically infeasible.

Our work as described above follows a similar approach in that a seed s is signaled bit by bit. And that a step of proving security is to add misinformation in by adding a counter signal in at positions $(\bar{s}_i, i)$. An important distinction is that in the work of Garg and Hajiabadi the signaling and inversion process is very tightly coupled in the one way function with encryption primitive. One could imagine trying to build an Attribute-Based version of one way function with encryption and then try to yield a CCA encryption from the resulting trapdoor. This runs into two problems. First, it would require a tailored construction for each type of ABE scheme that we want and then we are back to hacking CCA into each type of ABE variant. Second, since the GH scheme allows for ambiguous inputs, it can be difficult for mapping into chosen ciphertext secure schemes. In particular, this issue caused GH to need an adaptive version of one way function with encryption to bridge from TDFs to CCA security and this adaptive version was not realizable from the CDH assumption.

In our work the signaling strategy is decoupled from the recovery of the signals. In particular, the form of the signals comes from our computation of the (non-hinting) PRG, while recovery is realized from simply invoking the ABE decryption algorithm. We also get perfect correctness since a non-signal will be an encryption of the all 0's string. Also, with high probability our setup algorithm will choose parameters for which it is (information theoretically) impossible to create ambiguous signals. So once the ABE parameters are setup by an honest party (and with overwhelming probability, land in a good spot), there will be no further opportunity to take advantage of conflicting signals by an attacker via a decryption query.

We also believe that it might be interesting to swing some of our techniques back to the trapdoor function regime. For example, consider the GH TDF, but where we added values $a_1, \ldots, a_n$ to the public parameters. We could modify the evaluation algorithm such that at position i, the algorithm gives the one-way function with encryption output e_i if $s_i = 0$ and gives $e_i \oplus a_i$ if $s_i = 1$. This modification would allow us to drop the additional z_i values from the GH construction and make the output of the TDF shorter. In addition, while there would still be a negligible correctness error, it could be possible to rest this error solely in the choice of public parameters and for a "good" choice of parameters there would be no further error from evaluation. This last claim would require making sure that the a_i values were sufficiently long relative to y. We believe the techniques from [41] can be used here to achieve CCA security.

Independent Work. Independently, Garg, Gay and Hajiabadi [21] recently built upon the work of [22] to build trapdoors from one way function with encryption that has improved correctness properties. In particular, the base construction of [21] generates parameters that with high probability will allow inversion on all inputs, whereas any parameters generated from the [22] construction will always have inversion failure on some small fraction of inputs. They then build upon using erasure codes and a "smoothness" property to get CCA secure deterministic encryption with shorter ciphertexts. In addition, they show a modification to the Peikert-Waters [39] DDH-based Lossy TDF that gets a better ciphertext rate. The initial direction of getting better correctness in TDFs is similar to our "swinging techniques back" comment above, but otherwise the works pursue separate goals and techniques.

Subsequent Work. Subsequent to our work Kitagawa, Matsuda and Tanaka [29] proposed a variant of our CCA transformation for public key encryption. Their transformation had two significant differences (along with some minor ones) from ours. The first is that they showed how to execute the transformation with using just two public/private key pairs as opposed to the $2n$ public/private key pairs in our transformation. In our construction setup we generate $(\mathsf{cpa.sk}_{b,i}, \mathsf{cpa.pk}_{b,i}) \leftarrow \mathsf{CPA.Setup}(1^\lambda)$ for each $b \in \{0,1\}$, $i \in [n]$. They essentially show that one can replace this with a pair of calls to generate $(\mathsf{cpa.sk}_b, \mathsf{cpa.pk}_b) \leftarrow \mathsf{CPA.Setup}(1^\lambda)$ for each $b \in \{0,1\}$ where the 'i' subscript can be dropped in the construction and the keys essentially reused. Doing this requires a modified analysis where the hybrids are reordered. One will first change about half of the ciphertext components using IND-CPA security of the PKE scheme. Next, the decryption algorithm will be (undetectably) modified. Finally, IND-CPA security will be invoked a *second* time to change the other half of the ciphertexts.

The second major difference is that for the final "tie-off" step in the proof they will use a symmetric key encryption scheme with key-dependent message security as opposed to a hinting PRG. Like hinting PRGs these encryption schemes are also realizable from DDH, CDH and LWE, but also contain realizations from the Learning Parity with Noise (LPN) assumption for certain parameters. We remark that these two modifications (shorter keys and using key-dependent message security) appear to be orthogonal and one could choose adopt one without the other.

In other work Lombardi, Quach, Rothblum, Wichs and Wu [33] showed how to adapt our transformation to achieve a single key secure Attribute-Based Encryption scheme with a function hiding property. Suppose that a user has a secret key for a function f in an ABE system. The function hiding property roughly states that an attacker with access to decryption oracle cannot learn any more about what that user's function f is beyond what must be inherently learnable. The authors show that this property is sufficient for achieving designated verifier non-interactive zero knowledge proofs.

1.4 Toward Bridging Chosen Ciphertext Security in PKE

One classical open problem in cryptography is whether chosen plaintext security implies chosen ciphertext security in standard public key encryption. From a cursory glance one can see that it is easy to swap out the ABE system from our construction for a plain old public key encryption system and the same proof will go through—this time for obtaining chosen ciphertext secure public key encryption. Thus the "only" barrier for moving from IND-CPA to IND-CCA security is in the hinting PRG.

An interesting open question is just how strong this barrier is. From our viewpoint, the hinting security is something that most natural PRGs would likely have. In trying to understand whether it or something similar could be built from general assumptions (e.g. PKE or one way functions) it could be useful to first try to build a separation from our hinting PRG and a standard one. *Do there exist PRGs that do not meet the security definition of hinting PRG?*

As a first stab at the problem, one might consider PRGs where there is an initial trusted setup algorithm that produces a set of public parameters, which are then used for every subsequent evaluation. In this setting one could imagine a counterexample where the public parameters produced by the setup algorithm include an obfuscated program which will assist in breaking the hinting security, but not be helpful enough to break standard security. Using obfuscation in a similar manner has been useful for achieving other separation results. If we consider PRGs that do not allow for such setup, the task appears to be more challenging. One could try to embed such an obfuscated program in the first block of the PRG output, but this block would need to still look random for standard PRG security.

However, as it turns out there is a much simpler way to achieve a separation. Consider the case where $\ell = 1$ then the identity function on the seed will be a pseudorandom function for the trivial reason that it does not expand. However, this function will not be hinting secure. To get a separation with expansion one can consider a PRG G that takes as input an n bit seed s and outputs $z_0 z_1 \ldots z_n \ldots z_{2n}$. Now, let G' be a function that takes $2n$ bits as input, and maps (s', s) to $(z_0, s'_1 z_1, \ldots, s'_n z_n, z_{n+1}, \ldots, z_{2n})$. One can check that G' is a secure PRG, but is not a hinting PRG.

Altogether we believe that our work opens up a new avenue for exploring the connection of chosen plaintext and ciphertext security.

2   One-Sided Predicate Encryption

A predicate encryption (PE) scheme $\mathcal{PE}$, for set of attribute spaces $\mathcal{X} = \{\mathcal{X}_\lambda\}_{\lambda \in \mathbb{N}}$, predicate classes $\mathcal{C} = \{\mathcal{C}_\lambda\}_{\lambda \in \mathbb{N}}$ and message spaces $\mathcal{M} = \{\mathcal{M}_\lambda\}_{\lambda \in \mathbb{N}}$, consists of four polytime algorithms (Setup, Enc, KeyGen, Dec) with the following syntax.

Setup(1^λ) $\rightarrow$ (pp, msk). The setup algorithm takes as input the security parameter λ and a description of attribute space $\mathcal{X}_\lambda$, predicate class $\mathcal{C}_\lambda$ and message space $\mathcal{M}_\lambda$, and outputs the public parameters pp and the master secret key msk.

Enc(pp, m, x) $\rightarrow$ ct. The encryption algorithm takes as input public parameters pp, a message $m \in \mathcal{M}_\lambda$ and an attribute $x \in \mathcal{X}_\lambda$. It outputs a ciphertext ct.

KeyGen(msk, C) $\rightarrow$ sk$_C$. The key generation algorithm takes as input master secret key msk and a predicate $C \in \mathcal{C}_\lambda$. It outputs a secret key sk$_C$.

Dec(sk$_C$, ct) $\rightarrow m$ or $\perp$. The decryption algorithm takes as input a secret key sk$_C$ and a ciphertext ct. It outputs either a message $m \in \mathcal{M}_\lambda$ or a special symbol $\perp$.

Correctness. A key-policy predicate encryption scheme is said to be correct if for all $\lambda \in \mathbb{N}$, (pp, msk) $\leftarrow$ Setup(1^λ), for all $x \in \mathcal{X}_\lambda$, $C \in \mathcal{C}_\lambda$, $m \in \mathcal{M}_\lambda$, sk$_C \leftarrow$ KeyGen(msk, C), ct $\leftarrow$ Enc(pp, m, x), the following holds

Correctness for decryptable ciphertexts : $C(x) = 1 \Rightarrow \Pr\left[\text{Dec}(\text{sk}_C, \text{ct}) = m\right] = 1,$

Correctness for non-decryptable ciphertexts : $C(x) = 0 \Rightarrow \Pr\left[\text{Dec}(\text{sk}_C, \text{ct}) = \perp\right] \geq 1 - \text{negl}(\lambda),$

where $\text{negl}(\cdot)$ are negligible functions, and the probabilities are taken over the random coins used during key generation and encryption procedures.

Recovery from Randomness Property. A key-policy predicate encryption scheme is said to have *recovery from randomness property* if there is an additional algorithm Recover that takes as input public parameters pp, ciphertext ct, string r and outputs $y \in (\mathcal{M}_\lambda \times \mathcal{X}_\lambda) \cup \{\perp\}$ and satisfies the following condition: for all $\lambda \in \mathbb{N}$, (pp, msk) $\leftarrow$ Setup(1^λ), for all $x \in \mathcal{X}_\lambda$, $m \in \mathcal{M}_\lambda$, ct $=$ Enc(pp, $m, x; r$), Recover(pp, ct, r) $= (m, x)$. If there is no (m, x, r) tuple such that ct $=$ Enc(pp, $m, x; r$), then Recover(pp, ct, r) $= \perp$.

Security. In this work, we will be considering predicate encryption systems with one-sided security. One can consider both security against *chosen plaintext attacks* and *chosen ciphertext attacks*. First, we will present one-sided security against chosen plaintext attacks.

Definition 1 (One-Sided Security against Chosen Plaintext Attacks).
A predicate encryption scheme $\mathcal{PE} = $ (Setup, Enc, KeyGen, Dec) *is said to be one-sided secure against chosen plaintext attacks if for every stateful PPT adversary* $\mathcal{A}$, *there exists a negligible function* $\mathsf{negl}(\cdot)$, *such that the following holds:*

$$\left| \Pr \left[\mathcal{A}^{\mathsf{KeyGen}(\mathsf{msk}, \cdot)}(\mathsf{ct}) = b : \begin{array}{c} (\mathsf{pp}, \mathsf{msk}) \leftarrow \mathsf{Setup}(1^\lambda) \\ ((m_0, x_0), (m_1, x_1)) \leftarrow \mathcal{A}^{\mathsf{KeyGen}(\mathsf{msk}, \cdot)}(\mathsf{pp}) \\ b \leftarrow \{0, 1\}; \ \mathsf{ct} \leftarrow \mathsf{Enc}(\mathsf{pp}, m_b, x_b) \end{array} \right] - \frac{1}{2} \right| \leq \mathsf{negl}(\lambda)$$

where every predicate query C, *made by adversary* $\mathcal{A}$ *to the* $\mathsf{KeyGen}(\mathsf{msk}, \cdot)$ *oracle, must satisfy the condition that* $C(x_0) = C(x_1) = 0$.

The notion of one-sided security against chosen plaintext attacks could alternatively be captured by a simulation based definition [24]. Goyal et al. [25] showed that if a PE scheme satisfies Definition 1, then it also satisfies the simulation based definition of [24].

Next, we present the definition for capturing chosen ciphertext attacks on predicate encryption schemes. Here, we will assume that the key generation algorithm is deterministic.

Definition 2 (One-Sided Security against Chosen Ciphertext Attacks). *A predicate encryption scheme* $\mathcal{PE} = $ (Setup, Enc, KeyGen, Dec) *with deterministic key generation is said to be one-sided secure against chosen ciphertext attacks if for every stateful PPT adversary* $\mathcal{A}$, *there exists a negligible function* $\mathsf{negl}(\cdot)$, *such that the following event's probability is at most* $1/2 + \mathsf{negl}(\lambda)$:

$$\left[\mathcal{A}^{\mathsf{KeyGen}(\mathsf{msk}, \cdot), \mathcal{O}_{\mathsf{Dec}}(\mathsf{msk}, \cdot, \cdot)}(\mathsf{ct}^*) = b : \begin{array}{c} (\mathsf{pp}, \mathsf{msk}) \leftarrow \mathsf{Setup}(1^\lambda) \\ ((m_0, x_0), (m_1, x_1)) \leftarrow \mathcal{A}^{\mathsf{KeyGen}(\mathsf{msk}, \cdot), \mathcal{O}_{\mathsf{Dec}}(\mathsf{msk}, \cdot, \cdot)}(\mathsf{pp}) \\ b \leftarrow \{0, 1\}; \ \mathsf{ct}^* \leftarrow \mathsf{Enc}(\mathsf{pp}, m_b, x_b) \end{array} \right].$$

- *the oracle* $\mathcal{O}_{\mathsf{Dec}}(\mathsf{msk}, \cdot, \cdot)$ *takes as input a ciphertext* ct *and a circuit* C. *It computes* $\mathsf{sk}_C = \mathsf{KeyGen}(\mathsf{msk}, C)$ *and outputs* $\mathsf{Dec}(\mathsf{sk}_C, \mathsf{ct})$.
- *every predicate query* C, *made by adversary* $\mathcal{A}$ *to the* $\mathsf{KeyGen}(\mathsf{msk}, \cdot)$ *oracle, must satisfy the condition that* $C(x_0) = C(x_1) = 0$.
- *every post-challenge query* (C, ct) *made by the adversary* $\mathcal{A}$ *to* $\mathcal{O}_{\mathsf{Dec}}$ *must satisfy the condition that either* $\mathsf{ct} \neq \mathsf{ct}^*$ *or if* $\mathsf{ct} = \mathsf{ct}^*$, *then* $C(x_0) = C(x_1) = 0$.

Remark 1. Note that the above definition addresses chosen ciphertext attacks against systems with deterministic key generation. An analogous definition for general schemes (that is, with randomized key generation) would involve maintaining key handles and allowing the adversary to choose the key to be used for the decryption queries. We choose the simpler definition since any scheme's key generation can be made deterministic by using a pseudorandom function. In particular, the setup algorithm chooses a PRF key K which is included as part of the master secret key. To derive a key for circuit C, the algorithm first computes $r = \mathrm{PRF}(K, C)$ and then uses r as randomness for the randomized key generation algorithm.

2.1 PE Schemes with 'Recovery from Randomness' Property

Any PE scheme satisfying one-sided CPA security can be transformed into another PE scheme that is also one-sided CPA secure, and has the 'recovery from randomness' property. The encryption algorithm simply uses part of the randomness to compute a symmetric key encryption of the message and attribute, with part of the randomness as the encryption key.

More formally, let $E = (\mathsf{Setup}, \mathsf{Enc}, \mathsf{KeyGen}, \mathsf{Dec})$ be a PE scheme that satisfies one-sided CPA security (see Definition 1), and let $(\mathsf{SKE.Setup}, \mathsf{SKE.Enc}, \mathsf{SKE.Dec})$ be a symmetric key CPA secure encryption scheme. consider the following scheme $E' = (\mathsf{Setup}', \mathsf{Enc}', \mathsf{KeyGen}', \mathsf{Dec}', \mathsf{Recover})$, where $\mathsf{Setup}' = \mathsf{Setup}$ and $\mathsf{KeyGen}' = \mathsf{KeyGen}$.

$\mathsf{Enc}'(\mathsf{pk}, m, x)$: The encryption algorithm first samples three random strings r_1, r_2, r_3. It computes $\mathsf{ct}_1 = \mathsf{Enc}(\mathsf{pk}, m, x; r_1)$. Next, it computes $\mathsf{ske.sk} = \mathsf{SKE.Setup}(1^\lambda; r_2)$. Finally, it computes $\mathsf{ct}_2 = \mathsf{SKE.Enc}(\mathsf{ske.sk}, (m, x); r_3)$ and outputs $(\mathsf{ct}_1, \mathsf{ct}_2)$.

$\mathsf{Dec}'(\mathsf{sk}, (\mathsf{ct}_1, \mathsf{ct}_2))$: The decryption algorithm simply decrypts ct_1 using sk, and ignores ct_2. It outputs $\mathsf{Dec}(\mathsf{sk}, \mathsf{ct}_1)$.

$\mathsf{Recover}((\mathsf{ct}_1, \mathsf{ct}_2), r = (r_1, r_2, r_3))$: The recovery algorithm first computes $\mathsf{ske.sk} = \mathsf{SKE.Setup}(1^\lambda; r_2)$. It outputs $y \leftarrow \mathsf{SKE.Dec}(\mathsf{ske.sk}, \mathsf{ct}_2)$.

Assuming the symmetric key encryption scheme satisfies perfect correctness, this PE scheme has perfect recovery from randomness property. To argue CPA security, we can first use the security of the SKE scheme to switch ct_2 to an encryption of $0^{|m|+|x|}$. Then, we can use the one-sided CPA security.

3 Hinting PRGs

A hinting PRG scheme is a PRG with a stronger security guarantee than standard PRGs. A hinting PRG takes n bits as input, and outputs $n \cdot \ell$ output bits. In this security game, the challenger outputs $2n$ strings, each of ℓ bits. In one scenario, all these $2n$ strings are uniformly random. In the other case, half the strings are obtained from the PRG evaluation, and the remaining half are uniformly random. Moreover, these $2n$ strings are output as a $2 \times n$ matrix, where in the ith column, the top entry is pseudorandom if the ith bit of the seed is 0, else the bottom entry is pseudorandom. As a result, these $2n$ strings give a 'hint' about the seed, and hence this property is stronger than regular PRGs. Note, if this hint is removed and the top entries in each column were pseudorandom (and the rest uniformly random), then this can be achieved using regular PRGs.

Below, we define this primitive formally. The informal description above had two simplifications. First, the definition below considers PRGs with setup (although one can analogously define such a primitive without setup). Second, we assume the PRG outputs $(n + 1) \cdot \ell$ bits, where the first ℓ bits do not contain any extra hint about the seed. Finally, for our CCA application, we introduce some notation in order to represent the $n + 1$ blocks of the PRG output. Instead of describing the PRG as a function that outputs $(n + 1) \cdot \ell$ bits, we have an evaluation algorithm that takes as input an index $i \in \{0, 1, \ldots, n\}$, and outputs the ith block of the PRG output.

Let $n(\cdot, \cdot)$ be a polynomial. A n-hinting PRG scheme consists of two PPT algorithms Setup, Eval with the following syntax.

Setup($1^\lambda, 1^\ell$): The setup algorithm takes as input the security parameter λ, and length parameter ℓ, and outputs public parameters pp and input length $n = n(\lambda, \ell)$.

Eval (pp, $s \in \{0, 1\}^n, i \in [n] \cup \{0\}$): The evaluation algorithm takes as input the public parameters pp, an n bit string s, an index $i \in [n] \cup \{0\}$ and outputs an ℓ bit string y.

Definition 3. *A hinting PRG scheme* (Setup, Eval) *is said to be secure if for any PPT adversary $\mathcal{A}$, polynomial $\ell(\cdot)$ there exists a negligible function* negl$(\cdot)$ *such that for all $\lambda \in \mathbb{N}$, the following event's probability is at most $1/2 + $ negl(λ):*

$$\left[\beta \leftarrow A\left(\mathsf{pp}, \left(y_0^\beta, \left\{ y_{i,b}^\beta \right\}_{i \in [n], b \in \{0,1\}} \right) \right) : \begin{array}{l} (\mathsf{pp}, n) \leftarrow \mathsf{Setup}(1^\lambda, 1^{\ell(\lambda)}), s \leftarrow \{0, 1\}^n, \\ \beta \leftarrow \{0, 1\}, y_0^0 \leftarrow \{0, 1\}^\ell, y_0^1 = \mathsf{Eval}(\mathsf{pp}, s, 0), \\ y_{i,b}^0 \leftarrow \{0, 1\}^\ell \; \forall \, i \in [n], b \in \{0, 1\}, \\ y_{i,s_i}^1 = \mathsf{Eval}(\mathsf{pp}, s, i), y_{i,\overline{s_i}}^1 \leftarrow \{0, 1\}^\ell \; \forall \, i \in [n] \end{array} \right]$$

4   CCA Secure Public Key Encryption Scheme

Let $\mathsf{PKE_{CPA}} = (\mathsf{CPA.Setup}, \mathsf{CPA.Enc}, \mathsf{CPA.Dec})$ be a IND-CPA secure public key encryption scheme with randomness-decryptable ciphertexts and perfect decryption correctness, $\mathsf{S} = (\mathsf{ss.Setup}, \mathsf{ss.Sign}, \mathsf{ss.Verify})$ a strongly unforgeable one time signature scheme and $\mathsf{HPRG} = (\mathsf{HPRG.Setup}, \mathsf{HPRG.Eval})$ a hinting PRG scheme. We will assume that our encryption scheme has message space $\{0, 1\}^{\lambda+1}$. Let $\ell_{\mathsf{PKE}}(\cdot)$ be a polynomial representing the number of bits of randomness used by CPA.Enc, and $\ell_{\mathsf{vk}}(\cdot)$ the size of verification keys output by ss.Setup. For simplicity of notation, we will assume $\ell(\cdot) = \ell_{\mathsf{PKE}}(\cdot)$, $\ell_{\mathsf{out}}(\lambda) = \ell_{\mathsf{vk}}(\lambda) + 3\lambda$ and $\mathsf{PRG}_\lambda : \{0, 1\}^\lambda \to \{0, 1\}^{\ell_{\mathsf{out}}(\lambda)}$ a family of secure pseudorandom generators.

We will now describe our CCA secure public key encryption scheme $\mathsf{PKE_{CCA}} = (\mathsf{CCA.Setup}, \mathsf{CCA.Enc}, \mathsf{CCA.Dec})$ with message space $\mathcal{M}_\lambda = \{0, 1\}^{\ell(\lambda)}$. For simplicity of notation, we will skip the dependence of ℓ and ℓ_{out} on λ.

CCA.Setup(1^λ): The setup algorithm performs the following steps.

1. It chooses $(\mathsf{HPRG.pp}, 1^n) \leftarrow \mathsf{HPRG.Setup}(1^\lambda, 1^\ell)$.
2. It chooses $2n$ different $\mathsf{PKE_{CPA}}$ keys. Let $(\mathsf{cpa.sk}_{b,i}, \mathsf{cpa.pk}_{b,i}) \leftarrow \mathsf{CPA.Setup}(1^\lambda)$ for each $b \in \{0, 1\}$, $i \in [n]$.
3. It then chooses $a_i \leftarrow \{0, 1\}^{\ell_{\mathsf{out}}}$ for each $i \in [n]$ and $B \leftarrow \{0, 1\}^{\ell_{\mathsf{out}}}$.
4. It sets $\mathsf{cca.pk} = \left(\mathsf{HPRG.pp}, B, \left(a_i, \mathsf{cpa.pk}_{b,i} \right)_{b \in \{0,1\}, i \in [n]} \right)$ and $\mathsf{cca.sk} = \left(\mathsf{cpa.sk}_{0,i} \right)_{i \in [n]}$.

CCA.Enc(cca.pk, m, x): Let cca.pk $= \left(\mathsf{HPRG.pp}, B, (a_i, \mathsf{cpa.pk}_{b,i})_{b\in\{0,1\}, i\in[n]}\right)$. The encryption algorithm does the following:

1. It first chooses $s \leftarrow \{0,1\}^n$. It sets $c = \mathsf{HPRG.Eval}(\mathsf{HPRG.pp}, s, 0) \oplus m$.
2. Next, it chooses signature keys $(\mathsf{ss.sk}, \mathsf{ss.vk}) \leftarrow \mathsf{ss.Setup}(1^\lambda)$.
3. For each $i \in [n]$, it chooses $v_i \leftarrow \{0,1\}^\lambda$ and $r_i \leftarrow \{0,1\}^\ell$, sets $\widetilde{r}_i = \mathsf{HPRG.Eval}(\mathsf{HPRG.pp}, s, i)$.
4. Next, for each $i \in [n]$, it does the following:
    - If $s_i = 0$, it sets $c_{0,i} = \mathsf{CPA.Enc}(\mathsf{cpa.pk}_{0,i}, 1|v_i; \widetilde{r}_i)$, $c_{1,i} = \mathsf{CPA.Enc}(\mathsf{cpa.pk}_{1,i}, 0^{\lambda+1}; r_i)$ and $c_{2,i} = \mathsf{PRG}(v_i)$.
    - If $s_i = 1$, it sets $c_{0,i} = \mathsf{CPA.Enc}(\mathsf{cpa.pk}_{0,i}, 0^{\lambda+1}; r_i)$, $c_{1,i} = \mathsf{CPA.Enc}(\mathsf{cpa.pk}_{1,i}, 1|v_i; \widetilde{r}_i)$ and $c_{2,i} = \mathsf{PRG}(v_i) + a_i + B \cdot \mathsf{ss.vk}$.[4]
5. Finally, it sets $M = \left(c, (c_{0,i}, c_{1,i}, c_{2,i})_{i\in[n]}\right)$, computes $\sigma \leftarrow \mathsf{ss.Sign}(\mathsf{ss.sk}, M)$ and outputs $(\mathsf{ss.vk}, M, \sigma)$ as the ciphertext.

CCA.Dec(cca.sk, cca.pk, cca.ct): Let the ciphertext cca.ct be parsed as $\left(\mathsf{ss.vk}, M = \left(c, (c_{0,i}, c_{1,i}, c_{2,i})_{i\in[n]}\right), \sigma\right)$ and cca.sk $= \left((\mathsf{cpa.sk}_{0,i})_{i\in[n]}\right)$. The decryption algorithm does the following:

1. It first verifies the signature σ. It checks if $\mathsf{ss.Verify}(\mathsf{ss.vk}, M, \sigma) = 1$, else it outputs $\bot$.
2. Next, the decryption algorithm computes $d = \mathsf{PKE.Find}(\mathsf{cca.pk}, \mathsf{cca.sk}, \mathsf{cca.ct})$ (where PKE.Find is defined in Fig. 1), and outputs PKE.Check $(\mathsf{cca.pk}, \mathsf{cca.ct}, d)$ (where PKE.Check is defined in Fig. 2).

PKE.Find(cca.pk, cca.sk, cca.ct)

Inputs: Public Key cca.pk $= \left(\mathsf{HPRG.pp}, B, (a_i, \mathsf{cpa.pk}_{b,i})_{b\in\{0,1\}, i\in[n]}\right)$

Secret Key cca.sk $= (\mathsf{cpa.sk}_{0,i})_{i\in[n]}$

Ciphertext cca.ct $= \left(\mathsf{ss.vk}, M = \left(c, (c_{0,i}, c_{1,i}, c_{2,i})_{i\in[n]}\right), \sigma\right)$

Output: $d \in \{0,1\}^n$

- For each $i \in [n]$, do the following:
    1. Let $m_i = \mathsf{CPA.Dec}(\mathsf{cpa.sk}_{0,i}, c_{0,i})$.
    2. If $m_i = 1|v_i$ and $\mathsf{PRG}(v_i) = c_{2,i}$, set $d_i = 0$. Else set $d_i = 1$.
- Output $d = d_1 d_2 \ldots d_n$.

Fig. 1. Routine PKE.Find

---

[4] Here, we assume the verification key is embedded in $\mathbb{F}_{2^{\ell_{out}}}$, and the addition and multiplication are performed in $\mathbb{F}_{2^{\ell_{out}}}$. Also, the function $h(x) = a_i + B \cdot x$ serves as a pairwise independent hash function.

PKE.Check(cca.pk, cca.ct, d)

Inputs: Public Key cca.pk $= \left(\text{HPRG.pp}, B, \left(a_i, \text{cpa.pk}_{b,i}\right)_{b \in \{0,1\}, i \in [n]} \right)$

Ciphertext cca.ct $= \left(\text{ss.vk}, M = \left(c, (c_{0,i}, c_{1,i}, c_{2,i})_{i \in [n]} \right), \sigma \right)$

$d \in \{0,1\}^n$

Output: msg $\in \{0,1\}^\ell$

- Let flag = true. For $i = 1$ to n, do the following:
  1. Let $\widetilde{r}_i = \text{HPRG.Eval}(\text{HPRG.pp}, d, i)$.
  2. If $d_i = 0$, let $m \leftarrow \text{CPA.Recover}(\text{cpa.pk}_{0,i}, c_{0,i}, \widetilde{r}_i)$. Perform the following checks. If any of the checks fail, set flag = false and exit loop.
     - $m \neq \perp$.
     - $\text{CPA.Enc}(\text{cpa.pk}_{0,i}, m; \widetilde{r}_i) = c_{0,i}$.
     - $m = 1|v$ and $\text{PRG}(v) = c_{2,i}$.
  3. If $d_i = 1$, let $m \leftarrow \text{CPA.Recover}(\text{cpa.pk}_{1,i}, c_{1,i}, \widetilde{r}_i)$. Perform the following checks. If any of the checks fail, set flag = false and exit loop.
     - $m \neq \perp$.
     - $\text{CPA.Enc}(\text{cpa.pk}_{1,i}, m; \widetilde{r}_i) = c_{1,i}$.
     - $m = 1|v$ and $c_{2,i} = \text{PRG}(v) + a_i + B \cdot \text{ss.vk}$.
- If flag = true, output $c \oplus \text{HPRG.Eval}(\text{HPRG.pp}, d, 0)$. Else output $\perp$.

Fig. 2. Routine PKE.Check

4.1 Discussion

We will now make a few observations about our construction and then proceed to give a brief overview our proof that appears in the next subsection.

First, for each $i \in [n]$ if $s_i = 0$ the encryption algorithm will choose a random v_i and 'signal'[5] that this bit is a 0 by encrypting $1|v_i$ to the position $(0, i)$ and giving $c_{2,i} = \text{PRG}(v_i)$ in the clear. In the opposite position of $(1, i)$ it will encrypt the all 0's string. Likewise, if $s_i = 1$ it will signal a 1 by encrypting $1|v_i$ to the position $(1, i)$ and giving $c_{2,i} = \text{PRG}(v_i) + a_i + B \cdot \text{ss.vk}$ in the clear. With all but negligible probability it is impossible to signal both 0 and 1 simultaneously for an index i. This follows from the fact that a_i is chosen randomly and that the space of verification keys is much smaller than $2^{\ell_{\text{out}}(\lambda)}$. We observe that this argument has some flavor of Naor's bit commitment scheme [35].

Second, we observe that even though one is supposed to encrypt the all 0's string to position $(\bar{s}_i, i)$ the PKE.Find routine will not immediately quit if discovers something else. Instead it simply sets $d_i = 0$ if decryption outputs $1|v_i$

---

[5] By signaling, we mean that any party that has the secret key for decryption can learn the bits of s one after another, by using the ciphertext components $c_{0,i}, c_{1,i}, c_{2,i}$.

and $c_{2,i} = \mathsf{PRG}(v_i)$; otherwise it sets $d_i = 1$. Thus, the decryption routine may refrain from immediately aborting even though when it "knows" the ciphertext was not formed entirely correctly. This will be critical to a proof step.

Our proof of security will be organized as a sequence of security games which we show to be indistinguishable. In the first proof step we apply a standard argument using strongly unforgeable signatures to change the decryption oracle to reject all ciphertexts corresponding to $\mathsf{ss.vk}^*$ where $\mathsf{ss.vk}^*$ is the verification key used by the challenge ciphertext.

Next, for each i we choose the public parameter values a_i such that it is possible for one to signal both 0 and 1 at index i, but that this ambiguity is only possible for a ciphertext corresponding to $\mathsf{ss.vk}^*$. To do this it chooses uniformly random $w_i \leftarrow \{0,1\}^\lambda$, and sets $a_i = \mathsf{PRG}(v_i^*) - \mathsf{PRG}(w_i) - \mathsf{ss.vk}^* \cdot B$ if $s_i^* = 0$, else $a_i = \mathsf{PRG}(w_i) - \mathsf{PRG}(v_i^*) - \mathsf{ss.vk}^* \cdot B$. This change can be shown to be undetectable by a standard pseudorandom generator argument. The effect of this change is that it allows the possibility of ambiguous signaling at both 0 and 1 in the challenge ciphertext. However, for all possible decryption queries where $\mathsf{ss.vk} \neq \mathsf{ss.vk}^*$ this remains impossible.

Our next goal will be to use the IND-CPA security of the underlying PKE scheme to introduce signals on the opposite path $\overline{s^*}$. To do this, however, for all i where $s_i^* = 1$ we must first change the decryption routine to use $\mathsf{cpa.sk}_{1,i}$ to decrypt the sub-ciphertext at position $(1, i)$ instead of using $\mathsf{cpa.sk}_{0,i}$ (at position $(0, i)$). Consider a particular ciphertext query and let d_i be the bit reported by the original find algorithm on that ciphertext query and d_i' be the bit reported by a the new decryption procedure on that same ciphertext. We want to argue that if $d_i \neq d_i'$ then the PKE.Check procedure will abort and output $\bot$ on both encryptions. The first possibility is that $d_i = 0$ and $d_i' = 1$; however, that should be information theoretically impossible as it would entail signaling both a 0 and 1 for a query with $\mathsf{ss.vk} \neq \mathsf{ss.vk}^*$. The other possibility is that $d_i = 1$ and $d_i' = 0$; i.e. that there is not a signal present at either side. In this case the first decryption routine will have $d_i = 1$, but then when running PKE.Check it will fail to find a signal at position $(1, i)$ and abort. Likewise, the second decryption routine will have $d_i' = 0$, but then fail to find a signal at position $(0, i)$, so both routines will behave identically in this case as well.

Once the oracle decryption is set to follow the seed s^* we can straightforwardly use CPA security to introduce ambiguous signals in the messages for all positions $(\overline{s^*}_i, i)$. Once this change is made we can change the oracle decryption routine again. This time it will only decrypt at positions $(1, i)$ for all $i \in [n]$ and only use $\mathsf{cpa.sk}_{1,i}$. A similar argument to before can be applied to make this change.

All information about s is gone except to the lingering amount in the random coins used to encrypt. We can immediately apply the hinting PRG to change to a game where these values can be moved to be uniformly at random. At this point the message will be hidden.

4.2   Security Proof

We will now show that the above construction satisfies the CCA security definition. Our proof proceeds via a sequence of hybrids. First, we will describe all hybrids, and then show that the hybrids are computationally indistinguishable.

Hybrids

Hybrid H_0: This corresponds to the original security game.

- **Setup Phase**
    1. The challenger first chooses $(\mathsf{HPRG.pp}, 1^n) \leftarrow \mathsf{HPRG.Setup}(1^\lambda, 1^\ell)$.
    2. Next it chooses $2n$ different $\mathsf{PKE_{CPA}}$ keys. Let $(\mathsf{cpa.sk}_{b,i}, \mathsf{cpa.pk}_{b,i}) \leftarrow \mathsf{CPA.Setup}(1^\lambda)$ for each $i \in [n]$, $b \in \{0,1\}$.
    3. The challenger chooses $s^* \leftarrow \{0,1\}^n$, $v_i^* \leftarrow \{0,1\}^\lambda$ for each $i \in [n]$, and $(\mathsf{ss.sk}^*, \mathsf{ss.vk}^*) \leftarrow \mathsf{ss.Setup}(1^\lambda)$. It sets $\widetilde{r}_i^* = \mathsf{HPRG.Eval}(\mathsf{HPRG.pp}, s^*, i)$. (These components will be used during the challenge phase.)
    4. It then chooses $a_i \leftarrow \{0,1\}^{\ell_{\mathrm{out}}}$ for each $i \in [n]$ and $B \leftarrow \{0,1\}^{\ell_{\mathrm{out}}}$.
    5. It sends $\mathsf{cca.pk} = \left(\mathsf{HPRG.pp}, B, \left(a_i, \mathsf{cpa.pk}_{b,i}\right)_{b \in \{0,1\}, i \in [n]} \right)$ to $\mathcal{A}$, and sets the secret key $\mathsf{cca.sk} = (\mathsf{cpa.sk}_{0,i})_{i \in [n]}$.
- **Pre-challenge Query Phase**
    - *Decryption Queries*
        1. For each query $\left(\mathsf{ct} = \left(\mathsf{ss.vk}, M = \left(c, (c_{0,i}, c_{1,i}, c_{2,i})_i\right), \sigma\right)\right)$, the challenger first checks the signature σ.
        2. Next, the challenger first computes $d = \mathsf{PKE.Find}(\mathsf{cca.pk}, \mathsf{cca.sk}, \mathsf{cca.ct})$.
        3. It outputs $\mathsf{PKE.Check}(\mathsf{cca.pk}, \mathsf{cca.ct}, d)$.
- **Challenge Phase**
    1. The adversary sends two challenge messages (m_0^*, m_1^*).
    2. The challenger chooses a bit $\beta \in \{0,1\}$.
    3. It sets $c^* = \mathsf{HPRG.Eval}(\mathsf{HPRG.pp}, s, 0) \oplus m_\beta^*$.
    4. It sets $(c_{0,i}^*, c_{1,i}^*, c_{2,i}^*)$ as follows.
        - If $s_i^* = 0$, it sets $c_{0,i}^* = \mathsf{CPA.Enc}(\mathsf{cpa.pk}_{0,i}, 1|v_i^*; \widetilde{r}_i^*)$, $c_{1,i}^* \leftarrow \mathsf{CPA.Enc}(\mathsf{cpa.pk}_{1,i}, 0^{\lambda+1})$ and $c_{2,i}^* = \mathsf{PRG}(v_i^*)$.
        - If $s_i^* = 1$, it sets $c_{0,i}^* \leftarrow \mathsf{CPA.Enc}(\mathsf{cpa.pk}_{0,i}, 0^{\lambda+1})$, $c_{1,i}^* = \mathsf{CPA.Enc}(\mathsf{cpa.pk}_{1,i}, 1|v_i^*; \widetilde{r}_i^*)$ and $c_{2,i}^* = \mathsf{PRG}(v_i^*) + a_i + B \cdot \mathsf{ss.vk}^*$.
    5. Finally, it computes a signature σ^* on $M^* = \left(c^*, (c_{0,i}^*, c_{1,i}^*, c_{2,i}^*)\right)$ using $\mathsf{ss.sk}^*$ and sends $(\mathsf{ss.vk}^*, M^*, \sigma^*)$ to $\mathcal{A}$.
- **Post-challenge Query Phase**
    - *Decryption Queries.* These are handled as in the pre-challenge phase, with the restriction that all queries (ct, C) must satisfy that $\mathsf{ct} \neq \mathsf{ct}^*$.
- Finally, the adversary sends its guess b.

Hybrid H_1: This hybrid is similar to the previous one, except that during the decryption queries, the challenger checks if $\mathsf{ss.vk} = \mathsf{ss.vk}^*$. If so, it rejects. ***

Hybrid H_2: In this hybrid, the challenger changes Step 4 of the setup phase. It chooses uniformly random $w_i \leftarrow \{0,1\}^\lambda$, and sets $a_i = \mathsf{PRG}(v_i^*) - \mathsf{PRG}(w_i) - \mathsf{ss.vk}^* \cdot B$ if $s_i^* = 0$, else $a_i = \mathsf{PRG}(w_i) - \mathsf{PRG}(v_i^*) - \mathsf{ss.vk}^* \cdot B$.

Hybrid H_3: This hybrid is similar to the previous one, except that the challenger modifies the way decryption queries are handled. Instead of using PKE.Find, the challenger uses PKE.Find-1 (defined in Fig. 3). The PKE.Find routine decrypts only the $c_{0,i}$ values. If decryption works, it guesses $d_i = 0$, else it guesses $d_i = 1$. The PKE.Find-1 routine decrypts either $c_{0,i}$ or $c_{1,i}$, depending on the ith bit of s^*. Note that the PKE.Check routine is identical in both experiments.

$\mathsf{PKE.Find\text{-}1}(\mathsf{cca.pk}, (\mathsf{cpa.sk}_{s_i^*,i})_{b \in \{0,1\}, i \in [n]}, \mathsf{cca.ct}, s^*)$

Inputs: Public Key $\mathsf{cca.pk} = \left(\mathsf{HPRG.pp}, B, (a_i, \mathsf{cpa.pk}_{b,i})_{b \in \{0,1\}, i \in [n]}\right)$

Secret Keys $(\mathsf{cpa.sk}_{s_i^*,i})_{i \in [n]}$

Ciphertext $\mathsf{cca.ct} = \left(\mathsf{ss.vk}, \left(c, M = (c_{0,i}, c_{1,i}, c_{2,i})_{i \in [n]}\right), \sigma\right)$

String $s^* \in \{0,1\}^n$

Output: $d \in \{0,1\}^n$

- For each $i \in [n]$, do the following:
  - If $s_i^* = 0$,
    1. Let $m_i = \mathsf{CPA.Dec}(\mathsf{cpa.sk}_{0,i}, c_{0,i})$.
    2. If $m_i = 1|v_i$ and $\mathsf{PRG}(v_i) = c_{2,i}$, set $d_i = 0$. Else set $d_i = 1$.
  - Else if $s_i^* = 1$,
    1. Let $m_i = \mathsf{CPA.Dec}(\mathsf{cpa.sk}_{1,i}, c_{1,i})$.
    2. If $m_i = 1|v_i$ and $\mathsf{PRG}(v_i) + a_i + B \cdot \mathsf{ss.vk}^* = c_{2,i}$, set $d_i = 1$. Else set $d_i = 0$.
- Output $d = d_1 d_2 \ldots d_n$.

Fig. 3. Routine PKE.Find-1

Hybrid H_4: In this step, the challenger modifies the challenge ciphertext. For all $i \in [n]$ such that $s_i^* = 0$, the challenger sets $c_{1,i}^* \leftarrow \mathsf{CPA.Enc}(\mathsf{cpa.pk}_{1,i}, 1|w_i)$.

Hybrid H_5: In this step, the challenger modifies the challenge ciphertext. For all $i \in [n]$ such that $s_i^* = 1$, the challenger sets $c_{0,i}^* \leftarrow \mathsf{CPA.Enc}(\mathsf{cpa.pk}_{0,i}, 1|w_i)$.[6]

---

[6] Note that hybrids H_4 and H_5 could have been clubbed into a single hybrid. We chose this distinction so that the hybrids for the PKE CCA proof are similar to the hybrids for our Predicate Encryption security proof.

Hybrid H_6: This step is similar to the previous one, except for the decryption queries in the pre-challenge/post-challenge phase. Instead of using PKE.Find-1, the challenger uses PKE.Find-2 (defined in Fig. 4).[7]

PKE.Find-2(cca.pk, $(\text{cpa.sk}_{1,i})_{i\in[n]}$, cca.ct)

Inputs: Public Key $\text{cca.pk} = \left(\text{HPRG.pp}, B, \left(a_i, \text{cpa.pk}_{b,i}\right)_{b\in\{0,1\},i\in[n]}\right)$

　　　　　Secret Keys $(\text{cpa.sk}_{1,i})_{i\in[n]}$

　　　　　Ciphertext $\text{cca.ct} = \left(\text{ss.vk}, \left(c, M = (c_{0,i}, c_{1,i}, c_{2,i})_{i\in[n]}\right), \sigma\right)$

Output: $d \in \{0,1\}^n$

- For each $i \in [n]$, do the following:
  1. Let $m_i = \text{CPA.Dec}(\text{cpa.sk}_{1,i}, c_{1,i})$.
  2. If $m_i = 1|v_i$ and $\text{PRG}(v_i) + a_i + B \cdot \text{ss.vk}^* = c_{2,i}$, set $d_i = 1$. Else set $d_i = 0$.
- Output $d = d_1 d_2 \ldots d_n$.

Fig. 4. Routine PKE.Find-2

Hybrid H_7: This hybrid is identical to the previous one, and the only difference here is change of variable names. In particular, we will swap the variable names v_i^* and w_i if $s_i^* = 1$. This change affects the setup phase (where the a_i values are set), and the challenge phase (where we set $c_{0,i}^*$ and $c_{1,i}^*$). Also, we rename the $\widetilde{r}_i^*$ and r_i^* variables to $r_{i,0}^*$ and $r_{i,1}^*$, depending on s_i^*. For clarity, we present the entire setup and challenge phase in the full version of our paper.

Hybrid H_8: In this hybrid, the challenger chooses both $r_{i,b}^*$ uniformly at random from $\{0,1\}^\ell$. It also chooses c^* uniformly at random.

Analysis. Let $\text{adv}_{\mathcal{A}}^x$ denote the advantage of an adversary $\mathcal{A}$ in Hybrid H_x.

Lemma 1. *Assuming ss is a strongly unforgeable one-time signature scheme, for any PPT adversary $\mathcal{A}$, there exists a negligible function $\text{negl}(\cdot)$ such that for all $\lambda \in \mathbb{N}$, $|\text{adv}_{\mathcal{A}}^0 - \text{adv}_{\mathcal{A}}^1| \leq \text{negl}(\lambda)$.*

Proof. This proof follows from the security of ss. The only difference between these two hybrids is that the challenger, on receiving a decryption query,

---

[7] We could have simplified this step by using PKE.Find instead of using PKE.Find-2. However, looking ahead, our proof for ABE/PE systems will require an analogous PKE.Find-2 routine. Hence, we chose to add this minor additional complication here as well.

rejects if it contains ss.vk*. Suppose there exists a PPT adversary $\mathcal{A}$ such that $|\mathsf{adv}^0_{\mathcal{A}} - \mathsf{adv}^1_{\mathcal{A}}|$ is non-negligible. We can use $\mathcal{A}$ to break the security of ss. The reduction algorithm $\mathcal{B}$ receives a verification key vk* from the signature scheme's challenger. The reduction algorithm chooses all other components by itself. Next, during the pre-challenge decryption queries, if any decryption query has vk* in it and the signature verification passes, then the reduction algorithm outputs this as a forgery.

During the challenge phase, the reduction algorithm receives (m^*_0, m^*_1). It chooses β, and computes $M^* = \left(c^*_0, \left(c^*_{0,i}, c^*_{1,i}, c^*_{2,i}\right)\right)$ as in H_0. Finally, it sends M^* to the challenger, and receives signature σ^*. It sends $(\mathsf{vk}^*, M^*, \sigma^*)$ to $\mathcal{A}$.

The adversary then makes polynomially many decryption/key generation queries. If there exists some decryption query with verification key vk* that verifies, then the reduction algorithm outputs the corresponding message and signature as a forgery.

Clearly, $\mathcal{B}'s$ advantage is at least $\mathsf{adv}^1_{\mathcal{A}} - \mathsf{adv}^2_{\mathcal{A}}$.

Lemma 2. *Assuming* PRG *is a secure pseudorandom generator, for any PPT adversary* $\mathcal{A}$*, there exists a negligible function* $\mathsf{negl}(\cdot)$ *such that for all* $\lambda \in \mathbb{N}$*,* $|\mathsf{adv}^1_{\mathcal{A}} - \mathsf{adv}^2_{\mathcal{A}}| \leq \mathsf{negl}(\lambda)$*.*

Proof. The proof of this lemma follows from the security of PRG. The only difference between the two hybrids is the choice of a_i. In H_1, all a_i are chosen uniformly at random. In H_2, the challenger chooses $w_i \leftarrow \{0,1\}^\lambda$ for each i, and sets a_i as either $\mathsf{PRG}(v^*_i) - \mathsf{PRG}(w_i) - \mathsf{ss.vk}^* \cdot B$ or $\mathsf{PRG}(w_i) - \mathsf{PRG}(v^*_i) - \mathsf{ss.vk}^* \cdot B$, depending on s_i. Since w_i is not used anywhere else in both these hybrid experiments, we can use PRG security to argue that any PPT adversary has nearly identical advantage in H_1 and H_2.

Lemma 3. *Assuming correctness for decryptable ciphertexts for* PKE *scheme, for any adversary* $\mathcal{A}$*, there exists a negligible function* $\mathsf{negl}(\cdot)$ *such that for all* $\lambda \in \mathbb{N}$*,* $|\mathsf{adv}^2_{\mathcal{A}} - \mathsf{adv}^3_{\mathcal{A}}| \leq \mathsf{negl}(\lambda)$*.*

Proof. This is an information-theoretic step, and holds for all adversaries (not necessarily polynomial time). The only difference between these two hybrids is with respect to the decryption queries. In H_2, the challenger uses the routine PKE.Find to get a string d, and then checks if d is valid (using PKE.Check). In H_3, the challenger uses PKE.Find-1 to compute the string d. In fact, one can prove a more general statement: note that PKE.Find corresponds to PKE.Find-1 with last input set to be 0^n. We can show that for any two strings s^* and s', decryption using PKE.Find-1$(\cdot, \cdot, \cdot, s^*)$ is statistically indistinguishable from decryption using PKE.Find-1$(\cdot, \cdot, \cdot, s')$. For simplicity, we will present indistinguishability of H_2 and H_3, where in H_2, the challenger uses PKE.Find for decryption queries.

We will argue that with overwhelming probability, for any decryption query ct, either PKE.Find and PKE.Find-1 output the same d, or they output d and d' respectively but PKE.Check rejects both. In particular, it suffices to show that there exists a negligible function $\mathsf{negl}(\cdot)$ such that for all $\lambda \in \mathbb{N}$, $s^* \in [n]$ and ss.vk*, the following event's probability (denoted by p, parameterized by s^* and ss.vk*) is at most $\mathsf{negl}(\lambda)$:

$$\Pr\left[\begin{array}{l} \exists \mathsf{ct}\ \text{s.t.} \\ \mathsf{ct} = (\mathsf{ss.vk}, (c_0, (c_{0,i}, c_{1,i}, c_{2,i})), \sigma), \mathsf{ss.vk} \neq \mathsf{ss.vk}^* \\ \mathsf{PKE.Find}(\mathsf{pk}, \mathsf{sk}, \mathsf{ct}) = d \\ \mathsf{PKE.Find\text{-}1}(\mathsf{pk}, \mathsf{sk}', \mathsf{ct}, s^*) = d' \\ \mathsf{PKE.Check}(\mathsf{pk}, \mathsf{ct}, d) \neq \mathsf{PKE.Check}(\mathsf{pk}, \mathsf{ct}, d') \end{array} \middle| \begin{array}{l} \mathsf{HPRG.pp} \leftarrow \mathsf{HPRG.Setup}(1^\lambda, 1^\ell), B \leftarrow \{0,1\}^{\ell_{\mathrm{out}}} \\ v_i^*, w_i \leftarrow \{0,1\}^\lambda, \\ a_i = (\mathsf{PRG}(v_i^*) - \mathsf{PRG}(w_i)) \cdot (-1)^{s_i^*} - B \cdot \mathsf{ss.vk}^*, \\ (\mathsf{cpa.pk}_{b,i}, \mathsf{cpa.sk}_{b,i}) \leftarrow \mathsf{CPA.Setup}(1^\lambda) \\ \mathsf{sk} = (\mathsf{cpa.sk}_{0,i})_i, \mathsf{sk}' = \left(\mathsf{cpa.sk}_{s_i^*,i}\right)_i \end{array}\right]$$

where the probability is over the random coins used in $\mathsf{CCA.Setup}$. Now, $p \leq p_0 + p_1$, where p_b is defined as the following event's probability:

$$\Pr\left[\begin{array}{l} \exists \mathsf{ct}\ \text{s.t.} \\ \mathsf{ct} = (\mathsf{ss.vk}, (c_0, (c_{0,i}, c_{1,i}, c_{2,i})), \sigma), \mathsf{ss.vk} \neq \mathsf{ss.vk}^* \\ \mathsf{PKE.Find}(\mathsf{pk}, \mathsf{sk}, \mathsf{ct}) = d \\ \mathsf{PKE.Find\text{-}1}(\mathsf{pk}, \mathsf{sk}', \mathsf{ct}, s^*) = d' \\ i: \ \text{first index s.t.}\ s_i^* = 1, d_i = b, d_i' = \overline{b} \\ \mathsf{PKE.Check}(\mathsf{pk}, \mathsf{ct}, d) \neq \mathsf{PKE.Check}(\mathsf{pk}, \mathsf{ct}, d') \end{array} \middle| \begin{array}{l} \mathsf{HPRG.pp} \leftarrow \mathsf{HPRG.Setup}(1^\lambda, 1^\ell), B \leftarrow \{0,1\}^{\ell_{\mathrm{out}}} \\ v_i^*, w_i \leftarrow \{0,1\}^\lambda, \\ a_i = (\mathsf{PRG}(v_i^*) - \mathsf{PRG}(w_i)) \cdot (-1)^{s_i^*} - B \cdot \mathsf{ss.vk}^*, \\ (\mathsf{cpa.pk}_{b,i}, \mathsf{cpa.sk}_{b,i}) \leftarrow \mathsf{CPA.Setup}(1^\lambda) \\ \mathsf{sk} = (\mathsf{cpa.sk}_{0,i})_i, \mathsf{sk}' = \left(\mathsf{cpa.sk}_{s_i^*,i}\right)_i \end{array}\right]$$

We will show that $p_b \leq \mathsf{negl}(\cdot)$ for both $b \in \{0,1\}$. To prove this, let us first consider the following event:

$$p_{\mathsf{PRG}} = \Pr\left[\exists\ \alpha_1, \alpha_2 \in \{0,1\}^\lambda, i \in [n], \mathsf{ss.vk}\ \text{s.t.}\ \mathsf{PRG}(\alpha_1) = \mathsf{PRG}(\alpha_2) + a_i + B \cdot \mathsf{ss.vk}\right]$$

where the probability is over the choice of $B \leftarrow \{0,1\}^{\ell_{\mathrm{out}}}$ and $v_i^*, w_i \leftarrow \{0,1\}^\lambda$. Then $p_b \leq p_{\mathsf{PRG}} + p_b'$, where p_b' is like p_b, except for an additional condition that $\forall \gamma, \delta, \mathsf{PRG}(\gamma) \neq \mathsf{PRG}(\delta) + a_i + B \cdot \mathsf{ss.vk}$. It is formally defined as the following event's probability:

$$\Pr\left[\begin{array}{l} \exists \mathsf{ct}\ \text{s.t.} \\ \mathsf{ct} = (\mathsf{ss.vk}, (c_0, (c_{0,i}, c_{1,i}, c_{2,i})), \sigma), \mathsf{ss.vk} \neq \mathsf{ss.vk}^* \\ \mathsf{PKE.Find}(\mathsf{pk}, \mathsf{sk}, \mathsf{ct}) = d \\ \mathsf{PKE.Find\text{-}1}(\mathsf{pk}, \mathsf{sk}', \mathsf{ct}, s^*) = d' \\ i: \ \text{first index s.t.}\ s_i^* = 1, d_i = b, d_i' = \overline{b} \\ \forall \gamma, \delta, \mathsf{PRG}(\gamma) \neq \mathsf{PRG}(\delta) + a_i + B \cdot \mathsf{ss.vk} \\ \mathsf{PKE.Check}(\mathsf{pk}, \mathsf{ct}, d) \neq \mathsf{PKE.Check}(\mathsf{pk}, \mathsf{ct}, d') \end{array} \middle| \begin{array}{l} \mathsf{HPRG.pp} \leftarrow \mathsf{HPRG.Setup}(1^\lambda, 1^\ell), B \leftarrow \{0,1\}^{\ell_{\mathrm{out}}} \\ v_i^*, w_i \leftarrow \{0,1\}^\lambda, \\ a_i = (\mathsf{PRG}(v_i^*) - \mathsf{PRG}(w_i)) \cdot (-1)^{s_i^*} - B \cdot \mathsf{ss.vk}^*, \\ (\mathsf{cpa.pk}_{b,i}, \mathsf{cpa.sk}_{b,i}) \leftarrow \mathsf{CPA.Setup}(1^\lambda) \\ \mathsf{sk} = (\mathsf{cpa.sk}_{0,i})_i, \mathsf{sk}' = \left(\mathsf{cpa.sk}_{s_i^*,i}\right)_i \end{array}\right]$$

Hence, it suffices to show that $p_{\mathsf{PRG}} \leq \mathsf{negl}(\lambda)$, $p_0' \leq \mathsf{negl}(\lambda)$ and $p_1' \leq \mathsf{negl}(\lambda)$.

Claim 1. $p_{\mathsf{PRG}} \leq \mathsf{negl}(\lambda)$.

Proof. We will prove a stronger statement: for all $\mathsf{ss.vk}^*, s^*$ and $\{v_i, w_i\}_{i \in [n]}$, the following probability is at most $n \cdot 2^{-\lambda}$:

$$\Pr\left[\begin{array}{l} \exists\ \gamma, \delta \in \{0,1\}^\lambda, i \in [n], \mathsf{ss.vk} \neq \mathsf{ss.vk}^*\ \text{s.t.} \\ \mathsf{PRG}(\gamma) = \mathsf{PRG}(\delta) + (\mathsf{PRG}(v_i) - \mathsf{PRG}(w_i)) \cdot (-1)^{s_i^*} + B \cdot \mathsf{ss.vk} \end{array}\right]$$

where the probability is over the choice of B. Fix any integer $i \in [n]$. Consider the following sets.

$$S = \{\mathsf{PRG}(x) : x \in \{0,1\}^\lambda\}$$
$$S^- = \{\mathsf{PRG}(x) - \mathsf{PRG}(y) - (\mathsf{PRG}(v_i) - \mathsf{PRG}(w_i)) \cdot (-1)^{s_i^*} : x, y \in \{0,1\}^\lambda\}$$
$$S_{\mathsf{vk}}^- = \{(\mathsf{PRG}(x) - \mathsf{PRG}(y) - (\mathsf{PRG}(v_i) - \mathsf{PRG}(w_i)) \cdot (-1)^{s_i^*})/(\mathsf{ss.vk} - \mathsf{ss.vk}^*) :$$
$$x, y \in \{0,1\}^\lambda, \mathsf{ss.vk} \in \{0,1\}^{\ell_{\mathrm{vk}}}\}$$

The set S has size at most 2^λ. As a result, the set S^- has size at most $2^{2\lambda}$. Finally, the set S_{vk}^- has size at most $2^{2\lambda+\ell_{\mathsf{vk}}}$. If we choose a uniformly random element from $\{0,1\}^{\ell_{\mathsf{out}}} \equiv \{0,1\}^{3\lambda+\ell_{\mathsf{vk}}}$, then this element falls in S_{vk}^- with probability at most $2^{-\lambda}$. This concludes our proof.

Claim 2. $p'_0 = 0$.

Proof. This follows from the definitions of PKE.Find, PKE.Find-1 and p'_0. Note that PKE.Find sets $d_i = 0$ only if the decrypted value $1|v_i$ satisfies $\mathsf{PRG}(v_i) = c_{2,i}$, and PKE.Find-1 sets $d_i = 1$ only if the decrypted value $1|w_i$ satisfies $\mathsf{PRG}(w_i) + a_i + B \cdot \mathsf{ss.vk} = c_{2,i}$. This, together with the requirement in p'_0 that $\forall\ \gamma, \delta$, $\mathsf{PRG}(\gamma) \neq \mathsf{PRG}(\delta) + a_i + B \cdot \mathsf{ss.vk}$, implies that $p'_0 = 0$.

Claim 3. *Assuming correctness for decryptable ciphertexts , $p'_1 = 0$.*

Proof Intuition. We will first present an overview of the proof, and discuss a subtle but important point in the construction/proof.

Let E'_1 denote the event corresponding to p'_1. For this event to happen, there exists an index i such that $s^*_i = 1$, and the ith iteration of both PKE.Find and PKE.Find-1 fail to find a signal (that is, either the decryption fails, or the PRG check fails). Let d be the string output by PKE.Find, and d' the string output by PKE.Find-1 (therefore $d_i = \overline{d'_i} = 1$). We need to show that PKE.Check outputs $\perp$ for both d and d'. Suppose PKE.Check does not output $\perp$ for d. Then, this means that there exists a v such that $c_{1,i}$ is a PKE encryption of $1|v$ and $\mathsf{PRG}(v) + a_i + B \cdot \mathsf{ss.vk} = c_{2,i}$. In this case, the ith iteration of PKE.Find-1 should set $d'_i = 1$, which is a contradiction.

The other case, where PKE.Check does not output $\perp$ for d', is similar. This means there exists v, x such that $c_{0,i}$ is an encryption of $1|v$ for attribute x, $C(x) = 1$ and $\mathsf{PRG}(v) = c_{2,i}$. Using perfect correctness of the PKE scheme, we can argue that PKE.Find should have set $d_i = 0$, which is a contradiction.

Proof. Suppose $s^*_i = 1$, $d_i = 1$, $d'_i = 0$, and PKE.Check outputs different value for both d and d'. Let $\widetilde{r}_i = \mathsf{HPRG.Eval}(\mathsf{HPRG.pp}, d, i)$, $\widetilde{r}_i{}' = \mathsf{HPRG.Eval}(\mathsf{HPRG.pp}, d', i)$, $m \leftarrow \mathsf{CPA.Recover}(\mathsf{cpa.pk}_{1,i}, c_{1,i}, \widetilde{r}_i)$, $m' \leftarrow \mathsf{CPA.Recover}(\mathsf{cpa.pk}_{0,i}, c_{0,i}, \widetilde{r}_i{}')$. Since PKE.Check outputs different values for d and d', it does not output $\perp$ for at least one of them in the ith iteration. We will consider two cases.

Case 1: PKE.Check does not output $\perp$ for d in the ith iteration: As a result, $m = 1|v$, $c_{1,i} = \mathsf{CPA.Enc}(\mathsf{cpa.pk}_{1,i}, m; \widetilde{r}_i)$ and $\mathsf{PRG}(v) + a_i + B \cdot \mathsf{ss.vk} = c_{2,i}$. This means that $\mathsf{CPA.Dec}(\mathsf{sk}_{1,i}, c_{1,i}) = 1|v$ (by perfect correctness of the PKE decryption algorithm). However, this means $d'_i = 1$ (by definition of PKE.Find-1). Hence Case 1 cannot occur.

Case 2: PKE.Check does not output $\perp$ for d' in the ith iteration: As a result, $m = 1|v$, $c_{0,i} = \mathsf{CPA.Enc}(\mathsf{cpa.pk}_{0,i}, m; \widetilde{r}_i)$, and $\mathsf{PRG}(v) = c_{2,i}$. This means that $\mathsf{CPA.Dec}(\mathsf{cpa.sk}_{0,i}, c_{0,i}) = 1|v$ (since we have perfect correctness for PKE decryption). However, by definition of PKE.Find, $d_i = 0$. Hence Case 2 cannot occur.

Lemma 4. *Assuming* PKE *is* IND-CPA *secure, for any PPT adversary $\mathcal{A}$, there exists a negligible function* negl$(\cdot)$ *such that for all* $\lambda \in \mathbb{N}$, $|\mathsf{adv}_{\mathcal{A}}^3 - \mathsf{adv}_{\mathcal{A}}^4| \leq$ negl(λ).

Proof. The only difference in the two hybrids is with respect to the challenge ciphertext. In H_3, the challenger sets $c_{1,i}^*$ to be encryption of $0^{\lambda+1}$ for all $i \in [n]$ such that $s_i^* = 0$. In H_4, the challenger sets $c_{1,i}^*$ to be encryption of $1|w_i$. Note that the decryption queries require cpa.sk$_{1,i}$ only if $s_i^* = 1$. As a result, using the IND-CPA security of PKE, it follows that the two hybrids are computationally indistinguishable.

Lemma 5. *Assuming* PKE *is* IND-CPA *secure, for any PPT adversary $\mathcal{A}$, there exists a negligible function* negl$(\cdot)$ *such that for all* $\lambda \in \mathbb{N}$, $|\mathsf{adv}_{\mathcal{A}}^4 - \mathsf{adv}_{\mathcal{A}}^5| \leq$ negl(λ).

Proof. The proof of this lemma is similar to the proof of the previous lemma (Lemma 4). In H_4, the challenger sets $c_{0,i}^*$ to be encryption of $0^{\lambda+1}$ for all $i \in [n]$ such that $s_i^* = 1$. In H_5, the challenger sets $c_{0,i}^*$ to be encryption of $1|w_i$. Note that the decryption queries require cpa.sk$_{0,i}$ only if $s_i^* = 0$. As a result, using the IND-CPA security of PKE, it follows that the two hybrids are computationally indistinguishable.

Lemma 6. *Assuming correctness for decryptable ciphertexts for* PKE *scheme, for any adversary $\mathcal{A}$, there exists a negligible function* negl$(\cdot)$ *such that for all* $\lambda \in \mathbb{N}$, $|\mathsf{adv}_{\mathcal{A}}^5 - \mathsf{adv}_{\mathcal{A}}^6| \leq$ negl(λ).

Proof. This proof is similar to the proof of Lemma 3. In particular, recall that the proof of Lemma 3 works for any s^*, s', and note that PKE.Find-2 simply corresponds to PKE.Find-1$(\cdot, \cdot, \cdot, 1^n)$.

Lemma 7. $\mathsf{adv}_{\mathcal{A}}^6 = \mathsf{adv}_{\mathcal{A}}^7$.

Proof. This follows from the definition of the two hybrids. The only difference between H_6 and H_7 is that the variable names v_i^* and w_i are swapped if $s_i^* = 1$. As a result, any adversary has identical advantage in both hybrids.

Lemma 8. *Assuming* HPRG *satisfies Definition 3, for any PPT adversary $\mathcal{A}$, there exists a negligible function* negl$(\cdot)$ *such that for all* $\lambda \in \mathbb{N}$, $|\mathsf{adv}_{\mathcal{A}}^7 - \mathsf{adv}_{\mathcal{A}}^8| \leq$ negl(λ).

Proof. Suppose there exists a PPT adversary $\mathcal{A}$ such that $|\mathsf{adv}_{\mathcal{A}}^7 - \mathsf{adv}_{\mathcal{A}}^8| = \epsilon$. We will use $\mathcal{A}$ to build a PPT reduction algorithm $\mathcal{B}$ that breaks the security of HPRG.

The reduction algorithm first receives HPRG.pp and $\left(r_0^*, \left(r_{b,i}^*\right)_{i \in [n], b \in \{0,1\}}\right)$ from the challenger. It chooses $\{v_i^*, w_i\}$, (ss.sk*, ss.vk*), sets $\{a_i\}$, chooses $B \leftarrow$

$\{0,1\}^{\ell_{\text{out}}}$, $\{(\text{cpa.pk}_{b,i}, \text{cpa.sk}_{b,i}) \leftarrow \text{CPA.Setup}(1^{\lambda})\}$ and sends $(\text{HPRG.pp}, B,$ $(a_i, \text{cpa.pk}_{b,i}))$ to $\mathcal{A}$. Next, it receives decryption queries, which can be handled using $\{\text{cpa.sk}_{1,i}\}$ (as in H_6/H_7). For the challenge ciphertext, it chooses $\beta \leftarrow \{0,1\}$, sets $c_0^* = m_b^* \oplus r_0^*$, computes $c_{0,i}^* = \text{CPA.Enc}(\text{cpa.pk}_{0,i}, 1|v_i^*; r_{0,i}^*)$, $c_{1,i}^* = \text{CPA.Enc}(\text{cpa.pk}_{1,i}, 1|w_i; r_{1,i}^*)$, $c_{2,i}^* = \text{PRG}(v_i^*) + a_i + B \cdot \text{ss.vk}^*$ and finally computes a signature on $(c^*, (c_{0,i}^*, c_{1,i}^*, c_{2,i}^*))$. It sends the ciphertext to the adversary. The post-challenge queries are handled as the pre-challenge queries. Finally, the adversary sends its guess β'. If $\beta \neq \beta'$, the reduction algorithm guesses that all $r_{b,i}^*$ are uniformly random. This reduction algorithm has advantage ϵ in the hinting PRG security game.

Lemma 9. *For any adversary* $\mathcal{A}$, $\text{adv}_{\mathcal{A}}^8 = 0$.

Proof. Note that in hybrid H_8, there is no information about m_β in the challenge ciphertext, since c_0^* is uniformly random.

5 CCA Secure Predicate Encryption Scheme

Let $\text{PredE} = (\text{PredE.Setup}, \text{PredE.Enc}, \text{PredE.KeyGen}, \text{PredE.Dec})$ be a predicate encryption scheme with randomness-decryptable ciphertexts and one-sided security against chosen plaintext attacks, $\text{PKE} = (\text{CPA.Setup}, \text{CPA.Enc}, \text{CPA.Dec})$ an IND-CPA secure public key encryption scheme with randomness-decryptable ciphertexts, $\text{S} = (\text{ss.Setup}, \text{ss.Sign}, \text{ss.Verify})$ a strongly unforgeable one time signature scheme and $\text{HPRG} = (\text{HPRG.Setup}, \text{HPRG.Eval})$ a hinting PRG scheme. We will assume both our encryption schemes have message space $\{0,1\}^{\lambda+1}$. Let $\ell_{\text{PredE}}(\cdot)$ be a polynomial representing the number of bits of randomness used by PredE.Enc, $\ell_{\text{PKE}}(\cdot)$ the number of random bits used by CPA.Enc, and $\ell_{\text{vk}}(\cdot)$ the size of verification keys output by ss.Setup. For simplicity of notation, we will assume $\ell(\cdot) = \ell_{\text{PredE}}(\cdot) = \ell_{\text{PKE}}(\cdot)$,[8] $\ell_{\text{out}}(\lambda) = \ell_{\text{vk}}(\lambda) + 3\lambda$ and $\text{PRG}_\lambda : \{0,1\}^\lambda \rightarrow \{0,1\}^{\ell_{\text{out}}(\lambda)}$ a family of secure pseudorandom generators.

We will now describe our CCA-one-sided secure predicate encryption scheme $\text{PredE}_{\text{CCA}} = (\text{PredE}_{\text{CCA}}.\text{Setup}, \text{PredE}_{\text{CCA}}.\text{Enc}, \text{PredE}_{\text{CCA}}.\text{KeyGen}, \text{PredE}_{\text{CCA}}.\text{Dec})$ with message space $\mathcal{M}_\lambda = \{0,1\}^{\ell(\lambda)}$. For simplicity of notation, we will skip the dependence of ℓ and ℓ_{out} on λ.

$\text{PredE}_{\text{CCA}}.\text{Setup}(1^\lambda)$: The setup algorithm first chooses $(\text{HPRG.pp}, 1^n) \leftarrow \text{HPRG.Setup}(1^\lambda, 1^\ell)$. Next it chooses n different PredE keys and PKE keys. Let $(\text{pred.msk}_i, \text{pred.pk}_i) \leftarrow \text{PredE.Setup}(1^\lambda)$, $(\text{cpa.sk}_i, \text{cpa.pk}_i) \leftarrow \text{CPA.Setup}(1^\lambda)$ for each $i \in [n]$. It then chooses $a_i \leftarrow \{0,1\}^{\ell_{\text{out}}}$ for each $i \in [n]$ and $B \leftarrow \{0,1\}^{\ell_{\text{out}}}$. It sets $\text{pe.cca.pk} = \left(\text{HPRG.pp}, B, (a_i, \text{pred.pk}_i, \text{cpa.pk}_i)_{i \in [n]}\right)$ and $\text{pe.cca.msk} = (\text{pred.msk}_i, \text{cpa.sk}_i)_{i \in [n]}$.

---

[8] Alternatively, we could set ℓ to be max of these two polynomials.

$\mathsf{PredE}_{\mathsf{CCA}}.\mathsf{Enc}(\mathsf{pe.cca.pk}, m, x)$: Let $\mathsf{pe.cca.pk} = (\mathsf{HPRG.pp}, B, (a_i, \mathsf{pred.pk}_i,$
$\mathsf{cpa.pk}_i)_{i \in [n]})$. The encryption algorithm first chooses $s \leftarrow \{0,1\}^n$. It
sets $c_0 = \mathsf{HPRG.Eval}(\mathsf{HPRG.pp}, s, 0) \oplus m$. Next, it chooses signature keys
$(\mathsf{ss.sk}, \mathsf{ss.vk}) \leftarrow \mathsf{ss.Setup}(1^\lambda)$. For each $i \in [n]$, it chooses $v_i \leftarrow \{0,1\}^\lambda$ and
$r_i \leftarrow \{0,1\}^\ell$, sets $\tilde{r}_i = \mathsf{HPRG.Eval}(\mathsf{HPRG.pp}, s, i)$ and does the following:
- If $s_i = 0$, it sets $c_{0,i} = \mathsf{PredE.Enc}(\mathsf{pred.pk}_i, 1|v_i, x; \tilde{r}_i)$, $c_{1,i} = \mathsf{CPA.Enc}$
  $(\mathsf{cpa.pk}_i, 0^{\lambda+1}; r_i)$ and $c_{2,i} = \mathsf{PRG}(v_i)$.
- If $s_i = 1$, it sets $c_{0,i} = \mathsf{PredE.Enc}(\mathsf{pred.pk}_i, 0^{\lambda+1}, x; r_i)$, $c_{1,i} = \mathsf{CPA.Enc}$
  $(\mathsf{cpa.pk}_i, 1|v_i; \tilde{r}_i)$ and $c_{2,i} = \mathsf{PRG}(v_i) + a_i + B \cdot \mathsf{ss.vk}$.[9]

Finally, it sets $M = (c_0, (c_{0,i}, c_{1,i}, c_{2,i})_{i \in [n]})$, computes $\sigma \leftarrow \mathsf{ss.Sign}(\mathsf{ss.sk}, M)$
and outputs $(\mathsf{ss.vk}, M, \sigma)$ as the ciphertext.

$\mathsf{PredE}_{\mathsf{CCA}}.\mathsf{KeyGen}(\mathsf{pe.cca.msk}, C)$: Let $\mathsf{pe.cca.msk} = (\mathsf{pred.msk}_i, \mathsf{cpa.sk}_i)_{i \in [n]}$. The
key generation algorithm computes $\mathsf{pred.sk}_i \leftarrow \mathsf{PredE.KeyGen}(\mathsf{pred.msk}_i, C)$
and outputs $\mathsf{pe.cca.sk} = (C, (\mathsf{pred.sk}_i)_{i \in [n]})$.

$\mathsf{PredE}_{\mathsf{CCA}}.\mathsf{Dec}(\mathsf{pe.cca.sk}, \mathsf{pe.cca.pk}, \mathsf{pe.cca.ct})$: Let the ciphertext $\mathsf{pe.cca.ct}$ be
parsed as $(\mathsf{ss.vk}, M = (c_0, (c_{0,i}, c_{1,i}, c_{2,i})_{i \in [n]}), \sigma)$ and $\mathsf{pe.cca.sk} =$
$(C, (\mathsf{pred.sk}_i)_{i \in [n]})$. The decryption algorithm first verifies the signature σ.
It checks if $\mathsf{ss.Verify}(\mathsf{ss.vk}, M, \sigma) = 1$, else it outputs $\bot$.

Next, the decryption algorithm computes $d = \mathsf{Find}(\mathsf{pe.cca.pk}, \mathsf{pe.cca.sk},$
$\mathsf{pe.cca.ct})$ (where Find is defined in Fig. 5), and outputs $\mathsf{Check}(\mathsf{pe.cca.pk},$
$\mathsf{pe.cca.ct}, C, d)$ (where Check is defined in Fig. 6).

$\mathsf{Find}(\mathsf{pe.cca.pk}, \mathsf{pe.cca.sk}, \mathsf{pe.cca.ct})$

Inputs: Public Key $\mathsf{pe.cca.pk} = (\mathsf{HPRG.pp}, B, (a_i, \mathsf{pred.pk}_i, \mathsf{cpa.pk}_i)_{i \in [n]})$

Secret Key $\mathsf{pe.cca.sk} = (\mathsf{pred.sk}_i)_{i \in [n]}$

Ciphertext $\mathsf{pe.cca.ct} = (\mathsf{ss.vk}, M = (c_0, (c_{0,i}, c_{1,i}, c_{2,i})_{i \in [n]}), \sigma)$

Output: $d \in \{0,1\}^n$

- For each $i \in [n]$, do the following:
  1. Let $m_i = \mathsf{PredE.Dec}(\mathsf{pred.sk}_i, c_{0,i})$.
  2. If $m_i = 1|v_i$ and $\mathsf{PRG}(v_i) = c_{2,i}$, set $d_i = 0$. Else set $d_i = 1$.
- Output $d = d_1 d_2 \ldots d_n$.

Fig. 5. Routine Find

---

[9] Here, we assume the verification key is embedded in $\mathbb{F}_{2^{\ell_{\mathsf{out}}}}$, and the addition and
multiplication are performed in $\mathbb{F}_{2^{\ell_{\mathsf{out}}}}$.

Check(pe.cca.pk, pe.cca.ct, C, d)

Inputs: Public Key pe.cca.pk $= \left(\text{HPRG.pp}, B, (a_i, \text{pred.pk}_i, \text{cpa.pk}_i)_{i \in [n]}\right)$

Ciphertext pe.cca.ct $= \left(\text{ss.vk}, M = \left(c_0, (c_{0,i}, c_{1,i}, c_{2,i})_{i \in [n]}\right), \sigma\right)$

Circuit $C \in \mathcal{C}_\lambda$

$d \in \{0, 1\}^n$

Output: msg $\in \{0, 1\}^\ell$

- Let flag $=$ true. For $i = 1$ to n, do the following:
  1. Let $\widetilde{r}_i = \text{HPRG.Eval}(\text{HPRG.pp}, d, i)$.
  2. If $d_i = 0$, let $y \leftarrow \text{PredE.Recover}(\text{pred.pk}_i, c_{0,i}, \widetilde{r}_i)$. Perform the following checks. If any of the checks fail, set flag $=$ false and exit loop.
     - $y = (m, x) \neq \bot$.
     - $C(x) = 1$.
     - $\text{PredE.Enc}(\text{pred.pk}_i, m, x; \widetilde{r}_i) = c_{0,i}$.
     - $m = 1|v$ and $\text{PRG}(v) = c_{2,i}$.
  3. If $d_i = 1$, let $m \leftarrow \text{CPA.Recover}(\text{cpa.pk}_i, c_{1,i}, \widetilde{r}_i)$. Perform the following checks. If any of the checks fail, set flag $=$ false and exit loop.
     - $m \neq \bot$.
     - $\text{CPA.Enc}(\text{cpa.pk}_i, m; \widetilde{r}_i) = c_{1,i}$.
     - $m = 1|v$ and $c_{2,i} = \text{PRG}(v) + a_i + B \cdot \text{ss.vk}$.
- If flag $=$ true, output $c_0 \oplus \text{HPRG.Eval}(\text{HPRG.pp}, d, 0)$. Else output $\bot$.

Fig. 6. Routine Check

5.1 Security Proof

The security proof works via a sequence of hybrid experiments, and the hybrid experiments are very similar to the ones used for the PKE construction. Due to space constraints, the proof of security is included in the full version of our paper.

References

1. Attrapadung, N.: Dual system encryption via doubly selective security: framework, fully secure functional encryption for regular languages, and more. In: Nguyen, P.Q., Oswald, E. (eds.) EUROCRYPT 2014. LNCS, vol. 8441, pp. 557–577. Springer, Heidelberg (2014). https://doi.org/10.1007/978-3-642-55220-5_31
2. Attrapadung, N., Libert, B., de Panafieu, E.: Expressive key-policy attribute-based encryption with constant-size ciphertexts. In: Catalano, D., Fazio, N., Gennaro, R., Nicolosi, A. (eds.) PKC 2011. LNCS, vol. 6571, pp. 90–108. Springer, Heidelberg (2011). https://doi.org/10.1007/978-3-642-19379-8_6

3. Bellare, M., Rogaway, P.: Random oracles are practical: a paradigm for designing efficient protocols. In: ACM Conference on Computer and Communications Security, pp. 62–73 (1993)

4. Blömer, J., Liske, G.: Construction of fully CCA-secure predicate encryptions from pair encoding schemes. In: Sako, K. (ed.) CT-RSA 2016. LNCS, vol. 9610, pp. 431–447. Springer, Cham (2016). https://doi.org/10.1007/978-3-319-29485-8_25

5. Blum, M., Feldman, P., Micali, S.: Non-interactive zero-knowledge and its applications. In: STOC, pp. 103–112 (1988)

6. Boneh, D., et al.: Fully key-homomorphic encryption, arithmetic circuit ABE and compact garbled circuits. In: Nguyen, P.Q., Oswald, E. (eds.) EUROCRYPT 2014. LNCS, vol. 8441, pp. 533–556. Springer, Heidelberg (2014). https://doi.org/10.1007/978-3-642-55220-5_30

7. Boneh, D., Waters, B.: Conjunctive, subset, and range queries on encrypted data. In: Vadhan, S.P. (ed.) TCC 2007. LNCS, vol. 4392, pp. 535–554. Springer, Heidelberg (2007). https://doi.org/10.1007/978-3-540-70936-7_29. http://dl.acm.org/citation.cfm?id=1760749.1760788

8. Brakerski, Z., Lombardi, A., Segev, G., Vaikuntanathan, V.: Anonymous IBE, leakage resilience and circular security from new assumptions. In: Nielsen, J.B., Rijmen, V. (eds.) EUROCRYPT 2018, Part I. LNCS, vol. 10820, pp. 535–564. Springer, Cham (2018). https://doi.org/10.1007/978-3-319-78381-9_20

9. Canetti, R., Halevi, S., Katz, J.: Chosen-ciphertext security from identity-based encryption. In: Cachin, C., Camenisch, J.L. (eds.) EUROCRYPT 2004. LNCS, vol. 3027, pp. 207–222. Springer, Heidelberg (2004). https://doi.org/10.1007/978-3-540-24676-3_13

10. Chase, M.: Multi-authority attribute based encryption. In: Vadhan, S.P. (ed.) TCC 2007. LNCS, vol. 4392, pp. 515–534. Springer, Heidelberg (2007). https://doi.org/10.1007/978-3-540-70936-7_28

11. Chase, M., Chow, S.S.M.: Improving privacy and security in multi-authority attribute-based encryption. In: ACM Conference on Computer and Communications Security, pp. 121–130 (2009)

12. Chen, J., Gay, R., Wee, H.: Improved dual system ABE in prime-order groups via predicate encodings. In: Oswald, E., Fischlin, M. (eds.) EUROCRYPT 2015, Part II. LNCS, vol. 9057, pp. 595–624. Springer, Heidelberg (2015). https://doi.org/10.1007/978-3-662-46803-6_20

13. Dolev, D., Dwork, C., Naor, M.: Non-malleable cryptography (extended abstract). In: Proceedings of the 23rd Annual ACM Symposium on Theory of Computing, New Orleans, Louisiana, USA, 5–8 May 1991, pp. 542–552 (1991)

14. Döttling, N., Garg, S.: From selective IBE to full IBE and selective HIBE. In: Kalai, Y., Reyzin, L. (eds.) TCC 2017, Part I. LNCS, vol. 10677, pp. 372–408. Springer, Cham (2017). https://doi.org/10.1007/978-3-319-70500-2_13

15. Döttling, N., Garg, S.: Identity-based encryption from the Diffie-Hellman assumption. In: Katz, J., Shacham, H. (eds.) CRYPTO 2017, Part I. LNCS, vol. 10401, pp. 537–569. Springer, Cham (2017). https://doi.org/10.1007/978-3-319-63688-7_18

16. Döttling, N., Garg, S., Hajiabadi, M., Masny, D.: New constructions of identity-based and key-dependent message secure encryption schemes. In: Abdalla, M., Dahab, R. (eds.) PKC 2018, Part I. LNCS, vol. 10769, pp. 3–31. Springer, Cham (2018). https://doi.org/10.1007/978-3-319-76578-5_1

17. Dwork, C., Naor, M., Reingold, O.: Immunizing encryption schemes from decryption errors. In: Cachin, C., Camenisch, J.L. (eds.) EUROCRYPT 2004. LNCS, vol. 3027, pp. 342–360. Springer, Heidelberg (2004). https://doi.org/10.1007/978-3-540-24676-3_21

18. Feige, U., Shamir, A.: Witness indistinguishable and witness hiding protocols. In: Proceedings of the 22nd Annual ACM Symposium on Theory of Computing, Baltimore, Maryland, USA, 13–17 May 1990, pp. 416–426 (1990)
19. Fiat, A., Naor, M.: Broadcast encryption. In: Stinson, D.R. (ed.) CRYPTO 1993. LNCS, vol. 773, pp. 480–491. Springer, Heidelberg (1994). https://doi.org/10.1007/3-540-48329-2_40
20. Fujisaki, E., Okamoto, T.: Secure integration of asymmetric and symmetric encryption schemes. In: Wiener, M. (ed.) CRYPTO 1999. LNCS, vol. 1666, pp. 537–554. Springer, Heidelberg (1999). https://doi.org/10.1007/3-540-48405-1_34
21. Garg, S., Gay, R., Hajiabadi, M.: New techniques for efficient trapdoor functions and applications. Cryptology ePrint Archive, Report 2018/872 (2018). https://eprint.iacr.org/2018/872
22. Garg, S., Hajiabadi, M.: Trapdoor functions from the computational Diffie-Hellman assumption. In: Shacham, H., Boldyreva, A. (eds.) CRYPTO 2018, Part II. LNCS, vol. 10992, pp. 362–391. Springer, Cham (2018). https://doi.org/10.1007/978-3-319-96881-0_13
23. Gorbunov, S., Vaikuntanathan, V., Wee, H.: Attribute-based encryption for circuits. In: STOC (2013)
24. Gorbunov, S., Vaikuntanathan, V., Wee, H.: Predicate encryption for circuits from LWE. In: Gennaro, R., Robshaw, M. (eds.) CRYPTO 2015, Part II. LNCS, vol. 9216, pp. 503–523. Springer, Heidelberg (2015). https://doi.org/10.1007/978-3-662-48000-7_25
25. Goyal, R., Koppula, V., Waters, B.: Lockable obfuscation. In: 58th IEEE Annual Symposium on Foundations of Computer Science, FOCS 2017, pp. 612–621 (2017)
26. Goyal, V., Pandey, O., Sahai, A., Waters, B.: Attribute-based encryption for fine-grained access control of encrypted data. In: Proceedings of the 13th ACM Conference on Computer and Communications Security, CCS 2006 (2006)
27. Katz, J., Sahai, A., Waters, B.: Predicate encryption supporting disjunctions, polynomial equations, and inner products. In: Smart, N. (ed.) EUROCRYPT 2008. LNCS, vol. 4965, pp. 146–162. Springer, Heidelberg (2008). https://doi.org/10.1007/978-3-540-78967-3_9
28. Kiltz, E.: Chosen-ciphertext security from tag-based encryption. In: Halevi, S., Rabin, T. (eds.) TCC 2006. LNCS, vol. 3876, pp. 581–600. Springer, Heidelberg (2006). https://doi.org/10.1007/11681878_30
29. Kitagawa, F., Matsuda, T., Tanaka, K.: CCA security and trapdoor functions via key-dependent-message security. Cryptology ePrint Archive, Report 2019/291 (2019). https://eprint.iacr.org/2019/291
30. Lewko, A.B., Okamoto, T., Sahai, A., Takashima, K., Waters, B.: Fully secure functional encryption: attribute-based encryption and (hierarchical) inner product encryption. In: Gilbert, H. (ed.) EUROCRYPT 2010. LNCS, vol. 6110, pp. 62–91. Springer, Heidelberg (2010). https://doi.org/10.1007/978-3-642-13190-5_4
31. Lewko, A.B., Waters, B.: Decentralizing attribute-based encryption. In: Paterson, K.G. (ed.) EUROCRYPT 2011. LNCS, vol. 6632, pp. 568–588. Springer, Heidelberg (2011). https://doi.org/10.1007/978-3-642-20465-4_31
32. Lewko, A.B., Waters, B.: New proof methods for attribute-based encryption: achieving full security through selective techniques. In: Safavi-Naini, R., Canetti, R. (eds.) CRYPTO 2012. LNCS, vol. 7417, pp. 180–198. Springer, Heidelberg (2012). https://doi.org/10.1007/978-3-642-32009-5_12

33. Lombardi, A., Quach, W., Rothblum, R.D., Wichs, D., Wu, D.J.: New constructions of reusable designated-verifier NIZKs. In: Boldyreva, A., Micciancia, D. (eds.) CRYPTO 2019. LNCS, vol. 11694, pp. 670–700. Springer, Heidelberg (2019). https://eprint.iacr.org/2019/242

34. Nandi, M., Pandit, T.: Generic conversions from CPA to CCA secure functional encryption. Cryptology ePrint Archive, Report 2015/457 (2015). https://eprint.iacr.org/2015/457

35. Naor, M.: Bit commitment using pseudo-randomness. In: Brassard, G. (ed.) CRYPTO 1989. LNCS, vol. 435, pp. 128–136. Springer, New York (1990). https://doi.org/10.1007/0-387-34805-0_13

36. Naor, M., Yung, M.: Public-key cryptosystems provably secure against chosen ciphertext attacks. In: Proceedings of the 22nd Annual ACM Symposium on Theory of Computing, Baltimore, Maryland, USA, 13–17 May 1990, pp. 427–437 (1990)

37. Okamoto, T., Takashima, K.: Fully secure functional encryption with general relations from the decisional linear assumption. In: Rabin, T. (ed.) CRYPTO 2010. LNCS, vol. 6223, pp. 191–208. Springer, Heidelberg (2010). https://doi.org/10.1007/978-3-642-14623-7_11

38. Peikert, C., Shiehian, S.: Noninteractive zero knowledge for NP from (plain) learning with errors. Cryptology ePrint Archive, Report 2019/158 (2019). https://eprint.iacr.org/2019/158

39. Peikert, C., Waters, B.: Lossy trapdoor functions and their applications. In: Proceedings of the 40th Annual ACM Symposium on Theory of Computing, Victoria, British Columbia, Canada, 17–20 May 2008, pp. 187–196 (2008)

40. Rackoff, C., Simon, D.R.: Non-interactive zero-knowledge proof of knowledge and chosen ciphertext attack. In: Feigenbaum, J. (ed.) CRYPTO 1991. LNCS, vol. 576, pp. 433–444. Springer, Heidelberg (1992). https://doi.org/10.1007/3-540-46766-1_35

41. Rosen, A., Segev, G.: Chosen-ciphertext security via correlated products. SIAM J. Comput. **39**(7), 3058–3088 (2010)

42. Sahai, A., Waters, B.: Fuzzy identity-based encryption. In: Cramer, R. (ed.) EUROCRYPT 2005. LNCS, vol. 3494, pp. 457–473. Springer, Heidelberg (2005). https://doi.org/10.1007/11426639_27

43. Shoup, V.: Why chosen ciphertext security matters (1998)

44. Waters, B.: Dual system encryption: realizing fully secure IBE and HIBE under simple assumptions. In: Halevi, S. (ed.) CRYPTO 2009. LNCS, vol. 5677, pp. 619–636. Springer, Heidelberg (2009). https://doi.org/10.1007/978-3-642-03356-8_36

45. Wee, H.: Dual system encryption via predicate encodings. In: Lindell, Y. (ed.) TCC 2014. LNCS, vol. 8349, pp. 616–637. Springer, Heidelberg (2014). https://doi.org/10.1007/978-3-642-54242-8_26

46. Wichs, D., Zirdelis, G.: Obfuscating compute-and-compare programs under LWE. In: 58th IEEE Annual Symposium on Foundations of Computer Science, FOCS 2017, pp. 600–611 (2017)

47. Yamada, S., Attrapadung, N., Hanaoka, G., Kunihiro, N.: Generic constructions for chosen-ciphertext secure attribute based encryption. In: Catalano, D., Fazio, N., Gennaro, R., Nicolosi, A. (eds.) PKC 2011. LNCS, vol. 6571, pp. 71–89. Springer, Heidelberg (2011). https://doi.org/10.1007/978-3-642-19379-8_5

Match Me if You Can: Matchmaking Encryption and Its Applications

Giuseppe Ateniese[1], Danilo Francati[1(✉)], David Nuñez[2], and Daniele Venturi[3]

[1] Stevens Institute of Technology, Hoboken, NJ, USA
dfrancat@stevens.edu
[2] NuCypher, San Francisco, CA, USA
[3] Department of Computer Science, Sapienza University of Rome, Rome, Italy

Abstract. We introduce a new form of encryption that we name *matchmaking encryption* (ME). Using ME, sender S and receiver R (each with its own attributes) can both specify policies the other party must satisfy in order for the message to be revealed. The main security guarantee is that of privacy-preserving policy matching: During decryption nothing is leaked beyond the fact that a match occurred/did not occur.

ME opens up new ways of secretly communicating, and enables several new applications where both participants can specify fine-grained access policies to encrypted data. For instance, in social matchmaking, S can encrypt a file containing his/her personal details and specify a policy so that the file can be decrypted only by his/her ideal partner. On the other end, a receiver R will be able to decrypt the file only if S corresponds to his/her ideal partner defined through a policy.

On the theoretical side, we define security for ME, as well as provide generic frameworks for constructing ME from functional encryption. These constructions need to face the technical challenge of simultaneously checking the policies chosen by S and R, to avoid any leakage.

On the practical side, we construct an efficient identity-based scheme for equality policies, with provable security in the random oracle model under the standard BDH assumption. We implement and evaluate our scheme and provide experimental evidence that our construction is practical. We also apply identity-based ME to a concrete use case, in particular for creating an anonymous bulletin board over a Tor network.

Keywords: Secret handshake · Attribute-based encryption · Social matchmaking · Tor

1 Introduction

Intelligence operations often require secret agents to communicate with other agents from different organizations. When two spies meet to exchange secrets, they use a type of secret handshake to ensure that the parties participating in the exchange are the ones intended. For example, an FBI agent may want to communicate only with CIA agents, and if this is not the case, the communication

© International Association for Cryptologic Research 2019
A. Boldyreva and D. Micciancio (Eds.): CRYPTO 2019, LNCS 11693, pp. 701–731, 2019.
https://doi.org/10.1007/978-3-030-26951-7_24

should drop without revealing membership information and why the communication failed. This form of *live drop* communication,[1] when parties are online and interact, has been implemented in cryptography and it is referred to as secret handshake (SH) protocol [9]. In SH, two parties agree on the same secret key only if they are both from the same group. Privacy is preserved in the sense that, if the handshake fails, nobody learns anything relevant other than the participants are not in the same group. In SH with dynamic matching [6], groups and roles can even be determined just before the protocol execution.

SH can be thought of as an evolution of traditional key exchange protocols, where protecting privacy of the participants assumes an essential role. As any other key agreement protocol, SH is inherently interactive and its purpose is for the parties to converge on a secret key. A natural question is whether there exists a non-interactive version of SH, in a similar way as ElGamal public-key encryption can be interpreted as a non-interactive version of the classical Diffie-Hellman key exchange. This new cryptographic primitive would allow senders to encrypt messages offline given only the public key of the receiver, thus getting rid of real-time interactions, while at the same time providing strong privacy guarantees for time-delayed communications such as email. Non-interactivity mitigates or prevents *traffic analysis* which affects all SH protocols when deployed within a network environment (see, e.g., [6]). In particular, increased traffic between nodes may signal to an adversary that the SH protocol was successful, even though the nodes' group affiliations and roles remain private.

Non-interactive SH is even more relevant if we consider that the most common method of espionage tradecraft is the *dead drop* one, (See footnote 1) which maintains operational security by using a secret location for the exchange of information, thus relieving the agents from meeting in person. Unfortunately, dead-drop communication cannot be captured by any existing cryptographic primitive, since it requires a form of expressiveness that is not currently provided by encryption and its more advanced forms.

Matchmaking Encryption. In this paper, we are revamping the encryption primitive and introducing a new concept termed *"Matchmaking Encryption"*, or ME. In ME, a trusted authority generates encryption and decryption keys associated, respectively, to attributes of the sender and the receiver. The authority also generates an additional decryption key for the receiver, associated to an arbitrary policy of its choice. The sender of the message can specify on the fly an arbitrary policy the receiver must satisfy in order for the message to be revealed. The guarantee is now that the receiver will obtain the message if and only if a match occurs (i.e., the sender's attributes match the receiver's policy and vice-versa). Nothing beyond that is leaked; furthermore, the sender's attributes are certified by the authority, so that no malicious sender can forge a valid ciphertext which embeds fake attributes.

For instance, the sender, during encryption, can specify that the message is intended for an FBI agent that lives in NYC. The receiver, during decryption,

---

[1] See https://en.wikipedia.org/wiki/Dead_drop.

can also specify that he wants to read messages only if they come from CIA agents. If any of these two policies is not satisfied, the message remains secret, but nobody learns which policy failed. In this vein, ME can be seen as a non-interactive version of SH, but with much more enhanced functionality. Indeed, an SH works only for groups and roles, while attribute-based key agreements [25] do not consider privacy. We refer the reader to Sect. 1.3 for a comparison between ME and other primitives in the realm of attribute-based cryptography.

Other killer applications of ME are those where the receiver must be sheltered from the actual content of messages to avoid liability, inconvenience or inappropriateness. ME naturally tackles *social matchmaking* confidentiality, where potential partners open files intended for them but only if they contain the traits of the desired person; if decryption fails, nobody learns why, so that privacy is preserved. Encrypting bids (or votes) under ME provides an exciting twist to well-studied problems. Bidders send private bids to a collector and specify the conditions under which the encryption should be opened. The collector opens only the bids that match specific requirements. If decryption fails, the collector does not learn why, and the actual bid (or vote) remain sealed. ME avoids exposing information connected to unlooked-for bids which could influence the receiver and adversely affect the bidding process outcome.

ME also supports marginalized and dissident communities in authoritarian countries. It can act as an enabler for journalists, political activists and minorities in free-speech technical applications such as SecurePost [35] that provides verified group anonymity. Indeed, in their thorough study [35], the authors reveal that, in authoritarian countries, anonymous communication may not be credible and cannot be trusted since sources are unknown.[2] ME provides a comprehensive technical solution for censorship-resistant communication while providing source authenticity and strong privacy guarantees that cannot be obtained with existing tools. For instance, the ability to check ciphertexts against a policy before decryption allows journalists or activists to vet messages and avoid exposure to unwanted information that would make them liable. To this end, in Sect. 6, we introduce and implement a privacy-preserving bulletin board that combines Tor hidden services with ME to allow parties to collect information from anonymous but authentic sources.

1.1 Our Contributions

We initiate a systematic study of ME, both in terms of definitions and constructions. Our main contributions are summarized below.

Syntax of ME. In ME, a trusted authority publishes a master public key mpk, associated to a master secret key msk. The master secret key msk is used by the authority to generate three types of keys: (i) An encryption key ek_σ, associated with attributes σ for the sender (created using an algorithm SKGen); (ii) A decryption key dk_ρ, associated with attributes ρ for the receiver (created using

---

[2] See https://www.news.ucsb.edu/2019/019308/anonymous-yet-trustworthy.

an algorithm RKGen); (iii) A decryption key dk_S, associated to a policy S that the sender's attributes should satisfy, but that is chosen by the receiver (created using an algorithm PolGen).

A sender with attributes σ, and corresponding encryption key ek_σ obtained from the authority, can encrypt a plaintext m by additionally specifying a policy R (chosen on the fly), thus yielding a ciphertext c that is associated with both σ and R. Finally, the receiver can attempt to decrypt c using keys dk_ρ and dk_S: In case of a match (i.e., the attributes of both parties satisfy the counterparty's policy), the receiver obtains the plaintext, and otherwise an error occurs.

Security of ME. We consider two properties termed *privacy*, and *authenticity*. On rough terms, privacy looks at the secrecy of the sender w.r.t. the plaintext m, the chosen policy R, and its attributes σ, whenever a malicious receiver, possessing decryption keys for several attributes ρ and policies S:

- Can't decrypt the ciphertext ("mismatch condition"), i.e., either the sender's attributes do not satisfy the policies held by the receiver ($S(\sigma) = 0$), or the receiver's attributes do not satisfy the policy specified by the sender ($R(\rho) = 0$).
- Can decrypt the ciphertext ("match condition"), i.e., both the sender's and the receiver's attributes satisfy the corresponding policy specified by the counterpart ($R(\rho) = 1$ and $S(\sigma) = 1$). Of course, in such a case the receiver is allowed to learn the plaintext.

On the other hand, authenticity says that an attacker not possessing attributes σ should not be able to create a valid ciphertext (i.e., a ciphertext not decrypting to $\perp$) w.r.t. any access policy that is satisfied by σ.

Black-Box Constructions. It turned out that building matchmaking encryption is quite difficult. While a compiler turning key agreement into public-key encryption exists (e.g., Diffie-Hellman key exchange into ElGamal public-key encryption), there is no obvious way of building ME from SH, even by extending the model of SH to include attributes and policies in order to achieve something akin to attribute-based key agreement protocols. The main technical challenge is to ensure that the policies established by the sender and receiver are simultaneously checked to avoid any leakage. This simultaneity requirement is so elusive that even constructions combining attribute-based encryption (ABE) with authentication mechanisms fail to achieve it (more on this later).

Our first technical contribution is a construction of an ME for arbitrary policies based on three tools: (i) an FE scheme for randomized functionalities [1] (rFE), (ii) digital signatures, and (iii) non-interactive zero-knowledge (NIZK) proofs. When using the rFE scheme from [1], we can instantiate our scheme assuming the existence of *either* semantically secure public-key encryption schemes and low-depth pseudorandom generators, *or* concrete assumptions on multi-linear maps, *or* polynomially-secure indistinguishability obfuscation (iO).

This construction satisfies only security against bounded collusions, where there is an a-priori upper bound on the number of queries a malicious receiver can make to oracles RKGen and PolGen. We additionally give a simpler construction of ME for arbitrary policies that even achieves full security (i.e., security against unbounded collusions), albeit under stronger assumptions. In particular, we replace rFE with 2-input functional encryption (2FE) [24]. When using the 2FE scheme by Goldwasser et al. [24], we can instantiate this construction based on sub-exponentially secure iO.

Being based on strong assumptions, the above constructions should be mainly understood as feasibility results showing the possibility of constructing ME for arbitrary policies. It is nevertheless worth pointing out a recent construction of iO based on LWE, bilinear maps, and weak pseudorandomness [4], which avoids multi-linear maps. Additionally, Fisch et al. [20] show how to implement efficiently FE and 2FE using Intel's Software Guard Extensions (SGX), a set of processors allowing for the creation of isolated execution environments called *enclaves*. At a high level, in their practical implementation, a functional decryption key sk_f consists of a signature on the function f, while messages are encrypted using standard PKE. In order to run the decryption algorithm, a client sends sk_f together with ciphertext c to a *decryption enclave*, which first checks if the signature is valid (i.e., the function evaluation has been authorized by the authority), and if so it decrypts c by using the corresponding secret key, and outputs the function f evaluated on the plaintext. Lastly, the enclave erases its memory. This approach can be applied directly to FE, 2FE, and even rFE for arbitrary functionalities, which, thanks to our results, makes ME for arbitrary policies practical in the trusted hardware setting.

The Identity-Based Setting. Next, we turn to the natural question of obtaining efficient ME in restricted settings. In particular, we focus on the identity-based setting where access policies are simply bit-strings representing identities (as for standard identity-based encryption). This yields identity-based ME (IB-ME). For this setting, we provide an efficient construction that we prove secure in the random oracle model (ROM), based on the standard bilinear Diffie-Hellman assumption (BDH) over bilinear groups.

Recall that in ME the receiver needs to obtain from the authority a different key for each access policy $\mathbb{S}$. While this requirement is perfectly reasonable in the general case, where the policy might consist of the conjunction of several attributes, in the identity-based setting a receiver that wants to receive messages from several sources must obtain one key for each source. As this would not scale well in practice, we change the syntax of IB-ME and remove the PolGen algorithm. In particular, the receiver can now specify on the fly an identity string snd (playing the role of the access policy $\mathbb{S}$) that is directly input to the decryption algorithm (together with the secret key associated to the receiver's identity).

While the above modification yields much more efficient IB-ME schemes, it comes with the drawback that an adversary in the privacy game can try to unlock a given ciphertext using different target identities snd chosen on the fly. The latter yields simple attacks that required us to tweak the definition of privacy in the identity-based setting slightly. We refer the reader to Sect. 5 for more details.

Table 1. Results achieved in this work ([5] is the full version of this paper). † Security only holds in the identity-based setting. ‡ Security only holds in case of bounded collusions.

	Type	Privacy	Authenticity	Assumptions
Section 4	ME	$\checkmark^{\ddagger}$	$\checkmark^{\ddagger}$	rFE + Signatures + NIZK
Section 5	IB-ME	$\checkmark^{\dagger}$	$\checkmark^{\dagger}$	BDH (RO model)
[5]	ME	$\checkmark$	$\checkmark$	2FE + Signatures + NIZK
[5]	A-ME	$\checkmark$	$\checkmark$	FE + Signatures + NIZK

Concrete Use Case and Implementation. We give evidence of the practical viability of our IB-ME construction by providing a prototype implementation in Python. Our experimental evaluation can be found in Sect. 6. There, we also detail a concrete use case where IB-ME is used in order to realize a prototype of a new privacy-preserving bulletin board that is run on the Tor network [43]. Our system allows parties to communicate privately, or entities such as newspapers or organizations to collect information from anonymous sources.

A public bulletin board is essentially a broadcast channel with memory. Messages can be encrypted under ME so that their content is revealed only in case of a policy match. The privacy-preserving feature of ME ensures that, if decryption fails, nobody learns which policies were not satisfied. This effectively creates secure and private virtual rooms or sub-channels.

Arranged ME. In ME a receiver can obtain independent decryption keys for its attributes and policies. Note that these keys can be arbitrarily combined during decryption. For this reason, we also consider an alternative flavor of ME, called *arranged* matchmaking encryption (A-ME), where there is a single decryption key $\mathsf{dk}_{\rho,\mathbb{S}}$ that describes simultaneously the receiver's attributes ρ and the policy $\mathbb{S}$ chosen by the receiver. Thus, an A-ME scheme does not come with a PolGen algorithm. This feature makes sense in applications where a receiver has many attributes, each bearing different restrictions in terms of access policies. A-ME is simpler to construct, in fact we show how to obtain A-ME for arbitrary policies from FE for deterministic functionalities, digital signatures, and NIZK proofs.

See Table 1 for a summary of our constructions in terms of assumptions and for different flavors of ME.

1.2 Technical Approach

Below, we describe the main ideas behind our constructions of ME. We start by presenting two unsuccessful attempts, naturally leading to our secure constructions. Both attempts are based on FE. Recall that FE allows us to generate decryption keys dk_f associated to a functionality f, in such a way that decrypting a ciphertext c, with underlying plaintext x, under dk_f, yields $f(x)$ (and nothing more). Note that FE implies both ciphertext-policy ABE [12] (CP-ABE) and key-policy ABE [28] (KP-ABE).

First Attempt. A first natural approach would be to construct an ME scheme by combining two distinct FE schemes. The idea is to apply sequentially two functionalities f^1 and f^2, where the first functionality checks whether the sender's policy $\mathbb{R}$ is satisfied, whereas the second functionality checks whether the receiver's policy $\mathbb{S}$ is satisfied. More in details, let f^1 and f^2 be the following functions:

$$f^1_\rho(\mathbb{R}, c) = \begin{cases} c, & \text{if } \mathbb{R}(\rho) = 1 \\ \bot, & \text{otherwise} \end{cases} \qquad f^2_\mathbb{S}(\sigma, m) = \begin{cases} m, & \text{if } \mathbb{S}(\sigma) = 1 \\ \bot, & \text{otherwise} \end{cases}$$

where $\mathbb{R}(\rho) = 1$ (resp. $\mathbb{S}(\sigma) = 1$) means that receiver's attributes ρ (resp. sender's attributes σ) satisfy the sender's policy $\mathbb{R}$ (resp. receiver's policy $\mathbb{S}$). A sender now encrypts a message m under attributes σ by first encrypting (σ, m) under the second FE scheme, and thus it encrypts the corresponding ciphertext concatenated with the policy $\mathbb{R}$ under the first FE scheme. The receiver first decrypts a ciphertext using secret key dk_ρ associated with function f^1_ρ, and then it decrypts the obtained value using secret key $\mathsf{dk}_\mathbb{S}$ associated with function $f^2_\mathbb{S}$.

While "semantic security" of the underlying FE schemes computationally hides the plaintext of the resulting ME scheme, privacy is not guaranteed completely: In fact, when the first encrypted layer decrypts correctly (resp. does not decrypt correctly), a receiver infers that the sender's attributes σ match (resp. do not match) the policy $\mathbb{S}$.

Second Attempt. One could think to salvage the above construction as follows. Each function f^i returns a random key r_i in case the corresponding policy (i.e., the policy checked by function f^i) is satisfied, and otherwise it returns a random value generated by running a secure PRF F. Both partial keys r_1, r_2 are then needed to unmask the string $r_1 \oplus r_2 \oplus m$, which is included in the ciphertext.

More precisely, consider functions $f^1_\rho(\mathbb{R}, r_1, k_1)$ and $f^2_\mathbb{S}(\sigma, r_2, k_2)$, such that $f^1_\rho(\mathbb{R}, r_1, k_1)$ (resp. $f^2_\mathbb{S}(\sigma, r_2, k_2)$) returns r_1 (resp. r_2) if ρ satisfies $\mathbb{R}$ (resp. σ satisfies $\mathbb{S}$); otherwise, it returns $F_{k_1}(\rho)$ (resp. $F_{k_2}(\mathbb{S})$), where k_1 (resp. k_2) is a key for the PRF F. An encryption of message m w.r.t. attributes σ and policy $\mathbb{R}$ would now consist of three values (c_1, c_2, c_3), where c_1 is an encryption of $(\mathbb{R}, r_1, k_1)$ under the first FE scheme, c_2 is an encryption of (σ, r_2, k_2) under the second FE scheme, and finally $c_3 = r_1 \oplus r_2 \oplus m$. A receiver (with keys dk_ρ and $\mathsf{dk}_\mathbb{S}$ associated to functions f^1_ρ and $f^2_\mathbb{S}$ as before) would decrypt c_1 and c_2 using dk_ρ and $\mathsf{dk}_\mathbb{S}$, and finally xor the outputs between them and with c_3.

As before, "semantic security" still follows from the security of the two FE schemes. Furthermore, it might seem that privacy is also satisfied because, by security of the PRF, it is hard to distinguish whether the decryption of each c_i yields the random string r_i (i.e., there was a match) or an output of F_{k_i} (i.e., there was no match). However, a malicious receiver possessing distinct attributes ρ and ρ', such that both satisfy the policy $\mathbb{R}$, is able to figure out whether the sender's policy is matched by simply decrypting c_1 twice (using attributes ρ and ρ') and comparing if the decryption returns twice the same value (i.e., r_1). A similar attack can be carried out using two different keys for distinct policies $\mathbb{S}$ and $\mathbb{S}'$, such that both policies are satisfied by the attributes σ.

ME from 2FE. Intuitively, in order to avoid the above attacks, we need to check simultaneously that $\mathbb{S}(\sigma) = 1$ and $\mathbb{R}(\rho) = 1$. 2FE comes handy to solve this problem, at least if one is willing to give up on authenticity. Recall that in a 2FE scheme we can associate secret keys with 2-ary functionalities, in such a way that decrypting ciphertexts c_0, c_1 computed using independent keys $\mathsf{ek}_0, \mathsf{ek}_1$, and corresponding to plaintexts x_0, x_1, yields $f(x_0, x_1)$ (and nothing more).

Wlog., we reserve the 1st slot to the sender, while the 2nd slot is reserved to the receiver; the administrator gives the key ek_0 to the sender. The sender now encrypts a message m under attributes σ and policy $\mathbb{R}$ by computing $\mathsf{Enc}(\mathsf{ek}_0, (\sigma, \mathbb{R}, m))$, which yields a ciphertext c_0 for the first input of the function f. The receiver, as usual, has a pair of decryption keys $\mathsf{dk}_\rho, \mathsf{dk}_\mathbb{S}$ obtained from the administrator; here, $\mathsf{dk}_\mathbb{S} = \mathsf{Enc}(\mathsf{ek}_1, \mathbb{S}) = c_1$ is an encryption of $\mathbb{S}$ under key ek_1. Hence, the receiver runs $\mathsf{Dec}(\mathsf{dk}_\rho, c_0, c_1)$, where dk_ρ is associated to the function $f_\rho((m, \sigma, \mathbb{R}), \mathbb{S})$ that returns m if and only if both $\mathbb{R}(\rho) = 1$ and $\mathbb{S}(\sigma) = 1$ (i.e., a match occurs).

On rough terms, privacy follows by the security of the underlying 2FE scheme, which guarantees that the receiver learns nothing more than the output of f. Unfortunately, this construction does not immediately satisfy authenticity. To overcome this limitation, we tweak it as follows. First, we let the sender obtain from the authority a signature s on its own attributes σ; the signature is computed w.r.t. a verification key that is included in the public parameters of the scheme. Second, during encryption, the sender computes the ciphertext c_0 as above, but now additionally proves in zero knowledge that it knows a valid signature for the attributes that are hidden in the ciphertext. As we show, this modification allows us to prove authenticity, while at the same time preserving privacy. We refer the reader to the full version [5] for the formal proof.

ME from rFE. In Sect. 4, we give an alternative solution that combines rFE and FE (and thus can be instantiated from weaker assumptions). Recall that rFE is a generalization of FE that supports randomized functionalities. In what follows, we write f^1 for the randomized functionality supported by the rFE scheme, and f^2 for the deterministic functionality supported by the plain FE scheme. The main idea is to let the sender encrypt $(m, \sigma, \mathbb{R})$ under the rFE scheme. We then consider the randomized function f_ρ^1 that checks if ρ satisfies $\mathbb{R}$: In case a match occurs (resp. does not occur), it returns an encryption of (m, σ) (resp. of $(\bot, \bot)$, where $\bot$ denotes garbage) for the second function $f_\mathbb{S}^2$ that simply checks whether the policy $\mathbb{S}$ is satisfied or not. The receiver decryption keys are the keys $\mathsf{dk}_\rho, \mathsf{dk}_\mathbb{S}$ associated to the functions f_ρ^1 and $f_\mathbb{S}^2$.

Roughly speaking, since the randomized function f^1 passes encrypted data to f^2, a malicious receiver infers nothing about the satisfiability of policy $\mathbb{R}$. On the other hand, the satisfiability of $\mathbb{S}$ remains hidden, as long as the FE scheme for the function f^2 is secure.

While the above construction does not directly satisfy authenticity, we can show that the same trick explained above for the 2FE-based scheme works here as well.

A-ME from FE. Recall that the difference between ME and A-ME lies in the number of decryption keys: While in ME there are two distinct keys (one for the policy $\mathbb{S}$, and one for the attributes ρ), in A-ME there is a single decryption key $\mathsf{dk}_{\rho,\mathbb{S}}$ that represents both the receiver's attributes ρ and the policy $\mathbb{S}$.

As a result, looking at our construction of ME from 2FE, we can now hard-code the policy $\mathbb{S}$ (together with the attributes ρ) into the function, which allows us to replace 2FE with plain FE. This way, each A-ME decryption key $\mathsf{dk}_{\rho,\mathbb{S}}$ is the secret key corresponding to the function $f_{\rho,\mathbb{S}}$ for the FE scheme. The security proof, which appears in the full version [5], only requires FE with game-based security [12], which in turn can be instantiated under much weaker assumptions.

IB-ME. Above, we mentioned that the natural construction of ME where a ciphertext masks the plaintext m with two distinct pads r_1, r_2—where r_1, r_2 are re-computable by the receiver as long as a match occurs—is insecure. This is because the expressiveness of ME allows us to have two distinct attributes ρ and ρ' (resp. two distinct policies $\mathbb{S}$ and $\mathbb{S}'$) such that both satisfy the sender's policy $\mathbb{R}$ (resp. both are satisfied by the sender's attributes σ).

The main idea behind our construction of IB-ME (cf. Sect. 5) under the BDH assumption is that the above attack does not work in the identity-based setting, where each receiver's policy $\mathbb{S}$ (resp. receiver's policy $\mathbb{R}$) is satisfied only by the attribute $\sigma = \mathbb{S}$ (resp. $\rho = \mathbb{R}$). This means that an encryption $m \oplus r_1 \oplus r_2$ yields an efficient IB-ME as long as the random pad r_2 (resp. r_1) can be re-computed by the receiver if and only if its policy $\mathbb{S}$ is satisfied (resp. its attributes ρ satisfy the sender's policy). On the other hand, if $\mathbb{S}$ is not satisfied (resp. ρ does not satisfy the sender's policy), the receiver obtains a pad r_2' (resp. r_1') that is completely unrelated to the real r_2 (resp. r_1). In our scheme, we achieve the latter by following a similar strategy as in the Boneh-Franklin IBE construction [11].

1.3 Related Work

Secret Handshakes. Introduced by Balfanz *et al.* [9], an SH allows two members of the same group to secretly authenticate to each other and agree on a symmetric key. During the protocol, a party can additionally specify the precise group identity (e.g., role) that the other party should have.

SH preserves the privacy of the participants, meaning that when the handshake is successful they only learn that they both belong to the same group (yet, their identities remain secret), whereas they learn nothing if the handshake fails. Subsequent work in the area [6,13,29–32,41,42,46,47,49] focused on improving on various aspects of SH, including members' privacy and expressiveness of the matching policies (i.e., attribute-based SH).

In this vein, ME can be thought of as a *non-interactive* SH. Indeed, ME gives privacy guarantees similar to that of SH, but it provides a more efficient way to communicate (being non-interactive) and, at the same time, it is more flexible since a party is not constrained to a group.

Attribute-Based Encryption. The concept of ABE was first proposed by Sahai and Waters [40] in the setting of fuzzy identity-based encryption, where users are identified by a single attribute (or identity string), and policies consist of a single threshold gate. Afterwards, Bethencourt *et al.* [10] generalized this idea to the case where users are described by multiple attributes. Their ABE scheme is a CP-ABE, i.e., a policy is embedded into the ciphertext, whereas the attributes are embedded into the receiver's decryption keys. The first CP-ABE with non-monotonic access structures was proposed by Ostrovsky *et al.* [37]. Goyal *et al.* [28], instead, introduced KP-ABE, where ciphertexts contain the attributes, whereas the policy is embedded in the decryption keys. Several other CP-ABE and KP-ABE schemes have been proposed in the litterature, see, among others, [8, 14–16, 27, 36, 38, 48, 50–53].

In ABE, only one party can specify a policy, and thus only one entity has the power to select the source (or the destination) of an encrypted message. Motivated by this limitation, Attrapadung and Imai [7] introduced dual-policy ABE. Here, the sender encrypts a message by choosing both a policy and a set of attributes. The receiver can decrypt the ciphertext using a single decryption key that describes both the receiver's policy and attributes. Similarly to ME, if both policies are satisfied by the respective counterpart, the message is revealed.

Dual-policy ABE and ME differ in several aspects. First, on the syntactical level, in ME there are two distinct decryption keys: One for the attributes and one for the policy specified by the receiver. This yields improved flexibility, as receivers are allowed to choose attributes and policies independently. (Indeed, the syntax of dual-policy ABE is more similar to that of A-ME.) Second, on the security level, both ME and A-ME provide much stronger privacy guarantees than dual-policy ABE. In fact, the security definition for dual-policy ABE only protects the secrecy of the plaintext. Additionally, the actual constructions in [7, 8] are easily seen not to preserve privacy w.r.t. the sender's attributes/policy whenever a match does not occur. Intuitively, this is because the procedure that checks, during decryption, whether a match occurred or not, is not an atomic operation. Also note that dual-policy ABE does not directly provide authenticity, which instead is a crucial property for ME and A-ME (those being a type of non-interactive SH).

Attribute-Based Key Exchange. Gorantla *et al.* [25] introduced attribute-based authenticated key exchange (AB-AKE). This is essentially an interactive protocol which allows sharing a secret key between parties whose attributes satisfy a fixed access policy. Note that the policy must be the same for all the parties, and thus it must, e.g., be negotiated before running the protocol.

In a different work, Kolesnikov *et al.* [34] built a different AB-KE without bilateral authentication. In their setting, a client with some attributes (certificated by an authority) wants to authenticate himself to a server according to a fixed policy. The server will share a secret key with the client if and only if the client's attributes satisfy the server's policy.

Note that in ME both senders and receivers can choose their own policies, a feature not present in attribute-based key exchange protocols.

Access Control Encryption. Access control encryption (ACE) [19,21,33,44] is a novel type of encryption that allows fine-grained control over information flow. The actors are a set of senders, a set of receivers, and a sanitizer. The goal is to enforce *no-read* and *no-write* rules (described by a policy) over the communication, according to the sender's and receiver's identities.

The flow enforcement is done by the sanitizer, that applies a randomized algorithm to the incoming ciphertexts. The result is that only receivers allowed to communicate with the source will be able to decrypt the sanitized ciphertext correctly, obtaining the original message (*no-read* rule). On the other hand, if the source has not the rights to communicate with a target receiver (e.g., the sender is malicious), then the latter will receive a sanitized ciphertext that looks like an encryption of a random message (*no-write* rule).

ACE and ME accomplish orthogonal needs: The former enables cryptographic control over information flow within a system, whereas the latter enables both the sender and the receiver to specify fine-grained access rights on encrypted data. Furthermore, ACE inherently requires the presence of a trusted sanitizer, whereas ME involves no additional actor (besides the sender and the receiver).

2   Preliminaries

2.1   Notation

We use the notation $[n] \stackrel{\text{def}}{=} \{1, \ldots, n\}$. Capital boldface letters (such as $\mathbf{X}$) are used to denote random variables, small letters (such as x) to denote concrete values, calligraphic letters (such as $\mathcal{X}$) to denote sets, and serif letters (such as A) to denote algorithms. All of our algorithms are modeled as (possibly interactive) Turing machines; if algorithm A has oracle access to some oracle O, we often implicitly write $\mathcal{Q}_\mathsf{O}$ for the set of queries asked by A to O.

For a string $x \in \{0,1\}^*$, we let $|x|$ be its length; if $\mathcal{X}$ is a set, $|\mathcal{X}|$ represents the cardinality of $\mathcal{X}$. When x is chosen randomly in $\mathcal{X}$, we write $x \leftarrow_\$ \mathcal{X}$. If A is an algorithm, we write $y \leftarrow_\$ \mathsf{A}(x)$ to denote a run of A on input x and output y; if A is randomized, y is a random variable and $\mathsf{A}(x; r)$ denotes a run of A on input x and (uniform) randomness r. An algorithm A is *probabilistic polynomial-time* (PPT) if A is randomized and for any input $x, r \in \{0,1\}^*$ the computation of $\mathsf{A}(x; r)$ terminates in a polynomial number of steps (in the input size).

Negligible Functions. Throughout the paper, we denote by $\lambda \in \mathbb{N}$ the security parameter and we implicitly assume that every algorithm takes as input the security parameter. A function $\nu : \mathbb{N} \to [0,1]$ is called *negligible* in the security parameter λ if it vanishes faster than the inverse of any polynomial in λ, i.e. $\nu(\lambda) \in \mathcal{O}(()1/p(\lambda))$ for all positive polynomials $p(\lambda)$. We sometimes write $\mathsf{negl}(\lambda)$ (resp., $\mathsf{poly}(\lambda)$) to denote an unspecified negligible function (resp., polynomial function) in the security parameter.

2.2   Signature Schemes

A signature scheme is made of the following polynomial-time algorithms.

$\mathsf{KGen}(1^\lambda)$: The randomized key generation algorithm takes the security parameter and outputs a secret and a public key $(\mathsf{sk}, \mathsf{pk})$.

$\mathsf{Sign}(\mathsf{sk}, m)$: The randomized signing algorithm takes as input the secret key sk and a message $m \in \mathcal{M}$, and produces a signature s.

$\mathsf{Ver}(\mathsf{pk}, m, s)$: The deterministic verification algorithm takes as input the public key pk, a message m, and a signature s, and it returns a decision bit.

A signature scheme should satisfy two properties. The first property says that honestly generated signatures always verify correctly. The second property, called unforgeability, says that it should be hard to forge a signature on a fresh message, even after seeing signatures on polynomially many messages. See the full version [5] for formal definitions.

2.3   Functional Encryption

Functional Encryption for Randomized Functionalities. A functional encryption scheme for randomized functionalities [26] (rFE) $f : \mathcal{K} \times \mathcal{X} \times \mathcal{R} \to \mathcal{Y}$ consists of the following polynomial-time algorithms.[3]

$\mathsf{Setup}(1^\lambda)$: Upon input the security parameter, the randomized setup algorithm outputs a master public key mpk and a master secret key msk.

$\mathsf{KGen}(\mathsf{msk}, k)$: The randomized key generation algorithm takes as input the master secret key msk and an index $k \in \mathcal{K}$, and outputs a secret key sk_k for f_k.

$\mathsf{Enc}(\mathsf{mpk}, x)$: The randomized encryption algorithm takes as input the master public key mpk, an input $x \in \mathcal{X}$, and returns a ciphertext c_x.

$\mathsf{Dec}(\mathsf{sk}_k, c_x)$: The deterministic decryption algorithm takes as input a secret key sk_k and a ciphertext c_x, and returns a value $y \in \mathcal{Y}$.

Correctness of rFE intuitively says that decrypting an encryption of $x \in \mathcal{X}$ using a secret key sk_k for function f_k yields $f_k(x; r)$, where $r \leftarrow_\$ \mathcal{R}$. Since $f_k(x)$ is a random variable, the actual definition requires that whenever the decryption algorithm is invoked on a fresh encryption of a message x under a fresh key for f_k, the resulting output is computationally indistinguishable to $f_k(x)$.

Definition 1 (Correctness of rFE). *A rFE scheme Π = (Setup, KGen, Enc, Dec) for a randomized functionality $f : \mathcal{K} \times \mathcal{X} \times \mathcal{R} \to \mathcal{Y}$ is correct if the following distributions are computationally indistinguishable:*

$$\{\mathsf{Dec}(\mathsf{sk}_{k_j}, c_i)\}_{k_j \in \mathcal{K}, x_i \in \mathcal{X}} \qquad \{f_{k_j}(x_i; r_{i,j})\}_{k_j \in \mathcal{K}, x_i \in \mathcal{X}}$$

where $(\mathsf{mpk}, \mathsf{msk}) \leftarrow_\$ \mathsf{Setup}(1^\lambda)$, $\mathsf{sk}_{k_j} \leftarrow_\$ \mathsf{KGen}(\mathsf{msk}, k_j)$ *for* $k_j \in \mathcal{K}$, $c_i \leftarrow_\$ \mathsf{Enc}(\mathsf{mpk}, x_i)$ *for* $x_i \in \mathcal{X}$, *and* $r_{i,j} \leftarrow_\$ \mathcal{R}$.

---

[3] Often, and equivalently, FE schemes are parameterized by a function ensemble $\mathcal{F} = \{f_k : \mathcal{X} \times \mathcal{R} \to \mathcal{Y}\}_{k \in \mathcal{K}}$.

As for security, the setting of rFE tackles malicious encryptors. However, for our purpose, it will be sufficient to consider a weaker security guarantee that only holds for honest encryptors. In this spirit, the definition below is adapted from [1, Definition 3.3] for the special case of honest encryptors.

Definition 2 ($((q_1, q_c, q_2)$-NA-SIM-security of rFE). *A rFE scheme $\Pi =$ (Setup, KGen, Enc, Dec) for a randomized functionality $f : \mathcal{K} \times \mathcal{X} \times \mathcal{R} \rightarrow \mathcal{Y}$ is (q_1, q_c, q_2)-NA-SIM-secure if there exists an efficient (stateful) simulator $\mathsf{S} = (\mathsf{S}_1, \mathsf{S}_2, \mathsf{S}_3, \mathsf{S}_4)$ such that for all PPT adversaries $\mathsf{A} = (\mathsf{A}_1, \mathsf{A}_2)$ where A_1 makes at most q_1 key generation queries and A_2 makes at most q_2 key generation query, the output of the following two experiments are computationally indistinguishable:*

$\mathbf{REAL}_{\Pi, \mathsf{A}}(\lambda)$	$\mathbf{IDEAL}_{\Pi, \mathsf{A}}(\lambda)$
$(\mathsf{mpk}, \mathsf{msk}) \leftarrow\!\!{\scriptstyle\$}\; \mathsf{Setup}(1^\lambda)$	$(\mathsf{mpk}, \alpha') \leftarrow\!\!{\scriptstyle\$}\; \mathsf{S}_1(1^\lambda)$
$(x^*, \alpha) \leftarrow\!\!{\scriptstyle\$}\; \mathsf{A}_1^{\mathsf{O}_1(\mathsf{msk}, \cdot)}(1^\lambda, \mathsf{mpk})$	$(x^*, \alpha) \leftarrow\!\!{\scriptstyle\$}\; \mathsf{A}_1^{\mathsf{O}_1'(\alpha', \cdot)}(1^\lambda, \mathsf{mpk})$
$\quad$ *where* $x^* = (x_0, \ldots, x_{q_c})$	$\quad$ *where* $x^* = (x_0, \ldots, x_{q_c})$
$c_i \leftarrow\!\!{\scriptstyle\$}\; \mathsf{Enc}(\mathsf{mpk}, x_i)$ *for* $i \in [q_c]$	Let $\{k_1, \ldots, k_{q_1}\} = \mathcal{Q}_{\mathsf{O}_1'}$
$\mathsf{out} \leftarrow\!\!{\scriptstyle\$}\; \mathsf{A}_2^{\mathsf{O}_2(\mathsf{msk}, \cdot)}(1^\lambda, \{c_i\}, \alpha)$	For $i \in [q_c], j \in [q_1]$
return $(x, \{k\}, \mathsf{out})$	$\quad y_{i,j} = f_{k_j}(x_i; r_{i,j})$, *where* $r_{i,j} \leftarrow\!\!{\scriptstyle\$}\; \mathcal{R}$
	$(\{c_i\}, \alpha') \leftarrow\!\!{\scriptstyle\$}\; \mathsf{S}_3(\alpha', \{y_{i,j}\})$
	$\mathsf{out} \leftarrow\!\!{\scriptstyle\$}\; \mathsf{A}_2^{\mathsf{O}_2'(\alpha', \cdot)}(1^\lambda, \{c_i\}, \alpha)$
	return $(x, \{k'\}, \mathsf{out})$

where the key generation oracles are defined in the following way:

$\mathsf{O}_1(\mathsf{msk}, \cdot)$ **and** $\mathsf{O}_2(\mathsf{msk}, \cdot)$**:** *Are implemented with the algorithm* $\mathsf{KGen}(\mathsf{msk}, \cdot)$. *The ordered set* $\{k\}$ *is composed of the queries made to oracles* O_1 *and* O_2.

$\mathsf{O}_1'(\mathsf{st}', \cdot)$ **and** $\mathsf{O}_2'(\mathsf{st}', \cdot)$**:** *Are implemented with two simulators* $\mathsf{S}_2(\alpha', \cdot)$, $\mathsf{S}_4(\alpha', \cdot)$. *The simulator* S_4 *is given oracle access to* $\mathsf{KeyIdeal}(x^*, \cdot)$, *which, on input* k, *outputs* $f_k(x_i; r)$, *where* $r \leftarrow\!\!{\scriptstyle\$}\; \mathcal{R}$ *for every* $x_i \in x^*$. *The ordered set* $\{k'\}$ *is composed of the queries made to oracles* O_1' *and the queries made by* S_4 *to* $\mathsf{KeyIdeal}$.

Functional Encryption for Deterministic Functionalities. Functional encryption (FE) for deterministic functionalities $f : \mathcal{K} \times \mathcal{X} \rightarrow \mathcal{Y}$ can be cast as a special case of rFE. Since f is a deterministic functionality, correctness now simply says that whenever the decryption algorithm is invoked on a fresh encryption of a message x under a fresh key for f, the resulting output equals $f_k(x)$. The definition of security is also a simple adaptation of Definition 2, with the twist that the ideal functionality in the ideal experiment is deterministic. We refer the reader to the full version [5] for the details.

2.4 Bilinear Diffie-Hellman Assumption

Our practical implementation of IB-ME is provably secure under the BDH assumption, which we recall below.

Definition 3 (BDH assumption). *Let* $\mathbb{G}$ *and* $\mathbb{G}_T$ *be two groups of prime order* q. *Let* $e : \mathbb{G} \times \mathbb{G} \to \mathbb{G}_T$ *be an admissible bilinear map, and let* P *be a generator of* $\mathbb{G}$. *The BDH problem is hard in* $(\mathbb{G}, \mathbb{G}_T, e)$ *if for every PPT adversary* A:

$$\mathbb{P}\left[\mathsf{A}(q, \mathbb{G}, \mathbb{G}_T, e, P, P^a, P^b, P^c) = e(P,P)^{abc}\right] \leq \mathsf{negl}(\lambda),$$

where $P \leftarrow\!\!{}_\$ \mathbb{G}^*$, *and* $a, b, c \leftarrow\!\!{}_\$ \mathbb{Z}_q^*$.

2.5   Non-interactive Zero Knowledge

Let R be a relation, corresponding to an NP language L. A non-interactive zero-knowledge (NIZK) proof system for R is a tuple of polynomial-time algorithms $\Pi = (\mathsf{I}, \mathsf{P}, \mathsf{V})$ specified as follows. (i) The randomized algorithm I takes as input the security parameter and outputs a common reference string ω; (ii) The randomized algorithm $\mathsf{P}(\omega, (y, x))$, given $(y, x) \in R$ outputs a proof π; (iii) The deterministic algorithm $\mathsf{V}(\omega, (y, \pi))$, given an instance y and a proof π outputs either 0 (for "reject") or 1 (for "accept"). We say that a NIZK for relation R is *correct* if for all $\lambda \in \mathbb{N}$, every ω output by $\mathsf{I}(1^\lambda)$, and any $(y, x) \in R$, we have that $\mathsf{V}(\omega, (y, \mathsf{P}(\omega, (y, x)))) = 1$.

We define two properties of a NIZK proof system. The first property, called adaptive multi-theorem zero knowledge, says that honest proofs do not reveal anything beyond the fact that $y \in L$. The second property, called knowledge soundness, requires that every adversary creating a valid proof for some statement, must know the corresponding witness. We defer the formal definitions to the full version [5].

3   Matchmaking Encryption

As explained in the introduction, an ME allows both the sender and the receiver, characterized by their attributes, to choose fined-grained access policies that together describe the access rights both parties must satisfy in order for the decryption of a given ciphertext to be successful.

We present two flavors of ME. In the first, which is the standard one, the receiver's attributes and policy are independent of each other (i.e., a receiver with some given attributes can choose different policies). In the second flavor, dubbed A-ME, the receiver's attributes and policy are tighten together. For space reasons, we defer the formal definitions for A-ME to the full version [5].

3.1   Security Model

Formally, an ME is composed of the following polynomial-time algorithms:

Setup(1^λ): Upon input the security parameter 1^λ the randomized setup algorithm outputs the master public key mpk, the master policy key kpol, and the master secret key msk. We implicitly assume that all other algorithms take mpk as input.

SKGen(msk, σ): The randomized sender-key generator takes as input the master secret key msk, and attributes $\sigma \in \{0,1\}^*$. The algorithm outputs a secret encryption key ek_σ for attributes σ.

RKGen(msk, ρ): The randomized receiver-key generator takes as input the master secret key msk, and attributes $\rho \in \{0,1\}^*$. The algorithm outputs a secret decryption key dk_ρ for attributes ρ.

PolGen(kpol, $\mathbb{S}$): The randomized receiver policy generator takes as input the master policy key kpol, and a policy $\mathbb{S} : \{0,1\}^* \rightarrow \{0,1\}$ represented as a circuit. The algorithm outputs a secret decryption key $\mathsf{dk}_\mathbb{S}$ for the circuit $\mathbb{S}$.

Enc($\mathsf{ek}_\sigma, \mathbb{R}, m$): The randomized encryption algorithm takes as input a secret encryption key ek_σ for attributes $\sigma \in \{0,1\}^*$, a policy $\mathbb{R} : \{0,1\}^* \rightarrow \{0,1\}$ represented as a circuit, and a message $m \in \mathcal{M}$. The algorithm produces a ciphertext c linked to both σ and $\mathbb{R}$.

Dec($\mathsf{dk}_\rho, \mathsf{dk}_\mathbb{S}, c$): The deterministic decryption algorithm takes as input a secret decryption key dk_ρ for attributes $\rho \in \{0,1\}^*$, a secret decryption key $\mathsf{dk}_\mathbb{S}$ for a circuit $\mathbb{S} : \{0,1\}^* \rightarrow \{0,1\}$, and a ciphertext c. The algorithm outputs either a message m or $\bot$ (denoting an error).

Note that the decryption keys dk_ρ and $\mathsf{dk}_\mathbb{S}$ are independent, thus allowing a receiver with attributes ρ to obtain decryption keys for different policies $\mathbb{S}$. We also remark that the master policy key kpol could be considered as part of the master secret key msk, but we preferred to use distinct keys for clarity.

Correctness. The intuition for correctness is that the output of the decryption algorithm using decryption keys for receiver's attributes ρ and access policy $\mathbb{S}$, when decrypting an honestly generated ciphertext which encrypts a message m using sender's attributes σ and policy $\mathbb{R}$, should equal m if and only if the receiver's attributes ρ match the policy $\mathbb{R}$ specified by the sender, and at the same time the sender's attributes σ match the policy $\mathbb{S}$ specified by the receiver. On the other hand, in case of mismatch, the decryption algorithm returns $\bot$. More formally:

Definition 4 (Correctness of ME). *An ME with message space $\mathcal{M}$ is correct if $\forall \lambda \in \mathbb{N}$, $\forall(\mathsf{mpk}, \mathsf{kpol}, \mathsf{msk})$ output by* $\mathsf{Setup}(1^\lambda)$*, $\forall m \in \mathcal{M}$, $\forall \sigma, \rho \in \{0,1\}^*$, $\forall \mathbb{R}, \mathbb{S} : \{0,1\}^* \rightarrow \{0,1\}$:*

$$\mathbb{P}\left[\mathsf{Dec}(\mathsf{dk}_\rho, \mathsf{dk}_\mathbb{S}, \mathsf{Enc}(\mathsf{ek}_\sigma, \mathbb{R}, m)) = m\right] \geq 1 - \mathsf{negl}(\lambda),$$

whenever $\mathbb{S}(\sigma) = 1$ and $\mathbb{R}(\rho) = 1$, and otherwise

$$\mathbb{P}\left[\mathsf{Dec}(\mathsf{dk}_\rho, \mathsf{dk}_\mathbb{S}, \mathsf{Enc}(\mathsf{ek}_\sigma, \mathbb{R}, m)) = \bot\right] \geq 1 - \mathsf{negl}(\lambda),$$

where $\mathsf{ek}_\sigma \leftarrow_\$ \mathsf{SKGen}(\mathsf{msk}, \sigma)$, $\mathsf{dk}_\rho \leftarrow_\$ \mathsf{RKGen}(\mathsf{msk}, \rho)$, $\mathsf{dk}_\mathbb{S} \leftarrow_\$ \mathsf{PolGen}(\mathsf{kpol}, \mathbb{S})$.

Security. We now turn to defining security of an ME via two properties, that we dub *privacy* and *authenticity*. Intuitively, privacy aims at capturing secrecy of the sender's inputs (i.e., the attributes σ, the policy for the receiver $\mathbb{R}$, and the plaintext m), in two different conditions: In case of a match between the sender's and receiver's attributes/policy, and in case of mismatch. This is formalized by requiring that the distributions $\mathsf{Enc}(\mathsf{ek}_{\sigma_0}, \mathbb{R}_0, m_0)$ and $\mathsf{Enc}(\mathsf{ek}_{\sigma_1}, \mathbb{R}_1, m_1)$ be computationally indistinguishable to the eyes of an attacker with oracle access to $\mathsf{SKGen}, \mathsf{RKGen}, \mathsf{PolGen}$, where the values $(m_0, m_1, \mathbb{R}_0, \mathbb{R}_1, \sigma_0, \sigma_1)$ are all chosen by the adversary. The actual definition requires some care, as the adversary could, e.g., obtain a decryption key for attributes ρ and policy $\mathbb{S}$ such that $\mathbb{R}_0(\rho) = 0 \vee \mathbb{S}(\sigma_0) = 0$ but $\mathbb{R}_1(\rho) = 1 \wedge \mathbb{S}(\sigma_1) = 1$, which clearly allows him to distinguish by evaluating the decryption algorithm. In order to exclude such "trivial attacks", we quantify privacy over all *valid adversaries*, as explained below:

- In case of a mismatch, i.e., when the adversary cannot decrypt the challenge ciphertext, it must be the case that for each attribute ρ and policy $\mathbb{S}$ for which the adversary knows a valid decryption key: (i) Either ρ does not satisfy policies $\mathbb{R}_0$ and $\mathbb{R}_1$; (ii) or σ_0 and σ_1 do not satisfy policy $\mathbb{S}$; (iii) or ρ does not satisfy $\mathbb{R}_0$ and σ_1 does not satisfy $\mathbb{S}$; (iv) or ρ does not satisfy $\mathbb{R}_1$ and σ_0 does not satisfy $\mathbb{S}$.
- In case of match, i.e., when the adversary can decrypt the challenge ciphertext, it must be the case that $m_0 = m_1$, and additionally, for each attribute ρ and policy $\mathbb{S}$ for which the adversary knows a valid decryption key, it holds that both: (i) $\mathbb{R}_0$ and $\mathbb{R}_1$ have the same evaluation on attributes ρ (i.e., $\mathbb{R}_0(\rho) = \mathbb{R}_1(\rho)$); and (ii) $\mathbb{S}$ has the same evaluation on attributes σ_0 and σ_1 (i.e., $\mathbb{S}(\sigma_0) = \mathbb{S}(\sigma_1)$).

$\mathbf{G}^{\mathsf{priv}}_{\Pi,\mathsf{A}}(\lambda)$	$\mathbf{G}^{\mathsf{auth}}_{\Pi,\mathsf{A}}(\lambda)$
$(\mathsf{mpk}, \mathsf{kpol}, \mathsf{msk}) \leftarrow\!\!{\$}\ \mathsf{Setup}(1^\lambda)$	$(\mathsf{mpk}, \mathsf{kpol}, \mathsf{msk}) \leftarrow\!\!{\$}\ \mathsf{Setup}(1^\lambda)$
$(m_0, m_1, \mathbb{R}_0, \mathbb{R}_1, \sigma_0, \sigma_1, \alpha) \leftarrow\!\!{\$}\ \mathsf{A}_1^{\mathsf{O}_1, \mathsf{O}_2, \mathsf{O}_3}(1^\lambda, \mathsf{mpk})$	$(c, \rho, \mathbb{S}) \leftarrow\!\!{\$}\ \mathsf{A}^{\mathsf{O}_1, \mathsf{O}_2, \mathsf{O}_3}(1^\lambda, \mathsf{mpk})$
$b \leftarrow\!\!{\$}\ \{0, 1\}$	$\mathsf{dk}_\rho \leftarrow\!\!{\$}\ \mathsf{RKGen}(\mathsf{msk}, \rho)$
$\mathsf{ek}_{\sigma_b} \leftarrow\!\!{\$}\ \mathsf{SKGen}(\mathsf{msk}, \sigma_b)$	$\mathsf{dk}_{\mathbb{S}} \leftarrow\!\!{\$}\ \mathsf{PolGen}(\mathsf{kpol}, \mathbb{S})$
$c \leftarrow\!\!{\$}\ \mathsf{Enc}(\mathsf{ek}_{\sigma_b}, \mathbb{R}_b, m_b)$	$m = \mathsf{Dec}(\mathsf{dk}_\rho, \mathsf{dk}_{\mathbb{S}}, c)$
$b' \leftarrow\!\!{\$}\ \mathsf{A}_2^{\mathsf{O}_1, \mathsf{O}_2, \mathsf{O}_3}(1^\lambda, c, \alpha)$	If $\forall \sigma \in \mathcal{Q}_{\mathsf{O}_1} : (\mathbb{S}(\sigma) = 0) \wedge (m \neq \bot)$
If $(b' = b)$ **return** 1	**return** 1
Else **return** 0	Else **return** 0

Fig. 1. Games defining privacy and authenticity of ME. Oracles $\mathsf{O}_1, \mathsf{O}_2, \mathsf{O}_3$ are implemented by $\mathsf{SKGen}(\mathsf{msk}, \cdot)$, $\mathsf{RKGen}(\mathsf{msk}, \cdot)$, $\mathsf{PolGen}(\mathsf{kpol}, \cdot)$.

Definition 5 (Privacy of ME). *We say that an ME Π satisfies* privacy *if for all valid PPT adversaries* A:

$$\left| \mathbb{P}\left[\mathbf{G}^{\mathsf{priv}}_{\Pi,\mathsf{A}}(\lambda) = 1 \right] - \frac{1}{2} \right| \leq \mathsf{negl}(\lambda),$$

where game $\mathbf{G}^{\mathsf{priv}}_{\Pi,\mathsf{A}}(\lambda)$ *is depicted in Fig. 1. Adversary* A *is called* valid *if* $\forall \rho \in \mathcal{Q}_{\mathsf{O}_2}, \forall \mathbb{S} \in \mathcal{Q}_{\mathsf{O}_3}$ *it satisfies the following invariant:*

- *(Mismatch condition).* Either

$$(\mathbb{R}_0(\rho) = \mathbb{R}_1(\rho) = 0) \vee (\mathbb{S}(\sigma_0) = \mathbb{S}(\sigma_1) = 0)$$
$$\vee \, (\mathbb{R}_0(\rho) = \mathbb{S}(\sigma_1) = 0) \vee (\mathbb{R}_1(\rho) = \mathbb{S}(\sigma_0) = 0); \qquad (1)$$

- *(Match condition).* Or *(if $\exists \hat{\rho} \in \mathcal{Q}_{O_2}, \hat{\mathbb{S}} \in \mathcal{Q}_{O_3}$ s.t. Eq. (1) does not hold)*

$$(m_0 = m_1) \wedge (\mathbb{R}_0(\rho) = \mathbb{R}_1(\rho)) \wedge (\mathbb{S}(\sigma_0) = \mathbb{S}(\sigma_1)).$$

Note that in the above definition the challenge ciphertext is honestly computed. This is because privacy captures security against malicious receivers. Authenticity, on the other hand, demands that the only way to produce a valid ciphertext under attributes σ is to obtain an encryption key ek_σ from the authority, thus guaranteeing that if a ciphertext decrypts correctly, then it has been created by a sender with the proper encryption key. This captures security against malicious senders.

The latter is modeled by a game in which the attacker has oracle access to SKGen, RKGen, and PolGen. The attacker's goal is to output a tuple $(\rho, \mathbb{S}, c)$ such that $\mathsf{Dec}(\mathsf{dk}_\rho, \mathsf{dk}_\mathbb{S}, c) \neq \bot$, and none of the encryption keys ek_σ for attributes σ (obtained by the adversary via oracle queries) satisfies the policy $\mathbb{S}$. Observe that the adversary is not given access to an encryption oracle. The reason for this is that we only consider security in the presence of chosen-plaintext attacks, and thus ciphertexts might be malleable,[4] which makes it possible to forge in the authenticity game.

Definition 6 (Authenticity of ME). *We say that an ME Π satisfies authenticity if for all PPT adversaries A:*

$$\mathbb{P}\left[\mathbf{G}_{\Pi,\mathsf{A}}^{\mathsf{auth}}(\lambda) = 1\right] \leq \mathsf{negl}(\lambda),$$

where game $\mathbf{G}_{\Pi,\mathsf{A}}^{\mathsf{auth}}(\lambda)$ is depicted in Fig. 1.

Finally, a secure ME is an ME satisfying all the properties.

Definition 7 (Secure ME). *We say that an ME Π is secure, if Π satisfies privacy (Definition 5) and authenticity (Definition 6).*

Sometimes, we will also consider a weaker definition where there is an a priori upper bound on the number of queries an attacker can make to oracles RKGen and PolGen. We refer to this variant as security against bounded collusions. In particular, we say that an ME is (q_1, q_1', q_2, q_2')-secure if it has (q_1, q_1', q_2, q_2')-privacy and authenticity, where q_1, q_1' (resp. q_2, q_2') denote the number of queries to RKGen and PolGen allowed by A_1 (resp. A_2) in the privacy game.

---

[4] Note that malleability (and thus the authenticity property considered in our paper) might be a desirable feature in some scenarios, as it implies a form of deniability. It could also be useful in future extensions of ME (e.g., in the spirit of proxy re-encryption).

Relation to ABE. An ME for arbitrary policies can be used as a CP-ABE with the same expressiveness. The idea is to ignore the attributes of the sender and the policy of the receiver. It is sufficient to set the ABE master public key to $(\mathsf{mpk}, \mathsf{ek}_\sigma)$ and an ABE receiver's decryption key to $(\mathsf{dk}_\rho, \mathsf{dk}_\phi)$, where ek_σ is the encryption key generated for attributes $\sigma = 0^\lambda$, dk_ϕ is the policy key for a tautology ϕ (i.e., a circuit whose output is always 1 regardless of the input), and dk_ρ is the decryption key for attributes ρ. The encryption of a message m under a policy $\mathbb{R}$ works by running the ME encryption algorithm $\mathsf{Enc}(\mathsf{ek}_\sigma, \mathbb{R}, m)$. The receiver will decrypt the ciphertext by using the keys $(\mathsf{dk}_\rho, \mathsf{dk}_\phi)$. Since ϕ is a tautology, it does not matter under which attributes the message has been encrypted. Thus, the scheme will work as a normal CP-ABE.

Following a similar reasoning, ME implies KP-ABE. This is achieved by setting $\mathsf{ek}_\sigma = \sigma$, and by using the same approach described above (i.e., set the sender's policy circuit $\mathbb{R}$ to a tautology ϕ which ignores the receiver's attributes). Note that for this implication authenticity is not required, which is reminiscent of the fact that in ABE the attributes are not explicitly certified by an authority.

4 Black-Box Construction

We explore black-box constructions of ME and A-ME from several types of FE schemes. In particular, in Sect. 4.1 we give a construction of ME based on rFE and FE. As discussed in the introduction, such a construction allows us to obtain ME from weaker assumptions, at the price of achieving only security against bounded collusions. In the full version of the paper [5], we describe and analyze two additional schemes: (i) A construction of ME that is secure against unbounded collusions, based on 2FE (and thus on stronger assumptions); (ii) A construction of A-ME based on FE. All schemes additionally rely on digital signatures and on NIZK proofs.

4.1 ME from rFE

Our construction is based on the following two functionalities f^{FE} and f^{rFE}:

$$f^{\mathsf{FE}}_{\mathbb{S}}(\sigma, m) = \begin{cases} m, & \text{if } \sigma \neq \bot \wedge \mathbb{S}(\sigma) = 1 \\ \bot, & \text{otherwise} \end{cases}$$

and

$$f^{\mathsf{rFE}}_{(\rho, \mathsf{mpk}_{\mathsf{FE}})}(\mathbb{R}, \sigma, m; r) = \begin{cases} \mathsf{Enc}(\mathsf{mpk}_{\mathsf{FE}}, (\sigma, m); r), & \text{if } \mathbb{R}(\rho) = 1 \\ \mathsf{Enc}(\mathsf{mpk}_{\mathsf{FE}}, (\bot, \bot); r), & \text{otherwise.} \end{cases}$$

Construction 1 (ME for Arbitrary Policies). *Let* FE, rFE, SS, NIZK *be respectively an FE scheme for the deterministic functionality* f^{FE}, *a rFE scheme for the randomized functionality* f^{rFE}, *a signature scheme, and a NIZK proof system for the NP relation:*

$$R_1 \stackrel{def}{=} \left\{ ((c, \mathsf{pk}, \mathsf{mpk}_{\mathsf{rFE}}), (\sigma, s)) : \begin{array}{c} \exists r, m, \mathbb{R} \; s.t. \\ c = \mathsf{Enc}_{\mathsf{rFE}}(\mathsf{mpk}_{\mathsf{rFE}}, (\mathbb{R}, \sigma, m); r) \wedge \\ \mathsf{Ver}(\mathsf{pk}, s, \sigma) = 1 \end{array} \right\}.$$

We construct an ME scheme in the following way:

Setup(1^λ): *On input the security parameter 1^λ, the setup algorithm computes* $(\mathsf{mpk}_{\mathsf{FE}}, \mathsf{msk}_{\mathsf{FE}}) \leftarrow_\$ \mathsf{Setup}_{\mathsf{FE}}(1^\lambda)$, $(\mathsf{sk}, \mathsf{pk}) \leftarrow_\$ \mathsf{KGen}_{\mathsf{SS}}(1^\lambda)$, $(\mathsf{mpk}_{\mathsf{rFE}}, \mathsf{msk}_{\mathsf{rFE}}) \leftarrow_\$ \mathsf{Setup}_{\mathsf{rFE}}(1^\lambda)$, *and* $\omega \leftarrow_\$ \mathsf{I}(1^\lambda)$. *Finally, it outputs the master secret key* $\mathsf{msk} = (\mathsf{msk}_{\mathsf{rFE}}, \mathsf{sk})$, *the master policy key* $\mathsf{kpol} = \mathsf{msk}_{\mathsf{FE}}$, *and the master public key* $\mathsf{mpk} = (\mathsf{pk}, \omega, \mathsf{mpk}_{\mathsf{FE}}, \mathsf{mpk}_{\mathsf{rFE}})$. *Recall that all other algorithms are implicitly given* mpk *as input.*

SKGen(msk, σ): *On input the master secret key* $\mathsf{msk} = (\mathsf{msk}_{\mathsf{rFE}}, \mathsf{sk})$, *and attributes* $\sigma \in \{0,1\}^*$, *the algorithm returns the encryption key* $\mathsf{ek}_\sigma = (\sigma, s)$ *where* $s \leftarrow_\$ \mathsf{Sign}(\mathsf{sk}, \sigma)$ *(i.e., s is a signature on attributes $\sigma \in \{0,1\}^*$).*

RKGen(msk, ρ): *On input the master secret key* $\mathsf{msk} = (\mathsf{msk}_{\mathsf{rFE}}, \mathsf{sk})$, *and attributes* $\rho \in \{0,1\}^*$, *the algorithm computes the decryption key* $\mathsf{sk}_{(\rho, \mathsf{mpk}_{\mathsf{FE}})} \leftarrow_\$ \mathsf{KGen}_{\mathsf{rFE}}(\mathsf{msk}_{\mathsf{rFE}}, (\rho, \mathsf{mpk}_{\mathsf{FE}}))$. *Then, it outputs the decryption key* $\mathsf{dk}_\rho = \mathsf{sk}_{(\rho, \mathsf{mpk}_{\mathsf{FE}})}$.

PolGen($\mathsf{kpol}, \mathbb{S}$): *On input the master policy key* $\mathsf{kpol} = \mathsf{msk}_{\mathsf{FE}}$, *and policy $\mathbb{S}$ represented as a circuit, the algorithm computes the function key* $\mathsf{sk}_{\mathbb{S}}$ *by running* $\mathsf{KGen}_{\mathsf{FE}}(\mathsf{msk}_{\mathsf{FE}}, \mathbb{S})$. *Then, it outputs the decryption key* $\mathsf{dk}_{\mathbb{S}} = \mathsf{sk}_{\mathbb{S}}$.

Enc($\mathsf{ek}_\sigma, \mathbb{R}, m$): *On input an encryption key* $\mathsf{ek}_\sigma = (\sigma, s)$, *a policy $\mathbb{R}$ represented as a circuit, and a message m, the algorithm encrypt the message by computing* $c \leftarrow_\$ \mathsf{Enc}_{\mathsf{rFE}}(\mathsf{mpk}_{\mathsf{rFE}}, (\mathbb{R}, \sigma, m))$. *Finally, it returns the ciphertext* $\hat{c} = (c, \pi)$ *where* $\pi \leftarrow_\$ \mathsf{P}(\omega, (\mathsf{pk}, c, \mathsf{mpk}_{\mathsf{rFE}}), (\sigma, s))$.

Dec($\mathsf{dk}_\rho, \mathsf{dk}_{\mathbb{S}}, c$): *On input two keys* $\mathsf{dk}_\rho = \mathsf{sk}_{(\rho, \mathsf{mpk}_{\mathsf{FE}})}$, $\mathsf{dk}_{\mathbb{S}} = \mathsf{sk}_{\mathbb{S}}$, *and a ciphertext* $\hat{c} = (c, \pi)$, *the algorithm first checks whether* $\mathsf{V}(\omega, (\mathsf{pk}, c, \mathsf{mpk}_{\mathsf{rFE}}), \pi) = 1$. *If that is not the case, it returns $\perp$, and else it returns* $\mathsf{Dec}_{\mathsf{FF}}(\mathsf{sk}_{\mathbb{S}}, \mathsf{Dec}_{\mathsf{rFE}}(\mathsf{sk}_{(\rho, \mathsf{mpk}_{\mathsf{FE}})}, c))$.

Correctness of the scheme follows directly by the correctness of the underlying primitives. As for security, we establish the following result, whose proof appears in the full version [5].

Theorem 1. *Let* rFE, FE, SS, NIZK *be as above. If* rFE *is* $(q_1, 1, q_2)$-*NA-SIM-secure (Definition 2),* FE *is* (q_1', q_1, q_2')-*SIM-secure,* SS *is EUF-CMA, and* NIZK *satisfied adaptive multi-theorem zero knowledge and knowledge soundness, then the ME scheme Π from Construction 1 is* (q_1, q_1', q_2, q_2')-*secure.*

5   Identity-Based Matchmaking Encryption

In this section, we present a practical ME for the identity-based setting (i.e., equality policies). As in ME, attributes are encoded by bit strings, but now each attribute $x \in \{0,1\}^*$ satisfies only the access policy $\mathbb{A} = x$, which means that both the sender and the receiver specify a single identity instead of general policies (represented as a circuit). We will denote by snd and rcv, respectively, the target identities (i.e., the access policies) specified by the receiver and by the sender.

While any ME as defined in Sect. 3 perfectly works for this restricted setting, the problem is that in order to select the identity snd of the source, a receiver must ask to the administrator the corresponding key dk_{snd} such that $S = snd$. (Recall that the sender, instead, can already specify the target identity $R = rcv$ on the fly, during encryption.) In particular, if the receiver is interested in decrypting ciphertexts from several distinct sources, it must ask for several decryption keys dk_{snd}, which is impractical.[5]

We resolve this issue by removing algorithm PolGen from the syntax of an IB-ME, so that the decryption algorithm takes directly as input the description of the target identity snd (i.e., $Dec(dk_\rho, snd, c)$). This way, the receiver can specify the target identity the source must satisfy on the fly, without talking to the authority.

5.1 Security of IB-ME

The choice of removing the PolGen algorithm has an impact on the security properties for IB-ME. Below, we revisit each security guarantee in the identity-based setting and explain how (and why) the security definition has to be adapted. We refer the reader to Fig. 2 for the formal definitions.

Privacy of IB-ME. We cannot require that the sender's identity remains hidden in case of a decryption failure due to a mismatch condition. In particular, a malicious receiver can always change the sender's target identity in order to infer under which identity a ciphertext has been encrypted.

More formally, consider the adversary that chooses a tuple $(m, m, rcv, rcv, \sigma_0, \sigma_1)$, and receives a ciphertext c such that $c \leftarrow_s Enc(ek_{\sigma_b}, rcv, m)$, where the encryption key ek_{σ_b} corresponds to identity σ_b; the attacker can simply pick a target identity snd' such that, say, $\sigma_0 = snd'$ (whereas $\sigma_1 \neq snd'$), and thus distinguish σ_0 from σ_1 by decrypting c with dk_ρ and target identity snd'.[6] On the other hand, privacy might still hold in case of mismatch, as long as the keys dk_ρ held by the receiver correspond to identities ρ that do not match the receiver's target identity. Thus, in the security game, an attacker is now valid if for every decryption key dk_ρ obtained from the oracle, it holds that $\rho \neq rcv_0$ and $\rho \neq rcv_1$, where the target identities rcv_0, rcv_1 are chosen by the adversary. Lastly, note that in case of a match, if a receiver has identity ρ and specifies a policy snd, it can automatically infer that $\sigma = snd$ and $rcv = \rho$. For this reason, the privacy game does not consider any match condition.

This relaxed form of privacy is enough and desirable in many scenarios. Intuitively, it guarantees that nothing is leaked to an unintended receiver who doesn't match the sender's policy; on the other hand, an intended receiver can choose which ciphertexts to decrypt by trying different policies. This feature is essential in our bulletin board application (Sect. 6) because it allows parties, e.g.,

---

[5] This is *not* an issue for an ME that supports arbitrary policies, as in that case, a single policy encodes a large number of attributes.

[6] This attack can be generalized to show that privacy does not hold if the PolGen algorithm (and thus the policy key kpol) is made public.

journalists and political activists, to select which type of messages to read. IB-ME works well in this scenario since it provides enough flexibility to the intended receivers while protecting senders from possible attackers.

Finally, we note that the above security definition does not guarantee that the message m remains secret with respect to an *honest receiver* that chooses the "wrong" target identity snd. The latter is, however, a desirable feature that our practical scheme will satisfy (cf. Remark 1).

Authenticity of IB-ME. Turning to unforgeability in the identity-based setting, the forgery (c, ρ, snd) is considered valid if for all encryption keys ek_σ obtained by the adversary it holds that $\sigma \neq \mathsf{snd}$, and moreover the identity ρ is not held by the adversary (i.e., the adversary cannot "forge to itself").

$\mathbf{G}^{\mathsf{ib\text{-}priv}}_{\Pi,\mathsf{A}}(\lambda)$

$(\mathsf{mpk}, \mathsf{msk}) \leftarrow\!\!\$ \ \mathsf{Setup}(1^\lambda)$

$(m_0, m_1, \mathsf{rcv}_0, \mathsf{rcv}_1, \sigma_0, \sigma_1, \alpha) \leftarrow\!\!\$ \ \mathsf{A}_1^{O_1, O_2}(1^\lambda, \mathsf{mpk})$

$b \leftarrow\!\!\$ \ \{0, 1\}$

$\mathsf{ek}_{\sigma_b} \leftarrow\!\!\$ \ \mathsf{SKGen}(\mathsf{msk}, \sigma_b)$

$c \leftarrow\!\!\$ \ \mathsf{Enc}(\mathsf{ek}_{\sigma_b}, \mathsf{rcv}_b, m_b)$

$b' \leftarrow\!\!\$ \ \mathsf{A}_2^{O_1, O_2}(1^\lambda, c, \alpha)$

If $(b' = b)$ **return** 1

Else **return** 0

$\mathbf{G}^{\mathsf{ib\text{-}auth}}_{\Pi,\mathsf{A}}(\lambda)$

$(\mathsf{mpk}, \mathsf{msk}) \leftarrow\!\!\$ \ \mathsf{Setup}(1^\lambda)$

$(c, \rho, \mathsf{snd}) \leftarrow\!\!\$ \ \mathsf{A}^{O_1, O_2}(1^\lambda, \mathsf{mpk})$

$\mathsf{dk}_\rho \leftarrow\!\!\$ \ \mathsf{RKGen}(\mathsf{msk}, \rho)$

$m = \mathsf{Dec}(\mathsf{dk}_\rho, \mathsf{snd}, c)$

If $\forall \sigma \in \mathcal{Q}_{O_1} : (\sigma \neq \mathsf{snd}) \wedge (\rho \notin \mathcal{Q}_{O_2}) \wedge$

$(m \neq \perp)$

return 1

Else **return** 0

Fig. 2. Games defining privacy and authenticity security of IB-ME. Oracles O_1, O_2 are implemented by $\mathsf{SKGen}(\mathsf{msk}, \cdot)$, $\mathsf{RKGen}(\mathsf{msk}, \cdot)$.

Security Definitions. The definitions below capture the very same correctness and security requirements of an ME, but translated to the identity-based case.

Definition 8 (Correctness of IB-ME). *An IB-ME* $\Pi =$ (Setup, SKGen, RKGen, Enc, Dec) *is correct if* $\forall \lambda \in \mathbb{N}$, $\forall (\mathsf{mpk}, \mathsf{msk})$ *output by* Setup(1^λ), $\forall m \in \mathcal{M}$, $\forall \sigma$, ρ, rcv, snd $\in \{0, 1\}^*$:

$$\mathbb{P}\left[\mathsf{Dec}(\mathsf{dk}_\rho, \mathsf{snd}, \mathsf{Enc}(\mathsf{ek}_\sigma, \mathsf{rcv}, m)) = m\right] \geq 1 - \mathsf{negl}(\lambda),$$

whenever $\sigma = \mathsf{snd}$ *and* $\rho = \mathsf{rcv}$, *and otherwise*

$$\mathbb{P}\left[\mathsf{Dec}(\mathsf{dk}_\rho, \mathsf{snd}, \mathsf{Enc}(\mathsf{ek}_\sigma, \mathsf{rcv}, m)) = \perp\right] \geq 1 - \mathsf{negl}(\lambda),$$

where ek_σ, dk_ρ *are generated by* SKGen(msk, σ), *and* RKGen(msk, ρ).

Definition 9 (Privacy of IB-ME). *We say that an IB-ME* Π *satisfies* privacy *if for all valid PPT adversaries* A:

$$\left| \mathbb{P}\left[\mathbf{G}^{\mathsf{ib\text{-}priv}}_{\Pi,\mathsf{A}}(\lambda) = 1\right] - \frac{1}{2} \right| \leq \mathsf{negl}(\lambda),$$

where game $\mathbf{G}^{\mathsf{ib\text{-}priv}}_{\Pi,\mathsf{A}}(\lambda)$ *is depicted in Fig. 2. Adversary* A *is called valid if* $\forall \rho \in \mathcal{Q}_{O_2}$ *it satisfies the following invariant:*

– *(Mismatch condition).* $\rho \neq \text{rcv}_0 \wedge \rho \neq \text{rcv}_1$.

Definition 10 (Authenticity of IB-ME). *We say that an IB-ME Π satisfies authenticity if for all PPT adversaries A:*

$$\mathbb{P}\left[\mathbf{G}_{\Pi,\mathsf{A}}^{\text{ib-auth}}(\lambda) = 1\right] \leq \text{negl}(\lambda),$$

where game $\mathbf{G}_{\Pi,\mathsf{A}}^{\text{ib-auth}}(\lambda)$ is depicted in Fig. 2.

Definition 11 (Secure IB-ME). *We say that an IB-ME Π is secure if it satisfies privacy (Definition 9) and authenticity (Definition 10).*

5.2 The Scheme

We are now ready to present our practical IB-ME scheme.

Construction 2 (IB-ME). *The construction works as follows.*

Setup(1^λ): *Let $e : \mathbb{G} \times \mathbb{G} \to \mathbb{G}_T$ be a symmetric pairing, and P a generator of $\mathbb{G}$, with $\mathbb{G}$, and $\mathbb{G}_T$ of an order q that depends on λ. We also have three hash functions $H : \{0,1\}^* \to \mathbb{G}$, $H' : \{0,1\}^* \to \mathbb{G}$, $\hat{H} : \mathbb{G}_T \to \{0,1\}^\ell$, modeled as random oracles, and a polynomial-time computable padding function $\Phi : \{0,1\}^n \to \{0,1\}^\ell$. We require that for all $m \in \{0,1\}^n$ one can verify in polynomial time if m has been padded correctly, and moreover that $\Phi(m)$ is efficiently invertible. On input the security parameter 1^λ, the setup algorithm samples two random $r, s \in \mathbb{Z}_q$, and sets $P_0 = P^r$. Finally, it outputs the master public key $\mathsf{mpk} = (e, \mathbb{G}, \mathbb{G}_T, q, P, P_0, H, H', \hat{H}, \Phi)$ and the master secret key is $\mathsf{msk} = (r, s)$. Recall that all other algorithms are implicitly given mpk as input.*

SKGen(msk, σ): *On input the master secret key msk, and identity σ, the algorithm outputs $\mathsf{ek}_\sigma = H'(\sigma)^s$.*

RKGen($\mathsf{mpk}, \mathsf{msk}, \rho$): *On input the master secret key msk, and identity ρ, the algorithm outputs $\mathsf{dk}_\rho = (\mathsf{dk}_\rho^1, \mathsf{dk}_\rho^2, \mathsf{dk}_\rho^3) = (H(\rho)^r, H(\rho)^s, H(\rho))$.*

Enc($\mathsf{mpk}, \mathsf{ek}_\sigma, \mathsf{rcv}, m$): *On input an encryption key ek_σ, a target identity $\mathsf{rcv} = \rho$, and a message $m \in \{0,1\}^n$, the algorithm proceeds as follows:*

1. *Sample random $u, t \in \mathbb{Z}_q$.*
2. *Compute $T = P^t$ and $U = P^u$.*
3. *Compute $k_R = e(H(\rho), P_0^u)$ and $k_S = e(H(\rho), T \cdot \mathsf{ek}_\sigma)$.*
4. *Compute $V = \Phi(m) \oplus \hat{H}(k_R) \oplus \hat{H}(k_S)$.*
5. *Output ciphertext $C = (T, U, V)$.*

Dec($\mathsf{mpk}, \mathsf{dk}_\rho, \mathsf{snd}, c$): *On input the master public key mpk, a decryption key dk_ρ, a target identity $\mathsf{snd} = \sigma$, and a message m, the algorithm proceeds as follows:*

1. *Parse c as (T, U, V).*
2. *Compute $k_R = e(\mathsf{dk}_\rho^1, U)$ and $k_S = e(\mathsf{dk}_\rho^2, H'(\sigma)) \cdot e(\mathsf{dk}_\rho^3, T)$.*
3. *Compute $\Phi(m) = V \oplus \hat{H}(k_R) \oplus \hat{H}(k_S)$*
4. *If the padding is valid, return m. Otherwise, return $\perp$.*

Correctness. The correctness of the scheme only depends on the computation of k_R and k_S as evaluated by the decryption algorithm. Here, we require that the padding function Φ satisfies the property that a random string in $\{0,1\}^\ell$ has only a negligible probability to form a valid padding w.r.t. the function Φ.[7] Let k_R, k_S be the keys computed during encryption, and k'_R, k'_S the ones computed during decryption. The scheme is correct since $\forall \sigma, \rho, \mathsf{rcv}, \mathsf{snd} \in \{0,1\}^*$, $\mathsf{ek}_\sigma \leftarrow_\$ \mathsf{SKGen}(\mathsf{msk}, \sigma)$, $\mathsf{dk}_\rho \leftarrow_\$ \mathsf{RKGen}(\mathsf{msk}, \rho)$:

1. If $\sigma = \mathsf{snd}$ and $\rho = \mathsf{rcv}$:

$$k_R = e(H(\rho), P_0^u) = e(H(\rho)^r, P^u)$$
$$= e(\mathsf{dk}_\rho^1, U) = k'_R, \text{ and}$$
$$k_S = e(H(\rho), T \cdot \mathsf{ek}_\sigma) = e(H(\rho), T \cdot H'(\sigma)^s)$$
$$= e(H(\rho), T) \cdot e(H(\rho)^s, H'(\sigma)) =$$
$$= e(\mathsf{dk}_\rho^3, T) \cdot e(\mathsf{dk}_\rho^2, H'(\sigma)) = k'_S$$

2. Otherwise, if $\rho \neq \mathsf{rcv} = \rho'$ or $\sigma \neq \mathsf{snd} = \sigma$

$$k_R = e(H(\rho'), P_0^u) \neq e(H(\rho)^r, P^u)$$
$$= e(\mathsf{dk}_\rho^1, U) = k'_R, \text{ or}$$
$$k_S = e(H(\rho), T \cdot \mathsf{ek}_\sigma) = e(H(\rho), T \cdot H'(\sigma)^s)$$
$$= e(\mathsf{dk}_\rho^3, T) \cdot e(\mathsf{dk}_\rho^2, H'(\sigma)) \neq$$
$$= e(\mathsf{dk}_\rho^3, T) \cdot e(\mathsf{dk}_\rho^2, H'(\sigma')) = k'_S.$$

Since k'_R (resp. k'_S) is hashed by the random oracle $\hat{H}$, then $\hat{H}(k'_R)$ (resp. $\hat{H}(k'_S)$) is statistically close to a random string of length ℓ. Hence, with overwhelming probability, $V \oplus \hat{H}(k_R) \oplus \hat{H}(k'_S)$, where either $k_R \neq k'_R$ or $k_S \neq k'_S$, will produce an invalid padding, and the decryption algorithm returns $\perp$.

Remark 1 (Plaintext secrecy w.r.t. unauthorized-but-honest receivers). We note that the plaintext is information-theoretically hidden from the point of view of an honest receiver which specifies a target identity that does not match the sender's identity. Moreover, the latter holds even given the internal state of the receiver at the end of the decryption procedure. In fact, since $\hat{H}(k_S)$ is statistically close to uniform, and $|\hat{H}(k_S)| = |\Phi(m)| = \ell$, the decryption algorithm will compute a symmetric key k_S different to the one generated during encryption.[8]

---

[7] This can be achieved, e.g., by setting $\ell = n + \lambda + 1$, and by appending to each message the string $1||0^\lambda$.

[8] It is important to recall that a similar guarantee does not hold in the identity-based setting, when the receiver is semi-honest (cf. Sect. 5.1).

Security. As for security, we establish the following result, whose proof appears in the full version [5].

Theorem 2. *Let $\mathbb{G}$, $\mathbb{G}_T$ be two groups of prime order q, and let $e : \mathbb{G} \times \mathbb{G} \to \mathbb{G}_T$ be an admissible bilinear map. If the BDH problem is hard in $(\mathbb{G}, \mathbb{G}_T, e)$ (Definition 3), then the IB-ME scheme Π from Construction 2 is secure (Definition 11) in the random oracle model.*

6 IB-ME Performance Evaluation and Application to Tor

In this section, we demonstrate that our IB-ME is practical and we use it to implement a novel system for anonymous but authentic communication. We first show in Sect. 6.1 the performance evaluation of our IB-ME implementation. We then describe in Sect. 6.2 an application for IB-ME built on top of our implementation. The proposed application is a *bulletin board hidden service* that allows parties to collect or exchange anonymous messages that have an expected format and come from authentic sources. It allows users to exchange IB-ME messages over the Tor network, specifically, using the Tor Hidden Services feature (cf. Sect. 6.2). Our bulletin board prototype can be used for covert communication by journalists or activists under authoritarian governments. It improves upon systems such as SecurePost [35] for verified group anonymity by providing much stronger privacy guarantees since ciphertexts can be vetted *before* decryption.

6.1 Implementation and Evaluation of the IB-ME Cryptosystem

We provide an experimental evaluation of the IB-ME cryptosystem. To this end, we implemented a proof of concept in Python 3.6.5 using Charm 0.50 [2], a framework for prototyping pairing-based cryptosystems (among others). Since our IB-ME is defined using symmetric pairings (also called Type-I pairings), we instantiate it with a supersingular curve with a 512-bit base field (curve SS512 in Charm), which gives approximately 80 bits of security [39]. The execution environment is an Intel NUC7i7BNH with an Intel Core i7-7567U CPU @ 3.50 GHz and 16 GB of RAM, running Ubuntu 18.04 LTS.

Table 2. Performance of high- and low-level cryptographic operations of IB-ME

Operation	Minimum (ms)	Average (ms)
Setup	2.197	2.213
RKGen	2.200	2.225
SKGen	3.400	3.429
Encryption	6.942	7.012
Decryption	4.344	4.385

Table 2 shows the cost in milliseconds associated to the main high- and low-level cryptographic operations of IB-ME. We executed these experiments in 50 different runs of 10 times each and both the minimum and average timing was taken for each operation; we use the Python module `timeit` for these measurements. It can be seen that the average timings for the main high-level operations of IB-ME, namely Encryption and Decryption, are 7.012 ms and 4.385 ms, respectively. These results show that the scheme is highly practical.

It is worth mentioning that there is room for improvement in the implementation if we use optimizations such as pre-computation of some pairing operations when one of the arguments is fixed (which occurs in the two pairings during decryption since one argument is a decryption key) or is reused (the two pairings in the encryption function have $H(\rho)$ as an argument), which can lead to speeds-up around 30%, as reported in [18]. Another potential optimization is the use of multipairings in the decryption operation. A promising direction would be to redefine the scheme in a Type-III pairing setting, which allows for more performant curves [22].

Finally, Table 3 shows a summary of the space costs associated to different elements of our IB-ME. We analyze both the theoretical cost and the actual values with the parameters of the experiment. In addition to the use of Charm's curve SS512 (which implies that the size of $|\mathbb{G}| = 512$ bits and $|\mathbb{G}_T| = 1024$), we use for the size of identity bitstrings $|\mathbb{G}|$, for the size of messages $n = |\mathbb{G}_T|$, and for the padding output size $\ell = n + \lambda + 1 = 1105$.

Table 3. Space costs of IB-ME elements.

Element	Theoretical cost	Size (in bits)
Encryption key	$\|\mathbb{G}\|$	512
Decryption key	$3\|\mathbb{G}\|$	1536
Message	n	1024
Ciphertext	$2\|\mathbb{G}\| + \ell$	2129
Ciphertext expansion	$\frac{\ell}{n} + \frac{2\|\mathbb{G}\|}{n}$	≈ 2

6.2   An Anonymous Bulletin Board

Here, we describe the implementation of a bulletin board hidden service that is powered by our IB-ME scheme (cf. Sect. 5). In a nutshell, our application allows senders to post encrypted messages to an anonymous bulletin board, hosted by a Tor hidden service [45]. To this end, senders specify a target identity string that acts as the receiver's access policy, as well as the encryption key corresponding to their own identity. Conversely, receivers can fetch encrypted messages from the bulletin board, and try to decrypt them with their own decryption keys (associated with their identity) and the expected identity of the sender. Only those encrypted messages where there is a match between sender and receiver can be decrypted correctly.

Our system protects every party's privacy in several aspects. First of all, thanks to the nature of Tor hidden services, the IP addresses of each party and the connection between the client and the server remain hidden. Secondly, if decryption fails nothing is revealed to the parties.

Next, we will give a brief overview of Tor Hidden Services.

Tor and Hidden Services. Tor [43] is the most prominent P2P anonymous system, totaling more than 2 million users and 6,000 relays. It allows clients to access the Internet anonymously by hiding the final destination of their connections. It achieves this by creating random circuits between the client and the destination (e.g., web server), where every relay is aware only of its incoming and outgoing links.

Various services can be set up so that they are accessible only within the Tor network. These Tor *Hidden Services* [45], or HS, are run without revealing their IP addresses and can be reached with no prior information. In order to deploy an HS, the owner needs to initialize the service by choosing some relays that will act as introduction points (IPs). The service will keep an open Tor circuit to each IP that will be used as the entry points to access the HS. The IPs' identities are communicated to Tor by creating a service descriptor entry. This entry contains all the information needed to access the service (e.g., description ID, list of IPs, etc.). Then, the entry is uploaded to the hidden service directory (HSDir) which stores the description entries of all available HSs. A node that wants to connect to an HS will (1) retrieve from HSDirs the correct description entry, (2) establish a Tor circuit to a random relay known as the *rendezvous point*, RP in short, and (3) reveal to one of the hidden service's IP (contained in the description entry) the address of the RP. The HS can now open a Tor circuit to the RP, so that the node and the HS can communicate without revealing their respective IP addresses.

Our Anonymous Bulletin Board. Our application is composed of two parts: a web server implemented as a Tor hidden service, and a command line client that is used to upload and download data from the server.

A user that wants to post a message to the bulletin board can use the client to encrypt it (using their IB-ME encryption key ek_σ and an identity string policy rcv for the intended receiver), and upload the ciphertext to the web server through the Tor network. These ciphertexts are publicly available.

A receiver can now use the client to download all the ciphertexts and try to decrypt each of them, using the receiver's decryption key dk_ρ and the sender's identity policy snd (given as input to the client). The client will report to the user the outcome of the decryption phase, showing all the successfully decrypted messages. The role of the web server is to store encrypted messages and to offer a simple REST API that allows clients to post and read these messages. In our prototype, we do not include any additional security measure, but in a real-world deployment, specific countermeasures should be taken in order to protect against potential denial of service attacks from clients (e.g., by requiring a proof-of-work along with the request) and/or include some authentication mechanisms. We refer the reader to Fig. 3 for an overview of the system.

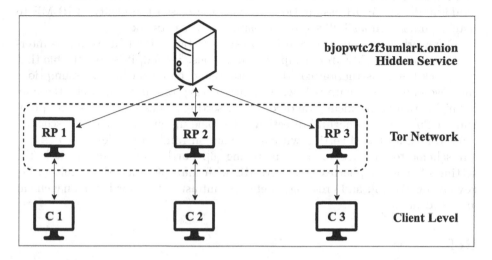

Fig. 3. Example of interaction between three clients C1, C2, C3 and the anonymous bulletin board (http://bjopwtc2f3umlark.onion) using Tor. The relays RP1, RP2, and RP3 are the rendezvous points shared between the service and the respective clients. Each party communicates with the respective RP using a Tor circuit.

As in any identity-based cryptosystem, key management requires a key generation service that generates and distributes encryption and decryption keys. This service could be implemented as another Tor hidden service, or even integrated with an existing HSDir (already assumed to be trusted because downloaded from legitimate servers), that automatically converts email addresses or phone numbers into keys. Another possibility is to assume the existence of an off-line authority so that users of the application obtain their keys through an out-of-band channel. In our prototype, we assume the latter option for simplicity.

Finally, note that the performance cost of our Tor application is dominated by the network latency of the Tor relays. Since the main focus of the paper is the new cryptographic primitive, we report only the performance evaluation of our IB-ME scheme (cf. Sect. 6.1).

7 Conclusions

We have proposed a new form of encryption, dubbed matchmaking encryption (ME), where both the sender and the receiver, described by their own attributes, can specify fine-grained access policies to encrypted data. ME enables several applications, e.g., communication between spies, social matchmaking, and more.

On the theoretical side, we put forward formal security definitions for ME and established the feasibility of ME supporting arbitrary policies by leveraging

FE for randomized functionalities in conjunction with other more standard cryptographic tools. On the practical side, we constructed and implemented practical ME for the identity-based setting, with provable security in the random oracle model under the BDH assumption. We also showcased the utility of IB-ME to realize an anonymous bulletin board using the Tor network.

Our work leaves open several important questions. First, it would be interesting to construct ME from simpler assumptions. Second, it is conceivable that our black-box construction could be instantiated based on better assumptions since we only need secure rFE w.r.t. honest encryptors; unfortunately, the only definition that is specifically tailored for this setting [3] has some circularity problems [1,26]. Third, a natural direction is to come up with efficient ME schemes for the identity-based setting without relying on random oracles, or to extend our scheme to the case of fuzzy matching [6]. Further extensions include the setting of chosen-ciphertext security, ME with multiple authorities, mitigating key escrow [17,23], and creating an efficient infrastructure for key management and revocation.

References

1. Agrawal, S., Wu, D.J.: Functional encryption: deterministic to randomized functions from simple assumptions. In: Coron, J.-S., Nielsen, J.B. (eds.) EUROCRYPT 2017. LNCS, vol. 10211, pp. 30–61. Springer, Cham (2017). https://doi.org/10.1007/978-3-319-56614-6_2
2. Akinyele, J.A., et al.: Charm: a framework for rapidly prototyping cryptosystems. J. Cryptogr. Eng. **3**(2), 111–128 (2013)
3. Alwen, J., et al.: On the relationship between functional encryption, obfuscation, and fully homomorphic encryption. In: Stam, M. (ed.) IMACC 2013. LNCS, vol. 8308, pp. 65–84. Springer, Heidelberg (2013). https://doi.org/10.1007/978-3-642-45239-0_5
4. Ananth, P., Jain, A., Khurana, D., Sahai, A.: Indistinguishability obfuscation without multilinear maps: iO from LWE, bilinear maps, and weak pseudorandomness. Cryptology ePrint Archive, Report 2018/615 (2018)
5. Ateniese, G., Francati, D., Nuñez, D., Venturi, D.: Match me if you can: Matchmaking encryption and its applications. Cryptology ePrint Archive, Report 2018/1094 (2018), https://eprint.iacr.org/2018/1094
6. Ateniese, G., Kirsch, J., Blanton, M.: Secret handshakes with dynamic and fuzzy matching. In: NDSS, vol. 7, pp. 1–19 (2007)
7. Attrapadung, N., Imai, H.: Dual-policy attribute based encryption. In: Abdalla, M., Pointcheval, D., Fouque, P.-A., Vergnaud, D. (eds.) ACNS 2009. LNCS, vol. 5536, pp. 168–185. Springer, Heidelberg (2009). https://doi.org/10.1007/978-3-642-01957-9_11
8. Attrapadung, N., Yamada, S.: Duality in ABE: converting attribute based encryption for dual predicate and dual policy via computational encodings. In: CT-RSA, pp. 87–105 (2015)
9. Balfanz, D., Durfee, G., Shankar, N., Smetters, D., Staddon, J., Wong, H.C.: Secret handshakes from pairing-based key agreements. In: IEEE S&P, pp. 180–196 (2003)
10. Bethencourt, J., Sahai, A., Waters, B.: Ciphertext-policy attribute-based encryption. In: IEEE S&P, pp. 321–334 (2007)

11. Boneh, D., Franklin, M.: Identity-based encryption from the Weil pairing. In: Kilian, J. (ed.) CRYPTO 2001. LNCS, vol. 2139, pp. 213–229. Springer, Heidelberg (2001). https://doi.org/10.1007/3-540-44647-8_13
12. Boneh, D., Sahai, A., Waters, B.: Functional encryption: definitions and challenges. In: Ishai, Y. (ed.) TCC 2011. LNCS, vol. 6597, pp. 253–273. Springer, Heidelberg (2011). https://doi.org/10.1007/978-3-642-19571-6_16
13. Castelluccia, C., Jarecki, S., Tsudik, G.: Secret handshakes from CA-oblivious encryption. In: Lee, P.J. (ed.) ASIACRYPT 2004. LNCS, vol. 3329, pp. 293–307. Springer, Heidelberg (2004). https://doi.org/10.1007/978-3-540-30539-2_21
14. Chase, M.: Multi-authority attribute based encryption. In: Vadhan, S.P. (ed.) TCC 2007. LNCS, vol. 4392, pp. 515–534. Springer, Heidelberg (2007). https://doi.org/10.1007/978-3-540-70936-7_28
15. Chase, M., Chow, S.S.: Improving privacy and security in multi-authority attribute-based encryption. In: CCS, pp. 121–130 (2009)
16. Cheung, L., Newport, C.: Provably secure ciphertext policy ABE. In: CCS, pp. 456–465 (2007)
17. Chow, S.S.M.: Removing escrow from identity-based encryption. In: Jarecki, S., Tsudik, G. (eds.) PKC 2009. LNCS, vol. 5443, pp. 256–276. Springer, Heidelberg (2009). https://doi.org/10.1007/978-3-642-00468-1_15
18. Costello, C., Stebila, D.: Fixed argument pairings. In: Abdalla, M., Barreto, P.S.L.M. (eds.) LATINCRYPT 2010. LNCS, vol. 6212, pp. 92–108. Springer, Heidelberg (2010). https://doi.org/10.1007/978-3-642-14712-8_6
19. Damgård, I., Haagh, H., Orlandi, C.: Access control encryption: enforcing information flow with cryptography. In: Hirt, M., Smith, A. (eds.) TCC 2016. LNCS, vol. 9986, pp. 547–576. Springer, Heidelberg (2016). https://doi.org/10.1007/978-3-662-53644-5_21
20. Fisch, B., Vinayagamurthy, D., Boneh, D., Gorbunov, S.: Iron: functional encryption using intel SGX. In: CCS, pp. 765–782 (2017)
21. Fuchsbauer, G., Gay, R., Kowalczyk, L., Orlandi, C.: Access control encryption for equality, comparison, and more. In: PKC, pp. 88–118 (2017)
22. Galbraith, S.D., Paterson, K.G., Smart, N.P.: Pairings for cryptographers. Discrete Appl. Math. 156(16), 3113–3121 (2008)
23. Garg, S., Hajiabadi, M., Mahmoody, M., Rahimi, A., Sekar, S.: Registration-based encryption from standard assumptions. In: Lin, D., Sako, K. (eds.) PKC 2019. LNCS, vol. 11443, pp. 63–93. Springer, Cham (2019). https://doi.org/10.1007/978-3-030-17259-6_3
24. Goldwasser, S., et al.: Multi-input functional encryption. In: Nguyen, P.Q., Oswald, E. (eds.) EUROCRYPT 2014. LNCS, vol. 8441, pp. 578–602. Springer, Heidelberg (2014). https://doi.org/10.1007/978-3-642-55220-5_32
25. Gorantla, M.C., Boyd, C., González Nieto, J.M.: Attribute-based authenticated key exchange. In: Steinfeld, R., Hawkes, P. (eds.) ACISP 2010. LNCS, vol. 6168, pp. 300–317. Springer, Heidelberg (2010). https://doi.org/10.1007/978-3-642-14081-5_19
26. Goyal, V., Jain, A., Koppula, V., Sahai, A.: Functional encryption for randomized functionalities. In: Dodis, Y., Nielsen, J.B. (eds.) TCC 2015. LNCS, vol. 9015, pp. 325–351. Springer, Heidelberg (2015). https://doi.org/10.1007/978-3-662-46497-7_13
27. Goyal, V., Jain, A., Pandey, O., Sahai, A.: Bounded ciphertext policy attribute based encryption. In: Aceto, L., Damgård, I., Goldberg, L.A., Halldórsson, M.M., Ingólfsdóttir, A., Walukiewicz, I. (eds.) ICALP 2008. LNCS, vol. 5126, pp. 579–591. Springer, Heidelberg (2008). https://doi.org/10.1007/978-3-540-70583-3_47

28. Goyal, V., Pandey, O., Sahai, A., Waters, B.: Attribute-based encryption for fine-grained access control of encrypted data. In: CCS, pp. 89–98 (2006)
29. Hou, L., Lai, J., Liu, L.: Secret handshakes with dynamic expressive matching policy. In: Liu, J.K.K., Steinfeld, R. (eds.) ACISP 2016. LNCS, vol. 9722, pp. 461–476. Springer, Cham (2016). https://doi.org/10.1007/978-3-319-40253-6_28
30. Jarecki, S., Kim, J., Tsudik, G.: Authentication for paranoids: multi-party secret handshakes. In: Zhou, J., Yung, M., Bao, F. (eds.) ACNS 2006. LNCS, vol. 3989, pp. 325–339. Springer, Heidelberg (2006). https://doi.org/10.1007/11767480_22
31. Jarecki, S., Kim, J., Tsudik, G.: Beyond secret handshakes: affiliation-hiding authenticated key exchange. In: Malkin, T. (ed.) CT-RSA 2008. LNCS, vol. 4964, pp. 352–369. Springer, Heidelberg (2008). https://doi.org/10.1007/978-3-540-79263-5_23
32. Jarecki, S., Liu, X.: Unlinkable secret handshakes and key-private group key management schemes. In: Katz, J., Yung, M. (eds.) ACNS 2007. LNCS, vol. 4521, pp. 270–287. Springer, Heidelberg (2007). https://doi.org/10.1007/978-3-540-72738-5_18
33. Kim, S., Wu, D.J.: Access control encryption for general policies from standard assumptions. In: Takagi, T., Peyrin, T. (eds.) ASIACRYPT 2017. LNCS, vol. 10624, pp. 471–501. Springer, Cham (2017). https://doi.org/10.1007/978-3-319-70694-8_17
34. Kolesnikov, V., Krawczyk, H., Lindell, Y., Malozemoff, A., Rabin, T.: Attribute-based key exchange with general policies. In: CCS, pp. 1451–1463 (2016)
35. Nekrasov, M., Iland, D., Metzger, M., Parks, L., Belding, E.: A user-driven free speech application for anonymous and verified online, public group discourse. J. Internet Serv. Appl. **9**(1), 21 (2018)
36. Nishide, T., Yoneyama, K., Ohta, K.: Attribute-based encryption with partially hidden encryptor-specified access structures. In: Bellovin, S.M., Gennaro, R., Keromytis, A., Yung, M. (eds.) ACNS 2008. LNCS, vol. 5037, pp. 111–129. Springer, Heidelberg (2008). https://doi.org/10.1007/978-3-540-68914-0_7
37. Ostrovsky, R., Sahai, A., Waters, B.: Attribute-based encryption with non-monotonic access structures. In: CCS, pp. 195–203 (2007)
38. Pirretti, M., Traynor, P., McDaniel, P., Waters, B.: Secure attribute-based systems. J. Comput. Secur. **18**(5), 799–837 (2010)
39. Rouselakis, Y., Waters, B.: Efficient statically-secure large-universe multi-authority attribute-based encryption. In: Böhme, R., Okamoto, T. (eds.) FC 2015. LNCS, vol. 8975, pp. 315–332. Springer, Heidelberg (2015). https://doi.org/10.1007/978-3-662-47854-7_19
40. Sahai, A., Waters, B.: Fuzzy identity-based encryption. In: Cramer, R. (ed.) EUROCRYPT 2005. LNCS, vol. 3494, pp. 457–473. Springer, Heidelberg (2005). https://doi.org/10.1007/11426639_27
41. Sorniotti, A., Molva, R.: Secret handshakes with revocation support. In: Lee, D., Hong, S. (eds.) ICISC 2009. LNCS, vol. 5984, pp. 274–299. Springer, Heidelberg (2010). https://doi.org/10.1007/978-3-642-14423-3_19
42. Sorniotti, A., Molva, R.: A provably secure secret handshake with dynamic controlled matching. Comput. Secur. **29**(5), 619–627 (2010)
43. Syverson, P., Dingledine, R., Mathewson, N.: Tor: the second generation onion router. In: Usenix Security (2004)
44. Tan, G., Zhang, R., Ma, H., Tao, Y.: Access control encryption based on LWE. In: International Workshop on ASIA Public-Key Cryptography, pp. 43–50 (2017)
45. Tor: Onion service protocol (2018). https://www.torproject.org/docs/onion-services.html.en

46. Tsudik, G., Xu, S.: A flexible framework for secret handshakes. In: Danezis, G., Golle, P. (eds.) PET 2006. LNCS, vol. 4258, pp. 295–315. Springer, Heidelberg (2006). https://doi.org/10.1007/11957454_17
47. Vergnaud, D.: RSA-based secret handshakes. In: Ytrehus, Ø. (ed.) WCC 2005. LNCS, vol. 3969, pp. 252–274. Springer, Heidelberg (2006). https://doi.org/10. 1007/11779360_21
48. Waters, B.: Ciphertext-policy attribute-based encryption: an expressive, efficient, and provably secure realization. In: Catalano, D., Fazio, N., Gennaro, R., Nicolosi, A. (eds.) PKC 2011. LNCS, vol. 6571, pp. 53–70. Springer, Heidelberg (2011). https://doi.org/10.1007/978-3-642-19379-8_4
49. Xu, S., Yung, M.: K-anonymous secret handshakes with reusable credentials. In: CCS, pp. 158–167 (2004)
50. Yamada, S., Attrapadung, N., Hanaoka, G., Kunihiro, N.: Generic constructions for chosen-ciphertext secure attribute based encryption. In: Catalano, D., Fazio, N., Gennaro, R., Nicolosi, A. (eds.) PKC 2011. LNCS, vol. 6571, pp. 71–89. Springer, Heidelberg (2011). https://doi.org/10.1007/978-3-642-19379-8_5
51. Yu, S., Ren, K., Lou, W.: Attribute-based content distribution with hidden policy. In: Secure Network Protocols, pp. 39–44 (2008)
52. Yu, S., Ren, K., Lou, W.: Attribute-based on-demand multicast group setup with membership anonymity. Comput. Netw. 54(3), 377–386 (2010)
53. Yu, S., Ren, K., Lou, W., Li, J.: Defending against key abuse attacks in KP-ABE enabled broadcast systems. In: Chen, Y., Dimitriou, T.D., Zhou, J. (eds.) SecureComm 2009. LNICST, vol. 19, pp. 311–329. Springer, Heidelberg (2009). https://doi.org/10.1007/978-3-642-05284-2_18

ABE for DFA from k-Lin

Junqing Gong[1(✉)], Brent Waters[2,4(✉)], and Hoeteck Wee[1,3(✉)]

[1] CNRS, ENS and PSL, Paris, France
{jgong,wee}@di.ens.fr
[2] University of Texas at Austin, Austin, USA
bwaters@cs.utexas.edu
[3] Algorand, Boston, USA
[4] NTT Research, Palo Alto, USA

Abstract. We present the first attribute-based encryption (ABE) scheme for deterministic finite automaton (DFA) based on static assumptions in bilinear groups; this resolves an open problem posed by Waters (CRYPTO 2012). Our main construction achieves selective security against unbounded collusions under the standard k-linear assumption in prime-order bilinear groups, whereas previous constructions all rely on q-type assumptions.

1 Introduction

Attribute-based encryption (ABE) [10,18] is a generalization of public-key encryption to support fine-grained access control for encrypted data. Here, ciphertexts are associated with a description value x and keys with a policy f, and decryption is possible when $f(x) = 1$. In many prior ABE schemes, the policy f is specified using a boolean formula, but there are many applications where we want the policy f to operate over arbitrary sized input data. For example, we could imagine a network logging application where x represents an arbitrary number of events logged. Another example is where x is a database of patient data that includes disease history paired with gene sequences where the number of participants is not apriori bounded or known.

Following the work of Waters in 2012 [20], we consider ABE for regular languages, where the policies f are specified using deterministic finite automata (DFA). This allows us to capture applications such as tax returns and virus scanners. In spite of the substantial progress made in the design and analysis of ABE schemes over the past decade, all known constructions of ABE for DFA rely on q-type assumptions in bilinear groups [1–3,20], where the complexity of the assumption grows with the length of the string x. In this work, we address the following open problem posed in the original work of Waters [20]:

J. Gong—Supported by ERC Project aSCEND (H2020 639554) and the French ANR ALAMBIC Project (ANR-16-CE39-0006). Part of this work was done while at ENS de Lyon.
B. Waters—Supported by NSF CNS-1908611, CNS-1414082, DARPA SafeWare and Packard Foundation Fellowship.
H. Wee—Supported by ERC Project aSCEND (H2020 639554).

© International Association for Cryptologic Research 2019
A. Boldyreva and D. Micciancio (Eds.): CRYPTO 2019, LNCS 11693, pp. 732–764, 2019.
https://doi.org/10.1007/978-3-030-26951-7_25

Can we build an ABE for DFA based on static assumptions in bilinear groups, notably the k-linear assumption in prime-order bilinear groups?

From both a practical and theoretical stand-point, we would like to base cryptography on weaker and better understood assumptions, as is the case with the k-linear assumption. This is also an intriguing problem from a conceptual standpoint because prior approaches exploit q-type assumptions in a fairly inherent manner. Waters' ABE for DFA was based on an "embedding paradigm" where the arbitrary-length challenge string was programmed into the public parameters, and embedding an arbitrary length string into fixed-size parameters seems to require a q-type assumption. The dual system encryption methodology developed in the context of ABE for boolean formula [6,14,15,17,19] allows us to overcome the latter limitation, provided the ciphertext or key size is allowed to grow with the size of the formula; this does not work in the DFA setting, since formula size roughly corresponds to $\ell \cdot Q$, where ℓ is the length of the string x and Q is the number of states in the DFA. Indeed, a key challenge that distinguishes ABE for DFA from ABE for boolean formula is that both the size of public parameters and the secret keys are independent of ℓ, which means that we cannot afford to unroll and embed the entire DFA computation path into the secret key.

This Work. We present the first ABE for DFA based on static assumptions in bilinear groups, thereby providing an affirmative answer to the above open problem. Our main construction achieves selective security against unbounded collusions under the standard k-linear assumption in prime-order bilinear groups. Our proof strategy departs significantly from prior ABEs for DFA in that we design a series of hybrids that traces through the computation. Our proof of security carefully combines a "nested, two-slot" dual system argument [6,11,14, 15,17,19] along with a novel combinatorial mechanism for propagating entropy along the computation path of a DFA.

We note that our high-level approach of tracing the computation path across hybrids is similar to that used in the recent ABE for boolean formula from static assumptions in [13], but we have to deal with the afore-mentioned challenge specific to DFAs. In a bit more detail, in our ABE for DFA, the secret keys contain random shares "in the exponent" corresponding to each state of the DFA; this is analogous to ABE for boolean formula where the random shares correspond to wires in a formula. Roughly speaking, in the i'th hybrid, we modify the distribution of the share corresponding to the state u_i reached upon reading the first i bits of the input string. In a DFA, a state could be reached many times throughout the DFA computation on a fixed input, which means that we need to modify the share corresponding to u_i (along with the challenge ciphertext) in such a way that it does not affect the functionality of the DFA. This difficulty does not arise in ABE for boolean formula, because each wire is only used once during the computation.

1.1   Technical Overview – Warm-Up

We present an overview of our ABE scheme for DFAs. Recall that a DFA is specified by a tuple (Q, Σ, δ, F) where the state space is $[Q] := \{1, 2, \ldots, Q\}$; 1 is the unique start state; $F \subseteq [Q]$ is the set of accept states, and $\delta : [Q] \times \Sigma \to [Q]$ is the state transition function.

Warm-Up Construction. The starting point of our construction is Waters' ABE scheme for DFA [20] over asymmetric composite-order bilinear groups (G_N, H_N, G_T, e) whose order N is the product of three primes p_1, p_2, p_3. (The original scheme is instantiated over prime-order bilinear groups, but relies on q-type assumptions.) Let g_i, h_i denote generators of order p_i in G_N and H_N, for $i = 1, 2, 3$, and let h be a generator for H_N. The scheme is as follows:

$$\mathsf{msk} = \left(h, \alpha, w_{\text{start}}, w_{\text{end}}, z, \{w_\sigma\}_{\sigma \in \Sigma} \right) \tag{1}$$

$$\mathsf{mpk} = \left(g_1, g_1^{w_{\text{start}}}, g_1^{w_{\text{end}}}, g_1^z, \{g_1^{w_\sigma}\}_{\sigma \in \Sigma}, e(g_1, h)^\alpha \right)$$

$$\mathsf{ct}_x = \begin{pmatrix} g_1^{s_0}, g_1^{s_0 w_{\text{start}}}, \\ \{g_1^{s_i}, g_1^{s_{i-1}z + s_i w_{x_i}}\}_{i \in [\ell]}, \\ g_1^{s_\ell}, g_1^{s_\ell w_{\text{end}}}, e(g_1, h)^{s_\ell \alpha} \cdot m \end{pmatrix}$$

$$\mathsf{sk}_f = \begin{pmatrix} h^{d_1 + w_{\text{start}} r_1}, h^{r_1}, \\ \{h^{-d_u + z r_u}, h^{d_v + w_\sigma r_u}, h^{r_u}\}_{u \in [Q], \sigma \in \Sigma, v = \delta(u, \sigma)}, \\ \{h^{\alpha - d_u + w_{\text{end}} r_u}, h^{r_u}\}_{u \in F} \end{pmatrix}$$

Decryption proceeds as follows:

(i) compute $e(g_1^{s_0}, h^{d_1})$;
(ii) for $i = 1, \ldots, \ell$, compute $e(g_1^{s_i}, h^{d_{u_i}})$, where u_i denotes the state reached upon reading $x_1, \ldots, x_i$.
(iii) compute $e(g_1, h)^{s_\ell \alpha}$ and thus m.

To go from $e(g_1^{s_{i-1}}, h^{d_{u_{i-1}}})$ to $e(g_1^{s_i}, h^{d_{u_i}})$ in step (ii), we rely on the identity: for all $u \in [Q], \sigma \in \Sigma$,

$$s_i d_{\delta(u,\sigma)} - s_{i-1} d_u = s_i \cdot (d_{\delta(u,\sigma)} + w_\sigma r_u) + s_{i-1} \cdot (-d_u + z r_u) - (s_{i-1}z + s_i w_\sigma) \cdot r_u$$

We note that our scheme differs from Waters' scheme in that we reuse r_u for all the transitions starting from u instead of a fresh $r_{u,\sigma}$ for each (u, σ). This modification yields a smaller secret key (roughly $Q \cdot |\Sigma| + 2Q$ vs $3Q \cdot |\Sigma|$ group elements), and also simplifies the notation.

Proof Strategy. At a very high level, the proof follows Waters' dual system encryption methodology [14,19]. This means that throughout the proof, we modify the ciphertext and key distributions but not mpk, and only in the p_2-subgroup generated by g_2, h_2 (which we also refer to as the p_2-components). In fact, we will rely on the "nested two-slot" variant of dual system encryption introduced in [6,11,15,17] for settings where the ciphertext uses independent randomness

$s_0, s_1, \ldots$, as is the case for our DFA scheme. Here, "nested" refers to the fact that the security proof interweaves a computational argument over ciphertexts with another over secret keys, whereas "two-slot" refers to the use of the p_3-subgroup to carry out this delicate interweaving. In contrast, the basic dual system encryption framework [2,21] applies a *single* computational argument over ciphertexts at the beginning and can be instantiated in asymmetric composite-order groups whose order is the product of *two* primes.

Proof – First Idea. For this proof overview, we will focus on the selective setting where the adversary first picks a challenge x^* before seeing mpk and making secret key queries. In addition, we consider a further simplification where the adversary only makes a single key query for some DFA f where $f(x^*) = 0$ (i.e. rejecting). Let $u_0 = 1$ denote the start state, and let $u_1, \ldots, u_\ell$ denote the state in f reached upon reading $x_1^*, \ldots, x_\ell^*$. In particular, $u_\ell \notin F$.

Recall that decryption computes $e(g_1^{s_i}, h^{d_{u_i}})$ for each $i = 0, \ldots, \ell$. A natural proof strategy would be design a series of games $\mathsf{G}_0, \ldots, \mathsf{G}_\ell$ such that in G_i, the quantity $e(g_1^{s_i}, h^{d_u})$ is pseudorandom for each $u \neq u_i$. In particular, since $u_\ell \notin F$, this means that $e(g_1^{s_\ell}, h^{d_u})$ is pseudorandom for all $u \in F$, which should imply that $e(g_1^{s_\ell}, h^\alpha)$ is pseudorandom.

Towards carrying out this strategy, we pick $\Delta \leftarrow \mathbb{Z}_N$ and define:

$$\Delta_{i,u} := \begin{cases} \Delta & \text{if } u \neq u_i \\ 0 & \text{otherwise} \end{cases}$$

In G_i, we switch the ciphertext-key distributions from $(\mathsf{ct}_{x^*}, \mathsf{sk}_f)$ to $(\mathsf{ct}_{x^*}^i, \mathsf{sk}_f^i)$ where

- $\mathsf{ct}_{x^*}^i$ is the same as ct_{x^*} except we replace $g_1^{s_i}$ with $(g_1 g_2)^{s_i}$;
- sk_f^i is the same as sk_f except we add a $h_2^{\Delta_{i,v}}$ term to $h^{d_v + w_\sigma r_u}$ for every u, σ.

Roughly speaking, this means that in G_i, the quantity $e(g_1^{s_i}, h^{d_u})$ would be masked by $e(g_2^{s_i}, h_2^{\Delta_{i,u}}) = e(g_2^{s_i}, h_2^\Delta)$ whenever $u \neq u_i$. In particular, the quantity $e(g_1^{s_\ell}, h^\alpha)$ would be masked by $e(g_2^{s_\ell}, h_2^\Delta)$.

Proof – Second Idea. As it turns out, we cannot hope to show that the quantity $e(g_1^{s_i}, h^{d_u})$ is pseudorandom for each $u \neq u_i$. Consider a DFA with $Q = 3, \Sigma = \{0\}$ and $\delta(1, 0) = 2, \delta(3, 0) = 2$. Then, given an encryption of $x = 0$, an adversary can compute

$$e(g_1^{s_0}, h^{d_3})$$

by first computing $e(g_1^{s_1}, h^{d_2})$ using the transition $1 \xrightarrow{0} 2$, and then "backtracking" along the transition $3 \xrightarrow{0} 2$; these are so-called "back-tracking attacks" in [20].

Instead, we will only argue that $e(g_1^{s_i}, h^{d_u})$ is pseudorandom, for $u \in F_{i,x^*}$ for some family of sets $F_{i,x^*} \subseteq [Q]$. (Our first attempt corresponds to setting

$F_{i,x^*} = [Q] \setminus \{u_i\}$.) In order to argue that $e(g_1^{s_\ell}, h^\alpha)$ is pseudorandom, we want $F_{\ell,x^*} = F$. For $i = 0, \ldots, \ell - 1$, we will define

$$F_{i,x^*} := \{ u \in [Q] : \delta(u, x_{i+1}^*, \ldots, x_\ell^*) \in F \}.$$

Here, we use δ to also denote the "extended transition" function, namely

$$\delta(u, \sigma_1, \sigma_2, \ldots, \sigma_{\ell'}) = \delta(\delta(\delta(u, \sigma_1), \sigma_2), \ldots, \sigma_{\ell'}).$$

That is, F_{i,x^*} is the set of states that are reachable from the accept states in F by back-tracking along $x_\ell^*, \ldots, x_{i+1}^*$. In particular, if $f(x^*) = 0$, then $1 \notin F_{0,x^*}$ (recall that 1 denotes the start state) and more generally, $u_i \notin F_{i,x^*}$ (recall that $u_i = \delta(1, x_1^*, \ldots, x_i^*)$). Finally, we modify $\Delta_{i,u}$ to be

$$\Delta_{i,u} := \begin{cases} \Delta & \text{if } u \in F_{i,x^*} \\ 0 & \text{otherwise} \end{cases}$$

Intuitively, the proof starts by introducing a unit of entropy captured by Δ to each state in F_{0,x^*} in G_0, and then propagates that entropy to the states in F_{1,x^*} in G_1, then F_{2,x^*} in G_2, and finally to $F_{\ell,x^*} = F$ in G_ℓ. We can then use Δ to mask α, upon which we can argue that the plaintext is perfectly hidden via an information-theoretic argument. Looking ahead, (5) captures precisely how we computationally propagate entropy from F_{i-1,x^*} in G_{i-1} to F_{i,x^*} in G_i. The key insight here is that these sets F_{i,x^*} are the states that are reachable by back-tracking from the accept states, and not the ones that are reachable from the start state.

Proof – Interlude. Now, we are ready to describe how to carry out the hybrid argument from G_0 to G_ℓ. As mentioned earlier, we focus on the setting with a single key query f. This means that we need to show that for each $i = 1, \ldots, \ell$, we have:

$$\mathsf{G}_{i-1} = (\mathsf{mpk}, \mathsf{ct}_{x^*}^{i-1}, \mathsf{sk}_f^{i-1}) \approx_c (\mathsf{mpk}, \mathsf{ct}_{x^*}^i, \mathsf{sk}_f^i) = \mathsf{G}_i$$

To prove this, we will introduce an additional ciphertext distribution $\mathsf{ct}_{x^*}^{i-1,i}$, where:

- $\mathsf{ct}_{x^*}^{i-1,i}$ is the same as ct_{x^*} except we replace $g_1^{s_{i-1}}, g_1^{s_i}$ with $(g_1 g_2)^{s_{i-1}}, (g_1 g_2)^{s_i}$

and move from G_{i-1} to G_i via the following hybrid arguments:

$$\begin{aligned} \mathsf{G}_{i-1} = \ & (\mathsf{mpk}, \ \mathsf{ct}_{x^*}^{i-1}, \ \mathsf{sk}_f^{i-1}) \\ \approx_c \ & (\mathsf{mpk}, \boxed{\mathsf{ct}_{x^*}^{i-1,i}}, \mathsf{sk}_f^{i-1}) \\ \approx_c \ & (\mathsf{mpk}, \ \mathsf{ct}_{x^*}^{i-1,i}, \boxed{\mathsf{sk}_f^i}) \\ \approx_c \ & (\mathsf{mpk}, \boxed{\mathsf{ct}_{x^*}^i}, \ \mathsf{sk}_f^i) = \mathsf{G}_i \end{aligned} \tag{2}$$

Note that the proof interweaves a computational argument over ciphertexts with another over secret keys. In the proof, we will rely on the following computational assumptions in composite-order bilinear groups:

- $\mathrm{SD}^{G_N}_{p_1 \mapsto p_1 p_2}$ subgroup assumption in G_N, which says that $g_1^s \approx_c (g_1 g_2)^s$;
- $\mathrm{DDH}^{H_N}_{p_2}$ in H_N (w.r.t. w), which implies that $(h_2^r, h_2^{wr}) \approx_c (h_2^r, h_2^{\Delta+wr})$ given (h_2, h_2^w) for all Δ.

Later on, we will describe how to instantiate the scheme and these assumptions using the k-linear assumption in prime-order bilinear groups.

Proof – Third Idea. We begin with the first computational transition in (2), namely:

$$(\mathsf{mpk}, \mathsf{ct}^{i-1}_{x^*}, \mathsf{sk}^{i-1}_f) \approx_c (\mathsf{mpk}, \boxed{\mathsf{ct}^{i-1,i}_{x^*}}, \mathsf{sk}^{i-1}_f)$$

The only difference between $\mathsf{ct}^{i-1}_{x^*}$ and $\mathsf{ct}^{i-1,i}_{x^*}$ is that we have $g_1^{s_i}$ in the former, and $(g_1 g_2)^{s_i}$ in the latter. Unfortunately, we cannot directly invoke the $\mathrm{SD}^{G_N}_{p_1 \mapsto p_1 p_2}$ assumption to carry out this transition, because we need h_2 to simulate the extra $h_2^{\Delta_{i-1,v}}$ terms in sk^{i-1}_f, and the $\mathrm{SD}^{G_N}_{p_1 \mapsto p_1 p_2}$ assumption is trivially broken in the presence of h_2. Instead, we crucially rely on the fact that the $h_2^{\Delta_{i-1,v}}$ terms appear in sk^{i-1}_f as:

$$h_2^{\Delta_{i-1,v}} \cdot h^{w_\sigma r_u}, \; h^{r_u}$$

where $\Delta_{i-1,v} \in \{0, \Delta\}$. In particular, we will prove a statement of the form:

$$g_1^s \approx_c (g_1 g_2)^s \quad \text{given} \quad g_1, g_1^w, g_2, g_2^w, h, h^w, h_2^\Delta \cdot h^{wr}, h^r \tag{3}$$

where $s, w, r, \Delta \in \mathbb{Z}_N$. We refer to this as the (s, w)-switching lemma. Note the presence of the term g_2^w, which we need in the reduction to simulate the $g_2^{s_{i-1} w^*_{i-1}}$ term in $\mathsf{ct}^{i-1,i}_{x^*}$, and which means that $(h_2^\Delta \cdot h^{w^*_{i-1} r_u}, h^{r_u})$ is not pseudorandom. We will prove the (s, w)-switching lemma by exploiting the third p_3-subgroup, using a "two slot" dual system argument:

$$
\begin{aligned}
\mathrm{LHS} \quad = \quad & g_1^s, & h^{wr} \cdot h_2^\Delta, & \quad h^r \\
\overset{p_1 \mapsto p_1 p_3}{\approx_c} \quad & g_1^s \cdot \boxed{g_3^s}, & h^{wr} \cdot h_2^\Delta, & \quad h^r \\
\overset{\mathrm{DDH}}{\approx_c} \quad & g_1^s \cdot g_3^s, & h^{wr} \cdot h_2^\Delta \cdot \boxed{h_3^\Delta}, & \quad h^r \\
\overset{p_3 \mapsto p_2}{\approx_c} \quad & g_1^s \cdot \boxed{g_2^s}, & h^{wr} \cdot h_2^\Delta \cdot h_3^\Delta, & \quad h^r \\
\overset{\mathrm{DDH}}{\approx_c} \quad & g_1^s \cdot g_2^s, & h^{wr} \cdot h_2^\Delta, & \quad h^r \quad = \mathrm{RHS}
\end{aligned}
\tag{4}
$$

We now clarify that there is in fact a catch here, namely that the (s, w)-switching lemma breaks down if the adversary is also given g_1^{sw}, which could indeed be the case due to the $g_2^{s_i w_{x^*_i}}$ term in $\mathsf{ct}^{i-1,i}_{x^*}$. We will circumvent this issue by modifying scheme (1) in the next section.

Looking ahead, we note that the same argument (once we fix the catch) would allow us to handle the third computational transition in (2), namely

$$(\mathsf{mpk}, \mathsf{ct}^{i-1,i}_{x^*}, \mathsf{sk}^i_f) \approx_c (\mathsf{mpk}, \boxed{\mathsf{ct}^i_{x^*}}, \mathsf{sk}^i_f).$$

Proof – Fourth Idea. Next, we handle the remaining computational transition in (2), namely

$$(\mathsf{mpk}, \mathsf{ct}_{x^*}^{i-1,i}, \mathsf{sk}_f^{i-1}) \approx_c (\mathsf{mpk}, \mathsf{ct}_{x^*}^{i-1,i}, \boxed{\mathsf{sk}_f^i})$$

By a standard argument based on the Chinese Remainder Theorem, it suffices to prove the statement for the p_2-components of the above expression, and since mpk has no p_2-components, this leaves us with:

$$(\mathsf{ct}_{x^*}^{i-1,i}[2], \mathsf{sk}_f^{i-1}[2]) \approx_c (\mathsf{ct}_{x^*}^{i-1,i}[2], \boxed{\mathsf{sk}_f^i[2]})$$

where xx[2] denotes the p_2-components of xx. That is, we will need to prove a statement of the form:

$$\left\{ h_2^{-d_u + z r_u}, h_2^{d_v + \boxed{\Delta_{i-1,v}} + w_\sigma r_u}, h_2^{r_u} \right\}_{u, \sigma, v = \delta(u, \sigma)}$$
$$\approx_c \left\{ h_2^{-d_u + z r_u}, h_2^{d_v + \boxed{\Delta_{i,v}} + w_\sigma r_u}, h_2^{r_u} \right\}_{u, \sigma, v = \delta(u, \sigma)}$$

given $\mathsf{ct}_{x^*}^{i-1,i}[2]$. Instead, we will sketch a proof that

$$\left\{ h_2^{-d_u + \boxed{\Delta_{i-1,u}} + z r_u}, h_2^{d_v + w_\sigma r_u}, h_2^{r_u} \right\}_{u, \sigma, v = \delta(u, \sigma)}$$
$$\approx_c \left\{ h_2^{-d_u + z r_u}, h_2^{d_v + \boxed{\Delta_{i,v}} + w_\sigma r_u}, h_2^{r_u} \right\}_{u, \sigma, v = \delta(u, \sigma)} \tag{5}$$

given $(s_{i-1}, s_i, s_{i-1}z + s_i w_{x_i^*})$. The latter will be useful for simulating the terms in $\mathsf{ct}_{x^*}^{i-1,i}[2]$, which is given by:

$$\mathsf{ct}_{x^*}^{i-1,i}[2] = (g_2^{s_{i-1}w_{x_{i-1}^*}}, g_2^{s_{i-1}}, g_2^{s_{i-1}z + s_i w_{x_i^*}}, g_2^{s_i}, g_2^{s_i z})$$

We can interpret (5) as the key computational step that "propagates" the entropy from the states in F_{i-1,x^*} to those in F_{i,x^*}. We will explain the connection between (5) and the statement $\mathsf{sk}_f^{i-1} \approx_c \mathsf{sk}_f^i$ we need later on in the overview.

The proof of (5) relies on the following three observations:

1. by the $\mathsf{DDH}_{p_2}^{H_N}$ assumption w.r.t. $w_{x_i^*} \bmod p_2$, we have

$$(h_2^{zr}, h_2^{w_{x_i^*}r}, h_2^r) \approx_c (h_2^{zr - s_i \gamma}, h_2^{w_{x_i^*}r + s_{i-1}\gamma}, h_2^r) \tag{6}$$

   given $(s_{i-1}, s_i, s_{i-1}z + s_i w_{x_i^*})$; this extends readily to the setting with many triplets corresponding to the r_u's. Note that the above triplets (X, Y, Z) satisfies a consistency check $X^{s_{i-1}} \cdot Y^{s_i} = Z^{s_{i-1}z + s_i w_{x_i^*}}$.

2. whenever $\sigma \neq x_i^*$, we can again invoke the $\mathsf{DDH}_{p_2}^{H_N}$ assumption, now w.r.t. $w_\sigma \bmod p_2$, to replace $h_2^{w_\sigma r_u}$ with $h_2^{\Delta_{i,v} + w_\sigma r_u}$ for all $u \in [Q], \sigma \neq x_i^*, v = \delta(u, \sigma)$.

3. for all x^* and $i \in [\ell], u \in [Q]$, we have

$$u \in F_{i-1,x^*} \iff \delta(u, x_i^*) \in F_{i,x^*}$$

This is one of two steps where we crucially relies on the definition of F_{i,x^*}.

We note that the analogue of (6) given also $g_2^{s_i z}$ in $\mathsf{ct}_x^{i-1,i}[2]$ is false due to the consistency check $e(g_2^{s_i}, h_2^{zr}) = e(g_2^{s_i z}, h_2^r)$. Again, we will circumvent this issue by modifying scheme (1) in the next section.

Proof – Fifth Idea. To make use of (5) in the proof, we introduce an additional key distribution $\mathsf{sk}_f^{i-1,i}$:

- $\mathsf{sk}_f^{i-1,i}$ is the same as sk_f except we add a $h_2^{\Delta_{i-1,u}}$ term to $h^{-d_u + z r_u}$ for every u.

Instead of

$$(\mathsf{mpk}, \mathsf{ct}_{x^*}^{i-1,i}, \mathsf{sk}_f^{i-1}) \approx_c (\mathsf{mpk}, \mathsf{ct}_{x^*}^{i-1,i}, \boxed{\mathsf{sk}_f^{i-1,i}}) \approx_c (\mathsf{mpk}, \mathsf{ct}_{x^*}^{i-1,i}, \boxed{\mathsf{sk}_f^i})$$

we will show:

$$(\mathsf{mpk}, \mathsf{ct}_{x^*}^{i-1}, \mathsf{sk}_f^{i-1}) \approx_c (\mathsf{mpk}, \mathsf{ct}_{x^*}^{i-1}, \boxed{\mathsf{sk}_f^{i-1,i}})$$
$$(\mathsf{mpk}, \mathsf{ct}_{x^*}^{i-1,i}, \boxed{\mathsf{sk}_f^{i-1,i}}) \approx_c (\mathsf{mpk}, \mathsf{ct}_{x^*}^{i-1,i}, \boxed{\mathsf{sk}_f^i})$$

That is, we will switch from sk_f^{i-1} to $\mathsf{sk}_f^{i-1,i}$ in the presence of $\mathsf{ct}_{x^*}^{i-1}$ instead of $\mathsf{ct}_{x^*}^{i-1,i}$ and employ the following strategy:

$$
\begin{aligned}
\mathsf{G}_{i-1} = \ & (\mathsf{mpk}, \quad \mathsf{ct}_{x^*}^{i-1}, \quad \mathsf{sk}_f^{i-1} \quad) \\
\approx_c \ & (\mathsf{mpk}, \quad \mathsf{ct}_{x^*}^{i-1}, \quad \boxed{\mathsf{sk}_f^{i-1,i}} \ ) \\
\approx_c \ & (\mathsf{mpk}, \quad \boxed{\mathsf{ct}_{x^*}^{i-1,i}}, \quad \mathsf{sk}_f^{i-1,i} \ ) && \text{similar to 1st transition in (2)} \\
\approx_c \ & (\mathsf{mpk}, \quad \mathsf{ct}_{x^*}^{i-1,i}, \quad \boxed{\mathsf{sk}_f^i} \quad) && \text{using (5)} \\
\approx_c \ & (\mathsf{mpk}, \quad \boxed{\mathsf{ct}_{x^*}^i}, \quad \mathsf{sk}_f^i \quad) = \mathsf{G}_i && \text{identical to 3rd transition in (2)}
\end{aligned}
$$
$$(7)$$

Here, the last three computational transitions can be handled as before. This leaves us with the first transition, namely to show that

$$(\mathsf{mpk}, \mathsf{ct}_{x^*}^{i-1}, \mathsf{sk}_f^{i-1}) \approx_c (\mathsf{mpk}, \mathsf{ct}_{x^*}^{i-1}, \boxed{\mathsf{sk}_f^{i-1,i}}).$$

Roughly, we focus on the p_2-components and prove it via the following hybrid arguments:

$$\mathsf{sk}_f^{i-1}[2] = \left(\begin{array}{c} h_2^{d_1+w_{\mathrm{start}}r_1}, h_2^{r_1}, \\ \{h_2^{-d_u+zr_u}, h_2^{d_v+\boxed{\Delta_{i-1,v}}+w_\sigma r_u}, h_2^{r_u}\}_{u,\sigma,v=\delta(u,\sigma)}, \\ \{h_2^{\alpha-d_u+w_{\mathrm{end}}r_u}, h_2^{r_u}\}_{u\in F} \end{array} \right)$$

$$\approx_s \left(\begin{array}{c} h_2^{d_1-\boxed{\Delta_{i-1,1}}+w_{\mathrm{start}}r_1}, h_2^{r_1}, \\ \{h_2^{-d_u+\boxed{\Delta_{i-1,u}}+zr_u}, h_2^{d_v+w_\sigma r_u}, h_2^{r_u}\}_{u,\sigma,v=\delta(u,\sigma)}, \\ \{h_2^{\alpha-d_u+\boxed{\Delta_{i-1,u}}+w_{\mathrm{end}}r_u}, h_2^{r_u}\}_{u\in F} \end{array} \right)$$

$$\approx_c \left(\begin{array}{c} h_2^{d_1-\Delta_{i-1,1}+w_{\mathrm{start}}r_1}, h_2^{r_1}, \\ \{h_2^{-d_u+\Delta_{i-1,u}+zr_u}, h_2^{d_v+w_\sigma r_u}, h_2^{r_u}\}_{u,\sigma,v=\delta(u,\sigma)}, \\ \{h_2^{\alpha-d_u+\Delta_{i-1,u}+w_{\mathrm{end}}r_u}, h_2^{r_u}\}_{u\in F} \end{array} \right) = \mathsf{sk}_f^{i-1,i}[2]$$

in the presence of $\mathsf{ct}_{x^*}^{i-1}[2]$, which is given by:

$$\mathsf{ct}_{x^*}^{i-1}[2] = \begin{cases} g_2^{s_0 w_{\mathrm{start}}}, g_2^{s_0}, g_2^{s_0 z} & \text{if } i = 1 \\ g_2^{s_{i-1} w_{x_{i-1}^*}}, g_2^{s_{i-1}}, g_2^{s_{i-1} z} & \text{if } 2 \leq i \leq \ell \end{cases}$$

The first statistical step simply relies on the change of variable

$$d_u \mapsto d_u - \Delta_{i-1,u} \quad \forall u \in [Q].$$

Then we handle the second computational step by arguing

$$h_2^{-\Delta_{i-1,1}+w_{\mathrm{start}}r_1} \approx_c h_2^{w_{\mathrm{start}}r_1} \quad \text{and} \quad h_2^{\Delta_{i-1,u}+w_{\mathrm{end}}r_u} \approx_c h_2^{w_{\mathrm{end}}r_u} \quad \forall u \in F$$

This is implied by $\mathrm{DDH}_{p_2}^{H_N}$ assumption w.r.t. $w_{\mathrm{start}}, w_{\mathrm{end}} \bmod p_2$ with an exception:

- when $i = 1$, the ciphertext $\mathsf{ct}_{x^*}^0$ leaks $w_{\mathrm{start}} \bmod p_2$ via $g_2^{s_0 w_{\mathrm{start}}}$ and $\mathrm{DDH}_{p_2}^{H_N}$ assumption w.r.t. $w_{\mathrm{start}} \bmod p_2$ does not hold. In this case, we use the fact that $\Delta_{0,1} = 0$ which is implied by $1 \notin F_{0,x^*}$.

This is the second step where we crucially rely on the definition of F_{i,x^*}.

1.2   Our Construction

Here is our final "alternating" construction, where we introduce two copies of $(z, \{w_\sigma\})$, and we alternate between the two copies in the ciphertext depending on the parity of i:

$$\mathsf{msk} = \left(h, \alpha, w_{\mathrm{start}}, w_{\mathrm{end}}, z_0, z_1, \{w_{\sigma,0}, w_{\sigma,1}\}_{\sigma \in \Sigma} \right) \qquad (8)$$

$$\mathsf{mpk} = \left(g_1, g_1^{w_{\mathrm{start}}}, g_1^{w_{\mathrm{end}}}, g_1^{z_0}, g_1^{z_1}, \{g_1^{w_{\sigma,0}}, g_1^{w_{\sigma,1}}\}_{\sigma \in \Sigma}, e(g_1, h)^{\alpha} \right)$$

$$\mathsf{ct}_x = \begin{pmatrix} g_1^{s_0}, g_1^{s_0 w_{\mathrm{start}}}, \\ \{g_1^{s_i}, g_1^{s_{i-1} z_i \bmod 2 + s_i w_{x_i, i \bmod 2}}\}_{i \in [\ell]}, \\ g_1^{s_\ell}, g_1^{s_\ell w_{\mathrm{end}}}, \ e(g_1, h)^{s_\ell \alpha} \cdot m \end{pmatrix}$$

$$\mathsf{sk}_f = \begin{pmatrix} h^{d_1 + w_{\mathrm{start}} r_1}, h^{r_1}, \\ \{h^{-d_u + z_b r_u}, h^{d_v + w_{\sigma,b} r_u}, h^{r_u}\}_{b \in \{0,1\}, u \in [Q], \sigma \in \Sigma, v = \delta(u,\sigma)}, \\ \{h^{\alpha - d_u + w_{\mathrm{end}} r_u}, h^{r_u}\}_{u \in F} \end{pmatrix}$$

Note the additional $i \bmod 2$ subscript in ct_x and the additional quantifier $b \in \{0,1\}$ in sk_f. Decryption proceeds essentially as before by computing $e(g_1^{s_i}, h^{d_{u_i}})$ for $i = 0, \dots, \ell$ and finally $e(g_1, h)^{s_\ell \alpha}$ and thus m.

Updating Auxiliary Distributions. The proof for the "alternating" construction still follows the strategy in (7). The distributions $\mathsf{ct}_{x^*}^i$ and $\mathsf{ct}_{x^*}^{i-1,i}$ are defined analogously; we update $\mathsf{sk}_f^i[2]$ and $\mathsf{sk}_f^{i-1,i}[2]$ for the "alternating" construction as follows:

$$\mathsf{sk}_f^i[2] = \begin{pmatrix} h_2^{d_1 + w_{\mathrm{start}} r_1}, h_2^{r_1}, \\ \{h_2^{-d_u + z_i \bmod 2 r_u}, h_2^{d_v + \boxed{\Delta_{i,v}} + w_{\sigma, i \bmod 2} r_u}, h_2^{r_u}\}_{u, \sigma, v = \delta(u,\sigma)}, \\ \{h_2^{-d_u + z_{i-1} \bmod 2 r_u}, h_2^{d_v + w_{\sigma, i-1} \bmod 2 r_u}, h_2^{r_u}\}_{u, \sigma, v = \delta(u,\sigma)}, \\ \{h_2^{\alpha - d_u + w_{\mathrm{end}} r_u}, h_2^{r_u}\}_{u \in F} \end{pmatrix}$$

$$\mathsf{sk}_f^{i-1,i}[2] = \begin{pmatrix} h_2^{d_1 + w_{\mathrm{start}} r_1}, h_2^{r_1}, \\ \{h_2^{-d_u + \boxed{\Delta_{i-1,u}} + z_i \bmod 2 r_u}, h_2^{d_v + w_{\sigma, i \bmod 2} r_u}, h_2^{r_u}\}_{u, \sigma, v = \delta(u,\sigma)}, \\ \{h_2^{-d_u + z_{i-1} \bmod 2 r_u}, h_2^{d_v + w_{\sigma, i-1} \bmod 2 r_u}, h_2^{r_u}\}_{u, \sigma, v = \delta(u,\sigma)}, \\ \{h_2^{\alpha - d_u + w_{\mathrm{end}} r_u}, h_2^{r_u}\}_{u \in F} \end{pmatrix}$$

As an example, we illustrate a complete game sequence for 3-bit input in Fig. 1.

How Alternation Helps. We briefly describe how the alternating structure circumvents two of the issues in the earlier proof overview:

- To switch from $\mathsf{ct}_{x^*}^{i-1}$ to $\mathsf{ct}_{x^*}^{i-1,i}$ given $\mathsf{sk}_f^{i-1,i}$, we will rely on $(s_i, z_i \bmod 2)$-switching lemma. The earlier issue with the terms $(g_1^{s_i}, g_1^{s_i z_{i+1} \bmod 2})$ in $\mathsf{ct}_{x^*}^{i-1,i}$ simply goes away because $z_i \bmod 2 \neq z_{i+1} \bmod 2$, thanks to the alternation. A similar trick works for switching from $\mathsf{ct}_{x^*}^{i-1,i}$ to $\mathsf{ct}_{x^*}^i$.
- To switch from $\mathsf{sk}_f^{i-1,i}$ to sk_f^i given $\mathsf{ct}_{x^*}^{i-1,i}$, we will rely on the analogue of (6) with $(z_i \bmod 2, w_{x_i^*, i \bmod 2})$ in place of $(z, w_{x_i^*})$. The extra term in $\mathsf{ct}_{x^*}^{i-1,i}$ that enables the earlier attack now corresponds to $g_2^{s_i z_{i+1} \bmod 2}$, and the attack is no longer applicable simply because $z_i \bmod 2 \neq z_{i+1} \bmod 2$, thanks again to the alternation.

Game	$\mathrm{sk}_f[2]$			$\mathrm{ct}_x[2]$
0	$\llbracket d_u \mapsto d_v \rrbracket_{z_0,w_\sigma,0}$	$\llbracket d_u \mapsto d_v \rrbracket_{z_1,w_\sigma,1}$	$\llbracket d_u - \alpha \mapsto 0 \rrbracket_{w_{\mathrm{end}},0}$	—
1	$\llbracket d_u \mapsto d_v \rrbracket_{z_0,w_\sigma,0}$	$\llbracket d_u \mapsto d_v \rrbracket_{z_1,w_\sigma,1}$	$\llbracket d_u - \alpha \mapsto 0 \rrbracket_{w_{\mathrm{end}},0}$	$s_0 w_{\mathrm{start}},\ \boxed{s_0},\ \boxed{s_0 z_1}$
2.1.0	$\llbracket d_u \mapsto d_v + \boxed{\Delta_{0,v}} \rrbracket_{z_0,w_\sigma,0}$	$\llbracket d_u \mapsto d_v \rrbracket_{z_1,w_\sigma,1}$	$\llbracket d_u - \alpha \mapsto 0 \rrbracket_{w_{\mathrm{end}},0}$	$\rightarrow$
2.1.1	$\llbracket d_u \mapsto d_v \rrbracket_{z_0,w_\sigma,0}$	$\llbracket d_u - \boxed{\Delta_{0,u}} \mapsto d_v \rrbracket_{z_1,w_\sigma,1}$	$\llbracket d_u - \alpha \mapsto 0 \rrbracket_{w_{\mathrm{end}},0}$	$\rightarrow$
2.1.2	$\llbracket d_u \mapsto d_v \rrbracket_{z_0,w_\sigma,0}$	$\llbracket d_u - \Delta_{0,u} \mapsto d_v \rrbracket_{z_1,w_\sigma,1}$	$\llbracket d_u - \alpha \mapsto 0 \rrbracket_{w_{\mathrm{end}},0}$	$s_0 w_{\mathrm{start}},\ s_0,\ s_0 z_1 + \boxed{s_1 w_{x_1^*,1}},\ \boxed{s_1},\ \boxed{s_1 z_0}$
2.1.3	$\llbracket d_u \mapsto d_v \rrbracket_{z_0,w_\sigma,0}$	$\llbracket d_u \mapsto d_v + \boxed{\Delta_{1,v}} \rrbracket_{z_1,w_\sigma,1}$	$\llbracket d_u - \alpha \mapsto 0 \rrbracket_{w_{\mathrm{end}},0}$	$\rightarrow$
2.1.4 (=2.2.0)	$\llbracket d_u \mapsto d_v \rrbracket_{z_0,w_\sigma,0}$	$\llbracket d_u \mapsto d_v + \Delta_{1,v} \rrbracket_{z_1,w_\sigma,1}$	$\llbracket d_u - \alpha \mapsto 0 \rrbracket_{w_{\mathrm{end}},0}$	$\cancel{s_0 w_{\mathrm{start}}},\ s_0,\ \cancel{s_0 z_1} + s_1 w_{x_1^*,1},\ s_1,\ s_1 z_0$
2.2.1	$\llbracket d_u - \boxed{\Delta_{1,u}} \mapsto d_v \rrbracket_{z_0,w_\sigma,0}$	$\llbracket d_u \mapsto d_v \rrbracket_{z_1,w_\sigma,1}$	$\llbracket d_u - \alpha \mapsto 0 \rrbracket_{w_{\mathrm{end}},0}$	$\rightarrow$
2.2.2	$\llbracket d_u - \Delta_{1,u} \mapsto d_v \rrbracket_{z_0,w_\sigma,0}$	$\llbracket d_u \mapsto d_v \rrbracket_{z_1,w_\sigma,1}$	$\llbracket d_u - \alpha \mapsto 0 \rrbracket_{w_{\mathrm{end}},0}$	$s_1 w_{x_1^*,1},\ s_1,\ s_1 z_0 + \boxed{s_2 w_{x_2^*,0}},\ \boxed{s_2},\ \boxed{s_2 z_1}$
2.2.3	$\llbracket d_u \mapsto d_v + \boxed{\Delta_{2,v}} \rrbracket_{z_0,w_\sigma,0}$	$\llbracket d_u \mapsto d_v \rrbracket_{z_1,w_\sigma,1}$	$\llbracket d_u - \alpha \mapsto 0 \rrbracket_{w_{\mathrm{end}},0}$	$\rightarrow$
2.2.4 (=2.3.0)	$\llbracket d_u \mapsto d_v + \Delta_{2,v} \rrbracket_{z_0,w_\sigma,0}$	$\llbracket d_u \mapsto d_v \rrbracket_{z_1,w_\sigma,1}$	$\llbracket d_u - \alpha \mapsto 0 \rrbracket_{w_{\mathrm{end}},0}$	$\cancel{s_1 w_{x_1^*,1}},\ \cancel{s_1},\ \cancel{s_1 z_0} + s_2 w_{x_2^*,0},\ s_2,\ s_2 z_1$
2.3.1	$\llbracket d_u \mapsto d_v \rrbracket_{z_0,w_\sigma,0}$	$\llbracket d_u - \boxed{\Delta_{2,u}} \mapsto d_v \rrbracket_{z_1,w_\sigma,1}$	$\llbracket d_u - \alpha \mapsto 0 \rrbracket_{w_{\mathrm{end}},0}$	$\rightarrow$
2.3.2	$\llbracket d_u \mapsto d_v \rrbracket_{z_0,w_\sigma,0}$	$\llbracket d_u - \Delta_{2,u} \mapsto d_v \rrbracket_{z_1,w_\sigma,1}$	$\llbracket d_u - \alpha \mapsto 0 \rrbracket_{w_{\mathrm{end}},0}$	$s_2 w_{x_2^*,0},\ s_2,\ s_2 z_1 + \boxed{s_3 w_{x_3^*,1}},\ \boxed{s_3},\ \boxed{s_3 w_{\mathrm{end}}}$
2.3.3	$\llbracket d_u \mapsto d_v \rrbracket_{z_0,w_\sigma,0}$	$\llbracket d_u \mapsto d_v + \boxed{\Delta_{3,v}} \rrbracket_{z_1,w_\sigma,1}$	$\llbracket d_u - \alpha \mapsto 0 \rrbracket_{w_{\mathrm{end}},0}$	$\rightarrow$
2.3.4	$\llbracket d_u \mapsto d_v \rrbracket_{z_0,w_\sigma,0}$	$\llbracket d_u \mapsto d_v + \Delta_{3,v} \rrbracket_{z_1,w_\sigma,1}$	$\llbracket d_u - \alpha \mapsto 0 \rrbracket_{w_{\mathrm{end}},0}$	$\cancel{s_2 w_{x_2^*,0}},\ \cancel{s_2},\ \cancel{s_2 z_1} + s_3 w_{x_3^*,1},\ s_3,\ s_3 w_{\mathrm{end}}$
3	$\llbracket d_u \mapsto d_v \rrbracket_{z_0,w_\sigma,0}$	$\llbracket d_u \mapsto d_v \rrbracket_{z_1,w_\sigma,1}$	$\llbracket d_u - \boxed{\Delta_{3,u}} - \alpha \mapsto 0 \rrbracket_{w_{\mathrm{end}},0} \downarrow$	

Fig. 1. Summary of game sequence for $\ell = 3$. We only describe the p_2-components here. Recall the notational short-hand $\llbracket d_u \mapsto d_v \rrbracket_{z,w} := (h_2^{-d_u + z r_u}, h_2^{d_v + w r_u}, h_2^{r_u})$ while secret key elements in the second and third columns are quantified over $u \in [Q], \sigma \in \Sigma, v = \sigma(u,\sigma)$ while those in the fourth column are over $u \in F$; we omit $\llbracket 0 \mapsto d_1 \rrbracket_{0,w_{\mathrm{start}}}$. For the ciphertext elements, we omitted the terms $e(g_2^{s_3}, h^\alpha)$ in games 2.3.$\star$ and 3. Throughout, a $\downarrow$ means "same as preceding row".

Handling Many Secret Keys. The proof extends to selective security for many keys, with fresh $\{d_u, r_u\}_{u \in [Q]}$ per key and the same Δ used across all the keys. Roughly speaking, the fresh r_u allows us to carry out the computational steps involving the $\mathrm{DDH}_{p_2}^{H_N}$ assumption, and in the final step, we rely on the fact that all the secret keys only leak $\alpha + \Delta$ and not α itself.

1.3 Prime-Order Groups

To complete the overview, we sketch our final ABE scheme which is secure under the k-Linear assumption in prime-order bilinear groups.[1] Here, we rely on the previous framework of Chen et al. [4–6,9] for simulating composite-order groups in prime-order ones. Let (G_1, G_2, G_T, e) be a bilinear group of prime order p. We start with our ABE scheme in composite-order groups (8) and carry out the following substitutions:

$$
\begin{aligned}
d_u, \alpha &\mapsto \mathbf{d}_u, \mathbf{k} & z_b, w_{\sigma,b} &\mapsto \mathbf{Z}_b, \mathbf{W}_{\sigma,b} \\
g_1^{s_i} &\mapsto [\mathbf{s}_i^\top \mathbf{A}_1^\top]_1 & h^{r_u} &\mapsto [\mathbf{r}_u]_2 \\
g_1^{s_i z_b}, g_1^{s_i w_{\sigma,b}} &\mapsto [\mathbf{s}_i^\top \mathbf{A}_1^\top \mathbf{Z}_b]_1, [\mathbf{s}_i^\top \mathbf{A}_1^\top \mathbf{W}_{\sigma,b}]_1 & h^{z_b r_u}, h^{w_{\sigma,b} r_u} &\mapsto [\mathbf{Z}_b \mathbf{r}_u]_2, [\mathbf{W}_{\sigma,b} \mathbf{r}_u]_2
\end{aligned}
$$

where

$$
\mathbf{A}_1 \leftarrow \mathbb{Z}_p^{(2k+1) \times k} \quad \text{and} \quad \mathbf{Z}_b, \mathbf{W}_{\sigma,b} \leftarrow \mathbb{Z}_p^{(2k+1) \times k}, \quad \mathbf{d}_u, \mathbf{k} \leftarrow \mathbb{Z}_p^{2k+1}, \quad \mathbf{s}_i, \mathbf{r}_u \leftarrow \mathbb{Z}_p^k
$$

and $[\cdot]_1, [\cdot]_2$ correspond respectively to exponentiations in the prime-order groups G_1, G_2. Note that $\mathbf{A}_1$ has height $2k + 1$: we will use k-dimensional random subspaces to simulate each of the p_1 and p_3 subgroups, and a 1-dimensional subspace to simulate the p_2 subgroup; these are sufficient to simulate the $\mathrm{SD}_{p_1 \mapsto p_1 p_2}^{G_N}$, $\mathrm{SD}_{p_1 \mapsto p_1 p_3}^{G_N}$ and $\mathrm{SD}_{p_3 \mapsto p_3 p_2}^{G_N}$ assumptions (we would need to modify the proof of the (s, w)-switching lemma in (4) to avoid $\mathrm{SD}_{p_3 \mapsto p_2}^{G_N}$ assumption). It is sufficient to use $\mathbf{Z}_b, \mathbf{W}_{\sigma,b}$ of width k since we only rely on the $\mathrm{DDH}_{p_2}^{H_N}, \mathrm{DDH}_{p_3}^{H_N}$ assumptions.

This yields the following prime-order ABE scheme for DFA:

$$
\mathsf{msk} = (\mathbf{k}, \mathbf{W}_{\mathrm{start}}, \mathbf{W}_{\mathrm{end}}, \mathbf{Z}_0, \mathbf{Z}_1, \{\mathbf{W}_{\sigma,0}, \mathbf{W}_{\sigma,1}\}_{\sigma \in \Sigma})
$$

$$
\mathsf{mpk} = ([\mathbf{A}_1^\top, \mathbf{A}_1^\top \mathbf{W}_{\mathrm{start}}, \mathbf{A}_1^\top \mathbf{W}_{\mathrm{end}}, \mathbf{A}_1^\top \mathbf{Z}_0, \mathbf{A}_1^\top \mathbf{Z}_1, \{\mathbf{A}_1^\top \mathbf{W}_{\sigma,0}, \mathbf{A}_1^\top \mathbf{W}_{\sigma,1}\}_{\sigma \in \Sigma}]_1, [\mathbf{A}_1^\top \mathbf{k}]_T)
$$

$$
\mathsf{ct}_x = \begin{pmatrix} [\mathbf{s}_0^\top \mathbf{A}_1^\top]_1, \ [\mathbf{s}_0^\top \mathbf{A}_1^\top \mathbf{W}_{\mathrm{start}}]_1 \\ \{[\mathbf{s}_i^\top \mathbf{A}_1^\top]_1, [\mathbf{s}_{i-1}^\top \mathbf{A}_1^\top \mathbf{Z}_{i \bmod 2} + \mathbf{s}_i^\top \mathbf{A}_1^\top \mathbf{W}_{x_i, i \bmod 2}]_1\}_{i \in [\ell]} \\ [\mathbf{s}_\ell^\top \mathbf{A}_1^\top]_1, [\mathbf{s}_\ell^\top \mathbf{A}_1^\top \mathbf{W}_{\mathrm{end}}]_1, [\mathbf{s}_\ell^\top \mathbf{A}_1^\top \mathbf{k}]_T \cdot m \end{pmatrix}
$$

$$
\mathsf{sk}_f = \begin{pmatrix} [\mathbf{d}_1 + \mathbf{W}_{\mathrm{start}} \mathbf{r}_1]_2, [\mathbf{r}_1]_2, \\ \{[-\mathbf{d}_u + \mathbf{Z}_b \mathbf{r}_u]_2, [\mathbf{d}_v + \mathbf{W}_{\sigma,b} \mathbf{r}_u]_2, [\mathbf{r}_u]_2\}_{b \in \{0,1\}, u \in [Q], \sigma \in \Sigma, v = \delta(u,\sigma)} \\ \{[\mathbf{k} - \mathbf{d}_u + \mathbf{W}_{\mathrm{end}} \mathbf{r}_u]_2, [\mathbf{r}_u]_2\}_{u \in F} \end{pmatrix}.
$$

Decryption proceeds as before by first computing

$$
[\mathbf{s}_i^\top \mathbf{A}_1^\top \mathbf{d}_{u_i}]_T \quad \forall i = 0, \ldots, \ell
$$

via the associativity relations $\mathbf{A}_1^\top \mathbf{Z} \cdot \mathbf{r}_u = \mathbf{A}_1^\top \cdot \mathbf{Z} \mathbf{r}_u$ (ditto $\mathbf{W}_{\mathrm{start}}, \mathbf{W}_{\sigma,b}, \mathbf{W}_{\mathrm{end}}$) [7]; and finally recovers $[\mathbf{s}_\ell^\top \mathbf{A}_1^\top \mathbf{k}]_T$ and thus m.

---

[1] e.g: $k = 1$ corresponds to the Symmetric External Diffie-Hellman Assumption (SXDH), and $k = 2$ corresponds to the Decisional Linear Assumption (DLIN).

1.4 Discussion

The main open problem arising in this work is to obtain an adaptively secure ABE scheme for DFA under the k-Lin assumption. One natural approach is to combine our techniques with the piecewise guessing framework in [12, 13] to obtain an adaptively secure ABE scheme for DFA under the k-Lin assumption. The main obstacle here is that in the intermediate hybrids, we need to know the sets F_{i,x^*}, for which there can be up to 2^Q possibilities, where Q is the maximal number of states in a DFA provided by the adversary in the secret key queries. As such, naively applying the piecewise guessing framework would incur a 2^Q security loss. Another potential approach is to appeal to the doubly selective framework in [2, 16], which reduces the problem to building a selectively secure ciphertext-policy ABE for DFA (alternatively, a co-selectively secure key-policy ABE for DFA) under the k-Lin assumption, in the single-key setting; again, naively applying the techniques in this work would incur a 2^Q security loss. To conclude, achieving adaptive security under the k-Lin assumption with only a polynomial loss appears to require new ideas that go beyond the state of the art.

Organization. The next section gives some background knowledge. We prove selective security of the composite-order scheme in the one-key setting in Sect. 3. We defer the prime-order scheme with proof in the many-key setting to the full paper.

2 Preliminaries

Notation. We denote by $s \leftarrow S$ the fact that s is picked uniformly at random from a finite set S. By PPT, we denote a probabilistic polynomial-time algorithm. Throughout this paper, we use 1^λ as the security parameter. We use lower case boldface to denote (column) vectors and upper case boldcase to denote matrices. We use $\approx_s$ to denote two distributions being statistically indistinguishable, and $\approx_c$ to denote two distributions being computationally indistinguishable.

Deterministic Finite Automaton (DFA). A deterministic finite automaton (DFA) f is defined by (Q, Σ, δ, F) where

- Q is the number of states and we take $[Q]$ as the state space;
- Σ is the alphabet;
- $\delta : [Q] \times \Sigma \to [Q]$ is a transition function;
- $F \subseteq [Q]$ is the set of accept states.

Here the (unique) start state is always state 1. We use $f(x) = 1$ to denote that an input $x = (x_1, \ldots, x_\ell) \in \Sigma^\ell$ is accepted by DFA f, which means that there exists a sequence of states $u_0, u_1, \ldots, u_\ell \in [Q]$ satisfying: (1) $u_0 = 1$; (2) for all $i = 1, \ldots, \ell$, we have $\delta(u_{i-1}, x_i) = u_i$; (3) $u_\ell \in F$. If input x is not accepted by DFA f, we write $f(x) = 0$.

2.1 Attribute-Based Encryption for Deterministic Finite Automaton

Syntax. An attribute-based encryption (ABE) scheme for DFA consists of four algorithms (Setup, Enc, KeyGen, Dec):

Setup$(1^\lambda, \Sigma) \rightarrow$ (mpk, msk). The setup algorithm gets as input the security parameter 1^λ and the alphabet Σ. It outputs the public parameter mpk and the master key msk. We assume mpk defines the message space $\mathcal{M}$.

Enc(mpk, x, m) $\rightarrow$ ct$_x$. The encryption algorithm gets as input mpk, an input $x \in \Sigma^*$ and a message $m \in \mathcal{M}$. It outputs a ciphertext ct$_x$. Note that x is public given ct$_x$.

KeyGen(mpk, msk, f) $\rightarrow$ sk$_f$. The key generation algorithm gets as input mpk, msk and a description of DFA f. It outputs a secret key sk$_f$. Note that f is public given sk$_f$.

Dec(mpk, sk$_f$, ct$_x$) $\rightarrow m$. The decryption algorithm gets as input sk$_f$ and ct$_x$ such that $f(x) = 1$ along with mpk. It outputs a message m.

Correctness. For all input x and DFA f with $f(x) = 1$ and all $m \in \mathcal{M}$, we require

$$\Pr \left[\text{Dec(mpk, sk}_f, \text{ct}_x) = m : \begin{array}{l} \text{(mpk, msk)} \leftarrow \text{Setup}(1^\lambda, \Sigma); \\ \text{sk}_f \leftarrow \text{KeyGen(mpk, msk, } f); \\ \text{ct}_x \leftarrow \text{Enc(mpk, } x, m) \end{array} \right] = 1.$$

Security Definition. For a stateful adversary $\mathcal{A}$, we define the advantage function

$$\text{Adv}^{\text{ABE}}_{\mathcal{A}}(\lambda) := \Pr \left[\beta = \beta' : \begin{array}{l} \text{(mpk, msk)} \leftarrow \text{Setup}(1^\lambda, \Sigma); \\ (x^*, m_0, m_1) \leftarrow \mathcal{A}^{\text{KeyGen(mpk,msk,}\cdot)}(\text{mpk}); \\ \beta \leftarrow \{0, 1\}; \text{ ct}_{x^*} \leftarrow \text{Enc(mpk, } x^*, m_\beta); \\ \beta' \leftarrow \mathcal{A}^{\text{KeyGen(mpk,msk,}\cdot)}(\text{ct}_{x^*}) \end{array} \right] - \frac{1}{2}$$

with the restriction that all queries f that $\mathcal{A}$ makes to KeyGen(mpk, msk, $\cdot$) satisfy $f(x^*) = 0$. An ABE scheme is *adaptively secure* if for all PPT adversaries $\mathcal{A}$, the advantage $\text{Adv}^{\text{ABE}}_{\mathcal{A}}(\lambda)$ is a negligible function in λ. The *selective security* is defined analogously except that the adversary $\mathcal{A}$ selects x^* before seeing mpk.

2.2 Composite-Order Groups

A generator $\mathcal{G}$ takes as input a security parameter 1^λ and outputs group description $\mathbb{G} := (N, G_N, H_N, G_T, e)$, where N is product of three primes p_1, p_2, p_3 of $\Theta(\lambda)$ bits, G_N, H_N and G_T are cyclic groups of order N and $e : G_N \times H_N \rightarrow G_T$ is a non-degenerate bilinear map. We require that the group operations in G_N, H_N and G_T as well the bilinear map e are computable in deterministic polynomial time with respect to λ. We assume that a random generator g (resp. h)

of G_N (resp. H_N) is always contained in the description of bilinear groups. For every divisor n of N, we denote by G_n the subgroup of G_N of order n. We use g_1, g_2, g_3 to denote random generators of subgroups $G_{p_1}, G_{p_2}, G_{p_3}$ respectively and define h_1, h_2, h_3 random generators of subgroups $H_{p_1}, H_{p_2}, H_{p_3}$ analogously.

Computational Assumptions. We review two static computational assumptions in the composite-order group, used e.g. in [8,14]. By symmetry, one may permute the indices for subgroups.

Assumption 1 ($SD^{G_N}_{p_1 \mapsto p_1 p_2}$). *We say that $(p_1 \mapsto p_1 p_2)$-subgroup decision assumption, denoted by $SD^{G_N}_{p_1 \mapsto p_1 p_2}$, holds if for all PPT adversaries $\mathcal{A}$, the following advantage function is negligible in λ.*

$$\mathsf{Adv}_{\mathcal{A}}^{SD^{G_N}_{p_1 \mapsto p_1 p_2}}(\lambda) := \left| \Pr[\mathcal{A}(\mathbb{G}, D, T_0) = 1] - \Pr[\mathcal{A}(\mathbb{G}, D, T_1) = 1] \right|$$

where $D := (g_1, g_2, g_3, h_1, h_3, h_{12})$ with $h_{12} \leftarrow H_{p_1 p_2}$ and

$$T_0 \leftarrow_{\mathrm{R}} \boxed{G_{p_1}}, \quad T_1 \leftarrow \boxed{G_{p_1 p_2}}.$$

Assumption 2 ($DDH^{H_N}_{p_1}$). *We say that p_1-subgroup Diffie-Hellman assumption, denoted by $DDH^{H_N}_{p_1}$, holds if for all PPT adversaries $\mathcal{A}$, the following advantage function is negligible in λ.*

$$\mathsf{Adv}_{\mathcal{A}}^{DDH^{H_N}_{p_1}}(\lambda) := \left| \Pr[\mathcal{A}(\mathbb{G}, D, T_0) = 1] - \Pr[\mathcal{A}(\mathbb{G}, D, T_1) = 1] \right|$$

where $D := (g_1, g_2, g_3, h_1, h_2, h_3)$ and

$$T_0 := (h_1^x, h_1^y, \boxed{h_1^{xy}}), \quad T_1 := (h_1^x, h_1^y, \boxed{h_1^{xy+z}}), \quad x, y, z \leftarrow \mathbb{Z}_N.$$

3   ABE for DFA in Composite-Order Groups

In this section, we present our ABE for DFA in composite-order groups. Here, we focus on selective security in the *one-key* setting under static assumptions.

3.1   Scheme

Our ABE for DFA in composite-order groups is described as follows:

- Setup($1^\lambda, \Sigma$) : Run $\mathbb{G} = (N = p_1 p_2 p_3, G_N, H_N, G_T, e) \leftarrow \mathcal{G}(1^\lambda)$ and pick generators $g_1 \leftarrow G_{p_1}, h \leftarrow H_N$. Sample $\alpha, w_{\mathrm{start}}, w_{\mathrm{end}}, z_0, z_1, w_{\sigma,0}, w_{\sigma,1} \leftarrow \mathbb{Z}_N$ for all $\sigma \in \Sigma$. Choose a pairwise-independent hash function H. Output

$$\mathsf{mpk} = \left(g_1, g_1^{w_{\mathrm{start}}}, g_1^{w_{\mathrm{end}}}, g_1^{z_0}, g_1^{z_1}, \{ g_1^{w_{\sigma,0}}, g_1^{w_{\sigma,1}} \}_{\sigma \in \Sigma}, e(g_1, h)^\alpha, \mathsf{H} \right) \quad \text{and}$$
$$\mathsf{msk} = \left(h, \alpha, w_{\mathrm{start}}, w_{\mathrm{end}}, z_0, z_1, \{ w_{\sigma,0}, w_{\sigma,1} \}_{\sigma \in \Sigma} \right)$$

The message space $\mathcal{M}$ is the image space of H.

– Enc(mpk, x, m) : Let $x = (x_1, \ldots, x_\ell) \in \Sigma^\ell$. Pick $s_0, s_1, \ldots, s_\ell \leftarrow \mathbb{Z}_N$ and output

$$\mathsf{ct}_x = \begin{pmatrix} g_1^{s_0}, g_1^{s_0 w_{\text{start}}}, \\ \{g_1^{s_i}, g_1^{s_{i-1} z_i \bmod 2 + s_i w_{x_i, i} \bmod 2}\}_{i \in [\ell]}, \\ g_1^{s_\ell}, g_1^{s_\ell w_{\text{end}}}, \mathsf{H}(e(g_1, h)^{s_\ell \alpha}) \cdot m \end{pmatrix}.$$

– KeyGen(mpk, msk, f) : Pick $d_u, r_u \leftarrow \mathbb{Z}_N$ for all $u \in [Q]$ and output

$$\mathsf{sk}_f = \begin{pmatrix} h^{d_1 + w_{\text{start}} r_1}, h^{r_1}, \\ \{h^{-d_u + z_b r_u}, h^{d_v + w_{\sigma, b} r_u}, h^{r_u}\}_{b \in \{0,1\}, u \in [Q], \sigma \in \Sigma, v = \delta(u, \sigma)}, \\ \{h^{\alpha - d_u + w_{\text{end}} r_u}, h^{r_u}\}_{u \in F} \end{pmatrix}.$$

– Dec(mpk, sk_f, ct_x) : Parse ciphertext for input $x = (x_1, \ldots, x_\ell)$ as

$$\mathsf{ct}_x = (\, C_{0,1}, C_{0,2}, \{C_{i,1}, C_{i,2}\}_{i \in [\ell]}, C_{\text{end},1}, C_{\text{end},2}, C \,)$$

and key for $f = (Q, \Sigma, \delta, F)$ as

$$\mathsf{sk}_f = (\, K_{0,1}, K_{0,2}, \{K_{b,u}, K_{b,u,\sigma}, K_u\}_{b,u,\sigma}, \{K_{\text{end},u}, K_u\}_{u \in F} \,).$$

If $f(x) = 1$, compute $(u_0 = 1, u_1, \ldots, u_\ell) \in [Q]^{\ell+1}$ such that $\delta(u_{i-1}, x_i) = u_i$ for $i \in [\ell]$ and $u_\ell \in F$, and proceed as follows:

1. Compute $B_0 = e(C_{0,1}, K_{0,1}) \cdot e(C_{0,2}, K_{0,2})^{-1}$;
2. For all $i = 1, \ldots, \ell$, compute

$$B_i = e(C_{i-1,1}, K_{i \bmod 2, u_{i-1}}) \cdot e(C_{i,1}, K_{i \bmod 2, u_{i-1}, x_i}) \cdot e(C_{i,2}, K_{u_{i-1}})^{-1}$$

3. Compute $B_{\text{end}} = e(C_{\text{end},1}, K_{\text{end},u_\ell}) \cdot e(C_{\text{end},2}, K_{u_\ell})^{-1}$ and

$$B = B_0 \cdot \prod_{i=1}^{\ell} B_i \cdot B_{\text{end}}$$

4. Output the message $m' \leftarrow C \cdot \mathsf{H}(B)^{-1}$.

Due to the lack of space, we defer the proof of correctness to the full paper.

Security. We will prove the following theorem for the *one-key* setting where the adversary asks for at most one secret key. We explain how to handle *many* keys in Sect. 3.9.

Theorem 1 (composite-order ABE for DFA). *The ABE scheme for DFA in composite-order bilinear groups described above is selectively secure (cf. Sect. 2.1) in the one-key setting under the following static assumptions:* $SD_{p_1 \mapsto p_1 p_2}^{G_N}$, $SD_{p_1 \mapsto p_1 p_3}^{G_N}$, $SD_{p_3 \mapsto p_3 p_2}^{G_N}$, $DDH_{p_2}^{H_N}$ *and* $DDH_{p_3}^{H_N}$.

3.2   Game Sequence

Let $x^* \in \Sigma^\ell$ denote the selective challenge and let $\bar{\ell} = \ell \bmod 2$. WLOG, we assume $\ell > 1$. Recall that g_2, h_2 denote random generators for G_{p_2}, H_{p_2} respectively.

Auxiliary Distributions. We describe the auxiliary ciphertext and secret key distributions that we use in the proof of security. Throughout, the distributions are the same as the original distributions except for the p_2-components. For notational simplicity, we will only write down the p_2-components and use $\mathsf{xx}[2]$ to denote p_2-components of xx.

Ciphertext distributions

- for $i = 0, 1, \ldots, \ell$: $\mathsf{ct}^i_{x^*}$ is the same as ct_{x^*} except we replace $g_1^{s_i}$ with $(g_1 g_2)^{s_i}$;
- for $i = 1, 2, \ldots, \ell$: $\mathsf{ct}^{i-1,i}_{x^*}$ is the same as ct_{x^*} except we replace $g_1^{s_{i-1}}, g_1^{s_i}$ with $(g_1 g_2)^{s_{i-1}}, (g_1 g_2)^{s_i}$.

That is, we have: writing $\tau = i \bmod 2$,

$$\mathsf{ct}^i_{x^*}[2] = \begin{cases} g_2^{s_0 w_{\mathsf{start}}}, g_2^{s_0}, g_2^{s_0 z_1} & \text{if } i = 0 \\ g_2^{s_i w_{x_i^*, \tau}}, g_2^{s_i}, g_2^{s_i z_{1-\tau}} & \text{if } 0 < i < \ell \\ g_2^{s_\ell w_{x_\ell^*, \bar\ell}}, g_2^{s_\ell}, g_2^{s_\ell w_{\mathsf{end}}}, e(g_2^{s_\ell}, h_2^\alpha) & \text{if } i = \ell \end{cases}$$

$$\mathsf{ct}^{i-1,i}_{x^*}[2] = \begin{cases} g_2^{s_0 w_{\mathsf{start}}}, g_2^{s_0}, g_2^{s_0 z_1 + s_1 w_{x_1^*, 1}}, g_2^{s_1}, g_2^{s_1 z_0} & \text{if } i = 1 \\ g_2^{s_{i-1} w_{x_{i-1}^*, 1-\tau}}, g_2^{s_{i-1}}, g_2^{s_{i-1} z_\tau + s_i w_{x_i^*, \tau}}, g_2^{s_i}, g_2^{s_i z_{1-\tau}} & \text{if } 1 < i < \ell \\ g_2^{s_{\ell-1} w_{x_{\ell-1}^*, 1-\bar\ell}}, g_2^{s_{\ell-1}}, g_2^{s_{\ell-1} z_{\bar\ell} + s_\ell w_{x_\ell^*, \bar\ell}}, g_2^{s_\ell}, g_2^{s_\ell w_{\mathsf{end}}}, e(g_2^{s_\ell}, h_2^\alpha) & \text{if } i = \ell \end{cases}$$

The Δ-distributions. Fix a DFA f. Let $F_{\ell, x^*} = F$; for $i = 0, \ldots, \ell - 1$, we will define

$$F_{i, x^*} := \{ u \in [Q] : \delta(u, x_{i+1}^*, \ldots, x_\ell^*) \in F \}.$$

Here, we use δ to also denote the "extended transition" function, namely

$$\delta(u, \sigma_1, \sigma_2, \ldots, \sigma_{\ell'}) = \delta(\delta(\delta(u, \sigma_1), \sigma_2), \ldots, \sigma_{\ell'}).$$

That is, F_{i, x^*} is the set of states that are reachable from the accept states by back-tracking along $x_\ell^*, \ldots, x_{i+1}^*$. In particular, if $f(x^*) = 0$, then $1 \notin F_{0, x^*}$ (recall that 1 denotes the start state) and more generally, $u_i \notin F_{i, x^*}$ (recall that $u_i = \delta(1, x_1^*, \ldots, x_i^*)$). Finally, we pick $\Delta \leftarrow \mathbb{Z}_N$ and define $\Delta_{i, u}$ to be

$$\Delta_{i, u} := \begin{cases} \Delta & \text{if } u \in F_{i, x^*} \\ 0 & \text{otherwise} \end{cases}$$

Secret key distributions

- for $i = 0, 1, \ldots, \ell$: sk^i_f is the same as sk_f except we add $h_2^{\Delta_{i, v}}$ to $h^{d_v + w_{\sigma, i \bmod 2} r_u}$ for every $u \in [Q], \sigma \in \Sigma$ and $v = \delta(u, \sigma)$.
- for $i = 1, 2, \ldots, \ell$: $\mathsf{sk}^{i-1,i}_f$ is the same as sk_f except we add $h_2^{\Delta_{i-1, u}}$ to $h^{-d_u + z_i \bmod 2 r_u}$ for every $u \in [Q]$.
- sk^*_f is the same as sk_f except we add $h_2^{\Delta_{\ell, u}}$ to $h^{\alpha - d_u + w_{\mathsf{end}} r_u}$ for every $u \in F$.

That is, we have: writing $\tau = i \bmod 2$,

$$
\mathsf{sk}_f^i[2] = \left(
\begin{array}{c}
h_2^{d_1 + w_{\mathrm{start}} r_1}, h_2^{r_1}, \\
\{h_2^{-d_u + z_\tau r_u}, h_2^{d_v + \boxed{\Delta_{i,v}} + w_{\sigma,\tau} r_u}, h_2^{r_u}\}_{u \in [Q], \sigma \in \Sigma, v = \delta(u,\sigma)}, \\
\{h_2^{-d_u + z_{1-\tau} r_u}, h_2^{d_v + w_{\sigma, 1-\tau} r_u}, h_2^{r_u}\}_{u \in [Q], \sigma \in \Sigma, v = \delta(u,\sigma)}, \\
\{h_2^{\alpha - d_u + w_{\mathrm{end}} r_u}, h_2^{r_u}\}_{u \in F}
\end{array}
\right)
$$

$$
\mathsf{sk}_f^{i-1,i}[2] = \left(
\begin{array}{c}
h_2^{d_1 + w_{\mathrm{start}} r_1}, h_2^{r_1}, \\
\{h_2^{-d_u + \boxed{\Delta_{i-1,u}} + z_\tau r_u}, h_2^{d_v + w_{\sigma,\tau} r_u}, h_2^{r_u}\}_{u \in [Q], \sigma \in \Sigma, v = \delta(u,\sigma)}, \\
\{h_2^{-d_u + z_{1-\tau} r_u}, h_2^{d_v + w_{\sigma, 1-\tau} r_u}, h_2^{r_u}\}_{u \in [Q], \sigma \in \Sigma, v = \delta(u,\sigma)}, \\
\{h_2^{\alpha - d_u + w_{\mathrm{end}} r_u}, h_2^{r_u}\}_{u \in F}
\end{array}
\right)
$$

$$
\mathsf{sk}_f^*[2] = \left(
\begin{array}{c}
h_2^{d_1 + w_{\mathrm{start}} r_1}, h_2^{r_1}, \\
\{h_2^{-d_u + z_b r_u}, h_2^{d_v + w_{\sigma,b} r_u}, h_2^{r_u}\}_{b \in \{0,1\}, u \in [Q], \sigma \in \Sigma, v = \delta(u,\sigma)}, \\
\{h_2^{\alpha - d_u + \boxed{\Delta_{\ell,u}} + w_{\mathrm{end}} r_u}, h_2^{r_u}\}_{u \in F}
\end{array}
\right)
$$

Game Sequence. We prove Theorem 1 via a series of games described below and summarized in Fig. 2.

- G_0: Identical to the real game.
- G_1: Identical to G_0 except that the challenge ciphertext is $\mathsf{ct}_{x^*}^0$.
- $\mathsf{G}_{2.i.0}$, $i = 1, \ldots, \ell$: In this game, the challenge ciphertext is $\mathsf{ct}_{x^*}^{i-1}$ and the secret key is sk_f^{i-1}. Note that $\mathsf{G}_{2.1.0}$ is identical to G_1 except that the secret key is sk_f^0 and we have $\mathsf{G}_{2.i.0} = \mathsf{G}_{2.i-1.4}$ for all $2 \leq i \leq \ell$.
- $\mathsf{G}_{2.i.1}$, $i = 1, \ldots, \ell$: Identical to $\mathsf{G}_{2.i.0}$ except that the secret key is $\mathsf{sk}_f^{i-1,i}$.
- $\mathsf{G}_{2.i.2}$, $i = 1, \ldots, \ell$: Identical to $\mathsf{G}_{2.i.1}$ except that the challenge ciphertext is $\mathsf{ct}_{x^*}^{i-1,i}$.
- $\mathsf{G}_{2.i.3}$, $i = 1, \ldots, \ell$: Identical to $\mathsf{G}_{2.i.2}$ except that the secret key is sk_f^i.
- $\mathsf{G}_{2.i.4}$, $i = 1, \ldots, \ell$: Identical to $\mathsf{G}_{2.i.3}$ except that the challenge ciphertext is $\mathsf{ct}_{x^*}^i$.
- G_3: Identical to $\mathsf{G}_{2.\ell.4}$ except that secret key is sk_f^*.

We use $\mathsf{Adv}_{\mathcal{A}}^{\mathsf{xxx}}(\lambda)$ to denote the advantage of adversary $\mathcal{A}$ in $\mathsf{G}_{\mathsf{xxx}}$ with parameter 1^λ.

3.3 Useful Lemmas

We begin with a few useful lemmas which will be used throughout the proof of security.

Basic Facts. We first state several facts which we will use in the proof.

Lemma 1. *For any $x^* \in \Sigma^\ell$ and f such that $f(x^*) = 0$, we have:*

Game	ct_{x*}	sk_f	p_2-components of sk_f			Remark
0	ct_{x*}	sk_f	$[\![d_u \mapsto d_v]\!]_{z_0,w_{\sigma,0}}$	$[\![d_u \mapsto d_v]\!]_{z_1,w_{\sigma,1}}$	$[\![d_u - \alpha \mapsto 0]\!]_{w_{end},0}$	Real game
1	$\boxed{\mathsf{ct}_{x*}^{0}}$	sk_f	$[\![d_u \mapsto d_v]\!]_{z_0,w_{\sigma,0}}$	$[\![d_u \mapsto d_v]\!]_{z_1,w_{\sigma,1}}$	$[\![d_u - \alpha \mapsto 0]\!]_{w_{end},0}$	SD
2.1.0	ct_{x*}^{0}	$\boxed{\mathsf{sk}_f^{0}}$	$[\![d_u \mapsto d_v + \boxed{\Delta_{0,v}}]\!]_{z_0,w_{\sigma,0}}$	$[\![d_u \mapsto d_v]\!]_{z_1,w_{\sigma,1}}$	$[\![d_u - \alpha \mapsto 0]\!]_{w_{end},0}$	DDH
2.i.0	ct_{x*}^{i-1}	sk_f^{i-1}	$[\![d_u \mapsto d_v]\!]_{z_\tau,w_{\sigma,\tau}}$	$[\![d_u \mapsto d_v + \boxed{\Delta_{i-1,v}}]\!]_{z_{1-\tau},w_{\sigma,1-\tau}}$	$[\![d_u - \alpha \mapsto 0]\!]_{w_{end},0}$	$G_{2.i.0}=G_{2.i-1.4} \wedge \ell \geq i \geq 2$
2.i.1	$\mathsf{ct}_{x*}^{i-1,i}$	$\mathsf{sk}_f^{i-1,i}$	$[\![d_u - \boxed{\Delta_{i-1,u}} \mapsto d_v]\!]_{z_\tau,w_{\sigma,\tau}}$	$[\![d_u \mapsto d_v]\!]_{z_{1-\tau},w_{\sigma,1-\tau}}$	$[\![d_u - \alpha \mapsto 0]\!]_{w_{end},0}$	"$d_u \mapsto d_u - \Delta_{i-1,u}$" + DDH (+ Lem 1-1)
2.i.2	$\boxed{\mathsf{ct}_{x*}^{i-1,i}}$	$\mathsf{sk}_f^{i-1,i}$	$[\![d_u - \Delta_{i-1,u} \mapsto d_v]\!]_{z_\tau,w_{\sigma,\tau}}$	$[\![d_u \mapsto d_v]\!]_{z_{1-\tau},w_{\sigma,1-\tau}}$	$[\![d_u - \alpha \mapsto 0]\!]_{w_{end},0}$	Lem 2
2.i.3	$\mathsf{ct}_{x*}^{i-1,i}$	sk_f^{i}	$[\![d_u \mapsto d_v + \boxed{\Delta_{i,v}}]\!]_{z_\tau,w_{\sigma,\tau}}$	$[\![d_u \mapsto d_v]\!]_{z_{1-\tau},w_{\sigma,1-\tau}}$	$[\![d_u - \alpha \mapsto 0]\!]_{w_{end},0}$	Lem 3 + DDH + Lem 1-2
2.i.4	$\boxed{\mathsf{ct}_{x*}^{i}}$	sk_f^{i}	$[\![d_u \mapsto d_v + \Delta_{i,v}]\!]_{z_0,w_{\sigma,0}}$	$[\![d_u \mapsto d_v]\!]_{z_{1-\tau},w_{\sigma,1-\tau}}$	$[\![d_u - \alpha \mapsto 0]\!]_{w_{end},0}$	Lem 2 + DDH
3	ct_{x*}^{ℓ}	$\boxed{\mathsf{sk}_f^{*}}$	$[\![d_u \mapsto d_v]\!]_{z_0,w_{\sigma,1}}$	$[\![d_u \mapsto d_v]\!]_{z_1,w_{\sigma,1}}$	$[\![d_u - \boxed{\Delta_{\ell,u}} - \alpha \mapsto 0]\!]_{w_{end},0}$	"$d_u \mapsto d_u - \Delta_{\ell,u}$" + DDH

Fig. 2. Game sequence for composite-order ABE for DFA with $i = 1, \ldots, \ell$. Recall that $\tau = i \bmod 2$. We only describe the p_2-components for keys with the notational short-hand $[\![d_u \mapsto d_v]\!]_{z,w} = d_v[\![z]\!]_{z,w} := (h_2^{-d_u+z r_u}, h_2^{d_u+w r_u}, h_2^{r_u})$. All secret key elements in the fourth and fifth columns are quantified over $u \in [Q]$, $\sigma \in \Sigma$, $v = \sigma(u,\sigma)$) while those in the sixth column are over $u \in F$; we omit $[\![0 \mapsto d_1]\!]_{0,w_{start}}$. In the "Remark" column, "SD" and "DDH" mean $\mathrm{SD}_{p_1 \mapsto p_1 p_2}^{G_N}$ assumption and $\mathrm{DDH}_{p_2}^{H_N}$ assumption, respectively, cf. Sect. 2.2; all lemmas will be described in Sect. 3.3; "Lemma 1-1" and "Lemma 1-2" indicate the two statements in Lemma 1, respectively. Note that we use Lemma 1 for "$G_{2.i.0} \mapsto G_{2.i.1}$" only when $i = 1$ which is indicating by brackets.

1. $\Delta_{0,1} = 0$;
2. *for all* $i \in [\ell], u \in [Q]$, *we have*

$$u \in F_{i-1,x^*} \iff \delta(u, x_i^*) \in F_{i,x^*}.$$

Proof. The first statement follows from the fact $1 \notin F_{0,x^*}$. The second one can be proved as follows: For direction $\Longrightarrow$, we know $\delta(u, x_i^*, x_{i+1}^*, \ldots, x_\ell^*) \in F$ for all $u \in F_{i-1,x^*}$. This means $\delta(\delta(u, x_i^*), x_{i+1}^*, \ldots, x_\ell^*) \in F$ and thus $\delta(u, x_i^*) \in F_{i,x^*}$ by the definition. The direction $\Longleftarrow$ can be proved analogously. $\square$

Ciphertext Switching. We use (s, w)-switching lemma (Lemma 2) when switching ciphertext distributions in Sect. 3.6. This extends the statement described in (3) by considering many tuples of form $(h^{wr} \cdot h_2^{\Delta}, h^r)$ each with fresh r. To prove Lemma 2, we follow hybrid arguments described in (4) except that (i) we use $\mathsf{SD}^{G_N}_{p_3 \mapsto p_3 p_2}$ instead of $\mathsf{SD}^{G_N}_{p_3 \mapsto p_2}$ assumption and (ii) we apply $\mathsf{SD}^{G_N}_{p_1 \mapsto p_1 p_3}$ assumption once more. Looking ahead, this allows us to derive a prime-order scheme with better parameters.

Lemma 2 ((s, w)-switching lemma). *For all* $Q \in \mathbb{N}$, *we have*

$$
\begin{aligned}
&\mathsf{aux}, g_1^s, &&\{ h^{w\bar{r}_u} \cdot h_2^{\bar{\Delta}}, h^{\bar{r}_u} \}_{u \in [Q]} \\
&\approx_c \mathsf{aux}, g_1^s \cdot \boxed{g_2^s}, &&\{ h^{w\bar{r}_u} \cdot h_2^{\bar{\Delta}}, h^{\bar{r}_u} \}_{u \in [Q]}
\end{aligned}
$$

where $\mathsf{aux} = (g_1, g_2, h, h^w, g_1^w, g_2^w)$ *and* $w, s, \bar{\Delta}, \bar{r}_u \leftarrow \mathbb{Z}_N$ *for all* $u \in [Q]$. *Concretely, the advantage function* $\mathsf{Adv}^{\mathrm{SWITCH}}_{\mathcal{B}}(\lambda)$ *is bounded by*

$$2 \cdot \mathsf{Adv}^{\mathsf{SD}^{G_N}_{p_1 \mapsto p_1 p_3}}_{\mathcal{B}_1}(\lambda) + 4 \cdot \mathsf{Adv}^{\mathsf{DDH}^{H_N}_{p_3}}_{\mathcal{B}_2}(\lambda) + \mathsf{Adv}^{\mathsf{SD}^{G_N}_{p_3 \mapsto p_3 p_2}}_{\mathcal{B}_3}(\lambda)$$

with $\mathsf{Time}(\mathcal{B}_1), \mathsf{Time}(\mathcal{B}_2), \mathsf{Time}(\mathcal{B}_3) \approx \mathsf{Time}(\mathcal{B})$.

Proof. We prove the lemma via the following hybrid arguments:

$$
\begin{aligned}
\mathsf{LHS} = \ &\mathsf{aux}, g_1^s, &&\{ h^{w\bar{r}_u} \cdot h_2^{\bar{\Delta}}, &&h^{\bar{r}_u} \}_u \\
\approx_c \ &\mathsf{aux}, g_1^s \cdot \boxed{g_3^s}, &&\{ h^{w\bar{r}_u} \cdot h_2^{\bar{\Delta}}, &&h^{\bar{r}_u} \}_u &&\text{using } \mathsf{SD}^{G_N}_{p_1 \mapsto p_1 p_3} \\
\approx_c \ &\mathsf{aux}, g_1^s \cdot g_3^s, &&\{ h^{w\bar{r}_u} \cdot h_2^{\bar{\Delta}} \cdot \boxed{h_3^{\bar{\Delta}}}, &&h^{\bar{r}_u} \}_u &&\text{using } \mathsf{DDH}^{H_N}_{p_3} \\
\approx_c \ &\mathsf{aux}, g_1^s \cdot \boxed{g_2^s} \cdot g_3^s, &&\{ h^{w\bar{r}_u} \cdot h_2^{\bar{\Delta}} \cdot h_3^{\bar{\Delta}}, &&h^{\bar{r}_u} \}_u &&\text{using } \mathsf{SD}^{G_N}_{p_3 \mapsto p_3 p_2} \\
\approx_c \ &\mathsf{aux}, g_1^s \cdot g_2^s \cdot g_3^s, &&\{ h^{w\bar{r}_u} \cdot h_2^{\bar{\Delta}} \cdot \cancel{h_3^{\bar{\Delta}}}, &&h^{\bar{r}_u} \}_u &&\text{using } \mathsf{DDH}^{H_N}_{p_3} \\
\approx_c \ &\mathsf{aux}, g_1^s \cdot g_2^s \cdot \cancel{g_3^s}, &&\{ h^{w\bar{r}_u} \cdot h_2^{\bar{\Delta}}, &&h^{\bar{r}_u} \}_u = \mathsf{RHS} \ \text{using } \mathsf{SD}^{G_N}_{p_1 \mapsto p_1 p_3}
\end{aligned}
$$

We proceed as follows:

– The first and the last $\approx_c$ rely on the $\mathsf{SD}^{G_N}_{p_1 \mapsto p_1 p_3}$ assumption stating that:

$$g_1^s \approx_c g_1^s \cdot g_3^s \quad \text{given } g_1, g_2, h, h_2$$

where $s \leftarrow \mathbb{Z}_N$. All reductions are straight-forward.

- The second and the fourth $\approx_c$ rely on the following statement implied by $\mathrm{DDH}_{p_3}^{H_N}$ assumption w.r.t. $w \bmod p_3$: for all $\bar{\Delta} \in \mathbb{Z}_N$, we have

$$\{ h_3^{w\bar{r}_u}, h_3^{\bar{r}_u} \}_{u\in[Q]} \approx_c \{ h_3^{w\bar{r}_u+\bar{\Delta}}, h_3^{\bar{r}_u} \}_{u\in[Q]}$$

given $g_1, g_2, g_3, h_1, h_2, h_3, h_3^w$ where $w, \bar{r}_u \leftarrow \mathbb{Z}_N$ for all $u \in [Q]$. All reductions are straight-forward.
- The third $\approx_c$ relies on the $\mathrm{SD}_{p_3 \mapsto p_3 p_2}^{G_N}$ assumption stating that:

$$g_3^s \approx_c g_2^s \cdot g_3^s \quad \text{given } g_1, g_2, h, h_{23} \tag{9}$$

where $s \leftarrow \mathbb{Z}_N$ and h_{23} is a random generator for $H_{p_2 p_3}$. The reduction works as follows: On input (S, g_1, g_2, h, h_{23}) where either $S = g_3^s$ or $S = g_2^s \cdot g_3^s$, we sample $w, \bar{\Delta}, \bar{r}_u, \tilde{s} \leftarrow \mathbb{Z}_N$ for all $u \in [Q]$. First, we can trivially compute aux and challenge term $g_1^{\tilde{s}} \cdot S$. Second, we simulate $h_2^{\bar{\Delta}} \cdot h_3^{\bar{\Delta}}$ with $h_{23}^{\bar{\Delta}}$ by the fact: $h_2^{\bar{\Delta}} \cdot h_3^{\bar{\Delta}} \approx_s h_{23}^{\bar{\Delta}}$ for all h_2, h_3, h_{23} when $\bar{\Delta} \leftarrow \mathbb{Z}_N$; this is sufficient for simulating all remaining terms.

Combining all five steps proves the lemma. □

Remark 1. Observe that the distributions in the lemma are easily distinguishable if the view also contains g_1^{sw} or $(g_1 g_2)^{sw}$ (on the LHS and RHS respectively).

Key Switching. We use (z, w)-transition lemma (Lemma 3) for switching key distributions (see Sect. 3.7), which captures the core argument in the statement (5) in the Introduction. Due to the lack of space, we defer the detailed proof to the full paper.

Lemma 3 $((z, w)$-transition lemma). *For all $Q \in \mathbb{N}$, $s_{i-1}, s_i \neq 0$ and $\bar{\Delta} \in \mathbb{Z}_N$, we have*

$$\text{aux, } s_{i-1}z + s_i w, \{ h_2^{\boxed{s_i\bar{\Delta}}+z\bar{r}_u}, \quad h_2^{w\bar{r}_u}, h_2^{\bar{r}_u} \}_{u\in[Q]}$$

$$\approx_c \text{aux, } s_{i-1}z + s_i w, \{ \quad h_2^{z\bar{r}_u}, h_2^{\boxed{s_{i-1}\bar{\Delta}}+w\bar{r}_u}, h_2^{\bar{r}_u} \}_{u\in[Q]}$$

where $\text{aux} = (g_1, g_2, h_1, h_2, h_3, h_2^z, h_2^w)$ and $z, w, \bar{r}_u \leftarrow \mathbb{Z}_N$ for all $u \in [Q]$. Concretely, the advantage function $\mathrm{Adv}_\mathcal{B}^{\mathrm{TRANS}}(\lambda)$ is bounded by $2 \cdot \mathrm{Adv}_{\mathcal{B}_1}^{\mathrm{DDH}_{p_2}^{H_N}}(\lambda)$ with $\mathrm{Time}(\mathcal{B}_1) \approx \mathrm{Time}(\mathcal{B})$.

3.4   Initialization: $\mathsf{G}_0 \mapsto \mathsf{G}_1, \mathsf{G}_1 \mapsto \mathsf{G}_{2.1.0}$

The first two transitions are straight-forward; we describe the following two lemmas with the first proof omitted.

Lemma 4 ($\mathsf{G}_0 \approx_c \mathsf{G}_1$). *There exists $\mathcal{B}$ with $\mathrm{Time}(\mathcal{B}) \approx \mathrm{Time}(\mathcal{A})$ such that*

$$|\mathrm{Adv}_\mathcal{A}^0(\lambda) - \mathrm{Adv}_\mathcal{A}^1(\lambda)| \leq \mathrm{Adv}_\mathcal{B}^{\mathrm{SD}_{p_1 \mapsto p_1 p_2}^{G_N}}(\lambda).$$

Lemma 5 ($G_1 \approx_c G_{2.1.0}$). *There exists $\mathcal{B}$ with* $\mathsf{Time}(\mathcal{B}) \approx \mathsf{Time}(\mathcal{A})$ *such that*

$$|\mathsf{Adv}^1_{\mathcal{A}}(\lambda) - \mathsf{Adv}^{2.1.0}_{\mathcal{A}}(\lambda)| \leq 2|\Sigma| \cdot \mathsf{Adv}^{\mathrm{DDH}^{H_N}_{p2}}_{\mathcal{B}}(\lambda).$$

Proof. This roughly means that

$$(\,\mathsf{mpk},\, \mathsf{ct}^0_{x^*},\, \mathsf{sk}_f\,) \approx_c (\,\mathsf{mpk},\, \mathsf{ct}^0_{x^*},\, \boxed{\mathsf{sk}^0_f}\,).$$

By the Chinese Reminder Theorem, it suffices to focus on the p_2-components; concretely, we prove that

$$\mathsf{sk}_f[2] = \begin{pmatrix} h_2^{d_1 + w_{\mathrm{start}} r_1},\, h_2^{r_1}, \\ \{h_2^{-d_u + z_0 r_u},\, h_2^{d_v + w_{\sigma,0} r_u},\, h_2^{r_u}\}_{u \in [Q], \sigma \in \Sigma, v = \delta(u,\sigma)}, \\ \{h_2^{-d_u + z_1 r_u},\, h_2^{d_v + w_{\sigma,1} r_u},\, h_2^{r_u}\}_{u \in [Q], \sigma \in \Sigma, v = \delta(u,\sigma)}, \\ \{h_2^{\alpha - d_u + w_{\mathrm{end}} r_u},\, h_2^{r_u}\}_{u \in F} \end{pmatrix}$$

$$\approx_c \begin{pmatrix} h_2^{d_1 + w_{\mathrm{start}} r_1},\, h_2^{r_1}, \\ \{h_2^{-d_u + z_0 r_u},\, h_2^{d_v + \boxed{\Delta_{0,v}} + w_{\sigma,0} r_u},\, h_2^{r_u}\}_{u \in [Q], \sigma \in \Sigma, v = \delta(u,\sigma)}, \\ \{h_2^{-d_u + z_1 r_u},\, h_2^{d_v + w_{\sigma,1} r_u},\, h_2^{r_u}\}_{u \in [Q], \sigma \in \Sigma, v = \delta(u,\sigma)}, \\ \{h_2^{\alpha - d_u + w_{\mathrm{end}} r_u},\, h_2^{r_u}\}_{u \in F} \end{pmatrix} = \mathsf{sk}^0_f[2]$$

given g_1, h_1, h_3 and

$$\mathsf{ct}^0_{x^*}[2] := (\, q_2^{s_0 w_{\mathrm{start}}},\, q_2^{s_0},\, q_2^{s_0 z_1} \,).$$

Here terms g_1, h_1, h_3 allow us to simulate the p_1- and p_3-components of $\mathsf{ct}^0_{x^*}$ and sk_f (or sk^0_f) as well as mpk, which is sufficient for proving the lemma. Furthermore, this statement immediately follows from the statement below which are implied by $\mathrm{DDH}^{H_N}_{p2}$ assumption w.r.t. $w_{\sigma,0} \bmod p_2$ with $\sigma \in \Sigma$: for all $\sigma \in \Sigma$ and $\Delta \in \mathbb{Z}_N$, we have

$$\{\, h_2^{r_u},\, h_2^{w_{\sigma,0} r_u} \,\}_{u \in [Q]} \approx_c \{\, h_2^{r_u},\, h_2^{\Delta + w_{\sigma,0} r_u} \,\}_{u \in [Q]}$$

given g_1, g_2, h_1, h_2, h_3 and $h_2^{w_{\sigma,0}}$ where $w_{\sigma,0}, r_u \leftarrow \mathbb{Z}_N$ for $u \in [Q]$. Here we crucially rely on the fact the ciphertext $\mathsf{ct}^0_{x^*}[2]$ does not leak $w_{\sigma,0} \bmod p_2$ with $\sigma \in \Sigma$. $\qquad\square$

3.5   Switching Secret Keys I: $G_{2.i.0} \mapsto G_{2.i.1}$

In this section, we prove the following lemma.

Lemma 6 ($G_{2.i.0} \approx_c G_{2.i.1}$). *For all $i = 1, \ldots, \ell$, there exists $\mathcal{B}$ with* $\mathsf{Time}(\mathcal{B}) \approx \mathsf{Time}(\mathcal{A})$ *such that*

$$|\mathsf{Adv}^{2.i.0}_{\mathcal{A}}(\lambda) - \mathsf{Adv}^{2.i.1}_{\mathcal{A}}(\lambda)| \leq 2(|\Sigma| + 3) \cdot \mathsf{Adv}^{\mathrm{DDH}^{H_N}_{p2}}_{\mathcal{B}}(\lambda).$$

Proof Organization. We need two auxiliary games $G_{2.i.1.a}$ and $G_{2.i.1.b}$ and prove that:

$$G_{2.i.0} \overset{\text{Lemma 7}}{\approx_s} G_{2.i.1.a} \overset{\text{Lemma 8}}{\approx_c} G_{2.i.1.b} \overset{\text{Lemma 9}}{\approx_c} G_{2.i.1}$$

where the p_2-components of the secret key in these games are recalled/defined as below

$$G_{2.i.0} : \begin{pmatrix} h_2^{d_1+w_{\text{start}}r_1}, h_2^{r_1}, \\ \{h_2^{-d_u+z_{\tau}r_u}, h_2^{d_v+w_{\sigma,\tau}r_u}, h_2^{r_u}\}_{u\in[Q],\sigma\in\Sigma,v=\delta(u,\sigma)}, \\ \{h_2^{-d_u+z_{1-\tau}r_u}, h_2^{d_v+\boxed{\Delta_{i-1,v}}+w_{\sigma,1-\tau}r_u}, h_2^{r_u}\}_{u\in[Q],\sigma\in\Sigma,v=\delta(u,\sigma)}, \\ \{h_2^{\alpha-d_u+w_{\text{end}}r_u}, h_2^{r_u}\}_{u\in F} \end{pmatrix} = \text{sk}_f^{i-1}[2]$$

$$G_{2.i.1.a} : \begin{pmatrix} h_2^{d_1-\boxed{\Delta_{i-1,1}}+w_{\text{start}}r_1}, h_2^{r_1}, \\ \{h_2^{-d_u+\boxed{\Delta_{i-1,u}}+z_{\tau}r_u}, h_2^{d_v-\boxed{\Delta_{i-1,v}}+w_{\sigma,\tau}r_u}, h_2^{r_u}\}_{u\in[Q],\sigma\in\Sigma,v=\delta(u,\sigma)}, \\ \{h_2^{-d_u+\boxed{\Delta_{i-1,u}}+z_{1-\tau}r_u}, h_2^{d_v+w_{\sigma,1-\tau}r_u}, h_2^{r_u}\}_{u\in[Q],\sigma\in\Sigma,v=\delta(u,\sigma)}, \\ \{h_2^{\alpha-d_u+\boxed{\Delta_{i-1,u}}+w_{\text{end}}r_u}, h_2^{r_u}\}_{u\in F} \end{pmatrix}$$

$$G_{2.i.1.b} : \begin{pmatrix} h_2^{d_1-\cancel{\Delta_{i-1,1}}+w_{\text{start}}r_1}, h_2^{r_1}, \\ \{h_2^{-d_u+\Delta_{i-1,u}+z_{\tau}r_u}, h_2^{d_v-\Delta_{i-1,v}+w_{\sigma,\tau}r_u}, h_2^{r_u}\}_{u\in[Q],\sigma\in\Sigma,v=\delta(u,\sigma)}, \\ \{h_2^{-d_u+\Delta_{i-1,u}+z_{1-\tau}r_u}, h_2^{d_v+w_{\sigma,1-\tau}r_u}, h_2^{r_u}\}_{u\in[Q],\sigma\in\Sigma,v=\delta(u,\sigma)}, \\ \{h_2^{\alpha-d_u+\Delta_{i-1,u}+w_{\text{end}}r_u}, h_2^{r_u}\}_{u\in F} \end{pmatrix}$$

$$G_{2.i.1} : \begin{pmatrix} h_2^{d_1+w_{\text{start}}r_1}, h_2^{r_1}, \\ \{h_2^{-d_u+\Delta_{i-1,u}+z_{\tau}r_u}, h_2^{d_v-\cancel{\Delta_{i-1,v}}+w_{\sigma,\tau}r_u}, h_2^{r_u}\}_{u\in[Q],\sigma\in\Sigma,v=\delta(u,\sigma)}, \\ \{h_2^{-d_u+\cancel{\Delta_{i-1,u}}+z_{1-\tau}r_u}, h_2^{d_v+w_{\sigma,1-\tau}r_u}, h_2^{r_u}\}_{u\in[Q],\sigma\in\Sigma,v=\delta(u,\sigma)}, \\ \{h_2^{\alpha-d_u+\cancel{\Delta_{i-1,u}}+w_{\text{end}}r_u}, h_2^{r_u}\}_{u\in F} \end{pmatrix} = \text{sk}_f^{i-1,i}[2]$$

and the p_2-components of ciphertext are recalled as follows

$$\text{ct}_{x^*}^{i-1}[2] = \begin{cases} g_2^{s_0 w_{\text{start}}}, g_2^{s_0}, g_2^{s_0 z_1} & \text{if } i=1 \\ g_2^{s_{i-1}w_{x_{i-1}^*,1-\tau}}, g_2^{s_{i-1}}, g_2^{s_{i-1}z_{\tau}} & \text{if } 2\le i\le\ell \end{cases}$$

The p_1- and p_3-components of secret key and ciphertext as well as mpk remain unchanged among all the four games.

Lemmas and Proofs. We describe and prove the following lemmas. Combining them together proves Lemma 6.

Lemma 7 ($G_{2.i.0} \approx_s G_{2.i.1.a}$). *For all $i = 1, \ldots, \ell$, we have*

$$\text{Adv}_{\mathcal{A}}^{2.i.0}(\lambda) = \text{Adv}_{\mathcal{A}}^{2.i.1.a}(\lambda).$$

Proof. This immediately follows from the change of variables: $d_u \mapsto d_u - \Delta_{i-1,u} \mod p_2$ for all $u \in [Q]$. □

Lemma 8. ($\mathsf{G}_{2.i.1.a} \approx_c \mathsf{G}_{2.i.1.b}$). *For all $i = 1, \ldots, \ell$, there exists $\mathcal{B}$ with* $\mathsf{Time}(\mathcal{B}) \approx \mathsf{Time}(\mathcal{A})$ *such that*

$$|\mathsf{Adv}_{\mathcal{A}}^{2.i.1.a}(\lambda) - \mathsf{Adv}_{\mathcal{A}}^{2.i.1.b}(\lambda)| \leq 2 \cdot \mathsf{Adv}_{\mathcal{B}}^{\mathsf{DDH}_{p_2}^{H_N}}(\lambda).$$

Proof. We prove the lemma via a case analysis for i:

- Case $i = 1$: The two games are exactly identical due to the fact that $\Delta_{0,1} = 0$, see Lemma 1.
- Case $i > 1$: The lemma follows from the statement below implied by $\mathsf{DDH}_{p_2}^{H_N}$ assumption w.r.t. $w_{\mathsf{start}} \bmod p_2$: for all $\Delta \in \mathbb{Z}_N$, we have

$$\{ h_2^{r_1}, h_2^{w_{\mathsf{start}} r_1} \} \approx_c \{ h_2^{r_1}, h_2^{-\Delta + w_{\mathsf{start}} r_1} \}$$

given g_1, g_2, h_1, h_2, h_3 and $h_2^{w_{\mathsf{start}}}$ where $w_{\mathsf{start}}, r_1 \leftarrow \mathbb{Z}_N$. Here we crucially rely on the fact the ciphertext $\mathsf{ct}_{x^*}^{i-1}[2]$ with $i > 1$ does not leak $w_{\mathsf{start}} \bmod p_2$. $\square$

Lemma 9 ($\mathsf{G}_{2.i.1.b} \approx_c \mathsf{G}_{2.i.1}$). *For all $i = 1, \ldots, \ell$, there exists $\mathcal{B}$ with* $\mathsf{Time}(\mathcal{B}) \approx \mathsf{Time}(\mathcal{A})$ *such that*

$$|\mathsf{Adv}_{\mathcal{A}}^{2.i.1.b}(\lambda) - \mathsf{Adv}_{\mathcal{A}}^{2.i.1}(\lambda)| \leq 2(|\Sigma| + 2) \cdot \mathsf{Adv}_{\mathcal{B}}^{\mathsf{DDH}_{p_2}^{H_N}}(\lambda).$$

Proof. This follows from statements below implied by $\mathsf{DDH}_{p_2}^{H_N}$ assumption w.r.t $w_{\sigma,\tau}, z_{1-\tau}, w_{\mathsf{end}} \bmod p_2$ with $\sigma \in \Sigma$:

- For all $\Delta \in \mathbb{Z}_N$, we have

$$\{ h_2^{r_u}, h_2^{z_{1-\tau} r_u}, h_2^{w_{\mathsf{end}} r_u} \}_{u \in [Q]} \approx_c \{ h_2^{r_u}, h_2^{\Delta + z_{1-\tau} r_u}, h_2^{\Delta + w_{\mathsf{end}} r_u} \}_{u \in [Q]}$$

given g_1, g_2, h_1, h_2, h_3 and $h_2^{z_{1-\tau}}, h_2^{w_{\mathsf{end}}}$ where $z_{1-\tau}, w_{\mathsf{end}}, r_u \leftarrow \mathbb{Z}_N$ for all $u \in [Q]$.
- For all $\sigma \in \Sigma$ and $\Delta \in \mathbb{Z}_N$, we have

$$\{ h_2^{r_u}, h_2^{w_{\sigma,\tau} r_u} \}_{u \in [Q]} \approx_c \{ h_2^{r_u}, h_2^{-\Delta + w_{\sigma,\tau} r_u} \}_{u \in [Q]}$$

given g_1, g_2, h_1, h_2, h_3 and $h_2^{w_{\sigma,\tau}}$ where $w_{\sigma,\tau}, r_u \leftarrow \mathbb{Z}_N$ for $u \in [Q]$.

Here we use the fact that $\mathsf{ct}_{x^*}^{i-1}[2]$ with $1 \leq i \leq \ell$ does not leak $w_{\sigma,\tau}, z_{1-\tau}, w_{\mathsf{end}} \bmod p_2$ with $\sigma \in \Sigma$. $\square$

3.6 Switching Ciphertexts: $\mathsf{G}_{2.i.1} \mapsto \mathsf{G}_{2.i.2}, \mathsf{G}_{2.i.3} \mapsto \mathsf{G}_{2.i.4}$

In this section, we prove the following two lemmas for $\mathsf{G}_{2.i.1} \mapsto \mathsf{G}_{2.i.2}$ and $\mathsf{G}_{2.i.3} \mapsto \mathsf{G}_{2.i.4}$, respectively. The proofs are similar, we give the details for the first proof and only sketch the differences in the second proof.

Lemma 10 ($\mathsf{G}_{2.i.1} \approx_c \mathsf{G}_{2.i.2}$). *For $i = 1, \ldots, \ell$, there exists $\mathcal{B}$ with* $\mathsf{Time}(\mathcal{B}) \approx \mathsf{Time}(\mathcal{A})$ *such that*

$$|\mathsf{Adv}_{\mathcal{A}}^{2.i.1}(\lambda) - \mathsf{Adv}_{\mathcal{A}}^{2.i.2}(\lambda)| \leq \mathsf{Adv}_{\mathcal{B}}^{\mathsf{SWITCH}}(\lambda).$$

Proof. This roughly means that

$$(\text{mpk}, \boxed{\text{ct}_{x^*}^{i-1}}, \text{sk}_f^{i-1,i}) \approx_c (\text{mpk}, \boxed{\text{ct}_{x^*}^{i-1,i}}, \text{sk}_f^{i-1,i}).$$

Recall that $\tau = i \bmod 2$. We prove the lemma using (s_i, z_τ)-switching lemma (see Lemma 2). On input

$$\text{aux}, S_i, \{h^{z_\tau \bar{r}_u} \cdot h_2^{\bar{\Delta}}, h^{\bar{r}_u}\}_{u \in [Q]}$$

with $\text{aux} = (g_1, g_2, h, h^{z_\tau}, g_1^{z_\tau}, g_2^{z_\tau})$ and

$$S_i = g_1^{s_i} \quad \text{or} \quad S_i = g_1^{s_i} \cdot g_2^{s_i}$$

where $z_\tau, s_i, \bar{\Delta}, \bar{r}_u \leftarrow \mathbb{Z}_N$ for all $u \in [Q]$, the reduction proceeds as follows:

(Simulating mpk). We sample $\alpha, w_{\text{start}}, w_{\text{end}}, z_{1-\tau}, w_{\sigma,\tau}, w_{\sigma,1-\tau} \leftarrow \mathbb{Z}_N$ for all $\sigma \in \Sigma$; then we can trivially simulate mpk with terms $g_1, h, g_1^{z_\tau}$ given out in aux.

(Simulating key for f). We want to simulate $\text{sk}_f^{i-1,i}$ in the form

$$\text{sk}_f^{i-1,i} = \begin{pmatrix} h^{d_1 + w_{\text{start}} r_1}, h^{r_1}, \\ \{\boxed{h^{-d_u + z_\tau r_u} \cdot h_2^{\Delta_{i-1,u}}}, h^{d_v + w_{\sigma,\tau} r_u}, \boxed{h^{r_u}}\}_{u \in [Q], \sigma \in \Sigma, v = \delta(u,\sigma)}, \\ \{h^{-d_u + z_{1-\tau} r_u}, h^{d_v + w_{\sigma,1-\tau} r_u}, h^{r_u}\}_{u \in [Q], \sigma \in \Sigma, v = \delta(u,\sigma)}, \\ \{h^{\alpha - d_u + w_{\text{end}} r_u}, h^{r_u}\}_{u \in F} \end{pmatrix}$$

On input f, we build $F_{i-1,x^*} \subseteq [Q]$ from f, then sample $d_u \leftarrow \mathbb{Z}_N$ for all $u \in [Q]$ and $r_u \leftarrow \mathbb{Z}_N$ for all $u \notin F_{i-1,x^*}$. We implicitly set

$$\Delta = \bar{\Delta} \quad \text{and} \quad r_u = \bar{r}_u \quad \text{for all} \ u \in F_{i-1,x^*}$$

and simulate $\text{sk}_f^{i-1,i}$ as follows:

– By the definition of $\{\Delta_{i-1,u}\}_u$ and our implicit setting, we can rewrite all terms in the dashed boxes as:

$$\begin{cases} h^{r_u}, h^{-d_u + z_\tau r_u} & \text{if } u \notin F_{i-1,x^*} \\ h^{\bar{r}_u}, h^{-d_u + z_\tau \bar{r}_u} \cdot h_2^{\bar{\Delta}} & \text{if } u \in F_{i-1,x^*} \end{cases}$$

Terms for $u \notin F_{i-1,x^*}$ can be computed honestly from $\{r_u, d_u\}_{u \notin F_{i-1,x^*}}$ we sampled and h, h^{z_τ} given in aux; terms for $u \in F_{i-1,x^*}$ can be computed from $\{d_u\}_{u \in F_{i-1,x^*}}$ we sampled and $\{h^{z_\tau \bar{r}_u} \cdot h_2^{\bar{\Delta}}, h^{\bar{r}_u}\}_{u \in F_{i-1,x^*}}$ given out in the input.

– All remaining terms can be trivially simulated using $\{r_u\}_{u \notin F_{i-1,x^*}}$ and $\{h^{r_u} = h^{\bar{r}_u}\}_{u \in F_{i-1,x^*}}$ as well as $\alpha, \{d_u\}_{u \in [Q]}, w_{\text{start}}, z_{1-\tau}, \{w_{\sigma,\tau}, w_{\sigma,1-\tau}\}_{\sigma \in \Sigma}, w_{\text{end}}$ we sampled.

(**Simulating ciphertext for x^***). We want to generate a ciphertext for x^* which is distributed as either $\mathsf{ct}_{x^*}^{i-1}$ or $\mathsf{ct}_{x^*}^{i-1,\boxed{i}}$:

$$
\begin{cases}
g_2^{s_0 w_{\mathsf{start}}}, g_2^{s_0}, g_2^{\boxed{s_0 z_1 + s_1 w_{x_1^*,1}}}, \boxed{g_2^{s_1}}, \boxed{g_2^{s_1 z_0}} & \text{if } i = 1 \\
g_2^{s_{i-1} w_{x_{i-1}^*,1-\tau}}, g_2^{s_{i-1}}, g_2^{\boxed{s_{i-1} z_\tau + s_i w_{x_i^*,\tau}}}, \boxed{g_2^{s_i}}, \boxed{g_2^{s_i z_{1-\tau}}} & \text{if } 1 < i < \ell \\
g_2^{s_{\ell-1} w_{x_{\ell-1}^*,1-\bar\ell}}, g_2^{s_{\ell-1}}, g_2^{\boxed{s_{\ell-1} z_{\bar\ell} + s_\ell w_{x_\ell^*,\bar\ell}}}, \boxed{g_2^{s_\ell}}, \boxed{g_2^{s_\ell w_{\mathsf{end}}}}, \boxed{e(g_2^{s_\ell}, h^\alpha)} & \text{if } i = \ell
\end{cases}
$$

On input $(m_0, m_1) \in \mathcal{M} \times \mathcal{M}$, we sample $\beta \leftarrow \{0,1\}$ and $s_j \leftarrow \mathbb{Z}_N$ for all $j \neq i$, and output the challenge ciphertext

$$
\begin{cases}
\left(\ldots, (g_1 g_2)^{s_0 z_1} \cdot S_1^{w_{x_1^*,1}}, S_1, S_1^{z_0} \cdot g_1^{s_2 w_{x_2^*,0}}, \ldots \right) & \text{if } i = 1 \\
\left(\ldots, (g_1 g_2)^{s_{i-1} z_\tau} \cdot S_i^{w_{x_i^*,\tau}}, S_i, S_i^{z_{1-\tau}} \cdot g_1^{s_{i+1} w_{x_{i+1}^*,1-\tau}}, \ldots \right) & \text{if } 1 < i < \ell \\
\left(\ldots, (g_1 g_2)^{s_{\ell-1} z_{\bar\ell}} \cdot S_\ell^{w_{x_\ell^*,\bar\ell}}, S_\ell, S_\ell^{w_{\mathsf{end}}}, \mathsf{H}(e(S_\ell, h^\alpha)) \cdot m_\beta \right) & \text{if } i = \ell
\end{cases}
$$

Here we use the fact that the ciphertext contains no term with $s_i z_\tau$ in the exponent (cf. Remark 1). All omitted terms can be honestly computed from aux and exponents $\{s_j\}_{j \neq i}$ sampled by ourselves. Clearly, when $S_i = g_1^{s_i}$, the output is identical to $\mathsf{ct}_{x^*}^{i-1}$; when $S_i = g_1^{s_i} \cdot g_2^{s_i}$, the output is identical to $\mathsf{ct}_{x^*}^{i-1,i}$. This completes the proof. $\qquad\square$

Lemma 11 ($\mathsf{G}_{2.i.3} \approx_c \mathsf{G}_{2.i.4}$). *For* $i = 1, \ldots, \ell$, *there exists* $\mathcal{B}_1, \mathcal{B}_2$ *with* $\mathsf{Time}(\mathcal{B}_1), \mathsf{Time}(\mathcal{B}_2) \approx \mathsf{Time}(\mathcal{A})$ *such that*

$$
|\mathsf{Adv}_{\mathcal{A}}^{2.i.3}(\lambda) - \mathsf{Adv}_{\mathcal{A}}^{2.i.4}(\lambda)| \leq \mathsf{Adv}_{\mathcal{B}_1}^{\mathrm{SWITCH}}(\lambda) + 4(|\Sigma| - 1) \cdot \mathsf{Adv}_{\mathcal{B}_2}^{\mathrm{DDH}_{p_2}^{H_N}}(\lambda).
$$

Proof. This roughly means that

$$
(\, \mathsf{mpk}, \boxed{\mathsf{ct}_{x^*}^{i-1,i}}, \mathsf{sk}_f^i \,) \approx_c (\, \mathsf{mpk}, \boxed{\mathsf{ct}_{x^*}^i}, \mathsf{sk}_f^i \,)
$$

We prove the lemma using $(s_{i-1}, w_{x_i^*,\tau})$-transition lemma (see Lemma 2). Recall that $\tau = i \bmod 2$. The reduction is analogous to that for Lemma 10: On input

$$
\mathsf{aux}, S_{i-1}, \{h^{w_{x_i^*,\tau} \bar r_u} \cdot h_2^{\bar A}, h^{\bar r_u}\}_{u \in [Q]}
$$

with $\mathsf{aux} = (g_1, g_2, h, h^{w_{x_i^*,\tau}}, g_1^{w_{x_i^*,\tau}}, g_2^{w_{x_i^*,\tau}})$ and

$$
S_{i-1} = g_1^{s_{i-1}} \quad \text{or} \quad S_{i-1} = g_1^{s_{i-1}} \cdot g_2^{s_{i-1}}
$$

where $w_{x_i^*,\tau}, s_{i-1}, \bar A, \bar r_u \leftarrow \mathbb{Z}_N$ for all $u \in [Q]$, we sample $\alpha, w_{\mathsf{start}}, w_{\mathsf{end}}, z_0, z_1$, $w_{\sigma,1-\tau} \leftarrow \mathbb{Z}_N$ for all $\sigma \in \Sigma$, $w_{\sigma,\tau} \leftarrow \mathbb{Z}_N$ for all $\sigma \neq x_i^*$ and $s_j \leftarrow \mathbb{Z}_N$ for all $j \neq i - 1$; then we can simulate mpk and the challenge ciphertext analogously. The main difference locates at the simulation of secret key.

(**Simulating key for** f). We want to simulate sk_f^i in the form:

$$\mathsf{sk}_f^i = \begin{pmatrix} h^{d_1+w_{\mathsf{start}}r_1}, h^{r_1}, \\ \{h^{-d_u+z_\tau r_u}, \boxed{h^{d_{\delta(u,x_i^*)}+w_{x_i^*,\tau}r_u} \cdot h_2^{\Delta_{i,\delta(u,x_i^*)}}, h^{r_u}}\}_{u\in[Q]}, \\ \boxed{\{h^{d_v+w_{\sigma,\tau}r_u} \cdot h_2^{\Delta_{i,v}}\}_{u\in[Q],\sigma\neq x_i^*,v=\delta(u,\sigma)}} \\ \{h^{-d_u+z_{1-\tau}r_u}, h^{d_v+w_{\sigma,1-\tau}r_u}, h^{r_u}\}_{u\in[Q],\sigma\in\Sigma,v=\delta(u,\sigma)}, \\ \{h^{\alpha-d_u+w_{\mathsf{end}}r_u}, h^{r_u}\}_{u\in F} \end{pmatrix}.$$

On input f, we sample $d_u \leftarrow \mathbb{Z}_N$ for all $u \in [Q]$ and implicitly set $\Delta = \bar{\Delta}$ as before but we set $\{r_u\}_{u\in[Q]}$ as follows:

- We build $F_{i,x^*} \subseteq [Q]$, sample $r_u \leftarrow \mathbb{Z}_N$ for all u such that $\delta(u,x_i^*) \notin F_{i,x^*}$ and implicitly set $r_u = \bar{r}_u$ for all u such that $\delta(u,x_i^*) \in F_{i,x^*}$.

Then we simulate sk_f^i as follows:

- By the definition of $\{\Delta_{i,u}\}_u$ and our implicit setting, we can rewrite all terms in the dashed box as below

$$\begin{cases} h^{r_u}, h^{d_{\delta(u,x_i^*)}+w_{x_i^*,\tau}r_u} & \text{if } \delta(u,x_i^*) \notin F_{i,x^*} \\ h^{\bar{r}_u}, h^{d_{\delta(u,x_i^*)}+w_{x_i^*,\tau}\bar{r}_u} \cdot h_2^{\bar{\Delta}} & \text{if } \delta(u,x_i^*) \in F_{i,x^*} \end{cases}$$

and simulate them from either $\{r_u\}_{\delta(u,x_i^*)\notin F_{i,x^*}}$ or $\{h^{w_{x_i^*,\tau}\bar{r}_u} \cdot h_2^{\bar{\Delta}}, h^{\bar{r}_u}\}_{\delta(u,x_i^*)\in F_{i,x^*}}$ with the help of $\{d_u\}_{u\in[Q]}$ and aux. This is similar to the simulation of terms in the dashed boxes in the proof for Lemma 10.

- The terms in the gray box are computationally simulated in the following form

$$\{h^{d_v+w_{\sigma,\tau}r_u} \cdot h_2^{\Delta_{i,v}}\}_{u\in[Q],\sigma\neq x_i^*,v=\delta(u,\sigma)}$$

using $\{d_u\}_{u\in[Q]}, \{w_{\sigma,\tau}\}_{\sigma\neq x_i^*}$ we sampled and $\{h^{r_u}\}_{u\in[Q]}$ we have simulated. This follows from $\mathsf{DDH}_{p_2}^{H_N}$ assumption w.r.t $w_{\sigma,\tau} \bmod p_2$ with $\sigma \neq x_i^*$ which implies that: for all $\sigma \neq x_i^*$ and $\Delta \in \mathbb{Z}_N$, we have

$$\{h_2^{r_u}, h_2^{w_{\sigma,\tau}r_u}\}_{u\in[Q]} \approx_c \{h_2^{r_u}, h_2^{\Delta+w_{\sigma,\tau}r_u}\}_{u\in[Q]}$$

given g_1, g_2, h_1, h_2, h_3 and $h_2^{w_{\sigma,\tau}}$ where $w_{\sigma,\tau}, r_u \leftarrow \mathbb{Z}_N$ for all $u \in [Q]$. Here we use the fact that both $\mathsf{ct}_{x^*}^{i-1,i}$ and $\mathsf{ct}_{x^*}^i$ does not leak $w_{\sigma,\tau} \bmod p_2$ with $\sigma \neq x_i^*$.

- All remaining terms can be easily handled as in the proof of Lemma 10.

This completes the proof.   □

3.7   Switching Key II: $\mathbf{G}_{2.i.2} \mapsto \mathbf{G}_{2.i.3}$

In this section we prove the following lemma.

Lemma 12 ($\mathsf{G}_{2.i.2} \approx_c \mathsf{G}_{2.i.3}$). *For all* $i = 1, \ldots, \ell$, *there exists* $\mathcal{B}_1, \mathcal{B}_2$ *with* $\mathsf{Time}(\mathcal{B}_1)$, $\mathsf{Time}(\mathcal{B}_2) \approx \mathsf{Time}(\mathcal{A})$ *such that*

$$|\mathsf{Adv}_{\mathcal{A}}^{2.i.2}(\lambda) - \mathsf{Adv}_{\mathcal{A}}^{2.i.3}(\lambda)| \leq \mathsf{Adv}_{\mathcal{B}_1}^{\mathrm{TRANS}}(\lambda) + 2(|\Sigma| - 1) \cdot \mathsf{Adv}_{\mathcal{B}_2}^{\mathrm{DDH}_{p_2}^{H_N}}(\lambda).$$

Proof. Recall $\tau = i \bmod 2$. By the Chinese Reminder Theorem, it suffices to focus on the p_2-components; concretely we prove

$$
\mathsf{sk}_f^{i-1,i}[2] = \begin{pmatrix}
h_2^{d_1 + w_{\mathrm{start}} r_1}, h_2^{r_1}, \\
\{h_2^{-d_u + \boxed{\Delta_{i-1,u}} + z_\tau r_u}, h_2^{d_{\delta(u, x_i^*)} + w_{x_i^*, \tau} r_u}, h_2^{r_u}\}_{u \in [Q]}, \\
\{h_2^{d_v + w_{\sigma, \tau} r_u}\}_{u \in [Q], \sigma \neq x_i^*, v = \delta(u, \sigma)}, \\
\{h_2^{-d_u + z_{1-\tau} r_u}, h_2^{d_v + w_{\sigma, 1-\tau} r_u}, h_2^{r_u}\}_{u \in [Q], \sigma \in \Sigma, v = \delta(u, \sigma)}, \\
\{h_2^{\alpha - d_u + w_{\mathrm{end}} r_u}, h_2^{r}\}_{u \in F}
\end{pmatrix}
$$

$$
\approx_c \begin{pmatrix}
h_2^{d_1 + w_{\mathrm{start}} r_1}, h_2^{r_1}, \\
\{h_2^{-d_u + z_\tau r_u}, h_2^{d_{\delta(u, x_i^*)} + \boxed{\Delta_{i, \delta(u, x_i^*)}} + w_{x_i^*, \tau} r_u}, h_2^{r_u}\}_{u \in [Q]}, \\
\{h_2^{d_v + w_{\sigma, \tau} r_u}\}_{u \in [Q], \sigma \neq x_i^*, v = \delta(u, \sigma)}, \\
\{h_2^{-d_u + z_{1-\tau} r_u}, h_2^{d_v + w_{\sigma, 1-\tau} r_u}, h_2^{r_u}\}_{u \in [Q], \sigma \in \Sigma, v = \delta(u, \sigma)}, \\
\{h_2^{\alpha - d_u + w_{\mathrm{end}} r_u}, h_2^{r_u}\}_{u \in F}
\end{pmatrix}
$$

$$
\approx_c \begin{pmatrix}
h_2^{d_1 + w_{\mathrm{start}} r_1}, h_2^{r_1}, \\
\{h_2^{-d_u + z_\tau r_u}, h_2^{d_{\delta(u, x_i^*)} + \Delta_{i, \delta(u, x_i^*)} + w_{x_i^*, \tau} r_u}, h_2^{r_u}\}_{u \in [Q]}, \\
\{h_2^{d_v + \boxed{\Delta_{i,v}} + w_{\sigma, \tau} r_u}\}_{u \in [Q], \sigma \neq x_i^*, v = \delta(u, \sigma)}, \\
\{h_2^{-d_u + z_{1-\tau} r_u}, h_2^{d_v + w_{\sigma, 1-\tau} r_u}, h_2^{r_u}\}_{u \in [Q], \sigma \in \Sigma, v = \delta(u, \sigma)}, \\
\{h_2^{\alpha - d_u + w_{\mathrm{end}} r_u}, h_2^{r_u}\}_{u \in F}
\end{pmatrix} = \mathsf{sk}_f^i[2]
$$

given g_1, h_1, h_3 and

$$
\mathsf{ct}_{x^*}^{i-1,i}[2] = \begin{cases}
g_2^{s_0 w_{\mathrm{start}}}, g_2^{s_0}, g_2^{s_0 z_1 + s_1 w_{x_1^*, 1}}, g_2^{s_1}, g_2^{s_1 z_0} & \text{if } i = 1 \\
g_2^{s_{i-1} w_{x_{i-1}^*, 1-\tau}}, g_2^{s_{i-1}}, g_2^{s_{i-1} z_\tau + s_i w_{x_i^*, \tau}}, g_2^{s_i}, g_2^{s_i z_{1-\tau}} & \text{if } 1 < i < \ell \\
g_2^{s_{\ell-1} w_{x_{\ell-1}^*, 1-\bar{\ell}}}, g_2^{s_{\ell-1}}, g_2^{s_{\ell-1} z_{\bar{\ell}} + s_\ell w_{x_\ell^*, \bar{\ell}}}, g_2^{s_\ell}, g_2^{s_\ell w_{\mathrm{end}}}, e(g_2^{s_\ell}, h_2^\alpha) & \text{if } i = \ell
\end{cases}
$$

Here terms g_1, h_1, h_3 allow us to simulate the p_1- and p_3-components of $\mathsf{ct}_{x^*}^{i-1,i}$ and $\mathsf{sk}_f^{i-1,i}$ (or sk_f^i) as well as mpk, which is sufficient for proving the lemma. We then proceed as follows:

- The first $\approx_c$ relies on $(z_\tau, w_{x_i^*, \tau})$-transition lemma (see Lemma 3). On input

$$
\mathsf{aux}, s_{i-1} z_\tau + s_i w_{x_i^*, \tau}, \{h_2^{\hat{\Delta}_0 + z_\tau \bar{r}_u}, h_2^{\hat{\Delta}_1 + w_{x_i^*, \tau} \bar{r}_u}, h_2^{\bar{r}_u}\}_{u \in [Q]}
$$

with $\mathsf{aux} = (g_1, g_2, h_1, h_2, h_3, s_{i-1}, s_i, h_2^{z_\tau}, h_2^{w_{x_i^*, \tau}})$ where $z_\tau, w_{x_i^*, \tau}, \bar{r}_u \leftarrow \mathbb{Z}_N$ for all $u \in [Q]$ and

$$
(\hat{\Delta}_0, \hat{\Delta}_1) \in \{(s_i \bar{\Delta}, 0), (0, s_{i-1} \bar{\Delta})\} \quad \text{with} \quad \bar{\Delta} \leftarrow \mathbb{Z}_N,
$$

we simulate p_2-components of the ciphertext and keys as follows:

(Simulating ciphertext). We sample $\alpha, w_{\text{start}}, w_{\text{end}}, z_{1-\tau}, w_{\sigma,1-\tau} \leftarrow \mathbb{Z}_N$ for all $\sigma \in \Sigma$, and $w_{\sigma,\tau} \leftarrow \mathbb{Z}_N$ for $\sigma \neq x_i^*$. It is straight-forward to simulate $\text{ct}_{x^*}^{i-1,i}[2]$ from $g_2, s_{i-1}, s_i, s_{i-1}z_\tau + s_i w_{x_i^*,\tau}$. This relies on the fact that neither $z_\tau \bmod p_2$ nor $w_{x_i^*,\tau} \bmod p_2$ appear elsewhere in $\text{ct}_{x^*}^{i-1,i}[2]$.

(Simulating key for f). We want to generate a challenge key which is either $\text{sk}_f^{i-1,i}[2]$ on the LHS or the key on the RHS depending on $(\hat{\Delta}_0, \hat{\Delta}_1)$. On input f, we build $F_{i-1,x^*} \subseteq [Q]$ from f and sample $d_u \leftarrow \mathbb{Z}_N$ for all $u \in [Q]$ and $r_u \leftarrow \mathbb{Z}_N$ for all $u \notin F_{i-1,x^*}$. We implicitly set

$$\Delta = \begin{cases} s_i \bar{\Delta} & \text{for the LHS} \\ s_{i-1}\bar{\Delta} & \text{for the RHS} \end{cases} \quad \text{and} \quad r_u = \bar{r}_u \text{ for all } u \in F_{i-1,x^*}$$

and proceed as follows:

o We rewrite all terms in the second row of keys on the two sides in terms of $s_{i-1}, s_i, \bar{\Delta}, \bar{r}_u$:

$$\text{LHS}_{\text{row 2}} = \begin{cases} h_2^{-d_u + \boxed{s_i\bar{\Delta}} + z_\tau \bar{r}_u}, \ h_2^{d_{\delta(u,x_i^*)} + w_{x_i^*,\tau}\bar{r}_u}, \ h_2^{\bar{r}_u} & \text{if } u \in F_{i-1,x^*} \\ h_2^{-d_u + z_\tau r_u}, \qquad\quad h_2^{d_{\delta(u,x_i^*)} + w_{x_i^*,\tau} r_u}, \ h_2^{r_u} & \text{if } u \notin F_{i-1,x^*} \end{cases}$$

$$\text{RHS}_{\text{row 2}} = \begin{cases} h_2^{-d_u + z_\tau \bar{r}_u}, h_2^{d_{\delta(u,x_i^*)} + \boxed{s_{i-1}\bar{\Delta}} + w_{x_i^*,\tau}\bar{r}_u}, \ h_2^{\bar{r}_u} & \text{if } \delta(u,x_i^*) \in F_{i,x^*} \\ h_2^{-d_u + z_\tau r_u}, h_2^{d_{\delta(u,x_i^*)} + w_{x_i^*,\tau} r_u}, \qquad\quad h_2^{r_u} & \text{if } \delta(u,x_i^*) \notin F_{i,x^*} \end{cases}$$

and generate the second row of the challenge key as

$$\begin{cases} h_2^{-d_u + \boxed{\hat{\Delta}_0} + z_\tau \bar{r}_u}, \ h_2^{d_{\delta(u,x_i^*)} + \boxed{\hat{\Delta}_1} + w_{x_i^*,\tau}\bar{r}_u}, \ h_2^{\bar{r}_u} & \text{if } u \in F_{i-1,x^*} \\ h_2^{-d_u + z_\tau r_u}, \qquad\quad h_2^{d_{\delta(u,x_i^*)} + w_{x_i^*,\tau} r_u}, \qquad\quad h_2^{r_u} & \text{if } u \notin F_{i-1,x^*} \end{cases}$$

where, with $\{d_u\}_{u \in [Q]}$, all terms for $u \in F_{i-1,x^*}$ can be built from terms $\{h_2^{\hat{\Delta}_0 + z_\tau \bar{r}_u}, h_2^{\hat{\Delta}_1 + w_{x_i^*,\tau}\bar{r}_u}, h_2^{\bar{r}_u}\}_{u \in F_{i-1,x^*}}$ provided in the input; all terms for $u \notin F_{i-1,x^*}$ can be built from $h_2, h_2^{z_\tau}, h_2^{w_{x_i^*,\tau}}$ in aux and $\{r_u\}_{u \notin F_{i-1,x^*}}$ we sampled.

o We can trivially generate all remaining terms in the challenge key which are identical to $\text{sk}_f^{i-1,i}[2]$ (and also the key on the RHS) using $\{r_u\}_{u \notin F_{i-1,x^*}}$ and $\{h_2^{r_u} = h_2^{\bar{r}_u}\}_{u \in F_{i-1,x^*}}$ as well as $\alpha, w_{\text{start}}, z_{1-\tau}, \{w_{\sigma,\tau}\}_{\sigma \neq x_i^*}, \{w_{\sigma,1-\tau}\}_{\sigma \in \Sigma}, w_{\text{end}}$.

Observe that,

o when $(\hat{\Delta}_0, \hat{\Delta}_1) = (s_i\bar{\Delta}, 0)$, the output distribution is identical to the LHS;

o when $(\hat{\Delta}_0, \hat{\Delta}_1) = (0, s_{i-1}\bar{\Delta})$, the output distribution is identical to the RHS; here we rely on the fact that $u \in F_{i-1,x^*} \iff \delta(u,x_i^*) \in F_{i,x^*}$ for all $u \in [Q]$, see Lemma 1.

This is sufficient for the proof of the first $\approx_c$.

- The second $\approx_c$ follows from $\mathrm{DDH}_{p_2}^{H_N}$ assumption w.r.t. $w_{\sigma,\tau} \bmod p_2$ with $\sigma \neq x_i^*$, which implies that: for all $\sigma \neq x_i^*$ and $\Delta \in \mathbb{Z}_N$, we have

$$\left\{h_2^{r_u}, h_2^{w_{\sigma,\tau} r_u}\right\}_{u \in [Q]} \approx_c \left\{h_2^{r_u}, h_2^{\Delta + w_{\sigma,\tau} r_u}\right\}_{u \in [Q]}$$

given g_1, g_2, h_1, h_2, h_3 and $h_2^{w_{\sigma,\tau}}$ where $w_{\sigma,\tau}, r_u \leftarrow \mathbb{Z}_N$ for all $u \in [Q]$. This relies on the fact that $\mathsf{ct}_{x^*}^{i-1,i}[2]$ does not leak $w_{\sigma,\tau} \bmod p_2$ with $\sigma \neq x_i^*$.

Combining the two steps proves the lemma. $\qquad\square$

3.8   Finalize: $\mathsf{G}_{2.\ell.4} \mapsto \mathsf{G}_3$

We first describe the following lemma. The proof is analogous to the proof for Lemma 6 and we defer more details to the full paper due to the lack of space.

Lemma 13 ($\mathsf{G}_{2.\ell.4} \approx \mathsf{G}_3$). *There exists $\mathcal{B}$ with $\mathsf{Time}(\mathcal{B}) \approx \mathsf{Time}(\mathcal{A})$ such that*

$$|\mathsf{Adv}_{\mathcal{A}}^{2.\ell.4}(\lambda) - \mathsf{Adv}_{\mathcal{A}}^3(\lambda)| \leq 2(|\Sigma| + 3) \cdot \mathsf{Adv}_{\mathcal{B}}^{\mathrm{DDH}_{p_2}^{H_N}}(\lambda).$$

Finally we prove the last lemma evaluating adversary's advantage in G_3. Combining this lemma with Lemmas 2, 3 and Lemmas 4, 5, 6, 10, 11, 12, 13 proves Theorem 1.

Lemma 14 (Advantage in G_3). *For all $\mathcal{A}$, we have $\mathsf{Adv}_{\mathcal{A}}^3(\lambda) \approx 0$.*

Proof. The definition of $\{\Delta_{\ell,u}\}_{u \in F}$ and $F_{\ell,x^*} = F$ imply that sk_f^* only leak $\alpha + \Delta \bmod p_2$. This means that secret keys perfectly hide $\alpha \bmod p_2$. Therefore, the term $e(g_2, h)^{s_\ell \alpha}$ in $\mathsf{ct}_{x^*}^\ell$ is independently and uniformly distributed and message m_β is statistically hidden by $\mathsf{H}(e(g_1, h)^{s_\ell \alpha} e(g_2, h)^{s_\ell \alpha})$ by the leftover hash lemma. Hence, $\mathsf{Adv}_{\mathcal{A}}^3(\lambda) \approx 0$. $\qquad\square$

3.9   Towards Many-Key Setting

Our proof for the one-key setting can be extended to the many-key setting in a straight-forward way. Without loss of generality, we assume that all key queries $f_1, \ldots, f_q$ share the same state space $[Q]$ and alphabet Σ, and extend notations δ, F and $F_{i,x^*}, d_u, r_u, \Delta_{i,u}$ for f_κ with an additional subscript κ. Then we sketch the changes that are needed to handle the many-key setting:

Game Sequence. We still employ the game sequence described in Sect. 3.2 except

- secret keys in $\mathsf{G}_{2.i.0}$, $\mathsf{G}_{2.i.1}$, $\mathsf{G}_{2.i.3}$ and G_3 are $\mathsf{sk}_{f_\kappa}^{i-1}$, $\mathsf{sk}_{f_\kappa}^{i-1,i}$, $\mathsf{sk}_{f_\kappa}^i$ and $\mathsf{sk}_{f_\kappa}^*$, respectively, for *all* $\kappa \in [q]$;
- in each game, $\{\Delta_{i,u,\kappa}\}_{u \in [Q]}$ for all $\kappa \in [q]$ are defined using the same $\Delta \leftarrow \mathbb{Z}_N$.

Useful Lemmas. All lemmas in Sect. 3.3 can be trivially extended to the many-key setting; in fact, the (s, w)-switching lemma (Lemma 2) and (z, w)-transition lemma (Lemma 3) hold when we replace index $u \in [Q]$ with $(u, \kappa) \in [Q] \times [q]$.

Lemmas and Proofs. Lemmas 4, 5, 6, 10, 11, 12, 13, 14 all hold in the many-key setting:

- The proof for Lemma 4 can be trivially extended to the many-key setting.
- The proofs for Lemmas 5, 6, 13 can work in the many-key setting due to the fact that
  - $\{d_{u,\kappa}\}_{u \in [Q]}$ are fresh for each $\kappa \in [q]$; this ensures that all changes of variables still hold with multiple keys;
  - $\{r_{u,\kappa}\}_{u \in [Q]}$ are fresh for each $\kappa \in [q]$; this ensures that all DDH-based arguments still hold with multiple keys.
- The proofs for Lemmas 10, 11, 12 can be extended using the many-key version of (s, w)-switching lemma or (z, w)-transition lemma; here we also need the fact that $\{r_{u,\kappa}\}_{u \in [Q]}$ are fresh for each $\kappa \in [q]$.
- To prove Lemma 14 with many keys, we argue that *all* secret keys $\mathsf{sk}^*_{f_1}, \ldots, \mathsf{sk}^*_{f_q}$ only leak $\alpha + \Delta \bmod p_2$.

References

1. Agrawal, S., Chase, M.: Simplifying design and analysis of complex predicate encryption schemes. In: Coron, J.-S., Nielsen, J.B. (eds.) EUROCRYPT 2017, Part I. LNCS, vol. 10210, pp. 627–656. Springer, Cham (2017). https://doi.org/10.1007/978-3-319-56620-7_22

2. Attrapadung, N.: Dual system encryption via doubly selective security: framework, fully secure functional encryption for regular languages, and more. In: Nguyen, P.Q., Oswald, E. (eds.) EUROCRYPT 2014. LNCS, vol. 8441, pp. 557–577. Springer, Heidelberg (2014). https://doi.org/10.1007/978-3-642-55220-5_31

3. Attrapadung, N.: Dual system encryption framework in prime-order groups via computational pair encodings. In: Cheon, J.H., Takagi, T. (eds.) ASIACRYPT 2016, Part II. LNCS, vol. 10032, pp. 591–623. Springer, Heidelberg (2016). https://doi.org/10.1007/978-3-662-53890-6_20

4. Blazy, O., Kiltz, E., Pan, J.: (Hierarchical) identity-based encryption from affine message authentication. In: Garay, J.A., Gennaro, R. (eds.) CRYPTO 2014, Part I. LNCS, vol. 8616, pp. 408–425. Springer, Heidelberg (2014). https://doi.org/10.1007/978-3-662-44371-2_23

5. Chen, J., Gay, R., Wee, H.: Improved dual system ABE in prime-order groups via predicate encodings. In: Oswald, E., Fischlin, M. (eds.) EUROCRYPT 2015, Part II. LNCS, vol. 9057, pp. 595–624. Springer, Heidelberg (2015). https://doi.org/10.1007/978-3-662-46803-6_20

6. Chen, J., Gong, J., Kowalczyk, L., Wee, H.: Unbounded ABE via bilinear entropy expansion, revisited. In: Nielsen, J.B., Rijmen, V. (eds.) EUROCRYPT 2018, Part I. LNCS, vol. 10820, pp. 503–534. Springer, Cham (2018). https://doi.org/10.1007/978-3-319-78381-9_19

7. Chen, J., Wee, H.: Fully, (almost) tightly secure IBE and dual system groups. In: Canetti, R., Garay, J.A. (eds.) CRYPTO 2013, Part II. LNCS, vol. 8043, pp. 435–460. Springer, Heidelberg (2013). https://doi.org/10.1007/978-3-642-40084-1_25

8. Chen, J., Wee, H.: Semi-adaptive attribute-based encryption and improved delegation for Boolean formula. In: Abdalla, M., De Prisco, R. (eds.) SCN 2014. LNCS, vol. 8642, pp. 277–297. Springer, Cham (2014). https://doi.org/10.1007/978-3-319-10879-7_16

9. Gong, J., Dong, X., Chen, J., Cao, Z.: Efficient IBE with tight reduction to standard assumption in the multi-challenge setting. In: Cheon, J.H., Takagi, T. (eds.) ASIACRYPT 2016, Part II. LNCS, vol. 10032, pp. 624–654. Springer, Heidelberg (2016). https://doi.org/10.1007/978-3-662-53890-6_21

10. Goyal, V., Pandey, O., Sahai, A., Waters, B.: Attribute-based encryption for fine-grained access control of encrypted data. In: Juels, A., Wright, R.N., Vimercati, S. (eds.) ACM CCS 2006, pp. 89–98. ACM Press, October/November 2006. Available as Cryptology ePrint Archive Report 2006/309

11. Hofheinz, D., Koch, J., Striecks, C.: Identity-based encryption with (almost) tight security in the multi-instance, multi-ciphertext setting. In: Katz, J. (ed.) PKC 2015. LNCS, vol. 9020, pp. 799–822. Springer, Heidelberg (2015). https://doi.org/10.1007/978-3-662-46447-2_36

12. Jafargholi, Z., Kamath, C., Klein, K., Komargodski, I., Pietrzak, K., Wichs, D.: Be adaptive, avoid overcommitting. In: Katz, J., Shacham, H. (eds.) CRYPTO 2017, Part I. LNCS, vol. 10401, pp. 133–163. Springer, Cham (2017). https://doi.org/10.1007/978-3-319-63688-7_5

13. Kowalczyk, L., Wee, H.: Compact adaptively secure ABE for NC^1 from k-Lin. In: Ishai, Y., Rijmen, V. (eds.) EUROCRYPT 2019. LNCS, vol. 11476, pp. 3–33. Springer, Cham (2019). https://doi.org/10.1007/978-3-030-17653-2_1

14. Lewko, A., Waters, B.: New techniques for dual system encryption and fully secure hibe with short ciphertexts. In: Micciancio, D. (ed.) TCC 2010. LNCS, vol. 5978, pp. 455–479. Springer, Heidelberg (2010). https://doi.org/10.1007/978-3-642-11799-2_27

15. Lewko, A., Waters, B.: Unbounded HIBE and attribute-based encryption. In: Paterson, K.G. (ed.) EUROCRYPT 2011. LNCS, vol. 6632, pp. 547–567. Springer, Heidelberg (2011). https://doi.org/10.1007/978-3-642-20465-4_30

16. Lewko, A., Waters, B.: New proof methods for attribute-based encryption: achieving full security through selective techniques. In: Safavi-Naini, R., Canetti, R. (eds.) CRYPTO 2012. LNCS, vol. 7417, pp. 180–198. Springer, Heidelberg (2012). https://doi.org/10.1007/978-3-642-32009-5_12

17. Okamoto, T., Takashima, K.: Fully secure unbounded inner-product and attribute-based encryption. In: Wang, X., Sako, K. (eds.) ASIACRYPT 2012. LNCS, vol. 7658, pp. 349–366. Springer, Heidelberg (2012). https://doi.org/10.1007/978-3-642-34961-4_22

18. Sahai, A., Waters, B.: Fuzzy identity-based encryption. In: Cramer, R. (ed.) EUROCRYPT 2005. LNCS, vol. 3494, pp. 457–473. Springer, Heidelberg (2005). https://doi.org/10.1007/11426639_27

19. Waters, B.: Dual system encryption: realizing fully secure IBE and HIBE under simple assumptions. In: Halevi, S. (ed.) CRYPTO 2009. LNCS, vol. 5677, pp. 619–636. Springer, Heidelberg (2009). https://doi.org/10.1007/978-3-642-03356-8_36

20. Waters, B.: Functional encryption for regular languages. In: Safavi-Naini, R., Canetti, R. (eds.) CRYPTO 2012. LNCS, vol. 7417, pp. 218–235. Springer, Heidelberg (2012). https://doi.org/10.1007/978-3-642-32009-5_14

21. Wee, H.: Dual system encryption via predicate encodings. In: Lindell, Y. (ed.) TCC 2014. LNCS, vol. 8349, pp. 616–637. Springer, Heidelberg (2014). https://doi.org/10.1007/978-3-642-54242-8_26

Attribute Based Encryption (and more) for Nondeterministic Finite Automata from LWE

Shweta Agrawal[1], Monosij Maitra[1], and Shota Yamada[2(✉)]

[1] IIT Madras, Chennai, India
{shweta.a,monosij}@cse.iitm.ac.in
[2] National Institute of Advanced Industrial Science and Technology (AIST),
Tokyo, Japan
yamada-shota@aist.go.jp

Abstract. Constructing Attribute Based Encryption (ABE) [56] for uniform models of computation from standard assumptions, is an important problem, about which very little is known. The *only* known ABE schemes in this setting that (i) avoid reliance on multilinear maps or indistinguishability obfuscation, (ii) support *unbounded length inputs* and (iii) permit *unbounded key requests* to the adversary in the security game, are by Waters from *Crypto, 2012* [57] and its variants. Waters provided the first ABE for Deterministic Finite Automata (DFA) satisfying the above properties, from a parametrized or "q-type" assumption over bilinear maps. Generalizing this construction to Nondeterministic Finite Automata (NFA) was left as an explicit open problem in the same work, and has seen no progress to date. Constructions from other assumptions such as more standard pairing based assumptions, or lattice based assumptions has also proved elusive.

In this work, we construct the first symmetric key attribute based encryption scheme for nondeterministic finite automata (NFA) from the learning with errors (LWE) assumption. Our scheme supports unbounded length inputs as well as unbounded length machines. In more detail, secret keys in our construction are associated with an NFA M of *unbounded* length, ciphertexts are associated with a tuple $(\mathbf{x}, m)$ where $\mathbf{x}$ is a public attribute of *unbounded* length and m is a secret message bit, and decryption recovers m if and only if $M(\mathbf{x}) = 1$.

Further, we leverage our ABE to achieve (restricted notions of) attribute hiding analogous to the circuit setting, obtaining the first *predicate encryption* and bounded key *functional encryption* schemes for NFA from LWE. We achieve machine hiding in the single/bounded key setting to obtain the first *reusable garbled NFA* from standard assumptions. In terms of lower bounds, we show that secret key *functional encryption* even for DFAs, with security against unbounded key requests implies indistinguishability obfuscation (iO) for circuits; this suggests a barrier in achieving full fledged functional encryption for NFA.

© International Association for Cryptologic Research 2019
A. Boldyreva and D. Micciancio (Eds.): CRYPTO 2019, LNCS 11693, pp. 765–797, 2019.
https://doi.org/10.1007/978-3-030-26951-7_26

1   Introduction

Attribute based encryption (ABE) [56] is an emerging paradigm of encryption that enables fine grained access control on encrypted data. In attribute based encryption, a ciphertext of a message m is labelled with a public attribute $\mathbf{x}$ and secret keys are labelled with a Boolean function f. Decryption succeeds to yield the hidden message m if and only if the attribute satisfies the function, namely $f(\mathbf{x}) = 1$. Starting with the seminal work of Sahai and Waters [56], ABE schemes have received a lot of attention in recent years [4,10,20,22,23,26,39–41, 43,45,49,57], yielding constructions for various classes of functions under diverse assumptions.

In most constructions, the function f embedded in the key is represented as a circuit. While powerful, circuits are a *non-uniform* model of computation which necessitates different representations for different input lengths, forcing the scheme to provide multiple function keys for the same functionality as the input length varies. This drawback poses a significant deployment barrier in many practical application scenarios, since data sizes in the real world are rarely of fixed length[1]. Attribute based encryption for uniform models of computation has also been studied, but so far, we have very few constructions from standard assumptions. Waters [57] provided a construction of ABE for Deterministic Finite Automata (DFA) from parametrized or "q-type" assumptions over bilinear maps. Generalizing this construction to Nondeterministic Finite Automata (NFA) was left as an explicit open problem[2] in [57], and has remained open to date. Constructions from other assumptions such as more standard pairing based assumptions, or lattice based assumptions has also proved elusive. Boyen and Li [24] provided a construction of ABE for DFA from the Learning With Errors (LWE) assumption but this was restricted to DFAs with *bounded* length inputs, rendering moot the primary advantage of a DFA over circuits. Agrawal and Singh [8] constructed a primitive closely related to ABE for DFA, namely *reusable garbled DFA* from LWE, but their construction is limited to a security game where the adversary may only request a single function key.

From strong assumptions such as the existence of multilinear maps [33], witness encryption [36] or indistinguishability obfuscation [18,34], attribute based encryption (indeed, even its more powerful generalization – *functional encryption*) has been constructed even for Turing machines [6,14,48], but these are not considered standard assumptions; indeed many candidate constructions have been broken [15,27–29,31,32,44,55]. Very recently, Ananth and Fan [10] constructed ABE for RAM programs from LWE achieving decryption complexity that is sublinear in the database length. However, the key sizes in their

---

[1] A trivial workaround would be to fix the input length to some fixed upper bound and pad all data to this bound; but this solution incurs substantial overhead (besides being inelegant).

[2] Note that an NFA can be converted to an equivalent DFA but this transformation incurs exponential blowup in machine size.

construction are massive and grow with the size of the entire database as well as with worst case running time of the program on any input. In particular, restricting the construction to any model of computation that reads the entire input string (e.g. DFA, TM) yields a bounded input solution, since the key size depends on the input length. Similarly, [26,42] construct attribute based encryption for "bundling functionalities" where the size of the public parameters does not depend on the size of the input chosen by the encryptor, say ℓ. However, the key generator must generate a key for a circuit with a fixed input length, say ℓ', and decryption only succeeds if $\ell = \ell'$. Thus, bundling functionalities do not capture the essential challenge of supporting dynamic data sizes; this was noted explicitly in [42].

Our Results. In this work, we construct the first symmetric key attribute based encryption scheme for nondeterministic finite automata (NFA) from the learning with errors (LWE) assumption. Our scheme supports unbounded length inputs as well as unbounded length machines. In more detail, secret keys in our construction are associated with an NFA M of *unbounded* length, ciphertexts are associated with a tuple $(\mathbf{x}, m)$ where $\mathbf{x}$ is a public attribute of *unbounded* length and m is a secret message bit, and decryption recovers m if and only if $M(\mathbf{x}) = 1$. Moreover our construction achieves succinct parameters, namely, the length of the function key and ciphertext grow only with the machine size and input length respectively (and do not depend on the input length and machine size respectively).

Further, we leverage our ABE to achieve (restricted notions of) attribute hiding analogous to the circuit setting, obtaining the first *predicate encryption* and bounded key *functional encryption* schemes for NFA. We achieve machine hiding in the single key[3] setting to obtain the first *reusable garbled NFA* from standard assumptions. This improves upon the result of [8], which can only support a *single* key request (as against bounded), and only DFAs (as against NFAs).

The above results raise the question of whether full fledged functional encryption, which achieves full attribute hiding for NFAs is possible under standard assumptions. However, we show that secret key functional encryption even for DFA with security against unbounded key requests implies indistinguishability obfuscation (iO) for circuits. Since constructing iO for circuits from standard assumptions is a central challenge in cryptography, this suggests that there is a barrier in further generalizing our result to achieve full attribute hiding.

We summarize our results in Table 1.

---

[3] This may be generalized to bounded key, for any a-priori fixed (polynomial) bound.

Table 1. Prior work and our results. Above, we say that input length supported by a construction is bounded if the parameters and key lengths depend on the input size. For attribute hiding, yes* indicates hiding in the restricted security games of predicate or bounded key functional encryption.

Construction	Model	Input Length	Number of Keys	Attribute and Function Hiding	Assumption
Waters [57]	DFA	unbounded	unbounded	(no, no)	q-type assumption on bilinear maps
Boyen-Li [24]	DFA	bounded	unbounded	(no, no)	LWE
Agrawal-Singh [8]	DFA	unbounded	single	(yes, yes)	LWE
Ananth-Fan [10]	RAM	bounded	unbounded	(no, no)	LWE
Section 4	NFA	unbounded	unbounded	(no, no)	LWE
Full version	NFA	unbounded	unbounded	(yes*, no)	LWE
Full version	NFA	unbounded	bounded	(yes, yes)	LWE

1.1   Our Techniques

In this section, we provide an overview of our techniques. Before we proceed, we discuss the technical barriers that arise in following the approaches taken by prior work. Since the construction by Waters [57] is the only one that supports unbounded attribute lengths and unbounded key requests by the adversary, [4] it is the most promising candidate for generalization to NFA. However, the challenges in generalizing this construction to support NFAs were explicitly discussed in the same work, and this has seen no progress in the last seven years to the best of our knowledge, despite the significant research attention ABE schemes have received. Moreover, even the solution for DFAs is not fully satisfactory since it relies on a non-standard parametrized or "q-type" assumption.

Boyen and Li [24] attempt to construct ABE for DFAs from the LWE assumption, but their construction crucially requires the key generator to know the length of the attribute chosen by the encryptor, since it must provide a fresh "trapdoor" for each row of the DFA transition table and each input position. Indeed, reusing the same trapdoor for multiple positions in the input leads to trivial "mix and match" attacks against their scheme. Thus, it is not even clear how to obtain ABE for DFA with support for unbounded lengths by following this route. The work of Agrawal and Singh [8] gives a construction of functional encryption for DFA from LWE that does handle unbounded length inputs, but

---

[4] The construction is later extended to be adaptively secure rather than selectively secure (e.g., [16]), but the basic structure of the construction is unchanged.

only in the limited single key setting. Their construction crucially relies on reusable garbled circuits [37] which is a single key primitive, and natural attempts to generalize their construction to support even two keys fails[5]. Similarly, the very recent construction of Ananth and Fan [10] is also inherently bounded length, for reasons similar as those discussed above for [24].

Thus, the handful of existing results in this domain all appear to pose fundamental barriers to generalization. To overcome this hurdle, we design completely new techniques to handle the challenge of unbounded length; these may be applicable elsewhere. We focus on the symmetric key setting, and proceed in two steps: i) we provide a secret key ABE scheme for NFA that supports unbounded length inputs but only supports bounded size NFA machines, and ii) we "bootstrap" the construction of step (i) to handle unbounded length machines. We additionally achieve various notions of attribute hiding as discussed above, but will focus on the ABE construction for the remainder of this overview. We proceed to describe each of these steps in detail.

Constructing NfaABE *for Bounded Size NFA.* Our first goal is to construct a secret key ABE scheme for NFA that supports unbounded length inputs but only supports bounded size NFA machines from the LWE assumption. Since ABE for circuits has received much success from the LWE assumption [22,39], our first idea is to see if we can run many circuit ABE schemes "in parallel", one for each input length. We refer to our resulting ABE scheme for NFAs as NfaABE and the ABE for circuits scheme simply as ABE, in order to differentiate them.

Naïve Approach : We start with the following naïve construction that uses a (public key) ABE for circuits as an ingredient. The master secret key of the NfaABE scheme is a PRF key K. This PRF key defines a set of key pairs $\{(\text{ABE.mpk}_j, \text{ABE.msk}_j)\}_{j \in [2^\lambda]}$ of the ABE scheme, where each $(\text{ABE.mpk}_j, \text{ABE.msk}_j)$ is sampled using randomness derived from the PRF key K and supports circuits with inputs of length j. When one encrypts a message for a ciphertext attribute $\mathbf{x}$, one chooses the master public key $\text{ABE.mpk}_{|\mathbf{x}|}$ and encrypts the message using the key, where $|\mathbf{x}|$ is the length of $\mathbf{x}$. We can encrypt for $\mathbf{x}$ with length at most 2^λ and therefore can deal with essentially unbounded length strings as ciphertext attributes. In order to generate a secret key for a machine M, one has to convert it into a circuit since our underlying ingredient is an ABE for circuits. The difference between an NFA machine M and a circuit is that while the former takes a string with arbitrary length as an input, the input length for the latter is fixed. To fill the gap, we prepare a circuit version of NFA M for all possible input lengths. Namely, we convert the machine M into an equivalent circuit $\widehat{M}_j$ with input length j for all $j \in [2^\lambda]$. Then, we generate ABE secret key associated with $\widehat{M}_j$ by running the key generation algorithm

---

[5] For the knowledgeable reader, bounded key variants of reusable garbled circuits exist, for instance by applying the compiler of [38], but using this in the aforementioned construction does not work due to the structure of their construction.

of the ABE for all j to obtain the NfaABE secret key $\{\mathsf{ABE.sk}_j\}_{j \in [2^\lambda]}$. When decrypting a ciphertext associated with $\mathbf{x}$, the decryptor chooses $\mathsf{ABE.sk}_{|\mathbf{x}|}$ and runs the decryption algorithm of the underlying ABE to retrieve the message.

Reducing the Number of Keys: Obviously, there are multiple problems with this approach. The first problem is that there are 2^λ instances of ABE and thus the secret key of NfaABE is exponentially large. To handle this, we thin out most of the instances and change the secret key to be $\{\mathsf{ABE.sk}_{2^j}\}_{j \in [0,\lambda]}$. In order to make sure that the decryption is still possible even with this change, we modify the encryption algorithm. To encrypt a message for an attribute $\mathbf{x}$, one chooses $i \in [0, \lambda]$ such that $2^{i-1} < |\mathbf{x}| \le 2^i$ and uses the i-th instance to encrypt the message, where if the length of $\mathbf{x}$ is not exactly 2^i, it is padded with blank symbols to adjust the length. This change reduces the number of instances down to be polynomial.

Reducing the Size of Keys: However, a bigger problem is that even though we reduced the *number* of secret keys, we did not reduce their size, which is still not polynomial. In particular, there is no guarantee on the size of $\mathsf{ABE.sk}_{2^\lambda}$ since the associated circuit $\widehat{M}_{2^\lambda}$ is of exponential size. Here, we leverage a crucial efficiency property that is enjoyed by the ABE for circuits constructed by Boneh et al. [22], namely, that the secret keys in this scheme are very short. The size of secret keys in their scheme is dependent only on the depth of the circuits being supported and *independent of the input length and size*. Thus, if we can ensure that the depth of $\widehat{M}_{2^\lambda}$ is polynomially bounded (even though the input is exponentially long), we are back in business.

However, converting the NFA to a circuit requires care. We note that implementing the trivial approach of converting an NFA to a circuit by keeping track of all possible states while reading input symbols results in circuit whose depth is linear in input length, which is exponential. To avoid this, we make use of a divide and conquer approach to evaluate the NFA, which makes the circuit depth poly-logarithmic in the input length. As a result, the size of the secret keys can be bounded by a polynomial as desired.

Efficiency of Key Generation: The final and the most difficult problem to be addressed is that even though we managed to make the size of $\{\mathsf{ABE.sk}_{2^j}\}_{j \in [0,\lambda]}$ polynomially bounded, computational time for generating it is still exponentially large, since so is the size of the associated circuits $\{\widehat{M}_{2^j}\}_{j \in [0,\lambda]}$. To resolve the problem, we note that the only algorithm which has the "space" to handle the unbounded input length is the encryption algorithm. Hence, we carefully divide the computation of generating $\{\mathsf{ABE.sk}_{2^j}\}_{j \in [0,\lambda]}$ into pieces so that the key generator only needs to do work proportional to the size of the machine, the encryptor does work proportional to the size of the input and the decryptor computes the requisite key on the fly.

To implement this idea, we use succinct single-key functional encryption (FE), which can be realized from the LWE assumption [2,37]. To support unbounded input length, we generate $\lambda + 1$ instances of the FE scheme to obtain $\{\mathsf{FE.mpk}_j, \mathsf{FE.msk}_j\}_{j \in [0,\lambda]}$. The secret key of NfaABE is $\{\mathsf{FE.ct}_j\}_{j \in [0,\lambda]}$, where $\mathsf{FE.ct}_j = \mathsf{FE.Enc}(\mathsf{FE.mpk}_j, (M, \mathsf{K}))$ is an encryption of a description of the associated NFA M and the PRF key K under the j-th instance of the FE scheme. To provide the matching secret key, the encryptor appends $\mathsf{FE.sk}_i = \mathsf{FE.KeyGen}(\mathsf{FE.msk}_i, C_i)$ to the ciphertext. Here, $\mathbf{x}$ is the attribute vector of unbounded length, i is an integer s.t. $2^{i-1} < |\mathbf{x}| \le 2^i$ and C_i is a circuit that takes as inputs the machine M and PRF key K and outputs an ABE secret key $\mathsf{ABE.sk}_{2^i}$ associated with M.

We are almost done – the decryptor chooses $\mathsf{FE.ct}_i$ with appropriate i from the received set $\{\mathsf{FE.ct}_j\}_{j \in [0,\lambda]}$ and decrypts it using $\mathsf{FE.sk}_i$ that is appended to the ciphertext to obtain an ABE secret key $\mathsf{ABE.sk}_{2^i}$. Then, it decrypts the ABE ciphertext also provided in the ciphertext to retrieve the message. Note that our construction is carefully designed so that we only require a *single* key of the succinct FE scheme.

Arguing the efficiency of the scheme requires care. In order to make the key generation algorithm run in polynomial time, we rely on the succinctness of the underlying FE. Recall that the succinctness property says that the running time of the encryption algorithm is independent of the size of the circuits being supported and only dependent on the depth and input and output length. In our construction, the computation of $\{\mathsf{FE.ct}_j = \mathsf{FE.Enc}(\mathsf{FE.mpk}_j, (M, \mathsf{K}))\}_{j \in [0,\lambda]}$ can be performed in polynomial time, since the input length $|M| + |\mathsf{K}|$ is bounded by a fixed polynomial[6] and so is the output length $|\mathsf{ABE.sk}_{2^j}|$. Note that we crucially use the succinctness of the FE here, since the size of the circuit C_{2^j}, which is supported by the j-th instance of FE, is polynomial in 2^j and thus exponential for $j = \lambda$.

Security: Our construction of NfaABE satisfies standard (selective) indistinguishability based security. The high level idea of the proof is outlined next. Intuitively, security follows from the security of the single key FE scheme and the underlying circuit ABE scheme. In the first step, we show that even though an adversary can obtain multiple FE ciphertexts and secret keys, it cannot obtain anything beyond their decryption results $\{\mathsf{FE.Dec}(\mathsf{FE.sk}_i, \mathsf{FE.ct}_i) = \mathsf{ABE.sk}_i\}$ by the security of the FE. Then, we leverage the security of the ABE to conclude that the message is indeed hidden. We note that in order to invoke the FE security, we need to ensure that only single secret key is revealed to the adversary for each instance of FE. This property is guaranteed, since the circuit for which a secret key of the j-th instance of FE is generated is fixed (i.e., C_{2^j}). Please see Sect. 3 for details.

Removing the Size Constraint on NFAs. So far, we have constructed NfaABE for NFA that can deal with unbounded input length and bounded size NFAs. Let us call such a scheme (u, b)-NfaABE, where "u" and "b" stand for "unbounded" and "bounded". We define (b, u)-NfaABE and (u, u)-NfaABE analogously, where the first parameter refers to input length and the second to machine size.

---

[6] Recall that we are only dealing with bounded size NFAs.

Our goal is to obtain (u, u)-NfaABE. At a high level, we compile (u, u)-NfaABE using two pieces, namely (u, b)-NfaABE which we have already constructed, and (b, u)-NfaABE, which we will instantiate next.

To construct (b, u)-NfaABE, our basic idea is to simply convert an NFA into an equivalent circuit and then use existing ABE for circuits schemes [22, 39]. This approach almost works, but we need to exercise care to ensure that the depth of these circuits can be bounded since we hope to support NFAs of unbounded size. To fill this gap, we show that an NFA can be converted into an equivalent circuit whose depth is poly-logarithmic in the size of the NFA by again using the divide and conquer approach we discussed previously. This enables us to bound the depth of the circuits by a fixed polynomial, even if the size of corresponding NFA is unbounded and allows us to use existing ABE schemes for circuits to construct (b, u)-NfaABE.

We are ready to construct (u, u)-NfaABE by combining (u, b)-NfaABE and (b, u)-NfaABE. The master secret key of the (u, u)-NfaABE is a PRF key K. This PRF key defines a set of keys $\{(u, b)\text{-NfaABE.msk}_j\}_{j \in [2^\lambda]}$ of the (u, b)-NfaABE scheme, where each (u, b)-NfaABE.msk$_j$ supports NFAs with size j. Similarly, the PRF key also defines keys $\{(b, u)\text{-NfaABE.msk}_j\}_{j \in [2^\lambda]}$ of the (b, u)-NfaABE scheme, where each (b, u)-NfaABE.msk$_j$ supports input strings with length j. To encrypt a message with respect to a ciphertext attribute $\mathbf{x}$, it encrypts the message for $\mathbf{x}$ using (u, b)-NfaABE.msk$_j$ to obtain (u, b)-NfaABE.ct$_j$ for all $j \in [\mathbf{x}]$. Furthermore, it also encrypts the message for $\mathbf{x}$ using (b, u)-NfaABE.msk$_{|\mathbf{x}|}$ to obtain (b, u)-NfaABE.ct$_{|\mathbf{x}|}$. The final ciphertext is

$$\left(\ \{(u, b)\text{-NfaABE.ct}_j\}_{j \in [|\mathbf{x}|]}, \ (b, u)\text{-NfaABE.ct}_{|\mathbf{x}|} \ \right).$$

To generate a secret key for a machine M, we essentially swap the roles of (u, b)-NfaABE and (b, u)-NfaABE. Namely, we generate a secret key (b, u)-NfaABE.sk$_j$ for M using (b, u)-NfaABE.msk$_j$ for all $j \in [|M|]$, where $|M|$ is the size of the machine M. We also generate (u, b)-NfaABE.sk$_{|M|}$ for M using (u, b)-NfaABE.msk$_{|M|}$. The final secret key is

$$\left(\ (u, b)\text{-NfaABE.sk}_{|M|}, \ \{(b, u)\text{-NfaABE.sk}_j\}_{j \in [|M|]} \ \right).$$

To decrypt a ciphertext for attribute $\mathbf{x}$ using a secret key for an NFA machine M, we first compare $|\mathbf{x}|$ and $|M|$. If $|\mathbf{x}| > |M|$, it decrypts (u, b)-NfaABE.ct$_{|M|}$ using (u, b)-NfaABE.sk$_{|M|}$. Otherwise, it decrypts (b, u)-NfaABE.ct$_{|\mathbf{x}|}$ using (u, b)-NfaABE.sk$_{|\mathbf{x}|}$. It is not hard to see that the correctness of the resulting scheme follows from those of the ingredients. Furthermore, the security of the scheme is easily reduced to those of the ingredients, as the construction simply runs them in parallel with different parameters. The proof is by a hybrid argument, where we change the encrypted messages in a instance-wise manner. In Sect. 4, we streamline the construction and directly construct (u, u)-NfaABE from (u, b)-NfaABE and ABE for circuits instead of going through (b, u)-NfaABE.

Generalizations and Lower Bounds. We further generalize our ABE construction to obtain predicate encryption and bounded key functional encryption for

NFAs along with the first construction of resuable garbled NFA. These constructions are obtained by carefully replacing the underlying ABE for circuits with predicate encryption, bounded key functional encryption for circuits or reusable garbled circuits. This compiler requires some care as we need to argue that the delicate balance of efficiency properties that enable our NfaABE construction are not violated, as well as ensure that the constructions and security proofs translate. In the full version, we show that we can indeed ensure this, sometimes by employing additional tricks as required. In Sect. 5 we show that secret key functional encryption (SKFE) for DFA with security against unbounded collusion implies indistinguishability obfuscation for circuits. There, we essentially show that we can convert an SKFE for DFA into an SKFE for NC_1 circuit, which implies indistinguishability obfuscation for circuits by previous results [9,47]. The conversion is by encoding and purely combinatorial – we first convert an NC_1 circuit into an equivalent branching program and then leverage the similarity between the branching program and DFA to obtain the result.

Organization of the Paper. In Sect. 2, we provide the definitions and preliminaries we require. In Sect. 3, we provide our ABE for NFA supporting unbounded input but bounded machine length. In Sect. 4, we enhance the construction to support both unbounded input and unbounded machine length. The extensions of our construction to the setting of bounded key functional encryption and reusable garbled circuits for NFA will appear in the full version. In Sect. 5 we show that secret key functional encryption for DFA with security against unbounded collusion implies indistinguishability obfuscation for circuits. We conclude in Sect. 6.

2   Preliminaries

In this section, we define some notation and preliminaries that we require.

Notation. We begin by defining the notation that we will use throughout the paper. We use bold letters to denote vectors and the notation $[a, b]$ to denote the set of integers $\{k \in \mathbb{N} \mid a \leq k \leq b\}$. We use $[n]$ to denote the set $[1, n]$. Concatenation is denoted by the symbol $\|$.

We say a function $f(n)$ is *negligible* if it is $O(n^{-c})$ for all $c > 0$, and we use $\mathrm{negl}(n)$ to denote a negligible function of n. We say $f(n)$ is *polynomial* if it is $O(n^c)$ for some constant $c > 0$, and we use $\mathrm{poly}(n)$ to denote a polynomial function of n. We use the abbreviation PPT for probabilistic polynomial-time. We say an event occurs with *overwhelming probability* if its probability is $1 - \mathrm{negl}(n)$. The function $\log x$ is the base 2 logarithm of x. For any finite set S we denote $\mathcal{P}(S)$ to be the power set of S. For a circuit $C : \{0, 1\}^{\ell_1 + \ell_2} \to \{0, 1\}$ and a string $\mathbf{x} \in \{0, 1\}^{\ell_1}$, $C[\mathbf{x}] : \{0, 1\}^{\ell_2} \to \{0, 1\}$ denotes a circuit that takes $\mathbf{y}$ and outputs $C(\mathbf{x}, \mathbf{y})$. We construct $C[\mathbf{x}]$ in the following specified way. Namely, $C[\mathbf{x}]$ is the circuit that takes as input $\mathbf{y}$ and sets

$$z_i = \begin{cases} y_1 \wedge \neg y_1 & \text{if } x_i = 0 \\ y_1 \vee \neg y_1 & \text{if } x_i = 1 \end{cases}$$

and then computes $C(\mathbf{z}, \mathbf{y})$, where x_i, y_i, and z_i are the i-th bit of $\mathbf{x}$, $\mathbf{y}$, and $\mathbf{z}$, respectively. In the above, it is clear that $z_i = x_i$ and we have $C(\mathbf{z}, \mathbf{y}) = C(\mathbf{x}, \mathbf{y})$. Furthermore, it is also easy to see that $\mathsf{depth}(C[\mathbf{x}]) \leq \mathsf{depth}(C) + O(1)$ holds.

2.1   Definitions: Non Deterministic Finite Automata

A Non-Deterministic Finite Automaton (NFA) M is represented by the tuple $(Q, \Sigma, T, q_{\mathsf{st}}, F)$ where Q is a finite set of states, Σ is a finite alphabet, $T :$ $\Sigma \times Q \rightarrow \mathcal{P}(Q)$ is the transition function (stored as a table), q_{st} is the start state, $F \subseteq Q$ is the set of accepting states. For states $q, q' \in Q$ and a string $\mathbf{x} = (x_1, \ldots, x_k) \in \Sigma^k$, we say that q' is reachable from q by reading $\mathbf{x}$ if there exists a sequence of states $q_1, \ldots, q_{k+1}$ such that $q_1 = q$, $q_{i+1} \in T(x_i, q_i)$ for $i \in [k]$ and $q_{k+1} = q'$. We say $M(\mathbf{x}) = 1$ iff there is a state in F that is reachable from q_{st} by reading $\mathbf{x}$.

Remark 1. As it is known, we can transform an NFA with ϵ-transitions into a one without them by a simple and efficient conversion. The conversion preserves the size of the NFA. For simplicity and without loss of generality, we do not deal with an NFA with ϵ-transitions in this paper.

2.2   Definitions: Secret-Key Attribute Based Encryption for NFA

A secret-key attribute-based encryption (SKABE) scheme NfaABE for a message space $\mathcal{M} = \{\mathcal{M}_\lambda\}_{\lambda \in \mathbb{N}}$ consists of four algorithms. In the following, we fix some alphabet $\Sigma = \Sigma_\lambda$ of size $2 \leq |\Sigma| \leq \mathsf{poly}(\lambda)$.

- NfaABE.Setup(1^λ) is a PPT algorithm takes as input the unary representation of the security parameter and outputs the master secret key NfaABE.msk.
- NfaABE.Enc(NfaABE.msk, $\mathbf{x}$, m) is a PPT algorithm that takes as input the master secret key NfaABE.msk, a string $\mathbf{x} \in \Sigma^*$ of arbitrary length and a message $m \in \mathcal{M}$. It outputs a ciphertext NfaABE.ct.
- NfaABE.KeyGen(NfaABE.msk, M) is a PPT algorithm that takes as input the master secret key NfaABE.msk and a description of an NFA machine M. It outputs a corresponding secret key NfaABE.sk$_M$.
- NfaABE.Dec(NfaABE.sk$_M$, M, NfaABE.ct, $\mathbf{x}$) is a deterministic polynomial time algorithm that takes as input the secret key NfaABE.sk$_M$, its associated NFA M, a ciphertext NfaABE.ct, and its associated string $\mathbf{x}$ and outputs either a message m' or $\perp$.

Remark 2. In our construction in Sect. 3.2, we will pass an additional parameter $\mathsf{s} = \mathsf{s}(\lambda)$ to the NfaABE.Setup, NfaABE.Enc, NfaABE.KeyGen algorithms denoting the description size of NFAs that the scheme can deal with. Later we give a construction in Sect. 4 which can support NFAs with arbitrary size.

Definition 1 (Correctness). *An SKABE scheme* NfaABE *is correct if for all NFAs M, all $\mathbf{x} \in \Sigma^*$ such that $M(\mathbf{x}) = 1$ and for all messages $m \in \mathcal{M}$,*

$$\Pr \begin{bmatrix} \mathsf{NfaABE.msk} \leftarrow \mathsf{NfaABE.Setup}(1^\lambda)\ , \\ \mathsf{NfaABE.sk}_M \leftarrow \mathsf{NfaABE.KeyGen}(\mathsf{NfaABE.msk}, M)\ , \\ \mathsf{NfaABE.ct} \leftarrow \mathsf{NfaABE.Enc}(\mathsf{NfaABE.msk}, \mathbf{x}, m)\ : \\ \mathsf{NfaABE.Dec}(\mathsf{NfaABE.sk}_M, M, \mathsf{NfaABE.ct}, \mathbf{x}) \neq m \end{bmatrix} = \mathrm{negl}(\lambda)$$

where the probability is taken over the coins of NfaABE.Setup, NfaABE.KeyGen, *and* NfaABE.Enc.

Definition 2 (Security for NfaABE). *The SKABE scheme* NfaABE *for a message space $\mathcal{M}$ is said to satisfy selective security if for any stateful PPT adversary* A, *there exists a negligible function* $\mathrm{negl}(\cdot)$ *such that* $\mathsf{Adv}_{\mathsf{NfaABE}, \mathsf{A}}$ $(1^\lambda, \Sigma) :=$

$$\left| \Pr[\mathsf{Exp}^{(0)}_{\mathsf{NfaABE}, \mathsf{A}}(1^\lambda) \to 1] - \Pr[\mathsf{Exp}^{(1)}_{\mathsf{NfaABE}, \mathsf{A}}(1^\lambda) = 1] \right| \leq \mathrm{negl}(\lambda),$$

where for each $b \in \{0, 1\}$ and $\lambda \in \mathbb{N}$, the experiment $\mathsf{Exp}^{(b)}_{\mathsf{NfaABE}, A}$, *modeled as a game between the adversary* A *and a challenger, is defined as follows:*

1. **Setup phase:** *At the beginning of the game,* A *takes as input 1^λ and declares its target $X \subset \Sigma^*$, which is a set of strings of arbitrary size. Then the challenger samples* NfaABE.msk $\leftarrow$ NfaABE.Setup(1^λ).
2. **Query phase:** *During the game,* A *adaptively makes the following queries, in an arbitrary order and unbounded many times.*
   (a) **Encryption queries:** A *submits to the challenger an attribute $\mathbf{x} \in X$ and a pair of messages $(m^{(0)}, m^{(1)}) \in (\mathcal{M}_\lambda)^2$. Then, the challenger replies with* NfaABE.ct $\leftarrow$ NfaABE.Enc(NfaABE.msk, $\mathbf{x}$, $m^{(b)}$) *in order.*
   (b) **Key queries:** A *submits to the challenger an NFA M such that $M(\mathbf{x}) = 0$ for all $\mathbf{x} \in X$. Then, the challenger replies with* NfaABE.sk$_M$ $\leftarrow$ NfaABE.KeyGen(NfaABE.msk, M) *in order.*
3. **Output phase:** A *outputs a guess bit b' as the output of the experiment.*

Remark 3. As noted in Remark 2, our construction in Sect. 3.2 is indexed with an additional parameter s that specifies the size of NFAs being dealt with. In that case, the above security definitions are modified so that A chooses 1^s in addition to X (or X and S, in the case of very selective security) at the beginning of the game and key generation queries are made only for machines with size s.

2.3 Definitions: Attribute Based Encryption and Functional Encryption for Circuits

Attribute Based Encryption for Circuits. For $\lambda \in \mathbb{N}$, let $\mathcal{C}_{\mathsf{inp},\mathsf{d}}$ denote a family of circuits with inp bit inputs, an a-priori bounded depth d, and binary output and $\mathcal{C} = \{\mathcal{C}_{\mathsf{inp}(\lambda),\mathsf{d}(\lambda)}\}_{\lambda \in \mathbb{N}}$. An attribute-based encryption (ABE) scheme ABE for $\mathcal{C}$ over a message space $\mathcal{M} = \{\mathcal{M}_\lambda\}_{\lambda \in \mathbb{N}}$ consists of four algorithms:

- ABE.Setup($1^\lambda, 1^{\mathsf{inp}}, 1^{\mathsf{d}}$) is a PPT algorithm takes as input the unary representation of the security parameter, the length $\mathsf{inp} = \mathsf{inp}(\lambda)$ of the input and the depth $\mathsf{d} = \mathsf{d}(\lambda)$ of the circuit family $\mathcal{C}_{\mathsf{inp}(\lambda),\mathsf{d}(\lambda)}$ to be supported. It outputs the master public key and the master secret key (ABE.mpk, ABE.msk).
- ABE.Enc(ABE.mpk, $\mathbf{x}, m$) is a PPT algorithm that takes as input the master public key ABE.mpk, a string $\mathbf{x} \in \{0,1\}^{\mathsf{inp}}$ and a message $m \in \mathcal{M}$. It outputs a ciphertext ABE.ct.
- ABE.KeyGen(ABE.mpk, ABE.msk, C) is a PPT algorithm that takes as input the master secret key ABE.msk and a circuit $C \in \mathcal{C}_{\mathsf{inp}(\lambda),\mathsf{d}(\lambda)}$ and outputs a corresponding secret key ABE.sk$_C$.
- ABE.Dec(ABE.mpk, ABE.sk$_C$, C, ABE.ct, $\mathbf{x}$) is a deterministic algorithm that takes as input the secret key ABE.sk$_C$, its associated circuit C, a ciphertext ABE.ct, and its associated string $\mathbf{x}$ and outputs either a message m' or $\bot$.

Definition 3 (Correctness). *An ABE scheme for circuits ABE is correct if for all $\lambda \in \mathbb{N}$, polynomially bounded inp and d, all circuits $C \in \mathcal{C}_{\mathsf{inp}(\lambda),\mathsf{d}(\lambda)}$, all $\mathbf{x} \in \{0,1\}^{\mathsf{inp}}$ such that $C(\mathbf{x}) = 1$ and for all messages $m \in \mathcal{M}$,*

$$\Pr \left[\begin{array}{l} (\mathsf{ABE.mpk, ABE.msk}) \leftarrow \mathsf{ABE.Setup}(1^\lambda, 1^{\mathsf{inp}}, 1^{\mathsf{d}}), \\ \mathsf{ABE.sk}_C \leftarrow \mathsf{ABE.KeyGen}(\mathsf{ABE.mpk, ABE.msk}, C), \\ \mathsf{ABE.ct} \leftarrow \mathsf{ABE.Enc}(\mathsf{ABE.mpk}, \mathbf{x}, m) : \\ \mathsf{ABE.Dec}\left(\mathsf{ABE.mpk, ABE.sk}_C, C, \mathsf{ABE.ct}, \mathbf{x} \right) \neq m \end{array} \right] = \mathsf{negl}(\lambda)$$

where the probability is taken over the coins of ABE.Setup, ABE.KeyGen, and ABE.Enc.

Definition 4 (Selective Security for ABE). *The ABE scheme ABE for a circuit family $\mathcal{C} = \{\mathcal{C}_{\mathsf{inp}(\lambda),\mathsf{d}(\lambda)}\}_{\lambda \in \mathbb{N}}$ and a message space $\{\mathcal{M}_\lambda\}_{\lambda \in \mathbb{N}}$ is said to satisfy selective security if for any stateful PPT adversary A, there exists a negligible function $\mathsf{negl}(\cdot)$ such that*

$$\mathsf{Adv}_{\mathsf{ABE,A}}(1^\lambda) = \left| \Pr[\mathsf{Exp}^{(0)}_{\mathsf{ABE,A}}(1^\lambda) = 1] - \Pr[\mathsf{Exp}^{(1)}_{\mathsf{ABE,A}}(1^\lambda) = 1] \right| \leq \mathsf{negl}(\lambda),$$

for all sufficiently large $\lambda \in \mathbb{N}$, where for each $b \in \{0,1\}$ and $\lambda \in \mathbb{N}$, the experiment $\mathsf{Exp}^{(b)}_{\mathsf{ABE,A}}$, modeled as a game between adversary A and a challenger, is defined as follows:

1. **Setup phase:** *On input 1^λ, A submits $(1^{\mathsf{inp}}, 1^{\mathsf{d}})$ and the target $X \subset \{0,1\}^{\mathsf{inp}}$, which is a set of binary strings of length inp, to the challenger. The challenger samples $(\mathsf{ABE.mpk, ABE.msk}) \leftarrow \mathsf{ABE.Setup}(1^\lambda, 1^{\mathsf{inp}}, 1^{\mathsf{d}})$ and replies to A with ABE.mpk.*
2. **Query phase:** *During the game, A adaptively makes the following queries, in an arbitrary order and unbounded many times.*
   (a) **Key Queries:** *A chooses a circuit $C \in \mathcal{C}_{\mathsf{inp},\mathsf{d}}$ that satisfies $C(\mathbf{x}) = 0$ for all $\mathbf{x} \in X$. For each such query, the challenger replies with $\mathsf{ABE.sk}_C \leftarrow \mathsf{ABE.KeyGen}(\mathsf{ABE.mpk, ABE.msk}, C)$.*

(b) **Encryption Queries:** A *submits a string* $\mathbf{x} \in X$ *and a pair of equal length messages* $(m_0, m_1) \in (\mathcal{M})^2$ *to the challenger. The challenger replies to A with* ABE.ct $\leftarrow$ ABE.Enc(ABE.mpk, $\mathbf{x}, m_b$).

3. **Output phase:** A *outputs a guess bit b' as the output of the experiment.*

Remark 4. The above definition allows an adversary to make encryption queries multiple times. More standard notion of the security for an ABE restricts the adversary to make only a single encryption query. It is well-known that they are actually equivalent, which is shown by a simple hybrid argument. We adopt the above definition since it is convenient for our purpose.

In our construction of SKABE for NFA in Sect. 3.2, we will use the ABE scheme by Boneh et al. [22] as a building block. The following theorem summarizes the efficiency properties of their construction.

Theorem 1 (Adapted from [22]). *There exists a selectively secure ABE scheme* ABE = (ABE.Setup, ABE.KeyGen, ABE.Enc, ABE.Dec) *with the following properties under the LWE assumption.*

1. *The circuit* ABE.Setup($\cdot, \cdot, \cdot; \cdot$), *which takes as input* $1^\lambda, 1^{\mathsf{inp}}, 1^{\mathsf{d}}$, *and a randomness* r *and outputs* ABE.msk = ABE.Setup($1^\lambda, 1^{\mathsf{inp}}, 1^{\mathsf{d}}; r$), *can be implemented with depth* poly(λ, d). *In particular, the depth of the circuit is independent of* inp *and the length of the randomness* r.
2. *We have* $|\mathsf{ABE.sk}_C| \leq$ poly(λ, d) *for any* $C \in \mathcal{C}_{\mathsf{inp,d}}$, *where* (ABE.mpk, ABE.msk) $\leftarrow$ ABE.Setup($1^\lambda, 1^{\mathsf{inp}}, 1^{\mathsf{d}}$) *and* $\mathsf{ABE.sk}_C \leftarrow$ ABE.KeyGen(ABE. mpk, ABE.msk, C). *In particular, the length of the secret key is independent of the input length* inp *and the size of the circuit* C.
3. *Let* $C : \{0,1\}^{\mathsf{inp}+\ell} \to \{0,1\}$ *be a circuit such that we have* $C[v] \in \mathcal{C}_{\mathsf{inp,d}}$ *for any* $v \in \{0,1\}^\ell$. *Then, the circuit* ABE.KeyGen($\cdot, \cdot, C[\cdot]; \cdot$), *that takes as input* ABE.mpk, ABE.msk, v, *and randomness* $\widehat{R}$ *and outputs* ABE.KeyGen (ABE.mpk, ABE.msk, $C[v]; \widehat{R}$), *can be implemented with depth* depth(C) $\cdot$ poly(λ, d).

Functional Encryption for Circuits. For $\lambda \in \mathbb{N}$, let $\mathcal{C}_{\mathsf{inp,d,out}}$ denote a family of circuits with inp bit inputs, depth d, and output length out and $\mathcal{C} = \{\mathcal{C}_{\mathsf{inp}(\lambda), \mathsf{d}(\lambda), \mathsf{out}(\lambda)}\}_{\lambda \in \mathbb{N}}$. A functional encryption (FE) scheme FE = (FE.Setup, FE.KeyGen, FE.Enc, FE.Dec) for $\mathcal{C}$ consists of four algorithms:

- FE.Setup($1^\lambda, 1^{\mathsf{inp}}, 1^{\mathsf{d}}, 1^{\mathsf{out}}$) is a PPT algorithm takes as input the unary representation of the security parameter, the length inp = inp(λ) of the input, depth d = d(λ), and the length of the output out = out(λ) of the circuit family $\mathcal{C}_{\mathsf{inp}(\lambda), \mathsf{d}(\lambda), \mathsf{out}(\lambda)}$ to be supported. It outputs the master public key FE.mpk and the master secret key FE.msk.
- FE.KeyGen(FE.mpk, FE.msk, C) is a PPT algorithm that takes as input the master public key FE.mpk, master secret key FE.msk, and a circuit $C \in \mathcal{C}_{\mathsf{inp}(\lambda), \mathsf{d}(\lambda), \mathsf{out}(\lambda)}$ and outputs a corresponding secret key FE.sk$_C$.

- FE.Enc(FE.mpk, $\mathbf{x}$) is a PPT algorithm that takes as input the master public key FE.mpk and an input message $\mathbf{x} \in \{0,1\}^{\mathsf{inp}(\lambda)}$ and outputs a ciphertext FE.ct.
- FE.Dec(FE.mpk, FE.sk$_C$, FE.ct) is a deterministic algorithm that takes as input the master public key FE.mpk, a secret key FE.sk$_C$ and a ciphertext FE.ct and outputs $C(\mathbf{x})$.

Definition 5 (Correctness). *A functional encryption scheme* FE *is correct if for all* $C \in \mathcal{C}_{\mathsf{inp}(\lambda),\mathsf{d}(\lambda),\mathsf{out}(\lambda)}$ *and all* $\mathbf{x} \in \{0,1\}^{\mathsf{inp}(\lambda)}$,

$$\Pr \left[\begin{array}{l} (\mathsf{FE.mpk}, \mathsf{FE.msk}) \leftarrow \mathsf{FE.Setup}(1^\lambda, 1^{\mathsf{inp}(\lambda)}, 1^{\mathsf{d}(\lambda)}, 1^{\mathsf{out}(\lambda)}); \\ \mathsf{FE.sk}_C \leftarrow \mathsf{FE.KeyGen}(\mathsf{FE.mpk}, \mathsf{FE.msk}, C); \\ \mathsf{FE.Dec}\Big(\mathsf{FE.mpk}, \mathsf{FE.sk}_C, \mathsf{FE.Enc}(\mathsf{FE.mpk}, \mathbf{x})\Big) \neq C(\mathbf{x}) \end{array} \right] = \mathsf{negl}(\lambda)$$

where the probability is taken over the coins of FE.Setup, FE.KeyGen, FE.Enc *and,* FE.Dec).

We then define full simulation based security for single key FE as in [37, Definition 2.13].

Definition 6 (FULL-SIM Security). *Let* FE *be a functional encryption scheme for a circuits. For a stateful PPT adversary* A *and a stateless PPT simulator* Sim, *consider the following two experiments:*

$\mathsf{Exp}^{\mathsf{real}}_{\mathsf{FE,A}}(1^\lambda)$:	$\mathsf{Exp}^{\mathsf{ideal}}_{\mathsf{FE,Sim}}(1^\lambda)$:
1: $(1^{\mathsf{inp}}, 1^{\mathsf{d}}, 1^{\mathsf{out}}) \leftarrow \mathsf{A}(1^\lambda)$	*1:* $(1^{\mathsf{inp}}, 1^{\mathsf{d}}, 1^{\mathsf{out}}) \leftarrow \mathsf{A}(1^\lambda)$
2: $(\mathsf{FE.mpk}, \mathsf{FE.msk})$	*2:* $(\mathsf{FE.mpk}, \mathsf{FE.msk})$
$\leftarrow \mathsf{FE.Setup}(1^\lambda, 1^{\mathsf{inp}}, 1^{\mathsf{d}}, 1^{\mathsf{out}})$	$\leftarrow \mathsf{FE.Setup}(1^\lambda, 1^{\mathsf{inp}}, 1^{\mathsf{d}}, 1^{\mathsf{out}})$
3: $C \leftarrow \mathsf{A}(\mathsf{FE.mpk})$	*3:* $C \leftarrow \mathsf{A}(\mathsf{FE.mpk})$
4: $\mathsf{FE.sk}_C$	*4:* $\mathsf{FE.sk}_C$
$\leftarrow \mathsf{FE.KeyGen}(\mathsf{FE.mpk}, \mathsf{FE.msk}, C)$	$\leftarrow \mathsf{FE.KeyGen}(\mathsf{FE.mpk}, \mathsf{FE.msk}, C)$
5: $\alpha \leftarrow \mathsf{A}^{\mathsf{FE.Enc}(\mathsf{FE.mpk}, \cdot)}(\mathsf{FE.mpk}, \mathsf{FE.sk}_C)$	*5:* $\alpha \leftarrow \mathsf{A}^{\mathsf{O}(\cdot)}(\mathsf{FE.mpk}, \mathsf{FE.sk}_C)$

Here, $\mathsf{O}(\cdot)$ is an oracle that on input $\mathbf{x}$ from A, runs Sim with inputs $(\mathsf{FE.mpk}, \mathsf{sk}_C, C, C(\mathbf{x}), 1^{\mathsf{inp}})$ to obtain a ciphertext FE.ct and returns it to the adversary A.

The functional encryption scheme FE is then said to be single query FULL-SIM secure if there exists a PPT simulator Sim such that for every PPT adversary A, the following two distributions are computationally indistinguishable:

$$\left\{ \mathsf{Exp}^{\mathsf{real}}_{\mathsf{FE,A}}(1^\lambda) \right\}_{\lambda \in \mathbb{N}} \overset{c}{\approx} \left\{ \mathsf{Exp}^{\mathsf{ideal}}_{\mathsf{FE,Sim}}(1^\lambda) \right\}_{\lambda \in \mathbb{N}}$$

Remark 5. The above definition allows an adversary to make encryption queries multiple times. In the security notion defined in [37], the adversary is allowed to make only a single encryption query. Similarly to the case of ABE, it is easy to see that these definitions are actually equivalent (See Remark 4). We adopt the above definition since it is convenient for our purpose.

In our construction of SKABE for NFA in Sect. 3.2, we will use the FE scheme by Goldwasser et al. [37] as a building block. The following theorem summarizes the efficiency properties of their construction.

Theorem 2 ([37]). *There exists an FE scheme* FE $=$ (FE.Setup, FE.KeyGen, FE.Enc, FE.Dec) *with the following properties.*

1. *For any polynomially bounded* $\mathsf{inp}(\lambda), \mathsf{d}(\lambda), \mathsf{out}(\lambda)$, *all the algorithms in* FE *run in polynomial time. Namely, the running time of* FE.Setup *and* FE.Enc *do not depend on the size of circuit description to be supported by the scheme.*
2. *Assuming the subexponential hardness of the LWE problem, the scheme satisfies full-simulation-based security.*

We note that the first property above is called succinctness or semi-compactness of FE. A stronger version of the efficiency property called compactness requires the running time of the encryption algorithm to be dependent only on the length of input message **x**. An FE with compactness is known to imply indistinguishability obfuscation [12,21].

3 Attribute-Based Encryption for NFA

3.1 NFA as NC Circuit

Here, we introduce a theorem that provides an efficient algorithm that converts an NFA into an equivalent circuit with shallow depth. The shallowness of the circuit will play a crucial role in our construction of SKABE for NFA. In the following, for ease of notation, we often input a string in Σ^* to a circuit with the understanding that the input is actually a binary string encoding a string in Σ^*. To do so, we set $\eta := \lceil \log(|\Sigma| + 1) \rceil$ and regard a symbol in Σ as a binary string in $\{0,1\}^\eta$ by a natural injection map from Σ to $\{0,1\}^\eta$. Furthermore, we also introduce a special symbol $\perp$ that is not in Σ and assign an unused symbol in $\{0,1\}^\eta$ to it. Intuitively, $\perp$ represents a blank symbol that will be used to adjust the length of a string. We will use alphabets $\{0,1\}^\eta$ and $\Sigma \cup \{\perp\}$ interchangeably.

Theorem 3. *Let Σ be an alphabet for NFAs. Then we have the following:*

1. *There exists a family of circuits* $\{\mathsf{To\text{-}Circuit}_{\mathsf{s},\ell}\}_{\mathsf{s},\ell \in \mathbb{N}}$ *where the circuit* $\mathsf{To\text{-}Circuit}_{\mathsf{s},\ell}$ *takes as input an NFA M with size s and outputs a circuit*

$\widehat{M_\ell} : (\Sigma \cup \{\bot\})^\ell \rightarrow \{0, 1\}$. *Furthermore, for all* $\ell, s \in \mathbb{N}$, *all string* $\mathbf{x} \in \Sigma^{\leq \ell}$, *and all NFA* M *with size* s, *we have*

$$\widehat{M_\ell}(\hat{\mathbf{x}}) = M(\mathbf{x}),$$

where $\widehat{M_\ell} = \text{To-Circuit}_{s,\ell}(M)$ *and* $\hat{\mathbf{x}} = \mathbf{x} \| \bot^{\ell - |\mathbf{x}|}$.

2. *The depths of the circuits* $\text{To-Circuit}_{s,\ell}$ *and* $\widehat{M_\ell} = \text{To-Circuit}_{s,\ell}(M)$ *for an NFA* M *of size* s *are bounded by* $\text{poly}(\log s, \log \ell)$. *Furthermore, the sizes of these circuits are bounded by* $\text{poly}(s, \ell)$.

The proof is by divide and conquer and will appear in the full version.

3.2 Construction: SKABE for Bounded Size NFA

We construct an SKABE scheme for NFA denoted by NfaABE = (NfaABE.Setup, NfaABE.KeyGen, NfaABE.Enc, NfaABE.Dec) from the following ingredients:

1. PRF = (PRF.Setup, PRF.Eval): a pseudorandom function, where a PRF key $K \leftarrow \text{PRF.Setup}(1^\lambda)$ defines a function $\text{PRF.Eval}(K, \cdot) : \{0, 1\}^\lambda \rightarrow \{0, 1\}$. We denote the length of K by $|K|$.
2. FE = (FE.Setup, FE.KeyGen, FE.Enc, FE.Dec): a functional encryption scheme for circuit with the efficiency property described in Item 1 of Theorem 2. We can instantiate FE with the scheme proposed by Goldwasser et al. [37].
3. ABE = (ABE.Setup, ABE.KeyGen, ABE.Enc, ABE.Dec): An ABE scheme that satisfies the efficiency properties described in Theorem 1. We can instantiate ABE with the scheme proposed by Boneh et al. [22].
4. $U(\cdot, \cdot)$: a universal circuit that takes as input a circuit C of fixed depth and size and an input $\mathbf{x}$ to the circuit and outputs $C(\mathbf{x})$. We often denote by $U[C](\cdot) = U(C, \cdot)$ a universal circuit U with the first input C being hardwired. We need to have $\text{depth}(U) \leq O(\text{depth}(C))$. For construction of such a universal circuit, we refer to [30].

Below we provide our construction for SKABE for NFA. In the description below, we abuse notation and denote as if the randomness used in a PPT algorithm was a key K of the pseudorandom function PRF. Namely, for a PPT algorithm (or circuit) A that takes as input x and a randomness $r \in \{0, 1\}^\ell$ and outputs y, $A(x; K)$ denotes an algorithm that computes $r := \text{PRF}(K, 1) \| \text{PRF}(K, 2) \| \cdots \| \text{PRF}(K, \ell)$ and runs $A(x; r)$. Note that if A is a circuit, this transformation makes the size of the circuit polynomially larger and adds a fixed polynomial overhead to its depth. In particular, even if we add this change to ABE.Setup and ABE.KeyGen, the efficiency properties of ABE described in Theorem 1 is preserved.

NfaABE.Setup($1^\lambda, 1^s$): On input the security parameter 1^λ and a description size s of an NFA, do the following:
    1. For $j \in [0, \lambda]$, sample PRF keys $\widehat{K}_j, R_j \leftarrow \text{PRF.Setup}(1^\lambda)$.

2. For $j \in [0, \lambda]$, sample $(\mathsf{FE.mpk}_j, \mathsf{FE.msk}_j) \leftarrow \mathsf{Setup}(1^\lambda, 1^{\mathsf{inp}(\lambda)}, 1^{\mathsf{out}(\lambda)}, 1^{\mathsf{d}(\lambda)})$.

   Here, we generate $\lambda + 1$ instances of FE. Note that all instances support a circuit class with input length $\mathsf{inp}(\lambda) = \mathsf{s} + 2|\mathsf{K}|$, output length $\mathsf{out}(\lambda)$, and depth $\mathsf{d}(\lambda)$, where $\mathsf{out}(\lambda)$ and $\mathsf{d}(\lambda)$ are polynomials in the security parameter that will be specified later.

3. Output $\mathsf{NfaABE.msk} = (\{\widehat{\mathsf{K}}_j, \mathsf{R}_j, \mathsf{FE.mpk}_j, \mathsf{FE.msk}_j\}_{j \in [0, \lambda]})$.

$\mathsf{NfaABE.Enc}(\mathsf{NfaABE.msk}, \mathbf{x}, m, 1^{\mathsf{s}})$: On input the master secret key $\mathsf{NfaABE.msk}$, an attribute $\mathbf{x} \in \Sigma^*$ of length at most 2^λ, a message m and the description size s of NFA, do the following:

1. Parse the master secret key as $\mathsf{NfaABE.msk} \rightarrow (\{\widehat{\mathsf{K}}_j, \mathsf{R}_j, \mathsf{FE.mpk}_j, \mathsf{FE.msk}_j\}_{j \in [0, \lambda]})$.

2. Set $\hat{\mathbf{x}} = \mathbf{x} \| \bot^{2^i - \ell}$, where $\ell = |\mathbf{x}|$ and $i = \lceil \log \ell \rceil$.

3. Compute an ABE key pair $(\mathsf{ABE.mpk}_i, \mathsf{ABE.msk}_i) = \mathsf{ABE.Setup}(1^\lambda, 1^{2^i \eta}, 1^{\hat{\mathsf{d}}}; \widehat{\mathsf{K}}_i)$ with $\widehat{\mathsf{K}}_i$ as the randomness.

   Here, we generate an instance of ABE that supports a circuit class with input domain $\{0, 1\}^{2^i \eta} \supseteq (\Sigma \cup \{\bot\})^{2^i}$ and depth $\hat{\mathsf{d}}$.

4. Compute $\mathsf{ABE.ct} \leftarrow \mathsf{ABE.Enc}(\mathsf{ABE.mpk}_i, \hat{\mathbf{x}}, m)$ as an ABE ciphertext for the message m under attribute $\hat{\mathbf{x}}$.

5. Obtain $\mathsf{FE.sk}_i = \mathsf{FE.KeyGen}(\mathsf{FE.mpk}_i, \mathsf{FE.msk}_i, C_{\mathsf{s}, 2^i}; \mathsf{R}_i)$, where $C_{\mathsf{s}, 2^i}$ is a circuit described in Fig. 1.

6. Output $\mathsf{NfaABE.ct} = (\mathsf{FE.sk}_i, \mathsf{ABE.mpk}_i, \mathsf{ABE.ct})$.

Function $C_{\mathsf{s}, 2^i}$

1. Parse the input $\mathbf{w} = (M, \widehat{\mathsf{K}}, \widehat{\mathsf{R}})$, where M is an NFA and $\widehat{\mathsf{K}}$ and $\widehat{\mathsf{R}}$ are PRF keys.
2. Compute $(\mathsf{ABE.mpk}, \mathsf{ABE.msk}) = \mathsf{ABE.Setup}(1^\lambda, 1^{2^i \eta}, 1^{\hat{\mathsf{d}}}; \widehat{\mathsf{K}})$.
3. Compute $\widehat{M}_{2^i} = \mathsf{To\text{-}Circuit}_{\mathsf{s}, 2^i}(M)$. (See Theorem 3 for the definition of To-Circuit.)
4. Compute and output $\mathsf{ABE.sk}_{U[\widehat{M}_{2^i}]} = \mathsf{ABE.KeyGen}(\mathsf{ABE.mpk}, \mathsf{ABE.msk}, U[\widehat{M}_{2^i}]; \widehat{\mathsf{R}})$.

Fig. 1. The description of the circuit.

$\mathsf{NfaABE.KeyGen}(\mathsf{NfaABE.msk}, M, 1^{\mathsf{s}})$: On input the master secret key $\mathsf{NfaABE.}$ msk, the description of an NFA M and a size s of the NFA, if $|M| \neq \mathsf{s}$, output $\bot$ and abort. Else, proceed as follows.

1. Parse the master secret key as $\mathsf{NfaABE.msk} \rightarrow (\{\widehat{\mathsf{K}}_j, \mathsf{R}_j, \mathsf{FE.mpk}_j, \mathsf{FE.msk}_j\}_{j \in [0, \lambda]})$.

2. Sample $\widehat{\mathsf{R}}_j \leftarrow \mathsf{PRF.Setup}(1^\lambda)$ for all $j \in [0, \lambda]$.

3. Compute $\mathsf{FE.ct}_j = \mathsf{FE.Enc}(\mathsf{FE.mpk}_j, (M, \widehat{\mathsf{K}}_j, \widehat{\mathsf{R}}_j))$ for all $j \in [0, \lambda]$.

4. Output $\mathsf{NfaABE.sk}_M = \{\mathsf{FE.ct}_j\}_{j \in [0, \lambda]}$.

$\mathsf{NfaABE.Dec}(\mathsf{NfaABE.sk}_M, M, \mathsf{NfaABE.ct}, \mathbf{x})$: On input a secret key for NFA M and a ciphertext encoded under attribute $\mathbf{x}$, proceed as follows:

1. Parse the secret key as $\mathsf{NfaABE.sk}_M \to \{\mathsf{FE.ct}_j\}_{j\in[0,\lambda]}$ and the ciphertext as $\mathsf{NfaABE.ct} \to (\mathsf{FE.sk}_i, \mathsf{ABE.mpk}_i, \mathsf{ABE.ct})$.
2. Set $\ell = |\mathbf{x}|$ and choose $\mathsf{FE.ct}_i$ from $\mathsf{NfaABE.sk}_M = \{\mathsf{FE.ct}_j\}_{j\in[0,\lambda]}$ such that $i = \lceil \log \ell \rceil < \lambda$.
3. Compute $y = \mathsf{FE.Dec}(\mathsf{FE.mpk}_i, \mathsf{FE.sk}_i, \mathsf{FE.ct}_i)$.
4. Compute and output $z = \mathsf{ABE.Dec}(\mathsf{ABE.mpk}_i, y, U[\widehat{M_{2^i}}], \mathsf{ABE.ct}_i, \hat{\mathbf{x}})$, where we interpret y as an ABE secret key and $\hat{\mathbf{x}} = \mathbf{x} \| \perp^{2^i - \ell}$.

3.3 Correctness of NfaABE

The following theorem asserts that our scheme is efficient. This directly follows from Theorem 3 and the efficiency of the underlying scheme NfaABE. We refer to full version for the formal proof.

Theorem 4. *Let $|\Sigma|$, $\mathsf{d}(\lambda)$, $\hat{\mathsf{d}}(\lambda)$, and $\mathsf{out}(\lambda)$, be polynomials in λ. Then, $\mathsf{NfaABE} = (\mathsf{NfaABE.Setup}, \mathsf{NfaABE.KeyGen}, \mathsf{NfaABE.Enc}, \mathsf{NfaABE.Dec})$ defined above runs in polynomial time.*

The following theorem addresses the correctness of the scheme.

Theorem 5. *For appropriately chosen $\hat{\mathsf{d}}(\lambda)$, $\mathsf{out}(\lambda)$, and $\mathsf{d}(\lambda)$, our scheme NfaABE is correct for any polynomially bounded $\mathsf{s}(\lambda)$.*

Proof. We have to show that if we set $\hat{\mathsf{d}}(\lambda)$, $\mathsf{out}(\lambda)$, and $\mathsf{d}(\lambda)$ appropriately, we have $z = m$ when $M(\mathbf{x}) = 1$, where z is the value retrieved in Step 3.2 of the decryption algorithm. To show this, let us set $\hat{\mathsf{d}}(\lambda) = \Omega(\lambda)$ and assume that

$$y = \mathsf{ABE.KeyGen}(\mathsf{ABE.mpk}_i, \mathsf{ABE.msk}_i, U[\widehat{M_{2^i}}]; \widehat{\mathsf{R}}_i) \tag{3.1}$$

holds for the moment, where y is the value retrieved in Step 3.2 of the decryption algorithm. Then, we have $z = m$ by the correctness of ABE if $U[\widehat{M_{2^i}}]$ is supported by the scheme, since we have

$$U[\widehat{M_{2^i}}](\hat{\mathbf{x}}) = \widehat{M_{2^i}}(\hat{\mathbf{x}}) = M(\mathbf{x}) = 1$$

by Item 1 of Theorem 3. We claim that the depth of $U[\widehat{M_{2^i}}]$ is at most $\hat{\mathsf{d}}$ and therefore $U[\widehat{M_{2^i}}]$ is indeed supported by the scheme. To see this, we observe that

$$\begin{aligned}
\mathsf{depth}(U[\widehat{M_{2^i}}]) &\leq \mathsf{depth}(U(\cdot, \cdot)) + O(1) \\
&\leq O(1) \cdot \mathsf{depth}(\widehat{M_{2^i}}) + O(1) \\
&\leq \mathsf{poly}(\log \mathsf{s}, \log 2^i) \\
&\leq \mathsf{poly}(\log \lambda) \\
&\leq \hat{\mathsf{d}} \tag{3.2}
\end{aligned}$$

holds, where the second inequality follows from the property of the depth preserving universal circuit U and the third from Item 2 of Theorem 3.

It remains to prove that Eq. (3.1) holds if we set $\mathsf{d}(\lambda)$ and $\mathsf{out}(\lambda)$ appropriately. To do so, we show that the depth and the output length of $C_{\mathsf{s},2^i}$ are bounded by some fixed polynomials. By taking $\mathsf{d}(\lambda)$ and $\mathsf{out}(\lambda)$ larger than these polynomials, we can ensure that the circuit $C_{\mathsf{s},2^i}$ is supported by the FE scheme and thus Eq. (3.1) follows from the correctness of the FE, since we have

$$C_{\mathsf{s},2^i}(M, \widehat{\mathsf{K}}_i, \widehat{\mathsf{R}}_i) = \mathsf{ABE.KeyGen}(\mathsf{ABE.mpk}_i, \mathsf{ABE.msk}_i, U[\widehat{M_{2^i}}]; \widehat{\mathsf{R}}_i),$$

where $(\mathsf{ABE.mpk}_i, \mathsf{ABE.msk}_i) = \mathsf{ABE.Setup}(1^\lambda, 1^{2^i\eta}, 1^{\hat{\mathsf{d}}}; \widehat{\mathsf{K}}_i)$ by the definition of $C_{\mathsf{s},2^i}$. We first bound the depth of $C_{\mathsf{s},2^i}$. To do so, we first observe that Step 2 of $C_{\mathsf{s},2^i}$ can be implemented by a circuit of depth $\mathrm{poly}(\lambda, \hat{\mathsf{d}}) = \mathrm{poly}(\lambda)$ by Item 1 of Theorem 1. We then observe that Step 3 of $C_{\mathsf{s},2^i}$ can be implemented by a circuit of depth $\mathrm{poly}(\log \mathsf{s}, \log 2^i) = \mathrm{poly}(\log \lambda)$ by Item 2 of Theorem 3. We then bound the depth of the circuit that implements Step 4 of $C_{\mathsf{s},2^i}$. This step is implemented by the circuit $\mathsf{ABE.KeyGen}(\cdot, \cdot, U[\cdot]; \cdot)$ that takes as input $\mathsf{ABE.mpk}_i, \mathsf{ABE.msk}_i, U[\widehat{M_{2^i}}]$ constructed in the previous step, and $\widehat{\mathsf{R}}$ and returns $\mathsf{ABE.KeyGen}(\mathsf{ABE.mpk}_i, \mathsf{ABE.msk}_i, U[\widehat{M_{2^i}}]; \widehat{\mathsf{R}})$. We have

$$\mathsf{depth}(\mathsf{ABE.KeyGen}(\cdot, \cdot, U[\cdot]; \cdot)) \leq \mathrm{poly}(\lambda, \hat{\mathsf{d}}) \cdot \mathsf{depth}(U(\cdot, \cdot))$$
$$\leq \mathrm{poly}(\lambda, \hat{\mathsf{d}}) \cdot \hat{\mathsf{d}}$$
$$\leq \mathrm{poly}(\lambda),$$

where the first inequality follows from Item 3 of Theorem 1 and the second from Eq. (3.2). To sum up, we have that the depth of the circuit $C_{\mathsf{s},2^i}$ is bounded by some fixed polynomial.

We next bound the output length of $C_{\mathsf{s},2^i}$. Since the output of the circuit is $\mathsf{ABE.sk}_{U[\widehat{M_{2^i}}]} = \mathsf{ABE.KeyGen}(\mathsf{ABE.mpk}_i, \mathsf{ABE.msk}_i, U[\widehat{M_{2^i}}]; \widehat{\mathsf{R}})$, we bound the length of the ABE secret key. We have

$$|\mathsf{ABE.sk}_{U[\widehat{M_{2^i}}]}| \leq \mathrm{poly}(\lambda, \hat{\mathsf{d}}) \leq \mathrm{poly}(\lambda, \mathrm{poly}(\lambda)) \leq \mathrm{poly}(\lambda)$$

as desired, where the first inequality follows from the Item 2 of Theorem 1. This completes the proof of the theorem.

3.4 Proof of Security for NfaABE

Here, we prove that NfaABE defined above is secure, if so are FE and ABE. Formally, we have the following theorem.

Theorem 6. *Assume that* FE *satisfies full simulation based security,* ABE *is selectively secure, and that* PRF *is a secure pseudorandom function. Then,* NfaABE *satisfies selective security.*

Proof. To prove the theorem, let us fix a PPT adversary A and introduce the following game $\textbf{Game}_i$ between the challenger and A for $i \in [0, \lambda]$.

$\textbf{Game}_i$: The game proceeds as follows.

   Setup phase. At the beginning of the game, A takes 1^λ as input and submits 1^s and the set of its target $X \subset \Sigma^*$ to the challenger. Then, the challenger chooses $\mathsf{NfaABE.msk} \leftarrow \mathsf{NfaABE.Setup}(1^\lambda, 1^s)$

   The challenger answers the encryption and key queries made by A as follows.

   Encryption queries. Given two messages $(m^{(0)}, m^{(1)})$ and $\mathbf{x} \in X$ from A, the challenger sets $\ell := |\mathbf{x}|$ and computes

$$\mathsf{NfaABE.ct} = \begin{cases} \mathsf{NfaABE.Enc}(\mathsf{NfaABE.msk}, \hat{\mathbf{x}}, m^{(0)}) & \text{If } \lceil \log \ell \rceil \geq i \\ \mathsf{NfaABE.Enc}(\mathsf{NfaABE.msk}, \hat{\mathbf{x}}, m^{(1)}) & \text{If } \lceil \log \ell \rceil \leq i - 1. \end{cases}$$

   Then, it returns $\mathsf{NfaABE.ct}$ to A.

   Key queries. Given an NFA M from A, the challenger runs $\mathsf{NfaABE.sk}_M \leftarrow \mathsf{NfaABE.KeyGen}(\mathsf{NfaABE.msk}, M)$ and returns $\mathsf{NfaABE.sk}_M$ to A.

   Finally, A outputs its guess b'.

In the following, let $\mathsf{E}_{\mathsf{xxx}}$ denote the probability that A outputs 1 in $\textbf{Game}_{\mathsf{xxx}}$. It suffices to prove $|\Pr[\mathsf{E}_0] - \Pr[\mathsf{E}_{\lambda+1}]| = \mathrm{negl}(\lambda)$, since $\textbf{Game}_0$ (resp., $\textbf{Game}_{\lambda+1}$) corresponds to the selective security game with $b = 0$ (resp., $b = 1$). Since we have

$$|\Pr[\mathsf{E}_0] - \Pr[\mathsf{E}_{\lambda+1}]| \leq \sum_{i \in [0,\lambda]} |\Pr[\mathsf{E}_i] - \Pr[\mathsf{E}_{i+1}]|$$

by the triangle inequality, it suffices to show $|\Pr[\mathsf{E}_i] - \Pr[\mathsf{E}_{i+1}]| = \mathrm{negl}(\lambda)$ for $i \in [0, \lambda]$. Let us define $\ell_{\max}$ and $i_{\max}$ as

$$\ell_{\max} := \max\{|\mathbf{x}| : \mathbf{x} \in X\} \qquad \text{and} \qquad i_{\max} := \lceil \log \ell_{\max} \rceil.$$

Note that $\ell_{\max}$ is bounded by the running time of A and thus is polynomial in λ. We then observe that for $i > i_{\max}$, we have $\textbf{Game}_i = \textbf{Game}_{\lambda+1}$ and thus $\Pr[\mathsf{E}_i] - \Pr[\mathsf{E}_{i+1}] = 0$. Therefore, in the following, we will show that $|\Pr[\mathsf{E}_i] - \Pr[\mathsf{E}_{i+1}]| = \mathrm{negl}(\lambda)$ holds for $i \leq i_{\max}$. To do so, we further introduce the following sequence of games for $i \in [0, i_{\max}]$:

$\textbf{Game}_{i,0}$: The game is the same as $\textbf{Game}_i$.

$\textbf{Game}_{i,1}$: In this game, we change the setup phase and the way encryption queries are answered as follows.

   Setup phase. Given $X \subset \Sigma^*$ from A, the challenger chooses $\mathsf{NfaABE.msk} \leftarrow \mathsf{NfaABE.Setup}(1^\lambda, 1^s)$ as in the previous game. In addition, it computes

$$(\mathsf{ABE.mpk}_i, \mathsf{ABE.msk}_i) \leftarrow \mathsf{ABE.Setup}(1^\lambda, 1^{2^i \eta}, 1^{\hat{d}}; \hat{\mathsf{K}}_i)$$

   and

$$\mathsf{FE.sk}_i \leftarrow \mathsf{FE.KeyGen}(\mathsf{FE.mpk}_i, \mathsf{FE.msk}_i, C_{\mathsf{s}, 2^i}; \mathsf{R}_i).$$

Encryption queries. Given two messages $(m^{(0)}, m^{(1)})$ and $\mathbf{x} \in X$ from A, the challenger sets $\ell := |\mathbf{x}|$ and computes NfaABE.ct as in the previous game if $\lceil \log \ell \rceil \neq i$. Otherwise, it computes

$$\mathsf{ABE.ct} \leftarrow \mathsf{ABE.Enc}(\mathsf{ABE.mpk}_i, \hat{\mathbf{x}}, m^{(0)})$$

and returns $\mathsf{NfaABE.ct} = (\mathsf{FE.sk}_i, \mathsf{ABE.mpk}_i, \mathsf{ABE.ct})$ to A, where $\mathsf{FE.sk}_i$ and $\mathsf{ABE.mpk}_i$ are the values that are computed in the setup phase.

Game$_{i,2}$: In this game, the challenger samples $\mathsf{FE.sk}_i$ as

$$\mathsf{FE.sk}_i \leftarrow \mathsf{FE.KeyGen}(\mathsf{FE.mpk}_i, \mathsf{FE.msk}_i, C_{\mathsf{s},2^i})$$

in the setup phase. Namely, it is sampled using true randomness instead of the pseudorandom bits derived from the PRF key R_i.

Game$_{i,3}$: We change the way key queries are answered as follows:

Key queries. Given an NFA M of size s from A, the challenger answers the query as follows. It first chooses $\widehat{\mathsf{R}}_j \leftarrow \mathsf{PRF.Setup}(1^\lambda)$ for $j \in [0, \lambda]$ and computes

$$\mathsf{ABE.sk}_{U[\widehat{M}_{2^i}]} = \mathsf{ABE.KeyGen}(\mathsf{ABE.mpk}_i, \mathsf{ABE.msk}_i, U[\widehat{M}_{2^i}]; \widehat{\mathsf{R}}_i),$$

where $\mathsf{ABE.mpk}_i$ and $\mathsf{ABE.msk}_i$ are the values that are computed in the setup phase. It then computes $\mathsf{FE.ct}_j \leftarrow$

$$\begin{cases} \mathsf{FE.Enc}(\mathsf{FE.mpk}_j, (M, \widehat{\mathsf{K}}_j, \widehat{\mathsf{R}}_j)) & \text{If } j \in [0, \lambda] \setminus \{i\} \\ \mathsf{Sim}(\mathsf{FE.mpk}_i, \mathsf{FE.sk}_i, C_{\mathsf{s},2^i}, \mathsf{ABE.sk}_{U[\widehat{M}_{2^i}]}, 1^{\mathsf{inp}(\lambda)}) & \text{If } j = i. \end{cases}$$

$$(3.3)$$

Then, it returns $\mathsf{NfaABE.sk}_M := \{\mathsf{FE.ct}_j\}_{j \in [0, \lambda]}$ to A.

Game$_{i,4}$: In this game, the challenger samples $(\mathsf{ABE.mpk}_i, \mathsf{ABE.msk}_i)$ in the setup phase as

$$(\mathsf{ABE.mpk}_i, \mathsf{ABE.msk}_i) \leftarrow \mathsf{ABE.Setup}(1^\lambda, 1^{2^i \eta}, 1^{\hat{d}}).$$

It also generates $\mathsf{ABE.sk}_{U[\widehat{M}_{2^i}]}$ as

$$\mathsf{ABE.sk}_{U[\widehat{M}_{2^i}]} \leftarrow \mathsf{ABE.KeyGen}(\mathsf{ABE.mpk}_i, \mathsf{ABE.msk}_i, U[\widehat{M}_{2^i}]).$$

when answering a key query. Namely, they are sampled using true randomness instead of the pseudorandom bits derived from the PRF keys $\widehat{\mathsf{K}}_i$ and $\widehat{\mathsf{R}}_i$.

Game$_{i,5}$: In this game, we change the way the encryption queries are answered as follows.

Encryption queries. Given two messages $(m^{(0)}, m^{(1)})$ and $\mathbf{x} \in X$ from A, the challenger sets $\ell := |\mathbf{x}|$ and computes NfaABE.ct as in the previous game if $\lceil \log \ell \rceil \neq i$. Otherwise, it computes

$$\mathsf{ABE.ct} = \mathsf{ABE.Enc}(\mathsf{ABE.mpk}_i, \hat{\mathbf{x}}, m^{(1)})$$

and returns $\mathsf{NfaABE.ct} = (\mathsf{FE.sk}_i, \mathsf{ABE.mpk}_i, \mathsf{ABE.ct})$ to A, where $\mathsf{FE.sk}_i$ and $\mathsf{ABE.mpk}_i$ are the values that are computed in the setup phase.

Game$_{i,6}$: The game is the same as **Game$_{i+1}$.**

Since we have

$$| \Pr[\mathsf{E}_i] - \Pr[\mathsf{E}_{i+1}]| \leq \sum_{j \in [6]} | \Pr[\mathsf{E}_{i,j-1}] - \Pr[\mathsf{E}_{i,j}]|$$

by the triangle inequality, it suffices to show $| \Pr[\mathsf{E}_{i,j-1}] - \Pr[\mathsf{E}_{i,j}]| = \mathsf{negl}(\lambda)$ for $j \in [6]$. To complete the proof of the theorem, it remains to prove the following lemmas.

Lemma 1. *We have* $\Pr[\mathsf{E}_{i,0}] = \Pr[\mathsf{E}_{i,1}]$.

Proof. The change introduced here is only conceptual, where ABE.mpk$_i$ and FE.sk$_i$ are computed beforehand. The lemma trivially follows.

Lemma 2. *We have* $| \Pr[\mathsf{E}_{i,1}] - \Pr[\mathsf{E}_{i,2}]| = \mathsf{negl}(\lambda)$.

Proof. We observe that R$_i$ is used only when generating FE.sk$_i$ in **Game$_{i,1}$**. Therefore, the lemma follows by a straightforward reduction to the security of PRF.

Lemma 3. *We have* $| \Pr[\mathsf{E}_{i,2}] - \Pr[\mathsf{E}_{i,3}]| = \mathsf{negl}(\lambda)$.

Proof. To prove the lemma, let us assume that $| \Pr[\mathsf{E}_{i,2}] - \Pr[\mathsf{E}_{i,3}]|$ is non-negligible and construct an adversary B that breaks the full simulation security of FE using A. B proceeds as follows.

Setup phase. At the beginning of the game, B inputs 1^λ to A and obtains 1^s and $X \subset \Sigma^*$ from A. Then B submits its target $(1^\lambda, 1^{\mathsf{inp}(\lambda)}, 1^{\mathsf{out}(\lambda)})$. Then, the experiment samples

$$(\mathsf{FE.mpk}, \mathsf{FE.msk}) \leftarrow \mathsf{FE.Setup}(1^\lambda, 1^{\mathsf{inp}(\lambda)}, 1^{\mathsf{out}(\lambda)})$$

and returns FE.mpk to B. B then sets FE.mpk$_i$:= FE.mpk. In the rest of the simulation, it implicitly sets FE.msk$_i$:= FE.msk without knowing the value. B then chooses $(\mathsf{FE.mpk}_j, \mathsf{FE.msk}_j) \leftarrow \mathsf{FE.Setup}(1^\lambda, 1^{\mathsf{inp}(\lambda)}, 1^{\mathsf{out}(\lambda)}, 1^{\mathsf{d}(\lambda)})$ for $j \in [0, \lambda] \backslash \{i\}$. It also chooses $\widehat{\mathsf{K}}_j, \mathsf{R}_j \leftarrow \mathsf{PRF.Setup}(1^\lambda)$ for $j \in [0, \lambda]$ and $(\mathsf{ABE.mpk}_i, \mathsf{ABE.msk}_i) \leftarrow \mathsf{ABE.Setup}(1^\lambda, 1^{2^i \eta}, 1^{\hat{\mathsf{d}}}; \widehat{\mathsf{K}}_i)$. Finally, it declares $C_{\mathsf{s},2^i}$ as a circuit for which it request a secret key. Then, the experiment runs

$$\mathsf{FE.sk} \leftarrow \mathsf{FE.KeyGen}(\mathsf{FE.mpk}, \mathsf{FE.msk}, C_{\mathsf{s},2^i})$$

and returns FE.sk to B. B sets FE.sk$_i$:= FE.sk.

B then handles the encryption and key queries as follows.

Encryption queries. Given two messages $(m^{(0)}, m^{(1)})$ and $\mathbf{x} \in X$ from A, B sets $\ell := |\mathbf{x}|$ and $i' = \lceil \log \ell \rceil$. If $i' \neq i$, B answers the query using $(\widehat{K}_{i'}, R_{i'}, \mathsf{FE.mpk}_{i'}, \mathsf{FE.msk}_{i'})$. Otherwise, it computes $\mathsf{ABE.ct} \leftarrow \mathsf{ABE.Enc}$ $(\mathsf{ABE.mpk}_i, \hat{\mathbf{x}}, m^{(0)})$ and returns $\mathsf{NfaABE.ct} = (\mathsf{FE.sk}_i, \mathsf{ABE.mpk}_i, \mathsf{ABE.ct})$ to A, where $\mathsf{ABE.mpk}_i$ (resp., $\mathsf{FE.sk}_i$) is the value sampled by itself (resp., by the experiment) in the setup phase.

Key queries. Given an NFA M of size s from A, B first chooses $\widehat{R}_j \leftarrow \mathsf{PRF.Setup}(1^\lambda)$ for $j \in [0, \lambda]$ and computes $\mathsf{FE.ct}_j = \mathsf{FE.Enc}(\mathsf{FE.mpk}_j, (M, \widehat{K}_j, \widehat{R}_j))$ for $j \in [0, \lambda] \setminus \{i\}$. B then submits $(M, \widehat{K}_i, \widehat{R}_i)$ to its encryption oracle. Then, the experiment computes $\mathsf{FE.ct} \leftarrow$

$$\begin{cases} \mathsf{FE.Enc}(\mathsf{FE.mpk}, (M, \widehat{K}_i, \widehat{R}_i)) & \text{If B is in } \mathsf{Exp}_{\mathsf{FE,B}}^{\mathsf{real}}(1^\lambda) \\ \mathsf{Sim}(\mathsf{FE.mpk}, \mathsf{FE.sk}, C_{\mathsf{s},2^i}, C_{\mathsf{s},2^i}(M, \widehat{K}_i, \widehat{R}_i), 1^{\mathsf{inp}(\lambda)}) & \text{If B is in } \mathsf{Exp}_{\mathsf{FE,Sim}}^{\mathsf{ideal}}(1^\lambda) \end{cases}$$
(3.4)

and returns $\mathsf{FE.ct}$ to B. B then sets $\mathsf{FE.ct}_i := \mathsf{FE.ct}$ and returns $\mathsf{NfaABE.sk}_M := \{\mathsf{FE.ct}_j\}_{j \in [0,\lambda]}$ to A.

Output phase: B outputs the same bit as A as its guess.

It is easy to see that B simulates $\mathbf{Game}_{i,2}$ if B is in the real game. We then claim that B simulates $\mathbf{Game}_{i,3}$ if B is in the simulated game. The only difference between these games is the way $\mathsf{FE.ct}_i$ is computed. In $\mathbf{Game}_{i,3}$, it is generated as Eq. (3.3) while in the simulation above, it is generated as Eq. (3.4) (with B being in $\mathsf{Exp}_{\mathsf{FE,Sim}}^{\mathsf{ideal}}$). However, they are equivalent because B has set $(\mathsf{FE.mpk}_i, \mathsf{FE.msk}_i) := (\mathsf{FE.mpk}, \mathsf{FE.msk})$ and $\mathsf{FE.sk}_i := \mathsf{FE.sk}$ and we have

$$C_{\mathsf{s},2^i}(M, \widehat{K}_i, \widehat{R}_i) = \mathsf{ABE.KeyGen}(\mathsf{ABE.mpk}_i, \mathsf{ABE.msk}_i, U[\widehat{M}_{2^i}]; \widehat{R}_i) = \mathsf{ABE.sk}_{U[\widehat{M}_{2^i}]}.$$

From the above observation, we can see that B breaks the security of FE if A distinguishes the two games. This completes the proof of the lemma.

Lemma 4. *We have* $|\Pr[\mathsf{E}_{i,3}] - \Pr[\mathsf{E}_{i,4}]| = \mathsf{negl}(\lambda)$.

Proof. Due to the change we introduced, $\widehat{K}_i$ is not used to answer the encryption queries any more and used only when generating $(\mathsf{ABE.mpk}_i, \mathsf{ABE.msk}_i)$ in $\mathbf{Game}_{i,3}$. We also observe that $\widehat{R}_i$ is used only when generating $\mathsf{ABE.sk}_{U[\widehat{M}_{2^i}]}$. Therefore, the lemma follows by straightforward reductions to the security of PRF.

Lemma 5. *We have* $|\Pr[\mathsf{E}_{i,4}] - \Pr[\mathsf{E}_{i,5}]| = \mathsf{negl}(\lambda)$.

Proof. To prove the lemma, let us assume that $|\Pr[\mathsf{E}_{i,4}] - \Pr[\mathsf{E}_{i,5}]|$ is non-negligible and construct an adversary B that breaks the selective security of ABE using A. B proceeds as follows.

Setup phase. At the beginning of the game, B inputs 1^λ to A and obtains 1^s and $X \subset \Sigma^*$ from A. Then, B sets $X_i := \{\hat{\mathbf{x}} = \mathbf{x} \| \perp^{2^i - |\mathbf{x}|} : \mathbf{x} \in X, \ 2^{i-1} < |\mathbf{x}| \leq 2^i\}$ and submits its target X_i and $(1^\lambda, 1^{2^i \eta}, 1^d)$ to its challenger. Then, the challenger samples

$$(\mathsf{ABE.mpk}, \mathsf{ABE.msk}) \leftarrow \mathsf{ABE.Setup}(1^\lambda, 1^{2^i \eta}, 1^d)$$

and returns ABE.mpk to B. B then sets $\mathsf{ABE.mpk}_i := \mathsf{ABE.mpk}$. In the rest of the simulation, it implicitly sets $\mathsf{ABE.msk}_i := \mathsf{ABE.msk}$ without knowing the value. It then chooses $\widehat{\mathsf{K}}_j, \mathsf{R}_j \leftarrow \mathsf{PRF.Setup}(1^\lambda)$ for $j \in [0, \lambda] \backslash \{i\}$ and $(\mathsf{FE.mpk}_j, \mathsf{FE.msk}_j) \leftarrow \mathsf{Setup}(1^\lambda, 1^{\mathsf{inp}(\lambda)}, 1^{\mathsf{out}(\lambda)}, 1^{d(\lambda)})$ for $j \in [0, \lambda]$. It also computes $\mathsf{FE.sk}_i \leftarrow \mathsf{FE.KeyGen}(\mathsf{FE.mpk}_i, \mathsf{FE.msk}_i, C_{s,2^i})$.

B then handles the encryption and key queries as follows.

Encryption queries. Given two messages $(m^{(0)}, m^{(1)})$ and $\mathbf{x} \in X$ from A, $\mathcal{B}$ sets $\ell := |\mathbf{x}|$ and $i' = \lceil \log \ell \rceil$. If $i' \neq i$, B answers the encryption query using $(\widehat{\mathsf{K}}_{i'}, \mathsf{R}_{i'}, \mathsf{FE.mpk}_{i'}, \mathsf{FE.msk}_{i'})$. Otherwise, $\mathcal{B}$ makes an encryption query for the attribute $\hat{\mathbf{x}} = \mathbf{x} \| \perp^{2^i - \ell}$ and messages $(m^{(0)}, m^{(1)})$ to its challenger. Then, the challenger runs

$$\mathsf{ABE.ct} \leftarrow \mathsf{ABE.Enc}(\mathsf{ABE.mpk}, \hat{\mathbf{x}}, m^{(b)})$$

and returns a ciphertext ABE.ct to B. Then, it returns $\mathsf{NfaABE.ct} = (\mathsf{FE.sk}_i, \mathsf{ABE.mpk}_i, \mathsf{ABE.ct})$ to A. Here, B uses $\mathsf{FE.sk}_i$ that is sampled in the setup phase.

Key queries. Given an NFA M of size s from A, B first chooses $\widehat{\mathsf{R}}_j \leftarrow \mathsf{PRF.Setup}(1^\lambda)$ for $j \in [0, \lambda] \backslash \{i\}$. It then queries a secret key for $U[\widehat{M}_{2^i}]$ to its challenger. Then, the challenger runs

$$\mathsf{ABE.sk}_{U[\widehat{M}_{2^i}]} \leftarrow \mathsf{ABE.KeyGen}(\mathsf{ABE.mpk}, \mathsf{ABE.msk}, U[\widehat{M}_{2^i}])$$

and returns $\mathsf{ABE.sk}_{U[\widehat{M}_{2^i}]}$ to B. It then computes $\mathsf{FE.ct}_j$ for $j \in [0, \lambda]$ as Eq. (3.3) and returns $\mathsf{NfaABE.sk}_M := \{\mathsf{FE.ct}_j\}_{j \in [0, \lambda]}$ to A.

Output phase: B outputs the same bit as A as its guess.

It is easy to see that B simulates $\mathbf{Game}_{i,4}$ if $b = 0$ and $\mathbf{Game}_{i,5}$ if $b = 1$. Therefore, B breaks the security of ABE if A distinguishes the two games. It remains to prove that B is a legitimate adversary (i.e., it does not make any prohibited key queries). For any attribute $\hat{\mathbf{x}}$ for which B makes an encryption query and for any circuit $U[\widehat{M}_{2^i}]$ for which B makes a key query, we have

$$U[\widehat{M}_{2^i}](\hat{\mathbf{x}}) = \widehat{M}_{2^i}(\hat{\mathbf{x}}) = M(\mathbf{x}),$$

where the second equality above follows from Item 1 of Theorem 3. Therefore, B is a legitimate adversary as long as so is A. This completes the proof of the lemma.

Lemma 6. *We have* $|\Pr[\mathsf{E}_{i,5}] - \Pr[\mathsf{E}_{i,6}]| = \mathrm{negl}(\lambda)$.

Proof. This follows as in the indistinguishability of **Game**$_{i,0}$ and **Game**$_{i,4}$, but in the reverse order. That is, we first change the random bits used in ABE.KeyGen to a pseudorandom one by invoking the security of PRF. We then generate FE.ct$_i$ by using FE.Enc instead of Sim by invoking the full-simulation security of FE. Finally, we change the random bits used in ABE.KeyGen to a pseudorandom one by invoking the security of PRF again.

This concludes the proof of Theorem 6.

3.5   Extensions

In the full version, we adapt our ABE construction to achieve (restricted versions of) attribute privacy. In more detail, we construct secret key predicate encryption and bounded key functional encryption for nondeterministic finite automata. We also additionally achieve machine privacy, improving the result of [8]. Intuitively, these results proceed by replacing the "inner" circuit ABE scheme in our compiler by predicate encryption or bounded key functional encryption scheme and arguing that the requisite efficiency requirements (Theorem 1) are not violated. We again refer to the full version for details.

4   Attribute Based Encryption for NFA with Unbounded Size Machines and Inputs

In this section we construct a secret-key attribute-based encryption scheme (SKABE) for nondeterministic finite automata of arbitrary sizes supporting inputs of arbitrary length. We denote our scheme by uNfaABE = (uNfaABE.Setup, uNfaABE.KeyGen, uNfaABE.Enc, uNfaABE.Dec) and its construction uses the following two ingredients.

1. NfaABE = (NfaABE.Setup, NfaABE.KeyGen, NfaABE.Enc, NfaABE.Dec): An SKABE for NFA supporting inputs of *unbounded length* but for *bounded size* machines. We instantiate NfaABE from our construction in Sect. 3.2.
2. ABE = (ABE.Setup, ABE.KeyGen, ABE.Enc, ABE.Dec): An ABE scheme for circuits that satisfies the efficiency properties described in Theorem 1. We can instantiate ABE with the scheme proposed by Boneh et al. [22].
3. PRF = (PRF.Setup, PRF.Eval): a pseudorandom function, where a PRF key K $\leftarrow$ PRF.Setup(1^λ) defines a function PRF.Eval(K, $\cdot$) : $\{0,1\}^\lambda \rightarrow \mathcal{R}$, where we assume $\mathcal{R}$ to be the randomness space of *both* NfaABE.Setup and ABE.Setup algorithms. Note that without loss of generality, we may assume $\mathcal{R} = \{0,1\}^{p(\lambda)}$ for some sufficiently large polynomial $p(\lambda)$.

Below we provide our construction for SKABE for NFA.

uNfaABE.Setup(1^λ): On input the security parameter 1^λ, do the following:
1. Sample two PRF keys $K_{NfaABE} \leftarrow PRF.Setup(1^\lambda)$, $K_{ABE} \leftarrow PRF.Setup(1^\lambda)$.
2. Output uNfaABE.msk $= (K_{NfaABE}, K_{ABE})$.

uNfaABE.Enc(uNfaABE.msk, $\mathbf{x}$, m): On input the master secret key uNfaABE.msk, an attribute as $\mathbf{x} \in \Sigma^*$ of length at most 2^λ and a message $m \in \mathcal{M}$, do the following:
1. Parse the master secret key as uNfaABE.msk $= (K_{NfaABE}, K_{ABE})$. Denote $\ell = |\mathbf{x}|$.
2. For all $i \in [\ell]$, do the following:
   (a) Sample NfaABE.msk$_i$ $\leftarrow$ NfaABE.Setup($1^\lambda, 1^i; r_i$) as an NfaABE master secret key, where $r_i = PRF.Eval(K_{NfaABE}, i)$.

   Note that i denotes the size of the NFAs that are supported by NfaABE.msk$_i$.

   (b) Compute NfaABE.ct$_i$ = NfaABE.Enc(NfaABE.msk$_i$, $\mathbf{x}$, m, 1^i).

3. Sample (ABE.mpk$_\ell$, ABE.msk$_\ell$) $\leftarrow$ ABE.Setup($1^\lambda, 1^\ell, 1^{\hat{d}}; r_\ell$) as an ABE key pair, where $r_\ell = PRF.Eval(K_{ABE}, \ell)$.
   Note that ℓ and $\hat{d}$ denotes the input length and the depth of the circuit respectively that (ABE.mpk$_\ell$, ABE.msk$_\ell$) supports.

4. Compute ABE.ct$_\ell$ = ABE.Enc(ABE.mpk$_\ell$, $\mathbf{x}$, m).

5. Output uNfaABE.ct $= (\{NfaABE.ct_i\}_{i \in [\ell]}, ABE.mpk_\ell, ABE.ct_\ell)$.

uNfaABE.KeyGen(uNfaABE.msk, M): On input the master secret key uNfaABE.msk and the description of a NFA $M = (Q, \Sigma, T, q_{st}, F)$, proceed as follows.
1. Parse the master secret key as uNfaABE.msk $= (K_{NfaABE}, K_{ABE})$. Denote $s = |M|$.
2. For all $i \in [s]$, do the following:
   (a) Let $\widehat{M_i} = $ To-Circuit$_{s,i}(M)$. (See Theorem 3 for the definition of To-Circuit.)

   (b) Sample (ABE.mpk$_i$, ABE.msk$_i$) $\leftarrow$ ABE.Setup($1^\lambda, 1^i, 1^{\hat{d}}; r_i$) as an ABE key pair, where $r_i = PRF.Eval(K_{ABE}, i)$.

   (c) Compute ABE.sk$_i$ = ABE.KeyGen(ABE.mpk$_i$, ABE.msk$_i$, $\widehat{M_i}$).
   Note that $\forall i \in [s]$, i and $\hat{d}$ denotes the input length and the depth of the circuit respectively that (ABE.mpk$_i$, ABE.msk$_i$) supports.

3. Sample NfaABE.msk$_s \leftarrow$ NfaABE.Setup($1^\lambda, 1^s; r_s$) as an NfaABE master secret key, where $r_s = PRF.Eval(K_{NfaABE}, s)$.

4. Compute NfaABE.sk$_s$ = NfaABE.KeyGen(NfaABE.msk$_s$, M).

5. Output uNfaABE.sk$_M$ = (NfaABE.sk$_s$, $\{ABE.mpk_i, ABE.sk_i\}_{i \in [s]}$).

uNfaABE.Dec(uNfaABE.sk$_M$, M, uNfaABE.ct, $\mathbf{x}$): On input a secret key for NFA M and a ciphertext encoded under some attribute $\mathbf{x}$, proceed as follows:

1. Parse the secret key as uNfaABE.sk$_M$ = (NfaABE.sk$_{|M|}$, {ABE.mpk$_i$, ABE.sk$_i$}$_{i \in [|M|]}$) and the ciphertext as uNfaABE.ct = ({NfaABE.ct$_i$}$_{i \in [|\mathbf{x}|]}$, ABE.mpk$_{|\mathbf{x}|}$, ABE.ct$_{|\mathbf{x}|}$).

2. If $|\mathbf{x}| \geq |M|$, compute and output NfaABE.Dec(NfaABE.sk$_{|M|}$, M, NfaABE.ct$_{|M|}$, $\mathbf{x}$).

3. Otherwise, compute and output ABE.Dec(ABE.mpk$_{|\mathbf{x}|}$, ABE.sk$_{|\mathbf{x}|}$, $\widehat{M}_{|\mathbf{x}|}$, ABE.ct$_{|\mathbf{x}|}$, $\mathbf{x}$), where $\widehat{M}_{|\mathbf{x}|}$ = To-Circuit$_{|M|,|\mathbf{x}|}(M)$.

The following theorems assert that our scheme is efficient, satisfies correctness, and is secure, as long as so are the underlying NfaABE and ABE schemes. Intuitively, these theorems follow since we simply run these underlying schemes in parallel. We refer to the full version for the formal proofs.

Theorem 7. *The scheme* uNfaABE = (uNfaABE.Setup, uNfaABE.KeyGen, uNfaABE.Enc, uNfaABE.Dec) *defined above runs in polynomial time, as long as* $\hat{\mathsf{d}}$ *and* $|\Sigma|$ *are polynomials in* λ.

Theorem 8. *For appropriately chosen* $\hat{\mathsf{d}} = \hat{\mathsf{d}}(\lambda)$, *our scheme* uNfaABE *is correct for any NFA.*

Theorem 9. *Assume that* NfaABE *and* ABE *both satisfy selective indistinguishability based security and* PRF *is a secure pseudorandom function. Then,* uNfaABE *satisfies selective security.*

5 FE for DFA Implies iO

Here, we show that secret key functional encryption (SKFE) for DFA with security against unbounded collusion implies indistinguishability obfuscation (iO). This result illuminates the difficulty of constructing such SKFE from a standard assumption, since no construction of iO from standard assumption is known despite the significant research effort in recent years [1–3,5,7,8,11–13,17,21,34,35,37–40,40,50,51,51–54].

5.1 Preliminaries on DFA and Branching Programs

Here, we first recall that a deterministic finite automaton (DFA) is a special case of NFA where for the transition function T, $T(\sigma, q)$ consists of a single element in Q for any $\sigma \in \Sigma$ and $q \in Q$. We then define branching program similarly to [25].

Definition 7 (Branching Programs). *A width-5 permutation branching program* BP *of length L with input space* $\{0,1\}^\ell$ *is a sequence of L tuples of the form* $(\mathsf{var}(t), \sigma_{t,0}, \sigma_{t,1})$ *where*

- $\mathsf{var} : [L] \to [\ell]$ *is a function that associates the t-th tuple with an input bit* $x_{\mathsf{var}(t)}$.
- $\sigma_{j,0}$ *and* $\sigma_{j,1}$ *are permutations on 5 elements. We will think of* $\sigma_{j,0}$ *and* $\sigma_{j,1}$ *as bijective functions from the set* $\{1,2,3,4,5\}$ *to itself.*

The computation of the program BP *on input* $\mathbf{x} = (x_1, \ldots, x_\ell)$ *proceeds as follows. The state of the computation at any point in time t is a number* $\zeta_t \in \{1,2,3,4,5\}$. *Computation starts with the initial state* $\zeta_0 = 1$. *The state* ζ_t *is computed recursively as*

$$\zeta_t = \sigma_{t, x_{\mathsf{var}(t)}}(\zeta_{t-1}). \tag{5.1}$$

Finally, after L steps, our state is ζ_L. *The output of the computation* BP$(\mathbf{x})$ *is* 1 *if* $\zeta_L = 1$ *and* 0 *otherwise.*

We will use the following theorem, which essentially says that an NC^1 circuit can be converted into an equivalent branching program.

Theorem 10 (Barrington's Theorem [19]). *Every Boolean NAND circuit C that acts on ℓ inputs and has depth d can be computed by a width-5 permutation branching program* BP *of length* 4^d. *Given the description of the circuit* BP, *the description of the branching program* BP *can be computed in* poly$(\ell, 4^d)$ *time. In particular, if C is a polynomial-sized circuit with logarithmic depth (i.e., if the circuit is in* NC^1), BP *can be computed in polynomial time.*

5.2   SKFE for DFA Implies iO

We first state the following theorem, which will be useful for our purpose. We refer to the full version for the proof.

Theorem 11. *Let* $d = d(\lambda)$ *and* $\ell = \ell(\lambda)$ *be integers. There exist deterministic algorithms* Encode *and* ToDFA *with the following properties.*

- Encode$(\mathbf{x}) \to \mathbf{y} \in \{0,1\}^n$, *where* $\mathbf{x} \in \{0,1\}^\ell$ *and n is a parameter determined by d and ℓ.*
- ToDFA$(C) \to M$, *where* $C : \{0,1\}^\ell \to \{0,1\}$ *is a circuit with depth bounded by d and M is a DFA over alphabet* $\Sigma = \{0,1\}$.

We have that $M(\mathbf{y}) = 1$ *if and only if* $C(\mathbf{x}) = 1$. *We also have that the running time of* Encode *and* ToDFA *is* poly$(\ell, 2^d)$. *In particular, if C is a polynomial-sized circuit with logarithmic depth (i.e., if the circuit is in* NC^1), Encode *and* ToDFA(C) *run in polynomial time.*

We then discuss that if there exists subexponentially secure SKFE for DFA that is very selectively secure against unbounded collusion, it can be converted into a secure indistinguishability obfuscation.

To do so, we first convert an SKFE for DFA into an SKFE for NC^1 circuits. The latter SKFE has the same setup algorithm as the former, but when generating a secret key for a circuit C, it first converts C into a DFA M using the algorithm in Theorem 11 and then invoke the key generation algorithm of the SKFE for DFA on input M. Similarly, when encrypting a message $\mathbf{x}$, it computes $\mathbf{y}$ as in Theorem 11 and then invoke the encryption algorithm of the SKFE for DFA on input $\mathbf{y}$. The decryption algorithm is defined naturally. It is easy to see that this conversion preserves the correctness and the security since we have $M(\mathbf{y}) = C(\mathbf{x})$ by Theorem 11.

Then, we apply the conversion given by [12,21] to the SKFE for NC^1 to obtain SKFE for all circuits. We then further apply the conversion by Kitagawa et al. [46,47] to the SKFE for all circuits to obtain iO. Note that while the former conversion incurs only polynomial loss, the latter conversion incurs subexponential security loss.

In summary, we obtain the following theorem.

Theorem 12. *If there exists a subexponentially secure SKFE scheme for DFA that is very selectively secure against unbounded collusion, then there exists an indistinguishability obfuscation.*

6 Conclusions

Several interesting questions arise from our work. The first is whether we may generalize our techniques to support more advanced models of computation. For the moment, we are restricted to NFAs, since we must bound the depth of the equivalent circuits by a fixed polynomial and this step fails for more general models such as Turing machines. Second, it would be interesting to design a public key variant of our scheme. Improving the security proof to satisfy adaptive rather than selective security is also a useful direction. Finally, it would be nice to find other applications for our techniques.

Acknowledgement. We thank anonymous reviewers of Crypto 2019 for their helpful comments. The third author is supported by JST CREST Grant Number JPMJCR19F6 and JSPS KAKENHI Grant Number 16K16068.

References

1. Abdalla, M., Bourse, F., Caro, A.D., Pointcheval, D.: Simple functional encryption schemes for inner products. Cryptology ePrint Archive, Report 2015/017 (2015). http://eprint.iacr.org/ To appear in PKC'15

2. Agrawal, S.: Stronger security for reusable garbled circuits, general definitions and attacks. In: Katz, J., Shacham, H. (eds.) CRYPTO 2017. LNCS, vol. 10401, pp. 3–35. Springer, Cham (2017). https://doi.org/10.1007/978-3-319-63688-7_1

3. Agrawal, S.: Indistinguishability obfuscation minus multilinear maps: new methods for bootstrapping and instantiation (2018)

4. Agrawal, S., Freeman, D.M., Vaikuntanathan, V.: Functional encryption for inner product predicates from learning with errors. In: Lee, D.H., Wang, X. (eds.) ASIACRYPT 2011. LNCS, vol. 7073, pp. 21–40. Springer, Heidelberg (2011). https://doi.org/10.1007/978-3-642-25385-0_2

5. Agrawal, S., Libert, B., Stehlé, D.: Fully secure functional encryption for inner products, from standard assumptions. In: Robshaw, M., Katz, J. (eds.) CRYPTO 2016. LNCS, vol. 9816, pp. 333–362. Springer, Heidelberg (2016). https://doi.org/10.1007/978-3-662-53015-3_12

6. Agrawal, S., Maitra, M.: FE and iO for turing machines from minimal assumptions. In: Beimel, A., Dziembowski, S. (eds.) TCC 2018. LNCS, vol. 11240, pp. 473–512. Springer, Cham (2018). https://doi.org/10.1007/978-3-030-03810-6_18

7. Agrawal, S., Rosen, A.: Functional encryption for bounded collusions, revisited. In: Kalai, Y., Reyzin, L. (eds.) TCC 2017. LNCS, vol. 10677, pp. 173–205. Springer, Cham (2017). https://doi.org/10.1007/978-3-319-70500-2_7

8. Agrawal, S., Singh, I.P.: Reusable garbled deterministic finite automata from learning with errors. In: ICALP, vol. 80. Schloss Dagstuhl-Leibniz-Zentrum fuer Informatik (2017)

9. Ananth, P., Brakerski, Z., Segev, G., Vaikuntanathan, V.: From selective to adaptive security in functional encryption. In: Gennaro, R., Robshaw, M. (eds.) CRYPTO 2015. LNCS, vol. 9216, pp. 657–677. Springer, Heidelberg (2015). https://doi.org/10.1007/978-3-662-48000-7_32

10. Ananth, P., Fan, X.: Attribute based encryption with sublinear decryption from LWE. Cryptology ePrint Archive, Report 2018/273 (2018). https://eprint.iacr.org/2018/273

11. Ananth, P., Jain, A., Sahai, A.: Indistinguishability obfuscation without multilinear maps: iO from LWE, bilinear maps, and weak pseudorandomness. Cryptology ePrint Archive, Report 2018/615 (2018)

12. Ananth, P., Jain, A.: Indistinguishability obfuscation from compact functional encryption. In: Gennaro, R., Robshaw, M. (eds.) CRYPTO 2015. LNCS, vol. 9215, pp. 308–326. Springer, Heidelberg (2015). https://doi.org/10.1007/978-3-662-47989-6_15

13. Ananth, P., Jain, A., Sahai, A.: Achieving compactness generically: indistinguishability obfuscation from non-compact functional encryption. IACR Cryptology ePrint Archive 2015/730 (2015)

14. Ananth, P., Sahai, A.: Projective arithmetic functional encryption and indistinguishability obfuscation from degree-5 multilinear maps. In: Coron, J.-S., Nielsen, J.B. (eds.) EUROCRYPT 2017. LNCS, vol. 10210, pp. 152–181. Springer, Cham (2017). https://doi.org/10.1007/978-3-319-56620-7_6

15. Apon, D., Döttling, N., Garg, S., Mukherjee, P.: Cryptanalysis of indistinguishability obfuscations of circuits over GGH13. eprint 2016 (2016)

16. Attrapadung, N.: Dual system encryption via doubly selective security: framework, fully secure functional encryption for regular languages, and more. In: Nguyen, P.Q., Oswald, E. (eds.) EUROCRYPT 2014. LNCS, vol. 8441, pp. 557–577. Springer, Heidelberg (2014). https://doi.org/10.1007/978-3-642-55220-5_31

17. Baltico, C.E.Z., Catalano, D., Fiore, D., Gay, R.: Practical functional encryption for quadratic functions with applications to predicate encryption. In: Katz, J., Shacham, H. (eds.) CRYPTO 2017. LNCS, vol. 10401, pp. 67–98. Springer, Cham (2017). https://doi.org/10.1007/978-3-319-63688-7_3

18. Barak, B., et al.: On the (im)possibility of obfuscating programs. In: Kilian, J. (ed.) CRYPTO 2001. LNCS, vol. 2139, pp. 1–18. Springer, Heidelberg (2001). https://doi.org/10.1007/3-540-44647-8_1

19. Barrington, D.A.: Bounded-width polynomial-size branching programs recognize exactly those languages in NC1. J. Comput. Syst. Sci. **38**(1), 150–164 (1989)

20. Bethencourt, J., Sahai, A., Waters, B.: Ciphertext-policy attribute-based encryption. In: IEEE Symposium on Security and Privacy, pp. 321–334 (2007)

21. Bitansky, N., Vaikuntanathan, V.: Indistinguishability obfuscation from functional encryption. In: FOCS 2015, 163 (2015). http://eprint.iacr.org/2015/163

22. Boneh, D., et al.: Fully key-homomorphic encryption, arithmetic circuit ABE and compact garbled circuits. In: Nguyen, P.Q., Oswald, E. (eds.) EUROCRYPT 2014. LNCS, vol. 8441, pp. 533–556. Springer, Heidelberg (2014). https://doi.org/10.1007/978-3-642-55220-5_30

23. Boneh, D., Waters, B.: Conjunctive, subset, and range queries on encrypted data. In: Vadhan, S.P. (ed.) TCC 2007. LNCS, vol. 4392, pp. 535–554. Springer, Heidelberg (2007). https://doi.org/10.1007/978-3-540-70936-7_29

24. Boyen, X., Li, Q.: Attribute-based encryption for finite automata from LWE. In: Au, M.-H., Miyaji, A. (eds.) ProvSec 2015. LNCS, vol. 9451, pp. 247–267. Springer, Cham (2015). https://doi.org/10.1007/978-3-319-26059-4_14

25. Brakerski, Z., Vaikuntanathan, V.: Lattice-based FHE as secure as PKE. In: Proceedings of the 5th Conference on Innovations in Theoretical Computer Science, ITCS 2014 (2014)

26. Brakerski, Z., Vaikuntanathan, V.: Circuit-ABE from LWE: unbounded attributes and semi-adaptive security. In: Robshaw, M., Katz, J. (eds.) CRYPTO 2016. LNCS, vol. 9816, pp. 363–384. Springer, Heidelberg (2016). https://doi.org/10.1007/978-3-662-53015-3_13

27. Cheon, J.H., Han, K., Lee, C., Ryu, H., Stehlé, D.: Cryptanalysis of the multilinear map over the integers. In: Oswald, E., Fischlin, M. (eds.) EUROCRYPT 2015. LNCS, vol. 9056, pp. 3–12. Springer, Heidelberg (2015). https://doi.org/10.1007/978-3-662-46800-5_1

28. Cheon, J.H., Fouque, P.A., Lee, C., Minaud, B., Ryu, H.: Cryptanalysis of the new CLT multilinear map over the integers. Eprint 2016/135

29. Cheon, J.H., Jeong, J., Lee, C.: An algorithm for NTRU problems and cryptanalysis of the GGH multilinear map without a low level encoding of zero. Eprint 2016/139 (2016)

30. Cook, S.A., Hoover, H.J.: A depth-universal circuit. SIAM J. Comput. **14**(4), 833–839 (1985). https://doi.org/10.1137/0214058

31. Coron, J.-S., et al.: Zeroizing without low-level zeroes: new MMAP attacks and their limitations. In: Gennaro, R., Robshaw, M. (eds.) CRYPTO 2015. LNCS, vol. 9215, pp. 247–266. Springer, Heidelberg (2015). https://doi.org/10.1007/978-3-662-47989-6_12

32. Coron, J.S., Lee, M.S., Lepoint, T., Tibouchi, M.: Zeroizing attacks on indistinguishability obfuscation over CLT13. Eprint 2016 (2016)

33. Garg, S., Gentry, C., Halevi, S.: Candidate multilinear maps from ideal lattices. In: Johansson, T., Nguyen, P.Q. (eds.) EUROCRYPT 2013. LNCS, vol. 7881, pp. 1–17. Springer, Heidelberg (2013). https://doi.org/10.1007/978-3-642-38348-9_1

34. Garg, S., Gentry, C., Halevi, S., Raykova, M., Sahai, A., Waters, B.: Candidate indistinguishability obfuscation and functional encryption for all circuits. In: FOCS (2013). http://eprint.iacr.org/

35. Garg, S., Gentry, C., Halevi, S., Sahai, A., Waters, B.: Attribute-based encryption for circuits from multilinear maps. In: Canetti, R., Garay, J.A. (eds.) CRYPTO 2013. LNCS, vol. 8043, pp. 479–499. Springer, Heidelberg (2013). https://doi.org/10.1007/978-3-642-40084-1_27

36. Goldwasser, S., Kalai, Y.T., Popa, R.A., Vaikuntanathan, V., Zeldovich, N.: How to run turing machines on encrypted data. In: Canetti, R., Garay, J.A. (eds.) CRYPTO 2013. LNCS, vol. 8043, pp. 536–553. Springer, Heidelberg (2013). https://doi.org/10.1007/978-3-642-40084-1_30

37. Goldwasser, S., Kalai, Y.T., Popa, R.A., Vaikuntanathan, V., Zeldovich, N.: Reusable garbled circuits and succinct functional encryption. In: STOC, pp. 555–564 (2013)

38. Gorbunov, S., Vaikuntanathan, V., Wee, H.: Functional encryption with bounded collusions via multi-party computation. In: Safavi-Naini, R., Canetti, R. (eds.) CRYPTO 2012. LNCS, vol. 7417, pp. 162–179. Springer, Heidelberg (2012). https://doi.org/10.1007/978-3-642-32009-5_11

39. Gorbunov, S., Vaikuntanathan, V., Wee, H.: Attribute based encryption for circuits. In: STOC (2013)

40. Gorbunov, S., Vaikuntanathan, V., Wee, H.: Predicate encryption for circuits from LWE. In: Gennaro, R., Robshaw, M. (eds.) CRYPTO 2015. LNCS, vol. 9216, pp. 503–523. Springer, Heidelberg (2015). https://doi.org/10.1007/978-3-662-48000-7_25

41. Gorbunov, S., Vinayagamurthy, D.: Riding on asymmetry: efficient abe for branching programs. In: Iwata, T., Cheon, J.H. (eds.) ASIACRYPT 2015. LNCS, vol. 9452, pp. 550–574. Springer, Heidelberg (2015). https://doi.org/10.1007/978-3-662-48797-6_23

42. Goyal, R., Koppula, V., Waters, B.: Semi-adaptive security and bundling functionalities made generic and easy. In: Hirt, M., Smith, A. (eds.) TCC 2016. LNCS, vol. 9986, pp. 361–388. Springer, Heidelberg (2016). https://doi.org/10.1007/978-3-662-53644-5_14

43. Goyal, V., Pandey, O., Sahai, A., Waters, B.: Attribute-based encryption for fine-grained access control of encrypted data. In: ACM Conference on Computer and Communications Security, pp. 89–98 (2006)

44. Hu, Y., Jia, H.: Cryptanalysis of GGH map. Cryptology ePrint Archive: Report 2015/301 (2015)

45. Katz, J., Sahai, A., Waters, B.: Predicate encryption supporting disjunctions, polynomial equations, and inner products. In: Smart, N. (ed.) EUROCRYPT 2008. LNCS, vol. 4965, pp. 146–162. Springer, Heidelberg (2008). https://doi.org/10.1007/978-3-540-78967-3_9

46. Kitagawa, F., Nishimaki, R., Tanaka, K.: Indistinguishability obfuscation for all circuits from secret-key functional encryption. IACR Cryptology ePrint Archive 2017/361 (2017)

47. Kitagawa, F., Nishimaki, R., Tanaka, K.: Obfustopia built on secret-key functional encryption. In: Nielsen, J.B., Rijmen, V. (eds.) EUROCRYPT 2018. LNCS, vol. 10821, pp. 603–648. Springer, Cham (2018). https://doi.org/10.1007/978-3-319-78375-8_20

48. Kitagawa, F., Nishimaki, R., Tanaka, K., Yamakawa, T.: Adaptively secure and succinct functional encryption: Improving security and efficiency, simultaneously. Cryptology ePrint Archive, Report 2018/974 (2018). https://eprint.iacr.org/2018/974

49. Lewko, A., Okamoto, T., Sahai, A., Takashima, K., Waters, B.: Fully secure functional encryption: attribute-based encryption and (hierarchical) inner product encryption. In: Gilbert, H. (ed.) EUROCRYPT 2010. LNCS, vol. 6110, pp. 62–91. Springer, Heidelberg (2010). https://doi.org/10.1007/978-3-642-13190-5_4

50. Lin, H.: Indistinguishability obfuscation from constant-degree graded encoding schemes. In: Fischlin, M., Coron, J.-S. (eds.) EUROCRYPT 2016. LNCS, vol. 9665, pp. 28–57. Springer, Heidelberg (2016). https://doi.org/10.1007/978-3-662-49890-3_2

51. Lin, H.: Indistinguishability obfuscation from SXDH on 5-linear maps and locality-5 PRGs. In: Katz, J., Shacham, H. (eds.) CRYPTO 2017. LNCS, vol. 10401, pp. 599–629. Springer, Cham (2017). https://doi.org/10.1007/978-3-319-63688-7_20

52. Lin, H., Matt, C.: Pseudo flawed-smudging generators and their application to indistinguishability obfuscation. Cryptology ePrint Archive, Report 2018/646 (2018)

53. Lin, H., Tessaro, S.: Indistinguishability obfuscation from trilinear maps and block-wise local PRGs. In: Katz, J., Shacham, H. (eds.) CRYPTO 2017. LNCS, vol. 10401, pp. 630–660. Springer, Cham (2017). https://doi.org/10.1007/978-3-319-63688-7_21

54. Lin, H., Vaikuntanathan, V.: Indistinguishability obfuscation from DDH-like assumptions on constant-degree graded encodings. In: FOCS (2016)

55. Miles, E., Sahai, A., Zhandry, M.: Annihilation attacks for multilinear maps: cryptanalysis of indistinguishability obfuscation over GGH13. In: Robshaw, M., Katz, J. (eds.) CRYPTO 2016. LNCS, vol. 9815, pp. 629–658. Springer, Heidelberg (2016). https://doi.org/10.1007/978-3-662-53008-5_22

56. Sahai, A., Waters, B.: Fuzzy identity-based encryption. In: Cramer, R. (ed.) EUROCRYPT 2005. LNCS, vol. 3494, pp. 457–473. Springer, Heidelberg (2005). https://doi.org/10.1007/11426639_27

57. Waters, B.: Functional encryption for regular languages. In: Safavi-Naini, R., Canetti, R. (eds.) CRYPTO 2012. LNCS, vol. 7417, pp. 218–235. Springer, Heidelberg (2012). https://doi.org/10.1007/978-3-642-32009-5_14

Foundations

The Distinction Between Fixed and Random Generators in Group-Based Assumptions

James Bartusek[1]([⊠]), Fermi Ma[1]([⊠]), and Mark Zhandry[2]

[1] Princeton University, Princeton, USA
bartusek.james@gmail.com, fermima1@gmail.com
[2] Princeton University & NTT Research, Princeton, USA
mzhandry@princeton.edu

Abstract. There is surprisingly little consensus on the precise role of the generator g in group-based assumptions such as DDH. Some works consider g to be a fixed part of the group description, while others take it to be random. We study this subtle distinction from a number of angles.

- In the generic group model, we demonstrate the plausibility of groups in which random-generator DDH (resp. CDH) is hard but fixed-generator DDH (resp. CDH) is easy. We observe that such groups have interesting cryptographic applications.
- We find that seemingly tight generic lower bounds for the Discrete-Log and CDH problems with preprocessing (Corrigan-Gibbs and Kogan, Eurocrypt 2018) are not tight in the sub-constant success probability regime if the generator is random. We resolve this by proving tight lower bounds for the random generator variants; our results formalize the intuition that using a random generator will reduce the effectiveness of preprocessing attacks.
- We observe that DDH-like assumptions in which exponents are drawn from low-entropy distributions are particularly sensitive to the fixed- vs. random-generator distinction. Most notably, we discover that the Strong Power DDH assumption of Komargodski and Yogev (Komargodski and Yogev, Eurocrypt 2018) used for non-malleable point obfuscation is in fact *false* precisely because it requires a fixed generator. In response, we formulate an alternative fixed-generator assumption that suffices for a new construction of non-malleable point obfuscation, and we prove the assumption holds in the generic group model. We also give a generic group proof for the security of fixed-generator, low-entropy DDH (Canetti, Crypto 1997).

1 Introduction

Starting with the seminal work of Diffie and Hellman [21], the *Computational Diffie-Hellman* (CDH) assumption in certain cyclic groups has become a core

The full version of this paper is available at iacr.org/2019/202 [3].

pillar of modern cryptography. For a finite cyclic group G and generator g, the assumption holds if it is hard to compute g^{ab} given (g, g^a, g^b) for random a, b. The corresponding *Decisional Diffie-Hellman* (DDH) assumption, introduced by Brands [12], is that given (g, g^a, g^b) for random a, b, it is hard to distinguish g^{ab} from g^c for random c.

A somewhat subtle issue is the precise role of g in these assumptions: is it fixed in the group description, or is it randomly chosen along with a and b? For CDH in groups where the totient of the order is known, a folklore equivalence between the fixed and random generator variants exists (e.g. see Chap. 21 of Galbraith's textbook [25]). For DDH, Shoup [40] observed that the fixed generator assumption appears to be a *stronger* assumption than the random generator version, though a formal separation between the two is unknown. Despite this apparent distinction, the cryptographic literature commonly refers to both the fixed and random generator variants simply as "DDH".[1]

A likely explanation for this practice is that in most applications of cryptographic groups, it is straightforward to switch between fixed and random generators. For example, in ElGamal encryption [22], users who want the additional security of random-generator DDH can easily specify a random generator in their public key.

Sadeghi and Steiner [37] observed that this justification does not apply in settings where the choice of group generator is left to a potentially untrusted party.[2] They give the example of a bank that offers its customers an anonymous payment system, claiming provable security under group-based assumptions. If the bank is free to choose parameters such as the group generator, then for security it is crucial that any underlying assumptions hold in their (stronger) fixed generator form. While Sadeghi and Steiner did not point to specific assumptions that can be broken simply by fixing the group generator, they stressed that continuing to conflate these distinct assumptions could lead to serious ambiguities and mistakes in the future.

In the nearly two decades since Sadeghi and Steiner [37] first called attention to the above issue, dozens of new and increasingly sophisticated group-based assumptions have been introduced. Accordingly, researchers have devoted significant effort to evaluating the plausibility of these assumptions (e.g. [2,20]), frequently in idealized models such as the generic group model [34,36,39]. We observe that these generic group justifications generally ignore the question of whether the generator is fixed or random, but that in most cases this distinction does not seem to affect real world security of these assumptions.

In this work, however, we will see that this is not *always* the case.

---

[1] For example, the Katz-Lindell textbook [29] defines DDH with a fixed generator, while Cramer-Shoup [19] defines DDH with a random generator.

[2] Sadeghi and Steiner [37] actually consider the more general possibility of the untrusted party choosing the group itself maliciously. This question is beyond the scope of our work, but in many cases it is an equally important consideration.

1.1   Our Results

We first examine how the fixed vs. random generator distinction affects the classical Discrete-Log, CDH, and DDH problems in a variety of different settings, obtaining the following results:

- **Generic Separations for CDH and DDH.** We prove that fixed- and random-generator DDH are *inequivalent* assumptions in the generic group model [34,36,39]. We show that for groups of *unknown order*, fixed- and random-generator CDH are also inequivalent assumptions in the generic group model. In addition, we give evidence (relying on a new assumption about arithmetic circuits) that they are inequivalent even if the group order is known but its factorization is not.[3]

- **Split-CDH and Split-DDH Groups.** We define Split-CDH (resp. Split-DDH) groups for which the fixed-generator variant of CDH (resp. DDH) is easy but the random-generator variant is hard, and we observe that such groups imply interesting cryptographic applications. A split-CDH group can be turned into a *self-bilinear map* [30,43] where the random-generator variant of the Multilinear CDH assumption holds. This implies powerful primitives such as multiparty non-interactive key agreement (with trusted setup).[4] A split-DDH group can be used to instantiate a variant of the Boneh-Franklin identity-based encryption [8] scheme. We stress here that giving candidate constructions of these groups is outside of the scope of this work. On the negative side, we prove that a natural class of non-interactive key exchange protocols (without trusted setup) are *insecure* in certain split-CDH groups.

- **Asymptotic Bounds for Discrete-Log and CDH with Preprocessing.** We revisit the recent work of Corrigan-Gibbs and Kogan [18], which seemingly resolves the generic hardness of Discrete-Log and CDH with preprocessing. We observe that while their lower bounds are tight for the fixed-generator variants, they leave a gap in the random-generator setting for algorithms with sub-constant success probability. We close these gaps by proving tight lower bounds for the random-generator variants. Our bounds suggest that using a random generator can reduce the impact of preprocessing attacks, and in turn group parameters can be set more aggressively than previously thought in situations where random-generator Discrete-Log or CDH are sufficient.

Next, we turn our attention to the class of Diffie-Hellman-like assumptions involving *non-uniform random exponents*. An example of such an assumption is Canetti's "DDH-II" assumption [13], which states that DDH remains hard even if the exponent a in (g, g^a, g^b, g^{ab}) is drawn from a well-spread distribution (so that a has super-logarithmic min-entropy). While these assumptions are somewhat undesirable due to their non-standard nature [27], Wee [42] showed that these assumptions (ones that require hardness given only super-logarithmic entropy) are *necessary* for applications such as point-function obfuscation.

---

[3] This inequivalence was also suggested by Saxena and Soh [38].

[4] A similar observation was also made in [38].

Before we rely on such assumptions, it is important to rule out idealized adversaries that attack the underlying structure of the assumption. The most common technique for achieving this is to prove the assumption holds in the generic group model [34,36,39]. Such proofs certainly do not imply the validity of the assumption; instead, these proofs are generally viewed as a *minimal level of guarantee* we need to gain confidence in an assumption [2].

Our central focus is on the recently proposed "Strong Power DDH" assumption of Komargodski and Yogev [31]. The assumption states that for x sampled from any arbitrary well-spread distribution $\mathcal{D}$, that $g^x, g^{x^2}, \ldots, g^{x^k}$ is indistinguishable from k uniformly random group elements. Our results are the following:

- **Strong Power DDH is False for a Fixed Generator.** We demonstrate the "Strong Power DDH" assumption underlying Komargodski and Yogev's non-malleable point obfuscator [31] as well as Fenteany and Fuller's non-malleable digital locker [23] is *false* in the fixed-generator setting.[5] This results from a subtle issue in the order of quantifiers; if g is fixed, an arbitrary well-spread distribution could depend on g. For example, x can come from the distribution that conditions on the bit-representation of g^x beginning with 0. Unfortunately, these constructions can only be instantiated with a fixed generator, so the original security proofs in [31] and [23] must rely on a false assumption.[6,7]

  In response to private communication from the authors of this work, Komargodski and Yogev have offered a simple fix [32] for their original construction through a new "Entropic Power DDH" assumption.[8] This new assumption suffices for non-malleable point obfuscation and is formulated precisely to address the vulnerability described above.

- **Fixing Non-Malleable Point Obfuscation and Justifying Assumptions in the Generic Group Model.** In this work, we offer an alternative resolution. We construct a new non-malleable point obfuscator that is qualitatively different from the one in [31]. Security of our construction relies on a newly formulated fixed-generator entropic assumption that we prove holds in the generic group model. Note that neither the Strong Power DDH Assumption [31] nor the revised Entropic Power DDH Assumption [32] come with generic group proofs of security.

  Along the way, we develop general techniques (based heavily on [16]) for proving generic security of non-standard, entropic assumptions. As a final

---

[5] The authors privately communicated these issues to the authors of [23,31].

[6] Relying on a random generator would require a common random string, which is not the model considered in [31] or in the version of [23] dated Jan 30, 2019 at eprint.iacr.org/2018/957/20190130:190441.

[7] This issue appears in the Eurocrypt 2018 version of [31], in an older ePrint version of [32] dated May 1, 2018 at eprint.iacr.org/2018/149/20180211:142746, and in the ePrint version of [23] dated Jan 30, 2019 at eprint.iacr.org/2018/957/20190130:190441.

[8] This refers to the newer ePrint version of [32] dated Feb 21, 2019 available at https://eprint.iacr.org/2018/149/20190221:133556.

contribution, we demonstrate the applicability of these techniques by showing that the fixed- and random-generator versions of Canetti's DDH-II assumption [13] hold in the generic group model.[9] This assumption has been used in both its fixed-generator form (e.g. [14,20,28]) and random-generator form (e.g. [6,13]).

1.2 Technical Overview

Part 1: Generic Separations and Split Groups

Formalizing the Distinction. We will assume some process for generating a group description G of order N. This group description is assumed to include a generator g. The *fixed-generator* DDH assumption, or f-DDH, states that the tuples (g^x, g^y, g^{xy}) and (g^x, g^y, g^z) are computationally indistinguishable, given the description of G. Here, x, y, z are chosen randomly in $\mathbb{Z}_N$. On the other hand, the *random-generator* DDH assumption, or r-DDH, states that the tuples (h, h^x, h^y, h^{xy}) and (h, h^x, h^y, h^z) are computationally indistinguishable. Here, x, y, z are chosen randomly in $\mathbb{Z}_N$, and h is a random generator of G (chosen, say, by setting $h = g^r$ for a random r in $\mathbb{Z}_N^*$). We can also define fixed- and random-generator variants of Computational Diffie-Hellman (CDH) and Discrete-Log (DLog). For example, f-CDH states that given (g^x, g^y) for random x, y, it is computationally infeasible to find g^{xy}.

We consider the following three settings of groups: known prime group order, known composite group order of *unknown* factorization, and unknown group order. For each of the three assumptions and three settings (for 9 instances in total) we explore the relationship between the fixed- and random-generator variants. Trivially, the f- variants of the assumptions are at least as strong as the r- variants. In the other direction, some instances have known or folklore reductions showing equivalence [25]. For each of the cases that do not have a proof of equivalence, we provide a separation. This is formalized by augmenting the generic group model [39] with an oracle for the f- variant, and showing (potentially under reasonable computational assumptions) that the r- variant still holds. Table 1 summarizes our findings.

Applications of Split Groups. Looking at Table 1, we see that in the case of DDH, there is the potential for a group where f-DDH is easy but r-DDH is hard. We will call such groups split-DDH groups. Similarly, if the group order is unknown, potentially f-CDH is easy but r-CDH is hard; we call such groups split-CDH groups. In this section, we will see that such split Diffie-Hellman groups have useful cryptographic applications.

---

[9] Previously, such proofs had been obtained by Bitanksy and Canetti [6] and Damgård, Hazay, and Zottarel [20], who considered the random- and fixed-generator versions, respectively. We observe that both of these proofs treat the well-spread distribution as independent of the generic group labeling. Our proof handles distributions with arbitrary dependence on the labels; for more discussion refer to Part 4 of Sect. 1.2.

Table 1. Generic equivalences and separations. FL denotes a folklore result. ✓ means that the fixed and random generator versions are equivalent. × means that the random generator version is harder than the fixed generator version (in the generic model). ×? means the result holds under a plausible conjecture. These results are all given in the full version [3].

	DLog	CDH	DDH
Known Order	✓ FL	✓ FL	×
Unknown Factorization	✓ FL	×?	×
Unknown order	✓ FL	×? [44]	×

First, we observe that a split-CDH group is very close to a self-bilinear map [43]. A self-bilinear map is a group G together with a pairing $e : G^2 \to G$ such that $e(g^x, g^y) = e(g,g)^{xy}$. Let $g_1 = g$ and $g_n = e(g, g_{n-1})$. A typical computational assumption on self-bilinear maps would be the multilinear CDH assumption [9]: for any $n > 1$, given $g^{x_0}, \ldots, g^{x_n}$, it is hard to compute $g_n^{\prod_{i=0}^n x_i}$. Notice that by applying the mapping $e(\cdot, \cdot)$, it is only possible to compute $g_{n+1}^{\prod_{i=0}^n x_i}$.

An f-CDH oracle gives such an oracle where $e(g, g) = g$. Therefore, a split-CDH group gives all the functionality of a self-bilinear map. But notice that since $e(g, g) = g$, $g_n = g$ for any n. Therefore, the multilinear CDH assumption is false. However, we observe that if we choose a random element h, then $e(h, h) = h^r$ where $h = g^r$. As such, the f-CDH oracle would also give a self-bilinear map with respect to the random generator h. We then show that multilinear CDH is actually hard relative to h, assuming r-CDH is hard. Thus, we obtain a self-bilinear map from any split-CDH group. As a consequence, following [43] we would immediately obtain multiparty non-interactive key agreement, broadcast encryption satisfying a distributed setup notion [10], and attribute-based encryption for circuits.

In the full version [3] we show that Split-DDH groups allow for a simple identity-based encryption (IBE) scheme based on the Boneh-Franklin [8] construction.

Part 2: Trusted Setup Assumptions. The previous sections demonstrated that the f- and r-DDH assumptions are distinct assumptions that may not both be true. But then which DDH assumption should be used? In practice, g is typically part of a standards library chosen by a trusted third party (e.g. NIST). As such, users have essentially three choices:

1. Believe that the trusted third party chose g at random, and use the r-DDH assumption.

2. Do not trust the third party, but instead assume that there are no bad g. In other words, rely on the f-DDH assumption for g.
3. Do not trust the third party, but instead have one of the users generate a random g and distribute it to everyone else. Then rely on r-DDH.

Option 1 means that users need to trust that no one could have subverted g and chosen a bad generator for which DDH is actually easy; history has shown such trust could very well be misplaced. Only Options 2 and 3 remove the need to trust a third party.

Remark 1. Note that to remove trusted setup assumptions entirely, we would need to ensure that G itself is guaranteed to satisfy f-DDH. One option is to assume that both G and g were generated by a deterministic process, so that all parties can calculate G, g for themselves without any setup. For groups based on finite fields, this requires deterministically generating large primes; while no polynomial-time provable algorithms are known, there are very simple heuristic algorithms. For elliptic curve-based groups, other options are available (e.g. using a field with small characteristic). For one approach to deterministic curve generation, see [11].

In most cases, it is straightforward to switch between Options 2 and 3. A scheme designed for f-DDH can often be converted into a scheme that relies only on r-DDH by having one of the parties choose a random generator. On the other hand, a scheme designed for r-DDH can often be converted into an f-DDH scheme by fixing a group element and not including it with the user's messages, saving slightly on transmission costs.

The above means slightly different parameter sizes for the two assumptions. For example, for public key schemes, the extra group element would naturally go in the public key. The result is that schemes secure under r-DDH naturally require one additional group element in the public key relative to the f-DDH analog. As authors often compare parameter sizes in terms of group elements (e.g. [24]), it is important that they clearly identify which assumption is used.

In some cases, however, switching between f-DDH and r-DDH will have a more profound impact. For example, in a protocol between mutually distrusting parties, which party will be entrusted to come up with the generator? While we are not aware of any instances of protocols in the literature that cannot be made to work with a random generator, it is straightforward to devise protocols where no single party can be trusted to choose the generator. As such, care must be taken when using the r-DDH assumption in these settings.

Diffie-Hellman Key Exchange. For the remainder of this section, we will focus on a concrete setting where it is not possible to trivially switch between f-DDH and r-DDH: Diffie-Hellman key exchange. In the protocol, Alice chooses a random $a \leftarrow \mathbb{Z}_N$ and computes $A = g^a$, and Bob chooses a random $b \leftarrow \mathbb{Z}_N$ and computes $B = g^b$. Then the two parties exchange A, B. In most treatments, Diffie-Hellman is a *non-interactive key exchange* (NIKE), which means that A and B are sent simultaneously. Alice then computes the secret key $K = g^{ab} = B^a$ and Bob computes $K = g^{ab} = A^b$. By the DDH assumption, an eavesdropper who learns A, B can learn nothing about K.

The key issue here is that Alice and Bob need to know g in order to generate their first message. So if we want one of them, say Alice, to come up with the generator, the result is an *interactive* protocol with Alice sending the first message, and only then can Bob send his. Therefore, in addition to requiring slightly more communication, Option 3 actually changes the nature of the protocol. What we see is that Diffie-Hellman can only remain a setupless NIKE under the f-DDH assumption.

Now, it is possible to alter Diffie-Hellman to work with CDH by extracting hardcore bits from the unpredictable key. By the equivalence of f-CDH and r-CDH in known prime-order groups, we can obtain a setupless NIKE protocol from r-CDH (and hence also r-DDH). In groups of unknown order, however, this does not apply. As our main technical result from this section, we give evidence that in groups where the totient of the order is *unknown*, r-CDH alone is *insufficient* for constructing setupless NIKE. This is formalized by assuming that f-CDH is easy and demonstrating an attack on a wide class of key agreement protocols that generalize the classical Diffie-Hellman protocol.

Part 3: Random-Generator Discrete-Log and CDH with Preprocessing. A recent line of works [5,16,18,33,35] have explored *non-uniform* attacks on various problems in cryptographic groups. Here, a computationally expensive offline pre-processing stage generates an advice string, which in a later online stage can be used to speed up computation in the group. We are interested in the relationship between the length S of the advice string, the running time T of the online stage, the group order N, and the success probability ϵ.

Very recently, Corrigan-Gibbs and Kogan [18] seemingly resolve the non-uniform hardness of the *discrete logarithm* problem. Namely, they show in the generic group model that $\epsilon = \widetilde{O}(ST^2/N)$, where the $\widetilde{O}$ hides logarithmic factors. This matches known upper bounds (attacks) up to logarithmic factors.

However, all the works in this line (both lower bounds and attacks) only consider the fixed generator version of discrete log. Corrigan-Gibbs and Kogan briefly mention this, concluding that "using a fixed generator is essentially without loss of generality" since a discrete log with respect to one generator can be solved by solving two discrete logs with respect to a different generator.

When considering just polynomial reductions between problems, the above is certainly true. However, when it comes to precisely quantifying hardness, the problem no longer remains identical for different generators. In particular, suppose we have an algorithm that solves discrete log with respect to generator g with probability ϵ and we want to solve a discrete log instance with respect to generator $h = g^r$. To do so, on input h^x, we apply the algorithm twice to find the discrete logs of h and h^x with respect to g. This gives r and rx, allowing us to solve for x. But since we needed to solve both instances correctly, our overall success probability is only ϵ^2. Of course if ϵ is a constant so is ϵ^2, but in the low success probability regime, squaring the advantage significantly changes the hardness of the problem.

We resolve the question of the hardness of random-generator discrete log in the pre-processing setting, showing that $\epsilon = \widetilde{\Theta}\left(\frac{T^2}{N} + \frac{S^2 T^4}{N^2}\right)$. The attack side is simple: there are two natural ways to attack a random-generator discrete log instance h, h^x. One is to ignore the pre-processing, and apply the Baby-step Giant-step algorithm, with success $\Omega(\frac{T^2}{N})$. The other is to use the pre-processing to solve two discrete log instances relative to some fixed generator g, in the manner described above. This gives success $\Omega((\frac{ST^2}{N})^2)$, as shown in [18]. By choosing which algorithm to use based on the parameters S, T, N, one obtains $\epsilon = \Omega\left(\frac{T^2}{N} + \frac{S^2 T^4}{N^2}\right)$.

On the other hand, to prove the lower bound we need to show, essentially, that the two algorithms above are the only possible algorithms. This does not follow from the analysis of [18]. Instead, we use the tools developed in subsequent works [16,17] (based on the earlier pre-sampling techniques developed by Unruh [41] for the Random Oracle model) to switch to a "bit-fixing" model, where we then show the optimality of the algorithms. In addition, we show that the same relationship holds as well for r-CDH. Generically, auxiliary input r-CDH is as hard as either using the auxiliary information to solve two discrete logarithms, or ignoring the input and solving one discrete logarithm.

1.3   Part 4: Low-Entropy Fixed-Generator Assumptions

Background: Point Obfuscation from Low-Entropy Assumptions. Our discussion thus far has focused on Discrete Log/Diffie-Hellman-type assumptions where g^a, g^b are uniformly random group elements. However, the security of many important cryptographic applications often relies on a stronger version of these assumptions in which a and/or b might not be drawn uniformly at random.

Canetti's construction of point function obfuscation is perhaps the most well-known example. A point function $f_x(\cdot)$ is a boolean function that accepts on x and rejects on all other inputs. Roughly speaking, an obfuscated point function $\mathcal{O}(f_x(\cdot))$ implements the same input/output functionality as $f_x(\cdot)$, but leaks no information about x beyond what can be learned through black-box oracle queries to $f_x(\cdot)$. In other words, the obfuscated program acts as a *virtual black box* for evaluating the function.[10] Canetti's point function obfuscator is simple: to obfuscate $f_x(\cdot)$, draw a random group element g^b and output (g^b, g^{xb}). Evaluation on input y is done by computing $(g^b)^y$ and accepting if it matches g^{xb}.

The security of this construction follows from an assumption Canetti refers to as DHI-II (in subsequent works it has been renamed to "DDH-II"; we will adopt this name), which states that $(g, g^a, g^b, g^{ab}) \approx_C (g, g^a, g^b, g^c)$ where g is a random generator, b, c are chosen uniformly at random, and a has super-logarithmic min-entropy, i.e. it is sampled from a *well-spread* distribution $\mathcal{D}$.

---

[10] We defer a more detailed discussion on virtual-black-box obfuscation to [1] (see [42] for specifics on point function obfuscation).

We stress that DDH-II is technically an infinite family of assumptions, since it requires indistinguishability if $\mathcal{D}$ is *any* well-spread distribution (even ones that are not efficiently sampleable).

Under DDH-II, the obfuscated program (g^b, g^{xb}) hides all information about the point x as long as x is drawn from a well-spread distribution, since g^{xb} is indistinguishable from g^c. This immediately implies a notion of average-case virtual-black-box (VBB) security. Canetti proves that if a point function obfuscator is average-case VBB for *any* well-spread distribution, this implies full (worst-case) VBB security. It was later shown by Wee ([42], Sect. 4.2) that Canetti's approach is essentially inherent: VBB-secure point function obfuscation *requires* strong assumptions that are hard for any well-spread distribution.

Background: Non-malleable Point Obfuscation. Canetti's original motivation for studying point obfuscation was to realize useful properties of random oracles [4] in the standard model. If $H(\cdot)$ is a random oracle, observe that $H(x)$ is a secure point obfuscation of $f_x(\cdot)$, where evaluation is a single random oracle call followed by a comparison. Komargodski and Yogev [31] observe that the random oracle obfuscator $H(x)$ satisfies a strong *non-malleability* property, in the sense that given $H(x)$ it is impossible to compute $H(f(x))$ for any (meaningfully) related point $f(x)$, without first recovering x. This property is missing from Canetti's point obfuscator [13], e.g. since given (g^b, g^{xb}), one can easily compute $(g^b, g^{(x+1)b})$, which is an obfuscation of the related point $f(x) = x + 1$.

Komargodski and Yogev [31] propose the following modification to Canetti's point obfuscator. To obfuscate the point x, sample a random b and output $(g^b, (g^b)^{g^{x^4+x^3+x^2+x}})$. Note that for this expression to make sense, $g^{x^4+x^3+x^2+x}$ must be mapped back into the exponent space under some fixed public mapping. Evaluation on input y is done by computing $g^{y^4+y^3+y^2+y}$, mapping this element back to the exponent space and raising g^b to that power, and finally comparing to $(g^b)^{g^{x^4+x^3+x^2+x}}$.

Komargodski and Yogev [31] argue their obfuscation resists bounded-degree polynomial *mauling* attacks, in which an adversary given an obfuscation of x attempts to produce an obfuscation of $P(x)$ for some bounded-degree polynomial $P(\cdot)$. Roughly, the intuition is that the adversary cannot replace g^b with any other $g^{b'}$, since generating $(g^{b'})^{g^{P(x)}}$ does not appear possible given only $(g^b)^{g^{x^4+x^3+x^2+x}}$. But if the adversary cannot change g^b, the argument is that the linear constraints imposed by the form of $x^4 + x^3 + x^2 + x$ make it impossible to replace x with $P(x)$.

Formally, security in [31] is proved under the newly introduced "Strong Power DDH" assumption, which states it is hard to distinguish $g^x, g^{x^2}, \ldots, g^{x^\ell}$ from ℓ random group elements, if x is drawn from any well-spread distribution.

Fixed-Generator Strong Power DDH is False. In stating the assumption, Komargodski and Yogev [31] do not specify how g is chosen or the relationship between g and the distribution over x. We observe that if g is a fixed generator, then their assumption is false. For a uniformly random group element, there must be some bit in its description with noticeable entropy. If it is bit i, we let $\mathcal{D}$ be the distribution over all points x such that the ith bit of the description of g^x is 0. Then $\mathcal{D}$ has high min-entropy, and moreover g^x for $x \leftarrow \mathcal{D}$ is distinguishable from a random group element by inspecting the ith bit.

If the assumption is taken in its random-generator formulation, the security proof in [31] breaks down, since an adversary can potentially replace g with a different generator g'. A natural idea to fix the construction would be to generate g using a public source of randomness.[11] However, this would move the construction into the CRS model, where strong non-malleability results were previously known [15].

Fixing Non-malleable Point Obfuscation. We remedy this situation by giving an alternative low-entropy fixed-generator assumption, and proving that this assumption is sufficient to achieve their notion of non-malleable point obfuscation. We formulate our assumption in a way that allows us to prove it holds in the generic group model. Our assumption is the following:

> Let $p \in [2^{\lambda-1}, 2^\lambda]$ and let n be at most $\mathsf{poly}(\lambda)$. Fix a group G of order p along with a generator g and any well-spread distribution $\mathcal{D}$ over $\mathbb{Z}_p$ (which can depend on G). Next sample $k_2, \ldots, k_n$ uniformly at random from $\mathbb{Z}_p$. Then no efficient adversary can distinguish $\{g^{k_i x + x^i}\}_{i \in \{2,\ldots,n\}}$ for $x \leftarrow \mathcal{D}$ from $n - 1$ uniformly random group elements, even given $k_2, \ldots, k_n$.[12]

The intuition for the design of this assumption is the following. We want to modify the group elements $g^x, g^{x^2}, \ldots$ in Strong Power DDH to block distributions $\mathcal{D}$ which "condition" on the fixed y, as we have already seen how such distributions falsify the assumption. However, we are restricted to modifications that preserve our ability to perform a security reduction for the proof of non-malleability, as in [31].

Without delving into the non-malleability security proof itself, the key requirement is that the reduction must be able to construct specific polynomials (in x) in the exponent. We tweak the construction so that the reduction can construct a polynomial of the form $ax + x^2 + x^3 + x^4 + x^5$, where a is an arbitrary but known scalar. Then by using terms of the form $g^{k_i x + x^i}$, we enable the reduction to construct this polynomial by simply multiplying the $i = 2, \ldots, 5$ terms; it will know a since the k_i's are given in the clear. Intuitively, the k_i scalars contribute enough randomness to prevent distributions $\mathcal{D}$ which make the $g^{k_i x + x^i}$ terms distinguishable from random.

---

[11] As noted in Sect. 1.1, Komargodski and Yogev have offered a fix through a new Entropic Power DDH Assumption in a revised ePrint posting [32], which does not come with a generic group proof. The goal of this section is to build non-malleable point obfuscation from an assumption that holds against generic adversaries.

[12] The assumption we actually use is slightly different: instead of stating indistinguishability from uniform, we require indistinguishability from $\{g^{k_i y + y^i}\}_{i \in \{2,\ldots,n\}}$ for the same $\{k_i\}_i$ but uniformly random y. We can prove both forms of this assumption hold in the GGM, but this second form yields a simpler proof of VBB security. For the purposes of this technical overview this distinction can be ignored.

Our resulting construction of non-malleable point obfuscation is (essentially) $a, g^{ax+x^2+x^3+x^4+x^5}$. We note that our construction does not require the "double exponentiation" of [31]. The full construction comes with two additional scalars and group elements that ensure that x is the only accepting input.

Discussion: Low-Entropy Fixed Generator Assumptions in the Generic Group Model. In order to gain confidence in our assumption, we prove it secure in the generic group model. As discussed in Sect. 1.1, this is usually viewed as a minimum requirement in order to gain confidence in a new group-based assumption. Recall that in the generic group model, group elements g^x are replaced with random "labels" $\sigma(x)$, where σ is a uniformly random injection from the space of exponents to some space of labels. An oracle stores the entire description of σ, and allows the generic adversary oracle access to honest group operations. For example, an adversary with labels $\sigma(x), \sigma(y)$ can request the label for $\sigma(x+y)$.

We find that in the setting of fixed generator lower entropy assumptions, the standard intuition for designing generic group model proofs falls short. Our goal is to prove no generic adversary can distinguish between $\{k_i, \sigma(k_i x + x^i)\}_{i \in \{2,...,n\}}$ and $\{k_i, \sigma(r_i)\}_{i \in \{2,...,n\}}$ for uniformly random k_i, r_i, and $x \leftarrow \mathcal{D}$. Since the group and generator are fixed in this assumption, we *must* consider distributions which depend on the group description itself. So in the generic model, any distribution $\mathcal{D}$ should be viewed as the output distribution of a potentially *inefficient* sampling algorithm $\mathcal{S}$ that is free to scan the entire labeling function σ. The only requirement we enforce is that given σ, the point $x \leftarrow \mathcal{S}(\sigma)$ has super-logarithmic entropy.

To illustrate the difference in this setting, suppose for a moment that the sampler $\mathcal{S}$ had to output x without seeing σ (as is the case when x is drawn uniformly at random from $\mathbb{Z}_p$). The standard generic group argument for indistinguishability would use the following structure:

> Imagine treating x as a formal variable instead of as a randomly drawn value. This replaces the group exponent space $\mathbb{Z}_p$ with formal polynomials $\mathbb{Z}_p[x]$, so the oracle now returns labels by sampling a uniformly random label from the image of σ each time it encounters a distinct formal polynomial. Observe that there are no (non-trivial) linear combinations of the $\{k_i x + x^i\}_i$ polynomials (taken as formal polynomials in x) that evaluate to identically zero polynomials over x. This implies that the adversary will never encounter non-trivial collisions in the labels it sees, and we can use the Schwartz-Zippel Lemma to argue that the adversary's view is identical in the world where x is random instead of a formal variable.

This type of argument breaks down if $\mathcal{S}$ can choose x *after* seeing the labeling function σ. Now $\mathcal{S}$ can try to pick x so that $\sigma(k_i x + x^i)$ conveys non-trivial distinguishing information to the adversary. In particular, it is no longer accurate to argue that we can produce an identical view for the adversary by replacing x with a formal variable.

We could intuitively hope that $\mathcal{S}$ is powerless to pick x that can bias the distribution of $\sigma(k_i x + x^i)$ away from uniform, as it does not know the random

k_i. However, this intuition proves tricky to formalize, especially since S is given unlimited computational power and access to the entire function σ.

Connection to Preprocessing Attacks. To solve this problem, we apply the "bit-fixing" technique from Coretti, Dodis, and Guo [16]. They consider generic algorithms which are given an additional advice string, computed beforehand using a computationally unbounded algorithm with access to σ. Conditioned on the advice string, it is no longer accurate to argue σ is a random labeling function. However, they show (roughly) that if we obtain at most P bits of advice about σ, this only leaks useful information about σ on $O(P)$ points. So for generic security proofs, this allows us to switch to a setting in which σ is a random labeling function on all but $O(P)$ inputs.

We apply these techniques to our setting by re-casting the sampler S outputting x as a computationally unbounded algorithm outputting x as "advice". However in our setting, the challenger is the one receiving the advice instead of the adversary. It turns out that the [16] techniques still apply here, allowing us to argue that σ can be re-sampled on all but polynomially many points. Once we perform this re-sampling, we show that the adversary will not be able to apply group operations to its set of initial group elements and produce a point that was not re-sampled, except with negligible probability. Once this is established, standard generic group techniques suffice to complete the proof.

Generic Hardness of DDH-II. As a final contribution, we also prove the generic hardness of Canetti's DDH-II assumption. We remark that previous proofs of DDH-II [6,20] operate in a highly idealized model that assumes the sampler is independent of the labeling function σ. Preventing the sampler from seeing the labels implicitly relies on the group itself being drawn at random, which in particular leads to counterexamples when dealing with fixed generator assumptions. For example, the Strong Power DDH assumption with fixed generator can be proven in this model even though it is false in the real world.

In the case of DDH-II, one of the elements the adversary receives is $\sigma(a)$ for low entropy a. We must show at a minimum that this does not allow the adversary to recover a (i.e. compute the discrete log), as distinguishing would then be trivial. Such a claim might not be immediately obvious, especially considering that we can *distinguish* $\sigma(a)$ from $\sigma(r)$ for uniform r for certain distributions on a. We observe that any adversary which succeeds in solving discrete log of $\sigma(a)$ with noticeable advantage for a well-spread distribution is also an adversary that solves discrete log (with much smaller advantage) for the uniform distribution. However, the resulting advantage exceeds the known generic bounds for discrete log algorithms [39]. The remainder of our proof makes use of bit-fixing techniques to reduce the problem of distinguishing the DDH-II instance to the problem of recovering a given just $\sigma(a)$.

2   Preliminaries

For $n \in \mathbb{N}$, let $[n]$ denote the set $\{1, \ldots, n\}$. We specify formal variables by bold letters $\mathbf{x}$. For a function f, let $im(f)$ denote the image of f.

Throughout, we let $\lambda \in \mathbb{N}$ be the security parameter. We use the usual Landau notations. A function $f(\lambda)$ is said to be negligible if it is $\lambda^{-\omega(1)}$ and we denote it by $f(\lambda) := \mathsf{negl}(\lambda)$. A function $f(\lambda)$ is said to have polynomial growth rate if it is $\lambda^{O(1)}$ and we denote it by $f(\lambda) := \mathsf{poly}(\lambda)$. A probability $p(\lambda)$ is said to be overwhelming if it is $1 - \lambda^{-\omega(1)}$. We refer to $\mathcal{A}$ as PPT if it is a probabilistic polynomial time algorithm. If $\mathcal{A}$ has access to an oracle $\mathcal{O}$, we write $\mathcal{A}^{\mathcal{O}}$.

The statistical distance between two distributions D_1 and D_2 over a countable support S is defined to be $\Delta(D_1, D_2) := \frac{1}{2} \sum_{x \in S} |D_1(x) - D_2(x)|$. Let $\gamma > 0$. We say that two distributions D_1 and D_2 are γ-close if $\Delta(D_1, D_2) \leq \gamma$. We let $x \leftarrow \mathcal{D}$ denote drawing x from the distribution $\mathcal{D}$. When X is a set, then $x \leftarrow X$ denotes drawing x *uniformly at random* from the set X. The following definition regarding infinite families of distributions will be used throughout.

Definition 1 (Well-Spread Distribution Ensemble). *An ensemble of distributions* $\{\mathcal{D}_\lambda\}_\lambda$ *over domains* $\{\mathcal{X}_\lambda\}_\lambda$ *is well-spread if for all large enough* $\lambda \in \mathbb{N}$,

$$H_\infty(\mathcal{D}_\lambda) = - \min_{x \in \mathcal{X}_\lambda} \log_2 \Pr[x \leftarrow \mathcal{D}_\lambda] = \omega(\log(\lambda)).$$

2.1   Generic Group Model

Definition 2 (Generic Group Model (GGM) [36,39]). *An application in the generic group model is defined as an interaction between a* T-*attacker* $\mathcal{A}$ *and a challenger* $\mathcal{C}$. *For a cyclic group of order* N *with fixed generator* g, *a random injective function* $\sigma : [N] \to [M]$ *is sampled, mapping group exponents in* $\mathbb{Z}_N$ *to a set of labels* $\mathcal{L}$. *Label* $\sigma(x)$ *for* $x \in \mathbb{Z}_N$ *corresponds to the group element* g^x.

$\mathcal{C}$ *initializes* $\mathcal{A}$ *with some set of labels* $\{\sigma(x_i)\}_i$. *It then implements the group operation oracle* $\mathcal{O}_G(\cdot, \cdot)$, *which on inputs* $\sigma_1, \sigma_2 \in [M]$ *does the following:*

- *If either of* σ_1 *or* σ_2 *is not in* $\mathcal{L}$, *return* $\perp$.
- *Otherwise, set* $x = \sigma^{-1}(\sigma_1)$ *and* $y = \sigma^{-1}(\sigma_2)$, *compute* $x + y \in \mathbb{Z}_N$, *and return* $\sigma(x + y)$.

$\mathcal{A}$ *is allowed at most* T *queries to the oracle, after which* $\mathcal{C}$ *outputs a bit indicating whether* $\mathcal{A}$ *was successful. We refer to the probability that this bit is 1 as* $\mathsf{Succ}_{\mathcal{C}}(\mathcal{A})$.

Remark 2. It will often be convenient to represent each query to $\mathcal{O}_G$ as a linear polynomial over the initial set of elements $\{x_i\}_i$ given to $\mathcal{A}$.

For an *indistinguishability* application, we define the *advantage* of attacker $\mathcal{A}$ as $\mathsf{Adv}_{\mathcal{C}}(\mathcal{A}) = 2|\mathsf{Succ}_{\mathcal{C}}(\mathcal{A}) - 1/2|$. For an *unpredictability* application, the advantage is defined as $\mathsf{Adv}_{\mathcal{C}}(\mathcal{A}) = \mathsf{Succ}_{\mathcal{C}}(\mathcal{A})$. An application with associated challenger $\mathcal{C}$ is (T, ϵ)-secure in the GGM is for every T-attacker $\mathcal{A}$, $\mathsf{Adv}_{\mathcal{C}}(\mathcal{A}) \leq \epsilon$.

Definition 3 (Auxiliary-Input Generic Group Model (AI-GGM)). *We now consider (S,T)-attackers $\mathcal{A} = (\mathcal{A}_1, \mathcal{A}_2)$. First $\sigma : [N] \rightarrow [M]$ is sampled. $\mathcal{A}_1$ receives σ as input and outputs an S-bit string* aux. *Then the challenger $\mathcal{C}$ operates as before, modeling interaction between $\mathcal{A}_2$ and $\mathcal{O}_G(\cdot, \cdot)$. Now $\mathcal{A}_2$ receives* aux *as input and is allowed T queries to the oracle. Success, advantage, and security are defined analogously.*

Definition 4 (Bit-Fixing Generic Group Model (BF-GGM)). *We now consider (S, T, P)-attackers $\mathcal{A} = (\mathcal{A}_1, \mathcal{A}_2)$. First $\sigma : [N] \rightarrow [M]$ is sampled. $\mathcal{A}_1$ receives σ as input and outputs an S-bit string* aux *along with a set $\mathcal{P} \subseteq \mathbb{Z}_N$ of size P. Then σ is uniformly re-sampled on all but the points $\mathcal{P}$ (conditioned on maintaining the same image), producing the injection σ'. We let $\text{im}(\mathcal{P})$ refer to the images under σ and σ' of the points in $\mathcal{P}$. Then the challenger $\mathcal{C}$ operates as before, modeling interaction between $\mathcal{A}_2$ and $\mathcal{O}_G(\cdot, \cdot)$, where $\mathcal{O}_G(\cdot, \cdot)$ uses σ' to answer queries. $\mathcal{A}_2$ receives* aux *as input and is allowed T queries to the oracle. Success, advantage, and security are defined analogously.*

Theorem 1 ([16]). *Let $N, M, P \in \mathbb{N}$, $N \geq 16$, and $\gamma > 0$. If an unpredictability application with challenger $\mathcal{C}$ that initializes $\mathcal{A}$ with T' group elements is $((S, T, P), \epsilon')$-secure in the BF-GGM for*

$$P \geq 18(S + \log(\gamma^{-1}))(T + T'),$$

then it is $((S, T, P), \epsilon)$-secure in the AI-GGM for $\epsilon \leq 2\epsilon' + \gamma$.

3   Lower Bounds for Random Generator Discrete Log and CDH

We proceed to give tight lower bounds (up to logarithmic factors) for r-DLog and r-CDH in the AI-GGM, making use of the following special case of a lemma due to Yun [45].

Lemma 1 (Search-by-Hyperplane-Queries [45] (SHQ)). *Consider drawing z_1, z_2 uniformly at random from $\mathbb{Z}_N$, and allowing an adversary $\mathcal{A}$ hyperplane queries of the form (a_1, a_2, b) where 1 is returned if $a_1 z_1 + a_2 z_2 = b$ and 0 otherwise. Then the probability that $\mathcal{A}$ outputs (z_1, z_2) after q hyperplane queries is at most q^2/N^2.*

Theorem 2. *The r-Dlog problem is $((S, T), \epsilon)$-secure in the AI-GGM for any prime $N \geq 16$ and*

$$\epsilon = \tilde{O}\left(\frac{T^2}{N} + \left(\frac{ST^2}{N}\right)^2\right).$$

Proof. In the r-Dlog game, the challenger $\mathcal{C}$ draws $x \leftarrow \mathbb{Z}_N^*, y \leftarrow \mathbb{Z}_N$ and initializes $\mathcal{A}$ with $(\sigma(1), \sigma(x), \sigma(xy))$. $\mathcal{A}$ is successful if it outputs y after at most T generic group queries. We show that r-Dlog is

$\left((S,T), O\left(\frac{T^2}{N} + \frac{T^2P^2 + T^3P}{N^2}\right)\right)$-secure in the BF-GGM. Then we can apply Theorem 1 with $\gamma = 1/N$ to get the result, noting that $T' = 3$ and $\log(1/\gamma) = \log(N)$, so $P = \widetilde{O}(ST)$.

$\mathcal{A} := \mathcal{A}_2$ takes as input the advice string aux generated by $\mathcal{A}_1$, makes T adaptive queries $\{c_1^{(t)}\sigma(x) + c_2^{(t)}\sigma(xy) + c_3^{(t)}\sigma(1)\}_{t \in [T]}$ to the generic group oracle and receives $\{\sigma(c_1^{(t)}x + c_2^{(t)}xy + c_3^{(t)})\}_{t \in [T]}$ in return. Let E be the event that there exists an $a \in \mathcal{P}$ and $t \in [T]$ such that $c_1^{(t)}x + c_2^{(t)}xy + c_3^{(t)} = a$ and $c_3^{(t)} \neq a$. Then

$$\Pr_{\sigma,x,y}\left[y \leftarrow \mathcal{A}^{\mathcal{O}_G}(\mathsf{aux})\right] \leq \Pr_{\sigma,x,y}\left[y \leftarrow \mathcal{A}^{\mathcal{O}_G}(\mathsf{aux}) \mid E\right] + \Pr_{\sigma,x,y}\left[y \leftarrow \mathcal{A}^{\mathcal{O}_G}(\mathsf{aux}) \mid \neg E\right].$$

We begin by analyzing the first probability in the sum. Condition on a particular image $\mathcal{L}$ of σ and a particular set of fixed points $\mathcal{P}$. The following holds for any such choice. We set up a reduction $\mathcal{B}$ which plays the SHQ game defined above and perfectly simulates the generic group game for $\mathcal{A}$. $\mathcal{B}$ has access to $\mathcal{L}, \mathcal{P}, im(\mathcal{P})$, and hyperplane query access to uniform values z_1, z_2 in $\mathbb{Z}_N$ which we implicitly set to be x, xy. We assume that $z_1 \neq 0$, which happens except with probability $1/N$. $\mathcal{B}$ operates as follows.

- Maintain a table mapping linear polynomials in $\mathbb{Z}_N[\mathbf{z_1}, \mathbf{z_2}]$ to $\mathcal{L}$. For each $a \in \mathcal{P}$, record the pair $(a, \sigma(a))$.
- Query the SHQ oracle on hyperplane $(1, 0, a)$ for each $a \in \mathcal{P}$. If any query returns 1, record the pair $(\mathbf{z_1}, \sigma(a))$, otherwise choose a uniform value r from all unused values in $\mathcal{L} \setminus im(\mathcal{P})$ and record $(\mathbf{z_1}, r)$. Do the same for $\mathbf{z_2}$. Next, store 1 along with its image. If $1 \in \mathcal{P}$ this is already done. If not, query $(1, 0, 1)$ to determine if $z_1 = 1$ and if so store 1 along with the image of $\mathbf{z_1}$. Do the same for $\mathbf{z_2}$. Otherwise, draw a uniform value r from all unused values in $\mathcal{L} \setminus im(\mathcal{P})$ and record $(1, r)$. Initialize $\mathcal{A}$ with the images of 1, $\mathbf{z_1}$, and $\mathbf{z_2}$.
- When $\mathcal{A}$ submits a query $c_1\mathbf{z_1} + c_2\mathbf{z_2} + c_3$, subtract each previously stored polynomial $Q(\mathbf{z_1}, \mathbf{z_2})$, resulting in some polynomial $k_1\mathbf{z_1} + k_2\mathbf{z_2} + k_3$. Query the SHQ oracle on $(k_1, k_2, -k_3)$. If 1 is returned, let s be the element stored along with $Q(\mathbf{z_1}, \mathbf{z_2})$, record $(c_1\mathbf{z_1} + c_2\mathbf{z_2} + c_3, s)$, and return s to $\mathcal{A}$. Otherwise, choose a uniform value r from all unused values in $\mathcal{L} \setminus im(\mathcal{P})$, record $(c_1\mathbf{z_1} + c_2\mathbf{z_2} + c_3, r)$ and return r.
- If E occurs, $\mathcal{B}$ will see a 1 returned by the SHQ oracle on a hyperplane query (k_1, k_2, k_3) for $k_3 \neq 0$, meaning at least one of $k_1, k_2 \neq 0$. Record this tuple. At the end of the interaction, $\mathcal{A}$ will return a $y \in \mathbb{Z}_N$. Now $\mathcal{B}$ outputs $(k_3(k_1 + k_2y)^{-1}, y)$.

Setting $z_1 = x$ and $z_2 = xy$, it is clear that $\mathcal{B}$ perfectly simulates the r-Dlog game for $\mathcal{A}$. If E occurs, we know that $k_3 = k_1x + k_2xy = x(k_1 + k_2y)$, and $k_3 \neq 0$, so $k_1 + k_2y \neq 0$. Thus if $\mathcal{A}$ is successful and returns y, $\mathcal{B}$ successfully computes $x = k_3(k_1 + k_2y)^{-1}$. Applying Lemma 1, and noting that $\mathcal{B}$ makes less than $2(P + 1) + T(P + T) = O(TP + T^2)$ queries, we get that

$$\Pr_{\sigma,x,y} [y \leftarrow \mathcal{A}^{\mathcal{O}_G}(\mathsf{aux}) \mid E] = O\left(\frac{T^2P^2 + T^3P + T^4}{N^2}\right).$$

To analyze the second probability, we move to a hybrid game in the BF-GGM where x and y are set to be formal variables $\mathbf{x}$ and $\mathbf{y}$ at the beginning of the game. The challenger implements group operations over $\mathbb{Z}_N[\mathbf{x}, \mathbf{y}]$, initializing its table with the points in $(a, \sigma(a))$ for all $a \in \mathcal{P}$. Every time $\mathcal{A}$ queries for a new polynomial, $\mathcal{C}$ chooses a uniform element in $\mathcal{L} \setminus im(\mathcal{P})$ among those unused so far. When $\mathcal{A}$ outputs a guess for y at the end of the game, the true value is chosen uniformly at random, so $\mathcal{A}$ wins with probability $1/N$. Given that E does not occur, $\mathcal{A}$'s probability of distinguishing these two games is bounded by the probability that in the original game, two of its T queries are different polynomials over $\mathbf{x}$ and $\mathbf{y}$ but evaluate to the same element, or there exists some query $c_1^{(j)}\mathbf{x} + c_2^{(j)}\mathbf{xy} + c_3^{(j)}$ such that $c_1^{(j)}x + c_2^{(j)}xy = 0$ and at least one of $c_1^{(j)}, c_2^{(j)} \neq 0$. So there are $O(T^2)$ possible equations that could be satisfied and by Schwartz-Zippel, each occurs with probability $O(1/N)$ over the random choice of x and y. Thus by a union bound, $\mathcal{A}$'s probability of distinguishing is $O(T^2/N)$.

Combining, we have that $\mathcal{A}$'s probability of success is

$$O\left(\frac{T^2P^2 + T^3P + T^4}{N^2}\right) + O\left(\frac{T^2}{N}\right) + O\left(\frac{1}{N}\right) = O\left(\frac{T^2}{N} + \frac{T^2P^2 + T^3P}{N^2}\right).$$

$\square$

In the full version [3], we use similar techniques to show the same bound for r-CDH, which again is tight.

Theorem 3. *The r-CDH problem is $((S,T), \epsilon)$-secure in the AI-GGM for any prime $N \geq 16$ and*

$$\epsilon = \tilde{O}\left(\frac{T^2}{N} + \left(\frac{ST^2}{N}\right)^2\right).$$

4 Non-malleable Point Obfuscation

In this section, we construct a non-malleable point obfuscator secure against *polynomial mauling attacks*, which were first considered by Komargodski and Yogev [31]. We first briefly review relevant definitions.

4.1 Definitions

Denote by $\mathcal{I}_x$ the function that returns 1 on input x and 0 otherwise.

Definition 5. *(Point Obfuscation). A point obfuscator for a domain $\{\mathcal{X}_\lambda\}_\lambda$ of inputs is a PPT Obf that takes as input a point $x \in \mathcal{X}_\lambda$ and outputs a circuit such that the following hold.*

- **Functionality Preservation:** *For all $\lambda \in \mathbb{N}$, there exists a negligible function μ such that for all $x \in \mathcal{X}_\lambda$,*

$$\Pr[\mathsf{Obf}(x) \equiv \mathcal{I}_x] = 1 - \mu(\lambda).$$

- **Virtual Black Box (VBB) Security:** *For all PPT $\mathcal{A}$ and any polynomial function p, there exists a PPT $\mathcal{S}$ such that for all $x \in \mathcal{X}_\lambda$ and any predicate $P : \mathcal{X}_\lambda \to \{0,1\}$, and all large enough λ,*

$$\left| \Pr[\mathcal{A}(\mathsf{Obf}(x)) = P(x)] - \Pr[\mathcal{S}^{\mathcal{I}_x}(1^\lambda) = P(x))] \right| \leq \frac{1}{p(\lambda)}.$$

We give another property of point obfuscators first considered in [13] and re-defined in [7].

Definition 6 (Distributional Indistinguishability). *Let $\{\mathcal{X}_\lambda\}_\lambda$ be a family of domains. Then a point obfuscator Obf for $\{\mathcal{X}_\lambda\}_\lambda$ satisfies Distributional Indistinguishability if for all PPT $\mathcal{A}$ and well-spread ensembles of distributions $\{\mathcal{D}_\lambda\}_\lambda$ over $\{\mathcal{X}_\lambda\}_\lambda$, there exists a negligble function $\mu(\lambda)$ such that*

$$|\Pr[\mathcal{A}(\mathsf{Obf}(x)) = 1] - \Pr[\mathcal{A}(\mathsf{Obf}(u)) = 1]| = \mu(\lambda),$$

where $x \leftarrow \mathcal{D}_\lambda$ and u is drawn from the uniform distribution over $\mathcal{X}_\lambda$.

[7,13] show that Distributional Indistiguishability is equivalent to VBB security for point obfuscators. Now we give the [31] definition of non-malleability. This definition involves the notion of a Verifier algorithm, which simply checks that the potentially mauled obfuscation is valid.

Definition 7. *(Verifier) A PPT $\mathcal{V}$ for a point obfuscator Obf for an ensemble of domains $\{\mathcal{X}_\lambda\}_\lambda$ is called a Verifier if for all $\lambda \in \mathbb{N}$ and $x \in \mathcal{X}_\lambda$, it holds that $\Pr[\mathcal{V}(\mathsf{Obf}(x)) = 1] = 1$, where the probability is taken over the randomness of $\mathcal{V}$ and Obf.*

Definition 8. *(Non-malleable Point Function Obfuscation). Let Obf be a point function obfuscator for an ensemble of domains $\{\mathcal{X}_\lambda\}_\lambda$ with an associated verifier $\mathcal{V}$. Let $\{\mathcal{F}_\lambda\}_\lambda = \{f : \mathcal{X}_\lambda \to \mathcal{X}_\lambda\}_\lambda$ be an ensemble of families of functions, and let $\{\mathcal{D}_\lambda\}_\lambda$ be an ensemble of distributions over $\mathcal{X}_\lambda$. Then Obf is a non-malleable point obfuscator for $\mathcal{F}$ and $\mathcal{D}$ if for any PPT $\mathcal{A}$, there exists a negligible function μ such that for any $\lambda \in \mathbb{N}$,*

$$\Pr[\mathcal{V}(C) = 1, f \in \mathcal{F}_\lambda, C \equiv \mathcal{I}_{f(x)} \mid x \leftarrow \mathcal{D}_\lambda, (C, f) \leftarrow \mathcal{A}(\mathsf{Obf}(x))] \leq \mu(\lambda).$$

In the following, we rely on the existence of a *pseudo-deterministic* GroupGen algorithm that may use randomness, but on input the security parameter 1^λ outputs a *unique* description of a group $\mathbb{G}_\lambda$ with a unique generator g and prime order $p(\lambda) \in [2^{\lambda-1}, 2^\lambda]$. As discussed in the introduction, this would involve psuedo-deterministic generation of large primes. This is not provably efficient, but we can rely for example on Cramer's conjecture to argue efficiency. See [26] for further discussion on psuedo-deterministic algorithms, including group generator generation.

4.2 Assumptions

Assumption 1. *Let* $\mathsf{GroupGen}(1^\lambda) = (\mathbb{G}_\lambda, g, p(\lambda))$, *where* $2^{\lambda-1} < p(\lambda) < 2^\lambda$. *Let* $\{\mathcal{D}_\lambda\}$ *be a family of well-spread distributions where the domain of* $\mathcal{D}_\lambda$ *is* $\mathbb{Z}_{p(\lambda)}$. *Then for any* $n = poly(\lambda)$, *for any PPT* $\mathcal{A}$,

$$\left| \Pr[\mathcal{A}(\{k_i, g^{k_i x + x^i}\}_{i \in [2,\dots,n]}) = 1] - \Pr[\mathcal{A}(\{k_i, g^{k_i r + r^i}\}_{i \in [2,\dots,n]}) = 1] \right| = \mathsf{negl}(\lambda),$$

where $x \leftarrow \mathcal{D}_\lambda$, $r \leftarrow \mathbb{Z}_{p(\lambda)}$, *and* $k_i \leftarrow \mathbb{Z}_{p(\lambda)}$.

Assumption 2. *Let* $\mathsf{GroupGen}(1^\lambda) = (\mathbb{G}_\lambda, g, p(\lambda))$, *where* $2^{\lambda-1} < p(\lambda) < 2^\lambda$. *Let* $\{\mathcal{D}_\lambda\}$ *be a family of well-spread distributions where the domain of* $\mathcal{D}_\lambda$ *is* $\mathbb{Z}_{p(\lambda)}$. *Then for any* $n = poly(\lambda)$, *for any PPT* $\mathcal{A}$ *(which outputs an element of* $\mathbb{G}_\lambda$*),*

$$\Pr[g^x = \mathcal{A}(\{k_i, g^{k_i x + x^i}\}_{i \in [2,\dots,n]})] = \mathsf{negl}(\lambda),$$

where $x \leftarrow \mathcal{D}_\lambda$ *and* $k_i \leftarrow \mathbb{Z}_{p(\lambda)}$.

We prove the following in the full version [3].

Lemma 2. *Assumption 1 implies Assumption 2.*

4.3 The Obfuscator

Our obfuscation consists of three scalars and three group elements. We remark that the first group element is sufficient for our proof on non-malleability, but that we include the next two to obtain functionality preservation.

- $\mathsf{Obf}(1^\lambda, x)$: Compute $\mathsf{GroupGen}(1^\lambda) = (\mathbb{G}_\lambda, g, p(\lambda))$. Draw $a, b, c \leftarrow \mathbb{Z}_{p(\lambda)}$ and output
$$a, b, c, g^{ax + x^2 + x^3 + x^4 + x^5}, g^{bx + x^6}, g^{cx + x^7}.$$

- $\mathsf{Eval}(1^\lambda, (a, b, c, h_a, h_b, h_c), x)$: Compute $\mathsf{GroupGen}(1^\lambda) = (\mathbb{G}_\lambda, g, p(\lambda))$. Accept if and only if
$$h_a = g^{ax + x^2 + x^3 + x^4 + x^5}, \ h_b = g^{bx + x^6}, \ h_c = g^{cx + x^7}.$$

Theorem 4. *The above point obfuscator satisfies functionality preservation.*

Proof. Fix a point $x \in \mathbb{Z}_{p(\lambda)}$. We show the probability that there exists a $y \neq x$ such that $\mathsf{Eval}(1^\lambda, \mathsf{Obf}(1^\lambda, x), y)$ accepts is at most $4/p(\lambda)^2$. Union bounding over all x completes the proof.

The randomness in Obf consists of the elements a, b, c. Fix just a for now and let $t = ax + x^2 + x^3 + x^4 + x^5$. Then any y which causes Eval to accept satisfies $ay + y^2 + y^3 + y^4 + y^5 = t$. This leaves four possible $y \neq x$. For each such y, we write $P(\mathbf{b}) = (x^6 - y^6) + (x - y)\mathbf{b}$ and $Q(\mathbf{c}) = (x^7 - y^7) + (x - y)\mathbf{c}$ which are linear polynomials over $\mathbf{b}$ and $\mathbf{c}$ respectively with non-zero linear coefficient. Then y only causes Eval to accept if $P(b) = 0$ and $P(c) = 0$. But these occur simultaneously with probability $1/p(\lambda)^2$ over the uniform randomness of b, c. So by a union bound, there exists a $y \neq x$ such that $\mathsf{Eval}(1^\lambda, \mathsf{Obf}(1^\lambda, x), y)$ accepts with probability at most $4/p(\lambda)^2$. $\square$

Theorem 5. *Under Assumption 1, the above point obfuscator satisfies Virtual Black Box Security.*

Proof. The obfuscator satisfies distributional indistinguishability, which follows directly from Assumption 1 with $n = 7$. A reduction simply receives $\{k_i, h_i\}_{i \in [2,...,7]}$ and forms the obfuscation $(\sum_{i=2}^{5} k_i, k_6, k_7, \prod_{i=2}^{5} h_i, h_6, h_7)$. As mentioned earlier, this is equivalent to VBB security.   □

Theorem 6. *Let $\{\mathcal{D}_\lambda\}$ be a well-spread distribution ensemble with domain $\{\mathbb{Z}_{p(\lambda)}\}_\lambda$. Let $\mathcal{F}_{poly} = \{f_\lambda : \mathbb{Z}_{p(\lambda)} \to \mathbb{Z}_{p(\lambda)}\}_\lambda$ be the ensemble of functions where f_λ is the set of non-constant, non-identity polynomials [13] in $\mathbb{Z}_{p(\lambda)}[x]$ with $\mathsf{poly}(\lambda)$ degree. Then under Assumption 1, the above obfuscator is non-malleable for $\mathcal{F}_{poly}$ and distribution ensemble $\{\mathcal{D}_\lambda\}$.*

Proof. First, we fix the verifier to check that the Eval circuit is using the g output by GroupGen(1^λ). Now we show that any mauling adversary $\mathcal{A}$ can be used to break Assumption 2, which as seen above follows from Assumption 1.

We first handle the case where $\mathcal{A}$ outputs an f of degree at least 2. Let $m \geq 2$ be the degree of $\mathcal{A}$'s polynomial. We define the following reduction $\mathcal{B}$.

- Receive $\{k_i, h_i\}_{i \in [2,...,7m]} := \{k_i, g^{k_i x + x^i}\}_{i \in [2,...,7m]}$ from the Assumption 2 challenger, where $x \leftarrow \mathcal{D}_\lambda$.
- Send $(\sum_{i=2}^{5} k_i, k_6, k_7, \prod_{i=2}^{5} h_i, h_6, h_7)$ to $\mathcal{A}$, which returns $(f, a, b, c, j_a, j_b, j_c)$ where $a, b, c \in \mathbb{Z}_{p(\lambda)}$ and j_a, j_b, j_c are group elements.
- Compute $cf(x) + f(x)^7 = \ell_0 + \ell_1 x + \cdots + \ell_{7m} x^{7m}$.
- Return $(j_c / (g^{\ell_0} \prod_{i=2}^{7m} (h_i^{\ell_i})))^{1/(\ell_1 - \sum_{i=2}^{7m} k_i \ell_i)}$.

$\mathcal{B}$ perfectly simulates the obfuscation for $x \leftarrow \mathcal{D}_\lambda$ for $\mathcal{A}$, which is guaranteed to return a valid obfuscation of $f(x)$ with $1/\mathsf{poly}(\lambda)$ probability. In this case, $f_c = g^{\ell_0 + \ell_1 x + \cdots + \ell_{7m} x^{7m}}$. Then $\mathcal{B}$ successfully computes g^x unless $\ell_1 - \sum_{i=2}^{7m} k_i \ell_i = 0$. We know that $\ell_{7m} \neq 0$ and that k_{7m} is uniformly random and independent of $\mathcal{A}$'s view, so this occurs with probability at most $1/p(\lambda) = \mathsf{negl}(\lambda)$. Thus, $\mathcal{B}$ breaks Assumption 2 with $1/\mathsf{poly}(\lambda)$ probability.

In the case that f is linear, we set up the same reduction $\mathcal{B}$, except for the last two steps.

- Compute $af(x) + f(x)^2 + f(x)^3 + f(x)^4 + f(x)^5 = \ell_0 + \ell_1 x + \cdots + \ell_5 x^5$.
- Return $(j_a / (g^{\ell_0} \prod_{i=2}^{5} (h_i^{\ell_i})))^{1/(\ell_1 - \sum_{i=2}^{5} k_i \ell_i)}$.

Like before, it suffices to argue that $\ell_1 - \sum_{i=2}^{5} k_i \ell_i \neq 0$ except with negligible probability. In this case, the adversary receives $z := k_2 + k_3 + k_4 + k_5$. Thus letting $k_5 = z - k_2 - k_3 - k_4$, there are 3 free variables k_2, k_3, k_4 in $\mathcal{A}$'s view. We can then re-write $\ell_1 - \sum_{i=2}^{5} k_i \ell_i \neq 0$ as

$$\ell_1 - \ell_5 z + (\ell_5 - \ell_2) k_2 + (\ell_5 - \ell_3) k_3 + (\ell_5 - \ell_4) k_4.$$

---

[13] Note that constant and identity polynomials correspond to "trivial" mauling attacks that cannot be prevented. A constant polynomial corresponds to picking an unrelated y and obfuscating y, while the identity polynomial corresponds to doing nothing.

So in order for this to evaluate to 0 with non-negligible probability, each of the coefficients on k_2, k_3, k_4 must be 0. Let $f(x) = rx + s$. Then writing out what the ℓ_i are, we see that the following must hold.

$$r^5 = 5r^4s + r^4 = 10r^3s^2 + 4r^3s + r^3 = 10r^2s^3 + 6r^2s^2 + 3r^2s + r^2$$

It is easily verified that the only solutions to the above system are when $r = 0$ or $(r = 1, s = 0)$. These correspond to when f is constant or the identity, so we can conclude that if $\mathcal{A}$ succeeds in breaking non-malleability, $\mathcal{B}$ breaks Assumption 2 with $1/\mathsf{poly}(\lambda)$ probability. $\qquad\qquad\square$

5   Justifying Assumptions in the Generic Group Model

We will need some additional background from [16], plus a couple of new simple lemmas. Note that while we make use of techniques from [16] that establish theorems relating the AI-GGM and BF-GGM, we never technically operate in the BF-GGM. We need a more fine-grained approach, starting in the plain GGM and modifying the labeling function and challenger's game incrementally.

5.1   Background

Definition 9 ([16]). *An (N, M)-injection source Σ is a random variable that takes on as value function tables corresponding to injections $\sigma : [N] \to [M]$. An (N, M)-injection source Σ is called $(P, \mathcal{L}, 1 - \delta)$-dense for $\mathcal{L} \subseteq [M]$ if it is fixed on at most P coordinates and if for every subset I of non-fixed coordinates,*

$$H_\infty(\Sigma_I) \geq (1 - \delta) \log \left(\frac{(N - P)!}{(N - P - |I|)!} \right),$$

where Σ_I is the random variable Σ restricted to the coordinates in I. When $\delta = 0$, the source is called $(P, \mathcal{L})$-fixed.

Remark 3. We denote by $\mathcal{A}^\Sigma$ an algorithm that has oracle access to an injection σ drawn from the source Σ. This means that $\mathcal{A}$ can perform forward queries where on input x the oracle returns $\sigma(x)$ or backward queries where on input x the oracle returns $\sigma^{-1}(x)$.

Lemma 3 ([16]). *Let Σ be a uniform (N, M)-injection source and $f : [M]^{[N]} \to \{0, 1\}^S$ a potentially randomized function. Let $\Sigma_{f,x,\mathcal{L}}$ be the random variable corresponding to the distribution of Σ conditioned on $f(\Sigma) = x$ and $\mathrm{im}(\Sigma) = \mathcal{L}$. Then for any $\gamma > 0, P \in \mathbb{N}$, there exists a family $\{Y_{x,\mathcal{L}}\}_{x,\mathcal{L}}$, indexed by values $x \in \{0, 1\}^S$ and size-N subsets $\mathcal{L}$ of $[M]$, of convex combinations $Y_{x,\mathcal{L}}$ of $(P, \mathcal{L}, 1 - \frac{S + \log(1/\gamma)}{P \log(N/e)})$-dense sources, such that $\Sigma_{f,x,\mathcal{L}}$ is γ-close to $Y_{x,\mathcal{L}}$. Furthermore, replacing each $Y_{x,\mathcal{L}}$ with its corresponding convex combination $Z_{x,\mathcal{L}}$ of $(P, \mathcal{L})$-fixed sources, we have that for any distinguisher $\mathcal{D}$ taking an S-bit input and making at most T queries to its injection oracle,*

$$|\Pr[\mathcal{D}^\Sigma(f(\Sigma)) = 1] - \Pr[\mathcal{D}^{Z_{f(\Sigma), \mathrm{im}(\Sigma)}}(f(\Sigma)) = 1]| \leq \frac{2(S + \log 1/\gamma) \cdot T}{P} + \gamma.$$

The above is actually slightly modified from the statement in [16], with the only difference being that we allow f to be randomized. The only place in their proof that makes use of f being deterministic is Claim 19, essentially that (where everything is conditioned on some range $\mathcal{L}$), $E_x[H_\infty(\Sigma|f(\Sigma) = x)] \geq \log(N!) - S$. Their proof of this claim can easily be adapted to allow randomized f. Say that f uses k uniformly random bits. Then define the deterministic function $f' : \{0,1\}^k \times [N]^{[N]} \to \{0,1\}^S$ that runs f using its first input as the randomness. Let K be the random variable corresponding to drawing a uniformly random string in $\{0,1\}^k$. Now by averaging, we have that for any x, $H_\infty(\Sigma|X = x) \geq H_\infty((K,\Sigma)|X = x) - k$. Then, following the proof in [16],

$$E_x[H_\infty(\Sigma|f(\Sigma) = x)] \geq E_x[H_\infty((K,\Sigma)|f'(K,\Sigma) = x)] - k$$
$$= E_x[H((K,\Sigma)|f'(K,\Sigma) = x)] - k \geq \log(N!) + k - S - k = \log(N!) - S,$$

where H is Shannon entropy, and the equality is due to the fact that conditioned on x, (K, Σ) is uniform over all values (r, σ) such that $f'(r, \sigma) = x$.

Lemma 4 ([16]). *For any $(P, N, 1 - \delta)$-dense (N, N)-injection (bijection) source Y and its corresponding (P, N)-fixed source Z, it holds that for any (adaptive) distinguisher $\mathcal{D}$ that makes at most T queries to its oracle,*

$$|\Pr[\mathcal{D}^Y = 1] - \Pr[\mathcal{D}^Z = 1]| \leq T\delta \log N.$$

Now we give two additional lemmas, useful for proving Theorem 7.

Lemma 5. *Let Σ be a uniform (N, N)-injection (bijection) source with $\log(N) = \Theta(\lambda)$ and $f : [N]^{[N]} \to \{0,1\}^S$ a potentially randomized function. Let Σ' be the random variable on σ' that results from drawing $\sigma \leftarrow \Sigma$, $x \leftarrow f(\sigma)$, and then $\sigma' \leftarrow \Sigma_{f,x,[N]}$ defined in Lemma 3. Say that for all σ, $H_\infty(X|\Sigma = \sigma) = \omega(\log(\lambda))$. Then*

$$E_{\Sigma'}[\max_x\{\Pr[X = x|\Sigma' = \sigma]\}] = \mathsf{negl}(\lambda).$$

Proof. With two applications of Bayes' Theorem, we see that for any $x \in \{0,1\}^S$

$$\Pr[X = x|\Sigma' = \sigma] = \frac{\Pr[\Sigma' = \sigma|X = x]\Pr[X = x]}{\Pr[\Sigma' = \sigma]} = \frac{\Pr[\Sigma = \sigma|X = x]\Pr[X = x]}{Pr[\Sigma' = \sigma]}$$

$$= \frac{\left(\frac{\Pr[X=x|\Sigma=\sigma]\Pr[\Sigma=\sigma]}{\Pr[X=x]}\right)\Pr[X = x]}{\Pr[\Sigma' = \sigma]} = \Pr[X = x|\Sigma = \sigma]\left(\frac{\Pr[\Sigma = \sigma]}{\Pr[\Sigma' = \sigma]}\right).$$

So plugging in,

$$E_{\Sigma'}[\max_x\{\Pr[X = x|\Sigma' = \sigma]\}] = \sum_\sigma \max_x\{\Pr[X = x|\Sigma' = \sigma]\}\Pr[\Sigma' = \sigma]$$

$$= \sum_\sigma \max_x\{\Pr[X = x|\Sigma = \sigma]\Pr[\Sigma = \sigma]\} \leq \max_{x,\sigma}\{\Pr[X = x|\Sigma = \sigma]\} = \mathsf{negl}(\lambda).$$

$\square$

Lemma 6. *Consider n events $X_1, \ldots, X_n$ such that each event occurs with probability at least α, where $\alpha > 2/n$. Then for a uniformly random $i, j \leftarrow [n]$, $\Pr[X_i \wedge X_j] \geq \frac{\alpha^2}{4}$.*

The proof can be found in the full version [3].

5.2 Proofs

Theorem 7. *Assumption 1 (Sect. 4) holds in the Generic Group Model.*

Proof. We define the following hybrid games.

- **Hybrid 0.** The Assumption 1 distinguishing game for generic adversary $\mathcal{A}$.
  Let $\mathsf{GroupGen}(1^\lambda) = (\mathbb{G}_\lambda, g, p(\lambda))$, where $2^{\lambda-1} < p(\lambda) < 2^\lambda$. Let $p := p(\lambda)$.
  Sample a uniformly random injection $\sigma : [p] \to [p']$ for an arbitrary $p' > p$.
  Let $S : [p']^{[p]} \to \mathbb{Z}_p$ be a possibly inefficient randomized algorithm such that $H_\infty(S(\sigma)|\sigma) = \omega(\log(\lambda))$. Sample $x \leftarrow S(\sigma)$.
  The challenger $\mathcal{C}$ receives as input $(\mathbb{G}_\lambda, g, p, \sigma, x)$, chooses $b \leftarrow \{0,1\}, r, k_i \leftarrow \mathbb{Z}_p$ for $i \in [2, \ldots, n]$, and initializes the adversary $\mathcal{A}$ with $\{k_i, \sigma(b(k_i x + x^i) + (1-b)(k_i r + r^i))\}_{i \in [2, \ldots n]}$. The challenger $\mathcal{C}$ proceeds to implement the generic group oracle for $\mathcal{A}$, after which $\mathcal{A}$ outputs a guess $b' \in \{0,1\}$. $\mathcal{A}$ wins if $b' = b$.
- **Hybrid 1.** In this hybrid, we switch to a "bit-fixing" labeling σ'.
  Let $\mathsf{GroupGen}(1^\lambda) = (\mathbb{G}_\lambda, g, p(\lambda))$, where $2^{\lambda-1} < p(\lambda) < 2^\lambda$. Let $p := p(\lambda)$.
  Sample a uniformly random injection $\sigma : [p] \to [p']$ for an arbitrary $p' > p$.
  Let $S : [p']^{[p]} \to \mathbb{Z}_p$ be a possibly inefficient randomized algorithm such that $H_\infty(S(\sigma)|\sigma) = \omega(\log(\lambda))$. Sample $x \leftarrow S(\sigma)$.
  Let $Z_{x,im(\sigma)}$ be the family defined as in Lemma 3 (parameterized by some $P \in \mathbb{N}$ and $\gamma := 1/2^\lambda$). Sample $\sigma' \leftarrow Z_{x,im(\sigma)}$
  The challenger $\mathcal{C}$ receives as input $(\mathbb{G}_\lambda, g, p, \sigma', x)$, chooses $b \leftarrow \{0,1\}, r, k_i \leftarrow \mathbb{Z}_p$ for $i \in [2, \ldots, n]$, and initializes the adversary $\mathcal{A}$ with $\{k_i, \sigma'(b(k_i x + x^i) + (1-b)(k_i r + r^i))\}_{i \in [2, \ldots n]}$. The challenger $\mathcal{C}$ proceeds to implement the generic group oracle for $\mathcal{A}$, after which $\mathcal{A}$ outputs a guess $b' \in \{0,1\}$. $\mathcal{A}$ wins if $b' = b$.

Now we assume the existence of an adversary $\mathcal{A}$ that makes $T(\lambda) = \mathsf{poly}(\lambda)$ queries and attains non-negligible advantage $\epsilon(\lambda)$ in **Hybrid 0**. Let $q(\lambda) = \mathsf{poly}(\lambda)$ be such that $q(\lambda) > 1/\epsilon(\lambda)$ for infinitely many λ. Let $T := T(\lambda)$ and $q := q(\lambda)$. Set $P = 30\lambda T^4 q = \mathsf{poly}(\lambda)$.

Claim. $\mathcal{A}$ attains advantage at least $1/2q$ in **Hybrid 1**.

Consider the following distinguisher $\mathcal{D}(x)$, which interacts with an oracle injection source mapping $[p] \to [p']$, and receives as input $x \leftarrow S(\sigma)$. $\mathcal{D}$ simulates the interaction between $\mathcal{C}$ and $\mathcal{A}$ described in **Hybrid 0** and outputs a bit indicating whether $\mathcal{A}$ was successful or not. If the injection source that $\mathcal{D}$ is interacting with is σ, then the simulation is exactly **Hybrid 0**. If it is $Z_{x,im(\sigma)}$, then the simulation is exactly **Hybrid 1**.

Applying Lemma 3 with the sampler $x \leftarrow S(\sigma)$ as the function f, we have that the success probability of $\mathcal{A}$ in **Hybrid 1** must be at least

$$\epsilon(\lambda) - \frac{2T(\log p + \log(1/\gamma))}{P} - \gamma \geq \frac{1}{q} - \frac{4\lambda T}{30\lambda T^4 q} - \frac{1}{2^\lambda} \geq \frac{1}{2q}.$$

We show that $\mathcal{A}$ obtaining this advantage leads to a contradiction. Condition on $im(\sigma) = \mathcal{L}$ for some $\mathcal{L}$ where $\mathcal{A}$ obtains at least advantage $1/2q$. Here Σ is defined as in Lemma 3, except $[M]$ is fixed to be $\mathcal{L}$, resulting in a bijection source. We drop subscripts from the associated distributions, so $Y_x := Y_{x,\mathcal{L}}$, $Z_x := Z_{x,\mathcal{L}}$, and $\Sigma_x := \Sigma_{S,x,\mathcal{L}}$. The distribution Z_x is a convex combination of bit-fixing distributions $\mathcal{B}_x^{(j)}$ with associated fixed points $\mathcal{P}_x^{(j)}$. Let this convex combination be $\mathcal{J}_x$. So to draw σ' from Z_x, we draw $j \leftarrow \mathcal{J}_x$, then $\sigma' \leftarrow \mathcal{B}_x^{(j)}$.

Now we analyze the adversary's generic group oracle queries. Any query $\mathcal{A}$ makes can be viewed as a linear polynomial over its challenge elements

$$\ell_1 + \sum_{i=2}^{n} \ell_i (b(k_i x + x^i) + (1-b)(k_i r + r^i)),$$

specified by coefficients $[\ell_1, ..., \ell_n]$. We split these queries into two parts based on whether the linear polynomial is constant or non-constant over the challenge elements (whether there is some $i \in [2, ..., n]$ such that $\ell_i \neq 0$). We will consider each initial handle that $\mathcal{A}$ receives as a non-constant query where $\ell_i = 1$ for some i and $\ell_j = 0$ for $j \neq i$. Assume without loss of generality that all of $\mathcal{A}$'s queries are distinct linear combinations.

Note that constant queries are identically distributed in the $b = 0$ and $b = 1$ cases. Let $\mathcal{T}_c$ denote the set of constants that are queried by $\mathcal{A}$ throughout its interaction. Then observe that if, for both settings of b, all of $\mathcal{A}$'s non-constant queries result in distinct group elements that each lie outside of the set $\mathcal{P}_x^{(j)} \cup \mathcal{T}_c$, the oracle responses are identically distributed in both cases. Now, for any T-query adversary that at some point queries two distinct non-constant linear polynomials that evaluate to the same point, we can define a T^2-query adversary that at some point queries a non-constant linear polynomial that evaluates to zero. Redefine $\mathcal{A}$ to be this latter adversary. Thus if $\mathcal{A}$ distinguishes, it must at some point form a non-constant query that evaluates to a value in $\mathcal{P}_x^{(j)} \cup \mathcal{T}_c \cup \{0\}$.

For a given query t, let $\mathcal{T}_c^{(t)}$ denote the set of constants among the first t queries made by $\mathcal{A}$. There must exist some query t such that both of the following hold with probability $1/(2qT^2)$.

- t is non-constant and evaluates to an element in $\mathcal{P}_x^{(j)} \cup \mathcal{T}_c^{(t)} \cup \{0\}$ OR t is a constant c and there exists an earlier non-constant query t' such that query t' evaluates to c
- all previous non-constant queries (except perhaps t') evaluate to an element outside of $\mathcal{P}_x^{(j)} \cup \mathcal{T}_c^{(t)} \cup \{0\}$

Otherwise, by a union bound, $\mathcal{A}$ could not obtain distinguishing success $1/(2q)$. Note that every non-constant query prior to t except perhaps t' is answered with a uniformly random value in $\mathcal{L} \setminus im(\mathcal{P}_x^{(j)} \cup \mathcal{T}_c^{(t)} \cup \{0\})$. Since $|\mathcal{P}_x^{(j)} \cup \mathcal{T}_c^{(t)} \cup \{0\}| = \mathsf{poly}(\lambda)$, we can imagine instead drawing each response uniformly from $\mathcal{L}$, which by a union bound will change $\mathcal{A}$'s view with negligible probability. Then $\mathcal{A}$ can simulate these answers itself with uniform randomness, with a negligible difference in success probability.

Now we are left with an adversary $\mathcal{A}$ that takes as input $\{k_i\} := \{k_i\}_{i \in [2,...,n]}$, makes at most T^2 queries to σ', and outputs a set of coefficients $[\ell_1, ..., \ell_n]$ (representing the non-constant query t or t'). Define $\mathcal{P}'^{(j)}_x := \mathcal{P}_x^{(j)} \cup \mathcal{T}_c^{(t)} \cup \{0\}$.

Now we break up the analysis into whether $b = 0$ or $b = 1$. If $b = 0$, we are guaranteed that with probability $1/(2qT^2) - \mathsf{negl}(\lambda) = 1/\mathsf{poly}(\lambda)$ over all randomness in the game setup, $\{k_i\}$, and $\mathcal{A}$, the following holds.

$$\ell_1 + \sum_{i=2}^{n} \ell_i(k_i r + r^i) \in \mathcal{P}'^{(j)}_x$$

But note that r is drawn uniformly at random from a set of size p, independently of $\mathcal{A}$'s view. Thus by Schwartz-Zippel and a union bound, the above holds with probability at most $(T^2 + P + 1)n/p = \mathsf{negl}(\lambda)$.

Now let $b = 1$. We are guaranteed that with probability $1/(2qT^2) - \mathsf{negl}(\lambda)$ over all randomness in the game setup, $\{k_i\}$, and $\mathcal{A}$, the following holds:

$$\ell_1 + \sum_{i=2}^{n} \ell_i(k_i x + x^i) \in \mathcal{P}'^{(j)}_x.$$

Redefine $\mathcal{A}$ to output the above polynomial $Q(x) \in \mathbb{Z}_p[x]$ on input $\{k_i\}$. Now accounting for all randomness during the course of the game, we have that

$$\Pr_{\substack{\sigma \leftarrow \Sigma, x \leftarrow S(\sigma), j \leftarrow \mathcal{J}_x, \\ \sigma' \leftarrow \mathcal{B}_x^{(j)}, \{k_i\} \leftarrow \mathbb{Z}_p^{n-1}, \mathcal{A}}} [Q(x) \in \mathcal{P}'^{(j)}_x : Q \leftarrow \mathcal{A}^{\sigma'}(\{k_i\})] = \frac{1}{2qT^2} - \mathsf{negl}(\lambda).$$

Now we switch the distribution on σ' from $Z = \{Z_x\}_x$ to $Y = \{Y_x\}_x$. We can still represent Y_x in the same way as Z_x except the $\mathcal{B}_x^{(j)}$'s are replaced by $(P, 1 - \delta)$-dense sources $\mathcal{D}_x^{(j)}$. Referring to the Lemma 3 statement, we have that

$$\delta \leq \frac{2\lambda + \log 1/\gamma}{P \log(p/e)} \leq \frac{1}{10T^4 q \log(p/e)}.$$

Now assume towards contradiction that this switch in distribution causes the adversary's success to become at most $1/(4qT^2)$. Then there must exist some fixed choice of σ, x and j such that $\mathcal{A}$'s difference in success over σ' and its input is at least $1/(4qT^2) - \mathsf{negl}(\lambda)$. So we have

$$\Pr_{\sigma' \leftarrow \mathcal{B}_x^{(j)}, \{k_i\} \leftarrow \mathbb{Z}_p^{n-1}, \mathcal{A}} [Q(x) \in \mathcal{P}'^{(j)}_x : Q \leftarrow \mathcal{A}^{\sigma'}(\{k_i\})] -$$

$$\Pr_{\sigma' \leftarrow \mathcal{D}_x^{(j)}, \{k_i\} \leftarrow \mathbb{Z}_p^{n-1}, \mathcal{A}} [Q(x) \in \mathcal{P}'^{(j)}_x : Q \leftarrow \mathcal{A}^{\sigma'}(\{k_i\})] \geq \frac{1}{4qT^2} - \mathsf{negl}(\lambda).$$

But now we can define a distinguisher that contradicts Lemma 4. The distinguisher knows the fixed x and the set of fixed points $\mathcal{P}_x^{(j)}$, and interacts with either $\mathcal{B}_x^{(j)}$ or $\mathcal{D}_x^{(j)}$, simulating $\mathcal{A}$ making T^2 queries. It can tell whether $\mathcal{A}$ succeeds by plugging x into the polynomial produced and comparing the result to the set of fixed points and the set of queries made by $\mathcal{A}$. Yet it can only distinguish with probability at most $T^2 \delta \log p \leq 1/(5qT^2)$ which is a contradiction.

Now we imagine picking c uniformly at random from $\mathcal{P}_x'^{(j)}$. Since $1/(4qT^2) = 1/\mathsf{poly}(\lambda)$ and $|\mathcal{P}_x'^{(j)}| \leq T^2 + P + 1 = \mathsf{poly}(\lambda)$, we can say that

$$\Pr_{\substack{\sigma \leftarrow \Sigma, x \leftarrow S(\sigma), j \leftarrow \mathcal{J}_x, \sigma' \leftarrow \mathcal{D}_x^{(j)}, \\ c \leftarrow \mathcal{P}_x'^{(j)}, \{k_i\} \leftarrow \mathbb{Z}_p^{n-1}, \mathcal{A}}} [Q(x) = c : Q \leftarrow \mathcal{A}^{\sigma'}(\{k_i\})] = \frac{1}{\mathsf{poly}(\lambda)}.$$

Now there must exist a $1/\mathsf{poly}(\lambda)$ fraction of $\{k_i\}$ such that the above holds with probability $1/\mathsf{poly}(\lambda)$ on each of those inputs. Denote this set $\mathcal{K}$, where $\mathcal{K}_i$ denotes the ith element of the set. We also now give σ' as an input to $\mathcal{A}$ rather than just giving it oracle access. So we have

$$\Pr_{\substack{\sigma \leftarrow \Sigma, x \leftarrow S(\sigma), j \leftarrow \mathcal{J}_x, \\ \sigma' \leftarrow \mathcal{D}_x^{(j)}, c \leftarrow \mathcal{P}_x'^{(j)}, \mathcal{A}}} [Q(x) = c : Q \leftarrow \mathcal{A}(\sigma', \mathcal{K}_i)] = \frac{1}{\mathsf{poly}(\lambda)} \ \forall i \in [|\mathcal{K}|].$$

Then by Lemma 6, noting that $|\mathcal{K}| = \omega(\mathsf{poly}(\lambda))$,

$$\Pr_{\substack{\sigma \leftarrow \Sigma, x \leftarrow S(\sigma), j \leftarrow \mathcal{J}_x, \sigma' \leftarrow \mathcal{D}_x^{(j)}, \\ c \leftarrow \mathcal{P}_x'^{(j)}, \mathcal{A}, i_1, i_2 \leftarrow [|\mathcal{K}|]}} \left[Q_1(x) = c = Q_2(x) : \begin{matrix} Q_1 \leftarrow \mathcal{A}(\sigma', \mathcal{K}_{i_1}) \\ Q_2 \leftarrow \mathcal{A}(\sigma', \mathcal{K}_{i_2}) \end{matrix} \right] = \frac{1}{\mathsf{poly}(\lambda)}.$$

Thus we can get rid of c, and are guaranteed that

$$\Pr_{\substack{\sigma \leftarrow \Sigma, x \leftarrow S(\sigma), j \leftarrow \mathcal{J}_x, \\ \sigma' \leftarrow \mathcal{D}_x^{(j)}, \mathcal{A}, i_1, i_2 \leftarrow [|\mathcal{K}|]}} \left[Q_1(x) - Q_2(x) = 0 : \begin{matrix} Q_1 \leftarrow \mathcal{A}(\sigma', \mathcal{K}_{i_1}) \\ Q_2 \leftarrow \mathcal{A}(\sigma', \mathcal{K}_{i_2}) \end{matrix} \right] = \frac{1}{\mathsf{poly}(\lambda)}.$$

Now since $\mathcal{K}$ is a $1/\mathsf{poly}(\lambda)$ fraction of the entire domain of $\{k_i\}$, we can instead pick these sets from the entire domain, and with $1/\mathsf{poly}(\lambda)$ probability they will both lie in $\mathcal{K}$. This gives

$$\Pr_{\substack{\sigma \leftarrow \Sigma, x \leftarrow S(\sigma), j \leftarrow \mathcal{J}_x, \sigma' \leftarrow \mathcal{D}_x^{(j)}, \\ \mathcal{A}, \{k_i^{(1)}\}, \{k_i^{(2)}\} \leftarrow \mathbb{Z}_p^{n-1}}} \left[Q_1(x) - Q_2(x) = 0 : \begin{matrix} Q_1 \leftarrow \mathcal{A}(\sigma', \{k_i^{(1)}\}) \\ Q_2 \leftarrow \mathcal{A}(\sigma', \{k_i^{(2)}\}) \end{matrix} \right] = \frac{1}{\mathsf{poly}(\lambda)}.$$

Now we look at the probability that Q_1 and Q_2 are distinct polynomials. For any fixed Q, there are at most a $1/p$ fraction of sets $\{k_i\}$ such that $\mathcal{A}(\{k_i\})$ could possibly output Q. This follows since given some $\{k_i\}$, the coefficients on $x^2, ..., x^n$ in Q determine the $\ell_2, ..., \ell_n$ in $\mathcal{A}$'s linear combination. Then there remains a $1/p$ chance that the $\{\ell_i\}$ and $\{k_i\}$ dot product to the correct linear coefficient in Q. So for uniformly random choice of the $\{k_i^{(1)}\}$ and $\{k_i^{(2)}\}$ sets, there is a $\mathsf{negl}(\lambda)$ chance that the resulting Q_1 and Q_2 output by $\mathcal{A}$ could possibly be equal.

Let E_1 be the event that $Q_1(x) - Q_2(x) = 0$ and E_2 be the event that $Q_1 \neq Q_2$. We want to say that $\Pr[E_1 \wedge E_2] = 1/\mathsf{poly}(\lambda)$. This follows from a simple union bound: $\Pr[E_1 \wedge E_2] = 1 - \Pr[\neg E_1 \vee \neg E_2] \geq 1 - \Pr[\neg E_1] - \Pr[\neg E_2] = 1 - (1 - 1/\mathsf{poly}(\lambda)) - \mathsf{negl}(\lambda) = 1/\mathsf{poly}(\lambda)$.

So we redefine $\mathcal{A}$ to generate two random sets $\{k_i^{(1)}\}$ and $\{k_i^{(2)}\}$ for itself, determine the polynomials Q_1 and Q_2, solve for the roots of $Q_1 - Q_2$, and output a uniformly random root. Note that the degree of $Q_1 - Q_2$ will be at most $n = \mathsf{poly}(\lambda)$. Thus the following holds:

$$\Pr_{\sigma \leftarrow \Sigma, x \leftarrow S(\sigma), \sigma' \leftarrow Y_x, \mathcal{A}}[x \leftarrow \mathcal{A}(\sigma')] = \frac{1}{\mathsf{poly}(\lambda)}.$$

Now we can switch Y_x to Σ_x, and claim that

$$\Pr_{\sigma \leftarrow \Sigma, x \leftarrow S(\sigma), \sigma' \leftarrow \Sigma_x, \mathcal{A}}[x \leftarrow \mathcal{A}(\sigma')] = \frac{1}{\mathsf{poly}(\lambda)}.$$

If instead $\mathcal{A}$'s success was negligible after this switch, then there exists a fixed x for which the difference in success is $1/\mathsf{poly}(\lambda)$. But Y_x and Σ_x are γ-close with $\gamma = 1/2^\lambda = \mathsf{negl}(\lambda)$ so this is impossible. Then, we can write

$$\Pr_{\sigma' \leftarrow \Sigma', \mathcal{A}}[x \leftarrow \mathcal{A}(\sigma')] = \frac{1}{\mathsf{poly}(\lambda)},$$

where Σ' is defined as in Lemma 5. This contradicts Lemma 5. □

Assumption 3 (f-DDH-II). *Let* $\mathsf{GroupGen}(1^\lambda) = (\mathbb{G}_\lambda, g, p(\lambda))$, *where* $2^{\lambda-1} < p(\lambda) < 2^\lambda$. *Let* $\{\mathcal{D}_\lambda\}_\lambda$ *be a family of well-spread distributions where the domain of* $\mathcal{D}_\lambda$ *is* $\mathbb{Z}_{p(\lambda)}$. *Then for any PPT* $\mathcal{A}$,

$$|\Pr[\mathcal{A}(g^x, g^r, g^{xr}) = 1] - \Pr[\mathcal{A}(g^x, g^r, g^s) = 1]| = \mathsf{negl}(\lambda),$$

where $x \leftarrow \mathcal{D}_\lambda$, *and* $r, s \leftarrow \mathbb{Z}_{p(\lambda)}$.

Theorem 8. *Assumption 3 holds in the Generic Group Model.*

We give the proof in the full version [3]. Note that this trivially implies generic security of r-DDH-II.

Acknowledgements. We thank Justin Holmgren for collaboration in the early stages of this work and for contributing a number of extremely valuable insights. We also thank Alon Rosen for helpful feedback regarding exposition and presentation.

This material is based upon work supported by the ARO and DARPA under Contract No. W911NF-15-C-0227. Any opinions, findings and conclusions or recommendations expressed in this material are those of the author(s) and do not necessarily reflect the views of the ARO and DARPA.

References

1. Barak, B., et al.: On the (Im)possibility of obfuscating programs. In: Kilian, J. (ed.) CRYPTO 2001. LNCS, vol. 2139, pp. 1–18. Springer, Heidelberg (2001). https://doi.org/10.1007/3-540-44647-8_1

2. Barthe, G., Fagerholm, E., Fiore, D., Mitchell, J.C., Scedrov, A., Schmidt, B.: Automated analysis of cryptographic assumptions in generic group models. In: Garay, J.A., Gennaro, R. (eds.) CRYPTO 2014. LNCS, vol. 8616, pp. 95–112. Springer, Heidelberg (2014). https://doi.org/10.1007/978-3-662-44371-2_6

3. Bartusek, J., Ma, F., Zhandry, M.: The distinction between fixed and random generators in group-based assumptions. Cryptology ePrint Archive, Report 2019/202 (2019). https://eprint.iacr.org/2019/202

4. Bellare, M., Rogaway, P.: Random oracles are practical: a paradigm for designing efficient protocols. In: Ashby, V. (ed.) ACM CCS 1993, pp. 62–73. ACM Press, November 1993

5. Bernstein, D.J., Lange, T.: Non-uniform cracks in the concrete: the power of free precomputation. In: Sako, K., Sarkar, P. (eds.) ASIACRYPT 2013. LNCS, vol. 8270, pp. 321–340. Springer, Heidelberg (2013). https://doi.org/10.1007/978-3-642-42045-0_17

6. Bitansky, N., Canetti, R.: On strong simulation and composable point obfuscation. In: Rabin, T. (ed.) CRYPTO 2010. LNCS, vol. 6223, pp. 520–537. Springer, Heidelberg (2010). https://doi.org/10.1007/978-3-642-14623-7_28

7. Bitansky, N., Canetti, R.: On strong simulation and composable point obfuscation. J. Cryptol. **27**(2), 317–357 (2014)

8. Boneh, D., Franklin, M.K.: Identity-based encryption from the Weil pairing. In: Kilian, J. (ed.) CRYPTO 2001. LNCS, vol. 2139, pp. 213–229. Springer, Heidelberg (2001). https://doi.org/10.1007/3-540-44647-8_13

9. Boneh, D., Silverberg, A.: Applications of multilinear forms to cryptography. Contemp. Math. **324**, 71–90 (2002)

10. Boneh, D., Zhandry, M.: Multiparty key exchange, efficient traitor tracing, and more from indistinguishability obfuscation. In: Garay, J.A., Gennaro, R. (eds.) CRYPTO 2014. LNCS, vol. 8616, pp. 480–499. Springer, Heidelberg (2014). https://doi.org/10.1007/978-3-662-44371-2_27

11. Bos, J.W., Costello, C., Longa, P., Naehrig, M.: Selecting elliptic curves for cryptography: an efficiency and security analysis. J. Crypt. Eng. **6**(4), 259–286 (2016). https://doi.org/10.1007/s13389-015-0097-y

12. Brands, S.: Untraceable off-line cash in wallet with observers. In: Stinson, D.R. (ed.) CRYPTO 1993. LNCS, vol. 773, pp. 302–318. Springer, Heidelberg (1994). https://doi.org/10.1007/3-540-48329-2_26

13. Canetti, R.: Towards realizing random oracles: hash functions that hide all partial information. In: Kaliski, B.S. (ed.) CRYPTO 1997. LNCS, vol. 1294, pp. 455–469. Springer, Heidelberg (1997). https://doi.org/10.1007/BFb0052255

14. Canetti, R., Dakdouk, R.R.: Extractable perfectly one-way functions. In: Aceto, L., Damgård, I., Goldberg, L.A., Halldórsson, M.M., Ingólfsdóttir, A., Walukiewicz, I. (eds.) ICALP 2008. LNCS, vol. 5126, pp. 449–460. Springer, Heidelberg (2008). https://doi.org/10.1007/978-3-540-70583-3_37

15. Canetti, R., Varia, M.: Non-malleable obfuscation. In: Reingold, O. (ed.) TCC 2009. LNCS, vol. 5444, pp. 73–90. Springer, Heidelberg (2009). https://doi.org/10.1007/978-3-642-00457-5_6

16. Coretti, S., Dodis, Y., Guo, S.: Non-uniform bounds in the random-permutation, ideal-cipher, and generic-group models. In: Shacham, H., Boldyreva, A. (eds.) CRYPTO 2018. LNCS, vol. 10991, pp. 693–721. Springer, Cham (2018). https://doi.org/10.1007/978-3-319-96884-1_23

17. Coretti, S., Dodis, Y., Guo, S., Steinberger, J.: Random oracles and non-uniformity. In: Nielsen, J.B., Rijmen, V. (eds.) EUROCRYPT 2018. LNCS, vol. 10820, pp. 227–258. Springer, Cham (2018). https://doi.org/10.1007/978-3-319-78381-9_9

18. Corrigan-Gibbs, H., Kogan, D.: The discrete-logarithm problem with preprocessing. In: Nielsen, J.B., Rijmen, V. (eds.) EUROCRYPT 2018. LNCS, vol. 10821, pp. 415–447. Springer, Cham (2018). https://doi.org/10.1007/978-3-319-78375-8_14

19. Cramer, R., Shoup, V.: A practical public key cryptosystem provably secure against adaptive chosen ciphertext attack. In: Krawczyk, H. (ed.) CRYPTO 1998. LNCS, vol. 1462, pp. 13–25. Springer, Heidelberg (1998). https://doi.org/10.1007/BFb0055717

20. Damgård, I., Hazay, C., Zottarel, A.: Short paper on the generic hardness of DDH-II (2014)

21. Diffie, W., Hellman, M.E.: New directions in cryptography. IEEE Trans. Inf. Theory 22(6), 644–654 (1976)

22. ElGamal, T.: A public key cryptosystem and a signature scheme based on discrete logarithms. In: Blakley, G.R., Chaum, D. (eds.) CRYPTO 1984. LNCS, vol. 196, pp. 10–18. Springer, Heidelberg (1985). https://doi.org/10.1007/3-540-39568-7_2

23. Fenteany, P., Fuller, B.: Non-malleable digital lockers for efficiently sampleable distributions. Cryptology ePrint Archive, Report 2018/957 (2018). https://eprint.iacr.org/2018/957

24. Fujisaki, E.: Improving practical UC-secure commitments based on the DDH assumption. In: Zikas, V., De Prisco, R. (eds.) SCN 2016. LNCS, vol. 9841, pp. 257–272. Springer, Cham (2016). https://doi.org/10.1007/978-3-319-44618-9_14

25. Galbraith, S.D.: Mathematics of Public Key Cryptography. Cambridge University Press, Cambridge (2012)

26. Gat, E., Goldwasser, S.: Probabilistic search algorithms with unique answers and their cryptographic applications. In: Electronic Colloquium on Computational Complexity (ECCC), vol. 18, p. 136 (2011)

27. Goldwasser, S., Tauman Kalai, Y.: Cryptographic assumptions: a position paper. In: Kushilevitz, E., Malkin, T. (eds.) TCC 2016. LNCS, vol. 9562, pp. 505–522. Springer, Heidelberg (2016). https://doi.org/10.1007/978-3-662-49096-9_21

28. Kalai, Y.T., Li, X., Rao, A., Zuckerman, D.: Network extractor protocols. In: 49th FOCS, pp. 654–663. IEEE Computer Society Press, October 2008

29. Katz, J., Lindell, Y.: Modern Cryptography, 2nd edn. (2014)

30. Kim, J., Kim, S., Seo, J.H.: Multilinear map via scale-invariant FHE: Enhancing security and efficiency. Cryptology ePrint Archive, Report 2015/992 (2015). https://ia.cr/2015/992

31. Komargodski, I., Yogev, E.: Another step towards realizing random oracles: non-malleable point obfuscation. In: Nielsen, J.B., Rijmen, V. (eds.) EUROCRYPT 2018. LNCS, vol. 10820, pp. 259–279. Springer, Cham (2018). https://doi.org/10.1007/978-3-319-78381-9_10

32. Komargodski, I., Yogev, E.: Another step towards realizing random oracles: non-malleable point obfuscation. Cryptology ePrint Archive, Report 2018/149 (2018). https://ia.cr/2018/149

33. Lee, H.T., Cheon, J.H., Hong, J.: Accelerating ID-based encryption based on trapdoor DL using pre-computation. Cryptology ePrint Archive, Report 2011/187 (2011). https://ia.cr/2011/187

34. Maurer, U.M.: Abstract models of computation in cryptography. In: Smart, N.P. (ed.) Cryptography and Coding 2005. LNCS, vol. 3796, pp. 1–12. Springer, Heidelberg (2005). https://doi.org/10.1007/11586821_1

35. Mihalcik, J.: An analysis of algorithms for solving discrete logarithms in fixed groups, master's thesis, Naval Postgraduate School (2010)

36. Nechaev, V.I.: Complexity of a determinate algorithm for the discrete logarithm. Math. Notes 55(2), 165–172 (1994)

37. Sadeghi, A.-R., Steiner, M.: Assumptions related to discrete logarithms: why subtleties make a real difference. In: Pfitzmann, B. (ed.) EUROCRYPT 2001. LNCS, vol. 2045, pp. 244–261. Springer, Heidelberg (2001). https://doi.org/10.1007/3-540-44987-6_16

38. Saxena, A., Soh, B.: A new cryptosystem based on hidden order groups. Cryptology ePrint Archive, Report 2006/178 (2006). https://ia.cr/2006/178

39. Shoup, V.: Lower bounds for discrete logarithms and related problems. In: Fumy, W. (ed.) EUROCRYPT 1997. LNCS, vol. 1233, pp. 256–266. Springer, Heidelberg (1997). https://doi.org/10.1007/3-540-69053-0_18

40. Shoup, V.: On formal models for secure key exchange. Technical report, RZ 3120, IBM (1999)

41. Unruh, D.: Random oracles and auxiliary input. In: Menezes, A. (ed.) CRYPTO 2007. LNCS, vol. 4622, pp. 205–223. Springer, Heidelberg (2007). https://doi.org/10.1007/978-3-540-74143-5_12

42. Wee, H.: On obfuscating point functions. In: Gabow, H.N., Fagin, R. (eds.) 37th ACM STOC, pp. 523–532. ACM Press, May 2005

43. Yamakawa, T., Yamada, S., Hanaoka, G., Kunihiro, N.: Self-bilinear map on unknown order groups from indistinguishability obfuscation and its applications. In: Garay, J.A., Gennaro, R. (eds.) CRYPTO 2014. LNCS, vol. 8617, pp. 90–107. Springer, Heidelberg (2014). https://doi.org/10.1007/978-3-662-44381-1_6

44. Yamakawa, T., Yamada, S., Hanaoka, G., Kunihiro, N.: Generic hardness of inversion on ring and its relation to self-bilinear map. Cryptology ePrint Archive, Report 2018/463 (2018). https://ia.cr/2018/463

45. Yun, A.: Generic hardness of the multiple discrete logarithm problem. In: Oswald, E., Fischlin, M. (eds.) EUROCRYPT 2015. LNCS, vol. 9057, pp. 817–836. Springer, Heidelberg (2015). https://doi.org/10.1007/978-3-662-46803-6_27

Unifying Computational Entropies via Kullback–Leibler Divergence

Rohit Agrawal$^{(\boxtimes)}$, Yi-Hsiu Chen$^{(\boxtimes)}$, Thibaut Horel$^{(\boxtimes)}$, and Salil Vadhan

John A. Paulson School of Engineering and Applied Sciences, Harvard University,
Cambridge, MA 02138, USA
{rohitagr,yhchen,thorel}@seas.harvard.edu, salil_vadhan@harvard.edu

Abstract. We introduce *hardness in relative entropy*, a new notion of hardness for search problems which on the one hand is satisfied by all one-way functions and on the other hand implies both *next-block pseudoentropy* and *inaccessible entropy*, two forms of computational entropy used in recent constructions of pseudorandom generators and statistically hiding commitment schemes, respectively. Thus, hardness in relative entropy unifies the latter two notions of computational entropy and sheds light on the apparent "duality" between them. Additionally, it yields a more modular and illuminating proof that one-way functions imply next-block inaccessible entropy, similar in structure to the proof that one-way functions imply next-block pseudoentropy (Vadhan and Zheng, STOC '12).

Keywords: One-way function · Pseudorandom generator ·
Pseudoentropy · Computational entropy · Inaccessible entropy ·
Statistically hiding commitment · Next-bit pseudoentropy

1 Introduction

1.1 One-Way Functions and Computational Entropy

One-way functions [3] are on one hand the minimal assumption for complexity-based cryptography [15], but on the other hand can be used to construct a remarkable array of cryptographic primitives, including such powerful objects as CCA-secure symmetric encryption, zero-knowledge proofs and statistical zero-knowledge arguments for all of **NP**, and secure multiparty computation with an

R. Agrawal—Supported by the Department of Defense (DoD) through the National Defense Science & Engineering Graduate Fellowship (NDSEG) Program.
Y.-H. Chen—Supported by NSF grant CCF-1763299.
T. Horel—Supported in part by the National Science Foundation under grants CAREER IIS-1149662, CNS-1237235 and CCF-1763299, by the Office of Naval Research under grants YIP N00014-14-1-0485 and N00014-17-1-2131, and by a Google Research Award.
S. Vadhan—Supported by NSF grant CCF-1763299.

A. Boldyreva and D. Micciancio (Eds.): CRYPTO 2019, LNCS 11693, pp. 831–858, 2019.
https://doi.org/10.1007/978-3-030-26951-7_28

honest majority [5–7,9,14,16,20]. All of these constructions begin by converting the "raw hardness" of a one-way function (OWF) to one of the following more structured cryptographic primitives: a pseudorandom generator (PRG) [1,22], a universal one-way hash function (UOWHF) [18], or a statistically hiding commitment scheme (SHC) [2].

The original constructions of these three primitives from arbitrary one-way functions [9,14,20] were all very complicated and inefficient. Over the past decade, there has been a series of simplifications and efficiency improvements to these constructions [8,11,12,21], leading to a situation where the constructions of two of these primitives—PRGs and SHCs—share a very similar structure and seem "dual" to each other. Specifically, these constructions proceed as follows:

1. Show that every OWF $f : \{0,1\}^n \rightarrow \{0,1\}^n$ has a gap between its "real entropy" and an appropriate form of "computational entropy". Specifically, for constructing PRGs, it is shown that the function $G(x) = (f(x), x_1, x_2, \ldots, x_n)$ has "next-block pseudoentropy" at least $n + \omega(\log n)$ while its real entropy is $H(G(U_n)) = n$ [21] where $H(\cdot)$ denotes Shannon entropy. For constructing SHCs, it is shown that the function $G(x) = (f(x)_1, \ldots, f(x)_n, x)$ has "next-block accessible entropy" at most $n - \omega(\log n)$ while its real entropy is again $H(G(U_n)) = n$ [11]. Note that the differences between the two cases are whether we break x or $f(x)$ into individual bits (which matters because the "next-block" notions of computational entropy depend on the block structure) and whether the form of computational entropy is larger or smaller than the real entropy.

2. An "entropy equalization" step that converts G into a similar generator where the real entropy in each block conditioned on the prefix before it is known. This step is exactly the same in both constructions.

3. A "flattening" step that converts the (real and computational) Shannon entropy guarantees of the generator into ones on (smoothed) min-entropy and max-entropy. This step is again exactly the same in both constructions.

4. A "hashing" step where high (real or computational) min-entropy is converted to uniform (pseudo)randomness and low (real or computational) max-entropy is converted to a small-support or disjointness property. For PRGs, this step only requires randomness extractors [14,19], while for SHCs it requires (information-theoretic) interactive hashing [4,17]. (Constructing full-fledged SHCs in this step also utilizes UOWHFs, which can be constructed from one-way functions [20]. Without UOWHFs, we obtain a weaker binding property, which nevertheless suffices for constructing statistical zero-knowledge arguments for all of **NP**.)

This common construction template came about through a back-and-forth exchange of ideas between the two lines of work. Indeed, the uses of computational entropy notions, flattening, and hashing originate with PRGs [14], whereas the ideas of using next-block notions, obtaining them from breaking $(f(x), x)$ into short blocks, and entropy equalization originate with SHCs [11]. All this leads to a feeling that the two constructions, and their underlying computational entropy notions, are "dual" to each other and should be connected at a formal level.

In this paper, we make progress on this project of unifying the notions of computational entropy, by introducing a new computational entropy notion that yields both next-block pseudoentropy and next-block accessible entropy in a clean and modular fashion. It is inspired by the proof of [21] that $(f(x), x_1, \ldots, x_n)$ has next-block pseudoentropy $n + \omega(\log n)$, which we will describe now.

1.2   Next-Block Pseudoentropy via Relative Pseudoentropy

We recall the definition of next-block pseudoentropy, and the result of [21] relating it to one-wayness.

Definition 1.1 (next-block pseudoentropy, informal). *Let n be a security parameter, and $X = (X_1, \ldots, X_m)$ be a random variable distributed on strings of length $\mathrm{poly}(n)$. We say that X has* next-block pseudoentropy *at least k if there is a random variable $Z = (Z_1, \ldots, Z_m)$, jointly distributed with X, such that:*

1. *For all $i = 1, \ldots, m$, $(X_1, \ldots, X_{i-1}, X_i)$ is computationally indistinguishable from $(X_1, \ldots, X_{i-1}, Z_i)$.*
2. *$\sum_{i=1}^{m} \mathrm{H}(Z_i | X_1, \ldots, X_{i-1}) \geq k$.*

Equivalently, for I uniformly distributed in $[m]$, X_I has conditional pseudoentropy at least k/m given $(X_1, \ldots, X_{i-1})$.

It was conjectured in [10] that next-block pseudoentropy could be obtained from any OWF by breaking its input into bits, and this conjecture was proven in [21]:

Theorem 1.2 ([21], informal). *Let $f : \{0,1\}^n \to \{0,1\}^n$ be a one-way function, let X be uniformly distributed in $\{0,1\}^n$, and let $X = (X_1, \ldots, X_m)$ be a partition of X into blocks of length $O(\log n)$. Then $(f(X), X_1, \ldots, X_m)$ has next-block pseudoentropy at least $n + \omega(\log n)$.*

The intuition behind Theorem 1.2 is that since X is hard to sample given $f(X)$, then it should have some extra computational entropy given $f(X)$. This intuition is formalized using the following notion of "relative pseudoentropy," which is a renaming of [21]'s notion of "KL-hard for sampling," to better unify the terminology with the notions introduced in this work.

Definition 1.3 (relative pseudoentropy). *Let n be a security parameter, and (X, Y) be a pair of random variables, jointly distributed over strings of length $\mathrm{poly}(n)$. We say that X has* relative pseudoentropy at least Δ given Y if for all probabilistic polynomial-time S, we have*

$$\mathrm{KL}(X, Y \parallel \mathsf{S}(Y), Y) \geq \Delta,$$

where $\mathrm{KL}(\cdot \parallel \cdot)$ denotes the relative entropy (a.k.a. Kullback–Leibler divergence).[1]

---

[1] Recall that for random variables A and B with $\mathrm{Supp}(A) \subseteq \mathrm{Supp}(B)$, the relative entropy is defined by $\mathrm{KL}(A \parallel B) = \mathrm{E}_{a \leftarrow A}[\log(\Pr[A = a] / \Pr[B = a])]$.

That is, it is hard for any efficient adversary S to sample the conditional distribution of X given Y, even approximately.

The first step of the proof of Theorem 1.2 is to show that one-wayness implies relative pseudoentropy (which can be done with a one-line calculation):

Lemma 1.4. *Let $f : \{0,1\}^n \to \{0,1\}^n$ be a one-way function and let X be uniformly distributed in $\{0,1\}^n$. Then X has relative pseudoentropy at least $\omega(\log n)$ given $f(X)$.*

Next, we break X into short blocks, and show that the relative pseudoentropy is preserved:

Lemma 1.5. *Let n be a security parameter, let (X,Y) be random variables distributed on strings of length $\mathrm{poly}(n)$, let $X = (X_1, \ldots, X_m)$ be a partition of X into blocks, and let I be uniformly distributed in $[m]$. If X has Δ relative pseudoentropy given Y, then X_I has relative pseudoentropy at least Δ/m given $(Y, X_1, \ldots, X_{I-1})$.*

Finally, the main part of the proof is to show that, once we have short blocks, relative pseudoentropy is *equivalent* to a gap between conditional pseudoentropy and real conditional entropy.

Lemma 1.6. *Let n be a security parameter, Y be a random variable distributed on strings of length $\mathrm{poly}(n)$, and X a random variable distributed on strings of length $O(\log n)$. Then X has relative pseudoentropy at least Δ given Y iff X has conditional pseudoentropy at least $\mathrm{H}(X|Y) + \Delta$ given Y.*

Putting these three lemmas together, we see that when f is a one-way function, and we break X into blocks of length $O(\log n)$ to obtain $(f(X), X_1, \ldots, X_m)$, on average, the conditional pseudoentropy of X_I given $(f(X), X_1, \ldots, X_{I-1})$ is larger than its real conditional entropy by $\omega(\log n)/m$. This tells us that the next-block pseudoentropy of $(f(X), X_1, \ldots, X_m)$ is larger than its real entropy by $\omega(\log n)$, as claimed in Theorem 1.2.

We remark that Lemma 1.6 explains why we need to break the input of the one-way function into short blocks: it is false when X is long. Indeed, if f is a one-way function, then we have already seen that X has $\omega(\log n)$ relative pseudoentropy given $f(X)$ (Lemma 1.4), but it does not have conditional pseudoentropy noticeably larger than $\mathrm{H}(X|f(X))$ given $f(X)$ (as correct preimages can be efficiently distinguished from incorrect ones using f).

1.3   Inaccessible Entropy

As mentioned above, for constructing SHCs from one-way functions, the notion of next-block pseudoentropy is replaced with next-block accessible entropy:

Definition 1.7 (next-block accessible entropy, informal). *Let n be a security parameter, and $Y = (Y_1, \ldots, Y_m)$ be a random variable distributed on strings of length $\mathrm{poly}(n)$. We say that Y has next-block accessible entropy at most k if the following holds.*

Let $\widetilde{\mathsf{G}}$ be any probabilistic poly(n)-time algorithm that takes a sequence of uniformly random strings $\widetilde{R} = (\widetilde{R}_1, \ldots, \widetilde{R}_m)$ and outputs a sequence $\widetilde{Y} = (\widetilde{Y}_1, \ldots, \widetilde{Y}_m)$ in an "online fashion" by which we mean that $\widetilde{Y}_i = \widetilde{\mathsf{G}}(\widetilde{R}_1, \ldots, \widetilde{R}_i)$ depends on only the first i random strings of $\widetilde{\mathsf{G}}$ for $i = 1, \ldots, m$. Suppose further that $\mathrm{Supp}(\widetilde{Y}) \subseteq \mathrm{Supp}(Y)$.

Then we require:

$$\sum_{i=1}^{m} \mathrm{H}\left(\widetilde{Y}_i | \widetilde{R}_1, \ldots, \widetilde{R}_{i-1}\right) \leq k.$$

(Next-block) accessible entropy differs from (next-block) pseudoentropy in two ways:

1. Accessible entropy is useful as an *upper* bound on computational entropy, and is interesting when it is *smaller* than the real entropy $\mathrm{H}(Y)$. We refer to the gap $\mathrm{H}(Y) - k$ as the *next-block inaccessible entropy* of Y.
2. The accessible entropy adversary $\widetilde{\mathsf{G}}$ is trying to *generate* the random variables Y_i conditioned on the history rather than recognize them. Note that we take the "history" to not only be the previous blocks $(\widetilde{Y}_1, \ldots, \widetilde{Y}_{i-1})$, but the coin tosses $(\widetilde{R}_1, \ldots, \widetilde{R}_{i-1})$ used to generate those blocks.

Note that one unsatisfactory aspect of the definition is that when the random variable Y is not *flat* (i.e. uniform on its support), then there can be an adversary $\widetilde{\mathsf{G}}$ achieving accessible entropy even *larger* than $\mathrm{H}(Y)$, for example by making $\widetilde{Y}$ uniform on $\mathrm{Supp}(Y)$.

Similarly to (and predating) Theorem 1.2, it is known that one-wayness implies next-block inaccessible entropy.

Theorem 1.8 ([11]). *Let $f : \{0,1\}^n \to \{0,1\}^n$ be a one-way function, let X be uniformly distributed in $\{0,1\}^n$, and let $(Y_1, \ldots, Y_m)$ be a partition of $Y = f(X)$ into blocks of length $O(\log n)$. Then $(Y_1, \ldots, Y_m, X)$ has next-block accessible entropy at most $n - \omega(\log n)$.*

Unfortunately, however, the existing proof of Theorem 1.8 is not modular like that of Theorem 1.2. In particular, it does not isolate the step of relating one-wayness to entropy-theoretic measures (like Lemma 1.4 does) or the significance of having short blocks (like Lemma 1.6 does).

1.4   Our Results

We remedy the above state of affairs by providing a new, more general notion of hardness in relative entropy that allows us to obtain next-block inaccessible entropy in a modular way while also encompassing what is needed for next-block pseudoentropy.

Like in relative pseudoentropy, we will consider a pair of jointly distributed random variables (Y, X). Following the spirit of accessible entropy, the adversary

$\widetilde{\mathsf{G}}$ for our new notion will try to *generate* Y together with X, rather than taking Y as input. That is, $\widetilde{\mathsf{G}}$ will take randomness $\widetilde{R}$ and output a pair $(\widetilde{Y}, \widetilde{X}) = \widetilde{\mathsf{G}}(\widetilde{R}) = (\widetilde{\mathsf{G}}_1(\widetilde{R}), \widetilde{\mathsf{G}}_2(\widetilde{R}))$, which we require to be always within the support of (Y, X). Note that $\widetilde{\mathsf{G}}$ need not be an online generator; it can generate both $\widetilde{Y}$ and $\widetilde{X}$ using the same randomness $\widetilde{R}$. Of course, if (Y, X) is efficiently samplable (as it would be in most cryptographic applications), $\widetilde{\mathsf{G}}$ could generate $(\widetilde{Y}, \widetilde{X})$ identically distributed to (Y, X) by just using the "honest" sampler G for (Y, X). So, in addition, we require that the adversary $\widetilde{\mathsf{G}}$ also come with a *simulator* S, that can simulate its coin tosses given only $\widetilde{Y}$. The goal of the adversary is to minimize the relative entropy

$$\mathrm{KL}\left(\widetilde{R}, \widetilde{Y} \,\middle\|\, \mathsf{S}(Y), Y\right)$$

for a uniformly random $\widetilde{R}$. This divergence measures both how well $\widetilde{\mathsf{G}}_1$ approximates the distribution of Y as well as how well S simulates the corresponding coin tosses of $\widetilde{\mathsf{G}}_1$. Note that when $\widetilde{\mathsf{G}}$ is the honest sampler G, the task of S is exactly to sample from the conditional distribution of $\widetilde{R}$ given $\mathsf{G}(\widetilde{R}) = Y$. However, the adversary may reduce the divergence by instead designing the sampler $\widetilde{\mathsf{G}}$ and simulator S to work in concert, potentially trading off how well $\mathsf{G}(\widetilde{R})$ approximates Y in exchange for easier simulation by S. Explicitly, the definition is as follows.

Definition 1.9 (hardness in relative entropy, informal version of Definition 3.4). *Let n be a security parameter, and (Y, X) be a pair of random variables jointly distributed over strings of length* $\mathrm{poly}(n)$. *We say that (Y, X) is Δ-hard in relative entropy if the following holds.*

Let $\widetilde{\mathsf{G}} = (\widetilde{\mathsf{G}}_1, \widetilde{\mathsf{G}}_2)$ and S be probabilistic $\mathrm{poly}(n)$-time algorithms such that $\mathrm{Supp}(\widetilde{\mathsf{G}}(\widetilde{R})) \subseteq \mathrm{Supp}((Y, X))$, *where $\widetilde{R}$ is uniformly distributed. Then writing $\widetilde{Y} = \widetilde{\mathsf{G}}_1(\widetilde{R})$, we require that*

$$\mathrm{KL}\left(\widetilde{R}, \widetilde{Y} \,\middle\|\, \mathsf{S}(Y), Y\right) \geq \Delta.$$

Similarly to Lemma 1.4, we can show that one-way functions achieve this notion of hardness in relative entropy.

Lemma 1.10. *Let $f : \{0,1\}^n \to \{0,1\}^n$ be a one-way function and let X be uniformly distributed in $\{0,1\}^n$. Then $(f(X), X)$ is $\omega(\log n)$-hard in relative entropy.*

Note that this lemma implies Lemma 1.4. If we take $\widetilde{\mathsf{G}}$ to be the "honest" sampler $\widetilde{\mathsf{G}}(x) = (f(x), x)$, then we have:

$$\mathrm{KL}\left(X, f(X) \,\|\, \mathsf{S}(Y), Y\right) = \mathrm{KL}\left(\widetilde{R}, \widetilde{Y} \,\middle\|\, \mathsf{S}(Y), Y\right),$$

which is is $\omega(\log n)$ by Lemma 1.10. That is, relative pseudoentropy (as in Definition 1.3 and Lemma 1.4) is obtained by fixing $\widetilde{\mathsf{G}}$ and focusing on the hardness for the simulator S, i.e. the divergence $\mathrm{KL}\left(X|Y \parallel S(Y)|Y\right)$. Furthermore, the step of breaking into short blocks (Lemma 1.5) is equivalent to requiring the simulator be *online* and showing that relative pseudoentropy implies the following notion of *next-block relative pseudoentropy*:

Definition 1.11 (next-block relative pseudoentropy, informal). *Let n be a security parameter, (X, Y) be jointly distributed random variables over strings of length* $\mathrm{poly}(n)$, *and let $X = (X_1, \ldots, X_m)$ be a partition of X into blocks. We say that X has* next-block relative pseudoentropy at least Δ given Y *if for all probabilistic polynomial-time* S, *we have*

$$\sum_{i=1}^{m} \mathrm{KL}\left(X_i|X_{<i}, Y \parallel S(X_{<i}, Y)|X_{<i}, Y\right) \geq \Delta,$$

where we use the notation $z_{<i} = (z_1, \ldots, z_{i-1})$.

Here, the simulator S *is required to be "online" in the sense that it cannot simulate* $(X_1, \ldots, X_m)$ *at once, but must simulate X_i only as a function of $X_{<i}$ and Y.*

In particular, Lemma 1.6 is thus equivalent to the statement that having Δ next-block relative pseudoentropy for blocks of length $O(\log n)$ is equivalent to having next-block pseudoentropy at least $\Delta + \sum_{i=1}^{m} \mathrm{H}\left(X_i|X_{<i}, Y\right)$ in the sense of Definition 1.1.

Conversely, we show that inaccessible entropy arises from hardness in relative entropy by first requiring the *generator* G to be online and breaking the relative entropy into blocks to obtain the following next-block hardness property.

Definition 1.12 (next-block hardness in relative entropy, informal). *Let n be a security parameter, and $Y = (Y_1, \ldots, Y_m)$ be a random variable distributed on strings of length* $\mathrm{poly}(n)$. *We say that Y is Δ next-block hard in relative entropy if the following holds.*

Let $\widetilde{G}$ be any probabilistic $\mathrm{poly}(n)$-time *algorithm that takes a sequence of uniformly random strings $\widetilde{R} = (\widetilde{R}_1, \ldots, \widetilde{R}_m)$ and outputs a sequence $\widetilde{Y} = (\widetilde{Y}_1, \ldots, \widetilde{Y}_m)$ in an "online fashion" by which we mean that $\widetilde{Y}_i = \widetilde{G}(\widetilde{R}_1, \ldots, \widetilde{R}_i)$ depends on only the first i random strings of $\widetilde{G}$ for $i = 1, \ldots, m$. Suppose further that* $\mathrm{Supp}(\widetilde{Y}) \subseteq \mathrm{Supp}(Y)$. *Additionally, let S be a probabilistic* $\mathrm{poly}(n)$-time *algorithms such for all $i = 1, \ldots, m$, S takes as input $\widehat{R}_1, \ldots, \widehat{R}_{i-1}$ and Y_i and outputs $\widehat{R}_i$, where $\widehat{R}_j$ has the same length as $\widetilde{R}_j$. Then we require that for all such $(\widetilde{G}, S)$, we have:*

$$\sum_{i=1}^{m} \mathrm{KL}\left(\widehat{R}_i, \widetilde{Y}_i|\widehat{R}_{<i}, \widetilde{Y}_{<i} \parallel \widehat{R}_i, Y_i|\widehat{R}_{<i}, Y_{<i}\right) \geq \Delta.$$

Observe that hardness in relative entropy can be seen as the specific case of next-block hardness in relative entropy when there is only one block (*i.e.*, setting $m = 1$ in the previous definition).

Next, we fix the *simulator*, analogously to how relative pseudoentropy was obtained by fixing the generator, and obtain *next-block inaccessible relative entropy*:

Definition 1.13 (next-block inaccessible relative entropy, informal).
Let n be a security parameter, and $Y = (Y_1, \ldots, Y_m)$ be a random variable distributed on strings of length $\mathrm{poly}(n)$. We say that Y has next-block inaccessible relative entropy *at least Δ if the following holds.*

Let $\widetilde{\mathsf{G}}$ be any probabilistic $\mathrm{poly}(n)$-time algorithm that takes a sequence of uniformly random strings $\widetilde{R} = (\widetilde{R}_1, \ldots, \widetilde{R}_m)$ and outputs a sequence $\widetilde{Y} = (\widetilde{Y}_1, \ldots, \widetilde{Y}_m)$ in an online fashion, and such that $\mathrm{Supp}(\widetilde{Y}) \subseteq \mathrm{Supp}(Y)$. Then we require that for all such $\widetilde{\mathsf{G}}$, we have:

$$\sum_{i=1}^{m} \mathrm{KL}\left(\widetilde{Y}_i | \widetilde{R}_{<i}, \widetilde{Y}_{<i} \,\middle\|\, Y_i | R_{<i}, Y_{<i}\right) \geq \Delta,$$

where $R = (R_1, \ldots, R_m)$ is a dummy random variable independent of Y.

That is, the goal of the online generator $\widetilde{\mathsf{G}}$ is to generate $\widetilde{Y}_i$ given the history of coin tosses $\widetilde{R}_{<i}$ with the same conditional distribution as Y_i given $Y_{<i}$. As promised, there is no explicit simulator in the definition of next-block inaccessible relative entropy, as we essentially dropped all $\widehat{R}$ variables from the definition of next-block hardness in relative entropy. Nevertheless we can obtain it from hardness in relative entropy by using sufficiently short blocks:

Lemma 1.14. *Let n be a security parameter, let Y be a random variable distributed on strings of length $\mathrm{poly}(n)$, and let $Y = (Y_1, \ldots, Y_m)$ be a partition of Y into blocks of length $O(\log n)$.*

If $(Y_1, \ldots, Y_m)$ is Δ next-block hard in relative entropy, then $(Y_1, \ldots, Y_m)$ has next-block inaccessible relative entropy at least $\Delta - \mathrm{negl}(n)$.

An intuition for the proof is that since the blocks are of logarithmic length, given Y_i we can simulate the corresponding coin tosses of $\widetilde{R}_i$ of G by rejection sampling and succeed with high probability in $\mathrm{poly}(n)$ tries.

A nice feature of the definition of next-block inaccessible relative entropy compared to inaccessible entropy is that it is meaningful even for non-flat random variables, as KL divergence is always nonnegative. Moreover, for flat random variables, it equals the inaccessible entropy:

Lemma 1.15. *Suppose $Y = (Y_1, \ldots, Y_m)$ is a flat random variable. Then Y has next-block inaccessible relative entropy at least Δ if and only if Y has accessible entropy at most $\mathrm{H}(Y) - \Delta$.*

Intuitively, this lemma comes from the identity that if Y is a flat random variable and $\mathrm{Supp}(\widetilde{Y}) \subseteq \mathrm{Supp}(Y)$, then $\mathrm{H}\left(\widetilde{Y}\right) = \mathrm{H}(Y) - \mathrm{KL}\left(\widetilde{Y} \,\middle\|\, Y\right)$. We stress that we do not require the individual blocks Y_i have flat distributions, only that the random variable Y as a whole is flat. For example, if f is a function and X is uniform, then $(f(X), X)$ is flat even though $f(X)$ itself may be far from flat.

Putting together Lemmas 1.10, 1.14, and 1.15, we obtain a new, more modular (and slightly tighter) proof of Theorem 1.8. The reduction implicit in the combination of these lemmas is the same as the one in [11], but the analysis is different. (In particular, [11] makes no use of KL divergence.) Like the existing proof of Theorem 1.2, this proof separates the move from one-wayness to a form of hardness involving relative entropies, the role of short blocks, and the move from hardness in relative entropy to computational entropy, as summarized in Fig. 1. Moreover, this further illumination of and toolkit for notions of computational entropy may open the door to other applications in cryptography.

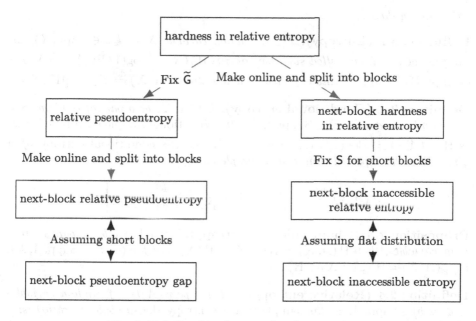

Fig. 1. Relationships between hardness notions.

We remark that another interesting direction for future work is to find a construction of universal one-way hash functions (UOWHFs) from one-way functions that follows a similar template to the above constructions of PRGs and SHCs. There is now a construction of UOWHFs based on a variant of inaccessible entropy [8], but it remains more complex and inefficient than those of PRGs and SHCs.

2   Preliminaries

Notations. For a tuple $x = (x_1, \ldots, x_n)$, we write $x_{\leq i}$ for $(x_1, \ldots, x_i)$, and $x_{<i}$ for $(x_1, \ldots, x_{i-1})$.

poly denotes the set of polynomial functions and negl the set of all negligible functions: $\varepsilon \in$ negl if for all $p \in$ poly and large enough $n \in \mathbb{N}$, $\varepsilon(n) \leq 1/p(n)$. We will sometimes abuse notations and write poly(n) to mean $p(n)$ for some $p \in$ poly and similarly for negl(n).

PPT stands for probabilistic polynomial time and can be either in the uniform or non-uniform model of computation. All our results are stated as uniform polynomial time oracle reductions and are thus meaningful in both models.

For a random variable X over $\mathcal{X}$, Supp$(X) \overset{\text{def}}{=} \{x \in \mathcal{X} : \Pr[X = x] > 0\}$ denotes the support of X. A random variable is *flat* if it is uniform over its support. Random variables will be written with uppercase letters and the associated lowercase letter represents a generic element from its support.

Information theory.

Definition 2.1 (Entropy). *For a random variable X and $x \in$ Supp(X), the sample entropy (also called surprise) of x is* $\text{H}_x^*(X) \overset{\text{def}}{=} \log(1/\Pr[X = x])$. *The entropy* $\text{H}(X)$ *of X is the expected sample entropy:* $\text{H}(X) \overset{\text{def}}{=} \text{E}_{x \leftarrow X}[\text{H}_x^*(X)]$.

Definition 2.2 (Conditional entropy). *Let (A, X) be a pair of random variables and consider $(a, x) \in$ Supp(A, X), the conditional sample entropy of (a, x) is* $\text{H}_{a,x}^*(A|X) \overset{\text{def}}{=} \log(1/\Pr[A = a \mid X = x])$ *and the conditional entropy of A given X is the expected conditional sample entropy:*

$$\text{H}(A|X) \overset{\text{def}}{=} \underset{(a,x) \leftarrow (A,X)}{\text{E}} \left[\log \frac{1}{\Pr[A = a \mid X = x]} \right].$$

Proposition 2.3 (Chain rule for entropy). *Let (A, X) be a pair of random variables, then* $\text{H}(A, X) = \text{H}(A|X) + \text{H}(X)$ *and for $(a, x) \in$ Supp(A, X), $\text{H}_{a,x}^*(A, X) = \text{H}_{a,x}^*(A|X) + \text{H}_x^*(X)$.*

Definition 2.4 (Relative entropy[2]). *For a pair (A, B) of random variables and $(a, b) \in$ Supp(A, B) the sample relative entropy (log-probability ratio) is:*

$$\text{KL}_a^*(A \parallel B) \overset{\text{def}}{=} \log \frac{\Pr[A = a]}{\Pr[B = a]},$$

and the relative entropy of A with respect to B is the expected sample relative entropy:

$$\text{KL}(A \parallel B) \overset{\text{def}}{=} \underset{a \leftarrow A}{\text{E}} \left[\log \frac{\Pr[A = a]}{\Pr[B = a]} \right].$$

---

[2] *Relative entropy* is also commonly referred to as *Kullback–Liebler divergence*, which explains the standard KL notation. We prefer to use relative entropy to have more uniformity across the notions discussed in this work.

Definition 2.5 (Conditional relative entropy). *For pairs of random variables* (A, X) *and* (B, Y), *and* $(a, x) \in \mathrm{Supp}(A, X)$, *the conditional sample relative entropy is:*

$$\mathrm{KL}^*_{a,x} \left(A|X \parallel B|Y \right) \overset{\text{def}}{=} \log \frac{\Pr\left[A = a | X = x\right]}{\Pr\left[B = a | Y = x\right]},$$

and the conditional relative entropy is:

$$\mathrm{KL} \left(A|X \parallel B|Y \right) \overset{\text{def}}{=} \underset{(a,x) \leftarrow (A,X)}{\mathrm{E}} \left[\log \frac{\Pr\left[A = a | X = x\right]}{\Pr\left[B = a | Y = x\right]} \right].$$

Proposition 2.6 (Chain rule for relative entropy). *For pairs of random variables* (X, A) *and* (Y, B):

$$\mathrm{KL} \left(A, X \parallel B, Y \right) = \mathrm{KL} \left(A|X \parallel B|Y \right) + \mathrm{KL} \left(X \parallel Y \right),$$

and for $(a, x) \in \mathrm{Supp}(A, X)$:

$$\mathrm{KL}^*_{a,x} \left(A, X \parallel B, Y \right) = \mathrm{KL}^*_{a,x} \left(A|X \parallel B|Y \right) + \mathrm{KL}^*_{x} \left(X \parallel Y \right).$$

Proposition 2.7 (Data-processing inequality). *Let* (X, Y) *be a pair of random variables and let* f *be a function defined on* $\mathrm{Supp}(Y)$, *then:*

$$\mathrm{KL} \left(X \parallel Y \right) \geq \mathrm{KL} \left(f(X) \parallel f(Y) \right).$$

Definition 2.8 (min relative entropy). *Let* (X, Y) *be a pair of random variables and* $\delta \in [0, 1]$. *We define* $\mathrm{KL}^{\delta}_{\min} \left(X \parallel Y \right)$ *to be the quantile of level* δ *of* $\mathrm{KL}^*_{x} \left(X \parallel Y \right)$, *equivalently it is the smallest* $\Delta \in \mathbb{R}$ *satisfying:*

$$\Pr_{x \leftarrow X} \left[\mathrm{KL}^*_{x} \left(X \parallel Y \right) \leq \Delta \right] \geq \delta,$$

and it is characterized by the following equivalence:

$$\mathrm{KL}^{\delta}_{\min} \left(X \parallel Y \right) > \Delta \iff \Pr_{x \leftarrow X} \left[\mathrm{KL}^*_{x} \left(X \parallel Y \right) \leq \Delta \right] < \delta.$$

Block generators.

Definition 2.9 (Block generator). *An* m-*block generator is a function* $\mathsf{G} : \{0, 1\}^s \to \prod_{i=1}^{m} \{0, 1\}^{\ell_i}$. $\mathsf{G}_i(r)$ *denotes the* i-*th block of* G *on input* r *and* $|\mathsf{G}_i| = \ell_i$ *denotes the bit length of the* i-*th block.*

Definition 2.10 (Online generator). *An* online m-*block generator is a function* $\widetilde{\mathsf{G}} : \prod_{i=1}^{m} \{0, 1\}^{s_i} \to \prod_{i=1}^{m} \{0, 1\}^{\ell_i}$ *such that for all* $i \in [m]$ *and* $r \in \prod_{i=1}^{m} \{0, 1\}^{s_i}$, $\widetilde{\mathsf{G}}_i(r)$ *only depends on* $r_{\leq i}$. *We sometimes write* $\widetilde{\mathsf{G}}_i(r_{\leq i})$ *when the input blocks* $i + 1, \ldots, m$ *are unspecified.*

Definition 2.11 (Support). *The support of a generator* G *is the support of the random variable* $\mathrm{Supp}\left(\mathsf{G}(R)\right)$ *for uniform input* R. *If* G *is an* $(m + 1)$-*block generator, and* Π *is a binary relation, we say that* G *is supported on* Π *if* $\mathrm{Supp}\left(\mathsf{G}_{\leq m}(R), \mathsf{G}_{m+1}(R)\right) \subseteq \Pi$.

When G is an $(m + 1)$-block generator supported on a binary relation Π, we will often use the notation $\mathsf{G}_{\mathsf{w}} \overset{\text{def}}{=} \mathsf{G}_{m+1}$ to emphasize that the last block corresponds to a witness for the first m blocks.

Cryptography.

Definition 2.12 (One-way Function). *Let n be a security parameter, $t = t(n)$ and $\varepsilon = \varepsilon(n)$. A function $f : \{0,1\}^n \to \{0,1\}^n$ is a (t, ε)-one-way function if:*

1. *For all time t randomized algorithm* A: $\Pr_{x \leftarrow U_n} \left[A(f(x)) \in f^{-1}(f(x)) \right] \leq \varepsilon$, *where U_n is uniform over $\{0,1\}^n$.*
2. *There exists a polynomial time algorithm* B *such that* $B(x, 1^n) = f(x)$ *for all $x \in \{0,1\}^n$.*

If f is $(n^c, 1/n^c)$-one-way for every $c \in \mathbb{N}$, we say that f is (strongly) *one-way.*

3   Search Problems and Hardness in Relative Entropy

In this section, we first present the classical notion of hard-on-average search problems and introduce the new notion of hardness in relative entropy. We then relate the two notions by proving that average-case hardness implies hardness in relative entropy.

3.1   Search Problems

For a binary relation $\Pi \subseteq \{0,1\}^* \times \{0,1\}^*$, we write $\Pi(y, w)$ for the predicate that is true iff $(y, w) \in \Pi$ and say that w is a *witness* for the *instance* y^3. To each relation Π, we naturally associate (1) a *search problem*: given y, find w such that $\Pi(y, w)$ or state that no such w exist and (2) the *decision problem* defined by the language $L_\Pi \overset{\text{def}}{=} \{y \in \{0,1\}^* : \exists w \in \{0,1\}^*, \Pi(y, w)\}$. **FNP** denotes the set of all relations Π computable by a polynomial time algorithm and such that there exists a polynomial p such that $\Pi(y, w) \Rightarrow |w| \leq p(|y|)$. Whenever $\Pi \in$ **FNP**, the associated decision problem L_Π is in **NP**. We now define average-case hardness.

Definition 3.1 (Distributional search problem). *A* distributional search problem *is a pair (Π, Y) where $\Pi \subseteq \{0,1\}^* \times \{0,1\}^*$ is a binary relation and Y is a random variable supported on L_Π.*

The problem (Π, Y) is (t, ε)- hard *if* $\Pr \left[\Pi(Y, A(Y)) \right] \leq \varepsilon$ *for all time t randomized algorithm* A, *where the probability is over the distribution of Y and the randomness of* A.

Example 3.2. For $f : \{0,1\}^n \to \{0,1\}^n$, the problem of inverting f is the search problem associated with the relation $\Pi^f \overset{\text{def}}{=} \{(f(x), x) : x \in \{0,1\}^n\}$. If f is a (t, ε)-one-way function, then the distributional search problem $(\Pi^f, f(X))$ of inverting f on a uniform random input $X \in \{0,1\}^n$ is (t, ε)-hard.

---

[3] We used the unconventional notation y for the instance (instead of x) because our relations will often be of the form Π^f for some function f; in this case an instance is some y in the range of f and a witness for y is any preimage $x \in f^{-1}(y)$.

Remark 3.3. Consider a distributional search problem (Π, Y). Without loss of generality, there exists a (possibly inefficient) two-block generator $\mathsf{G} = (\mathsf{G}_1, \mathsf{G}_\mathsf{w})$ supported on Π such that $\mathsf{G}_1(R) = Y$ for uniform input R. If G_w is polynomial-time computable, it is easy to see that the search problem $(\Pi^{\mathsf{G}_1}, \mathsf{G}_1(R))$ is at least as hard as (Π, Y). The advantage of writing the problem in this "functional" form is that the distribution $(\mathsf{G}_1(R), R)$ over (instance, witness) pairs is flat, which is a necessary condition to relate hardness to inaccessible entropy (see Theorem 4.10).

Furthermore, if G_1 is also polynomial-time computable and (Π, Y) is $(\mathrm{poly}(n), \mathrm{negl}(n))$-hard, then $R \mapsto \mathsf{G}_1(R)$ is a one-way function. Combined with the previous example, we see that the existence of one-way functions is equivalent to the existence of $(\mathrm{poly}(n), \mathrm{negl}(n))$-hard search problems for which (instance, witness) pairs can be efficiently sampled.

3.2   Hardness in Relative Entropy

Instead of considering an adversary directly attempting to solve a search problem (Π, Y), the adversary in the definition of hardness in relative entropy comprises a pair of algorithm $(\widetilde{\mathsf{G}}, \mathsf{S})$ where $\widetilde{\mathsf{G}}$ is a two-block generator outputting valid (instance, witness) pairs for Π and S is a *simulator* for $\widetilde{\mathsf{G}}$: given an instance y, the goal of S is to output randomness r for $\widetilde{\mathsf{G}}$ such that $\widetilde{\mathsf{G}}_1(r) = y$. Formally, the definition is as follows.

Definition 3.4 (hardness in relative entropy). *Let (Π, Y) be a distributional search problem. We say that (Π, Y) is (t, Δ)-hard in relative entropy if:*

$$\mathrm{KL}\left(\widetilde{R}, \widetilde{\mathsf{G}}_1(\widetilde{R}) \,\big\|\, \mathsf{S}(Y), Y\right) > \Delta,$$

for all pairs $(\widetilde{\mathsf{G}}, \mathsf{S})$ of time t algorithms where $\widetilde{\mathsf{G}}$ is a two-block generator supported on Π and $\widetilde{R}$ is uniform randomness for $\widetilde{\mathsf{G}}_1$. Similarly, for $\delta \in [0, 1]$, (Π, Y) is (t, Δ)-hard in δ-min relative entropy if for all such pairs:

$$\mathrm{KL}^\delta_{\min}\left(\widetilde{R}, \widetilde{\mathsf{G}}_1(\widetilde{R}) \,\big\|\, \mathsf{S}(Y), Y\right) > \Delta.$$

Note that a pair $(\widetilde{\mathsf{G}}, \mathsf{S})$ achieves a relative entropy of zero in Definition 3.4 if $\widetilde{\mathsf{G}}_1(R)$ has the same distribution as Y and if $\widetilde{\mathsf{G}}_1(\mathsf{S}(y)) = y$ for all $y \in \mathrm{Supp}(Y)$. In this case, writing $\widetilde{\mathsf{G}}_\mathsf{w} \stackrel{\mathrm{def}}{=} \widetilde{\mathsf{G}}_2$, we have that $\widetilde{\mathsf{G}}_\mathsf{w}(\mathsf{S}(Y))$ is a valid witness for Y since $\widetilde{\mathsf{G}}$ is supported on Π.

More generally, the composition $\widetilde{\mathsf{G}}_\mathsf{w} \circ \mathsf{S}$ solves the search problem (Π, Y) whenever $\widetilde{\mathsf{G}}_1(\mathsf{S}(Y)) = Y$. When the relative entropies in Definition 3.4 are upper-bounded, we can lower bound the probability of the search problem being solved (Lemma 3.7) This immediately implies that hard search problems are also hard in relative entropy.

Theorem 3.5. *Let (Π, Y) be a distributional search problem. If (Π, Y) is (t, ε)-hard, then it is (t', Δ')-hard in relative entropy and (t', Δ'')-hard in δ-min relative entropy for every $\delta \in [0, 1]$ where $t' = \Omega(t)$,[4] $\Delta' = \log(1/\varepsilon)$ and $\Delta'' = \log(1/\varepsilon) - \log(1/\delta)$.*

Remark 3.6. As we see, a "good" simulator S for a generator $\widetilde{\mathsf{G}}$ is one for which $\widetilde{\mathsf{G}}_1(\mathsf{S}(Y)) = Y$ holds often. It will be useful in Sect. 4 to consider simulators S which are allowed to fail by outputting a failure string $r \notin \mathrm{Supp}(\widetilde{R})$, (e.g. $r = \perp$) and adopt the convention that $\widetilde{\mathsf{G}}_1(r) = \perp$ whenever $r \notin \mathrm{Supp}(\widetilde{R})$. With this convention, we can without loss of generality add the requirement that $\widetilde{\mathsf{G}}_1(\mathsf{S}(Y)) = Y$ whenever $\mathsf{S}(Y) \in \mathrm{Supp}(\widetilde{R})$: indeed, S can always check that it is the case and if not output a failure symbol. For such a simulator S, observe that for all $r \in \mathrm{Supp}(\widetilde{R})$, the second variable on both sides of the relative entropy in Definition 3.4 is obtained by applying $\widetilde{\mathsf{G}}_1$ on the first variable and can thus be dropped, leading to a simpler definition of hardness in relative entropy:
$\mathrm{KL}\left(\widetilde{R} \,\middle\|\, \mathsf{S}(Y)\right) > \Delta$.

Theorem 3.5 is an immediate consequence of the following lemma.

Lemma 3.7. *Let (Π, Y) be a distributional search problem and $(\widetilde{\mathsf{G}}, \mathsf{S})$ be a pair of algorithms with $\widetilde{\mathsf{G}} = (\widetilde{\mathsf{G}}_1, \widetilde{\mathsf{G}}_{\mathsf{w}})$ a two-block generator supported on Π. Define the linear-time oracle algorithm $\mathsf{A}^{\widetilde{\mathsf{G}}_{\mathsf{w}}, \mathsf{S}}(y) \overset{\text{def}}{=} \widetilde{\mathsf{G}}_{\mathsf{w}}(\mathsf{S}(y))$. For $\Delta \in \mathbb{R}^+$ and $\delta \in [0, 1]$:*

1. *If $\mathrm{KL}\left(\widetilde{R}, \widetilde{\mathsf{G}}_1(\widetilde{R}) \,\middle\|\, \mathsf{S}(Y), Y\right) \leq \Delta$ then $\Pr\left[\Pi(Y, \mathsf{A}^{\widetilde{\mathsf{G}}_{\mathsf{w}}, \mathsf{S}}(Y))\right] \geq 1/2^{\Delta}$.*
2. *If $\mathrm{KL}^{\delta}_{\min}\left(\widetilde{R}, \widetilde{\mathsf{G}}_1(\widetilde{R}) \,\middle\|\, \mathsf{S}(Y), Y\right) \leq \Delta$ then $\Pr\left[\Pi(Y, \mathsf{A}^{\widetilde{\mathsf{G}}_{\mathsf{w}}, \mathsf{S}}(Y))\right] \geq \delta/2^{\Delta}$.*

Proof. We have:

$$
\begin{aligned}
\Pr\left[\Pi(Y, \mathsf{A}^{\widetilde{\mathsf{G}}_{\mathsf{w}}, \mathsf{S}}(Y))\right] &= \Pr\left[\Pi(Y, \widetilde{\mathsf{G}}_{\mathsf{w}}(\mathsf{S}(Y)))\right] \\
&\geq \Pr\left[\widetilde{\mathsf{G}}_1(\mathsf{S}(Y)) = Y\right] \qquad (\widetilde{\mathsf{G}} \text{ is supported on } \Pi) \\
&= \sum_{r \in \mathrm{Supp}(\widetilde{R})} \Pr\left[\mathsf{S}(Y) = r \wedge Y = \widetilde{\mathsf{G}}_1(r)\right] \\
&= \mathop{\mathrm{E}}_{r \leftarrow \widetilde{R}} \left[\frac{\Pr\left[\mathsf{S}(Y) = r \wedge Y = \widetilde{\mathsf{G}}_1(r)\right]}{\Pr\left[\widetilde{R} = r\right]}\right] \\
&= \mathop{\mathrm{E}}_{\substack{r \leftarrow \widetilde{R} \\ y \leftarrow \widetilde{\mathsf{G}}_1(r)}} \left[2^{-\mathrm{KL}^*_{r,y}\left(\widetilde{R}, \widetilde{\mathsf{G}}_1(\widetilde{R}) \,\middle\|\, \mathsf{S}(Y), Y\right)}\right].
\end{aligned}
$$

---

[4] For the theorems in this paper that relate two notions of hardness, the notation $t' = \Omega(t)$ means that there exists a constant C depending *only* on the computational model such that $t' \geq C \cdot t$.

Now, the first claim follows by Jensen's inequality (since $x \mapsto 2^{-x}$ is convex) and the second claim follows by Markov' inequality when considering the event that the sample relative entropy is smaller than Δ (which occurs with probability at least δ by assumption).

Relation to Relative Pseudoentropy. In [21], the authors introduced the notion of relative pseudoentropy[5]: for jointly distributed variables (Y, W), W has relative pseudoentropy given Y if it is hard for a polynomial time adversary to approximate—measured in relative entropy—the conditional distribution W given Y. Formally:

Definition 3.8 (Relative pseudoentropy, Definition 3.4 in [21]). *Let* (Y, W) *be a pair of random variables, we say that* W *has* relative pseudoentropy (t, Δ) *given* Y *if for all time* t *randomized algorithm* S, *we have:*

$$\mathrm{KL}\left(Y, W \,\|\, Y, \mathsf{S}(Y)\right) > \Delta .$$

As discussed in Sect. 1.2, it was shown in [21] that if $f : \{0,1\}^n \to \{0,1\}^n$ is a one-way function, then $(f(X), X_1, \ldots, X_n)$ has next-bit pseudoentropy for uniform $X \in \{0,1\}^n$ (see Theorem 1.2). The first step in proving this result was to prove that X has relative pseudoentropy given $f(X)$ (see Lemma 1.4).

We observe that when (Y, W) is of the form $(f(X), X)$ for some function $f : \{0,1\}^n \to \{0,1\}^n$ and variable X over $\{0,1\}^n$, then relative pseudoentropy is implied by hardness in relative entropy by simply fixing $\widetilde{\mathsf{G}}$ to be the "honest sampler" $\widetilde{\mathsf{G}}(X) = (f(X), X)$. Indeed, in this case we have:

$$\mathrm{KL}\left(X, \widetilde{\mathsf{G}}_1(X) \,\middle\|\, \mathsf{S}(Y), Y\right) = \mathrm{KL}\left(X, f(X) \,\|\, \mathsf{S}(Y), Y\right) .$$

We can thus recover Lemma 1.4 as a direct corollary of Theorem 3.5.

Corollary 3.9. *Consider a function* $f : \{0,1\}^n \to \{0,1\}^n$ *and define* $\Pi^f \stackrel{\mathrm{def}}{=} \{(f(x), x) : x \in \{0,1\}^n\}$ *and* $Y \stackrel{\mathrm{def}}{=} f(X)$ *for* X *uniform over* $\{0,1\}^n$. *If* f *is* (t, ε)-*one-way, then* (Π^f, Y) *is* $(t', \log(1/\varepsilon))$-*hard in relative entropy and* X *has* $(t', \log(1/\varepsilon))$ *relative pseudoentropy given* Y *with* $t' = \Omega(t)$.

Witness Hardness in Relative Entropy. We also introduce a relaxed notion of hardness in relative entropy called witness hardness in relative entropy. In this notion, we further require $(\widetilde{\mathsf{G}}, \mathsf{S})$ to approximate the joint distribution of (instance, witness) pairs rather than only instances. For example, the problem of inverting a function f over a random input X is naturally associated with the distribution $(f(X), X)$. The relaxation in this case is analogous to the notion of *distributional one-way function* for which the adversary is required to approximate the uniform distribution over preimages.

---

[5] As already mentioned in the introduction, this notion was in fact called "KL-hardness for sampling" in [21] but we rename it here to unify the terminology between the various notions discussed here.

Definition 3.10 (Witness hardness in relative entropy). *Let Π be a binary relation and (Y, W) be a pair of random variables supported on Π. We say that (Π, Y, W) is (t, Δ) witness hard in relative entropy if for all pairs of time t algorithms $(\widetilde{\mathsf{G}}, \mathsf{S})$ where $\widetilde{\mathsf{G}}$ is a two-block generator supported on Π, for uniform $\widetilde{R}$:*

$$\mathrm{KL}\left(\widetilde{R}, \widetilde{\mathsf{G}}_1(\widetilde{R}), \widetilde{\mathsf{G}}_{\mathsf{w}}(\widetilde{R}) \,\middle\|\, \mathsf{S}(Y), Y, W\right) > \Delta \,.$$

Similarly, for $\delta \in [0, 1]$, (Π, Y, W) is (t, Δ)-witness hard in δ-min relative entropy, if for all such pairs:

$$\mathrm{KL}^{\delta}_{\min}\left(\widetilde{R}, \widetilde{\mathsf{G}}_1(\widetilde{R}), \widetilde{\mathsf{G}}_{\mathsf{w}}(\widetilde{R}) \,\middle\|\, \mathsf{S}(Y), Y, W\right) > \Delta \,.$$

We introduced hardness in relative entropy first, since it is the notion which is most directly obtained from the hardness of distribution search problems. Observe that by the data processing inequality for relative entropy (Proposition 2.7), dropping the third variable on both sides of the relative entropies in Definition 3.10 only decreases them. Hence, hardness in relative entropy implies witness hardness as stated in (Theorem 3.11). As we will see in Sect. 4 witness hardness in relative entropy is the "correct" notion to obtain inaccessible entropy from: it is in fact equal to inaccessible entropy up to $1/\operatorname{poly}$ losses.

Theorem 3.11. *Let Π be a binary relation and (Y, W) be a pair of random variables supported on Π. If (Π, Y) is (t, ε)-hard, then (Π, Y, W) is (t', Δ') witness hard in relative entropy and (t', Δ'') witness hard in δ-min relative entropy for every $\delta \in [0, 1]$ where $t' = \Omega(t)$, $\Delta' = \log(1/\varepsilon)$ and $\Delta'' = \log(1/\varepsilon) - \log(1/\delta)$.*

Remark 3.12. The data processing inequality does not hold exactly for $\mathrm{KL}_{\min}$, hence the statement about δ-min relative entropy in Theorem 3.11 does not follow with the claimed parameters in a black-box manner from Theorem 3.5. However, an essentially identical proof given in Appendix A yields the result.

4   Inaccessible Entropy and Hardness in Relative Entropy

In this section, we relate our notion of witness hardness in relative entropy to the inaccessible entropy definition of [13]. Roughly speaking, we "split" the relative entropy into blocks and obtain the intermediate notion of next-block inaccessible relative entropy (Sect. 4.1) that we then relate to inaccessible entropy (Sect. 4.2). Together, these results show that if f is a one-way function, the generator $\mathsf{G}^f(X) = \left(f(X)_1, \ldots, f(X)_n, X\right)$ has superlogarithmic inaccessible entropy.

4.1   Next-Block Hardness and Rejection Sampling

Consider a binary relation Π and a pair of random variables (Y, W) supported on Π. Let $\widetilde{\mathsf{G}}$ be an online $(m+1)$-block generator supported on Π and write $\widetilde{Y}_{\leq m} \overset{\text{def}}{=} \widetilde{\mathsf{G}}(\widetilde{R}_{\leq m})$ for uniform $\widetilde{R}_{\leq m}$. For such a generator $\widetilde{\mathsf{G}}$, it is natural to consider simulators operating in an online manner. Specifically, an online simulator in this context is a PPT algorithm S such that on input $(\widehat{R}_{<i}, Y_i)$, S outputs $\widehat{R}_i$ of the same length as $\widetilde{R}_i$. The goal of S is to output random coins such that $(\widetilde{R}_i, \widetilde{Y}_i)$ is "close" to $(\widehat{R}_i, Y_i)$ conditioned on the past. This leads to the following natural blockwise notion of hardness in relative entropy for online generators and simulators.

Definition 4.1 (Next-block hardness in relative entropy). *The joint distribution* $(Y_1, \ldots, Y_m)$ *is* (t, Δ) *next-block hard in relative entropy if the following holds.*

Let $\widetilde{\mathsf{G}}$ *be any time* t *online* m-block generator supported on $Y_{\leq m}$ and write $\widetilde{Y}_{\leq m} \overset{\text{def}}{=} \widetilde{\mathsf{G}}(\widetilde{R}_{\leq m})$ for uniform $\widetilde{R}_{\leq m}$. Let S be an online simulator and define inductively $\widehat{R}_i \overset{\text{def}}{=} \mathsf{S}(\widehat{R}_{<i}, Y_i)$ with $\widehat{R}_i$ having the same length as $\widetilde{R}_i$, where S is a probabilistic algorithm that uses time at most t to compute $\widehat{R}_{\leq m}$.

Then we require:

$$\sum_{i=1}^{m} \mathrm{KL}\left(\widetilde{R}_i, \widetilde{Y}_i | \widetilde{R}_{<i}, \widetilde{Y}_{<i} \,\middle\|\, \widehat{R}_i, Y_i | \widehat{R}_{<i}, Y_{<i} \right) > \Delta.$$

Similarly, for $\delta \in [0,1]$, *we say that* $(Y_1, \ldots, Y_m)$ *is* (t, Δ)-next-block hard in δ-min relative entropy if, with the same notations as above:

$$\Pr_{\substack{i \leq m, \, \widetilde{R}_{\leq m} \\ y_{\leq m} \leftarrow \widetilde{\mathsf{G}}(r_{\leq m})}} \left[\sum_{i=1}^{m} \mathrm{KL}^*_{y_i, r_{<i}, y_{<i}} \left(\widetilde{R}_i, \widetilde{Y}_i | \widetilde{R}_{<i}, \widetilde{Y}_{<i} \,\middle\|\, \widehat{R}_i, Y_i | \widehat{R}_{<i}, Y_{<i} \right) \leq \Delta \right] < \delta.$$

Observe that using the chain rule for relative entropy, the sum of relative entropies appearing in Definition 4.1 is exactly equal to the relative entropies appearing in Definition 3.4. Since, furthermore considering an online generator $\widetilde{\mathsf{G}}$ and online simulator S is only less general than arbitrary pairs $(\widetilde{\mathsf{G}}, \mathsf{S})$, we immediately obtain the following theorem.

Theorem 4.2. *Let* (Π, Y) *be a distributional search problem. If* (Π, Y) *is* (t, Δ)- *hard in relative entropy then* $(Y_1, \ldots, Y_m)$ *is* (t, Δ) *next-block hard in relative entropy.*

Similarly, for any $\delta \in [0,1]$, *if* (Π, Y) *is* (t, Δ)-*hard in* δ-*min relative entropy then* $(Y_1, \ldots, Y_m)$ *is* (t, Δ) *next-block hard in* δ-*min relative entropy.*

Proof. Immediate using the chain rule for relative (sample) entropy.

The next step is to obtain a notion of hardness that makes no reference to simulators by considering, for an online block generator $\widetilde{\mathsf{G}}$, a specific simulator $\mathsf{Sim}^{\widetilde{\mathsf{G}}, T}$ which on input $(\widehat{R}_{<i}, Y_i)$, generates $\widehat{R}_i$ using rejection sampling until $\widetilde{\mathsf{G}}_i(\widehat{R}_{\leq i}) = Y_i$. The superscript T is the maximum number of attempts after which $\mathsf{Sim}^{\widetilde{\mathsf{G}}, T}$ gives up and outputs $\bot$. The formal definition of $\mathsf{Sim}^{\widetilde{\mathsf{G}}, T}$ is given in Algorithm 1.

Algorithm 1. Rejection sampling simulator $\mathrm{Sim}^{\widetilde{G},T}$ for $1 \leq i \leq m$

Input: $y_i \in \{0,1\}^*$, $\widehat{r}_{<i} \in (\{0,1\}^v \cup \{\bot\})^{i-1}$
Output: $\widehat{r}_i \in \{0,1\}^v \cup \{\bot\}$
  if $\widehat{r}_{i-1} = \bot$ **then**
    $\widehat{r}_i \leftarrow \bot$; **return**
  end if
  repeat
    sample $\widehat{r}_i \leftarrow \{0,1\}^v$
  until $\widetilde{G}_i(\widehat{r}_{\leq i}) = y_i$ or $\geq T$ attempts
  if $\widetilde{G}_i(\widehat{r}_{\leq i}) \neq y_i$ **then**
    $\widehat{r}_i \leftarrow \bot$
  end if

For the rejection sampling simulator $\mathrm{Sim}^{\widetilde{G},T}$, we will show in Lemma 4.5 that the next-block hardness in relative entropy in Definition 4.1 decomposes as the sum of two terms:

1. A term measuring how well $\widetilde{G}_{\leq m}$ approximates the distribution Y in an online manner, without any reference to a simulator.
2. An error term measuring the failure probability of the rejection sampling procedure due to having a finite time bound T.

As we show in Lemma 4.6, the error term can be made arbitrarily small by setting the number of trials T in $\mathrm{Sim}^{\widetilde{G},T}$ to be a large enough multiple of $m \cdot 2^\ell$ where ℓ is the length of the blocks of $\widetilde{G}_{\leq m}$. This leads to a poly(m) time algorithm whenever ℓ is logarithmic in m. That is, given an online block generator $\widetilde{G}$ for which $\widetilde{G}_{\leq m}$ has short blocks, we obtain a corresponding simulator "for free". Thus, considering only the first term leads to the following clean definition of next-block inaccessible relative entropy that makes no reference to simulators.

Definition 4.3 (Next-block inaccessible relative entropy). *The joint distribution* $(Y_1, \ldots, Y_m)$ *has* (t, Δ) *next-block inaccessible relative entropy, if for every time* t *online* m-*block generator* $\widetilde{G}$ *supported on* $Y_{\leq m}$, *writing* $\widetilde{Y}_{\leq m} \stackrel{\mathrm{def}}{=} \widetilde{G}(\widetilde{R}_{\leq m})$ *for uniform* $\widetilde{R}_{\leq m}$, *we have:*

$$\sum_{i=1}^{m} \mathrm{KL}\left(\widetilde{Y}_i | \widetilde{R}_{<i}, \widetilde{Y}_{<i} \,\middle\|\, Y_i | R_{<i}, Y_{<i}\right) > \Delta,$$

where R_i *is a "dummy" random variable over the domain of* $\widetilde{G}_i$ *and independent of* $Y_{\leq m+1}$. *Similarly, for* $\delta \in [0,1]$, *we say that* $(Y_1, \ldots, Y_{m+1})$ *has* (t, Δ)-*next-block inaccessible* δ-*min relative entropy if for every* $\widetilde{G}$ *as above:*

$$\Pr_{\substack{r_{\leq m} \leftarrow \widetilde{R}_{\leq m} \\ y_{\leq m} \leftarrow \widetilde{G}(r_{\leq m})}} \left[\sum_{i=1}^{m} \mathrm{KL}^*_{y_i, r_{<i}, y_{<i}}\left(\widetilde{Y}_i | \widetilde{R}_{<i}, \widetilde{Y}_{<i} \,\middle\|\, Y_i | R_{<i}, Y_{<i}\right) \leq \Delta\right] < \delta,$$

where $(\widetilde{Y}_{\leq m}, \widetilde{R}_{\leq m})$ are defined as above.

Remark 4.4. Since $\widetilde{Y}_{<i}$ is a function of $\widetilde{R}_{<i}$, the first conditional distribution in the KL is effectively $\widetilde{Y}_i|\widetilde{R}_{<i}$. Similarly the second distribution is effectively $Y_i|Y_{<i}$. The extra random variables are there for syntactic consistency.

With this definition in hand, we can make formal the claim that, even as sample notions, the next-block hardness in relative entropy decomposes as next-block inaccessible relative entropy plus an error term.

Lemma 4.5. *For a joint distribution $(Y_1, \ldots, Y_m)$, let $\widetilde{G}$ be an online m-block generator supported on $Y_{\leq m}$. Define $(\widetilde{Y}_1, \ldots, \widetilde{Y}_m) \overset{\text{def}}{=} \widetilde{G}(\widetilde{R})$ for uniform random variable $\widetilde{R} = (\widetilde{R}_1, \ldots, \widetilde{R}_m)$ and let R_i be a "dummy" random variable over the domain of $\widetilde{G}_i$ and independent of $Y_{\leq m+1}$. We also define $\widehat{R}_i \overset{\text{def}}{=} \text{Sim}^{\widetilde{G},T}(\widehat{R}_{<i}, Y_i)$ and $\widehat{Y}_i = \widetilde{G}(\widehat{R}_{\leq i})$. Then, for all $r \in \text{Supp}(\widetilde{R})$ and $y \overset{\text{def}}{=} \widetilde{G}(r)$:*

$$\sum_{i=1}^{m} \text{KL}^*_{r,y}\left(\widetilde{R}_i, \widetilde{Y}_i|\widetilde{R}_{<i}, \widetilde{Y}_{<i} \,\middle\|\, \widehat{R}_i, Y_i|\widehat{R}_{<i}, Y_{<i}\right)$$

$$= \sum_{i=1}^{m} \text{KL}^*_{r,y}\left(\widetilde{Y}_i|\widetilde{R}_{<i}, \widetilde{Y}_{<i} \,\middle\|\, Y_i|R_{<i}, Y_{<i}\right)$$

$$+ \sum_{i=1}^{m} \log\left(\frac{1}{\Pr\left[\widehat{Y}_i = y_i|Y_i = y_i, \widehat{R}_{<i} = r_{<i}\right]}\right).$$

Moreover, the running time of $\text{Sim}^{\widetilde{G},T}$ on input $\widehat{R}_{<i}, Y_i$ is $O(|r_i| \cdot T)$, with at most T oracle calls to $\widetilde{G}$.

Proof. Consider $r \in \text{Supp}(\widetilde{R})$ and $y \overset{\text{def}}{=} \widetilde{G}(r)$. Then:

$$\sum_{i=1}^{m} \text{KL}^*_{r,y}\left(\widetilde{R}_i, \widetilde{Y}_i|\widetilde{R}_{<i}, \widetilde{Y}_{<i} \,\middle\|\, \widehat{R}_i, Y_i|\widehat{R}_{<i}, Y_{<i}\right)$$

$$= \sum_{i=1}^{m} \text{KL}^*_{r,y}\left(\widetilde{R}_i, \widetilde{Y}_i|\widetilde{R}_{<i}, \widetilde{Y}_{<i} \,\middle\|\, \widehat{R}_i, \widehat{Y}_i|\widehat{R}_{<i}, \widehat{Y}_{<i}\right)$$

$$= \sum_{i=1}^{m} \left(\text{KL}^*_{r,y}\left(\widetilde{R}_i|\widetilde{R}_{<i}, \widetilde{Y}_{\leq i} \,\middle\|\, \widehat{R}_i|\widehat{R}_{<i}, \widehat{Y}_{\leq i}\right) + \text{KL}^*_{r,y}\left(\widetilde{Y}_i|\widetilde{R}_{<i}, \widetilde{Y}_{<i} \,\middle\|\, \widehat{Y}_i|\widehat{R}_{<i}, \widehat{Y}_{<i}\right)\right)$$

$$= \sum_{i=1}^{m} \text{KL}^*_{r,y}\left(\widetilde{Y}_i|\widetilde{R}_{<i}, \widetilde{Y}_{<i} \,\middle\|\, \widehat{Y}_i|\widehat{R}_{<i}, \widehat{Y}_{<i}\right)$$

$$= \sum_{i=1}^{m} \text{KL}^*_{r,y}\left(\widetilde{Y}_i|\widetilde{R}_{<i} \,\middle\|\, \widehat{Y}_i|\widehat{R}_{<i}\right),$$

The first equality is because $Y_i = \widehat{Y}_i$ since we are only considering non-failure cases ($r_i \neq \perp$). The second equality is the chain rule. The penultimate equality is by definition of rejection sampling: $\widehat{R}_i | \widetilde{R}_{<i}, \widetilde{Y}_{\leq i}$ and $\widehat{R}_i | \widehat{R}_{<i}, \widehat{Y}_{\leq i}$ are identical on $\mathrm{Supp}(\widetilde{R}_i)$ since conditioning on $\widehat{Y}_i = y$ implies that only non-failure cases ($r_i \neq \perp$) are considered. The last equality is because $\widetilde{Y}_{<i}$ (resp. $\widehat{Y}_{<i}$) is a deterministic function of $\widetilde{R}_{<i}$ (resp. $\widehat{R}_{<i}$).

We now relate $\widehat{Y}_i | \widehat{R}_{<i}$ to $Y_i | Y_{<i}$:

$$\Pr\left[\widehat{Y}_i = y_i | \widehat{R}_{<i} = r_{<i}\right]$$

$$= \Pr\left[\widehat{Y}_i = y_i, Y_i = y_i | \widehat{R}_{<i} = r_{<i}\right] \qquad (\widehat{Y}_i = y_i \Leftrightarrow \widehat{Y}_i = y_i \wedge Y_i = y_i)$$

$$= \Pr\left[\widehat{Y}_i = y_i | Y_i = y_i, \widehat{R}_{<i} = r_{<i}\right] \cdot \Pr\left[Y_i = y_i | \widehat{R}_{<i} = r_{<i}\right] \quad \text{(Bayes' Rule)}$$

$$= \Pr\left[\widehat{Y}_i = y_i | Y_i = y_i, \widehat{R}_{<i} = r_{<i}\right] \cdot \Pr\left[Y_i = y_i | Y_{<i} = y_{<i}\right],$$

where the last equality is because when $r \in \mathrm{Supp}(\widetilde{R})$, $\widehat{R}_{<i} = r_{<i} \Rightarrow Y_{<i} = y_{<i}$ and because Y_i is independent of $\widehat{R}_{<i}$ given $Y_{<i}$ (as $\widehat{R}_{<i}$ is simply a randomized function of $Y_{<i}$). The conclusion of the lemma follows by combining the previous two derivations.

Observe that taking expectations with respect to a uniform $\widetilde{R}$ on both sides in the conclusion of Lemma 4.5, we get that next-block hardness in relative entropy is equal to the sum of next-block inaccessible relative entropy and the expectation of the error term coming from the rejection sampling procedure. The following lemma upper bounds this expectation.

Lemma 4.6. *Let $\widetilde{\mathsf{G}}$ be an online m-block generator, and let $L_i \stackrel{\text{def}}{=} 2^{|\widetilde{\mathsf{G}}_i|}$ be the size of the codomain of $\widetilde{\mathsf{G}}_i$, $i \in [m]$. Then for all $i \in [m]$, $r_{<i} \in \mathrm{Supp}(\widetilde{R}_{<i})$ and uniform $\widetilde{R}_i$:*

$$\operatorname*{E}_{y_i \leftarrow \widetilde{\mathsf{G}}_i(r_{<i}, \widetilde{R}_i)}\left[\log \frac{1}{\Pr\left[\widehat{Y}_i = y_i | Y_i = y_i, \widehat{R}_{<i} = r_{<i}\right]}\right] \leq \log\left(1 + \frac{L_i - 1}{T}\right).$$

Proof (Proof of Lemma 4.6). By definition of $\mathsf{Sim}^{\widetilde{\mathsf{G}}, T}$, we have:

$$\Pr\left[\widehat{Y}_i = y_i | Y_i = y_i, \widehat{R}_{<i} = r_{<i}\right] = 1 - \left(1 - \Pr\left[\widetilde{\mathsf{G}}_i(r_{<i}, \widetilde{R}_i) = y_i\right]\right)^T.$$

Applying Jensen's inequality, we have:

$$
\mathop{\mathrm{E}}_{y_i \leftarrow \widetilde{\mathsf{G}}_i(r_{<i}, \widetilde{R}_i)} \left[\log \left(\frac{1}{\Pr\left[\widehat{Y}_i = y_i | Y_i = y_i, \widehat{R}_{<i} = r_{<i} \right]} \right) \right]
$$

$$
\leq \log \mathop{\mathrm{E}}_{y_i \leftarrow \widetilde{\mathsf{G}}_i(r_{<i}, \widetilde{R}_i)} \left[\frac{1}{\Pr\left[\widehat{Y}_i = y_i | Y_i = y_i, \widehat{R}_{<i} = r_{<i} \right]} \right]
$$

$$
= \log \left(\sum_{y \in \mathrm{Im}(\widetilde{\mathsf{G}}_i(r_{<i}, \cdot))} \frac{p_y}{1 - (1 - p_y)^T} \right)
$$

where $p_y = \Pr\left[\widetilde{\mathsf{G}}_i(r_{<i}, \widetilde{R}_i) = y \right]$. Since the function $x / \left(1 - (1 - x)^T\right)$ is convex (see Lemma A.1 in the appendix), the maximum of the expression inside the logarithm over probability distributions $\{p_y\}$ is achieved at the extremal points of the standard probability simplex. Namely, when all but one $p_y \to 0$ and the other one is 1. Since $\lim_{x \to 0} x / 1 - (1 - x)^T = 1/T$:

$$
\log \left(\sum_{y \in \mathrm{Im}(\widetilde{\mathsf{G}}_i)} \frac{p_y}{1 - (1 - p_y)^T} \right) \leq \log \left(1 + (L_i - 1) \cdot \frac{1}{T} \right).
$$

By combining Lemmas 4.5 and 4.6, we are now ready to state the main result of this section, relating witness hardness in relative entropy to next-block inaccessible relative entropy.

Theorem 4.7. *Let Π be a binary relation and let (Y, W) be a pair of random variables supported on Π. Let $Y = (Y_1, \ldots, Y_m)$ where the bit length of Y_i is at most ℓ. Then we have:*

1. *if (Π, Y, W) is (t, Δ) witness hard in relative entropy, then for every $0 < \Delta' \leq \Delta$, $(Y_1, \ldots, Y_m, W)$ has $(t', \Delta - \Delta')$ next-block inaccessible relative entropy where $t' = \Omega(t\Delta'/(m^2 2^\ell))$.*
2. *if (Π, Y, W) is (t, Δ) witness hard in δ-min relative entropy then for every $0 < \Delta' \leq \Delta$ and $0 \leq \delta' \leq 1 - \delta$, we have that $(Y_1, \ldots, Y_m, W)$ has $(t', \Delta - \Delta')$ next-block inaccessible $(\delta + \delta')$-min relative entropy where $t' = \Omega(t\delta'\Delta'/(m^2 2^\ell))$.*

Proof. We consider an online generator $\widetilde{\mathsf{G}}$ supported on $(Y_1, \ldots, Y_m, W)$ and the simulator $\mathsf{Sim}^{\widetilde{\mathsf{G}}, T}$. For convenience, we sometimes write Y_{m+1} for W. Define $\widetilde{R} \overset{\mathrm{def}}{=} \widetilde{R}_{\leq m}$ where $\widetilde{R}_{\leq m}$ is a sequence of independent and uniformly random variables, $\widetilde{Y}_{\leq m+1} \overset{\mathrm{def}}{=} \widetilde{\mathsf{G}}(\widetilde{R})$, $\widetilde{\mathsf{G}}_1(\widetilde{R}) \overset{\mathrm{def}}{=} \widetilde{Y}_{\leq m}$ and $\widetilde{\mathsf{G}}_w(\widetilde{R}) \overset{\mathrm{def}}{=} \widetilde{Y}_{m+1}$. We also write for $1 \leq i \leq m$, $\widehat{R}_i \overset{\mathrm{def}}{=} \mathsf{Sim}^{\widetilde{\mathsf{G}}, T}(\widehat{R}_{<i}, Y_i)$, $\widehat{Y}_i \overset{\mathrm{def}}{=} \widetilde{\mathsf{G}}(\widehat{R}_{\leq i})_i$. Finally we define $\mathsf{S}^{\widetilde{\mathsf{G}}, T}(Y) \overset{\mathrm{def}}{=} \widehat{R}_{\leq m}$.

Observe that $(\widetilde{\mathsf{G}}_1, \widetilde{\mathsf{G}}_w)$ is a two-block generator supported on Π, so the pair $(\widetilde{\mathsf{G}}, \mathsf{S}^{\widetilde{\mathsf{G}}, T})$ forms a pair a algorithms as in the definition of witness hardness in relative entropy (Definition 3.10). We focus on sample notions first, and consider $r \in \text{Supp}(\widetilde{R})$, $y \in \text{Supp}(\widetilde{Y}_{\leq m})$ and $w \in \text{Supp}(\widetilde{Y}_{m+1})$. First we use the chain rule to isolate the witness block:

$$
\begin{aligned}
\text{KL}^*_{r,y,w} &\left(\widetilde{R}, \widetilde{\mathsf{G}}_1(\widetilde{R}), \widetilde{\mathsf{G}}_w(\widetilde{R}) \,\middle\|\, \mathsf{S}^{\widetilde{\mathsf{G}},T}(Y), Y, W \right) \\
&= \text{KL}^*_{r,y,w} \left(\widetilde{\mathsf{G}}_w(\widetilde{R}) | \widetilde{R}, \widetilde{\mathsf{G}}_1(\widetilde{R}) \,\middle\|\, W | \mathsf{S}^{\widetilde{\mathsf{G}},T}(Y), Y \right) \\
&\quad + \text{KL}^*_{r,y,w} \left(\widetilde{R}, \widetilde{\mathsf{G}}_1(\widetilde{R}) \,\middle\|\, \mathsf{S}^{\widetilde{\mathsf{G}},T}(Y), Y \right) \\
&= \text{KL}^*_{r,y,w} \left(\widetilde{Y}_{m+1} | \widetilde{R}_{\leq m}, \widetilde{Y}_{\leq m} \,\middle\|\, Y_{m+1} | R_{\leq m}, Y_{\leq m} \right) \\
&\quad + \text{KL}^*_{r,y,w} \left(\widetilde{R}, \widetilde{\mathsf{G}}_1(\widetilde{R}) \,\middle\|\, \mathsf{S}^{\widetilde{\mathsf{G}},T}(Y), Y \right) .
\end{aligned}
$$

Next, as in Theorem 4.2 we apply the chain rule to decompose the second term on the right-hand side and obtain next-block hardness in relative entropy:

$$
\begin{aligned}
\text{KL}^*_{r,y,w} &\left(\widetilde{R}, \widetilde{\mathsf{G}}_1(\widetilde{R}) \,\middle\|\, \mathsf{S}^{\widetilde{\mathsf{G}},T}(Y), Y \right) \\
&= \sum_{i=1}^m \text{KL}^*_{r,y,w} \left(\widetilde{R}_i, \widetilde{Y}_i | \widetilde{R}_{<i}, \widetilde{Y}_{<i} \,\middle\|\, \widehat{R}_i, Y_i | \widehat{R}_{<i}, Y_{<i} \right) .
\end{aligned}
$$

Finally, we use Lemma 4.5 to further decompose the right-hand side term into inaccessible relative entropy and the rejection sampling error:

$$
\begin{aligned}
\sum_{i=1}^m &\text{KL}^*_{r,y,w} \left(\widetilde{R}_i, \widetilde{Y}_i | \widetilde{R}_{<i}, \widetilde{Y}_{<i} \,\middle\|\, \widehat{R}_i, Y_i | \widehat{R}_{<i}, Y_{<i} \right) \\
&= \sum_{i=1}^m \text{KL}^*_{r,y} \left(\widetilde{Y}_i | \widetilde{R}_{<i}, \widetilde{Y}_{<i} \,\middle\|\, Y_i | R_{<i}, Y_{<i} \right) \\
&\quad + \sum_{i=1}^m \log \left(\frac{1}{\Pr\left[\widehat{Y}_i = y_i | Y_i = y_i, \widehat{R}_{<i} = r_{<i} \right]} \right) .
\end{aligned}
$$

Combining the previous derivations, we obtain:

$$
\begin{aligned}
\sum_{i=1}^{m+1} &\text{KL}^*_{r,y} \left(\widetilde{Y}_i | \widetilde{R}_{<i}, \widetilde{Y}_{<i} \,\middle\|\, Y_i | R_{<i}, Y_{<i} \right) \\
&= \text{KL}^*_{r,y,w} \left(\widetilde{R}, \widetilde{\mathsf{G}}_1(\widetilde{R}), \widetilde{\mathsf{G}}_w(\widetilde{R}) \,\middle\|\, \mathsf{S}^{\widetilde{\mathsf{G}},T}(Y), Y, W \right) \\
&\quad - \sum_{i=1}^m \log \left(\frac{1}{\Pr\left[\widehat{Y}_i = y_i | Y_i = y_i, \widehat{R}_{<i} = r_{<i} \right]} \right) .
\end{aligned}
$$

Now, the first claim of the theorem follows by taking expectations on both sides and observing that when $T = m \cdot 2^\ell / (\Delta' \ln 2)$, Lemma 4.6 implies that the expected value of the rejection sampling error is smaller than Δ'.

For the second claim, we first establish using Lemma 4.6 and Markov's inequality that:

$$\Pr_{\substack{y_{\leq m+1} \leftarrow \widetilde{Y}_{\leq m+1} \\ r \leftarrow \widetilde{R}}} \left[\sum_{i=1}^{m} \log \left(\frac{1}{\Pr\left[\widehat{Y}_i = y_i | \widehat{R}_{<i} = r_{<i}, \widehat{Y}_{<i} = y_{<i} \right]} \right) \geq \frac{m \cdot 2^{\ell}}{T \delta' \ln 2} \right] \leq \delta'$$

and we reach a similar conclusion by setting $T = m \cdot 2^{\ell}/(\delta' \Delta' \ln 2)$.

Remark 4.8. For fixed distribution and generators, in the limit where T grows to infinity, the error term caused by the failure of rejection sampling in time T vanishes. In this case, hardness in relative entropy implies next-block inaccessible relative entropy without any loss in the hardness parameters.

4.2 Next-Block Inaccessible Relative Entropy and Inaccessible Entropy

We first recall the definition from [13], slightly adapted to our notations.

Definition 4.9 (Inaccessible Entropy). *Let $(Y_1, \ldots, Y_{m+1})$ be a joint distribution.[6] We say that $(Y_1, \ldots, Y_{m+1})$ has t-inaccessible entropy Δ if for all $(m + 1)$-block online generators $\widetilde{G}$ running in time t and consistent with $(Y_1, \ldots, Y_{m+1})$:*

$$\sum_{i=1}^{m+1} \left(\mathrm{H}(Y_i|Y_{<i}) - \mathrm{H}(\widetilde{Y}_i|\widetilde{R}_{<i}) \right) > \Delta .$$

where $(\widetilde{Y}_1, \ldots, \widetilde{Y}_{m+1}) = \widetilde{G}(\widetilde{R}_1, \ldots, \widetilde{R}_{m+1})$ for a uniform $\widetilde{R}_{\leq m+1}$. We say that $(Y_1, \ldots, Y_{m+1})$ has (t, δ)-max-inaccessible entropy Δ if for all $(m + 1)$-block online generators $\widetilde{G}$ running in time t and consistent with $(Y_1, \ldots, Y_{m+1})$:

$$\Pr_{\substack{r_{\leq m+1} \leftarrow \widetilde{R}_{\leq m+1} \\ y_{\leq m+1} \leftarrow \widetilde{G}(r_{\leq m+1})}} \left[\sum_{i=1}^{m+1} \left(\mathrm{H}^*_{y_i, y_{<i}}(Y_i|Y_{<i}) - \mathrm{H}^*_{y_i, r_{<i}}\left(\widetilde{Y}_i|\widetilde{R}_{<i} \right) \right) \leq \Delta \right] < \delta .$$

Unfortunately, one unsatisfactory aspect of Definition 4.9 is that inaccessible entropy can be negative since the generator $\widetilde{G}$ could have more entropy than $(Y_1, \ldots, Y_{m+1})$: if all the Y_i are independent biased random bits, then a generator $\widetilde{G}$ outputting unbiased random bits will have negative inaccessible entropy. On the other hand, next-block inaccessible relative entropy (Definition 4.3) does not suffer from this drawback.

Moreover, in the specific case where $(Y_1, \ldots, Y_{m+1})$ is a flat distribution[7], then no distribution with the same support can have higher entropy and in this case Definitions 4.3 and 4.9 coincide as stated in the following theorem.

---

[6] We write $m+1$ the total number of blocks, since in this section we will think of Y_{m+1} (also written as W) as the witness of distributional search problem and $(Y_1, \ldots, Y_m)$ are the blocks of the instance as in the previous section.

[7] For example, the distribution $(Y_{\leq m}, Y_{m+1}) = (f(U), U)$ for a function f and uniform input U is always a flat distribution even if f itself is not regular.

Theorem 4.10. *Let $(Y_1,,\ldots,Y_{m+1})$ be a flat distribution and $\widetilde{\mathsf{G}}$ be an $(m+1)$-block generator consistent with $Y_{\leq m+1}$. Then for $\widetilde{Y}_{\leq m+1} = \widetilde{\mathsf{G}}(\widetilde{R}_{\leq m+1})$ for uniform $\widetilde{R}_{\leq m+1}$:*

1. *For every $y_{\leq m+1}, r_{\leq m+1} \in \mathrm{Supp}(\widetilde{Y}_{\leq m+1}, \widetilde{R}_{\leq m+1})$, it holds that*

$$\sum_{i=1}^{m+1} \left(\mathrm{H}^*_{y_i, y_{<i}} \left(Y_i | Y_{<i} \right) - \mathrm{H}^*_{y_i, r_{<i}} \left(\widetilde{Y}_i | \widetilde{R}_{<i} \right) \right)$$

$$= \sum_{i=1}^{m+1} \mathrm{KL}^*_{y_i, y_{<i}, r_{<i}} \left(\widetilde{Y}_i | \widetilde{R}_{<i}, \widetilde{Y}_{<i} \,\middle\|\, Y_i | R_{<i}, Y_{<i} \right)$$

   In particular, $(Y_1,\ldots,Y_{m+1})$ has (t,Δ) next-block inaccessible δ-min relative entropy if and only if it has (t,δ)-max-inaccessible entropy at least Δ.

2. *Furthermore,*

$$\sum_{i=1}^{m+1} \left(\mathrm{H}\left(Y_i | Y_{<i}\right) - \mathrm{H}\left(\widetilde{Y}_i | \widetilde{R}_{<i}\right) \right) = \sum_{i=1}^{m+1} \mathrm{KL}\left(\widetilde{Y}_i | \widetilde{R}_{<i}, \widetilde{Y}_{<i} \,\middle\|\, Y_i | R_{<i}, Y_{<i} \right),$$

   so in particular, $(Y_1,\ldots,Y_{m+1})$ has (t,Δ) next-block inaccessible relative entropy if and only if it has t-inaccessible entropy at least Δ.

Proof. For the sample notions, the chain rule (Proposition 2.6) gives:

$$\sum_{i=1}^{m+1} \mathrm{H}^*_{y_i, y_{<i}} \left(Y_i | Y_{<i} \right) = \mathrm{H}^*_y \left(Y_{\leq m+1} \right) = \log | \mathrm{Supp}(Y_{\leq m+1})|$$

for all y since Y is flat. Hence:

$$\log|\mathrm{Supp}(Y_{\leq m+1})| - \sum_{i=1}^{m+1} \mathrm{H}^*_{y_i, y_{<i}} \left(\widetilde{Y}_i | \widetilde{R}_{<i} \right)$$

$$= \sum_{i=1}^{m+1} \left(\mathrm{H}^*_{y_i, y_{<i}} \left(Y_i | Y_{<i} \right) - \mathrm{H}^*_{y_i, r_{<i}} \left(\widetilde{Y}_i | \widetilde{R}_{<i} \right) \right)$$

$$= \sum_{i=1}^{m+1} \mathrm{KL}^*_{y_i, y_{<i}, r_{<i}} \left(\widetilde{Y}_i | \widetilde{R}_{<i}, \widetilde{Y}_{<i} \,\middle\|\, Y_i | R_{<i}, Y_{<i} \right),$$

so the second claim follows by taking the expectation over $(\widetilde{Y}_{\leq m+1}, \widetilde{R}_{\leq m+1})$ on both sides.

By chaining the reductions between the different notions of hardness considered in this work (hardness in relative entropy, next-block inaccessible relative entropy and inaccessible entropy), we obtain a more modular proof of the theorem of Haitner *et al.* [13], obtaining inaccessible entropy from any one-way function.

Theorem 4.11. *Let n be a security parameter, $f : \{0,1\}^n \to \{0,1\}^n$ be a (t, ε)-one-way function, and X be uniform over $\{0,1\}^n$. For $\ell \in \{1, \ldots, n\}$, decompose $f(X) \overset{\text{def}}{=} (Y_1, \ldots, Y_{n/\ell})$ into blocks of length ℓ. Then:*

1. *For every $0 \le \Delta \le \log(1/\varepsilon)$, $(Y_1, \ldots, Y_{n/\ell}, X)$ has t'-inaccessible entropy at least $(\log(1/\varepsilon) - \Delta)$ for $t' = \Omega\left(t \cdot \Delta \cdot \ell^2 / (n^2 \cdot 2^\ell)\right)$.*
2. *For every $0 < \delta \le 1$ and $0 \le \Delta \le \log(1/\varepsilon) - \log(2/\delta)$, $(Y_1, \ldots, Y_{n/\ell}, X)$ has (t', δ)-max-inaccessible entropy at least $(\log(1/\varepsilon) - \log(2/\delta) - \Delta)$ for $t' = \Omega\left(t \cdot \delta \cdot \Delta \cdot \ell^2 / (n^2 \cdot 2^\ell)\right)$.*

Proof. Since f is (t, ε)-one-way, the distributional search problem $\left(\Pi^f, f(X)\right)$ where $\Pi^f = \{(f(x), x) : x \in \{0,1\}^n\}$ is (t, ε)-hard. Clearly, $(f(X), X)$ is supported on Π^f, so by applying Theorem 3.11, we have that $(\Pi^f, f(X), X)$ is $(\Omega(t), \log(1/\varepsilon))$ witness hard in relative entropy and $(\Omega(t), \log(1/\varepsilon) - \log(2/\delta))$ witness hard in $\delta/2$-min relative entropy. Thus, by Theorem 4.7 we have that $(Y_1, \ldots, Y_{n/\ell}, X)$ has $\left(\Omega\left(t \cdot \Delta \cdot \ell^2 / (n^2 \cdot 2^\ell)\right), \log(1/\varepsilon) - \Delta\right)$ next-block inaccessible relative entropy and $\left(\Omega\left(t \cdot \delta \cdot \Delta \cdot \ell^2 / (n^2 \cdot 2^\ell)\right), \log(1/\varepsilon) - \log(2/\delta) - \Delta\right)$ next-block inaccessible δ-min relative entropy, and we conclude by Theorem 4.10.

Remark 4.12. For comparison, the original proof of [13] shows that for every $0 < \delta \le 1$, $(Y_1, \ldots, Y_{n/\ell}, X)$ has (t', δ)-max-inaccessible entropy at least $(\log(1/\varepsilon) - 2\log(1/\delta) - O(1))$ for $t' = \tilde{\Omega}\left(t \cdot \delta \cdot \ell^2 / (n^2 \cdot 2^\ell)\right)$, which in particular for fixed t' has quadratically worse dependence on δ in terms of the achieved inaccessible entropy: $\log(1/\varepsilon) - 2 \cdot \log(1/\delta) - O(1)$ rather than our $\log(1/\varepsilon) - 1 \cdot \log(1/\delta) - O(1)$.

Corollary 4.13 (Theorem 4.2 in [13]). *Let n be a security parameter, $f : \{0,1\}^n \to \{0,1\}^n$ be a strong one-way function, and X be uniform over $\{0,1\}^n$. Then for every $\ell = O(\log n)$, $(f(X)_{1 \ldots \ell}, \ldots, f(X)_{n-\ell+1 \ldots n}, X)$ has $n^{\omega(1)}$-inaccessible entropy $\omega(\log n)$ and $(n^{\omega(1)}, \text{negl}(n))$-max-inaccessible entropy $\omega(\log n)$.*

Acknowledgements. We thank Muthuramakrishnan Venkitasubramaniam for an inspiring conversation which sparked this work.

A   Missing Proofs

Lemma A.1. *For all $t \ge 1$, $f : x \mapsto \frac{x}{1-(1-x)^t}$ is convex over $[0,1]$.*

Proof. We instead show convexity of $\tilde{f} : x \mapsto f(1-x)$. A straightforward computation gives:

$$\tilde{f}''(x) = \frac{x^{t-2}t\left(t(1-x)(x^t+1) - (1+x)(1-x^t)\right)}{(1-x^t)^3}$$

so that it suffices to show the non-negativity of $g(x) = t(1-x)(x^t+1) - (1+x)(1-x^t)$ over $[0,1]$. The function g has second derivative $t(1-x)(t^2-1)x^{t-2}$, which is non-negative when $x \in [0, 1]$, and thus the first derivative g' is non-decreasing. Also, the first derivative at 1 is equal to zero, so that g' is non-positive over $[0, 1]$ and hence g is non-increasing over this interval. Since $g(1) = 0$, this implies that g is non-negative over $[0, 1]$ and f is convex as desired.

Theorem A.2 (Theorem 3.11 **restated).** *Let Π be a binary relation and let (Y, W) be pair of random variables supported on Π. If (Π, Y) is (t, ε)-hard, then (Π, Y, W) is (t', Δ') witness hard in relative entropy and (t', Δ'') witness hard in δ-min relative entropy for every $\delta \in [0, 1]$ where $t' = \Omega(t)$, $\Delta' = \log(1/\varepsilon)$ and $\Delta'' = \log(\delta/\varepsilon)$.*

Proof. We proceed similarly to the proof of Theorem 3.5. Let $(\widetilde{G}, S)$ be a pair of algorithms with $\widetilde{G} = (\widetilde{G}_1, \widetilde{G}_w)$ a two-block generator supported on Π. Define the linear-time oracle algorithm $A^{\widetilde{G}_w, S}(y) \overset{\text{def}}{=} \widetilde{G}_w(S(y))$. Then

$$
\Pr\left[\Pi\left(Y, A^{\widetilde{G}_w, S}(Y)\right)\right] = \Pr\left[\Pi(Y, \widetilde{G}_w(S(Y)))\right]
$$

$$
\geq \Pr\left[\widetilde{G}_1(S(Y)) = Y\right] \qquad (\widetilde{G} \text{ is supported on } \Pi)
$$

$$
= \sum_{r \in \text{Supp}(\widetilde{R})} \Pr\left[S(Y) = r \wedge Y = \widetilde{G}_1(r)\right]
$$

$$
\geq \sum_{\substack{r \in \text{Supp}(\widetilde{R}) \\ w \in \text{Supp}(\widetilde{G}_2(\widetilde{R}))}} \Pr\left[S(Y) = r \wedge Y = \widetilde{G}_1(r) \wedge W = w\right]
$$

$$
= \underset{\substack{r \leftarrow \widetilde{R} \\ w \leftarrow \widetilde{G}_2(r)}}{E}\left[\frac{\Pr\left[S(Y) = r \wedge Y = \widetilde{G}_1(r) \wedge W = w\right]}{\Pr\left[\widetilde{R} = r \wedge \widetilde{G}_2(r) = w\right]}\right]
$$

$$
= \underset{\substack{r \leftarrow \widetilde{R} \\ y \leftarrow \widetilde{G}_1(r) \\ w \leftarrow \widetilde{G}_2(r)}}{E}\left[2^{-\text{KL}^*_{r, y, w}\left(\widetilde{R}, \widetilde{G}_1(\widetilde{R}), \widetilde{G}_2(\widetilde{R}) \,\|\, S(Y), Y, W\right)}\right],
$$

The witness hardness in relative entropy then follows by applying Jensen's inequality (since 2^{-x} is convex) and the witness hardness in δ-min relative entropy follows by Markov's inequality by considering the event that the sample relative entropy is smaller than Δ (this event has density at least δ).

References

1. Blum, M., Micali, S.: How to generate cryptographically strong sequences of pseudo random bits. In: Proceedings of the 23th Annual Symposium on Foundations of Computer Science (FOCS), pp. 112–117 (1982)
2. Brassard, G., Chaum, D., Crépeau, C.: Minimum disclosure proofs of knowledge. J. Comput. Syst. Sci. **37**(2), 156–189 (1988)
3. Diffie, W., Hellman, M.E.: New directions in cryptography. IEEE Trans. Inf. Theor. **22**(6), 644–654 (1976)

4. Ding, Y.Z., Harnik, D., Rosen, A., Shaltiel, R.: Constant-round oblivious transfer in the bounded storage model. In: Naor, M. (ed.) TCC 2004. LNCS, vol. 2951, pp. 446–472. Springer, Heidelberg (2004). https://doi.org/10.1007/978-3-540-24638-1_25

5. Goldreich, O., Goldwasser, S., Micali, S.: How to construct random functions. J. ACM **33**(4), 792–807 (1986)

6. Goldreich, O., Micali, S., Wigderson, A.: How to play any mental game or a completeness theorem for protocols with honest majority. In: Proceedings of the 19th Annual ACM Symposium on Theory of Computing (STOC), pp. 218–229. ACM Press (1987)

7. Goldreich, O., Micali, S., Wigderson, A.: Proofs that yield nothing but their validity or all languages in NP have zero-knowledge proof systems. J. ACM **38**(1), 691–729 (1991)

8. Haitner, I., Holenstein, T., Reingold, O., Vadhan, S.P., Wee, H.: Universal one-way hash functions via inaccessible entropy. In: Gilbert, H. (ed.) EUROCRYPT 2010. LNCS, vol. 6110, pp. 616–637. Springer, Heidelberg (2010). https://doi.org/10.1007/978-3-642-13190-5_31

9. Haitner, I., Nguyen, M., Ong, S.J., Reingold, O., Vadhan, S.: Statistically hiding commitments and statistical zero-knowledge arguments from any one-way function. SIAM J. Comput. **39**(3), 1153–1218 (2009)

10. Haitner, I., Reingold, O., Vadhan, S.: Efficiency improvements in constructing pseudorandom generators from one-way functions. In: Proceedings of the 42nd Annual ACM Symposium on Theory of Computing (STOC), pp. 437–446 (2010)

11. Haitner, I., Reingold, O., Vadhan, S., Wee, H.: Inaccessible entropy. In: Proceedings of the 41st Annual ACM Symposium on Theory of Computing (STOC 2009), pp. 611–620, 31 May–2 June 2009

12. Haitner, I., Reingold, O., Vadhan, S.P.: Eciency improvements in constructing pseudorandom generators from one-way functions. SIAM J. Comput. **42**(3), 1405–1430 (2013). https://doi.org/10.1137/100814421

13. Haitner, I., Reingold, O., Vadhan, S.P., Wee, H.: Inaccessible entropy I: inaccessible entropy generators and statistically hiding commitments from one-way functions (2016). www.cs.tau.ac.il/~iftachh/papers/AccessibleEntropy/IE1.pdf. To appear. Preliminary version, named Inaccessible Entropy, appeared in STOC 2009

14. Håstad, J., Impagliazzo, R., Levin, L.A., Luby, M.: A pseudorandom generator from any one-way function. SIAM J. Comput. **28**(4), 1364–1396 (1999)

15. Impagliazzo, R., Luby, M.: One-way functions are essential for complexity based cryptography. In: Proceedings of the 30th Annual Symposium on Foundations of Computer Science (FOCS), pp. 230–235 (1989)

16. Naor, M.: Bit commitment using pseudorandomness. J. Cryptol. **4**(2), 151–158 (1991)

17. Naor, M., Ostrovsky, R., Venkatesan, R., Yung, M.: Perfect zero-knowledge arguments for NP using any one-way permutation. J. Cryptol. **11**(2), 87–108 (1998). Preliminary version in CRYPTO 1992

18. Naor, M., Yung, M.: Universal one-way hash functions and their cryptographic applications. In: Proceedings of the 21st Annual ACM Symposium on Theory of Computing (STOC), pp. 33–43. ACM Press (1989)

19. Nisan, N., Zuckerman, D.: Randomness is linear in space. J. Comput. Syst. Sci. **52**(1), 43–52 (1996)

20. Rompel, J.: One-way functions are necessary and sufficient for secure signatures. In: Proceedings of the 22nd Annual ACM Symposium on Theory of Computing (STOC), pp. 387–394 (1990)

21. Vadhan, S.P., Zheng, C.J.: Characterizing pseudoentropy and simplifying pseudo-random generator constructions. In: Proceedings of the 44th Symposium on Theory of Computing Conference, STOC 2012, pp. 817–836 (2012). http://doi.acm.org/10.1145/2213977.2214051
22. Yao, A.C.: Theory and applications of trapdoor functions. In: Proceedings of the 23th Annual Symposium on Foundations of Computer Science (FOCS), pp. 80–91 (1982)

Author Index

Printed in the United States
By Bookmasters